FOURTH CANADIAN
EDITION

sociology
in our times

Diana Kendall
Baylor University

Jane Lothian Murray
University of Winnipeg

Rick Linden
University of Manitoba

THOMSON
✴ ™
NELSON

Australia   Canada   Mexico   Singapore   Spain   United Kingdom   United States

THOMSON

NELSON

Sociology in Our Times, Fourth Canadian Edition
by Diana Kendall, Jane Lothian Murray, and Rick Linden

Associate Vice-President, Editorial Director:
Evelyn Veitch

Publisher:
Joanna Cotton

Acquisitions Editor:
Cara Yarzab

Marketing Managers:
Lenore Taylor
Kelly Smyth

Senior Developmental Editor:
Rebecca Rea

Permissions Coordinator:
Cindy Howard

Production Editor:
Lara Caplan

Copy Editor:
Kelli Howey

Proofreader:
Joan Rawlin

Indexer:
Belle Wong

Senior Production Coordinator:
Hedy Sellers

Design Director:
Ken Phipps

Interior Design:
Lisa Delgado

Cover Design:
Sasha Moroz

Cover Image:
Daly & Newton/Stone/Getty Images

Compositor:
Integra

Printer:
Quebecor World

Library and Archives Canada Cataloguing in Publication

Kendall, Diana Elizabeth
    Sociology in our times/Diana Kendall, Jane Lothian Murray, Rick Linden.—4th Canadian ed.

Includes bibliographical references and index.
ISBN 0-17-640668-9

1. Sociology—Textbooks.
I. Lothian Murray, Jane, 1960–
II. Linden, Rick III. Title

HM586.K45 2006   301
C2005-906908-2

Rick Linden would like to dedicate this edition to the memory of his mother-in-law, Mildred Cormack. She was a great friend who taught him the value of storytelling as a way of understanding the world (as well as keeping her grandchildren amused).

B R I E F C O N T E N T S

CONTENTS

BOXES

■ CRITICAL THINKING

■ SOCIOLOGY AND THE MEDIA

■ SOCIOLOGY AND THE LAW

■ SOCIOLOGY AND TECHNOLOGY

■ SOCIOLOGY IN GLOBAL PERSPECTIVE

■ YOU CAN MAKE A DIFFERENCE

PREFACE

Welcome to the fourth Canadian edition of *Sociology in Our Times*! As this edition was being written, we all became acutely aware of how our country and the world have changed in recent years. However, even as some things change others remain the same, and one thing that has not changed is the significance of education and the profound importance of understanding how and why people act the way they do, how societies grapple with issues and major problems, and why many of us are reassured by social institutions—including family, religion, education, government, and the media—even at times when we might like to see certain changes occur in these institutions.

Like previous editions of this widely read text, the fourth Canadian edition of *Sociology in Our Times* is a cutting-edge book in at least two ways: (1) by including a diversity of classical and contemporary theory, interesting and relevant research, and lived experiences that accurately mirror the diversity in society itself, and (2) by showing students that sociology involves important questions and issues that they confront both personally and vicariously (for example, through the media). This text speaks to a wide variety of Canadian students and captures their interest by taking into account their concerns and perspectives. The research used in this text includes the best work of classical and established contemporary sociologists, and it weaves an inclusive treatment of all people into the examination of sociology.

Although a number of introductory sociology texts give the appearance of inclusion, most existing texts were initially written with class, race, and gender neatly compartmentalized into their "appropriate" chapters, and perhaps an occasional "diversity" box. That approach not only marginalizes an increasing proportion of the students in introductory sociology classes—as well as in the Canadian population—but also leads many students to view class, race, and gender as nothing more than variables in sociological research (e.g., statistics on welfare, crime, and homelessness).

That approach downplays the significance of the interlocking nature of class, race, and gender in all topics examined by sociologists.

By using the latest theory and research, *Sociology in Our Times* not only provides students with the most relevant information about sociological thinking, but also helps students consider the significance of the interlocking nature of class, race, and gender in all aspects of life.

We encourage you to read our text and judge the writing style for yourself. We have sought to make the research accessible and engaging for both students and instructors. Concepts and theories are presented in a straightforward and understandable way, and the wealth of concrete examples and lived experiences woven throughout the chapters makes the relevance of sociological theory and research abundantly clear to students.

New Features

Applying Sociological Knowledge to Help Improve Society

We have added to this edition a series of **"You Can Make a Difference"** boxes, which help get students involved by finding out how they can use the knowledge gained from a particular chapter to improve society. Topics include using sociological theories to reduce crime, getting involved with organizations that try to reduce global stratification, helping to reduce medical costs by living a healthy lifestyle, and helping with the resettlement of immigrants to Canada.

Census Profiles

The **"Census Profile"** is a new feature that provides information highlighting changes in Canadian society based on Census data. Each unique box uses recent statistics, ensuring students are up-to-date and informed about the topics discussed.

Changes in the Fourth Canadian Edition

The fourth Canadian edition of *Sociology in Our Times* provides us with the opportunity to continue to improve a text that has been very well received by students and teachers. We have added several hundred new references that incorporate the most recent Census data available as well as reflecting new developments in sociological research. The fourth Canadian edition builds on the best from previous editions while providing students with insights for their times.

Chapter 1 opens with a narrative from one of the authors regarding the sociological imagination. The chapter introduces students to the main theoretical perspectives used in sociology and applies them to the study of suicide. The concept of the sociological imagination is examined in various boxes throughout the chapter.

Chapter 2 includes a new discussion on content analysis and new material on ethnography. The ethnographic material includes a discussion of Jack Haas's well-known ethnography of high steel workers. There is also a new section on triangulation through the use of multiple methods.

Chapter 3 has the most recent Census data on language diversity, ethnicity, and Aboriginal peoples in Canada. A new box examines the *Idol* phenomenon in popular culture and the issue of cultural diffusion.

Chapter 4 has shifted focus somewhat to examine the effects of positive socialization and early childhood development. A new box deals with the issue of stay-at-home dads across the world and how they are coping with their new roles. Sociological theories of human development are now highlighted, with an emphasis on the primary socialization agents.

Chapter 5 includes recent research on homelessness among youth in Canada.

Chapter 6 has been extensively revised. One of the themes of the chapter is the shortcomings of bureaucracies, and we have included the flawed rescue efforts in New Orleans after Hurricane Katrina as an example of bureaucratic inflexibility. Ritzer's work on McDonaldization is now linked with the postmodernist view that groups and organizations are typically characterized by superficiality and shallow social relationships. The chapter now

also points out the methodological problems with Milgram's studies of obedience and the small-world phenomenon, and there is an expanded discussion of the importance of informal networks within bureaucracies. A new "Sociology and the Law" box discusses how bureaucratic inefficiency contributed to the Air India bombing and to the 9/11 attacks. The most significant revision is that the discussion of the Japanese organizational model has been replaced by a new section on the network organization. Based on Castells's work, this section explores the way in which global network enterprises, such as Dell, are coming to dominate the world of business. Included in this new section is a discussion of how al-Qaeda and other terrorist organizations have adopted a networked organizational structure that makes them very difficult to deal with.

Chapter 7 includes a new lived experience that involves testimony from the trial of Hells Angels leader Mom Boucher, which illustrates the level of violence involved in organized crime. The revised section on feminist perspectives incorporates the view that the roots of female criminality lie in a social structure characterized by inequalities of class, race, and gender. The section on postmodern theories of crime and deviance now explores the role of modern surveillance technologies. The new "You Can Make a Difference" box links several of the most important deviance theories with different types of volunteer opportunities for students.

Crime statistics have been updated to 2004 and there is a new discussion of research on racial profiling by police in Toronto and Kingston. Finally, there is an extensive new discussion of the globalization of crime that focuses on organized crime networks and on the blurring of boundaries between organized crime and terrorism. Among the examples discussed in this section are the case of Ahmed Ressam, who was stopped at the U.S. border with a car full of explosives that he intended to use to blow up part of the Los Angeles airport; the international system of money laundering; and the problem of organized crime groups moving into weak or failed states.

Chapter 8 has incorporated the most current research on the distribution of wealth and income in today's society.

Chapter 9 has a new graphic from the United Nations Development Programme that contrasts the aid provided to dairy and cotton producers in industrialized countries with the per capita income and aid provided to people in sub-Saharan Africa. We have also added a new section on gender and inequality in which we explain why women suffer from global inequality more than men. A new "You Can Make a Difference" box tells students how they can contribute to the betterment of people in other countries. Finally, we have added a section on the Millennium Development Goals and Targets that explores the kinds of policies that can help improve the lives of people in low-income countries.

Chapter 10 takes a closer look at the significance of ethnic diversity with an emphasis on various forms of racism. A postmodernist perspective introduces the idea that ethnic and racial identities are socially constructed and constantly evolving. A new "You Can Make a Difference" box highlights various ways that readers can engage in the fight against racism.

Chapter 11 has incorporated a more comprehensive discussion of sexuality, including information on sexual orientation and transsexuality. A new "Critical Thinking" box tells the tragic story of the gender reassignment of David Reimer to highlight the complexity of the concepts of gender and sex.

In **Chapter 12** a new chapter introduction illustrates different perspectives on aging using the voices of three older Canadians. A major addition to this chapter is a discussion of postmodern perspectives on aging. A central theme of postmodernism is the view that identity is a social construct, which implies that we can alter the way our culture thinks about aging. The new section explores some of the ways in which changing attitudes and modern medical technology are giving seniors the freedom to experiment with identities that are no longer restricted by stereotyped views of appropriate roles for older people.

Chapter 13 provides updated statistics on work and the economy and now includes a new section on feminist perspectives on work and labour.

In **Chapter 14** the section on totalitarian regimes has been expanded to include a discussion of life under the Taliban in Afghanistan. We have also added a new section on interactionist perspectives in the political process that looks at Joseph Gusfield's work on symbolic crusades. A box has been added that discusses the history of terrorism in Canada. The box on nationalism now includes a section on the ways in which international organizations are attempting to deal with the civil conflicts that have resulted from nationalist movements.

Chapter 15 opens with a new narrative from a gay man talking about his "out family," an example that is used to highlight the increasing variety and diversity in this primary social institution. This chapter also has a new "Sociology and the Law" box that examines same-sex marriages and the state of these new unions.

Chapter 16 examines changes in the education system, the rising costs of education, and the positive changes that have occurred in recent decades that will benefit students in the future.

Chapter 17 now includes a section on the postmodern perspective on religion. The postmodern perspective is used to analyze the debate between those who think that the world is becoming more secular and those who believe that religion is more influential than ever. A Concept Table has been added to help students understand the different theories of the role of religion in society. The chapter also includes a new box dealing with the important issue of religious terrorism.

Chapter 18 has a new section examining feminist perspectives on health and health care that focuses on the issue of the medicalization of women's lives. The discussion of HIV/AIDS now has an expanded look at the reasons why Uganda has been more successful than most other African countries in reducing the incidence of the disease and why the U.S. emphasis on abstinence-only programs has put this progress at risk. Finally, there is a new "You Can Make a Difference" box on improving your own health.

Because **Chapter 19** deals with population issues, there are extensive changes to update population data for Canada and the many other countries discussed in the chapter. An expanded discussion of the demographic consequences of China's one-child-per-family policy looks at the gender imbalance that has resulted from the preference that a family's one child be male. The new "You Can Make a Difference" box describes how students can help with the resettlement of immigrants.

There have been two major additions to the urban section of the chapter. The interactionist perspective is used to highlight the ways in which people manage to live in an urban world of strangers. The work of Lyn Lofland, Erving Goffman, Jane Jacobs, and Tracy Nielsen is used to illustrate how we interact in the urban environment. A new section on postmodern cities includes a discussion of changes, such as the loss of public space in contemporary cities, and outlines John Hannigan's notion of the Fantasy City. Finally, a Concept Table outlines the different theoretical approaches to urban life.

Chapter 20 opens with a new personal narrative on environmental activism and continues with this theme in a "You Can Make a Difference" box.

Unique Features

The following special features are specifically designed to reflect the themes of relevance and diversity in *Sociology in Our Times,* as well as to support student learning.

Providing Interesting and Engaging Lived Experiences Throughout

Authentic first-person accounts are used as opening vignettes and throughout each chapter to create interest and give concrete meaning to the topics being discussed. Lived experiences including racism, child abuse, environmental activism, eating disorders, suicide, disability, and homelessness provide opportunities for students to examine social life beyond their own experiences and to examine class, ethnicity, gender, and age from diverse perspectives. An unusually wide range of diverse experiences—both positive and negative—is systematically incorporated to expose students to a multiplicity of viewpoints. The lived experiences have been selected for their ability to speak to students, to assist them in learning concepts and theories, and to illustrate how they can be applied to other situations.

Focusing on the Relationship Between Sociology and Everyday Life

Each chapter has a brief "Sociology and Everyday Life" quiz that relates the sociological perspective to the pressing social issues presented in the opening vignette. (Answers are provided on the subsequent page.) Do official statistics accurately reflect crime rates in Canada? Does increasing cultural diversity lead to an increasing incidence of hate crimes and racism? Do welfare benefits provide enough income for recipients to live comfortably? Topics such as these will pique the interest of students.

Applying the Sociological Imagination to Contemporary Issues and the Law

Based on the latest legal research, "Sociology and the Law" boxes encourage students to think critically about the many ties between the law and sociology, and provide a springboard for discussion. Topics include child abuse, assisted suicide, obscenity and women's equality, Quebec and the Constitution, and AIDS and public health.

Using the Media to Encourage Critical Thinking

Like most people in our society, students get much of their information about the social world from the media. A significant benefit of a sociology course is the encouragement to think critically about such information. Focusing on various types of media depictions—including television shows, cartoons, movies, and mainstream and alternative presses— "Sociology and the Media" boxes provide an overview of sociological topics as seen through the eye of the media. Topics range from racism in the media to news coverage of diverse topics, such as immigration and people living with AIDS.

Emphasizing the Importance of a Global Perspective

In our interconnected world, the sociological imagination must extend beyond national borders. The global implications of topics are examined throughout each chapter and in "Sociology in Global Perspective" boxes. Topics include the Grameen Bank; child abuse in Asia; global advertising; and wealth, poverty, and aging in Russia.

Analyzing the Sociological Implications of Technology

As computers become an increasingly important part of our everyday lives, they change how we communicate, how we learn, and how we perceive ourselves in relation to others. "Sociology and Technology" box topics include seniors in cyberspace, the Internet and urban legends, technology in the classroom, technology and crime, and cyberdating.

Encouraging Students to Use Their Sociological Knowledge to Think Critically

From homeless rights to reproductive technology to reverse racism, "Critical Thinking" boxes encourage students to use their sociological knowledge to grapple with some of today's most hotly contested issues.

Looking Ahead to Sociology in the Future

In addition to highlighting the contemporary relevance of sociology, students are encouraged to consider the sociological perspective as it might be in the future. The concluding section of Chapters 3 through 20 looks into the future and suggests how our social lives may look in the years to come. Environmental issues, homelessness, technology, population, deviance and crime, and the economy and work are among the topics discussed.

In-Text Learning Aids

Sociology in Our Times includes a number of pedagogical aids to promote students' mastery of sociological concepts and terminology.

- *Chapter Outlines.* A concise outline at the beginning of each chapter gives students an overview of major topics and a convenient aid for review.
- *Questions and Issues.* After the opening lived experience in each chapter, a series of introductory questions invites students to think about the major topics discussed in the chapter.
- *Integrated Running Glossary.* Major concepts and key terms are concisely defined and highlighted in bold print within the text flow to avoid disrupting students' reading. These concepts and terms are also listed at the end of the chapters and in the glossary at the back of the book.
- *End-of-Chapter Study Aids.* The Chapter Review provides a concise summary of key points and theoretical perspectives, along with a list of Key Terms. Questions for Critical Thinking encourage students to assess their knowledge of the chapter and apply insights they have gained to other issues. The Suggested Readings describe recent publications related to the chapter. This list also is a good source for book review suggestions.

- *Net Links.* Net Links, found at the end of every chapter, encourage students to explore the Internet. The Net Links list research articles found on the Internet that can be used for further study or in-class discussion.

Fully Integrated Support Package for Students and Instructors

Materials that enhance teaching and learning are an important feature of a textbook. The supplements offered with *Sociology in Our Times,* Fourth Canadian Edition, ensure that the themes of diversity, inclusiveness, and contemporary issues are consistent with the text. These pieces work together as an effective and integrated teaching package.

For Students

Study Guide

The *Study Guide for use with Sociology in Our Times,* Fourth Canadian Edition, gives students further opportunity to think sociologically. Each chapter includes a chapter summary, a list of key terms and key people, a list of learning objectives, and multiple-choice and true–false questions. (ISBN: 0-17-610283-3)

Sociology on the Web

http://www.sociologyinourtimes4e .nelson.com

Sociology in Our Times features a companion Web site designed for both students and instructors. Features of the Web site include online material linked directly to the text, plus interactive quizzes, study resources, and a career centre.

ThomsonNOW™

ThomsonNOW™ is an **online learning and homework assessment program** created in concert with *Sociology in Our Times* to present a seamless, integrated learning tool.

With ThomsonNOW™, instructors can dramatically affect student success. Assigning text specific tutorials requires no instructor set-up. Or faculty can use the same system to **create tailored homework assignments, quizzes, and tests that auto-grade and flow directly into your gradebook!** This means you can actually assign marks to homework assignments, motivating students to study the material and come to class prepared.

Students can improve their grades and save study time with ThomsonNOW™. It isn't just reading—it provides a **customized study plan that lets students master what they need to know without wasting time on what they already know!** The study plan provides a road map to interactive exercises, videos, e-books, and other resources that help students master the subject. Pre-tests and post-tests allow students to monitor their progress and focused studying via ThomsonNOW™ will minimize student efforts and yet maximize results.

InfoTrac® College Edition

Ignite discussions or augment your lectures with the latest developments in sociology and societal change. Create your own course reader by selecting articles or by using the search keywords provided at the end of each chapter. InfoTrac® College Edition gives you and your students four months of free access to an easy-to-use online database of reliable, full-length articles (not abstracts) from hundreds of top academic journals and popular sources. Among the journals available twenty-four hours a day, seven days a week are: *Canadian Review of Sociology and Anthropology, Canadian Journal of Sociology, Canadian Ethnic Studies, Public Policy, American Journal of Sociology, Social Forces, Social Research,* and *Sociology.* Contact your Thomson Nelson representative for more information.

Society in Question, Fourth Edition

Society in Question, Fourth Edition, by Robert J. Brym, is the only introductory sociology reader that combines Canadian and international readings. This reader provides balanced coverage of the approaches and methods in current sociology as well as unique and surprising perspectives on many major sociological topics. All readings have been chosen for their ability to speak directly to contemporary Canadian students about how sociology can enable them to make sense of their lives in a rapidly changing world. (ISBN: 0-17-622538-2)

Classic Readings in Sociology, Fourth Edition

Classic Readings in Sociology, Fourth Edition, edited by Eve Howard, is a series of classic articles written by key sociologists and social thinkers that will complement any introductory sociology textbook. This reader serves as a foundation where students can read original works that teach the fundamental ideas of sociology. At only 128 pages, this brief reader is a convenient and painless way to introduce the "great thinkers." (ISBN: 0-495-18739-9)

Thomson Nelson Guide to Success in Social Science: Writing Papers and Exams

Thomson Nelson Guide to Success in Social Science: Writing Papers and Exams by Diane Symbaluk is an indispensable resource for any social science student. *Thomson Nelson Guide to Success in Social Science* is a roadmap to the often unfamiliar terrain of university or college academia. Leveraging best practices of master students, author Diane Symbaluk has created a book that will help students achieve their goals of excellence in writing and research. (ISBN: 0-17-625182-0)

Thomson Nelson Canadian Dictionary for the Social Sciences

Thomson Nelson Canadian Dictionary for the Social Sciences by Gary Parkinson and Robert Drislane has over 1400 entries covering the fields of anthropology, sociology, and political science. This dictionary is designed for undergraduate students and covers the main concepts, names, and events in social sciences in Canada. Each entry is designed to provide sufficient information to grasp the basic content of a concept, how the term is used, and its connection to other concepts. (ISBN: 0-17-625237-1)

For Instructors

Instructor's Resource Manual

The Instructor's Resource Manual provides lecture outlines, chapter summaries, and teaching tips, as well as a list of further print and video resources. In addition, guest speaker suggestions, student learning objectives, student projects, and essay questions are included. (ISBN: 0-17-640680-8)

Test Bank

A completely revised Test Bank is available with more than 2,000 multiple-choice and true–false items. Each question is categorized as testing conceptual understanding, concept application, or factual knowledge, and a page reference is provided for each answer. The **Computerized Test Bank,** found on the **Instructor's Resource CD** (information on the next page), is available to facilitate the creation of your own tests. (ISBN: 0-17-640681-6)

ExamView Computerized Test Bank

Create, deliver, and customize tests in minutes with this easy-to-use assessment and tutorial system. *ExamView* offers both a *Quick Test Wizard* and an *Online Test Wizard* that guide you step-by-step through the process of creating tests. The test appears on screen exactly as it will print or display online. Using ExamView's complete word processing capabilities, you can enter an unlimited number of new questions or edit existing questions. The ExamView Computerized Test Bank is available on the Instructor's Resource CD-ROM. (0-17-640682-4)

PowerPoint™ Lecture Slides

The PowerPoint lecture slides have been completely revised and updated for the Fourth Canadian Edition, containing focus questions, reviews of outlines, selected figures and tables from the textbook, review of key sections, topics, and theories. Our PowerPoint slides are a beneficial resource for new and experienced professors and are downloadable from the password-protected instructor's resource centre available at **http://www.sociologyinourtimes4e.nelson.com.**

Instructor's Resource CD (IRCD)

This *all in one* ancillary for the instructor contains the IM, TB, CTB, and PPTs all on one easy-to-use-and-store CD-ROM. (ISBN: 0-17-640682-4)

Multimedia Manager for Introductory Sociology

The easy way to get great multimedia lectures! This one-stop digital library and presentation tool helps you assemble, edit, and present custom lectures. The CD-ROM brings together art (figures, tables, and illustrations) from the text itself, pre-assembled PowerPoint™ lecture slides, and sources from many other texts. You can use these materials as they are, or add your own materials for a truly customized lecture presentation. (ISBN: 0-17-610429-1)

Nelson Videos for Introductory Sociology, Think Outside the Book

This 5 volume set of 34 video segments, each is 5 to 27 minutes in length, was created to stimulate discussion of topics raised in sociology. Produced in conjunction with Face to Face Media (Vancouver), the selections have been edited to optimize their impact in the classroom. Many of the selections are taken from films that have won national and international awards. Six of the selections are from the celebrated work of Gwynne Dyer, one of Canada's leading media intellectuals. Videos and an accompanying Video Guide and Instructor's Manual are available from your local Thomson Nelson sales and editorial representative. Visit **www.thinkoutsidethebook.nelson.com** for more information.

CNN Today Sociology Video Series

The *CNN Today* Sociology Video Series is an exclusive series jointly created by Thomson Wadsworth and *CNN* for the introduction to sociology course. Each video in the series consists of approximately 45 minutes of footage originally broadcast on *CNN* within the last several years and selected specifically to illustrate important sociological concepts. The videos are broken into short, 2- to 7-minute segments that are perfect for classroom use as lecture launchers or to illustrate key sociological concepts. An annotated table of contents accompanies each video, with descriptions of the segments and suggestions for their possible use within the course.

JoinIn™ on TurningPoint®

Book-specific JoinIn™ content from *Sociology in Our Times* for classroom response systems, allows you to transform your classroom and assess your students' progress with instant in-class quizzes and polls. Our exclusive agreement to offer TurningPoint® software lets you pose book-specific questions and display students' answers seamlessly within the Microsoft® PowerPoint® slides of your own lecture, in conjunction with the "clicker" hardware of your choice. Enhance how your students interact with you, your lecture, and each other. For college and university adopters only. Contact your local Thomson Nelson representative to learn more.

Opposing Viewpoints Resource Center

This online centre helps you expose your students to all sides of today's most compelling social and scientific issues, from genetic engineering to environmental policy, prejudice, abortion, health care reform, violence in the media, and much more. The Opposing

Viewpoints Resource Center draws on Greenhaven Press's acclaimed social issues series, popular periodicals and newspapers, and core reference content from other Thomson Gale and Macmillan Reference USA sources. The result is a dynamic online library of current events topics—the facts as well as the arguments as articulated by the proponents and detractors of each position. Special sections focus on critical thinking (walking students through the critical evaluation of point-counterpoint arguments) and researching and writing papers. To take a quick tour of the OVRC, visit **http://www.gale.com/OpposingViewpoints**. For college and university adopters only and is not sold separately. (ISBN: 0-534-12853-X)

Acknowledgments

This edition of *Sociology in Our Times* would not have been possible without the insightful critiques of these colleagues, who have reviewed some or all of this book or its previous editions. Our profound thanks to each reviewer for engaging in this time-consuming process:

Francis Adu-Febiri, Camosun College
Bernie Hammond, King's University College
Ronald M. Joudrey, Red Deer College
Tracy Nielsen, Mount Royal College
Alice Propper, York University
B. Bryan Puk, University of Saskatchewan
Diane Symbaluk, Grant MacEwan College

We would also like to express our appreciation to the many individuals at Nelson involved in the development and production of the fourth Canadian edition of *Sociology in Our Times*. Among them, Joanna Cotton gave us encouragement and sound advice for the first three editions, and Cara Yarzab has continued to act as a mentor and friend throughout the preparation of this edition. We are pleased that Rebecca Rea joined our team for this edition, and we appreciated her guidance with the revision plan, her eye for compelling photos, and her ability to make schedules to help us create the most up-to-date book in a timely fashion. Lara Caplan, Kelli Howey, and Joan Rawlin worked diligently to ensure that the manuscript was a product that teachers and students would enjoy. We would also like to thank Lenore Taylor and the sales and marketing staff for their great work in ensuring there would be a fourth edition of this book. As always, the commitment, good humour, and hard work of the Nelson team have made this a very enjoyable experience.

Finally, we would like to thank our families for ensuring we were stolen away on a regular basis to enjoy the important things in life, and for their encouragement—mostly in the form of "Are you finished the book yet?"—when we were working on deadlines for this project.

FOURTH CANADIAN
EDITION

sociology
in our times

The Sociological Perspective

More than forty years ago sociologist Peter Berger first introduced what he called "an invitation to sociology." In his classic work by the same name, he writes:

People who like to avoid shocking discoveries, who prefer to believe that society is just what they were taught in Sunday school, who like the safety of the rules and the maxims of what Alfred Schuetz called the "world-taken-for-granted," should stay away from sociology. People who feel no temptation before closed doors, who have no curiosity about human beings, who are content to admire scenery without wondering about the people who live in those houses on the other side of the river, should probably stay away from sociology. They will find it unpleasant or, at any rate, unrewarding. People who are interested in human beings only if they can change, convert, or reform them should also be warned, for they will find sociology much less useful than they had hoped. And people whose interest is mainly their own conceptual constructions will do just as well to turn to the study of little white mice. Sociology will be satisfying, in the long run, only to those who can think of nothing more entrancing than to watch men [and women] and to understand things human. (Berger, 1963:24)

Berger is writing about what may be described as a passion for sociology, a fascination with human social interaction. In my first year of university I discovered this passion sitting in the Arts building gazing out the window observing, watching, analyzing this new social world (campus life) around me. It was also during this first year that I learned another valuable lesson from reading Berger's works. As he explained, "The first wisdom of sociology is this—things are not what they seem. This too is a deceptively simple statement. It ceases to be simple after a while. Social reality turns out to have many layers of meaning. The discovery of each new layer changes the perception of the whole" (1963:24).

Throughout this text you will be invited to use the sociological perspective and to apply your sociological imagination to re-examine your social world and explore important social issues and problems you may not have considered before.

QUESTIONS AND ISSUES

Chapter Focus Question: Why is it important to use your sociological imagination when studying such issues as suicide?

What is the sociological imagination?

Why were early thinkers concerned with social order and stability?

Why were later social thinkers concerned with change?

What are the assumptions behind each of the contemporary theoretical perspectives?

PUTTING SOCIAL LIFE INTO PERSPECTIVE

Sociology **is the systematic study of human society and social interaction.** It is a *systematic* study because sociologists apply both theoretical perspectives and research methods (or orderly approaches) to examinations of social behaviour. Sociologists study human societies and their social interactions in order to develop theories of how human behaviour is shaped by group life and how, in turn, group life is affected by individuals.

Why Study Sociology?

Sociology helps us gain a better understanding of ourselves and our social world. It enables us to see how behaviour is largely shaped by the groups to which we belong and the society in which we live.

Most of us take our social world for granted and view our lives in very personal terms. Because of our culture's emphasis on individualism, we often do not consider the complex connections between our own lives and the larger, recurring patterns of the society and world in which we live. Sociology helps us look beyond our personal experiences and gain insights into society and the larger world order. A *society* **is a large social grouping that shares the same geographical territory and is subject to the same political authority and dominant cultural expectations,** such as Canada, the United States, or Mexico. Examining the world order helps us understand that each of us is affected by *global interdependence*—**a relationship in which the lives of all people are closely intertwined and any one nation's problems are part of a larger global problem.**

Individuals can make use of sociology on a more personal level. Sociology enables us to move beyond established ways of thinking, thus allowing us to gain new insights into ourselves and to develop a greater awareness of the connection between our own "world" and that of other people. According to sociologist Peter Berger (1963:23), sociological inquiry helps us see that "things are not what they seem." Sociology provides new ways of approaching problems and making decisions in everyday life. Sociology promotes understanding and tolerance by enabling each of us to look beyond our personal experiences. (See Figure 1.1.)

Many of us rely on intuition or common sense gained from personal experience to help us understand our daily lives and other people's behaviour. *Commonsense knowledge* **guides ordinary conduct in everyday life.** We often rely on common sense— or "what everybody knows"—to answer key questions about behaviour: Why do people behave the way they do? Who makes the rules? Why do some people break rules and why do others follow them?

Many commonsense notions actually are myths. A *myth* is a popular but false notion that may be used, either intentionally or unintentionally, to perpetuate certain beliefs or "theories" even in the light of conclusive evidence to the contrary. Before reading on, take the quiz in Box 1.1, which includes a number of commonsense notions we may share.

The media are the source of much of our commonsense knowledge. Television talk show hosts and news anchors, journalists for magazines and newspapers, and authors of the many books in print all provide us with information about family life, sexual assault, homelessness, AIDS, violence, and thousands of related sociological topics. With all of this information readily available, why should we study sociology? What can we learn that is better than relying on common sense or information from an alleged expert on a talk show?

The answer is that sociologists strive to use scientific standards, not popular myths or hearsay, in studying society and social interaction. They use systematic research techniques and are accountable to

Figure 1.1	Fields That Use Social Science Research

In many careers, including jobs in academia, business, communications, health and human services, and law, the ability to analyze social science research is an important asset.

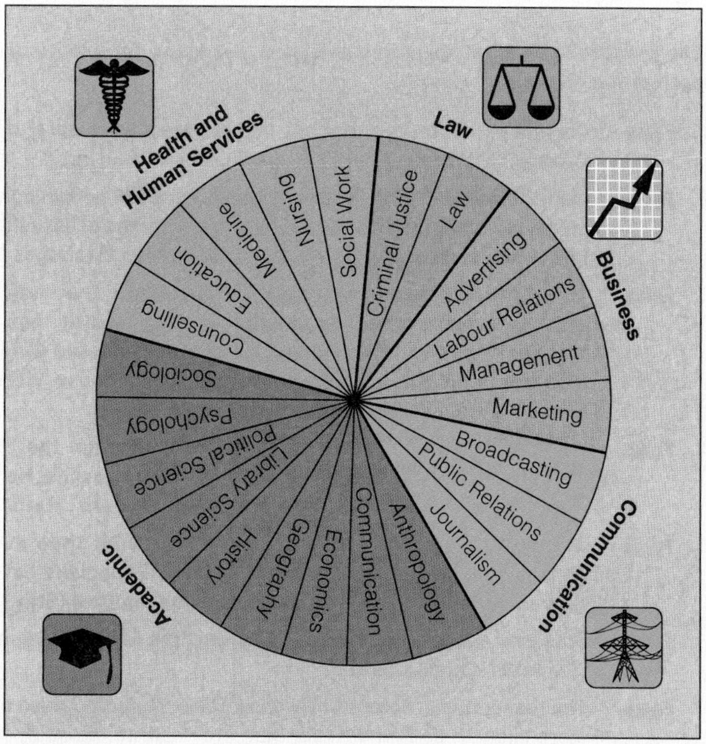

Source: Based on Katzer, Cook, and Crouch, 1991.

BOX 1.1 SOCIOLOGY AND EVERYDAY LIFE

Test Your Commonsense Knowledge

True	False	
T	F	1. One in two marriages ends in divorce.
T	F	2. Women are more likely to be assaulted than men.
T	F	3. Individuals who are abused as children will most likely grow up to abuse their own children.
T	F	4. Rates of murder and other violent crimes have steadily increased over the past twenty years.
T	F	5. Most Canadians have a postsecondary education.
T	F	6. The majority of poor children in Canada come from single-mother households.
T	F	7. Children who grow up in a family with gay parents are more likely to be gay.
T	F	8. Most people with AIDS are gay men.

Answers on page 6.

BOX 1.1 SOCIOLOGY AND EVERYDAY LIFE

Answers to the Sociology Quiz on Commonsense Knowledge

The answers to all of the questions are false. See below for a more detailed explanation of each of the answers.

1. **False.** Current estimates are that one in three marriages will end in divorce (Statistics Canada, 2003h).

2. **False.** Men and women stand about the same chance of becoming a victim of a *personal* crime. However, men are more likely to be victims of assault, with a rate of 92 per 1,000 men compared with 70 per 1,000 women (Statistics Canada, 2000a).

3. **False.** This myth is an oversimplification of a statistic that indicates a large number of parents who abuse their children were abused by their parents as children. This does not mean that individuals who were abused *will become* abusers. The research indicates a large number of child abuse victims do not become abusers as adults (Department of Justice, 2002).

4. **False.** While violent crime rates generally rose through the 1980s, they declined steadily throughout the 1990s and continue to decline. Homicide rates in 2004 were the lowest they had been in thirty-five years (Statistics Canada, 2004b).

5. **False.** Although Canadians today are more educated than ever, the most recent Census indicates that 20 percent of adult Canadians have university credentials and another 16 percent have a college diploma (Statistics Canada, 2001a).

6. **False.** Just over half of the children in low-income families live in two-parent families (Statistics Canada, 2002j).

7. **False.** The research has consistently shown that children raised by gay parents are no more likely to be homosexual than are children raised by heterosexual parents (Schlesinger, 1998).

8. **False.** The World Health Organization estimates that about 75 percent of the people with AIDS worldwide are heterosexual (UNAIDS, 2002).

the scientific community for their methods and the presentation of their findings. Although some sociologists argue that sociology must be completely value free—without distorting subjective (personal or emotional) bias—others do not think that total objectivity is an attainable or desirable goal when studying human behaviour. This issue will be discussed in Chapter 2 ("Sociological Research").

Sociologists attempt to discover patterns or commonalities in human behaviour. For example, when they study suicide, they look for patterns of behaviour even though *individuals* usually commit suicide and other *individuals* suffer as a result of these actions. Consequently, sociologists seek out the multiple causes and effects of suicide or other social issues. They analyze the impact of the problem not only from the standpoint of suicide victims but also from the standpoint of the effects of such behaviour on a given society. For some students of sociology, this perspective becomes a way of understanding their social world.

The Sociological Imagination

Sociologist C. Wright Mills (1959b) described sociological reasoning as the ***sociological imagination*—the ability to see the relationship between individual experiences and the larger society.** This awareness enables us to understand the link between our personal experiences and the social contexts in which they occur. The sociological imagination helps us distinguish between personal troubles and social (or public) issues. *Personal troubles* are private problems of individuals and the networks of people with whom they associate regularly. As a result, those problems must be solved by individuals within their immediate social settings. For example, one person being unemployed may be a personal trouble. *Public issues* are matters beyond an individual's own control that are caused by problems at the societal level. Widespread unemployment as a result of economic changes, such as plant closings, is an example of a public issue. The sociological imagination helps us place seemingly personal troubles, such as contemplating suicide or losing one's job, into a larger social context, where we can distinguish whether and how personal troubles may be related to public issues.

Suicide as a Personal Trouble Many of our individual experiences may be largely beyond our own control. They are determined by society as a whole—by its historical development and its organization. In everyday life, we do not define personal experiences in these terms. If a person commits suicide, many people consider it the result of the individual's personal problems. Historical explanations of suicide focused on suicide as personal trouble, viewing the act as sinful or criminal (Evans and Farberow, 1988). Suicide was believed to be part of an evolutionary process whereby "weak-brained individuals were sorted by insanity and voluntary death" (Morselli, 1975/1881).

Today, many experts who study suicide continue to focus on explanations of suicide that look to the individual's personal problems, psyche, or state of mind. For example, the Suicide Information & Education Centre explains that, "a suicidal person is feeling so much pain that they can see no other option. They feel they are a burden to others and in desperation see death as a way to escape their overwhelming pain and anguish" (2002).

BOX 1.2 SOCIOLOGY IN GLOBAL PERSPECTIVE

The Importance of a Global Sociological Imagination

Although existing sociological theory and research provide the foundation for sociological thinking, we must reach beyond past studies that have focused primarily on North America to develop a more comprehensive global approach for the future. In the twenty-first century, we face important challenges in a rapidly changing nation and world. The world's *high-income countries* are countries with highly industrialized economies, technologically advanced industrial, administrative, and service occupations, and relatively high levels of national and personal income. Examples include Australia, New Zealand, Japan, the European nations, Canada, and the United States. As compared with other countries of the world, most high-income countries offer a high standard of living and a lower death rate due to good nutrition and advances in medical technology.

In contrast, *middle-income countries* are countries with industrializing economies, particularly in urban areas, and moderate levels of national and personal income. Examples include the countries of Eastern Europe and many in Latin America, where countries, such as Brazil and Mexico, are industrializing rapidly. However, generalizations are difficult to make because these nations vary widely in levels of economic development and standards of living (see Chapter 9, "Global Stratification").

Low-income countries are primarily agrarian, with little industrialization and low levels of national and personal income. Examples include many of the countries of Africa and Asia, particularly the People's Republic of China and India, where people typically work the land and are among the poorest in the world. Suicide patterns in these countries vary widely from those in the most developed nations. For example, some social analysts suggest that the recent increase in suicides among the Kaiowá Indians in Brazil can be linked to the loss of their land (which previously was used to grow crops to feed their families) to large, foreign-owned agribusinesses. With loss of land has come loss of culture, because to the Kaiowá land is more than a means of surviving; it is the support for a social life that is directly linked to their system of belief and knowledge (Schemo, 1996).

Throughout this text, we will continue to develop our sociological imaginations by examining social life in Canada and other nations. The future of this country is deeply intertwined with the future of all nations of the world on economic, political, environmental, and humanitarian levels. We buy many goods and services that were produced in other nations, and sell much of what we produce to the people of other nations. Peace in other nations is important if we are to ensure peace within our own borders. Famine, unrest, and brutality in other regions of the world must be of concern to people in Canada. Global problems such as these contribute to the large influx of immigrants who arrive in this country annually. These immigrants bring with them a rich diversity of language, customs, religions, and previous life experiences; they also contribute to dramatic population changes that will have a long-term effect on this country. Developing a better understanding of diversity and tolerance for people who are different from us is important for our personal, social, and economic well-being in the twenty-first century.

Suicide as a Public Issue   We can use the sociological imagination to look at the problem of suicide as a public issue—a societal problem. For example, we may use our sociological imagination to understand why suicide rates are so high in some Aboriginal communities in Canada.

Early sociologist Émile Durkheim refused to accept commonsense explanations of suicide, such as the notion that suicide is an isolated act that can be understood only by studying individual personalities or inherited tendencies. Rather, he related suicide to the issue of cohesiveness (or lack of cohesiveness) in a society. In *Suicide* (1964b/1897), Durkheim documented his contention that a high suicide rate was symptomatic of large-scale social problems. In the process, he developed an approach that influences researchers to this day. Mills' *The Sociological Imagination* (1959a) remains useful for examining issues in the twenty-first century because it helps integrate microlevel (individual and small group) troubles with compelling issues of our day. Recently, his ideas have been applied at the global level as well.

Whatever your race/*ethnicity, class,* sex, or age, are you able to include in your thinking the perspectives of people who are different from you in experiences and points of view?

In forming your own sociological imagination and in seeing the possibilities for sociology, it will be helpful to understand the development of the discipline, beginning about one hundred years ago.

THE ORIGINS OF SOCIOLOGICAL THINKING

Throughout history, social philosophers and religious authorities have made countless observations about human behaviour, but the first systematic analysis of society is found in the philosophies of early Greek philosophers, such as Plato (c. 427–347 B.C.E.) and Aristotle (384–322 B.C.E.). For example, Aristotle was concerned with developing a system of knowledge, and he engaged in theorizing and empirical analysis of data collected from people in Greek cities regarding their views about social life when ruled by kings or aristocracies or when living in democracies (Collins, 1994). However, early thinkers, such as Plato and Aristotle, provided thoughts on what they believed society *ought* to be like, rather than describing how society actually *was.*

Social thought began to change rapidly in the seventeenth century with the scientific revolution. Like their predecessors in the natural sciences, social thinkers sought to develop a scientific understanding of social life, believing that their work might enable people to reach their full potential. The contributions of Isaac Newton (1642–1727) to modern science, including the discovery of the laws of gravity and motion and the development of calculus, inspired social thinkers to believe that similar advances could be made in systematically studying human behaviour. As Newton advanced the cause of physics and the natural sciences, he was viewed by many as the model of a true scientist. Moreover, his belief that the universe is an orderly, self-regulating system strongly influenced the thinking of early social theorists.

Sociology and the Age of Enlightenment

The origins of sociological thinking as we know it today can be traced to the scientific revolution in the late seventeenth and mid-eighteenth centuries and to the Age of Enlightenment. In this period of European thought, emphasis was placed on the individual's possession of critical reasoning and experience. There was also widespread skepticism of the primacy of religion as a source of knowledge and heartfelt opposition to traditional authority. A basic assumption of the Enlightenment was that scientific laws had been designed with a view to human happiness and that the "invisible hand" of either Providence or the emerging economic system of capitalism would ensure that the individual's pursuit of enlightened self-interest would always be conducive to the welfare of society as a whole.

In France, the Enlightenment (also referred to as the Age of Reason) was dominated by a group of thinkers referred to collectively as the *philosophes.* The philosophes included such well-known intellectuals as Charles Montesquieu (1689–1755), Jean-Jacques Rousseau (1712–1778), and Jacques Turgot (1727–1781). They defined a *philosophe* as one who, trampling on prejudice, tradition, universal consent, and authority—in a word, all that enslaves most minds—dares to think for himself, to go back and search for the clearest general principles, and to admit nothing except on the testimony of his experience and reason (Kramnick, 1995). For the most part, these men were optimistic about the future, believing that human society could be improved through scientific discoveries. In this view, if people

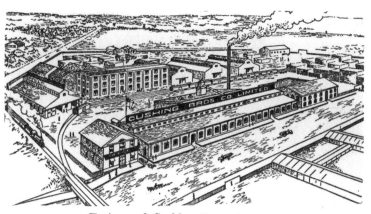

Factory of Cushing Bros. Co., Ltd.

As the Industrial Revolution swept through North America in the nineteenth century, sights such as this became increasingly common. The emerging factory system shifted the economic base in Canada from agriculture toward manufacturing.

were free from the ignorance and superstition of the past, they could create new forms of political and economic organization, such as democracy and capitalism, which would eventually produce wealth and destroy aristocracy and other oppressive forms of political leadership.

Although women were categorically excluded from much of public life in France because of the sexism of the day, some women strongly influenced the philosophes and their thinking through their participation in the *salon*—an open house held to stimulate discussion and intellectual debate. Salons provided a place for intellectuals and authors to discuss ideas and opinions and for women and men to engage in witty repartee regarding the issues of the day, but the "brotherhood" of philosophes typically viewed the women primarily as good listeners or mistresses more than as intellectual equals, even though the men sometimes later adopted the women's ideas as if they were their own. However, the writings of Mary Wollstonecraft (1759–1797) reflect the Enlightenment spirit, and her works have recently received recognition for influencing people's thoughts on the idea of human equality, particularly as it relates to social equality and women's right to education.

For women and men alike, the idea of observing how people lived in order to find out what they thought, and doing so in a systematic manner that could be verified, did not take hold until sweeping political and economic changes in the late eighteenth and early nineteenth centuries caused many people to realize that many of the answers provided by philosophers and theologians to some very pressing questions no longer seemed relevant. Many of these questions concerned the social upheaval brought about by the age of revolution, particularly the American Revolution of 1776 and the French Revolution of 1789, and the rapid industrialization and urbanization that occurred first in Britain, then in Western Europe, and later in the United States.

Sociology and the Age of Revolution, Industrialization, and Urbanization

Several types of revolution that took place in the eighteenth century had a profound influence on the origins of sociology. The Enlightenment produced an intellectual revolution in how people thought about social change, progress, and critical thinking. The optimistic views of the philosophes and other social thinkers regarding progress and equal opportunity (at least for some people) became part of the impetus for political and economic revolutions, first in America and then in France. The Enlightenment thinkers had emphasized a sense of common purpose and hope for human progress; the French Revolution and its aftermath replaced these ideals with discord and overt conflict (see Schama, 1989; Arendt, 1973a).

During the nineteenth and early twentieth centuries, another form of revolution also occurred: the Industrial Revolution. **Industrialization is the process by which societies are transformed from dependence on agriculture and handmade products to an emphasis on manufacturing and related industries.** This process first occurred during the Industrial Revolution in Britain between 1760 and 1850 and was soon repeated throughout Western Europe. By the mid-nineteenth century, industrialization was well under way in Canada and the United States. Massive economic, technological, and social changes occurred as machine technology and the factory system shifted the economic base of these nations from agriculture to manufacturing. A new social

As Canada continues to become increasingly diverse, sociologists need to recognize the importance of taking all people's experiences into account as we confront public issues.

class of industrialists emerged in textiles, iron smelting, and related industries. Many people who had laboured on the land were forced to leave their tightly knit rural communities and sacrifice well-defined social relationships to seek employment as factory workers in the emerging cities, which became the centres of industrial work.

Urbanization accompanied modernization and the rapid process of industrialization. *Urbanization* **is the process by which an increasing proportion of a population lives in cities rather than in rural areas.** Although cities existed long before the Industrial Revolution, the development of the factory system led to a rapid increase in both the number of cities and the size of their populations. People from very diverse backgrounds worked together in the same factory. At the same time, many people shifted from being *producers* to being *consumers*. For example, families living in the cities had to buy food with their wages because they could no longer grow their own crops to consume or to barter for other resources. Similarly, people had to pay rent for their lodging because they could no longer exchange their services for shelter.

These living and working conditions led to the development of new social problems: inadequate housing, crowding, unsanitary conditions, poverty, pollution, and crime. Wages were so low that entire families—including very young children—were forced to work, often under hazardous conditions and with no job security. As these conditions became more visible, a new breed of social thinkers turned its attention to trying to understand why and how society was changing.

THE DEVELOPMENT OF MODERN SOCIOLOGY

At the same time that urban problems were growing worse, natural scientists had been using reason, or rational thinking, to discover the laws of physics and the movement of the planets. Social thinkers started to believe that by applying the methods developed by the natural sciences, they might discover the laws of human behaviour and apply these laws to solve social problems. Historically, the time was ripe for such thoughts because the Age of Enlightenment had produced a belief in reason and humanity's ability to perfect itself.

Early Thinkers: A Concern with Social Order and Stability

Early social thinkers—such as Auguste Comte, Harriet Martineau, Herbert Spencer, and Émile Durkheim—were interested in analyzing social order and stability, and many of their ideas had a dramatic influence on modern sociology.

Auguste Comte French philosopher Auguste Comte (1798–1857) coined the term *sociology* from the Latin *socius* ("social, being with others") and the Greek *logos* ("study of") to describe a new science that would engage in the study of society. Even though he never actually conducted sociological research, Comte is considered by some to be the "founder of sociology." Comte's theory that societies contain *social statics* (forces for social order and stability) and *social dynamics* (forces for conflict and change) continues to be used, although not in these exact terms, in contemporary sociology.

Drawing heavily on the ideas of his mentor, Count Henri de Saint-Simon, Comte stressed that the methods of the natural sciences should be applied to the objective study of society. Saint-Simon's primary interest in studying society was social reform, but Comte sought to unlock the secrets of society so that intellectuals like himself could become the new secular (as contrasted with religious) "high priests" of society (Nisbet, 1979). For Comte, the best policies involved order and authority. He envisioned that a new consensus would emerge on social issues and that the new science of sociology would play a significant part in the reorganization of society (Lenzer, 1998).

Comte's philosophy became known as ***positivism***— **a belief that the world can best be understood through scientific inquiry.** Comte believed that

Auguste Comte

objective, bias-free knowledge was attainable only through the use of science, rather than religion. However, scientific knowledge was "relative knowledge," not absolute and final. Comte's positivism had two dimensions: (1) methodological—the application of scientific knowledge to both physical and social phenomena—and (2) social and political—the use of such knowledge to predict the likely results of different policies so that the best one could be chosen.

What did Comte actually mean by positivism? Some recent scholars have suggested that Comte's ideas regarding positivism are often misinterpreted. They believe he was arguing that we should limit what we consider to be "valid knowledge" to those testable statements that have proved to be true. In this view, Comte was not advocating that the social sciences should merely imitate the methods of the natural sciences; rather, he was developing a historical and differential theory of science based upon distinguishing levels of complexity (Heilbron, 1995).

The ideas of Saint-Simon and Comte regarding the objective, scientific study of society are deeply embedded in the discipline of sociology. Of particular importance is Comte's idea that the nature of

human thinking and knowledge passed through several stages as societies evolved from simple to more complex. Comte described how the idea systems and their corresponding social structural arrangements changed according to what he termed the *law of the three stages:* the theological, metaphysical, and scientific (or positivistic) stages. Comte believed that knowledge began in the *theological stage*—explanations were based on religion and the supernatural. Next, knowledge moved to the *metaphysical stage*—explanations were based on abstract philosophical speculation. Finally, knowledge would reach the *scientific* or *positive stage*—explanations are based on systematic observation, experimentation, comparison, and historical analysis. Shifts in the forms of knowledge in societies were linked to changes in the structural systems of society. In the theological stage, kinship was the most prominent unit of society; however, in the metaphysical stage, the state became the prominent unit, and control shifted from small groups to the state, military, and law. In the scientific or positive stage, industry became the prominent structural unit in society, and scientists became the spiritual leaders, replacing in importance the priests and philosophers of the previous stages of knowledge. For Comte, this progression through the three stages constituted the basic law of social dynamics, and, when coupled with the laws of statics (which emphasized social order and stability), constituted the new science of sociology, which could bring about positive social change.

Social analysts have praised Comte for his advocacy of sociology and his contributions to positivism. His insights regarding linkages between the social structural elements of society (such as family, religion, and government) and social thinking in specific historical epochs were useful to later sociologists. However, a number of contemporary sociologists argue that Comte, among others, brought about an overemphasis on the "natural science model" that has been detrimental to sociology (Vaughan, Sjoberg, and Reynolds, 1993). Still others state that sociology, while claiming to be "scientific" and "objective," has focused on the experiences of a privileged few, to the exclusion by class, gender, race, ethnicity, and age of all others (Harding, 1986; Collins, 1990).

Harriet Martineau Comte's works were made more accessible for a wide variety of scholars through the efforts of British sociologist Harriet Martineau (1802–1876). Until recently, Martineau received no recognition in the field of sociology, partly because she was a woman in a male-dominated discipline and society. Not only did she translate and condense Comte's work, but she also was an active sociologist in her own right. Martineau studied the social customs of Britain and the United States, and analyzed the consequences of industrialization and capitalism. In *Society in America* (1962/1837), she examined religion, politics, child rearing, slavery, and immigration in the United States, paying special attention to social distinctions based on class, race, and gender. Her works explore the status of women, children, and "sufferers" (persons who were considered to be criminal, mentally ill, handicapped, poor, or alcoholic).

Based on her reading of Mary Wollstonecraft's *A Vindication of the Rights of Women* (1974/1797), Martineau advocated racial and gender equality. She was also committed to creating a science of society that would be grounded in empirical observations and widely accessible to people. She argued that sociologists should be impartial in their assessment of society but that it is entirely appropriate to compare the existing state of society with the principles on which it was founded (Lengermann and Niebrugge-Brantley, 1998).

Recently, some scholars have argued that Martineau's place in the history of sociology should be as a founding member of this field of study,

Harriet Martineau

not just as the translator of Auguste Comte's work (Hoecker-Drysdale, 1992; Lengermann and Niebrugge-Brantley, 1998). Others have highlighted her influence in spreading the idea that societal progress could be brought about by the spread of democracy and the growth of industrial capitalism (Polanyi, 1944). Martineau believed that a better society would emerge if women and men were treated equally, enlightened reform occurred, and cooperation existed among people in all social classes (but led by the middle class).

In keeping with the sociological imagination, Martineau not only analyzed large-scale social structures in society but also explored how these factors influenced the lives of people, particularly women, children, and those who were marginalized by virtue of being criminal, mentally ill, disabled, poor, or alcoholic (Lengermann and Niebrugge-Brantley, 1998). She remained convinced that sociology, the "true science of human nature," could bring about new knowledge and understanding, enlarging people's capacity to create a just society and live heroic lives (Hoecker-Drysdale, 1992).

Herbert Spencer   Unlike Comte, who was strongly influenced by the upheavals of the French Revolution, British social theorist Herbert Spencer (1820–1903) was born in a more peaceful and optimistic period in his country's history. Spencer's major contribution to sociology was an evolutionary perspective on social order and social change. Although the term *evolution* has various meanings, evolutionary theory should be taken to mean "a theory to explain the mechanisms of organic/social change" (Haines, 1997:81). According to Spencer's theory of general evolution, society, like a biological organism, has various interdependent parts (such as the family, the economy, and the government) that work to ensure the stability and survival of the entire society.

Spencer believed that societies developed through a process of "struggle" (for existence) and "fitness" (for survival), which he referred to as the "survival of the fittest." Because this phrase is often attributed to Charles Darwin, Spencer's view of society is known as ***social Darwinism—the belief that those species of animals (including human beings) best adapted to their environment survive and prosper, whereas those poorly adapted die out.*** Spencer equated this process of *natural selection* with progress, because only the "fittest" members of society would survive the competition; the "unfit" would be filtered out of society. Based on this belief, he strongly opposed any social reform that might interfere with the natural selection process and, thus, damage society by favouring its least worthy members.

Critics have suggested that many of Spencer's ideas had serious flaws. For one thing, societies are not the same as biological systems; people are able to create and transform the environment in which they live. Moreover, the notion of the survival of the fittest can easily be used to justify class, racial–ethnic, and gender inequalities and to rationalize the lack of action to eliminate harmful practices that contribute to such inequalities. Not surprisingly, Spencer's "hands-off" view was applauded by wealthy industrialists of his day. John D. Rockefeller, who gained monopolistic control of much of the U.S. oil industry early in the twentieth century, maintained that the growth of giant businesses was merely the "survival of the fittest" (Feagin and Feagin, 1997).

Social Darwinism served as a rationalization for some people's assertion of the superiority of the white race. After the American Civil War, it was used to justify the repression and neglect of African Americans as well as the policies that resulted in the annihilation of Native American populations. Although some social reformers spoke out against these justifications, "scientific" racism continued to exist (Turner, Singleton, and Musick, 1984). In both positive and negative ways, many of Spencer's ideas and concepts have been deeply embedded in social thinking and public policy for over a century.

Émile Durkheim French sociologist Émile Durkheim (1858–1917) criticized some of Spencer's views while incorporating others into his own writing. Durkheim stressed that people are the product of their social environment and that behaviour cannot be fully understood in terms of *individual* biological and psychological traits. He believed that the limits of human potential are *socially*, not *biologically*, based. As Durkheim saw religious traditions evaporating in his society, he searched for a scientific, rational way to provide for societal integration and stability (Hadden, 1997).

In his work *The Rules of Sociological Method* (1964a/1895), Durkheim set forth one of his most important contributions to sociology: the idea that societies are built on social facts. **Social facts are patterned ways of acting, thinking, and feeling that exist outside any one individual** but that exert social control over each person. Durkheim believed that social facts must be explained by other social facts— by reference to the social structure rather than to individual attributes.

Émile Durkheim

Durkheim was concerned with social order and social stability because he lived during the period of rapid social changes in Europe resulting from industrialization and urbanization. His recurring question was this: How do societies manage to hold together? In *The Division of Labor in Society* (1933/1893), Durkheim concluded that preindustrial societies were held together by strong traditions and by members' shared moral beliefs and values. As societies industrialized, more specialized economic activity became the basis of the social bond because people became interdependent on one another.

Durkheim observed that rapid social change and a more specialized division of labour produce *strains* in society. These strains lead to a breakdown in traditional organization, values, and authority and to a dramatic increase in ***anomie***—**a condition in which social control becomes ineffective as a result of the loss of shared values and of a sense of purpose in society.** According to Durkheim, anomie is most likely to occur during a period of rapid social change. In *Suicide* (1964b/1897), he explored the relationship between anomic social conditions and suicide, as discussed in Chapter 2.

Durkheim's contributions to sociology are so significant that he has been referred to as "*the* crucial figure in the development of sociology as an academic discipline [and as] one of the deepest roots of the socio-logical imagination" (Tiryakian, 1978:187). He has long been viewed as a proponent of the scientific approach to examining social facts that lie outside individuals. He is also described as the founding figure of the functionalist theoretical tradition. Recently, scholars have acknowledged Durkheim's influence on contemporary social theory, including the structuralist and postmodernist schools of thought. Like Comte, Martineau, and Spencer, Durkheim emphasized that sociology should be a science based on observation and the systematic study of social facts rather than on individual characteristics or traits.

Although they acknowledge Durkheim's impor-tant contributions, some critics note that his emphasis on societal stability, or the "problem of order"—how society can establish and maintain social stability and cohesiveness—obscures the *subjective meaning* that individuals give to social phenomena, such as religion, work, and suicide. In this view, overemphasis on *structure* and the determining power of "society" resulted in a corre-sponding neglect of *agency,* the beliefs and actions of the actors involved, in much of Durkheim's theorizing (Zeitlin, 1997).

Differing Views on the Status Quo: Stability versus Change

Together with Karl Marx, Max Weber, and Georg Simmel, Durkheim established the course for modern sociology. We will look first at Marx's and Weber's divergent thoughts about conflict and social change in societies, and then at Simmel's analysis of society.

Karl Marx   In sharp contrast to Durkheim's focus on the stability of society, German economist and philosopher Karl Marx (1818–1883) stressed that his-tory is a continuous clash between conflicting ideas and forces. He believed that conflict—especially class conflict—is necessary in order to produce social change and a better society. For Marx, the most important changes were economic. He concluded that the capitalist economic system was responsible for the overwhelming poverty that he observed in London at the beginning of the Industrial Revolution (Marx and Engels, 1967/1848).

In the Marxian framework, **class conflict is the struggle between the capitalist class and the working class.** The capitalist class, or **bourgeoisie, comprises those who own and control the *means***

Karl Marx

of production*—the tools, land, factories, and money for investment that form the economic basis of a society.** The working class, or ***proletariat, **is composed of those who must sell their labour because they have no other means to earn a liveli-hood.** From Marx's viewpoint, the capitalist class controls and exploits the masses of struggling workers by paying less than the value of their labour. This exploitation results in workers' ***alienation*—a feeling of powerlessness and estrangement from other people and from oneself.** Marx predicted that the working class would become aware of its exploitation, overthrow the capitalists, and establish a free and classless society.

Marx's theories provide a springboard for neo-Marxist analysts and other scholars to examine the economic, political, and social relations embedded in production and consumption in historical and con-temporary societies. But what is Marx's place in the history of sociology? Marx is regarded as one of the most profound sociological thinkers, one who com-bined ideas derived from philosophy, history, and the social sciences into a new theoretical configuration. However, his social and economic analyses have also inspired heated debates among generations of social scientists. Central to his views was the belief that society should not just be studied but should also be changed, because the status quo (the existing state of society) involved the oppression of most of the population by a small group of wealthy people. Those who believe that sociology should be value free are uncomfortable with Marx's advocacy of what some perceive to be radical social change. Scholars who examine society through the lens of race, gender, and class believe that his analysis places too much emphasis on class relations, often to the exclusion of issues regarding race/ethnicity and gender. In regard to power differences between women and men, Marx believed that the primary form of oppression was rooted in *class divisions*. He justified his explanation by noting that gender and class divisions were not present in the earliest forms of human society; men first came into power over women when class divisions emerged. Then the institution of marriage established that women were a form of "private property" to be owned by men. According to Marx, women would become free from this bondage only when class divisions were overcome. Some scholars have criticized this notion, arguing that it does not fully reflect the nature of men's and women's power relations (see Hartmann, 1981). Marx also viewed power differentials across racial–ethnic lines as being primarily *class* divisions. Critics disagree with the notion that racial–ethnic inequalities can be reduced to class divisions, meaning that racism can be eradicated only after the class struggle has been won (Martin and Cohen, 1980).

In recent decades, scholars have shown renewed interest in Marx's *social theory,* as opposed to his radical ideology (see Postone, 1997; Lewis, 1998). Throughout this text, we will continue to explore Marx's various contributions to sociological thinking.

Max Weber   German social scientist Max Weber (pronounced VAY-ber) (1864–1920) was also concerned about the changes brought about by the Industrial Revolution. Although he disagreed with Marx's idea that economics is *the* central force in social change, Weber acknowledged that economic interests are important in shaping human action. Even so, he thought that economic systems are heavily influenced by other factors in a society. As we will see in Chapter 17 ("Religion"), one of Weber's most important works, *The Protestant Ethic and the Spirit of Capitalism* (1976/1904–1905), evaluated the role of the Protestant Reformation in producing a social climate in which capitalism could exist and flourish.

Unlike many early analysts, who believed that values could not be separated from the research process, Weber emphasized that sociology should be

Max Weber

value free—that is, research should be conducted in a scientific manner and should exclude the researcher's personal values and economic interests (Turner, Beeghley, and Powers, 1998). However, Weber realized that social behaviour cannot be analyzed by the objective criteria that we use to measure such things as temperature or weight. Although he recognized that sociologists cannot be totally value free, Weber stressed that they should employ *verstehen* (German for "understanding" or "insight") to gain the ability to see the world as others see it. In contemporary sociology, Weber's idea has been incorporated into the concept of the sociological imagination (discussed earlier in this chapter).

Weber was also concerned that large-scale organizations (bureaucracies) were becoming increasingly oriented toward routine administration and a specialized division of labour, which he believed were destructive to human vitality and freedom. According to Weber, rational bureaucracy, rather than class struggle, was the most significant factor in determining the social relations among people in industrial societies. In this view, bureaucratic domination can be used to maintain powerful (capitalist) interests in society. As we will see in Chapter 6 ("Groups and Organizations"), Weber's work on bureaucracy has had a far-reaching impact.

According to the sociologist Georg Simmel, society is a web of patterned interactions among people. If we focus on the behaviour of individuals in isolation, such as any one of the members of this women's rowing team, we may miss the underlying forms that make up the "geometry of social life."

Weber made significant contributions to modern sociology by emphasizing the goal of value-free inquiry and the necessity of understanding how others see the world. He also provided important insights on the process of rationalization, bureaucracy, religion, and many other topics. In his writings, Weber was more aware of women's issues than were many of the scholars of his day. Perhaps his awareness at least partially resulted from the fact that his wife, Marianne Weber, was an important figure in the women's movement in Germany in the early twentieth century (Roth, 1988).

Georg Simmel   At about the same time that Durkheim was developing the field of sociology in France, the German sociologist Georg Simmel (pronounced ZIM-mel) (1858–1918) was theorizing about society as a web of patterned interactions among people. The main purpose of sociology, according to Simmel, should be to examine these social interaction processes within groups. In *The Sociology of Georg Simmel* (1950/1902–1917), he analyzed how social interactions vary depending on the size of the social group. He concluded that interaction patterns differed between a *dyad,* a social group with two members, and a *triad,* a social group with three members. He developed *formal sociology,* an approach that focuses attention on the universal, recurring social forms that underlie the varying content of social interaction. Simmel referred to these forms as the "geometry of social life." He also distinguished between the *forms* of social interaction (such as cooperation or conflict) and the *content* of social interaction in different contexts (for example, between leaders and followers).

Like the other social thinkers of his day, Simmel analyzed the impact of industrialization and urbanization on people's lives. He concluded that class conflict was becoming more pronounced in modern industrial societies. He also linked the increase in individualism, as opposed to concern for the group, to the fact that people now had many cross-cutting "social spheres"— membership in a number of organizations and voluntary associations—rather than having the singular community ties of the past. Simmel also assessed the costs of "progress" on the upper-class city dweller, who, he believed, had to develop certain techniques to survive the overwhelming stimulation of the city. Simmel's ultimate concern was to protect the autonomy of the individual in society.

The Development of Sociology in North America

From Western Europe, sociology spread in the 1890s to the United States, and in the early 1900s to Canada. It thrived in both countries as a result of the intellectual climate and the rapid rate of social change. The first department of sociology in the United States was established at the University of Chicago in 1892. Robert E. Park (1864–1944), an original member of the Chicago School, assisted in the development of the sociology of urban life (see Chapter 19, "Population and Urbanization").

George Herbert Mead (1863–1931), a sociologist and social psychologist, became one of the best-known members of the Chicago School and the founder of the symbolic interaction perspective, which is discussed later in this chapter. The University of Chicago continues to be an important centre for sociological research and instruction.

In the early years, women were welcomed to sociology departments, such as the University of Chicago's. However, as the departments became more established, a number of its male members became disenchanted with their own earlier radical ideas, including feminism. When many of the women were unable to gain more than a temporary foothold in academic sociology, they sought employment in the emerging field of social work. This change marked the beginning of a dual system of sex-segregated labour, whereby sociology became male-dominated and social work became female-dominated (Deegan, 1988).

Jane Addams (1860–1935) is one of the best-known early women sociologists because she founded Hull House, one of the most famous settlement houses, in an impoverished area of Chicago. Throughout her career she actively engaged in sociological endeavours. She lectured at numerous colleges, was a charter member of the American Sociological Society, and published a number of articles and books. Although Addams was awarded a Nobel Peace Prize for her contributions to the field of social work and her assistance to the underprivileged, her sociological work was not acknowledged until recently.

The second department of sociology in the United States was founded by W. E. B. Du Bois (1868–1963) at Atlanta University. Du Bois's classic work *The Philadelphia Negro: A Social Study* (1967/1899), was based on his research into Philadelphia's African American community and stressed the strengths and weaknesses of a community wrestling with overwhelming social problems. Over the years, he became frustrated with the lack of progress in race relations and helped found the National Association for the Advancement of Colored People (NAACP).

The first sociology department in Canada was established in 1925 at McGill University in Montreal. The faculty consisted of Carl A. Dawson and Everett Hughes. Dawson modelled the McGill sociology department after the University of Chicago's, at which he was trained. Although other Canadian universities offered sociology courses through other departments, particularly history and economics, McGill had the only independent sociology department until the early 1960s (Denton and Hunter, 1995).

The University of Toronto, although equally influential in the field, had a very different approach to sociology than McGill. Sociology courses were taught as part of the department of political economy and did not form an independent department until 1963. Modelled on British sociology, the sociology taught at the University of Toronto focused on how issues of political and economic history affected Canadian society. The works of Harold A. Innis and S. D. Clark laid the groundwork for the political economy perspective, which is central to Canadian sociology today.

By the late 1960s, sociology departments had been established across the country. The first Canadian sociology journal, the *Canadian Review of Sociology*

George H. Mead

Patricia Marchak

and Anthropology, began publication in 1964. The Canadian Sociology and Anthropology Association was established in 1965 with a membership of under 200. However, at this time no significant government or private agency for sociological research existed in Canada, and only about a dozen books had been written by accredited Canadian sociologists (Brym and Fox, 1989).

The 1970s was a period of "Canadianization" of sociology in Canada. Prior to this time, Canadian sociology departments had tended to hire sociologists trained in the United States and to use American textbooks. During the 1970s, pressure was put on universities to hire sociologists trained in Canada. As a result, graduate programs across Canada were developed and expanded. A unique sociology was developed that focused on Canadian issues such as regionalism, ethnic relations, multiculturalism, and national identity, as well as issues common to all societies such as social inequalities created by social class, race and ethnicity, or gender. Canadian works such as John Porter's 1965 book *The Vertical Mosaic* and Patricia Marchak's *Ideological Perspectives on Canadian Society,* published in 1975, became landmarks in Canadian sociology (Denton and Hunter, 1995).

BOX 1.3 CRITICAL THINKING

From Sociological Illiteracy to Sociological Imagination

By Judith Shapiro

At one point in the mid-1980's, when I was teaching, I started paying attention to a common phrase, repeated like a mantra by students there and elsewhere: "racism, sexism, and classism." I had heard the phrase so often that I had become quite used to it, but it suddenly struck me as odd.

The terms racism and sexism seemed unproblematic enough, referring to discrimination based on what we take to be physical differences of one kind of another. But what did classism really mean? Although my 1960's ears were expecting to hear students talk about class, instead I was hearing about classism. Had the students been talking about class, they would have discussed the structure of our society, and how socioeconomic inequalities were built into it. In fact, talk of that kind was relatively rare in students' political conversations. Rather, they seemed to be concerned about individuals—prejudice against individuals belonging to less-privileged socioeconomic groups.

That discovery led me to wonder how the students saw race and gender. Were they also viewing racism and sexism exclusively in terms of individual identities and interpersonal relationships? If so, what did that say about the students' chances for improving the world? Had the goal of creating a more just society dwindled down into a matter of sensitivity training?

I realized, however, that I was being unfair to the students. For one thing, they were living in a far more diverse community than I had known in my undergraduate days; navigating a culturally complex universe of fellow students was for them a significant task. Although some were retreating from that project, and spending most of their time with those who were most like them, others were reaching out, realizing that the reason a college assembles a diverse group of students is to extend their horizons.

Moreover, our success in transforming the liberal-arts college into a kind of utopia was insulating our students from certain realities and decisions. To give them the freedom to explore intellectual, professional, and social options, we were housing and feeding them, and providing them with health care.

And yet, those students of the 1980's were missing something important, something we should have given them during their college years. Too many of them were deficient in the skills needed for analyzing society in economic, political, and structural terms. They seemed unable to move beyond their immediate experience to see how that experience was shaped by larger social and historical forces. They were suffering from a lack of what the eminent sociologist C. Wright Mills called "the sociological imagination"—which is in short supply among today's students as well.

I have come to refer to that condition as sociological illiteracy. Just as a person may be illiterate in the most literal sense (unable to read or write), or scientifically illiterate, or innumerate (as we have come to call someone who lacks quantitative skills), so a person may be uneducated in the social sciences, and thus unable to make use of the insights and tools that those disciplines provide.

When people are ignorant about quantum mechanics or medieval literature, they are generally aware of their ignorance, readily admit it, and understand that the remedy for their ignorance is serious and systematic study. When, however, the subject is how societies operate, or why people behave the way they do, the situation is different. Confusing their folk beliefs with knowledge, people typically don't realize their ignorance.

We all walk around with theories in our heads about the social world in which we move—indeed, we could not operate without them. In that sense, we are all social scientists. But most of us are bad ones.

Because they question familiar assumptions, and also because they sometimes seem to be making heavy weather of things we all think we understand already, social scientists are the folks that people love to hate. Anthropologists get blamed for the fact that culture now refers not only to *Paradise Lost* and Beethoven's Ninth Symphony, but also to nose rings and televised wrestling. Sociologists generally fare even worse in public esteem, because they lack the redeeming features of being exotic and entertaining. Besides, they have a habit of trying to get us to think about unpleasant matters, such as urban poverty and teenage pregnancy.

Given the level of estrangement between social scientists and the public, it is not surprising that sociological illiteracy is revealed in a number of the major policy debates currently engaging our national attention—for example, affirmative action. Whenever I hear the policy described as a form of reverse racism, I know that I am in the presence of someone who is, at best, semiliterate—sociologically speaking. There is, in fact, no form of discrimination against white people in our society that mirrors the systemic, pervasive, and often unconscious discrimination that persists against Black people, despite the considerable progress we have made since the end of slavery.

Returning to our students: Many undergraduates today demonstrate impressive levels of civic engagement in the form of community service. They serve meals in soup kitchens, work in homeless shelters, and staff AIDS hot lines. They work as interns in a variety of social agencies. Too few of them, however, are able to raise their eyes to the level of policy and social structure. They need the sociological imagination to see how their on-the-ground activities fit into a bigger picture, so that more of them can cross the bridge from serious moral commitment to effective political participation.

As teachers, we must admit our share of responsibility for that state of affairs. We need to adjust the focus between what we want to teach and what our students need to learn. Those of us who are faculty members in the social sciences must be sure that we are providing to all of our students, majors and nonmajors alike, basic tools of social and cultural understanding, as they have evolved over time in our various disciplines.

As faculty members, we must remember that our responsibilities extend beyond the academy. Sociologists such as Mills wrote with a force and grace that enabled them to reach a wide audience. We have not seen their like in years—too many years. More of us must follow their example and write for the general reader. And we should encourage our students—so full of energy, intelligence, and commitment—to move beyond the *personal* to the political.

CONTEMPORARY THEORETICAL PERSPECTIVES

Given the many and varied ideas and trends that influenced the development of sociology, how do contemporary sociologists view society? Some see it as basically a stable and ongoing entity; others view it in terms of many groups competing for scarce resources; still others describe it as based on the everyday, routine interactions among individuals. Each of these views represents a method of examining the same phenomena. Each is based on general ideas as to how social life is organized and represents an effort to link specific observations in a meaningful way. Each utilizes *theory*—**a set of logically interrelated statements that attempts to describe, explain, and (occasionally) predict social events.** Each theory helps interpret reality in a distinct way by providing a framework in which observations may be logically ordered. Sociologists refer to this theoretical framework as a *perspective*—**an overall approach to or viewpoint on some subject.** The major theoretical perspectives that have emerged in sociology include the functionalist, conflict, feminist, and interactionist perspectives. Other perspectives, such as postmodernism, have emerged and gained acceptance among some social thinkers more recently. Before turning to the specifics of these perspectives, we should note that some theorists and theories do not fit neatly into any of these perspectives. Nevertheless, these perspectives will be used throughout this book to show you how sociologists try to understand many of the issues affecting Canadian society.

Functionalist Perspectives

Also known as *functionalism* and *structural functionalism*, **functionalist perspectives are based on the assumption that society is a stable, orderly system.** This stable system is characterized by **societal consensus, whereby the majority of members share a common set of values, beliefs, and behavioural expectations.** According to this perspective, a society is composed of interrelated parts, each of which serves a function and (ideally) contributes to the overall stability of the society. Since this approach was influenced by Comte, Spencer, and Durkheim, who often drew on the work of natural scientists, early functionalists compared society to a living, evolving organism. Societies develop social structures, or institutions, that persist because they play a part in helping society survive. These institutions include the family, education, government, religion, and the economy. If anything adverse happens to one of these institutions or parts, all other parts are affected and the system no longer functions properly. As Durkheim noted, rapid social change and a more specialized division of labour produce *strains* in society that lead to a breakdown in these traditional institutions and may result in social problems, such as increased rates of crime and suicide.

Talcott Parsons and Robert Merton

Talcott Parsons (1902–1979), a founder of the sociology department at Harvard University, was perhaps the most influential contemporary advocate of the functionalist perspective. He stressed that all societies must make provisions for meeting social needs in order to survive (Parsons, 1951; Parsons and Shils, 1951). For example, Parsons (1955) suggested that a division of labour (distinct, specialized functions) between husband and wife is essential for family stability and social order. The husband/father performs the *instrumental tasks,* which involve leadership and decision-making responsibilities in the home and employment outside the home to support the family. The wife/mother is responsible for the *expressive tasks,* including housework, caring for the children, and providing emotional support for the entire family. Parsons believed that other institutions, including school, church, and government, must function to assist the family and that all institutions must work together to preserve the system over time (Parsons, 1955). Although Parsons's analysis has been criticized for its conservative bias, his work still influences sociological thinking about gender roles and the family.

Functionalism was refined further by a student of Parsons, Robert K. Merton (1910–2003), who distinguished between manifest and latent functions of social institutions. **Manifest functions are intended and/or overtly recognized by the participants in a social unit.** In contrast, *latent functions* **are unintended functions that are hidden and remain unacknowledged by participants.** For example, a manifest function of education is the transmission of knowledge and skills from one generation to the next; a latent function is the establishment of social relations and networks. Merton noted that all features of a social system may not be functional at all times; *dysfunctions* **are the undesirable consequences of any element of a society.** A dysfunction of education can be the perpetuation of gender, racial, and class inequalities. Such dysfunctions may threaten the capacity of a society to adapt and survive (Merton, 1968).

Between 1945 and 1960, the functionalist perspective flourished in sociology; however, social strife during the 1960s exposed the limitations of this perspective. Critics questioned Parsons's rigid differentiation of gender roles and his assumption that the public sphere belonged to men and the private sphere to women. The functional perspective also was criticized for its tendency to legitimize the status quo without effectively examining conflict and social change. Recently, functionalism has experienced a resurgence and now is referred to by some as "neofunctionalism" (see Alexander, 1985).

Applying a Functionalist Perspective to Suicide

How might functionalists analyze the problem of suicide, which we examined at the beginning of this chapter? Although a number of possible functionalist explanations exist, we will look briefly at only one. Most functionalists emphasize the importance of shared moral values and strong social bonds to a society. When rapid social change or other disruptive conditions occur, moral values may erode, people may become more uncertain about how to act, and suicide rates may therefore increase.

In his classic study of suicide, functionalist Émile Durkheim (1964b/1897) argued that suicide rates are a reflection of the degree in a society of *social solidarity*—**that is, the state of having shared beliefs and values among members of a social group, along with intense and frequent interaction among group members.** According to Durkheim, people are most likely to kill themselves when social solidarity is either very weak or very strong.

Durkheim collected data from vital statistics for approximately 26,000 suicides and classified them according to variables, such as age, sex, marital status, family size, religion, geographic location, and method of suicide. From this analysis, he was able to identify four distinct categories of suicide: egoistic, anomic, altruistic, and fatalistic. *Egoistic suicide* occurs among people who are isolated from any social group. For example, Durkheim concluded that suicide rates were relatively high in Protestant countries in Europe because Protestants were more loosely tied to the church than were Catholics. Similarly, single people had proportionately higher suicide rates than married persons because they had a low degree of social integration, which contributed to their loneliness. In contrast, *altruistic suicide* occurs among individuals who are excessively integrated into society. An example is soldiers who kill themselves after defeat in battle because they have so strongly identified with their cause that they believe they cannot live with the shame of defeat.

Durkheim recognized that the degree of social integration is not the only variable that influences the suicide rate. In keeping with the functionalist perspective, Durkheim emphasized the importance of social stability and social consensus. Rapid social change and shifts in moral values make it difficult for people to know what is right and wrong. *Anomic suicide* results from a lack of shared values or purpose and from the absence of social regulation. In contrast, excessive regulation and oppressive discipline may contribute to *fatalistic suicide,* as in the suicide of slaves.

Although Durkheim's analysis of suicide was developed in the nineteenth century, it can be used to understand suicide rates among categories of people in Canada today. For example, the rate of suicide among Aboriginal people in Canada is two to three times higher than that of non-Aboriginal people (see Figure 1.2). Centuries of attempts to assimilate Aboriginal people have resulted in a weakening of traditional Aboriginal cultures. Government intervention in the form of such policies as relocating First Nations people to reserves, prohibiting traditional religious or spiritual practices, sending Aboriginal children to residential schools, and destroying Aboriginal people's economic base have resulted in social breakdown and disorganization in many Aboriginal communities.

| Figure 1.2 | Aboriginal and Non-Aboriginal Suicide Rates, 1979–1991 |

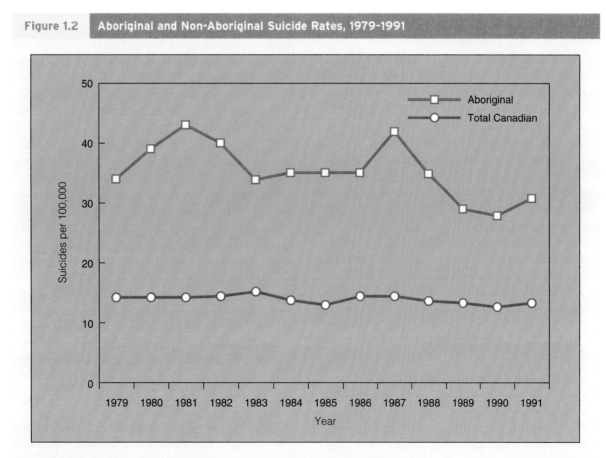

Source: Royal Commission Report on Aboriginal Peoples, 1995.

Choosing Life: Special Report on Suicide among Aboriginal Peoples, prepared by the Royal Commission on Aboriginal Peoples, includes the following comments:

> We believe that suicide is a special issue. It is first and foremost a matter of life and death for that minority of Aboriginal people whose inner despair threatens daily to overwhelm them. But, like other forms of violence and self-destructive behaviour in Aboriginal communities, it is also the expression of a kind of collective anguish— part grief, part anger—tearing at the minds and hearts of many people. This anguish is the cumulative effect of 300 years of colonial history: lands occupied, resources seized, beliefs and cultures ridiculed, children taken away, power concentrated in distant capitals, hopes for honourable co-existence dashed over and over again. (1995:x)

Today, suicide rates are epidemic in some Aboriginal communities. Suicides due to social breakdown and normlessness are an example of what Durkheim defined as anomic suicides (Kirmayer, 1994). Using Durkheim's theoretical framework, these suicides can be best understood as indicative of social, rather than personal, problems.

The functionalist analysis of suicide (or other social problems) has been criticized for its assumption that shared values and beliefs are equally beneficial for everyone. For example, if a society values men more than women or ties being a "man" to sexual aggression, these values may contribute to the victimization of women and children. Likewise, the law-and-order solution to crime may have inherent class, race, gender, and age biases, as discussed in Chapter 7 ("Crime and Deviance"). However, proponents of functionalism point out that this perspective demonstrates the importance of social bonds for the stability of society and the well-being of individuals. For example, in communities where there is no shared sense of community, suicide rates will be higher.

Conflict Perspectives

According to **conflict perspectives, groups in society are engaged in a continuous power struggle for control of scarce resources.** Conflict may take the form of politics, litigation, negotiations, or family discussions about financial matters. Simmel, Marx, and Weber contributed significantly to this perspective by focusing on the inevitability of clashes between social

groups. Today, advocates of the conflict perspective view social life as a continuous power struggle among competing social groups.

Max Weber and C. Wright Mills
As previously discussed, Marx focused on the exploitation and oppression of the proletariat (the workers) by the bourgeoisie (the owners or capitalist class). Weber recognized the importance of economic conditions in producing inequality and conflict in society but added *power* and *prestige* as other sources of inequality. Weber (1968/1922) defined power as the ability of a person within a social relationship to carry out his or her own will despite resistance from others. Prestige ("status group" to Weber) is a positive or negative social estimation of honour (Weber, 1968/1922).

Other theorists have looked at conflict among many groups and interests (such as employers and employees) as a part of everyday life in any society. Ralf Dahrendorf (1959), for example, observed that conflict is inherent in *all* authority relationships, not just that between the capitalist class and the working class. To Dahrendorf, *power* is the critical variable in explaining human behaviour. People in positions of authority benefit from the conformity of others; those who are forced to conform feel resentment and demonstrate resistance, much as a child may resent parental authority. The advantaged group that possesses authority attempts to preserve the status quo— the existing set of social arrangements—and may use coercion to do so.

C. Wright Mills (1916–1962), a key figure in the development of contemporary conflict theory, encouraged sociologists to get involved in social reform. He contended that value-free sociology was impossible because social scientists must make value-related choices—including the topics they investigate and the theoretical approaches they adopt. He encouraged others to look beneath everyday events in order to observe the major resource and power inequalities that exist in society. He believed that the most important decisions are made largely behind the scenes by the ***power elite*— a small clique composed of the top corporate, political, and military officials.** Mills's power elite theory is discussed in Chapter 14 ("Power, Politics, and Government").

Applying Conflict Perspectives to Suicide
How might advocates of a conflict approach explain patterns of suicide among young people in Canada?

Social Class   Although many other factors may be present, social class pressures can affect rates of suicide among young people. According to some conflict theorists, North American teenagers are confronted with a capitalist economy predicated on consumption and waste and on the need to achieve high levels of economic success. Some young people may perceive that they have no future because they see few educational or employment opportunities in our technologically oriented society. Some researchers suggest that young people from low-income or working-class backgrounds are among the most powerless people in society. Low levels of family income and education and financial uncertainty associated with unemployment are known risk factors associated with suicide among Canadian youth (Health Canada, 1997).

Race   Racial oppression may explain the high suicide rates of some minority groups. This fact is more glaringly reflected in the extremely high rate of suicide among some Aboriginal communities. Canadian children and youth living in Aboriginal reserve communities have a suicide rate almost five times that of children and youth in the general population (Health Canada, 1997:272). Most research has focused on individualistic reasons why some young Aboriginal people commit suicide. However, analysts using a conflict framework focus on the effect of social inequality and racial discrimination on suicidal behaviour. The *Special Report on Suicide among Aboriginal Peoples* (Royal Commission on Aboriginal Peoples, 1995) makes frequent references to oppression as a significant factor in Aboriginal suicide. For example, Sarah MacKay of the Shibogama First Nations Council comments:

> Many reports written today about the suicides of youth . . . outline in great detail the contributing factors that lead to suicide. Yet these reports fail to clearly identify the reasons why the suicides occur. The contributing factors, such as sexual abuse, family violence, alcohol and drug abuse, solvent abuse . . . are only symptoms of a bigger and more devastating cycle of oppression and deprivation . . . first initiated with colonial contact in 1492 . . . We must stop the immoral behaviours caused by oppressions . . . [That's how] to stop the suicides that are occurring amongst our youth today. (Royal Commission on Aboriginal Peoples, 1995:19)

The various conflict approaches help clarify the connections between social arrangements in society and problems such as violent crimes and suicide. However, these perspectives have been criticized for giving little attention to social stability and shared values. Critics contend that conflict perspectives have lost at least some claim to scientific objectivity. Advocates of conflict perspectives respond that all social approaches have inherent biases, as will be discussed in Chapter 2 ("Sociological Research").

Feminist Perspectives

In the past several decades, feminists have radically transformed the discipline of sociology. Feminist theory first emerged as a critique of traditional sociological theory and methodology. The primary criticism was that sociology did not acknowledge the experiences of women. Written by men, sociology involved the study of men and not humankind, much less women; sociology examined only half of social reality (Fox, 1989). Feminist scholar Dorothy Smith (1974) argued that sociological methods, concepts, and analyses were products of the "male social universe." If women appeared at all, it was as men saw them and not as they saw themselves. In this way, feminist sociologists argued, sociology actually contributed to the subordination and exploitation of women (Anderson, 1996). The first task of feminist sociology was to provide the missing half of social reality by generating research and theory "by, for, and about women" (Smith, 1987). In doing so, feminist sociology brought the personal problems of women, including violence against women, the poverty of women, and the invisibility of women's reproductive labour, into the public forum.

***Feminist perspectives* focus on the significance of gender in understanding and explaining inequalities that exist between men and women in the household, in the paid labour force, and in the realms of politics, law, and culture** (Armstrong and Armstrong, 1994; Luxton, 1995; Marshall, 1995). Feminism is not one single unified approach. Rather, there are different approaches among feminist writers, namely the liberal, radical, and socialist strains (discussed in Chapter 11, "Sex and Gender"). Feminist sociology incorporates both microlevel and macrolevel analysis in studying the experiences of women. For example, some feminist theorists, such as Margrit Eichler, have used a structural approach to explain how gender inequality is created and maintained in a society dominated by men (Armstrong and Armstrong, 1994; Eichler, 1988b). Other feminist research has focused on the interpersonal relationships between men and women in terms of verbal and nonverbal communication styles, attitudes, and values in explaining the dynamics of power and social control in the private sphere (Mackie, 1995). For example, "Who eats first, sits last, or talks back reflects the micro-politics of gender" (Coltrane, 1992:104). All of these approaches share the belief that "women and men are equal and should be equally valued as well as have equal rights" (Basow, 1992). According to feminists (including many men as well as women), we live in a *patriarchy,* a hierarchical system of power in which males possess greater economic and social privilege than females (Saunders, 1999). Feminist perspectives assume that gender roles are socially created, rather than determined by one's biological inheritance, and that change is essential in order for people to achieve their human potential without limits based on gender. Feminism assumes that society reinforces social expectations through social learning: what we learn is a social product of the political and economic structure of the society in which we live (Renzetti and Curran, 1995). Feminists argue that women's subordination can end only after the patriarchal system of male dominance is replaced with a more egalitarian system.

Applying a Feminist Perspective to Suicide

Feminist research on suicide has examined the role of gender on attitudes toward suicide. Specifically, feminist analysts have found that gender plays a significant role in a person's risk for suicidal behaviour and how the

Margrit Eichler

suicidal behaviour is evaluated. In North America, non-fatal suicidal behaviour is more common in women and fatal suicides are more common among men (Canetto and Sakinofsky, 1998:1). Feminists describe this phenomenon as the "gender paradox" in suicide. Researchers utilizing a feminist perspective focus on differences in gender socialization to explain this pattern. For example, Canetto explains that cultural expectations about gender and suicidal behaviour are like scripts that individuals refer to as a model for their behaviour. She argues that in North American culture suicide is viewed as a masculine behaviour. Killing oneself may be perceived as a powerful act for a male in response to particular life circumstances, such as a debilitating illness or a serious achievement failure (such as a job loss). In contrast, "attempting suicide" is regarded as feminine. Although this behaviour is viewed negatively, it may be expected in females in some circumstances. Non-fatal suicidal behaviour may be viewed as an understandable "feminine" response to relationship problems, such as the loss of a boyfriend, lover, or husband. Some analysts suggest that the gender paradox in suicidal behaviour is a reflection of the fact that women and men will tend to adopt the self-destructive behaviours that are congruent with the gender scripts of their culture (Canetto and Sakinofsky, 1998:17).

Other feminist theorists have emphasized that we must examine social–structural pressures that are brought to bear on young women and look at how these may contribute to their behaviour—for example, cultural assumptions about women and what their multiple roles should be in the family, in education, and in the workplace. Women also experience unequal educational and employment opportunities that may contribute to feelings of powerlessness and alienation. Recent research shows there are persistent gender gaps in employment, politics, education, and other areas of social life that tend to adversely affect women more than men. Feminist theorists would suggest that the higher rate of attempted suicide among women of all age groups may be an expression of their sense of powerlessness in a male-dominated society.

Symbolic Interactionist Perspectives

The functional and the conflict perspectives have been criticized for focusing primarily on macrolevel analysis. A *macrolevel analysis* examines whole societies, large-scale social structures, and social systems instead of looking at important social dynamics in individuals' lives. Our final perspective, symbolic interactionism, fills this void by examining people's day-to-day interactions and their behaviour in groups.

Thus, symbolic interactionist approaches are based on a *microlevel analysis,* **which focuses on small groups rather than large-scale social structures.**

We can trace the origins of this perspective to the Chicago School, especially George Herbert Mead and Herbert Bloomer (1900–1986), who is credited with coining the term *symbolic interactionism.* According to *symbolic interactionist perspectives,* **society is the sum of the interactions of individuals and groups.** Theorists using this perspective focus on the process of *interaction*—defined as immediate reciprocally oriented communication between two or more people—and the part that *symbols* play in giving meaning to human communication. A *symbol* **is anything that meaningfully represents something else.** Examples of symbols include signs, gestures, written language, and shared values. Symbolic interaction occurs when people communicate through the use of symbols; for example, a gift of food—a cake or a casserole—to a newcomer in a neighbourhood is a symbol of welcome and friendship. Symbolic communication occurs in a variety of forms, including facial gestures, posture, tone of voice, and other symbolic gestures (such as a handshake or a clenched fist).

Symbols are instrumental in helping people derive meanings from social situations. In social encounters, each person's interpretation or definition of a given situation becomes a *subjective reality* from that person's viewpoint. We often assume that what we consider to be "reality" is shared; however, this assumption is often incorrect. Subjective reality is acquired and shared through agreed-upon symbols, especially language. If a person shouts, "Fire!" in a crowded movie theatre, for example, that language produces the same response (attempting to escape) in all of those who hear and understand it. When people in a group do not share the same meaning for a given symbol, however, confusion results; for example, people who did not know the meaning of the word *fire* would not know what the commotion was about. How people *interpret* the messages they receive and the situations they encounter becomes their subjective reality and may strongly influence their behaviour.

Symbolic interactionists attempt to study how people make sense of their life situations and the way they go about their activities, in conjunction with others, on a day-to-day basis (Prus, 1996). How do people develop the capacity to think and act in socially prescribed ways? According to symbolic interactionists, our thoughts and behaviour are shaped by our social interactions with others. Early theorists, such as Charles Horton Cooley and George Herbert Mead, explored how individual personalities are developed from social experience and concluded that we could not have an identity, a "self," without communication from other people. This idea is developed in Cooley's notion of the *looking-glass self* and Mead's *generalized other,* as discussed in Chapter 4 ("Socialization"). From this perspective, the attainment of language is essential not only for the development of self but also for establishing common understandings about social life.

How do symbolic interactionists view social organization and the larger society? According to symbolic interactionists, social organization and society are possible only through people's everyday interactions. In other words, group life takes its shape as people interact with one another (Blumer, 1969). Although macrolevel factors such as economic and political institutions constrain and define the forms of interaction that we have with others, the social world is dynamic and always changing. Chapter 5 ("Society, Social Structure, and Interaction") explores two similar approaches—rational choice and exchange theories—that focus specifically on how people rationally try to get what they need by exchanging valued resources with others.

As we attempt to present ourselves to others in a particular way, we engage in behaviour that the sociologist Erving Goffman (1959) referred to as "impression management." Chapter 5 also presents some of Goffman's ideas, including *dramaturgical analysis,* which envisions that individuals go through their life somewhat like actors performing on a stage, playing out their roles before other people. Symbolic interactionism involves both a theoretical perspective and specific research methods, such as observation, participant observation, and interviews, that focus on the individual and small group behaviour (see Chapter 2, "Sociological Research").

Applying Symbolic Interactionist Perspectives to Suicide

Sociologists applying a symbolic interactionist framework to the study of suicide would primarily focus on a microlevel analysis of suicidal persons' face-to-face interactions with others and the roles that people play in society. In our efforts to interact with others, we define particular situations according to our own subjective reality. This theoretical viewpoint applies to suicide just as it does to other types of conduct. In studying suicide, the interactionist focuses on the various meanings that are attributed to the act of suicide.

There is a great deal of variation among different cultures around the world regarding the meaning of suicide. For example, in Japan, where suicide has traditionally been accepted, the words used to describe it reflect tolerance toward suicide. In English, the word *suicide* is derived from a Latin word meaning "murder." In contrast, the Japanese have thirty-five different expressions for suicide, but none meaning self-murder (Fuse, 1997). The meaning attached to suicide in Japan is closely related to Japanese views of death. These include that death is something to be welcomed and that it allows one to have a continuing life through one's children and their children (Leenaars et al., 1998).

How might a symbolic interactionist perspective be applied to understand the pattern of suicide among youth in some Aboriginal communities? Once again, the symbolic interactionist perspective focuses on the meaning of suicide in attempting to understand patterns or variations in suicide rates. These patterns may be an indication of the redefinition among Aboriginal youth of the meaning of suicide. A young Aboriginal student from New Brunswick discusses how suicide is viewed by some of his peers:

> Too many [North] American Indian youths find this life devoid of meaning and worth little, whereas death is a way of finding peace and reunion with glorified ancestors. Suicide is often viewed as a brave, heroic act. Self-destructive behaviour becomes a learned and rewarded pattern. Those who die by suicide become idols of their peer group. (Royal Commission on Aboriginal Peoples, 1995:10)

From this point of view, suicide is seen as a way of gaining peer approval and acceptance. When suicide becomes defined as a brave or heroic act, we can expect an increase in suicide rates.

This helps to explain why clusters of suicide have become more common among Aboriginal Canadian youth in recent years. For example, the Inuit of the East Coast of Hudson Bay experienced a dramatic increase in suicide between 1987 and 1991. Most of this increase was the result of a cluster of suicides in 1991. Furthermore, more than 90 percent of these suicides occurred in the 15 to 25 age group (Kirmayer, 1994:10). The symbolic interactionist perspective would view this as learned behaviour. Suicide becomes viewed by some youth as a socially acceptable solution to life's problems (Health Canada, 1997).

As this symbolic interactionist analysis of suicide makes clear, social learning is important in how we define ourselves and our relationship to others. Because symbolic interactionist perspectives focus on the microlevel of society, they help us see how individuals interact in their daily lives and interpret their experiences. However, this approach also is limited in that it basically ignores the larger social context in which behaviour takes place. If we focus primarily on the individual and small-group context of behaviour, we may overlook important macrolevel societal forces that are beyond the control of individuals, such as the effects of socially imposed definitions of race–ethnicity, gender, class, and age on people's lives.

Postmodern Perspectives

According to *postmodern perspectives*, **existing theories have been unsuccessful in explaining social life in contemporary societies that are characterized by postindustrialization, consumerism, and global communications.** Postmodern social theorists reject the theoretical perspectives we have previously discussed, as well as how those thinkers created the theories (Ritzer, 1996). These theorists oppose the grand narratives that characterize modern thinking and believe that boundaries should not be placed on academic disciplines—such as philosophy, literature, art, and the social sciences—where much could be learned by sharing ideas.

Just as functionalist, conflict, and symbolic interactionist perspectives emerged in the aftermath of the Industrial Revolution, postmodern theories emerged after World War II (in the late 1940s) and reflected the belief that some nations were entering a period of postindustrialization. Postmodern (or postindustrial) societies are characterized by an *information explosion* and an economy in which large numbers of people either provide or apply information or are employed in service jobs (such as fast-food server or health care worker). There is a corresponding *rise of a consumer society* and the emergence of a *global village*, in which people around the world communicate with one another by electronic technologies, such as television, telephone, fax, e-mail, and the Internet. Today, postmodern theory remains an emerging perspective in the social sciences. How influential will this approach be? It remains to be seen what influence postmodern thinkers will have on the social sciences. Although this approach opens up broad new avenues of inquiry by challenging existing perspectives and questioning current belief systems, it also tends to ignore many of the central social problems of our time—such as inequalities based on race, class, and gender, and global political and economic oppression (Ritzer, 1996).

Applying Postmodern Perspectives to Suicide   Do information technologies, such as computers and the Internet, bind people together, or do they create a world where people feel only tenuously

involved in the collective life and interpersonal relations? Such questions might be asked by postmodern analysts in a study of people's suicidal behaviour.

According to some postmodern thinkers, we face a high-tech world in which images, ideas, and identity-forming material pass before our eyes at an accelerated pace. As a result, we are required to develop our own coherent narrative order by which we understand ourselves and the social events that take place around us (Gergen, 1991; Harvey, 1989). In the aftermath of the 1997 Heaven's Gate mass suicide in California, for example, some social analysts highlighted what they perceived to be the role of the media, the Internet, and the World Wide Web in that event. Media representations of the mass suicide often depicted the Internet and cyberspace as having *agency* (as possessing motives and being able to "act" as if they were human beings). Referring to the Heaven's Gate group as a "computer cult," CNN Interactive titled its story "The Internet as a God and Propaganda Tool for Cults." From a postmodern approach, representations such as this reflect a world in which individuals and the media may establish "fake" realities and pseudo-explanations in the absence of *real* knowledge about events or their causes. In future chapters, we use a postmodern framework to examine topics such as cultural ideas, language use, issues of race/class/gender, the political economy, and individual self-conceptions.

Each of the sociological perspectives we have examined involves different assumptions. Consequently, each leads us to ask different questions and to view the world somewhat differently. Different aspects of reality are the focus of each approach. While functionalism emphasizes social cohesion and order, conflict and feminist approaches focus primarily on social conflict and change. In contrast, symbolic interactionism primarily examines people's interactions and shared meanings in everyday life. Concept Table 1.A reviews the major perspectives. Throughout this book, we will be using these perspectives as lenses through which to view our social world. Each approach also will be helpful in developing your own sociological imagination.

USING YOUR SOCIOLOGICAL IMAGINATION IN THE FUTURE

Having acquired or developed your own sociological imagination, how will you use it in the future? For some, sociology may become a profession. This century may be the most exciting period in sociology's

Concept Table 1.A	THE MAJOR THEORETICAL PERSPECTIVES	
PERSPECTIVE	**ANALYSIS LEVEL**	**NATURE OF SOCIETY**
Functionalist	Macrolevel	Society is composed of interrelated parts that work together to maintain stability within society. This stability is threatened by dysfunctional acts and institutions.
Conflict	Macrolevel	Society is characterized by social inequality; social life is a struggle for scarce resources. Social arrangements benefit some groups at the expense of others.
Feminist	Macrolevel/Microlevel	Society is based on patriarchy—a hierarchical system of power in which males possess greater economic and social privilege than females.
Symbolic Interactionist	Microlevel	Society is the sum of the interactions of people and groups. Behaviour is learned in interaction with other people; how people define a situation becomes the foundation for how they behave.
Postmodernist	Macrolevel/Microlevel	Societies characterized by postindustrialization, consumerism, and global communications bring into question existing assumptions about social life and the nature of reality.

history. More than ever before, we are aware of the need to understand, alleviate, and solve problems that affect individuals, such as substance abuse and unemployment, and address problems that affect societies, such as ethnic conflict, war, and environmental destruction. Some of the best employment opportunities may lie in policy research and administration or clinical and applied research as well as the more traditional areas of teaching and basic research (American Sociological Association, 2005:1). See Table 1.1 for a detailed list of career opportunities for individuals with degrees in sociology.

Table 1.1 CAREERS IN SOCIOLOGY

Sociology, the study of human society, is a fascinating and exciting area of inquiry. Some students develop a deep interest in the subject of sociology and decide that they wish to major in it. Since the vast majority of university students look upon their education as a "gateway" to a career, it is desirable to examine what type of career opportunities exist for university graduates with a degree in sociology.

In general, a career specifically in sociology consists of employment in an academic setting as a researcher or teacher. With the exception of a few high school teaching positions, most teaching and research positions require graduate (master's or Ph.D.) degrees. There are a number of careers for which sociology offers valuable preparation. Many career opportunities require a bachelor's degree, and a sociology degree provides entry into a wide array of such occupations. Listed below are some of the careers for sociology majors:

Admissions Counsellor / Director of Admissions
Affirmative Action Coordinator
College Placement Officer
Community Planner (urban development work)
Correctional Officer
Counsellor (alcoholism, career, drug abuse, for the disabled, for independent living)
Criminology Researcher
Demographer
Employment Counsellor / Interviewer
Environmental Analyst / Planner
Equal Opportunity Specialist (Employment Equity Officer)
Graduate Student / Professor
Grants Officer / Assistant
Group Worker (in a social service agency or hospital)
Health Researcher
Health and Safety Education Specialist
Human Rights Worker
Labour Relations Specialist
Marketing Researcher / Assistant
Park and Recreation Program Planner
Personnel Management / Personnel Relations Assistant
Police Officer
Policy Planner / Policy Analyst / Policy Evaluator
Probation Officer
Public Information Specialist
Public Relations Supervisor
Recreation Director / Aide
Recreation Supervisor
Rehabilitation Counsellor
Research Analyst / Assistant
Social Activist
Social Researcher
Social Service Worker / Aide
Statistician / Statistical Assistant
Urban Planner / Urban Analyst
Vocational Development Specialist

Source: University of Winnipeg, 2002, Department of Sociology.

For others, sociology will not become a profession but rather, as sociologist Peter Berger describes it, a worldview—a way of seeing "the strange in the familiar." This view however, is often more than a way of interpreting or understanding one's social world. For many it is a precipitant for social change. Sociologist Allan G. Johnson explains one of the many effects of "practising sociology":

> It is impossible to study social life for very long without coming up against the consequences that social life produces, and a lot of these consequences do such damage to people's lives that, unless we find ways to deny or ignore the reality of it, we feel compelled to ask "why?" And once we ask that question, we need tools to help make sense of where it leads and to imagine how we might go from there toward something better. We can't help but be part of the problem; practicing sociology is a way to also be part of the solution. This not only helps the world, but it makes it easier to live in, especially given how crazy a place can seem. It helps to be able to see how one thing is connected to another, and, in that, how to find ways to make some small difference. We can't change the world all by ourselves, but we can make informed decisions about how to participate in it, and how that can help turn the world toward something better, even if it's just in our neighborhoods or families or where we work. (Johnson, 2005:9)

Throughout the text, several boxes entitled "You Can Make a Difference" provide suggestions and opportunities for you to "practise sociology" in this manner. Join us as we examine specific ways in which sociology creates its own realm of knowledge in order to provide new information and personal insights that we can use in our everyday lives.

CHAPTER REVIEW

■ **What is sociology and how can it help us understand ourselves and others?**

Sociology is the systematic study of human society and social interaction. We study sociology to understand how human behaviour is shaped by group life and, in turn, how group life is affected by individuals. Our culture tends to emphasize individualism, and sociology pushes us to consider more complex connections between our personal lives and the larger world.

■ **What is the sociological imagination?**

According to C. Wright Mills, the sociological imagination helps us understand how seemingly personal troubles, such as suicide, are actually related to larger social forces. It allows us to see the relationship between individual experiences and the larger society. It is important to have a global sociological imagination because the future of this country is deeply intertwined with the future of all nations of the world on economic, political, environmental, and humanitarian levels.

■ **What factors contributed to the emergence of sociology as a discipline?**

Industrialization and urbanization increased rapidly in the late eighteenth century, and social thinkers began to examine the consequences of these powerful forces. Auguste Comte coined the term sociology to describe a new science that would engage in the study of society.

■ **What are the major contributions of the early sociologists Durkheim, Marx, Weber, and Simmel?**

The ideas of Émile Durkheim, Karl Marx, Max Weber, and Georg Simmel helped lead the way to contemporary sociology. Durkheim argued that societies are built on social facts, that rapid social change produces strains in society, and that the loss of shared values and purpose can lead to a condition of anomie. Marx stressed that within society there is a continuous clash between the owners of the means of production and the workers, who have no choice but to sell their labour to others. According to Weber, it is necessary to acknowledge the meanings that individuals attach to their own actions. Simmel explored small social groups and argued that society was best seen as a web of patterned interactions among people.

■ What are the major contemporary sociological perspectives?

Functionalist perspectives assume that society is a stable, orderly system characterized by societal consensus; however, this perspective has been criticized for overlooking the importance of change in societies. Conflict perspectives argue that society is a continuous power struggle among competing groups, often based on class, race, ethnicity, or gender. Critics of conflict theory note that it minimizes the importance of social stability and shared values in society. Feminist perspectives focus on the significance of gender in understanding and explaining inequalities that exist between men and women in the household, in the paid labour force, and in politics, law, and culture. Symbolic interactionist perspectives focus on how people make sense of their everyday social interactions, which are made possible by the use of mutually understood symbols. However, this approach focuses on the microlevel of society and tends to ignore the larger macrolevel social context. From an alternative perspective, postmodern theorists believe that entirely new ways of examining social life are needed and that it is time to move beyond functionist, conflict, and interactionist perspectives.

KEY TERMS

alienation 14
anomie 13
bourgeoisie 14
class conflict 14
commonsense knowledge 4
conflict perspectives 22
dysfunctions 20
feminist perspectives 23
functionalist perspectives 20
global interdependence 4
industrialization 9
latent functions 20
macrolevel analysis 24
manifest functions 20
means of production 14
microlevel analysis 25
perspective 19
positivism 10
postmodern perspectives 26

power elite 22
proletariat 14
social Darwinism 12
social facts 13
social solidarity 20
societal consensus 20
society 4
sociological imagination 6
sociology 4
symbol 25
symbolic interactionist perspectives 25
theory 19
urbanization 10

NET LINKS

The SocioWeb is a guide to sociological resources on the Web. It is located at:
http://www.socioweb.com/~markbl/ socioweb/

A social sciences reference library is located at:
http://web.clas.ufl.edu/users/gthursby/ socsci/index.htm

Nelson has a Web site that includes study resources, chapter quizzes, degree and career information, and Web links for additional information on a variety of topics in sociology. Go to:
http://sociology.nelson.com

The Canadian Sociology and Anthropology Association has a Web site at:
http://www.csaa.ca/

QUESTIONS FOR CRITICAL THINKING

1. What does C. Wright Mills mean when he says the sociological imagination helps us "grasp history and biography and the relations between the two within society" (Mills, 1959b:6)? How might this idea be applied to various trends in suicide in today's society?

2. As a sociologist, how would you remain objective and yet see the world as others see it? Would you make subjective decisions when trying to understand the perspectives of others?

3. Early social thinkers were concerned about stability in times of rapid change. In our more global world, is stability still a primary goal? Or is constant conflict important for the well-being of all humans? Use the conflict and feminist perspectives to support your analysis.

4. According to the functionalist perspective, what would happen to society if one of its institutions—say, the educational system—were to break down?

SUGGESTED READINGS

These two classics describe sociological thinking and implementation of the sociological imagination:

Peter L. Berger. *Invitation to Sociology: A Humanistic Perspective.* New York: Anchor, 1963.

C. Wright Mills. *The Sociological Imagination.* London: Oxford University Press, 1959.

The following books examine various aspects of sociological theory in more depth:

Randall Collins. *Four Sociological Traditions.* New York: Oxford University Press, 1994.

George Ritzer. *Sociological Theory* (3rd ed.). New York: Knopf, 1992.

Dorothy Smith. *The Everyday World as Problematic: A Feminist Sociology.* Toronto: University of Toronto Press, 1987.

To find out about career possibilities in sociology, contact the Canadian Sociology and Anthropology Association, Concordia University, 1455 Boul. de Maisonneuve Ouest, Montreal, Quebec M3G 1M8. Ask for the publication *Opportunities in Sociology.*

ONLINE STUDY AND RESEARCH TOOLS

THOMSONNOW™ Thomson NOW!

Go to **http://hed.nelson.com** to link to ThomsonNOW for *Sociology in Our Times,* Fourth Canadian Edition, your online study tool. First take the **Pre-Test** for this chapter to get your personalized **Study Plan,** which will identify topics you need to review and direct you to the appropriate resources. Then take the **Post-Test** to determine what concepts you have mastered and what you still need work on.

INFOTRAC®

InfoTrac College Edition is included free with every new copy of this text. Explore this online library for additional readings, review, and a handy resource for assignments. Visit **www.infotrac-college.com** to access this online database of full-text articles. Enter the key terms from this chapter to start your search.

Sociological Research

On October 31, 1991, a Canadian Armed Forces Hercules transport plane with eighteen passengers and crew was preparing to land at Canadian Forces Station Alert on Ellesmere Island in the Northwest Territories. Just 800 kilometres from the North Pole, Alert is the world's most northerly permanent settlement. In the dark Arctic night, sixteen kilometres short of the runway, the left wing of the Hercules struck the peak of a small mountain and the aircraft crashed onto a barren Arctic plateau. Fourteen survivors, many of them seriously injured, waited for help in the twisted wreckage.

Thirty-two hours later, another Hercules, with a team of Search and Rescue Technicians (SARtechs) on board, was circling the crash site. The SARtechs were hoping conditions would allow them to parachute into the site to help the survivors. The temperature was –66°C, visibility on the ground was limited, and the winds of 35 to 40 knots were more than three times the permissible limit for parachuting. Because of the terrible weather conditions, a U.S. Air Force crew had just cancelled their attempt at a jump onto the crash site. In the back of the Canadian Hercules, Warrant Officer Arnie Macauley, the SARtech team leader, addressed his men:

"Okay, guys, you know the situation. The winds are pretty stiff. They've blown away all our marker lights . . .

It looks like a snowfield down there, but ground conditions are unknown. We'll be landing at a good clip. We'll try for flare illumination but I can't promise you anything.

"One more thing. Once we're down there, we're down for good. Marv will try for a supply drop, but we can expect the survival gear to be blown away. We'll have no way of extracting ourselves or the survivors . . .

"That's the situation, men. We can expect casualties. I have to inform you that the jump involves a knowing risk of life. I can't ask any of you to do this."

Some of the SARtechs studied their boots, others looked out the open door into the howling void. One by one, they looked back at him. "Arnie," one said, "you know how we feel."

Good guys, Arnie thought. I hope like hell I'm doing the right thing.

Arnie checked the closures on his padded orange jumpsuit and the fasteners of his parachute harness. He pulled on his gloves. The jumpmaster clipped their static lines to the overhead cable, and the men crowded around the open door. There were six of them. They squeezed into the opening and grabbed one another by the legs, arms, waist. They would go together. (Mason Lee, 1991:229-231)

he rescuers completed their harrowing jump with relatively minor injuries and immediately began caring for the survivors.

Thirteen people are alive today because of the heroism of the SARtechs and the rest of the aircrew and technicians involved in this rescue. Why do people like Warrant Officer Macauley and his men risk their lives in order to save others? This question has been asked by sociologists who have studied **altruism—behaviour intended to help others and done without any expectation of personal benefit.**

In this chapter, we will see how sociological research methods can help us understand social phenomena, such as altruism. How do sociologists determine what to study? How do they go about conducting research with human subjects? What factors determine the appropriate method to use in social research? These are all questions pertaining to the process of "doing research"—questions that will be addressed in this chapter. Conducting sociological research is an interesting, exciting, and at times difficult process. Why? Because sociological research is directed at understanding human social interaction and solving problems in our social world.

Sociological research offers the challenge of going as a "stranger" into a familiar world.

Several researchers have conducted studies that try to help us understand altruistic behaviour, and their work will be used to illustrate the different research methods used by sociologists. Before reading on, test your knowledge of altruism by answering the questions in Box 2.1.

QUESTIONS AND ISSUES

Chapter Focus Question: How does social research add to our knowledge of human societies?

What is the relationship between theory and research?

What are the main steps in the sociological research process?

Why is it important to have different research methods?

What has research contributed to our understanding of altruism?

Why is a code of ethics for sociological research necessary?

WHY IS SOCIOLOGICAL RESEARCH NECESSARY?

Sociologists obtain their knowledge of human behaviour through research, which results in a body of information that helps us move beyond guesswork and common sense in understanding society. Throughout this text, you will learn that commonsense beliefs about society are often wrong. The sociological perspective incorporates theory and research to arrive at a more informed understanding of the "hows" and "whys" of human social interaction. Social research, then, is a key part of sociology.

Many Nova Scotians contributed their time to help search for bodies and debris following the crash of Swissair Flight 111 off the Nova Scotia coast.

Five Ways of Knowing the World

Sociologists try to understand social behaviour. People have always sought to bring order to the chaotic world of experience by trying to understand the social and physical realm in which they live. Understanding is the major goal of science, but this goal is shared by other fields, including philosophy,

religion, the media, and the arts. Our ways of knowing the world include the following:

1. *Personal experience.* We have discovered for ourselves many of the things we know. If we put our tongue on a frozen doorknob, we learn that removing it can be very painful.
2. *Tradition.* People hold firmly to a belief because "everyone knows" it to be true. Tradition tells us that something is correct because it has always

been done that way. We accept what has always been believed rather than finding out the answers by ourselves.

3. *Authority.* Experts tell us that something is true. We do not need to go to the moon to discover its mineral composition, but instead accept the judgment of space scientists. In practice, much of what we know about medicine, crime, and many other phenomena is based on what authorities have told us.

4. *Religion.* A specific type of authority is religious authority. We accept the truths that our particular scriptures and religious officials advocate. Factors as diverse as morality, diet, dress, and hair styles are based on religious authority.

5. *Science.* The scientific way of knowing involves controlled, systematic observation. Scientists insist that all statements be tested and that testing procedures be open to public inspection.

Personal experience, tradition, authority, and religion are all valid sources of understanding. However, a major difficulty with these ways of knowing is that there is no way to resolve differences or disagreements between those who have had different experiences, or who believe in different religions, traditions, or authorities. For example, if two religious groups have different views concerning the activities that are permissible on the Sabbath, the role that women should play in society, or the regulation of abortion, there is no institutionalized way of reconciling these contrary positions. Scientific explanations differ from the other ways of knowing in several fundamental ways. These characteristics allow scientists to resolve differences in their understanding of the social and physical world.

First, science uses the **empirical approach; that is, its findings are based on the assumption that knowledge is best gained by direct, systematic observation.** By contrast, the **normative approach uses religion, tradition, or authority to answer important questions.** It is based on strong beliefs about what is right and wrong, and what is desirable in a society.

Second, scientific knowledge is *systematic and public.* The procedures used by scientists are organized, public, and recognized by other scientists. The scientific community will not accept claims that

BOX 2.1 SOCIOLOGY AND EVERYDAY LIFE

How Much Do You Know About Altruism?

True	False	
T	F	1. It is nice to help other people, but altruistic behaviour has little impact on the nature of society.
T	F	2. People who behave altruistically often had parents who also actively helped others.
T	F	3. Helping others after a disaster can be a way of helping oneself recover from the shock of having lived through a traumatic event.
T	F	4. Research has found significant personality differences between altruists and non-altruists.
T	F	5. Good Samaritan laws require that Canadians assist those they see in danger or in need of assistance.
T	F	6. People are more likely to help in an emergency in small towns than in big cities.
T	F	7. Experiments in laboratories and in natural settings have shown that the likelihood of bystanders intervening in situations where someone needs help is reduced as the number of people who are aware of the incident increases.
T	F	8. Canada has always had a system that supplied blood free of charge.
T	F	9. People donate blood because they expect to get something in return.
T	F	10. Most Canadians have made a commitment to donate their organs after their deaths.

Answers on page 36.

BOX 2.1 SOCIOLOGY AND EVERYDAY LIFE

Answers to the Sociology Quiz on Altruism

1. **False.**   Durkheim and other sociologists have shown that even in complex, large-scale societies, such as ours, altruism has a significant role to play in maintaining the social order.

2. **True.**   Studies of the rescuers of Jews during the Holocaust, freedom riders in the American South in the 1960s, and blood donation have shown that many of those showing altruism had parents with similar commitments.

3. **True.**   In his participant observation study of a volunteer work crew following a severe tornado, Louis Zurcher found that helping other victims acted as a form of catharsis for the men on the crew. Thus helping others can benefit both the helper and the community.

4. **False.**   Researchers have found very few personality differences between altruists and those less inclined to help others.

5. **False.**   In most cases there is no obligation to help those in distress.

6. **True.**   The anonymity of city life apparently reduces the likelihood that a bystander will help someone in trouble.

7. **True.**   In experimental situations, subjects who were the only witnesses to an emergency felt they had to intervene because nobody else knew of the victim's distress. However, those in larger groups showed concern for the victim but were also concerned about making fools of themselves by overreacting. Therefore, they often waited to see if others would respond before deciding what, if anything, they would do.

8. **False.**   Prior to 1947, Canadian patients had to pay for or replace the blood they used.

9. **False.**   A British survey found that only a small percentage of blood donors expected to get anything—directly or indirectly—in return.

10. **False.**   Canada has a very low rate of organ donation compared with other industrial countries. Our rate of organ donation is fourteen donors per million population compared with thirty per million for Spain and twenty-two per million in the United States. As a result, a shortage of organs exists and many people die each year because they are unable to obtain organs for transplants.

cannot be publicly verified. This means that both the findings and the methods by which scientists reached those findings must be open to scrutiny.

Third, science has a built-in mechanism for *self-correction*. Scientists do not claim that their findings represent eternal truths, but rather they present *hypotheses*—**tentative statements of the relationship between two or more concepts or variables**—that are subject to verification by themselves and by others. What is accepted as scientific truth changes over time as more evidence accumulates. By contrast, it can be very difficult to make changes in understandings based on tradition, authority, or religious belief.

Fourth, science is *objective*: **scientists try to ensure that their biases and values do not affect their research.** In some situations, this criterion seems easily met. For example, two scientists measuring the

length of time it takes for a ball to fall from a height of three hundred metres should arrive at the same answer despite having different biases and values. However, things are not always this clear, particularly in the social sciences, and complete objectivity is not possible. Sociologists Sandra Kirby and Kate McKenna tell us that "our interaction with the social world is affected by such variables as gender, race, class, sexuality, age, physical ability . . ." and conclude that "this does not mean that facts about the social world do not exist, but that what we see and how we go about constructing meaning is a matter of interpretation" (1989:25). That is, marriage may mean different things for men and for women, and people with disabilities may experience the world differently than those without disabilities. This does not mean that the observers lack objectivity, but rather that they experience social life in different ways. Because of this, researchers must always carefully describe the methods they have used in their research so that others can decide for themselves how the researcher's subjectivity has affected his or her conclusions.

Descriptive and Explanatory Studies

Sociologists typically use two types of empirical studies: descriptive and explanatory. **Descriptive studies attempt to describe social reality or provide facts about some group, practice, or event.** Studies of this type are designed to find out what is happening to whom, where, and when. For example, a descriptive study of altruism might attempt to determine what percentage of people would return a lost wallet or help a stranger in distress. The Canadian Census provides a wealth of information about the people of Canada, including such things as age, marital status, and place of residence. For example, we can use the census to tell us what proportion of Canadians are living in common-law relationships and what age groups are most likely to be living common-law. By contrast, **explanatory studies attempt to explain relationships and to**

provide information on why certain events do or do not occur. In an explanatory study of altruism, we might ask, Why are some people more likely than others to offer help? or, Why do some countries rely on volunteer blood donations while others feel they must pay donors? Sociologists engage in the research process to provide answers to questions such as these.

The Theory and Research Cycle

The relationship between theory and research has been referred to as a continuous cycle, as shown in Figure 2.1 (Wallace, 1971). As we saw in Chapter 1, **a theory is a set of logically interrelated statements that attempts to describe, explain, and (occasionally) predict social events.** A theory attempts to explain why something is the way it is. **Research is the process of systematically collecting information for the purposes of testing an existing theory or generating a new one.** The theory and research cycle consists of deductive and inductive approaches. In the **deductive approach, the researcher begins with a theory and uses research to test the theory.** This approach proceeds as follows: (1) theories generate

| Figure 2.1 | The Theory and Research Cycle |

The theory and research cycle can be compared to a relay race; although all participants do not necessarily start or stop at the same point, they share a common goal: to examine all levels of social life.

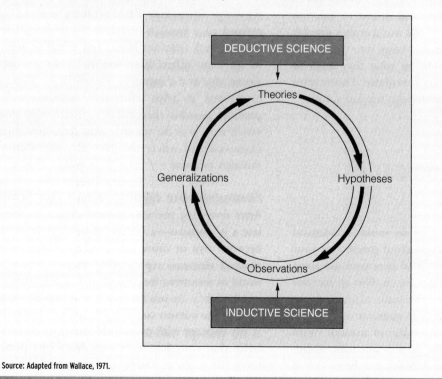

Source: Adapted from Wallace, 1971.

hypotheses; (2) hypotheses lead to observations (data gathering); (3) observations lead to the formation of generalizations; and (4) generalizations are used to support the theory, to suggest modifications to it, or to refute it. To illustrate, if we use the deductive method to answer the question, Why do people help others?, we start by formulating a theory about the "causes" of altruism and then test our theory by collecting and analyzing data (for example, experiments on helping behaviour, or surveys to determine if men or women are more likely to offer assistance).

In the *inductive approach,* **the researcher collects information or data (facts or evidence) and then generates theories from the analysis of those data.** Under the inductive approach, we would proceed as follows: (1) specific observations suggest generalizations; (2) generalizations produce a tentative theory; (3) the theory is tested through the formation of hypotheses; and (4) hypotheses may provide suggestions for additional observations. Using the inductive approach to study altruism, we might start by simultaneously collecting and analyzing data related to helping behaviour and then generate a theory (see Glaser and Strauss, 1967; Reinharz, 1992). The actual process of research is rarely as tidy as the diagram in Figure 2.1 would suggest. Instead, it typically moves back and forth from theory to data throughout the course of the inquiry. In fact, researchers rarely, if ever, begin with either just a theory or data. Inductive theorists need at least rudimentary theories in order to guide their data collection, and deductive theorists must refer constantly to the real world as they develop their theories. Researchers may break into the cycle at different points depending on what they want to know and what information is available. Theory gives meaning to research; research helps support theory.

THE SOCIOLOGICAL RESEARCH PROCESS

Suppose you were going to do some sociological research. How would you go about conducting your study? The procedure outlined here provides some guidelines for sociological research. Not all sociologists conduct research in the same manner. Some researchers engage primarily in *quantitative* research, whereas others engage in *qualitative* research. With quantitative research, the goal is scientific objectivity, and the focus is on data that can be measured numerically. With qualitative research, interpretive description (words) rather than statistics (numbers) is used to analyze underlying meanings and patterns of social relationships.

The Quantitative Research Model

Research models are tailored to the specific problem being investigated and to the focus of the researcher. Both quantitative research and qualitative research contribute to our knowledge of society and social interaction. We will now trace the steps in the quantitative research model; then we will look at an alternative model that emphasizes qualitative research.

Select and Define the Research Problem
The first step is to select a research topic. Sometimes, a personal experience can trigger interest in a topic. At other times, you might select topics to fill gaps or challenge misconceptions in existing research or to test a specific theory (Babbie, 2001). Many sociologists choose topics related to their concerns about social policy issues. You will read about the researchers' reasons for selecting a topic in each of the four case studies of research methods that appear later in this chapter.

Once a topic is selected, you must ask yourself, What do I want to know about this topic? For example, consider the issue of Good Samaritan laws discussed in Box 2.2. As a researcher, how would you approach the questions raised in the box?

Review Previous Research   Once you have defined your research problem, you need to review the literature (relevant books and scholarly articles) to see what others have written about the topic. Knowledge of the literature is essential for a number of reasons. It helps refine the research problem, provides possible theoretical approaches, indicates which aspects of the research topic have already been examined and where the gaps are, and identifies mistakes to avoid.

Formulate the Hypothesis (If Applicable)
After reviewing previous research, you may formulate a hypothesis—a statement of the relationship between two or more concepts. Concepts are the abstract elements representing some aspect of the world in simplified form (such as "social integration" or "altruism"). As you formulate your hypothesis, you will need to convert concepts to variables. A *variable* **is any concept with measurable traits or characteristics that can change or vary from one person, time, situation, or society to another.** Variables are the observable and/or measurable counterparts of

BOX 2.2 SOCIOLOGY AND THE LAW

Does the Law Require Us to Help?

Following Princess Diana's death in a Paris automobile crash in 1997, many people in Canada were surprised to learn that France has a law requiring people to help others in distress. Such laws are referred to as Good Samaritan laws after the biblical story of altruistic behaviour. Because of their failure to help the princess, nine photographers and a press motorcyclist were placed under formal investigation—one step short of being charged—for failing to come to the aid of a person in danger. What about Canada? Does the law require that we intervene in situations where others are in danger? Will we be compensated if we are injured when trying to help others?

In most cases, the answer to these questions is no—Canadian law does little to encourage or to protect Good Samaritans. In fact, under some circumstances Canadians have been penalized for trying to help others. For example, in March 1998, a Manitoba man stopped to help three teenagers after their car had crashed. When he let them into his car, he was stabbed in the face. His attackers then tried to steal his van. Not only was the man permanently scarred, but Manitoba's public insurance corporation also made him pay the $500 deductible cost for repairing his vehicle. In other cases, people have been sued for injuries suffered by the person they had assisted.

Most provinces do have Good Samaritan laws that protect health care professionals from liability if they stop and offer assistance outside a hospital or office setting. Some provinces extend this protection to all citizens who provide emergency medical services or aid. However, only Quebec *requires* people to assist others. The Quebec Charter of Human Rights and Freedoms states:

> Every human being whose life is in peril has a right to assistance. Every person must come to the aid of anyone whose life is in peril either personally or calling for aid, by giving him the necessary and immediate physical assistance, unless it involves danger to himself or a third person, or he has another valid reason.

What is your view of this issue? Should we be compelled to help each other, or should we rely on people's altruism? Can the law help to encourage altruism, or is it more a function of our backgrounds and social relationships?

How could sociological research help society's understanding of this issue? How could you assess the need for Good Samaritan laws and the impact of such laws on altruistic behaviour? Do you think most people are aware that such laws are—or are not—on the books? What are public attitudes concerning the need for such laws?

Sources: Nairne, 1998; Quinton, 1989.

concepts. For example, "altruism" is a concept; the "percentage of the population who donate blood" is a variable.

Now you are ready to answer two important questions: What are the essential variables? and What are the relations between them? (Hoover, 1992:48). The most fundamental relationship in a hypothesis is between a dependent variable and one or more independent variables. The ***independent variable* is presumed to cause or determine a dependent variable.** Sociologists often use characteristics, such as age, sex, race, and ethnicity, as independent variables. The ***dependent variable* is assumed to depend on or be caused by the independent variable(s).** The dependent variable can also be known as the outcome or effect. Several researchers have tested the hypothesis that women are

more likely to be altruistic than men. In this research, gender is the independent variable and the degree of altruism is the dependent variable. Whether a variable is dependent or independent depends on the context in which it is used, and a variable that is independent in one study may be dependent in another. For example, in a study in which a researcher is investigating the relationship between a family's income and the likelihood of their child graduating from university, the dependent variable is university education. In another study looking at the relationship between university education and voting behaviour, university education is the independent variable.

To use variables in the research process, sociologists create operational definitions. An ***operational definition* is an explanation of an abstract concept**

in terms of observable features that are specific enough to measure the variable. Suppose, for example, your goal is to earn an "A" in this course. Your professor may have created an operational definition by defining an "A" as "having a final grade of 85 percent or above" (Babbie, 2001).

Some variables can be very difficult to operationalize. For example, how do we distinguish between "criminals" and "noncriminals" when virtually all of us have broken the law? One way might be to define "criminals" as those who have been convicted of a crime. However, what do we do about people who have committed crimes, but who have been found not guilty at a trial because the evidence against them was obtained illegally? What about corporate offenders whose behaviour may have injured people but which violates government regulations rather than the criminal law? These are some of many measurement issues with which criminologists must deal.

The operational definition of altruism has also been debated. At the beginning of this chapter we defined altruism as actions intended to help others and done without any expectation of personal benefit. However, Warrant Officer Macauley and the other SARtechs were paid to rescue people and their heroism was publicly recognized. Blood donors may someday receive the benefits of a transfusion. Mother Teresa received personal satisfaction from working with the poor and may become a saint someday. Thus we must consider altruism a matter of degree rather than an attribute that some people have and others do not.

Not all social research makes use of hypotheses. If you plan to conduct an explanatory study, you likely will want to formulate one or more hypotheses to test theories. If you plan to conduct a descriptive study, however, you will be less likely to do so, since you may want only to describe social reality or provide facts.

Develop the Research Design

During the research design phase, you will decide on one or more of the research methods—including experiments, survey research, field research, and secondary analysis of data, all of which are described in this chapter. In developing the research design, it is important to carefully consider the advantages and disadvantages of each of these methods.

In developing the research design, you must consider the units of analysis. *Units of analysis* are the *what* or *whom* being studied (Babbie, 2001). In social science research, individuals are the most typical unit of analysis. Social groups (such as families, cities, or geographic regions), organizations (such as clubs,

What if one of these people suddenly had a heart attack or were stabbed by another person? Under what conditions would others intervene to help? Social research has helped us answer this question.

labour unions, or political parties), and social artifacts (such as books, paintings, or weddings) also may be units of analysis.

Collect and Analyze the Data

Your next step is to collect and analyze the data. In the next section, you will learn about the most common methods of collecting social science data. No matter which of these methods is chosen, researchers must consider the reliability and validity of their data when designing a specific research project.

Reliability **is the extent to which a study or research instrument yields consistent results** when applied to different individuals at one time or to the same individual over time. For example, a ruler is a very reliable measure of length because it consistently gives the same results. In the social realm, an IQ test can be considered reliable if a person receives the same score when he or she takes the test more than one time. *Validity* **is the extent to which a study or research instrument accurately measures what it is supposed to measure.** While IQ tests are quite reliable, their validity as a measure of intelligence is more controversial. Proponents are convinced they are good measures of people's natural abilities. However, some social scientists feel the tests measure only some components of intelligence, while others criticize their use among people whose language and cultural backgrounds are different from those of the researchers who designed the tests.

Once you have collected your data, they must be analyzed. *Analysis* **is the process through which data are organized so that comparisons can be made and conclusions drawn.** Sociologists use many techniques to analyze data. The process for each type of research method is discussed later in this chapter.

Draw Conclusions and Report the Findings

After analyzing the data, your first step in drawing conclusions is to return to your hypothesis or research objective to clarify how the data relate both to the hypothesis and to the larger issues being addressed. At this stage, you note the limitations of the study, such as problems with the sample, the influence of variables over which you had no control, or variables that your study was unable to measure.

Reporting the findings is the final stage. The report generally includes a review of each step taken in the research process in order to make the study available for *replication*—**the repetition of the investigation in substantially the same way that it originally was conducted.** This means that other researchers will see if they get the same results when they repeat your study. If your findings are replicated, the research community will have more faith in your conclusions. Social scientists generally present their findings in papers at professional meetings and publish them in academic journals and books.

The Qualitative Research Model

Although the same underlying logic is involved in both quantitative and qualitative sociological research, the *styles* of these two models are very different. Qualitative research is more likely to be used where the research question does not easily lend itself to numbers and statistical methods. Compared to a quantitative model, a qualitative approach often involves a different type of research question and a smaller number of cases. As a result, the outcome of a qualitative study can be a more detailed picture of some particular social phenomenon or social problem (King, Keohane, and Verba, 1994; Creswell, 1998).

Conducting surveys or polls is an international means of gathering data. This investigator is conducting his research in Mexico City.

As you will read later in this chapter (in the section on field research), qualitative researchers typically do not initially define their research problem in as much detail as quantitative researchers. The first step in qualitative research often consists of *problem formulation* to clarify the research question and formulate questions of concern and interest to the research participants (Reinharz, 1992). The next step is to collect and analyze data to assess the validity of the starting proposition. Qualitative researchers typically gather data in natural settings, such as places where people live or work, rather than in a laboratory or research setting. In this environment, the researcher can play a background rather than a foreground role, and the data analysis often uses the language of the people being studied, not that of the researcher. This means that the qualitative approach can generate new theories and innovative findings that incorporate the perspectives of the research subjects themselves.

Although the qualitative approach follows the conventional research approach in presenting a problem, asking a question, collecting and analyzing

Natural disasters, such as the tsunami in Sri Lanka, may be "living laboratories" for sociologists.

data, and seeking to answer the research question, it also has several unique features (Creswell, 1998; Kvale, 1996):

1. *The researcher begins with a general approach rather than a highly detailed plan.* Flexibility is necessary because of the nature of the research question. The topic needs to be explored so that we can know "how" or "what" is going on, but we may not be able to explain "why" a particular social phenomenon is occurring.

2. *The researcher has to decide when the literature review and theory application should take place.* Initial work may involve redefining existing concepts or reconceptualizing how existing studies have been conducted. The literature review may take place at an early stage, before the research design is fully developed, or it may occur after development of the research design and after the data collection has already occurred.

3. *The study presents a detailed view of the topic.* Qualitative research usually involves a smaller number of cases and many variables, whereas quantitative researchers typically work with a few variables and many cases (Creswell, 1998).

■ RESEARCH METHODS

How do sociologists know which research method to use? Are some approaches better than others for particular research problems? **Research methods are specific strategies or techniques for conducting research.** *Qualitative* researchers frequently use field observation studies to help them to understand the social world from the point of view of the people they are studying. *Quantitative* researchers generally use experimental designs, surveys, and secondary analysis of existing data. We will now look at these research methods.

Experiments

An *experiment* **is a carefully designed situation in which the researcher studies the impact of certain variables on subjects' attitudes or behaviour.** Experiments are designed to create "real-life" situations, ideally under controlled circumstances, in which the influence of different variables can be modified and measured.

Types of Experiments   Conventional experiments require that subjects be divided into two groups: an experimental group and a control group. The *experimental group* **contains the subjects who are exposed to an independent variable** (the experimental condition) to study its effect on them. The *control group* **contains the subjects who are not exposed to the independent variable.** In an experiment, the independent variable is manipulated by the researcher and the dependent variable is what the researcher measures. The members of the two groups are matched for similar characteristics or randomly assigned to each group so that comparisons may be made between the groups. This is done to ensure that the two groups are equivalent at the beginning of the study. In the simplest experimental design, (1) subjects are pretested (measured in terms of the dependent variable in the hypothesis); (2) those in the experimental group are then exposed to a stimulus representing an independent variable; and (3) subjects are post-tested (remeasured) in terms of the dependent variable. The experimental and control groups then are compared to see if they differ in relation to the dependent variable, and the hypothesis about the relationship of the two variables is confirmed or rejected.

In a *laboratory experiment*, subjects are studied in a closed setting, such as an animal's cage or a room in a university building, so researchers can maintain as much control as possible over the research. But not all experiments occur in laboratory settings. *Natural experiments* are real-life occurrences, such as floods and other disasters, that provide researchers with "living laboratories." In other circumstances, researchers might stage events in a natural setting by conducting a *field experiment*. Can you think of how you might design a field experiment to help determine the value of microcredit programs, such as the one described in Box 2.3?

Experimental Research: Would You Help Another Person?

At 3 a.m. on March 13, 1964, Kitty Genovese was stabbed to death in the street near her home in New York City. Vincent Mosely, her attacker, assaulted her three times over a period of half an hour. At one point he left her on the street and returned a few minutes later. During the assault, Ms. Genovese screamed "Oh, my God, he stabbed me! Please help me!" However, she received no help from at least 38 neighbours who saw the attack and heard her cries for help. These neighbours did not turn away or ignore the attack; they continued to watch the murder from their apartment windows without coming to her assistance or calling the police. At Mosely's trial, several of these witnesses said they simply didn't want to get involved. Mosely himself said, "I knew they wouldn't do anything—they never do."

This case received worldwide attention as people tried to understand the failure of the bystanders to act. In addition to attracting public comment, the killing raised questions for researchers who sought to address the troubling questions raised by the tragedy: Why did Ms. Genovese's neighbours fail to act altruistically? Under what conditions will people be more or less likely to help others?

Among those who addressed these important issues were social psychologists Bibb Latané and John Darley (1970). They conducted initial field experiments and found that in routine situations people were very willing to help. The vast majority willingly gave directions, told inquirers the time of day, and provided change for a quarter. However, their willingness to help could be changed by manipulating simple conditions, such as the wording of the request for assistance and the number of people asking for help.

Given the general willingness of the public to help in nonemergency situations, the question of why they often fail to respond to emergencies is difficult to understand. Latané and Darley rejected the view that this failure is due to apathy, indifference, or alienation. Instead they developed a *theoretical model* of the intervention process. Before a bystander will intervene in an emergency, he or she must notice that something is happening; interpret this event as an emergency; and decide that he or she has the personal responsibility to help. Latané and Darley proposed the hypothesis that the presence of other people will make people less likely to take each of these steps. They predicted that the presence of others would inhibit the impulse to help for several reasons: each of the potential helpers may look to the others for guidance rather than act quickly; potential helpers might be afraid of failing in front of other bystanders; and potential helpers may feel they are not obliged to help because one of the other bystanders could take care of the problem.

Latané and Darley did a series of experiments to test this hypothesis. Each of these experiments was scripted and designed like a short play. However, rather than entertaining, the goal of experimental research is to allow us to understand social life. One of Latané and Darley's studies was designed to simulate an emergency. Fifty-two university students were asked to take part in an experiment as part of a course requirement. These participants were randomly assigned to groups of three different sizes: a two-person group (the subject and the victim); a three-person group; and a six-person group. Each of the students was seated at a table in a room, given a pair of headphones with an attached microphone, and told to listen for instructions. Over the intercom, each of the subjects was told that they were to participate in a study concerning the personal problems facing students in a high-pressure urban environment. They were also told that in order to maintain their anonymity when discussing personal matters, they had been placed in individual rooms and would talk and listen to others only through an intercom. The discussion would be controlled by a mechanical switching device that would turn each student's microphone on for two minutes at a time, then turn it off while the other students were talking. Thus only one student could be heard at a time and students

BOX 2.3 SOCIOLOGY IN GLOBAL PERSPECTIVE

Altruism and Finance: The Grameen Bank

Many rich nations, including Canada, provide foreign aid to poorer countries. Much of this aid is spent on large projects, such as dams, power plants, and transportation systems. Many critics have claimed that these infrastructure projects have done little to benefit the poor people these countries are trying to help (see Chapter 9, "Global Stratification"). However, in recent years the problem of development has been approached in a new way.

Mohammad Yunus has invented a novel form of aid that directly benefits the poorest of the world's people. In the early 1970s, Yunus was the head of the economics department at Chittagong University in the newly independent country of Bangladesh. In 1974, a terrible famine killed 1.5 million Bangladeshis and changed Yunus's life. Disturbed by the contrast between the economic theories he was teaching in his classes and the terrible poverty that surrounded him, he decided to take his students to the affected towns and villages and try to find solutions to their poverty. On one of these visits, he met a woman who said her profit from making bamboo stools was the equivalent of only 2 cents per day. She explained to Yunus that because she had no money, she could not buy the bamboo herself, even though it cost only 20 cents for a day's worth of the raw material. Instead, she had to get it from a trader who required that she sell the stools to him for a very low price. Yunus spoke with others in the same village and found forty-two self-employed people in similar circumstances who together needed a total of $27 to become self-sufficient. Yunus lent them the money and then also tried to convince local banks to lend money to the poor. The banks refused, saying that people would not repay the money and that such small sums were not worth the trouble. So, Yunus borrowed money himself and lent it to people in many different villages.

After several years of lobbying, Yunus convinced the government to allow him to set up a bank called the Grameen Bank ("rural bank" in Bengali). The bank was funded through preferential loans and through grants from international donors. Unlike most banks that lend money only to people who have money or property they can use as collateral, the Grameen Bank deals solely with the destitute. Yunus lends mainly to women, as he finds that they are more likely to give the benefits to their families and to repay the money. The bank charges interest and has several interesting requirements. For example, the bank will lend money only to groups of five borrowers. The five do not necessarily have to be in business together, but are responsible for one another's loans. The group provides both peer support and peer pressure to ensure the loans are repaid. Grameen also requires borrowers to adhere to several principles that are essentially personal commitments to things like improving sanitation practices and sending their children to school. In addition to business loans, the bank also provides housing loans.

The Grameen Bank has been phenomenally successful. About 98 percent of its loans are repaid, a much higher rate than that of other banks. The bank has expanded dramatically since it began operating in 1979. There are nearly four million borrowers in Bangladesh, almost all of whom are women, and it is lending more than half a billion dollars each year. Because of the high repayment rate, the bank is now self-sustaining.

Yunus's idea of microcredit has spread around the globe and is operating in more than fifty countries. In Canada, there are hundreds of microcredit programs. Among the most notable are those run by Martin Connell's Calmeadow Foundation. Connell has established several microcredit programs including the First People's Fund. Calmeadow provided half the money for this program, with First Nations communities and the five largest chartered banks sharing the remainder. The fund has now been spun off into a number of separate funds, based on reserves and run by Aboriginal people themselves.

Yunus is a very unusual bank president. He is paid only $500 per month for this job, does not own a car, and has never charged anything on a credit card. However, his work has been widely recognized and he has won countless awards and honours, including an honorary doctorate from the University of Toronto. Several observers, including former U.S. president Bill Clinton, have suggested that Yunus be awarded a Nobel Prize for his revolutionary ideas and for the altruism he has shown in devoting his life to ending poverty.

What do you think would be the best way to study the impact of microcredit programs? One way would be to conduct an observational study involving extensive interviews with those who have received loans. You might also set up a field experiment in which microcredit programs were introduced into some communities that were then compared with communities that did not have the programs.

Sources: Grameen Bank, 2005; Jolis, 1996; Mitchell, 1997; Stackhouse, 1998; and Yunus, 1997.

could not have conversations with each other. To ensure spontaneity, the experimenter would not listen to the students' discussion but would get their reactions later.

All these instructions were part of an elaborate script designed to see how the participants would respond to an emergency, in this case an epileptic seizure by one of the respondents. The script had been acted out and tape-recorded. After receiving the instructions, each subject heard a taped simulation that began with the future seizure victim discussing his difficulties adjusting to university and to big-city life. In the course of this discussion, he mentioned that he was prone to seizures during studying and exams. Each of the other people in the group, including the subject, then took their turns talking about their own adjustment problems.

The emergency occurred when it was again the victim's turn to talk. After beginning normally, he began to show obvious distress, then asked repeatedly for help, then made choking sounds and said he was going to die. After that, the intercom went quiet.

You will recall that Latané and Darley proposed the hypothesis that the presence of others would inhibit a helping response when people were faced with an emergency. The dependent variable in this experiment was the time that elapsed from the start of the victim's seizure until the participant left the experiment room to get help. The major independent variable was the number of other people each participant believed had also heard the victim's distress.

Did the experiment support the hypothesis? Figure 2.2 shows the results. Clearly, the number of bystanders had a significant effect on the likelihood of the student reporting the emergency. All of the participants in the two-person groups reported the emergency, compared with 85 percent of the subjects in the three-person groups and only 62 percent of the subjects in the six-person groups. The participants in the two-person groups also responded more quickly than those in the larger groups.

What about those who failed to respond? Were they apathetic or unconcerned about the victim? You might be surprised to learn that this was not the case. Those who did not respond were clearly upset by the episode.

| Figure 2.2 | A Study of Altruistic Behaviour |

Cumulative proportion of subjects reporting seizure who think they alone hear the victim, or that one to four others also are present.

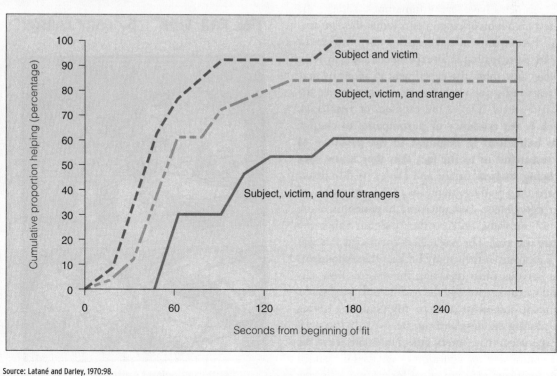

Source: Latané and Darley, 1970:98.

When the researcher entered the experiment room to end the study, the students who had not reported the seizure were often nervous and emotionally aroused. Many asked the experimenter to confirm that the victim was "all right." While the students in the two-person groups clearly felt they had to intervene because nobody else knew of the victim's distress, those in the larger groups did worry about the victim but were also concerned about making fools of themselves by overreacting and about ruining the experiment. Knowledge that others also knew of the emergency made it less likely that they would resolve this conflict by helping the victim. However, according to Latané and Darley it would not be fair to say that their failure to intervene was due to apathy or a lack of concern.

Strengths and Weaknesses of Experiments

The major advantage of the controlled experiment is the researcher's control over the environment and the ability to isolate the experimental variable. Because the researcher controls the independent variable, experiments are the best way of testing cause-and-effect relationships. A second advantage is that since many experiments require relatively little time and money and can be conducted with limited numbers of participants, it is possible for researchers to replicate an experiment several times by using different groups of participants. Replication strengthens claims about the validity and generalizability of the original research findings (Babbie, 2001).

Experiments have several limitations. Perhaps the greatest limitation of experiments is that they are artificial. Participants in a laboratory obviously know they are participating in an experiment and may react to what they think the experiment is about or may not react realistically because they do not believe the scenario is real. This is the problem of *reactivity,* **which is the tendency of participants to change their behaviour in response to the presence of the researcher or to the fact that they know they are being studied.** Latané and Darley tried to determine if their findings were due to the artificiality of their experiment. Perhaps some respondents chose not to intervene because they did not think the seizure was real. The researchers concluded this was not a problem in their study because the respondents were nervous when reporting the seizure, were surprised when they learned the true nature of the study, and made comments such as "My God, he's having a fit" during the simulated seizure.

Experiments have several other limitations. First, the rigid control and manipulation of variables demanded by experiments may not allow for a more collective approach to data gathering that would allow input from the research participants. Second, social scientists frequently rely on volunteers or captive audiences, such as students. As a result, the subjects of most experiments may not be representative of a larger population, and the findings cannot be generalized to other groups. Third, experiments are limited in scope, as only a small number of variables can be manipulated.

Surveys

Survey research is the method of data collection perhaps most often associated with the discipline of sociology. In a *survey,* **a number of respondents are asked identical questions through a systematic questionnaire or interview.** Researchers frequently select a representative sample (a small group of respondents) from a larger population (the total group of people) to answer questions about their attitudes, opinions, or behaviour. **Respondents are persons who provide data for analysis through interviews or questionnaires.** The Gallup and Ipsos-Reid polls are among the most widely known large-scale surveys. Government agencies, such as Statistics Canada, conduct a variety of surveys as well, including the census, which attempts to gain information from

This cartoon illustrates the problem of reactivity. People may change their behaviours in response to the presence of a researcher.

THE FAR SIDE®   BY GARY LARSON

© 1984 FarWorks, Inc. All Rights Reserved/Dist. by Creators Syndicate

"Anthropologists! Anthropologists!"

all persons in Canada. Surveys are an important research method because they make it possible to study things that are not directly observable—such as people's attitudes and beliefs—and to describe a population too large to observe directly (Babbie, 2001).

Types of Surveys   Survey data are collected by using self-administered questionnaires, personal interviews, and/or telephone surveys. A **questionnaire is a research instrument containing a series of items to which subjects respond.** Questionnaires may be administered by interviewers in face-to-face encounters, by telephone, over the Internet, or by self-administered questionnaires.

Self-administered questionnaires have certain strengths. They are relatively simple and inexpensive to administer, they allow for rapid data collection and analysis, and they permit respondents to remain anonymous (an important consideration when the questions are of a personal nature). A major disadvantage is the low response rate. Mailed surveys sometimes have a response rate as low as 10 percent—and a 50-percent response rate is considered by some to be minimally adequate (Babbie, 2001). The response rate usually is somewhat higher if the survey is handed out to a group, such as a school class, that is asked to fill it out on the spot.

Survey data may also be collected by interviews. An **interview is a data collection encounter in which an interviewer asks the respondent questions and records the answers.** Survey research often uses structured interviews, in which the interviewer asks questions from a standardized questionnaire.

Interviews have specific advantages. They usually are more effective in dealing with complicated issues and provide an opportunity for face-to-face communication between the interviewer and respondent.

When open-ended questions are used, the researcher may gain new perspectives. The major disadvantage of interviews is the cost and time involved in conducting them.

Questionnaires may also be administered by *telephone surveys,* which are becoming an increasingly popular way to collect data for a number of reasons. Telephone surveys save time and money compared to face-to-face interviews. Some respondents may be more honest than when they are facing an interviewer. Telephone surveys also give greater control over data collection and provide greater personal safety for respondents and researchers than do personal encounters. They usually have much higher response rates than questionnaires that are mailed out. However, telephone answering machines, caller identification systems, and cell phones have made telephone surveys more difficult since some people now are less accessible to researchers.

Sampling Considerations   Survey research usually involves some form of sampling. Researchers begin by identifying the population they want to study. They then determine what constitutes a representative sample of that population.

The **population consists of those persons about whom we want to be able to draw conclusions.** A **sample is the people who are selected from the population to be studied.** A *representative sample* **is a selection from a larger population that has the essential characteristics of the total population.** For example, if you have to interview five students selected haphazardly from your sociology class, they would not be representative of your school's total student body. By contrast, if five hundred students were selected from the total student body using a random sampling method, they would very likely be representative of your school's students. A simple

Computer-assisted telephone interviewing is an easy and cost-efficient method of conducting research. The widespread use of answering machines, cell phones, and caller ID may make this form of research more difficult in the twenty-first century.

random sample **is chosen by chance: every member of an entire population being studied has the same chance of being selected.** For example, you might draw a sample of the total student body by placing all the students' names in a rotating drum and drawing names from it.

Survey Research: The Gift of Blood

To what degree should we be responsible for the lives of others? Should an economic value be placed on human life? Can social policy influence moral behaviour? Richard Titmuss of the University of London addressed these very important questions in his study of blood donation. Titmuss's concerns were much broader than blood; he was interested in society's spirit of altruism and he used blood donation as an indicator of social values and human relationships. He wished to understand why people would donate blood to strangers in a world that often seems characterized by self-interest and greed.

Policies regarding the donation and distribution of blood vary widely around the world. In many countries at least some donors are paid, and the collection and distribution of blood is a business. In others, including Canada and the United Kingdom, blood is not treated as a commodity to be bought and sold, but as a voluntary gift. For Titmuss, donating blood is a special kind of gift because the recipient is an anonymous stranger and because the donor may never receive anything in return. He refers to such gifts as "creative altruism" and suggests they are an important component of caring communities. In his research, he wished to determine what types of people became blood donors and to ask them about their motivations for donating.

At the time of Titmuss's research, Britain's National Blood Transfusion Service did not record statistics about the age, sex, marital status, or social class of its donors. To learn about the characteristics of blood donors and their reasons for giving blood, Titmuss distributed 8,000 questionnaires to current blood donors. Respondents were asked to complete the surveys and to personally return them at meetings with the researchers. To see how Titmuss presented his data, see Box 2.4.

BOX 2.4 SOCIOLOGY AND EVERYDAY LIFE

Presenting Sociological Data

As you have read in this chapter, sociologists have a variety of ways of gathering data. These data are often presented numerically, and in this book you will find many tables that give the results of sociological studies. It will be helpful to you to learn how to understand these tables and to develop the skill of presenting your own data.

The simplest table shows how a single variable is distributed. For example, in his study of blood donors in England, Richard Titmuss was interested in finding out whether there were social class differences in willingness to donate blood. Titmuss looked at the distribution of incomes reported by the 3,699 people who responded to his survey. While he could have simply listed each of the reported incomes, the resulting table would have been very large. To make the data more manageable, Titmuss provided a *frequency distribution*—he put each respondent into one of five income categories (see Table 1).

Table 1 SOCIAL CLASS OF BLOOD DONORS IN ENGLAND

	Upper		Middle		Lower	Total
	I	II	III	IV	V	
Percentage of Respondents	10	20	55	12	3	100 (3699)

When you look at the line of percentages, you see that 55 percent of all blood donors were from Class III compared with 20 percent from Class II and lower percentages from each of the other class categories. This seems to tell us that middle-class people are far more likely than others to donate blood. However, before you can come to this conclusion, you must know one additional piece of information—the percentage of the general population that is in each class. While it is true that 55 percent of the blood donated in England comes from the middle class (people in Class III), this figure would have a different meaning if 80 percent of the population were middle class than it would if 30 percent were in this category.

Ideally, Titmuss would have compared the percentage of those who donated blood in each social class category with the percentage of those in the same category who did not donate blood. However, because he had not collected data on nondonors, he compared the percentage of donors in each class with the class distribution of the British census. This enabled him to determine if the various classes included more or fewer blood donors than would be expected based on their proportion in the general population.

Now, looking at Table 2, we can see that while it is true that most blood is donated by members of the middle class, we can also see that upper-class members were disproportionately more likely to donate blood than those in the other classes. Those in Class I made up 3 percent of the population but 10 percent of all blood donors. By contrast, those in Class V (the lowest-income earners) made up 8 percent of the population but accounted for

only 3 percent of blood donors. While the middle class does contribute more than its share of blood donors, their overcontribution is actually rather small, as they make up 48 percent of the population and 55 percent of the blood donors.

If you look at Table 2, you can see the basic elements of a table:

1. *Title or heading*: This is a brief description of the *content* of the table.
2. *Variables*: In this case, the variable is "Social Class."
3. *Categories of the variables*: The variable of Social Class is divided into five categories based on reported income.
4. *Percentages*: The information given in our table is stated in percentages. Using the raw numbers would make comparisons very difficult for the reader. For example, the raw numbers for Class I are 370 blood donors and approximately 163,500 people from the general population. Using percentages enables us to compare the two figures very quickly. By comparing the 10 percent of blood donors with the 3 percent of the population we can easily determine that people in Class I are disproportionately likely to donate blood.
5. *Totals*: Since the numbers in the table are percentages, we need to know the total number of cases in each category in order to be able to calculate the raw numbers in each cell of the table. In this case, the total number of blood donors in Titmuss's sample was 3,699; the population of England at that time was 54,350,000.

Table 2	COMPARISON OF SOCIAL CLASS OF BLOOD DONORS WITH GENERAL POPULATION, ENGLAND AND WALES					
	SOCIAL CLASS					
	Upper		Middle		Lower	Total
	I	II	III	IV	V	
Percentage of Respondents	10	20	55	12	3	100 (3699)
Percentage of Census Population	3	16	48	25	8	100 (54,350,000)

Source: Data adapted from Titmuss, 1971.

The British donors came from all segments of society, but were somewhat more likely to be young, male, and from the middle and upper middle classes. Most were long-service donors; over

half had donated blood fifteen or more times. When asked why they had decided to become blood donors, respondents clearly supported Titmuss's hypothesis that their motivation was altruistic.

They spoke of their desire to help, their awareness of the need for blood, and their sense of duty toward others. These quotations from the surveys are typical of the responses:

> I thought it just a small way to help people—as a blind person other opportunities are limited.

> At the age of 18 I decided that it was a good thing for anyone capable and healthy to donate blood for the good of other people and the advancement of medical science.

> My son was killed on the road, he was a blood donor and I knew they did their best to save him and because I know he would be pleased I am carrying on as long as I can to help someone I hope. (Titmuss, 1971: 227–229)

Most donors explained their behaviour in moral terms. They felt they had responsibilities and obligations beyond their own immediate gratification. Titmuss concluded that these obligations help sustain a feeling of community membership. You will recall from Chapter 1, "The Sociological Perspective," that Émile Durkheim discussed how preindustrial societies were held together by strong traditions and by members' shared moral beliefs and values. As societies industrialized, economic activity increasingly became the basis of the social bond. Titmuss's work demonstrates that even in complex, large-scale societies altruism plays a significant role in maintaining the social order.

Strengths and Weaknesses of Surveys

Survey research has several important strengths. First, it is useful in describing the characteristics of a large population without having to interview each person in that population. Second, survey research enables the researcher to assess the relative importance of a number of variables. Unfortunately, Titmuss gave his surveys only to those who had donated blood, so his work does not allow us to examine the differences between donors and nondonors without bringing in additional data, such as the census data presented in Table 2 in Box 2.4. The best way to study these differences would be to conduct a survey of a sample of the general population in which respondents would be asked if they had donated blood. We could then look at the effect of demographic variables (such as age, sex, and income level) and attitudinal variables on the decision to donate blood. This would allow us to determine which of these independent variables

influences altruism the most and how influential each is relative to the others.

Survey research also has several weaknesses. One is that the use of standardized questions tends to force responses into categories in which they may or may not belong. Another weakness concerns validity. People's opinions on issues seldom take the form of a standard response ranging from "strongly agree" to "strongly disagree." Moreover, as in other types of research, people may be less than truthful, especially on emotionally charged issues or on issues, such as altruism, that have a strong element of social desirability. They may also be unwilling to provide information on sensitive issues and may simply forget relevant information. Some possible reasons for error are shown in Table 2.1. This can make reliance on self-reported attitudes and behaviour problematic.

Secondary Analysis of Existing Data

In **secondary analysis, researchers use existing material and analyze data originally collected by others.** Existing data sources include public records, official reports of organizations or government agencies, and surveys conducted by researchers in universities and private corporations. Research data gathered from studies are available in data banks. Many Canadian university libraries have recently joined the Data Liberation Initiative, which gives members of the university community access to a wide variety of databases. Other sources of data for secondary analysis are books, magazines, newspapers, radio and television programs, and personal documents. Secondary analysis is referred to as *unobtrusive research* because it includes a variety of nonreactive research techniques— that is, techniques that have no impact on the people being studied. In Durkheim's study of suicide (discussed in Chapter 1), for example, his analysis of existing statistics on suicide did nothing to increase or decrease the number of people who *actually* committed suicide.

The case study in the next section shows how data collected for other purposes can be used to shed light on the phenomenon of altruism.

Secondary Analysis: Good Neighbours and Saints

Sociologist Pitirim Sorokin had a remarkable life and career, and his background played an important role in shaping his work on altruism. Sorokin was born in

Table 2.1 STATISTICS: WHAT WE KNOW (AND DON'T KNOW)

	TOPIC		
	Homelessness	Gay Men	Domestic Violence
Research Finding	More than 200,000 people in this country are homeless.	At least 1 percent of Canadian men are exclusively homosexual.	Some surveys have reported that women are as likely as men to engage in domestic violence.
Possible Problem	Does that badly underestimate the total number of homeless people?	Does this under-estimate the gay population? Is the actual figure higher?	Are the results of these surveys accurate, or should we believe other data, such as homicide statistics, that show domestic violence is predominantly committed by males?
Explanation	The homeless are diffi-cult to count. They may avoid interviews with census takers. The 1996 census was the first attempt to count the number of homeless in Canada. However, these numbers will not be released by Statistics Canada.	Many people are reluctant to tell interviewers the truth about their sexuality; people often are hesitant to report their sexual orientation. This may result in estimates being too low.	There may be differences in the willingness of males and females to report abusing their partners; the surveys ignore the context of the violence; and the surveys do not consider the degree of injury.

1889 into a poor peasant family in northern Russia, but by 1930 he had become the first chairman of Harvard University's sociology department. As a youth he was part of the active resistance against the Russian czar and spent much of the time between 1906 and 1917 in jail. He was a senior official in the Kerensky government after the czar fell, but once again became a political target when his party was replaced by the Bolsheviks, who imprisoned Sorokin for opposing Lenin. Throughout these difficult times, his strong commitment to the Orthodox church helped him retain a positive view of life and a strong sense of duty and obligation.

Sorokin's work on altruism was driven by his view that Western culture had become increasingly negativistic. He was particularly critical of the mass media's emphasis on crime, sex scandals, and hypocrisy. In words that predated Jerry Springer and Howard Stern by almost fifty years, Sorokin expressed his disgust with a popular culture that "dwells mainly in the region of subsocial sewers;

breathes mainly their foul air; and drags down into their turbid muck everything heroic, positive, true, good and beautiful" (1950:3). He was also critical of social scientists who concentrated their efforts on studying the negative aspects of society:

The criminal has been "researched" incomparably more thoroughly than the saint or the altruist; the idiot has been studied much more carefully than the genius; perverts and failures have been investigated much more intensely than inte-grated persons or heroes. In accordance with the total nature of our negativistic culture, our social science has been semi-blind about all positive types and actions and very sharp-eyed about all negative types and actions. It seems to have enjoyed moving in the muck of social sewers; it has been reluctant to move in the fresh air of high social peaks. It has stressed the pathological and neglected the sound and heroic. (1950:4)

Sorokin wanted to redress this one-sided perspective by studying altruistic behaviour. He felt that increasing the incidence of altruism was the key to transforming the culture and hoped his research on altruists would facilitate this transformation. In his book *Altruistic Love,* he looked at two very different groups of people: "good neighbours" and saints. He chose these groups because of the rich secondary data that were made available to him.

In the first part of his study, rather than looking at dramatic acts of kindness or heroism, Sorokin chose to study the behaviour of ordinary people. During the 1940s, a radio program called *Breakfast in Hollywood* rewarded what it called "good neighbours" with an orchid and a citation on the show. These people were chosen from letters of recommendation sent in by listeners from across the United States. The show's producers had kept the letters on file and Sorokin was able to analyze five hundred nominations of people who had quietly served their communities with no expectation of any benefit to themselves.

The majority of the good neighbours were females. Sorokin attributed this to the socialization of women into nurturing roles, to the tendency of men to express their altruistic spirit through financial donations rather than through direct service, and to the fact that many of the nominations were received during World War II, when millions of men were serving overseas. Most were middle-aged married people from rural communities. The vast majority were frequent churchgoers. Not surprisingly, most were very optimistic, friendly people who belonged to a wide variety of community organizations.

Because of the many wartime nominations, the largest category of persons helped were members of the military. Other common recipients of assistance were the sick, charitable organizations, children, and the elderly. In many respects, those helped were the opposites of their helpers—they were most often male, unmarried, and either aged or children. Many different types of help were offered, including recreational and social activities, activities to help alleviate loneliness and grief, and more tangible things, such as money, food, shelter, and clothing.

In the second part of his study, Sorokin turned to the lives of Catholic saints. Unlike the good neighbours, whose activities usually went unrecognized outside their communities, saints had been singled out for unique recognition by the Catholic church. For many, saints represent the epitome of selfless love and goodness. They are visible examples of the highest human qualities and are held out to other church members as examples of the highest form of altruistic love. In this study, Sorokin drew from the very rich resource provided by a twelve-volume work called *The Lives of the Saints,* which provided biographical information on 3,090 saints.

Unlike the good neighbours, who were predominantly female, more than 80 percent of the saints were males. However, the proportion of women achieving sainthood has changed dramatically over time. From the first to the twelfth centuries, the proportion of women who became saints rarely exceeded 20 percent. Since the thirteenth century, the proportion of women saints has fallen below 20 percent in only the sixteenth and seventeenth centuries, and in the eighteenth century women made up almost half the new saints. This suggests that as women moved toward becoming the social equals of men, their representation in the sainthood rose. Similarly, the proportion of saints from royal or noble backgrounds has declined, and by the nineteenth century most saints were drawn from the lower classes of peasants and urban workers.

Sorokin was able to distinguish several different paths to sainthood. The largest number (44 percent) were what he called "fortunate saints," who showed signs of religiosity and devotion to God from a very early age. They continued to show this devotion until death, so their whole lives were examples of goodness and purity. Another 37 percent achieved sainthood through martyrdom—they showed courage and devotion by not renouncing their faith despite their imminent death at a time of either religious persecution or religious war. Perhaps the most interesting finding was that 11 percent led distinctly unsaintly lives until they experienced a crisis such as sickness, a death, or an unexpected, extraordinary kindness that precipitated a complete reorientation in their lives.

Through his use of data collected for other purposes, Sorokin was able to tell us a great deal about the lives and work of altruistic people. However, his observation that social scientists are more interested in bad behaviour than in good works still holds true, and very few sociologists have followed his lead in studying the lives of exemplary people.

Analyzing Content **Content analysis** **is the systematic examination of cultural artifacts or various forms of communication to extract thematic data and draw conclusions about social life.** *Cultural artifacts* **are products of individual activity, social organizations, technology, and cultural patterns** (Reinharz, 1992). Among the materials studied are *written records,* such as diaries, love letters, poems, books, and graffiti, and *narratives and visual texts,* such as movies, television programs, advertisements, and greeting cards. Also studied are *material culture,* such as music, art, and even garbage, and *behavioural residues,* such as patterns of wear and tear on the floors in front of various exhibits at museums to determine which exhibits are the most popular (see Webb, 1966). Harriet Martineau stated that more could be learned about a society in a day by studying "things" than by talking with individuals for a year (Martineau, 1988/1838).

Strengths and Weaknesses of Secondary Analysis
One strength of secondary analysis is that data are readily available and often are inexpensive to obtain. Another is that, because the researcher usually does not collect the data personally, the chances of bias may be reduced. In addition, the use of existing sources makes it possible to analyze longitudinal data to provide a historical context within which to locate original research. However, secondary analysis has inherent problems. For one thing, the data may be incomplete, inauthentic, or inaccurate. Sorokin found that even basic data, such as age at death and social class of origin, were not available for many of the early saints. Also, secondary data are often collected for administrative purposes, so the categories may not reflect variables of interest to the researcher. Sorokin could not find information in the records about the motivation of either the good neighbours or the saints, so he could not explain why they behaved altruistically.

Field Research

Field research **is the study of social life in its natural setting: observing and interviewing people where they live, work, and play.** Some kinds of behaviour can be studied best by "being there"; a fuller understanding can be developed through observations, face-to-face discussions, and participation in events. Researchers use these methods to generate *qualitative* data: observations that are best described verbally rather than numerically. Although field research is less structured and more flexible than the other methods we have discussed, it also places many demands on the researcher. To engage in field research, sociologists must select the method or combination of methods that will best reveal what they want to know. For example, they must decide how to approach the target group, whether to identify themselves as researchers, and whether to participate in the events they are observing.

Canadians have always shown a strong willingness to help in natural disasters, such as the 1997 Red River flood.

Observation Sociologists who are interested in observing social interaction as it occurs may use either complete observation or participant observation. In ***complete observation,* the researcher systematically observes a social process but does not take part in it.** Observational research can take place just about anywhere. For example, sociologists David Karp and William Yoels (1976) became interested in why many students do not participate in discussions in university classrooms. Observers sat in on various classes and took notes that included the average number of students who participated, the number of times they talked during one class session, and the sex of the instructor and of the students who talked in class. From their observational data, Karp and Yoels found that, on average, a very small number of students are responsible for the majority of all discussion that occurs in class on any given day.

Suppose you wanted to study your own class to identify the "talkers" and the "silent ones." You would need to develop a game plan before you started to observe. A game plan typically is guided by a research question, such as, "Why don't more university students participate in class discussions?" Subjects in observation studies may not realize that they are being studied, especially if the researcher remains unobtrusive. Observation helps us view behaviour as it is taking place; however, it provides limited opportunities to learn why people do certain things. One way for researchers to remain unobtrusive is through *participant observation*—**collecting systematic observations while being part of the activities of the group they are studying.** Participant observation generates more "inside" information than simply asking questions or observing from the outside. As sociologist William Whyte noted in his classic participant observation study of a Boston low-income neighbourhood: "As I sat and listened, I learned the answers to questions I would not have had the sense to ask" (1957:303).

Field Research: Responding to Disaster

During the spring of 1997, two of this book's authors observed altruistic behaviour first-hand when they witnessed the phenomenal response to the massive Red River floods. Tens of thousands of Manitobans devoted several weeks of their time to sandbagging; volunteers flew in from as far away as Newfoundland at their own expense to help; the Canadian military sent in more than 8,000 soldiers, sailors, and air force members who worked day and night to save Manitoba communities; and people from all parts of Canada donated millions of dollars to help pay for the cleanup. While the flooding was very costly and disrupted the lives of thousands of people in Manitoba and North Dakota, it was also an event that created bonds among the people involved and reinforced a sense of community.

The Manitoba experience is not unique. Natural disasters have brought people together in many parts of the world and have often shown human behaviour at its altruistic best. This was illustrated once again in 2005, when individual Canadians donated more than $150 million to help survivors of the Indian Ocean tsunami. What motivates people to get involved in helping after natural disasters? How do groups of strangers come together and work effectively to help others? How do communities restore their cohesiveness after a tragic loss? Sociologist Louis Zurcher (1968) tried to answer these questions when he took part in the cleanup following a severe tornado that destroyed parts of Topeka, Kansas. The tornado killed 17 persons, injured 550 others, and made 2,500 people homeless.

Zurcher, a resident of Topeka, joined a volunteer work crew that spent several days cleaning up after the tornado. He joined the crew in order to help his community recover from the disaster, but he also took the opportunity to carry out an observational research study. In addition to the physical work he was doing—largely removing fallen tree limbs and trees from houses—he systematically observed what was happening and recorded these observations in detailed notes made on the scene and at the end of each work day. He supplemented these observations with unstructured interviews with members of his work crew conducted after the cleanup.

One of the most important research questions for Zurcher was why individuals gave up their time and took the risks involved in helping their fellow residents. In his interviews, he found that all the volunteers in his workcrew felt they simply had to do something. The stress of living through the tornado and, for some, the guilt at having survived unscathed motivated the workers to get out and to help the community recover from the disaster.

The crew members, most of whom did not know each other prior to the disaster, seemed to find the first day of hard work a way of working off the emotions raised by the tornado. By the end of the day, the men had begun to form a cohesive group in which each member had a specific role. On the second day, the roles became more formalized and group identity became stronger as the men took on some challenging tasks. Outside social status meant little, as people from a broad range of occupations worked together. The workcrew quickly evolved from a group of strangers into a cohesive group with a well-defined division of labour and its own history, loyalty to other members, a great deal of humour, and its own specialized language. The group ended its work after the third day, but some of the men met socially for years after the disaster.

Zurcher felt that the manner in which group solidarity and cohesiveness developed in his workcrew would also develop in other social settings. Following a disaster, people initially come together because of shared concerns and common experiences. However, in our complex world, a division of labour quickly evolves, and people are also bound together by their mutual dependence as they carry out specialized tasks. You will learn more about these processes in Chapter 5 ("Society, Social Structure, and Interaction") when you read about Émile Durkheim's important distinction between mechanical and organic solidarity. Durkheim's insights about the change in the source of social solidarity as societies become more complex were tested by Zurcher in the real-life social laboratory provided by the Kansas tornado.

Case Studies Most participant observation research takes the form of a *case study*, an in-depth, multifaceted investigation of a single event, person, or social grouping (Feagin, Orum, and Sjoberg, 1991). Case studies often involve more than one method of research, such as participant observation, unstructured or in-depth interviews, and life histories.

How do social scientists decide to do case studies? Initially, some researchers have only a general idea of what they wish to investigate. In other cases, they literally "back into" the research. They may find themselves in proximity to interesting people or situations. For example, just as Zurcher "backed into" his study of helping when he joined a volunteer workcrew cleaning up after a tornado, anthropologist Elliot Liebow got the idea for his study of single, homeless women living in emergency shelters after becoming a volunteer at a shelter. As he got to know the women, Liebow became fascinated with their lives and survival strategies. Prior to Liebow's research, most studies of the homeless focused primarily on men. These studies typically asked questions such as, "How many homeless are there?" and "What proportion of the homeless are chronically mentally ill?" By contrast, Liebow wanted to know more about the homeless women themselves, wondering such things as, "What are they carrying in those [shopping] bags?" (Coughlin, 1993:A8). Liebow spent the next four years engaged in participant observation research that culminated in his book *Tell Them Who I Am* (1993).

In participant observation studies, the researcher must decide whether to let people know they are being studied. After Liebow decided that he would like to take notes on informal conversations and conduct interviews with the women, he asked the shelter director and the women for permission and told them that he would like to write about them. Liebow's findings are discussed in Chapter 5.

Ethnography An ***ethnography* is a detailed study of the life and activities of a group of people by researchers who may live with that group over a period of years** (Feagin, Orum, and Sjoberg, 1991). Although this approach is similar in some ways to participant observation, these studies typically take place over much longer periods of time. In fact, ethnography has been referred to as "the study of the way of life of a group of people" (Prus, 1996). For example, the books *Middletown* and *Middletown in Transition* describe Robert Lynd and Helen Lynd's (1929, 1937) study in Muncie, Indiana. The Lynds, who lived in this Midwestern town for a number of

years, applied ethnographic research to the daily lives of residents, conducting interviews and reading newspaper files in order to build a historical base for their own research. The Lynds showed how a dominant family "ruled" the city and how the working class developed as a result of industry moving into Muncie. They concluded that the people had strong beliefs about the importance of religion, hard work, self-reliance, and civic pride. When a team of sociologists returned to Muncie in the late 1970s, they found that the people there still held these views (Bahr and Caplow, 1991).

In another classic study, *Street Corner Society*, William F. Whyte (1988/1943) conducted long-term participant observation studies in Boston's low-income Italian neighbourhoods. Whereas "outsiders" generally regarded these neighbourhoods as disorganized slums with high crime rates, Whyte found the residents to be hardworking people who tried to take care of one another. More recently, Elijah Anderson (1990) conducted a study in two Philadelphia neighbourhoods—one populated by low-income African Americans, the other racially mixed but becoming increasingly middle- to upper-income and white. Over the course of fourteen years Anderson spent numerous hours on the streets, talking and listening to the people (Anderson, 1990:ix). In this longitudinal study, Anderson was able to document the changes brought about by drug abuse, loss of jobs, decreases in city services despite increases in taxes, and the eventual exodus of middle-income people. As these examples show, ethnographic work involves not only immersing oneself into the group or community that the researcher studies but also engaging in dialogue to learn more about social life through ongoing interaction with others (Burawoy, 1991).

Case studies of homeless persons have added to our insights on the causes and consequences of this major social concern. Women often are the "invisible homeless."

Unstructured Interviews An *unstructured interview* **is an extended, open-ended interaction between an interviewer and an interviewee.** The interviewer has a general plan of inquiry but not a specific set of questions that must be asked, as is often the case with surveys. Unstructured interviews are essentially conversations in which interviewers establish the general direction by asking open-ended questions, to which interviewees may respond flexibly. Interviewers have the ability to "shift gears" and pursue specific topics raised by interviewees, because answers to one question are used to suggest the next question or new areas of inquiry.

Even in unstructured interviews, researchers must prepare a few general or "lead-in" questions to get the interview started. Following the interviewee's initial responses, the interviewer may wish to ask additional questions on the same topic, probe for more information (by using questions, such as "In what ways?" or "Anything else?"), or introduce a new line of inquiry. At all points in the interview, *careful listening* is essential. It provides the opportunity to introduce new questions as the interview proceeds while simultaneously keeping the interview focused on the research topic. It also enables the interviewer to envision interviewees' experiences and to glean multiple levels of meaning.

Interviews and Theory Construction

In-depth interviews, along with participant observation and case studies, frequently are used to develop theories through observation. The term *grounded theory* was developed by sociologists Barney Glaser and Anselm Strauss (1967) to describe this inductive method of theory construction. Researchers who use grounded theory collect and analyze data simultaneously. For example, after in-depth interviews with 106 suicide attempters, researchers in one study concluded that half of the individuals who attempted suicide wanted both to live and to die at the time of their attempt. From these unstructured interviews, it became obvious that ambivalence led about half of "serious" suicidal attempters to "literally gamble with death" (Kovacs and Beck, 1977, quoted in Taylor, 1982:144).

Strengths and Weaknesses of Field Research

Field research provides opportunities for researchers to view from the inside what may not be obvious to an outside observer. Field methods are useful when attitudes and behaviours can be understood best within their natural setting or when the researcher wants to study social processes and change over a period of time. They provide a wealth of information about the reactions of people and give us an opportunity to generate theories from the data collected (Whyte, 1989).

Participant observation can also be very difficult. Jack Haas describes his first day in the field in his study of high steel ironworkers:

> My traumatic introduction to the workday realities of high steel ironworking came the day the construction superintendent passed me through the construction gate, gave me a hard hat, and wished me good luck. Directly ahead were five incomplete levels of an emerging 21 storey office building. From my vantage point I observed a variety of workers engaged in the construction process. The most visible and immediately impressive group of workers were those on the upper level who were putting steel beams into place. These were the ironworkers I had come to participate with and observe. This chilling reality filled me with an almost overwhelming anxiety. I began to experience a trepidation that far exceeded any usual observer anxiety encountered in the first days of field research . . . the risks of firsthand observation were profoundly obvious. It was with fearful anticipation that I moved toward the job site. (1977:148)

Haas's understandable fear over the prospect of walking on ten-centimetre-wide steel beams hundreds of metres above city streets led to the central focus of his research. He eventually learned that while the ironworkers did not talk publicly about their fears and while they worked daily far above the ground in very difficult conditions, they also shared his concerns. Despite this they were careful not to let their colleagues know they were afraid and often took risks in order to prove themselves to the other workers. Like other people in dangerous occupations, the ironworkers had developed a work culture that helped them to deal with the risks inherent in their work. They try to control their work environment through practices like deciding on their own whether it is too dangerous to work rather than going along with the demands of their supervisors, and by following a rather strict informal code of what types of behaviour are appropriate for their co-workers:

> Workers who perceive physical danger develop mechanisms to control their reactions and the reactions of others. . . . Symbolic or real threats bind workers together in an effort to protect themselves. Part of the defense, however, lies

in controlling one's personal trepidations and insecurities and maintaining an appearance of fearlessness. (1977:168)

While most field research does not involve this degree of danger, field research often involves spending large blocks of time with very different types of people, long periods of time away from home, work schedules that respond to the activities being observed rather than the wishes of the researcher, and a host of other difficulties.

Despite these concerns, there is really no other way of experiencing the world of your research subjects. It is far different to have someone describe what it is like to stand on a piece of steel with nothing below you than to actually be there yourself.

Through unstructured interviews, researchers gain access to "people's ideas, thoughts, and memories in their own words rather than in the words of the researcher" (Reinharz, 1992:19). Research of this type is important for the study of race, ethnicity, and gender because it lets people who previously have had no "voice" describe their experiences and provides researchers with an opportunity to explore people's views of reality.

Social scientists who believe that quantitative research methods (such as survey research) provide the most scientific and accurate means of measuring attitudes, beliefs, and behaviour often are critical of data obtained through field research. They argue that what is learned from a specific group or community cannot be generalized to a larger population. They also suggest that the data collected in natural settings are descriptive and do not lend themselves to precise measurement.

Feminist Research Methods

During the past two decades, feminist social scientists have focused a critical eye on traditional sociological research, as well as on the research methodologies and findings of other disciplines. Margrit Eichler (1988b) has identified several limitations in research that relate to gender, including *androcentricity* (which means approaching an issue from a male perspective or viewing women only in terms of how they relate to men); sexist language or concepts; research methods that are biased in favour of men (for example, in sampling techniques or questionnaire design); and research results that overgeneralize (which means that results that focus on members of one sex are used to support conclusions about both sexes).

Most writers on feminist research issues agree that there is no one method that can be termed *the* feminist methodology. However, qualitative methods and, in particular, in-depth interviews tend to be associated with feminist research. Although feminist research may involve the same basic methods for collecting data as other research, the way in which feminists use these methods is very different. First, women's experiences are important and, to understand them, women's lives need to be addressed in their own terms (Edwards, 1993). Feminist research is woman centred; that is, "it puts women at the center of research that is nonalienating, nonexploitive, and potentially emancipating" (Scully, 1990:2–3). Second, the goal of feminist research is to provide explanations of women's lives that are useful to them in terms of improving their situations. It is important, therefore, to ensure that women's experiences are not objectified or treated as merely "research data." In fact, feminist sociologist Dorothy Smith (1987) suggests that "giving voice" to disadvantaged and marginalized groups in society should be a primary goal of sociology. Finally, feminist research methods challenge the traditional role of the researcher as a detached, "value-free," objective observer. Rather, the researcher is seen as central to the research process and her feelings and experiences should be analyzed as an integral part of the research process (Edwards, 1993; Kirby and McKenna, 1989).

In a discussion of her study of marital rape, Raquel Kennedy Bergen has shown the need for the researcher's personal involvement in the research process. Bergen took care to ensure that the women she interviewed knew that she was supportive and interested in helping them, and was not simply exploiting their experiences for her own purposes. She was willing to share her own views and experiences with her research subjects and was careful to deal with any emotional distress that was caused by her interviews:

> During the most emotionally difficult interview, I spent a long time offering support to a woman who became extremely upset when she described her husband . . . raping her in front of her child. This experience emphasized the need for researchers . . . to interview with conscious partiality. If I had been a detached and objective researcher merely collecting data, I might have either terminated the interview and discarded the data or possibly suggested that the woman receive outside counseling. As a feminist researcher, however, I was interacting with this woman on a personal level and her distress was deeply affecting. (1993:208)

Multiple Methods: Triangulation   What is the best method for studying a particular topic? Concept Table 2.A compares the various social research methods. There is no one best research method; each method has its own strengths and weaknesses, so many sociologists believe that it is best to combine multiple methods in a given study. Triangulation is the term used to describe this approach (Denzin, 1989). *Triangulation* refers not only to research methods **but also to multiple data sources, investigators, and theoretical perspectives in a study.** Multiple data sources include persons, situations, contexts, and time (Snow and Anderson, 1991). For example, in a study of "unattached homeless men and women living in and passing through Austin, Texas, in the mid-1980s," David Snow and Leon Anderson (1991:158) used as their primary data sources "the homeless themselves and the array of settings, agency personnel, business

Concept Table 2.A   STRENGTHS AND WEAKNESSES OF SOCIAL RESEARCH

RESEARCH METHOD	STRENGTHS	WEAKNESSES
Experiments		
Laboratory	Control over research	Artificial by nature
Field	Ability to isolate experimental factors	Frequent reliance on volunteers or captive audiences
Natural	Relatively little time and money required; replication possible, except for natural experiments	Ethical questions of deception; problem of reactivity
Survey Research		
Self-administered questionnaire	Useful in describing features of a large population without interviewing everyone	Potentially forced answers
Interview	Relatively large samples possible	Respondent untruthfulness on emotional issues
Telephone survey	Multivariate analysis possible	Data that are not always "hard facts" presented as such in statistical analyses
Secondary Analysis of Existing Data		
Existing statistics	Data often readily available, inexpensive to collect	Difficulty in determining accuracy of some of the data
Content analysis	Longitudinal and comparative studies possible; replication possible	Failure of data gathered by others to meet goals of current research; questions of privacy when using diaries or other personal documents
Field Research		
Observation	Opportunity to gain insider's view	Problems in generalizing results to a larger population
Participant observation	Useful for studying attitudes and behaviour in natural settings	Nonprecise data measurements
Case study	Longitudinal/comparative studies possible; documentation of important social problems of excluded groups possible	Inability to demonstrate cause/ effect relationships or test theories
Unstructured interviews	Access to people's ideas in their words; forum for previously excluded groups	Difficult to make comparisons because of lack of structure; not representative sample

proprietors, city officials, and neighborhood activities relevant to the routines of the homeless." Snow and Anderson gained a detailed portrait of the homeless and their experiences and institutional contacts by tracking more than seven hundred homeless individuals through a network of seven institutions with which they had varying degrees of contact.

The study also tracked a number of the individuals over a period of time and used a variety of methods, including "participant observation and informal, conversational interviewing with the homeless; participant and nonparticipation observation, coupled with formal and informal interviewing in street agencies and settings; and a systematic survey of agency records" (Snow and Anderson, 1991:158–169). This study is discussed in depth in Chapter 5 ("Society, Social Structure, and Interaction").

Multiple methods and approaches provide a wider scope of information and enhance our understanding of critical issues. Many researchers also use multiple methods to validate or refine one type of data by use of another type.

ETHICAL ISSUES IN SOCIOLOGICAL RESEARCH

The study of people ("human subjects") raises vital questions about ethical concerns in sociological research. Researchers are now required by a professional code of ethics to weigh the societal benefits of research against the potential physical and emotional costs to participants. Researchers are required to obtain written "informed consent" statements from the persons they study. However, these guidelines have produced many new questions, such as, What constitutes "informed consent"? What constitutes harm to a person? How do researchers protect the identity and confidentiality of their sources?

The Canadian Sociology and Anthropology Association has outlined the basic standards sociologists must follow in conducting research. Social research often involves intrusions into people's lives—surveys, interviews, field observations, and participation in experiments all involve personally valuable commodities: time, energy, and privacy. Participation in research must be voluntary. No one should be enticed, coerced, or forced to participate. Researchers must not harm the research subjects in any way—physically, psychologically, or personally. For example,

the researcher must be careful not to reveal information that would embarrass the participants or damage their personal relationships. Researchers must respect the rights of research subjects to anonymity and confidentiality.

A respondent is *anonymous* when the researcher cannot identify a given response with a given respondent. Anonymity is often extremely important in terms of obtaining information on "deviant" or illegal activities. For example, in a study on physician-assisted suicides conducted by the Manitoba Association of Rights and Liberties (Searles, 1995), ensuring the anonymity of the physicians responding to the survey was crucial because the doctors were being asked about their participation in illegal acts.

Maintaining *confidentiality* means that the researcher is able to identify a given person's responses with that person but essentially promises not to do so. Whether the researcher should reveal his or her identity is also a difficult issue. In some cases, it is useful to identify yourself as a researcher to obtain cooperation from respondents. However, there are other instances when revealing your identity can affect the content and quality of your research. It is not acceptable to use deception to obtain informed consent. For example, not informing a research subject of potential risk or harm constitutes deception.

Sociologists are committed to adhering to ethical considerations and to protecting research participants; however, many ethical issues arise that cannot be resolved easily. Research ethics is a difficult and often ambiguous topic and there are often disagreements among researchers concerning ethical issues. For example, is it ethical to give students extra marks in a course if they participate in an experiment? Is it ethical to persuade institutionalized young offenders to be interviewed about their crimes by offering payment? Different researchers might make different judgments for each of these questions.

How honest do researchers have to be with potential participants? Let's look at a specific case. Where does the "right to know" end and the "right to privacy" begin in this situation?

The Humphreys Research

Laud Humphreys (1970), then a sociology graduate student, decided to study homosexual behaviour for his doctoral dissertation. His research focused on homosexual acts between strangers meeting in "tearooms," public restrooms in parks. He did not ask permission of his subjects, nor did he inform them that they were being studied. Instead, he took advantage of the typical tearoom encounter, which involved three men: two who engaged in homosexual acts, and a third who kept a lookout for police and other unwelcome strangers. To conduct his study, Humphreys showed up at public restrooms that were known to be tearooms and offered to be the lookout. Then he systematically recorded details of the encounters that took place.

Humphreys was interested in the fact that the tearoom participants seemed to live "normal" lives apart from these encounters, and he decided to learn more about their everyday lives. To determine who they were, he wrote down their car licence numbers and tracked down their names and addresses. Later, he arranged for these men to be included in a medical survey so that he could go out and interview them personally. He wore different disguises and drove a different car so that they would not recognize him. From these interviews, he collected personal information and determined that most of the men were married and lived very conventional lives.

Humphreys probably would not have gained access to these subjects if he had identified himself as a researcher; nevertheless, the fact that he did not do so produced widespread criticism from sociologists and journalists. The police became very interested in his notes, but he refused to turn any information over to the authorities. His award-winning study, *Tearoom Trade* (1970), dispelled many myths about homosexual behaviour; however, the controversy surrounding his study has never been resolved. Do you think Humphreys's research was ethical? Would these men willingly have agreed to participate in Humphreys's research if he had identified himself as a researcher? What psychological harm might have come to these married men if people, outside of those involved in the encounters, knew about their homosexual behaviour? Today's university ethics committees would never permit this type of research to be conducted. Ethical issues continue to arise in sociological research. A recent case involved a different sort of question than the Humphreys case.

The Ogden Case

What should social scientists do when the ethical principles of confidentiality and not harming subjects conflict with the law? In 1992, Simon Fraser University student Russel Ogden began work on his master's thesis, which was to be a study on euthanasia (mercy killing) and assisted suicide involving AIDS patients (Ogden, 1994). Both euthanasia and assisted suicide are crimes in Canada. The university's ethics committee approved his research proposal, which included a promise to maintain the "absolute confidentiality" of any information provided to him by those he interviewed (Palys, 1997).

Ogden defended his M.A. thesis in 1994. Shortly afterward, he was subpoenaed to give evidence at a coroner's inquest that was investigating the possible assisted suicide of an AIDS victim. Ogden refused to testify, citing the guarantee of confidentiality he had given to his respondents. The coroner charged Ogden with contempt of court. After a lengthy legal battle, the coroner agreed that Ogden's guarantee of confidentiality was in the public good and dropped the charges. Despite this precedent, researchers do not know if other courts will support their right to maintain confidentiality, as academics do not have any legal exemption similar to that which exists between a lawyer and client. Without this exemption, decisions are made on a case-by-case basis. In the United States, researchers have gone to prison for refusing to testify about their research.

An interesting issue in the Ogden case is the role played by the university. Since the cornerstone of a university is the protection of academic freedom, and since Ogden's research had been approved by the university, one might have expected the university to support Ogden and to pay his legal fees. However, the $2,000 the university gave him covered only part of his legal costs, and they took no responsibility for his actions. On top of this, a clause was added to the university's ethics review policy whereby researchers would be required to tell their subjects that "the researcher may be required to divulge information obtained in the course of this research to a court or other legal body." This clause subordinates ethics to law and may have a dramatic impact on the ability of social scientists to conduct research on sensitive topics (Palys and Lowman, 1998).

Ogden later sued the university for $9,000 to recover his legal costs. While rejecting Ogden's claim, the judge took the unusual step of stating he felt the university's president and vice-president "demonstrated a surprising lack of courage" when they failed to support the university's principle of academic freedom because they were afraid defending Ogden would be interpreted as supporting assisted suicide. Ultimately, under a new president, Simon Fraser University accepted the recommendation of a review committee and acknowledged its responsibility in the matter. The university paid Ogden's legal fees, compensated him for lost wages, and formally apologized to him.

In this chapter, we have looked at the research process and the methods used to pursue sociological knowledge. The important thing to realize is that research is the lifeblood of sociology. Without research, sociologists would be unable to test existing theories and develop new ones. Research takes us beyond common sense and provides opportunities for us to use our sociological imagination to generate new knowledge.

CHAPTER REVIEW

■ **What are the five ways of knowing?**

The five ways of knowing are personal experience, tradition, authority, religion, and science.

■ **What is the empirical approach to knowledge? What are the two types of empirical studies conducted by sociologists?**

Sociological research is based on an empirical approach that answers questions through a direct, systematic collection and analysis of data. Sociologists generally use two types of empirical studies. Descriptive studies attempt to describe social reality or provide facts. Explanatory studies attempt to explain relationships and the reasons certain events do or do not occur.

■ **What are the inductive and deductive approaches to research?**

Theory and research form a continuous cycle that encompasses both deductive and inductive approaches. With the deductive approach, the researcher begins with a theory and then collects and analyzes research to test it. With the inductive approach, the researcher collects and analyzes data and then generates a theory based on that analysis.

■ **What are the key steps in the quantitative research process?**

The quantitative research process has these key steps: (1) selecting and defining the research problem; (2) reviewing previous research; (3) formulating the hypothesis, which involves constructing variables; (4) developing the research design; (5) collecting and analyzing the data; and (6) drawing conclusions and reporting the findings.

■ **What are the major sociological research methods?**

Research methods are systematic techniques for conducting research. Through experiments, researchers study the impact of certain variables on their subjects. Surveys are polls used to gather facts about people's attitudes, opinions, or behaviours; a sample of respondents provides data through questionnaires or interviews. In secondary analysis, researchers analyze existing data, such as a government census, or cultural artifacts, such as a diary. In field research, sociologists study social life in its natural setting through participant and complete observation, case studies, unstructured interviews, and ethnography.

KEY TERMS

altruism 33
analysis 41
complete observation 53
content analysis 52
control group 42
cultural artifacts 52
deductive approach 37
dependent variable 39
descriptive studies 37
empirical approach 35
ethnography 55
experiment 42
experimental group 42
explanatory studies 37
field research 53
hypotheses 36
independent variable 39

NET LINKS

The Web site for Statistics Canada's Data Liberation Initiative gives you access to other Statistics Canada data and provides links to statistical agencies in many other parts of the world:
http://www.statcan.ca/english/Dli/dli.htm

Carleton University sociologist Craig McKie has designed a Web site that has a rich variety of Internet links for researchers:
http://www.socsciresearch.com/

The code of ethics that applies to all Canadian universities can be accessed at:
http://pre.ethics.gc.ca

For some online advice about academic writing, go to:
http://www.utoronto.ca/writing/advise.html

One of Canada's leading social research organizations is the Institute for Social Research at York University:
http://www.isr.yorku.ca/

Public Agenda Online is designed to provide background information on issues for journalists:
http://www.publicagenda.org/

If you would like to read about some of the statistics used by social scientists, go to:
http://www.statsoft.com/textbook/stathome.html

QUESTIONS FOR CRITICAL THINKING

1. The agency that funds the local suicide clinic has asked you to study the clinic's effectiveness in preventing suicide. What would you need to measure? What *can* you measure? What research method(s) would provide the best data for analysis?
2. Together with a group of students, perform a content analysis on the photographs in your textbooks. First, determine whether to sample texts from various fields of study or just one field. Try to follow the steps in the sociological research process.
3. You have been assigned a research study that examines possible discrimination against men in child custody cases. What will be the population(s) you will study? How will you sample the population(s)? How will you account for sex, race, age, income level, and other characteristics in your population(s)?
4. For a class project, you want to study the relationship between students' grades and their willingness to cheat on examinations. What are some of the ethical issues you must consider before you administer a survey to the other students in your class?

SUGGESTED READINGS

The following books provide in-depth information about research methods:

Earl Babbie. *The Practice of Social Research* (9th ed.). Belmont, Calif.: Wadsworth, 2001.

Therese L. Baker. *Doing Social Research* (3rd ed.). New York: McGraw-Hill, 1999.

Margrit Eichler. *Nonsexist Research Methods: A Practical Guide.* Boston: Allen & Unwin, 1988.

Sandra Kirby and Kate McKenna. *Experience Research Social Change*: *Methods from the Margins.* Toronto: Garamond, 1989.

Shulamit Reinharz. *Feminist Methods in Social Research.* New York: Oxford University Press, 1992. (Provides excellent information and examples of qualitative research using methods such as oral histories, content analysis, case studies, action research, and multiple-method research.)

Janice L. Ristock and Joan Pennell. *Research as Empowerment: Feminist Links, Postmodern Interruptions.* Don Mills, Ont.: Oxford University Press, 1996.

To find out more about writing a sociology term paper or report, see:

Richard Floyd. *Success in the Social Sciences: Writing and Research for Canadian Students.* Toronto: Harcourt Brace, 1995.

Margot Northey. *Making Sense: A Student's Guide to Research, Writing and Style.* Don Mills, Ont.: Oxford University Press, 1993. (Takes the reader from the initial steps of choosing a topic to doing research and writing the final paper. Describes the types of social science literature and makes suggestions about writing a research paper and preparing an oral presentation.)

ONLINE STUDY AND RESEARCH TOOLS

THOMSONNOW™ Thomson NOW!

Go to **http://hed.nelson.com** to link to ThomsonNOW for *Sociology in Our Times,* Fourth Canadian Edition, your online study tool. First take the **Pre-Test** for this chapter to get your personalized **Study Plan,** which will identify topics you need to review and direct you to the appropriate resources. Then take the **Post-Test** to determine what concepts you have mastered and what you still need work on.

INFOTRAC®

Infotrac College Edition is included free with every new copy of this text. Explore this online library for additional readings, review, and a handy resource for assignments. Visit **www.infotrac-college.com** to access this online database of full-text articles. Enter the key terms from this chapter to start your search.

Culture

Crown attorney and author Rupert Ross describes the difficulties he had in learning to understand and accept the cultural traditions of the Ojibway. According to Ross, this story demonstrates how easy it is to misread people who have a "different understanding" of the world (1996:51):

"My own cultural eyes have often tricked me into seeing things that Aboriginal people did not—or completely missing things they thought too obvious to point out. One of the most significant came one day when I was having coffee with an Ojibway friend. I asked her about something I often saw in the North: older couples walking along with the man twelve paces out in front, his wife bringing up the rear. I asked her how that behaviour fit with what I was being taught about equality between men and women in traditional times. She laughed, then said something like 'Rupert, Rupert, that's only your eyes again! You have to look at it the way we do!'

"She began by asking me to remember where those old people had spent their lives, to imagine walking a narrow trail through the bush with my own family. She asked me to think about who I would prefer to have out in front, my wife or myself, to be the first to face whatever dangers the bush presented. In one way, she said, it could be compared to wartime. 'Where,' she asked, 'do you put your general? Are they out in front or are they in the rear, where they have time to see and plan and react?'

"Viewed in that way, things appeared to be the opposite of what I had first supposed. Instead of occupying an inferior position, the woman was seen as the organizer and director, while the man out front was counted on for his capacity to take action under her direction. Instead of remembering the bush context in which they had lived their lives, I had put them in my own urban context where such a formation might indicate the opposite. 'So,' I said, 'she's really the general and her husband is just the footsoldier!'

"There was a pause then, and she chuckled again, shaking her head. 'Not really,' she said. 'The problem is . . . you see everything in terms of hierarchies, don't you? Why do you do that?' . . . She tried to express her way then, the way she understood from the teaching of her people. In those teachings, all things have a purpose, and unless these are fulfilled, the strength of the whole is weakened. The jobs of the husband and of the wife were just that, their jobs, assumed on the basis of their having different skills and capacities— different *gifts*—none of which had to be compared with each other in terms of worth or importance. Comparison itself was seen as a strange thing to do.

"As she spoke, I was flooded with recollections of other events that raised the issue of our Western dependence on hierarchies of worth and power." (Ross, 1996:52-53)

To what extent does our own culture "blind" us; that is, keep us from understanding, accepting, or learning from other cultures? Is intolerance toward "outsiders"—people who are viewed as being different from one's own group or way of life—accepted by some people in Canada? As our world appears to grow increasingly smaller because of rapid transportation, global communications, and international business transactions and political alliances—and sometimes because of hostility, terrorism, and warfare—learning about cultural diversity, within our own nation and globally, is extremely important for our individual and collective well-being. Although the world's population shares a common humanity—and perhaps some components of culture—cultural differences pose crucial barriers to our understanding of others. Sociology provides us with

65

a framework for examining and developing a greater awareness of culture and cultural diversity, and how cultures change over time and place.

What is culture? Why is it so significant to our personal identities? What happens when others are intolerant of our culture? *Culture* **is the knowledge, language, values, customs, and material objects that are passed from person to person and from one generation to the next in a human group or society.** As previously defined, a *society* is a large social grouping that occupies the same geographic territory and is subject to the same political authority and dominant cultural expectations. While a society is made up of people, a culture is made up of ideas, behaviour, and material possessions. Society and culture are interdependent; neither could exist without the other.

If we look within our own country, culture can be an enormously stabilizing force for a society, and it can provide a sense of continuity. However, culture can also be a force that generates discord, conflict, and even violence. How people view culture is intricately related to their location in society with regard to their race/ethnicity, class, sex, and age. From one perspective, Canadian culture does not condone intolerance or *hate crimes*—attacks against people because of their race, religion, colour, disability, sexual orientation, ethnic origin, or ancestry. In fact, we have laws against such behaviour, and persons apprehended and convicted of hate crimes may be punished. From another perspective, however, intolerance and hatred may be the downside of some "positive" cultural values—such as individualism, competition, and consumerism—found in Canadian society. Just as attitudes of love and tolerance may be embedded in societal values and teachings, beliefs that reinforce acts of intolerance and hatred may also be embedded in culture.

If we look across the cultures of various nations, we may see opportunities for future cooperation based on our shared beliefs, values, and attitudes, or we may see potential for lack of understanding, discord, and conflict based on divergent ideas and worldviews.

In this chapter we examine society and culture, with special attention to the components of culture and the relationship between cultural change and diversity. We will also analyze culture from functionalist, conflict, feminist, interactionist, and postmodern perspectives. Before reading on, test your knowledge of the relationship between culture and intolerance toward others by answering the questions in Box 3.1.

QUESTIONS AND ISSUES

Chapter Focus Question: What part does culture play in shaping people and the social relations in which they participate?

What are the essential components of culture?

To what degree are we shaped by popular culture?

How do subcultures and countercultures reflect diversity within a society?

How do the various sociological perspectives view culture?

CULTURE AND SOCIETY IN A CHANGING WORLD

Understanding how culture affects our lives helps us develop a sociological imagination. When we meet someone from a culture vastly different from our own, or when we travel in another country, it may be easier to perceive the enormous influence of culture on people's lives. However, as our society has become more diverse, and communication among members of international cultures more frequent, the need to appreciate diversity and to understand how people in other cultures view their world has also increased (Samovar and Porter, 1991b). For example, many international travellers and businesspeople have learned the importance of knowing what gestures mean in various nations. In Argentina, rotating one's index finger around the front of the ear means "You have a telephone call," but in North American culture it usually suggests that a person is "crazy" (Axtell, 1991). Similarly, making a circle with your thumb and index finger indicates "OK", but in Tunisia it means "I'll kill you!" (Samovar and Porter, 1991a).

BOX 3.1 SOCIOLOGY AND EVERYDAY LIFE

How Much Do You Know About Culture and Intolerance Toward Others?

True	False	
T	F	1. Canadians generally see themselves as tolerant of other cultures and intolerant of racism.
T	F	2. In recent years, the number of reported attacks in Canada against persons because of their race, religion, or ethnic origin has increased.
T	F	3. It is illegal to be a member of a racist organization.
T	F	4. As the rate of immigration to Canada has increased in recent years, anti-immigrant feelings have risen.
T	F	5. The majority of hate crimes in Canada are directed against racial minorities.
T	F	6. Communities with greater proportions of visible-minority immigrants are generally more tolerant of racial and ethnic differences.
T	F	7. It is illegal to disseminate hate literature on the Internet.
T	F	8. A recent national survey found that the majority of respondents accept the concept of Canada as a multicultural mosaic.

Answers on page 68.

CULTURE AND SOCIETY

The Importance of Culture

How important is culture in determining how people think and act on a daily basis? Simply stated, culture is essential for our individual survival and for our communication with other people. We rely on culture because we are not born with the information we need to survive. We do not know how to take care of ourselves, how to behave, how to dress, what to eat, which gods to worship, or how to make or spend money. We must learn about culture through interaction, observation, and imitation in order to participate as members of the group (Samovar and Porter, 1991a). Sharing a common culture with others simplifies day-to-day interactions. However, we must also understand other cultures and the world views therein.

Just as culture is essential for individuals, it is also fundamental for the survival of societies. Culture has been described as "the common denominator that makes the actions of individuals intelligible to the group" (Haviland, 1993:30). Some system of rule making and enforcing necessarily exists in all societies. What would happen, for

example, if *all* rules and laws in Canada suddenly disappeared? At a basic level, we need rules in order to navigate our bicycles and cars through traffic. At a more abstract level, we need laws to establish and protect our rights. To survive, societies need rules about civility and tolerance toward others. We are not born knowing how to express kindness or hatred toward others, although some people may say "Well, that's just human nature" when explaining someone's behaviour. Such a statement is built on the assumption that what we do as human beings is determined by *nature* (our biological and genetic makeup) rather than *nurture* (our social environment)—in other words, that our behaviour is instinctive. An *instinct* is an unlearned, biologically determined behaviour pattern common to all members of a species that predictably occurs whenever certain environmental conditions exist. For example, spiders do not learn to build webs. They build webs because of instincts that are triggered by basic biological needs, such as protection and reproduction.

Humans do not have instincts. What we most often think of as instinctive behaviour can actually be attributed to reflexes and drives. A *reflex* is an unlearned, biologically determined involuntary

BOX 3.1 SOCIOLOGY AND EVERYDAY LIFE

Answers to the Sociology Quiz on Culture and Intolerance Toward Others

1. **True.** Canadians generally see themselves as tolerant of other cultures, yet they are also aware that racism is a serious problem in Canada. Sociologists identify this as a paradox of Canadian society (Henry et al., 2000).

2. **True.** Even though such incidents are seriously underreported in Canada, statistics indicate that the number of reported hate or bias crimes has increased in recent years (Galloway, 1999).

3. **False.** As provided for in the *Charter of Rights and Freedoms*, individuals have the right to belong to any organization they choose to join.

4. **True.** Polls show that high rates of immigration, combined with the tightening economy, are related to an increase in anti-immigrant sentiment.

5. **True.** Recent statistics indicate that in one year, 61 percent of hate crime incidents reported to police were directed against racial minorities, 23 percent against religious minorities, 11 percent against gays or lesbians, and 5 percent against ethnic minorities (Henry et al., 2000).

6. **True.** According to the Economic Council of Canada's report on changing attitudes toward prejudice, the communities with more visible minorities expressed the most tolerant attitudes.

7. **False.** In fact, according to one watchdog site (http://www.hatewatch.org), there are currently approximately 500 "hardcore" hate sites and as many as 1,750 other sites that are problematic (HateWatch, 2000).

8. **False.** Nearly 75 percent of 1,200 Canadians surveyed in a recent poll rejected the concept of Canada as a multicultural mosaic.

response to some physical stimuli (such as a sneeze after breathing some pepper in through the nose, or the blinking of an eye when a speck of dust gets in it). *Drives* are unlearned, biologically determined impulses common to all members of a species that satisfy needs, such as sleep, food, water, and sexual gratification. Reflexes and drives do not determine how people will behave in human societies; even the expression of these biological characteristics is channelled by culture. For example, we may be taught that the "appropriate" way to sneeze (an involuntary response) is to use a tissue or turn our head away from others (a learned response). Similarly we may learn to sleep on mats or in beds. Most contempo-rary sociologists agree that culture and social learning, not nature, account for virtually all of our behaviour patterns.

Since humans cannot rely on instincts in order to survive, culture is a "tool kit" for survival. According to the sociologist Ann Swidler (1986:273), culture is a "tool kit of symbols, stories, rituals, and world views, which people may use in varying configurations to solve different kinds of problems." The tools we choose will vary according to our own personality and the situations we face. We are not puppets on a string; we make choices from among the items in our own "tool box."

Material and Nonmaterial Culture

Our cultural toolbox is divided into two major parts: *material* and *nonmaterial* culture (Ogburn, 1966/1922). **Material culture consists of the physical or tangible creations that members of a society make, use, and share.** Initially, items of material culture begin as raw materials or resources, such as ore, trees, and oil. Through technology, these raw materials are transformed into usable items (ranging from books and computers to guns and bombs). Sociologists define **technology as the knowledge, techniques, and tools that make it possible for people to transform resources into usable forms,**

Shelter is a universal type of material culture, but it comes in a wide variety of shapes and forms. What might some of the reasons be for the similarities and differences you see in these cross-cultural examples?

and the knowledge and skills required to use them after they are developed. From this standpoint, technology is both concrete and abstract. For example, technology includes a pair of scissors and the knowledge and skill necessary to make them from iron, carbon, and chromium (Westrum, 1991). At the most basic level, material culture is important because it is our buffer against the environment. For example, we create shelter to protect ourselves from the weather and to provide ourselves with privacy. Beyond the survival level, we make, use, and share objects that are interesting and important to us. Why are you wearing the particular clothes you have on today? Perhaps you're communicating something

about yourself, such as where you attend school, what kind of music you like, or where you went on vacation.

Nonmaterial culture **consists of the abstract or intangible human creations of society that influence people's behaviour.** Language, beliefs, values, rules of behaviour, family patterns, and political systems are examples of nonmaterial culture. A central component of nonmaterial culture is *beliefs*—the mental acceptance or conviction that certain things are true or real. Beliefs may be based on tradition, faith, experience, scientific research, or some combination of these. Faith in a supreme being, conviction that education is the key to success, and

The customs and rituals associated with weddings are one example of nonmaterial culture. What can you infer about beliefs and attitudes concerning marriage in the societies represented by these photographs?

the opinion that smoking causes cancer are examples of beliefs. We also have beliefs in items of material culture. For example, most students believe that computers are the key to technological advancement and progress.

Cultural Universals

Because all humans face the same basic needs (such as food, clothing, and shelter), we engage in similar activities that contribute to our survival. Anthropologist George Murdock (1945:124) compiled a list of more than seventy *cultural universals*—**customs and practices that occur across all societies.** His categories included appearance (such as bodily adornment and hairstyles), activities (such as sports, dancing, games, joking, and visiting), social institutions (such as family, law, and religion), and customary practices (such as cooking, folklore, gift giving, and hospitality). These general customs and practices may be present in all cultures, but their specific forms vary from one group to another and from one time to another within the same group. For example, while

telling jokes may be a universal practice, what is considered a joke in one society may be an insult in another.

How do sociologists view cultural universals? In terms of their functions, cultural universals are useful because they ensure the smooth and continual operation of society (Radcliffe-Brown, 1952). A society must meet basic human needs by providing food, shelter, and some degree of safety for its members so that they will survive. Children and other new members (such as immigrants) must be taught the ways of the group. A society also must settle disputes and deal with people's emotions. All the while, the self-interest of individuals must be balanced with the needs of society as a whole. Cultural universals help to fulfil these important functions of society.

From another perspective, however, cultural universals are not the result of functional necessity; these practices may have been *imposed* by members of one society on members of another. Similar customs and practices do not necessarily constitute cultural universals. They may be an indication that a conquering

Symbols are powerful sources of communication. What messages do these two pictures communicate to you?

nation used its power to enforce certain types of behaviour on those who were defeated (Sargent, 1987). Sociologists might ask questions, such as Who determines the dominant cultural patterns? For example, although religion is a cultural universal, traditional religious practices of indigenous peoples (those who first live in an area) often have been repressed and even stamped out by subsequent settlers or conquerors who hold political and economic power over them.

COMPONENTS OF CULTURE

Even though the specifics of individual cultures vary widely, all cultures have four common nonmaterial cultural components: symbols, language, values, and norms. These components contribute to both harmony and conflict in a society.

Symbols

A *symbol* **is anything that meaningfully represents something else.** Culture could not exist without symbols because there would be no shared meanings among people. Symbols can simultaneously produce loyalty and animosity, and love and hate. They help us communicate ideas, such as love or patriotism, because they express abstract concepts with visible objects. To complicate matters, however, the interpretation of various symbols varies in different cultural contexts. For example, for some Indo-Canadians, the colour green rather than white symbolizes purity or virginity. Similarly, although a swastika represents hate to most Canadians, to a member of the Aryan Nations Church of Jesus Christ, a swastika represents love.

Flags can stand for patriotism, nationalism, school spirit, or religious beliefs held by members of a group or society. They also can be a source of discord and strife among people, as evidenced by recent controversies over the Canadian flag. In 1996, a retired Canadian couple, vacationing in a Florida trailer park, decided to fly the Canadian flag on their trailer. Their neighbours, patriotic Americans, objected so strenuously that the Canadians were forced to take their flag down. One of the neighbours even claimed (mistakenly) that it was against the law to fly a foreign flag on American soil. In our technology-oriented society *emoticons* are a new system of symbols used to express emotions when people are communicating on their computers via chat lines or e-mail. (See Figure 3.1.)

Symbol can stand for love (a heart or a valentine), peace (a dove), or hate (a Nazi swastika), just as words can be used to convey meanings. Symbols also can transmit other types of ideas. A siren is a symbol that denotes an emergency situation and sends the message to clear the way immediately. Gestures also are a symbolic form of communication—a movement of the head, body, or hands can express our ideas or feelings to others. For example, in Canada, pointing toward your chest with your thumb or

Figure 3.1	Emoticons

The symbols shown here are examples of "emoticons" or "smileys," a symbolic way to express moods in e-mail or text messages. Turn the page sideways and the meaning of each emotion will be clear.

:) = SMILE

:D = SMILE/LAUGHING/BIG GRIN

;) = WINK

:X = MY LIPS ARE SEALED

:P = STICKING OUT TONGUE

{ } = HUG

:(= FROWN

:'(= CRYING

0:) = ANGEL

}:> = DEVIL

finger is a symbol for "me." We are also all aware of how useful our middle finger can be in communicating messages to inconsiderate drivers.

Symbols affect our thoughts about class. For example, how a person is dressed or the kind of car that he or she drives is often at least subconsciously used as a measure of that individual's economic standing or position. With regard to clothing, although many people wear casual clothes on a daily basis, where the clothing was purchased is sometimes used as a symbol of social status. Were the items purchased at Zellers, Old Navy, Club Monaco, or Holt-Renfrew? What indicators are there on the items of clothing—such as the Nike swoosh, some other logo, or a brand name—that say something about the status of the product? Automobiles and their logos are also symbols that have cultural meaning beyond the shopping environment in which they originate.

Language

Language is a set of symbols that expresses ideas and enables people to think and communicate with one another. Verbal (spoken) and nonverbal (written or gestured) language help us describe reality. One of our most important human attributes is the ability to use language to share our experiences, feelings, and knowledge with others. Language can create visual images in our head, such as "the kittens look like little cotton balls" (Samovar and Porter, 1991a). Language also allows people to distinguish themselves from outsiders and maintain group boundaries and solidarity (Farb, 1973).

Language is not solely a human characteristic. Other animals use sounds, gestures, touch, and smell to communicate with one another, but they use signals with fixed meanings that are limited to the immediate situation (the present) and cannot encompass past or future situations. For example, chimpanzees can use elements of Standard American Sign Language and manipulate physical objects to make "sentences," but they are not physically endowed with the vocal apparatus needed to form the consonants required for verbal language. As a result, nonhuman animals cannot transmit the more complex aspects of culture to their offspring. Humans have a unique ability to manipulate symbols to express abstract concepts and rules and thus to create and transmit culture from one generation to the next.

Language and Social Reality   One key issue in sociology is whether language *creates* or simply *communicates* reality. For example, consider the terms used by organizations involved in the abortion debate: pro-life and pro-choice. Do such terms create or simply express a reality? Anthropological linguists Edward Sapir and Benjamin Whorf have suggested that language not only expresses our thoughts and perceptions but also influences our perception of reality. According to the **Sapir–Whorf hypothesis, language shapes the view of reality of its speakers** (Whorf, 1956; Sapir, 1961). If people are able to think only through language, language must precede thought.

If language shapes the reality we perceive and experience, some aspects of the world are viewed as important and others are virtually neglected because people know the world only in terms of the vocabulary and grammar of their own language. For example, most Aboriginal languages focus on describing relationships between things rather than using language to judge or evaluate. One Aboriginal author explains, "No, we don't have any gender. It's a relationship . . . The woman who cares for your heart—that's your wife. Your daughters are the ones who enrich your heart. Your sons are the ones that test your heart!" (Ross, 1996:116). Consequently, many Aboriginal languages do not have any personal pronouns based on gender (such as words for *she* or *he*). As writer Rupert Ross explains:

> Because they don't exist there, searching for the correct ones often seems an artificial and unreasonable exercise. As a result, Aboriginal people are often as careless about getting them right as I am when speaking French and trying to remember whether a noun has "le" or "la" in front of it . . . On the more humorous side, my Aboriginal friends appear heartily amused by the frenzied Western debate over whether God is a "He" or a "She." (1996:117)

According to Ross, language does have a dramatic impact on our perception of the world. He describes two very different worlds experienced by English-speaking Canadians and Aboriginal peoples:

> I've struggled for some time to find a way to express how I perceive the difference between my English-speaking world and the world my Aboriginal friends tell me is given to them by their languages. I have this sense that if you decide that the first reality is constant change, if you discard your belief in the usefulness of judgmental absolutes like "good" and "bad" and choose to speak in terms of relative

movement like "towards harmony" instead, then a lot of other things change as well. You start to sit in a room differently, in a car differently, everywhere differently. (1996:125)

Similarly, Sapir and Whorf explain that the Hopi language does not contain past, present, and future tenses of verbs, or nouns for times, days, or years (Carroll, 1956); however, scholars recently have argued that this assertion is incorrect (see Edgerton, 1992). By contrast, English speakers in North America perceive time as something that can be kept, saved, lost, or wasted; therefore, "being on time" or "not wasting time" are important. Many English words divide time into units (years, months, weeks, days, hours, minutes, seconds, and milliseconds) and into the past, present, and future (yesterday, today, and tomorrow) (Samovar and Porter, 1991a).

If language does create reality, are we trapped by our language? Many social scientists agree that the Sapir–Whorf hypothesis overstates the relationship between language and our thoughts and behaviour patterns. While acknowledging that language has many subtle meanings and that the words used by people reflect their central concerns, most sociologists contend that language may *influence* our behaviour and interpretation of social reality but does not *determine* it.

Language and Gender

What is the relationship between language and gender? What cultural assumptions about women and men does language reflect? Scholars have suggested several ways in which language and gender are intertwined:

- The English language ignores women by using the masculine form to refer to human beings in general (Basow, 1992). For example, the word *man* is used generically in words like *chairman* and *mankind*, which allegedly include both men and women. However, *man* can mean either "all human beings" or "a male human being" (Miller and Swift, 1993:71).
- Use of the pronouns *he* and *she* affects our thinking about gender. Pronouns show the gender of the person we *expect* to be in a particular occupation. For instance, nurses, secretaries, and schoolteachers usually are referred to as *she,* while doctors, engineers, electricians, and presidents are referred to as *he* (Baron, 1986).

■ Words have positive connotations when relating to male power, prestige, and leadership; when related to women, they carry negative overtones of weakness, inferiority, and immaturity (Epstein, 1988:224). Table 3.1 shows how gender-based language reflects the traditional acceptance of men and women in certain positions, implying that the jobs are different when filled by women rather than men.

■ A language-based predisposition to think about women in sexual terms reinforces the notion that women are sexual objects. Women often are described by terms, such as *fox, broad, bitch, babe,* or *doll,* which ascribe childlike or even petlike characteristics to them. By contrast, men have performance pressures placed on them by being defined in terms of their sexual prowess, such as *dude, stud,* and *hunk* (Baker, 1993).

Gender in language has been debated and studied extensively in recent years, and greater awareness and some changes have been the result. For example, the desire of many women to have *Ms.* (rather than *Miss* or *Mrs.,* which indicate their marital status) precede their names has received a degree of acceptance in public life and the media (Tannen, 1995). Many organizations and publications have established guidelines for the use of nonsexist language and have changed titles, such as

Does the language people use influence their perception of reality? According to social scientists, the words we use strongly influence our relationships with other people. What kind of interaction is taking place in this photo?

chairman to *chair* or *chairperson.* "Men Working" signs in many areas have been replaced with ones that say "People Working" (Epstein, 1988). Some occupations have been given "genderless" titles, such as *firefighter* and *flight attendant* (Maggio, 1988). Yet many people resist change, arguing that the English language is being ruined (Epstein,

Table 3.1 LANGUAGE AND GENDER

MALE TERM	FEMALE TERM	NEUTRAL TERM
teacher	teacher	teacher
chairman	chairwoman	chair, chairperson
policeman	policewoman	police officer
fireman	lady fireman	firefighter
airline steward	airline stewardess	flight attendant
race car driver	woman race car driver	race car driver
wrestler	lady/woman wrestler	wrestler
professor	female/woman professor	professor
doctor	lady/woman doctor	doctor
bachelor	spinster/old maid	single person
male prostitute	prostitute	prostitute
male nurse	nurse	nurse
welfare recipient	welfare mother	welfare recipient
worker/employee	working mother	worker/employee
janitor/maintenance man	maid/cleaning lady	custodial attendant

Sources: Adapted from Korsmeyer, 1981:122; Miller and Swift, 1991.

1988). Many scholars suggest that a more inclusive language is needed to develop a more inclusive and equitable society (see Basow, 1992).

Language, Race, and Ethnicity

Language may create and reinforce our perceptions about race and ethnicity by transmitting preconceived ideas about the superiority of one category of people over another. Let's look at a few images conveyed by words in the English language in regard to race and ethnicity.

■ Words may have more than one meaning and create and reinforce negative images. Terms, such as *black-hearted* (malevolent), and expressions, such as "a black mark" (a detrimental fact) and "Chinaman's chance of success" (unlikely to succeed), give the words *black* and *Chinaman* negative associations and derogatory imagery. By contrast, expressions, such as "That's white of you" and "The good guys wear white hats," reinforce positive associations with the colour white.

■ Overtly derogatory terms, such as *nigger, kike, gook, honkey, chink, squaw, savage,* and other racial–ethnic slurs, have been "popularized" in movies, music, comic routines, and so on. Such derogatory terms often are used in conjunction with physical threats against persons.

■ Words frequently are used to create or reinforce perceptions about a group. For example, Aboriginal peoples have been referred to as "savages" and described as "primitive," while Blacks have been described as "uncivilized," "cannibalistic," and "pagan."

■ The "voice" of verbs may minimize or incorrectly identify the activities or achievements of members of various minority groups. For example, use of the passive voice in the statement "Chinese Canadians *were given* the right to vote" ignores how Chinese Canadians *fought* for that right. Active-voice verbs also may inaccurately attribute achievements to people or groups. Some historians argue that cultural bias is shown by the very notion that "Cabot discovered Canada"—given that Canada already was inhabited by people who later became known as Aboriginal Canadians (see Stannard, 1992; Takaki, 1993).

In addition to these concerns about the English language, problems also arise when more than one language is involved.

Language Diversity in Canada

Canada is a linguistically diverse society. The existence of Aboriginal languages, the presence of French- and English-speaking populations, and the increasing number of other languages commonly spoken are all evidence. Language has been referred to as the keystone to culture because of the fact that language is the chief vehicle for understanding and experiencing one's culture (McVey and Kalbach, 1995).

Bilingualism In 1969, the federal government passed the *Official Languages Act,* making both French and English the official languages. In doing so, Canada officially became a bilingual society. However, this action by no means resolved the complex issues regarding language in our society. According to a recent census, 67 percent of Canadians speak English only, another 14 percent speak French only, and 17 percent are bilingual. Only 2 percent, or 473,475 Canadians, indicated they lacked the skills to converse in either French or English (Statistics Canada, 2003i). This census also indicated that bilingualism has continued to gain ground across the country. Although French-versus-English language issues have been a significant source of conflict, bilingualism remains a distinct component of Canadian culture, as the following comments demonstrate:

> Most people I talk to do not want a divided country. Nor do they deny the right of Québécois to preserve their language and culture . . . having two languages doesn't split up the country, it *makes* it. Without Quebec and their French language I would feel lost as a Canadian. ("Citizen's Forum," 1991:55)

Although it may be easy for members of the English-speaking majority to display such acceptance and tolerance of bilingualism, francophones are concerned that this policy is not enough to save their culture. Efforts to protect French language and culture have resulted in some exclusionary policies. For example, Quebec's controversial Bill 178 specifies that exterior signs on stores, restaurants, and offices are to be in French only. As the following incident demonstrates, this law has increased the tension between our two charter linguistic groups:

> I went to meet some friends at a downtown bar . . . As I arrived, a solemn middle-aged man was taking photographs of the blackboard mounted on the outside steps. He was intent on a notice scrawled in chalk on the board: TODAY'S SPECIAL—PLOUGHMAN'S LUNCH. This notice happened to be a blatant violation of Quebec's Bill 178 . . . and the photographer was one of a number of self-appointed vigilantes

who . . . dutifully search the downtown streets for English language or bilingual commercial signs . . . They photograph the evidence and then lodge an official complaint with the Commission de Protection de la Langue Française. (Richler, 1992:1)

As this example demonstrates, the Québécois feel that their language and culture is threatened and that these types of defensive strategies are essential to the survival of their culture.

Aboriginal Languages   Canada's Aboriginal languages are many and diverse. These languages, tangible symbols of Aboriginal culture and group identity, are tremendously important to Canada's indigenous people. Aboriginal people's cultures are *oral cultures*; that is, cultures that are transmitted through speech rather than the written word. Many Aboriginal stories can be passed on only in the Aboriginal language in which they originated. Language is not only a means of communication, but also a link that connects people with their past and grounds their social, emotional, and spiritual vitality. Although loss of language doesn't necessarily lead to the death of a culture, it can severely handicap the transmission of that culture (Norris, 1998:8). For Aboriginal people, huge losses have already occurred as a result of the assimilationist strategies of missionaries and Jesuit priests running residential schools. At these schools, Aboriginal children were forbidden to speak their language. An Ojibway woman from northwestern Ontario describes her experience:

Boarding school was supposed to be a place where you forgot everything about being Anishinabe. And our language too. But I said, "I'm going to talk to myself"—and that's what I did, under my covers—talked to myself in Anishinabe. If we were caught, the nuns would make us stand in a corner and repeat over and over, "I won't speak my language." (Ross, 1996:122)

Despite the efforts of Canadian Aboriginal peoples to maintain their languages, these languages are among the most endangered in the world. Only three of the approximately fifty Aboriginal languages in Canada are in a healthy state; many have already disappeared or are near extinction. In the 2001 census, only 24 percent of Aboriginal persons reported an Aboriginal language as their first language and even fewer spoke it at home (Statistics Canada, 2001a).

Loss of their languages will have a profound effect on the cultural survival of Aboriginal peoples. According to Eli Taylor, a Dakota-Sioux from Manitoba:

Our native language embodies a value system about how we ought to live and relate to each other . . . Now if you destroy our language, you not only break down these relationships, but you also destroy other aspects of our Indian way of life and culture, especially those that describe man's connection with nature, the Great Spirit, the order of things. Without our language, we will cease to exist as a separate people. (Fleras and Elliott, 1992:151)

Aboriginal elders, teachers, and other leaders are well aware of the gravity of the language situation and have taken steps to preserve the few remaining indigenous languages. These steps include the introduction of Aboriginal language courses in schools and universities, Aboriginal media programming, and the recording of elders' stories, songs, and accounts of history in Aboriginal language (Ponting, 1997). According to social analyst Mary Jane Norris, if these languages vanish, "they take with them unique ways of looking at the world, explaining the unknown and making sense of life" (Norris, 1998:8).

Theoretical Interpretations of Language Diversity   How does the presence of all of these different languages affect Canadian culture? From the functionalist perspective, a shared language is essential to a common culture; language is a stabilizing force in society and is an important means of cultural transmission. Through language, children learn about their cultural heritage and develop a sense of personal identity in relation to their group.

Conflict theorists view language as a source of power and social control; it perpetuates inequalities between people and between groups because words are used (intentionally or not) to "keep people in their place." As linguist Deborah Tannen (1993:B5) has suggested, "The devastating group hatreds that result in so much suffering in our own country and around the world are related in origin to the small intolerances in our everyday conversations—our readiness to attribute good intentions to ourselves and bad intentions to others." Furthermore, different languages themselves are associated with inequalities. Consider this Aboriginal language instructor's comments on the lure of the English language: "It's to do with the perception of power. People associate English with prestige and power. We don't have movies in [Aboriginal language], we don't have hardcover books . . . or neon signs in our language" (Martin, 1996:A8). Language, then, is a reflection of our feelings and values.

Values

Values **are collective ideas about what is right or wrong, good or bad, and desirable or undesirable in a particular culture** (Williams, 1970). Values do not dictate which behaviours are appropriate and which are not, but they provide us with the criteria by which we evaluate people, objects, and events. Values typically come in pairs of positive and negative values, such as being brave or cowardly, hardworking or lazy. Since we use values to justify our behaviour, we tend to defend them staunchly (Kluckhohn, 1961).

Core Canadian Values

Do we have shared values in Canada? Sociologists disagree about the extent to which all people in this country share a core set of values. Functionalists tend to believe that shared values are essential for societies and have conducted most of the research on core values. More than a decade ago, approximately 400,000 respondents were asked what it meant to be Canadian. The following list summarizes the core values that emerged most strongly from participants in all regions of Canada. As you read this list, evaluate the extent to which these values fit with what you think it means to be Canadian.

1. *Equality and fairness in a democratic society.* Equality and fairness were not seen as mutually exclusive values. As one respondent said: "My hope for the future of Canada is for . . . a country where people feel comfortable with one another, are tolerant and understanding with one another, and where each person recognizes they have the same opportunities, responsibilities and privileges" ("Citizen's Forum," 1991:37).
2. *Consultation and dialogue.* Canadians view themselves as people who settle their differences peaceably and in a consultative rather than confrontational manner. The view was widely held that Canadians must work together to solve their problems and remedy the apparent lack of understanding among different groups, regions, and provinces.
3. *Accommodation and tolerance.* The forum participants recognized the existence of different groups in Canadian society and their need to sustain their own culture while attaching themselves to the country's society, values, and institutions.
4. *Support for diversity.* This diversity has a number of facets, including linguistic, regional, ethnic, and cultural differences. Again, the respondents spoke of the difficulty of achieving a balance between a multicultural Canada and a secure sense of a Canadian identity.
5. *Compassion and generosity.* Respondents deeply valued Canada's compassion and generosity as exemplified in our universal and extensive social services, health care and pension systems, immigration policies, and commitment to regional economic equalization.
6. *Canada's natural beauty.* Canada's unspoiled natural beauty was identified as very important. Respondents noted that this may be threatened by inadequate attention to environmental protection issues.
7. *Canada's world image: Commitment to freedom, peace, and nonviolent change.* Canada's role as a nonviolent, international peacekeeper was summed up in one respondent's comments: "Canada should not try to be a world power like the U.S.A. We should be the same kind of nation that we have always been, a peaceful and quiet nation" ("Citizen's Forum," 1991:44).

More recently, sociologist and pollster Michael Adams examined Canadian social values and concluded that the consensus on social values is breaking down. He explains that this has resulted in

a culture that has few illusions about its uniformity. In the past, most Canadians had a fairly well-defined stereotype of what constituted a "Canadian." Now we have to ask ourselves, "Which one?" or "Which tribe?" "A typical Albertan? Is that Preston Manning or k.d. lang?" (1998:132)

According to Adams, when Canadians are divided according to their social values, twelve distinct social value groups emerge: three groups among those over 50, four groups among the baby boomers (aged 30 to 49), and five groups of Canadians under 30 (Generation X). The fact that there are more social value groups among the Generation Xers reflects a trend toward increasingly diverse Canadian values. Adams (1998) attributes this trend largely to the effects of advances in technology, such as computers and the Internet, which allow Canadians to cross cultural boundaries and explore a diverse spectrum of values.

Value Contradictions

All societies have value contradictions. *Value contradictions* **are values that conflict with one another or are mutually exclusive** (achieving one makes it difficult, if not impossible, to achieve another). For example, core values of morality and humanitarianism may conflict with values of individual achievement and success. In the 1990s, for example, humanitarian values reflected in welfare and other government aid programs have come into conflict with values emphasizing hard work and personal achievement. Similarly, despite the fact that 84 percent of Canadians feel that "people who are poor have a right to an adequate income to live on" (Bibby, 1995a), they have also shown strong support for governments that have dramatically cut budgets in order to reduce financial deficits. Can you identify any value contradictions in the list of Canadian core values outlined previously?

Ideal versus Real Culture

What is the relationship between values and human behaviour? Sociologists stress that a gap always exists between ideal culture and real culture in a society.

Ideal culture **refers to the values and standards of behaviour that people in a society profess to hold.** *Real culture* **refers to the values and standards of behaviour that people actually follow.** For example, we may claim to be law-abiding (ideal cultural value) but smoke marijuana (real cultural behaviour), or we may regularly drive over the speed limit but think of ourselves as "good citizens."

The degree of discrepancy between ideal and real culture is relevant to sociologists investigating social change. Large discrepancies provide a foothold for demonstrating hypocrisy (pretending to be what one is not or to feel what one does not feel). These discrepancies often are a source of social problems; if the discrepancy is perceived, leaders of social movements may utilize them to point out people's contradictory behaviour. For example, preserving our natural environment may be a core value, but our behaviour (such as littering highways and lakes) contributes to its degradation, as is further discussed in Chapter 20 ("Collective Behaviour").

Norms

Values provide ideals or beliefs about behaviour but do not state explicitly how we should behave. Norms, on the other hand, do have specific behavioural expectations. *Norms* **are established rules of behaviour or standards of conduct.** *Prescriptive norms* state what behaviour is appropriate or acceptable. For example, persons making a certain amount of money are expected to file a tax return and pay any taxes

they owe. Norms based on custom direct us to open a door for a person carrying a heavy load. By contrast, *proscriptive norms* state what behaviour is inappropriate or unacceptable. Laws that prohibit us from driving over the speed limit and "good manners" that preclude reading a newspaper during class are examples. Prescriptive and proscriptive norms operate at all levels of society, from our everyday actions to the formulation of laws.

Formal and Informal Norms

Not all norms are of equal importance; those that are most crucial are formalized. *Formal norms* are written down and involve specific punishments for violators. Laws are the most common type of formal norms; they have been codified and may be enforced by sanctions. *Sanctions* **are rewards for appropriate behaviour or penalties for inappropriate behaviour.** Examples of *positive sanctions* include praise, honours, or medals for conformity to specific norms. *Negative sanctions* range from mild disapproval to life imprisonment. In the case of law, formal sanctions are clearly defined and can be administered only by persons in certain official positions (such as police officers and judges) who are given the authority to impose the sanctions.

Norms considered to be less important are referred to as *informal norms*—unwritten standards of behaviour understood by people who share a common identity. When individuals violate informal norms, other people may apply informal sanctions. *Informal sanctions* are not clearly defined and can be applied by any member of a group (such as frowning at someone or making a negative comment or gesture).

Folkways

Norms are also classified according to their relative social importance. *Folkways* **are informal norms or everyday customs that may be violated without serious consequences within a particular culture** (Sumner, 1959/1906). They provide rules for conduct but are not considered to be essential to society's survival. In Canada, folkways include using underarm deodorant, brushing one's teeth, and wearing appropriate clothing for a specific occasion. Folkways are not often enforced; when they are enforced, the resulting sanctions tend to be informal and relatively mild.

Folkways are very culture specific; they are learned patterns of behaviour that can vary markedly from one society to another. In Japan, for example, where the walls of restroom stalls reach to the floor, folkways dictate that a person should knock on the door before entering a stall (you cannot tell if anyone is inside without knocking). People in Canada find it disconcerting, however, when someone knocks on the door of the stall (Collins, 1991).

Mores   Other norms are considered highly essential to the stability of society. ***Mores* (pronounced MOR-ays) are strongly held norms with moral and ethical connotations that may not be violated without serious consequences in a particular culture.** Since mores are based on cultural values and are considered crucial for the well-being of the group, violators are subject to more severe negative sanctions (such as ridicule, loss of employment, or imprisonment) than are those who fail to adhere to folkways. The strongest mores are referred to as taboos. ***Taboos are mores so strong that their violation is considered to be extremely offensive and even unmentionable.*** Violation of taboos is punishable by the group or even, according to certain belief systems, by a supernatural force. The incest taboo, which prohibits sexual or marital relations between certain categories of kin, is an example of a nearly universal taboo.

Folkways and mores provide structure and security in a society. They make everyday life more predictable and provide people with some guidelines for appearance and behaviour. As individuals travel in countries other than their own, they become aware of cross-cultural differences in folkways and mores. For example, women from Canada travelling in Muslim nations quickly become aware of mores, based on the *sharia* (the edicts of the Koran), that prescribe the dominance of men over women. In Saudi Arabia, for instance, women are not allowed to mix with men in public. Banks have branches with only women tellers—and only women customers. In hospitals, female doctors are supposed to tend only to children and other women (Alireza, 1990; Ibrahim, 1990).

Laws   **Laws are formal, standardized norms that have been enacted by legislatures and are enforced by formal sanctions.** Laws may be either civil or criminal. *Civil law* deals with disputes among persons or groups. Persons who lose civil suits may encounter negative sanctions, such as having to pay compensation to the other party or being ordered to stop certain conduct. *Criminal law,* on the other hand, deals with public safety and well-being. When criminal laws are violated, fines and prison sentences are the most likely negative sanctions.

As with material objects, all of the nonmaterial components of culture—symbols, language, values, and norms—are reflected in the popular culture of contemporary society.

TECHNOLOGY, CULTURAL CHANGE, AND DIVERSITY

Cultures do not generally remain static. There are many forces working toward change and diversity. For example, the Internet links material and non-material cultures across the world, thus accelerating cultural change. Some societies and individuals adapt to this change, whereas others suffer culture shock and succumb to ethnocentrism.

Cultural Change

Societies continually experience cultural change at both material and nonmaterial levels. Changes in technology continue to shape the material culture of society. Although most technological changes are primarily modifications of existing technology, *new technologies* are changes that make a significant difference in many people's lives. Examples of new technologies include the introduction of the printing press more than 500 years ago and the advent of computers and electronic communications in the twentieth century. The pace of technological change has increased rapidly in the past 150 years, as contrasted with the 4,000 years prior to that, during which humans advanced from digging sticks and hoes to the plow.

All parts of culture do not change at the same pace. When a change occurs in the material culture of a society, nonmaterial culture must adapt to that change. Frequently, this rate of change is uneven, resulting in a gap between the two. Sociologist William F. Ogburn (1966/1922) referred to this disparity as ***cultural lag— a gap between the technical development of a society and its moral and legal institutions.*** In other words, cultural lag occurs when material culture changes faster than nonmaterial culture, thus creating a lag between the two cultural components. For example, at the material cultural level, the personal computer and electronic coding have made it possible to create a unique health identifier for each person in Canada. Based on available technology (material culture), it would be possible to create a national data bank that includes everyone's individual medical records from birth to death.

With the widespread accessibility of television and the Internet, popular culture is increasingly accessible for both children and adults in their own homes. Studies show that many children spend more time watching television than they spend attending school.

Using this identifier, health providers and insurance companies could rapidly transfer medical records around the globe, and researchers could access unlimited data on people's diseases, test results, and treatments. However, the availability of this technology does not mean that it will be accepted by people who believe (nonmaterial culture) that such a national data bank would constitute an invasion of privacy and could easily be abused by others. The failure of nonmaterial culture to keep pace with material culture is linked to social conflict and societal problems. As in the above example, such changes are often set in motion by discovery, invention, and diffusion.

Discovery **is the process of learning about something previously unknown or unrecognized.** Historically, discovery involved unearthing natural elements or existing realities, such as "discovering" fire or the true shape of the earth. Today, discovery most often results from scientific research. For example, the discovery of a polio vaccine virtually eliminated one of the major childhood diseases. A future discovery of a cure for cancer or the common cold could result in longer and more productive lives for many people.

As more discoveries have occurred, people have been able to reconfigure existing material and nonmaterial cultural items through invention. *Invention* **is the process of reshaping existing cultural items into a new form.** Guns, video games, airplanes, and the *Charter of Rights and Freedoms* are examples of inventions that positively or negatively affect our lives today.

When diverse groups of people come into contact, they begin to adapt one another's discoveries, inventions, and ideas for their own use. *Diffusion* **is the transmission of cultural items or social practices from one group or society to another** through such means as exploration, military endeavours, the media, tourism, and immigration. To illustrate, piñatas can be traced back to the twelfth century, when Marco Polo brought them back from China, where they were used to celebrate the springtime harvest, to Italy, where they were filled with costly gifts in a game played by the nobility. When the piñata travelled to Spain, it became part of Lenten traditions. In Mexico, it was used to celebrate the birth of the Aztec god Huitzilopochtli (Burciaga, 1993). Today, children in many countries squeal with excitement at parties as they swing a stick at a piñata. In today's "shrinking globe," cultural diffusion moves at a very rapid pace as countries continually seek new markets for their products. (See Box 3.2.)

Cultural Diversity

Cultural diversity refers to the wide range of cultural differences found between and within nations. Cultural diversity between countries may be the result of natural circumstances (such as climate and geography) or social circumstances (such as level of technology and composition of the population). Some countries—such as Sweden—are referred to as *homogeneous societies,* meaning they include people who share a common culture and are typically from similar social, religious, political, and economic backgrounds. By contrast, other countries—including Canada—are referred to as *heterogeneous societies,* meaning they include people who are dissimilar in regard to social characteristics, such as nationality, race, ethnicity, class, occupation, or education (See Figure 3.2).

BOX 3.2 SOCIOLOGY AND THE MEDIA

Cultural Diffusion or Cultural Confusion: Advertising—The Global Market

Selling a product in a foreign culture requires that attention be paid to cultural differences. The world's smartest advertising minds have sometimes forgotten to do so and, as the examples below demonstrate, they have consequently come off as village idiots. Costly—often amusing—mistakes have been made by advertisers who have misread cultural attitudes, sensitivities, or superstitions, or something has simply been lost in the translation to the global marketplace. Here are a few examples:

- When the makers of Coca-Cola were launching their drink in China, they found a phrase that sounded perfect: "Ko-kou-ke-la." After printing thousands of signs, the Coke masterminds discovered that they had christened their drink "Bite the wax tadpole."
- When Colgate introduced a toothpaste called "Cue" in France, it turned out to be the same name as a well-known pornographic magazine.
- Most North Americans know the slogan for Kentucky Fried Chicken as "Finger-lickin' good." In China, after translation, the slogan became "Eat your fingers off."
- The American Dairy Council ran a "Got milk?" campaign that featured celebrities sporting milk moustaches. In converting the message to Spanish, the council ended up asking its Mexican consumers, "Are you lactating?"
- "Come alive with the Pepsi Generation" was a perfectly good slogan—until it got translated into

Taiwanese as "Pepsi will bring your ancestors back from the dead."
- The makers of Coors Light beer hired an agency to develop promotional materials aimed at Hispanics in the United States. In trying to translate the ad's catchphrase "Turn it loose" into Spanish, a copywriter ended up inviting customers to "Drink Coors and get diarrhea."

The lack of cultural awareness of corporate North America is obvious in the following blunders:

- When Coca-Cola introduced its two-litre bottles in Japan, it was unaware of the fact that few Japanese refrigerators are roomy enough to store such a large bottle.
- Trying to market its cake mixes in Japan in the 1960s, Betty Crocker discovered that most Japanese homes were missing a necessary ingredient: an oven.
- When McDonald's ventured into China, corporate mascot Ronald McDonald was in tow to clown around at the launch. Talk about a bozo move: to the Chinese, the clown is a symbol of death.
- A toothpaste company ran a commercial in Southeast Asia proclaiming that its product helped whiten teeth. The problem was that the people in the local target market were in the habit of chewing betel nut in order to achieve darkly stained teeth—a social sign of prestige.

Source: Snyder and Foxman, 1998.

Canada has always been characterized by at least three main cultures. Cultural diversity in our country is not the result only of immigration. However, immigration has certainly had a significant impact on the development of this nation's culturally diverse society. Over the past 150 years, more than 13 million "documented" (i.e., legal) immigrants have arrived here; innumerable people also have entered the country as undocumented immigrants. Immigration can cause feelings of frustration and hostility, especially in people who feel threatened by the changes that large numbers of immigrants may produce. Often, people are intolerant of those who are different from themselves. When societal tensions

rise, people may look for others on whom they can place blame—or single out persons because they are the "other," the "outsider," the one who does not belong. Sociologist Adrienne Shadd described her experience of being singled out as an "other":

Routinely I am asked, "Where are you from?" or "What nationality are you?" as if to be Black, you have to come from somewhere else. I respond that I'm "Canadian" . . . I play along. The scenario usually unfolds as follows:

"But where are you *originally* from?"

"Canada."

| Figure 3.2 | Heterogeneity of Canadian Society |

Throughout history, Canada has been heterogeneous. Today, Canada is represented by a wide variety of social categories, including our religious affiliations and ethnic origins.

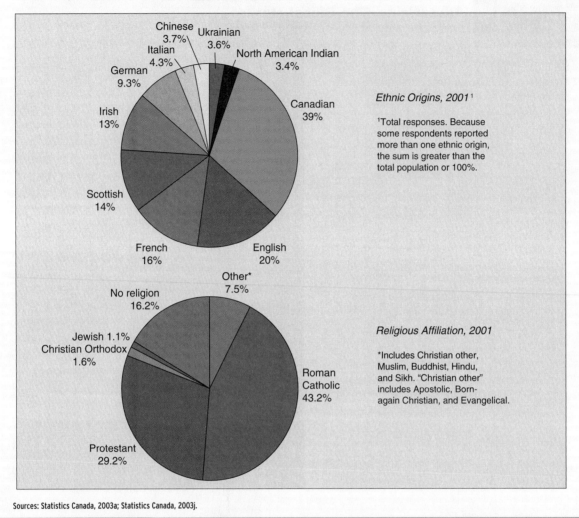

Ethnic Origins, 2001[1]

[1]Total responses. Because some respondents reported more than one ethnic origin, the sum is greater than the total population or 100%.

Religious Affiliation, 2001

*Includes Christian other, Muslim, Buddhist, Hindu, and Sikh. "Christian other" includes Apostolic, Born-again Christian, and Evangelical.

Sources: Statistics Canada, 2003a; Statistics Canada, 2003j.

"Oh, *you* were born here. But where are your parents from?"

"Canada."

"But what about your grandparents?"

As individuals delve further into my genealogy to find out where I'm "really" from, their frustration levels rise.

"No, uh, I mean . . . your *people.* Where do your *people* come from?"

At this point, questioners are totally annoyed and/or frustrated. After all, Black people in

Canada are supposed to come from "the islands," aren't they? For those of us living in large urban centres, there are constant reminders that we are not regarded as truly "Canadian." (1994:11)

Have you ever been made to feel like an "outsider"? Each of us receives cultural messages that may make us feel good or bad about ourselves or may give us the perception that we "belong" or "do not belong." However, in heterogeneous societies, such as Canada, cultural diversity is inevitable. In Canada, this diversity has created some unique problems in terms of defining and maintaining our distinct

Christmas trees and other holiday symbols exemplify the ways in which elements from diverse cultures take on new meanings through the process of diffusion. For instance, notice the European-looking Joseph and Mary, as well as the Greek columns, in this depiction of a manger in Bethlehem. Even the traditional date chosen to celebrate the birth of Jesus (to Christians, the "light of the world") is an adaptation of an ancient pagan celebration of the winter solstice (when the light of the returning sun conquers the darkness of winter).

Technology and tradition meet at the Fairholme Hutterite Colony as these young women try out a new digital camera at school.

Canadian culture. In fact, what is unique to Canada is the number of distinct subcultures that together make up our Canadian culture.

It has been suggested that complex societies are more likely to produce subcultures. This is certainly the case in Canada, where regional, ethnic, class, language, and religious subcultures combine to produce a highly diverse society.

Subcultures   A *subculture* **is a group of people who share a distinctive set of cultural beliefs and behaviours that differ in some significant way from that of the larger society.** Emerging from the functionalist tradition, this concept has been applied to categories ranging from ethnic, religious, regional, and age-based categories to those categories presumed to be "deviant" or marginalized from the larger society. In the broadest use of the concept, thousands of categories of people residing in Canada might be classified as belonging to one or more subcultures, including Muslims, Italian Canadians, Orthodox Jews, Generation Xers, and bikers. However, many sociological studies of subcultures have limited the scope of inquiry to more visible distinct subcultures, such as the Hutterites, to see how subcultural participants interact with the dominant culture.

The Hutterites   This subculture has fought for many years to maintain its distinct identity. They are the largest family-type communal grouping in the Western world, with more than 20,000 members living in approximately 200 settlements (Curtis and Lambert, 1994). The Hutterites live on farms, called "colonies," in Western Canada and the United States, where they practise their religious beliefs and maintain a relatively closed social network. Colonies strive to be self-sufficient—doing everything themselves, from making their own soap to pouring concrete and raising new buildings (Lyons, 1998).

The Hutterites are considered a subculture because their values, norms, and appearance differ significantly from those of members of the dominant culture. They have a strong faith in God and reject worldly concerns. Their core values include the joy of work, the primacy of the home, faithfulness, thriftiness, tradition, and humility. Hutterites hold conservative views of the family, believing that women are subordinate to men, birth control is unacceptable, and wives should remain at home. Children are cherished and seen as an economic asset: they help with the farming and other work.

Hutterite life is centred on the community rather than on the individual. Significant life decisions, such as whether a high-school graduate will attend university, are made on the basis of what is best for the entire community. All aspects of day-to-day life are based on sharing, right down to eating every meal in a community hall. Members of this group also have communal rather than private property; nobody is permitted to individually own as much as a pair of shoes (Curtis and Lambert, 1994). The Hutterites also have a distinctive mode of dress that makes this subculture readily identifiable.

The Hutterites are aware that their values are distinct from those of most other Canadians and that they look different from other people. However, these differences provide them with a collective identity and make them feel close to one another (Peter, 1987). A predominant tenet of Hutterite faith is *nonassimilation;* that is, they wish to maintain their separatist status. They do not wish to be absorbed into the dominant culture, and their colonies are usually located far from towns, cities, and highways to emphasize this. However, the Hutterites do not attempt to achieve complete social isolation from the wider society. Although this subculture strictly adheres to centuries-old traditions, the Hutterites don't hesitate to take advantage of twenty-first century advancements (Lyons, 1998). They are successful farmers who trade with people in the surrounding communities, and they buy modern farm machinery. They also read newspapers, use home computers and telephones, and utilize the services of non-Hutterite professionals (Curtis and Lambert, 1994). Yet there are many items we take for granted that are considered unacceptable in their society (Kephart, 1982).

Applying the concept of subculture to our study of social life helps us understand how cultural differences may influence people. However, subcultural theory and research have been criticized for overstating the within-category similarities and making the assumption that most people primarily identify with others who are similar to themselves in ethnicity, religion, age, or other categories. Until recently, most studies of subcultures did not acknowledge that the experiences of women might be quite different from those of men in the same subcultural setting. Finally, some contemporary theorists argue that information technologies and the plurality and fragmentation of life in the twenty-first century have contributed to the creation of new subcultures in cyberspace and the larger global community that are no longer geographically specific or limited by time and space.

Countercultures   Some subcultures actively oppose the larger society. A ***counterculture* is a group that strongly rejects dominant societal values and norms and seeks alternative lifestyles** (Yinger, 1960, 1982). Young people are most likely to join countercultural groups, perhaps because younger persons generally have less invested in the existing culture. Examples of countercultures include the beatniks of the 1950s, the flower children of the 1960s, the drug enthusiasts of the 1970s, and members of non-mainstream religious sects, or cults. Some countercultures (such as the Ku Klux Klan and the neo-Nazi skinheads) engage in revolutionary political activities.

One of the countercultures closely associated with hate crimes is the skinheads, sometimes referred to as "neo-Nazi skinheads," who have been present in North America since the early 1980s. Skinheads primarily are young, white, working-class males who express group identity by wearing boots, jeans, suspenders, green flight jackets, and chains, and by shaving their heads or sporting "burr" haircuts. Core values of "hardcore" skinheads include racial group superiority, patriotism, a belief in the traditional roles of women and men, and justification of physical violence as a means of expressing anger toward immigrants, gay men and lesbians, people of colour, and Jews (Wooden, 1995). Some skinhead groups are highly organized and motivated. These groups select leaders, hold regular meetings, distribute racist propaganda, and attend rallies sponsored by groups, such as the Ku Klux Klan and the White Aryan Resistance (Barrett, 1987).

Recent research by sociologist Stephen Baron (1997) with skinhead subculture in Edmonton disputes the characterization of this group as highly organized and politically motivated. Although Baron found that the youth had grown up as highly aggressive individuals who targeted racial and sexual minorities, he also found that their violent behaviour was "unorganized and unfocused and totally lacked any kind of political coherence" (quoted in Tanner, 2001:146).

Canadian neo-Nazi countercultural groups also believe that the survival of white society in this country is in jeopardy because of the practice of allowing "non-Aryans" into Canada. Skinheads, consequently, have been involved in a number of violent assaults and murders. For example, in 1993, three Tamil refugees were beaten in Toronto. One died as a result of the injuries inflicted and one was paralyzed (Henry et al., 2000). Hardcore skinheads are a counter-cultural group because they focus on "white power" and other racist views that contradict the norms and values of mainstream Canadian culture. However, not all skinheads share racist views; some identify themselves as SHARPs (Skinheads Against Racial Prejudice) or SARs (Skinheads Against Racism) (Young and Curry, 1997). Members of these groups have been attacked by hardcore skinheads because they refused to participate in violence against members of "out" groups.

Culture Shock

Culture shock **is the disorientation that people feel when they encounter cultures radically different from their own** and believe they cannot depend on their own taken-for-granted assumptions about life. When people travel to another society, they may not know how to respond to that setting. For example, Napoleon Chagnon (1992) was initially shocked at the sight of the Yanomamö (pronounced yah-noh-MAH-mah) tribe of South America for the first time in 1964.

The Yanomamö (also referred as the "Yanomami") are a tribe of about 20,000 South American Indians who live in the rain forest. Although Chagnon travelled in a small aluminum motorboat for three days to reach these people, he was not prepared for the sight that met his eyes when he arrived:

> I looked up and gasped to see a dozen burly, naked, sweaty, hideous men staring at us down the shafts of their drawn arrows. Immense wads of green tobacco were stuck between their lower

teeth and lips, making them look even more hideous, and strands of dark-green slime dripped from their nostrils—strands so long that they reached down to their pectoral muscles or drizzled down their chins and stuck to their chests and bellies. We arrived as the men were blowing *ebene,* a hallucinogenic drug, up their noses. As I soon learned, one side effect of the drug is a runny nose. The mucus becomes saturated with the drug's green powder, and the Yanomamö usually just let it dangle freely from their nostrils to plop off when the strands become too heavy.

> Then the stench of decaying vegetation and filth hit me, and I was almost sick to my stomach. I was horrified. What kind of welcome was this for someone who had come to live with these people and learn their way of life? (Chagnon, 1992:12–14)

The Yanomamö have no written language, system of numbers, or calendar. They lead a nomadic lifestyle, carrying everything they own on their backs. They wear no clothes and paint their bodies; the women insert slender sticks through holes in the lower lip and through the pierced nasal septum. In other words, the Yanomamö—like the members of thousands of other cultures around the world—live in a culture very different from that of Canada.

Ethnocentrism and Cultural Relativism

When observing people from other cultures, many of us use our own culture as the yardstick by which we judge the behaviour of others. Sociologists refer to this

Even as global travel and the media make us more aware of people around the world, the distinctiveness of the Yanomamö in South America remains apparent.

approach as *ethnocentrism*—**the tendency to regard one's own culture and group as the standard, and thus superior, whereas all other groups are seen as inferior.** Ethnocentrism is based on the assumption that one's own way of life is superior to all others. For example, most schoolchildren are taught that their own school and country are the best. The school song and the national anthem are forms of *positive ethnocentrism*. However, *negative ethnocentrism* can also result from constant emphasis on the superiority of one's own group or nation. Negative ethnocentrism is manifested in derogatory stereotypes that ridicule recent immigrants whose customs, dress, eating habits, or religious beliefs are markedly different from those of dominant group members. Long-term Canadian residents who are members of racial and ethnic minority groups, such as Native Canadians and Indo-Canadians, have also been the target of ethnocentric practices by other groups.

An alternative to ethnocentrism is *cultural relativism*—**the belief that the behaviours and customs of any culture must be viewed and analyzed by the culture's own standards.** For example, the anthropologist Marvin Harris (1974, 1985) uses cultural relativism to explain why cattle, which are viewed as sacred, are not killed and eaten in India, where widespread hunger and malnutrition exist. From an ethnocentric viewpoint, we might conclude that cow worship is the cause of the hunger and poverty in India. However, according to Harris, the Hindu taboo against killing cattle is very important to their economic system. Live cows are more valuable than dead ones because they have more important uses than as a direct source of food. As part of the ecological system, cows consume grasses of little value to humans. Then they produce two valuable resources—oxen (the neutered offspring of cows), to power the plows, and manure (for fuel and fertilizer)—as well as milk, floor covering, and leather. As Harris's study reveals, culture must be viewed from the standpoint of those who live in a particular society.

Cultural relativism also has a downside. It may be used to excuse customs and behaviour (such as cannibalism) that may violate basic human rights. Cultural relativism is a part of the sociological imagination; researchers must be aware of the customs and norms of the society they are studying and then spell out their background assumptions, so that others can spot possible biases in their studies. However, according to some social scientists, issues surrounding ethnocentrism and cultural relativism may become less distinct in the future as people around the globe increasingly share a common popular culture.

A GLOBAL POPULAR CULTURE

Before taking this course, what was the first thing you thought about when you heard the term *culture*? In everyday life, culture often is used to describe the fine arts, literature, or classical music. When people say that a person is "cultured," they may mean that the individual has a highly developed sense of style or aesthetic appreciation of the "finer" things.

High Culture and Popular Culture

Some sociologists use the concepts of high culture and popular culture to distinguish between different cultural forms. These ideal types are differentiated by their content, style, expressed values, and respective audiences (Gans, 1974; DiMaggio and Useem, 1978; Bourdieu, 1984; DiMaggio, 1987). *High culture* consists of classical music, opera, ballet, live theatre, and other activities usually patronized by elite audiences, composed primarily of members of the upper-middle and upper classes, who have the time, money, and knowledge assumed to be necessary for its appreciation. *Popular culture* **consists of activities, products, and services that are assumed to appeal primarily to members of the middle and working classes.** These include rock concerts, spectator sports, movies, television soap operas, situation comedies, and, more recently, the Internet. Although we will distinguish between high and popular culture in our discussion, it is important to note that some social analysts believe that the rise of a consumer society in which luxury items have become more widely accessible to the masses has significantly reduced the great divide between activities and possessions associated with wealthy people or a social elite and the rest of the society (see Huyssen, 1984; Lash and Urry, 1994).

However, most sociological examinations of high culture and popular culture focus primarily on the link between culture and social class. French sociologist Pierre Bourdieu's (1984) *cultural capital theory* views high culture as a device used by the dominant class to exclude the subordinate classes. According to Bourdieu, people must be trained to appreciate and understand high culture. Individuals learn about high culture in upper-middle and upper-class families and in elite education systems, especially higher education. Once they acquire this trained capacity, they possess a form of cultural capital.

Persons from poor and working-class backgrounds typically do not acquire this cultural capital. Since knowledge and appreciation of high culture is considered a prerequisite for access to the dominant class, its members can use their cultural capital to deny access to subordinate group members and thus preserve and reproduce the existing class structure (but see Halle, 1993).

Unlike high culture, popular culture is assumed to be far more widespread and accessible to everyone; for this reason, it is sometimes referred to as "mass culture." The primary purpose of popular culture is entertainment, but it also provides an avenue for people to express their hopes, fears, and anger. However, popular culture also may include racism, sexism, and nativism (hostility toward immigrants by native-born citizens) (Mukerji and Schudson, 1991). "Cruising the Internet" has become a new form of popular culture. Although this medium is for most Canadians a source of education and entertainment, it has also become a medium for hate groups to disseminate racist and homophobic ideology. For example, on the World Wide Web there are White Nationalist and One World Government resource pages (Chidley, 1995). For sociologists, popular culture provides a window into the public consciousness. At times the view can be disturbing.

Forms of Popular Culture

Three prevalent forms of popular culture are fads, fashions, and leisure activities. A *fad* is a temporary but widely copied activity followed enthusiastically by large numbers of people. Most fads are short-lived novelties (Garreau, 1993). According to the sociologist John Lofland (1993), fads can be divided into

Activity fads, such as moshing, are particularly popular with young people. Why are such fads often short-lived?

four major categories. First, *object fads* are items that people purchase despite the fact that they have little use or intrinsic value. Recent examples include Beanie Babies, Harry Potter characters, and Pokémon games, toys, trading cards, clothing, cartoons, and snack foods. Second, *activity fads* include pursuits, such as body piercing, "surfing" the Internet, and raves. Third are *idea fads,* such as New Age ideologies. Fourth are *personality* fads, such as those surrounding celebrities such as Jennifer Lopez, Tiger Woods, and Brad Pitt (see Box 3.3).

A *fashion* is a currently valued style of behaviour, thinking, or appearance that is longer lasting and more widespread than a fad. Examples of fashion are found in many areas, including child rearing, education, arts, clothing, music, and sports. Soccer is an example of a fashion in sports. Until recently, only schoolchildren played soccer in Canada. Now it has become a popular sport, perhaps in part because of immigration from European countries and other areas of the world where soccer is widely played.

Like soccer, other forms of popular culture move across nations. Sadly, in Canada we often assess the quality of popular culture on the basis of whether it is a Canadian or American product. Canadian artists, musicians, and entertainers often believe they have "made it" only when they become part of American popular culture. Music, television shows, novels, and street fashions from the United States have become a part of our Canadian culture (see Box 3.3). People in this country continue to be strongly influenced by popular culture from nations other than the United States. For example, Canada's contemporary music and clothing reflect African, Caribbean, and Asian cultural influences, among others.

Will the spread of popular culture produce a homogeneous global culture? Critics argue that the world is not developing a global culture; rather, other cultures are becoming westernized. Political and religious leaders in some nations oppose this process, which they view as **cultural imperialism—the extensive infusion of one nation's culture into other nations.** For example, some view the widespread infusion of the English language into countries that speak other languages as a form of cultural imperialism. On the other hand, the concept of cultural imperialism may fail to take into account various cross-cultural influences. For example, cultural diffusion of literature, music, clothing, and food has occurred on a global scale. A global culture, if it comes into existence, will most likely include components from many societies and cultures.

BOX 3.3 CRITICAL THINKING

American Idol and the Diffusion of Popular Culture

The hot topic at this year's Passover Seder was *American Idol.* It was Wednesday night, and the show was down to the final six. Every 10 minutes, the somber proceedings of the annual ritual were interrupted to check in with Ryan, Paula, Randy, and Simon [the show's judges]. Sometime between the 4 questions and the 10 plagues [in the Passover Seder], the week's loser was announced and dinner continued. Our voices were speaking the *Haggadah* [the text that is recited at the Seder], but our minds were still reeling: *Who would be next? I'm so glad Kimberly was kicked off and Clay is gonna be back. Josh's performance was horrible!*

–Russell Brown (2003), writing for *The Simon,* an Internet commentary on current issues

In this personal commentary about his family's celebration of the Jewish Passover, Internet columnist Russell Brown describes the fascination that he and millions of other viewers have with *American Idol,* the Fox television series that searches for a new national solo pop idol. The competition allows viewers to be involved in the process of selecting the next "star" because (in addition to celebrity judges who evaluate each contestant and render an opinion about their performance) television viewers call in and vote for their favourite contestant. According to Brown (2003), it is this illusion of choice and of supposedly having the power to help decide who might be the next new musical star that makes *American Idol* a hit with viewers.

Although the success of *American Idol* is an interesting sociological study in itself, the prominence of this TV show is actually part of a larger story of cultural diffusion—the transmission of cultural items or social practices from one group or society to another. In fact, the story of *American Idol* does not start in the United States: The program originated in the United Kingdom as *Pop Idol.* After that show received high viewer ratings in Britain, versions of *Idol* were adapted for the United States, Germany, the Netherlands, Poland,

and South Africa. Among adults aged sixteen to forty-nine in these countries, the various *Idols* swept the TV ratings week after week. In North America, more than 30-million viewers watched the final show of *American Idol*'s second season, and interest has been sustained by competition for the next season and the release of the movie *From Justin to Kelly,* a teen musical starring the winner and runner-up from the first *American Idol* (Stein, 2003). However, the story does not end there. By 2003, *Idols* had popped up in other countries including our *Canadian Idol* in Canada, *Superstar* on Lebanon-based TV, *Idool 2003* in Belgium, *A la Recherche de la Nouvelle Star* in France, *Idol* in Norway, and *Idols* in Finland, to name only a few.

Is this show highly successful across nations strictly because of corporate marketing strategies used by the various television networks? Although the show's hype in various countries no doubt plays a part in generating contestants and millions of viewers, there is a larger cultural appeal to the program that cannot be ignored. Brown (2003) believes that part of the appeal of *Idol* is that even though the program is produced by powerful media industries, viewers believe that they can take culture into their own hands, defy what the judges think, and help determine the outcome. Perhaps a more enduring cultural appeal of the show around the world is that viewers believe that they are connecting with other people—that they are developing new sets of friends and that they are choosing how they will be entertained.

How long will the *Idols* be popular in various nations? These shows may just be fads that temporarily catch some people's interest, or they may produce offshoots (contests involving younger would-be-stars, for example) that help such reality-based programming remain popular for some more extended period of time.

What kinds of television programming do you believe will have the widest appeal to diverse viewers around the world? Which popular North American programs are least likely to survive the process of cultural diffusion? Why?

U.S. contestants during a recent season of *American Idol* were not alone in their pursuit of fame and fortune in the entertainment industry. Similar "Idol" programs are popular with television audiences in many other countries. Above is a photo of *Canadian Idol* contestants.

SOCIOLOGICAL ANALYSIS OF CULTURE

Sociologists regard culture as a central ingredient in human behaviour. Although all sociologists share a similar purpose, they typically see culture through somewhat different lenses as they are guided by different theoretical perspectives in their research. What do these perspectives tell us about culture?

Functionalist Perspectives

As previously discussed, functionalist perspectives are based on the assumption that society is a stable, orderly system with interrelated parts that serve specific functions. Anthropologist Bronislaw Malinowski (1922) suggested that culture helps people meet their *biological needs* (including food and procreation), *instrumental needs* (including law and education), and *integrative needs* (including religion and art). Societies in which people share a common language and core values are more likely to have consensus and harmony.

How might functionalist analysts view popular culture? According to many functionalist theorists, popular culture serves a significant function in society in that it may be the "glue" that holds society together. Regardless of race, class, sex, age, or other characteristics, many people are brought together (at least in spirit) to cheer teams competing in major sporting events, such as the Grey Cup or the Olympic Games. Television and the

Internet help integrate recent immigrants into the mainstream culture, whereas longer-term residents may become more homogenized as a result of seeing the same images and being exposed to the same beliefs and values (Gerbner et al., 1987).

However, functionalists acknowledge that all societies have dysfunctions that produce a variety of societal problems. When a society contains numerous subcultures, discord results from a lack of consensus about core values. In fact, popular culture may undermine core cultural values rather than reinforce them (Christians, Rotzoll, and Fackler, 1987). For example, movies may glorify crime, rather than hard work, as the quickest way to get ahead. According to some analysts, excessive violence in music videos, movies, and television programs may be harmful to children and young people (Medved, 1992). From this perspective, popular culture may be a factor in antisocial behaviour as seemingly diverse as hate crimes and fatal shootings in public schools.

A strength of the functionalist perspective on culture is its focus on the needs of society and the fact that stability is essential for society's continued survival. A shortcoming is its overemphasis on harmony and cooperation. This approach also fails to fully account for factors embedded in the structure of society—such as class-based inequalities, racism, and sexism—that may contribute to conflict strife.

Conflict Perspectives

Conflict perspectives are based on the assumption that social life is a continuous struggle in which members of powerful groups seek to control scarce resources. According to this approach, values and norms help create and sustain the privileged position of the powerful in society while excluding others. As early conflict theorist Karl Marx stressed, ideas are *cultural creations* of a society's most powerful members. Thus, it is possible for political, economic, and social leaders to use *ideology*—an integrated system of ideas that is external to, and coercive of, people—to maintain their positions of dominance in a society. As Marx stated,

> The ideas of the ruling class are in every epoch the ruling ideas, i.e., the class which is the ruling material force in society, is at the same time, its ruling intellectual force. The class, which has the means of material production at its disposal, has control at the same time over the means of mental production . . . The ruling ideas are nothing more than the ideal expression of the

dominant material relationships, the dominant material relationships grasped as ideas. (Marx and Engels, 1970/1845–1846:64)

Many contemporary conflict theorists agree with Marx's assertion that ideas, a nonmaterial component of culture, are used by agents of the ruling class to affect the thoughts and actions of members of other classes.

How might conflict theorists view popular culture? Some conflict theorists believe that popular culture, which originated with everyday people, has been largely removed from their domain and has become nothing more than a part of the North American capitalist economy (Gans, 1974; Cantor, 1980, 1987). From this approach, U.S. media conglomerates, such as AOL Time Warner, Disney, and Viacom, create popular culture, such as films, television shows, and amusement parks, in the same way that they would produce any other product or service. Creating new popular culture also promotes consumption of *commodities*—objects outside ourselves that we purchase to satisfy our human needs or wants (Fjellman, 1992). Recent studies have shown that moviegoers spend more money on popcorn, drinks, candy, and other concession-stand food than they do on tickets to get into the theatre. Similarly, park-goers at Disneyland and Walt Disney World spend as much money on merchandise—such as Magic Kingdom pencils, Mickey Mouse hats, kitchen accessories, and clothing—as they do on admission tickets and rides (Fjellman, 1992).

From this perspective, people come to believe that they *need* things they ordinarily would not purchase. Their desire is intensified by marketing techniques that promote public trust in products and services provided by a corporation, such as the Walt Disney Company. Sociologist Pierre Bourdieu (1984:291) refers to this public trust as *symbolic capital:* "the acquisition of a reputation for competence and an image of respectability and honourability." Symbolic capital consists of culturally approved intangibles—such as honour, integrity, esteem, trust, and goodwill—that may be accumulated and used for tangible (economic) gain. Thus, people buy products at Walt Disney World (and Disney stores throughout the world) because they believe in the trustworthiness of the item ("These children's pajamas are bound to be flame retardant; they came from the Disney Store") and the integrity of the company ("I can trust Disney; it has been around for a long time").

Other conflict theorists examine the intertwining relationship among race, gender, and popular culture. According to the sociologist K. Sue Jewell (1993), popular cultural images are often linked to negative stereotypes of people of colour, particularly Black women. Jewell believes that cultural images depicting Black women as mammies or domestics—such as those previously used in Aunt Jemima Pancake ads and recent resurrections of films like *Gone with the Wind*—affect contemporary Black women's economic prospects in profound ways (Jewell, 1993).

A strength of the conflict perspective is that it stresses how cultural values and norms may perpetuate social inequalities. It also highlights the inevitability of change and the constant tension between those who want to maintain the status quo and those who desire change. A limitation is its focus on societal discord and the divisiveness of culture.

Symbolic Interactionist Perspectives

Unlike functionalists and conflict theorists, who focus primarily on macrolevel concerns, symbolic interactionists engage in a microlevel analysis that views society as the sum of all people's interactions. From this perspective, people create, maintain, and modify culture as they go about their everyday activities. Symbols make communication with others possible because they provide us with shared meanings.

According to some symbolic interactionists, people continually negotiate their social realities. Values and norms are not independent realities that automatically determine our behaviour. Instead,

Is this Japanese amusement park a sign of a homogeneous global culture or of cultural imperialism?

we reinterpret them in each social situation we encounter. However, the classical sociologist Georg Simmel warned that the larger cultural world—including both material culture and nonmaterial culture—eventually takes on a life of its own apart from the actors who daily re-create social life. As a result, individuals may be more controlled by culture than they realize. Simmel (1990/1907) suggested that money is an example of how people may be controlled by their culture. According to Simmel, people initially create money as a means of exchange, but then money acquires a social meaning that extends beyond its purely economic function. Money becomes an end in itself, rather than a means to an end. Today, we are aware of the relative "worth" not only of objects but also of individuals. Many people revere wealthy entrepreneurs and highly paid celebrities, entertainers, and sports figures for the amount of money they make, not for their intrinsic qualities. According to Simmel (1990/1907), money makes it possible for us to *relativize* everything, including our relationships with other people. When social life can be reduced to money, people become cynical, believing that anything—including people, objects, beauty, and truth—can be bought if we can pay the price. Although Simmel acknowledged the positive functions of money, he believed that the social interpretations people give to money often produce individual feelings of cynicism and isolation.

A symbolic interactionist approach highlights how people maintain and change culture through their interactions with others. However, interactionism does not provide a systematic framework for analyzing how we shape culture and how it, in turn, shapes us. It also does not provide insight into how shared meanings are developed among people, and it does not take into account the many situations in which there is disagreement on meanings. Whereas the functional and conflict approaches tend to overemphasize the macrolevel workings of society, the interactionist viewpoint often fails to take these larger social structures into account.

Postmodern Perspectives

Postmodern theorists believe that much of what has been written about culture in the Western world is Eurocentric—that it is based on the uncritical assumption that European culture (including its dispersed versions in countries such as Canada, the United States, Australia, and South Africa) is the true, universal culture in which all the world's people ought

to believe (Lemert, 1997). By contrast, postmodernists believe that we should speak of *cultures,* rather than *culture.*

However, Jean Baudrillard, one of the best-known French social theorists, believes that the world of culture today is based on *simulation,* not reality. According to Baudrillard, social life is much more a spectacle that simulates reality than reality itself. Many people gain "reality" from the media or cyberspace. For example, consider the many North American children who, upon entering school for the first time, have already watched more hours of television than the total number of hours of classroom instruction they will encounter in their entire school careers (Lemert, 1997). Add to this the number of hours that some will have spent playing computer games or surfing the Internet. Baudrillard refers to this social creation as *hyperreality*—a situation in which the *simulation* of reality is more real than the thing itself. For Baudrillard, everyday life has been captured by the signs and symbols generated to represent it, and we ultimately relate to simulations and models as if they were reality. Baudrillard (1983) uses Disneyland as an example of a simulation that conceals the reality that exists outside rather than inside the boundaries of the artificial perimeter. According to Baudrillard, Disney-like theme parks constitute a form of seduction that substitutes symbolic (seductive) power for real power, particularly the ability to bring about social change. From this perspective, amusement park "guests" may feel like "survivors" after enduring the rapid speed and gravity-defying movements of the roller coaster rides or see themselves as "winners" after surviving fights with hideous cartoon villains on the "dark rides" when they have actually experienced the substitution of an *appearance* of power over their lives for the *absence* of real power. Similarly, Stephen M. Fjellman (1992) studied Disney World in Orlando, Florida, and noted that people may forget, at least briefly, that the outside world can be threatening while they stroll Disney World's streets without fear of crime or automobiles. Although this freedom may be temporarily empowering, it also may lull people into accepting a "worldview that presents an idealized United States as heaven . . . How nice if they could all be like us—with kids, a dog, and General Electric appliances—in a world whose only problems are avoiding Captain Hook, the witch's apple, and Toad Hall weasels" (Fjellman, 1992:317).

In their examination of culture, postmodern social theorists make us aware of the fact that no single perspective can grasp the complexity and

New technologies have made educational opportunities available to a wider diversity of students, including persons with disabilities.

diversity of the social world. They also make us aware that reality may not be what it seems. According to the postmodern view, no one authority can claim to know social reality, and we should deconstruct—take apart and subject to intense critical scrutiny—existing beliefs and theories about culture in hopes of gaining new insights (Ritzer, 1997).

Although postmodern theories of culture have been criticized on a number of grounds, we will examine only three. One criticism is postmodernism's lack of a clear conceptualization of ideas. Another is the tendency to critique other perspectives as being "grand narratives," whereas postmodernists offer their own varieties of such narratives. Finally, some analysts believe that postmodern analyses of culture lead to profound pessimism about the future.

CULTURE IN THE FUTURE

As we have discussed in this chapter, many changes are occurring in our Canadian culture. Increasing cultural diversity can either cause long-simmering racial and ethnic antagonisms to come closer to the boiling point or result in the creation of a truly multicultural society in which diversity is respected and encouraged. According to our ideal culture, Canada will "prosper in diversity." The *Multicultural Act* has legislated cultural freedom. However, it has been suggested that this freedom is more "symbolic" than real (Roberts and Clifton, 1999). In the real culture, anti-immigration sentiment has risen in response to the estimated one-and-a-half million newcomers who

have arrived in Canada over the past decade. Cultural diversity and global immigration are affecting economic and employment perceptions. Many people accuse newcomers of stealing jobs and overutilizing the social service safety net at the Canadian taxpayers' expense.

In the future, the issue of cultural diversity will increase in importance, especially in schools. Multicultural education that focuses on the contributions of a wide variety of people from different backgrounds will continue to be an issue from kindergarten through university. Some public schools have incorporated heritage languages into their curriculum. These schools will face the challenge of embracing widespread cultural diversity while conveying a sense of community and national identity to students.

Technology will continue to have a profound effect on culture. Television and radio, films and videos, and electronic communications will continue to accelerate the flow of information and expand cultural diffusion throughout the world. Global communication devices will move images of people's lives, behaviour, and fashions instantaneously among almost all nations (Petersen, 1994). Increasingly, computers and cyberspace will become people's window on the world and, in the process, promote greater integration or fragmentation among nations. Integration occurs when there is a widespread acceptance of ideas and items—such as democracy, rock music, blue jeans, and McDonald's hamburgers—among cultures. By contrast, fragmentation occurs when people in one culture disdain the beliefs and actions of other cultures. As a force for both cultural integration and fragmentation, technology will continue to revolutionize communications, but most of the world's population will not participate in this revolution (Petersen, 1994).

From a sociological perspective, the study of culture helps us not only understand our own "toolbox" of symbols, stories, rituals, and world views but also expand our insights to include those of other people of the world who also seek strategies for enhancing their lives. If we understand how culture is used by people, how cultural elements constrain or facilitate certain patterns of action, what aspects of our cultural heritage have enduring effects on our actions, and what specific historical changes undermine the validity of some cultural patterns and give rise to others, we can apply our sociological imagination not only to our own society but also to the entire world (see Swidler, 1986).

Concept Table 3.A THEORETICAL ANALYSIS OF CULTURE

Components of Culture	Symbol	Anything that meaningfully represents something else.
	Language	A set of symbols that expresses ideas and enables people to think and communicate with one another.
	Values	Collective ideas about what is right or wrong, good or bad, and desirable or undesirable in a particular culture.
	Norms	Established rules of behaviour or standards of conduct.
Sociological Analysis of Culture	Functionalist Perspectives	Culture helps people meet their biological, instrumental, and expressive needs.
	Conflict Perspectives	Ideas are a creation of society's most powerful members and can be used by the ruling class to affect the thoughts and actions of members of other classes.
	Symbolic Interactionist Perspectives	People create, maintain, and modify culture during their everyday activities; however, cultural creations can take on a life of their own and end up controlling people.
	Postmodern Perspectives	Much of culture today is based on simulation of reality (e.g., what we see on television) rather than reality itself.

CHAPTER REVIEW

■ What is culture?

Culture encompasses the knowledge, language, values, and customs passed from one generation to the next in a human group or society. Culture is essential for our individual survival because, unlike nonhuman animals, we are not born with instinctive information about how to behave and how to care for ourselves and others.

Culture can be a stabilizing force for society; it can provide a sense of continuity. However, culture also can be a force that generates discord, conflict, and violence.

There are both material and nonmaterial expressions of culture. Material culture consists of the physical creations of society. Nonmaterial culture is more abstract and reflects the ideas, values, and beliefs of a society.

■ What are cultural universals?

Cultural universals are customs and practices that exist in all societies and include activities and institutions, such as storytelling, families, and laws. Specific forms of these universals vary from one cultural group to another, however.

■ What are the four nonmaterial components of culture common to all societies?

These components are symbols, language, values, and norms. Symbols express shared meanings; through them, groups communicate cultural ideas and abstract concepts. Language is a set of symbols through which groups communicate. Values are a culture's collective ideas about what is or is not acceptable. Norms are the specific behavioural expectations within a culture.

■ What are the main types of norms?

Folkways are norms that express the everyday customs of a group, while mores are norms with strong moral and ethical connotations that are essential to the stability of a culture. Laws are formal, standardized norms that are enforced by formal sanctions.

■ What are high culture and popular culture?

High culture consists of classical music, opera, ballet, and other activities usually patronized by elite audiences. Popular culture consists of the activities, products, and services of a culture that appeal primarily to members of the middle and working classes.

■ **What causes cultural change in societies?**

Cultural change takes place in all societies. Change occurs through discovery and invention and through diffusion, which is the transmission of culture from one society or group to another.

■ **How is cultural diversity reflected in society?**

Cultural diversity is reflected through race, ethnicity, age, sexual orientation, religion, occupation, and so forth. A diverse culture also includes subcultures and countercultures. A subculture has distinctive ideas and behaviours that differ from the larger society to which it belongs. A counterculture rejects the dominant societal values and norms.

■ **What are culture shock, ethnocentrism, and cultural relativism?**

Culture shock refers to the anxiety people experience when they encounter cultures radically different from their own. Ethnocentrism is the assumption that one's own culture is superior to other cultures. Cultural relativism counters culture shock and ethnocentrism by viewing and analyzing another culture in terms of its own values and standards.

■ **How do the major sociological perspectives view culture?**

A functional analysis of culture assumes that a common language and shared values help produce consensus and harmony. According to some conflict theorists, culture may be used by certain groups to maintain their privilege and exclude others from society's benefits. Symbolic interactionists suggest that people create, maintain, and modify culture as they go about their everyday activities. Postmodern thinkers believe that there are many cultures within Canada alone. In order to gain a better understanding of how popular culture may simulate reality rather than being reality, postmodernists believe that we need a new way of conceptualizing culture and society.

■ **What cultural changes can we expect in the future?**

While increasing cultural diversity in Canada has expanded the thinking of some individuals, it has also increased racial–ethnic antagonisms. As we look toward even more diverse and global cultural patterns in the future, it is important to keep our sociological imaginations actively engaged.

KEY TERMS

counterculture 84
cultural imperialism 87
cultural lag 79
cultural relativism 86
cultural universals 70
culture 66
culture shock 85
diffusion 80
discovery 80
ethnocentrism 86
folkways 78
ideal culture 78
invention 80
language 72
laws 79
material culture 68
mores 79
nonmaterial culture 69
norms 78
popular culture 86
real culture 78
sanctions 78
Sapir–Whorf hypothesis 73
subculture 83
symbol 71
taboos 79
technology 68
values 77
value contradictions 77

NET LINKS

The federal government has a Web site called "Facts on Canada" that contains information related to society and culture, including multiculturalism, Aboriginal culture and heritage, and national cultural institutions; go to:

http://canada.gc.ca/acanada/acPubHome .jsp?lang=eng

The Department of Heritage has a site entitled "Multiculturalism" that includes current research on hate-motivated activities in Canada; go to:

http://www.pch.gc.ca/progs/multi/index_e.cfm

For information on what you can do about hate crime go to:

http://www.stop-the-hate.org/

QUESTIONS FOR CRITICAL THINKING

1. Would it be possible today to live in a totally separate culture in Canada? Could you avoid all influences from the mainstream popular culture or from the values and norms of other cultures? How would you be able to avoid any change in your culture?

2. Do fads and fashions in popular culture reflect and reinforce, or challenge and change the values and norms of a society? Consider a wide variety of fads and fashions: musical styles; computer and video games and other technologies; literature; and political, social, and religious ideas.

3. What do you consider to be uniquely Canadian symbols? Generate a list of three or four. Can you identify examples of symbols that represent other countries?

SUGGESTED READINGS

An interesting functionalist analysis of culture is provided by this anthropologist:

Marvin Harris. *Cannibals and Kings: The Origins of Cultures.* New York: Random House, 1977.

Marvin Harris. *Good to Eat: Riddles of Food and Culture.* New York: Simon & Schuster, 1985.

These authors analyze aspects of culture from diverse perspectives:

Michael Adams. *Sex in the Snow: Canadian Social Values at the End of the Millennium.* Toronto: Penguin, 1998.

Reginald W. Bibby. *Mosaic Madness: The Poverty and Potential of Life in Canada.* Toronto: Stoddart, 1990.

bell hooks. *Outlaw Culture: Resisting Representations.* New York: Routledge, 1994.

These books provide interesting insights on culture and demonstrate how fieldwork can be carried out in a wide variety of settings:

Napoleon A. Chagnon. *Yanamamö: The Last Days of Eden.* San Diego: Harcourt Brace Jovanovich, 1992.

Stephen M. Fjellman. *Vinyl Leaves: Walt Disney World and America.* Boulder, Colo.: Westview Press, 1992.

To find out more about subcultures, countercultures, and hate crimes, see the following:

Stanley R. Barrett. *Is God a Racist? The Right Wing in Canada.* Toronto: University of Toronto Press, 1987.

William M. Kephart and William W. Zellner. *Extraordinary Groups: An Examination of Unconventional Life-Styles* (5th ed.). New York: St. Martin's Press, 1994.

ONLINE STUDY AND RESEARCH TOOLS

THOMSONNOW™

Go to **http://hed.nelson.com** to link to ThomsonNOW for *Sociology in Our Times,* Fourth Canadian Edition, your online study tool. First take the **Pre-Test** for this chapter to get your personalized **Study Plan,** which will identify topics you need to review and direct you to the appropriate resources. Then take the **Post-Test** to determine what concepts you have mastered and what you still need work on.

INFOTRAC®

Infotrac College Edition is included free with every new copy of this text. Explore this online library for additional readings, review, and a handy resource for assignments. Visit **www.infotrac-college.com** to access this online database of full-text articles. Enter the key terms from this chapter to start your search.

Socialization

"Child care is a divisive issue—there's no question about it. To stay at home and care for your own children, or to do paid work and hire a caregiver? Either way it's a complex decision, with costs on both sides. I call it the Child Care Equation. Every parent has to determine for themselves the value of each variable in the equation.

"When my first baby was born, I welcomed the opportunity to stay home, having been unhappy in my paid work position. Still, by the time my daughter was nine months old. I felt isolated—despite the baby 'playgroups' I had optimistically joined. So I accepted a temporary contract and arranged for day-care. Never have I wept so hard as I did on the second day—not when I dropped off my baby, but when I arrived at the caregiver's house at the end of the day only to learn we had effectively been 'fired' because my daughter cried too much. Luckily I was able to find another caregiver. My daughter was treated with kindness and affection—yet, throughout the entire six months of my contract work, I was always concerned that she was in a less than ideal situation, although *she* seemed fairly content.

"When my contract expired, I seriously questioned the sense in leaving my child in a stranger's care so that I could work for other strangers for little reward, monetary or otherwise . . . After a few months of unsuccessful job searching, I decided to stay at home and open a family daycare to help ends meet. Once again I cried, only this time it was from fear that the world would pass me by.

"Admittedly, there are days when I feel a little sad and out of the loop, when I long to restart my career, when I miss going to an office and ploughing through an in basket with no little voice whining 'Mommeeeeeeeee' in the background. But there are many more days when it is pure joy and privilege to be at home experiencing every single moment of my children's discovery of the world. . . .

"Life is full of trade-offs, especially once you add children to the mix. I can't speak for all stay at home parents, and I know there are many who experience loneliness, frustration, boredom, and even depression. Yet, in spite of the toll it takes on their emotions and self-esteem, they choose to be at home with their children. Some mothers (yes, I'll come right out and identify the female sex here because in most cases when a parent stays at home it is the mother) delay returning to the outside workforce until their children enter school full-time. Others wait a little longer, while others never re-enter the outside workforce, happily complementing their mothering with equally valuable volunteer work.

"So, for the present, my Child Care Equation involves two parents, two kids, one moderate-income household, a growing

pile of bills, a healthy supply of fun, and an endless excitement about what the future may bring." (Sutin, 2002:14)

What this young mother is considering in her contemplation of what she refers to as the "child care equation" is what is best for her children's healthy socialization. Today more than ever before, parents are aware of the lasting impact of a child's early socialization. What is the formula to maximize a child's social, psychological, and intellectual potential? There are no easy answers, as parents are finding out. As sociologist Linda Quirke explains, "parents today are a formidable cohort" who are more educated, older, and with fewer children than previous generations (Ferguson,

2004:30). This may result in more effective parenting, with more intensive focus on meeting the early socialization needs of individual children. However, there are potentially a negative results as well—what has been referred to as "hyperparenting" (Rosenfeld and Wise, 2000). The choices are endless: home care, daycare, parent care, preschool, private school, home school, private tutoring, hockey, gymnastics, dance, music, Scouts, Girl Guides. Some of the results of these well intentioned efforts present some disturbing outcomes in our "hyperparenting culture." Examples include a 60-percent increase in some provinces in private tutoring services in the past decade, two-hour homework sessions for Grade 1 students, flashcards for preschoolers, and crazed hockey parents expelled from games for attacking referees. Some experts have

suggested that children today are overprogrammed, overscheduled, and have lost the ability to play. What will be the effects of these early socialization efforts on this new generation of children?

The process of socialization is of major significance to sociologists. We look to the answer to this question and many others regarding the lifelong process of socialization from the discipline of sociology.

In this chapter, we examine why socialization is so crucial, and we discuss both sociological and psychological theories of human development. We look at the dynamics of socialization—how it occurs and what shapes it. Throughout the chapter, we focus on positive and negative aspects of the socialization process. Before reading on, test your knowledge of early socialization and child care by taking the quiz in Box 4.1.

QUESTIONS AND ISSUES

Chapter Focus Question: What happens when children do not have an environment that supports positive socialization?

What purpose does socialization serve?

How do individuals develop a sense of self?

How does socialization occur?

Who experiences resocialization?

What are the consequences to children of isolation and physical abuse, as contrasted with social interaction and parental affection? Sociologists emphasize that social environment is a crucial part of an individual's socialization.

WHY IS SOCIALIZATION IMPORTANT?

Socialization **is the lifelong process of social interaction through which individuals acquire a self-identity and the physical, mental, and social skills needed for survival in society.** It is the essential link between the individual and society. Socialization enables each of us to develop our human potential and learn the ways of thinking, talking, and acting that are essential for social living.

Socialization is essential for the individual's survival and for human development. The many people who met the early material and social needs of each of us were central to our establishing our own identity. During the first three years of our life, we begin to develop a unique identity and the ability to manipulate things and to walk. We acquire sophisticated cognitive tools for thinking and analyzing a wide variety of situations, and we learn effective communication skills. In the process, we begin a relatively long socialization process that culminates in our integration into a complex social and cultural system (Garcia Coll, 1990).

Socialization is also essential for the survival and stability of society. Members of a society must be socialized to support and maintain the existing social structure. From a functionalist perspective, individual conformity to existing norms is not taken for granted; rather, basic individual needs and desires must be balanced against the needs of the social structure. The socialization process is most effective when people conform to the norms of society because they believe this is the best course of action. Socialization enables a society to "reproduce" itself by passing on this cultural content from one generation to the next.

Although the techniques used to teach beliefs, values, and rules of behaviour are somewhat similar in many countries, the content of socialization differs greatly from society to society. How people walk, talk, eat, make love, and wage war are all functions of the culture in which they are raised. At the same time, we also are influenced by our exposure to subcultures of class, ethnicity, religion, and gender. In addition, each of us has unique experiences in our families and friendship groupings. The kind of human being that we become depends greatly on the particular society and social groups that surround us at birth and

BOX 4.1 SOCIOLOGY AND EVERYDAY LIFE

How Much Do You Know About Early Socialization and Child Care?

True	False	
T	F	1. A child who experiences substantial amounts of child care especially in the first year of life is more likely to experience attachments problems with its mother.
T	F	2. Children cared for exclusively at home are better prepared for school.
T	F	3. There is considerable evidence that good-quality child care can play an important role in protecting young children from family-based risk.
T	F	4. Because of inadequate parental-leave programs, most Canadian mothers who work outside the home return to work when their children are less than a year old.
T	F	5. Social science confirms that children raised in daycare centres are often emotionally maladjusted.
T	F	6. Currently in Canada, more than half of preschool children spend time in some form of daycare.
T	F	7. In recent years there has been an increase in the number of stay-at-home dads.
T	F	8. The majority of children attend daycare in regulated daycare centres.

Answers on page 100.

during early childhood. What we believe about ourselves, our society, and the world is largely a product of our interactions with others.

Human Development: Biology and Society

What does it mean to be "human"? To be human includes being conscious of ourselves as individuals with unique identities, personalities, and relationships with others. As humans, we have ideas, emotions, and

values. We have the capacity to think and to make rational decisions. But what is the source of "humanness"? Are we born with these human characteristics, or do we develop them through our interactions with others?

When we are born, we are totally dependent on others for our survival. We cannot turn ourselves over, speak, reason, plan, or do many of the things that are associated with being human. Although we can nurse, wet, and cry, most small mammals also can do those things. As discussed in Chapter 3, we humans differ

BOX 4.1 SOCIOLOGY AND EVERYDAY LIFE

Answers to the Sociology Quiz on Early Socialization and Child Care

1. **False.** The most recent and comprehensive study to examine this issue found that this negative role of child care for infants occurs only when extensive or poor-quality child care is combined with insensitive maternal care (Cleveland & Krashinsky, 2003).

2. **False.** Results from analysis of data from the latest National Longitudinal Survey of Children and Youth (Statistics Canada, 1999c) suggest that children who are enrolled in early childhood programs and daycare centres appear to get a head start in school over youngsters who stay at home with a parent.

3. **True.** For example, good-quality child care can reduce the negative effects of poverty and maternal depression on the development of infants and older preschoolers (Cleveland & Krashinsky, 2003).

4. **False.** In Canada, the Employment Insurance program provides one year of income-replacing maternity and parental benefits—15 weeks exclusively to the mother, and another 35 weeks that can be divided between the mother and father (Cleveland & Krashinsky, 2003).

5. **False.** Controlled studies of good child care for preschool children found that children were not, in general, harmed in their emotional development by daily short-term separations from their parents and indeed benefited in many ways from the experience (Cleveland & Krashinsky, 2003).

6. **True.** According to the National Longitudinal Survey of Children and Youth, the rate has increased from 42 percent in 1994/95 to more than 53 percent today. Of all children in child care, approximately 25 percent were enrolled in a daycare centre as their main care arrangement, up from about 20 percent six years earlier. The proportion of children who were looked after in their own home by a relative rose from 8 percent to 14 percent (HRSDC, 2003).

7. **True.** The proportion of families with stay-at-home fathers has increased from 1 percent in 1976 to approximately 6 percent (Marshall, 1998).

8. **False.** While the number of regulated daycare spaces has increased dramatically, it is estimated that fewer than 20 percent of children whose mothers work can be accommodated. The majority of children in nonparental care continue to be cared for in unregulated homes or centres (Friendly & Beach, 2005).

For a detailed discussion of the above responses, see Gordon Cleveland and Michael Krashinsky's 2003 report *Eight Myths About Early Childhood Education and Care*, at http://www.childcarecanada.org/pubs/other/FF/FactandFantasy.pdf.

from nonhuman animals because we lack instincts and must rely on learning for our survival. Human infants have the potential for developing human characteristics if they are exposed to an adequate socialization process.

Every human being is a product of biology, society, and personal experiences—that is, of heredity and environment or, in even more basic terms, "nature" and "nurture." How much of our development can be explained by socialization? How much by our genetic heritage? Sociologists focus on how humans design their own culture and transmit it from generation to generation through socialization. By contrast, sociobiologists assert that nature, in the form of our genetic makeup, is a major factor in shaping human behaviour. *Sociobiology* **is the systematic study of how biology affects social behaviour** (Wilson, 1975). According to zoologist Edward O. Wilson, who pioneered sociobiology, genetic inheritance underlies many forms of social behaviour, such as war and peace, envy and concern for others, and competition and cooperation. Most sociologists disagree with the notion that biological principles can be used to explain all human behaviour. Obviously, however, some aspects of our physical makeup—such as eye colour, hair colour, height, and weight—largely are determined by our heredity.

How important is social influence ("nurture") in human development? There is hardly a behaviour that is not influenced socially. Except for simple reflexes, most human actions are social, either in their causes or in their consequences. Even solitary actions, such as crying or brushing our teeth, are ultimately social. We cry because someone has hurt us. We brush our teeth because our parents (or dentist) told us it was important. Social environment probably has a greater effect than heredity on the way we develop and the way we act. However, heredity does provide the basic material from which other people help to mould an individual's human characteristics.

Our biological and emotional needs are related in a complex equation. Children whose needs are met in settings characterized by affection, warmth, and closeness see the world as a safe and comfortable place and other people as trustworthy and helpful. By contrast, infants and children who receive less than adequate care or who are emotionally rejected or abused often view the world as hostile and have feelings of suspicion and fear.

Social Isolation and Maltreatment

Social environment, then, is a crucial part of an individual's socialization. Even nonhuman primates, such as monkeys and chimpanzees, need social contact with others of their species in order to develop properly. As we will see, appropriate social contact is even more important for humans.

Isolation and Nonhuman Primates Researchers have attempted to demonstrate the effects of social isolation on nonhuman primates raised without contact with others of their own species. In a series of laboratory experiments, psychologists Harry and Margaret Harlow (1962, 1977) took infant rhesus monkeys from their mothers and isolated them in separate cages. Each cage contained two nonliving "mother substitutes" made of wire, one with a feeding bottle attached and the other covered with soft terry cloth but without a bottle. The infant monkeys instinctively clung to the cloth "mother" and would not abandon it until hunger drove them to the bottle attached to the wire "mother." As soon as they were full, they went back to the cloth "mother" seeking warmth, affection, and physical comfort.

The Harlows' experiments show the detrimental effects of isolation on nonhuman primates. When the young monkeys later were introduced to other members of their species, they cringed in the corner. Having been deprived of social contact with other monkeys during their first six months of life, they never learned how to relate to other monkeys or to become well-adjusted adult monkeys—they were fearful of or hostile toward other monkeys (Harlow and Harlow, 1962, 1977).

Because humans rely more heavily on social learning than do monkeys, the process of socialization is even more important for us.

Isolated Children Of course, sociologists would never place children in isolated circumstances so that they could observe what the effects were. However, some cases have arisen in which parents or other caregivers failed to fulfil their responsibilities, leaving children alone or placing them in isolated circumstances. From analysis of these situations, social scientists have documented cases in which children were deliberately raised in isolation. A look at the lives of two children who suffered such emotional abuse provides insights into the importance of a positive socialization process and the negative effects of social isolation.

Anna Born in 1932 to an unmarried, mentally impaired woman, Anna was an unwanted child. She was kept in an attic-like room in her grandfather's house. Her mother, who worked on the farm all day and often went out at night, gave Anna just enough care to keep her alive; she received no other care. Sociologist Kingsley Davis (1940) described her condition when she was found in 1938:

> [Anna] had no glimmering of speech, absolutely no ability to walk, no sense of gesture, not the least capacity to feed herself even when the food was put in front of her, and no comprehension of cleanliness. She was so apathetic that it was hard to tell whether or not she could hear. And all of this at the age of nearly six years.

When she was placed in a special school and given the necessary care, Anna slowly learned to walk, talk, and care for herself. Just before her death at the age of 10, Anna reportedly could follow directions, talk in phrases, wash her hands, brush her teeth, and try to help other children (Davis, 1940).

Genie   Almost four decades after Anna was discovered, Genie was found in 1970 at the age of 13. She had been locked in a bedroom alone, alternately strapped down to a child's potty chair or straitjacketed into a sleeping bag, since she was 20 months old. She had been fed baby food and beaten with a wooden paddle when she whimpered. She had not heard the sounds of human speech because no one talked to her and there was no television or radio in her home (Curtiss, 1977; Pines, 1981). Genie was placed in a pediatric hospital where one of the psychologists described her condition:

> At the time of her admission she was virtually unsocialized. She could not stand erect, salivated continuously, had never been toilet-trained and had no control over her urinary or bowel functions. She was unable to chew solid food and had the weight, height and appearance of a child half her age. (Rigler, 1993:35)

In addition to her physical condition, Genie showed psychological traits associated with neglect, as described by one of her psychiatrists:

> If you gave [Genie] a toy, she would reach out and touch it, hold it, caress it with her fingertips, as though she didn't trust her eyes. She would rub it against her cheek to feel it. So when I met her and she began to notice me standing beside her bed, I held my hand out and she reached out and took my hand and carefully felt my thumb and fingers individually, and then put my hand against her cheek. She was exactly like a blind child. (Rymer, 1993:45)

Extensive therapy was used in an attempt to socialize Genie and develop her language abilities (Curtiss, 1977; Pines, 1981). These efforts met with limited success: In the early 1990s, Genie was living in a board-and-care home for mentally challenged adults (see Angier, 1993; Rigler, 1993; Rymer, 1993).

Child Maltreatment   What do the terms *child maltreatment* and *child abuse* mean to you? When asked what constitutes child maltreatment, many people first think of cases that involve severe injuries or sexual abuse. In fact, these terms refer to the violence, mistreatment, or neglect that a child may experience while in the care of someone he or she trusts or depends on, such as a parent, relative, caregiver, or guardian. There are many different forms of abuse, including physical abuse, sexual abuse or exploitation, neglect, and emotional abuse. A child who is abused often experiences more than one form of abuse. Recent studies indicate that neglect is the most frequent form of child abuse. Child neglect occurs when a child's basic needs—including emotional warmth and security, adequate shelter, food, health care, education, clothing, and protection—are not met, regardless of the cause (Trocmé et al., 2001). The neglect usually involves repeated incidents over a lengthy period of time.

Child abuse is a complex problem involving individual, familial, and social factors. Any child—regardless of age, gender, race, ethnicity, socioeconomic status, sexual orientation, physical or mental abilities, and personality—may be at risk of being abused. Sociologists argue that child abuse is linked to inequalities in our society and the power imbalance that exists between adults and children. A child is usually dependent on his or her abuser and has little power to control the abusive circumstances. There is increasing understanding that a child's risk of being abused may be increased by other identifiable social factors, such as racism, sexism, homophobia, poverty, and social isolation. For example, historically, many children who were sent to institutions were abused. The majority of these children were from marginalized groups: Aboriginal children, children from racial and ethnic minorities, children with physical or mental disabilities, and children living in poverty (Department of Justice, 2002c).

Throughout history and across cultures, perceptions of what constitutes abuse or neglect have differed. What might have been considered appropriate disciplinary action by parents in the past (such as following the adage "Spare the rod, spoil the child"), today is viewed by many as child abuse.

Still, many parents choose to use spanking as a form of discipline. A recent Canadian study conducted in three cities found that between 70 and 75 percent of parents had spanked their children at least once. However, most of the respondents also indicated that they felt guilty after spanking. Many Canadian parents have begun to redefine physical punishment as an act of violence. This social change may constitute one of the most significant contributions to the prevention of child abuse in recent history (Durrant, 2002:1). (For further discussion of this issue, see Box 4.2.)

BOX 4.2 CRITICAL THINKING

Redefining Physical Punishment: Spanking or Abuse?

The results of the Canadian Incidence Study of Reported Child Abuse and Neglect revealed that in 1998 there were close to 16,000 substantiated incidents of physical abuse of children. In close to 70 percent of these cases, the physical abuse occurred as a result of inappropriate punishment, such as hitting with a hand or object, that led to physical harm (Trocmé et al., 2001). What these results tell us is that physical abuse is not an aberration but rather a predictable outcome of child-rearing practices that include the use of physical punishment as a form of parental discipline (Durrant, 2002).

Twenty years ago, spanking was considered by many to be an effective approach to disciplining children. Today, this practice is increasingly recognized as ineffective, unnecessary, and harmful (Durrant, Broberg, and Rose-Krasnor, 2000). Why? According to child-rearing experts and parent educators, there are a number of reasons for discouraging the use of physical punishment on children. First of all, spanking leads to increased tolerance of violence. Second, this increased tolerance often translates into a greater propensity to use violence when one becomes a parent. As one expert comments, "What are kids learning from us when we spank about how to handle frustration, how to handle conflict?" (Bennett, 1997:51). The strongest predictor of one's use of physical punishment is the degree to which one was physically abused as a child. Therefore, the acts of violence we experience as children may be used to define our personal tolerance of violence as adults and our cutoff points as parents for making distinctions between "discipline" and "abuse" (Buntain-Ricklefs et al., 1994). The research evidence clearly supports this premise. Abusive parents are more likely to have received physical punishment as children than are nonabusive parents (Straus and Smith, 1992).

Section 43 of the *Criminal Code* (referred to as the corporal punishment law) provides legal immunity for parents who physically discipline their children. It states:

Every schoolteacher, parent or person standing in the place of a parent is justified in using force by way of correction toward a pupil or child, as the case may be, who is under his care, if force does not exceed what is reasonable under the circumstances. (*Criminal Code*, Section 43)

Children' rights advocates have tried unsuccessfully in recent years to have this law repealed. In June 2003, the Supreme Court of Canada heard an application by the Canadian Foundation for Children, Youth and Law to strike down s.43 arguing that it infringes on children's rights to security of the person, or equality rights under the Canadian *Charter of Rights and Freedoms*, and is therefore unconstitutional. A year later, the Supreme Court delivered its 30-page written decision. By a narrow margin, it ruled that s.43 did not violate the *Charter* rights of children and therefore was constitutional. It did, however, place further restrictions to allow for mild to moderate spanking on children between the ages of 2 and 12. In this case the result may be to "further public confusion on just when, where, and how parents and teachers can hit a child as a method of discipline" (Robertshaw, 2003).

According to clinical psychologist Joan Durrant, one of the difficulties we have in confronting the issue of physical punishment is the absence of a clear distinction between corporal punishment and abuse. Some argue that there is no distinction; any use of physical force against a child is abusive by definition. Others argue that defining a tap on a child's hand as abusive inflames the debate and trivializes abuse that involves more serious injury (Durrant, 2002). Other countries around the world have taken a more definitive stance on this issue. For example, in 1979 Sweden banned parental use of corporal punishment. Since that time, seven other countries (Israel, Germany, Croatia, Latvia, Cyprus, Austria, and Norway) have defined corporal punishment as an act of violence that is prohibited by law. As Durrant (2002:5) explains:

> These laws serve as important symbols that set a standard for non-violent child rearing and render moot the question of whether striking a child is an act of discipline or abuse. Their purpose is not to wield the power of the State against a frustrated, well-intentioned parent. Rather, their purpose is to make it clear that parental use of violence of any kind is not condoned by the State.

In Canada, there is a clear message mandated in law and sanctioned by society that violence as a means of resolving problems is not tolerated with respect to partners, peers, and strangers. If a clear message rejecting the use of physical punishment of children prevented even 10 percent of physical abuse cases, we would see close to 1,600 fewer cases of child physical abuse each year (Durrant, 2002:5). Is this not reason enough to make the message clear?

What do you think? How do you define child abuse? Is spanking included in your definition? Do you think Section 43 of the *Criminal Code* should be repealed? Do you think you will use physical punishment in disciplining your children? Why or why not?

For more detailed information on the Section 43 debate, go to: Repeal 43 Committee at http://www .repeal43.org/the-law.html. The Court's decision is available at www.lexum.umontreal.ca/csc-scc/en/ rec/index.html. The written argument filed by the Canadian Foundation for Children, Youth and the Law is available at www.jfcy.org/corporalp/corporalp.html.

AGENTS OF SOCIALIZATION

Agents of socialization **are the persons, groups, or institutions that teach us what we need to know in order to participate in society.** We are exposed to many agents of socialization throughout our lifetime; in turn, we have an influence on those socializing agents and organizations. Here, we look at those that are most pervasive in childhood—the family, the school, peer groups, and the mass media.

The Family

The family is the most important agent of socialization in all societies. As the discussion of child maltreatment has demonstrated, the initial love and nurturance we receive from our families are central to our cognitive, emotional, and physical development. From infancy, our families transmit cultural and social values to us. As we will discuss in Chapter 15 ("Families and Intimate Relationships"), families in Canada vary in size and structure. Some families consist of two parents and their biological children, while others consist of a single parent and one or more children. Still other families reflect changing patterns of divorce and remarriage, and an increasing number are made up of same-sex partners and their children.

Theorists using a functionalist perspective emphasize that families serve important functions in society because they are the primary focus for the procreation and socialization of children. Most of us form an emerging sense of self and acquire most of our beliefs and values within the family context. We also learn about the larger dominant culture (including language, attitudes, beliefs, values, and norms) and the primary subcultures to which our parents and other relatives belong.

Families also are the primary source of emotional support. Ideally, people receive love, understanding, security, acceptance, intimacy, and companionship within families (Benokraitis, 1999). The role of the family is especially significant because young children have little social experience beyond its boundaries; they have no basis for comparison or for evaluating how they are treated by their own family.

To a large extent, the family is where we acquire our specific social position in society. From birth, we are a part of the specific ethnic, economic, religious, and regional subcultural grouping of our family. Studies show that families socialize their children somewhat differently based on ethnicity and class (Kohn, 1977; Kohn et al., 1990; Kurian, 1991; Harrison et al., 1990). For example, sociologist Melvin Kohn (1977; Kohn et al., 1990) has suggested that social class (as measured by parental occupation) is one of the strongest influences on what and how parents teach their children. On the one hand, working-class parents who are closely supervised and expected to follow orders at work typically emphasize to their children the importance of obedience and conformity. On the other hand, parents from the middle and professional classes, who have more freedom and flexibility at work, tend to give their children more freedom to make their own decisions and to be creative. Kohn concluded that differences in the parents' occupations were a better predictor of child-rearing practices than was social class itself.

Conflict theorists stress that socialization attributes to false consciousness—a lack of awareness and a distorted perception of reality of class as it affects all aspects of social life. As a result, socialization reaffirms and reproduces the class structure in the next generation rather than challenging the conditions that currently exist. For example, children in poor and low-income families may be unintentionally socialized to believe that acquiring an education and aspiring to lofty ambitions are pointless because of existing economic conditions in the family (Ballantine, 1999). By contrast, middle- and upper-income families typically instil ideas of monetary and social success in children, as well as emphasizing the necessity of thinking and behaving in "socially acceptable" ways.

The social constructionist/symbolic interactionist perspective helps us recognize that children affect their parents' lives and change the overall household environment. When we examine the context in which family life takes place, we also see that grandparents and other relatives have a strong influence on how parents socialize their children. In turn, the children's behaviour may have an effect on how parents, siblings, and grandparents get along with one another. For example, in families where there is already intense personal conflict, the birth of an infant may intensify the stress and discord, sometimes resulting in child maltreatment, spousal battering, or elder abuse. By contrast, in families where partners feel happiness and personal satisfaction, the birth of an infant may contribute to the success of the marriage and bring about positive interpersonal communications among relatives (Ambert, 1992).

The School

As the amount of specialized technical and scientific knowledge has expanded rapidly, and the amount of time children are in educational settings has increased, schools continue to play an enormous role in the socialization of young people. For many people, the formal education process is an undertaking that lasts up to twenty years.

Daycare centres have become important agents of socialization for increasing numbers of children. Today, approximately 70 percent of all Canadian preschool children are in daycare of one kind or another.

The number of one-parent families and families in which both parents work outside the home has increased dramatically, and the number of children in daycare and preschool programs also has grown rapidly. Currently, approximately 70 percent of Canadian preschool children are in daycare, either in private homes or institutional settings, and this percentage continues to climb. Studies generally have found that daycare and preschool programs may have a positive effect on the overall socialization of children. These programs are especially beneficial for children from less-advantaged backgrounds in that they provide these children with valuable learning experiences not available at home. Many researchers also have found that children from all social classes and family backgrounds may benefit from learning experiences in early childhood education programs that they have not had in their homes (Cleveland and Krashinksy, 2003).

Schools teach specific knowledge and skills; they also have a profound effect on children's self-image, beliefs, and values. As children enter school for the first time, they are evaluated and systematically compared with one another by the teacher. A permanent, official record is kept of each child's personal behaviour and academic activities. From a functionalist perspective, schools are responsible for (1) socialization, or teaching students to be productive members of society, (2) transmission of culture, (3) social control and personal development, and (4) the selection, training, and placement of individuals on different rungs in the society (Ballantine, 1997).

In contrast, conflict theorists assert that students have different experiences in the school system depending on their social class, their ethnic background, the neighbourhood in which they live, their gender, and other factors. According to sociologist Stephen Richer (1988), much of what happens in school amounts to teaching a *hidden curriculum* in which children learn to value competition, materialism, work over play, obedience to authority, and attentiveness. Richer's study of Ottawa classrooms indicated that success in school may be based more on students' ability to conform to the hidden curriculum than on their mastery of the formal curriculum. Therefore, students who are destined for leadership or elite positions acquire different skills and knowledge than those who will enter working-class and middle-class occupations (see Cookson and Persell, 1985).

Symbolic interactionists examining socialization in the school environment might focus on how daily interactions and practices in schools affect the construction of students' beliefs regarding such things as patriotism, feelings of aggression or cooperation, and gender practices as they influence boys and girls. For example, recent studies have shown that the school environment continues to foster high degrees of gender segregation, including having boys and girls line up separately to participate in different types of extracurricular activities in middle, junior high, and high schools (Eder, 1985; Thorne, 1993).

Peer Groups

As soon as we are old enough to have acquaintances outside the home, most of us begin to rely heavily on peer groups as a source of information and approval about social behaviour (Lips, 1989). A *peer group* **is a group of people who are linked by common interests, equal social position, and (usually) similar age.** In early childhood, peer groups often are composed of classmates in daycare, preschool, and elementary school. Recent studies have found that preadolescence—the latter part of the elementary school years—is an age in which the child's peer culture has an important effect on how the child perceives himself or herself and how he or she internalizes society's expectations (Adler and Adler, 1998). In adolescence, peer groups are typically composed of people with similar interests and social activities. As adults, we

The pleasure of participating in activities with friends is one of the many attractions of adolescent peer groups. What groups have contributed the most to your own sense of belonging and self-worth?

continue to participate in peer groups of people with whom we share common interests and comparable occupations, income, and/or social position.

Peer groups function as agents of socialization by contributing to our sense of "belonging" and our feelings of self-worth. Unlike families and schools, peer groups provide children and adolescents with some degree of freedom from parents and other authority figures (Corsaro, 1992). Peer groups also teach and reinforce cultural norms while providing important information about "acceptable" behaviour. As a result, the peer group is both a product of culture and one of its major transmitters (Elkin and Handel, 1989). Peer groups simultaneously reflect the larger culture and serve as a conduit for passing on culture to young people.

Is there such a thing as "peer pressure"? Individuals must earn their acceptance with their peers by conforming to a given group's own norms, attitudes, speech patterns, and dress codes. When we conform to our peer group's expectations, we are rewarded; if we do not conform, we may be ridiculed or even expelled from the group. Conforming to the demands of peers frequently places children and adolescents at cross purposes with their parents. Sociologist William A. Corsaro (1992) notes that children experience strong peer pressure even during their preschool years. For example, children frequently are under pressure to obtain certain valued material possessions (such as toys, DVDs, clothing, or athletic shoes); they then pass this pressure on to their parents through emotional pleas to purchase the desired items. In this way, adult caregivers learn about the latest fads and fashions from children, and they may contribute to the peer culture by purchasing the items desired by the children (Corsaro, 1992). Socialization is not a one-way process from adults to children. Adults also learn from children.

Mass Media

An agent of socialization that has a profound impact on both children and adults is the *mass media,* composed of large-scale organizations that use print or electronic means (such as radio, television, film, and the Internet) to communicate with large numbers of people. The media function as socializing agents in several ways: (1) they inform us about events, (2) they introduce us to a wide variety of people, (3) they provide an array of viewpoints on current issues, (4) they make us aware of products and services that, if we purchase them, supposedly will help us to be accepted by others, and (5) they entertain us by providing the opportunity to live vicariously (through other people's experiences). Although most of us take for granted that the media play an important part in contemporary socialization, we frequently underestimate the enormous influence this agent of socialization may have on children's attitudes and behaviour.

Recent studies have shown that North American children are spending increasingly more time in front of TV sets, computers, and video games than they have in the past. According to media educator Arlene Moscovitch (1998:2), there is no doubt that media encounters are an inescapable part of everyday family life:

> TVs flicker in the kitchens and bedrooms, children's thumbs flash as they career through the latest video game landscape, families use the computer in a myriad of ways: for budgets and banking and e-mail and surfing the Internet and homework and computer games and chat rooms and e-commerce. Music pours out of radios and CD players and tape recorders, teens tote cell phones and pagers so their parents can stay in touch with them. The media influence is a given.

It is estimated that Canadian children spend two and a half hours per day watching television and an additional two hours with computers, video games, or a VCR. All of this adds up to more than 1,600 hours per year per child interacting with these media influences. By contrast, Canadian children spend about 1,200 hours per year in school. This means that the average sixteen-year-old will have spent more time in front of a television or computer than attending school. With this information at hand, it comes as no surprise that a recent study in the United States found that 93 percent of children between the ages of ten and seventeen know that Homer, Bart, and Maggie are characters on the animated series *The Simpsons,* whereas only 63 percent could name the current vice-president of the United States (Dart, 1999).

Parents, educators, social scientists, and public officials have widely debated the consequences of young people watching that much television. Television has been praised for offering numerous positive experiences to children. Some scholars suggest that television (when used widely) can enhance children's development by improving their language abilities, concept-formation skills, and reading skills and by encouraging prosocial development (Winn, 1985). However, other studies have shown that children and adolescents who spend a lot of time watching television often have lower grades in school, read fewer books, exercise less, and are overweight (Moscovitch, 1998).

Of special concern to many people is the issue of television violence. It is estimated that the typical young person who watches 28 hours of television a week will have seen 16,000 simulated murders and 200,000 acts of violence by the time he or she reaches age 18. A report by the American Psychological Association states that about 80 percent of all television programs contain acts of violence and that commercial television for children is 50 to 60 times more violent than prime-time television for adults. For example, some cartoons average more than 80 violent acts per hour (APA Online, 2000). The violent content of media programming and the marketing and advertising practices of mass media industries that routinely target children under age seventeen have come under the scrutiny of government agencies, such as the U.S. Federal Trade Commission, due to concerns raised by parents and social analysts.

In addition to concerns about violence in television programming, motion pictures, and electronic games, television shows have been criticized for projecting negative images of women and people of colour. Although the mass media have changed some of the roles that they depict women as playing (such as showing characters like Cat Woman and Charlie's Angels, who are able to vanquish everything that stands in their way), even these newer images tend to reinforce existing stereotypes of women as sex symbols because of the clothing they wear in their action adventures. Throughout this text, we will look at additional examples of how the media—ranging from advertising and television programs to video games and the Internet—socialize all of us, particularly when we are young, in ways that we may or may not realize. Television and other forms of media may have a positive influence on young children, introducing them to a world beyond their home and family. However, the media may also have a negative influence on children, especially when they are exposed to many hours of violent content.

Other researchers are finding that more affluent teenagers continue their peer group involvement via the Internet, particularly through chat rooms and on buddy lists, where they can spend their afternoon hours "visiting" with several friends at a time. According to one recent study, about 90 percent of adolescents aged 15 to 19 spend some time online, and young people make up the fastest growing segment of Internet users (Statistics Canada, 2001c).

Undoubtedly, all mass media socialize us in many ways we may or may not realize. Cultural studies scholars and some postmodern theorists believe that "media culture" has in recent years dramatically changed the socialization process for very young children.

SOCIOLOGICAL THEORIES OF HUMAN DEVELOPMENT

Although social scientists acknowledge the contributions of psychoanalytic and psychologically based explanations of human development, sociologists focus on sociological perspectives in understanding how people develop an awareness of self and learn about the culture in which they live. From a sociological perspective, we cannot form a sense of self or personal identity without intense social contact with others. The self represents the sum total of perceptions and feelings that an individual has of being a distinct, unique person—a sense of who and what one is. When we speak of the "self," we typically use words such as *I, me, my, mine,* and *myself* (Cooley, 1998/2002). This sense of self (also referred to as self-concept) is not present at birth; it arises in the process of social experience. **Self-concept is the totality of our beliefs and feelings about ourselves** (Gecas, 1982). Four components comprise our self-concept: (1) the physical self ("I am tall"), (2) the active self ("I am good at soccer"), (3) the social self ("I am nice to others"), and (4) the psychological self ("I believe in world peace"). Between early and late childhood, a child's focus tends to shift from the physical and active dimensions of self toward the social and psychological aspects (Lippa, 1994). Self-concept is

the foundation for communication with others; it continues to develop and change throughout our lives (Zurcher, 1983).

Our *self-identity* is our perception about what kind of person we are. As we have seen, socially isolated children do not have typical self-identities because they have had no experience of "humanness." According to symbolic interactionists, we do not know who we are until we see ourselves as we believe others see us. We gain information about the self largely through language, symbols, and interaction with others. Our interpretation and evaluation of these messages is central to the social construction of our identity. However, we are not just passive reactors to situations, programmed by society to respond in fixed ways. Instead, we are active agents who develop plans out of the pieces supplied by culture and attempt to execute these plans in social encounters (McCall and Simmons, 1978).

Cooley, Mead, and Symbolic Interactionist Perspectives

Social constructionism is a term that is applied to theories that emphasize the socially created nature of social life. This perspective is linked to symbolic interactionist theory, and its roots can be traced to the Chicago school and early theorists, such as Charles Horton Cooley and George Herbert Mead.

Cooley and the Looking-Glass Self
According to sociologist Charles Horton Cooley (1864–1929), the *looking-glass self* **refers to the way in which a person's sense of self is derived from the perceptions of others.** Our looking-glass self is not who we actually are or what people actually think about us; it is based on our perception of how other people think of us (Cooley, 1922/1902). Cooley asserted that we base our perception of who we are on how we think other people see us and on whether this seems good or bad to us.

As Figure 4.1 shows, the looking-glass self is a self-concept derived from a three-step process:

1. We imagine how our personality and appearance will look to other people. We may imagine that we are attractive or unattractive, heavy or slim, friendly or unfriendly, and so on.
2. We imagine how other people judge the appearance and personality that we think we present. This step involves our *perception* of how we think they are judging us. We may be correct or incorrect!

Our self-concept continues to be influenced by our interactions with others throughout our lives.

3. We develop a self-concept. If we think the evaluation of others is favourable, our self-concept is enhanced. If we think the evaluation is unfavourable, our self-concept is diminished (Cooley, 1998/1902).

According to Cooley, we use our interactions with others as a mirror for our own thoughts and actions; our sense of self depends on how we interpret what they do and say. Consequently, our sense of self is not permanently fixed; it is always developing as we interact with others.

Mead and Role-Taking George Herbert Mead (1863–1931) extended Cooley's insights by linking the idea of self-concept to ***role-taking***—**the process by which a person mentally assumes the role of another person in order to understand the world from that person's point of view.** Role-taking often occurs through play and games, as children try out different roles (such as being mommy, daddy, doctor, or teacher) and gain an appreciation of them. By taking the roles of others, the individual hopes to ascertain the intention or direction of the acts of others. Then the person begins to construct his or her own roles (role-making) and to anticipate other individuals' responses. Finally, the person plays at her or his particular role (role-playing) (Marshall, 1998).

Figure 4.1   How the Looking-Glass Self Works

According to Mead (1934/1962), in the early months of life children do not realize that they are separate from others. However, they do begin early on to see a mirrored image of themselves in others. Shortly after birth, infants start to notice the faces of those around them, especially the significant others, whose faces start to have meaning because they are associated with experiences, such as feeding and cuddling. **Significant others are those persons whose care, affection, and approval are especially desired and who are most important in the development of the self.** Gradually, we distinguish ourselves from our caregivers and begin to perceive ourselves in contrast to them. As we develop language skills and learn to understand symbols, we begin to develop a self-concept. When we can represent ourselves in our own minds as objects distinct from everything else, our self has been formed.

Mead divided the self into the "I" and the "me." The "I" is the subjective element of the self that represents the spontaneous and unique traits of each person. The "me" is the objective element of the self, which is composed of the internalized attitudes and demands of other members of society and the individual's awareness of those demands. Both the "I" and the "me" are needed to form the social self. The unity of the two constitutes the full development of the individual. According to Mead, the "I" develops first, and the "me" takes form during the three stages of self development:

1. During the *preparatory stage,* up to about age three, interactions lack meaning, and children largely imitate the people around them. At this stage, children are preparing for role-taking.
2. In the *play stage,* from about age three to five, children learn to use language and other symbols, which enable them to pretend to take the roles of specific people. At this stage, children begin to see themselves in relation to others, but they do not see role-taking as something they have to do.

According to sociologist George Herbert Mead, the self develops through three stages. In the preparatory stage, children imitate others; in the play stage, children pretend to take the roles of specific people; and in the game stage, children become aware of the "rules of the game" and the expectations of others.

3. During the *game stage,* which begins in the early school years, children understand not only their own social position but also the positions of others around them. In contrast to play, games are structured by rules, often are competitive, and involve a number of other "players." At this time, children become concerned about the demands and expectations of others and of the larger society. Mead used the example of a baseball game to describe this stage because children, like baseball players, must take into account the roles of all the other players at the same time. Mead's concept of the **generalized other refers to the child's awareness of the demands and expectations of the society as a whole or of the child's subculture.**

Is socialization a one-way process? Not according to Mead. Socialization is a two-way process between society and the individual. Just as the society in which we live helps determine what kind of individuals we will become, we have the ability to shape certain aspects of our social environment and perhaps even the larger society.

How useful are symbolic interactionist perspectives, such as Cooley's and Mead's, in enhancing our understanding of the socialization process? Certainly, this approach contributes to our understanding of how the self develops. Cooley's idea of the looking-glass self makes us aware that our perception of how we *think* others see us is not always correct. Mead extended Cooley's ideas by emphasizing the cognitive skills acquired through role-taking. He stressed the importance of play and games, as children try out different roles and gain an appreciation of them. His concept of the generalized other helps us see that the self is a social creation. According to Mead (1962/1934:196), "Selves can only exist in definite relations to other selves. No hard-and-fast line can be drawn between our own selves and the selves of others."

The viewpoints of symbolic interactionists, such as Cooley and Mead, have certain limitations, however. Some conflict theorists have argued that these theories are excessively conservative because they assume that what is good for dominant group members is good for everyone. Sociologist Anne Kaspar (1986) suggests that Mead's ideas about the social self may be more applicable to men than women because women are more likely to experience inherent conflicts between the meanings they derive from their personal experiences and those they take from culture, particularly in regard to balancing the responsibilities of family life and paid employment.

Recent Symbolic Interactionist Perspectives

The symbolic interactionist approach emphasizes that socialization is a collective process in which children are active and creative agents, not passive recipients of the socialization process. From this view, childhood is a *socially constructed* category (Adler and Adler, 1998). Children are capable of actively constructing their own shared meanings as they acquire language skills and accumulate interactive experiences (Qvortrup, 1990). According to the sociologist William A. Corsaro's (1985, 1997) "orb web model," children's cultural knowledge reflects not only the beliefs of the adult world but also the unique interpretations and aspects of the children's own *peer culture.* Corsaro (1992:162) states that peer culture is "a stable set of activities or routines, artifacts, values, and concerns that children produce and share." This peer culture emerges through interactions as children "borrow" from the adult culture but transform it so that it fits their own situation. Based on ethnographic studies of U.S. and Italian preschoolers, Corsaro found that very young children engage in predictable patterns of interaction. For example, when playing together, children often permit some children to gain access to their group and play area while preventing others from becoming a part of their group. Children also play "approach–avoidance" games in which they alternate between approaching a threatening person or group and then running away. In fact, Corsaro (1992) believes that the peer group is the most significant public realm for children. This approach contributes to our knowledge about human development because it focuses on group life rather than individuals. Researchers using this approach "look at social relations, the organization and meanings of social situations, and the collective practices through which children create and recreate key constructs in their daily interactions" (Adler and Adler, 1998:10; see also Thorne, 1993; Eder, 1995).

PSYCHOLOGICAL THEORIES OF HUMAN DEVELOPMENT

Up to this point, we have discussed sociologically oriented theories; we now turn to psychological theories that have influenced contemporary views of human development.

Freud and the Psychoanalytic Perspective

The basic assumption in Sigmund Freud's (1924) psychoanalytic approach is that human behaviour and personality originate from unconscious forces within individuals. Sigmund Freud (1856–1939), who is known as the founder of psychoanalytic theory, lived in the Victorian era, when biological explanations of human behaviour were prevalent. It also was an era of extreme sexual repression and male dominance when compared to contemporary North American standards. Freud's theory was greatly influenced by these cultural factors, as reflected in the importance he assigned to sexual motives in explaining behaviour.

For example, Freud based his ideas on the belief that people have two basic tendencies: the urge to survive and the urge to procreate. According to

Freud (1924), human development occurs in three stages that reflect different levels of the personality, which he referred to as the *id, ego,* and *superego*. The ***id*** **is the component of personality that includes all of the individual's basic biological drives and needs that demand immediate gratification.** For Freud, the newborn child's personality is all id, and from birth the child finds that urges for self-gratification—such as wanting to be held, fed, or changed—are not going to be satisfied immediately. However, the id remains with people throughout their lives in the form of *psychic energy,* the urges and desires that account for behaviour. By contrast, the second level of the personality, the ego, develops as infants discover their most basic desires are not always going to be met by others. **The *ego* is the rational, reality-oriented component of personality that imposes restrictions on the innate pleasure-seeking drives of the id.** The ego

Figure 4.2   Freud's Theory of Personality

This illustration shows how Freud might picture a person's internal conflict over whether to commit an antisocial act, such as stealing a candy bar. In addition to dividing personality into three components, Freud theorized that our personalities are largely unconscious—hidden away outside our normal awareness. To dramatize his point, Freud compared conscious awareness (portions of the ego and superego) to the visible tip of an iceberg. Most of personality—including all of the id, with its raw desires and impulses—lies submerged in our subconscious.

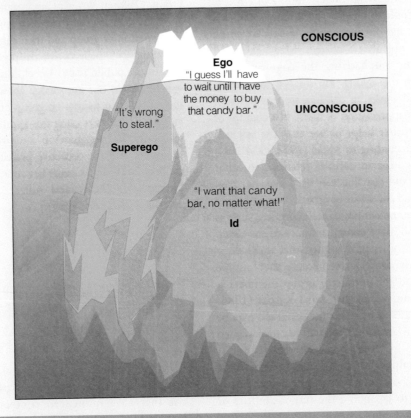

channels the desire of the id for immediate gratification into the most advantageous direction for the individual. The third level of the personality, the superego, is in opposition to both the id and the ego. The *superego,* **or conscience, consists of the moral and ethical aspects of personality.** It is first expressed as the recognition of parental control and eventually matures as the child learns that parental control is a reflection of the values and moral demands of the larger society. When a person is well adjusted, the ego successfully manages the opposing forces of the id and the superego. Figure 4.2 illustrates Freud's theory of personality.

Although subject to harsh criticism, Freud's theories made people aware of the significance of early childhood experiences, including abuse and neglect. His theories have also had a profound influence on contemporary mental health practitioners and on other human development theories.

Piaget and Cognitive Development

Unlike psychoanalytic approaches, which focus primarily on personality development, cognitive approaches emphasize the intellectual (cognitive) development of children. The Swiss psychologist Jean Piaget (1896–1980) was a pioneer in the field of cognitive development. Cognitive theorists are interested in how people obtain, process, and use information—that is, in how we think. Cognitive development relates to changes over time in how we think.

According to Piaget (1954), in each stage of development (from birth through adolescence), children's activities are governed by their perception of the world around them. His four stages of cognitive development are organized around specific tasks that, when mastered, lead to the acquisition of new mental capacities, which then serve as the basis for the next level of development. Piaget emphasized that all children must go through each stage in sequence before moving on to the next one, although some children move through them faster than others.

1. *Sensorimotor stage* (birth to age 2). Children understand the world only through sensory contact and immediate action; they cannot engage in symbolic thought or use language. Children gradually comprehend *object permanence*—the realization that objects continue to exist even when the items are placed out of their sight.
2. *Preoperational stage* (ages 2 to 7). Children begin to use words as mental symbols and to form mental images. However, they still are limited in their ability to use logic to solve problems or to realize that physical objects may change in shape or appearance but still retain their physical properties.
3. *Concrete operational stage* (ages 7 to 11). Children think in terms of tangible objects and actual events. They can draw conclusions about the likely physical consequences of an action without always having to try the action out. Children begin to take the role of others and start to empathize with the viewpoints of others.
4. *Formal operational stage* (age 12 through adolescence). Adolescents have the potential to engage in highly abstract thought and understand places, things, and events they have never seen. They can think about the future and evaluate different options or courses of action.

Using this cognitive model, Piaget (1932) also investigated moral development. In one study, he told children stories and asked them to judge how "good" or "bad" the consequences were. One story involved a child who *accidentally* broke fifteen cups while another *deliberately* broke one cup. Piaget asked the children if they thought one child's behaviour was worse than the other's. He concluded that younger children (up to the age of 8 or 10) believe that it is more evil to break a large number of cups (or steal large sums of money) than to break one cup (or steal small sums of money) for whatever reason. In contrast, older children (beginning at about age 11) are more likely to consider principles, including the intentions and motives behind other people's behaviour.

Piaget's stages of cognitive development provide us with useful insights into children's logical thinking and how they invent or construct the rules that govern their understanding of the world. Piaget asserted that children move from being totally influenced by external factors, such as parental and other forms of moral authority, to being more autonomous, thinking and acting based on their own moral judgments about behaviour. However, critics have pointed out that Piaget's theory fails to address individual differences, including how gender or culture may influence children's beliefs and actions.

Kohlberg and the Stages of Moral Development

Lawrence Kohlberg (b. 1927) elaborated on Piaget's theories of cognitive reasoning by conducting a series of studies in which respondents were presented with moral dilemmas that took the form of stories. Based on their responses, Kohlberg classified moral reasoning into three levels (Kohlberg, 1969, 1981).

1. *Preconventional level* (ages 7 to 10). Children's perceptions are based on punishment and obedience. Evil behaviour is that which is likely to be punished; good conduct is based on obedience and avoidance of unwanted consequences.
2. *Conventional level* (age 10 through adulthood). People are most concerned with how they are perceived by their peers and with how one conforms to rules.
3. *Postconventional level* (few adults reach this stage). People view morality in terms of individual rights; "moral conduct" is judged by principles based on human rights that transcend government and laws.

Although Kohlberg presents interesting ideas about the moral judgments of children, some critics have challenged the universality of his stages of moral development. They have also suggested that the elaborate "moral dilemmas" he used are too abstract for children. In one story, for example, a husband contemplates stealing medicine for his critically ill wife. When questions are made simpler, or when children and adolescents are observed in natural settings, they often demonstrate sophisticated levels of moral reasoning (Darley and Schultz, 1990; Lapsley, 1990).

Gilligan's View on Gender and Moral Development

Psychologist Carol Gilligan (b. 1936) is one of the major critics of Kohlberg's theory of moral development. According to Gilligan (1982), Kohlberg's model was developed solely on the basis of research with male respondents. She suggested that women and men often have diverging views on morality based on differences in socialization and life experiences. Gilligan believes that men become more concerned with law and order, while women analyze social relationships and the social consequences of behaviour. For example, in Kohlberg's story about a man who is thinking about stealing medicine for his wife, Gilligan argues that male respondents are more likely to use *abstract standards of right and wrong*, whereas female respondents are more likely to be concerned about what *consequences* his stealing the drug might have on the man and his family. Does this constitute a "moral deficiency" on the part of either gender? Not according to Gilligan.

To correct what she perceived to be a male bias in Kohlberg's research, Gilligan (1982) examined morality in women by interviewing twenty-eight pregnant women who were contemplating having an abortion. Based on her research, Gilligan concluded that Kohlberg's stages do not reflect the ways many women think about moral problems. As a result, Gilligan identified three stages in female moral development. In stage 1, the woman is motivated primarily by selfish concerns ("This is what I want . . . this is what I need"). In stage 2, she increasingly recognizes her responsibility to others. In stage 3, she makes her decision based on her desire to do the greatest good for both herself and for others. Gilligan argued that men are socialized to make moral decisions based on a justice perspective ("What is the fairest to do?"), while women are socialized to make such decisions on a responsibility and care perspective ("Who will be hurt least?").

Subsequent research that directly compared women's and men's reasoning about moral dilemmas has supported some of Gilligan's assertions but not others. For example, some researchers have not found women to be more compassionate than men (Tavris, 1993). Overall, however, Gilligan's argument that people make moral decisions according to both abstract principles of justice and principles of compassion and care contributes to our knowledge about moral reasoning.

Although the sociological and psychological perspectives we have examined often have been based on different assumptions and have reached somewhat different conclusions, an important theme emerges from these models of cognitive and moral development—through the process of socialization, people learn how to take into account other people's perspectives.

GENDER AND RACIAL-ETHNIC SOCIALIZATION

If you had only one child, would you prefer for the child to be a boy or a girl? In most societies, parents prefer male children to female children based on cultural assumptions about sex differences (Steinbacher and Holmes, 1987). Is this because males inherently are superior to females? Not at all; parents acquire these gender preferences through **gender socialization, the aspect of socialization** that contains specific messages and practices concerning the nature of being female or male in a specific group or society. Gender socialization is important in determining what we *think* the "preferred" sex of a child should be and in influencing our beliefs about acceptable behaviours for males and females.

In some families, gender socialization starts before birth. Parents who learn the sex of the fetus through ultrasound or amniocentesis often purchase colour-coded and gender-typed clothes, toys, and nursery decorations in anticipation of their daughter's or son's arrival. After birth, parents may respond differently toward male and female infants; they often play more roughly with boys and talk more lovingly to girls (Eccles, Jacobs, and Harold, 1990). Throughout childhood and adolescence, boys and girls typically are assigned different household chores and given different privileges (such as how late they may stay out at night).

When we look at the relationship between gender socialization and social class, the picture becomes more complex. Although some studies have found less rigid gender stereotyping in higher-income families (Seegmiller, Suter, and Duviant, 1980; Brooks-Gunn, 1986), others have found more (Bardwell, Cochran, and Walker, 1986). One study found that higher-income families are more likely than low-income families to give "male-oriented" toys (which develop visual–spatial and problem-solving skills) to children of both sexes (Serbin et al., 1990). Working-class families tend to adhere to more rigid gender expectations than middle-class families (Canter and Ageton, 1984; Brooks-Gunn, 1986).

Schools, peer groups, and the media also contribute to our gender socialization. From kindergarten through university, teachers and peers reward gender-appropriate attitudes and behaviour. Sports reinforce traditional gender roles through a rigid division of events into male and female categories. The media also are a powerful source of gender socialization; from an early age, children's books, television programs, movies, and music provide subtle and not-so-subtle messages about "masculine" and "feminine" behaviour. Gender socialization is discussed in more depth in Chapter 11 ("Sex and Gender").

Scholars may be hesitant to point out differences in socialization practices among diverse ethnic and social class groupings because such differences typically have been interpreted by others to be a sign of inadequate (or inferior) socialization practices.

SOCIALIZATION THROUGH THE LIFE COURSE

Why is socialization a lifelong process? Throughout our lives, we continue to learn. Each time we experience a change in status (such as becoming a university student or getting married), we learn a new set of rules, roles, and relationships. Even before we achieve a new status, we often participate in *anticipatory socialization*—the process by which knowledge and skills are learned for future roles. Many societies organize social experience according to age. Some have distinct *rites of passage,* based on age or other factors, that publicly dramatize and validate changes in a person's status. In Canada and other industrialized societies, the most common categories of age are infancy, childhood, adolescence, and adulthood (often subdivided into young adulthood, middle adulthood, and older adulthood). (See Census Profile on page 116.)

Infancy and Childhood

Some social scientists believe that a child's sense of self is formed at a very early age and that it is difficult to change this view later in life. Interactionists emphasize that during infancy and early childhood, family support and guidance are crucial to a child's developing self-concept. In some families, children are provided with emotional warmth, feelings of mutual trust, and a sense of security. These families come closer to our ideal cultural belief that childhood should be a time of carefree play, safety, and freedom from economic, political, and sexual responsibilities. However, other families reflect the discrepancy between cultural ideals and reality—children grow up in a setting characterized by fear, danger, and risks that are created by parental neglect, emotional abuse, or premature economic and sexual demands (Knudsen, 1992).

Abused children often experience low self-esteem, an inability to trust others, feelings of isolation and powerlessness, and denial of their feelings. However, the manner in which parental abuse affects children's ongoing development is subject to much debate and uncertainty. For example, some scholars and therapists assert that the intergenerational hypothesis—the idea that abused children will become abusive parents—is valid, but others have found little support for this hypothesis (Knudsen, 1992).

According to developmental psychologist Urie Bronfenbrenner (1990), mutual interaction with a

CENSUS ✦ PROFILE

Age of the Canadian Population

Just as age is a crucial variable in the socialization process, Statistics Canada gathers data about people's age so that the government and other interested parties will know how many individuals residing in this country are in different age categories. This chapter examines how a person's age is related to socialization and one's life experiences. The table

below shows a depiction of the nation's population in the year 2001, separated into three broad age categories.

Can age be a source of social cohesion among people? Why might age differences produce conflict among individuals in different age groups? What do you think?

PERCENTAGE DISTRIBUTION FOR BOTH SEXES, PROVINCES AND TERRITORIES

NAME	AGE GROUP			TOTAL
	0-19	20-64	65+	
Canada	25.9%	61.1%	13.0%	100.0%
Newfoundland and Labrador	25.0%	62.7%	12.3%	100.0%
Prince Edward Island	27.3%	59.0%	13.7%	100.0%
Nova Scotia	25.0%	61.1%	13.9%	100.0%
New Brunswick	24.8%	61.7%	13.6%	100.0%
Quebec	24.2%	62.5%	13.3%	100.0%
Ontario	26.3%	60.8%	12.9%	100.0%
Manitoba	28.1%	58.0%	14.0%	100.0%
Saskatchewan	29.2%	55.8%	15.1%	100.0%
Alberta	28.3%	61.4%	10.4%	100.0%
British Columbia	25.0%	61.4%	13.6%	100.0%
Yukon Territory	29.0%	64.9%	6.0%	100.0%
Northwest Territories	35.0%	60.7%	4.4%	100.0%
Nunavut	46.5%	51.2%	2.2%	100.0%

caring adult—and preferably a number of nurturing adults—is essential for a child's emotional, physical, intellectual, and social growth. However, he also emphasizes that at the macrosystem level, it is necessary for communities and the major economic, social, and political institutions of a society to provide the policies, practices, and services that support healthy child-rearing practices.

Adolescence

In industrialized societies, the adolescent (or teenage) years represent a buffer between childhood and adulthood. In Canada, no specific rites of passage exist to

mark children's move into adulthood; therefore, young people have to pursue their own routes to self-identity and adulthood. Anticipatory socialization often is associated with adolescence, whereby many young people spend much of their time planning or being educated for future roles they hope to occupy. However, other adolescents (such as eleven- and twelve-year-old mothers) may have to plunge into adult responsibilities at this time. Adolescence often is characterized by emotional and social unrest. In the process of developing their own identities, some young people come into conflict with parents, teachers, and other authority figures who attempt to restrict their freedom. Adolescents also may find themselves caught

An important rite of passage for many Jewish Canadians is the bar mitzvah or bat mitzvah—a celebration of the adolescent's passage into manhood or womanhood. Can you see how this might be a form of anticipatory socialization?

between the demands of adulthood and their own lack of financial independence and experience in the job market. The experiences of individuals during adolescence vary according to their ethnicity, class, and gender. Based on their family's economic situation, some young people move directly into the adult world of work. However, those from upper-middle- and upper-class families may extend adolescence into their late twenties or early thirties by attending graduate or professional school and then receiving additional advice and financial support from their parents as they start their own families, careers, or businesses.

Adulthood

One of the major differences between child and adult socialization is the degree of freedom of choice. If young adults are able to support themselves financially, they gain the ability to make more choices about their own lives. In early adulthood (usually until about age forty), people work toward their own goals of creating meaningful relationships with others, finding employment, and seeking personal fulfillment. Of course, young adults continue to be socialized by their parents, teachers, peers, and the media, but they also learn new attitudes and behaviours. For example, when we marry or have children, we learn new roles as partners or parents. Adults often learn about fads and fashions in clothing, music, and language from their children. Parents in one study indicated that they had learned new attitudes and behaviours about drug use, sexuality, sports, leisure, and ethnic issues from their university-aged children (Peters, 1985).

Workplace (or *occupational*) *socialization* is one of the most important types of adult socialization. Sociologist Wilbert Moore (1968) divided occupational socialization into four phases: (1) career choice, (2) anticipatory socialization (learning different aspects of the occupation before entering it), (3) conditioning and commitment (learning the ups and downs of the occupation and remaining committed to it), and (4) continuous commitment (remaining committed to the work even when problems or other alternatives may arise). This type of socialization tends to be most intense immediately after a person makes the transition from school to the workplace; however, this process continues throughout our years of employment. Nowadays, many people experience continuous workplace socialization as a result of individuals having more than one career in their lifetime (Lefrançois, 1999).

Between the ages of 40 and 60, people enter middle adulthood, and many begin to compare their accomplishments with their earlier expectations. This is the point at which people either decide that they have reached their goals or recognize that they have attained as much as they are likely to achieve.

In older adulthood, some people are quite happy and content; others are not. Erik Erikson noted that difficult changes in adult attitudes and behaviour occur in the last years of life, when people experience decreased physical ability, lower prestige, and the prospect of death. Older adults in industrialized societies have experienced *social devaluation*—**wherein a person or group is considered to have less social value than other individuals or groups.** Social devaluation is especially acute when people are leaving roles that have defined their sense of social identity and provided them with meaningful activity (Achenbaum, 1978).

It is important to note that not everyone goes through passages or stages of a life course at the same age. Sociologist Alice Rossi (1980) suggests that human experience is much more diverse than life-course models suggest. She also points out that young people growing up today live in a different world, with a different set of opportunities and problems, than did the young people of previous generations (Epstein, 1988). Rossi further suggests that women's and men's experiences are not identical throughout the life course and that the life course of women today is remarkably different from that of their mothers and grandmothers because of changing societal roles and expectations. Life-course patterns are strongly influenced by ethnicity and social class as well.

■ RESOCIALIZATION

Resocialization is the process of learning a new and different set of attitudes, values, and behaviours from those in one's previous background and experience. It may be voluntary or involuntary.

In either case, people undergo changes that are much more rapid and pervasive than the gradual adaptations that socialization usually involves. For many new parents, the process of resocialization involved in parenting is the most dramatic they will experience in their lifetimes. See Box 4.3 for a discussion of the trend toward stay-at-home fathers.

Voluntary Resocialization

Resocialization is voluntary when we assume a new status (such as becoming a student, an employee, or a retiree) of our own free will. Sometimes, voluntary resocialization involves medical or psychological treatment or religious conversion, in which case the person's existing attitudes, beliefs, and behaviours must undergo strenuous modification to a new regime and a new way of life. For example, resocialization for adult survivors of emotional or physical child abuse includes extensive therapy in

BOX 4.3 SOCIOLOGY IN GLOBAL PERSPECTIVE

Stay-at-Home Dads: Socialization for Kids and Resocialization for Parents

"You want to do what?!" came the reply from my boss, when told of my plans to leave work and stay home with my boys. I had been employed with the company for some six years as a buyer and was assured a successful career, in the fullness of time. All this was about to change! As my wife Lucy was due to return to work following her maternity leave, we set about investigating our options for childcare and quickly discovered that in real terms we didn't have any. Childcare placements for two babies were scarce, expensive, and not very flexible in relation to the unpredictability of two working parents. The decision was obvious ... it was time to join the new breed of Homedads!

–Karl Betschwar (2002), a father in the United Kingdom, describing his boss's reaction when he quit his job to become the family's primary daytime caregiver

Recent media reports about the growing number of men who are assuming full-time child care responsibilities rather than being employed outside the home (Horsburgh, 2003), along with the release of the Eddie

Murphy film *Daddy Day Care*, have made us aware that more fathers in two-parent families have now assumed the role of primary caregivers for their young children. In 2002, about 105,000 stay-at-home dads in the United States were caring for 189,000 children under age 15 (Horsburgh, 2003). In the United Kingdom, the numbers were similar: About 100,000 dads were bringing up their children, and it was estimated that this number had more than doubled in recent years (Cavender, 2001). In Canada there are approximately 80,000 families with a stay-at-home father (Marshall, 1998). What contributes to this trend? Recent accounts suggest that a man is more likely to become a stay-at-home dad when his wife has a high-paying job that she really likes, when the husband's job pays less and is viewed as less psychologically rewarding, or when the husband is laid off from his job (Horsburgh, 2003; Tyre and McGinn, 2003).

What do children learn from having a father as their primary caregiver? First, children may learn that much housework is gender neutral, meaning that neither women nor men are necessarily "better" at performing certain tasks at home. As Brian Fogg, a stay-at-home dad, told a journalist, "I think I'm a better housekeeper than any mother out there." According to Fogg, he does a great job of dusting, ironing, and cooking fettuccine Alfredo, but he doesn't do a good job of styling hair for his four daughters (qtd. in Horsburgh, 2003:79). Second, children may learn that men's and women's paid employment roles can be flexible: In some families, the mother leaves home for work while the father remains at home; in others, the father leaves for work, and the mother remains at home; and in still other families, both parents go off to work. (Of course, in single-parent families, all the work within the home and in the paid workplace typically falls most heavily on the parent who lives at home with the children.) Finally, if children who are cared for by their fathers receive adequate nurturing and have a variety of positive learning experiences, there is no indication that the children experience any detrimental effects—and may even experience many positive effects—from having their father present in their everyday lives.

In regard to socialization, perhaps the greatest adjustments are not for the children but rather for the mothers and fathers. Some fathers have to resocialize themselves for the role of stay-at-home dad, and some mothers have to resocialize themselves for assuming the role of the family's only breadwinner. This is because many men have been taught from an early age that they are supposed to be their family's primary breadwinner and because many women view themselves as possibly one of the wage earners in the family but not necessarily the only breadwinner (Tyre and McGinn, 2003). Further confounding the problem of adjusting are the lag in public perception and the lag in public accommodations: Some people do not believe that a woman should be the primary wage earner in a family (Tyre and McGinn, 2003), and many public accommodations are not geared to the role of men as child care providers. Stay-at-home dads are particularly frustrated when they need to change children's diapers in shopping and leisure centres. As one stay-at-home father in the United Kingdom commented, "Many shops in leisure centres still don't cater for men with young children. It's amazing how many baby changing facilities are found only in the ladies' toilets, so dads end up having to change nappies on the floor in the gents (never a pleasant situation) or in the back of the car." But, as he concluded, "Being

a man out with young children does have its advantages, however. Older men will open doors for me, older women will stand aside and let me go first, and I always get my bags packed at Waitrose [a grocery store]" (qtd. in Cavender, 2001).

Because they view their situation as unique, some stay-at-home dads around the world have joined online support groups. Web sites such as the United Kingdom's "HomeDad" (http://www.homedad .org.uk), the United States's Slowlane (http://www .slowlane.com), and "House Fathers" in Japan provide information on child rearing and food preparation, as well as offering online discussion forums where the men can communicate about child care issues and personal concerns.

In the future, will there be more flexible roles for women and men in the socialization of infants and young children? According to some analysts, today's university students are typically more open than their parents are in regard to roles in marriage and the family. Economic conditions, including the recent downturn in employment opportunities and problematic family finances, may contribute to a belief that greater flexibility will be necessary in work and family roles in the future (Kantrowitz, 2003). It is also possible that as today's infants and children see their parents assuming more flexible roles, including that of "Home Dad," they will not view these roles as unique.

■ Many fathers around the world are assuming full-time responsibility for their children. In some families, this is a matter of choice, but in others it is a matter of necessity. How do changes in family life affect our perceptions of the roles of men and women?

Sources: Based on Betschwar, 2002; Cavender, 2001; Horsburgh, 2003; Kantrowitz, 2003; and Tyre and McGinn, 2003.

---

order to form new patterns of thinking and action, somewhat like Alcoholics Anonymous and its twelve-step program that has become the basis for many other programs dealing with addictive behaviour (Parrish, 1990).

Involuntary Resocialization

Involuntary resocialization occurs against a person's wishes and generally takes place within a ***total institution***—a place where people are isolated from the rest of society for a set period of time and come under the control of the officials who run the institution (Goffman, 1961a). Military boot camps, jails and prisons, concentration camps, and some mental hospitals are total institutions. In these settings, people are totally stripped of their former selves—or depersonalized—through a *degradation ceremony* (Goffman, 1961a). Inmates entering prison, for example, are required to strip, shower, and wear assigned institutional clothing. In the process, they are searched, weighed, fingerprinted, photographed, and given no privacy even in showers and restrooms. Their official identification becomes not a name but a number. In this abrupt break from their former existence, they must leave behind their personal possessions and their family and friends. The depersonalization process continues as they are required to obey rigid rules and to conform to their new environment.

After stripping people of their former identities, the institution attempts to build a more compliant person. A system of rewards and punishments (such as providing or withholding cigarettes and television or exercise privileges) encourages conformity to institutional norms. Some individuals may be rehabilitated; others become angry and hostile toward the system that has taken away their freedom. Although

the assumed purpose of involuntary resocialization is to reform persons so that they will conform to societal standards of conduct after their release, the ability of total institutions to modify offenders' behaviour in a meaningful manner has been widely questioned. In many prisons, for example, inmates may conform to the norms of the prison or of other inmates, but little relationship exists between those norms and the laws of society.

SOCIALIZATION IN THE FUTURE

In the future, the family is likely to remain the institution that most fundamentally shapes and nurtures personal values and self-identity. However, parents increasingly may feel overburdened by this responsibility, especially without societal support—such as high-quality, affordable child care—and more education in parenting skills. Some analysts have suggested that there will be an increase in known cases of child abuse and in the number of children who experience delayed psychosocial development,

Concept Table 4.A THEORETICAL PERSPECTIVES ON HUMAN DEVELOPMENT

PERSPECTIVE	THEORIST	KEY ELEMENTS
Sociological		
Symbolic interactionist	C. H. Cooley	Our sense of self is based on how others perceive and treat us.
Symbolic interactionist	G. H. Mead	Our self-concept is developed through role playing and learning the rules of social interaction through others.
Symbolic interactionist	W. A. Corsaro	Children's socialization reflects not only knowledge from the adult world but also the unique interpretations of children's peer culture.
Psychological		
Psychoanalytic	S. Freud	The self is comprised of three interrelated components: id, ego, and superego. When a person is well adjusted, the three forces are in balance.
Cognitive Moral Development	L. Kohlberg	Classified moral development into six stages. Certain levels of cognitive development must occur before moral reasoning can develop.
	C. Gilligan	Men and women have different views on morality based on differences in socialization.
	J. Piaget	From birth through adolescence, children move through four states of cognitive development, which are organized around acquisition and mastery of specific tasks.

learning difficulties, and emotional and behavioural problems. They attribute these increases to the dramatic changes occurring in the size, structure, and economic stability of families.

A central value-oriented issue facing parents and teachers as they attempt to socialize children is the growing dominance of the mass media and other forms of technology. For example, interactive television and computer networking systems will enable children to experience many things outside their own homes and schools and to communicate regularly with people around the world. If futurists are correct in predicting that ideas and information

and access to them will be the basis for personal, business, and political advancement in this century, people without access to computers and other information technology will become even more disadvantaged. This prediction raises important issues about the effects of social inequality on the socialization process. Socialization—a lifelong learning process—can no longer be viewed as a "glance in the rearview mirror" or a reaction to some previous experience. With the rapid pace of technological change, we must not only learn about the past but also learn how to anticipate—and consider the consequences of—the future (Westrum, 1991). (See Box 4.4.)

BOX 4.4 YOU CAN MAKE A DIFFERENCE

Helping a Child Reach Adulthood

After Tina—one of your best friends—moves into a large apartment complex near her university, she keeps hearing a baby cry at all hours of the day and night. Although the crying is coming from the apartment next to Tina's, she never sees anyone come or go from it. On several occasions, she knocks on the door, but no one answers. At first Tina tries to ignore the situation, but eventually she can't sleep or study because the baby keeps crying. Tina decides she must take action and asks you, "What do you think I ought to do?" What advice could you give Tina?

Like Tina, many of us do not know if we should get involved in other people's lives. We also do not know how to report child maltreatment. However, social workers and researchers suggest that bystanders must be willing to get involved in cases of possible abuse or neglect to save a child from harm by others. They also note the importance of people knowing how to report incidents of maltreatment:

- *Report child maltreatment.* Cases of child maltreatment can be reported to any social service or law enforcement agency.
- *Identify yourself to authorities.* Although most agencies are willing to accept anonymous reports, many staff members prefer to know your name, address, telephone number, and other basic information so that they can determine that you are not a self-interested person, such as a hostile relative, ex-spouse, or vindictive neighbour.
- *Follow up with authorities.* Once an agency has validated a report of child maltreatment, the

agency's first goal is to stop the neglect or abuse of that child, whose health and safety are paramount concerns. However, intervention also has long-term goals. Sometimes, the situation can be improved simply by teaching the parents different values about child rearing or by pointing them to other agencies and organizations that can provide needed help. Other times, it may be necessary to remove the child from the parents' custody and place the child in a foster home, at least temporarily. Either way, the situation for the child will be better than if he or she had been left in an abusive or neglectful home environment.

So the best advice for Tina—or anyone else who has reason to believe that child maltreatment is occurring—is to report it to the appropriate authorities. In most telephone directories, the number can be located in the government listings section. Here are some other resources for help:

- Child Welfare Resouce Centre at: http://www .childwelfare.ca/cwrcabus.shtml
- Child Abuse Prevention Network at: http:// child-abuse.com/

On the Internet:

- The National Center for Missing and Exploited Children provides brochures about child safety and child protection upon request: http://www .missingkids.com/missingkids/servlet/Pageservlet ?LanguageCountry=en_US&PageId=200

C H A P T E R   R E V I E W

■ What is socialization, and why is it important for human beings?

Socialization is the lifelong process through which individuals acquire their self-identity and learn the physical, mental, and social skills needed for survival in society. The kind of person we become depends greatly on what we learn during our formative years from our surrounding social groups and social environment.

■ To what degree are our unique physical and human characteristics based on heredity and to what degree are they based on social environment?

As individual human beings, we have unique identities, personalities, and relationships with others. Individuals are born with some of their unique physical and human characteristics; other characteristics and traits are gained during the socialization process. Each of us is a product of two forces: (1) heredity, referred to as "nature," and (2) the social environment, referred to as "nurture." While biology dictates our physical makeup, the social environment largely determines how we develop and behave.

■ Why is social contact essential for human beings?

Social contact is essential in developing a self, or self-concept, which represents an individual's perceptions and feelings of being a distinct or separate person. Much of what we think about ourselves is gained from our interactions with others and from what we perceive others think of us.

■ What are the most important agents of socialization?

The people, groups, and institutions that teach us what we need to know in order to participate in society are called agents of socialization. The agents include the family, schools, peer groups, the media, the workplace, and so on. Families, which transmit cultural and social values to us, are the most important agents of socialization in all societies and have these roles: (1) procreating and socializing children, (2) providing emotional support, and (3) assigning social position. Schools are another key agent of socialization; they not only teach knowledge and skills but also deeply influence the self-image, beliefs, and values of children. Peer groups contribute to our sense of belonging and self-worth; they teach and reinforce cultural norms; and they are a key source of information about acceptable behaviour. The media function as socializing agents by (1) informing us about world events, (2) introducing us to a wide variety of people, and (3) providing an opportunity to live vicariously through other people's experiences.

■ How do sociologists explain our development of a self-concept?

Charles Horton Cooley developed the image of the looking-glass self to explain how people see themselves through the perceptions of others. Our initial sense of self is typically based on how families perceive and treat us. George Herbert Mead linked the idea of self-concept to role playing and to learning the rules of social interaction. According to Mead, the self is divided into the "I" and the "me." The "I" represents the spontaneous and unique traits of each person. The "me" represents the internalized attitudes and demands of other members of society.

■ What are the main psychological theories on human development?

According to Sigmund Freud, the self emerges from three interrelated forces (id, ego, and superego). When a person is well adjusted, the three forces act in balance. Jean Piaget identified four cognitive stages of development; at each stage, children's activities are governed by how they understand the world around them. Lawrence Kohlberg classified moral development into six stages; certain levels of cognitive development are essential before corresponding levels of moral reasoning may occur. Carol Gilligan suggested that there are male–female differences regarding morality and identified three stages in female moral development.

■ What factors determine socialization practices?

Social class, gender, and ethnicity are all determining factors in socialization practices. Social class is one of the strongest influences on what and how parents teach their children. Gender socialization strongly influences what we believe to be acceptable behaviour for females and males.

■ When does socialization end?

Socialization is ongoing throughout the life course. We learn knowledge and skills for future roles through anticipatory socialization. Parents are socialized by their own children, and adults learn through workplace socialization. Resocialization is the process of learning new attitudes, values, and behaviours, either voluntarily or involuntarily.

KEY TERMS

agents of socialization 104
anticipatory socialization 115
ego 112
gender socialization 114
generalized other 111
id 112
looking-glass self 108
peer group 106
resocialization 118
role-taking 109
self-concept 108
significant others 110
social devaluation 117
socialization 99
sociobiology 101
superego 113
total institution 119

NET LINKS

For current and expert knowledge about healthy socialization and development, visit the Voices for Children site at:
http://www.voices4children.org

To see an Internet journal on the development, care, and education of young children, go to:
http://www.ecrp.uiuc.edu

The International Society for the Prevention of Child Abuse and Neglect works toward the prevention and treatment of child abuse, neglect, and exploitation; go to:
http://www.ispcan.org

QUESTIONS FOR CRITICAL THINKING

1. Consider the concept of the looking-glass self. How do you think others perceive you? Do you think most people perceive you correctly?
2. What are your "I" traits? What are your "me" traits? Which ones are stronger?
3. What are some different ways you might study the effect of toys on the socialization of children? How could you isolate the toy variable from other variables that influence children's socialization?

4. How might functionalist, conflict, symbolic interactionist, and postmodernist analysis view the role of television and computers in childhood socialization? What influence do you think television and computers have on your own socialization?

SUGGESTED READINGS

These books provide in-depth information on various aspects of socialization:

Carol Gilligan. *In a Different Voice: Psychological Theory and Women's Development.* Cambridge, Mass.: Harvard University Press, 1982.

Erving Goffman. *Asylums: Essays on the Social Situation of Mental Patients and Other Inmates.* Chicago: Aldine, 1961.

Bernice Lott. *Women's Lives: Themes and Variations in Gender Learning* (2nd ed.). Pacific Grove, Calif.: Brooks/Cole, 1994.

George Herbert Mead. *Mind, Self, and Society from the Standpoint of a Social Behaviourist.* Charles W. Morris (ed.). Chicago: University of Chicago Press, 1962; orig. pub. 1934.

David A. Wolfe. *Child Abuse: Implications for Child Development and Psychopathology.* Newbury Park, Calif.: Sage, 1987.

ONLINE STUDY AND RESEARCH TOOLS

THOMSONNOW™ Thomson NOW!

Go to **http://hed.nelson.com** to link to ThomsonNOW for *Sociology in Our Times,* Fourth Canadian Edition, your online study tool. First take the **Pre-Test** for this chapter to get your personalized **Study Plan,** which will identify topics you need to review and direct you to the appropriate resources. Then take the **Post-Test** to determine what concepts you have mastered and what you still need work on.

INFOTRAC®

Infotrac College Edition is included free with every new copy of this text. Explore this online library for additional readings, review, and a handy resource for assignments. Visit **www.infotrac-college.com** to access this online database of full-text articles. Enter the key terms from this chapter to start your search.

Society, Social Structure, and Interaction

For most homeless persons living on the streets of Canada's major cities, the days end the same way they begin—searching for the basic necessities of life that many of us take for granted: food, shelter, work, and money. These circumstances are captured in the comments of Nancy, who describes her daily routine of survival living on the streets—sleeping "in the rough" (i.e., outdoors), securing food, and panhandling. She also describes the camaraderie among long-term street people.

It is not always safe. Sometimes you can get robbed. Sometimes you can get knocked out even before you wake up. It is not that safe but when you have somebody around you we can protect each other. I have learned to make street friends. Sometimes, like most people, we get sick of each other so we have to look for other friends.

If you are panhandling sometimes people go by and give you money. Sometimes they just go by. Mostly we eat at soup kitchens. We go to missions. Sometimes when you are panhandling, people will give you food. In their minds, it is better to give me food than money because money, I might spend on alcohol and drugs. So they buy the food and give it to me. I think these people are smart. Sometimes the police harass you. Sometimes they can be very nice. I had one bring me a sandwich and ask me how I was feeling. I said "I'm okay and I'm going to be out of here soon. I am about $1.50 short of a sub sandwich." He says "Come with me, I'll buy you one."

Sometimes restaurants won't even serve you. They won't let you pass through the door. That is how we learn to get food from fast food chains. We can order it out and eat outside without having everyone stare at you or whisper about you under their breath.

I sleep in the park, underneath the overpass or behind the library or downtown beneath the restaurant . . . as long as you find a spot where the cops won't bother you or people won't bother you. . . . Sometimes you have to walk miles to find a spot where you can sleep. I find good clean cardboard and I always carry my own sleeping bag. The most important thing is to have blankets. We learn to carry those blankets. We learn to because this is our home. (Neal, 2004:20)

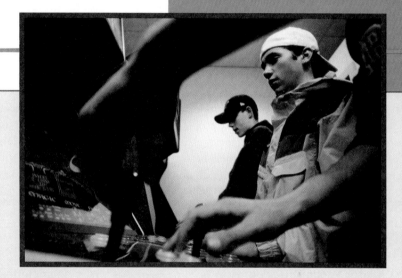

The activities of this homeless woman reflect a specific pattern of social behaviour. All activities in life—including sleeping in the rough or living on the streets—are social in nature. Homeless persons and domiciled persons (those with homes) live in social worlds that have predictable patterns of social interaction. *Social interaction* **is the process by which people act toward or respond to other people and is the foundation for all relationships and groups in society.** In this chapter, we look at the relationship between social structure and social interaction. Homelessness is used as an example of how social problems occur and may be perpetuated within social structures and patterns of interaction.

Social structure **is the stable pattern of social relationships that exists within a particular group or society.** This structure is essential for the survival of society and for the well-being of individuals because it provides a social web of familial support and social relationships that connects each of us to the larger society. Many homeless people have lost this vital linkage. As a result, they often experience a loss of personal dignity and sense of moral worth because of their "homeless" condition (Hagan and McCarthy, 1998; Lankenau, 1999). Consider the comments of Sally, a homeless woman in Toronto: "It is extremely demeaning to be treated like a zero every day of your life. No one knows the whole story and quite frankly, no one cares. All they see is a poorly dressed waste of human life" (Toronto Healthy City Office, 1998).

Who are the homeless? Before reading on, take the quiz on homelessness in Box 5.1. The profile of Canada's homeless has changed dramatically in recent years. Although there have always been homeless people, there has been a significant increase in the number of Canadians with no place to live. Our stereotypical image of single, alcoholic, or drug-using males who are "down on their luck" is far from an accurate reflection of our country's homeless population. Now included in the homeless category are people who have never before had to depend on social assistance for food, clothing, and a roof over their heads. Today's homeless include increasing numbers of women and children, adolescents, and Aboriginal people. The fastest growing segment of the homeless population is women and children. In fact, single mothers head 37 percent of homeless families (Golden, 1999).

Also startling is the overrepresentation of Aboriginal people in Canada's homeless population. *Relative homelessness*—**being housed in a dwelling that fails to meet basic living standards**—is disturbingly common in both the urban and rural Aboriginal population. Although most of the research has been done in Western Canada, large numbers of Aboriginal homeless also populate eastern cities, such as Toronto and Montreal. Refugees and visible minorities are also overrepresented among the homeless (Murdie, 1999).

Homeless people come from all walks of life. They live in cities, suburbs, and rural areas. Contrary to popular myth, most of the homeless are not on the streets by choice or because they were de-institutionalized by mental hospitals. Not all of the homeless are unemployed. Many homeless people hold full- or part-time jobs but earn too little to afford housing (Hargrave, 2005).

QUESTIONS AND ISSUES

Chapter Focus Question: How is homelessness related to the social structure of a society?

How do societies change over time?

What are the components of social structure?

Why do societies have shared patterns of social interaction?

How are daily interactions similar to being onstage?

Do positive changes in society occur through individual or institutional efforts?

All activities in life—including panhandling and living "on the streets"—are social in nature.

SOCIAL STRUCTURE: THE MACROLEVEL PERSPECTIVE

Social structure provides the framework within which we interact with others. This framework is an orderly, fixed arrangement of parts that together comprise the whole group or society (see Figure 5.1). As defined in Chapter 1, a *society* is a large social grouping that shares the same geographical territory and is subject to the same political authority and dominant cultural expectations. At the macrolevel, the social structure of a society has several essential elements: social institutions, groups, statuses, roles, and norms.

BOX 5.1 SOCIOLOGY AND EVERYDAY LIFE

How Much Do You Know About Homelessness?

True	False	
T	F	1. Most homeless people choose to be homeless.
T	F	2. The number of homeless persons in Canada has gradually declined over the past thirty years.
T	F	3. Homelessness is often caused by racism and discrimination.
T	F	4. Most homeless people are mentally ill.
T	F	5. Older men over the age of fifty make up most of Canada's homeless population.
T	F	6. Most homeless people are alcoholics and substance abusers.
T	F	7. The number of homeless adolescents has increased in the past decade.
T	F	8. Canada has the resources to end homelessness.
T	F	9. One out of every four homeless people is a child.
T	F	10. There are approximately 20,000 homeless persons in Canada.

Answers on page 128.

Functional theorists emphasize that social structure is essential because it creates order and predictability in a society (Parsons, 1951). Social structure also is important for our human development. As we saw in Chapter 4, we develop a self-concept as we learn the attitudes, values, and behaviours of the people around us. When these attitudes and values are part of a predictable structure, it is easier to develop that self-concept.

Social structure gives us the ability to interpret the social situations we encounter. For example, we expect our families to care for us, our schools to

Figure 5.1   Social Structure Framework

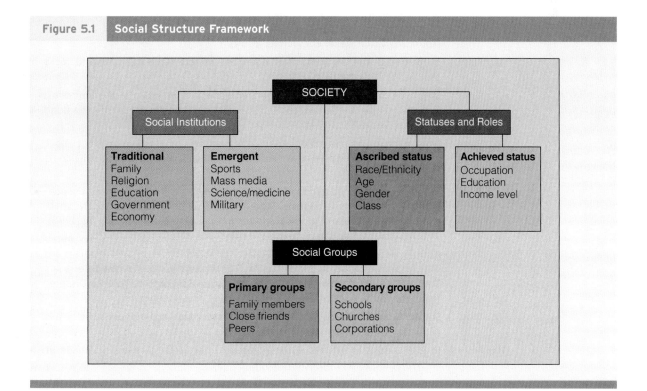

educate us, and our police to protect us. When our circumstances change dramatically, most of us feel an acute sense of anxiety because we do not know what to expect or what is expected of us. For example, newly homeless individuals may feel disoriented because they do not know how to function in their new setting. The person is likely to wonder, "How will I survive on the streets?" "Where do I go to get help?" "Should I stay at a shelter?" and "Where can I get a job?" Social structure helps people make sense of their environment, even when they find themselves on the streets.

In addition to providing a map for our encounters with others, social structure may limit our options and place us in arbitrary categories not of our own choosing. Conflict theorists maintain that there is more to the

social structure than is readily visible and that we must explore the deeper, underlying structures that determine social relations in a society. Karl Marx suggested that the way economic production is organized is the most important structural aspect of any society. In capitalistic societies where a few people control the labour of many, the social structure reflects a system of relationships of domination among categories of people (for example, owner–worker and employer–employee).

Social structure creates boundaries that define which persons or groups will be the "insiders" and which will be the "outsiders." **Social marginality is the state of being part insider and part outsider in the social structure.** Sociologist Robert Park (1928) coined this term to refer to persons (such as immigrants) who simultaneously share the life and traditions

BOX 5.1 SOCIOLOGY AND EVERYDAY LIFE

Answers to the Sociology Quiz on Homelessness

1. **False.** This myth is an example of "blaming the victim." Homelessness is the result of a number of social factors, namely poverty, changes in the housing market, and growing rates of unemployment (National Anti-Poverty Organization, 2005).

2. **False.** Surveys and statistics have shown that the number of homeless in Canada has grown over the past three decades (HRSDC, 2003).

3. **True.** Approximately one-quarter of homeless persons are Aboriginal. About 15 percent of Toronto's hostel users are immigrants and refugees. Some landlords refuse to rent apartments to families with children or to people on social assistance (Toronto Disaster Relief Committee, 2004).

4. **False.** Between 20 and 35 percent of homeless people have been treated for a psychiatric disorder (HRSDC, 2003).

5. **False.** Men over the age of fifty no longer represent the majority of the homeless. Now young men, teenagers, and families with children are predominant among homeless Canadians (HRSDC, 2003).

6. **False.** Most homeless people are not heavy drug users. Estimates suggest that about one-fourth of the homeless are substance abusers. Many of these individuals are also mentally ill.

7. **True.** The growth in this population of "street youth" has significantly altered the population of homeless Canadians. More than 70 percent of these youth report leaving home because of physical and sexual abuse (Hagan and McCarthy, 1998).

8. **True.** According to the *Report on Homelessness in Canada* submitted to the United Nations, adequate housing and adequate support services for all Canadians are well within Canada's financial means. The United Nations termed Canada's treatment of its homeless population a "national disgrace" (Toronto Disaster Relief Committee, 2004).

9. **True.** Further, women and children make up the fastest growing category of homeless people in North America (National Anti-Poverty Organization, 2005).

10. **False.** In 2000, experts estimated the number of homeless persons in Canada at between 35,000 and 40,000 (HRSDC, 2003).

of two distinct groups. Social marginality results in stigmatization. A *stigma* **is any physical or social attribute or sign that so devalues a person's social identity that it disqualifies that person from full social acceptance** (Goffman, 1963b). A convicted criminal, wearing a prison uniform, is an example of a person who has been stigmatized; the uniform says that the person has done something wrong and should not be allowed unsupervised outside the prison walls.

COMPONENTS OF SOCIAL STRUCTURE

The social structure of a society includes its social positions, the relationships among those positions, and the kinds of resources attached to each of the positions. Social structure also includes all of the groups that make up society and the relationships among those groups (Smelser, 1988). We begin by examining the social positions that are closest to the individual.

Status

A *status* **is a socially defined position in a group or society characterized by certain expectations, rights, and duties.** Statuses exist independently of the specific people occupying them (Linton, 1936); the statuses of professional athlete, rock musician, professor, university student, and homeless person all exist exclusive of the specific individuals who occupy these social positions. For example, although thousands of new students arrive on university campuses each year to occupy the status of first-year student, the status of university student and the expectations attached to that position have remained relatively unchanged.

Does the term *status* refer only to high-level positions in society? No, not in a sociological sense. Although many people equate the term *status* with high levels of prestige, sociologists use it to refer to *all* socially defined positions—high- and low-rank. For example, both the position of director of Health Canada in Ottawa and that of a homeless person who is paid about five dollars a week (plus bed and board) to clean up the dining room at a homeless shelter are social statuses.

Take a moment to answer the question, Who am I? To determine who you are, you must think about your social identity, which is derived from the statuses you occupy and is based on your status set. A *status* *set* **is made up of all the statuses that a person occupies at a given time.** For example, Marie may be a psychologist, a professor, a wife, a mother, a Catholic, a school volunteer, an Alberta resident, and a French Canadian. All of these socially defined positions constitute her status set.

Ascribed and Achieved Status   Statuses are distinguished by the manner in which we acquire them. An *ascribed status* **is a social position conferred at birth or received involuntarily later in life,** based on attributes over which the individual has little or no control, such as ethnicity, age, and gender. Marie, for example, is a female born to French Canadian parents; she was assigned these statuses at birth. An *achieved status* **is a social position a person assumes voluntarily as a result of personal choice, merit, or direct effort.** Achieved statuses (such as occupation, education, and income) are thought to be gained as a result of personal ability or successful competition. Most occupational positions in modern societies are achieved statuses. For instance, Marie voluntarily assumed the statuses of psychologist, professor, wife, mother, and school volunteer. However, not all achieved statuses are positions most people would want to attain: being a criminal, a drug addict, or a homeless person, for example, is a negative achieved status.

Ascribed statuses have a significant influence on the achieved statuses we occupy. Ethnicity, gender, and age affect each person's opportunity to acquire certain achieved statuses. Those who are privileged by their positive ascribed statuses are more likely to achieve the more prestigious positions in a society. Those who are disadvantaged by their ascribed statuses may more easily acquire negative achieved statuses.

Master Status   If we occupy many different statuses, how can we determine which is the most important? Sociologist Everett Hughes has stated that societies resolve this ambiguity by determining master statuses. A *master status* **is the most important status a person occupies;** it dominates all of the individual's other statuses and is the overriding ingredient in determining a person's general social position (Hughes, 1945). Being poor or rich is a master status that influences many other areas of life, including health, education, and life opportunities. Historically, the most common master statuses for women have related to positions in the family, such as daughter, wife, and mother. For men, occupation usually has been the most important status, although occupation increasingly is a master status for many women as well. "What do you do?" is one of the first questions many

How does your perception of Beverley McLachlin's master status change when you compare these photographs?

people ask when meeting one another. Occupation provides important clues to a person's educational level, income, and family background. An individual's ethnicity also may constitute a master status in a society in which dominant group members single out members of other groups as "inferior" on the basis of real or alleged physical, cultural, or nationality characteristics (see Feagin and Feagin, 1999).

Master statuses are vital to how we view ourselves, how we are seen by others, and how we interact with others. Beverley McLachlin is both the Chief Justice of the Supreme Court and a mother. Which is her master status? Can you imagine how she would react if lawyers arguing a case before the Supreme Court of Canada treated her as if she were a mother rather than a justice? Lawyers wisely use "Honourable Madam Justice" as her master status and act accordingly.

Master statuses confer high or low levels of personal worth and dignity on people. Those are not characteristics that we inherently possess; they are derived from the statuses we occupy. For those who have no residence, being a homeless person readily becomes a master status regardless of the person's other attributes. Homelessness is a stigmatized master status that confers disrepute on its occupant because domiciled people often believe a homeless person has a "character flaw." The circumstances under which someone becomes homeless determine the extent to which that person is stigmatized. For example, individuals who become homeless as a result of natural disasters (such as floods or ice storms) are not seen as causing their homelessness or as being a threat to the community. Thus, they are less likely to be stigmatized. However, in cases in which homeless persons are viewed as the cause of their own problems, they are more likely to be stigmatized and marginalized

by others. Twenty-six-year-old Guy, who is from Canada's East Coast, has been homeless in Vancouver for three years, during which time he has been living in shelters and looking for work. According to Guy, the homeless have to overcome a double stigma, that of being homeless and that of being dependent on welfare:

> I hate going to welfare. I hate asking for money. If there's a soup kitchen I'll go to a soup kitchen. Last time I went, I went home cause my dad had died and came back here and had to get started over again. I said to this woman is there any way I can get an emergency cheque so I can get started over? She looks at me and says, "You don't deserve one. If you don't leave here I'll call the police cause you're tryin' to rip us off." I said, "I was away, my dad had died and I need to get started again." She said, "Well we need to see a death certificate." I said, "The hell with you, I don't need this shit," and I walked out.
> (O'Reilly-Fleming, 1993:129)

Status Symbols   When people are proud of a particular social status they occupy, they often choose to use visible means to let others know about their position. ***Status symbols* are material signs that inform others of a person's specific status.** For example, just as wearing a wedding ring proclaims that a person is married, owning a Rolls-Royce announces that one has "made it." In North American society, people who have "made it" frequently want symbols to inform others of their accomplishments.

In our daily lives, status symbols both announce our statuses and facilitate our interactions with others. In hospitals affiliated with medical schools, the length and colour of a person's uniform in a hospital indicate the individual's status within the medical centre. Physicians wear longer white coats, medical students wear shorter white coats, laboratory technicians wear short blue coats, and so forth (Haas and Shaffir, 1995).

Status symbols for the domiciled and for the homeless may have different meanings. Among affluent persons, a full shopping cart in the grocery store and bags of merchandise from expensive department stores indicate a lofty financial position. By contrast, among the homeless, bulging shopping bags and overloaded grocery carts suggest a completely different status. Carts and bags are essential to street life; there is no other place to keep things, as shown by this description of Tamara, a homeless woman living in a city in Ontario:

> I don't care much for the police. I get in fights with them a lot. They tell me to "move along" and I tell them I have a right to be there just like anyone else. One time in the subway station I was carrying two shopping bags full of clothes. I hadn't had a chance to wash them in a while, so they were a little dirty, but they were my clothes! A policeman, or it may have been a company cop, grabbed my bags and put them in the garbage. I put up a fight and told him to give them back to me. We ended up wrestling on the platform! Finally, he let his hands fall to his sides and I again demanded that he give me back my things. He went over to the garbage and took them out. (Harman, 1989:95)

For homeless women and men, possessions are not status symbols so much as they are a link with the past, a hope for the future, and a potential source of immediate cash. As Snow and Anderson (1993:147) note, selling personal possessions is not uncommon among most social classes; members of the working and middle classes hold garage sales, and those in the upper classes have estate sales. However, when homeless persons sell their personal possessions, they do so to meet their immediate needs, not because they want to "clean house."

Roles

A role is the dynamic aspect of a status. Whereas we *occupy* a status, we *play* a role (Linton, 1936). A **role is a set of behavioural expectations associated with a given status.** For example, a carpenter (employee) hired to remodel a kitchen is not expected to sit down uninvited and join the family (employer) for dinner.

Role expectation **is a group's or society's definition of the way a specific role ought to be played.** By contrast, *role performance* **is how a person actually plays the role.** Role performance does not always match role expectation. Some statuses have role expectations that are highly specific, such as that of surgeon or university professor. Other statuses, such as friend or significant other, have less structured expectations. The role expectations tied to the status of student are more specific than those for being a friend. Role expectations typically are based on a range of acceptable behaviour rather than on strictly defined standards.

Our roles are relational (or complementary); that is, they are defined in the context of roles performed by others. We can play the role of student because someone else fulfils the role of professor. Conversely, to perform the role of professor, the teacher must have one or more students.

Role ambiguity occurs when the expectations associated with a role are unclear. For example, it is not always clear when the provider–dependant aspect of the parent–child relationship ends. Should it end at age 18 or 21? When a person is no longer in school? Different people will answer these questions differently depending on their experiences and socialization, as well as on the parents' financial capability and willingness to continue contributing to the welfare of their adult children.

Role Conflict and Role Strain   Most people occupy a number of statuses, each of which has numerous role expectations attached. For example, Charles is a student who attends morning classes at the university, and he is an employee at a fast-food restaurant where he works from 3 p.m. to 10 p.m. He also is Stephanie's boyfriend, and she would like to see him more often. On December 7, Charles has a final exam at 7 p.m., when he is supposed to be working. Meanwhile, Stephanie is pressuring him to take her to a movie. To top it off, his mother calls, asking him to fly home because his father is going to have emergency surgery. How can Charles be in all of these places at once? Such experiences of role conflict can be overwhelming.

Role conflict **occurs when incompatible role demands are placed on a person by two or more statuses held at the same time.** When role conflict occurs, we may feel pulled in different directions. To deal with this problem, we may prioritize our roles and first complete the one we consider to be most important. Or we may compartmentalize our lives and "insulate" our various roles (Merton, 1968). That is, we may perform the activities linked to one role for part of the day, and then engage in the activities associated with another role in some other time period or elsewhere. For example, under routine circumstances, Charles would fulfil his student role for part of the day and his employee role for another part of the day. In his current situation, however, he is unable to compartmentalize his roles.

What are the competing demands of working parents in contemporary societies? What sociological term best describes this situation?

Role conflict may occur as a result of changing statuses and roles in society. Research has found that women who engage in behaviour that is gender-typed as "masculine" tend to have higher rates of role conflict than those who engage in traditional "feminine" behaviour (Basow, 1992). According to sociologist Tracey Watson (1987), role conflict sometimes can be attributed not to the roles themselves but to the pressures people feel when they do not fit into culturally prescribed roles. In her study of women athletes in university sports programs, Watson found role conflict in the traditionally incongruent identities of being a woman and being an athlete. Even though

the women athletes in her study wore makeup and presented a conventional image when they were not on the basketball court, their peers in school still saw them as "female jocks," thus leading to role conflict.

Whereas role conflict occurs between two or more statuses (such as being homeless and being a temporary employee of a social services agency), role strain takes place within one status. **Role strain occurs when incompatible demands are built into a single status that a person occupies** (Goode, 1960). For example, many women experience role strain in the labour force because they hold jobs that are "less satisfying and more stressful than men's jobs since they involve less money, less prestige, fewer job openings, more career roadblocks, and so forth" (Basow, 1992:192). Similarly, married women may experience more role strain than married men, because of work overload, marital inequality with their spouse, exclusive parenting responsibilities, unclear expectations, and lack of emotional support.

Recent social changes may have increased role strain in men. In the family, men's traditional position of dominance has eroded as more women have entered the paid labour force and demanded more assistance in child-rearing and homemaking responsibilities. High rates of unemployment have produced problems for many men whose major role in the past was centred on their occupation.

Sexual orientation, age, and occupation frequently are associated with role strain. Lesbians and gay men often experience role strain because of the pressures associated with having an identity heavily stigmatized by the dominant cultural group (Basow, 1992). Women in their thirties may experience the highest levels of role strain; they face a large amount of stress in terms of role demands and conflicting work and family expectations. Dentists, psychiatrists, and police officers have been found to experience high levels of occupation-related role strain, which may result in suicide. (The concepts of role expectation, role performance, role conflict, and role strain are illustrated in Figure 5.2.)

Individuals frequently distance themselves from a role they find extremely stressful or otherwise problematic. *Role distancing* occurs when people consciously foster the impression of a lack of commitment or attachment to a particular role and merely go through the motions of role performance (Goffman, 1961b). People use distancing techniques when they do not want others to take them as the "self" implied in a particular role, especially if they think the role is "beneath them." While Charles is working in the fast-food restaurant, for example, he does not want

What are the competing demands of working parents in contemporary societies? What sociological term best describes this situation?

Figure 5.2　Role Expectation, Performance, Conflict, and Strain

When playing the role of "student," do you sometimes personally encounter these concepts?

The Role of "Student"

Role Expectation: a group's or society's definition of the way a specific role *ought* to be played.

Role Performance: how a person *actually* plays a role.

Role Conflict: occurs when incompatible demands are placed on a person by two or more statuses held at the same time.

Role Strain: occurs when incompatible demands are built into a single status that the person holds.

people to think of him as a "loser in a dead-end job." He wants them to view him as a university student who is working there just to "pick up a few bucks" until he graduates. When customers from the university come in, Charles talks to them about what courses they are taking, what they are majoring in, and what professors they have. He does not discuss whether the bacon cheeseburger is better than the chili burger. When Charles is really involved in role distancing, he tells his friends that he "works there but wouldn't eat there." Role distancing is most likely to occur when people find themselves in roles in which the social identities implied are inconsistent with how they think of themselves or how they want to be viewed by others.

Role Exit

Role exit **occurs when people disengage from social roles that have been central to their self-identity** (Ebaugh, 1988). Sociologist Helen Rose Fuchs Ebaugh studied this process by interviewing ex-convicts, ex-nuns, retirees, divorced men and women, and others who had exited voluntarily from significant social roles. According to Ebaugh, role exit occurs in four stages. The first stage is doubt, in which people experience frustration or burnout when they reflect on their existing roles. The second stage involves a search for alternatives; here, people may take a leave of absence from their work or temporarily separate from their marriage partner. The third stage is the turning point at which people realize that they must take some final action, such as quitting their job or getting a divorce. The fourth and final stage involves the creation of a new identity.

Exiting the "homeless" role often is very difficult. The longer a person remains on the streets, the more difficult it becomes to exit this role. Personal resources diminish over time. Personal possessions often are stolen, lost, sold, or pawned. Work experience and skills become outdated, and physical disabilities that prevent individuals from working are likely to develop on the streets.

However, a number of homeless people are able to exit this role. For example, Travis, a former addict who lived on the streets of Toronto and had been unemployed for almost a decade, was able to get off the streets after completing a job-training program:

I stopped taking drugs, and that's when I got faced with reality. Bam, right in the face! And I was like, wow! There's a lot more to give my thought to than I thought. I have a lot more resources that I can use to my advantage. I just said that's it. I'm going to pull all my resources together and see what I can come up with. I made up my mind, no more fooling around. No more of this street crap. I'm getting my life back together. The first few steps are more psychological stuff. You think it's your fault that you are on the streets. If you don't stop, or you think it's a party, you're going to stay on the streets. You're going to end up like one of those bums with long beards and hats on. (Hagan and McCarthy, 1998:222)

Of course, many of the homeless do not beat the odds and exit this role. Instead, they shift their focus from role exiting to survival on the streets.

Groups

Groups are another important component of social structure. To sociologists, a **social group consists of two or more people who interact frequently and share a common identity and a feeling of interdependence.** Throughout our lives, most of us participate in groups, from our families and childhood friends, to our university classes, to our work and community organizations, and even to society.

Primary and secondary groups are the two basic types of social groups. A **primary group is a small, less specialized group in which members engage in face-to-face, emotion-based interactions over an extended period of time.** Typically, primary groups include our family, close friends, and school or work-related peer groups. By contrast, a **secondary group is a larger, more specialized group in which members engage in more impersonal, goal-oriented relationships for a limited period of time.** Schools, churches, and corporations are examples of secondary groups. In secondary groups, people have few, if any, emotional ties to one another. Instead, they come together for some specific, practical purpose, such as getting a degree or a paycheque. Secondary groups are more specialized than primary ones; individuals relate

to one another in terms of specific roles (such as professor and student) and more limited activities (such as course-related endeavours).

As discussed in Chapter 1, *social solidarity,* or cohesion, relates to a group's ability to maintain itself in the face of obstacles. Social solidarity exists when social bonds, attractions, or other forces hold members of a group in interaction over a period of time (Jary and Jary, 1991). For example, if a local church is destroyed by fire and congregation members still worship together in a makeshift setting, then they have a high degree of social solidarity.

Many of us build social networks from our personal friends in primary groups and our acquaintances in secondary groups. A **social network is a series of social relationships that link an individual to others.** Social networks work differently for men and women, for different ethnic groups, and for members of different social classes. Traditionally, people of colour and women have been excluded from powerful "old-boy" social networks (Kanter, 1977; McPherson and Smith-Lovin, 1982, 1986). At the middle- and upper-class levels, individuals tap social networks to find employment, make business deals, and win political elections. However, social networks typically do not work effectively for poor and homeless individuals.

Hagan and McCarthy's research on homeless youth in Toronto and Vancouver revealed that informal social networks that the youth described as "street families" tended to form around issues of survival and support. Individuals within these groups often assumed specialized roles that were defined in family terms, including references to street brothers and sisters, and even fathers and mothers. One youth, Brenda, describes how these social networks are formed and their importance to her survival on the street:

You just kinda start hanging out with the same people, and you get together, and you each have your, you know, you each have certain expectations of each person, as to what their roles are. Like as in protecting each other or finding the squat to stay in . . . And, uh, you know, just, uh, basically that's how I ended up in it. I just started hangin' out with people that were sort of a group and just—I had a role. (Hagan and McCarthy, 1998:162)

Sociological research on the homeless has noted the social isolation experienced by people on the streets. Hagan and McCarthy (1998) found that a high degree of social isolation exists because the homeless are separated from their extended family and former friends. They noted that among the homeless who did have families, most either did not wish to return or believed that they would not be welcome. Most of the avenues for exiting the homeless role and acquiring housing are intertwined with the large-scale, secondary groups that sociologists refer to as formal organizations.

A *formal organization* **is a highly structured group formed for the purpose of completing certain tasks or achieving specific goals.** Many of us spend most of our time in formal organizations, such as universities, corporations, or the government. In Chapter 6 ("Groups and Organizations"), we analyze the characteristics of bureaucratic organizations; however, at this point, we should note that these organizations are a very important component of social structure in all industrialized societies. We expect such organizations to educate us, solve our social problems (such as crime and homelessness), and provide work opportunities.

Many formal organizations today have been referred to as "people-processing" organizations. For example, the Salvation Army and other caregiver groups provide services for the homeless and others in need. However, these organizations must work with limited monetary resources and at the same time maintain some control of their clientele. This control is necessary in order to provide their services in an orderly and timely fashion. However, according to some of Hagan and McCarthy's respondents, these policies may indirectly encourage youth to hang out on the street. This sentiment is evident in this youth's assessment of hostel policies:

> In a hostel you get kicked out in the morning, right? Like at 8:30, they say, "We don't care what you do, just come back at four." So you walk around, and you find places where people hang out, and you talk to them, you know, 'cause they know you're in the same situation, and they gotta pass the time, the time somehow. So, you just, meet different people, and everybody's in the same situation. (Hagan and McCarthy, 1998:43)

Likewise, a number of the women's shelters have restrictions and regulations that some of the women feel deprive them of their personhood. One shelter used to require a compulsory gynecological examination of its residents (Golden, 1992). Another required that the women be out of the building by 7 a.m. and not return before 7 p.m. Fearful of violence among shelter residents or between residents and staff, many

shelters use elaborate questionnaires and interviews to screen out potentially disruptive clients. Those who are supposed to benefit from the services of such shelters often find the experience demeaning and alienating. Nevertheless, organizations, such as the Salvation Army and women's shelters, do help people within the limited means they have available.

For many years, capitalism has been dominated by powerful "old-boy" social networks.

Professional women have increasingly turned to sporting activities, such as golf and tennis, to create social networks that enhance their business opportunities.

Social Institutions

At the macrolevel of all societies, certain basic activities routinely occur—children are born and socialized, goods and services are produced and distributed, order is preserved, and a sense of purpose is maintained (Aberle et al., 1950; Mack and Bradford, 1979). Social institutions are the means by which these basic needs are met. A *social institution* **is a set of organized beliefs and rules that establish how a society will attempt to meet its basic social needs.** In the past, these needs have centred around five basic social institutions: the family, religion, education, the economy, and the government or politics. Today, mass media, sports, science and medicine, and the military are also considered to be social institutions.

What is the difference between a group and a social institution? A group is composed of specific, identifiable people; an institution is a standardized way of doing something. The concept of "family" helps distinguish between the two. When we talk about your family or my family, we are referring to a family. When we refer to the family as a social institution, we are talking about ideologies and standardized patterns of behaviour that organize family life. For example, the family as a social institution contains certain statuses organized into well-defined relationships, such as husband–wife, parent–child, brother–sister, and so forth. Specific families do not always conform to these ideologies and behaviour patterns.

Functional theorists emphasize that social institutions exist because they perform five essential tasks:

1. *Replacing members.* Societies and groups must have socially approved ways of replacing members who move away or die. The family provides the structure for legitimated sexual activity—and thus procreation—between adults.
2. *Teaching new members.* People who are born into a society or move into it must learn the group's values and customs. The family is essential in teaching new members, but other social institutions educate new members as well.
3. *Producing, distributing, and consuming goods and services.* All societies must provide and distribute goods and services for their members. The economy is the primary social institution fulfilling this need; the government is often involved in the regulation of economic activity.
4. *Preserving order.* Every group or society must preserve order within its boundaries and protect itself from attack by outsiders. The government legitimates the creation of law enforcement agencies to preserve internal order and some form of military for external defence.
5. *Providing and maintaining a sense of purpose.* In order to motivate people to cooperate with one another, a sense of purpose is needed.

Although this list of functional prerequisites is shared by all societies, the institutions in each society perform these tasks in somewhat different ways depending on their specific cultural values and norms.

Conflict theorists agree with functionalists that social institutions originally are organized to meet basic social needs. However, they do not agree that social institutions work for the common good of everyone in society. For example, the homeless lack the power and resources to promote their own interests when they are opposed by dominant social groups. This is a problem not only in Canada, but for homeless people, especially children and youth, throughout the world (see Box 5.3). From the conflict perspective, social institutions, such as the government, maintain the privileges of the wealthy and powerful while contributing to the powerlessness of others (see Domhoff, 1983, 1990). For example, government policies in urban areas have benefited some people but exacerbated the problems of others. Urban renewal and transportation projects caused the destruction of low-cost housing and put large numbers of people "on the street" (Canadian Public Health Association, 1997). Similarly, the shift in governmental policies toward the mentally ill and welfare recipients resulted in more people struggling—and often failing—to find affordable housing. Meanwhile, many wealthy and privileged bankers, investors, developers, and builders benefited at the expense of the low-income casualties of those policies.

Functionalist and conflict perspectives provide a macrosociological overview because they concentrate on large-scale events and broad social features. For example, sociologists using the macrosociological approach to study the homeless might analyze how social institutions have operated to produce current conditions. By contrast, the interactionist perspective takes a microsociological approach, asking how social institutions affect our daily lives. We will discuss the microlevel perspective in detail later in this chapter.

STABILITY AND CHANGE IN SOCIETIES

Changes in social structure have a dramatic impact on individuals, groups, and societies. Social arrangements in contemporary societies have grown more complex with the introduction of new technology, changes in values and norms, and the rapidly shrinking "global village." How do societies maintain some degree of social solidarity in the face of such changes? Sociologists Émile Durkheim and Ferdinand Tönnies developed typologies to explain the processes of stability and change in the social structure of societies. A *typology* is a classification scheme containing two or more mutually exclusive categories that are used to compare different kinds of behaviour or types of societies.

Durkheim: Mechanical and Organic Solidarity

Early sociologist Émile Durkheim (1933/1893) was concerned with the question, How do societies manage to hold together? Durkheim asserted that preindustrial societies were held together by strong traditions and by the members' shared moral beliefs and values. As societies industrialized and developed more specialized economic activities, social solidarity came to be rooted in the members' shared dependence on one another. From Durkheim's perspective, social solidarity derives from a society's social structure, which, in turn, is based on the society's division of labour. *Division of labour* refers to how the various tasks of a society are divided up and performed. People in diverse societies (or in the same society at different points in time) divide their tasks somewhat differently, however, based on their own history, physical environment, and level of technological development.

To explain social change, Durkheim developed a typology that categorized societies as having either mechanical or organic solidarity. **Mechanical solidarity refers to the social cohesion in preindustrial societies, in which there is minimal division of labour and people feel united by shared values and common social bonds.** Durkheim used the term *mechanical solidarity* because he believed that people in such preindustrial societies feel a more or less automatic sense of belonging. Social interaction is characterized by face-to-face, intimate, primary-group relationships. Everyone is engaged in similar work, and little specialization is found in the division of labour.

Organic solidarity refers to the social cohesion found in industrial (and perhaps postindustrial) societies, in which people perform very specialized tasks and feel united by their mutual dependence. Durkheim chose the term *organic solidarity* because

he believed that individuals in industrial societies come to rely on one another in much the same way that the organs of the human body function interdependently. Social interaction is less personal, more status-oriented, and more focused on specific goals and objectives. People no longer rely on morality or shared values for social solidarity; instead, they are bound together by practical considerations.

Tönnies: *Gemeinschaft* and *Gesellschaft*

Sociologist Ferdinand Tönnies (1855–1936) used the terms *Gemeinschaft* and *Gesellschaft* to characterize the degree of social solidarity and social control found in societies. He was especially concerned about what happens to social solidarity in a society when a "loss of community" occurs.

The **Gemeinschaft (guh-MINE-shoft) is a traditional society in which social relationships are based on personal bonds of friendship and kinship and on intergenerational stability.** These relationships are based on ascribed rather than achieved status. In such societies, people have a commitment to the entire group and feel a sense of togetherness. Tönnies used the German term *Gemeinschaft* because it means "commune" or "community"; social solidarity and social control are maintained by the community. Members have a strong sense of belonging, but they also have very limited privacy.

By contrast, the **Gesellschaft (guh-ZELL-shoft) is a large, urban society in which social bonds are based on impersonal and specialized relationships, with little long-term commitment to the group or consensus on values.** In such societies, most people are "strangers" who perceive that they have very little in common with most other people. Consequently, self-interest dominates, and little consensus exists regarding values. Tönnies selected the German term *Gesellschaft* because it means "association"; relationships are based on achieved statuses, and interactions among people are both rational and calculated (see Figure 5.3).

Social Structure and Homelessness

In *Gesellschaft* societies, such as Canada, a prevailing core value is that people should be able to take care of themselves. Thus, many people view the homeless as "throwaways"—as beyond help or as having already had enough done for them by society. Some argue that the homeless made their own bad decisions, which led

Figure 5.3 *Gemeinschaft* and *Gesellschaft* Societies

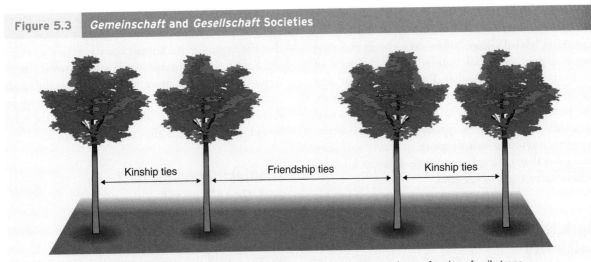

Kinship ties   Friendship ties   Kinship ties

If we compare societies to trees, a *Gemeinschaft* society would be made up of various family trees (clans or kinship groups) and their relationships to one another.

By contrast a *Gesellschaft* society would be made up of clumps of trees (kinship/friendship ties) that are important, but each clump would have a more specialized relationship and might not be committed to the others, just as an individual tree and the pot it is growing in could be moved to somewhere else.

them into alcoholism or drug addiction, and should be held responsible for the consequences of their own actions. In this sense, homeless people serve as a visible example to others to "follow the rules" lest they experience a similar fate (see White, 1992).

Alternative explanations for homelessness in *Gesellschaft* societies have been suggested. Elliot Liebow (1993) notes that homelessness is rooted in poverty; homeless people overwhelmingly are poor people who come from poor families. Homelessness is a "social class phenomenon, the direct result of a steady, across-the-board lowering of the standard of living of the working class and lower class" (Liebow, 1993:224). As the standard of living falls, those at the bottom

rungs of society are plunged into homelessness. The problem is exacerbated by a lack of jobs. Of those who find work, a growing number work full-time, year-round, but remain poor because of substandard wages. Households living below the poverty line use most of their income for rent—if they are able to find accommodations that they can afford at all (Canadian Council on Social Development, 2003). Clearly, there is no simple answer to the question about what should be done to help the homeless. Nor, as discussed in Box 5.2, is there any consensus as to what legal rights the homeless have in public areas. The answers we derive as a society and as individuals often are based on our social construction of this reality of life.

BOX 5.2 CRITICAL THINKING

Homeless Rights versus Public Space

Should homeless people be allowed to support themselves by panhandling on the public streets? Should homeless people be allowed to sleep in parks and other public areas? *Panhandling* is defined as the act of stopping people on the street to ask for assistance in the form of food or money. Over the past several years, cities across Canada have witnessed a dramatic increase in the amount of panhandling and the number of homeless persons living on the streets.

This issue has been the source of controversy in a numbers of cities, including Winnipeg, Vancouver, and Toronto. One common response among municipal governments is to introduce anti-panhandling legislation, which attempts to restrict where, when, and how one person can ask another for assistance. For example, the city of Vancouver passed a law that targets squeegee kids by making it illegal to ask anyone in a stopped car for money. Violators face a fine of up to $2,000. Winnipeg took the issue a step further, issuing a citywide ban on squeegee kids and a maximum fine of $1,000. In Toronto, police handed out hundreds of tickets after motorists complained about aggressive panhandling and topless squeegee girls. An Ontario MPP actually went so far as to suggest that he would outlaw homelessness if he became premier. He also pledged to create an army of "special constables" to corral homeless people into shelters, hospitals, and, in some cases, jail. "Call it tough love if you will. It will be illegal to live on the street, and it will be illegal to live in public places . . . and in the parks," he said, posing in front of downtown benches in Toronto covered in the possessions of homeless people (Benzie, 2002:1).

Advocates for the homeless and civil liberties groups have challenged the validity of these new anti-panhandling bylaws, claiming that the rights of the homeless are being violated. Specifically, the National Anti-Poverty Organization (NAPO) argues:

These laws discriminate against people who are poor. It is only the poor who are being restricted from parts of a city that are supposed to be open to full public access. In a free and democratic society, public spaces should be accessible to all citizens provided that they are not engaging in behaviour that is harmful to others—we are not free to threaten others or cause public disturbances. (2002:1)

Advocates also argue that panhandling does not harm anyone and is a legitimate means of livelihood for some of the homeless. In addition, they accuse public and law-enforcement officials of seeking to punish the homeless on the basis of their status. Poor people are perceived to be more of a threat simply because they may not look or act the same as people who are not poor. The wording of the anti-panhandling bylaws makes it clear that it is the visibility of poor people on the streets that people are objecting to, rather than the act of panhandling (NAPO, 2002:1). No question, the sight of people begging on the street is not a pretty one. Some people may feel annoyed by panhandlers who continually approach them on the street. Advocates for the homeless argue that maybe they should be annoyed. Why? Because maybe it is through being annoyed that more people will begin to recognize and acknowledge that the current economic and social policy options that our governments are pursuing are having a negative effect on the health and well-being of a large number of Canadian citizens (NAPO, 2002:2).

According to University of Manitoba ethics professor Arthur Schafer, sweeping the existence of panhandlers under a "coercive legal carpet" is the wrong way to go about dealing with this issue. In his paper "Down and Out in Winnipeg and Toronto: The Ethics of Legislating against Panhandling," Schafer raises a number of important ethical issues with respect to these new anti-panhandling laws:

Do we, as a society, really want to rely upon still more laws to deal with the serious social problems of poverty, homelessness, and panhandling? Are we convinced that legal coercion, with its use of physical force backed by weapons, lawyers, courts and jails, will be effective in addressing what is essentially a social problem? Are we prepared to violate fundamental rights to freedom of expression and add further burdens to the least advantaged members of our society? (1998:1)

Do you agree? What strategies would you recommend to address the issues of homelessness and panhandling on our city streets?

Sources: Schafer, 1998; NAPO, 2002; Benzie, 2002.

SOCIAL INTERACTION: THE MICROLEVEL PERSPECTIVE

So far in this chapter, we have focused on society and social structure from a macrolevel perspective. We have seen how the structure of society affects the statuses we occupy, the roles we play, and the groups and organizations to which we belong. Functionalist and conflict perspectives provide a macrosociological overview because they concentrate on large-scale events and broad social features. For example, sociologists using a macrosociological approach to study the homeless might analyze how social institutions have operated to produce current conditions. By contrast, the symbolic interactionist perspective takes a microsociological approach, asking how social institutions affect our daily lives. We will now look at society from the microlevel perspective, which focuses on social interaction among individuals, especially face-to-face encounters.

Social Interaction and Meaning

When you are with other people, do you often wonder what they think of you? If so, you are not alone! Because most of us are concerned about the meanings others ascribe to our behaviour, we try to interpret their words and actions so that we can plan how we will react toward them (Blumer, 1969). We know that others have expectations of us. We also have certain expectations about them. For example, if we enter an elevator that has only one other person in it, we do not expect that individual to confront us and stare into our eyes. As a matter of fact, we would be quite upset if the person did so.

This woman is displaying what Goffman referred to as civil inattention.

Social interaction within a given society has certain shared meanings across situations. For instance, our reaction would be the same regardless of *which* elevator we rode in *which* building. Sociologist Erving Goffman (1963b) described these shared meanings in his observation about two pedestrians approaching each other on a public sidewalk. He noted that each will tend to look at the other just long enough to acknowledge the other's presence. By the time they are about two and a half metres away from each other, both individuals will tend to look downward. Goffman referred to this behaviour as *civil inattention*—the ways in which an individual shows an awareness that others are present without making them the object of particular attention. The fact that people engage in civil inattention demonstrates that interaction does have a pattern, or *interaction order,* which regulates the form and processes (but not the content) of social interaction.

Does everyone interpret social interaction rituals in the same way? No. Ethnicity, gender, and social class play a part in the meanings we give to our interactions with others, including chance encounters on elevators or the street. Our perceptions about the meaning of a situation vary widely based on the statuses we occupy and our unique personal experiences. Social encounters have different meanings for men and women, and for individuals from different social classes and ethnic groups. For example, sociologist Carol Brooks Gardner (1989) found that women frequently do not perceive street encounters to be "routine" rituals. They fear for their personal safety and try to avoid comments and propositions that are sexual in nature when they walk down the street.

In another example, members of the dominant classes regard the poor, unemployed, and working class as less worthy of attention, frequently subjecting them to subtle yet systematic "attention deprivation" (Derber, 1983). The same can certainly be said about how members of the dominant classes "interact" with the homeless. A recent survey of Canadians' attitudes toward the homeless showed that more than 60 percent of respondents felt uncomfortable when they encountered homeless people (Canada Mortgage and Housing Corporation, 1998).

The Social Construction of Reality

If we interpret other people's actions so subjectively, can we have a shared social reality? Some interaction theorists believe that there is very little shared reality beyond that which is socially created. Interactionists refer to this as the *social construction of reality*—**the process by which our perception of reality is shaped largely by the subjective meaning that we give to an experience** (Berger and Luckmann, 1967). This meaning strongly influences what we "see" and how we respond to situations.

Our perceptions and behaviour are influenced by how we initially define situations: We act on reality as we see it. Sociologists describe this process as the *definition of the situation,* meaning that we analyze a social context in which we find ourselves, determine what is in our best interest, and adjust our attitudes and actions accordingly. This can result in a *self-fulfilling prophecy*—**a false belief or prediction that produces behaviour that makes the originally false belief come true** (Thomas and Thomas, 1928:72). An example would be a person who has been told repeatedly that she or he is not a good student; eventually, this person might come to believe it to be true, stop studying, and receive failing grades.

People may define a given situation in very different ways, a tendency demonstrated by sociologist Jacqueline Wiseman (1970) in her study of "Pacific City's" skid row. She wanted to know how people who live or work on skid row (a run-down area found in all cities) felt about it. Wiseman found that homeless people living on skid row evaluated it very differently from the social workers who dealt with them there. On the one hand, many of the social workers saw skid row as a smelly, depressing area filled with men who were "down-and-out," alcoholic, and often physically and mentally ill. On the other hand, the men who lived on skid row did not see it in such a negative light. They experienced some degree of satisfaction with their "bottle clubs [and a] remarkably indomitable and creative spirit"—at least initially (Wiseman, 1970:18). Also consider sociologist Lesley Harman's initial reaction to her field research site, a facility for homeless women in an Ontario city:

> The initial shock of facing the world of the homeless told me much about what I took for granted . . . The first day I lasted two very long hours. I went home and woke up severely depressed, weeping uncontrollably. (Harman, 1989:42)

In contrast, many of the women who lived there defined the situation of living in a hostel in very different terms. For example, one resident commented,

"This is home to me because I feel so comfortable. I can do what I really want, the staff are very nice to me, everybody is good to me, it's home, you know?" (1989:91). As these studies show, we define situations from our own frame of reference, based on the statuses that we occupy and the roles that we play.

Dominant group members with prestigious statuses may have the ability to establish how other people define "reality" (Berger and Luckmann, 1967:109). For example, the media often set the tone for our current opinions about homelessness, either with negative stories about the problems the homeless "cause" or with "human interest" stories.

Ethnomethodology

How do we know how to interact in a given situation? What rules do we follow? Ethnomethodologists are interested in the answers to these questions. *Ethnomethodology* **is the study of the commonsense knowledge that people use to understand the situations in which they find themselves** (Heritage, 1984:4). Sociologist Harold Garfinkel (1967) initiated this approach and coined the term: *ethno* for "people" or "folk" and *methodology* for "a system of methods." Garfinkel was critical of mainstream sociology for not recognizing the ongoing ways in which people create reality and produce their own world. Consequently, ethnomethodologists examine existing patterns of conventional behaviour in order to uncover people's *background expectancies*; that is, their shared interpretation of objects and events, as well as their resulting actions (Zimmerman, 1992). According to ethnomethodologists, interaction is based on assumptions of shared expectancies. For example, when you are talking with someone, what expectations do you have that you will take turns? Based on your background expectancies, would you be surprised if the other person talked for an hour and never gave you a chance to speak?

To uncover people's background expectancies, ethnomethodologists frequently break "rules" or act as though they do not understand some basic rule of social life so that they can observe other people's responses. In a series of *breaching experiments,* Garfinkel assigned different activities to his students to see how breaking the unspoken rules of behaviour created confusion. In one experiment, when students participating in the study were asked, "How are you?" by persons not in the study, they were

BOX 5.3 SOCIOLOGY IN GLOBAL PERSPECTIVE

Homelessness as an International Problem: The Plight of the "Street Children"

The eyes of the homeless, those who really need help, are the same eyes in any country—eyes that can see every door is closed to them.

—Valery Sokolov, a journalist and president of the Nochlyazhka Charitable Foundation in St. Petersburg, Russia, at the time he made this statement, knows what it means to be homeless: During six years of homelessness, he slept in a railroad station and sometimes in the forest (qtd. in Spence, 1997).

Homelessness is a widespread problem around the globe. In cities, such as St. Petersburg, Vancouver, Tokyo, Paris, Sydney, and New York, some homeless individuals and families are quite visible to others as they sleep in train stations, on the sidewalks, in doorways, and near warm air vents. But not all homeless people are so highly visible: Some reside in temporary shelters, sleep on the spare beds or sofas of friends and relatives, or are the "hidden homeless" who, in nations like Australia, camp in caravans or live in cars. Who are the homeless in other nations? A partial answer is that homeless people share many commonalities regardless of where they reside. According to recent reports from a variety of nations, the faces of homelessness have changed in recent decades. As a study of homelessness in Australia stated, "The old, derelict wino on the park bench has been joined by younger men, unemployed, and hopeless; by the confused and mentally ill, frightened by the pace of activity surrounding them; by women and children, desperate to escape violent and destructive domestic situations; by young people, cast off by families who can't cope or don't care" (Harrison, 2001). As this statement suggests, people from all walks of life may be affected by homelessness. A particularly pressing issue in many countries is the growing number of families with children and the "chronically homeless children," typically between the ages of twelve and eighteen, who reside on the streets or move between shelters, street life, and squatting (Harrison, 2001). Let's specifically focus our attention on the plight of the so-called "street children."

The World Health Organization's Street Children Project identified four categories of young people who fit the definition:

1. Children living on the streets, whose immediate concerns are survival and shelter.
2. Children who are detached from their families and living in temporary shelter, such as abandoned houses and other buildings (hostels/refuges/shelters), or moving about between friends.
3. Children who remain in contact with their families but because of poverty, overcrowding, or sexual or physical abuse within the family will spend some nights, or most days, on the streets.
4. Children who are in institutional care, who come from a situation of homelessness and are at risk of returning to a homeless existence.

If our children are the future of our nations, what can be said for those children who do not have a home to call their own? Some analysts believe that the plight of "street children" is especially dire in that they experience alienation and exclusion from society's mainstream structures and systems, including schools, churches, and other organizations that may provide stability and hope to youth. In addition, "street children" may participate in significant antisocial and self-destructive behaviour, and have a profound distrust for social services and welfare systems that might, in some cases, make it possible for them to leave a life of homelessness. Whether in England, Australia, Russia, Norway, Canada, the United States, or other nations of the world, homelessness, particularly of children and youth, marks the failure of existing social institutions to adequately provide for the next generation and puts people in a devalued master status in which they lack the power and resources to promote their own interests and in which survival becomes their primary objective.

Do nations have a responsibility to take care of homeless people within their borders? What about homeless children? Is there a difference between homeless adults and homeless children when we talk about social responsibility?

instructed to respond with very detailed accounts of their health and personal problems, as in this example:

> ACQUAINTANCE: How are you?
>
> STUDENT: How am I in regard to what? My health, my finances, my school work, my peace of mind, my . . .
>
> ACQUAINTANCE (red in the face and suddenly out of control): Look! I was just trying to be polite. Frankly, I don't give a damn how you are. (Garfinkel, 1967:44)

In this encounter, the acquaintance expected the student to use conventional behaviour in answering the question. By acting unconventionally, the student violated background expectancies and effectively "sabotaged" the interaction.

The ethnomethodological approach contributes to our knowledge of social interaction by making us aware of subconscious social realities in our daily lives. However, a number of sociologists regard ethnomethodology as a frivolous approach to studying human behaviour because it does not examine the impact of macrolevel social institutions—such as the economy and education—on people's expectancies. Women's studies scholars suggest that ethnomethodologists fail to do what they claim to: look at how social realities are created. Rather, they take ascribed statuses (such as ethnicity, class, gender, and age) as "givens," not as *socially created* realities. For example, in the experiments Garfinkel assigned to his students, he did not account for how gender affected their experiences. When Garfinkel asked students to reduce the distance between themselves and a nonrelative to the point that "their noses were almost touching," he ignored the fact that gender was as important to the encounter as

According to Erving Goffman, our day-to-day interactions have much in common with a dramatic production.

was the proximity of the two persons. Scholars recently have emphasized that our expectations about reality are strongly influenced by our assumptions relating to gender, ethnicity, and social class (see Bologh, 1992).

Dramaturgical Analysis

Erving Goffman suggested that day-to-day interactions have much in common with being on stage or in a dramatic production. ***Dramaturgical analysis is the study of social interaction that compares everyday life to a theatrical presentation.*** Members of our "audience" judge our performance and are aware that we may slip and reveal our true character (Goffman, 1959, 1963a). Consequently, most of us attempt to play our role as well as possible and to control the impressions we give to others. ***Impression management* or presentation of self refers to people's efforts to present themselves to others in ways that are most favourable to their own interests or image.***

For example, suppose that a professor has returned graded exams to your class. Will you discuss the exam and your grade with others in the class? If you are like most people, you probably play your student role differently depending on whom you are talking to and what grade you received on the exam. In a study at the University of Manitoba, Daniel and Cheryl Albas (1988) analyzed how students "presented themselves" or "managed impressions" when exam grades were returned. Students who all received high grades ("Ace–Ace encounters") willingly talked with one another about their grades and sometimes engaged in a little bragging about how they had "aced" the test. However, encounters between students who had received high grades and those who had received low or failing grades ("Ace–Bomber encounters") were uncomfortable. The Aces felt as if they had to minimize their own grade. Consequently, they tended to attribute their success to "luck" and were quick to offer the Bombers words of encouragement. On the other hand, the Bombers believed that they had to praise the Aces and hide their own feelings of frustration and disappointment. Students who received low or failing grades ("Bomber–Bomber encounters") were more comfortable when they talked with one another because they could share their negative emotions. They often indulged in self-pity and relied on face-saving excuses (such as an illness or an unfair exam) for their poor performances (Albas and Albas, 1988).

In Goffman's terminology, *face-saving behaviour* refers to the strategies we to rescue our performance when we experience a potential or actual loss of face. When the Bombers made excuses for their low scores, they were engaged in face-saving; the Aces attempted to help them save face by asserting that the test was unfair or that it was only a small part of the final grade. Why would the Aces and Bombers both participate in face-saving behaviour? In most social interactions, all role players have an interest in keeping the "play" going so that they can maintain their overall definition of the situation in which they perform their roles.

Goffman noted that people consciously participate in *studied nonobservance,* a face-saving technique in which one role player ignores the flaws in another's performance to avoid embarrassment for everyone involved. Most of us remember times when we have failed in our role and know that it is likely to happen again; thus, we may be more forgiving of the role failures of others.

Social interaction, like a theatre, has a front stage and a back stage. The *front stage* is the area where a player performs a specific role before an audience. The *back stage* is the area where a player is not required to perform a specific role because it is out of view of a given audience. For example, when the Aces and Bombers were talking with each other at school, they were on the "front stage." When they were in the privacy of their own residences, they were in "back stage" settings—they no longer had to perform the Ace and Bomber roles and could be themselves.

The need for impression management is most intense when role players have widely divergent or devalued statuses. As we have seen with the Aces and Bombers, the participants often play different roles under different circumstances and keep their various audiences separated from one another. If one audience becomes aware of other roles that a person plays, the impression being given at that time may be ruined. For example, homeless people may lose jobs or the opportunity to get them when their homelessness becomes known. One woman, Kim, had worked as a receptionist in a doctor's office for several weeks but was fired when the doctor learned that she was living in a shelter. According to Kim, the doctor told her, "If I had known you lived in a shelter, I would never have hired you. Shelters are places of disease" (Liebow, 1993:53–54). The homeless do not passively accept the roles into which they are cast. For the most part, they attempt—as we all do—to engage in impression management in their everyday life.

The dramaturgical approach helps us think about the roles we play and the audiences who judge our presentation of self. Like all other approaches, it has its critics. Sociologist Alvin Gouldner (1970) criticized this approach for focusing on appearances and not the underlying substance. Others have argued that Goffman's work reduces the self to "a peg on which the clothes of the role are hung" (see Burns, 1992) or have suggested that this approach does not place enough emphasis on the ways in which our everyday interactions with other people are influenced by occurrences within the larger society. For example, if a political official belittles the homeless as being lazy and unwilling to work, it may become easier for people walking down a street to do likewise. Goffman's defenders counter that he captured the essence of society because social interaction "turns out to be not only where most of the world's work gets done, but where the solid buildings of the social world are in fact constructed" (Burns, 1992:380). Goffman's work was influential in the development of the sociology of emotions, a relatively new area of theory and research.

The Sociology of Emotions

Why do we laugh, cry, or become angry? Are these emotional expressions biological or social in nature? To some extent, emotions are a biologically given sense (like hearing, smell, and touch), but they also are social in origin. We are socialized to feel certain emotions, and we learn how and when to express (or not express) those emotions (Hochschild, 1983).

How do we know which emotions are appropriate for a given role? Sociologist Arlie Hochschild (1983) suggests that we acquire a set of *feeling rules,* which shape the appropriate emotions for a given role or specific situation. These rules include how, where, when, and with whom an emotion should be expressed. For example, for the role of a mourner at a funeral, feeling rules tell us which emotions are required (sadness and grief, for example), which are acceptable (a sense of relief that the deceased no longer has to suffer), and which are unacceptable (enjoyment of the occasion expressed by laughing out loud) (see Hochschild, 1983:63–68).

Feeling rules also apply to the role of student. Albas and Albas (1988) examined the rules that exist regarding the emotions or feelings students experience at exam time. They concluded that when students believe that their level of anxiety is not at the "optimal level," they will engage in *emotional labour.* This term refers to the work that students will do to suppress or enhance the intensity, duration, or direction of their emotions (in this case, anxiety). The emotional labour done by students appears overwhelmingly to be in reducing the emotion rather than enhancing it. Students learn the feeling rules regarding "exam anxiety" informally through their interactions with other students (Albas and Albas, 1988).

Emotional labour may produce feelings of estrangement from one's "true" self. C. Wright Mills (1956) suggested that when we "sell our personality" in the course of selling goods or services, we engage in a seriously self-alienating process. Hochschild uses the following case to demonstrate the potential negative effects of emotional labour:

> A businessman asked a flight attendant, "Why aren't you smiling?" She looked at him in the eye. "I'll tell you what. You smile first, and then I'll smile." The businessman smiled at her. "Good," she replied. "Now freeze and hold that for fifteen hours." Then she walked away. (Hochschild, 1983:192)

In other words, the "commercialization" of our feelings may dehumanize our work role performance and create alienation and contempt that spills over into other aspects of our life (Smith and Kleinman, 1989).

Those who are unemployed and homeless also are required to engage in emotional labour. Panhandlers, for example, often rely on a regular clientele of contributors and must minimize reactions to gain support of passersby. Richard, a homeless man, makes reference to emotional labour in his description of the difficulties underlying panhandling:

> A lot of these people don't like me for one reason or another, right. And yet, I'm still more or less dependent upon them for money, you know. And they'll sit here and downgrade me, but I still have to be half-ass polite and ask them for the change. That's the most difficult part—dealing with people. (Lankenau, 1999:297)

Typically, over time, a panhandler becomes skilled at handling emotions, as he or she becomes hardened to abusive treatment and learns the value of remaining tightlipped. Eventually, the panhandler learns to view the abuse as less personal. Nate, a 45-year-old man who supports himself by panhandling, talks about how he manages the daily humiliations:

> I used to lash right back at them right, but I ain't never curse a person for it right. When people say negative things, I don't even respond to them.

> See, I'm not lookin' for no trouble, and I know they are, so I ain't gonna feed into that. They can say what they want to say, and I just let them go about their business. I'm used to all that ignorance. (Lankenau, 1999:298)

Do all people experience and express emotions the same way? It is widely believed that women express emotions more readily than men. However, very little research has been conducted to determine the accuracy of this belief. In fact, women and men may differ more in the way they express their emotions than in their actual feelings (Fabes and Martin, 1991). Differences in emotional expression also may be attributed to socialization; the extent to which men and women have been taught that a given emotion is appropriate (or inappropriate) to their gender no doubt plays an important part in their perceptions (Lombardo et al., 1983).

Social class also is a determinant in managed expression and emotion management. Emotional labour is emphasized in middle- and upper-class families. Since middle- and upper-class parents often work with people, they are more likely to teach their children the importance of emotional labour in their own careers than are working-class parents, who tend to work with things, not people (Hochschild, 1983). Ethnicity is also an important factor in emotional labour. Members of minority groups spend much of their life engaged in emotional labour because racist attitudes and discrimination make it continually necessary for them to manage their feelings.

Clearly, Hochschild's contribution to the sociology of emotions helps us understand the social context of our feelings and the relationship between the roles we play and the emotions we experience. However, her thesis has been criticized for overemphasizing the cost of emotional labour and the emotional controls that exist outside the individual (Wouters, 1989). The context in which emotions are studied and the specific emotions examined are important factors in determining the costs and benefits of emotional labour.

Nonverbal Communication

In a typical stage drama, the players not only speak their lines but also convey information by nonverbal communication. In Chapter 3, we discussed the importance of language; now we will look at the messages we communicate without speaking. *Nonverbal communication* **is the transfer of information between persons without the use of speech.** It includes not only visual cues (gestures, appearances) but also vocal features (inflection, volume, pitch) and environmental factors (use of space, position) that affect meanings (Wood, 1999). Facial expressions, head movements, body positions, and other gestures carry as much of the total meaning of our communication with others as our spoken words do (Wood, 1999).

Nonverbal communication may be intentional or unintentional. Actors, politicians, and salespersons may make deliberate use of nonverbal communication to convey an idea or "make a sale." We also may send nonverbal messages through gestures or facial expressions or even our appearance without intending to let other people know what we are thinking.

Functions of Nonverbal Communication

Nonverbal communication often supplements verbal communication (Wood, 1999). Head and facial movements may provide us with information about other people's emotional states, and others receive similar information from us (Samovar and Porter, 1991a). We obtain first impressions of others from various kinds of nonverbal communication, such as the clothing they wear and their body positions.

Our social interaction is regulated by nonverbal communication. Through our body posture and eye contact, we signal that we do or do not wish to speak to someone. For example, we may look down at the sidewalk or off into the distance when we pass homeless persons who look as if they are going to ask for money.

Nonverbal communication establishes the relationship between people in terms of their responsiveness to and power over one another (Wood, 1999). For example, we show that we are responsive toward or like another person by maintaining eye contact and attentive body posture and perhaps by touching and standing close. By contrast, we signal to others that we do not wish to be near them or that we dislike them by refusing to look them in the eye or stand near them. We can even express power or control over others through nonverbal communication. Goffman (1956) suggested that *demeanour* (how we behave or conduct ourselves) is relative to social power. People in positions of dominance are allowed a wider range of permissible actions than are their subordinates, who are expected to show deference. *Deference* is the symbolic means by which subordinates give a required permissive response to those in power; it confirms the existence of inequality and reaffirms each person's relationship to the other (Rollins, 1985).

Facial Expression, Eye Contact, and Touching

Deference behaviour is important in regard to facial expression, eye contact, and touching.

This type of nonverbal communication is symbolic of our relationships with others. Who smiles? Who stares? Who makes and sustains eye contact? Who touches whom? All of these questions relate to demeanour and deference; the key issue is the status of the person who is *doing* the smiling, staring, or touching relative to the status of the recipient (Goffman, 1967).

Facial expressions, especially smiles, also reflect gender-based patterns of dominance and subordination in society. Women typically have been socialized to smile and frequently do so even when they are not actually happy (Halberstadt and Saitta, 1987). Jobs held predominantly by women (including flight attendant, secretary, elementary school teacher, and nurse) are more closely associated with being pleasant and smiling than are "men's jobs." In addition to smiling more frequently, many women tend to tilt their heads in deferential positions when they are talking or listening to others. By contrast, men tend to display less emotion through smiles or other facial expressions and instead seek to show that they are reserved and in control (Wood, 1999).

Women are more likely to sustain eye contact during conversations (but not otherwise) as a means of showing their interest in and involvement with others. By contrast, men are less likely to maintain prolonged eye contact during conversations but are more likely to stare at other people (especially men) in order to challenge them and assert their own status (Pearson, 1985).

Eye contact can be a sign of domination or deference. For example, in a participant observation study of domestic (household) workers and their employers, sociologist Judith Rollins (1985) found that the domestics were supposed to show deference by averting their eyes when they talked to their employers. Deference also required that they present an "exaggeratedly subservient demeanour" by standing less erect and walking tentatively.

Touching is another form of nonverbal behaviour that has many different shades of meaning. Gender and power differences are evident in tactile communication from birth. Studies have shown that touching has variable meanings to parents: boys are touched more roughly and playfully, while girls are handled more gently and protectively (Condry, Condry, and Pogatshnik, 1983). This pattern continues into adulthood, with women touched more frequently than men. Sociologist Nancy Henley (1977) attributed this pattern to power differentials between men and women and to the nature of women's roles as mothers, nurses, teachers, and secretaries. Clearly, touching has

Nonverbal communication may be thought of as an international language. What message do you receive from the facial expression and gestures of each of these people? Is it possible to misinterpret their messages?

a different meaning to women than to men (Stier and Hall, 1984). Women may hug and touch others to indicate affection and emotional support, while men are more likely to touch others to give directions, assert power, and express sexual interest (Wood, 1999).

Personal Space   Physical space is an important component of nonverbal communication. Anthropologist Edward Hall (1966) analyzed the physical distance between people speaking to one another and found that the amount of personal space people prefer varies from one culture to another. ***Personal space* is the immediate area surrounding a person that the person claims as private.** Our personal space is contained within an invisible boundary surrounding our body, much like a snail's shell. When others invade our space, we may retreat, stand our ground, or even lash out, depending on our cultural background (Samovar and Porter, 1991a). Hall (1966) observed that North Americans have different "distance zones":

1. *Intimate distance* (contact to about 0.5 metre): reserved for spouses, lovers, and close friends, for purposes of lovemaking, comforting, and protecting.
2. *Personal distance* (0.5 metre to 1.2 metres): reserved for friends and acquaintances, for purposes of ordinary conversation, card playing, and similar activities.
3. *Social distance* (1.2 metres to 3.6 metres): marks impersonal or formal relationships, such as in job interviews and business transactions.

4. *Public distance* (over 3.6 metres): marks an even more formal relationship and makes interpersonal communication nearly impossible. This distance often denotes a status difference between dignitaries or speakers and their audience or the general public.

Hall makes the distinction between "contact" and "noncontact" cultures and emphasizes that people from different cultures have different distance zones. *Contact cultures* are characterized by closer physical distance in interaction, more frequent eye contact and touch, and greater voice volume. Representatives of contact cultures include Arabs, Southern Europeans, and the French. Canadians, Asians, and the British are examples of representatives of *noncontact cultures*, which typically interact at greater distances with less eye contact and touch and lower voice volume (Hall, 1966).

What happens to personal distance when individuals from contact and noncontact cultures interact? This question is particularly important in our multicultural society, where members of different ethnic subcultures interact on a regular basis. One study examined this question by observing members of a contact culture (Franco-Manitobans) and those of a noncontact culture (Anglo-Manitobans) interacting in one another's natural setting. Albas and Albas (1989) reported that the subjects, in an attempt to comply with the expectations of others, would adjust their "distance zone" when interacting with someone from a different cultural group.

Age, gender, kind of relationship, and social class also impact on the allocation of personal space. Power differentials are reflected in personal space and privacy issues. With regard to age, adults generally do not hesitate to enter the personal space of a child (Thorne, Kramarae, and Henley, 1983). Similarly, young children who invade the personal space of an adult tend to elicit a more favourable response than do older uninvited visitors (Dean, Willis, and la Rocco, 1976). The need for personal space appears to increase with age (Baxter, 1970; Aiello and Jones, 1971), although it may begin to decrease at about age forty (Heshka and Nelson, 1972).

For some people, the idea of privacy or personal space is an unheard of luxury afforded only to those in the middle and upper classes. As we have seen in this chapter, the homeless may have no space to call their own. Some may try to "stake a claim" on a heat grate or on the same bed in a shelter for more than one night, but such claims have dubious authenticity in a society in which the homeless are assumed to own nothing and have no right to lay claim to anything in the public domain.

In sum, all forms of nonverbal communication are influenced by gender, ethnicity, social class, and the personal contexts in which they occur. While it is difficult to generalize about people's nonverbal behaviour, we still need to think about our own nonverbal communication patterns. Recognizing that differences in social interaction exist is important. We should be wary of making value judgments—the differences are simply differences. Learning to understand and respect alternative styles of social interaction enhances our personal effectiveness by increasing the range of options we have for communicating with different people in diverse contexts and for varied reasons (Wood, 1999).

FUTURE CHANGES IN SOCIETY, SOCIAL STRUCTURE, AND INTERACTION

The social structure in North America has been changing rapidly in recent decades. Currently, there are more possible statuses for persons to occupy and roles to play than at any other time in history. Although achieved statuses are important, ascribed statuses still have a significant impact on the options and opportunities people have.

Ironically, at a time when we have more technological capability, more leisure activities and types of entertainment, and more quantities of material goods available for consumption than ever before, many people experience high levels of stress, fear for their lives because of crime, and face problems such as homelessness. In a society that can send astronauts into space to perform complex scientific experiments, is it impossible to solve some of the problems that plague us here on earth?

Individuals and groups often show initiative in trying to solve some of our pressing problems (see Box 5.4). We have recently seen the beginning of militant action by groups supporting the homeless. For example, the Ontario Coalition Against Poverty has held protest marches at the businesses of people who have objected to the presence of drop-in centres for the homeless, moved into abandoned buildings that could be used as emergency housing, and picketed the homes of government officials who have not supported the coalition's views (Philp, 1997). However, these initiatives alone will not solve all our social problems in the twenty-first century. Large-scale, formal organizations must become more responsive to society's needs.

At the microlevel, we need to regard social problems as everyone's problem; if we do not, they have a way of becoming everyone's problem anyway. When we think about "the homeless," for example, we are thinking in a somewhat misleading manner. "The homeless" suggests a uniform set of problems and a single category of poor people. Jonathan Kozol (1988:92) emphasizes that "their miseries are somewhat uniform; the squalor is uniform; the density of living space is uniform. [However, the] uniformity is in their mode of suffering, not in themselves."

What can be done about homelessness in the future? We must first become dissatisfied with explanations that see personal problems as the cause of homelessness. Many people in the past have experienced poverty, mental illness, alcoholism, physical disability, and drug addiction, but they have not become homeless. Only changes in structural factors can explain why we have a homelessness crisis in Canada today. Unless these factors are addressed, homelessness will continue to flourish and be a national disgrace. In sum, the future of this country rests on our collective ability to deal with major social problems at both the macrolevel and the microlevel of society.

BOX 5.4 YOU CAN MAKE A DIFFERENCE

One Person's Trash May Be Another Person's Treasure: Recycling for Good Causes

The average college student tosses out 640 pounds of trash through the year, and almost 30 percent of that is at the end of the year.

–Lisa K. Heller, founder of Dump & Run, a national nonprofit organization that helps colleges collect discarded items and organize sales for local charities and campus groups. (qtd. in Crawford, 2003:A6)

Lars Eighner (1993) pointed out that in his years as a Dumpster diver, he was able to find many useful things in large garbage bins because the area he "worked" was inhabited by many affluent university students. As you will recall, he stated that students are prone to throw away valuable items at certain times in the school year–particularly when they move out at the end of a semester. Although Eighner's Dumpster diving was a random process, Lisa K. Heller has organized a systematic way in which discarded items can be turned into cash to benefit organizations, such as soup kitchens and Head Start programs.

Heller's Dump & Run program has been successful at schools, such as Brown University, in the United States. Students at still other U.S. schools,

including Texas Christian University and Wilkes University, do not turn trash into cash but instead recycle unwanted items, such as furniture and half-full bottles of detergent, so that these items may be used at food banks, soup kitchens, and resale shops (Crawford, 2003).

Would you like an opportunity to participate in a similar program in your community? If none currently exists, perhaps you could start a group to take on a similar project. Even if there is no large college or university campus near you, no doubt many people throw away items that might be useful to others. In some cities, people put pieces of furniture, used household goods, and items of clothing out by their trash cans to be recycled. Some of these items may not be as "fancy" as the George Foreman grills, designer clothing, blenders, and cappuccino machines that Ms. Heller and others have found near university campuses through the Dump & Run program; however, even less flashy items can benefit many individuals and families.

To learn more about Dump & Run, visit http://www.dumpandrun.org.

CHAPTER REVIEW

■ **How does social structure shape our social interactions?**

The stable patterns of social relationships within a particular society make up its social structure. Social structure is a macrolevel influence because it shapes and determines the overall patterns in which social interaction occurs. Social interaction refers to how people within a society act and respond to one another. This interaction is a microlevel dynamic—between individuals and groups— and is the foundation of meaningful relationships in society. Social structure provides an ordered framework for society and for our interactions with others.

■ **What are the main components of social structure?**

Social structure comprises statuses, roles, groups, and social institutions. A status is a specific position in a group or society and is characterized by certain expectations, rights, and duties. Ascribed statuses, such as gender, class, and ethnicity, are acquired at birth or involuntarily later in life. Achieved statuses, such as education and occupation, are assumed voluntarily as a result of personal choice, merit, or direct effort. We occupy a status, but a role is a set of behavioural expectations associated with a given status. A social group consists of two or more people who interact frequently and share a common identity and sense of interdependence. A formal organization is a highly structured group formed to complete certain tasks or achieve specific goals. A social institution is a set of organized beliefs and rules that establish how a society attempts to meet its basic needs.

■ What are the functionalist and conflict perspectives on social institutions?

According to functionalist theorists, social institutions perform several prerequisites of all societies: replace members; teach new members; produce, distribute, and consume goods and services; preserve order; and provide and maintain a sense of purpose. Conflict theorists, however, note that social institutions do not work for the common good of all individuals. Institutions may enhance and uphold the power of some groups but exclude others, such as the homeless.

■ How do societies maintain stability in times of social change?

According to Durkheim, although changes in social structure may dramatically affect individuals and groups, societies manage to maintain some degree of stability. Mechanical solidarity refers to social cohesion in preindustrial societies, in which people are united by shared values and common social bonds. Organic solidarity refers to the cohesion in industrial societies, in which people perform specialized tasks and are united by mutual dependence.

■ How do Gemeinschaft and Gesellschaft societies differ in social solidarity?

According to Ferdinand Tönnies, the *Gemeinschaft* is a traditional society in which relationships are based on personal bonds of friendship and kinship and on intergenerational stability. The *Gesellschaft* is an urban society in which social bonds are based on impersonal and specialized relationships, with little group commitment or consensus on values.

■ Is all social interaction based on shared meanings?

Social interaction within a society, particularly face-to-face encounters, is guided by certain shared meanings of how we should behave. Social interaction also is marked by nonverbal communication, which is the transfer of information between people without using speech. Ethnicity, gender, and social class often influence perceptions of meaning, however.

■ What is the dramaturgical perspective?

According to Erving Goffman's dramaturgical analysis, our daily interactions are similar to dramatic productions. Impression management refers to efforts to present our self to others in ways that are most favourable to our own interests or self-image.

■ Why are feeling rules important?

Feeling rules shape the appropriate emotions for a given role or specific situation. Our emotions are not always private, and specific emotions may be demanded of us on certain occasions.

KEY TERMS

achieved status 129
ascribed status 129
dramaturgical analysis 143
ethnomethodology 141
formal organization 135
Gemeinschaft 137
Gesellschaft 137
impression management 143
master status 129
mechanical solidarity 137
nonverbal communication 145
organic solidarity 137
personal space 147
primary group 134
relative homelessness 126
role 131
role conflict 131
role exit 133
role expectation 131
role performance 131
role strain 132
secondary group 134
self-fulfilling prophecy 141
social construction of reality 141
social group 134
social institution 136
social interaction 125
social marginality 128
social network 134
social structure 125
status 129
status set 129
status symbol 130
stigma 129

NET LINKS

To learn more about Erving Goffman's book *The Presentation of Self in Everyday Life,* go to:
http://people.brandeis.edu/~teuber/ goffmanbio.html#Writings

What changes can we expect to see in our everyday social interactions as a result of new electronic technologies? The paper "The Presentation of Self in Electronic Life: Goffman on the Internet" addresses this question: **http://ess.ntu.ac.uk/miller/cyberpsych/ goffman.htm**

The Canadian Mortgage and Housing Corporation has current research on homeless women and homelessness among Aboriginal peoples, as well as a 1998 survey of Canadians' attitudes toward homelessness available at: **http://www.cmhc-schl.gc.ca/en/imquaf/ho/**

Raising the Roof is a national charity dedicated to funding long-term solutions to homelessness in Canada. Its primary activities involve developing, finding, and/or maintaining homes for homeless people. Questions and answers, as well as current articles on homelessness, are available on this site: **http://www.raisingtheroof.org/**

The National Homelessness Initiative is at work helping governments and community organizations come together to alleviate homelessness: **http://www21.hrdc-drhc.gc.ca/**

QUESTIONS FOR CRITICAL THINKING

1. Think of a person you know well who often irritates you or whose behaviour grates on your nerves (it could be a parent, friend, relative, or teacher). First, list that person's statuses and roles. Then, analyze his or her possible role expectations, role performance, role conflicts, and role strains. Does anything you find in your analysis help to explain his or her irritating behaviour? (If not, change your method of analysis!) How helpful are the concepts of social structure in analyzing individual behaviour?
2. Are structural problems responsible for homelessness, or are homeless individuals responsible for their own situation?
3. You are conducting field research on gender differences in nonverbal communication styles. How are you going to account for variations in age, ethnicity, and social class?
4. When communicating with other genders, ethnic groups, and ages, is it better to express and acknowledge different styles or to develop a common, uniform style?

SUGGESTED READINGS

These books provide interesting insights on social interaction and the social construction of reality:

Peter L. Berger and Thomas Luckmann. *The Social Construction of Reality: A Treatise in the Sociology of Knowledge.* Garden City, N.Y.: Anchor Books, 1967.

Erving Goffman. *The Presentation of Self in Everyday Life.* New York: Doubleday, 1959.

David A. Karp and William C. Yoels. *Sociology and Everyday Life.* Itasca, Ill.: Peacock, 1986.

The process of leaving a significant role and establishing a new identity is examined in this book:

Helen Rose Fuchs Ebaugh. *Becoming an EX: The Process of Role Exit.* Chicago: University of Chicago Press, 1988.

To find out more about the problem of homelessness:

Lars Eighner. *Travels with Lizbeth.* New York: St. Martin's Press, 1993.

David A. Snow and Leon Anderson. *Down on Their Luck: A Case Study of Homeless Street People.* Berkeley: University of California Press, 1993.

Lesley D. Harman. *When a Hostel Becomes a Home: Experiences of Women.* Toronto: Garamond Press, 1989.

Thomas O'Reilly-Fleming. *Down and Out in Canada: Homeless Canadians.* Toronto: Canadian Scholars' Press, 1993.

ONLINE STUDY AND RESEARCH TOOLS

THOMSONNOW™ Thomson NOW!

Go to **http://hed.nelson.com** to link to ThomsonNOW for *Sociology in Our Times,* Fourth Canadian Edition, your online study tool. First take the **Pre-Test** for this chapter to get your personalized **Study Plan,** which will identify topics you need to review and direct you to the appropriate resources. Then take the **Post-Test** to determine what concepts you have mastered and what you still need work on.

INFOTRAC®

Infotrac College Edition is included free with every new copy of this text. Explore this online library for additional readings, review, and a handy resource for assignments. Visit **www.infotrac-college.com** to access this online database of full-text articles. Enter the key terms from this chapter to start your search.

Groups and Organizations

Kenneth Payne describes his journey through a bureaucratic maze:

"Since November, I have spent six to eight hours a day trying to persuade the authorities to accommodate me, but it just goes around in a circle . . . It's George Orwell's Big Brother, 14 years after his book *1984* . . . The bureaucracy is making me prove a negative and it turns 'innocent until proven guilty' on its head . . . There's no common sense here. It's an inflexible bureaucracy where nobody takes any responsibility." (Reed, 1998:A11)

What is Mr. Payne's problem? The former carpenter wants to be a school teacher. He has a degree in education and has taught as a substitute. However, he is unable to get a permanent job teaching because he has a skin disease that causes the skin on his hands to blister and peel. Why should this disqualify Mr. Payne from teaching? Because the disease has removed his fingerprints and legislators in his home state of California have passed a law requiring that all teachers be fingerprinted so their criminal records can be checked. Of course, because Mr. Payne has never had proper fingerprints, there would be nothing on file to check against even if they could read his prints. But this has not discouraged the bureaucrats. He has appealed to the state and offered to prove

in other ways that he has no criminal record, but he has been unable to get an exemption from the rule.

Why do people in organizations behave in such unreasonable ways? Some rules are necessary for all organizations to function. Even in small groups, such as families or friendship groups, informal rules help to ensure that people interact smoothly. In a large bureaucracy, an explicit system of rules and regulations means that employees and clients know what is expected of them. These rules can also help to ensure that everyone receives equal treatment from the organization. Unfortunately, adherence to a set of rules can stifle individual judgment, and some bureaucrats become so inflexible that they hurt the organization and its clients. In Mr. Payne's case, it made sense for the school system to do its best to protect the children in its care by establishing background checks for prospective teachers. However, in this case the bureaucrats focused their concern on fingerprinting, which is just one way of ensuring that people without criminal records are hired as teachers. An official who was concerned with the goal of the policy (protecting children) rather than with one of the means of achieving that goal (fingerprinting) would have been willing to accept the other ways in which Mr. Payne could have proved he was not an offender. The

unthinking adherence to rules shown by the bureaucrats in this case accomplishes little other than alienating the people whom the bureaucrats are supposed to serve.

While Mr. Payne suffered some hardship, the consequences of bureaucratic inflexibility can be much more severe. In August 2005, Hurricane Katrina devastated the historic city of New Orleans. Tens of thousands of evacuees were not properly cared for and there was a total breakdown of law and order in the city immediately after Katrina had passed. The massive failures in planning for the disaster and in coordinating the response after the city was flooded will be studied for many years. While the most serious flaw was probably a lack of coordination among the local, state, and federal agencies responsible for the emergency, bureaucratic inflexibility was also pervasive.

Several relatively small incidents show that even in the face of the largest natural disaster ever to hit North America, the people running bureaucracies can be focused more on rules and regulations than on saving lives. Despite the desperate need for water for hurricane survivors, there were incidents where truckloads of water were turned back because the drivers didn't have the proper paperwork

(Lipton et al., 2005). A group of doctors were evacuated from their hospital and taken to the New Orleans airport. They offered to help tend the many sick people who had also been taken to the airport, but federal authorities were worried about liability issues and told them they could best help by mopping floors (CNN, 2005). While the doctors cleaned floors, patients died because of the lack of medical care. Another example of goal displacement occurred when hundreds of firefighters from around the U.S. were forced by the U.S. Federal Emergency Management Agency to delay their deployment into the emergency zone to take several days of community relations and sexual harassment training. Finally, two Navy helicopter pilots were counselled (a minor disciplinary procedure) by their commanding officer for delaying their return to their base in Pensacola, Florida, from a cargo mission the day after the hurricane in order to save 110 people who were stranded on rooftops in New Orleans (Kaczor, 2005).

We have all been treated badly by some bureaucracy. In fact, many of us think of bureaucracies in a very negative way because of their red tape and impersonal nature. However, while bureaucracies can be inflexible and inhumane, they are also a very powerful type of social organization and are essential to modern life. Bureaucracies have been the best way of managing large numbers of people who must accomplish a common task, so they are an essential part of our industrialized global society. Much of our time is spent dealing with bureaucratic organizations. Most of us are born in hospitals, educated in schools, fed by restaurants and supermarket chains, entertained by communications companies, employed by corporations, and buried by funeral companies.

In this chapter, you will learn about different types of groups and organizations including bureaucracies. As social beings, we live our lives in groups and they constantly affect our behaviour. Before reading on, test your knowledge about bureaucracies by taking the quiz in Box 6.1.

QUESTIONS AND ISSUES

Chapter Focus Question: How can we explain the behaviour of people who work in bureaucracies?

What constitutes a social group?

How are groups and their members shaped by group size, leadership style, and pressures to conform?

What purposes does bureaucracy serve?

What are some of the characteristics of bureaucracies?

How might an alternative form of organization differ from existing ones?

Napoleon's defeat at Waterloo in 1815 showed that massive armies could not be led in the traditional way, by a single commander responsible for everything. Subsequently, armies developed more effective organizational structures.

■ SOCIAL GROUPS

Three strangers are standing at a street corner waiting for a traffic light to change. Do they constitute a group? Five hundred women and men are first-year students at a university. Do they constitute a group? In everyday usage, we use the word *group* to mean any collection of people. According to sociologists, however, the answer to these questions is no; individuals who happen to share a common feature or to be in the same place at the same time do not constitute social groups.

Groups, Aggregates, and Categories

As we saw in Chapter 5, a *social group* is a collection of two or more people who interact frequently with one another, share a sense of belonging, and have a feeling of interdependence. Several people waiting for a traffic light to change constitute an *aggregate*—**a collection of people who happen to be in the same place at the same time but have little else in common.** Shoppers in a department store and passengers on an airplane flight also are examples of aggregates. People in aggregates share a common purpose (such as purchasing items or arriving at their destination) but generally do not interact with one another, except perhaps briefly. The first-year students, at least initially, constitute a *category*—**a number of people who may never have met one another but share a similar characteristic** (such as education level, age, ethnicity, and gender). Men and women make up categories, as do First Nations peoples and victims of sexual or racial harassment. Categories are not social groups because the people in them usually do not create a social structure or have anything in common other than a particular trait.

Occasionally, people in aggregates and categories form social groups. People within the category known as "students," for instance, become an aggregate when they get together for an orientation. Some of them may form social groups as they interact with one

another in classes and seminars, find that they have mutual interests and concerns, and develop a sense of belonging to the group. The number and diversity of social groups within society is enormous, especially when you consider that a social group may contain as few as two members and that the purposes for which they are formed are so wide-ranging.

Social groups can change and evolve over time. For example, an aggregate or category of people over time may become a formal organization with a specific structure and clear-cut goals. A *formal organization*, you will recall, is a highly structured group formed for the purpose of achieving specific goals in the most efficient manner. Universities, factories, corporations, the military, and government agencies are examples of formal organizations. Before we examine formal organizations, we need to know more about groups in general and the ways in which they function.

Types of Groups

As you will recall from Chapter 5, groups have varying degrees of social solidarity and structure. This structure is flexible in some groups and more

BOX 6.1 SOCIOLOGY AND EVERYDAY LIFE

How Much Do You Know About Bureaucracy?

True	False	
T	F	1. Large bureaucracies have existed for about a thousand years.
T	F	2. Because of the efficiency and profitability of the new factory bureaucracies, people were eager to leave the farms to work in the factories.
T	F	3. Bureaucracies are deliberately impersonal.
T	F	4. One of the first modern bureaucratic organizations was the Prussian army.
T	F	5. The rise of Protestantism helped create the social conditions favourable to the rise of modern bureaucracies.
T	F	6. In addition to their formal structure, bureaucracies also have an "other face"—an informal structure that is also important in analyzing their operation.
T	F	7. Because people in bureaucracies follow the direction of their superiors, bringing about change in large organizations is easy.
T	F	8. Businesses in Japan have developed an organizational model that is different from the one prevalent in North America.
T	F	9. The comic strip *Dilbert* has become popular because it is a reflection of the way many people feel about the bureaucracies in which they work.
T	F	10. The organizational principles used by McDonald's restaurants are being adopted by other sectors of the global economy.

Answers on page 156.

BOX 6.1 SOCIOLOGY AND EVERYDAY LIFE

Answers to the Sociology Quiz on Bureaucracy

1. **False.**   While not all sociologists agree on the specific origins of bureaucracies, many feel that modern bureaucracies began with the development of large factories in England during the nineteenth century. Large-scale organizations had existed prior to this time, but they were not organized on bureaucratic principles. As organizations grew in size, they became difficult to manage, so new organizing principles were required.

2. **False.**   Commenting on the eighteenth-century factory, Charles Perrow has observed that "the unnaturalness of working for someone else's profit twelve hours a day, seven days a week was so pronounced that the early factories had to rely on criminals and paupers to do the work" (1986:49).

3. **True.**   Bureaucracies are designed to be efficient and productive. In order to do this, they take a detached approach to clients and employees so that personal feelings do not interfere with organizational decisions.

4. **True.**   Napoleon's defeat at Waterloo in 1815 by the allied armies of Prussia (now part of Germany), Britain, Austria, and Russia showed that mass armies could not be led in the traditional way, by a single commander responsible for everything (Stark, 1998). The Prussian military, having learned from observing Napoleon's defeat, set about designing a more effective organization. Field Marshal Helmuth von Moltke, who took command of the Prussian army in 1857, was responsible for two major innovations. He developed a general staff made up of carefully selected and trained officers who could carry out the leader's commands, and he divided his army into standard-sized "divisions" that could be detached to fight as self-sufficient units. These innovations, which still guide contemporary armies, also influenced the development of industrial bureaucracies.

5. **True.**   According to Max Weber, Protestantism, with its emphasis on worldliness and commitment to long-term goals, helped create the social conditions that led to the rise of the modern bureaucracy.

6. **True.**   All bureaucracies have an informal structure that is composed of activities and interactions that do not correspond with the official rules and procedures of the bureaucracy.

7. **False.**   It is extremely difficult to bring about change in bureaucracies because people become comfortable with the way things have been done in the past.

8. **True.**   The main differences between Japanese and North American corporations are that Japanese employees can expect lifetime employment and are encouraged to participate in management decisions. This has begun to change, however, as the recession of the 1990s led some Japanese companies to rethink their guarantee of lifetime employment.

9. **True.**   Thousands of workers have posted *Dilbert* cartoons on their cubicle and office walls, and many of the ideas you see in *Dilbert* actually come from their suggestions.

10. **True.**   George Ritzer (1993) coined the term *McDonaldization* to describe the highly rationalized business process used by the restaurant chain. According to Ritzer, this process is characterized by efficiency; an emphasis on speed and quantity rather than quality; predictability; control; and dehumanization. Research done by Ritzer and others suggests this model is spreading to other types of business and to other parts of the world.

rigid in others. Some groups are small and personal; others are large and impersonal. We more closely identify with the members of some groups than we do others.

Primary and Secondary Groups

Sociologist Charles H. Cooley (1962/1909) used the term *primary group* to describe a small, less specialized group in which members engage in face-to-face, emotion-based interactions over an extended period of time. We have primary relationships with other individuals in our primary groups—that is, with our *significant others,* who frequently serve as role models.

In contrast, you will recall, a *secondary group* is a larger, more specialized group in which the members engage in more impersonal, goal-oriented relationships for a limited period of time. The size of a secondary group may vary. Twelve students in a university seminar may start out as a secondary group but eventually become a primary group as they get to know one another and communicate on a more personal basis. Formal organizations are secondary groups, but they also contain many primary groups within them. For example, how many primary groups do you think there are within the secondary group setting of your university?

Ingroups and Outgroups

All groups set boundaries by distinguishing between insiders who are members and outsiders who are not. Sociologist William Graham Sumner (1959/1906) coined the terms *ingroup* and *outgroup* to describe people's feelings toward members of their own and other groups. An **ingroup is a group to which a person belongs and with which the person feels a sense of identity.** An **outgroup is a group to which a person does not belong and toward which the person may feel a sense of competitiveness or hostility.** Distinguishing between our ingroups and our outgroups helps us establish our individual identity and self-worth. Likewise, groups are solidified by ingroup and outgroup distinctions; the presence of an enemy or hostile group may bind members more closely together (Coser, 1956).

Group boundaries may be formal, with clearly defined criteria for membership. For example, a country club that requires applicants for membership to be recommended by four current members, to pay a $25,000 initiation fee, and to pay $1,000 per month membership dues has clearly set requirements for its members. The club may even post a sign at its entrance that states "Members Only," and use security personnel to ensure that nonmembers

These Olympic teams graphically illustrate the concept of ingroups and outgroups. Each Olympic team can be seen as an ingroup that helps to give its members a sense of belonging and identity—feelings that are strengthened by the presence of clearly defined outgroups (competing teams).

do not encroach on its grounds. Boundary distinctions often are reflected in symbols, such as emblems or clothing. Members of the country club are given membership cards to gain access to the club's facilities and to charge food to their account. They may wear sun visors and shirts with the country club's logo on them. All of these symbols denote that the bearer/wearer is a member of the ingroup. They are status symbols.

Group boundaries are not always as formal as they are in a private club. Friendship groups, for example, usually do not have clear guidelines for membership. Rather, the boundaries tend to be very informal and vaguely defined.

Ingroup and outgroup distinctions may encourage social cohesion among members, but they also may promote classism, racism, sexism, and ageism. Ingroup members typically view themselves positively and members of outgroups negatively. These feelings of group superiority, or *ethnocentrism,* are somewhat inevitable. However, members of some groups feel more free than others to act on their beliefs. If groups are embedded in larger groups and organizations, the large organization may discourage such beliefs and their consequences (Merton, 1968). Conversely, organizations may foster these ingroup/outgroup distinctions by denying their existence or by failing to take action when misconduct occurs. For example:

In Winnipeg, Manitoba, recently two male employees were fired from a Canada Safeway bread plant for accusations of sexual harassment against female employees. One of the men allegedly exposed himself, stalked, and gave photographs of his anatomy to a female employee. Accusations against the other man include repeatedly making lewd and suggestive comments to female employees and inappropriately touching them. The female employee said that 10 or 12 women on the work floor have taken stress leave from work over the last five years because of the abuse. Men outnumber women on the shop floor by about eight to one. The United Food and Commercial Workers union spokesperson explained that, "the system of dealing with sexual-harassment complaints failed in this case because of the influential position one of the accused men held with the union." These incidents were not brought to the attention of the union management. Female employees say that the atmosphere at the plant discouraged women from coming forward to report incidents of harassment. (Owen, 1996)

In this case, male co-workers seem to have developed an ingroup from which the female employees were categorically excluded and were also made the object of the group's ridicule. In a work environment, ingroups can provide support for group members. Those who are denied membership in the group, however, may find it impossible to perform their job effectively.

Reference Groups

Ingroups provide us not only with a source of identity but also with a point of reference. A **reference group** **is a group that strongly influences a person's behaviour and social attitudes, regardless of whether that individual is an actual member.** When we attempt to evaluate our appearance, ideas, or goals, we automatically refer to the standards of some group. Sometimes, we will refer to our membership groups, such as family or friends. Other times, we will rely on groups to which we do not currently belong but that we might wish to join in the future, such as a social club or a profession. We also may have negative reference groups. For many people, the Ku Klux Klan and neo-Nazi skinheads are examples of negative reference groups because most people's racial attitudes compare favourably with such groups' blatantly racist behaviour.

Reference groups help explain why our behaviour and attitudes sometimes differ from those of our membership groups. We may accept the values and norms of a group with which we identify rather than one to which we belong. We also may act more like members of a group we want to join than members of groups to which we already belong. In this case, reference groups are a source of anticipatory socialization. Many people have more than one reference group and often receive conflicting messages from them about how they should view themselves. For most of us, our reference group attachments change many times during our life course, especially when we acquire a new status in a formal organization.

Networks

A *network* is a web of social relationships that links one person with other people and, through them, with additional people those people know. Frequently, networks connect people who share common interests but who otherwise might not identify and interact with one another. For example, if A is tied to B and B is tied to C, then a network may be formed among individuals A, B, and C. Think of the experiences that you and your friends have had looking for summer jobs. If your friend works at a company that needs more people, he or she may recommend you to the potential employer. This recommendation helps you get a job and gives the employer the assurance that you are likely to be a good employee. Research has found that networks play a very important role for graduating students in finding employment (Granovetter, 1994).

It's a Small World: Networks of Acquaintances

On September 11, 2001, nearly 3,000 people died when terrorists crashed two planes into the North and South towers of New York's World Trade Center and a third into the Pentagon. A fourth plane crashed into a field when passengers foiled the attempt to fly it into another target. Following the disaster, many people around the world were surprised to learn that they, or some of their friends and acquaintances, knew someone who had been personally touched by the tragedy. Social scientists were not surprised by this because of a fascinating research project done more than thirty years ago by psychologist Stanley Milgram (1967).

Milgram sent packages of letters to people in the Midwestern United States. The objective was to get the letters to one of two target recipients in Boston using personal contacts. Those originating the chain were given the name of the target recipient and told that the person was either a Boston stockbroker or the wife of a Harvard divinity student. They were asked to mail the letter to an acquaintance who they felt would be able to pass it on to another acquaintance even closer to the intended target. Milgram found that it took an average of five contacts to get the letters to the intended recipient. Many people learned about the "small world" concept through John Guare's play *Six Degrees of Separation,* which has been made into a film. In addition, the research led to the popular trivia game *Six Degrees of Kevin Bacon,* in which the objective is to link actors to other actors who have appeared in films with Kevin Bacon. Thus Nicole Kidman has a Kevin Bacon Number of 2, as she appeared in *Eyes Wide Shut* with Tom Cruise, who worked with Kevin Bacon in the film *A Few Good Men.* Since virtually no American actor has a Bacon Number larger than 4 (Saulnier, 1998), the challenge for movie trivia experts is to figure out the linkages. You can find out more about this game at the Oracle of Bacon Web site at http://www.cs.virginia.edu/oracle.

While the "small world" research has been most often used for entertainment, it may have more important implications. Steve Strogatz and Duncan Watts (1998) have worked out the mathematics behind the phenomenon and have documented the importance of "bridges"—that is, people who bridge very different social worlds. For example, in Milgram's study the Boston stockbroker received 64 letters, 16 of which were delivered by a person who owned a clothing store in Boston. Perhaps you can think of friends or acquaintances who come from other countries or who have unusual interests, hobbies, or jobs that would enable them to bridge vast distances or widely different social groups. The study of networks and the role of bridges has important implications for researchers in many fields, including *epidemiology,* which is the study of the spread of disease. For example, the spread of HIV/AIDS was hastened by a Canadian flight attendant (Patient X) whose travels meant that he bridged several different networks of gay males (Saulnier, 1998).

While Milgram's research was very influential and has some useful implications, upon re-examining Milgram's research material, Kleinfeld (2002) found that the vast majority of the letters that were initially sent never reached their intended destination. We do not know if the connections failed because the participants were unable to think of anyone who could act as the next link in the chain, or simply because they did not try to move the letter along toward the intended recipient. However, a recent study using e-mail contacts had somewhat lower failure rates and had similar results to Milgram. Dodds and his colleagues (2003) found that those who continued the chain needed an average of five to seven contacts to reach their targets even when in another country.

The research by Milgram and the later work of Dodds and his colleagues points out an interesting aspect of social networks. Korte and Milgram (1970) found that there was a significantly higher number of completed chains when both the sender and the recipient were the same race, and Dodds et al. found that people most frequently contacted persons of the same gender. Dodds et al. found that workplace and educational contacts were most likely to be used in completing chains. These findings imply that members of groups that are less powerful and less educated may be disadvantaged in a world that is increasingly dependent upon geographically dispersed social networks. Why is this important? We live in a world where many things get done through networks. Mark Granovetter (1995) has shown that social contacts and networks are very important both for employers and for people looking for work. Most people get their jobs through personal contacts rather than through formal job-search mechanisms. This means that those who have developed good networks will have the advantage in their search for work, while those without extensive networks or those whose networks are not oriented to the labour market will be at a great disadvantage. If most of your friends are unemployed, they will not be able to help you to find a job. This can perpetuate unemployment among groups, such as visible minorities and women, who may not have had the opportunity to build up strong networks.

We expect network analysis to become much more important in sociology. For example, e-mail patterns may tell us a great deal about the way in which organizations work. How do ideas spread within an organization? Do e-mail messages frequently pass between different levels of an organization, or are communications restricted to one level? Are there cliques that rarely communicate with others or are communications more broadly based? Do women and visible minorities have the same interaction patterns as white males, and are they able to bridge different parts of their organizations? On a broader level, can genuine communities flourish in cyberspace or does the Internet reduce community by reducing the personal contact between people?

GROUP CHARACTERISTICS AND DYNAMICS

What purpose do groups serve? Why are individuals willing to relinquish some of their freedom to participate in groups? According to functionalists, people form groups to meet instrumental and expressive needs. *Instrumental,* or task-oriented, needs cannot always be met by one person, so the group works cooperatively to fulfil a specific goal. For example, think of how hard it would be to function as a one-person football team or to single-handedly build a skyscraper. Groups help members do jobs that are impossible to do alone or that would be very difficult and time-consuming at best. In addition to instrumental needs, groups also help people meet their *expressive,* or emotional, needs, especially for self-expression and support from family, friends, and peers.

While not disputing that groups ideally perform such functions, conflict theorists suggest that groups also involve a series of power relationships whereby the needs of individual members may not be equally served. Symbolic interactionists focus on how the size of a group influences the kind of interaction that takes place among members.

To many postmodernists, groups and organizations—like other aspects of postmodern societies—are generally characterized by superficiality and by shallow social relationships (Jameson, 1984). One postmodern thinker who focuses on this issue is the literary theorist Fredric Jameson, whose works continue to have a significant influence on contemporary sociology. According to Jameson (1984), postmodern organizations (and societies as a whole) are characterized not only by superficial relations and lack of depth; people also experience a waning of emotion because the world, and the people in it, have become more fragmented (Ritzer, 1997). For example, George Ritzer (1997) examined fast-food restaurants using a postmodern approach and concluded that both restaurant employees and customers interact in extremely superficial ways that are largely scripted by large-scale organizations: The employees learn to follow scripts in taking and filling customers' orders (Leidner, 1993), while customers also respond with their own "recipied" action (Schutz, 1967/1932). According to Ritzer (1997: 226), "[C]ustomers are mindlessly following what they consider tried-and-true social recipes, either learned or created by them previously, on how to

deal with restaurant employees and, more generally, how to work their way through the system associated with the fast-food restaurant."

We now will look at certain characteristics of groups, such as how size affects group dynamics.

Group Size

The size of a group is one of its most important features. Interactions are more personal and intense in a *small group,* **a collectivity small enough for all members to be acquainted with one another and to interact simultaneously.**

Georg Simmel (1950/1902–1917) suggested that small groups have distinctive interaction patterns that do not exist in larger groups. According to Simmel, in a *dyad*—**a group composed of two members**—the active participation of both members is crucial for the group's survival. If one member withdraws from interaction or "quits," the group ceases to exist. Examples of dyads include two people who are best friends, married couples, and domestic

Our most intense relationships occur in dyads—groups composed of two members. How might the interaction of these two people differ if they were with several other people?

Figure 6.1   Growth of Possible Social Interactions Based on Group Size

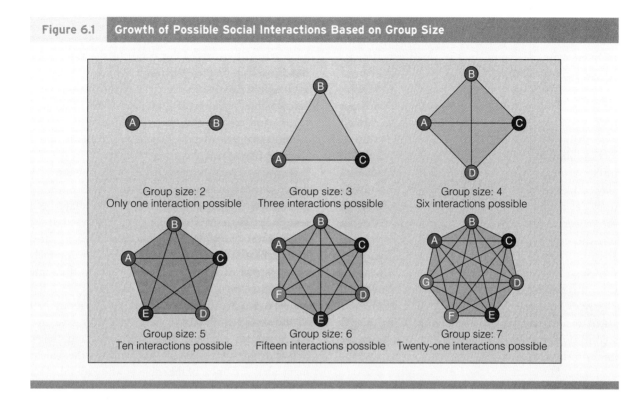

Group size: 2
Only one interaction possible

Group size: 3
Three interactions possible

Group size: 4
Six interactions possible

Group size: 5
Ten interactions possible

Group size: 6
Fifteen interactions possible

Group size: 7
Twenty-one interactions possible

partnerships. Dyads provide members with an intense bond and a sense of unity not found in most larger groups.

When a third person is added to a dyad, a ***triad, a group composed of three members,*** is formed. The nature of the relationship and interaction patterns changes with the addition of the third person. In a triad even if one member ignores another or declines to participate, the group can still function. In addition, two members may unite to create a coalition that can subject the third member to group pressure to conform. A *coalition* is an alliance created in an attempt to reach a shared objective or goal. If two members form a coalition, the other member may be seen as an outsider or intruder.

As the size of a group increases beyond three people, members tend to specialize in different tasks, and everyday communication patterns change. For instance, in groups of more than six or seven people, it becomes increasingly difficult for everyone to take part in the same conversation; so, several conversations likely will take place simultaneously. Members also are likely to take sides on issues and form a number of coalitions. In groups of more than ten or twelve people, it becomes virtually impossible for all members to participate in a single conversation unless

one person serves as moderator and facilitates the discussion. As shown in Figure 6.1, when the size of the group increases, the number of possible social interactions also increases.

Group Conformity

To what extent do groups exert a powerful influence in our lives? As discussed in Chapters 3 and 4, groups have a significant amount of influence over our values, attitudes, and behaviour. To gain and then retain our membership in groups, most of us are willing to exhibit a high level of conformity to the wishes of other group members. ***Conformity is the process of maintaining or changing behaviour to comply with the norms established by a society, subculture, or other group.*** We often experience powerful pressure from other group members to conform. In some situations, this pressure may be almost overwhelming.

In several studies researchers found that the pressure to conform may cause group members to say they see something that is contradictory to what they actually are seeing or to do something they otherwise would be unwilling to do. As we look at two of these studies, ask yourself what you might have done if you had been involved in this research.

Asch's Research   Pressure to conform is especially strong in small groups in which members want to fit in with the group. In a series of experiments conducted by Solomon Asch (1955, 1956), the pressure toward group conformity was so great that participants were willing to contradict their own best judgment if the rest of the group disagreed with them.

One of Asch's experiments involved groups of undergraduate men (seven in each group) who allegedly were recruited for a study of visual perception. All the men were seated in chairs. However, the person in the sixth chair did not know that he was the only actual subject; all of the others were assisting the researcher. The participants first were shown a large card with a vertical line on it and then a second card with three vertical lines (see Figure 6.2). Each of the seven participants was asked to indicate which of the three lines on the second card was identical in length to the "standard line" on the first card.

Figure 6.2	Asch's Cards

Although Line 2 is clearly the same length as the line in the lower card, Solomon Asch's research assistants tried to influence "actual" participants by deliberately picking Line 1 or Line 3 as the correct match. Many of the participants went along rather than risking the opposition of the "group."

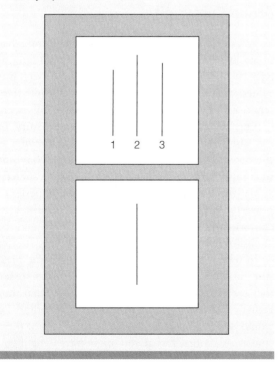

In the first test with each group, all seven men selected the correct matching line. In the second trial, all seven still answered correctly. In the third trial, however, the subject became very uncomfortable when all of the others selected the incorrect line. The actual subject could not understand what was happening and became even more confused as the others continued to give incorrect responses on eleven out of the next fifteen trials.

If you had been in the position of the subject, how would you have responded? Would you have continued to give the correct answer, or would you have been swayed by the others? When Asch (1955) averaged the responses of the fifty actual subjects who participated in the study, he found that about 33 percent routinely chose to conform to the group by giving the same (incorrect) responses as Asch's assistants. Another 40 percent gave incorrect responses in about half of the trials. Although 25 percent always gave correct responses, even they felt very uneasy and "knew that something was wrong." In discussing the experiment afterward, most of the subjects who gave incorrect responses indicated that they had known the answers were wrong but decided to go along with the group in order to avoid ridicule or ostracism. Figure 6.3 shows how group size was related to conformity.

In later studies, Asch found that if even a single assistant did not agree with the others, the subject was reassured by hearing someone else question the accuracy of incorrect responses and was much less likely to give a wrong answer himself.

One contribution of Asch's research is the dramatic way in which it calls our attention to the power that groups have to produce conformity among members. *Compliance* is the extent to which people say (or do) things so that they may gain the approval of other people. Certainly, Asch demonstrated that people will bow to social pressure in small-group settings.

Milgram's Research   How willing are we to do something because someone in a position of authority has told us to do it? How far are we willing to go in following the demands of that individual? Stanley Milgram (1963, 1974) conducted a series of controversial experiments to find answers to these questions about people's obedience to authority. *Obedience* is a form of compliance in which people follow direct orders from someone in a position of authority. Milgram wanted to do this research to help him understand atrocities, such as the Holocaust, where ordinary citizens behaved brutally when they were ordered to do so.

| Figure 6.3 | Effect of Group Size in the Asch Conformity Studies |

As more people are added to the "incorrect" majority, subjects' tendency to conform by giving wrong answers increases—but only up to a point. Adding more than seven people to the incorrect majority does *not* further increase subjects' tendency to conform—perhaps because subjects are suspicious about why so many people agree with one another.

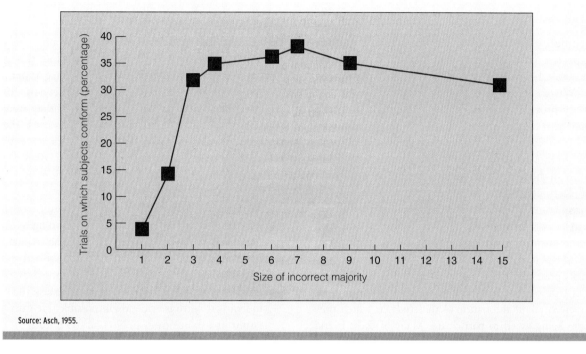

Source: Asch, 1955.

Milgram's subjects were men who had responded to an advertisement for participants in an experiment. When the first (actual) subject arrived, he was told that the study concerned the effects of punishment on learning. After the second subject (an assistant of Milgram's) arrived, the two men were instructed to draw slips of paper from a hat to get their assignments as either the "teacher" or the "learner." Because the drawing was rigged, the actual subject always became the teacher, and the assistant the learner. Next, the learner was strapped into a chair with protruding electrodes that looked something like an electric chair. The teacher was placed in an adjoining room and given a realistic-looking but nonoperative shock generator. The "generator's" control panel showed levels that went from "Slight Shock" (15 volts) on the left, to "Intense Shock" (255 volts) in the middle, to "DANGER: SEVERE SHOCK" (375 volts), and finally "XXX" (450 volts) on the right.

The teacher was instructed to read aloud a pair of words and then repeat the first of the two words. At that time, the learner was supposed to respond with the second of the two words. If the learner could not provide the second word, the teacher was instructed to press the lever on the shock generator so that the learner would be punished for forgetting the word. Each time the learner gave an incorrect response, the teacher was supposed to increase the shock level by 15 volts. The alleged purpose of the shock was to determine whether punishment improves a person's memory.

What was the maximum level of shock that a "teacher" was willing to inflict on a "learner"? The learner had been instructed (in advance) to beat on the wall between himself and the teacher as the experiment continued, pretending that he was in intense pain. The teacher was told that the shocks might be "extremely painful" but that they would cause no permanent damage. At about 300 volts, when the learner quit responding at all to questions, the teacher often turned to the experimenter to see what he should do next. When the experimenter indicated that the teacher should give increasingly painful shocks, 65 percent of the teachers administered shocks all the way up to the "XXX" (450-volt) level (see Figure 6.4). By this point in the process, the teachers frequently were sweating, stuttering, or biting on their lip. According to Milgram, the teachers (who were free to leave whenever they wanted to) continued in the experiment because they were being given directions by a person in a position of authority (a university scientist wearing a white coat). This finding was a surprise, because most people questioned by Milgram before the study expected that the teacher would stop the experiment at about 140 volts.

What can we learn from Milgram's study? The study provides evidence that obedience to authority may be more common than most of us would like to believe. None of the "teachers" challenged the process before they had applied 300 volts. Almost two-thirds went all the way to what could have been a deadly jolt of electricity if the shock generator had been real. For many years, Milgram's findings were found to be consistent in a number of different settings and with variations in the research design (Miller, 1986).

This research once again raises some questions originally posed in Chapter 2 concerning research ethics. As was true of Asch's research, Milgram's subjects were deceived about the nature of the study in which they were being asked to participate. Many of them found

the experiment extremely stressful and some suffered anxiety so severe that the experimental sessions had to be terminated (Milgram, 1963). Such conditions cannot be ignored by social scientists because subjects may receive lasting emotional scars from such research. It would be virtually impossible today to obtain permission to replicate this experiment in a university setting, though such studies were common in the 1960s.

In addition to ethical problems, Milgram's study may also be methodologically flawed. While this is one of the most widely cited social science experiments, Brannigan (2004) has raised the issue of whether the subjects actually believed that they were hurting people. The more realistic Milgram made the experiment, the more likely the subjects were to refuse to proceed. One critic explains why he does not take the results of Milgram's study very seriously:

> Every experiment was basically preposterous . . . the entire experimental procedure from beginning to end could make no sense at all, even to the laymen. A person is strapped to a chair and immobilized and is explicitly told he is going to be exposed to extremely painful electric shocks. . . . The task the student is to learn is evidently impossible. He can't learn it in a short time. . . . No one could learn

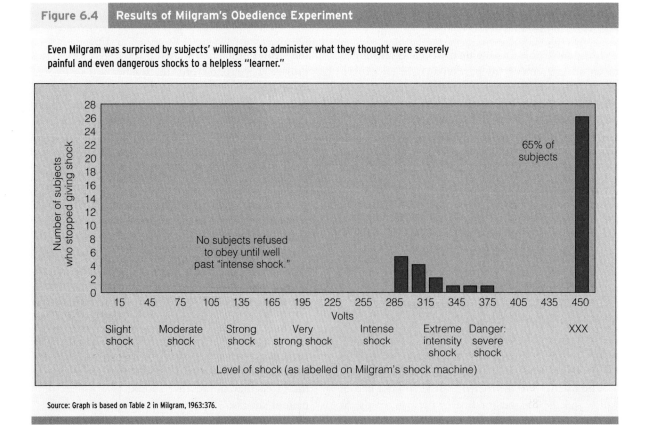

Figure 6.4   Results of Milgram's Obedience Experiment

Even Milgram was surprised by subjects' willingness to administer what they thought were severely painful and even dangerous shocks to a helpless "learner."

Source: Graph is based on Table 2 in Milgram, 1963:376.

it. . . . This experiment becomes more incredulous and senseless the further it is carried. (Mantell, 1971:110–111)

Because of the artificiality of the laboratory situation, Brannigan is very doubtful that this experiment tells us anything about why German citizens were willing to participate in the atrocities of the Holocaust. The issue of artificiality means that we should always be cautious when we consider the findings of laboratory experiments involving human behaviour.

Group Conformity and Sexual Harassment

Psychologist John Pryor (1995; PBS, 1992) has conducted behavioural experiments on university campuses to examine the social dynamics of sexual harassment. In one of his studies, a graduate student (who was actually a member of the research team) led research subjects to believe that they would be training undergraduate women to use a computer. The actual purpose of the experiment was to observe whether the trainers (subjects) would harass the women if given the opportunity and encouraged to do so. By design, the graduate student purposely harassed the women (who were also part of the research team), setting an example for the subjects to follow.

Pryor found that when the "trainers" were led to believe that sexual harassment was condoned and then were left alone with the women, they took full advantage of the situation in 90 percent of the experiments. Shannon Hoffman, one of the women who participated as a member of the research team, felt vulnerable because of the permissive environment created by the men in charge:

> So it kind of made me feel a little bit powerless as far as that goes because there was nothing I could do about it. But I also realized that in a business setting, if this person really was my boss, that it would be harder for me to send out the negative signals or whatever to try to fend off that type of thing. (Pryor, 1995)

This research suggests a relationship between group conformity and harassment. Behaviour such as sexual harassment or racism is more likely to occur when it is encouraged (or at least not actively discouraged) by others. This shows why organizations should not tolerate this sort of behaviour.

Groupthink

As we have seen, individuals often respond differently in a group context than they might if they were alone. Social psychologist Irving Janis (1972, 1989) examined group decision making among political experts and found that major blunders may be attributed to pressure toward group conformity. To describe this phenomenon, he coined the term *groupthink*—**the process by which members of a cohesive group arrive at a decision that many individual members privately believe is unwise.** Why not speak up at the time? Members usually want to be "team players." They may not want to be the ones who undermine the group's consensus or who challenge the group's leaders. Consequently, members often limit or withhold their opinions and focus on consensus rather than on exploring all of the options and determining the best course of action. Figure 6.5 summarizes the dynamics and results of groupthink.

Investigators attributed the explosion of the space shuttle *Columbia* to poor decision making by officials who were influenced by "groupthink."

Figure 6.5   Janis's Description of Groupthink

In Janis's model, prior conditions, such as a highly homogeneous group with committed leadership, can lead to potentially disastrous "groupthink," which short-circuits careful and impartial deliberation. Events leading up to the tragic 1986 launch of the space shuttle *Challenger* have been cited as an example of this process.

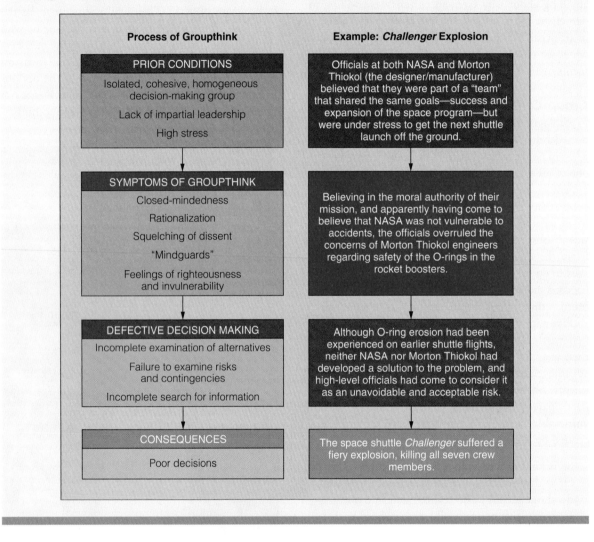

The tragic 1986 launch of the space shuttle *Challenger*, which exploded 73 seconds into its flight, killing all seven crew members, has been cited as an example of groupthink. On the day preceding the launch, engineers at the company responsible for designing and manufacturing the shuttle's rocket boosters became concerned that freezing temperatures at the launch site would interfere with the proper functioning of the O-ring seals in the boosters. But when they expressed their misgivings, they were over-ruled by higher-level officials at the company and with NASA (the government agency that administers the U.S. space program), where executives were impatient as a result of earlier delays. A presidential commission that investigated the tragedy concluded that neither the manufacturer nor NASA responded adequately to warnings about the seals (Lippa, 1994).

You may wonder why people agreed to the launch despite their safety concerns. After all, it is one thing to doubt your judgment about the length of a line as in the Asch experiments and quite another to send seven people to their deaths. The engineers closest to the situation were almost unanimous in opposing the launch. However, the decision was ultimately made by NASA and contractor managers who were more focused on the schedule than on safety concerns. NASA managers were under great pressure to keep the shuttle flights on schedule because they feared congressional budget cuts.

When the contractor suggested that the launch be delayed until air temperatures were above 53°F, NASA managers responded angrily. One said "My God . . . when do you want me to launch, next April?" (President's Commission, 1986:96). Another said, "I'm appalled by your recommendation" (President's Commission, 1986:94). Faced with this pressure, the contractor, who was about to begin negotiating a new billion-dollar agreement with NASA, had second thoughts. Senior managers overruled the recommendations of their engineers and recommended launch. NASA managers and the contractor managers were prepared to risk other people's lives in order to accomplish their own bureaucratic goals.

Despite the clear analysis of NASA's errors in the *Challenger* case, the 2003 crash of the space shuttle *Columbia* raises further questions of groupthink at NASA. The preliminary report of the Columbia Accident Investigation Board concluded that the shuttle broke up just before landing because some foam broke off an external fuel tank during the launch and damaged one of the wings. This damage led to a catastrophic failure of the wing during the initial stages of the reentry into the earth's atmosphere (Smith, 2003). Foam strikes had occurred on at least seven previous occasions but the problem had been ignored by senior administrators despite the fact that NASA engineers had been concerned about the problem. Communication about the problem was limited because a NASA office in Alabama was responsible for the fuel tank while the Houston office was responsible for the shuttle itself. Senior NASA personnel also ignored numerous requests from their staff to try to assess the damage during *Columbia*'s flight to see whether in-flight repairs were required. One of the investigation board members concluded that dissent was not welcome at NASA, even concerning matters of safety.

FORMAL ORGANIZATIONS

Over the past century, the number of formal organizations has increased dramatically in Canada and other industrialized nations. Everyday life previously was centred in small, informal, primary groups, such as the family and the village. With the advent of industrialization and urbanization (as discussed in Chapter 1), people's lives became increasingly dominated by large, formal, secondary organizations. A *formal organization* is a

Although telephone- and computer-based procedures have streamlined the registration process at many schools, for many students registration exemplifies the worst aspects of academic bureaucracy. Yet students and other members of the academic community depend upon the "bureaucracy" to establish and administer procedures that enable the complex system of the university to operate smoothly.

highly structured secondary group formed for the purpose of achieving specific goals in the most efficient manner. Formal organizations (such as corporations, schools, and government agencies) usually keep their basic structure for many years in order to meet their specific goals.

Bureaucracies

The bureaucratic model of organization is the most universal organizational form in government, business, education, and religion. A *bureaucracy* is an **organizational model characterized by a hierarchy of authority, a clear division of labour, explicit rules and procedures, and impersonality in personnel matters.**

When we think of a bureaucracy, we may think of "buck-passing," such as occurs when we are directed from one office to the next without receiving an answer to our question or a solution to our problem. We also may view a bureaucracy in terms of red tape because of the situations in which there is so much paperwork and so many incomprehensible rules that no one really understands what to do. However, the bureaucracy originally was not intended to be this way; it was seen as a way to make organizations *more* productive and efficient.

As noted in Chapter 1, German sociologist Max Weber (1968/1922) was interested in the historical trend toward bureaucratization that accelerated during the Industrial Revolution. To Weber, the bureaucracy was the most "rational" and efficient means of attaining organizational goals because it contributed to coordination and control. According to Weber, *rationality* **is the process by which traditional methods of social organization, characterized by informality and spontaneity, are gradually replaced by efficiently administered formal rules and procedures.** It can be seen in all aspects of our lives, from small organizations to multinational corporations employing many thousands of workers worldwide.

Why Bureaucracy?

While much of the rest of this chapter focuses on how bureaucracies work, it is also important to understand why they exist. The simple answer to this question is that they exist because organizations grew too large to be managed in any other way. However, large organizations existed for thousands of years before the birth of bureaucracy, so we must also consider social conditions to explain why the modern bureaucratic form of social organization arose in the nineteenth century in Europe and North America.

Rodney Stark (1998) has provided two examples of the development of modern bureaucracies. The first is the bureaucratization of the Prussian army. Even very large armies had traditionally been controlled by a single commander. However, armies had grown so large by the nineteenth century that even a brilliant general like Napoleon was unable to directly control the actions of 600,000 troops. The scale of battle was too large for one man to manage, but the structure of armies in Napoleon's time did not allow for the effective delegation of the commander's authority. Napoleon saw his army devastated in Russia, where he lost more than 400,000 men, and met his final defeat at Waterloo in 1815. The lessons of Napoleon's defeat were not lost on the Prussians. Field Marshal Helmuth von Moltke, who took command of the Prussian army in 1857, built an army based on new organizational principles. Von Moltke developed a General Staff made up of carefully selected and highly trained officers who could operate independently in battle while still following their commander's wishes. He also borrowed an idea from the Duke of Wellington, who had defeated Napoleon at Waterloo. Wellington had divided his army into several standard-sized "divisions" that could be detached to fight as self-sufficient units. Von Moltke placed these divisions under the command of his staff officers. Prussia's quick defeat of the more experienced French army in the 1871 Franco-Prussian War validated his methods, which were quickly adopted by other nations. Von Moltke's innovations still guide contemporary armies and have also influenced the development of industrial bureaucracies.

Stark's second example was one of the pioneering corporate bureaucracies, the meat-packing empire established by Gustavus Swift. In the 1870s, the American meat industry was composed of small, local firms, and getting the meat to market was a very difficult and inefficient process. The challenge faced by wholesale butchers like Swift was that most Americans lived in the East, while most of the livestock was produced on the Great Plains. Swift came up with the idea of shipping meat in the then newly invented refrigerated railroad cars. This required that he build refrigerated storage facilities. He also needed massive packing plants to kill the animals and process the meat. To sell the product, he set up sales and distribution systems. Swift did not raise cattle—he purchased them from ranchers—but he controlled each of the steps between purchase of the live cattle and the production of the packaged meat that would be bought by the consumer. Each step was carried out by a different division of the company. Unlike von Moltke's military divisions that were essentially complete armies, Swift's corporate divisions were based on different functions, such as meat packing, shipping, and sales. Each was headed by a manager who reported to a centralized corporate headquarters that was responsible for coordinating their activities. Swift's organizational model was highly successful, and his business empire is still a powerful force in the food industry. Several decades later, Henry Ford took Swift's organizational model a step further by creating the moving automobile assembly line, which has been the pattern for industrial production for nearly a hundred years (see Chapter 13, "The Economy and Work").

It seems clear that a bureaucratic structure is the key to effectively managing organizations that are large in size and scope. We can turn to the work of Max Weber to explain why the modern bureaucracy did not develop until the nineteenth century. Weber suggested that the growth of the modern bureaucracy required both cultural and structural changes that did not occur until the nineteenth century.

The cultural change was the rejection of *traditional authority* and the acceptance of *rational-legal authority* as the basis of conduct. This means that people were less willing to accept rules based on tradition, and more willing to grant legitimacy to a set of rules intended to achieve certain ends (Weber, 1947). Weber's influential work on the relationship between the rise of Protestantism and the development of capitalism (Weber, 1976) analyzes the factors that led to this change.

The structural change that facilitated the modern bureaucracy was the shift to an economic system in which people were forced to work for somebody else (Perrow, 1986). The social conditions for factory bureaucracies were established during the Industrial Revolution when peasants were forced off the farms. The former peasants became the first large labour pool for the factories, as they had no alternative but to work for whatever the owners would pay them. The system of wage employment gave the profits from the workers' labour to the factory owner while the workers were paid only a subsistence wage. This cheap labour provided a tremendous incentive for the factory owners to expand their enterprises. Owners used the capital their factories generated to mechanize the factories and they also developed the systems of specialization and standardization that most efficiently achieved the goals of productivity and profitability. Of course, breaking down production into specialized tasks required managers to coordinate activities, so the factories quickly became hierarchical organizations. The success of the factory bureaucracy was important because it encouraged other organizations to adopt the same principles. The bureaucratic form quickly spread to governments, schools, churches, and farms. Even today, we find pressure for other organizations to follow the lead of industry. Governments are continually urged to become more "business-like," and universities face pressure to become more efficient and to meet the specialized needs of industry rather than to provide students with a broader education.

Formal Characteristics of Bureaucracy

Weber set forth several characteristics of bureaucratic organizations. Although real bureaucracies may not feature all of these ideal characteristics, Weber's model highlights the organizational efficiency and productivity that bureaucracies strive for.

Division of Labour   Bureaucratic organizations are characterized by specialization, and each member has a specific status with certain assigned tasks to fulfil. This division of labour requires the employment of specialized experts who are responsible for the effective performance of their duties.

In a university, for example, a distinct division of labour exists between the faculty and the administration. Faculty members primarily are responsible for teaching students and conducting research. Administrators are responsible for the day-to-day operations of the school, external relations with business and

community leaders, fundraising activities, and internal governance, such as control of the budget, allocation of space, and appointments of deans, department heads, and faculty.

Hierarchy of Authority   In the sense that Weber described hierarchy of authority, or chain of command, it includes each lower office being under the control and supervision of a higher one. Charles Perrow (1986) has noted that all groups with a division of labour are hierarchically structured. Although the chain of command is not always followed, "in a crunch, the chain is there for those higher up to use it." Authority that is distributed hierarchically takes the form of a pyramid. Those few individuals at the top have more power and exercise more control than do the many at the lower levels. Hierarchy inevitably influences social interaction. Those who are lower in the hierarchy report to (and often take orders from) those above them in the organizational pyramid. Persons at the upper levels are responsible not only for their own actions but also for those of the individuals they supervise.

In a university, student–faculty relationships are based on both hierarchical and professional authority patterns. Professors have power based on their academic credentials and knowledge. Faculty members also have some degree of academic freedom and self-governance. At the same time, they are hierarchically arranged within the faculty in ranks of instructor, assistant professor, associate professor, and full professor. In the university's vertical chain of command, they also have a position. Suppose that a student has a complaint about an instructor. The chain of command in most universities would require that the student first speak with the department head, then to the dean of the faculty, and, occasionally, even to the vice president of academic affairs, provost, or president.

Rules and Regulations   Weber asserted that rules and regulations establish authority within an organization. These rules are typically standardized and provided to members in a written format. In theory, written rules and regulations offer clear-cut standards for determining satisfactory performance. They also provide continuity so that each new member does not have to reinvent the necessary rules and regulations.

In higher education, student handbooks, catalogues, and course syllabuses provide students with information about the school's rules, regulations, and academic expectations. Faculty and administrators also are provided with policy and procedures manuals that spell out their rights and obligations.

Qualification-based Employment   Bureaucracies hire staff members and professional employees based on specific qualifications. Favouritism, family connections, and other subjective factors not relevant to organizational efficiency are not acceptable criteria for employment. Individual performance is evaluated against specific standards, and promotions are based on merit as spelled out in personnel policies.

In universities, faculty members and administrators are hired based on their academic background and technical qualifications.

Impersonality   A detached approach should prevail toward clients so that personal feelings do not interfere with organizational decisions. Officials must interact with subordinates based on their official status, not on their personal feelings about them.

Impersonality can be seen in standardization of test scores for admission to graduate and professional schools across North America. Standardized examinations for graduate and professional schools include the Graduate Records Exam (GRE), Law School Admission Test (LSAT), and the Medical College Admission Test (MCAT). These criteria supposedly are impartially applied, and individuals are admitted based on their ability to perform in a given academic setting. However, questions may have a class, ethnic, or gender bias, and thus make it harder for some to achieve a high score.

Informal Structure in Bureaucracies
As researchers began to study how bureaucracies really operated, they found that these organizations did not always operate according to Weber's ideal principles. When we look at an organizational chart, we can easily see the official, formal structure of a bureaucracy. However, bureaucracies are more than just organization charts and rulebooks. Organizations are made up of people and people do not exist just to serve organizational goals. They bring with them their concerns about things like careers, friendships, and emotions, and these concerns lead to patterns of activities and interactions that cannot be accounted for by an organizational chart and formal rules. In addition to its formal structure, every bureaucracy has an informal structure, which has been called "bureaucracy's other face" (Page, 1946).

An organization's ***informal structure* comprises those aspects of participants' day-to-day activities and interactions that ignore, bypass, or do not correspond with the official rules and procedures of the bureaucracy.** An example is an informal "grapevine" that spreads information (with varying degrees of accuracy) much faster than do official channels of communication, which tend to be slow and unresponsive. The informal structure also includes the ideology and practices of workers on the job. It is the "informal, customary values and rules [that] mediate the formal authority structure of the workplace and distance workers from its impact" (Benson, 1983:185). Workers create this work culture in order to confront, resist, or adapt to the constraints of their jobs, as well as to guide and interpret social relations on the job (Zavella, 1987).

Hawthorne Studies and Informal Networks
The existence of informal networks was first established by researchers in the Hawthorne studies, which first made social scientists aware of the effect of informal networks on workers' productivity.

In this study, researchers observed fourteen men in the "bank wiring room" who were responsible for making parts of switches for telephone equipment. Although management had offered financial incentives to encourage the men to work harder, the men persisted in working according to their own informal rules and sanctions. For example, they tended to work rapidly in the morning and ease off in the afternoon. They frequently stopped their own work to help another person who had fallen behind. When they got bored, they swapped tasks so that their work was more varied. They played games and made bets on the horse races and on baseball. Two competing cliques formed in the room, each with its own separate games and activities.

Why did these men insist on lagging behind even when they had been offered financial incentives to work harder? Perhaps they feared that the required productivity levels would increase if they showed that they could do more. Some of them also may have feared that they would lose their jobs if the work was finished more rapidly. One fact stood out in the study: The men's productivity level was clearly related to the pressure they received from other members of their informal networks. Those who worked too hard were called "speed kings" and "rate busters"; individuals who worked too slowly were referred to as "chiselers." Those who broke the informal norm against telling a supervisor about someone else's shortcomings were called "squealers." Negative sanctions in the form of "binging" (striking a person on the shoulder) made the workers want to adhere to the informal norms of their clique. Ultimately, the level of productivity was determined by the workers' informal networks, not by the levels set by management (Roethlisberger and Dickson, 1939; Blau and Meyer, 1987).

Positive and Negative Aspects of Informal Structure

Is informal structure good or bad? Should it be controlled or encouraged? Two schools of thought have emerged with regard to these questions. One approach emphasizes control (or eradication) of informal groups; the other suggests that they should be nurtured. Traditional management theories are based on the assumption that people basically are lazy and motivated by greed. Consequently, informal groups must be controlled (or eliminated) in order to ensure greater worker productivity. Proponents of this view cite the bank wiring room study as an example of the importance of controlling informal networks.

By contrast, the other school of thought asserts that people are capable of cooperation. Thus, organizations should foster informal groups that permit people to work more efficiently toward organizational goals. Chester Barnard (1938), an early organizational theorist, focused on the functional aspects of informal groups. He suggested that organizations are cooperative systems in which informal groups "oil the wheels" by providing understanding and motivation for participants. In other words, informal networks serve as a means of communication and cohesion among individuals, as well as protecting the integrity of the individual (Barnard, 1938; Perrow, 1986).

The aftermath of the 9/11 terrorist attacks on the United States provided an interesting example of the importance of informal networks in the functioning of bureaucracies. John Kelly and David Stark (2002) studied how a large financial services firm recovered after the loss of its offices and many employees. While the company had its information systems backed up at a remote site, the passwords necessary to access the system had been lost when those who knew the passwords died. One of the executives of the company described how the passwords were rediscovered:

> The way they got into those systems? They sat around the group, they talked about where they went on vacation, what their kids' names were, what their wives' names were, what their dogs' names were, you know, every imaginable thing about their personal life. And the fact that we knew things about their personal life to break into those IDs and into the systems to be able to get the technology up and running before the bond market

opened, I think [that] is probably the number one connection between technology, communication, and sociology." (Kelly and Stark, 2002)

This is just one of the many ways in which the informal networks formed in the work environment can help bureaucratic organizations accomplish their objectives. A great deal of research on soldiers in combat has shown that bonds with other soldiers in each small squad or platoon have much more impact on performance than abstract notions of patriotism and love for one's country (Marshall, 1947). Thus, even in very large organizations it is close interpersonal relationships that provide meaning and a sense of belonging to individual workers.

Research has confirmed the importance of informal networks in bureaucracies. Exclusion from these networks can have a negative impact on employees. While some scholars have argued that women and visible

Captain Boni Prokopetz is a Burnaby firefighter who has complained of sexual harassment and discrimination at work. Sociologists have found that women in male-dominated fields are less likely than men to be included in informal networks and more likely to be harassed on the job. Are these two factors related? What steps could be taken to reduce the problems of harassment and lack of networks?

minorities receive fairer treatment in larger bureaucracies than they do in smaller organizations, others have stressed that they may be excluded from networks that are important for survival and advancement in the organization (Kanter, 1977; South et al., 1982; Benokraitis and Feagin, 1986; Feagin, 1991).

White women and visible minorities who are employed in positions traditionally held by white men (such as firefighters, police officers, and factory workers) often experience categoric exclusion from the informal structure. Not only do they lack an informal network to "grease the wheels," they also may be harassed and endangered by their co-workers. For example, Captain Boni Prokopetz, a firefighter in Burnaby, B.C., recently claimed that she suffered

sexual harassment, gender discrimination, exposure to pornography, and equipment tampering over an 11-year period (CBC, 2004). In sum, the informal structure is critical for employees—whether they are allowed to participate in it or not.

Shortcomings of Bureaucracies

Weber's description of bureaucracy was intentionally an abstract, idealized model of a rationally organized institution. However, the very characteristics that make up this "rational" model have a dark side that frequently has given this type of organization a bad name (see Figure 6.6). Two of the major problems of bureaucracies are inefficiency and rigidity, and resistance to change.

Figure 6.6	Characteristics and Effects of Bureaucracy

The very characteristics that define Weber's idealized bureaucracy can create or worsen the problems that many people associate with this type of organization.

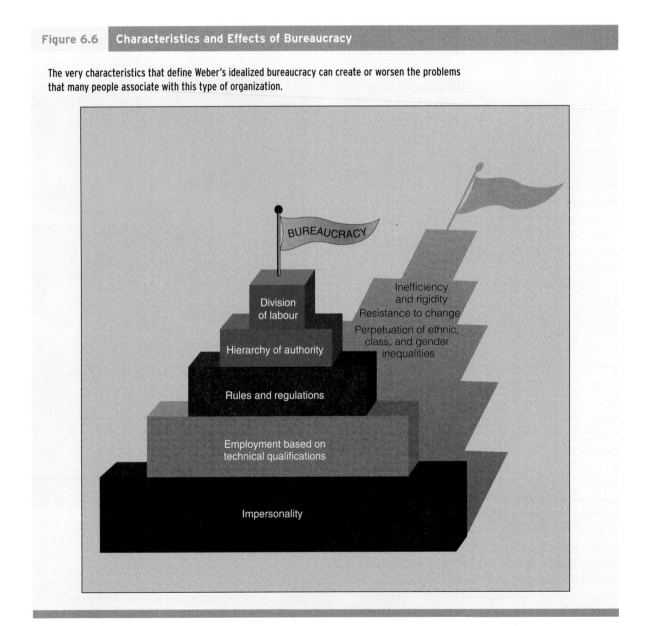

Inefficiency and Rigidity   Bureaucracies experience inefficiency and rigidity at both the upper and lower levels of the organization. The self-protective behaviour of officials at the top may render the organization inefficient. One type of self-protective behaviour is the monopolization of information in order to maintain control over subordinates and outsiders. Information is a valuable commodity in organizations. Budgets and long-range plans theoretically are based on relevant information, and decisions are made based on the best available data. However, those in positions of authority may guard information because it is a source of power for them—others cannot second-guess their decisions without access to relevant (and often confidential) information (Blau and Meyer, 1987).

This information blockage is intensified by the hierarchical arrangement of officials and workers. While those at the top tend to use their power and authority to monopolize information, they also fail to communicate with workers at the lower levels. As a result, they are often unaware of potential problems facing the organization and of high levels of worker frustration. Meanwhile, those at the bottom of the structure hide their mistakes from supervisors, a practice that ultimately may result in disaster for the organization.

Policies and procedures also contribute to inefficiency and rigidity. Peter M. Blau and Marshall W. Meyer (1987) have suggested that bureaucratic regulations are similar to bridges and buildings in that they are designed to withstand far greater stresses than they will ever experience. Accordingly, bureaucratic regulations are written in far greater detail than is necessary, in order to ensure that almost all conceivable situations are covered. **Goal displacement occurs when the rules become an end in themselves rather than a means to an end, and organizational survival becomes more important than achievement of goals** (Merton, 1968). Administrators tend to overconform to the rules because their expertise is knowledge of the regulations, and they are paid to enforce them. Officials are most likely to emphasize rules and procedures when they fear that they may lose their jobs or a "spoils system" that benefits them. They also fear that if they bend the rules for one person, they may be accused of violating the norm of impersonality and engaging in favouritism (Blau and Meyer, 1987).

Bureaucrats may also be inflexible because they fear criticism or liability if they do not follow the rules closely. In the case of Kenneth Payne, the aspiring teacher you read about at the beginning of this chapter, bureaucrats were afraid to waive the need for fingerprints because they were wary of public concern

The "organization man" of the computer age varies widely in manner and appearance, as shown in the contrast between the dark-suited chairman of Microsoft, Bill Gates, and this casually clad employee at Apple Computer.

about the possibility of sexual offenders working in the schools. Even though it made no sense to demand fingerprints from a man who had none, and even though Mr. Payne offered other ways of demonstrating he did not have a criminal record, bureaucrats were not willing to bend the rules to enable him to teach. These bureaucrats were also able to avoid taking responsibility for their stupid decision by saying that they were "just following the rules." Mistakes can be blamed on the bureaucracy rather than on the individuals who run it.

Inefficiency and rigidity occur at the lower levels of the organization as well. Workers often engage in ritualism; that is, they become most concerned with "going through the motions" and "following the rules." According to Robert Merton (1968), the term *bureaucratic personality* **describes those workers who are more concerned with following correct procedures than they are with getting the job done correctly.** Such workers usually are able to handle routine situations effectively but frequently are incapable of handling a unique problem or an emergency. Thorstein Veblen (1967/1899) used the term *trained incapacity* to characterize situations in which workers have become so highly specialized, or have been given such fragmented jobs to do, that they are unable to come up with creative solutions to problems. Workers who have reached this point also tend to experience bureaucratic alienation— they really do not care what is happening around them. In Box 6.2, you can learn how bureaucratic inefficiency contributed to serious terrorist attacks in Canada and the United States.

Resistance to Change   Resistance to change occurs in all bureaucratic organizations. This resistance can make it very difficult for organizations to adapt to new circumstances. Many workers are

BOX 6.2 SOCIOLOGY AND THE LAW

How Bureaucratic Inefficiency Contributed to Terrorist Attacks

Since Max Weber's time, sociologists have studied how the characteristics of bureaucracies can contribute to or impede information flow within and between large-scale organizations. Interest in this topic has increased because of failures of governmental organizations to properly utilize information that might have prevented major terrorist strikes in Canada and the United States.

In 1985, an explosion destroyed Air India Flight 182 and killed 329 people. The flight had originated in Vancouver and most of the victims were Canadians. After nearly two decades of investigation, two Sikh militants were tried for the crime, but they were acquitted in 2005. Following the trial, many of the victims' families were critical of the work of the RCMP and the Canadian Security and Intelligence Service (CSIS). While little official information has been made available, it is clear that the investigation into the bombing was seriously flawed and that there was little cooperation between the RCMP and CSIS. Some observers have claimed that CSIS had information that could have prevented the attack but that no action was taken on this information. While a more detailed examination is needed before blame can be assigned, it is likely that bureaucratic inefficiencies facilitated the attack and certainly hindered the subsequent investigation. One specific problem is that CSIS and the RCMP have separate and distinct roles.

CSIS is responsible for collecting intelligence on possible terrorist activity, while the RCMP is responsible for investigating criminal matters and assisting in the prosecution of accused persons. There is a history of poor relationships between these agencies, and without close cooperation there is a very real danger that information collected by one agency will not be made available to the other. Responding to RCMP claims that CSIS was negligent in destroying taped wiretap records of conversations prior to the attack involving the men who may have been responsible, the CSIS Director General of Counter Terrorism said that "it is important to bear in mind that the Service [CSIS] does not set out to collect evidence but rather intelligence and that the RCMP did have at least eight days before the erasure of the tapes to indicate to the Service their evidentiary value. This was not done and so . . . it is difficult for me to conceive how this . . . incident can in any way be construed as a lack of cooperation by this Service with the police investigation" (Warren, 1986). While each bureaucracy may believe that it has done its job, the failure to properly assess and share this evidence may have contributed to the murder of hundreds of people.

These problems are certainly not unique to Canada. Following the 2001 terrorist attacks on the United States, the Federal Bureau of Investigation, the Central Intelligence Agency, and other U.S.

governmental organizations faced similar criticism about how they used and shared information before these attacks. The U.S. Senate Judiciary Committee conducted hearings in an effort to learn what information about terrorist activities and possible U.S. targets had been available to federal agencies, such as the Federal Bureau of Investigation and the Central Intelligence Agency in advance of September 11, and why the government had not acted on available information in a manner that might have prevented the attacks. The Judiciary Committee interviewed FBI agent Coleen Rowley, who identified information known by the FBI that might have prevented the attacks if it had been used properly. She discussed her belief that the culture of the FBI had prevented the organization from acting on what it knew (*New York Times*, 2002b):

AGENT ROWLEY: We have a culture in the FBI that there's a certain pecking order, and it's pretty strong. And it's very rare that someone picks up the phone and calls a rank or two above themselves. It would have to be only on the strongest reasons. Typically, you would have to . . . pick up

the phone and talk to somebody who is at your rank. So when you have an item that requires review by a higher level, it's incumbent for you to go to a higher-level person in your office and then for that person to make a call. . . .

SENATOR GRASSLEY: In your letter [to the FBI director], you mention a culture of fear, especially a fear of taking action, and the problem of careerism. Could you talk about how this hurts investigations in the field, what the causes are, and what you think might fix these problems?

AGENT ROWLEY: [W]hen I looked up the definition [of careerism], I really said [it's] unbelievable how appropriate that is. I think the FBI does have a problem with that. And if I remember right, it means, "promoting one's career over integrity." So, when people make decisions, and it's basically so that [they] can get to the next level and not rock—either it's not rock the boat or do what a boss says without question. And either way that works, if you're making a decision to try to get to the next level, but you're not making that decision for the real right reason, that's a problem. . . .

reluctant to change because they have adapted their professional and personal lives to the old way of doing their jobs. Also, workers in some fields have seen previous change efforts fail and may not want to make a commitment to the latest effort at transforming their organization. Those trying to implement change can have a difficult task breaking through this resistance.

The structure of bureaucracies can make this situation worse. The traditional bureaucracy has a very hierarchical structure with many layers of authority and reporting lines that run from bottom to top. Management is separated from labour, clerical workers from professional workers, and people doing one function from those doing another function. This structure creates structural barriers to communication and to joint problem solving. People become defined by their positions. Information is restricted and problems are dealt with in a segmented way that may have more to do with the goals of a subunit than of the organization as a whole. People are rewarded for not taking risks and punished when they try to make changes. Often, people have no structural way of getting innovative ideas from the bottom to the top, so they give up trying. Writing

about a textile company that for decades had been putting up with frequent and costly yarn breakages, Rosabeth Moss Kanter provides an example of this kind of blockage:

A new plant manager interested in improving employee communication and involvement discovered a foreign-born worker with an ultimately successful idea for modifying the machine to reduce breakage—and was shocked to learn that the man had wondered about the machine modification for thirty-two years. "Why didn't you say something before?" the manager asked. The reply: "My supervisor wasn't interested and I had no one else to tell it to." (Kanter, 1983:70)

Organizations that resist change, rather than adapt to it, are not likely to survive and certainly will not flourish. Thus leaders of many different organizations face the task of developing new organizational models that are better suited to today's environment. Consider the challenges faced by leaders of corporations such as those discussed in Box 6.5, "The Internet and the Organization," on page 182.

Bureaucracy and Oligarchy

Max Weber believed that bureaucracy was necessary because it achieved coordination and control and thus efficiency in administration (Blau and Meyer, 1987). Sociologist Charles Perrow (1986) has suggested that bureaucracy produces a high standard of living for persons living in industrialized countries because of its superiority as a "social tool over other forms of organization."

Weber, however, was not completely favourable toward bureaucracies. He believed such organizations stifle human initiative and creativity, thus producing an "iron cage." Bureaucracy also places an enormous amount of unregulated and often unperceived social power in the hands of a very few leaders. Such a situation is referred to as an *oligarchy*—the rule of the many by the few.

Why do a small number of leaders at the top make all of the important organizational decisions? According to German political sociologist Robert Michels (1949/1911), all organizations encounter the **iron law of oligarchy**—**the tendency to become a bureaucracy ruled by the few.** His central idea was that those who control bureaucracies not only wield power but also have an interest in retaining their power. In his research, Michels studied socialist parties and labour unions in Europe before World War I and concluded that even some of the most radical leaders of these organizations had a vested interest in clinging to their power. In this case, if the leaders lost their power positions, they once again would become manual labourers.

Is the iron law of oligarchy correct? Many scholars believe that Michels overstated his case. The leaders in most organizations do not have unlimited power. Divergent groups within a large-scale organization often compete for power, and informal networks can be used to "go behind the backs" of leaders. In addition, members routinely challenge, and sometimes remove, their leaders when they are not pleased with their actions. However, the concentration of power and restricted communication discussed by Michels leads to a degree of inflexibility that makes it difficult for organizations to operate effectively in today's competitive and rapidly changing environment. The company that employs Dilbert would not likely last very long in the real world (see Box 6.3).

McDonaldization

Weber's work on bureaucracy was based on his view that rationalization was an inevitable part of the social world. George Ritzer has updated Weber's work by looking at what he calls McDonaldization—"the process by which the principles of the fast-food restaurant are coming to dominate more and more sectors of American society, as well as of the rest of the world" (1993:292). Ritzer feels that McDonald's restaurants embodied the principles of rationalization and established a model that has been emulated by many other types of organizations. To Ritzer, fast-food restaurants go beyond the Weberian model of bureaucracy. The basic elements of McDonaldization are

- *Efficiency.* Fast-food restaurants operate like an assembly line. Food is cooked, assembled, and served according to a standardized procedure. Customers line up or move quickly past a drive-through window. Despite the McDonald's slogan, "We do it all for you," it is the customer who picks up the food, takes it to the table, and cleans up the garbage at the end of the meal.
- *Calculability.* The emphasis is on speed and quantity rather than quality. Cooking and serving operations are precisely timed, and the emphasis on speed often results in poor employee morale and high rates of turnover. Customers are expected to play their part by finishing their meals as soon as possible, and restaurants are designed to encourage customers to leave quickly.
- *Predictability.* Standard menus and scripted encounters with staff make the experience predictable for customers. The food is supposed to taste the same wherever it is served.
- *Control.* Fast-food restaurants have never allowed individual employees much discretion; instead, employees must follow detailed procedures. The degree of control has been enhanced through technology. For example, automatic french-fry cookers and other devices ensure a standardized product. Nobody pretends to be a chef in a fast-food restaurant.
- *Irrationalities of rationality.* Fast-food restaurants are dehumanizing for both customers and employees.

Ritzer feels that McDonaldization is expanding to other parts of our lives and to other parts of the world. We can see that characteristics, such as efficiency and calculability, have spread to many different settings, including government, health care, and the business world. Can you think of examples from your own experience?

BOX 6.3 SOCIOLOGY AND THE MEDIA

Dilbert and the Bureaucracy

Sociologist Robert Merton has pointed out that successful bureaucracies must attain a high degree of reliability of behaviour. Thus, bureaucratic structures exert pressure on officials to be "methodical, prudent, disciplined" (1968:198) and follow the rules in order to accomplish the goals of the organization. However, Merton has also shown that goal displacement can occur and for some bureaucrats the rules become an end in themselves rather than just a means to an end. When this occurs, organizations become rigid and inflexible.

Our experiences with red tape and other bureaucratic inefficiencies have been satirized by cartoonist (and disillusioned bureaucrat) Scott Adams. In the late 1980s, Adams began passing his humorous cartoons around the office at Pacific Bell. Since then, *Dilbert* has become a phenomenal success and is read in more than 1,700 papers in thirty-nine countries. *Dilbert* ridicules many of the worst features of bureaucracy, including stupid bosses, reliance on technology instead of people, cubicles, management consultants, pointless meetings, and inflexibility. (For examples of the cartoon, go to http://www.unitedmedia.com/comics/dilbert).

Readership is not the only sign that *Dilbert* strikes a responsive chord with workers. The cartoons are posted on doors, walls, and desks in thousands of offices, and many of Adams's ideas come

from readers' suggestions. The British magazine *The Economist* attributes *Dilbert's* popularity to the fact that the comic strip taps into three trends that are troubling workers:

1. The obsession with work as employees are forced to labour harder to compensate for the effects of downsizing;
2. Fear in the workplace as workers are laid off or see their wage increases falling far behind those of their managers; and
3. A growing cynicism about new management fads that have led to constant reorganization but that seem to have had little impact on efficiency or on job satisfaction.

Ironically, while many workers feel *Dilbert* says what they are thinking about stupid and uncaring managers, the leaders of many of North America's largest corporations have used the cartoons for training and corporate communications.

Sources: *The Economist*, 1997; Merton, 1968; Whitaker, 1997. DILBERT reprinted by permission of United Features Syndicate, Inc.

ORGANIZATIONS OF THE FUTURE: THE NETWORK ORGANIZATION

As you learned in the discussion of the rise of bureaucracies, the form of organizations changes over time to accommodate other kinds of social change. While we can never be certain about the future, broad social trends, such as globalization, technological innovation, and the increased prevalence of a service economy (see Chapter 13, "The Economy and Work") make it likely that networks will be the

dominant organization of the future. One of the leading proponents of this view is social theorist Manuel Castells, who argues that "the old order, governed by discrete individual units in the pursuit of money, efficiency, happiness, or power, is being replaced by a novel one in which motives, decisions, and actions flow from ever more fluid, yet ever-present networks. It is networks, not the firm, bureaucracy, or the family that gets things done" (Esping Anderson, 2000:68).

You can get an idea of how global networks operate by reading about the structure of terrorist organizations in Box 6.4, or by thinking about the ways in which illicit drugs get from the coca fields of

Colombia and the poppy fields of Thailand to users on the streets of Halifax, Toronto, and Victoria. Large bureaucracies are not involved in either of these complex global enterprises, as terrorists and drug dealers operate very effectively through decentralized networks that extend around the globe. One reason why drug suppression strategies have not succeeded is because there is no company called Global Drugs Incorporated that can be easily located and destroyed by law enforcement agencies. Instead there are shifting, fluid networks of people who are difficult to identify and who are easily replaced when the legal system takes them out of the network. Similar problems face those who are trying to deal with the threat of terrorism.

Another example of the operation of a flexible global network is the production of open source software, such as the Linux operating system and the Firefox Internet browser. This software was not produced by a large profit-making corporation, such as Microsoft, but by networks of people working together with no expectation of profit. The product is available freely to anyone who wishes to download it,

and programmers all over the world can work on improvements in the software. While some coordination is necessary to develop a product that can be used by the public, no large bureaucracy is required and individual users are free to modify programs to suit their own needs.

Networks have always had an advantage over other organizational forms because they are very agile and can quickly adapt to new circumstances. However, the ability to coordinate network activities has been very weak compared to hierarchical bureaucratic organizations that have well-specified lines of communication and means of coordination. This has meant that bureaucracies have had a competitive advantage in handling complex tasks (Castells, 2000b). Von Moltke's nineteenth-century Prussian army could not have operated as a network because proper communication and coordination would have been impossible. However, modern information and communication technology has now provided networks with a competitive advantage. Each part of a network can communicate instantly with other parts and those responsible for the network can constantly

BOX 6.4 SOCIOLOGY IN GLOBAL PERSPECTIVE

The Structure of Terrorist Networks

Earlier in this chapter, we described how the growth of large armies contributed to the development of the bureaucratic form of organization. These large armies represented the governments of established states. Recent terrorist attacks in the United States, Spain, Russia, Indonesia, England, and elsewhere and the difficulties in maintaining order in Iraq following the U.S. invasion in 2003 have drawn attention to what military planners refer to as *asymmetrical warfare*. This term refers to attacks by small groups of people who usually do not represent states or governments upon much larger and stronger opponents. Terrorists do not directly confront their opponents since they would be quickly defeated in such a confrontation. Rather, they use covert tactics, such as car bombs and suicide bombings, that are very difficult to prevent.

In order to work effectively against larger and more powerful opponents, terrorist groups must develop organizational structures that are very difficult to identify and to fight against. Rather than

trying to form large hierarchical armies, terrorist groups, such as al-Qaeda, have evolved quite sophisticated network structures. These networks are made up of loosely coupled cells, each of which has only a few members. This structure allows for a high level of secrecy, flexibility, and innovation. Participants in the network can operate in a coordinated way because they have relationships with other members of the network with whom they share a common vision of the future, not because they are controlled by a bureaucracy. Al-Qaeda network members are linked by a common religious background and philosophy and through the leadership of Osama bin Laden and his associates.

The two diagrams in this box illustrate the nature of terrorist networks. Figure 6.7 is a simplified diagram of the al-Qaeda network (Marion and Uhl-Bien, 2003). This structure is very different from the hierarchical organization charts of the military and security organizations that are trying to defeat al-Qaeda. Their loose and flexible network structure makes it very difficult to deal a major blow to terrorist organizations. For example, the network has roots in many different countries and information and funds can flow relatively freely from one jurisdiction to another. On the other hand, security and intelligence agencies are based in individual countries and for a variety of reasons find it very difficult to work cooperatively (Arquilla and Ronfeldt, 2001). You can contrast the fluid network of al-Qaeda shown in Figure 6.7 with the hierarchical, vertical structure of the armies and governments opposing it. Using modern communications technology, including the Internet, information can flow to all parts of the network much more easily than can information that must be filtered through national governments and their internal bureaucracies (see Box 6.2).

Figure 6.8 (Krebs, 2002) represents an attempt to map the network of the hijackers responsible for the September 11 attacks on the United States. The grey lines indicate trusted prior contacts among the hijackers, while the gold lines represent contacts made at meetings in which the attacks were coordinated. You can see the central role of Mohamed Atta, who was the leader of the September 11 operation. The strategy of minimizing ties among members of the network is a deliberate one—if security personnel identify or apprehend one or two members of the network, they can provide only limited information about other members so the entire network would not be jeopardized. In a videotape that was found at an al-Qaeda training camp in Afghanistan, Osama bin Laden said that, "Those who were trained to fly didn't know the others. One group of people did not know the other group" (Department of Defense, 2001 cited in Krebs, 2002:46). It is very difficult for those opposing such networks to be able to target more than a limited part of the terrorist organization.

Figure 6.7	Simplified Representation of the al-Qaeda Network

Subcategories identify the given component's functions; arrows indicate direction of moderately to tightly coupled dependency. Al-Qaeda refers to bin Laden's leadership core. Each component is itself comprised of numerous aggregates linked in loose to tightly coupled networks of interdependency.

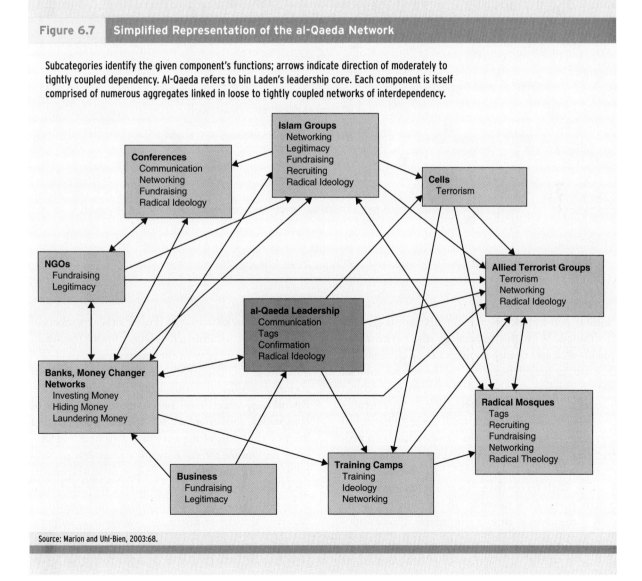

Source: Marion and Uhl-Bien, 2003:68.

| Figure 6.8 | Trusted Prior Contacts and Meeting Ties of al-Qaeda Members Involved in the 9/11 Terror Attacks |

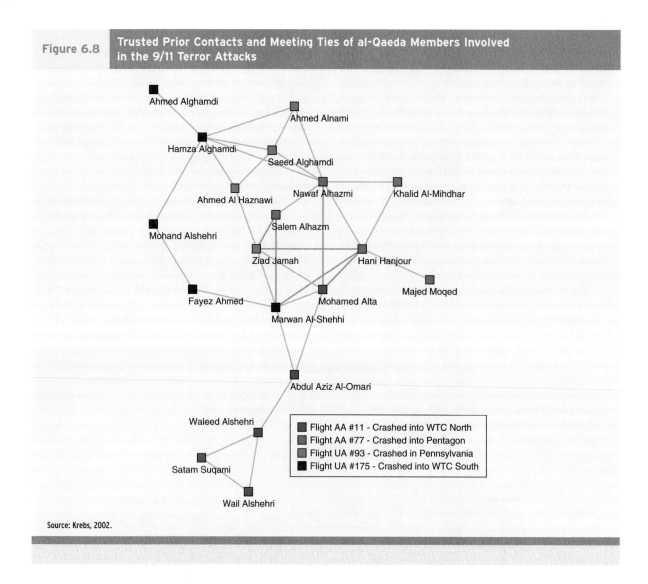

Source: Krebs, 2002.

monitor performance even if the network is globally distributed. With this technology, the network can quickly shift and change as pieces can be eliminated if they are no longer useful or can be temporarily set aside if they are not needed for a particular project (Castells, 2000b). It is more difficult to centrally control a network than a traditional hierarchical organization because once the network has been programmed and set in motion it may be difficult for anyone, even those who started the network, to shut it down. With no central communication and control system, parts of the network can continue to operate even if the central core is eliminated. Thus, opponents of al-Qaeda could not shut down the network by simply closing down some of its pieces. Even Osama bin Laden would have difficulty closing down

the network or changing its goals if other members of al-Qaeda and its affiliated groups around the world wanted to continue with their activities.

Castells (2000a, 2000b) speaks of a new type of economic organization called the **network enterprise. Businesses, which may be companies or parts of companies, join together for specific projects that become the focus of the network**. This structure gives those responsible for the network a great deal of flexibility, as they can select and change network partners based upon factors, such as cost, efficiency, and technological innovation. Automobile manufacturing illustrates this network structure. While large corporations, such as Ford and Toyota, still do the final assembly of vehicles, their factories do not produce most of the components that make up the vehicle. This manufacturing is done by hundreds of smaller companies around the world that deliver completed modules to the assembly plants where the vehicles are put together. The Dell laptop computer that you may be working on is also the product of a network enterprise (Friedman, 2005). Dell sells its products over the Internet and by telephone rather than in stores, so your order may be taken by a person in Bangalore, India rather by a clerk in your own city. The hardware that makes up the computer was manufactured by companies in Israel, the Philippines, Malaysia, Costa Rica, China, Taiwan, South Korea, Germany, Japan, Mexico, Singapore, Indonesia, India, and Thailand. The computers are assembled in Dell factories located in Ireland, China, Brazil, Malaysia, and the United States. Thomas Friedman describes how the company fills its orders:

> "In an average day, we sell 140,000 to 150,000 computers," explained Dick Hunter, one of Dell's three global production managers. "Those orders come over Dell.com or over the telephone. As soon as these orders come in, our suppliers know about it. They get a signal based on every component in the machine you ordered, so the supplier knows just what he has to deliver. If you are supplying power cords for desktops, you can see minute by minute how many power cords you are going to have to deliver." Every two hours, the Dell factory in Penang [Malaysia] sends an e-mail to the various SLCs [supplier logistics centres] nearby, telling each one what parts and what quantities of those parts it wants delivered within the next ninety minutes—and not one minute later. Within ninety minutes, trucks from the various SLCs around Penang pull up to the Dell manufacturing plant and unload the parts needed for all those notebooks ordered in the last two hours. This goes on all day, every two hours. As soon as those parts arrive at the factory, it takes thirty minutes for Dell employees to unload the parts, register their bar codes, and put them into bins for assembly. "We know where every part in the SLC is in the Dell system at all times," said Hunter. (2005:415)

This efficient supply and management system is a major reason why Dell is such a formidable competitor in the computer manufacturing business and has helped to dramatically reduce computer prices over the past decade.

While Castells mainly discusses business corporations in his analysis of network enterprises, the network form of organization is becoming more prevalent in other fields as well. Only a few years ago, academic research was typically conducted by individual researchers or by teams of researchers at one or two universities working on projects together. However, governments are now using their funding to promote research that involves large teams of researchers exploring broad topics related to government priorities. One example is the AUTO21 Network of Centres of Excellence (http://www.auto21.ca) that was set up to look at the Automobile of the 21st Century. The AUTO21 network involves more than 200 researchers and 300 graduate students from 44 different Canadian universities. Nearly 80 corporations and 44 provincial and federal government departments are also affiliated with the network. The researchers represent a wide variety of disciplines including engineering, physics, chemistry, history, medicine, and sociology, and are all doing work on topics related to the automobile of the future. Groups of researchers move in and out of the network as projects end and new ones begin. Two major functions of the network are to break down barriers among people from different disciplines and to share information with corporations and government agencies. A small staff at the University of Windsor administers and coordinates the network and distributes funding to the researchers, but virtually all of the research is done elsewhere. This structure enables the government and industry partners who fund the network to benefit from the work of the best researchers in Canada, but the loose network structure means that new research topics and researchers can easily be added; when research priorities change or when funding runs out the researchers can simply move on to other projects and there is no large bureaucracy that would need to be shut down.

A critical factor in the development of widely dispersed network organizations has been the development of modern communications technology. Networks are held together by the rapid flow of information rather than by bricks and mortar and a rigid organizational chart like that of the industrial organization. The globalized production processes used by Toyota and Dell would not be possible without instant global communication, and even the AUTO21 network, with all its components in Canada, would be very difficult to coordinate without the Internet. It is worth noting that the Internet itself is a decentralized and loosely coupled structure. The Internet was originally designed as way of ensuring that communications systems would survive an attack targeted at the central hubs of information systems. Instead of flowing from a central hub, information on the Internet is transmitted in small packets that can follow a wide range of electronic routes and are put together at the destination computer (Castells, 2000a).

Nobody owns the Internet, so it is universally accessible to anyone who has a computer and a connection. While the Internet is vulnerable to a variety of threats, including computer hacking, it would be almost impossible to completely shut it down. This flexibility and resilience is what makes the Internet such a valuable tool for networks. (See Box 6.5 for a discussion of how the Internet is transforming the retail industry).

However, Castells (2004) points out that it is not simply the technology that is critical, but also the cultural and organizational means of using the technology. This means that simply having computers is not enough to guarantee access to the networked global economy. Countries that have ineffective systems of government, that cannot provide trained workers, and that do not have an entrepreneurial culture that supports innovation will be excluded from these networks. While India has been very successful in getting involved in network enterprises because of an entrepreneurial culture, a democratic government, and the presence of a well-educated workforce with English

language skills, many parts of Africa and Latin America have virtually no involvement in the new economy.

Sociologists are also concerned with assessing the impact of network enterprises on people. While this network structure can help corporations to become more profitable, the impact upon workers has not always been as positive. For example, unions lose much of their power when production at one plant can be quickly moved to another part of the network in a different country. Thus a strike may result in the permanent closure of a factory and the movement of jobs offshore. You will read about the impact of these changes upon the workforce in Chapters 9 ("Global Stratification") and 13 ("The Economy and Work"). It is quite likely that the work lives of today's university students will be affected in many ways—some positive but others negative—by the shift to networked organizations. Because network enterprises are very fluid and can quickly transform themselves, you should anticipate that your working lives may also change very rapidly after you enter the labour market.

BOX 6.5 SOCIOLOGY AND TECHNOLOGY

The Internet and the Organization

Do you enjoy going to the grocery store, standing in line at the checkout counter, and carrying your groceries to the car? What if you could order your groceries on the Internet and have them delivered to your home for less than what it would cost to buy them at the store? The Internet may have a major impact on the organizational structure of many businesses, including the food industry, by simplifying product distribution. One company, Grocery Gateway (http://www.grocerygateway.com), sells groceries over the Internet in Ontario, and other Canadian companies have also entered the business. If large numbers of people begin to shop on the Internet, we may see what some analysts have called *disintermediation*–or removing the middleman. An Internet transaction is made directly between the producer and the consumer. The Internet will allow manufacturers to sell their products faster and more cheaply without going through wholesalers and retailers. This may have a major impact on the structure of organizations that deal with consumer goods.

The greeting card business shows us how the Internet can provide new ways of serving customer needs. For the past century, companies have designed and produced greeting cards and have sold the cards to wholesalers, who distributed them to retail outlets. Customers bought the cards, bought stamps, and mailed them to the recipient through Canada Post. A new approach taken by Blue Mountain (http://www.bluemountain.com) eliminates the need for printing and for wholesalers and retailers. Blue Mountain designs are sent electronically over the Internet. If this method of sending greetings becomes popular, several bureaucracies will be significantly affected. Can you think through some of the consequences of such a change?

Electronic commerce has become common in areas, such as banking, travel services, selling stocks, and selling goods, such as automobiles, flowers, and pizza. It is much cheaper for these organizations to transact business over the Internet. What do you think will happen to the jobs of those who sell stocks and work in banks and travel agencies? How will the change affect the bureaucracies in which they work?

If disintermediation because of Internet commerce becomes a trend, there will also be a new need for electronic intermediaries who can provide guidance and assistance for consumers and provide marketing services and transaction assistance for producers. Are such intermediaries likely to work within traditional bureaucratic organizations? One clue to the future may come from currently successful intermediary organizations such as Amazon.ca, an Internet bookseller. Amazon.ca is an intermediary between publisher and consumer, but rather than being a large, formal bureaucracy, it is a virtual company with little presence outside of cyberspace. Despite calling itself "The Earth's Biggest Bookstore" with its list of over a million titles, Amazon.ca keeps only a very small stock of books on hand. The rest are ordered electronically and shipped from traditional book wholesalers. Because of its low overhead costs, it can sell books more cheaply than traditional retailers. This means that many of these businesses may be in jeopardy.

Internet commerce now represents only a small portion of consumer sales. However, several factors suggest that Internet commerce will continue to expand very rapidly: use of the Internet is growing; those who use the Internet tend to be well-educated people with high incomes who are attractive to marketers; and secure payment mechanisms are making people more comfortable about providing their credit card numbers to Internet vendors. Because of this growth, we should soon be able to get a better indication of how Internet commerce will develop and of how it will affect the structure of traditional bureaucracies.

The Internet also provides opportunities for illegal transactions. For example, the music industry is threatened by the development of technology that allows people to download music from the Internet without paying royalties to the companies or musicians. Many different programs can be used to download music, which can then be played on conventional stereo systems, stored on players designed to hold MP3 music, or recorded on a custom CD. While some people use MP3 technology to purchase music online or to record songs that are in the public domain, many others use it to record illegally. Services, such as iTunes, have been successful in selling music over the Internet, but unauthorized downloading (which in 2005 was still legal in Canada if done for personal use) will be very difficult to stop.

The development of software such as Morpheus, Kazaa, and Gnutella has made downloading very easy. Ian Clarke, the developer of Freenet, has said he thinks that in twenty to forty years people will "look at the idea that you can own information in the same way as gold or real estate the way we look at witch burning today" (Markoff, 2000:B14).

Even if there were no illegal copying, the music industry is still threatened by the fact that Internet technology allows artists to sell their music directly to the public without going through the intermediary of the music companies.

CHAPTER REVIEW

■ How do sociologists distinguish among social groups, aggregates, and categories?

Sociologists define a social group as a collection of two or more people who interact frequently, share a sense of belonging, and depend on one another. People who happen to be in the same place at the same time are considered an aggregate. Those who share a similar characteristic are considered a category. Neither aggregates nor categories are considered social groups.

■ How do sociologists classify groups?

Primary groups are small and personal, and members engage in emotion-based interactions over an extended period. Secondary groups are larger and more specialized, and members have less personal and more formal, goal-oriented relationships. Ingroups are groups to which we belong and with which we identify. Outgroups are groups we do not belong to or perhaps feel hostile toward.

■ What is the significance of group size?

In small groups, all members know one another and interact simultaneously. In groups with more than three members, communication dynamics change and members tend to assume specialized tasks.

■ What is a bureaucracy?

A bureaucracy is a formal organization characterized by hierarchical authority, division of labour, explicit procedures, and impersonality. According to Max Weber, bureaucracy supplies a rational means of attaining organizational goals because it contributes to coordination and control.

■ What is "bureaucracy's other face"?

"Bureaucracy's other face" is the informal structure of daily activities and interactions that bypass the official rules and procedures. Informal networks may enhance productivity or may be counterproductive to the organization. Informal networks also may be detrimental to those who are excluded from them, typically any minority within the organization.

■ What are the weaknesses of bureaucracies?

There are two major shortcomings of bureaucracies. They may be inefficient and rigid, particularly when an organization's survival becomes more important than the achievement of its goals. They may resist change, which can lead to bureaucratic enlargement or incompetence.

■ What is an oligarchy?

An oligarchy is the rule of the many by the few. In bureaucracies with an oligarchical structure, those in control have not only power but also a great interest in maintaining that power.

■ What form will large organizations likely take in the future?

While we can never be certain about the future, broad social trends, such as globalization, technological innovation, and the increased prevalence of a service economy, make it likely that networks will be the dominant organization of the future. Networked organizations, which are made possible by modern communications technology, are very flexible and can respond very quickly to social change.

KEY TERMS

aggregate 155
bureaucracy 167
bureaucratic personality 174
category 155

conformity 161
dyad 160
goal displacement 173
groupthink 165
informal structure 170
ingroup 157
iron law of oligarchy 176
network enterprise 180
outgroup 157
rationality 168
reference group 158
small group 160
triad 161

NET LINKS

To read about the latest research in the area of formal organizations, see the Web site for the journal *Administrative Science Quarterly* at:
http://www.johnson.cornell.edu/publications/asq/

Government is a very complex bureaucracy. To see the number of departments in the Canadian federal government, go to:
http://www.canada.gc.ca/

Read more about Stanley Milgram's work on obedience and hear audio clips from one of his experiments at:
http://elvers.stjoe.udayton.edu/history/people/Milgram.html

To read an interview with George Ritzer concerning his view of the McDonaldization of society, go to:
http://www.mcspotlight.org/people/interviews/ritzer_george.html

QUESTIONS FOR CRITICAL THINKING

1. Who might be more likely to conform in a bureaucracy, those with power or those wanting more power?
2. Do you think the insights gained from Milgram's research on obedience outweigh the elements of deception and stress that were forced on his subjects?
3. Many students have worked at a McDonald's or at some other fast-food restaurant. Relate your experience (or that of your friends) to George Ritzer's analysis of "McDonaldization."
4. Downloading music and movies from the Internet has become very popular in Canada and in other countries. The film and music industries are trying very hard to convince the government to pass new legislation to combat this downloading. What are the arguments of those who think that this material

should be widely available on the Internet? What are the counter-arguments of those who wish to see downloading regulated? Which side do you support in this debate?

SUGGESTED READINGS

Organizations are examined from a variety of perspectives in these interesting books:

Harvey Krahn and Graham S. Lowe. *Work, Industry and Canadian Society* (4th ed.). Toronto: Thomson Nelson, 2002.

Manuel Castells. *The Rise of the Network Society* (2nd ed.). Oxford, UK: Blackwell Publishers. 2000.

Wallace Clement. *The Canadian Corporate Elite.* Toronto: McClelland and Stewart, 1975.

Kathy E. Ferguson. *The Feminist Case Against Bureaucracy.* Philadelphia: Temple University Press, 1984.

Richard H. Hall. *Organizations: Structures, Processes, and Outcomes.* Englewood Cliffs, N.J.: Prentice-Hall, 1991.

Rosabeth Moss Kanter. *Men and Women of the Corporation.* New York: Basic Books, 1993; orig. pub. 1977.

Gifford Pinchot and Elizabeth Pinchot. *The End of Bureaucracy and the Rise of the Intelligent Organization.* San Francisco: Berrett-Koehler, 1993.

ONLINE STUDY AND RESEARCH TOOLS

THOMSONNOW™

Go to **http://hed.nelson.com** to link to ThomsonNOW for *Sociology in Our Times*, Fourth Canadian Edition, your online study tool. First take the **Pre-Test** for this chapter to get your personalized **Study Plan,** which will identify topics you need to review and direct you to the appropriate resources. Then take the **Post-Test** to determine what concepts you have mastered and what you still need work on.

INFOTRAC®

Infotrac College Edition is included free with every new copy of this text. Explore this online library for additional readings, review, and a handy resource for assignments. Visit **www.infotrac-college.com** to access this online database of full-text articles. Enter the key terms from this chapter to start your search.

Crime and Deviance

Maurice "Mom" Boucher was the most powerful Hells Angels leader in Canada. President of the Quebec Nomads chapter, Boucher was consolidating his power over organized crime in Quebec. In 1997, he decided to go to war against the justice system. His first act in this war was to order the killing of some prison guards. Stephane "Godasse" Gagné was ordered to carry out the killings. Gagne was a member of the Rockers, one of the Hells Angels puppet gangs that did much of the Angels' dirty work. For several years he enforced drug debts and served as a bodyguard and did other jobs for members of the Hells Angels. In two separate operations, Gagné and another gang member killed guards Diane Lavigne and Pierre Rondeau. Gagné was eventually arrested and confessed to the murders. In exchange for some relatively minor concessions, he also agreed to testify against Mom Boucher for ordering the murders.

Boucher was tried in 1998. While Boucher was acquitted at this trial, the Crown successfully appealed the acquittal because the judge's instructions to the jury were biased. At his second trial in 2002, Boucher was found guilty and is currently serving a life sentence.

At Boucher's first trial, Gagné testified about his leader's role in the killing of the prison guards. In his cross-examination, Boucher's lawyer, Jacques Larochelle, tried to discredit Gagné's testimony by highlighting his criminal past. Gagné's responses illustrate the brutality of organized crime:

"During this entire time, you evidently had no respect for authority?"

"No."

"No respect for other people's property."

"No."

"No respect for the truth?"

"No."

Larochelle then tried to show Gagné's readiness to do anything he thought would please the Hells Angels. He recalled a hunger strike at Sorel prison that Mom ordered because he was sick of eating shepherd's pie. One inmate broke ranks and ate the meal.

"And without anyone asking you to do it," Larochelle asked, "you went over and beat him up?"

"Yes."

"In fact you courageously waited until he was asleep and you went to attack him in his bed, is that correct?"

"Yes."

"You hit him so hard with your fist that the bone came out his nose—all so that you would be noticed, is that correct?"

"Yes."

Larochelle also elicited the sordid details of Gagné's attempted murder of the drug dealer Christian Bellemare. He showed how Gagné acted alone, deciding to kill him because he owed him money.

"The first two bullets hit Bellemare in the throat or in that area. But the other bullets didn't fire, and Bellemare was still alive?" Larochelle said, taking the jurors back to the scene of the crime.

"Yes," Gagne agreed.

"You went running up to Bellemare and you put your fingers around his neck, your two hands around his neck, and squeezed?"

"Yes."

"He tries to talk, is that correct?" Larochelle pushed. "You have a good idea of what he is trying to tell you, I imagine?"

"Yes."

"Don't kill me, or something like that?" the lawyer suggested.

"Something like that, yes," said Gagné.

"That didn't impress you?"

"I had a job to do," he admitted. (Sher and Marsden, 2003:147-148)

Despite the Hells Angels' attempts to convince the public that they are just a social club, supporting the community through events such as toy runs, they are Canada's most powerful criminal organization. The violence of

Godasse Gagné is typical of the methods used by organized criminals and explains why one in every seven Canadian homicides—84 killings in 2003—is gang-related (Dauvergne, 2004).

The problem of organized crime is certainly not unique to Canada. This problem has existed for centuries and today such gangs operate around the world. As you will learn, organized crime is one of a wide range of behaviours that society has defined as deviant or criminal. For many years, crime and deviance have been of special interest to sociologists. Many of the issues they have examined remain important today: What is deviant behaviour, and how does it differ from criminal behaviour? Why are some people considered to be "deviants" or "criminals" while others are not? In this chapter, we look at the relationship between conformity, deviance, and crime. Before reading on, take the quiz on organized crime, deviance, and crime in Box 7.1.

QUESTIONS AND ISSUES

Chapter Focus Question: What are the causes and consequences of organized crime in Canada?

What is deviant behaviour?

How do sociologists explain deviant and criminal behaviour?

When is deviance considered a crime?

How do sociologists classify crime?

How does the criminal justice system deal with crime?

How can we begin to solve the crime problem?

According to sociologists, deviance is relative—in other words, it varies according to time, place, group, and circumstance. In this controlled aggression program for youth gang members in Toronto, aggression has been defined as normative rather than deviant.

■ WHAT IS DEVIANCE?

How do societies determine what behaviour is acceptable and unacceptable? As discussed in previous chapters, all societies have norms that govern acceptable behaviour. If we are to live and to work with others, these rules are necessary. We must also have a reasonable expectation that other people will obey the rules. Think of the chaos that would result if each driver decided which side of the road she would drive on each day, or which stop sign he would decide to obey. Most of us usually conform to the norms our group prescribes. Of course, not all members of the group obey all the time. All of us have broken many rules, sometimes even important ones. These violations are dealt with through various mechanisms of *social control*—systematic **practices developed by social groups to encourage**

conformity and to discourage deviance. One form of social control takes place through the process of socialization, whereby individuals *internalize* societal norms and values. A second form of social control occurs through the use of negative sanctions to punish rule-breakers and nonconforming acts. Although the purpose of social control is to ensure some level of conformity, all societies still have some degree of *deviance*—**any behaviour, belief, or condition that violates cultural norms in the society or group in which it occurs** (Adler and Adler, 1994).

We are most familiar with *behavioural* deviance; that is, a person's intentional or inadvertent actions. For example, a person may engage in intentional deviance by drinking too much or shoplifting, or in inadvertent deviance by losing the rent money at a video lottery terminal or laughing during a solemn occasion.

Although we usually think of deviance as a type of behaviour, people may be regarded as deviant if they express radical or unusual beliefs. For example, members of cults (such as Moonies and satanists) and of far-right- or far-left-wing political groups may be considered deviant when their religious or political beliefs become known to people with more conventional cultural views. For instance, Canadian schoolteachers James Keegstra and Malcolm Ross were removed from their classrooms for expressing anti-Semitic beliefs, including denying that the Holocaust actually occurred.

People may be regarded as deviant because of specific *characteristics* or *conditions* that they have had since birth (such as a physical disability or minority status in a racist society) or have acquired (such as contracting AIDS) (Adler and Adler, 1994). Rose Weitz (1993) has suggested that persons with AIDS live with a stigma that affects their relationships with family members, friends, lovers, colleagues, and health care workers. To avoid or reduce stigma, many people with AIDS attempt to conceal their illness, learn when and to whom they should reveal their illness, change their social networks, or work to convince others that they are still functioning social beings (Weitz, 1993). As Weitz's observation suggests, individuals considered "deviant" by one group may be conformists in another group. Organized crime gangs are no exception; members who shun mainstream cultural beliefs and values

BOX 7.1 SOCIOLOGY AND EVERYDAY LIFE

How Much Do You Know About Crime and Organized Crime?

True	False	
T	F	1. Official statistics accurately reflect the amount of crime in Canada.
T	F	2. Most organized criminals are affiliated with the Italian Mafia.
T	F	3. Organized crime exists largely to provide goods and services demanded by "respectable" members of the community.
T	F	4. Rates of murder and other violent crimes have been steadily rising for the past twenty years.
T	F	5. Because of their concern with a variety of charitable causes, biker gangs, such as the Hells Angels, have become less of a social threat.
T	F	6. During Canada's great cigarette smuggling epidemic of 1992 and 1993, our major cigarette companies exported cigarettes to the United States that they knew would be smuggled back into Canada.
T	F	7. Canada's most prolific serial killer was a Hells Angel who killed forty-three people but served only seven years of a sentence for manslaughter.
T	F	8. Many organized crime groups are made up of people from the same ethnic group.
T	F	9. In Russia, organized crime is so pervasive that it is a threat to the future economic and political life of that country.
T	F	10. Most of the money made by organized criminals comes from gambling and loan-sharking.

Answers on page 190.

may conform routinely to codes of dress, attitude (such as defiant individualism), and behaviour (Jankowski, 1991). The Hells Angels provide a graphic example of such conformity within a group of people who consider themselves nonconformists.

Defining Deviance

According to sociologists, deviance is *relative*—that is, an act becomes deviant when it is socially defined as such. Definitions of deviance vary widely from place to place, from time to time, and from group to group. For example, you may have played the Pick 3 lottery. To win, you must pick a three-digit number matching the one drawn by the government lottery agency. Television commercials encourage us to risk our money on this game from which the government profits. Several years ago, the same game was called the numbers racket and was the most popular form of gambling in many low-income neighbourhoods. The two main differences between now and then are that the game used to be run by organized criminals, and

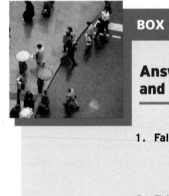

BOX 7.1 SOCIOLOGY AND EVERYDAY LIFE

Answers to the Sociology Quiz on Crime and Organized Crime

1. **False.** Although official statistics provide a variety of information about crime in Canada, they reflect only crimes that are *reported* to police, not all the offences that are *committed*. Studies have shown that fewer than half of all crimes are reported to the police (Evans and Himelfarb, 2004).

2. **False.** The Italian Mafia has a global influence on organized crime. However, it is one of many different organized crime groups (Stamler, 2004).

3. **True.** If not for public demand for illegal drugs, gambling, tax-free liquor and cigarettes, and the other goods and services supplied by organized crime, illegal profits would largely disappear (Stamler, 2004).

4. **False.** While crime rates generally rose through the 1980s, they declined steadily throughout the 1990s and continue to decline (Evans and Himelfarb, 2004).

5. **False.** The Hells Angels have used high-profile activities like toy runs for children to improve their public image. However, they are one of the most ruthless and profitable criminal organizations in North America (Lavigne, 1987).

6. **True.** The vast majority of cigarettes smuggled into Canada were legally manufactured here and exported into the United States. Executives of one of Canada's largest manufacturers, Imperial Tobacco, said explicitly that they wanted to ensure that their cigarettes were the ones smuggled back into Canada.

7. **True.** Yves "Apache" Trudeau was a contract killer who received a lenient sentence in exchange for information about other Montreal underworld figures (Lavigne, 1987). (For more on this case, see Box 7.3 on page 213.)

8. **True.** Many different nationalities are involved in Canadian organized crime, including Russian, Iranian, Chinese, Vietnamese, Colombian, Jamaican, and Italian. Restricting membership to one's own group provides a number of advantages. For one thing, interpersonal ties based on ethnic communities and language differences make it difficult for law enforcement to infiltrate the groups. The ethnic ties also facilitate the development of international crime networks (Stamler, 2004).

9. **True.** After the fall of communism, the lack of meaningful economic institutions and the failure of the criminal justice system created conditions favourable to organized crime. Organized criminals control many of the new businesses in Russia and have powerful links to the government (Jamieson, 2001).

10. **False.** The importation and distribution of illegal drugs is the main source of funds for organized crime (Stamler, 2004).

these criminals paid the winners a higher share of the take than the government now does. While the profits now go to social services rather than to the pockets of criminals, the example illustrates the point that the way societies define behaviour can be more important than the actual harm caused by that behaviour, as legalized gambling involves far more people suffering losses than was the case when gambling was illegal.

Definitions of deviance are continually changing. Several hundred thousand "witches" were executed in Europe during the middle ages; now the crime doesn't exist. Racist comments used to be socially acceptable; now they are not. Tattoos and piercings are now common among students, but twenty years ago they were almost unknown.

Deviance can be difficult to define. Good and evil are not two distinct categories. The two overlap, and the line between deviant and non-deviant can be very *ambiguous*. For example, how do we decide someone is mentally ill? What if your brother begins to behave in a strange fashion? You notice that he occasionally yells at people for no apparent reason and keeps changing topics when you talk to him. He begins to wear clothes that don't match and phones you in the middle of the night to talk about people on the street who are threatening him. How would you respond to this change in behaviour? Would it make any difference if you knew that your brother was drinking heavily at the time or that he was under a lot of stress at work? Would it make a difference if he behaved this way once a year or twice a week? When would you decide that he had a problem and should seek help? What is the difference between someone who is eccentric and someone who is mentally ill? These questions reflect the difficulty we have in defining deviance.

Deviant behaviour also varies in its degree of seriousness, ranging from mild transgressions of folkways, to more serious infringements of mores, to quite serious violations of the law. Have you kept a library book past its due date or cut classes? If so, you have violated folkways. Others probably view your infraction as relatively minor; at most, you might have to pay a fine or receive a lower grade. Violations of mores—such as falsifying a university application or cheating on an examination—are viewed as more serious infractions and are punishable by stronger sanctions, such as academic probation or expulsion. Some forms of deviant behaviour are officially defined as crimes. A **crime is an act that violates criminal law and is punishable with fines, jail terms, and other sanctions.** Crimes range from minor (such as running an illegal bingo game or

disorderly conduct) to major offences (such as sexual assault and murder). A subcategory, *juvenile delinquency,* **refers to a violation of law by young people under the age of 18.**

When sociologists study deviance, they attempt to learn what types of behaviour are defined as deviant, who does the defining, how and why people become deviants, and how society deals with deviants (Schur, 1983). In this chapter, we present several sociological explanations of deviance. While each focuses on the role of social groups in creating deviance, these theories are quite different from one another. However, each contributes in its own way to our understanding of deviance. No one perspective provides a comprehensive explanation of all deviance. In many respects the theories presented in this chapter can be considered complementary.

FUNCTIONALIST PERSPECTIVES ON CRIME AND DEVIANCE

Strain Theory: Goals and the Means to Achieve Them

According to Robert Merton (1938, 1968), in a smoothly functioning society deviance will be limited because most people share common cultural goals and agree upon the appropriate means for reaching them. However, societies that do not provide sufficient avenues to reach these goals may also lack agreement about the appropriate means by which people may achieve their aspirations. Deviance may be common in such societies because people may be willing to use whatever means they can to achieve their goals. According to *strain theory,* **people feel strain when they are exposed to cultural goals that they are unable to obtain because they do not have access to culturally approved means of achieving those goals.** The goals may be material possessions and money; the approved means may include an education and jobs. When denied legitimate access to these goals, some people seek access through deviant means.

Margaret Beare (1996a) has used Merton's strain theory to explain the involvement of Canadian Mohawks in the organized crime of smuggling in the early 1990s. In order to raise revenue and to discourage smoking, Canadian governments had for decades imposed high taxes on cigarettes. As a result, the cost of cigarettes had become much higher in this country than in the United States. To save money, many of those addicted to cigarettes turned to the contraband market. By 1993, more than one-quarter of the cigarettes consumed in Canada were purchased illegally. In Ontario and Quebec, residents of some First Nations communities were among the major sources of these contraband cigarettes.

Because of high unemployment and lack of legitimate opportunities in most First Nations communities, deviance had become an attractive option to some community members, who saw smuggling as a means of achieving the goal of financial success. Akwesasne Chief Mike Mitchell described the financial opportunity in a CBC interview:

> The money—it's unbelievable the money you can make and it's so easy . . . You can buy a pack of cigarettes on the American side of the reservation for $1.58 and you go across here in Cornwall and you have to buy it for close to $7.00 a pack, same pack, within a short distance of each other, so no one is surprised that all this is happening. (cited in Beare, 1996b:272)

The business of getting the cigarettes into Canada was facilitated by a number of factors. First, Canadian cigarette manufacturers were eager to ship Canadian brands into the United States, knowing that the cigarettes would be smuggled back into Canada. Second, the location of some reserves was ideal. The Mohawk reserve at Akwesasne, for example, straddles the Ontario–Quebec and Canada–U.S. borders (see Map 7.1), and the geography of the St. Lawrence River at Akwesasne makes detection difficult. Third, First Nations peoples can purchase for personal use unlimited amounts of tax-free tobacco in the United States. While this tobacco is supposed to remain on the reserve, at the height of the smuggling epidemic much of it became part of the contraband trade. Some residents argued that they had the legal right to sell this tobacco to whoever wished to buy it. Finally, jurisdictional disputes over law enforcement reduced the ability of the police to work effectively. In Beare's opinion, the smuggling was also facilitated by feelings of injustice against federal and provincial governments on the part of the Mohawks, which some felt justified their deviant behaviour.

Reductions in Canadian taxes on cigarettes and substantial increases in the cost of cigarettes in the United States have dramatically reduced the incidence of cigarette smuggling. However, the networks and expertise developed by the smugglers have remained, and many, having made linkages with other organized criminals, have turned to smuggling other commodities, including drugs, alcohol, and firearms. This has helped create illegitimate opportunity structures on some reserves that may attract others into the world of organized smuggling.

It is not only the poor who turn to illegal ways of achieving their goals. Some sociologists feel that strain theory can help explain upper-class deviance as

---

Map 7.1   Smuggling Routes

Two of the many smuggling routes into Canada through the Akwesasne reserve. [Before the taxes were reduced, police estimated] $1 million in illegal cigarettes [were] shipped daily.

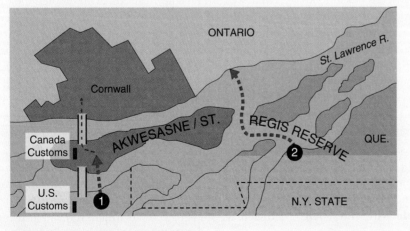

1. Cigarettes are loaded onto boats from marinas on the U.S. side of reserve. This route bypasses Canadian Customs, which is housed on the island.

2. When the St. Lawrence is frozen, contraband is shipped across the river by truck and snowmobile to landings on the north side.

Source: Reprinted with permission—The Toronto Star Syndicate.

well. For example, pressure to increase corporate profits may lead executives to turn to illegal ways of doing business. Company documents suggest that the president of Imperial Tobacco knowingly supplied tobacco to smugglers. The federal government filed a $1-billion lawsuit against RJR-Macdonald Canada and the Canadian Tobacco Manufacturers Council because of their alleged involvement in similar activities. In February 2003, criminal charges were filed against RJR-MacDonald Canada and several of its senior executives. These companies were motivated by their desire to maintain their market share by ensuring that their cigarettes were the ones smuggled back into Canada and by their desire to undermine the government's policy of reducing tobacco use by increasing the price of cigarettes.

Opportunity Theory: Access to Illegitimate Opportunities

Expanding on Merton's strain theory, sociologists Richard Cloward and Lloyd Ohlin (1960) have suggested that for deviance to occur people must have access to **illegitimate opportunity structures— circumstances that provide an opportunity for people to acquire through illegitimate activities what they cannot get through legitimate channels.** For example, members of some communities may have insufficient legitimate means to achieve conventional goals of status and wealth but have much greater access to illegitimate opportunity structures—such as theft, drug dealing, or robbery— through which they can achieve these goals. The situation at Akwesasne provided a very lucrative opportunity structure for the minority of community members who chose to use it. However, more typically, illegitimate opportunities are often situational and small-scale, as the following description an East Coast youth gave of his delinquent behaviour demonstrates:

We used to break into places. I was drunk on every one of them jobs. We never really planned it, we just broke in. The one I remember most clearly is when we broke into the Lougheed Drive-In. I was drunk then so I can't remember everything. We just wanted to do a break, so we did a break to get more booze for the next day. It was after dark and hardly anybody was there— this was 3:00 in the morning. We busted open the door, because there's no alarm system in it— we checked all that out—we just busted the door with a crowbar. We got in there and we searched

everywhere and we didn't find nothing, there wasn't no money there. Then we saw the cigarette machine so we said, "Let's take this." So the six of us picked it up and threw it in the back of the trunk—we had an old shitbox of a car—and took off. We got $35.00 out of it and around 200 packs of cigarettes. We dumped it in a field in there by Kmart on Ryerson Road. We bought a bottle of Seagram's—I know it was Seagram's because I drank half—I just drank it all down. You just get drunk, you get blackouts. You're nervous doing breaks. I never really wanted to be involved with them: mostly I just told them I'd be lookout. One time we all broke in this place: I was out watching and the boys went in, and then a cop car and two paddy wagons came down the road. I said, "Boys, the cops are coming," and I beat it. The boys all got caught. (Leyton, 1979:124)

According to Cloward and Ohlin (1960), three different forms of delinquent subcultures—criminal, conflict, and retreatist—emerge based on the type of illegitimate opportunities available in a specific area. The criminal subculture focuses on economic gain and includes acts such as theft, extortion, and drug dealing. Elijah Anderson (1990) suggested that the "drug economy [is an] employment agency superimposed on the existing gang network" for many young men who lack other opportunities. For young men who grow up in a gang subculture, running drug houses and selling drugs on street corners becomes a source of illegitimate opportunity. Using the money from these "jobs," they can support themselves and their families as well as purchase material possessions to impress others. When illegitimate economic opportunities are not available, gangs may become conflict subcultures that fight over turf (territory) and adopt a value system of toughness, courage, and similar status-enhancing qualities. Those who lack the opportunity or ability to join one of these gangs may turn to retreatist forms of deviance, such as drinking and drug use.

Opportunity theory expands strain theory by pointing out the relationship between deviance and the availability of illegitimate opportunity structures. Some recent studies of gangs have supported this premise by pointing out that gang membership provides some women and men in low-income central-city areas with an illegitimate means to acquire money, entertainment, refuge, physical protection, and an escape from living like their parents (Jankowski, 1991; Esbensen and Huizinga, 1993).

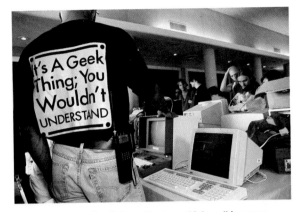

For some people, the "information superhighway" is a new avenue of illegitimate opportunity. While only a fraction of hackers engage in deviant behaviour, computer mischief and crime demonstrate how new opportunity structures can elicit new forms of deviance.

Control Theory: Social Bonding

Like strain theory, social control theory has its roots in Durkheim's anomie theory. In *Suicide* (1964), Durkheim pointed out the importance of social bonds to the understanding of deviant behaviour. Anomic suicide occurs when a lack of social regulation, caused by factors such as rapid economic change, creates a situation in which social organization is weak and the individual lacks moral guidance. The earliest social control theories explained how some types of social structures led to high rates of deviance. Communities characterized by poverty, physical deterioration, and internal conflict were too disorganized to exert effective control over the behaviour of residents. These communities often had high rates of suicide, mental illness, substance abuse, and crime. Most of the research documenting the correlation between community disorganization and crime has been done in large, urban areas. However, Linda Deutschmann (2002) has applied the theory to frontier areas as well. Many small Canadian communities were created solely to develop an economic resource. Such towns have grown up around mines, railroads, pulp mills, and hydro dams. These towns may be lasting or short-lived depending on the nature of the project or the life of the resource. Deutschmann notes that in these towns' early stages of development, the absence of controls, such as families and churches, means that deviant behaviour, such as fighting and alcohol abuse, may be common. In later stages of development, the strains of a booming town may also facilitate deviance.

While work in this tradition continues, much of the recent work on control theory has focused on the individual rather than on the community. In doing so, it has posed the fundamental question about causes of deviance in a new way.

Most theories of deviance ask the question, Why do they do it? Control theorists reverse this question, asking, Why don't we *all* do it? That is, Why do people *not* engage in deviant behaviour? In an effort to answer this question, Walter Reckless (1967) developed a theory of social control, which states that certain factors draw people toward deviance while others "insulate" them from such behaviour. According to Reckless, people are drawn to deviance by poverty, unemployment, and lack of educational opportunity. They also may be influenced by members of deviant subcultures, media depictions of deviant behaviour, and their own feelings of frustration, hostility, or inferiority. However, many people do not turn to deviance because they are insulated by *outer containments,* such as supportive family and friends, reasonable social expectations, and supervision by others, and by *inner containments,* such as self-control, a sense of responsibility, and resistance to unlawful diversions.

Extending Reckless's containment theory, Travis Hirschi (1969) developed a theory suggesting that deviant behaviour is minimized when people have strong bonds that bind them to families, school, peers, churches, and other social institutions. ***Social bond theory*** **holds that the probability of deviant behaviour increases when a person's ties to society are weakened or broken.** According to Hirschi, social bonding consists of (1) *attachment* to other people; (2) *commitment* to conventional lines of behaviour, such as schooling and job success; (3) *involvement* in conventional activities; and (4) *belief* in the legitimacy of conventional values and norms. The variables of attachment and commitment are much more strongly related to delinquency than involvement and belief. Although Hirschi did not include females in his study, others who have replicated it with both females and males have found that the theory appears to explain the delinquency of both (see Linden and Fillmore, 1981).

While Hirschi's theory did not differentiate between bonds to conventional and to deviant others, several researchers have modified the theory and have suggested that the probability of crime or delinquency increases when a person's social bonds are weak and when peers promote antisocial values and deviant behaviour (see Figure 7.1). Gang members

Figure 7.1	Model of the Impact of Social Bonds on Delinquency

The work of Linden and Fillmore supported control theory in its finding that youth with weak social bonds to parents, law-abiding friends, and schools were more likely to be delinquent. However, Linden and Fillmore also found that youth with weak social bonds were more likely to associate with delinquent friends and that this association further increased their chances of becoming delinquent. This model combines elements of social control theory and differential association theory.

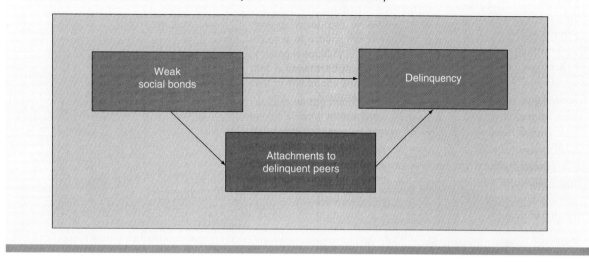

may bond with one another rather than with persons who subscribe to dominant cultural values. As one gang member explains:

> Before I joined the gang, I could see that you could count on your boys to help in times of need and that meant a lot to me. And when I needed money, sure enough they gave it to me. Nobody else would have given it to me; my parents didn't have it, and there was no other place to go. The gang was just like they said they would be, and they'll continue to be there when I need them. (Jankowski, 1991:42)

SYMBOLIC INTERACTIONIST PERSPECTIVES ON CRIME AND DEVIANCE

As we discussed in Chapter 4, symbolic interactionists focus on how people develop a self-concept and learn conforming behaviour through the process of socialization. According to symbolic interactionists, deviance is learned in the same way as conformity—through interaction with others.

Differential Association Theory

More than sixty years ago, Edwin Sutherland (1939) developed a theory to explain how people learn deviance through social interaction. ***Differential association theory* states that individuals have a greater tendency to deviate from societal norms when they frequently associate with persons who favour deviance over conformity.** According to Sutherland, people learn the necessary techniques and the motives, drives, rationalizations, and attitudes of deviant behaviour from people with whom they associate. Peter Letkemann (1973), for example, described how a former Canadian penitentiary resident learned the now-obsolete art of safecracking:

> Prior to doing his first "can" [safe] [he] bugged an older safecracker in prison "until he finally divulged how to do it." This instruction, he added was "not like a teacher–student, it was just a matter of discussion during work."
>
> When he left the prison he went back to his regular partner and described to him what he had learned about safes. His partner said this was ridiculous but [he] persuaded him to come along: "I followed the instructions to the letter. It opened—we were both overcome with it all— the ease of it all!"

This first job had been a punch job [breaking into a safe without explosives]—technically the simplest. Following this [he] and his partner "opened many doors by trial and error." . . . This went on for four years; they had not yet used explosives, nor had they ever been caught punching safes. They became increasingly eager to try explosives since they found so many safes that couldn't be opened any other way.

During this time, [he] was associating with other safecrackers . . . He eventually asked another safecracker whether he could borrow some grease [nitroglycerine]. "I wouldn't admit that I knew nothing about it." He obtained the grease and chose a small safe, but was unsuccessful. The next day, he discussed his problem with some more experienced safecrackers. He found he had used too long a fuse and was advised to use electric knockers [detonators]. This he did with success. (Letkemann, 1973:136)

Differential association is most likely to result in deviant activity when a person has frequent, intense, and long-lasting interaction with others who violate the rules. When there are more factors favouring violation of the law than there are opposing it, the person is more likely to become a criminal. Ties to other deviants can be particularly important in the world of organized crime, where the willingness of peers to stand up for one another can be critical in maintaining power in the face of violent opposition from competitors. Daniel Wolf, an anthropologist who rode with the Rebels, an Edmonton biker gang, describes this solidarity:

For an outlaw biker, the greatest fear is not of the police; rather, it is a slight variation of his own mirror image: the patch holder [full-fledged member] of another club. Under slightly different circumstances those men would call each other "brother." But when turf is at stake, inter-club rivalry and warfare completely override any considerations of the common bonds of being a biker—and brother kills brother. None of the outlaws that I rode with enjoyed the prospect of having to break the bones of another biker. Nor did they look forward to having to live with the hate–fear syndrome that dominates a conflict in which there are no rules. I came to realize that the willingness of an outlaw to lay down his life in these conflicts goes beyond a belligerent masculinity that brooks no challenge. When a patch holder defends his colours, he defends his personal identity, his community, his lifestyle. When a war is on, loyalty to the club and one another arises out of the midst of danger, out of apprehension of possible injury, mutilation, or worse. Whether one considers this process as desperate, heroic, or just outlandishly foolish and banal does not really matter. What matters is that, for patch holders, the brotherhood emerges as a necessary feature of their continued existence as individuals and as a group. (1996:11)

Group ties are important not just in highly organized crime groups, such as motorcycle gangs. Think of the different subcultural groups that are involved in deviant activities in many Canadian high schools. Whether the focus of the group is graffiti, body piercing, punk music or dress, or using drugs, the encouragement and support of peers is vital to recruiting and teaching new members and to sustaining the group.

Differential association theory contributes to our knowledge of how deviant behaviour reflects the individual's learned techniques, values, attitudes, motives, and rationalizations. However, critics question why many individuals who have had extensive contact with people who violate the law still conform most of the time. They also assert that the theory does not adequately assess possible linkages between social inequality and criminal behaviour.

Labelling Theory

Two complementary processes are involved in the definition of deviance. First, some people act (or are believed to act) in a manner contrary to the expectations of others. Second, others disapprove of and try to control this contrary behaviour. Part of this social control process involves labelling people as deviants. A very important contribution to the study of deviance was made by sociologists who asked the question, Why are some people labelled as deviants while others are not? *Labelling theory suggests that deviants are those people who have been successfully labelled as such by others.* The process of labelling is directly related to the power and status of those persons who do the labelling and those who are being labelled. Behaviour, then, is not deviant in and of itself; it is defined as such by a social audience (Erikson, 1962). According to sociologist Howard Becker (1963), *moral entrepreneurs* are persons who use their own views of right and wrong to establish rules and label others as deviant. These rules are enforced on persons with less power.

William Chambliss (1973) witnessed the labelling process when he observed members of two groups of high school boys: the Saints and the Roughnecks. Both groups were "constantly occupied with truancy, drinking, wild parties, petty theft, and vandalism." Overall, the Saints committed more offences than the Roughnecks, but the Roughnecks were labelled as troublemakers by school and law enforcement officials while the Saints were seen as being likely to succeed. Unlike the Roughnecks, none of the Saints was ever arrested.

Chambliss attributed this contradictory response by authorities to the fact the Saints came from "good families," did well in school, and thus were forgiven for their "boys will be boys"–type behaviour. By contrast, the Roughnecks came from lower-income families, did poorly in school, and generally were viewed negatively. Although both groups engaged in similar behaviour, only the Roughnecks were stigmatized by a deviant label.

The concept of secondary deviance is important to labelling theory because it suggests that when people accept a negative label or stigma that has been applied to them, the label may contribute to the type of behaviour it initially was meant to control (see Figure 7.2). According to sociologist Edwin Lemert (1951), ***primary deviance* is the initial act of rule breaking. *Secondary deviance* occurs when a person who has been labelled deviant accepts that new identity and continues the deviant behaviour.** For example, a person may shoplift, not be labelled deviant, and subsequently decide to forgo such acts in the future. Secondary deviance occurs if the person steals from a store, is labelled a "shoplifter," accepts that label, and then continues to steal.

Labelling theorists have made an important contribution to our understanding of the process by which society defines behaviours and individuals as deviant and of the consequences of that definition. Let us first look at the impact of labelling on a person who is defined as deviant. Robert Scott (1969) conducted a fascinating study that examined the effects of two different ways of treating blind people. One agency defined the blind as helpless, dependent people and developed programs to accommodate them. For example, their clients were driven to the agency's offices, where they worked in sheltered workshops and ate food that had been cut before being served. Staff and volunteers helped them with many activities. Not surprisingly, the clients had a great deal of trouble adapting to life outside the agency. Another agency, which dealt mainly with veterans of the Vietnam War, used a restorative approach with its clients. The goal was to reintegrate clients into the community. Instead of being driven places, they were trained to take public transit. They were given confidence training and encouraged to live on their own and work in normal job settings. Scott concluded that these different approaches, with different labels for the visually impaired clients, had a significant impact on the self-image and social adjustment of the blind clients.

You can think of the impact that other labels can have on a person's self-concept and on their life chances. Being labelled a drug addict can lead to

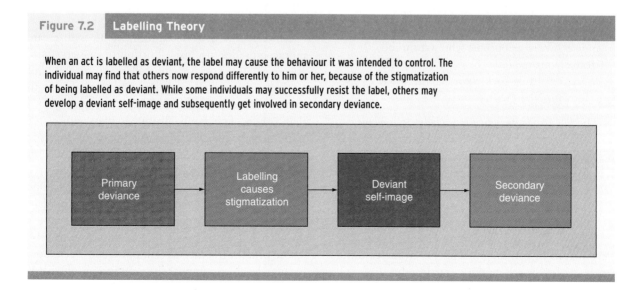

Figure 7.2   **Labelling Theory**

When an act is labelled as deviant, the label may cause the behaviour it was intended to control. The individual may find that others now respond differently to him or her, because of the stigmatization of being labelled as deviant. While some individuals may successfully resist the label, others may develop a deviant self-image and subsequently get involved in secondary deviance.

Primary deviance → Labelling causes stigmatization → Deviant self-image → Secondary deviance major difficulties in getting a job even after successful treatment. If the label prevents the former addict from reintegrating into the conventional community, he or she may accept this deviant status and return to his or her friends in the drug world. Similar problems come with other deviant labels. Many of us have done things in the past of which others would not approve, but if we have not been labelled, then we will not suffer some of the consequences of our behaviour. The impact of the label of "mentally ill" is clearly described by Tom, an ex-patient:

> Having been diagnosed as a psychiatric patient with psychotic tendencies is the worst thing that has ever happened to me. It's shitty to be mentally ill; it's not something to be proud of. It makes you realize just how different you are from everybody else—they're normal and you're not. Things are easy for them; things are hard for you. Life's a ball for them; life's a bitch for you. I'm like a mental cripple! I'm a failure for life! (Herman, 1996:310).

We should not assume that everyone just passively submits to the labelling process. Some people are successful at resisting the imposition of a label. This can be done individually or by working with others. The leader of one Ontario group of former psychiatric patients described the aims of his group:

> Simply put, we're tired of being pushed around. We reject everything society says about us, because it's just not accurate . . . We don't like the meaning of the words [people] use to describe us—"mentals" and "nuts." We see ourselves differently, just as good and worthy as everybody out there. In our newsletter, we're trying to get across the idea that we're not the stereotypical mental patient you see in movies. We're real people who want to be treated equally under the Charter of Rights. We're not sitting back, we're fighting back! (Herman, 1996:323).

The view that deviance is socially defined draws our attention to the question of why particular behaviours are defined as deviant and others are not. One of the answers highlights the role of ***moral entrepreneurs*—people or groups who take an active role in trying to have particular behaviours defined as deviant.** Think of the role that groups, such as Mothers Against Drunk Driving (MADD), have played in getting governments to increase the penalties for drunk driving and in educating the public about the dangers of this behaviour. We have seen a similar process in recent years in many of our communities as health advocates try to stigmatize cigarette smoking and to pass legislation banning smoking in most public places. A few decades ago, there was little opposition to smoking; people smoked on buses, in airplanes, in classrooms, in offices, and in virtually all other public places. When society became more aware of the health risks of smoking, an antismoking movement grew and was able to overcome the lobbying of tobacco companies and convince governments to impose more and more restrictions on smoking. According to Tuggle and Holmes (2000), the antismoking movement has moved from efforts to educate people about the dangers of smoking, to more coercive bans on smoking in public places, to a new definition of the smoker as a deviant who is threatening public health. Thus smoking has moved from a normative behaviour to a stigmatized behaviour over a period of about thirty years.

Moral entrepreneurs often create ***moral crusades*— public and media awareness campaigns that help generate public and political support for their causes.** You can read about an example of a moral crusade in Box 19.4, "Immigration and the Media," on page 607. The moral entrepreneurs promoting the Canadian antidrug movement in the 1920s focused most of their attention on nonwhite immigrants. Their attempt to protect the Canadian way of life from these immigrants was one reason why the legal penalties for possession and sale of drugs are so harsh; it also helped support racially biased immigration policies. Chinese and Black residents were labelled as villainous threats to Canada. The racist rhetoric of some of Canada's most prominent citizens made it much easier for members of the public to stigmatize these racial minorities.

More recently, we have seen attempts to create moral crusades against abortion providers, wife abusers, squeegee kids, panhandlers, prostitutes, and a wide variety of other real or perceived threats to society. Some crusades have been more successful than others. The campaign by women's groups for zero-tolerance policies mandating arrest in domestic violence cases has been successful. Anti-abortion groups have drawn attention to their cause but have not been able to bring about changes in the law. One of the major reasons why some groups succeed in changing perceptions and laws and others do not is the distribution of power and resources in society. Those who control the levers of power are much more likely to be able to impose their definitions of what is right and wrong on the rest of society.

Labelling theory has had an important impact on the justice system and has led to an increased use of diversion for minor offences so a formal label would not be applied. Critics argue that this theory does not explain what causes the original acts that make up primary deviance. Nor does it provide insight into why some people accept deviant labels and others do not (Cavender, 1995).

While symbolic interactionist perspectives are concerned with how people learn deviant behaviour, identities, and social roles through interaction with others, *conflict theorists* are interested in how certain kinds of people and behaviour, and not others, come to be defined as deviant.

CONFLICT PERSPECTIVES ON CRIME AND DEVIANCE

Who determines what kinds of behaviour are deviant or criminal? According to conflict perspectives, people in positions of power maintain their advantage by using the law to protect their own interests. Conflict theorists suggest that lifestyles considered deviant by political and economic elites often are defined as illegal. They note that the activities of poor and lower-income individuals are more likely to be defined as criminal than those of persons from middle- and upper-income backgrounds. For example, those who commit welfare fraud are more likely to face criminal charges than are professionals whose misconduct is generally dealt with by disciplinary committees of their peers rather than by the criminal courts. The relative degree of social harm caused by either of these groups seems to have little relevance in the determination of who is defined as criminal; what matters more may be the power of some groups to resist sanctions.

The Conflict Approach

Although Karl Marx wrote very little about deviance and crime, many of his ideas influenced a critical approach that is based on the assumption that the criminal justice system protects the power and privilege of the capitalist class.

As we saw in Chapter 1, Marx based his critique of capitalism on the inherent conflict that he believed existed between the capitalists and the working class. According to Marx, social institutions (such as law, politics, and education) make up a superstructure in society that legitimizes the class structure and maintains the capitalists' superior position in it. Crime is an expression of the individual's struggle against the unjust social conditions and inequality produced by capitalism.

According to Richard Quinney (1980), people with economic and political power define as criminal any behaviour that threatens their own interests. The powerful use law to control those who are without power. For example, drug laws enacted early in the twentieth century were passed and enforced in an effort to control immigrant workers, particularly Chinese workers, who were more inclined than most other residents of Canada to smoke opium. The laws were motivated by racism more than by a real concern with drug use (Cook, 1969). By contrast, while the Canadian government passed anticombines legislation in 1889 in response to concerns expressed by labour and small-business people about the growing power of monopoly capitalists, the law had no impact on major companies engaged in price-fixing and other means of limiting competition. Having symbolic anticombines laws on the books merely shored up the government's legitimacy by making it appear responsive to public concerns about big business (Smandych, 1985).

Why do people commit crimes? Some conflict theorists believe that the affluent commit crimes because they are greedy and want more than they have. Corporate or white-collar crimes, such as stock market manipulation, land speculation, and fraudulent bankruptcies and crimes committed on behalf of organizations, often involve huge sums of money and harm many people. By contrast, street crimes, such as robbery and aggravated assault, generally involve small sums of money and cause harm to limited numbers of victims (Bonger, 1969). According to conflict theorists, the poor commit street crimes in order to survive; they find that they cannot afford the necessary essentials, such as food, clothing, shelter, and health care. Thus, some crime represents a rational response by the poor to the unequal distribution of resources in society (Gordon, 1973). Further, living in poverty may lead to violent crime and victimization *of the poor by the poor*. For example, violent gang activity may be a collective response of young people to seemingly hopeless poverty (Quinney, 1979).

In sum, the conflict approach argues that the law protects the interests of the affluent and powerful. The way laws are written and enforced benefits the capitalist class by ensuring that individuals at the bottom of the social class structure do not infringe on the property or threaten the safety of those at the top (Reiman, 1984).

However, this theory explains some types of laws, but not others. People of all classes share a consensus about the criminality of certain acts. For example, laws that prohibit murder, rape, and armed robbery protect not only middle- and upper-income people but also low-income people, who frequently are the victims of such violent crimes (Klockars, 1979). While some laws do protect the rich and powerful, others reflect the interests of all citizens.

FEMINIST PERSPECTIVES ON CRIME AND DEVIANCE

Can theories developed to explain male behaviour help us understand female deviance and crime? According to some feminist scholars, the answer is no. The few early studies that were conducted on "women's crimes" focused almost exclusively on prostitution and attributed the cause of this crime to women's biological or psychological "inferiority." As late as the 1980s, researchers were still looking for unique predisposing factors that led women to commit crime, which was often seen as individual psychopathology rather than as a response to their social environment. These theories, which reinforce existing female stereotypes, have had a negative impact on both our understanding and our treatment of female offenders.

A new interest in women and deviance developed in 1975 when two books—Freda Adler's *Sisters in Crime* and Rita James Simons's *Women and Crime*—declared that women's crime rates were going to increase significantly as a result of the women's liberation movement. Although this so-called emancipation theory of female crime has been strongly criticized by subsequent analysts (Comack, 2000), Adler's and Simons's works encouraged feminist scholars (both women and men) to examine the relationship between gender, deviance, and crime more closely.

Feminist scholars have concluded the roots of female criminality lie in a social structure that is "characterized by inequalities of class, race, and gender" (Comack, 2004:173). Some theorists explain women's deviance and crime as a rational response to gender discrimination experienced in work, marriage, and interpersonal relationships. Some female crimes are attributed to women's lack of job opportunities and to stereotypical expectations about what roles women should have in society. For example, a woman is even less likely to be a big-time drug dealer or an organized crime boss

than she is to be a corporate director (Daly and Chesney-Lind, 1998; Simpson, 1989). Other theorists feel that women are exploited by capitalism and patriarchy. Because most females have had relatively low-wage jobs and few economic resources, minor crimes, such as prostitution, shoplifting, and passing bad cheques, became a means to earn money or to acquire consumer products. As you will read later in this chapter, increases in women's criminality during the 1970s and 1980s reflect the fact that the number of single female parents living in poverty grew significantly during this period.

Some of the most interesting recent work on female criminality has focused on the simultaneous effects of race, class, and gender on deviant behaviour. Regina Arnold (1990) attributes many of the women's offences to living in families in which sexual abuse, incest, and other violence left them few choices except to engage in deviance. Economic marginality and racism also contributed to their victimization. These conclusions are reinforced by a recent study in which Elizabeth Comack examined the relationship between women's earlier victimization and their subsequent involvement in Manitoba's criminal justice system. The incidence of prior victimization was pervasive among women incarcerated in a provincial jail. To examine the problem in detail, Comack interviewed twenty-four women. The abuse suffered by the women was connected to their criminal behaviour in several ways. Some women turned to crime as a means of coping with their histories of abuse. "Meredith" had been sexually abused by her father since the age of four or five. She was in jail for fraud and had been involved in drug use and prostitution:

> Some people are violent, some people take it out in other ways, but that was my only way to release it. It was like, it's almost orgasmic, you know, you'd write the cheques, and you'd get home and you'd go through all these things and it's like, "There's so much there. I have all these new things to keep my mind off. I don't have to deal with the old issues." And so you do it. And it becomes an escape. (Comack, 1996b:86)

Others break the law in the course of resisting abuse. "Janice" had been raped as a teenager and turned to alcohol as a means of coping. Serving time for manslaughter, she recounts the circumstances of the offence:

> . . . well I was at a party, and this guy, older, older guy, came, came on to me. He tried telling me, "Why don't you go to bed with me. I'm getting

some money, you know." And I said, "No." And then he started hitting me and then he raped me and then (pause) I lost it. Like I just, I went, I got very angry and I snapped. And I started hitting him. I threw a coffee table on top of his head and then I stabbed him, and then I left. (Comack, 1996b:96)

While abuse was strongly related to the women's law violations, Comack also found that race and class were factors contributing to the criminal behaviour of many of the women; most were Aboriginal and poor.

Feminist theorists feel that women who violate the law are not "criminal women" but "criminalized women" (Laberge, 1991). This means that they commit acts of crime and deviance because they have been forced into difficult situations that are not of their own making. The women interviewed by Comack faced many social pressures caused by race, class, and gender and had few options for escaping their situations and improving their lives.

POSTMODERN PERSPECTIVES ON CRIME AND DEVIANCE

How might postmodernists view deviance and social control? Although the works of social theorist Michel Foucault defy simple categorization, *Discipline and Punish* (1979) might be considered somewhat postmodern in its approach to explaining the intertwining nature of power, knowledge, and social control. In his study of prisons from the mid-1800s to the early 1900s, Foucault found that many penal institutions ceased torturing prisoners who disobeyed the rules and began using new surveillance techniques to maintain social control. Although the prisons appeared to be more humane in the post-torture era, Foucault contends that the new means of surveillance impinged more on prisoners and brought greater power to prison officials. To explain, he described the *Panopticon*—a structure that gives prison officials the possibility of complete observation of criminals at all times. For example, the Panopticon might be a tower located in the centre of a circular prison from which guards can see all the cells. Although the prisoners know they can be observed at any time, they do not actually know when their behaviour is being

scrutinized. As a result, prison officials are able to use their knowledge as a form of power over inmates. Eventually, the guards would not even have to be present all the time because prisoners would believe that they were under constant scrutiny by officials in the observation post. In this case, the social control and discipline are based on the use of knowledge, power, and technology.

How does Foucault's perspective explain social control in the larger society? According to Foucault, technologies, such as the Panopticon, make widespread surveillance and disciplinary power possible in many settings, including the police network, factories, schools, and hospitals. Modern technology has the potential to expand surveillance far more broadly than Foucault could have imagined. The computer can act as a modern Panopticon that gives workplace supervisors virtually unlimited capabilities for surveillance over subordinates (Zuboff, 1988). Paul Lashmar has described recent technological developments that will broaden the capacity of governments and corporations to control our behaviour:

> A Japanese company has already developed a toilet—targeted for use in large companies—that can analyse whether an employee has recently used illegal recreational drugs, such as cocaine or heroin. Numberplate recognition cameras are in place in a number of key British motorways, enabling police to track suspect or stolen vehicles. Facial recognition for [closed circuit surveillance television] is still in the early stages of development but has already been tried out in the London borough of Newham . . . Leeds University's Institute for Transport Studies has developed a communication box that could be fitted to all vehicles to regulate traffic speed and flow. (2004:1)

These technologies are all very useful and can be valuable tools in improving our safety and well-being. Closed-circuit television cameras in the subway were used to identify the people who carried out the July 2005 bombings that took more than 50 lives in London. Numberplate recognition cameras have enabled the British police to get many auto thieves and suspended drivers off the road. DNA technology has freed many people who had been unjustly convicted of serious crimes and has enabled the justice system to imprison others who had committed crimes, such as sexual assault and murder. A system that would allow us to log on to our computers by scanning the iris of our eyes or our fingerprints would eliminate the confusing number of passwords that each of us must remember and would help to ensure that our computers were secure.

BOX 7.2 YOU CAN MAKE A DIFFERENCE

Preventing Delinquency and Crime

Think about the crime-prevention implications of the sociological theories you have studied. Most of them suggest ways in which you might intervene to help reduce the amount of crime in your community and to help the lives of young people who might get involved in delinquency.

Merton's strain theory and Cloward's and Ohlin's differential opportunity theory suggest that increasing the legitimate opportunities available for young people will help to reduce delinquency. One way of doing this is by improving their school experience. Many schools are looking for university and college students to act as volunteer tutors for young people. The volunteers help with school work and act as role models to the young people.

Hirschi's social control theory tells us that people with strong bonds to other people and to conventional social institutions will be less likely to be deviant. As a volunteer, you could work with Big Brothers and Big Sisters to provide a young person with such a bond. You can find out more at the Big Brothers Big Sisters of Canada Web site at: http://www.bbbsc.ca/.

You could also help by getting involved with recreational programs involving groups such as Boys and Girls Clubs of Canada. You can contact them at their Web site: http://www.bgccan.com/index.asp.

Labelling theory was responsible for drawing attention to the need to avoid labelling young people as "delinquents" or "criminals" wherever possible. This led the Canadian government to pass young-offender legislation that emphasized diverting young people from the youth justice system. Many of these diversion programs require volunteers to help monitor alternative dispositions in the community. You can find out about these programs by contacting a criminology instructor at your local college or university or through provincial justice officials.

One other very good source of information about ways you can help to prevent crime is the Virtual Library of the National Crime Prevention Strategy. You can find the Web site at http://www.prevention.gc.ca/en/library/index.html.

While there are benefits, these technologies raise important issues of privacy and individual rights. As these technologies continue to develop, our society will have to decide the degree to which greater protection is worth the loss of our personal privacy. Foucault did not believe that discipline would sweep uniformly through society, due to opposing forces that would use their power to oppose such surveillance. What are your views on this issue? Where do you feel the balance lies between collective security and individual rights?

We have examined functionalist, interactionist, conflict, feminist, and postmodern perspectives on deviance and crime (see Concept Table 7.A). These explanations help us understand the causes and consequences of certain kinds of behaviour; however, they also make us aware of the limitations of our knowledge about deviance and crime. Many of these theories provide us with guidance concerning how we might reduce crime and deviance. Box 7.2 shows you how you can apply your knowledge in a practical way to help prevent crime.

CRIME CLASSIFICATION AND STATISTICS

The law divides crime into different categories. We will look first at the legal classifications of crime and then at categories typically used by sociologists and criminologists.

How the Law Classifies Crime

The law divides crime into summary conviction and indictable offences. The distinction between the two is based on the seriousness of the crime. *Indictable offences* include serious crimes, such as homicide, sexual assault, robbery, and break and enter. *Summary conviction offences* are relatively minor offences, including fraudulently obtaining food from a restaurant, causing a disturbance, and wilfully committing an indecent act. Summary conviction offences are punishable by a fine of up to $2,000 and/or six months in jail.

Concept Table 7.A   THEORETICAL PERSPECTIVES ON DEVIANCE

PERSPECTIVE	THEORY	KEY ELEMENTS
Functionalist		
Robert Merton	Strain Theory	Deviance occurs when access to the approved means of reaching culturally approved goals is blocked.
Richard Cloward/Lloyd Ohlin	Opportunity Theory	For deviance to occur, people must have the opportunity. Access to illegitimate opportunity structures varies, and this helps determine the nature of the deviance in which a person will engage.
Travis Hirschi	Social Control/Social Bonding	Social bonds keep people from becoming criminals. When ties to family, friends, and others become weak, an individual is most likely to engage in criminal behaviour.
Symbolic Interactionist		
Edwin Sutherland	Differential Association	Deviant behaviour is learned in interaction with others. A person becomes delinquent when exposure to law-breaking attitudes is more extensive than exposure to law-abiding attitudes.
Howard Becker	Labelling Theory	Acts are deviant or criminal because they have been labelled as such. Powerful groups often label less powerful individuals.
Edwin Lemert	Primary/Secondary Deviance	Primary deviance is the initial act. Secondary deviance occurs when a person accepts the label of "deviant" and continues to engage in the behaviour that initially produced the label.
Conflict		
Karl Marx Richard Quinney	Conflict Approach	The powerful use law and the criminal justice system to protect their own class interests.
Feminist		
Kathleen Daly Meda Chesney-Lind Elizabeth Comack	Feminist Approach	Historically, women have been ignored in research on crime. Current feminist theories suggest that structured inequalities of race, class, and gender lead to the criminalization of women.
Postmodern		
Michel Foucault	Knowledge as Power	Power, knowledge, and social control are intertwined. In prisons, for example, new means of surveillance that make prisoners think they are being watched all the time give officials knowledge that inmates do not have. Thus, the officials have a form of power over the inmates.

How Sociologists Classify Crime

Sociologists categorize crimes based on how they are committed and how society views the offences. We will examine four types: (1) street crime; (2) occupational, or white-collar, and corporate crime; (3) organized crime; and (4) political crime. As you read about these types of crime, ask yourself how you feel about them. Should each be a crime? How severe should the sanctions be against each type?

Street Crime When people think of crime, the images that most commonly come to mind are of *street crime,* **which includes all violent crime, certain property crimes, and certain morals crimes.** Examples are robbery, assault, and break and enter. These are the crimes that occupy most of the time and attention of the criminal justice system. Obviously, all street crime does not occur on the street; it frequently occurs in the home, workplace, and other locations.

Violent crime consists of actions involving force or the threat of force against others, including murder, sexual assault, robbery, and aggravated assault. Violent crimes are probably the most anxiety-provoking of all criminal behaviour. Victims often are physically injured or even lose their lives; the psychological trauma may last for years after the event (Parker, 1995). Violent crime receives the most sustained attention from law-enforcement officials and the media (see Warr, 1995). And, while much attention may be given to the violent stranger, the vast majority of violent crime victims actually are injured by someone whom they know: family members, friends, neighbours, or co-workers (Silverman and Kennedy, 1993).

Property crimes include break and enter, theft, motor vehicle theft, and arson. While violent crime receives the most publicity, property crime is much more common. In most property crimes, the primary motive is to obtain money or some other desired valuable.

Morals crimes involve an illegal action voluntarily engaged in by the participants, such as prostitution, illegal gambling, the private use of illegal drugs, and illegal pornography. Many people assert that such conduct should not be labelled as a crime; these offences often are referred to as "victimless crimes" because they involve exchanges of illegal goods or services among willing adults (Schur, 1965).

Occupational and Corporate Crime

Although Edwin Sutherland (1949) developed the concept of white-collar crime more than fifty years ago, it was not until the 1980s that the public really became aware of its nature. *Occupational* or *white-collar crime* **consists of illegal activities committed by people in the course of their employment or in dealing with their financial affairs.**

At the heart of much white-collar crime is a violation of positions of trust in business or government (Shapiro, 1990). These activities include pilfering (employee theft of company property or profits), soliciting bribes or kickbacks, and embezzling. In the past decade, computers have created even greater access to such illegal practices. Some white-collar criminals set up businesses for the sole purpose of victimizing the general public, engaging in activities such as land swindles, securities thefts, and consumer fraud.

In addition to acting for their own financial benefit, some white-collar offenders become involved in criminal conspiracies designed to improve the market share or profitability of their companies. This is known as *corporate crime*—**illegal acts committed by corporate employees on behalf of the corporation and with its support.** Examples include antitrust violations; false advertising; infringements on patents, copyrights, and trademarks; price-fixing; and financial fraud. These crimes are a result of deliberate decisions made by corporate personnel to enhance resources or profits at the expense of competitors, consumers, and the general public.

The cost of white-collar and corporate crimes far exceeds that of street crime. Gabor (1994) reports that tax evasion costs Canadians about $30 billion a year. In one of the world's biggest white-collar crimes, investors in Calgary's Bre-X gold-mining company lost around $5 billion when it was learned that geologist Michael de Guzman had salted core samples with gold to make a worthless mining property look like the world's biggest gold find. At the individual level, while few bank robbers get away with more than a few thousand dollars, Julius Melnitzer (a London, Ontario, lawyer) defrauded Canadian banks of $90 million in order to support his lavish lifestyle.

Corporate crimes can also be very costly in terms of lives lost and injury. Laureen Snider (1988) found that occupational accidents and illnesses were the third leading cause of death in Canada. She attributes at least half of these deaths to unsafe and illegal working conditions. Working conditions in the mining industry, for example, have been especially dangerous. Decades ago, large numbers of Canadian miners died because their employers failed to protect them from mine hazards. Coal miners died of black lung, a condition caused by inhaling coal dust, and fluorspar miners died from the effects of inhaling silica dust in unventilated mineshafts. Not only did the mine owners fail to provide safe working conditions, but company doctors were also told not to advise the miners of the seriousness of their illnesses (Leyton, 1997). The loss of twenty-six miners in a preventable explosion at Nova Scotia's Westray mine in 1992 suggests some mine owners have yet to put their employees' lives above profits (Richard, 1997).

Michael de Guzman (right), a geologist for the Bre-X gold-mining company, is one of those responsible for one of the world's largest stock frauds. De Guzman committed suicide by jumping from a helicopter while travelling to the Bre-X property in Indonesia.

One reason why many employers have been reluctant to implement required safety measures is because the penalties for violating workplace health and safety laws are so light. Consider the case of Silco, an Edmonton-based construction company. A Silco employee fell to his death from a homemade man-basket attached to an unstable crane boom. The company had received three different orders to improve safety practices earlier that year, but had ignored all of them, including a stop-work order the month of the accident. Despite Silco's obvious negligence, the company received a fine of only $6,000 for its part in the employee's death (Ward, 1996).

Although people who commit occupational and corporate crimes can be arrested, fined, and sent to prison, many people do not regard such behaviour as "criminal." People who tend to condemn street crime

are less sure of how their own (or their friends') financial and corporate behaviour should be judged. At most, punishment for such offences is usually a fine or a relatively brief prison sentence at a minimum-security facility.

In many corporate crimes, it is more difficult to attach individual blame than it is in street crimes. It is far easier to determine who was responsible for a sexual assault or a robbery than to determine the specific individuals who are responsible for complex price-fixing arrangements between companies. For example, a scheme by Canada's largest flour-milling companies to fix prices on flour sold to the government for food aid to Third World countries continued for more than a decade and involved very complex business arrangements. In some respects, individual blame is legally irrelevant in most corporate crimes because usually it is the corporation that is prosecuted, not the individual manager. This, of course, makes corporate officials less accountable for their actions.

One final point that can be made about white-collar crime is that the concept also fits people who wear blue collars. Because of this, some have suggested that *occupational crime* may be a more accurate term. Many tradespeople defraud the government by doing work "off the books" in order to avoid provincial sales tax and the goods and services tax. Some blue-collar businesses have bad records of consumer fraud. Robert Sikorsky (1990) travelled across Canada and visited 152 automobile repair shops. While doing so, he documented an appalling degree of misconduct in this business. Before each visit, he disconnected the idle air control in his car, which triggered a warning light on the instrument panel. The repair needed was obvious and simple—reinsert the connector. But more than half the shops Sikorsky visited performed unnecessary work, overcharged him for work, or lied about the work that had been done. In one case, he was presented with an estimate of $570.

Organized Crime ***Organized crime* is a business operation that supplies illegal goods and services for profit.** Organized crime includes drug trafficking, prostitution, liquor and cigarette smuggling, loan-sharking, money laundering, and large-scale theft, such as truck hijacking (Simon and Eitzen, 1993). No single organization controls all organized crime, but many groups operate at all levels of society. Organized crime thrives because there is great demand for illegal goods and services. This public demand has produced illicit supply systems with global connections. These activities are highly profitable, since groups that have a monopoly over goods and services the public strongly desires can set their own price. Legitimate competitors are excluded because of the illegality; illegitimate competitors are controlled by force.

The deadly nature of organized crime has been shown in Montreal, which has been the scene of a major turf war between two rival biker gangs: the Rock Machine and the Hells Angels. The two gangs have been engaged in a battle for control of a large segment of the city's illegal drug market. During January and February of 1995, the battle took a particularly bloody turn as rival gang members died at a rate of almost one a week as a result of car bombings, shootings, and stabbings. Gang-related murders have continued to increase in Canada, climbing from twenty-one in 1995 to eighty-four in 2003 (Dauvergne, 2004).

Along with their illegal enterprises, organized crime groups have infiltrated the world of legitimate business. Linkages between legitimate businesses and organized crime exist in banking, hotels and motels, immigration consulting, real estate, garbage collection, vending machines, construction, delivery and long-distance hauling, garment manufacturing, insurance, stocks and bonds, vacation resorts, and funeral parlours. In addition, law-enforcement and government officials may be corrupted through bribery, campaign contributions, and favours intended to buy them off, although this has been much less of a problem in Canada than in many other countries.

Political Crimes   The term ***political crime refers to illegal or unethical acts involving the misuse of power by government officials, or illegal or unethical acts perpetrated against the government by outsiders seeking to make a political statement, undermine the government, or overthrow it.*** Government officials may use their authority unethically or illegally for material gain or political power. They may engage in graft (taking advantage of political position to gain money or property) through bribery, kickbacks, or "insider" deals that financially benefit them. While Canadian governments have a better record than those of most other countries, there have been a number of scandals. Most recently, in the late 1990s twenty politicians and forty members of former premier Grant Devine's Saskatchewan government were charged with fraud and many—including the former deputy premier—received prison sentences for misusing

government funds (Hagan, 2004). The 2005 Gomery Inquiry has exposed serious wrongdoing by some members of Prime Minister Jean Chrétien's Liberal government who illegally funnelled millions of dollars to Quebec advertising agencies in exchange for their political support.

Political crimes also include illegal or unethical acts perpetrated against the government by outsiders seeking to make a political statement or to undermine or overthrow the government. Examples include treason, acts of political sabotage, and certain types of environmental protests. During the 1960s, the Front de Libération du Québec (FLQ) tried to bring about an independent Quebec through terrorism (Corrado, 1996). Several people were killed in bombings, and in 1970 the FLQ precipitated the October Crisis by kidnapping James Cross, a British trade official, and Pierre Laporte, a provincial cabinet minister. Laporte was killed, and the federal government invoked the *War Measures Act,* which suspended certain civil liberties in order to deal with the crisis. While the FLQ's acts were clearly criminal, debate continues about whether the government was justified in using the *War Measures Act,* or whether invoking it also constituted a political crime aimed at defeating the Quebec nationalist movement.

Crime Statistics

While citizens, police, and policy makers all wish to know how much crime there is and what forms this crime takes, those who commit crimes normally try to conceal their actions. It is always difficult to gather statistics about crime and to get access to the social worlds of criminals. Thus our information about crime will always be incomplete and we can never be certain that it is completely accurate. Our main sources of information about crime are police statistics and victimization surveys.

Offical Statistics   Our most important source of crime data is the Canadian Uniform Crime Reports (CUCR) system, which summarizes crimes reported to all Canadian police departments. The CUCR is compiled by the Canadian Centre for Justice Statistics, which is part of Statistics Canada. Most of our public information about crime comes from the CUCR. When we read that the homicide rate in British Columbia is higher than the national average, or that in 2004 more than 2.6 million offences were reported to the police, the information is usually based on CUCR data. Figure 7.3 shows trends in

Figure 7.3   Canadian Crime Rates, 1962-2004

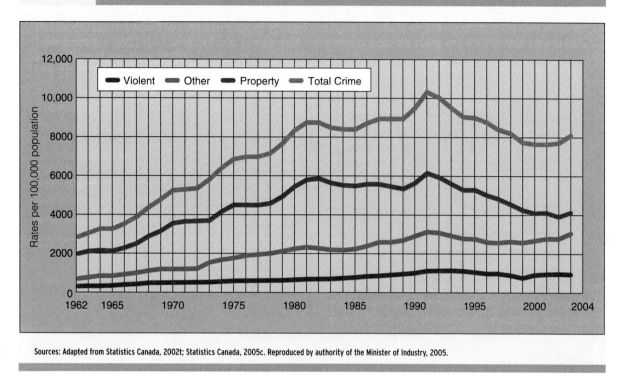

Sources: Adapted from Statistics Canada, 2002t; Statistics Canada, 2005c. Reproduced by authority of the Minister of Industry, 2005.

violent and property crimes, and Figure 7.4 shows Canada's homicide rates. While most Canadians think that crime is increasing, these charts show that it has declined significantly over the past decade. The decline is particularly significant in the case of homicide, where rates are now the lowest they have been in more than thirty years.

Crime figures should be interpreted very cautiously. While one can have confidence in homicide statistics, the accuracy of other crime statistics is less certain. Since many policy decisions by governments, as well as decisions by individuals about their personal safety, are based on CUCR statistics, it is important to recognize their limitations.

The major weakness of the CUCR is that police statistics always underreport the actual amount of crime. The vast majority of offences reported in the CUCR come to the attention of the police from the reports of victims of crime, and victims do not report all crimes. Furthermore, reporting of crime is inconsistent from place to place and from time to time. Official crime rates are the result of a criminal act, a complaint by a victim or witness, and a response by the criminal justice system. A change in any of these will lead to an increase or decrease in crime rates. This makes it very difficult to make sense of crime patterns and trends.

For example, Figure 7.3 shows that rates of reported violent crimes increased significantly in Canada during the late 1980s and early 1990s. In fact, they almost doubled between 1980 and 1990. While we don't know the real number of these crimes, we do know that at least part of the increase in reported crime is due to the fact that violence against women is now reported more often than it used to be (Linden, 1994). In the mid-1980s, many provincial governments directed police in their provinces to lay charges in all suspected cases of domestic violence. These zero-tolerance policies have been made progressively more effective since they were first implemented. This visible support by the justice system may have encouraged more victims to report spousal assaults. The impact of these changes can be seen in Winnipeg, where the police have instituted a mandatory charging policy and where the province has set up a special family violence court to facilitate the processing of spouse abuse cases. The number of domestic violence cases dealt with by this court rose from 1,444 in 1990, the first year of the court's operation, to 3,387 three years later (Ursel, 1996). It is likely that this increase was entirely due to changes in the reporting and recording of domestic assaults and not to any actual increase in family violence.

Figure 7.4   Canadian Homicide Rates, 1961-2004

As of 1971, population estimates were adjusted to reflect new methods of calculation.

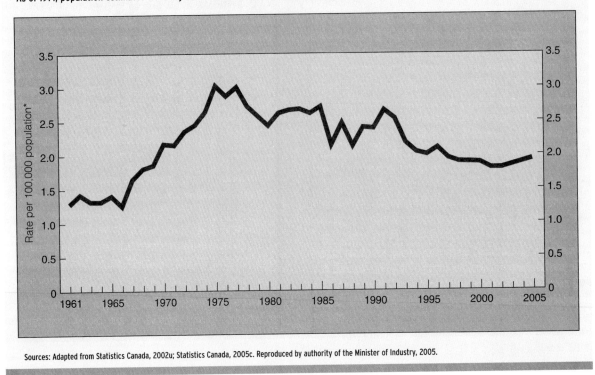

Sources: Adapted from Statistics Canada, 2002u; Statistics Canada, 2005c. Reproduced by authority of the Minister of Industry, 2005.

Another weakness of official statistics is that many crimes committed by persons of higher socioeconomic status are routinely handled by administrative or quasi-judicial bodies or by civil courts. To avoid negative publicity, many companies prefer to deal privately with offences like embezzlement committed by their employees, and these cases are never reported to the police. As a result, many elite crimes are never classified as "crimes," nor are the business people who commit them labelled as "criminals."

Victimization Surveys   The weaknesses of the CUCR have led to the development of other methods of measuring crime, the most important of which is the *victimization survey*. Because a major problem with the CUCR is the fact that many people do not report their victimization, some governments carried out surveys in which members of the public were directly asked whether they had been victims of crime. In the largest Canadian survey, fewer than 42 percent of the victimizations reported by respondents had been reported to the police (Evans and Himelfarb, 1996). Thus, reported crimes are only the tip of the iceberg. People told interviewers they did

not report a crime because they considered the incident too minor, because they felt it was a personal matter, because they preferred to deal with the problem in another way, or because they did not feel the police could do anything about the crime. Victimization surveys provide us with information about crimes that have not been officially reported, so they provide more accurate crime statistics than do police records. However, these surveys do have some weaknesses: people may not remember minor types of victimization; they may not report honestly to the interviewer; and they do not provide any information about "victimless crimes," such as drug use and illegal gambling. Despite these flaws, victimization surveys have shed new light on the extent of criminal behaviour and are a valuable complement to other ways of counting crimes.

For example, victimization surveys have provided additional information that has helped to confirm that the rise in violent crime during the 1980s and early 1990s was due to an increase in the reporting and recording of domestic assaults. Assaults did not likely increase during this period, we just did a better job of counting them.

Street Crimes and Criminals

Given the limitations of official statistics, is it possible to determine who commits crimes? We have much more information available about conventional or street crime than elite crime. Therefore, statistics do not show who commits all types of crime. Age, gender, class, and race are important factors in official statistics pertaining to street crime. These are known as *correlates of crime*. That is, they are factors associated with criminal activity. One method of testing theories of crime is to see how well they explain these correlates.

Age and Crime The age of the offender is one of the most significant factors associated with crime and most other kinds of deviance. Arrests increase from early adolescence, peak in young adulthood, and steadily decline with age. There is some variation in this pattern—for example, violent crimes peak at a later age than property crimes—but the general pattern is almost always the same. Crime is a young person's game. Property crimes peak between the ages of 15 and 18, while violent crimes are most common between 15 and 18 but are also frequently committed by offenders in their 20s and 30s.

The relationship between age and criminality exists in every society for which we have data (Hirschi and Gottfredson, 1983). The same finding holds true for most other types of high-risk behaviours, some of which are considered to be deviant. Adolescence and early adulthood are the peak times for both offending and victimization. Possible explanations for the decline in crime and deviance rates after early adulthood are the physical effects of aging, which make some criminal activity more difficult, and the realization by older chronic offenders that further arrests will result in very long jail sentences. Perhaps the best explanation for maturational reform, though, is related to the different social positions of youth and adults. Adolescents are between childhood and adult life. They have few responsibilities and no clear social role. Adolescence is also a time when young people are breaking away from the controls of their parents and others and preparing to live on their own. As we age, we begin to acquire commitments and obligations that limit our freedom to choose a lifestyle that includes crime and other forms of deviance.

Gender and Crime Another consistent correlate of crime is gender. Most crimes are committed by males. Females are more likely to be victims than offenders. As with age and crime, this relationship has existed in almost all times and cultures. However, while the age distribution is remarkably stable, considerably more variation in male/female crime ratios exists in different places, at different times, and for different types of crime.

Men make up more than 80 percent of those charged with crimes in Canada. As Figure 7.5 shows, the degree of involvement of males and females varies substantially for different crimes. The most important gender differences in arrest rates are reflected in the proportionately greater involvement of men in violent crimes and major property offences.

The difference between male and female involvement in crime has narrowed over the past three decades. Hartnagel (2004) found that the percentage of *Criminal Code* offences committed by females nearly doubled from 9 percent to 17 percent between 1968 and 2000. While there was virtually no change in the percentage of homicides committed by women (11 percent versus 10 percent), women's involvement in serious theft (9 percent versus 23 percent), fraud (11 percent versus 30 percent), and minor theft (22 percent versus 28 percent) increased substantially.

What has caused this change in the sex distribution of crime? One clue comes from cross-cultural data showing very large differences in sex ratios of criminal involvement in different parts of the world. While the ratio of male to female crime in North America and Western Europe is between 5:1 and 10:1, ratios as high as 20,000:1 have been reported elsewhere. The ratios are highest (meaning that male rates of crime are much higher than those of females) in countries having the greatest differences between the roles of men and women. Where women follow traditional roles in which their lives are centred exclusively on the home, their crime rates are very low. On the other hand, where women's lives are more similar to men's, their crime rates will be higher. This is consistent with the change in women's crime rates over the past several decades in Canada, where the role of women has come to resemble that of men.

While role convergence may explain some of the reduction in the gap between male and female crime rates, the convergence in crime rates has almost stopped over the past decade, and it does not seem likely that women will ever become as involved in crime as men, or that they will adopt male patterns of crime, particularly for violent crime. The increase in female crime has been greatest for property crimes, such as theft and fraud. These two categories include offences commonly committed by females, such as shoplifting, credit card fraud, and passing bad cheques, which are among the least serious property

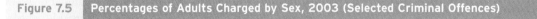

Figure 7.5　Percentages of Adults Charged by Sex, 2003 (Selected Criminal Offences)

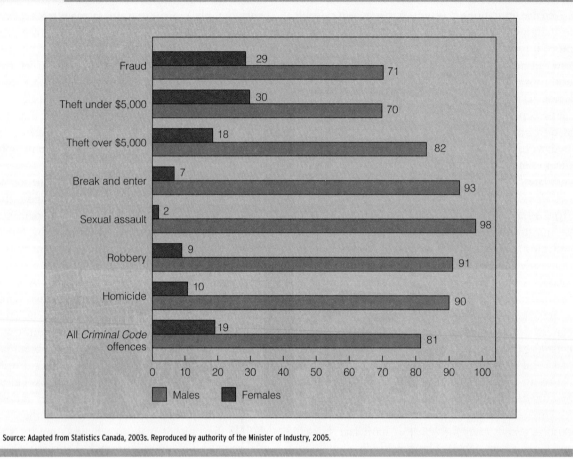

Source: Adapted from Statistics Canada, 2003s. Reproduced by authority of the Minister of Industry, 2005.

offences. Comack (2004) has concluded that this reflects the feminization of poverty rather than any convergence of men's and women's roles. As you will see in Chapter 8, the number of poor, female single parents is growing, and some of these women may commit crime in order to support themselves and their children. Thus, much of the increase in female crime may simply reflect the increased economic marginalization of poor women.

While female crime rates have increased more rapidly than male crime rates, it is important to remember that the numbers seem more dramatic than they are because the percentage changes are based on very low numbers of female crimes in earlier decades. Women have a long way to go to reach equality in crime with men.

Social Class and Crime

Criminologists have long debated the relationship between social class and crime. Many theories of crime are based on the assumption that crime is economically motivated and that poverty will lead to criminal behaviour.

Unfortunately, the evidence concerning the impact of economic factors on crime is not entirely clear. We do know that persons from lower socioeconomic backgrounds are more likely to be arrested for violent and property crimes. However, we also know that these types of crimes are more likely to come to the attention of the police than are the white-collar and corporate crimes that are more likely to be committed by members of the upper class. Because the vast majority of white-collar and corporate crimes are never reported, we do not have the data to adequately assess the relationship between class and crime.

Before looking at some of the data on social class and crime we do have, let us briefly consider several other economic variables. Does crime increase during times of high unemployment? Do poor cities, provinces, and countries have higher crime rates than richer communities? The answer to both these questions is no. Historically, crime rates are at least as likely to rise during periods of prosperity as during recessionary times (Nettler, 1984). We are also as likely to find high crime rates in rich countries as in poor ones.

The world's wealthiest countries, the United States and Japan, have very different crime rates. Compared with other countries, crime in the United States is very high and crime in Japan is very low. Within Canada, the poor provinces of Newfoundland and New Brunswick have crime rates far lower than the rich provinces of British Columbia and Alberta (see Map 7.2). Hartnagel (2004) has concluded that the *degree of inequality*—poverty amid affluence—is a better predictor of crime than is the amount of poverty.

Little research on this issue has been done in Canada, but researchers have found that homicide rates are correlated with the degree of inequality of provinces (Daly et al., 2001) and cities (Kennedy et al., 1991). These studies concluded that the size of the gap between rich and poor is more strongly correlated with homicide rates than are the actual income levels. Thus relative deprivation is a better predictor of homicide than absolute deprivation.

We know that lower-class people are overrepresented in arrest and prison admission statistics. However, we do not know if this is because lower-class people commit more crimes, or because the justice system treats them more harshly. To get closer to actual behaviour, researchers developed self-report surveys in which respondents were asked to report the number of deviant acts they had committed during a specified period of time. There is some disagreement about the conclusions that should be drawn from this research, most of which has used adolescent subjects. Some feel that self-report research shows almost no correlation between class and delinquency and crime, and attributes class differences in official measures to bias in the criminal justice system (Tittle et al., 1978). However, other research (Elliott and Ageton, 1980; Thornberry and Farnworth, 1982) has supported the view that crime is more frequent in the lower class. Based on the results of these and many other studies, the most likely conclusion is that for the vast majority of people, class and crime or delinquency are not related. People from all classes break the law, at least occasionally. However, those who engage in frequent and serious offending are most likely to come from the very bottom of the class ladder—from an underclass that is severely disadvantaged economically, educationally, and socially. There is also some evidence that other forms of deviance, such as suicide, alcoholism, mental illness, and drug addiction, are also more common among the underclass.

This conclusion is supported by the work of several researchers who have conducted field studies among street youth in several countries, including Canada, the United States, and Britain. U.S. research has focused on the role of chronic unemployment and discrimination in the development of street gangs in Hispanic (Vigil, 1990) and African American (Anderson, 1994) communities. Subcultures that encourage and facilitate crime have developed in response to the long-term poverty so common in many American communities. Compared to the bleak legitimate opportunities available to them, criminal opportunities, particularly from the drug trade, can be very attractive. The Canadian research involved studies of street youth in Toronto (Hagan and McCarthy, 1992) and Edmonton (Baron, 1994). These studies found that many street youth were from lower-class families and were on the streets because of poor relationships at home and at school. Their life on the streets often leads to delinquency because of the need to survive and also because engaging in crime provides them with a sense of control they do not get in other facets of their lives.

A unique victimization survey further reinforces this conclusion. In 1993, Statistics Canada conducted the national Violence Against Women Survey, for which more than 12,000 women were interviewed (Johnson, 1996). Several findings supported the view that violence is greatest in the lower class. First, men with high-school educations assaulted their wives at twice the rate of men with university degrees. Second, men who were out of work committed assaults at twice the rate of men who were employed. Third, men in the lowest income category (less than $15,000 a year) assaulted their wives at twice the rate of men with higher incomes. However, above this $15,000 level, there was no relationship between income and crime. This again suggests that the highest crime rates can be found at the very bottom of the economic ladder, but that above this level there is no relationship.

Race and Ethnicity and Crime

In societies with culturally heterogeneous populations, some ethnic and racial groups will have higher crime rates than others (Nettler, 1984). For example, in the United States, African Americans and Hispanics are overrepresented in arrest data.

However, because Statistics Canada does not routinely collect data about racial and ethnic correlates of crime, we know relatively little about the situation in Canada. In addition to data about Aboriginal Canadians, which will be discussed later, there have been three studies dealing with minorities and crime. The first of these studies, which examined race and ethnicity in the federal prison system, found that offenders from non-Aboriginal visible ethnic minorities were *underrepresented* in the federal correctional system's population (Thomas, 1992). Specifically, the study found that in 1989, 5.2 percent of the federal corrections population were members of ethnic minority groups, while these groups made up more than 6.3 percent of the general population. The second study, which examined provincial youth and adult correctional centres in British Columbia, arrived at similar findings. Only 8.2 percent of the prison population were members of non-Aboriginal visible ethnic minorities, yet these groups made up 13.5 percent of the province's population. Contrary to the common view that immigrants have high crime rates, only 11 percent of B.C. inmates were not born in Canada, compared with 22 percent of the population of the province. Finally, the Commission on Systemic Racism in the Ontario Criminal Justice System (1995) reported that the rate of imprisonment for Black adults in Ontario was five times higher than the rate for white adults. Black adults were also more likely to be imprisoned while awaiting trial, particularly for discretionary charges, such as drug possession and drug trafficking.

While statistics on other minorities are limited, there are extensive data on Aboriginal peoples. This is due in part to the documentation that resulted from special inquiries held to find out whether actions toward Aboriginal people by the justice system in several provinces have been discriminatory. Many studies have demonstrated the overinvolvement of Aboriginal people (Hartnagel, 2004). A typical finding is that while Aboriginal people made up about 2 percent of the population in 1991, they made up about 24 percent of persons held in custody after being convicted of a crime (Brantingham, Mu, and Verma, 1995). In their study of Canadian homicides, Silverman and Kennedy found that Aboriginal people are involved in homicides in proportions that are at least five times greater than their representation in the population (1993). Hyde and LaPrairie (1987) showed that Aboriginal and non-Aboriginal people had different patterns, as well as different rates, of crime. Aboriginal people had more social disorder offences (many of which were alcohol-related), fewer property offences, and more violent offences. Other researchers found a great deal of variation in Aboriginal crime rates among different communities and parts of the country (Wood and Griffiths, 1996).

What is the reason for these racial and ethnic differences in crime rates? One answer is that there has often been discrimination against minority groups. The treatment of Blacks in South Africa and in the southern United States are obvious examples. Discrimination against Aboriginal people in Canada, Australia, and New Zealand has also been well-documented by commissions of inquiry. Members of minority groups, who tend to be poor, may go to prison for minor offences if they are unable to pay fines. A report by the Law Reform Commission of Canada (1974) found that in 1970 and 1971 more than half of all Aboriginal people admitted to Saskatchewan jails were incarcerated for nonpayment of fines. While this type of discrimination may be unintentional, it is nonetheless real. The justice system also tends to focus its efforts on the types of crimes that are committed by low-income people rather than on white-collar and corporate crimes, so members of poor minority groups may be overrepresented in crime statistics. Discrimination likely accounts for some, but not all, of the high rates of criminality of some minority groups.

To provide a further explanation, consider again the case of Canada's Aboriginal people. Their situation is, of course, unique, but the same kinds of factors may apply in other contexts. While a number of theories have been advanced to explain Aboriginal overinvolvement (Hartnagel, 2004; Wood and Griffiths, 2000), consider the following explanation, which has been drawn from conflict and social control theories. Canada's Aboriginal people have far less power and fewer resources than other Canadians. They must cope with systems of education and religion that have been imposed on them from outside their cultural communities and that are incompatible with their customs and traditions. In the past, forced attendance at residential schools and forced adoption outside the community have weakened family ties. Crippling rates of unemployment in many areas mean no job ties, and school curricula that are irrelevant to the lives of Aboriginal students mean that children do not become attached to their schools. Under these conditions, strong social bonds are difficult to develop and high rates of crime can be predicted. As Manitoba's Aboriginal Justice Inquiry concluded: "From our review of the information available to us . . . we believe that the relatively high rates of crime among Aboriginal people are a result of the despair, dependency, anger, frustration and sense of injustice prevalent in Aboriginal communities, stemming from the cultural and community breakdown that has occurred over the past century" (Hamilton and Sinclair, 1991:91).

Region and Crime   Crime is not evenly distributed around the globe. Some countries have much higher crime rates than others, and within countries there are often significant differences among regions. Unfortunately, because different countries have such varying methods of reporting and recording crime, international comparisons are difficult. The most reliable measure for comparison is homicide rates, which are reported in a reasonably similar fashion in most countries. Canada's homicide rate of about 1.8 per

BOX 7.3 SOCIOLOGY AND THE MEDIA

"If It Bleeds, It Leads": Fear of Crime and the Media

Most Canadians learn about crime through the media rather than from first-hand experience. Stories on television and radio and in newspapers, magazines, and books shape our views about crime and criminals. However, the media do not simply "report" the news. Editors and reporters select the crime news we hear about and construct the way in which this news is presented to us.

Unfortunately, the picture of crime we receive from the media is very inaccurate. For example, while most crime is property crime, most stories in the media deal with violent crime. Gabor (1994) reviewed all the crime-related stories reported over two months in an Ottawa newspaper. More than half the stories focused on violent crimes, particularly murders. However, violent crimes actually made up only 7 percent of reported crimes in Ottawa, and the city averaged just six murders per year. While violent crimes were over-reported, property crimes rarely received much attention, and white-collar and political crimes were almost never written about. Between 1990 and 1996, the homicide rate in Canada declined by almost 20 percent while murder coverage on CBC and CTV national news programs increased by 300 percent. Calgary had twelve murders in 1996, a year in which the *Calgary Herald* published 1,667 murder-related stories (National Media Archive, 1997).

■ Members of the media pursue a vehicle containing convicted murderer Karla Homolka following a court hearing.

Why do the media misrepresent crime? The primary goal of the media is to make profits by selling advertising. Stories that attract viewers or readers will boost ratings and circulation, even if these stories do not represent the reality of crime. The informal media rule, "If it bleeds, it leads," reflects the fact that the public are fascinated by sensationalized, bloody stories, such as those of mass murders or attacks against helpless senior citizens. Commenting on his experience with the media, the executive director of a provincial legal society said, "If there's no blood and gore, or there's no sex, it's not newsworthy. And if it falls into the category of being newsworthy, then they have to show the dead body. They've got to show the corpse" (McCormick, 1995:182).

The media's misrepresentation of crime has several consequences. First, Canadians greatly overestimate the amount of violent crime that is committed and have a fear of crime that is more intense than the risk of victimization justifies. One survey found that the vast majority of Canadians (75 percent) felt that most crimes are accompanied by violence, though the true figure is fewer than 10 percent (Doob and Roberts, 1983). Our fears are reinforced by the global coverage of violence. Television can instantly bring us events from anywhere and violent crimes, such as mass murders in Australia and in Scotland are reported as immediately and as thoroughly as if they had happened in our own communities.

The media also provide us with a distorted stereotype of offenders. Violent crimes are most often committed by relatives, friends, and acquaintances, not by the anonymous stranger so many of us fear. Corporate and white-collar criminals are responsible for a great deal of social harm, but except for the most dramatic cases—such as Bre-X in Canada, and Martha Stewart and Enron in the U.S.—their activities rarely receive much attention in the media. Reporting of these cases is typically limited to the business section rather than the headlines.

Map 7.2 2004 Crime Rates per 100,000 Population (*Criminal Code* Excluding Traffic Offences)

Yukon
Territory
23,125
Northwest
Territories
42,126
Nunavut
36,685
Atlantic
Ocean
Newfoundland
6320
Hudson
Bay
British
Columbia
12,522
Pacific
Ocean
Labrador
Alberta
10,390
Saskatch-
ewan
15,159
Manitoba
12,753
Quebec
6493
Ontario
5702
Prince
Edward
Island
8220
Nova
Scotia
8764
New
Brunswick
7313

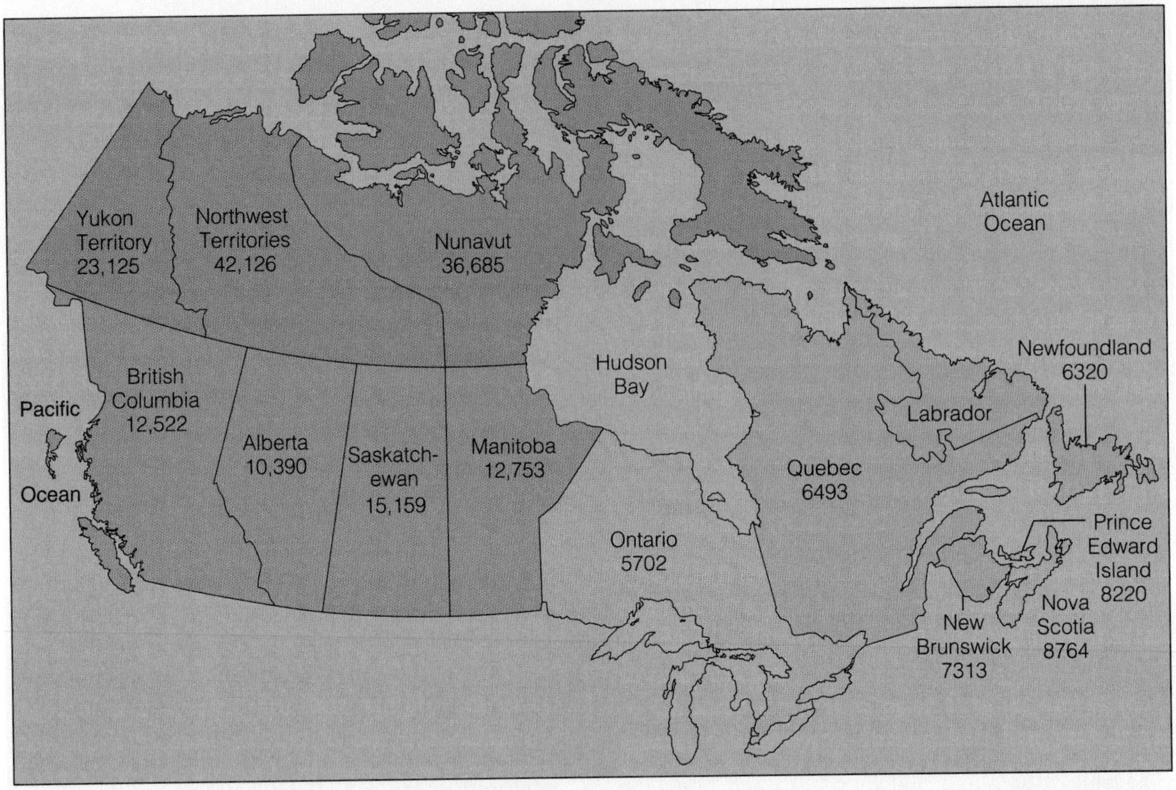

Source: Adapted from Statistics Canada, 2005c. Reproduced by authority of the Minister of Industry, 2005.

100,000 people is relatively low by world standards. It is about one-third of the U.S. rate, but about one and a half times that of the United Kingdom. The highest rates of homicide are typically found in the less economically developed countries, although the high rate in the United States is a notable exception.

Major regional differences in crime rates exist within Canada. As shown in Map 7.2, crime rates are highest in the West and the North, and lowest in Central Canada. Crime rates used to be lowest in Atlantic Canada, but have increased in those provinces over the past few years.

THE CRIMINAL JUSTICE SYSTEM

The criminal justice system includes the police, the courts, and prisons. However, the term *criminal justice system* is misleading because it implies that law enforcement agencies and courts constitute one large, integrated system, when it is actually a collection of "somewhat interrelated, semi-autonomous bureaucracies," each of which possesses considerable discretion to do as it wishes (Sheley, 1991:334). *Discretion* refers to the use of personal judgment by police officers, prosecutors, judges, and other criminal justice system officials regarding whether and how to proceed in a given situation.

The Police

Most people think the main function of the police is to enforce the law. That is indeed one of their functions, but there are several others, including order maintenance and the provision of social services. Order maintenance refers to keeping the peace. For example, stopping arguments, controlling the areas where skid-row alcoholics drink, and making a group of boisterous teenagers move away from the parking lot of a convenience store are all order-maintenance activities. While the main concern in law enforcement is arresting a suspect, the main concern in order maintenance is restoring peace in the community. In difficult situations, arrest may be one means of doing this, but arresting someone may be only a means to an end rather than an end in itself. The service role is also an important one and consists of many different activities, including finding lost children, counselling crime victims, and notifying next of kin in fatal accidents.

Two questions you might ask are: Why do the police have such a broad range of responsibilities? and What, if anything, do these activities have in common? To answer the first question, there are several reasons why the police have the broad responsibilities they do:

1. The police are one of the few public agencies open twenty-four hours a day.
2. In many cases, the police are serving clients that other agencies may not be interested in. The poor, the homeless, and the mentally ill may become police clients almost by default. If no other agency will look after intoxicated people who pass out on downtown streets, the police must do it.
3. The police may not know about, or have access to, other agencies that could handle some of their cases.
4. Historically, the role of the police has been to keep the peace. Sir Robert Peel, the founder of the first municipal police force, in London, England, stressed a service-oriented philosophy, and this tradition has persisted.

The second question—What ties these diverse activities together?—is best answered by looking at two dimensions of the police role. First, the police have the *authority* (and often the duty) to intervene in situations where something must be done immediately. This authority is the same whether the incident is an armed robbery in progress, a naked man standing on a busy street screaming at people, or a complaint that someone's pet boa constrictor has just appeared in someone else's bedroom. Second, the authority is backed up by *non-negotiable force*. If someone refuses to go along with what a police officer suggests, the officer can use force (usually arrest) to back up his or her demands. Even professional caregivers may resort to calling the police when clients refuse to cooperate with them. Once the situation gets into the hands of the police, there may be nobody else to call, so they have to resolve the situation themselves. Egon Bittner has nicely summed up the role of the patrol officer: "What policemen do appears to consist of rushing to the scene of any crisis whatever, judging its needs in accordance with canons of common sense reasoning, and imposing solutions upon it without regard to resistance or opposition" (1980:137).

Does the justice system discriminate against members of racial minority groups? CITY-TV assignment editor Dwight Drummond attends a public inquiry into his wrongful arrest during a drug bust in October 1993.

Given the enormous range of activities with which the police are involved, you can see that the police have a high degree of discretion. Police managers, for one thing, have *administrative discretion* over how they organize their department and use their resources. If few resources are dedicated to commercial crime, few white-collar offenders will be apprehended. If a department rewards its members only for law-enforcement tasks, they will not do as good a job on order maintenance and service activities. Second, police officers exercise a great deal of *individual discretion* in that they often have to decide which rules to apply and how to apply them. Many of the situations in which the police use their discretion have very low visibility. Their supervisors are unlikely to observe them or to find out many details about how individual officers use their discretion. For example, if a police officer stops a driver for speeding and the driver has alcohol on his or her breath, several outcomes are possible. The police officer may warn the person and tell them to go straight home, write a speeding ticket, or administer a breathalyzer and lay charges of impaired driving. If the officer elects not to administer the breathalyzer, the supervisor will never know how that officer has used discretion.

The use of discretion by the police is unavoidable. This is not a problem if discretion is dispensed equitably and in a manner consistent with both community standards and the rule of law. However, if it is based on extra-legal factors, such as race or class, or if it is used to favour certain individuals over others, it can be considered *discriminatory* and an abuse of police powers. Issues of racial discrimination have generated the most discussion in Canada in recent years as inquiries have been held in many cities following police shootings of minority group members.

Earlier in this chapter we discussed some of the ways in which the justice system discriminates against Aboriginal people. Similar conclusions may also apply to other groups. Many Blacks, particularly young people, feel that they are often harassed by the police and that they are stopped and questioned because of their race. Carl James interviewed a number of Black youth in several Ontario cities about their experiences with the police. Their comments show that they do not feel they have been treated equitably by the police:

> "You can't win. As long as you're Black you are a target."
>
> "They drive by. They don't glimpse your clothes, they glimpse your colour. That's the first thing they look at. If they judge the clothes so much why don't they go and stop those white boys that are wearing those same things like us?"
>
> No matter what the situation that you're in, what your dress is like . . . they will find a negative way of thinking about you, because you're Black, and secondly because you're Somali, and thirdly because you're an immigrant and you speak a different language." (James, 1998:165–168)

A survey conducted for the Commission on Systemic Racism in the Ontario Criminal Justice System (1995) also found that Black respondents were much more likely than white and Chinese respondents to report that they had been stopped by the police and were more likely to report feeling that the police had treated them unfairly the last time they were stopped. These perceptions of racial profiling have been supported by research done in Toronto (Wortley and Tanner, 2003) that has shown that Black drivers are more likely to be stopped by the police than drivers of other races, and by a later study in Kingston that showed Blacks were more likely to be stopped by the police than members of other races

(CTV, 2005). While not all researchers agree that these studies actually demonstrate racial profiling (see Melchers, 2003) there is little doubt that being more frequently stopped does contribute to the perception of police harassment felt by many Black people. If the police do selectively stop members of racial minorities and if they focus their enforcement activities on minority members, these actions will contribute to the overrepresentation of these minorities in the justice system (Quigley, 1994).

The Courts

Criminal courts decide the guilt or innocence of those accused of committing a crime. In theory, justice is determined in an adversarial process in which the prosecutor (a lawyer who represents the state) argues that the accused is guilty and the defence lawyer asserts that the accused is innocent. Proponents of the adversarial system feel this system best provides a just decision about guilt or innocence.

The essence of the adversarial system can be seen in the defence lawyer's role, which is to do all he or she can do to help the accused. This role was described by Lord Brougham, who was the defence lawyer in an 1821 case that could have had disastrous consequences for the British government had his defence been successful:

> An advocate, in the discharge of his duty, knows but one person in all the world, and that person is his client. To save that client by all means and expedients, and at all hazards and costs to their persons, and amongst them, to himself, is his first and only duty; and in performing this duty he must not regard the alarm, the torments, the destruction which he may bring upon others. Separating the duty of a patriot from that of an advocate, he must go on reckless of the consequences, though it should be his unhappy fate to involve his country in confusion. (cited in Greenspan, 1982:201)

We can add to Lord Brougham's comment that in an adversarial system the defence lawyer is obliged to fulfil this duty to the client without concern for the client's actual guilt or innocence.

Most of those working in the courts strongly defend the adversarial system and see it as one of the cornerstones of a free and democratic society. Many of the procedures that seem to restrict the ability of the court to get at the "truth," such as the rule that accused persons cannot be forced to testify against themselves, were adopted to prevent the arbitrary use of state power against the accused. However, some critics feel that our

BOX 7.4 CRITICAL THINKING

Let's Make a Deal: Bargaining for Justice

The image most of us have of the court process is that those who are arrested and charged will go to trial. This trial will be held in a courtroom packed with spectators and will be contested by highly trained and articulate lawyers arguing the fine points of law before a judge and jury. However, this image is far from the truth. Trials are relatively rare and most cases are decided by guilty pleas. A high proportion, probably the majority, of these guilty pleas result from plea bargaining.

Plea bargaining is the process of negotiating a guilty plea. Informal, private discussions are held between the defence and the prosecution in an attempt to reach a mutually agreeable outcome in which both parties receive concessions. For the accused, plea bargaining may mean that the severity of the penalty will be reduced. A negotiated guilty plea also relieves the anxiety of waiting for sentencing, as the outcome of the case is agreed on ahead of time. The accused may also wish to save the expense and publicity of a trial, especially if the likely result is conviction. For the prosecution, plea bargaining saves time, which is crucial in our overloaded courts. If all cases went to trial, the backlog would be endless. It is likely that busier courts will give more lenient deals as the accused will have more bargaining power. The Crown, or prosecuting, attorney may also bargain if the prosecution's case is weak. For example, if a key witness is very reluctant to testify or would not make a good impression on a judge or jury, the prosecution may bargain to ensure the defendant does not get off (Griffiths and Verdun-Jones, 1994).

Plea bargaining has been widely criticized on the grounds that it subverts the aims of the criminal justice system by rewarding the guilty and penalizing those who elect to maintain their innocence and go to trial. The Law Reform Commission of Canada, among other groups, has recommended its abolition. However, despite this criticism the practice continues, and some argue that the system could not work without it.

Plea bargaining has been particularly criticized in cases where guilty people are given light sentences in exchange for testimony against their partners in crime. The twelve-year sentence given to Karla Homolka in exchange for her testimony against Paul Bernardo is an example of this type of bargaining. While the Homolka case was controversial because of her direct involvement with Bernardo's killings (Williams, 2004), some cases are even more questionable because someone heavily involved in criminal activity receives a lenient disposition in exchange for information about others who are less involved.

Consider the case of Yves "Apache" Trudeau, for example (Lavigne, 1987). A former Hells Angel, of the notorious Laval, Quebec, chapter, Trudeau is one of the most prolific killers in Canada's history. In 1985 Trudeau admitted to forty-three gang-related killings carried out in the 1970s and 1980s and was able to negotiate a plea bargain in which the Crown accepted guilty pleas to forty-three counts of manslaughter and gave a commitment that he would be released with a new identity after serving seven years in jail. Trudeau agreed to cooperate with the police after learning he was the target of other Hells Angels who had already killed six members of his chapter. In exchange for police protection, a comfortable cell, and a light sentence, Trudeau agreed to tell what he knew about the operation of the Hells Angels and other Montreal organized crime groups. Two other members of the Laval chapter, Michel Blass and Gilles Lachance, also received plea bargains in exchange for their testimony against other gang members. As a result of this testimony, five Hells Angels were found guilty of murder and received life sentences. While the police and prosecutors would argue that plea bargaining was the only way to convict other Hells Angels and to reduce the influence of the gang, the practice of making deals with killers raises some difficult moral and ethical questions.

What are your views about plea bargaining? Do you think that justice is served when deals are made?

---

system does not deal adequately with crime because it places more emphasis on winning than on doing what is best for the accused, for the victim, and for society. The plea bargaining described in Box 7.4 is an aspect of our justice system that has drawn much criticism.

Not all Western countries use the adversarial court system. Several European countries use systems in which the judge takes a much more active role in ensuring that justice is done. Jim Hackler (1994), one of the most articulate critics of Canada's courts, has described the court process in Switzerland, for example. In Switzerland, the police investigation is directed by a magistrate and the police gather information relevant to both sides of the case. While the accused lacks some of the protection of our system, the defence has access to all information about the case and can request through the magistrate that the police gather additional information. At the trial, the judge leads the questioning and there is much more concern with getting at the truth, and less on legal constraints of the kind that exist in our system. The holistic approach to justice advocated by many Aboriginal people is another alternative to the very technical and legalistic system that now prevails in our courts. This approach takes into account the needs of the victim, the accused, and the community, rather than simply applying formal legal rules and procedures.

Punishment

Punishment is any action designed to deprive a person of things of value (including liberty) because of some offence the person is thought to have committed (Barlow, 1987:421). Punishment can serve four functions:

1. *Retribution* imposes a penalty on the offender. Retribution is based on the premise that the punishment should fit the crime: the greater the degree of social harm, the more the offender should be punished. An individual who murders, for example, should be punished more severely than one who steals.
2. *Social protection* results from restricting offenders so they cannot commit further crimes. If someone is in prison, he or she is no longer a threat to those of us on the outside. However, there is a high rate of offending within the prison, so imprisonment does not necessarily put an end to criminal behaviour.
3. *Rehabilitation* seeks to return offenders to the community as law-abiding citizens. However, rehabilitation programs are not a priority for governments or prison officials and the few rehabilitation programs that exist are typically underfunded. While many Canadian prisons offer some training to inmates, the job skills that may be learned in prison often do not transfer to the outside world, nor are offenders given much assistance in finding work that fits their skills once they are released.
4. *Deterrence* seeks to reduce criminal activity by instilling a fear of punishment. *Specific deterrence* is intended to deter the individual offender from reoffending. For example, a judge may sentence a wife abuser to six months in jail to teach him not to repeat his abuse. *General deterrence* is intended to deter all of us who see the example set by the justice system. For example, a judge may decide that convenience store robberies are getting out of hand and give one offender a severe sentence to set an example for others.

There is no question that the law deters. You do not deliberately park where you know your car will be towed away, and you do not speed if you see a police car behind you. However, the law does not deter as well as we might hope because the *certainty* of being arrested and convicted for most crimes is low. Most crimes do not result in arrests and most arrests do not result in convictions. It is difficult to increase the certainty of punishment, so we try to tinker with the severity of punishment instead. Most "law and order" politicians talk about getting tough on crime by increasing penalties rather than by making punishment more certain. However, increasing the average penalty for robbery by a year will not likely reduce robbery rates if most robberies do not result in a conviction and a jail sentence.

We know less about the impact of law as a specific deterrent. That is, does serving a prison sentence make it less likely that a person will commit a crime in the future? While we do know that a large proportion of criminals are *recidivists* (repeat offenders), we do not know how many would repeat if they had not been in prison.

Most convicted criminals today are out on either *probation* (supervision in the community instead of serving a prison term) or *parole* (early release from prison). If offenders violate the conditions of their probation or parole, they may be required to serve their full sentence in prison.

The disparate treatment of the poor and some racial minorities is evident in the prison system. We have seen that incarceration rates for Aboriginal people are disproportionately higher than those for whites. Disparate treatment of women also is evident. Women make up only a small minority of Canada's prison population—in 1996 there were 13,585 male inmates in federal penitentiaries compared with 277 females (Robinson et al., 1998). These small numbers mean that in some respects men are treated better than women in prison. Women's prisons, for example, offer far fewer educational and training programs than do men's prisons. The small number of women inmates makes it difficult to offer a wide range of programs. The small number of women's prisons means they are often imprisoned far from family and friends. Since the majority of female inmates are single parents (which is not true of male inmates), long periods of incarceration far away from home and family place a special burden on female inmates (Comack, 1996a).

Restorative Justice

For many years, we have relied on the formal justice system to deal with crime. Community members have been discouraged from participating in their own protection and have had little say in the services they received. After the victim called the police dispatcher, the police would soon arrive to take care of the problem, and if an arrest was made, case processing was left in the hands of the formal justice system. Many of those found guilty by the court were removed from the community and sent away to jail. Professionals have controlled each step in the system, and victims and other community members have had little involvement.

While most people have come to accept this as the proper way of dealing with crime, many of those who have been involved with the justice system feel it has failed them. Victims feel left out, as their role as the aggrieved party is forgotten and they are relegated to the role of witnesses. They have no control over the process; often they are not even informed about the disposition of the case. Offenders are also dealt with impersonally. Their crimes become the focus of concern, and their individual circumstances and needs are not considered. Offenders are rarely reminded of the personal harm they have done. Instead, many offenders are sent to costly prisons that result more in alienation than rehabilitation. In addition, the public is often dissatisfied with a justice system that does not respond to their concerns.

Many critics of the present justice system have advocated returning to a fundamentally different way of approaching criminal justice, to a system that is intended to restore social relationships rather than simply to punish (Church Council on Justice and Corrections, 1996). Advocates of *restorative justice* seek to return the focus of the justice system to repairing the harm that has been done to the victim and to the community. A key element of restorative justice is the involvement of the victim and other members of the community as active participants in the process. The focus of the restorative justice approach is to reconcile offenders with those they have harmed and to help communities reintegrate victims and offenders. Restorative justice has its roots in traditional societies where the restoration of order was

crucial to society's survival. In Canada, Aboriginal communities used a variety of different methods, including *circle sentencing,* which brings an offender together with the victims and other community members, to resolve disputes and are leading the way in the return to the use of restorative justice practices. In recent years, traditional practices have been revived and modified in innovative ways. Two of the most widespread contemporary restorative justice methods are *victim–offender reconciliation* and *family group conferencing.*

Victim–offender reconciliation is a program that was devised in Elmira, Ontario, in 1974 as an initiative by two individuals to persuade a judge to deal in a positive fashion with two youths who had vandalized property belonging to twenty-two different victims. Rather than a normal court disposition that may well have involved incarceration, the offence was handled in the community. Mediators worked with the victims and the offenders to reach a resolution that was acceptable to all parties. As a result, the boys had to deal personally with each of their victims and to make restitution for the damage they had caused. The restorative process gave victims a chance to have a say in what happened, and gave offenders the chance to make amends.

Family group conferencing (sometimes called community justice conferencing) is a restorative justice technique that had its origins in New Zealand and is a variation of circle sentencing. The RCMP has selected family group conferencing as one of the ways its detachments will work with communities to try to reduce crime, so use of this method of conflict resolution should become common in Canada. Family group conferencing typically applies to young offenders and normally involves the victim, the offender, and as many of their family and friends as possible. Professional or community workers may also participate. A typical family group conference involves about a dozen people. When adult offenders are involved in the process, it is more likely to involve community members than families. The goal of the conference is to allow those affected by the crime the opportunity to resolve the case in an environment that is supportive of both victim and offender. A coordinator allows all parties to speak about the case, and then leads the conference into a discussion of what might be done to repair the harm done to the victim. Victims and their family and friends outline their expectations, and offenders and their family and friends respond. Negotiation continues until a plan is agreed on and written down. The coordinator then establishes mechanisms for enforcing the plan. The family and friends of both the victim and the offender are encouraged to offer continuing help to ensure the resolution arrived at during the conference is actually carried out in the community.

Evaluations of restorative justice methods have identified concerns about the enforcement of negotiated agreements, the possible conflict with the due-process rights of the accused, the potential for net-widening through including offenders who might otherwise be dealt with in less formal ways, conflicts over jurisdiction among various professional groups, and the inability to address the conditions that cause crime, such as unemployment, poverty, and the breakdown of family support networks. Despite these concerns, restorative justice programs now provide us with a valuable alternative to the formal justice system.

Community Corrections

A major focus of the restorative justice approach is reducing the number of people in prison. Diversion programs and community corrections reduce the likelihood of imprisonment and replace formal consequences with more meaningful community-based sanctions. Community corrections, an important component of the restorative justice approach, shifts responsibility for corrections back to the community and minimizes the separation of the offender from society at a number of different stages in the correctional process.

The incarceration rate in Canada in 2002 was 116 per 100,000 people. This is lower than the rates in the United States (702) and England and Wales (139), but higher than many other countries including Italy (100), Germany (95), France (85), and Denmark (64) (Public Safety and Emergency Preparedness Canada, 2004). Because our rates are higher than those of many other countries, some have suggested that Canada should move toward a greater use of community corrections. These dispositions include programs, such as community probation, community service orders, intensive probation supervision, and bail supervision, as alternatives to incarceration. The movement toward community-based sanctions has been driven by three major concerns. First, these program, are much cheaper than incarceration. It costs more than $85,000 to keep a person in a federal penitentiary for a year (Statistics Canada, 2004a), so governments can achieve significant savings by increasing the use of community corrections. The second concern is humanitarian. Prison life is very unpleasant and it can be unfair to send people

to jail for relatively minor offences. Finally, an offender may benefit from being able to maintain ties with family and community, and these ties may make subsequent involvement in crime less likely.

The move toward community corrections has been supported by federal legislation. In addition to the conventional objectives of protection of the public, deterrence, and rehabilitation, recent sentencing legislation sets out the objectives of making reparations to victims and to the community, and promoting a sense of responsibility in offenders. In announcing the legislation, the government has explicitly stated that alternatives to imprisonment should be used where appropriate (Department of Justice, 1994). The legislation also added conditional sentences to the *Criminal Code*. Conditional sentences allow convicted offenders to serve their sentences in the community under greater control (e.g., house arrest and electronic monitoring) and represent an important step in the direction of community corrections. The use of conditional sentences has led to a reduction in Canada's incarceration rate (Statistics Canada, 2004a).

DEVIANCE AND CRIME IN THE FUTURE

Among the questions pertaining to deviance and crime facing us are: Is the solution to our "crime problem" more law and order? What impact will the global economy have on crime? and How will technology change the nature of crime in the future?

Although many Canadians agree that crime is one of our most important problems, they are divided over what to do about it. Some of the frustration about crime might be based on unfounded fears that the crime rate has been rising in the past few years, whereas it has actually declined. However, it is still far too high.

One thing is clear. The existing criminal justice system cannot solve the "crime problem." If most crimes do not result in arrest, most arrests do not result in convictions, and most convictions do not result in a jail term, the "lock 'em up and throw away the key" approach has little chance of succeeding. Nor does the high rate of recidivism among those who have been incarcerated speak well for the rehabilitative efforts of our existing correctional facilities. We can look to the United States to see a very expensive social experiment. Massive numbers of people are being locked up for very long

In recent years, military-style boot camps have been used as an alternative to prison and long jail terms for nonviolent offenders under age 30. Critics argue that structural solutions—not stopgap measures—are needed to reduce crime.

periods of time, and prison populations are increasing much more rapidly than in other countries. Between 1980 and 1990, the American prison population grew by 121 percent, while in Canada the increase was 14 percent (Mihorean and Lipinski, 1992). Since 1990, American prison populations have continued to increase. Several states have passed "three strikes and you're out" laws that impose a mandatory life sentence on anyone convicted of a third felony. Each inmate convicted under these laws will cost about $1.5 million to keep in prison for the rest of his or her life. In many U.S. states, particularly California, the prison systems are so overcrowded and underfunded that the courts have ordered increased spending to pay for improvements.

An alternative to this approach begins with the realization that the best way to deal with crime is to ensure that it doesn't happen. Instead of longer sentences, military-style boot camps, or other stopgap measures, *structural solutions*—such as more and better education and jobs, affordable housing, more equality and less discrimination, and socially productive activities—are needed to reduce street crime in the future. The best approach for reducing delinquency and crime ultimately would be prevention: to work with young people *before* they become juvenile offenders, to help them establish family relationships, build self-esteem, choose a career, and get an education that will help them pursue that career.

Perhaps the major trend that will affect the type of crime we will see in the future is the globalization of the economy and of communications. Organized crime has spread from one country to another as the drug trade became a vast international business. With the aid of satellites and computers, financial crimes can be committed from anywhere in the world, and may be almost impossible to punish because of competing jurisdictions and different laws. The reduction of border controls in trading alliances, such as the European Union, makes it easier for criminals to move from one country to another. For a more detailed look at global crime, see Box 7.5.

Globalization may affect crime in many other ways. The transition to a global economy has devastated the job market in many countries. Traditional, secure manufacturing jobs have either been moved to countries in which lower wages are paid or they have disappeared altogether, and poorly paid and insecure jobs in the service sector are the jobs that remain. This loss of good jobs has, in turn, affected families and communities and may result in increased criminality. In many countries, changes in taxation and social welfare policies, intended to increase global competitiveness, have increased social inequality. This inequality may also lead to crime.

Finally, much of the future growth of crime lies in the Internet and other new technologies. High-technology crimes are increasing quickly (Etter, 2002). Computer hackers are responsible for many different types of crimes including the spread of viruses and attacks that are intended to shut down specific Web sites. While many of these are simply intended to create chaos on the Internet, some hackers have tried to extort money from corporations by threatening to disrupt their communications systems. Other computer experts have used the Internet to steal people's identifying information and credit card numbers in order to obtain money by fraud. Company Web sites have also been hacked in order to find information about new products that can be used by competing businesses. Individuals can also be victimized by cyberstalking and by bullying over the Internet. These crimes are difficult to deal with because technology provides an anonymity that is not present in many other types of offences. The global nature of the Internet also means that many jurisdictions can be involved, some of which are not willing to investigate their own citizens. The nature of many of these crimes and the expertise required to investigate them mean that investigations are expensive.

The potential for criminals to exploit other new technologies, such as biotechnology and nanotechnology, means that we have only begun to see the potential of new discoveries to shape the crimes of the future.

BOX 7.5 SOCIOLOGY IN GLOBAL PERSPECTIVE

The Globalization of Crime

We should not be surprised to learn that crime is becoming a global phenomenon. The increasing prevalence of global crime raises many issues. Consider the following two examples:

> Con men operating out of Amsterdam sell bogus U.S. securities by telephone to Germans; the operation is controlled by an Englishman residing in Monaco whose profits go to a bank based in Panama. (United Nations Development Programme, 1999:104)

> When Yugoslavia disintegrated during the 1990s, the largely-Albanian province of Kosovo sought to break free of Serbian control. The United Nations intervened, but the agreement ending the fighting did not provide for a functioning justice system (Linden et al., forthcoming). Instead, United Nations personnel were responsible for policing and the rest of the justice system was barely functioning. It was not clear what criminal laws would apply. The Kosovo Liberation Army took advantage of this situation to become a major global player in trafficking heroin to many different countries and used their profits to buy weapons to help support their political cause. (Dishman, 2001)

As these examples show, international criminal activity poses new and interesting challenges not only for those who are victims of such crimes but also for the governmental agencies that are mandated to control crime. Among these issues are questions, such as: Which police forces should investigate? In which jurisdiction should a prosecution be mounted? What organizations can facilitate cooperation among justice agencies from different countries?

Global crime refers to the networking of powerful criminal organizations and their associates in shared activities around the world (Castells, 1998). Just as with legitimate businesses, these global networks are very fluid and are constantly changing. There have been formal strategic alliances between groups, such as the Sicilian Mafia and the Medellín drug cartel in Colombia (Jamieson, 2001), but more often the relationships are less formal. Many of these networks are involved in smuggling a wide range of things including drugs, weapons, intellectual property, such as DVDs, counterfeit watches, human organs needed for transplants, endangered animal and plant species, illegal immigrants, and

toxic waste. This requires groups that have a presence in a number of countries or that have alliances with local groups.

While organized-crime groups are among those most involved in global crime, there has also been a blurring of the boundaries between organized crime and terrorism (Jamieson, 2001). It has become common for terrorist groups to use transnational crime to raise the money to fund their other activities. This will almost certainly increase as states, such as Libya, that formerly sponsored and financed terrorist organizations withdraw this support and leave the groups to raise their own money. Many terrorist groups have used their international links to smuggle drugs, guns, illegal immigrants, and diamonds. The Irish Republican Army is involved in a broad range of organized crime activities (Dishman, 2001), and in 2004 was blamed for a bank robbery in which more than $60 million was stolen. Many groups, including al-Qaeda–linked networks in Canada, have used credit card fraud and forgery to fund their operations. For example, Ahmed Ressam had been given political asylum in Canada in 1994 and in December of 1999 was arrested at the U.S. border with a car full of explosives that he was intending to detonate at the Los Angeles airport to mark the millennium on January 1, 2000. Ressam later testified about some of his fund-raising activities:

Q. How did you support yourself during that four-year period [when you lived in Montreal]?

A. I lived on welfare and theft.

Q. What do you mean by "theft"?

A. I used to steal tourists, [sic] rob tourists. I used to go to hotels and find their suitcases and steal them when they're not paying attention.

Q. And what would you do with the contents of those suitcases?

A. I used to take the money, keep the money, and if there are passports, I would sell them, and if there are Visa credit cards, I would use them up, and if there were any traveler's checks, I would use them or sell them. (PBS, 2001:2)

Ressam and his accomplices had equipment to counterfeit credit cards and to forge cheques. They were also involved in passport-fraud networks that were linked with Osama bin Laden's terrorist training camps in Afghanistan.

While conventional organized crime groups rarely get involved with terrorists, they are often closely linked to the international business community, particularly to financial institutions. Organized crime is so lucrative that it has a major problem hiding the money. One of the keys to unravelling the Hells Angels drug operation run by Mom Boucher was surveillance of several apartments that were used to count and to store vast sums of money (Sher and Marsden, 2003); the same problems exist at the global level, where at least $500 billion per year in organized crime proceeds enter the financial system (United Nations, 2005a). Jamieson has described the global financial scene: "Thanks to the speed and ease of capital transfers, 'money' has become part of a network that includes stocks, bonds, futures, currency, interest rates, and a variety of financial instruments. Financial de-regulation and the globalization of these markets have created new profitable opportunities for licit and illicit traders, but have made control and monitoring virtually impossible. Because the global financial system has an infinite number of points of access, it is possible to trade anonymously, move money rapidly and easily, and obscure the origin and ownership of capital" (2001:379). Countries with very lax reporting regulations, such as the Cayman Islands, have become the home of huge numbers of global financial corporations. With these opportunities available, it is inevitable that some legitimate organizations will become involved with organized crime as well as initiating their own criminal activities. Organized crime groups, such as the Russian Mafia and the U.S. Mafia, have also broadened their activities by moving into white-collar crimes, such as fraudulent stock market schemes (Etter, 2002).

Political and corporate corruption also plays a major role in global crime. When governments failed in places, such as the Soviet Union and Yugoslavia, a power vacuum was created that was quickly filled by organized criminals. In the economic chaos that followed these political events, those who were willing and able to use force were in a strong position to make huge amounts of money and to have a great deal of influence over the political process through bribery and threats of violence. In Russia, organized criminals may control as much as half the economy and are using their secure base in Russia to expand their networks to many other countries including Canada.

Global crime will continue to be a major problem in the future. The opportunities to make money are simply too great and the global justice system too weak to deter potential criminals. As Naim has said, the fight against global organized crime "pits bureaucracies against networks" (2003:35), and law-enforcement agencies have not been able to keep up with the criminals. As with the terrorist groups you read about in Chapter 6, the networks are so flexible that if one part is closed the rest of the network can make small adjustments and continue to operate. To make things even more difficult, international policing organizations are reluctant to cooperate with one another, and their countries are often more concerned with protecting their own sovereignty than with breaking up crime networks.

CHAPTER REVIEW

■ What is deviance?

Deviant behaviour is any act that violates established norms. Deviance varies from culture to culture and in degree of seriousness. Crime is seriously deviant behaviour that violates written laws and that is punishable by fines, incarceration, or other sanctions.

■ What is the strain theory of deviance?

Strain theory focuses on the idea that the structure of a society can produce pressures that result in deviant behaviour. When denied legitimate access to cultural goals, such as a good job or nice home, people may engage in illegal behaviour to obtain them. Opportunity theory suggests that access to illegitimate opportunity structures varies, and this access helps determine the nature of deviance in which a person will engage.

■ How does social control theory explain crime?

According to social control theory, everyone is capable of committing crimes, but social bonding keeps many from doing so. People bond to society through their attachments to family and to other social institutions, such as the church and school. When a person's bonds to society are weakened or broken, the probability of deviant behaviour increases.

■ How do symbolic interactionists view the causes of crime?

Differential association theory states that individuals have a greater tendency to deviate from societal norms when they frequently associate with persons who tend toward deviance instead of conformity. According to labelling theory, deviant behaviour is that which is labelled deviant. The process of labelling is related to the relative power and status of those persons who do the labelling and those who are labelled. Those in power may use their power to label the behaviour of others as deviant.

■ How do conflict and feminist perspectives explain deviance?

Conflict perspectives on deviance examine inequalities in society. According to the critical approach, the legal order protects those with political and economic power and exploits persons from lower classes. Feminist approaches to deviance examine the relationship between gender and deviance. Some feminist scholars have concluded that the roots of female criminality lie in a social structure that is characterized by inequalities of class, race, and gender. Women's deviance and crime is a response to gender discrimination experienced in work, marriage, and interpersonal relationships.

■ How do postmodern theorists approach crime and deviance?

Some postmodern theorists focus on social control and discipline based on the use of knowledge, power, and technology. While most social control agencies no longer use harsh methods of social control, such as torture, newer techniques allow constant surveillance over individuals. The techniques that began in prison now exist in many parts of society, including factories, schools, and hospitals.

■ What are the major types of crime?

Street crime, which includes violent crimes, property crimes, and morals crimes, is a major type of crime. Another is occupational, or white-collar, crimes, which are illegal activities committed by people in the course of their employment or financial dealings. Other major types are corporate crimes, which are illegal acts committed by company employees on behalf of the corporation and with its support; organized crime, which is a business operation that supplies illegal goods and services for profit; and political crimes, which are illegal or unethical acts involving the misuse of power by government officials or illegal or unethical acts perpetrated against the government by those seeking to make a political statement, undermine the government, or overthrow it.

■ What are our main sources of crime statistics?

Official crime statistics are taken from the Canadian Uniform Crime Reporting survey, which lists crimes reported to the police. We also collect information about crime through victimization surveys that interview households to determine the incidence of crimes, including those not reported to police. Studies show that many more crimes are committed than are officially reported.

■ How are age, sex, and social class related to crime?

Age is a key factor in crime. Persons under 25 have the highest rates of crime. Persons arrested for assault and homicide generally are older, and white-collar criminals usually are older because it takes time to acquire the professional position and skill needed to commit occupational crime. Women have much lower rates of crime than men. Persons from lower socioeconomic backgrounds are more likely to be arrested for violent and property crimes; corporate crime is more likely to occur among upper socioeconomic classes.

■ How is discretion used in the justice system?

The criminal justice system includes the police, the courts, and prisons. These agencies often have considerable discretion in dealing with offenders. The police often use discretion in deciding whether to act on a situation. Prosecutors and judges use discretion in deciding which cases to pursue and how to handle them.

KEY TERMS

corporate crime 204
crime 191
deviance 189
differential association theory 195
illegitimate opportunity structures 193
juvenile delinquency 191
labelling theory 196
moral crusades 198
moral entrepreneurs 198
occupational or white-collar crime 204
organized crime 205
political crime 206
primary deviance 197

NET LINKS

Blue Line magazine is intended for police audiences and looks at a variety of issues concerning Canadian policing; go to:
http://www.blueline.ca/

Many jurisdictions still have outdated or strange laws on their books. Read some of them at:
http://www.dumblaws.com

Look at Canada's *Criminal Code.* You can read the way each offence is defined and look at the maximum penalties at:
http://laws.justice.gc.ca/en/C-46/index.html

Read recent news about criminal justice and Canadian research in policing and corrections at the Web site of Public Safety and Emergency Preparedness Canada:
http://www.psepc-sppcc.gc.ca/

See also the site for the Correctional Service of Canada.
http://www.csc-scc.gc.ca/

To read about some crimes that have been widely publicized in the media, go to:
http://www.crimelibrary.com/

QUESTIONS FOR CRITICAL THINKING

1. Consider the role of power in defining what acts are deviant and what acts are not. Can you think of examples where the definition of deviance has been changed because formerly stigmatized groups have achieved the power necessary to resist being labelled as deviant?
2. Should so-called victimless crimes, such as prostitution and recreational drug use, be decriminalized? Do these crimes harm society?
3. Several commissions have recommended that Aboriginal people have a separate justice system. Do you agree? How do you think such a system would operate?
4. As a sociologist armed with a sociological imagination, how would you propose to deal with the problem of crime in Canada? What programs would you suggest enhancing? What programs would you reduce?
5. Do you agree with the move toward community involvement in criminal justice through alternative measures? Do you feel these techniques can help restore social relationships? In your opinion, who should (and should not) be allowed access to restorative justice measures?

SUGGESTED READINGS

These books provide additional insights on many of the crime and justice issues discussed in this chapter:

Margaret Beare. *Criminal Conspiracies: Organized Crime in Canada.* Toronto: Nelson Canada, 1996.

James Dubro. *Mob Rule: Inside the Canadian Mafia.* Toronto: Macmillan, 1985.

Thomas Fleming. *The New Criminologies in Canada: State, Crime and Control.* Toronto: Oxford University Press, 1985.

Thomas Gabor. *Everybody Does It! Crime by the Public.* Toronto: University of Toronto Press, 1994.

Curt T. Griffiths and Simon N. Verdun-Jones. *Canadian Criminal Justice* (2nd ed.). Toronto: Harcourt Brace and Company, 1994.

James C. Hackler. *Crime and Canadian Public Policy.* Scarborough, Ont.: Prentice Hall, 1994.

Allen C. Hamilton and C. Murray Sinclair. *Report of the Aboriginal Justice Inquiry of Manitoba,* Vol. 1. Winnipeg: Queen's Printer, 1994.

Holly Johnson. *Dangerous Domains: Violence Against Women in Canada.* Toronto: Nelson Canada, 1996.

Leslie W. Kennedy and Vincent F. Sacco. *Crime Counts: A Criminal Event Analysis.* Toronto: Nelson Canada, 1997.

Yves Lavigne. *Hells Angels: Taking Care of Business.* Toronto: Ballantine Books, 1987.

Rick Linden. *Criminology: A Canadian Perspective* (5th ed.). Toronto: Harcourt Brace and Company, 2004.

Chris McCormick. *Constructing Danger: The Mis/Representation of Crime in the News.* Halifax: Fernwood Publishing, 1995.

Robert Silverman and Leslie Kennedy. *Deadly Deeds: Murder in Canada.* Scarborough, Ont.: Nelson Canada, 1993.

Laureen Snider. *Bad Business: Corporate Crime in Canada.* Scarborough, Ont.: Nelson Canada, 1993.

Daniel Wolf. *The Rebels: A Brotherhood of Outlaw Bikers.* Toronto: University of Toronto Press, 1991.

ONLINE STUDY AND RESEARCH TOOLS

THOMSONNOW™ Thomson NOW!

Go to **http://hed.nelson.com** to link to ThomsonNOW for *Sociology in Our Times,* Fourth Canadian Edition, your online study tool. First take the **Pre-Test** for this chapter to get your personalized **Study Plan,** which will identify topics you need to review and direct you to the appropriate resources. Then take the **Post-Test** to determine what concepts you have mastered and what you still need work on.

INFOTRAC®

Infotrac College Edition is included free with every new copy of this text. Explore this online library for additional readings, review, and a handy resource for assignments. Visit **www.infotrac-college.com** to access this online database of full-text articles. Enter the key terms from this chapter to start your search.

Social Class

Financial wealth—or, in more technical terms, "net worth"—is an important element of Canadian society. Most Canadians aspire to get some of it in order to help them live long and well. Others want it to help care for the less fortunate. Whether it is fair or not, wealth is also one of the ways used to measure people and their achievements. Advertisers push "the dream" of wealth . . . and what it can bring. For some, the dream and the reality do become one. There are nearly 500,000 millionaire households in Canada, and the richest 10 percent of Canadian households control 45 percent of the country's wealth.

For many, however, the dream never does become the reality. Their reality regarding wealth may consist of having enough to live just above the poverty line. The poorest 10 percent of Canadian households have a median net worth of only $150. The bottom half of all households control only 10 percent of the wealth (Sauvé, 2002:1). Grade 4 and 5 students in North Bay, Ontario, were asked to respond to the question, *What does poverty mean?* Following are their responses.

Poverty is . . .

Not being able to go to McDonald's.

Getting a basket from the Santa Fund.

Feeling ashamed when my dad can't get a job.

Not buying books at the book fair.

Not getting to go to birthday parties.

Hearing my mom and dad fight over money.

Not ever getting a pet because it costs too much.

Wishing you had a nice house.

Not being able to go camping.

Not getting a hot dog on hot dog day.

Not getting pizza on pizza day.

Not being able to have your friends sleep over.

Pretending you forgot your lunch.

Being afraid to tell your mom that you need gym shoes.

Not having breakfast sometimes.

Not being able to play hockey.

Sometimes really hard because my mom gets scared and she cries.

Not being able to go to Cubs or play soccer.

Not being able to take swimming lessons.

Not being able to afford a holiday.

Not having pretty barrettes for your hair.

Not having your own private backyard.

Being teased for the way you are dressed.

Not getting to go on school trips.
—Interfaith Social Assistance Reform Coalition, 1998:107

In Canadian society we are socialized to believe that hard work is the key to personal success. Conversely, we are also taught that individuals who fail—who do not achieve success–do so as a result of their own personal inadequacies. Poverty is attributable to personal defect and it is up to the individual to find a way to break the "cycle of poverty." Do you agree? Or do you think structural factors in Canadian society affect the degree of success individuals achieve? Anthropologist Katherine Newman (1993:11) has identified several social and structural factors that affect the level of material success an individual achieves. She attributes the downward mobility to "escalating housing prices, occupational insecurity, blocked mobility on the job, and the cost-of-living squeeze that has penalized the boomer generation, even when they have more education and better jobs than their parents." Ascribed statuses, such as race/ethnicity, gender, and religion also affect people's *social mobility*. We will look at the ideals versus the realities of social mobility when we examine the class structure in Canada.

Before reading on, test your knowledge of wealth and poverty in Canada by taking the quiz in Box 8.1.

QUESTIONS AND ISSUES

Chapter Focus Question: How are the lives of Canadians affected by social inequality?

How do prestige, power, and wealth determine social class?

What role does occupational structure play in a functionalist perspective on class structure?

What role does ownership of resources play in a conflict perspective on class structure?

How are social stratification and poverty linked?

What is the extent of social inequality in Canada?

INCOME AND WEALTH DIFFERENCES IN CANADA

Throughout human history, people have argued about the distribution of scarce resources in society. Disagreements often concentrate on whether the share we get is a fair reward for our effort and hard work (Braun, 1991). Recently, social analysts have pointed out that the old maxim "the rich get richer" continues to be valid in Canada. To understand how this happens, we must take a closer look at income and wealth inequality in this country.

Comparing Income and Wealth

When many people discuss financial well-being—and, thus, a person's place in the Canadian class structure—they are usually referring to income. However, it is important to distinguish between income and wealth. **Income is the economic gain derived from wages, salaries, income transfers (governmental aid), and ownership of property** (Beeghley, 2000). Or, to put it another way, "income refers to money, wages, and payments that periodically are received as returns from an occupation or investment" (Kerbo, 2000:19). For most of us living in a class system, our major sources of income are a wage or salary, although some people live entirely off the earnings on their investments. But income is only one aspect of wealth. Wealth, or net worth, is the difference between your assets and your debts. In other words, your personal wealth is the amount of money you'd have if you sold all your assets, such as your house, and paid off all your debts (Sauvé, 2003:2).

As this definition suggests, wealth refers to accumulated assets in the form of various types of valued goods, including property, such as buildings, land, farms, houses, factories, and cars, as well as other assets, such as bank accounts, corporate stocks, bonds, and insurance policies. Wealth can be used to generate income that is used to purchase necessities (such as food, clothing, and shelter) or luxuries (such as a diamond ring or a yacht). It has been said that "wealth generates more wealth" (Keister, 2000:7), meaning that wealthy people may acquire even more wealth as a result of their investments. Wealth makes it possible for people to "buy leisure," in that the owner of wealth can decide whether he or she will work or not. Similarly, wealth can be used to help people gain an advantage that they otherwise would not have. Such advantages include, but are not limited to, gaining high social prestige, political influence, improved opportunities and greater safety for oneself and one's family, high-quality health care, and enhanced life chances (Keister, 2000).

The idea of "making it" is linked to both wealth and income, and one's chances of succeeding are therefore threatened in periods of economic problems and political unrest, particularly for those persons who must rely on income alone for their family's economic survival.

BOX 8.1 SOCIOLOGY AND EVERYDAY LIFE

How Much Do You Know About Wealth and Poverty in Canada?

True	False	
T	F	1. There is less child poverty in Canada today than there was a decade ago.
T	F	2. Individuals over the age of sixty-five have the highest rate of poverty.
T	F	3. Men account for two out of every three impoverished adults in Canada.
T	F	4. Most poor children live in female-headed, single-parent households.
T	F	5. Age plays a key role in wealth accumulation in Canada.
T	F	6. The richest 10 percent of Canadian households account for approximately one-third of all wealth.
T	F	7. Fewer than 1 percent of Canadian households have a net worth of at least a million dollars.
T	F	8. Between 1984 and 2001 the rich got richer and the poor got poorer.

Answers on page 232.

People's life chances are enhanced by access to important societal resources, such as education. How will the life chances of students who have the opportunity to pursue a university degree differ from those of young people who do not have the chance to go to university?

DISTRIBUTION OF INCOME AND WEALTH

Money is essential for acquiring goods and services. People without money cannot purchase food, shelter, clothing, legal services, education, and the other things they need or desire. Money—in the form of both income and wealth—is very unevenly distributed in Canada (see Census Profile on page 233). Among the industrialized nations of North America and Europe, Canada has one of the worst records of income inequality, following only the United States and the United Kingdom (Picot and Myles, 2004).

Income Inequality

According to economist Paul Samuelson, "If we made an income pyramid out of a child's blocks, with each layer portraying $500 of income, the peak would be far higher than Mount Everest, but most people would be within a few feet of the ground" (quoted in Samuelson and Nordhaus, 1989:644).

One common method of analyzing the distribution of income is through the concept of income *quintiles*. Imagine lining up all of the families in Canada, beginning with those having the lowest incomes and ending with those having the highest incomes. You then divide the line into five groups, each with the same number of families. Each of the five groups is called an income quintile. At the end of the line is the quintile

BOX 8.1 SOCIOLOGY AND EVERYDAY LIFE

Answers to the Sociology Quiz on Wealth and Poverty

1. **False.** Despite the House of Commons' unanimous decision to "eliminate child poverty among Canadian children by the year 2000," there has been close to a 39-percent increase, from 936,000 children living in poverty to 1.3 million (Campaign 2000, 2002a).

2. **False.** As a group, children have a higher rate of poverty than the elderly. Government programs such as Old Age Security are indexed to inflation, while many of the programs for the young have been scaled back or eliminated. However, many elderly individuals do live in poverty (Canadian Council on Social Development, 2002b).

3. **False.** Women, not men, account for two out of three impoverished adults in Canada. Reasons for this include the lack of job opportunities for women, lower pay for women than men for comparable jobs, lack of affordable daycare for children, sexism in the workplace, and a number of other factors (Lee, 2000).

4. **False.** In 2000, just over half of the children in low-income families lived in two-parent families. However, the *rate* of poverty for female-headed single-parent families is 34 percent, as compared to a rate of 8.5 percent for children living in two-parent families (Canadian Council on Social Development, 2002b).

5. **True.** Groups that are older, such as senior families, naturally tend to have more wealth since they have had more years to accumulate assets and pay off debt (Sauvé, 2002).

6. **False.** The richest 10 percent of all households held 45 percent of all wealth and had average net worth of $872,000. The total wealth held by this group exceeds the combined wealth of the first eight groups (Sauvé, 2002).

7. **False.** In 1999 (the latest year for which the data is available) there were close to 500,000 Canadian households with at least $1 million. This millionaire group represents approximately 4 percent of all households (Sauvé, 2002).

8. **True.** The poorest 10 percent of households had a negative (owed more than they owned) net worth in 1984, and the situation worsened further (–216 percent) by 1999. The second poorest group experienced an 85-percent decline in wealth, and the third poorest group experienced a 12-percent decline. Each of the other seven groups had an actual increase in wealth ranging from 6 percent for the fourth wealth group to about 35 percent for each of the top two wealthiest groups (Sauvé, 2002).

containing the 20 percent of families with the lowest incomes, and the quintile at the other end contains the 20 percent of families with the highest incomes. Another useful way of conceptualizing the quintiles is in terms of a ladder with the richest families on the top rung and the poorest families on the bottom (Lochhead and Shalla, 1996). For example, as shown in Figure 8.1, in 2001 the richest families—the top quintile—had an average family income of $106,083, and the lowest quintile—the poorest families—had incomes of $19,844 (Sauvé, 2003).

Gilbert and Kahl (1998) compare the distribution of income to a national pie that has been cut into portions ranging from stingy to generous, for distribution among segments of the population. In 2001, the wealthiest 20 percent of households received approximately 40 percent of the total income "pie," while the poorest received just over 5 percent—a ratio of approximately 8:1 (Statistics Canada, 2003m). Analysts further report that incomes have remained remarkably stable over time. Using inflation-adjusted dollars, average family income was $52,756 in 1989, and by 2001 it increased only slightly, to $58,016 (Sauvé, 2003). However, a closer examination of the data reveals that focusing on the overall average family income tends to conceal wide variations between different segments of the populations and hides increasing inequities in the distribution of income in Canada. Overall, the average family income of the three lowest quintiles has declined in the past decade, while that of the two highest quintiles continues to increase (Sauvé, 2002; Statistics Canada, 2003m).

CENSUS ✦ PROFILE

Regional Variation in Annual Family Income, 2000

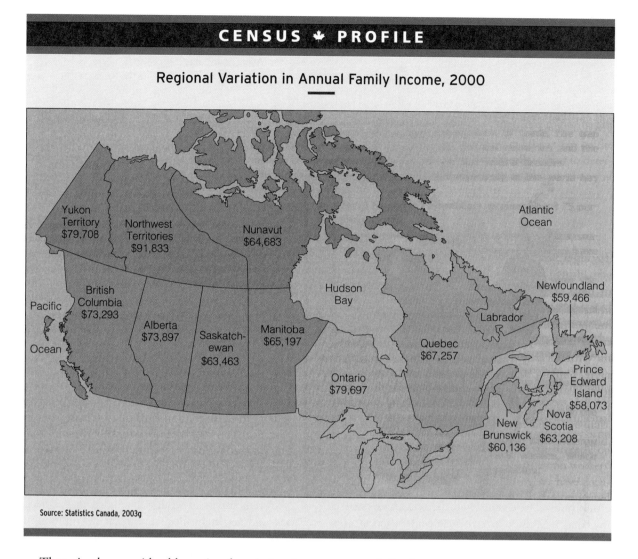

Yukon Territory $79,708

Northwest Territories $91,833

Nunavut $64,683

Atlantic Ocean

British Columbia $73,293

Pacific

Hudson Bay

Newfoundland $59,466

Alberta $73,897

Saskatchewan $63,463

Manitoba $65,197

Labrador

Ocean

Ontario $79,697

Quebec $67,257

Prince Edward Island $58,073

New Brunswick $60,136

Nova Scotia $63,208

Source: Statistics Canada, 2003g

There is also considerable regional variation in income across the country. As shown in the Census Profile, family income is highest in Ontario, the Northwest Territories, Alberta, and the Yukon, and lowest in the Atlantic provinces and Nunavut (Statistics Canada, 2003m). There is also significant income variation among particular racial–ethnic groups. For example, recent statistics indicate that 36 percent of visible minorities are in the low-income group, as compared to 20 percent of the general population. The data also clearly demonstrate the inequities in income distribution experienced by Aboriginal peoples in Canada, whose average income is less than two-thirds the average income of the general population (Statistics Canada, 2004f).

Wealth Inequality

Income is only one aspect of wealth. **Wealth includes property, such as buildings, land, farms, houses, factories, and cars, as well as other assets, such as money in bank accounts, corporate stocks, bonds, and insurance policies.** Wealth is computed by subtracting all debt obligations and converting the remaining assets into cash. The terms *wealth* and *net worth,* therefore, are used interchangeably. For most people in Canada, wealth is invested primarily in property that generates no income, such as a house or a car. In contrast, the wealth of an elite minority often is in the form of income-producing property.

Research on the distribution of wealth in Canada reveals that wealth is more unevenly distributed among the Canadian population than is income. The most recent year for this kind of information is 1999; in 1999, Statistics Canada collected detailed information about the financial assets, debts, and wealth of Canadian households. Before that, the last survey of this type had been conducted in 1984 (Sauvé, 2003).

Although the term *wealthy,* like the term *poor,* is a relative one, analysts generally define the wealthy as those whose total assets after debt payments are more than $250,000. Millionaire status can now be

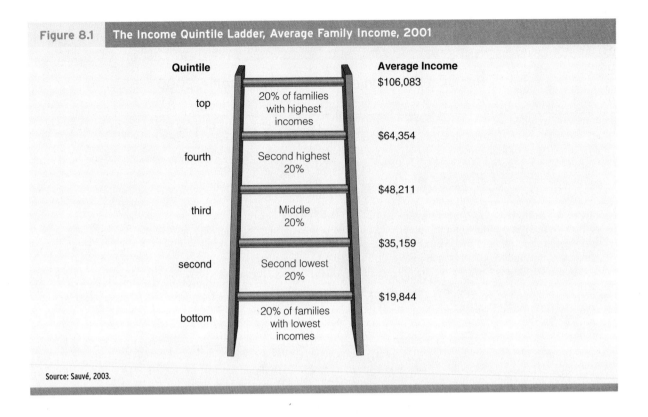

Figure 8.1   The Income Quintile Ladder, Average Family Income, 2001

Quintile		Average Income
top	20% of families with highest incomes	$106,083
fourth	Second highest 20%	$64,354
third	Middle 20%	$48,211
second	Second lowest 20%	$35,159
bottom	20% of families with lowest incomes	$19,844

Source: Sauvé, 2003.

claimed by 484,000 Canadian households, all with a net worth of at least $1 million. While they make up only 4 percent of all households, this millionaire group holds 31 percent of all the household wealth in Canada. Millionaires are most evident in Ontario (232,000 households), Quebec (85,100 households) and British Columbia (81,200 households). About 1.1 million households have a net worth of $500,000 to $1 million. This group represents 9 percent of all households and holds 26 percent of the wealth.

While these two groups together comprise only 13 percent of all households, they hold 57 percent of all the household wealth. Their wealth totalled $1,721,490,000,000 ($1.7 trillion) in 1999, and if cashed out could have bought all the consumer goods and services purchased in Canada during the previous three years.

The majority of the wealthiest people in Canada are inheritors, with some at least three or four generations removed from the original fortune (Dyck, 1996). The combined wealth of Canada's richest families, as shown in Table 8.1, totals approximately 46 billion, 21 billion of which is accounted for by Canada's richest person, former newspaper publisher Kenneth Thomson (*Canadian Business,* 2004). The combined wealth of Canada's super wealthy in 2002 was $111 billion

(*Canadian Business,* 2003). Clearly, a limited number of people own or control a very large portion of the wealth in Canada.

A recent survey of wealth concluded that there is "gross and persistent inequality in the distribution of wealth in Canada. A surprisingly small number of Canadians have huge slices of the wealth pie, and a surprisingly large number of Canadians have no more than a few crumbs" (Kerstetter, 2002:6).

Whether we consider distribution of income or wealth, though, it is relatively clear that social inequality is a real, consistent, and enduring feature of life in Canadian society.

CLASSICAL PERSPECTIVES ON SOCIAL CLASS

Early sociologists grappled with the definition of class and the criteria for determining people's location within the class structure. Both Karl Marx and Max Weber viewed class as an important determinant of social inequality and social change, and their works have had a profound influence on contemporary class theory.

Table 8.1 WEALTHIEST CANADIANS, 2004	
NAME	**WEALTH ($ BILLION)**
Kenneth Thomson and Family	21.67
Galen Weston	9.27
Jeff Skoll	4.63
James (J.R.), Arthur, and John (Jack) Irving	3.88
Bernard (Barry) Sherman	3.24
James (Jimmy) Pattison	3.19
Paul Desmarais Sr.	2.59

Source: *Canadian Business*, 2004.

Karl Marx: Relation to Means of Production

For Karl Marx, class position is determined by people's work situation, or relationship to the means of production. Marx based his concept of class on the assumption of antagonistic class relations. In preindustrial societies, slave masters exploit slaves, and lords exploit serfs. In industrial societies, capitalists exploit workers (Wright, 1997). In keeping with this, Marx suggested that capitalistic societies are made up of two classes—the capitalists and the workers. The *capitalist class* (*bourgeoisie*) consists of those who own the means of production—the land and capital necessary for factories and mines, for example. The *working class* (*proletariat*) consists of those who must sell their labour to the owners in order to earn enough money to survive (see Figure 8.2).

According to Marx, class relationships involve inequality and exploitation. The workers are exploited as capitalists maximize their profits by paying workers less than the resale value of what they produce but do not own. Marx believed that a deep level of antagonism exists between capitalists and workers because of extreme differences in the *material interests* of the people in these two classes. According to the sociologist Erik O. Wright (1997:5), material interests are "the interests people have in their material standard of living, understood as the package of toil, consumption, and leisure. Material interests are thus not interests of maximizing consumption *per se,* but rather interests in the trade-off between toil, leisure, and consumption." Wright suggests that *exploitation* is the key concept for understanding Marx's assertion that *interests* are generated by class relations: "In an exploitative relation, the exploiter needs the exploited since the exploiter depends upon the effort of the exploited." In other words, the capitalists *need* the workers to derive profits; therefore, capitalists benefit when workers do not have adequate resources to provide for themselves and hence must sell their labour power to the capitalist class. As Marx suggests, exploitation involves ongoing interactions between the two antagonistic classes, which are structured by a set of social relations that binds together the exploiter and the exploited (Wright, 1997).

Continual exploitation results in workers' *alienation*—**a feeling of powerlessness and estrangement from other people and from oneself.** In Marx's view, alienation develops as workers manufacture goods that embody their creative talents but the goods do not belong to them. Workers are also alienated from the work itself because they are forced to perform it in order to live. Because the workers' activities are not their own, they feel self-estrangement. Moreover, the workers are separated from others in the factory because they individually sell their labour power to the capitalists as a commodity.

In Marx's view, the capitalist class maintains its position at the top of the class structure by control of the society's *superstructure,* which is composed of the government, schools, churches, and other social institutions that produce and disseminate ideas perpetuating the existing system of exploitation. Marx predicted that the exploitation of workers by the capitalist class would ultimately lead to *class conflict*—**the struggle between the capitalist class and the working class.** According to Marx, when the workers realized that capitalists were the source of their oppression, they would overthrow the capitalists and their agents of social control, leading to the end of capitalism. The workers would then take over the government and create a more egalitarian society.

Why has no workers' revolution occurred? According to the sociologist Ralf Dahrendorf (1959), capitalism may have persisted because it has changed significantly since Marx's time. Individual capitalists no longer own and control factories and other means of production; today, ownership and control have largely been separated. For example, contemporary transnational corporations are owned by a multitude of shareholders but

Figure 8.2   Marx's View of Social Class

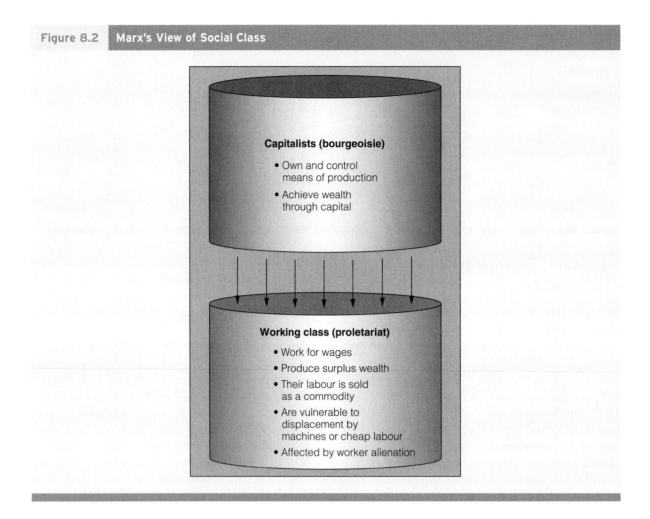

run by paid officers and managers. Similarly, many (but by no means all) workers have experienced a rising standard of living, which may have contributed to a feeling of complacency. Moreover, many people have become so engrossed in the process of consumption—including acquiring more material possessions and going on outings to shopping malls, movie theatres, and amusement parks, such as Canada's Wonderland—that they are less likely to engage in workers' rebellions against the system that has brought them a relatively high standard of living (Gottdiener, 1997).

Marx had a number of important insights about capitalist societies. First, he recognized the economic basis of *class systems* (Gilbert and Kahl, 1998). Second, he noted the relationship between people's location in the class structure and their values, beliefs, and behaviour. Finally, he acknowledged that classes may have opposing (rather than complementary) interests. For example, capitalists' best interests are served by a decrease in labour costs and other expenses and a corresponding increase in profits; workers' best interests are served by well-paid jobs, safe working conditions, and job security.

Max Weber: Wealth, Prestige, and Power

Max Weber's analysis of class builds upon earlier theories of capitalism (particularly those by Marx). Living in the late nineteenth and early twentieth centuries, Weber was in a unique position to see the transformation that occurred as individual, competitive, entrepreneurial capitalism went through the process of shifting to bureaucratic, industrial, corporate capitalism. As a result, Weber had more opportunity than Marx to see how capitalism changed over time.

Weber agreed with Marx's assertion that economic factors are important in understanding individual and group behaviour. However, he emphasized that no one factor (such as economic divisions between capitalists and workers) was sufficient for defining people's location within the class structure. For Weber, the access that people have to important societal resources (such as economic, social, and political power) is crucial in determining people's *life chances*. To highlight the importance of life chances for

The attempt by workers to improve their place in the stratification system has led to numerous labour strikes. Here, Ontario public-sector workers fight with police in an attempt to move their protests to the provincial legislature.

categories of people, Weber developed a multidimensional approach to *social stratification* that reflects the interplay among wealth, prestige, and power. In his analysis of these dimensions of class structure, Weber viewed the concept of "class" as an *ideal type* (which can be used to compare and contrast various societies), rather than as a specific category of "real" people (Bourdieu, 1984).

Weber placed people who have a similar level of wealth and income in the same class. For example, he identified a privileged commercial class of *entrepreneurs*—wealthy bankers, ship owners, professionals, and merchants who possess similar financial resources. He also described a class of *rentiers*— wealthy individuals who live off their investments and do not have to work. According to Weber, entrepreneurs and rentiers have much in common. Both are able to purchase expensive consumer items, control other people's opportunities to acquire wealth and property, and monopolize costly status privileges (such as education) that provide contacts and skills for their children.

Weber divided those who work for wages into two classes: the middle class and the working class. The middle class consists of white-collar workers, public officials, managers, and professionals. The working class consists of skilled, semiskilled, and unskilled workers.

The second dimension of Weber's system of social stratification is *prestige*—**the respect with which a person or status position is regarded by others.** Fame, respect, honour, and esteem are the most common forms of prestige. A person who has a high level of prestige is assumed to receive deferential and respectful treatment from others. Weber suggested that individuals who share a common level of social prestige belong to the same status group regardless of their level of wealth. They tend to socialize with one another, marry within their own group of social equals, spend their leisure time together, and safeguard their status by restricting outsiders' opportunities to join their ranks (Beeghley, 1996). Style of life, formal education, and occupation are often significant factors in establishing and maintaining prestige in industrial and postindustrial societies.

The other dimension of Weber's system is *power*— **the ability of people or groups to achieve their goals despite opposition from others.** The powerful shape society in accordance with their own interests and direct the actions of others (Tumin, 1953). According to Weber, social power in modern societies is held by bureaucracies; individual power depends on a person's position within the bureaucracy. Weber suggested that the power of modern bureaucracies was so strong that even a workers' revolution (as predicted by Marx) would not lessen social inequality (Hurst, 1998).

Wealth, prestige, and power are separate continuums on which people can be ranked from high to low. As shown in Figure 8.3, individuals may be high in one dimension while being low in another. For example, people may be very wealthy but have little political power (for example, a recluse who has inherited a large sum of money). They also may have prestige but not wealth (for instance, a university professor who receives teaching excellence awards but lives on a relatively low income). In Weber's multidimensional approach, people are ranked in all three dimensions. Sociologists often use the term *socioeconomic status* (SES) **to refer to a combined measure that attempts to classify individuals, families, or households in terms of factors, such as income, occupation, and education, to determine class location.**

What important insights does Weber provide in regard to social stratification and class? Weber's analysis of social stratification contributes to our understanding by emphasizing that people behave according to both their economic interests and their values. He also added to Marx's insights by developing a multidimensional explanation of the class structure and identifying additional classes.

A distinct advantage of Weber's theory is that it has allowed for empirical investigation of the class structure in North America (Blau and Duncan, 1967). Through his distinctions among wealth, power, and prestige, Weber makes it possible for researchers to examine the different dimensions of social stratification.

Figure 8.3	Weber's Multidimensional Approach to Social Stratification

According to Max Weber, wealth, power, and prestige are separate continuums. Individuals may rank high in one dimension and low in another, or they may rank high or low in more than one dimension. Also, individuals may use their high rank in one dimension to achieve a comparable rank in another.

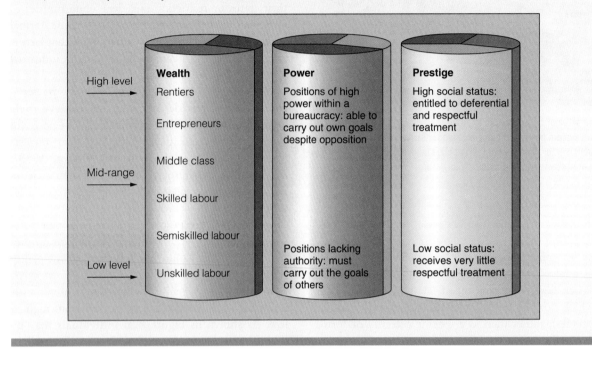

Weber's enlarged conceptual formulation of stratification is the theoretical foundation for mobility research by sociologists such as Peter Blau and Otis Duncan. Blau and Duncan (1967) measure the three dimensions from Weber's theory through a study of the occupational positions that individuals hold. According to Blau and Duncan, a person's occupational position is not identical to either economic class or prestige, but rather is closely related to both. As you might expect, different occupations have significantly different levels of status or prestige (see Table 8.2). Between 1963 and 1996 (the most recent year for which data are available), occupational ratings by prestige were fairly consistent. Do you think these rankings would be the same today? These rankings have become the foundation for *status attainment research,* which uses sophisticated statistical measurements to assess the influence of family background and education on people's occupational mobility and success (see Blau and Duncan, 1967; Duncan, 1968). Status attainment research focuses on the process by which people ultimately reach their position in the class structure. Based largely on studies of men, this research uses the father's occupation and the son's education and first job as primary determinants of the eventual class position of the son. Obviously, family background is the central factor in this process because the son's education and first job are linked to the family's economic status. In addition, the family's location in the class system is related to the availability of social ties that may open occupational doors for the son.

Although they have been widely employed in some prestigious sociological research, status attainment models have several serious limitations. One is the focus of this research on the occupational prestige of traditionally male jobs and the exclusion of women's work, which has often been unpaid. Moreover, the status attainment model is unable to take into account power differentials rooted in inequalities based on race, ethnicity, or gender.

A significant limitation of occupational prestige rankings is that the level of prestige accorded to a position may not actually be based on the importance of the position to society. The highest ratings may be given to professionals—such as physicians and lawyers—because they have many years of training in their fields and some control their own work, not because these positions contributed the most to society.

Table 8.2 PRESTIGE RATINGS FOR SELECTED OCCUPATIONS, 1996 AND 1963

Respondents were asked to evaluate a list of occupations according to their prestige; the individual rankings were averaged and then converted into scores, with 1 the lowest possible score and 99 the highest possible score (Gilbert and Kahl, 1998).

Occupation	SCORE 1996	1963	Occupation	SCORE 1996	1963
Physician	86	93	Police officer	60	72
Lawyer	75	89	Electrician	51	76
University professor	74	90	Mail carrier	47	66
Dentist	72	88	Garbage collector	28	39
Accountant	65	81	Janitor	22	48
Elementary school teacher	64	82	Shoe shiner	9	34

Sources: Hodge, Siegel, and Rossi, 1964; National Opinion Research Center, 1996.

SOCIOLOGICAL MODELS OF THE CLASS STRUCTURE IN CANADA

How many social classes exist in Canada today? What criteria are used for determining class membership? No broad consensus exists about how to characterize the class structure of this country. Canadians do not like to talk about social class. Some even deny that class distinctions exist, leading social analysts to describe class as the "last dirty secret" (see Forcese, 1986). Most people like to think of themselves as middle class; it puts them in a comfortable middle position—neither rich nor poor. Sociologists have developed several models of the class structure. One is broadly based on a Weberian approach, the second on a Marxian approach, and the third on a study of society today. We will examine each of these models briefly.

A Weberian Model of Class Structure

Expanding on Weber's analysis of the class structure, sociologists Dennis Gilbert and Joseph A. Kahl (1998) developed a widely used model of social classes based on three elements: (1) education, (2) occupation of the family head, and (3) family income. This model can be used to describe the social class structure in Canadian society.

The Upper Class   The upper class is the wealthiest and most powerful class in Canada. Members of the upper class own substantial income-producing assets (such as real estate, stocks, and bonds) and operate at both the national and international level. It is difficult to determine the exact size and composition of this group because information about the very rich is difficult to obtain. However, it has been estimated that approximately 3 percent of the population is included in this class, which owns and controls the major economic assets in Canada (Naiman, 2000).

Some models further divide the upper class into *upper-upper class* ("old money") and *lower-upper class* ("new money"). Because such a small number (approximately 1 percent) are members of the upper-upper class, many analysts have referred to this class as the *elite* class (Clement, 1975; Clement and Myles, 1994). Members of this class come from prominent families that possess tremendous wealth that they have held for several generations. For example, the net worth of the Thomson family was recently estimated at close to $15 billion (*Forbes,* 2002). Family names, such as Irving (oil), Bronfman (distilleries), and Eaton (retail stores), are well known and often held in high esteem. Wallace Clement, in his analysis of the "corporate elite" in Canada, notes that "more than one quarter of the present elite had inherited important positions from previous generations" (Clement, 1975:220).

Numerous scholars have examined the distribution of wealth and power in Canada with one consistent result: a small number of individuals—in the upper-upper classes—yield an enormous amount of power. For example, Porter's classic study identified just over 900 individuals who controlled all of the major corporations in Canada (1965:579). Author Peter Newman identified just under 1,000 individuals as members of what he described as "the Canadian establishment." As Newman points out, members of the upper-upper class share more than wealth and power; they tend to have strong feelings of in-group solidarity. They belong to the same exclusive clubs, share social activities, and support high culture (such as the symphony, opera, ballet, and art museums). Their children are educated at prestigious private schools and universities. In general, children of the upper class are socialized to view themselves as different from others; they may also learn that they are expected to marry within their own class (Warner and Lunt, 1941; Mills, 1959a; Johnson, 1974). As Johnson (1974:166) notes:

> For the super-elites of earners, the advantages gained by inherited wealth, attendance at the right schools, membership in the best clubs, and relationships with and marriage into other wealthy and powerful families, all determine that they will be real winners in any competition for income.

As Clement argues, "it is differential access to advantages based on a hierarchically structured society which serves to perpetuate inequality" (1975:206).

While some members of the lower-upper class have it all (i.e., money and prestige), most are extremely wealthy but have not attained as much prestige as the members of the upper-upper class. The "new rich" have earned most of their money in their lifetime as entrepreneurs, presidents of major corporations, sports or entertainment celebrities, or top-level professionals.

The Middle Class In his classic work *The Vertical Mosaic,* John Porter (1965) described Canada as a predominantly middle-class society with a certain uniformity of possessions, lifestyles, earnings, and access to opportunities. Subsequent research confirms this middle-class image of Canadian society. When questioned about their social class, most Canadians will deny class distinctions or take the middle ground, identifying themselves as middle class. For example, in a recent national survey of Canadian adults, close to 80 percent of respondents rated themselves as middle class. Of course, these data reflect a subjective method of assessing one's social class (Curtis and Grabb, 1999), which may not provide the most accurate description of the class structure in Canadian society. New studies have shown that Canada's rich really are getting richer, and the poor poorer, as the middle class erodes. The middle class remains, however, the largest group: an estimated 40 to 50 percent

of Canada's population is in this class. This group is sometimes further divided into the *lower-middle class* and the *upper-middle class.*

Upper-Middle Class Persons in the upper-middle class are often highly educated professionals who have established careers as physicians, lawyers, stockbrokers, or corporate managers. Others have derived their income from family-owned businesses. A combination of three factors qualifies people for the upper-middle class: a university education, authority and independence on the job, and high income. Of all the class categories, the upper-middle class is the one that is most influenced by education.

Across racial–ethnic and class lines, children are encouraged to acquire the higher education necessary for upper-middle-class positions that typically have high prestige in the community. However, many social analysts point out that racism still diminishes the life chances of people of colour even when they achieve a high income and a prestigious career (see Cose, 1993; Takaki, 1993; Hou and Balakrishnan, 1999).

Lower-Middle Class In the past decades, a high school diploma was required to qualify for most middle-class jobs. Today, undergraduate university degrees or college programs have replaced the high school diploma as an entry-level requirement for employment in many middle-class occupations, including medical technicians, nurses, legal and medical secretaries, lower-level managers, semiprofessionals, and nonretail salespersons. As economist Thomas Courchene points out, "Now if we want to earn middle-class wages, we have to have middle-class skills. And that means bringing up the education and skills of the lower half of the population" (quoted in Janigan, 2000).

Traditionally, most middle-class positions have been relatively secure and provided more opportunities for advancement (especially with increasing levels of education and experience) than working-class positions. Recently, however, four factors have diminished the chances for material success for members of this class: (1) escalating housing prices, (2) occupational insecurity, (3) blocked upward mobility on the job, and (4) the cost-of-living squeeze that has penalized younger workers, even when they have more education and better jobs than their parents (Newman, 1993). Class distinctions between the middle and working classes are sometimes blurred as a result of increasingly overlapping characteristics (Gilbert and Kahl, 1998).

The Working Class

The core of this class comprises people who hold relatively unskilled blue-collar and white-collar jobs. An estimated 30 percent of the Canadian population is in the working class. As a result of new technologies and increased productivity, the proportion of workers in this sector has been declining both in Canada and globally (Naiman, 2000:151). Members of the working class include retail salespeople and some members of the service sector who have jobs involving routine, mechanized tasks, which typically involve a short period of job training. Also included in the working class are *pink-collar occupations—relatively low-paying, non-manual, semiskilled positions primarily held by women,* such as daycare workers, checkout clerks, cashiers, and waitresses.

How does life in the working-class family compare with that of individuals in middle-class families? According to sociologists, working-class families not only earn less than middle-class families, but they also have less financial security, particularly with high rates of layoffs and corporate downsizing in some parts of the country. Few people in the working class have more than a high school diploma, which makes job opportunities increasingly scarce in our "high-tech" society (Gilbert and Kahl, 1998). Others find themselves in low-paying jobs in the service sector of the economy, particularly fast-food restaurants, a condition that often places them among the working poor.

The Working Poor

The working poor account for about 20 percent of the Canadian population. Members of the working-poor class live from just above to just below the poverty line. They typically hold unskilled jobs, seasonal jobs, lower-paid factory jobs, and service jobs (such as counter help at restaurants). Employed single mothers often belong to this class; consequently, children are overrepresented in this category. Members of some visible minority groups, Aboriginal peoples, and recent immigrants are also overrepresented among the working poor (Ross, Scott, and Smith, 2000). For the working poor, living from paycheque to paycheque makes it impossible to save money for emergencies, such as periodic or seasonal unemployment, which is a constant threat to any economic stability they may have.

Social critic and journalist Barbara Ehrenreich (2001) left her upper-middle-class lifestyle for a period of time to see if it was possible for the working poor to live on the wages that they were being paid as restaurant servers, sales clerks at discount department stores, aides in nursing homes, house cleaners for franchise maid services, and other similar jobs. She conducted her research by actually holding those jobs for periods of time and seeing if she could live on the wages that she received. Through her research, Ehrenreich persuasively demonstrated that people who work full-time, year-round for poverty-level wages must develop survival strategies that include such things as help from relatives or constant moves from one residence to another in order to have a place to live. Like many other researchers, Ehrenreich found that minimum-wage jobs cannot cover the full cost of living, such as rent, food, and the rest of an adult's monthly needs, even without taking into consideration the needs of children or other family members. According to Ehrenreich (2001:221),

> The "working poor," as they are approvingly termed, are in fact the major philanthropists of our society. They neglect their own children so that the children of others will be cared for; they live in substandard housing so that other homes will be shiny and perfect; they endure deprivation so that inflation will be low and stock prices high. To be a member of the working poor is to be an anonymous donor, a nameless benefactor, to everyone else.

The Underclass

According to Gilbert and Kahl (1998), people in the underclass are poor, seldom employed, and caught in long-term deprivation that results from low levels of education and income and high rates of unemployment. Some are unable to work because of age or disability; others experience discrimination based on race/ethnicity. Single mothers are overrepresented in this class because of lack of jobs, affordable child care, and many other impediments to the mother's future and the future of her children. People without a "living wage" often must rely on public or private assistance programs for their survival.

Whereas some young people in the underclass are hopeful that they can escape poverty, others view their futures with pessimism and uncertainty. Researchers at the Human Resources Development Corporation have concluded that "there is an increasing risk of an underclass that is trapped in persistent poverty, geographically concentrated in particular regions of Canada, and more likely to experience intergenerational transmission of disadvantage" (deGroot-Maggetti, 2002:16).

Studies by various social scientists have found that satisfactory employment opportunities are the critical missing link for people on the lowest rungs of the social class ladder. According to these analysts, job creation is essential in order for people to have the opportunity to earn a decent wage; have medical coverage; live meaningful, productive lives; and raise their children in a safe environment (see Fine and Weis, 1998; Nelson and Smith, 1999; Newman, 1999; Wilson, 1996).

A Marxian Model of Class Structure

The earliest Marxian model of class structure identified ownership or nonownership of the means of production as the distinguishing feature of classes. From this perspective, classes are social groups organized around property ownership, and social stratification is created and maintained by one group in order to protect and enhance its own economic interests. Moreover, societies are organized around classes in conflict over scarce resources. Inequality results from the more powerful exploiting the less powerful.

Contemporary Marxian (or conflict) models examine class in terms of people's relationships with others in the production process. For example, conflict theorists attempt to determine what degree of control workers have over the decision-making process and the extent to which they are able to plan and implement their own work. They also analyze the type of supervisory authority, if any, that a worker has over other workers. According to this approach, most employees are a part of the working class because they do not control either their own labour or that of others.

Erik Olin Wright's conflict model of the class system emphasizes the differing interests of the capitalist class, exemplified by the small-business class (top left); the managerial class (top right); Phil Knight, the founder of Nike (bottom left); and the working class (bottom right).

Erik Olin Wright (1979, 1985, 1997), one of the leading stratification theorists to examine social class from a Marxian perspective, has concluded that Marx's definition of "workers" does not fit the occupations found in advanced capitalist societies. For example, many top executives, managers, and supervisors who do not own the means of production (and thus would be "workers" in Marx's model) act like capitalists in their zeal to control workers and maximize profits. Likewise, some experts hold positions in which they have control over money and the use of their own time even though they are not owners. Wright views Marx's category of "capitalist" as being too broad as well. For instance, small-business owners might be viewed as capitalists because they own their own tools and have a few people working for them, but they have little in common with large-scale capitalists and do not share the interests of factory workers. Figure 8.4 compares Marx's model and Wright's model.

Wright (1979) argues that classes in modern capitalism cannot be defined simply in terms of different levels of wealth, power, and prestige, as in the Weberian model. Consequently, he outlines four criteria for placement in the class structure: (1) ownership of the means of production, (2) purchase of the labour of others (employing others), (3) control of the labour of others (supervising others on the job), and (4) sale of one's own labour (being employed by someone else). Wright (1978) assumes that these criteria can be used to determine the class placement of all workers, regardless of race/ethnicity, in a capitalist society. Let's take a brief look at Wright's (1979, 1985) four classes—(1) the capitalist

Figure 8.4 Comparison of Marx's and Wright's Models of Class Structure

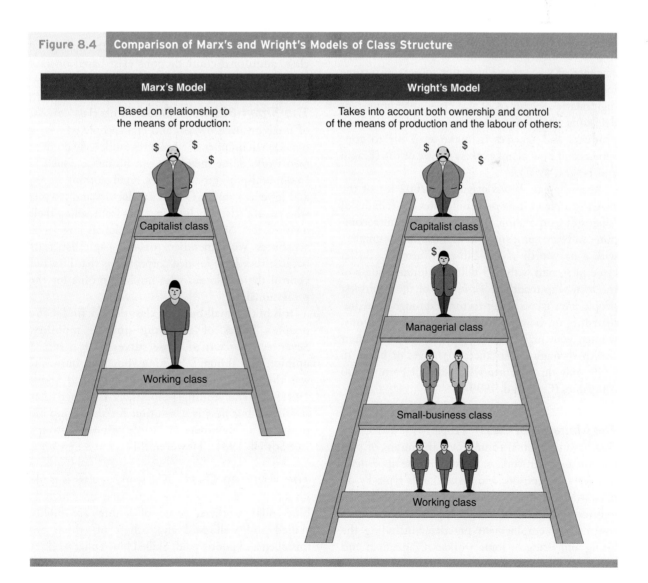

class, (2) the managerial class, (3) the small-business class, and (4) the working class—so that you can compare them to those found in the Weberian model.

The Capitalist Class

According to Wright, this class holds most of the wealth and power in society through ownership of capital—for example, banks, corporations, factories, mines, news and entertainment industries, and agribusiness firms. The "ruling elites," or "ruling class," within the capitalist class hold political power and are often elected or appointed to influential political and regulatory positions (Parenti, 1994).

This class is composed of individuals who have inherited fortunes, own major corporations, or are top corporate executives with extensive stock holdings or control of company investments. Even though many top executives have only limited *legal ownership* of their corporations, they have substantial economic ownership and exert extensive control over investments, distribution of profits, and management of resources. The major sources of income for the capitalist class are profits, interest, and very high salaries. Members of this class make important decisions about the workplace, including which products and services to make available to consumers and how many workers to hire or fire (Feagin and Feagin, 1997).

According to *Forbes* magazine's 2002 list of the richest people in the world, Bill Gates (co-founder of Microsoft Corporation, the world's largest microcomputer software company) was the wealthiest capitalist, with a net worth of $53 billion. Warren E. Buffet came in second with $35 billion. Although some of the men who made the *Forbes* list of the wealthiest people have gained their fortunes through entrepreneurship or being CEOs of large corporations, women who made the list typically acquired their wealth through inheritance, marriage, or both. In 1999, only three women were heads of Fortune 500 companies (Greenfeld, 1999).

The Managerial Class

People in the managerial class have substantial control over the means of production and over workers. However, these upper-level managers, supervisors, and professionals typically do not participate in key corporate decisions, such as how to invest profits. Lower-level managers may have some control over employment practices, including the hiring and firing of some workers (Vanneman and Cannon, 1987).

Top professionals, such as physicians, lawyers, accountants, and engineers, may control the structure of their own work; however, they typically do not own the means of production and may not have supervisory authority over more than a few people. Even so, they may influence the organization of work and the treatment of other workers. Members of the capitalist class often depend on these professionals for their specialized knowledge.

As previously discussed, members of the managerial class occupy a contradictory class location between the capitalist and working classes (Wright, 1979). Like members of the working class, persons in the managerial class do not own the means of production, and they usually earn a regular salary. However, they typically have control over the work of others and may exercise considerable authority over the organization of production. They also may invest in corporate stock and gain significant unearned income. As a result, they tend to align themselves with the basic interests of the capitalist class. For people of colour and white women in the managerial class, additional contradictions exist based on race and/or gender.

The Small-Business Class

This class consists of small-business owners and craftspeople who may hire a small number of employees but largely do their own work. Some members own businesses, such as "mom-and-pop" grocery stores, retail clothing stores, and jewellery stores. Others are doctors and lawyers who receive relatively high incomes from selling their own services. Some of these professionals now share attributes with members of the capitalist class because they have formed corporations that hire and control the employees who produce profits for the professionals.

It is in the small-business class that we find many people's hopes of achieving upward mobility. Seventeen percent of those surveyed in a recent opinion poll thought "owning your own business" was the essence of this dream (Feagin and Sikes, 1994). Several leading scholars have argued that starting a business is a solution for the economic problems of members of visible minority groups (see Sowell, 1981). However, this is not a new idea.

The Working Class

The working class is made up of a number of subgroups, one of which is blue-collar workers, some of whom are highly skilled and well paid and others of whom are unskilled and poorly paid. Skilled blue-collar workers include electricians, plumbers, and carpenters;

unskilled blue-collar workers include janitors and gardeners.

White-collar workers are another subgroup of the working class. Referred to by some as a "new middle class," these workers are actually members of the working class because they do not own the means of production, do not control the work of others, and are relatively powerless in the workplace. Secretaries, other clerical workers, and sales workers are members of the white-collar faction of the working class. They take orders from others and tend to work under constant supervision. Thus, these workers are at the bottom of the class structure in terms of domination and control in the workplace. The working class consists of about half of all employees in Canada.

A New Class Society?

According to the sociologists Robert Perrucci and Earl Wysong (1999), the beginning of this century is characterized by a new class society in which transnational corporations, high technology, and disposable workers encounter new and increasingly polarized class lines. Perrucci and Wysong believe that class membership is based on access to a new mix of critical resources, including income, investment capital, credentialled skills verified by elite schools, and social connections to organizational leaders. Like Marx, Perrucci and Wysong view the two largest classes—the privileged class and the working class—as possessing fundamentally different and opposed interests; consequently, when the situation of one class improves, the other class loses. For example, significantly improving the income, benefits, or job security of the working class would cut into the capital that members of the privileged class have used for consumption and investment.

To picture Perrucci and Wysong's model of the class structure, think of a figure that looks like a double diamond, with a small diamond on the top and a much larger diamond on the bottom. The small, top diamond is made up of the *privileged class* (about 20 percent of the population), and the much larger, bottom diamond is made up of the *new working class* (about 80 percent of the population).

The Privileged Class The top part of the privileged class is the *superclass* (about 1 to 2 percent of the population), which comprises wealthy owners and employers who make a living from investments or business ownership. Six- and seven-figure incomes are customary, and many make far more, which provides them with large sums of capital for consumption and investment. Beneath the superclass is the *credentialled class,* which consists of managers (13 to 15 percent) in mid- and upper-level management positions and the CEOs of corporations and public organizations. This class also includes professionals (4 to 5 percent of the population), who use their professional degrees and organizational ties to advance their interests even as they solidify the position of those in the superclass.

The New Working Class Perrucci and Wysong divide the new working class into the *comfort class* (10 percent), which is made up of nurses, teachers, civil servants, and skilled workers, such as carpenters and electricians, and the *contingent class.* Wage earners (such as people in clerical and sales jobs and personal services or crafts jobs) are located in the contingent class, along with those who are self-employed and hire no employees. At the bottom of the new working class is the *excluded class*—people who are in and out of the labour force and whose only source of employment is a variety of unskilled, low-wage, temporary jobs.

Is the new class society an accurate model of the Canadian class structure? What about dreams of rags to riches? These are difficult questions to answer; however, if Perrucci and Wysong are correct, Canada currently does not have a middle class: Many people do not have stable, secure resources over time, such as a steady job that provides an adequate income, health insurance, and a pension. According to this approach, the growing division in power and resources between the privileged class and the new working class gives the class structure an intergenerational permanence, and the balance of class power continues to shift toward the privileged class, which is able to "devise, disguise, and legitimate corporate practices and government policies that serve its interests but are destructive to working-class interests" (Perrucci and Wysong, 1999:244). Moreover, institutional classism serves to perpetuate privileged-class dominance. **Classism refers to the belief that persons in the upper or privileged class are superior to those in the lower or working class, particularly in regard to values, behaviour, and lifestyles.** However, some people resist classism by standing up against policies they believe will contribute to economic, political, and cultural inequalities. Perrucci and Wysong describe a "structural democracy" approach that seeks to revitalize participation in politics and government, as well as encourage people to place demands on corporate structures to enhance democratic governance so that the interests of the working class are not neglected. As Perrucci and Wysong (1999:273) state, it is necessary to reduce class-based inequalities between the privileged and working classes so that democracy in North America does not topple to a "permanent resting spot at the bottom of history."

Although Marxian and Weberian models of class structure show differences in people's occupations and access to valued resources, neither fully reflects the nature and extent of inequality in the United States and Canada. In the next section, we will take a closer look at the unequal distribution of income and wealth in Canada and the effects of inequality on people's opportunities and life chances.

CONSEQUENCES OF INEQUALITY

Income and wealth are not simply statistics; they are intricately related to our individual life chances. Persons with a high income or substantial wealth have more control over their lives. They have greater access to goods and services; they can afford better housing, more education, and a wider range of medical services. Similarly, as discussed in Box 8.2, those with greater access to economic resources fare better when dealing with the criminal justice system (Reiman, 1979; Gabor, 1994; Linden, 1995). Persons with less income, especially those living in poverty, must spend their limited resources on the basic necessities of life.

Physical and Mental Health and Nutrition

People who are wealthy and well educated and who have high-paying jobs are much more likely to be healthy than are poor people. As people's economic status increases, so does their health status (Health Canada, 1999). The poor have shorter life expectancies and are at greater risk for chronic illnesses, such as diabetes, heart disease, and cancer, as well as for infectious diseases, such as tuberculosis. (See Chapter 18, "Health, Health Care, and Disability.") For example, a recent report by Professor Dennis Raphael at York University concluded that the economic and social conditions under which Canadians live their lives are greater determinants of whether

they develop heart disease than medical and lifestyle factors (such as poor diet, lack of activity, and smoking). If all Canadians had the cardiovascular health of the wealthiest Canadians, there would be approximately 6,000 fewer deaths a year from heart disease. According to Raphael's (2001) report, the economic and social conditions that most contribute to heart disease are poverty and low income. Specifically, poverty and low income lead to heart disease in three ways:

1. People on low incomes live under conditions of material deprivation that produce a cardiovascular heart burden that accumulates over the life span.
2. Living on low incomes creates excessive stress that damages the cardiovascular system.
3. The stressful conditions associated with low incomes lead to unhealthy behaviours, such as smoking. (Raphael, 2001)

There is also increasing evidence that societies with large income gaps between the wealthy and the poor are the most likely to produce the conditions that lead to heart disease.

Children born into poor families are at much greater risk of dying during their first year of life. Some die from disease, accidents, or violence. Others are unable to survive because they are born with low birth weight, a condition linked to birth defects and increased probability of infant mortality (Canadian Institute of Child Health, 1994; Health Canada, 1997). Low birth weight in infants is attributed, at least in part, to the inadequate nutrition received by many low-income pregnant women. Most of the poor do not receive preventive medical and dental checkups; many do not receive adequate medical care after they experience illness or injury. Furthermore, many high-poverty areas lack an adequate supply of doctors and medical facilities. The higher death rates among Aboriginal peoples in Canada are partly attributable to unequal access to medical care and nutrition (Tjepkema, 2002).

Although the precise relationship between class and health is not known, analysts suggest that people with higher incomes and greater wealth tend to smoke less, exercise more, maintain a healthy body weight, and eat nutritious meals. As a category, affluent people tend to be less depressed and face less psychological stress, conditions that tend to be directly proportional to income, education, and job status (Ross and Roberts, 1997).

Good health is basic to good life chances, and adequate amounts of nutritious food are essential for good health. Hunger is related to class position and

BOX 8.2 SOCIOLOGY AND THE LAW

The Rich Get Richer and the Poor Get Prison

How does social class affect the likelihood of being sent to prison? Are there different sets of rules operating in the criminal justice system—one for the rich and one for the poor? According to Jeffery Reiman, author of *The Rich Get Richer and the Poor Get Prison: Ideology, Class and Criminal Justice* (1979), economic power is the central factor in determining whether a person will go to prison for a criminal offence. Reiman supports this premise with data that reveal that in the United States the prison populations are overwhelmingly from the ranks of society's disadvantaged. He states

> For the same criminal behavior, the poor are more likely to be arrested; if arrested, they are more likely to be charged; if charged, more likely to be convicted; if convicted, more likely to be sentenced to prison; and if sentenced, more likely to be given longer prison terms than members of the middle and upper classes. In other words, the image of the criminal population one sees in our nation's jails and prisons is an image distorted by the shape of the criminal justice system itself. It is the face of evil reflected in a carnival mirror, but it is no laughing matter. (1979:97)

What effect does social class play in the processing of accused persons in the Canadian criminal justice system? According to criminologist Thomas Gabor, the justice system in Canada also favours the middle and upper classes—those who have the financial resources to protect their best interests. For example, in the case of young offenders, police are more likely to refer lower-class youths to juvenile court. Youth from wealthier homes are more likely to be dealt with informally. Poor defendants are less likely to be able to afford bail and are therefore more likely to remain in jail until their case goes to trial (this may be several months). The poor must rely on legal-aid lawyers who have large caseloads and little time to prepare cases for trial. The sentencing stage also favours individuals of higher social standing. Crimes committed by middle- and upper-class persons—for example, embezzlement, fraud, and income tax evasion—usually earn lighter sentences

than those more likely to be committed by the poor (e.g., robbery and burglary).

In short, white-collar criminals have been very successful in ensuring that their interests are reflected in the law and its enforcement. According to one of the authors of this textbook, criminologist Rick Linden (2000), the crimes committed by higher-status criminals are much less likely to be labelled criminal:

> A storekeeper who sells a turkey labelled 12 kg which actually weighs 11 kg may not be prosecuted; if he or she actually is, the charge will be breach of a regulatory offence with relatively minor penalties. However, someone caught stealing a kilogram of turkey meat will be charged with the criminal offence of theft. Doctors who fraudulently bill provincial health insurance plans are usually disciplined by their professional body, while someone who fraudulently receives welfare is subject to criminal prosecution. (1994:219)

It is evident that social class plays a significant role in terms of the type of punishment, if any, offenders receive for their crime. However, as Gabor notes, other factors, such as the type and severity of the offence, are also important considerations:

> Even poor people are selectively punished. The poor people we find in prisons have been incarcerated for murder, robbery, theft, burglary, drug offences and the like; they are rarely punished for assaulting their wives, abusing their children, or stealing from their employers. Thus, the type of infraction one commits, too, is important in the selection of people for legal proceedings.

Arrest, detention, and sentencing decisions are extremely complex and involve a number of legal (prior record, severity of offence, type of offence) and nonlegal (social class, age, demeanour, gender) factors. Therefore, although we can say that social class affects an individual's chances of going to prison, it is difficult to determine the degree of influence this nonlegal factor has.

Sources: Gabor, 1994; Reiman, 1979; Linden, 2000.

income inequality. After spending 60 percent of their income on housing, low-income families are often unable to provide enough food for their children. Consider the following comments by a mother on her attempts to manage her food budget:

> I remember opening up the fridge just to see what was in there. There was a green pepper, an onion in the drawer and a bag of frozen rhubarb in the freezer, and that was all the food we had in the entire house. We used to eat peanut butter by the spoonful, if we had any peanut butter. We used to make rhubarb soup. And we'd throw in whatever we could find. (Canadian Council on Social Development, 1996:21)

A recent report of the Canadian Association of Food Banks (CAFB) shows that the number of people who are reliant on food banks has more than doubled since 1989. This increase clearly indicates that many Canadians are unable meet their nutritional needs (Sarick, 1999; Wilson and Steinman, 2000). The report estimates that every month at least 750,000 people, or about 2.5 percent of Canadians, are forced to turn to food banks for assistance. Recent estimates indicate that more than 50,000 Canadian children experience hunger due to lack of food or money in any given year. Lack of adequate nutrition has been linked to children's problems in school. To make matters worse, in a typical month fully half of those using food banks are families with children, meaning that children account for 40 percent of all food bank users. In addition to the overall increase in the use of food banks, the survey points to disturbing changes in the social composition of those compelled to turn to charity to meet their basic needs. More than half of food bank users are parents, single parents, and their dependants. Food bank use among students has risen sharply, a consequence no doubt of rising tuition fees and cuts to student aid. According to the Canadian Association of Food Banks, "Over 90 percent of universities have some type of food bank." The percentage of those using food banks who come from the "working poor"—those who name employment as their primary source of income yet whose incomes are insufficient to cover their food needs—is growing. Nearly 13 percent of food bank users in 2003 were employed, up from under 12 percent in 2002 (Parsons, 2003). For more information on food banks, see Box 8.3, "You Can Make a Difference: Helping Feed Canada's Hungry."

Education

Educational opportunities and life chances are directly linked. Some functionalist theorists view education as the "elevator" to social mobility. Improvements in the educational achievement levels (measured in number of years of schooling completed) of the poor, visible minorities, and women have been cited as evidence that students' abilities now are more important than their class, race, or gender. From this perspective, inequality in education is declining, and students have an opportunity to achieve upward mobility through achievements at school (see Hauser and Featherman, 1976). Functionalists generally see the education system as flexible, allowing most students the opportunity to attend university if they apply themselves (Ballantine, 1993).

In contrast, most conflict theorists stress that schools are agencies for reproducing the capitalist class system and perpetuating inequality in society (Bowles and Gintis, 1976; Bowles, 1977). From this perspective, education perpetuates poverty. Parents with limited income are not able to provide the same educational opportunities for their children as are families with greater financial resources. Today, great disparities exist in the distribution of educational resources. Because funding for education comes primarily from local property taxes, school districts in wealthy suburban areas generally pay higher teachers' salaries, have newer buildings, and provide state-of-the-art equipment. By contrast, schools in poorer areas have a limited funding base. Students in core-area schools and poverty-stricken rural areas often attend schools that lack essential equipment and teaching resources. Author Jonathan Kozol (1991, quoted in Feagin and Feagin, 1994:191) documented the effect of educational inequality on students:

> Kindergartners are so full of hope, cheerfulness, high expectations. By the time they get into fourth grade, many begin to lose heart. They see the score, understanding they're not getting what others are getting . . . They see suburban schools on television . . . They begin to get the point that they are not valued much in our society. By the time they are in junior high, they understand it. "We have eyes and we can see; we have hearts and we can feel . . . We know the difference."

Poverty exacts such a toll that many young people will not have the opportunity to finish high school, much less enter university, which subsequently affects job prospects, employment patterns, and potential earnings. As a report by the National Council of

BOX 8.3 YOU CAN MAKE A DIFFERENCE

Helping Feed Canada's Hungry

Consider the comments of these young single mothers discussing their efforts to feed their children:

> "We ate macaroni and cheese five nights a week. There was a Safeway special for 39 cents a box. We could eat seven dinners for $3.00 a week. . . . I think that's all we ate for months."

> "I opted for welfare. . . . It was the worst experience of my life. . . . I never dreamed that I, a middle-class housewife, would ever be in a position like that. It was humiliating . . . they make you feel it. . . . But we were desperate, and I had to feed my kids."

> "You name it, I tried it—food stamps, soup kitchens, shelters. It just about killed me to have the kids live like that." (Weitzman, 1999:205)

Hunger is an increasing problem in Canada. Much needs to be done to feed the hungry and combat the problem in the long term. The Canadian Association of Food Banks (CAFB) is an umbrella organization representing approximately 235 food banks across every Canadian province and territory. Member food banks and their agencies serve about 90 percent of people who use food banks.

In the short term, their main focus is feeding hungry Canadians. In the longer term, the organization is working together toward a hunger-free Canada. To do what it does, CAFB relies on a nationwide network of hard-working volunteers, corporations, and donations from Canadians. The CAFB Board of Directors is made up of two food bank representatives from each province. The CAFB operates according to a strict code of ethics that has received international acclaim.
The CAFB

- Represents foods banks across Canada
- Acts as advocates for food bank users
- Works with food banks, corporations and government to solve Canada's growing hunger problem
- Conducts research on hunger, including *Hunger-Count*, an annual survey of food bank use in Canada
- Distributes large food donations to member banks through the National Food Sharing System (NFSS)
- Promotes the dignity of food bank users
- Promotes the ethical stewardship of donated food
- Surveys Canadians' perceptions of the problem of hunger

Do you want to help fight hunger? The Canadian Association of Food Banks suggests a number of ways you can help:

- Run a fundraising event in your community
- Make or organize donations of money, products, or transportation
- Offer administrative help in food bank offices
- Help in food bank warehouses

For more information go to http://www.cafb-acba .ca/english/GetInvolved.html.

Source: Reprinted by permission of Canadian Association of Food Banks, 2005.

Welfare indicated, "To be born poor in Canada does not make it a certainty that you will live poor and die poor—but it makes it very likely" (quoted in Bolaria, Singh, and Wotherspoon, 1991:470).

Crime and Lack of Safety

Along with diminished access to quality health care, nutrition, and housing and unequal educational opportunities, crime and lack of safety are other consequences of inequality. As discussed in Chapter 7 ("Crime and Deviance"), although people from all classes commit crimes, they commit different kinds of crime. Capitalism and the rise of the consumer society may be factors in the criminal behavior of some upper-middle-class and upper-class people, who may be motivated by greed or the competitive desire to stay ahead of others in their reference group. By contrast, crimes committed by people in the lower classes may be motivated by feelings of anger, frustration, and hopelessness.

According to Marxist criminologists, capitalism produces social inequalities that contribute to criminality among people, particularly those who are outside the economic mainstream. Poverty and violence are also linked. In his recent ethnographic study of inner-city life, sociologist Elijah Anderson (1999:33) suggests that what some people refer to as "random, senseless street violence" is often not random at all, but instead a response to profound social inequalities in the inner city:

> The inclination to violence springs from the circumstances of life among the ghetto poor—the lack of jobs that pay a living wage, limited basic public services (police response in emergencies, building maintenance, trash pickup, lighting, and other services that middle-class neighborhoods take for granted), the stigma of race, the fallout from rampant drug use and drug trafficking, and the resulting alienation and absence of hope for the future. Simply living in such an environment places young people at special risk of falling victim to aggressive behavior. . . . [T]his environment means that even youngsters whose home lives reflect mainstream values—and most of the homes in the community do—must be able to handle themselves in a street-oriented environment. (Anderson, 1999: 32–33)

As Anderson states, consequences of inequality include both crime and lack of safety on the streets, particularly for people who feel a profound sense of alienation from mainstream society and its institutions. Those who are able to take care of themselves and protect their loved ones against aggression are accorded deference and regard by others. However, Anderson believes that it is wrong to place blame solely on individuals for the problems that exist in urban ghettos; instead, he asserts that the focus should be on the socioeconomic structure and public policy that have threatened the well-being of people who live in poverty.

■ POVERTY IN CANADA

When many people think about poverty, they think of people who are unemployed or on welfare. However, many hardworking people with full-time jobs live in poverty. In the United States, the government established an *official poverty line,* which is based on what is considered to be the minimum amount of money required for living at a subsistence level. The poverty level is computed by determining the cost of a minimally nutritious diet and multiplying this figure by three to allow for nonfood costs. Canada, however, has no official definition of poverty, no official method for measuring poverty, and no official set of poverty lines (Pohl, 2002). As a result, there is ongoing and

contentious debate with respect to how prevalent and how serious the problem of poverty is in Canada. The most accepted and commonly used definition of poverty is Statistics Canada's before-tax *low-income cutoff*—**the income level at which a family may be in "straitened circumstances" because it spends considerably more on the basic necessities of life (food, shelter, and clothing) than the average family.** The low-income cutoffs depend on family and community size (Statistics Canada, 2002j). According to this measure, any individual or family that spends more than 70 percent of their income on the three essentials of life—food, clothing, and shelter—is considered to be living in poverty. There is no single cutoff line for all of Canada, because living costs vary by family size and place of residence. In 2000, the income cutoffs for a family of four ranged from $18,928 in rural areas to $28,870 in cities of more than 500,000. Based on these low-income cutoffs, nearly 5 million children, women, and men—one in every six Canadians—were living in poverty (Lee, 2000). It should be noted that these data exclude a number of groups, including Aboriginal persons living on reserves or in the Yukon and Northwest Territories. Given that Aboriginal persons constitute one of the poorest groups in Canada, the full extent of poverty is underestimated by this Statistics Canada measure (Naiman, 2000).

When sociologists define poverty, they distinguish between absolute and relative poverty. **Absolute poverty exists when people do not have the means to secure the most basic necessities of life.** This definition comes closest to that used by the corporate think tanks, such as the Fraser Institute. Using this measure, there are relatively few poor people in Canada (Naiman, 2000:229). Absolute poverty often has life-threatening consequences, such as when a homeless person freezes to death on a park bench. By comparison, *relative poverty* **exists when people may be able to afford basic necessities but still are unable to maintain an average standard of living** (Lee, 2000). The relative approach is based on equity—that is, on some acknowledgment of the extent to which society should tolerate or accept inequality in the distribution of income and wealth. This definition recognizes that people who have so little that they stand out in relation to their community will feel deprived (Canadian Council on Social Development, 1996:3). In short, regardless of how it is defined, poverty is primarily about deprivation, as this woman's comments reveal:

> There are times when I am so scared that I'm not going to find a job, I think, "What the hell is wrong with me?" . . . I can get scared to

The "feminization of poverty" refers to the fact that two out of three impoverished adults in North America are women. Should we assume that poverty is primarily a women's issue? Why or why not?

death . . . I have periods of insomnia. I'll get very short tempered with my husband and with the children. (Burman, 1998:195)

With the exception of a small percentage of the Canadian population that is living at a bare subsistence level or below, most of the poor in our society suffer the effects of a relentless feeling of being boxed in, a feeling that life is dictated by the requirements of simply surviving each day. If something unexpected happens, such as sickness, accident, family death, fire, theft, or a rent increase, there is no buffer to deal with the emergency. Life is just today, because tomorrow offers no hope (Ross, Scott, and Smith, 2000). Perhaps one of the best ways to understand poverty is to describe a family's income after it pays for food, shelter, and clothing.

How much money does a typical poor family, consisting of two adults and two children and living in a large urban area, have at its disposal? In 1997, while the traditional Statistics Canada low-income cutoff line for such a family was set at $28,100, the average two-parent family with two children was in fact below this line by an amount equal to $10,050, leaving it with $18,050 annually on which to live (Ross, Scott, and Smith, 2000).

Compare this to the family's basic expenditures on shelter, food, and clothing. Using the Canadian Mortgage and Housing Corporation (CMHC) survey of shelter costs across the country, the median rent for a three-bedroom apartment amounted to $8,495 per year (weekly equivalent of $40.84 per person). To adhere to Agriculture Canada's Nutritious Food Basket as a guide to basic food costs, the family required $6,885 (weekly equivalent of $33.10 per person). Using the Montreal Diet

Dispensary guidelines for basic living, estimated clothing costs totalled $2,206 (weekly equivalent of $10.61 per person). This amounts to $17,538 per year for the typical poor four-member family. Deducting this from its gross income of $18,060 leaves a surplus of only $462 for the year, or $2.22 per person per week. This $2.22 per week must be used to meet all other needs, such as personal care, household needs, furniture, telephone, transportation, school supplies, health care, and so on. There is no money for entertainment, recreation, reading material, insurance, or charitable or religious donations (Ross, Scott, and Smith, 2000).

Who Are the Poor?

As might be expected, those who are society's most vulnerable, most disadvantaged, and least equipped to compete in a highly competitive, fast-polarizing labour market are most likely to be living in poverty (Pohl, 2002). Poverty in Canada is not randomly distributed, but rather is highly concentrated among certain groups of people—specifically, women, children, persons with disabilities, and Aboriginal peoples. When people belong to more than one of these categories—for example, Aboriginal children—their risk of poverty is even greater.

Age   Today, children are at much greater risk of living in poverty than are older persons (Statistics Canada, 2003l). A generation ago, persons over age 65 were at greatest risk of being poor; however, increased government transfer payments and an increase in the number of elderly individuals retiring with private pension plans have led to a decline in poverty among the elderly.

While approximately 17 percent of the elderly are still below the low-income cutoffs, the age group now most likely to be poor is children (Statistics Canada, 2003l). Recent statistics indicate that while the overall poverty rate is about 16 percent, the rate for children under age 18 is approximately 18 percent (Canadian Council on Social Development, 2002b). This means that more than 1 million Canadian children are living in poverty. A large number of children hover just above the official poverty line. The precarious position of Aboriginal children is even more striking. Approximately 50 percent of Aboriginal children (both on and off reserves) are living in poverty (Campaign 2000, 2003).

Children as a group are poorer now than they were at the beginning of the 1980s, and this is true whether they live in one- or two-parent families.

BOX 8.4 SOCIOLOGY IN GLOBAL PERSPECTIVE

How Does Child Poverty in Canada Compare with Child Poverty in Other Nations?

The UNICEF report *Child Poverty in Rich Nations* ranks Canada a lowly 17 (see the figure below) out of the 23 rich nations belonging to the Organisation for Economic Co-operation and Development (OECD).

The international rankings show that a nation's level of wealth does not predetermine its ability to prevent children from falling into poverty. Countries with higher economic growth do not necessarily have a lower poverty ranking. Many of the countries with the lowest poverty rates have relatively lower wealth rankings. The wealthiest nation, the United States, has the second highest poverty ranking. The

contention that child poverty can be addressed only through increased economic growth is contradicted by the available evidence.

UNICEF states that the reason why countries are able to address child poverty with such varying degrees of success relates to how each chooses to set priorities according to its wealth. Most of the nations that have been more successful than Canada at keeping low levels of child poverty are willing to counterbalance the effects of unemployment and low-paid work with substantial investments in family policies. The comprehensive

Child Poverty in Selected OECD Nations, 2000

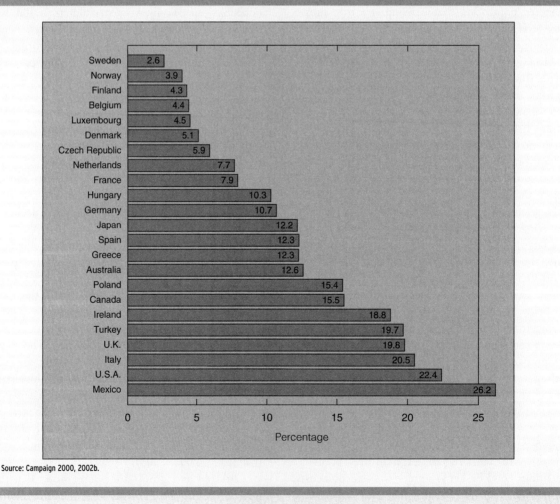

Source: Campaign 2000, 2002b.

approach to the well-being of children adopted by many European countries includes generous income security and unemployment benefits, national affordable housing programs, as well as widely accessible early childhood education and care.

The contrast of early childhood education and care services in Canada and in Europe is instructive. A recent OECD review of twelve nations found that early childhood education and care had experienced a "surge of policy attention" in Europe during the past decade. This has not been true in Canada. While the nations of Western Europe now provide universal full-day early childhood education and care for all three- to five-year olds, Canada has not even begun to consider this. Yet there is widespread agreement, including among Canadian researchers, that early childhood education and care is a critical component of comprehensive family policy and of an effective antipoverty strategy.

Source: UNICEF Innocenti Research Centre, 2000.

Although more than half of all poor children live in two-parent families, the number of poor children living in single-parent households is increasing. Despite the promise made by the House of Commons in 1989 to alleviate child poverty by the year 2000, the future for poor children does not look bright. These children are poor because their parents are poor, and one of the main reasons for poverty among adults is a lack of good jobs. Government cuts to unemployment insurance benefits, employment programs, income supports, and social services for families and children will affect not only those who need these services but also the children of these individuals. See Box 8.4 for a look at child poverty in Canada and other wealthy nations.

Gender About two-thirds of all adults living in poverty in Canada are women. Women in all categories are at greater risk for poverty than men, but the risk is particularly significant in single-parent families headed by women (Naiman, 2000). As Figure 8.5 shows, in 2001 single-parent families headed by women had a 56-percent poverty rate compared with a rate of 12 percent for two-parent families. Furthermore, women are among the poorest of the poor. Poor single mothers with children under 18 are the worst off, struggling on incomes more than $9,000 below the low-income cutoff (Campaign 2002a, 2002). Sociologist Diana Pearce (1978) coined a term to describe this problem. The ***feminization of poverty* refers to the trend in which women are disproportionately represented among individuals living in poverty.** According to Pearce (1978), women have a higher risk of being poor because they bear the major economic burden of raising children as single heads of households but earn only 70 cents for every dollar a male worker earns—a figure that has changed little over four decades. More women than men are unable to obtain regular, full-time, year-round employment, and the lack of adequate, affordable daycare exacerbates this problem (Schellenberg and Ross, 1997). As discussed in Chapter 9, the feminization of poverty is a global phenomenon.

Does the feminization of poverty explain poverty in Canada today? Is poverty primarily a women's issue? On one hand, this thesis highlights a genuine problem—the link between gender and poverty. On the other hand, several major problems exist with this argument. First, women's poverty is not a new phenomenon. Women have always been more susceptible to poverty (see Katz, 1989). Second, all women are not equally susceptible to poverty. For example, some women experience what has been described as *event-driven poverty* as a result of marital separation, divorce, or widowhood (Bane, 1986). A Statistics Canada report indicated that women's incomes (adjusted for family size) dropped by about 23 percent one year after divorce or separation, while men reported a 10-percent gain in the same time period (Statistics Canada, 1997d). Many in the upper and upper-middle classes have the financial resources, education, and skills to support themselves regardless of the presence of a man in the household. Third, event-driven poverty does not explain the realities of poverty for many visible-minority women, who instead may experience *reshuffled poverty*—a condition of deprivation that follows them regardless of their marital status or the type of family in which they live. Some women experience *multiple jeopardies,* a term that refers to the even greater risk of poverty experienced by women who are immigrants, visible minorities, or Aboriginal, or by women who have disabilities (Gerber, 1990).

| Figure 8.5 | Poverty Rate by Family Type, 2001 |

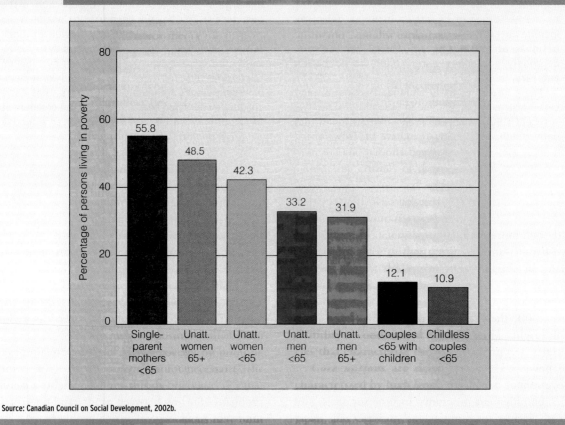

Source: Canadian Council on Social Development, 2002b.

Finally, poverty is everyone's problem, not just women's. When women are impoverished, so are their children. Moreover, many of the poor in our society are men, especially the chronically unemployed, older persons, the homeless, persons with disabilities, and visible-minority men. These men have spent their adult lives without hope of finding work (Ross, Scott, and Smith, 2000).

Race/Ethnicity

According to some stereotypes, most of the poor and virtually all welfare recipients are visible minorities. Such stereotypes are perpetuated because a disproportionate percentage of the impoverished in Canada are Aboriginal persons and recent immigrants. Aboriginal people in Canada are among the most severely disadvantaged persons. About one-half live below the poverty line, and some live in conditions of extreme poverty. The average income for Aboriginal persons is just over $17,000— 34 percent below the national average income of $26,000 (Minister of Indian Affairs and Northern Development, 2000). According to a study by the

Department of Indian Affairs, the quality of life for Aboriginal persons living on reserves—about 380,000 people—ranks worse than in countries such as Mexico and Thailand. For the 270,000 registered Aboriginal persons living off reserves, the quality of life is slightly better (Tjepkema, 2002). According to the United Nations Human Development Index, their living conditions are in line with those in Russia (Anderssen, 1998). Also, the unemployment rate for Aboriginal persons in Canada ranges from 40 to 60 percent, while the national average is about 10 percent. In short, the erosion of Canada's social safety net has had a particularly negative impact on those who have historically experienced exclusion and disadvantage in Canadian society (Campaign 2000, 2002a).

Persons with Disabilities

Awareness that persons with disabilities are discriminated against in the job market has increased in recent years. As a result, they now constitute one of the recognized "target groups" in efforts to eliminate discrimination in the workplace. People with disabilities have more opportunities to work today than they had a decade ago. Today, although more than 50 percent of people with disabilities are in the labour force, many continue to be excluded from the workplace not because of the disability itself, but because of environmental barriers in the workplace (Fawcett, 2000). The effects of this systemic discrimination continue to be felt by disabled persons, as they are still as a group vulnerable to poverty (Fawcett, 1996). As discussed in Chapter 18 ("Health, Health Care, and Disability"), adults with disabilities have significantly lower incomes than non-disabled Canadians. Recent estimates indicate that close to half of employed persons with disabilities had incomes below $10,000 (Canadian Council on Social Development, 2002a). Once again, when gender and disability are combined, we find that women with disabilities are doubly disadvantaged (Fawcett, 2000).

Economic and Structural Sources of Poverty

Poverty has both economic and structural sources. The low wages paid for many jobs is the major cause: more than half of all families living in poverty are headed by someone who is employed either full or part time (Naiman, 2000; National Council of Welfare, 2002). In 1972, minimum-wage legislation meant that a worker who worked 40 hours a week, 52 weeks a year could earn a yearly income 20 percent over the poverty line. By today's standards, the same worker would have to earn more than $10 per hour simply to reach the poverty line. Minimum wages across Canada range from just over $5 per hour to a high of approximately $7 per hour. In other words, a person with full-time employment in a minimum-wage job cannot keep a family of four above the official poverty line.

Structural problems contribute to both unemployment and underemployment. Today, a rapid worldwide transformation is taking place that is changing our societies from industrial-based ones to information-based ones. Automation in the industrial heartland of Quebec and Ontario has made the skills and training of thousands of workers obsolete. Many of these workers have become unemployable and poor. Corporations have been deinvesting in Canada, displacing millions of people from their jobs. Economists refer to this displacement as the *deindustrialization of North America* (Bluestone and Harrison, 1982). Even

as they have closed their Canadian factories and plants, many corporations have opened new facilities in other countries where "cheap labour" exists because people of necessity will work for lower wages. **Job deskilling—a reduction in the proficiency needed to perform a specific job that leads to a corresponding reduction in the wages for that job—**has resulted from the introduction of computers and other technology (Hodson and Parker, 1988). The shift from manufacturing to service occupations has resulted in the loss of higher-paying positions and their replacement with lower-paying and less secure positions that do not offer the wages, job stability, or advancement potential of the disappearing manufacturing jobs. Conse-quently, there are simply not enough good jobs available in Canada to enable families to lift themselves out of poverty. In addition, the lack of affordable, high-quality daycare for women who need to earn an income means that many jobs are inaccessible, especially to women who are single parents. The problems of unemployment, underemployment, and poverty-level wages are even greater for visible minorities and young people (Ross, Shillington, and Lochhead, 1994).

SOCIOLOGICAL EXPLANATIONS OF SOCIAL INEQUALITY

Obviously, some people are disadvantaged as a result of social inequality. Is inequality therefore always harmful to a society? Why are all societies stratified? The functionalist perspective sees inequality as an inevitable and even necessary feature of society. The conflict perspective, influenced by Karl Marx, sees inequality as avoidable, unnecessary, and the source of most human conflict. Gerhard Lenski (1966) has offered a third approach that combines elements of both functionalism and conflict theory.

Functionalist Perspectives

Fifty years ago, sociologists Kingsley Davis and Wilbert Moore developed a theory of social stratification that has been debated ever since. Davis and Moore (1945) suggested that social inequality not only is universal but also is necessary for the smooth functioning of society. How can social inequality be beneficial to a society? The *Davis–Moore thesis,* which has become the definitive functionalist explanation for social inequality, can be summarized as follows:

1. All societies have important tasks that must be accomplished and certain positions that must be filled.
2. Some positions are more important for the survival of society than others.
3. The most important positions must be filled by the most qualified people.
4. The positions that are the most important for society and that require scarce talent, extensive training, or both, must be the most highly rewarded.
5. The most highly rewarded positions should be those that are functionally unique (no other position can perform the same function) and on which other positions rely for expertise, direction, or financing.

Davis and Moore use the physician as an example of a functionally unique position. Doctors are very important to society and require extensive training, but individuals would not be motivated to go through years of costly and stressful medical training without incentives to do so. The Davis–Moore thesis assumes that social stratification results in **meritocracy**—**a hierarchy in which all positions are rewarded based on people's ability and credentials.**

Critics have suggested that the Davis–Moore thesis ignores inequalities based on inherited wealth and intergenerational family status (Rossides, 1986). The thesis assumes that economic rewards and prestige are the only effective motivators for people, and fails to take into account other intrinsic aspects of work, such as self-fulfillment (Tumin, 1953). It also does not adequately explain how such a reward system guarantees that the most qualified people will gain access to the most highly rewarded positions.

What about people who have not been able to maximize their talents and skills because they were born in impoverished circumstances and received a substandard education (see Kozol, 1991)? The functionalist approach generally ignores such questions because it does not consider structural factors (such as racial discrimination, lack of job opportunities, and inadequate funding of schools) that may contribute to the persistence of inequality in society.

The Davis–Moore thesis has also been subject to criticism around the idea that some occupations command greater social rewards because they are seen as more functionally important. Should an actor, entertainer, or star athlete earn $50 million a year for his or her scarce talent when other more important (in terms of the survival of society) jobs, such as elementary school teacher, police officer, or health care professional, pay so little by comparison?

Conflict Perspectives

From a conflict perspective, people with economic and political power are able to shape and distribute the rewards, resources, privileges, and opportunities in society for their own benefit. Conflict theorists do not believe that inequality serves as a motivating force for people; they argue that powerful individuals and groups use ideology to maintain their favoured positions at the expense of others. A stratified social system is accepted because of the dominant ideology of the society, the set of beliefs that explain and justify the existing social order (Marchak, 1975). Core values in Canada emphasize the importance of material possessions, hard work, and individual initiative to get ahead, and behaviour that supports the existing social structure. These same values support the prevailing resource distribution system and contribute to social inequality.

Conflict theorists note that laws and informal social norms also support inequality in Canada. For the first half of the twentieth century, for example, both legalized and institutionalized segregation and discrimination reinforced employment discrimination and produced higher levels of economic inequality. Although laws have been passed to make these overt acts of discrimination illegal, many forms of discrimination still exist in educational and employment opportunities.

Why is inequality growing in Canada? According to critical conflict (Marxist) theorists, the answer to this question partially lies in the concept of *surplus value*—the value produced, or the profit created, when the *cost of labour* is less than the *cost of the goods or services* that are produced by the workers. Thus, surplus value is created by the workers' labour powers, which is bought and employed by members of the capitalist and managerial classes, who work on behalf of the capitalist class. When profits are made, they are either reinvested in the business or used for the enrichment of members of the capitalist class, which includes wealthy shareholders who are not involved in the day-to-day operations of a particular corporation but nevertheless control vast quantities of stock or other interests in that corporation. However, since capitalists deem it necessary to continually increase the rate of surplus value, owners and managers must continue to find new ways to make more profits. These methods are typically at the expense of workers (employees) and their families. In the contemporary workplace, employees are the first to feel the brunt of corporate reorganizations, layoffs, downsizing activities, and production demands that require them to work longer hours, sometimes without additional compensation. In certain situations, employees are replaced by labour saving machines or technology, such as computers and robots. Even in a "booming economy," social inequality persists because not everyone benefits from economic growth and development. The wealth of the upper classes, particularly those at the top of the ladder, continues to increase, whereas the rank-and-file employee has limited opportunities, and the size of the marginal working class and the poor population swells. Other workplace factors that contribute to social inequality, such as minimum-wage jobs and part-time or "temp" work, are discussed in Chapter 13 ("The Economy and Work"). How the class structure is reproduced generation after generation through social institutions, such as education, is described in Chapter 16 ("Education").

Feminist Perspectives

According to feminist scholars, the quality of an individual's life experiences is a reflection of both their class position and their gender. These scholars examine the secondary forms of inequality and oppression occurring *within* each class that have been overlooked by the classical theorists. Feminist theorists focus on the combined effect that gender has on class inequality. Some feminist scholars view class and gender as reinforcing one another and creating groups that are "doubly oppressed." This combined effect of one's class and gender may manifest itself in the workplace or the home or both. Subsequently, feminist authors have identified such terms as the "double ghetto" (Armstrong & Armstrong, 1994) and the "double shift" or "second shift" (Hochschild, 1989) to describe women's experiences in the segregated workforce or the home (see Chapters 11 and 15). Rather than male and female spouses maintaining similar class positions within a family unit, women hold a subordinate position. A feminist perspective emphasizes that within any class, women

are less advantaged than men in their access to material goods, power, status, and possibilities for self-actualization. The causes of the inequality lie in the organization of capitalism itself (Ritzer, 1996:321). For example, upper-class women are wealthy but often remain secondary to their husbands in terms of power. Middle-class women may be financially well off, but often lack property or labour force experience and are vulnerable to financial instability in cases of divorce or separation. The position of working-class women varies based on their participation in the paid labour force. Typically the working-class woman has little income, primary responsibility for the household work, and an inferior position in terms of power and independence to her husband. As a result, the female spouse may become "the slave of a slave" (Mackinnon, 1982:8), allowing the working-class male to compensate for his lower class position in society. The family is viewed as an institution that supports capitalism and encourages or exacerbates the exploitation of women. By keeping women in the home with responsibility for family subsistence, emotional support, and reproduction, the family assists in the exploitation of women's labour and serves to maintain class and gender oppression.

Symbolic Interactionist Perspectives

Symbolic interactionists focus on microlevel concerns and usually do not analyze larger structural factors that contribute to inequality and poverty. However, many significant insights on the effects of wealth and poverty on people's lives and social interactions can be derived from applying a symbolic interactionist approach. Using qualitative research methods and influenced by a symbolic interactionist approach, researchers have collected the personal narratives of people across all social classes, ranging from the wealthiest to the poorest people.

Microlevel studies of the wealthy have examined issues, such as the social and psychological factors that influence members of the upper class to contribute vast sums of money to charitable and arts organizations (Odendahl, 1990; Ostrower, 1997). Other studies have focused on the social interactions involved in "male bonding" rituals of elite men's organizations, such as the Bohemian Club, which has annual two-week retreats at the "Bohemian Grove" in Northern California. Several decades ago, the sociologist G. William Domhoff (1974) engaged in participant observation research (serving as a waiter) at the Bohemian Grove to examine how the interactions of wealthy business executives and powerful political leaders partaking in games, rituals, and other activities helped bind these male members of the upper class into a socially cohesive group. Domhoff (1974) concluded that one of the ways the upper class perpetuates its position is through social cohesion, which is furthered by a wide variety of small groups that encourage face-to-face interaction and ensure status and security for members. Similarly, other social scientists have looked at the social and psychological aspects of life in the middle class (Newman, 1988, 1993; Rubin, 1994) or the working and lower classes (Anderson, 1999; Fine and Weis, 1998; Nelson and Smith, 1999; Newman, 1999).

A few studies provide rare insights into the social interactions between people from vastly divergent class locations. Sociologist Judith Rollins's (1985) study of the relationship between household workers and their employers is one example. Based on in-depth interviews and participant observation, Rollins examined rituals of deference that were often demanded by elite white women of their domestic workers, who were frequently women of colour. According to the sociologist Erving Goffman (1967), *deference* is a type of ceremonial activity that functions as a symbolic means whereby appreciation is regularly conveyed to a recipient. In fact, deferential behaviour between nonequals (such as employers and employees) confirms the inequality of the relationship and each party's position in the relationship relative to the other. Rollins identified three types of linguistic deference between domestic workers and their employers: use of the first names of the workers, contrasted with titles and last names (Mrs. Adams) of the employers; use of the term *girls* to refer to female household workers regardless of their age; and deferential references to employers, such as "Yes, ma'am." Spatial demeanour, including touching and how close one person stands to another, is an additional factor in deference rituals across class lines. Rollins (1985: 232) concludes that

> The employer, in her more powerful position, sets the essential tone of the relationship; and that tone . . . is one that functions to reinforce the inequality of the relationship, to strengthen the employer's belief in the rightness of her

advantaged class and racial position, and to provide her with justification for the inegalitarian social system.

Many concepts introduced by the sociologist Erving Goffman (1959, 1967) could be used as springboards for examining microlevel relationships between inequality and people's everyday interactions. What could you learn about class-based inequality in Canada by using a symbolic interactionist approach to examine a setting with which you are familiar?

SOCIAL CLASS IN THE FUTURE

Will social inequality in Canada increase in the future? Many social scientists predict that existing trends point to an increase. First, the purchasing power of the dollar has stagnated or declined since the early 1970s. As families started to lose ground financially, more family members (especially women) entered the labour force in an attempt to support themselves and their families. Economist Robert Reich (1993:145) has noted that the employed have been travelling as though on two escalators—one going up and the other going down—in recent years. The gap between the earnings of workers and the income of managers and top executives has widened (Feagin and Feagin, 1994).

Second, wealth continues to become more concentrated at the top of the Canadian class structure. As the rich have grown richer, more people have found themselves among the ranks of the poor. Third, federal tax laws in recent years have benefited corporations and wealthy families at the expense of middle- and lower-income families. Finally, structural sources of upward mobility are shrinking, whereas the rate of downward mobility has increased.

Are we sabotaging our future if we do not work constructively to eliminate poverty? It has been said that a chain is no stronger than its weakest link. If we apply this idea to the problem of poverty, it is to our advantage to see that those who cannot find work or do not have a job that provides a living wage receive adequate training and employment. Innovative programs can combine job training with producing something useful

Concept Table 8.A SOCIOLOGICAL EXPLANATIONS OF SOCIAL INEQUALITY

PERSPECTIVE	KEY ELEMENTS
Functionalist	Inequality is necessary for the smooth functioning of society. Social stratification leads to *meritocracy:* a hierarchy in which all positions are rewarded based on ability and credentials.
Conflict	Dominant groups maintain and control the distribution of rewards, resources, privileges, and opportunities at the expense of others. Marxist conflict theorists explain that growing inequality is a result of the *surplus value*, profit that is generated when the cost of labour is less than the cost of the goods and services being produced.
Symbolic Interactionist	Focus is on the microlevel effects of wealth and poverty on people's social interactions. For example, in its various forms *deference* confirms inequality between individuals in differing social class positions.
Feminist	Class and gender reinforce one another and create inequalities and oppressions for women "within" different social classes.

to meet the immediate needs of people living in poverty. Children of today—the adults of tomorrow—need education, health care, and nutrition as they grow up.

The growth in single-parent, lower-income families cannot continue to be used as an explanation for the widening gap between the rich and the poor. Rather, social analysts argue that the persistence of economic inequality is related to profound global economic changes. In this chapter, we have focused primarily on social stratification in Canada; however, in Chapter 9 ("Global Stratification"), we examine the connections between wealth and poverty in high-income nations (such as Canada and the United States) and in the lower-income nations of the world.

As mentioned at the beginning of this chapter, the House of Commons established a goal of eliminating poverty among children by the year 2000. Are we getting any closer to reaching this goal? Canada's response to poverty has been contradictory. One would expect that in working toward eliminating poverty, action would be taken to address the structural causes of poverty—high unemployment and an inadequate set of child and family social policies. Instead, the federal government has cut federal social supports (such as subsidized daycare, unemployment benefits, and family allowance) (Campaign 2000, 2002a), leaving families to bear the burden of poverty.

As Canadians, we take pride in our international reputation for fairness and compassion. The United Nations has ranked Canada one of the best countries in the world in which to live. However, the United Nations has also been harshly critical of Canada over its treatment of the poor. Almost one-fifth of the children in this country continue to grow up poor, in circumstances that seriously jeopardize their chances of becoming happy and productive citizens. As Greg deGroot-Maggetti, the socioeconomic concerns coordinator for Citizens for Public Justice, so poignantly concludes in his report entitled *A Measure of Poverty in Canada* (2002:16):

Ultimately, the discussion of poverty lines reflects the values we hold for our society. Do we value a society in which all people possess the means to participate fully in the life of their communities? Are we comfortable with having large differences in income levels? Are we willing to accept increasing reliance on emergency food and shelter by a growing proportion of our population? What social outcomes do we value—do they include improved prospects for long-term health? The measure of poverty we choose can serve as an indicator of how close or far we are as a society from meeting objectives. However, it does not provide a road map for reaching those objectives. That remains a challenge to all levels of society—from businesses and households, to local communities, municipalities, provincial and federal governments.

CHAPTER REVIEW

■ **How did classical sociologists, such as Karl Marx and Max Weber, view social class?**

Karl Marx and Max Weber acknowledged social class as a key determinant of social inequality and social change. For Marx, people's relationship to the means of production determines their class position. Weber developed a multidimensional concept of stratification that focuses on the interplay of wealth, prestige, and power.

■ **What are some of the consequences of inequality in Canada?**

The stratification of society into different social groups results in wide discrepancies in income and wealth and in variable access to available goods and services. People with high incomes or wealth have a greater opportunity to control their own lives. People with lower incomes have fewer life chances and must spend their limited resources to acquire basic necessities.

■ **How do sociologists define poverty?**

Sociologists distinguish between absolute poverty and relative poverty. Absolute poverty exists when people do not have the means to secure the basic necessities of life. Relative poverty exists when people may be able to afford basic necessities but still are unable to maintain an average standard of living.

■ **Who are the poor in Canada?**

Age, gender, race/ethnicity, and disability tend to be factors in poverty. Children have a greater risk of being poor than do the elderly, while women have a higher rate of poverty than do men. Although whites account for approximately two-thirds of those below the poverty line, Aboriginal peoples and visible minorities account for a share of the impoverished in Canada that is disproportionate to their numbers. As the gap between rich and poor and between employed and unemployed widens, social inequality clearly will increase in the future if we do nothing.

■ **What is the functionalist view of social inequality?**

According to the Davis–Moore thesis, stratification exists in all societies, and some inequality is not only inevitable but also necessary for the ongoing functioning of society. The positions that are most important within society and that require the most talent and training must be highly rewarded.

■ **What is the conflict view of social inequality?**

Conflict perspectives on inequality are based on the assumption that social stratification is created and maintained by one group in order to enhance and protect its own economic interests. Conflict theorists measure inequality according to people's relationships with others in the production process.

KEY TERMS

absolute poverty 250
alienation 235
class conflict 235
classism 245
feminization of poverty 253
income 230
job deskilling 255
low-income cutoff 250
meritocracy 256
pink-collar occupations 241
power 237
prestige 237
relative poverty 250
socioeconomic status (SES) 237
wealth 233

NET LINKS

The Canadian Council on Social Development is one of the leading organizations speaking for Canada's poor; see:
http://www.ccsd.ca

To see the details of the Campaign 2000 to end child poverty in Canada, check out the 2004 Report Card on Child Poverty in Canada at
http://cafb-acba.ca/documents/04National ReportCard.pdf

To see a list of the wealthiest people in Canada ranked by name, industry, and net worth, as well as individual profiles, go to
http://www.canadianbusiness.com/rich100/ index.htm

QUESTIONS FOR CRITICAL THINKING

1. Based on the functionalist model of class structure, what is the class location of each of your ten closest friends or acquaintances? What is their location in relation to yours? to one another? What does their location tell you about friendship and social class?

2. Should employment be based on merit, need, or affirmative action policies?

3. What might happen in Canada in the future if the gap between rich and poor continues to widen?

SUGGESTED READINGS

These texts provide more in-depth information about social stratification:

Wallace Clement. *The Canadian Corporate Elite: An Analysis of Economic Power.* Toronto: McClelland & Stewart, 1975.

Wallace Clement and John Myles. *Relations of Ruling Class and Gender in Postindustrial Societies.* Montreal: McGill–Queen's University Press, 1994.

Dennis Forcese. *The Canadian Class Structure.* Toronto: McGraw-Hill Ryerson, 1986.

E. G. Grabb. *Theories of Social Inequality: Classical and Contemporary Perspectives* (3rd ed.). Toronto: Harcourt Brace, 1996.

John Porter. *The Vertical Mosaic: An Analysis of Social Class and Power in Canada.* Toronto: University of Toronto Press, 1965.

A wide diversity of viewpoints on the intertwining of race, class, and gender in social stratification are found in this reader:

James E. Curtis, Edward Grabb, and Neil Guppy (eds). *Social Inequality in Canada: Patterns, Problems, Policies* (3rd ed.). Toronto: Pearson Education, 1999.

For more information on poverty in Canada, see:

The Canadian Fact Book on Poverty. Ottawa: Canadian Council on Social Development, 2002.

ONLINE STUDY AND RESEARCH TOOLS

THOMSONNOW™ Thomson NOW!

Go to **http://hed.nelson.com** to link to ThomsonNOW for *Sociology in Our Times,* Fourth Canadian Edition, your online study tool. First take the **Pre-Test** for this chapter to get your personalized **Study Plan,** which will identify topics you need to review and direct you to the appropriate resources. Then take the **Post-Test** to determine what concepts you have mastered and what you still need work on.

INFOTRAC®

Infotrac College Edition is included free with every new copy of this text. Explore this online library for additional readings, review, and a handy resource for assignments. Visit **www.infotrac-college.com** to access this online database of full-text articles. Enter the key terms from this chapter to start your search.

Global Stratification

The following is an excerpt from a letter a mother in the Philippines wrote to her daughters explaining her commitment to political activism:

"Today, both of you are in University. In less than five years, you will join the ranks of the 40–50 percent unemployed and under-employed Filipinos. If you are lucky and do find jobs, you will painfully experience the discrepancy between the daily cost of living at 354 pesos and the minimum wage pegged by the government at 150 pesos. I won't be surprised if you find yourselves in the 70 percent of the population considered below the poverty line and the 40 percent below the food threshold. Even now, that is what we see happening.

"I fear that very soon, even the environment will no longer be a dependable support system. What with biologically dead rivers, contaminated drinking water, and depleted marine resources because of the mine tailings spewed by mining companies, the likes of Marcopper and its Canadian partner, Placer Dome, what with dry rice fields that have to be abandoned due to the lack of water for irrigation brought about by open pit mining operations of giant establishments . . . What with 2/3 of the whole Cordillera region apportioned to Australian, American, and Canadian mining companies . . .

"This government has launched a grandiose plan it calls Philippines 2000. President Fidel Ramos ... wants to take the Philippines down the road to NIC-hood (Newly Industrialized Country) by the year 2000. That is why our agricultural lands which 75 percent of our population was tilling have now been converted into industrial enclaves, called Regional Industrial Centers. Is it any wonder, then, that thousands of peasants have been displaced?

"... The road is long that leads to progress—too long in fact, that hope could easily be snuffed out. But this one thing I can say, Mitzi May and Lily Joyce: I HAVE NOT LOST HOPE. This is why I have opted to leave you for a while—to join the many hopeful Filipinos who have put their lives on the line. And I will continue to put my life on the line for as long as this insensitive government rides roughshod on our people's God-given rights." (Ruiz-Duremdes, n.d.)

You might be surprised to learn that of all the narratives that we used to open the twenty chapters in this book, this was the most difficult to find. The world's poorest people have no voice. Even researchers who study global stratification rarely let them tell their own stories. Books are full of statistics that tell the stories of nations that cannot feed their citizens and of researchers' compassionate descriptions of the lives of people living at the margins of survival. However, the poor themselves remain faceless. If not for the haunting images of famine or civil war that we see on television news programs or the occasional story about problems in low-income countries on the radio or in the newspaper, most of us would know nothing about the more than one billion people who live out their lives in abject poverty. They are equally invisible to those managing the global corporations and the international organizations whose decisions have life-and-death consequences for those at the bottom of the global stratification system.

Even the quotation we did select is not really representative of the world's poor. The mother writing to her children is educated, articulate, and a member of an activist political organization. While her country, the Philippines, is poor, it is far wealthier than many other nations. However, her letter does articulate many of the problems of people in developing countries including unemployment, foreign control of resources, environmental degradation, economic restructuring, and political discontent.

Poverty and inequality know no political boundaries or international borders. In this chapter, we examine global stratification and inequality, and discuss the perspectives that have been developed to explain this problem. It is often difficult to connect the lives of people living in poverty in distant countries to our own lives in one of the world's wealthiest countries. When television shows us thousands of people starving in Somalia or babies being treated for dehydration at aid stations in Rwanda, it is sometimes hard to realize that the people we see are individual human beings just like us and our friends. The global

stratification system determines who will live long, prosperous lives like those of most Canadians and who will live short, miserable lives, eking out a marginal existence in subsistence agriculture and subject to the vagaries of rain, floods, and political instability.

Why do these inequities persist? In this chapter, you will learn about some of the reasons why the life prospects of billions of people remain so dismal. When you read the explanations of global stratification, you should remember that these are not just dry academic theories. Rather, these are the ideas shaping the way governments and international organizations, such as the United Nations, deal with this very complex and difficult problem. As you will see, decisions based on the wrong theories can be disastrous for the poor.

Before reading on, test your knowledge of global wealth and poverty by taking the quiz in Box 9.1.

QUESTIONS AND ISSUES

Chapter Focus Question: What is global stratification, and how does it contribute to economic inequality?

How are global poverty and human development related?

What is modernization theory, and what are its stages?

How do conflict theorists explain patterns of global stratification?

What is world systems theory?

How is the new system of global trade affecting people in poor countries?

WEALTH AND POVERTY IN GLOBAL PERSPECTIVE

What do we mean by global stratification? *Global stratification* refers to the unequal distribution of wealth, power, and prestige on a global basis, resulting in people having vastly different lifestyles and life chances both within and among the nations of the world. Just as Canada can be divided into classes, the world can be divided into unequal segments characterized by extreme differences in wealth and poverty. For example, the income gap between the richest and the poorest 20 percent of the world population continues to widen (see Figure 9.1). When we compare social and economic inequality *within* other nations, we find gaps that are more pronounced

than they are in Canada. *High-income countries* are countries characterized by highly industrialized economies; technologically advanced industrial, administrative, and service occupations; and relatively high levels of national and per-person income. In contrast, *low-income countries* are countries that are undergoing the transformation from an agrarian to an industrial economy and have lower levels of income. Within some nations, the poorest one-fifth of the population has an income that is only a slight fraction of the overall per capita income for that country. For example, in Brazil, Bolivia, and Honduras, less than 3 percent of total national income accrues to the poorest one-fifth of the population (World Bank, 2003).

Between 1960 and 2000, the gap in global income differences between rich and poor countries continued to widen. In 1960, the wealthiest 20 percent

BOX 9.1 SOCIOLOGY AND EVERYDAY LIFE

How Much Do You Know About Global Wealth and Poverty?

True	False	
T	F	1. Because of foreign aid and the globalization of trade, the gap between the incomes of people in the poorest countries and the richest countries has narrowed over the past several decades.
T	F	2. The number of people living in extreme poverty in the world has declined since 1981.
T	F	3. The richest one-fifth of the world's population receives about 75 percent of the total world income.
T	F	4. The political role of governments in policing the activities of transnational corporations has expanded as companies' operations have become more globalized.
T	F	5. Most analysts agree that the World Bank was created to serve the poor of the world and their borrowing governments.
T	F	6. In low-income countries, the problem of poverty is unequally shared between men and women.
T	F	7. Income and standard of living have increased significantly for most Russians as the transition from a centrally planned economy to a market orientation has taken place in recent years.
T	F	8. Poverty levels have declined somewhat in East Asia, the Middle East, and North Africa in recent years.
T	F	9. The majority of people with incomes below the poverty line live in the rural areas of the world.
T	F	10. Poor people in low-income countries meet most of their energy needs by burning wood, dung, and agricultural wastes, which increases health hazards and environmental degradation.

Answers on page 266.

of the world's population had more than thirty times the income of the poorest 20 percent. By 2000, the wealthiest 20 percent of the world's population had seventy-four times the income of the poorest 20 percent (United Nations Development Programme, 2001, 2003).

However, when examining the income gap, it is important to note that economic inequality is not the only dimension of global stratification. For example, in an earlier study on world poverty, Swedish economist Gunnar Myrdal (1970:56) distinguished between social and economic inequality:

Social inequality is clearly related to status and can perhaps best be defined as an extreme lack of social mobility and a severely hampered possibility of competing freely . . . Economic inequality . . . is related to differences in wealth and income . . . But there is a close relation between the two, since

social inequality stands as a main cause of economic inequality, while, at the same time, economic inequality supports social inequality.

Many of the things we buy are produced in low-income countries. Many workers in these countries are poorly paid and work in very harsh conditions.

BOX 9.1 SOCIOLOGY AND EVERYDAY LIFE

Answers to the Sociology Quiz on Global Wealth and Poverty

1. False. Since 1960, the gap between the incomes of the richest 20 percent of the world's population and the poorest 20 percent has been steadily growing. The ratio of the income of the top 20 percent of the population to that of the poorest 20 percent rose from 30:1 in 1960 to 74:1 in 2000 (United Nations Development Programme, 2001, 2003).

2. True. Data from the World Bank indicate that the percentage of the world's people living in absolute poverty has declined since the mid-1980s, particularly in Asia. Between 1981 and 2001, about 400 million people climbed out of extreme poverty (living on less than $1 per day). However, 1.1 billion people, or 21 percent, of the world's population remain below this level (World Bank, 2005a).

3. True. According the United Nations Development Programme, the richest one-fifth receive 75 percent of total world income, while the poorest one-fifth receive only 1.5 percent of world income. The poorest 40 percent of the world's population receive only 5 percent of world income (United Nations Development Programme, 2005:36).

4. False. As companies have globalized their operations, governmental restrictions have become less effective in controlling their activities. Transnational corporations have very little difficulty sidestepping governmental restrictions based on old assumptions about national economies and foreign policy. For example, Honda is able to circumvent import restrictions that the governments of Taiwan, South Korea, and Israel have placed on its vehicles by shipping vehicles made in Ohio to those locations (Korten, 1996).

5. False. Some analysts point out the linkages between the World Bank and the transnational corporate sector on both the borrowing and lending ends of its operation. Although the bank is supposedly owned by its members' governments and lends money only to governments, many of its projects involve vast financial dealings with transnational construction companies, consulting firms, and procurement contractors (see Korten, 1996).

6. True. In almost all low-income countries (as well as middle- and high-income countries), poverty is a more chronic problem for women due to sexual discrimination, resulting in a lack of educational and employment opportunities (Hauchler and Kennedy, 1994).

7. False. Not all Russians have shared equally in the transition to the market economy.

8. True. These have been the primary regions in which poverty has decreased somewhat and infant mortality rates have fallen. Factors, such as economic growth, oil production, foreign investment, and overall development, have been credited with the decrease in poverty in East Asia, the Middle East, and North Africa (United Nations Development Programme, 2005).

9. True. The majority of people with incomes below the poverty line live in the rural areas of the world; however, the number of poor people residing in urban areas is growing rapidly (United Nations DPCSD, 1997).

10. True. Poor people in low-income countries meet most of their energy needs by burning wood, dung, and agricultural wastes. Although these fuels are inefficient and harmful to health, many low-income people cannot afford appliances, connection charges, and so forth. In some areas, electric hookups are not available (United Nations DPCSD, 1997).

Figure 9.1	Income Gap Between the World's Richest and Poorest People

The income gap between the richest and poorest people in the world continued to grow between 1960 and 2000. As this figure shows, in 1960 the highest-income 20 percent of the world's population received an income of $30 for each dollar received by the lowest-income 20 percent. By 1997, the disparity had increased so that the richest 20 percent of the population each received $74 for each dollar of income received by those in the poorest 20 percent.

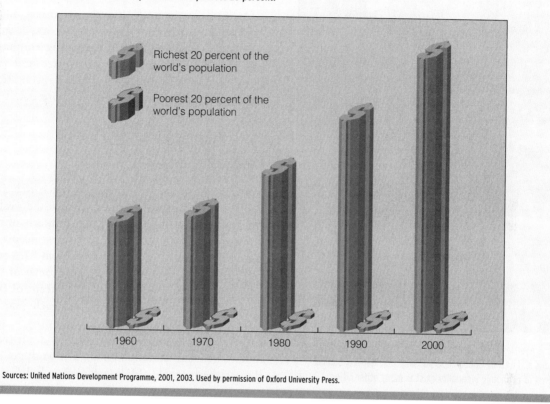

Sources: United Nations Development Programme, 2001, 2003. Used by permission of Oxford University Press.

Social inequality, which may result from factors, such as discrimination based on race, ethnicity, gender, or religion, exacerbates problems of economic inequality. According to Myrdal, social inequality is a main cause of the poverty of a nation. Therefore, a society must have greater social equality among its citizens as a precondition for the entire country getting out of poverty.

Many people have sought to address the issue of world poverty and to determine ways in which resources can be used to meet the urgent challenge of poverty. However, not much progress has been made on this front (Lummis, 1992), despite a great deal of talk and billions of dollars in "foreign aid" flowing from high-income to low-income nations. The notion of "development" has become the primary means used in attempts to reduce social and economic inequalities and to alleviate the worst effects of poverty in the less industrialized nations

of the world. Often, the nations that have been unable to reduce or eliminate poverty are chastised for not establishing the necessary social and economic reforms to make change possible. However, as other social analysts have suggested,

The *problem* of inequality lies not in poverty, but in excess. "The problem of the world's poor," defined more accurately, turns out to be "the problem of the world's rich." This means that the solution to the problem is not a massive change in the culture of poverty so as to place it on the path of development, but a massive change in the culture of superfluity in order to place it on the path of counter-development. It does not call for a new value system forcing the world's majority to feel shame at their traditionally moderate consumption habits, but for a new value

Vast inequalities in income and lifestyle are shown in this photo of slums and nearby upper-class housing in Singapore. Similar patterns of economic inequality exist in many other cities.

system forcing the world's rich to see the shame and vulgarity of their overconsumption habits, and the double vulgarity of standing on other people's shoulders to achieve those consumption habits. (Lummis, 1992:50)

As this statement suggests, the increasing interdependency of all the world's nations was largely overlooked or ignored until increasing emphasis was placed on the global marketplace and the global economy. The linkage between consumption and global poverty is explored in more detail in Box 9.2.

Inequality and Individuals

Nothing illustrates the disparity between rich and poor better than the difference between the wealth amassed by a few individuals and the poverty of the poorest nations. In 1998, the 225 richest people in the world had a net worth of more than $1.3 trillion. This was equal to the annual incomes of the poorest 2.5 billion people. Only 4 percent of this amount ($53 billion) was required each year to achieve reproductive health care for all women, and basic education, basic medical care, and adequate food, water, and sanitation for all. The wealth of the three richest people (Microsoft owner Bill Gates,

BOX 9.2 **SOCIOLOGY IN GLOBAL PERSPECTIVE**

Consumption and Global Poverty

The United Nations *Human Development Report* has played a major role in drawing attention to the need to eradicate poverty. The 1998 edition of the report focused on the ways in which some aspects of consumption have affected global stratification. Excessive consumption in developed countries threatens the environment, depletes natural resources, and wastes money that might otherwise provide for the needs of the desperately poor in developing countries.

Global consumption is concentrated among the wealthy. The wealthiest 20 percent of the world's people account for 86 percent of private consumption, while the poorest 20 percent account for only

1.3 percent (see the figure in this box). While some argue that money now used to buy luxuries might be better spent on the world's poor, others would claim that conspicuous consumption does buy happiness for those who can afford it. Though very limited, the evidence does not support the view that consumption beyond basic needs necessarily makes people happier. According to the *Human Development Report*, the percentage of Americans who describe themselves as "happy" peaked in 1957, even though consumption has more than doubled since that time. Unfortunately, as we spend more, we find more things to spend on. If we are able to keep up with the Joneses next door, we shift our horizons to the rich

Share of World Consumption[1]

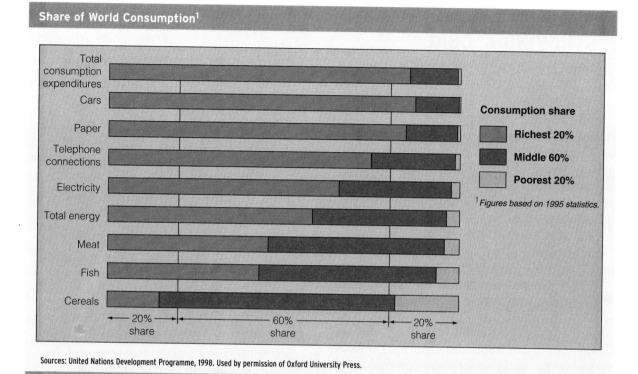

Consumption share
- Richest 20%
- Middle 60%
- Poorest 20%

[1] Figures based on 1995 statistics.

Total consumption expenditures
Cars
Paper
Telephone connections
Electricity
Total energy
Meat
Fish
Cereals

20% share   60% share   20% share

Sources: United Nations Development Programme, 1998. Used by permission of Oxford University Press.

and famous whose lifestyles we know about from newspapers and television. When American consumers were asked in 1986 how much they would need to earn to "fulfil all their dreams," the answer was $50,000. By 1994, this had increased to $102,000 (United Nations Development Programme, 1998). Theoretically at least, our wants are limitless.

But aren't the world's needs so great that channelling some of the money we spend on excessive consumption would make little difference in the lives of the world's poor? Surprisingly, the amount of money required to meet some basic human needs is not that great. *The Hindu,* an Indian newspaper, has put these needs in perspective:

> Consumers in Europe and the U.S. spend $17 billion every year on pet foods. Yet, the world cannot find the additional $13 billion that is needed every year to provide basic health services to all people in developing countries. Consumers in Europe and the U.S. annually spend $12 billion on perfumes. This is the additional amount needed to meet the basic reproductive health needs of the women in developing countries. Consumers in Europe spend $11 billion every year buying ice cream, which is more than the extra $9 billion required to provide universal access to drinking water and sanitation in the developing countries. (*The Hindu,* 1998:25)

Excessive consumption hurts the poor in another way. Rising consumption is harmful to the environment, and the poor are more vulnerable to environmental damage than the wealthy. Environmental degradation in countries where people depend on subsistence agriculture can mean malnutrition and starvation for huge numbers of people.

As we consume more, there is less for people in poor countries. Do you think we will ever have the political will to donate more of our surplus wealth to low-income countries?

Sources: United Nations Development Programme, 1998; *The Hindu,* 1998.

investor Warren Buffett, and the oil-rich Sultan of Brunei) was greater than the gross domestic product of the forty-eight least developed countries (United Nations Development Programme, 1998).

In 2002, the wealthiest 1 percent of the world's people received the same amount of income as the poorest 57 percent (United Nations Development Programme, 2003).

PROBLEMS IN STUDYING GLOBAL INEQUALITY

One of the primary problems encountered by social scientists studying global stratification and social and economic inequality is what terminology should be used to refer to the distribution of resources in various nations. During the past fifty years, major changes have occurred in the way that inequality is addressed by organizations, such as the United Nations. Most definitions of *inequality* are based on comparisons of levels of income or economic development, whereby countries are identified in terms of the "three worlds" or upon their levels of economic development.

The "Three Worlds" Approach

After World War II, the terms "First World," "Second World," and "Third World" were introduced by social analysts to distinguish among nations on the basis of their levels of economic development and the standard of living of citizens. First World countries included the advanced industrial countries, such as Britain, France, Germany, Japan, and Canada. Second World countries were the communist industrial countries, such as Poland, Czechoslovakia, and China. According to social analysts, although the quality of life in Second World nations was not comparable to that of life in the First World, it was far greater than that of people living in the Third World—the poorest countries, with little or no industrialization and the lowest standards of living, shortest life expectancies, and highest rates of mortality. The majority of these countries were either colonies or economic dependencies or had emerged from colonial status. The language of the "three worlds" was closely linked to terminology based on levels of development.

Is the "three worlds" approach an accurate representation of global inequality? According to Manual Castells (1998), the Second World has disintegrated with the advent of the Information Age, a period in which industrial capitalism is being superseded by global informational capitalism. Likewise, the Third World is no longer clearly identifiable in regard to specific geographic regions or political regimes as nations have become more diversified in their economic and social development (Castells, 1998). Instead, Castells (1998:164) adopts the term *Fourth World* to describe the "multiple black holes of social exclusion" that he believes exist throughout the planet in areas ranging from much of sub-Saharan Africa and the impoverished rural areas of Latin America and Asia to Spanish enclaves of mass youth unemployment in U.S. inner-city ghettoes. A term first used in the 1970s, the Fourth World originally designated indigenous people who are descended from a country's aboriginal population (such as First Nations in Canada, or Native Americans in the United States) and who are completely or partly deprived of the right to their own territory and its resources. Castells (1998:165) describes the contemporary Fourth World as follows:

> [The Fourth World] is populated by millions of homeless, incarcerated, prostituted, criminalized, brutalized, stigmatized, sick, and illiterate persons. They are the majority in some areas, the minority in others, and a tiny minority in a few privileged contexts. But, everywhere, they are growing in number and increasing in visibility, as the selective triage of information capitalism, and the political breakdown of the welfare state, intensify social exclusion. In the current historical context, the rise of the Fourth World is inseparable from the rise of international, global capitalism.

Thus, whether we embrace the concept of the "three worlds" approach or shift to the idea of the Fourth World, the central idea is the extent to which social exclusion occurs. According to Castells, **social exclusion is the process by which certain individuals and groups are systematically barred from access to positions that would enable them to have an autonomous livelihood in keeping with the social standards and values of a given social context.** For Castells, social exclusion is a process, not a condition. As informational capitalism grows around the world, the lack of regular work as a source of income is increasingly a key mechanism in social exclusion. Among persons with a disability or those who are too ill to work, social exclusion means not having health coverage or other benefits that incorporate them into the larger community. At the bottom line, Castells sees global financial markets and their networks of management as the central players in the twenty-first century because they control capital flows on a global scale. According to Castells (1998), rather than the "three worlds" approach, the future will be based on a global economy governed by a set of multilateral institutions, networked among themselves, and at the core of this network will be the International Monetary Fund, the World Bank, and the G-7 nations, such as Canada, as described in "High-Income Countries" later in this chapter.

The Levels of Development Approach

Among the most controversial terminology used for describing world poverty and global stratification has been the language of development. Terminology based on levels of development includes concepts such as developed nations, developing nations, less developed nations, and underdevelopment. Let's look first at the contemporary origins of the idea of "underdevelopment" and "underdeveloped nations."

Following World War II, the concepts of *underdevelopment* and *underdeveloped nations* emerged out of the Marshall Plan (named after U.S. Secretary of State George C. Marshall), which provided massive sums of money in direct aid and loans to rebuild the European economic base destroyed during World War II. Given the Marshall Plan's success in rebuilding much of Europe, U.S. political leaders decided that Southern Hemisphere nations that had recently been released from European colonialism could also benefit from a massive financial infusion and rapid economic development. Leaders of the developed nations argued that urgent problems, such as poverty, disease, and famine, could be reduced through the transfer of finance, technology, and experience from the developed nations to less developed countries. From this viewpoint, economic development is the primary way to solve the poverty problem. Hadn't economic growth brought the developed nations to their own high standard of living? Moreover, "self-sustained development" in a nation would require that people in the less developed nations accept the beliefs and values of people in the developed nations, so the development movement had an explicitly political component.

Ideas regarding *underdevelopment* were popularized by U.S. President Harry S. Truman in his 1949 inaugural address. According to Truman, the nations in the Southern Hemisphere were "underdeveloped areas" because of their low **gross national income (GNI)— a term that refers to all the goods and services produced in a country in a given year, plus the income earned outside the country by individuals or corporations.** If nations could increase their GNI, then social and economic inequality among the citizens within the country could also be reduced. Accordingly, Truman believed that it was necessary to assist the people of economically underdeveloped areas to raise their *standard of living,* by which he meant material well-being that can be measured by the quality of goods and services that may be purchased by the per capita national income (Latouche, 1992). Thus, an increase in the standard of living meant that a nation was moving toward economic development, which typically included the increased exploitation of natural resources by industrial development.

What has happened to the issue of development since the post–World War II era? After several decades of economic development fostered by organizations, such as the United Nations and the World Bank, it became apparent by the 1970s that improving a country's GNI did not tend to reduce the poverty of the poorest people in that country. In fact, global poverty and inequality were increasing, and the initial optimism of a speedy end to underdevelopment faded. Although many developing countries had achieved economic growth, it was not shared by everyone in the nation. For example, the poorest 40 percent of the Brazilian population receives less than 3 percent of the total national income, whereas the richest 20 percent of the population receives more than 63 percent (World Bank, 2003).

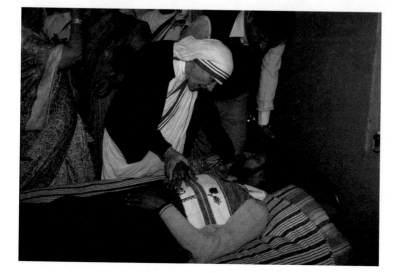

In 1997, people around the world were saddened by the death of Mother Teresa, who had dedicated her life to ministering to the poor and unfortunate in low-income nations, especially India. According to Mother Teresa, people who are not poor have much to learn from the poor.

Based on the assumption that economic development is the primary way to reduce poverty in low-income nations, the United Nations has funded projects, such as this paper company in Nepal.

CLASSIFICATION OF ECONOMIES BY INCOME

An alternative way of describing the global stratification system is simply to measure a country's per capita income. The World Bank (2005a) classifies nations into four economic categories: ***low-income economies*** (a GNI per capita of $765 U.S. or less), ***lower-middle-income economies*** (a GNI per capita between $766 and $3,035), ***upper-middle-income economies*** (a GNI per capita between $3,036 and $9,385), and ***high-income economies*** (a GNI per capita of $9,386 or more).

Low-Income Economies

About half of the world's population lives in the sixty-one low-income economies, where most people engage in agricultural pursuits, reside in nonurban areas, and are impoverished (World Bank, 2005a). As shown on Map 9.1, low-income economies are found primarily in countries in Asia and Africa. Included are such nations as Rwanda, Mozambique, Ethiopia, Nigeria, Cambodia, Vietnam, Afghanistan, and Bangladesh. Caribbean and Latin American nations with low-income economies include Haiti and Nicaragua.

Why did inequality increase even with greater economic development? Many attribute this to the actions of the industrialized countries. Later in this chapter we will consider the impact of foreign aid programs and policies to control debt on the economies of developing nations. Other analysts in the developed nations began to link growing social and economic inequality on a global basis to relatively high rates of population growth taking place in the poorest nations. Organizations, such as the United Nations and the World Health Organization, stepped up their efforts to provide family-planning services to the populations so that they could control their own fertility.

| Map 9.1 | **High-, Middle-, and Low-Income Economies in Global Perspective** |

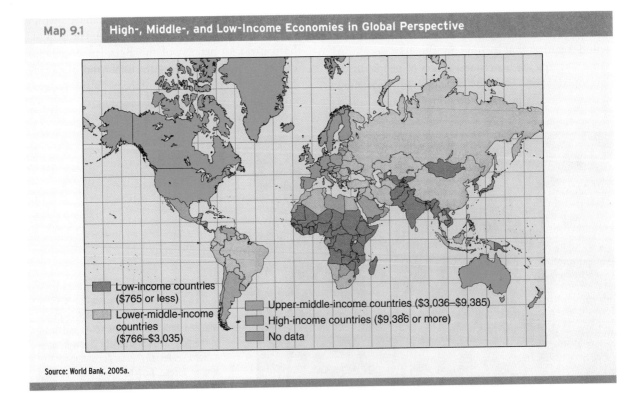

Low-income countries ($765 or less)

Lower-middle-income countries ($766–$3,035)

Upper-middle-income countries ($3,036–$9,385)

High-income countries ($9,386 or more)

No data

Source: World Bank, 2005a.

Among those most affected by poverty in low-income economies are women and children. Mayra Buvinic´, chief of the women in development program unit at the Inter-American Development Bank, describes the plight of one Nigerian woman as an example:

> On the outskirts of Ibadan, Nigeria, Ade cultivates a small, sparsely planted plot with a baby on her back and other visibly undernourished children nearby. Her efforts to grow an improved soybean variety, which could have improved her children's diet, failed because she lacked the extra time to tend the new crop, did not have a spouse who would help her, and could not afford hired labor. (Buvinic´, 1997:38)

According to Buvinic´, Ade's life is typical of many women worldwide who face obstacles to increasing their economic power because they do not have the time to invest in the additional work that could bring in more income.

Additionally, many poor women worldwide do not have access to commercial credit and have been trained only in traditionally female skills that produce low wages. All these factors have contributed to the *global feminization of poverty,* whereby women around the world tend to be more impoverished than men (Durning, 1993). Despite the fact that women have made some gains in terms of well-being, the income gap between men and women continues to grow wider in the low-income, developing nations.

Middle-Income Economies

About one-third of the world's population resides in the ninety-three nations with middle-income economies (World Bank, 2005). The World Bank divides middle-income economies into lower middle-income and upper middle-income. Countries classified as lower middle-income include the Latin American nations of Bolivia, Colombia, Guatemala, El Salvador, and Honduras. However, even though these countries are referred to as "middle-income," more than half of the people residing in countries, such as Bolivia and Guatemala, live in poverty, defined as $1 per day in purchasing power (World Bank, 2003).

Other lower-middle-income economies include Russia, Ukraine, and Romania. These areas had centrally planned (i.e., socialist) economies until dramatic political and economic changes occurred in the late 1980s and early 1990s. Since then, these nations have been going through a transition to a market economy. Some nations have been more successful than others in implementing key elements of change and bringing about a higher standard of living for their citizens. Among other factors, high rates of inflation, the growing gap between the rich and the poor, low life-expectancy rates, and homeless children have been visible signs of problems in the transition toward a free-market economy in countries such as Russia.

Compared with lower-middle-income economies, nations having upper-middle-income economies typically have a somewhat higher standard of living and export diverse goods and services, ranging from manufactured goods to raw materials and fuels. Nations with upper-middle-income economies include Argentina, Saudi Arabia, Chile, Hungary, and Mexico. Although these nations are referred to as middle-income economies, many of them have extremely high levels of indebtedness, leaving them with few resources for fighting poverty or developing their economies.

High-Income Economies

High-income economies are found in fifty-four nations, including Canada, the United States, Japan, Australia, Portugal, Ireland, Israel, Italy, Norway, and Germany (World Bank, 2005b). Nations with high-income economies dominate the world economy.

The only significant group of middle- and lower-income economies to close the gap with the high-income, industrialized economies over the past few decades has been the nations of East Asia. South Korea has recently been reclassified from a middle-income to a high-income economy, and growth in other countries, including China, has dramatically increased over the past two decades. Despite its recent economic growth, the East Asian region remains home to approximately 260 million poor people (United Nation Development Programme, 2004).

In developing nations, such as Turkey, many families support themselves by creating hand-made products, such as rugs. The loom in this living room is a common sight throughout Turkey.

THE IMPACT OF DEBT AND FOREIGN AID

Debt and Global Stratification

The gap between rich and poor countries has grown over the past forty years for many reasons. One is the problem of debt, which has made it virtually impossible for some countries to move out of poverty. Private banks, governments, and international organizations have lent more money to poor countries than these countries can afford to pay back, especially when cyclical reductions in commodity prices have dramatically reduced their incomes. Much of the borrowed money was spent on military hardware and other nonproductive investments, so little went to building the productive capacity that would have allowed the poor countries to develop. As a result of the debt crisis, many countries were forced by the International Monetary Fund and the World Bank to restructure their economies by cutting back on social spending, devaluing their currencies, and reducing the funds spent on economic development. In many respects, these governments have lost whatever power they once had to control their own economic destinies because they must follow the dictates of the lenders. This happened to most Latin American economies during the 1980s and to many East Asian and Eastern European economies during the late 1990s.

In many countries, the consequences of this externally imposed structural adjustment have been disastrous. Debt repayment takes money that could otherwise be used to provide social services and health care and to expand the country's economic base. In addition, debt repayment and economic restructuring have caused massive unemployment, reduced incomes, and soaring prices that have led to drastically reduced living standards, declines in investment, and political instability. This has represented a major setback in the progress of development. The problem has been summarized by Michel Chossudovsky:

> The movement of the global economy is "regulated" by "a world wide process of debt collection" which constricts the institutions of the national state and contributes to destroying employment and economic activity. In the developing world, the burden of external debt has reached two trillion dollars: entire countries have been destabilized as a consequence of the collapse

of national currencies, often resulting in the outbreak of social strife, ethnic conflicts and civil war (1997:15) . . . Internal purchasing power has collapsed, famines have erupted, health clinics and schools have been closed down, hundreds of millions of children have been denied the right to a primary education. In several regions of the developing world, the reforms have been conducive to resurgence of infectious diseases including tuberculosis, malaria, and cholera. (1997:33)

Many countries, particularly those in sub-Saharan Africa, have no chance of progressing economically unless the burden of debt repayment is eased by the richer debtholder countries.

In 2005, the wealthy countries agreed to cancel $40 billion in debt to allow some of the poor countries to spend on education, agriculture, health care, and infrastructure money that would otherwise have gone to interest payments. While this was a significant step, hundreds of billions of dollars in debt remain to be repaid. Some of the most indebted nations, including Nigeria, Sudan, and Congo, were not included in the deal because their governments were considered too corrupt and the donor countries were concerned that the benefits of debt cancellation would go to a few powerful rulers rather than to the poorest citizens.

Foreign Aid and Global Stratification

Few of us have not been moved by the compelling images of starving people in developing countries where droughts or floods have destroyed the annual harvest. Most of us support the emergency exports of food to these countries in order to prevent famine. However, some analysts have begun to ask whether this type of aid hurts more than it helps. For example, consider the recent history of Somalia, now one of the world's poorest and most politically unstable countries. While Somalia's troubles are commonly blamed on drought and clan rivalries, some analysts feel that economic restructuring and food aid are the real causes (Chossudovsky, 1997). Because of droughts and other internal problems, food aid to Somalia increased dramatically from the mid-1970s to the mid-1980s. This donated food was sold into local markets very cheaply and undercut the price of locally grown food. At the same time, a currency devaluation demanded by the

International Monetary Fund as a condition for restructuring Somalia's foreign debt made the cost of farm equipment and fuel more expensive. The combined result of the financial restructuring and the lower food prices was the virtual destruction of Somalia's agricultural system. While we normally think that a shortage of food is the cause of starvation, the global oversupply of grain may actually be contributing to famine by destroying the agricultural base of developing countries, making them vulnerable to future food shortages (Chossudovsky, 1997).

Foreign aid can also be damaging to low-income countries in other ways. First, aid can be tied to specific projects or objectives that may meet the interests of the donor country more than the interests of the recipients. For example, military aid will do little to help the lives of the poor and may do them great harm. Similarly, aid devoted to large infrastructure projects, such as dams, may cause more problems than it solves. Second, aid may be given to achieve political objectives. For example, the Soviet Union provided extensive aid to Cuba to maintain an ally just off the coast of the United States. The United States did the same thing in countries of strategic interest, including several Latin American countries. In these situations, aid is dependent on the low-income country's continuing political support for the activities of the donor country. This can severely constrain the power of governments to make decisions based on their own interests. Third, even when aid is targeted to individuals, it may not filter down to the poor. For example, donor countries may intend food aid to be distributed to the poor without payment, but elites may simply take the food, sell it, and keep the money.

The other problem is that there is not enough aid to help low-income countries solve health, nutrition, and employment problems. According to the head of the United Nations Children's Fund, foreign aid donations from the world's wealthiest countries declined by 30 percent between 1992 and 1997, despite the enormous growth of their economies over that time (Stackhouse, 1999). This has meant major reductions of assistance to the most needy countries. Canada has been one of the countries that have reduced aid donations over the past decade. Although Canada has a target of donating 0.7 percent of its gross domestic product (GDP) to foreign aid, the amount donated in 2005 was only 0.28 percent of GDP. During the 1990s, Canada's foreign aid budget declined by about 20 percent.

Thus there is not enough aid, and the aid that is provided is often not spent very effectively. However, there are signs of change. Many aid agencies have changed their focus away from large infrastructure programs, such as dams and railroads, to programs that focus directly on the poor. New ideas include using labour-intensive technologies and other strategies to create employment; providing basic social services, such as health care, nutrition, and education; and giving assistance directly to the poorest people in low-income countries (Martinussen, 1997). Above all, the poor themselves must have a say in aid programs and should be empowered to make decisions about how aid money is spent. Otherwise, foreign aid can be a double-edged sword that creates more problems than it solves. Not only do the poorest countries need more help from the industrialized world, but the aid that is provided needs to be administered in a manner than recognizes the needs of the countries receiving aid.

Finally, developed countries need to recognize that their trade policies are often devastating to the economies of poor countries and can negate the benefits of the aid that is provided. For example, in the mid-1990s, Canada gave an average of $44 million per year in aid to Bangladesh. However, Canadian quotas that restricted the export of textiles from Bangladesh cost the Bangladeshi people $36 for every $1 in aid provided (Oxfam, 2001). These quotas were designed to protect Canadian manufacturers from foreign competition, but they have had the effect of preventing developing nations from building a viable economic base. Even worse, developed countries

A young Hong Kong woman wearing a dust mask sews in a garment sweatshop under poor conditions.

Figure 9.2 | **Cows and Cotton Receive More Aid Than People, 2000**

In order to protect their agricultural industries, high-income countries provide enormous subsidies to farmers and to large agricultural corporations. In the United States, the subsidy provided to cotton growers is greater than the cash value of the entire cotton crop. The amount provided in subsidies by high-income countries to their own farmers far exceeds the foreign aid donated to the low-income countries and can have devastating effects on countries that are heavily dependent upon the export of commodities.

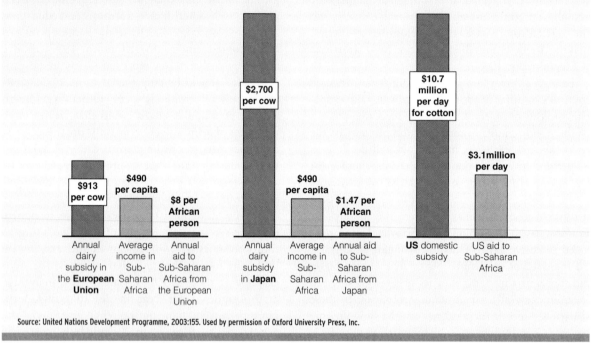

Source: United Nations Development Programme, 2003:155. Used by permission of Oxford University Press, Inc.

often force poor countries to liberalize their own trade laws, then sell heavily subsidized products into the poor countries' internal markets. The United States seriously harmed Haiti's rice farmers by forcing Haiti to reduce its tariffs on imported rice and selling Haiti large quantities of subsidized American-grown rice. This depressed local prices and resulted in a 40-percent reduction in Haitian rice production (Oxfam, 2001). By 2002, the U.S. and the countries making up the European Union were spending more than $450 billion to subsidize their farmers, making it impossible for farmers in poor countries to compete, particularly in the export market. At the same time, the aid given by wealthy countries to poor countries was only $75 billion. Policies such as these demonstrate that the high-income countries are not yet serious about helping to alleviate global poverty. Figure 9.2 illustrates the size of agricultural subsidies in the European Union, Japan, and the United States compared to the average income in sub-Saharan Africa and the aid given to these countries.

MEASURING GLOBAL WEALTH AND POVERTY

Absolute, Relative, and Subjective Poverty

How is poverty defined on a global basis? Isn't it more a matter of comparison than an absolute standard? According to social scientists, defining poverty involves more than comparisons of personal or household income; it also involves social judgments made by researchers. From this point of view, *absolute poverty*—previously defined as a condition in which people do not have the means to secure the most basic necessities of life—would be measured by comparing personal or household income or expenses with the cost of buying a given quantity of goods and services. The World Bank (2005) has defined absolute poverty as living on less than a dollar a day, and this definition is commonly used by international organizations, including the United Nations. Similarly, *relative poverty*—which exists when people may be able to afford basic necessities but are still unable to maintain an average standard of living—would be measured by comparing one person's income with the incomes of others. Finally, *subjective poverty* would be measured by comparing the actual income against the income earner's expectations and perceptions. However, for low-income nations in a state of economic transition, data on income and levels of consumption are typically difficult to obtain and often ambiguous when they are available. Defining levels of poverty involves several dimensions: (1) how many people are poor, (2) how far below the poverty line people's incomes fall, and (3) how long they have been poor (is the poverty temporary or long-term?) (World Bank, 2003).

GLOBAL POVERTY AND HUMAN DEVELOPMENT ISSUES

Most of the early work on global stratification focused on incomes as a measure of well-being. However, income disparities are not the only factor that defines poverty and its effect on people. Work by prominent economists, such as Amaryta Sen and Mahbub ul Haq, has led to a shift toward human welfare as a measure of development.

In 1990, the United Nations Development Programme introduced the Human Development Index (HDI), establishing three new criteria—in addition to GNI—for measuring the level of development in a country: life expectancy, education, and living standards. According to the United Nations, human development is "the process of increasing people's options to lead a long and healthy life, to acquire knowledge, and to find access to the assets needed for a decent standard of living" (Pietilä and Vickers, 1994:45).

Table 9.1 shows the difference between Canada and several other countries on the Human Development Index. While Canadians can be justifiably proud that they were at the top of the Human Development Index through much of the 1990s, and still remain very close to the top, the picture is not completely positive. The United Nations Development Programme also publishes a Human Poverty Index for industrial countries that measures the percentage of people not expected to survive to age 60, the percentage of the population that is functionally illiterate, the population below the

Table 9.1 HUMAN DEVELOPMENT INDEX

COUNTRY	RANK	INDEX	PER CAPITA GDP*
Norway	1	.963	37,670
Iceland	2	.956	31,243
Australia	3	.955	29,632
Luxembourg	4	.949	62,298
Canada	**5**	**.949**	**30,677**
Sweden	6	.949	26,750
United States	10	.944	37,562
Mexico	53	.814	9,168
Russia	62	.795	9,230
Brazil	63	.792	7,790
Thailand	73	.778	7,595
China	85	.755	5,003
Turkey	94	.750	6,772
India	127	.602	2,892
Kenya	154	.474	1,037
Nigeria	158	.453	1,050
Sierra Leone	176	.298	548

*In comparing GDP, the *Human Development Report* uses purchasing power parities (PPP) in U.S. dollars. PPP is a measure that accounts for different levels of purchasing power within different countries.

Source: United Nations Development Programme, 2005.

Table 9.2 HUMAN POVERTY INDEX (HPI) FOR INDUSTRIAL COUNTRIES

Countries	HUMAN POVERTY INDEX Human poverty index for industrial countries HPI (rank)	DEPRIVATION IN SURVIVAL People not expected to survive to age 60 (%)	DEPRIVATION IN KNOWLEDGE People who are functionally illiterate (% age 16-65)	DEPRIVATION IN INCOME Population below the income poverty line (%)	SOCIAL EXCLUSION Long-term unemployment, 12 months or more (as % of total labour force)
Sweden	1	7.2	7.5	6.5	0.9
Norway	2	8.4	7.9	6.4	0.3
Netherlands	3	8.2	8.7	7.3	1.2
Finland	4	9.7	10.4	5.4	2.2
Denmark	5	10.4	9.6	9.2	1.1
Germany	6	8.8	14.4	8.3	4.6
Switzerland	7	7.8	15.9	9.3	1.1
Luxembourg	8	9.7	–	6.0	1.0
Canada	**9**	**8.1**	**14.6***	**12.8**	**0.8**
France	10	9.8	–	8.0	4.2
Spain	11	8.7	–	10.1	4.5
Japan	12	7.1	–	11.8	1.8
Belgium	13	9.4	18.4	8.0	3.7
Australia	14	7.7	17.0	14.3	1.4
United Kingdom	15	8.7	21.8	12.5	1.2
Ireland	16	8.7	22.6	12.3	1.6
United States	17	11.8	20.8	17.0	0.7

*You might be surprised to learn that the illiteracy rate is this high in a country like Canada, with universal access to education. This is due to a relatively high proportion of people who have not finished high school and to the immigration into Canada of people without full literacy skills (Hoddnott, 1998). Functional literacy does not just mean the ability to read and to write, but also the ability to apply these skills. For example, can the person determine the proper dosage of medicine to give to a child by reading the information on the package? (ABC Canada, 2005).

Source: United Nations Development Programme, 2005.

poverty line, and the percentage of the labour force that has suffered long-term unemployment. Rankings on this index are shown in Table 9.2. You can see that Canada ranks only ninth on this index, because of a high rate of functional illiteracy and a high proportion of the population with incomes below the poverty level. The United Nations has been critical of the quality of life among Canada's Aboriginal people, who rank far below other Canadians on the Human Development Index.

Life Expectancy

Although some advances have been made in middle- and low-income countries regarding life expectancy, major problems still exist (see Figure 9.3). On the positive side, average life expectancy has increased by about one-third in the past three decades and is now more than seventy years in eighty-seven countries (United Nations Development Programme, 2003). On a less positive note, the average life expectancy at birth of people in middle-income countries remains about twelve years less than that of people in high-income countries. Moreover, the life expectancy of people in low-income nations is as much as twenty-three years less than that of people in high-income nations. Especially striking are the differences in life expectancies in high-income economies and low-income economies, such as sub-Saharan Africa, where estimated life expectancy has dropped significantly in many countries, largely because of HIV/AIDS (see Chapter 18, "Health, Health Care, and Disability"). While the Safe Motherhood Initiative has had some success, 530,000 women still die each year in pregnancy and childbirth (United Nations Development Programme, 2005).

One major cause of shorter life expectancy in low-income nations is the high rate of infant mortality. The infant mortality rate is more than eight times

Figure 9.3 **Improvements in Living Conditions**

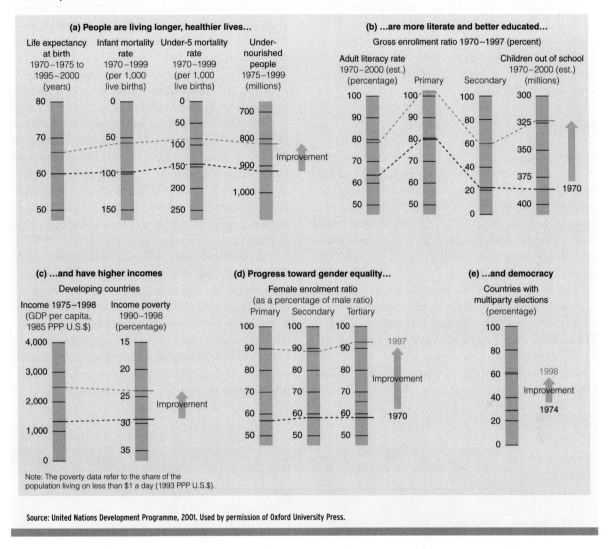

Source: United Nations Development Programme, 2001. Used by permission of Oxford University Press.

higher in low-income countries than in high-income countries (World Bank, 2003). Low-income countries typically have higher rates of illness and disease, and they do not have adequate health care facilities. Malnutrition is a common problem among children, many of whom are underweight, stunted, and have anemia—a nutritional deficiency with serious consequences for child mortality. Consider this journalist's description of a child she saw in Haiti:

Like any baby, Wisly Dorvil is easy to love. Unlike others, this 13-month-old is hard to hold.

That's because his 10-pound frame is so fragile that even the most minimal of movements can dislocate his shoulders.

As lifeless as a rag doll, Dorvil is starving. He has large, brown eyes and a feeble smile, but a stomach so tender that he suffers from ongoing bouts of vomiting and diarrhea.

Fortunately, though, Dorvil recently came to the attention of U.S. aid workers. With round-the-clock feeding, he is expected to survive.

Others are not so lucky. (Emling, 1997:A17)

The world's poorest 600 million people suffer from chronic malnutrition, and more than 40 million people die each year from hunger-related diseases (Kidron and Segal, 1995). To put this figure in perspective, the number of people worldwide dying from hunger-related diseases is the equivalent of more than 300 jumbo-jet crashes a day with no survivors, and half the passengers are children (Kidron and Segal, 1995). However, some progress has been made. Since the 1960s life expectancy has increased by sixteen years and infant mortality has been cut in half in low-income countries. Basic immunization—a simple measure—saves more than 3 million lives each year (United Nations Development Programme, 1998).

Health

Health is defined by the World Health Organization as "a state of complete physical, mental and social well-being and not merely the absence of disease or infirmity" (Smyke, 1991:2). Because of their poverty, many people in low-income nations are far from having physical, mental, and social well-being. About 4.6 billion people live in developing countries. Of those, 2.7 billion do not have proper sanitation and 1.2 billion do not have safe water. Many do not have adequate housing or access to modern health services (United Nations Development Programme, 2004). About 12 million people die each year from HIV/AIDS, diarrhea, malaria, tuberculosis, and other infectious and parasitic illnesses (World Health Organization, 2004). According to the World Health Organization, infectious diseases are far from under control in many nations due to such factors as unsanitary or overcrowded living conditions. Despite the possible eradication of diseases such as poliomyelitis, leprosy, guinea-worm disease, and neonatal tetanus in the near future, at least thirty new diseases—for which there is no treatment or vaccine—have recently emerged. Among these are AIDS and Ebola (see Chapter 18, "Health, Health Care, and Disability").

Some middle-income countries are experiencing rapid growth in degenerative diseases, such as cancer and coronary heart disease, and many more deaths are expected from smoking-related diseases. Despite the decrease in tobacco smoking in high-income countries, there has been an increase in per capita consumption of tobacco in low- and middle-income countries, many of which have been targeted for free samples and promotional advertising by U.S. tobacco companies (United Nations Development Programme, 1997).

Despite these problems, progress has been made. Figure 9.3a shows that from 1970 to 1999 there have been significant improvements in life expectancy at birth, infant and child mortality, and malnutrition. Most of this improvement has been in poorer countries. However, infant mortality rates remain high in many of these countries. Comparison of Map 9.2 with Map 9.1 on page 272 shows a very high correlation between income and infant mortality.

Map 9.2	Infant Mortality Rates, 2004

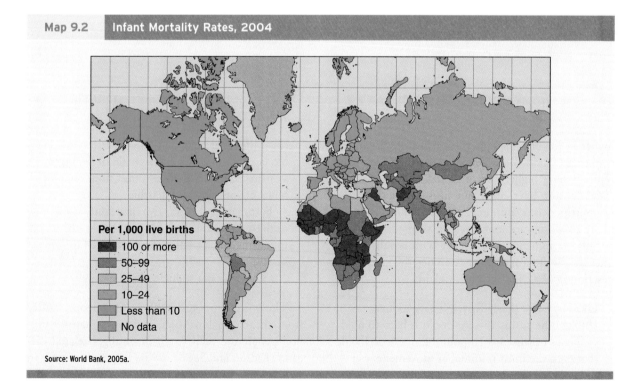

Per 1,000 live births
- 100 or more
- 50–99
- 25–49
- 10–24
- Less than 10
- No data

Source: World Bank, 2005a.

Malnutrition is a widespread health problem in many low-income nations. On the left, a Rwandan refugee child waits for help in a field hospital in Zaire; on the right, people in Sahel line up to receive food aid.

Education and Literacy

According to the *Human Development Report* (United Nations Development Programme, 2003), education is fundamental to reducing both individual poverty and national poverty. As a result, school enrolment is used as one measure of human development. The United Nations Educational, Scientific and Cultural Organization (UNESCO) defines a *literate* person as "someone who can, with understanding, both read and write a short, simple statement on their everyday life" (United Nations, 1997a:89). Based on this definition, people who can write only their name or a memorized phrase are not considered literate. The adult literacy rate in low-income countries is about half that of the high-income countries, and for women the rate is even lower (United Nations, 1997a).

Gender and Equality

According to the World Bank, women suffer more than men from global inequality:

Women have an enormous impact on the well-being of their families and societies—yet their potential is not realized because of discriminatory social norms, incentives, and legal institutions. And while their status has improved in recent decades, gender inequalities remain pervasive.

Gender inequality starts early and keeps women at a disadvantage throughout their lives. In some countries, infant girls are less likely to survive than infant boys because of parental discrimination and neglect—even though biologically infant girls should survive in greater numbers. Girls are more likely to drop out of school and to receive less education than boys because of discrimination, education expenses, and household duties. (2004:1)

Although more women have paid employment than in the past, more and more women are still finding themselves in poverty because of increases in single-person and single-parent households headed by women, and the fact that low-wage work is often the only source of livelihood available to them. According to an analyst for the Inter-American Development Bank, women experience sexual discrimination not only in terms of employment but also in wages:

In Honduras, for example, coffee and tobacco farmers prefer to hire girls and women as laborers because they are willing to accept low wages and are more reliable workers. Especially in poor countries, female labor is primarily sought for low-paid positions in services, agriculture, small-scale commerce, and in the growing, unregulated manufacturing and agribusiness industries, which pay their workers individual rather than family wages, offer seasonal or part-time employment, and carry few or no benefits. Hence, this explains the seemingly contradictory trends of women's increased economic participation alongside their growing impoverishment. (Buvinic´, 1997:47)

Researchers have concluded that women play a critical role in development. Women's education is particularly important because it has an impact on many other factors that contribute to human development (United Nations Development Programme, 2003). Figure 9.4 illustrates how the educated girls marry later and have smaller families. They also do a better job feeding their families and getting medical care, which means that more of their children survive. The children of illiterate mothers have an under-five mortality rate that is twice as high as the mortality rate for the children of mothers who have a middle-school education (United Nations Development Programme, 2005:31). This in turn leads to a reduction in birth rates, which allows better child care and less strain on the educational system. In societies where educated women are allowed to work outside the home, they make a significant contribution to family income, which improves the family's well-being.

Some progress is being made in improving women's education. Between 1990 and 2001, the ratio of literate females to literate males in low-human-development countries increased from 70 women per 100 men to 81 women per 100 men, and between 1990 and 2000 the ratio of girls to boys in primary education rose from 86 girls per 100 boys to 92 girls per 100 boys. However, at this rate it will take another two decades to achieve gender equality (United Nations Development Programme, 2003). Also, while most countries have seen improvement in women's education, some countries, such as India, Afghanistan, Ethiopia, and Pakistan, have ratios that are far below

Researchers have found that the education of girls is one of the most important factors in increasing development in low-income countries.

average and this may hamper their future development. Literacy is crucial for women because it has been closely linked to decreases in fertility, improved child health, and increased earnings potential (Hauchler and Kennedy, 1994).

THEORIES OF GLOBAL INEQUALITY

Why is the majority of the world's population growing richer while the poorest 20 percent—more than one billion people—are so poor that they are effectively excluded from even a moderate standard of

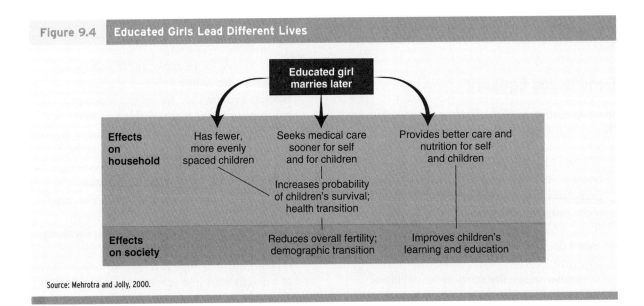

Figure 9.4   Educated Girls Lead Different Lives

Educated girl marries later

Effects on household

Has fewer, more evenly spaced children

Seeks medical care sooner for self and for children

Provides better care and nutrition for self and children

Increases probability of children's survival; health transition

Effects on society

Reduces overall fertility; demographic transition

Improves children's learning and education

Source: Mehrotra and Jolly, 2000.

living? Social scientists have developed many theories, which view the causes and consequences of global inequality somewhat differently. We will examine the development approach and modernization theory, dependency theory, world systems theory, and the new international division of labour theory. Modernization theory is part of the functionalist tradition, while the other perspectives are rooted in the conflict approach. These approaches are depicted in Figure 9.5.

Development and Modernization Theories

According to some social scientists, global wealth and poverty are linked to the level of industrialization and economic development in a given society. These theorists maintain that low-income nations have progressed less than the wealthier industrial countries. They feel that industrialization and economic development are essential steps that nations must go

| Figure 9.5 | Approaches to Studying Global Inequality |

What causes global inequality? Social scientists have developed a variety of explanations, including the four theories shown here.

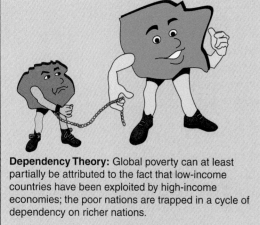

Modernization Theory: Low-income, less-developed countries can move to middle- and high-income economies by achieving self-sustained economic growth.

Dependency Theory: Global poverty can at least partially be attributed to the fact that low-income countries have been exploited by high-income economies; the poor nations are trapped in a cycle of dependency on richer nations.

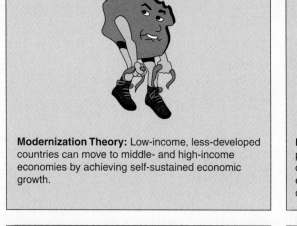

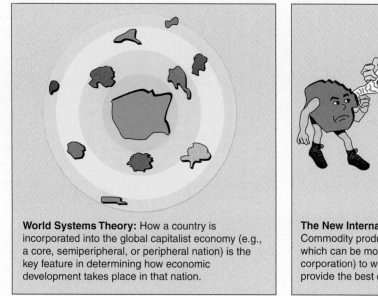

World Systems Theory: How a country is incorporated into the global capitalist economy (e.g., a core, semiperipheral, or peripheral nation) is the key feature in determining how economic development takes place in that nation.

The New International Division of Labour Theory: Commodity production is split into fragments, each of which can be moved (e.g., by a transnational corporation) to whichever part of the world can provide the best combination of capital and labour.

through in order to reduce poverty and improve the living conditions of their citizens.

The most widely known development theory is *modernization theory*—**a perspective that links global inequality to different levels of economic development and suggests that low-income economies can move to middle- and high-income economies by achieving self-sustained economic growth.** According to Trent University economist Steven Langdon, modernization theory holds that undeveloped countries must follow the road travelled by successful Western capitalist, democratic societies, such as Britain, the United States, and France:

> The usually implicit assumption was that economic development and growth involved a process of becoming like those societies and would be achieved essentially as those societies had achieved it: through economic change focused around industrialization, through social changes that would introduce Western institutions based on universalism and merit/achievement, and through political changes marked by secularization and the bureaucratic efficiency of the state. (1999:41)

Just as Max Weber had concluded that the adoption of a "spirit of capitalism" was an important factor in facilitating economic development, modernization theorists felt the development process would be accompanied by changes in people's beliefs, values, and attitudes toward work. As a result of modernization, the values of people in developing countries should become more similar to those of people in high-income nations.

Perhaps the most widely known modernization theory is that of Walt W. Rostow (1971, 1978). To Rostow, one of largest barriers to development in low-income nations was the traditional cultural values held by people, particularly fatalistic beliefs such as, viewing extreme hardship and economic deprivation as inevitable and unavoidable facts of life. Fatalistic people do not see any need to work in order to improve their lot in life: It is predetermined for them, so why bother? According to modernization theory, poverty can be attributed to people's cultural failings, which are further reinforced by governmental policies interfering with the smooth operation of the economy.

Rostow suggested that all countries go through four stages of economic development with identical content, regardless of when these nations started the process of industrialization. He compares the stages of economic development to an airplane ride. The first stage is the *traditional stage,* in which very little social

change takes place, and people do not think much about changing their circumstances. According to Rostow, societies in this stage are slow to change because the people hold a fatalistic value system, do not subscribe to the work ethic, and save very little money. The second stage is the *take-off stage*—a period of economic growth accompanied by a growing belief in individualism, competition, and achievement. During this stage, people start to look toward the future, to save and invest money, and to discard traditional values. According to Rostow's modernization theory, the development of capitalism is essential for the transformation from a traditional, simple society to a modern, complex one. With the financial help and advice of the high-income countries, low-income countries eventually will be able to "fly" and enter the third stage of economic development. In the third stage, the country moves toward *technological maturity.* At this point, the country improves its technology, reinvests in new industries, and embraces the beliefs, values, and social institutions of the high-income, developed nations. In the fourth and final stage, the country reaches the phase of *high mass consumption* and a corresponding high standard of living.

Modernization theory has had both its advocates and its critics. According to proponents of this approach, studies have supported the assertion that economic development occurs more rapidly in a capitalist economy. The countries that have been most successful in moving from low- to middle-income status typically have been those most centrally involved in the global capitalist economy. For example, the nations of East Asia have successfully made the transition from low-income to higher-income economies through factors such as a high rate of savings, an aggressive work ethic among employers and employees, and the fostering of a market economy.

Critics of modernization theory point out that it tends to be Eurocentric in its analysis of low-income countries, which it implicitly labels as backward (see Evans and Stephens, 1988). In many respects, modernization was equated with westernization, as modernization theorists assumed that the problems of low-income countries would be alleviated only once they adopted Western values, culture, and economic models. Modernization theory does not take into account the possibility that all nations do not industrialize in the same manner. For example, Anton Allahar (1989) points out that leading industrial countries, such as the United States, Britain, and Japan, followed very dissimilar paths to industrialization. Thus we might also assume that the modernization of low-income nations in the early twenty-first century will require novel policies, sequences, and ideologies that are not accounted for in Rostow's approach (see Gerschenkron, 1962). The theory also does not tell us what actually causes the move from one stage to another, but simply assumes they are natural stages that must be followed as societies advance economically and socially.

One of the most influential critics of modernization theory was Andre Gunder Frank (1969). Frank's research in Latin America convinced him that modernization theory was badly flawed. While Rostow felt that all societies had to move in a linear fashion from underdevelopment to industrialization, Frank pointed out that underdevelopment was not an original stage, but a condition created by the imperial powers that had created dependency through actions, such as the deindustrialization of India, the damage done to African societies during the years of the slave trade, and the destruction of Native civilizations in Central and Latin America (Hettne, 1995). All societies were *un*developed at one time, but not all became *under*developed. While some countries moved from being undeveloped to development, others moved from being undeveloped to a condition of underdevelopment in which they were dependent on other nations. These dependent countries had structures and institutions that effectively blocked any further development (Allahar, 1989).

Frank's critique of modernization theory was also a critique of the social policies that grew out of the theory. Rostow was a particular target, because he had been an adviser to U.S. President John Kennedy and as such had been instrumental in shaping U.S. policy in Latin America during the 1960s. Frank and others felt that the Western powers, particularly the United States, were imposing their views of development through both political and military means. Modernization theory was linked to the fight against communism. Because communism was an obstacle on the road to modernization, it was necessary to persuade or force countries to adopt alternative forms of government. Many critics felt that modernization theory contributed to the problem of underdevelopment by encouraging policies that perpetuated global inequality (Langdon, 1999). The inadequacies of modernization theory and the political injustices that resulted from policies based on the theory moved the next generation of development theorists to *dependency theory,* an approach that was based on the conflict perspective.

Dependency Theory

According to dependency theorists, rich countries have an interest in maintaining the dependent status of poor countries, as this ensures them a source of raw materials and an essentially captive market for manufactured goods exported to the dependent nations. Business and political leaders in the poor nations find it in their interests to accept dependence and willingly work with the advanced nations to impose policies that maintain the dependent relationship. Any surpluses created in the dependent country will be taken by the affluent capitalist country rather than being used to build up production infrastructure or raise the standard of living in the dependent nations. Unless this situation changes, poor countries will never reach the sustained economic growth patterns of the more advanced capitalist economies.

Dependency theory states that global poverty can at least partially be attributed to the fact that the low-income countries have been exploited by the high-income countries. Analyzing events as part of a particular historical process—the expansion of global capitalism—dependency theorists see the greed of the rich countries as a source of increasing impoverishment of the poorer nations and their people. Dependency theory disputes the notion of the development approach—and modernization theory specifically—that economic growth is the key to meeting important human needs in societies. In contrast, the poorer nations are trapped in a cycle of structural dependency on the richer nations due to their need for infusions of foreign capital and external markets for their raw materials, which makes it impossible for the poorer nations to pursue their own economic and human development agendas. Frank and other scholars believed that the best way for low-income countries to move ahead was to break their links with the industrialized countries and to establish independent socialist governments.

A variety of factors—such as foreign investment and the presence of transnational corporations—has contributed to the economic growth of nations such as Singapore.

Dependency theory has been most often applied to the newly industrializing countries (NICs) of Latin America, but scholars examining the NICs of East Asia have found that dependency theory has little or no relevance to economic growth and development in that part of the world. Therefore, dependency theory has had to be expanded to encompass transnational economic linkages that affect developing countries, including foreign aid, foreign trade, foreign direct investment, and foreign loans. On the one hand, in Latin America and sub-Saharan Africa, transnational linkages, such as foreign aid, investments by transnational corporations, foreign debt, and export trade, have been significant impediments to development within a country. On the other hand, East Asian countries, such as Hong Kong, Taiwan, South Korea, and Singapore, have also had high rates of dependency on foreign aid, foreign trade, and interdependence with transnational corporations but have still experienced high rates of economic growth despite dependency.

Dependency theory makes a positive contribution to our understanding of global poverty by pointing out that "underdevelopment" is not necessarily the cause of inequality. Rather, this theory points out that exploitation not only of one country by another but of countries by transnational corporations may limit or retard economic growth and human development in some nations.

What remains unexplained is how some East Asian countries had successful "dependency management" whereas many Latin American countries did not (Gereffi, 1994). In fact, over the past decade the annual economic growth in East Asia (excluding Japan) has averaged 8.5 percent, which was four times the rate of the West. Currently, the World Bank forecasts an annual growth rate of 6 percent in the region during the next decade (World Bank, 2003), which would be much higher than in the rest of the world.

While dependency theory has made a significant contribution to our understanding of global stratification, even its proponents feel it is no longer adequate. In addition to the problem of explaining the success of the East Asian economies that were closely linked with global capitalist structures, the dependency theorists' faith in development through socialist revolution has been shaken by the failure of many socialist economies, including that of the Soviet Union (Frank, 1981). Most have concluded that the global economy is so pervasive that it is impossible for low-income countries to disconnect themselves from the industrialized world and proceed with their own development (Martinussen, 1997).

World Systems Theory

Drawing on Karl Marx's ideas about global imperialism and capitalist exploitation, world systems theory suggests that what exists under capitalism is a truly global system held together by economic ties. From this approach, global inequality does not emerge solely as a result of the exploitation of one country by another. Instead, economic domination involves a complex world system in which the industrialized, high-income nations benefit from other nations and exploit the citizens of those nations. This theory is most closely associated with Immanuel Wallerstein (1979, 1984), who believed that a country's mode of incorporation into the capitalist work economy is the key feature in determining how economic development takes place in that nation. According to **world systems theory, the capitalist world economy is a global system divided into a hierarchy of three major types of nations—core, semiperipheral, and peripheral—in which upward or downward mobility is conditioned by the resources and obstacles that characterize the international system.**

Core nations are **dominant capitalist centres characterized by high levels of industrialization and urbanization.** Core nations, such as the United States, Japan, and Germany, possess most of the world's capital and technology. Even more importantly for their position of domination, they exert massive control over world trade and economic agreements across national boundaries. Some cities in core nations are referred to as *global cities* because they serve as international centres for political, economic, and cultural concerns. New York, Tokyo, and London are the largest global cities, and they are often referred to as the "command posts" for the world economy (Sassen, 1991, 1995).

Most low-income countries in Africa, South America, and the Caribbean are **peripheral nations— nations that are dependent on core nations for capital, have little or no industrialization (other than what may be brought in by core nations), and have uneven patterns of urbanization.** According to Wallerstein (1979, 1984), the wealthy in peripheral nations benefit from the labour of poor workers and from their economic relations with core nation capitalists, whom they uphold in order to maintain their own wealth and position. At a global level, uneven economic growth results from capital investment by core nations. Disparity between the rich and the poor within the major cities in these nations is increased in the process. The United States–Mexico border is an example of disparity and urban growth: Transnational corporations have built *maquiladora* plants just over the border in Mexico so that goods can be assembled by low-wage workers to keep production costs down. Because of a demand for a large supply of low-wage workers, thousands of people have moved from the rural regions of Mexico to urban areas along the border in hope of earning a higher wage. This influx has pushed already overcrowded cities far beyond their capacity. Many people live on the edge of the city in shantytowns made from discarded materials or in low-cost rental housing in central-city slums because their wages are low and affordable housing is nonexistent (Flanagan, 1999). In fact, housing shortages are among the most pressing problems in many peripheral nations. According to most world systems theorists, it will be very difficult for peripheral countries to change their structural position in the capitalist world economy (Wallerstein, 1979).

***Semiperipheral nations* are more developed than peripheral nations but less developed than core nations.** Nations in this category typically provide labour and raw materials to core nations within the world system. These nations constitute a

midpoint between the core and peripheral nations that promotes the stability and legitimacy of the three-tiered world economy. These nations include South Korea and Taiwan in East Asia, Mexico and Brazil in Latin America, India in South Asia, and Nigeria and South Africa in Africa. According to Wallerstein, semiperipheral nations exploit peripheral nations, just as the core nations exploit both the semiperipheral and the peripheral.

Not all social analysts agree with Wallerstein's (1979, 1984) perspective on the hierarchical position of nations in the global economy. However, most scholars acknowledge that nations throughout the world are influenced by a relatively small number of cities and transnational corporations that have prompted a shift from an international to a more global economy (see Knox and Taylor, 1995; Wilson, 1997). Even Wallerstein (1991) acknowledges that world systems theory is an "incomplete, unfinished critique" for long-term, large-scale social change that influences global inequality.

The New International Division of Labour Theory

Although the term *world trade* has long implied that there is a division of labour between societies, the nature and extent of this division were reassessed in the late 1990s based on the changing nature of the world economy. According to the ***new international division of labour theory*, commodity production is being split into fragments that can be assigned to whichever part of the world can provide the most profitable combination of capital and labour.** Consequently, the new international division of labour has changed the pattern of geographic specialization between countries, whereby high-income countries have become dependent on low-income countries for labour. The low-income countries, especially, provide transnational corporations with a situation in which they can pay lower wages and taxes and face fewer regulations regarding workplace conditions and environmental protection (Waters, 1995).

This new division of labour is part of a global economy based on free trade among countries. Multilateral trade agreements, such as the General Agreement on Tariffs and Trade (GATT) and the North American Free Trade Agreement (NAFTA), have allowed the freer transfer of goods and services among countries, and global corporations now view the whole world both as potential markets and as potential locations for production.

Tiger Woods makes more money for endorsing Nike products than the combined salaries of thousands of the workers who manufacture the products. According to Nike's chief executive officer, marketing is more important to the company's success than is the manufacturing of their products (Klein, 2000).

These trade liberalization agreements would appear to be beneficial for poor countries, as the movement of production into developing countries brings jobs to countries with chronically high unemployment. However, few of the profits remain in these countries. For example, a study of garment manufacturing in Bangladesh found that less than 2 percent of the final value of the product went to production workers and that 1 percent went to the local producer. The rest of the money went to profit those who owned the company, and to pay expenses, such as shipping and storage costs, and customs duties and sales taxes in high-income countries (Chossudovsky, 1997). There is little hope of higher wages for workers, as the jobs are unskilled and can quickly be moved to another poor country if workers begin to put pressure on the companies (Klein, 2000).

As you learned in the discussion of network enterprises in Chapter 6, many corporations have global operations. Typically, labour-intensive manufacturing operations, ranging from textiles to computers, are established in low-wage countries. Even service industries—such as completing income tax forms, taking computer orders, and processing insurance claims forms—that were formerly thought to be less mobile have become exportable through electronic transmission and the Internet. The global nature of these activities has been referred to as *global commodity chains,* a complex pattern of international labour and production processes that results in a finished commodity ready for sale in the marketplace.

This type of commodity chain is most common in labour-intensive consumer goods industries, such as toys, garments, and footwear (Gereffi, 1994). Athletic footwear companies, such as Nike and Reebok, and clothing companies, such as The Gap and Liz Claiborne, are examples of this model. Since these products tend to be labour-intensive at the manufacturing stage, the factory system is typically very competitive and globally decentralized. Workers in commodity chains are often exploited by low wages, long hours, and poor working conditions. In fact, most workers cannot afford the products they make. Tini Heyun Alwi, who works on the assembly line of the shoe factory in Indonesia that makes Reebok sneakers, is an example: "I think maybe I could work for a month and still not be able to buy one pair" (quoted in Goodman, 1996:F1). Since Tini earned only 2,600 Indonesian rupiah ($1.28) per day working a ten-hour shift six days a week, her monthly income would fall short of the retail price of the athletic shoes (Goodman, 1996).

Gereffi explains the problem with studying the new global patterns as follows:

> The difficulty may lie in the fact that today we face a situation where (1) the political unit is *national,* (2) industrial production is *regional,* and (3) capital movements are *international.* The rise of Japan and the East Asian [newly industrializing countries] in the 1960s and 1970s is the flip side of the "deindustrialization" that occurred in the United States and much of Europe. Declining industries in North America have been the growth industries in East Asia. (1994:225)

As other analysts suggest, these changes have had a mixed impact upon people residing in these countries. For example, Indonesia has been able to woo foreign business into the country, but workers have experienced poverty despite working full-time in factories making such consumer goods as Nike shoes (Gargan, 1996). As employers feel pressure from workers to raise wages, clashes erupt between the workers and managers or owners. Similarly, the governments in these countries fear that rising wages and labour strife will drive away the businesses, leaving behind workers who have no other hopes for employment and become more impoverished than they previously were. What will be the future of global inequality given this current set of conditions in countries such as Indonesia?

GLOBAL INEQUALITY IN THE FUTURE

As we have seen, social inequality is a major issue within and among the countries of the world. Even in high-income nations, where wealth is highly concentrated, many poor people coexist with the affluent. In middle- and low-income countries, there are small pockets of wealth in the midst of poverty and despair.

What are the future prospects for greater equality across and within nations? Not all social scientists agree on the answer to this question. Depending on their theoretical framework, social analysts may describe either an optimistic or a pessimistic scenario for the future.

In some regions, persistent and growing poverty continues to undermine human development and future possibilities for socioeconomic change. In many poor countries, economic development has stalled. According to the United Nations, "For many countries the 1990s were a decade of despair. Some 54 countries are poorer now than in 1990. In 21, a larger proportion of people is going hungry. In 14, more children are dying before age five. In 12, primary school enrolments are shrinking. In 34, life expectancy has fallen. Such reversals in survival were previously rare" (United Nations Development Programme, 2003:2). Most of the countries where human development has worsened are in sub-Saharan Africa and in Eastern Europe. Many of the countries where human development has reversed have been affected by the HIV/AIDS epidemic or are adjusting to the collapse of the former Soviet Union. Others have suffered from low prices for the agricultural products that are their main source of income in the global economy. The situation of coffee farmers provides a good illustration of how low-income producers fail to benefit from rising prices in high-income countries. Canadians have become used to paying $2 or $3 for a cup of coffee at chains, such as Second Cup and Starbucks. Many of us assume that the people who grow the coffee receive a fair share of this price. However, according to the United Nations, since 1990 the retail value of coffee sold in high-income countries has increased from $30 billion to $80 billion (United Nations Development Programme, 2005). Over the same period, the income received by coffee exporters has dropped from $12 billion to $5.5 billion even though the amount of coffee exported has increased. The farmer receives only one cent of each dollar you pay for your cup of coffee. The reduction in income has had devastating effects on human development in countries such as Ethiopia, Uganda, and Nicaragua, which rely heavily on coffee exports. At the same time, chains that serve coffee have been enormously profitable because they can charge high prices while paying almost nothing for their raw materials. While consumers in North America and Europe are content to pay high prices for their double-espresso low-fat lattes, coffee retailers have taken advantage of an oversupply of coffee beans to reduce their costs.

Gross inequality has high financial and quality-of-life costs to people, even among those who are not the poorest of the poor. In the future, continued population growth, urbanization, and environmental degradation threaten even the meagre living conditions of those residing in low-income nations. From this perspective, the future looks dim not only for people in low- and middle-income countries but also for those in high-income countries, who will see their quality of life diminish as natural resources are depleted, the environment is polluted, and high

rates of immigration and global political unrest threaten the elevated standard of living that many have enjoyed since the second half of the twentieth century. According to some social analysts, transnational corporations and financial institutions, such as the World Bank and the International Monetary Fund, will further solidify their control over a globalized economy, which will transfer the power to make significant choices to these organizations and away from the people and their governments. As a result, further loss of resources and means of livelihood will affect people and countries around the globe. Adding to the problem, industrialized countries have cut back on foreign aid despite their increased wealth.

On the other hand, a more optimistic scenario is also possible. Figure 9.3 shows how conditions have improved since 1970. Health is better, a higher proportion of people are educated, incomes have increased, far more females are enrolled in schools, and more countries are holding democratic elections. Most of this improvement has been in East Asia—particularly in China—where the number of people living in absolute poverty was reduced by nearly half during the 1990s (United Nations Development Programme, 2003), and it will be challenging to maintain these improvements and to make similar progress in areas such as sub-Saharan Africa that have largely been left behind.

These improvements show that it will be possible to alleviate global poverty, but if this positive change is to continue, the practices of global corporations, foreign aid donors, and international lending organizations must begin to focus on the needs of low-income countries rather than solely on the perceived demands of the marketplace.

The number of people living in absolute poverty was reduced by nearly half during the 1990s.

These needs were formally recognized in 2000, when most of the world's heads of state adopted the UN Millennium Declaration that committed countries to make dramatic improvements in the lives of the poor. The Declaration contains a series of specific goals and targets that are being monitored to track the progress that is being made (see Figure 9.6).

The United Nations has suggested six broad types of policy changes that will help low-income countries to improve their situations (United Nations Development Programme, 2003:4):

■ Investing in basic education and health and encouraging the equality of women will help to encourage economic growth;

■ Helping to improve the productivity of small farmers;

■ Improving roads, ports, communications systems, and the other infrastructure necessary for production and trade;

■ Promoting the development of small- and medium-sized businesses to help countries move away from dependence on exporting commodities;

■ Promote democratic governance and human rights, which will help to ensure that economic growth benefits the poorest people within low-income countries rather than just the elite;

■ Ensure environmental sustainability and urban planning.

Making these changes is beyond the capability of the poorest countries, so progress will depend on the willingness of the rest of the world to work with them to meet and then to exceed the Millennium Development Goals. Even individuals can help. While a few wealthy people, such as CNN founder Ted Turner and Microsoft's Bill Gates, have each contributed billions of dollars to improve human development, even very modest

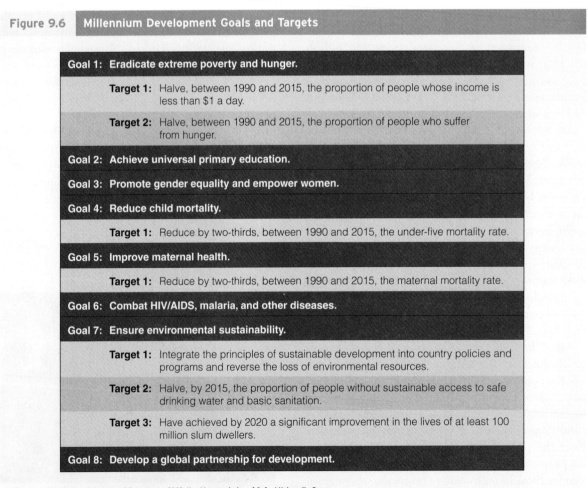

Figure 9.6   Millennium Development Goals and Targets

Goal 1: Eradicate extreme poverty and hunger.

Target 1: Halve, between 1990 and 2015, the proportion of people whose income is less than $1 a day.

Target 2: Halve, between 1990 and 2015, the proportion of people who suffer from hunger.

Goal 2: Achieve universal primary education.

Goal 3: Promote gender equality and empower women.

Goal 4: Reduce child mortality.

Target 1: Reduce by two-thirds, between 1990 and 2015, the under-five mortality rate.

Goal 5: Improve maternal health.

Target 1: Reduce by two-thirds, between 1990 and 2015, the maternal mortality rate.

Goal 6: Combat HIV/AIDS, malaria, and other diseases.

Goal 7: Ensure environmental sustainability.

Target 1: Integrate the principles of sustainable development into country policies and programs and reverse the loss of environmental resources.

Target 2: Halve, by 2015, the proportion of people without sustainable access to safe drinking water and basic sanitation.

Target 3: Have achieved by 2020 a significant improvement in the lives of at least 100 million slum dwellers.

Goal 8: Develop a global partnership for development.

Source: United Nations Development Programme, 2003. Used by permission of Oxford University Press.

contributions can make a big difference in the lives of the most impoverished people (see Box 9.3, "You Can Make a Difference: Global Networking to Reduce World Hunger and Poverty"). Achieving the Millennium Development Goals is very important to the world's poorest people. To give just one example, if the goals are not met, 41 million more children will die before their fifth birthday between 2005 and 2015 than would be the case if they were achieved (United Nations Development Programme, 2005).

We will continue to focus on issues pertaining to global inequality in subsequent chapters as we discuss such topics as race, gender, education, health and medicine, population, urbanization, social change, and the environment.

BOX 9.3 YOU CAN MAKE A DIFFERENCE

Global Networking to Reduce World Hunger and Poverty

◼ CARE water trucks, like this one, help provide clean drinking water to more than a quarter-million residents of Kabul, Afghanistan.

We, the people of the world, will mobilize the forces of transnational civil society behind a widely shared agenda that binds our many social movements in pursuit of just, sustainable, and participatory human societies. In so doing we are forging our own instruments and processes for redefining the nature and meaning of human progress and for transforming those institutions that no longer respond to our needs. We welcome to our cause all people who share our commitment to peaceful and democratic change in the interest of our living planet and the human societies it sustains.

–International NGO Forum, United Nations Conference on Environment and Development, Rio de Janeiro, Brazil, June 12, 1992 (qtd. in Korten, 1996:333)

If everyone lit just one little candle, what a bright world this would be.

–line from the 1950s theme song for Bishop Fulton J. Sheen's television series *Life Is Worth Living* (Sheen, 1995:245)

When many of us think about problems, such as world poverty, we tend to see ourselves as powerless to bring about change in so vast an issue. However, a recurring message from social activists is that each person can contribute something to the betterment of other people and sometimes the entire world.

An initial way for each of us to become involved is to become more informed about global issues and to learn how we can contribute time and resources to organizations seeking to address social issues, such as illiteracy and hunger. We can also find out about meetings and activities of organizations and participate in online discussion forums where we can express our opinions, ask questions, share information, and interact with other people interested in topics, such as international relief and development. At first, it may not feel like you are doing much to address global problems; however, information and education are the first steps to promoting greater understanding of social problems and of the world's people.

You can assist by fundraising or by working as a volunteer. Many relief organizations offer opportunities to volunteer internationally. If you would like to get involved, you can learn how to proceed by gathering information from organizations that seek to reduce problems, such as poverty, and to provide forums for interacting with other people. Here are a few starting points for your information search:

CARE Canada is part of an international network that was established to assist the world's poor in their efforts to achieve social and economic well-being. CARE provides emergency relief in disasters such as the 2004 tsunami in South Asia, but also supports a wide variety of long-term development projects. Like other successful aid and development organizations, CARE places a particular emphasis on community participation in its projects. One of CARE's rather unusual projects involves working

with small Honduran coffee producers to import gourmet coffee to Canada.
http://www.care.ca
Other organizations fighting world poverty and hunger include:
The Canadian Red Cross
http://www.redcross.ca
Mennonite Central Committee
http://www.mcc.org
Oxfam Canada
http://www.oxfam.ca
UNICEF Canada
http://www.unicef.ca

BOX 9.4 SOCIOLOGY AND TECHNOLOGY

The Digital Third World

There is little doubt that information and communications technologies are changing our world. However, there is considerable debate about the impact of these technologies on the poor. Some feel that the ability to share information from around the globe will hasten the development of low-income countries, as they will be able to become knowledge societies that can compete with the industrialized nations. The new technologies will allow them to rapidly streamline their governments and industries, and their competitive advantage in wages will allow them to attract business from richer nations. Technology can also speed the pace of educational reform and help build a more participatory civil society through the sharing of information and ideas. India is one country that has generated hundreds of thousands of jobs based on new information and communication technologies (Friedman, 2005). However, there is also a danger that the move to a world linked by new information and communications technology will lead to a greater polarization between the rich, who can exploit the new technologies, and the poor, who do not even have access to them. In other words, the poor will likely be excluded from the global information society—and this includes the poor in industrialized countries, as the "digital Third World" does not follow international borders.

Why is it unlikely that the information revolution will reduce global stratification? There are many barriers to the spread of information and communications technology. The major obstacle is cost.

To become part of the "digital world," low-income countries must build very expensive communications infrastructures. The costs of installing a phone line in places like rural Africa are about $5000, and existing phone lines in most low-income countries cannot handle the transmission speeds necessary to use the Internet effectively (Wresch, 1996). Thus, high-income residents of high-income countries are most likely to have access to the Internet. In 2005, 68 percent of North Americans had access to the Internet compared with 8.3 percent of people in the Middle East and only 1.8 percent of residents of Africa (Internet World Stats, 2005).

One response to the high fixed-line cost has been to move directly to mobile phones. Middle-income countries now have more mobile phones than fixed-line phones, and low-income countries are moving in the same direction. However, only about 1 percent of residents of low-income countries have access to mobile phones and fixed-line phones (Galbi, 2002), compared with almost all residents of high-income countries, so it's clear that progress in this area has been very slow.

In a world in which global communications and access to the Internet are becoming critical to business and trade, countries that cannot afford to build communications networks or to train people in how to use computers will be at a great competitive disadvantage. It is most unlikely that countries that are deeply in debt and have other pressing needs, such as health care and nutrition, will be able to create a communications infrastructure without a great deal of help. It is hard to conceive of the "wired classroom" in a country that cannot afford to build schools or train teachers.

A second reason for the lack of Internet access in most parts of the world is language. The vast majority of content on the Internet is in English. Without multilingual sites, the name, the World Wide Web, will never be accurate. A Web that is dominated linguistically by English and technologically and culturally by the United States will never reflect the point of view of people in low-income countries. (For a rare example of an Internet site that uses several African languages, see the Channel Africa site at http://www.channelafrica.org, where you can listen to African news in English on Internet radio). The magnitude of this problem was demonstrated by Kenny (2003), who searched for Web pages in Igbo, a language spoken by 17 million Nigerians. The Internet would be of little use to these people, as he found only five sites that used the Igbo language.

A final reason for lack of access is government censorship. Totalitarian countries are afraid of the free flow of information. It is easier to restrict the freedom of people who are unable to share ideas with each other and with people in other countries. As a result, many governments, including China and Algeria, have restricted their citizens' access to new forms of communications technology.

While low-income countries continue to fall further behind in the development of information technology, some small steps have been taken to reduce the gap. One model project has been undertaken by Canada's International Development Research Centre (IDRC). Project Acacia is an international effort led by the IDRC to provide sub-Saharan communities with the ability to apply information and communication technologies to their own social and economic development (for more information, go to http://www.idrc.ca/acacia). Its partners in the project include the African Information Society Initiative, which is trying to provide an African perspective on the opportunities and challenges of that continent in an emerging information age. The project has placed a priority on working with rural and disadvantaged communities, and particularly with women and youth groups in these communities. For example, a Senegalese women's fishing cooperative has developed a Web site that enables it to sell fish to overseas buyers and to monitor prices in other parts of the world.

While this project is promising, it is a very small step toward the solution of a very large problem. Much more must be done if low-income countries are to build on-ramps to the information superhighway. Rather than following the North American model involving individual access to communications technology, it is likely that solutions in low-income countries will involve shared infrastructure and public access facilities, such as Internet cafés and computers in local post offices. In many countries, technology, such as mobile phones, is accessed through individuals who make their living by sharing their phones with neighbours rather than through individuals who own the equipment. These intermediaries help to share the financial burden and are also important in helping unskilled people to utilize complex technology (Jensen, 2002).

CHAPTER REVIEW

■ **What is global stratification, and how does it contribute to economic inequality?**

Global stratification refers to the unequal distribution of wealth, power, and prestige on a global basis, which results in people having vastly different lifestyles and life chances both within and among the nations of the world. Today, the income gap between the richest and the poorest 20 percent of the world population continues to widen, and within some nations the poorest 20 percent of the population has an income that is only a slight fraction of the overall per capita income for that country.

■ **Why is it difficult to study global inequality?**

Terminology is a major problem in studying global inequality. Most definitions of inequality are based on comparisons of levels of income or economic development, whereby countries are identified in terms of the "three worlds" or upon their levels of economic development. Today, many sociologists use the World Bank's classification of nations into three economic categories: low-income economies, middle-income economies, and high-income economies.

■ **How are global poverty and human development related?**

Income disparities are not the only factor that defines poverty and its effect on people. The United Nations' Human Development Index measures the level of development in a country through indicators such as life expectancy, infant mortality rate, proportion of underweight children under age five (a measure of nourishment and health), and adult literacy rate for low-income, middle-income, and high-income countries.

■ **What is modernization theory, and what stages did Rostow believe all societies go through?**

Modernization theory is a perspective that links global inequality to different levels of economic development and suggests that low-income economies can move to middle- and high-income economies by achieving self-sustained economic growth. According to Rostow, all countries go through four stages of economic development: (1) the traditional stage, in which very little social change takes place; (2) the take-off stage, a period of economic growth accompanied by a growing belief in individualism, competition, and achievement; (3) technological maturity, a period of improving technology, reinvesting in new industries, and embracing the beliefs, values, and social institutions of the high-income, developed nations; and (4) the phase of high mass consumption, accompanied by a high standard of living.

■ **How does dependency theory differ from modernization theory?**

Dependency theory states that global poverty can at least partially be attributed to the fact that the low-income countries have been exploited by the high-income countries. Whereas modernization theory focuses on how societies can reduce inequality through industrialization and economic development, dependency theorists see the greed of the rich countries as a source of increasing impoverishment of the poorer nations and their people.

■ **What is world systems theory, and how does it view the global economy?**

According to world systems theory, the capitalist world economy is a global system divided into a hierarchy of three major types of nations: core nations are dominant capitalist centres characterized by high levels of industrialization and urbanization; peripheral nations are those countries that are dependent on core nations for capital, that have little or no industrialization (other than what may be brought in by core nations), and that have uneven patterns of urbanization; and semiperipheral nations are more developed than peripheral nations but less developed than core nations.

■ **What is the new international division of labour theory?**

The new international division of labour theory is based on the assumption that commodity production is split into fragments that can be assigned to whichever part of the world can provide the most profitable combination of capital and labour. This division of labour has changed the pattern of geographic specialization among countries, whereby high-income countries have become dependent on low-income countries for labour. The low-income countries provide transnational corporations with a situation in which they can pay lower wages and taxes and face fewer regulations regarding workplace conditions and environmental protection.

KEY TERMS

core nations 286
dependency theory 285
gross national income 271
high-income economies 272
low-income economies 272
lower-middle-income economies 272
modernization theory 284
new international division of labour theory 287
peripheral nations 286
semiperipheral nations 287
social exclusion 270
upper-middle-income economies 272
world systems theory 286

NET LINKS

The United Nations Development Programme has done an excellent job in focusing public attention on global inequality issues. To find out more about the world's poorest people and to learn what can be done to help them, visit the program's Web site, where you can find the Human Development Report, at:
http://www.undp.org/

World Factbook contains demographic information from around the globe; go to:
http://www.odci.gov/cia/publications/ factbook/

You can monitor the progress the world is making toward achieving the Millennium Development Goals at:
http://www.un.org/millenniumgoals/

A number of reports from the World Bank are available at:
http://www.worldbank.org/

Boycotts have been held against Nike and other sporting goods companies because of their treatment of workers in low-wage countries. Read about reasons for the boycott at:

http://www.saigon.com/~nike/

QUESTIONS FOR CRITICAL THINKING

1. You have decided to study global wealth and poverty. How would you approach your study? What research methods would provide the best data for analysis? What might you find if you compared your research data with popular presentations—such as films and advertising—of everyday life in low- and middle-income countries?
2. What are some of the positive aspects of globalization? How might the globalization of manufacturing and service industries benefit the world's poorest people?
3. Discuss why educating women is such an important strategy for improving the lives of people living in poor countries that it is one of the Millennium Development Goals.
4. Using the theories discussed in this chapter, devise a plan to alleviate poverty. Assume that you have the necessary wherewithal, including wealth, political power, and natural resources. Share your plan with others in your class and create a consolidated plan that represents the best ideas and suggestions presented.

SUGGESTED READINGS

For more information on issues, such as economic development and the global economy, the following books are recommended:

Michel Chossudovsky. *The Globalization of Poverty.* Penang: Third World Network, 1997.

James M. Cypher and James L. Dietz. *The Process of Economic Development.* New York: Routledge, 1997.

David C. Korten. *When Corporations Rule the World.* West Hartford, Conn: Kumarian Press, 1995.

John Martinussen. *Society, State and Market: A Guide to Competing Theories of Development.* Halifax: Fernwood Books, 1997.

United Nations Development Programme. *Human Development Report, 1997.* New York: Oxford University Press, 1997.

Malcolm Waters. *Globalization.* New York: Routledge, 1995.

World Bank. *World Development Report 1996: From Plan to Market.* New York: Oxford University Press, 1996.

ONLINE STUDY AND RESEARCH TOOLS

THOMSONNOW™

Go to **http://hed.nelson.com** to link to ThomsonNOW for *Sociology in Our Times,* Fourth Canadian Edition, your online study tool. First take the **Pre-Test** for this chapter to get your personalized **Study Plan,** which will identify topics you need to review and direct you to the appropriate resources. Then take the **Post-Test** to determine what concepts you have mastered and what you still need work on.

INFOTRAC®

Infotrac College Edition is included free with every new copy of this text. Explore this online library for additional readings, review, and a handy resource for assignments. Visit **www.infotrac-college.com** to access this online database of full-text articles. Enter the key terms from this chapter to start your search.

Race and Ethnicity

Professor Carl James has more than fifteen years' experience teaching at colleges and universities in southern Ontario. In the following personal narrative, he discusses how preconceived ideas of students inform their expectations of and interactions with him as a racial minority teacher (2001:53–54):

"Within either the first hour of my class or the first two weeks, students usually ask me, 'Where are you from?' or 'Are you from Jamaica?' In earlier years, I used to say, 'I am from the Caribbean,' and to the Jamaica question I would say, 'I'm not from Jamaica.' And when I ask, 'Why the question?' or 'Why do you assume that I am not Canadian, but an immigrant?' the response is, 'Because you have an accent.'

"Nowadays usually I do not answer the question, because I want to challenge the tendency of students, like many other Canadians, to associate being Black with being an immigrant. That tendency is an example of how individuals, consciously or unconsciously, reaffirm difference and remind those of us who are constructed as 'other'—because we do not 'look and/or sound Canadian'—of our 'outsider status.' Is it any wonder, then, that, when asked, we mention our ethnocultural origins, hyphenate our identities, and/or continue to identify ourselves as immigrants rather than Canadians? In doing so, we avoid the further questions, 'But where are you really from?'

"In some circles the question 'Where are you from?' is considered a 'friendly' way of initiating a conversation, of indicating an interest in the background and experiences of the person, and/or of showing that the questioner sees 'difference' and is not 'colour-blind.' I am aware that students sometimes ask this question because they are interested in establishing a 'friendly' rapport with me. But my response (or non-response) to the question does not mean that I am being unfriendly; rather, it is a way to have students, and whites in particular, recognize that all of our interactions, and indeed the educational process we engage in, are mediated by our race and other identities—their own as well as mine. Race and racial difference, then, are not the only, or even the most, significant factors around which interactions are built. I am not suggesting that students ignore our differences with regard to race—surely, we all see colour—but I want them to recognize, in my reactions to the question, my resistance to how my 'otherness' is reinscribed and the not-so-subtle ways in which they make evident their privilege and power in our encounters.

"In my experience with racial minority students, and Blacks in particular, the question is sometimes a way of establishing a connection or creating distance. In attempting to create distance, the question

would be a way of demonstrating to their peers that there is a difference between us—I talk with an 'accented' voice and they do not, because they are Canadian (born)."

C anada is a diverse and complex society composed of racially and ethnically different groups. Our country has a reputation as a tolerant and compassionate country whose success in race and ethnic relations has received worldwide admiration. Canada is widely renowned for emphasizing achievement and merit rather than skin colour as the basis for recognition, reward, and relationships (Fleras and Elliott, 1999:43). From a distance, Canada maintains its enviable status. However, upon closer examination, we see evidence of a country that has little to boast about with respect to the treatment of minority women and men (Walker, 1997). Despite our claims that Canadians are "colour-blind," racist ideas and practices affect individuals and groups in very real ways. Racism is something that not only is part of Canada's history, but also is an important aspect of current circumstances (Satzewich, 1998:13). In this chapter, racism will be central to the discussion of race and ethnicity. One of the most important and reliable sources of data on racism is the individuals who have experienced it directly (Henry et al., 2000). Therefore, we will explore the subjective impact of race and ethnicity on people's lives—and examine whether those effects are changing. Before reading on, test your knowledge about racism in Canada by taking the quiz in Box 10.1.

QUESTIONS AND ISSUES

Chapter Focus Question: What is the significance of race in Canadian society?

How do race and ethnicity differ?

How does discrimination differ from prejudice?

How are racial and ethnic relations analyzed according to the main theoretical perspectives?

What are the unique experiences of racial and ethnic groups in Canada?

Elijah was at the centre of a bitter custody battle between parents Kimberly van de Perre and Theodore "Blue" Edwards. A key issue in the custody battle, which ended up before the Supreme Court, was "race."

■ RACE AND ETHNICITY

What is "race"? Some people think it refers to skin colour (the Caucasian "race"); others use it to refer to a religion (the Jewish "race"), nationality (the British "race"), or the entire human species (the human "race") (Marger, 2000).

Popular usages of race have been based on the assumption that a race is a grouping or classification based on *genetic* variations in physical appearance, particularly skin colour. However, social scientists and biologists dispute the idea that biological race is a meaningful concept (Johnson, 1995). In fact, the idea of race has little meaning in a biological sense because of the enormous amount of interbreeding that has taken place within the human population. For these reasons, sociologists sometimes place "race" in quotation marks to show that categorizing individuals and population groups on biological characteristics is neither accurate nor based on valid distinctions between the genetic makeup of differently identified "races" (Marshall, 1998). Today, sociologists emphasize that race is a *socially constructed reality,* not a biological one (Feagin and Feagin, 2003). From this approach, the social significance that people accord to race is more significant than any biological differences that might exist among people who are placed in arbitrary categories.

A *race* **is a category of people who have been singled out as inferior or superior, often on the basis of real or alleged physical characteristics, such as skin colour, hair texture, eye shape, or other subjectively selected attributes** (Feagin and Feagin, 2003). Categories of people frequently thought of as racial groups include Asian Canadians, African Canadians, and Native or Aboriginal peoples. This classification is rooted in nineteenth-century distinctions made by some biologists, who divided the world's population into three racial categories: *Caucasian*—people characterized as having relatively light skin and fine hair; *Negroid*—people with darker skin and coarser, curlier hair; and *Mongoloid*—people with yellow or brown skin and distinctively shaped eyelids. However, racial categorization based on phenotypical differences (such as facial characteristics or skin colour) does not correlate with genotypical differences (differences in genetic makeup). As anthropologists and biologists have acknowledged for some time, most of us have more in common genetically with individuals from another "race" than we have with the genetic average of people from our own "race." Moreover, throughout human history, extensive interbreeding has made such classifications unduly simplistic.

How do you classify yourself with regard to race? For an increasing number of people, this is a difficult question to answer. What if you were asked about your ethnic origin or your ethnicity? The Canadian census, unlike that of the United States, collects information on ethnic origin rather than race. Whereas race refers only to *physical* characteristics, the concept of ethnicity refers to *cultural* features. An *ethnic group* **is a collection of people distinguished, by others or by themselves, primarily on the basis of cultural or nationality characteristics** (Feagin and Feagin, 2003). Ethnic groups share five main characteristics: (1) *unique cultural traits,* such as language, clothing, holidays, or religious practices; (2) *a sense of community;* (3) *a feeling of ethnocentrism;* (4) *ascribed membership from birth;* and (5) *territoriality,* or the tendency to occupy a distinct geographic area. Although some people do not identify with any ethnic group, others participate in social interaction with the individuals in their group and feel a sense of common identity based on cultural characteristics, such as language, religion, or politics. However, ethnic groups are influenced not only by their own past history but also by patterns of ethnic domination and subordination in societies (Marshall, 1998).

The Social Significance of Race and Ethnicity

How important are race and ethnicity in Canada? Sociologists Augie Fleras and Jean Leonard Elliott (1999) point out that ethnicity and race have been a fundamental source of meaning and recognition throughout human history and they remain so at the start of this century.

It is easy to suggest that race is insignificant if one is not a member of a racial minority. But, whether we like to acknowledge it or not, race does matter. Race and ethnicity take on great social significance because how

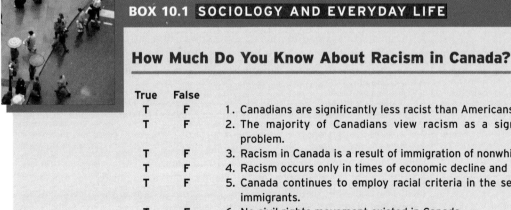

BOX 10.1 SOCIOLOGY AND EVERYDAY LIFE

How Much Do You Know About Racism in Canada?

True	False	
T	F	1. Canadians are significantly less racist than Americans.
T	F	2. The majority of Canadians view racism as a significant social problem.
T	F	3. Racism in Canada is a result of immigration of nonwhites.
T	F	4. Racism occurs only in times of economic decline and recession.
T	F	5. Canada continues to employ racial criteria in the selection of new immigrants.
T	F	6. No civil rights movement existed in Canada.
T	F	7. Affirmative action programs directed at hiring visible minorities are a form of reverse discrimination.
T	F	8. Slavery has never existed in Canada.

Answers on page 300.

people act in regard to these terms drastically affects other people's lives, including what opportunities they have, how they are treated, and even how long they live. It matters because it provides privilege and power for some. Fleras and Elliott (1999:33) discuss the significance of being white and enjoying what has sometimes been referred to as *white privilege:*

> Think for a moment about the privileges associated with whiteness, many of which are taken for granted and unearned by accident of birth. Being white means you can purchase a home in any part of town and expect cordial treatment rather than community grumblings about a plummeting in real estate values. Being white saves you the embarrassment of going into a shopping mall with fears of being followed, frisked, monitored, or finger printed. Being white means you can comment on a variety of topics without having someone question your objectivity or second-guess your motives. Being white provides a peace of mind in that your actions are judged not as a betrayal of or a credit to your race, but in terms of individual idiosyncracies . . . Finally, being white ensures one the satisfaction of socializing at night, without being pulled over by the police or patted down.

Ethnicity, like race, is a basis of hierarchical ranking in society. John Porter (1965) described Canada as a "vertical mosaic," made up of different ethnic groups wielding varying degrees of social and economic power, status, and prestige. Porter's analysis of ethnic groups in

BOX 10.1 SOCIOLOGY AND EVERYDAY LIFE

Answers to the Sociology Quiz on Racism

1. **False.** A comparative study of public opinion in both countries revealed that Canadians and Americans are roughly similar in their attitudes and behaviour toward racial minorities.

2. **True.** A recent poll indicated that 75 percent of Canadians consider racism a serious social problem (Reitz & Breton, 1994).

3. **False.** The argument here is that if immigration is curbed, racism will decrease. However, even before Canada began allowing large-scale immigration, racism existed in the relationship between white colonial settlers and Aboriginal peoples (Henry and Tator, 2006).

4. **False.** Racism has been practised systematically in Canada since this country was formed—even in times of economic prosperity. For example, in the early 1950s, despite an economic boom, Chinese and Japanese citizens were regarded as "enemy aliens" (Henry and Tator, 2006).

5. **False.** Canada officially abandoned racial criteria in the selection of new immigrants in the mid-1960s, when the points system was first introduced (Henry and Tator, 2006).

6. **False.** In the 1940s and 1950s, organizations, such as the Windsor Council on Group Relations, the National Unity Association of Chatham-Dresden-North Buxton, and the Negro Citizens' Association of Toronto, fought segregation in housing and employment, as well as fighting racist immigration laws (Fleras and Elliot, 2003).

7. **False.** For affirmative action policies to be a form of reverse discrimination, they would have to require employers to discriminate against better-qualified whites and give an unfair advantage to visible minorities. Affirmative action is directed not at discrimination, but at elimination of a long history of employment practices that result in preferential treatment toward white candidates (Fleras and Elliot, 2003).

8. **False.** Indeed, slavery was legal and practised by Europeans in Canada since almost the first European settlement of New France. Sixteen legislators in the first Parliament of Upper Canada owned slaves. Slavery existed in Quebec, New Brunswick, Nova Scotia, and Ontario until the early nineteenth century (Satzewich, 1998).

Canada revealed a significant degree of ethnic stratification, with some ethnic groups heavily represented in the upper strata, or elite, and other groups heavily represented in the lower strata. The dominant group holds power over other (subordinate) ethnic groups. Ethnic stratification is one dimension of a larger system of structured social inequality, as examined in Chapter 8. See Census Profile below for the percentages of Canadians belonging to different ethnicities.

Majority and Minority Groups

The terms *majority group* and *minority group* are widely used, but what do they actually mean? To sociologists, a **majority (or dominant) group is one that is advantaged and has superior resources and rights in a society** (Feagin and Feagin, 2003). In Canada, whites with northern European ancestry (often referred to as Euro-Canadians, white Anglo-Saxon Protestants, or WASPs) are considered the majority group. A **minority (or subordinate) group is one whose members, because of physical or cultural characteristics, are disadvantaged and subjected to unequal treatment by the dominant group and who regard themselves as objects of collective discrimination** (Wirth, 1945). All visible minorities and white women are considered minority-group members in Canada. The term **visible minority refers to an official government category of nonwhite, non-Caucasian individuals.** Included in this category are Chinese, Japanese, Koreans, Filipinos, Indo-Pakistanis, West Asians and Arabs,

Southeast Asians, Blacks, Latin Americans, and Pacific Islanders (Statistics Canada, 2003b). Aboriginal people form a separate category of individuals with minority group status. The 1996 census was the first census to collect data on persons who are members of visible minorities. This was an important objective due to the increasing number of recent immigrants from China, Asia, and Africa. In 2001, almost 4 million Canadians—more than 13 percent of the Canadian population—identified themselves as members of a visible minority (Statistics Canada, 2003f).

Although the terms *majority group* and *minority group* are widely used, their actual meanings are not clear. In the sociological sense, *group* is misleading because people who merely share ascribed racial or ethnic characteristics do not constitute a group. Further, *majority* and *minority* have meanings associated with both numbers and domination. Numerically speaking, *minority* means that a group is smaller in number than a dominant group. However, in countries such as South Africa and India, this has not historically been true. Those running the country were of a race (in South Africa) or caste (in India) with far fewer members than the masses that they ruled. Consequently, the use of these terms from a standpoint of dominance is more accurate. In this context, majority and minority refer to relationships of advantage/disadvantage and power/exploitation. Many sociologists prefer to use the terms *dominant group* and *subordinate group* because they more precisely reflect the importance of power in the relationships (Feagin and Feagin, 2003).

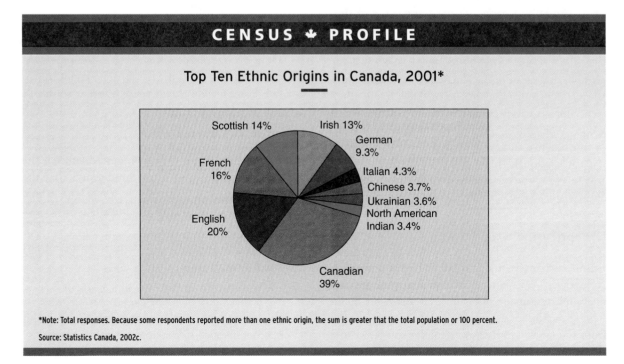

CENSUS ✦ PROFILE

Top Ten Ethnic Origins in Canada, 2001*

Scottish 14%
Irish 13%
German 9.3%
Italian 4.3%
Chinese 3.7%
Ukrainian 3.6%
North American Indian 3.4%
French 16%
English 20%
Canadian 39%

*Note: Total responses. Because some respondents reported more than one ethnic origin, the sum is greater that the total population or 100 percent.

Source: Statistics Canada, 2002c.

■ PREJUDICE

Prejudice **is a negative attitude based on preconceived notions about members of selected groups.** The term *prejudice* comes from the Latin words *prae* ("before") and *judicium* ("judgment"), which means that people may be biased either for or against members of other groups before they have had any contact with them (Cashmore, 1996). Although prejudice can be either *positive* (bias in favour of a group—often our own) or *negative* (bias against a group—one we deem less worthy than our own), it most often refers to the negative attitudes people may have about members of other racial or ethnic groups. To some extent, all people have prejudiced feelings against members of other groups. In this case, prejudice is not restricted to racial or ethnic groups but may be applied to virtually any category of people, including an entire nation or continent, to which negative generalizations are applied (Cashmore, 1996). During World War II, for example, Japan was an enemy of the United States and Canada (Isajiw, 1999). *Racial prejudice* **involves beliefs that certain racial groups are innately inferior to others or have a disproportionate number of negative traits.**

Ethnocentrism

Prejudice is rooted in stereotypes and ethnocentrism. When used in the context of racial and ethnic relations, *ethnocentrism* **refers to the tendency to regard one's own culture and group as the standard, and thus superior, whereas all other groups are seen as inferior.** What is wrong with believing that your cultural values are preferable to those of others? Such a belief is, after all, a source of pride. The problem with ethnocentrism is that your standards are used as a frame of reference for negatively evaluating the behaviour of other groups. Not surprisingly, these groups will be evaluated in this negative context as backward, immoral, primitive, or irrational. In short, although ethnocentrism may serve to promote group cohesion and morale, it is also a major source of intergroup hostility and conflict.

Stereotypes

Ethnocentrism is maintained and perpetuated by *stereotypes*—**overgeneralizations about the appearance, behaviour, or other characteristics of members of particular groups.** The term *stereotype* comes from the Greek word *stereos* ("solid") and refers to a fixed mental impression (Cashmore, 1996). Although

all stereotypes are hurtful, negative stereotypes are particularly harmful to members of minority groups. Consider the following conversation:

Sabra: So you think I'm not like the rest of them.

Alex: Yes, you are different. Well, you know what I mean.

Sabra: No, I don't. Tell me exactly what you do mean.

Alex: Well, when I see you, I don't see your colour. I don't see you as a South Asian. You're not like the rest of them. I'd like to think that I judge you through my own personal experiences with you. I don't judge you on the basis of your culture, colour, or class for that matter. I refuse to see you as being different. You're just another human being.

Sabra: First you tell me that I'm different, and then you say that you refuse to see me as being different. So which is it? Let's try to unravel this.

Alex: Well, I meant that you're more like me, you know, like one of us.

Sabra: Oh, so, I'm more like you and less like, should I say it, "a real South Asian." You see, although you're not saying it, your statement reveals that you have some preconceived ideas of South Asians, the people that I'm supposed to be so unlike. This means that whatever your preconceived ideas are of South Asians, they make South Asians less acceptable, less attractive, and less appealing to you than I. Well, this is not just stereotyping, it is racist stereotyping. (Desai, 2001:241–242)

How do people develop these stereotypes? As discussed in Box 10.2, the media are a major source of racial and ethnic stereotypes. Another source of stereotypes is ethnic jokes that portray minorities in a derogatory manner. Take a moment and think of an ethnic joke you have heard recently. Do you think this joke is harmful? Would you tell the joke to the member of the ethnic group that the joke is about? Paul, a student in a race and ethnic relations course at a Canadian university, discusses this issue:

I laugh at a joke that uses a Black . . . because I associate a stereotype with what has been said, I am a bigot. For example, what do you call a Black guy in a new car? A thief. Funny, eh? No, the joke itself is not funny, but it makes reference to a stereotype about Blacks that they're all thieves, which I do not find funny . . . That kind of joke is not funny. It does not point out a funny stereotype of a certain race . . . it is pure malice and cruelty against a specific group. (James, 1999:107)

Theories of Prejudice

Are some people more prejudiced than others? To answer this question, some theories focus on how individuals may transfer their internal psychological problems onto an external object or person. Others look at factors, such as social learning and personality types.

The frustration–aggression hypothesis states that people who are frustrated in their efforts to achieve a highly desired goal will respond with a pattern of aggression toward others (Dollard et al., 1939). The object of their aggression becomes the **scapegoat— a person or group that is incapable of offering resistance to the hostility or aggression of others** (Marger, 2003). Scapegoats are often used as substitutes for the actual source of the frustration. For example, members of subordinate racial and ethnic groups are often blamed for societal problems (such as unemployment or an economic recession) over which they have no control.

According to some symbolic interactionists, prejudice results from social learning; in other words, it is learned from observing and imitating significant others, such as parents and peers. Initially, children do not have a frame of reference from which to question the prejudices of their relatives and friends. When they are rewarded with smiles or laughs for telling derogatory jokes or making negative comments about outgroup members, children's prejudiced attitudes may be reinforced.

Psychologist Theodor W. Adorno and his colleagues (1950) concluded that highly prejudiced individuals tend to have an **authoritarian personality, which is characterized by excessive conformity, submissiveness to authority, intolerance, insecurity, a high level of superstition, and rigid, stereotypic thinking** (Adorno et al., 1950). It is most likely to develop in a family environment in which dominating parents who are anxious about status use physical discipline but show very little love in raising their children (Adorno et al., 1950). Other scholars have linked prejudiced attitudes to traits, such as submissiveness to authority, extreme anger toward outgroups, and conservative religious and political beliefs (Altemeyer, 1981, 1988; Weigel and Howes, 1985).

Measuring Prejudice

To measure levels of prejudice, some social scientists use the concept of **social distance, which refers to the extent to which people are willing to interact and establish relationships with members of racial and ethnic groups other than their own** (Park and Burgess, 1921). Sociologist Emory Bogardus (1925, 1968) developed a scale to measure social distance in specific situations. Using the scale, he asked respondents to answer yes or no to the following seven questions with regard to members of various racial and ethnic groups:

1. I would marry or accept as a close relative.
2. I would accept as a close friend.
3. I would accept as a next-door neighbour.
4. I would accept in my school or church.
5. I would accept in my community but would not have contact with.
6. I would accept as a resident of my country but not in my community.
7. I would not accept at all even as a resident of my country.

He concluded that some groups were consistently ranked as more desirable than others for close interpersonal contact. More recent social distance studies also suggest that Canadians display varying levels of "comfort" when interacting with members of different racial and ethnic groups. For example, a 1991 study conducted by the Angus Reid Group showed that Canadian-born respondents indicated greater levels of "comfort" when interacting with Canadians of British, Italian, French, Ukrainian, German, and Jewish origin. Respondents reported significantly less "comfort" when interacting with Canadians of West Indian, Black, Muslim, Arab, Indo-Pakistani, and Sikh origin or religion (Angus Reid, 1991:51).

But can prejudice really be measured? Existing research does not provide us with a conclusive answer to this question. Most social distance research has examined the perceptions of whites; few studies have measured the perceptions of people of colour about their interactions with members of the dominant group.

▌ DISCRIMINATION

Whereas prejudice is an attitude, **discrimination involves actions or practices of dominant group members (or their representatives) that have a**

harmful impact on members of a subordinate group (Feagin and Feagin, 2003). For example, people who are prejudiced toward South Asian, Jewish, or Aboriginal people may refuse to hire them, rent an apartment to them, or allow their children to play with them. In these instances, discrimination involves the differential treatment of minority group members not because of their ability or merit, but because of irrelevant characteristics, such as skin colour or language preference. Discriminatory actions vary in severity from the use of derogatory labels to violence against individuals and groups. Discrimination takes two basic forms: *de jure,* or legal discrimination, which is encoded in laws; and *de facto,* or informal discrimination, which is entrenched in social customs and institutions. De jure discrimination has been supported with explicitly discriminatory laws, such as the *Chinese Exclusionary Act*, which restricted immigration to Canada on the basis of race, or the Nuremberg laws passed in Nazi Germany, which imposed restrictions on Jews. The *Indian Act* provides other examples of *de jure* discrimination. According to the act, a Native woman who married a non-Native man automatically lost her Indian status rights and was no longer allowed to live on a reserve. Native men had no such problem. The *Indian Act* also specified that Native people who graduated from university, or who became doctors, lawyers, or ministers before 1920, were forced to give up their status rights. An amendment to the *Indian Act* in 1985 ended this legalized discrimination. The *Charter of Rights and Freedoms* prohibits discrimination on the basis of race, ethnicity, or religion. As a result, many cases of *de jure* discrimination have been eliminated. De facto discrimination is more subtle and less visible to public scrutiny and, therefore, much more difficult to eradicate.

Prejudiced attitudes do not always lead to discriminatory behaviour. This was demonstrated in a classic study conducted in the early 1930s. Richard LaPiere travelled around the United States with a Chinese

BOX 10.2 SOCIOLOGY AND THE MEDIA

Racism in the Media

The media are one of the most powerful sources of information in society, influencing the way we look at the world, how we understand it, and the manner in which we experience and relate to it. In other words, the media provide a "window on the world." For many Canadians, the media are the primary source of information about racial and ethnic groups. Racial minorities have accused Canada's mass media of slanted coverage; descriptions of the coverage have ranged from unfair and inadequate to overtly racist. These charges are not as obvious as we might expect. Rather, one's evaluation of media racism is contingent upon how racism is defined—as race or culture or power. The following vignettes from *Media and Minorities: Representing Diversity in a Multicultural Canada* (Fleras and Kunz, 2001) provide some insight into the complexity of racism when applied to media representations of minority men and women.

1. Do mainstream papers provide balanced coverage of minority issues? Not according to a major study of three Toronto newspapers (*The Globe and Mail*, the *Toronto Star*, and the *Toronto Sun*) conducted by Frances Henry between 1994 and 1997. Of the 2,622 references to Jamaican Canadians, 45 percent were about sports or entertainment, while 39 percent referred to crime, justice, immigration, and deportation. Only 2 percent were positive.

2. Diversity rules? On the basis of 114 hours of TV viewing by a *Toronto Star* television critic, minorities remain underrepresented in relation to their population and relative to whites. Advertisers justify this discrepancy on the grounds that minority images may offend their mainstream customers.

3. Prime-time segregation? Of the twenty-six series that were to premier on the top four U.S. networks in 1999 (CBS, ABC, NBC, and FOX), none featured a person of colour in a major role. Some modest changes resulted when the NAACP voiced its outrage and threatened a boycott. Of the twenty-one new sitcoms that premiered in 1997 in the United States, sixteen had white casts, four had all-Black casts, and only one had a mixed cast. Factor in the twenty-seven returning all-white sitcoms with the

twelve all-Black sitcoms, and allegations of prime-time segregation become more difficult to refute (Weintraub, 2000).

4. A six-month study of five major Canadian papers confirmed how the mainstream media routinely stereotype Muslims as barbaric fanatics. Muslims were repeatedly typecast as violent persons or terrorists who happen to believe in a fundamentalist religion that condones acts of inhumanity.

5. When Paul Bernardo tortured and killed two young women, no one in the media asked, "What's wrong with blue-eyed, blond-haired men of Italian descent?" When people of colour commit a crime, including the widely publicized shooting of a white woman in a Just Desserts café, collective responsibility is imposed on an entire race. Meanwhile, white criminal violence is a matter of individual responsibility, with the result that the "race" card stays in the deck no matter how horrific the crime.

6. A CTV newscaster accidentally blurted out a self-deprecating employment equity "joke" about lesbians, Blacks, people with disabilities, and stutterers. She was subsequently fired for her impertinent remarks. For some, this incident was proof that racism was alive and well in Canada's mainstream media; for others, the draconian response simply confirmed the degree of political correctness that was compromising society, despite Canada's reputation as one of the world's most tolerant countries. For still others, the issue was not about the attitude of one broadcaster, but a reflection of a bias that pervades the structure and culture of media organizations (Tator and Henry, 1999).

Source: Fleras and Kunz, 2001.

What do these vignettes have in common? In each of these media-related incidents, the media have been accused of reflecting, reinforcing, and advancing mainstream racism. Yet the racist dimensions behind each of these accusations are neither entirely transparent nor self-explanatory. Exactly what is meant by racism in the media? Are media racist and, if so, how? Is it more accurate to say that the media are the sites of racist incidents by racist individuals? Or are the media racist by definition, given their priorities, agenda, operational values, and practices? What would nonracist media look like?

Race relations scholars Frances Henry and Carol Tator's recent analysis of racism in the media suggests that "there appears to be a lack of awareness, understanding, or concern on the part of those who work in the media and that they may be contributing to racism" (2006:1). They argue that the media need to engage more fully in the issues of racial and ethnic diversity and equity. What is the cost to the media of more inclusive, less biased reporting?

In October 2002, the *Toronto Star* ran a series of stories on racial profiling in the Toronto Police Service. The reports raised serious questions about the practice of racial profiling and its impact on Black communities in Toronto. Toronto Police Chief Julian Fantino emphatically denied the allegations and the Toronto Police Association launched a $2.7-billion lawsuit against the *Toronto Star*. The lawsuit was later dismissed. This series prompted a "Summit on Policing, Race Relations, and Racial Profiling," held later that year in Toronto. Based on the political and legal impact of this series do you think we will see more of this type of media coverage?

---

couple, stopping at more than 250 restaurants and hotels along the way. The pervasive anti-Oriental prejudice of the time led LaPiere to assume that the travellers would be refused service in most of the hotels and restaurants at which they intended to stop. However, LaPiere was wrong—only one establishment refused service to LaPiere and his friends. Several months later, LaPiere sent letters to all the establishments they had visited, asking if they would serve "members of the Chinese race" as guests in their establishments. Ninety-two percent of the establishments that had earlier accepted LaPiere and his guests replied that Chinese people would not be welcome. This study is one of many examples of sociological research that reveals the discrepancy between what people say and what they do (Robertson, 1977).

Sociologist Robert Merton (1949) identified four combinations of attitudes and responses. *Unprejudiced nondiscriminators* are not personally prejudiced and do not discriminate against others. These are individuals who believe in equality for all. *Unprejudiced discriminators* may have no personal prejudices but still engage in discriminatory behaviour because of peer group pressure or economic, political, or social interests—for example, an employee who has no personal hostility toward members of certain groups but is encouraged not to hire them by senior management. *Prejudiced nondiscriminators* hold personal prejudices but do not discriminate due to peer pressure, legal demands, or a desire for profits. Such individuals are often referred to as "timid bigots" because they are reluctant to translate their attitudes into action (especially when prejudice is considered to be "politically incorrect"). Finally, *prejudiced discriminators* hold personal prejudices and actively discriminate against others—for example, the landlord who refuses to rent an apartment to an Aboriginal couple and then readily justifies his actions on the basis of racist stereotypes.

Discriminatory actions vary in severity from the use of derogatory labels to violence against individuals and groups. The ultimate form of discrimination occurs when people are considered to be unworthy to live because of their race or ethnicity. **Genocide is the deliberate, systematic killing of an entire people or nation** (Schaefer, 1993:23). Examples of genocide include the killing of thousands of Native Americans by white settlers in North America and the extermination of six million European Jews by Nazi Germany. More recently, the term *ethnic cleansing* has been used to define a policy of "cleansing" geographic areas (such as in Yugoslavia) by forcing persons of other races or religions to flee—or die (Schaefer, 1995).

Merton's typology shows that some people may be prejudiced but not discriminate against others. Do you think it is possible for a person to discriminate against some people without holding a prejudiced attitude toward them? Why or why not?

RACISM

Racism **is a set of ideas that implies the superiority of one social group over another on the basis of biological or cultural characteristics, together with the power to put these beliefs into practice in a way that denies or excludes minority women and men** (Fleras and Kunz, 2001).

Racism involves elements of prejudice, ethnocentrism, stereotyping, and discrimination. For example, racism is present in the belief that some racial or ethnic groups are superior while others are inferior; this belief is a prejudice. Racism may be the basis for unfair treatment toward members of a racial or ethnic group. In this case the racism involves discrimination.

Fleras and Elliott (1999) make distinctions among a number of diverse types of racism (see Table 10.1). **Overt racism may take the form of public statements about the "inferiority" of members of a racial or ethnic group.** Examples of overt racism are available in Canada. The 1998 beating death of a sixty-five-year-old Sikh temple employee in Surrey, B.C. prompted suggestions that Vancouver is the racism capital of Canada. Racist, white supremacist groups including the White Aryan Nation, the Western Guard, and the Ku Klux Klan are active in Canada. These groups have relied on violence to create an environment of fear and hatred against minorities throughout Canada and the United States. These groups are committed to an ideology of racial supremacy in which the white "race" is seen as superior to other races on the basis of physical and cultural characteristics (Fleras and Elliott, 2003). (See Chapter 3 for more on hate groups.)

However, research also suggests that this type of overt racism is becoming increasingly unacceptable in Canadian society, and few people today will tolerate the open expression of racism. Both the *Charter of Rights and Freedoms,* as previously mentioned, and human rights legislation have served to limit the expression of racist ideology or active racial discrimination. In Canada, overt acts of discrimination are now illegal. While blatant forms of racism have dissipated to some extent, less obvious expressions of bigotry and stereotyping remain in our society.

Table 10.1 THE FACES OF RACISM				
	WHAT: CORE SLOGAN	**WHY:** DEGREE OF INTENT	**HOW:** STYLE OF EXPRESSION	**WHERE:** MAGNITUDE AND SCOPE
Overt Racism	"X, get out."	Conscious	Personal and explicit	Interpersonal
Polite Racism	"Sorry, the job is taken."	Moderate	Discreet and subtle	Personal
Subliminal Racism	"I'm not racist, but . . ."	Ambivalent	Oblique	Cultural
Institutional Racism	"X need not apply."	Deliberate	Blatant	Institutional
Systemic Racism	"We treat everyone the same here."	Unintentional	Impersonal	Societal

Source: Fleras and Elliott, 1996:84.

Polite racism **is an attempt to disguise a dislike of others through behaviour that outwardly is nonprejudicial.** This type of racism may be operating when members of visible minority groups are ignored or turned down for jobs or promotions on a regular basis. A number of studies over the past two decades have examined the extent of racial prejudice and discrimination in the workplace. In the well-known study *Who Gets Work?* by Henry and Ginzberg (1984), Black and white job seekers with similar job qualifications were sent to apply for entry positions advertised in a major newspaper. After several hundred applications were received and interviews held, it was revealed that whites received job offers three times more often than did Black job applicants. In addition, telephone callers with accents, particularly those from South Asia and the Caribbean, were often screened out when they phoned to inquire about a job vacancy. This study was replicated in 1989 and the findings were much more favourable, with Blacks slightly favoured in job offers: twenty compared with eighteen offers to whites. However, individuals with accents were still more likely to be screened out prior to being selected for an interview (Economic Council of Canada, 1991).

Subliminal racism **involves an unconscious criticism of minorities.** Subliminal racism is not directly expressed, but is demonstrated in opposition to progressive minority policies (such as Canada's immigration policy) or programs (such as employment equity or affirmative action). For example, refugees are not condemned in blunt racist terminology, but their entry into Canada is viewed by some as taking unfair advantage of Canada's generosity. The decision by the Royal Canadian Mounted Police (RCMP) to allow

Sikh officers to wear turbans while on duty resulted in petitions that were signed by 250,000 Canadians. The petitioners said they had nothing against Sikhs, but that turbans were "un-Canadian," "an affront to majority values," "excessively demanding," and "too costly," among other things. Racist pins and calendars with depictions of turban-clad Mounties began appearing across Canada (Henry et al., 1996).

Subliminal racism, more than any other type of racism, demonstrates the ambiguity concerning racism. Values that support racial equality are publicly affirmed, while at the same time resentment at the prospect of moving over and making space for newcomers is also present. Subliminal racism enables individuals to maintain two apparently conflicting values—one rooted in the egalitarian virtues of justice and fairness, the other in beliefs that result in resentment and selfishness (Fleras and Elliott, 1999).

Institutionalized racism **is made up of the rules, procedures, and practices that directly and deliberately prevent minorities from having full and equal involvement in society.** In 1991, the Canadian Civil Liberties Association (CCLA) examined institutionalized discrimination in employment agencies. The CCLA randomly selected agencies in four cities in Ontario and asked whether the agencies would agree to refer only white people for the jobs that needed to be filled. Eleven of the fifteen agencies surveyed agreed to accept discriminatory job orders. The following are examples of the agencies' responses:

> It is discrimination, but it can be done discreetly without anyone knowing. No problem with that.

Members of white supremacy groups, such as the Ku Klux Klan, are overt racists; they often use members of subordinate racial and ethnic groups as scapegoats for societal problems over which they have no control.

The decision by the RCMP to allow Sikh officers to wear turbans in uniform resulted in subliminal racism. Racist pins and calendars with turban-clad Mounties appeared across Canada, and 250,000 Canadians signed a petition protesting that the turbans were "un-Canadian."

That's no problem. It's between you and me. I don't tell anyone; you don't tell anyone.

You are paying to see the people you want to see.

Absolutely—definitely . . . that request is pretty standard here.

That's not a problem. Appearance means a lot, whether it's colour or overweight people. (Rees, 1991, quoted in Henry et al., 2000:108)

What happens in actual cases of agencies using such discriminatory employment practices? Recently a complaint laid with the Ontario Human Rights Commission against two employment agencies in Toronto drew public attention to this issue. A settlement was reached in which the agencies agreed to develop policies against accepting discriminatory job requests, and employees received training in race relations and employment equity. As these incidents demonstrate, although institutions can no longer openly discriminate against minorities without attracting legal sanctions, negative publicity, or consumer resistance, this type of racism nevertheless continues to exist (Fleras and Kunz, 2001).

Systemic racism **refers to the practices, rules, and procedures of social institutions that have the unintended consequence of excluding minority group members.** Institutions are systematically racist when their organizational practices and structures reinforce white experiences as "normal" and necessary while perceiving minority realities as inferior or irrelevant (Fleras and Kunz, 2001). For example, occupations, such as police officer and firefighter, had minimum weight, height, and educational requirements for job applicants. These criteria resulted in discrimination because they favoured white applicants over members of many minority groups, as well as males over females. Other examples of systemic racism include the requirement of a college or university degree for nonspecialized jobs, employment regulations that require people to work on their Sabbath, and the policy of recognizing only university degrees and trade diplomas obtained in North America.

Systemic racism is normally reflected in statistical underrepresentation of certain groups within an institution or organization. For example, a given group may represent 15 percent of the general population but only 2 percent of those promoted to upper-management positions in a large company. Efforts to eliminate this kind of disproportionate representation are the focus of employment equity legislation. The target groups for employment equity in Canada are visible minorities, women, persons with disabilities, and Aboriginal

peoples. Strategies include modified admissions tests and requirements, enhanced recruitment of certain target groups, establishment of hiring quotas for particular minority groups, or specialized training or employment programs for specific target groups. Consideration of affirmative action strategies inevitably leads to claims of reverse discrimination by some individuals who enjoy majority group status. For a detailed examination of this claim, see Box 10.3. The most recent analysis of employment equity programs indicates that these programs have had the most significant effect on women and Aboriginal peoples, while people with disabilities have made the fewest gains. As for members of visible minorities, although they have higher levels of education on average than do other Canadians and very high labour-force participation rates, they continue to be concentrated in low-status, low-paying occupations (Henry et al., 2000). It is important to note that effects of systemic discrimination on specific visible minority groups in Canada vary substantially, with Blacks experiencing the greatest disadvantage in income and Asian groups the least (Reitz, 2001).

SOCIOLOGICAL PERSPECTIVES ON RACE AND ETHNIC RELATIONS

Symbolic interactionist, functionalist, conflict, feminist, and analysts examine race and ethnic relations in different ways. Symbolic interactionists examine how microlevel contacts between people may produce either greater racial tolerance or increased levels of hostility. Functionalists focus on the macrolevel intergroup processes that occur among members of majority and minority groups in society. Conflict theorists analyze power and economic differentials between the dominant group and subordinate groups. Feminists highlight the interactive effects of racism and sexism on the exploitation of women who are members of visible minorities.

Symbolic Interactionist Perspectives

What happens when people from different racial and ethnic groups come into contact with one another? In the *contact hypothesis,* symbolic interactionists point out that contact between people from divergent groups should lead to favourable attitudes and behaviour when

BOX 10.3 CRITICAL THINKING

What About Reverse Racism?

One of the most common questions put forth by students when they first examine the issue of racism and the diverse forms it takes concerns reverse racism. Class discussions regarding employment equity, affirmative action, and equality rights inevitably provoke a discussion about whether members of minorities can also be racist. For example, can ethnic minorities be racist toward other ethnic minorities? Is it a case of reverse racism when non-Aboriginal writers are discouraged from filming or writing fiction about Aboriginal themes? Is it racist for Aboriginal peoples to accuse whites of genocide because of the dominant society's undermining of the political, social, and cultural structure of Aboriginal society? Is it racist for Black militants to openly display hatred toward whites as an inferior race? Are Black leaders who make defamatory remarks about Jewish people acting in a racist manner (D'Sousa, 1996)? According to sociologist Augie Fleras, these are difficult questions that may never be answered to everyone's satisfaction, but the very asking promotes a clearer understanding of racism.

Consider the suggestion of reverse racism when the Writers' Union of Canada sponsored a conference in Vancouver in 1994 that barred white Canadians from activities. This conference, "Writing Thru 'Race': A Conference for First Nations Writers and Writers of Colour" sought a forum for minorities to explore the experiences of racism in a world

where, national myths notwithstanding, race matters. The conference justified its decision to exclude whites from one session on the grounds of improving dialogue among the historically oppressed, in the same way women's consciousness-raising movements excluded men. Critics saw this as a reverse discrimination on the basis of race. They resented the idea that people could be singled out and denied participation on the basis of race.

Would you agree that this is a case of reverse racism? Your answer will depend largely on how you define racism. If race is seen simply as biology—recourse to innate differences as criteria for differential treatment of others—then the answer would probably be yes. Majority members, it seems appear to have been excluded on the basis of their race (skin colour).

A more comprehensive view of racism as power suggests a different conclusion. Accusations of reverse racism must go beyond superficial appearances. There is a world of difference between using race to create equality (employment equity) and using it to limit opportunity (discrimination), even if the rhetoric sounds the same. Emphasis must be instead on the context of the actions and on their social consequences. The essence of racism resides not in treating others differently because they are different but in different treatment in contexts of power.

Source: Fleras and Elliott, 2003:62–63.

certain factors are present. Members of each group must (1) have equal status, (2) pursue the same goals, (3) cooperate with one another to achieve their goals, and (4) receive positive feedback when they interact with one another in positive, nondiscriminatory ways (Allport, 1958; Coakley, 1998). Does participation in interracial sports teams, for example, promote intergroup cohesion and reduce prejudice? Scholars have found that increased contact may have little or no effect on existing prejudices and, in some circumstances, can even lead to an increase in prejudice and conflict. If racial tension between players on teams is high enough, violence may erupt (Edwards, 1973; Lapchick, 1991). Why might sports contribute to prejudice? Sports events are highly competitive, and prejudice may be aggravated by the actions of players or spectators.

What happens when individuals meet someone who does not conform to their existing stereotype? Frequently, they ignore anything that contradicts the stereotype or interpret the situation to support their prejudices (Coakley, 1998). For example, a person who does not fit the stereotype may be seen as an exception— "You're not like other [persons of a particular race]."

When a person is seen as conforming to a stereotype, he or she may be treated simply as one of "you people." Former Los Angeles Lakers basketball star Earvin "Magic" Johnson (1992:31–32) described how he was categorized along with all other African Americans when he was bused to a predominantly white school:

On the first day of [basketball] practice, my teammates froze me out. Time after time I was wide open, but nobody threw me the ball. At first I thought they just didn't see me. But I woke up after a kid named Danny Parks looked right at me and then took a long jumper. Which he missed.

I was furious, but I didn't say a word. Shortly after that, I grabbed a defensive rebound and took the ball all the way down for a basket. I did it again and a third time, too.

Finally Parks got angry and said, "Hey, pass the [bleeping] ball."

That did it. I slammed down the ball and glared at him. Then I exploded. "I *knew* this would happen!" I said. "That's why I didn't want to come to this [bleeping] school in the first place!"

"Oh, yeah? Well, you people are all the same," he said. "You think you're gonna come in here and do whatever you want? Look, hotshot, your job is to get the rebound. Let us do the shooting."

The interaction between Johnson and Parks demonstrates that when people from different racial and ethnic groups come into contact with one another, they may treat one another as stereotypes, not as individuals.

Symbolic interactionist perspectives make us aware of the importance of intergroup contact and the fact that it may either intensify or reduce racial and ethnic stereotyping and prejudice.

Functionalist Perspectives

How do members of subordinate racial and ethnic groups become a part of the dominant group? To answer this question, early functionalists studied immigration and patterns of majority and minority group interaction.

Assimilation *Assimilation* **is a process by which members of subordinate racial and ethnic groups become absorbed into the dominant culture.** To some analysts, assimilation is functional because it contributes to the stability of society by minimizing group differences that otherwise might result in hostility and violence (Gordon, 1964).

Assimilation occurs at several distinct levels, including the cultural, structural, biological, and psychological stages. *Cultural assimilation,* or *acculturation,* occurs when members of an ethnic group adopt dominant group traits, such as language, dress, values, religion, and food preferences. Cultural assimilation in this country initially followed an "Anglo-conformity" model; members of subordinate ethnic groups were expected to conform to the culture of the dominant

white Anglo-Saxon population (Gordon, 1964). However, members of some groups, such as Aboriginal peoples and Québécois, refused to be assimilated and sought to maintain their unique cultural identity.

Structural assimilation, or *integration,* occurs when members of subordinate racial or ethnic groups gain acceptance in everyday social interaction with members of the dominant group. This type of assimilation typically starts in large, impersonal settings, such as schools and workplaces, and only later (if at all) results in close friendships and intermarriage. *Biological assimilation,* or *amalgamation,* occurs when members of one group marry those of other social or ethnic groups. Biological assimilation has been more complete in some other countries, such as Mexico and Brazil, than in Canada.

Psychological assimilation involves a change in racial or ethnic self-identification on the part of an individual. Rejection by the dominant group may prevent psychological assimilation by members of some subordinate racial and ethnic groups, especially those with visible characteristics, such as skin colour or facial features that differ from those of the dominant group.

Ethnic Pluralism Instead of complete assimilation, many groups share elements of the mainstream culture while remaining culturally distinct from both the dominant group and other social and ethnic groups. **Ethnic pluralism is the co-existence of a variety of distinct racial and ethnic groups within one society.**

Equalitarian pluralism, or *accommodation,* is a situation in which ethnic groups coexist in equality with one another. Switzerland has been described as a model of equalitarian pluralism; more than six million people with French, German, and Italian cultural heritages peacefully coexist there (Simpson and Yinger, 1972).

The members of this adult education class are learning English as their second language. What type of assimilation does this represent?

Has Canada achieved equalitarian pluralism? The *Canadian Multiculturalism Act* of 1988 stated that "All Canadians are full and equal partners in Canadian society." The Department of Multiculturalism and Citizenship was established in 1991 with the goal of encouraging ethnic minorities to participate fully in all aspects of Canadian life while at the same time maintaining their distinct ethnic identities and cultural practices. The objective of multiculturalism is to "promote unity through diversity." Multiculturalism programs provide funding for education, consultative support, and a range of activities, including heritage language training, race relations training, ethnic policing and justice, and ethnic celebrations. In recent years, multiculturalism policies have been under increasing attack. Neil Bissoondath, author of *Selling Illusions: The Cult of Multiculturalism in Canada* (1994), suggests that multiculturalism does not promote equalitarian pluralism. Rather, he argues, multiculturalism is divisive; it ghettoizes visible minorities, fosters racial animosity, and detracts from national unity.

Inequalitarian pluralism, or *segregation,* exists when specific ethnic groups are set apart from the dominant group and have unequal access to power and privilege (Marger, 2000). **Segregation is the spatial and social separation of categories of people by race, ethnicity, class, gender, and/or religion.** Segregation may be enforced by law (*de jure*) or by custom (*de facto*). An example of *de jure* segregation was the Jim Crow laws, which legalized the separation of the races in all public accommodations (including hotels, restaurants, transportation, hospitals, jails, schools, churches, and cemeteries) in the southern United States after the Civil War (Feagin and Feagin, 2003).

De jure segregation of Blacks is also part of the history of Canada. Blacks in Canada lived in largely segregated communities in Nova Scotia, New Brunswick, and Ontario, where racial segregation was evident in the schools, government, the workplace, residential housing, and elsewhere. Segregated schools continued in Nova Scotia until the 1960s. Residential segregation was legally enforced through the use of racially restrictive covenants attached to deeds and leases. Separation and refusal of service were common in restaurants, theatres, and recreational facilities (Henry and Tator, 2006). Sociologist Adrienne Shadd (1991:11) describes her experiences growing up in North Buxton, Ontario, in the 1950s and 1960s:

> When we would go into the local ice cream parlour, the man behind the counter would serve us last, after all the Whites had been served, even if they came into the shop after us.

Caribana Parade marchers in Toronto exemplify the concept of ethnic pluralism—maintaining their distinct identity even as they share in many elements of mainstream culture.

Southwestern Ontario may as well have been below the Mason-Dixon line in those days. Dresden, home of the historic Uncle Tom's cabin, made national headlines in 1954 when Blacks tested the local restaurants after the passage of the *Fair Accommodation Practices Act* and found that two openly refused to serve them. This came as no surprise, given that for years certain eateries, hotels, and recreational clubs were restricted to us, and at one time Blacks could only sit in designated sections of movie theatres (usually the balcony) if admitted at all.

One of the most blatant examples of segregation in Canada is the federal government's reserve system for status Indians, which resulted in segregation of Aboriginal peoples on reserves in remote areas across the country.

Although legally sanctioned forms of racial segregation have been all but eliminated, de facto segregation, which is enforced by custom, still exists. Although functionalist explanations provide a description of how some early white ethnic immigrants assimilated into the cultural mainstream, they do not adequately account for the persistent racial segregation and economic inequality experienced by some minority group members.

Conflict Perspectives

Why do some ethnic groups continue to experience subjugation after many years? Conflict theorists focus on economic stratification and access to power in their analysis of race and ethnic relations.

Internal Colonialism   Conflict theorists use the term ***internal colonialism* to refer to a situation in**

which members of a racial or ethnic group are conquered or colonized and forcibly placed under the economic and political control of the dominant group. Groups that have been subjected to internal colonialism often remain in subordinate positions longer than groups that voluntarily migrated to North America.

Aboriginal peoples in Canada were colonized by Europeans and others who invaded their lands and conquered them. In the process, Aboriginal peoples lost property, political rights, aspects of their culture, and often their lives (Frideres, 1998). The capitalist class acquired cheap labour and land through this government-sanctioned racial exploitation. The effects of past internal colonialism are reflected today in the number of Aboriginal people who live in extreme poverty on government reserves (Frideres, 1998).

The experiences of internally colonized groups are unique in three ways: (1) they have been forced to exist in a society other than their own; (2) they have been kept out of the economic and political mainstream, so that it is difficult for them to compete with dominant group members; and (3) they have been subjected to severe attacks on their own culture, which may lead to its extinction (Blauner, 1972).

The internal colonialism model is rooted in historical foundations of racial and ethnic inequality in North America. However, it tends to view all voluntary immigrants as having many more opportunities than do members of colonized groups. Thus, this model does not explain the continued exploitation of some immigrant groups, such as Chinese, Filipinos, and Vietnamese, and the greater acceptance of others, primarily those from northern Europe (Cashmore, 1996).

The Split-Labour-Market Theory Who benefits from the exploitation of visible minorities? Dual or split-labour-market theory states that both white workers and members of the capitalist class benefit from the exploitation of visible minorities. *Split labour market* **refers to the division of the economy into two areas of employment: a primary sector or upper tier, composed of higher-paid (usually dominant group) workers in more secure jobs, and a secondary sector or lower tier, made up of lower-paid (often subordinate group) workers in jobs with little security and hazardous working conditions** (Bonacich, 1972, 1976). According to this perspective, white workers in the upper tier may use racial discrimination against nonwhites to protect their positions. These actions most often occur when upper-tier workers feel threatened by lower-tier

Ethnic hatred in Kosovo, Serbia brought about the deaths of thousands of ethnic Albanians. Thousands of refugees fled to Canada and the United States.

workers hired by capitalists to reduce labour costs and maximize corporate profits. In the past, immigrants were a source of cheap labour that employers could use to break strikes and keep wages down. Agnes Calliste (1987) applied the split-labour-market theory in her study of sleeping-car porters in Canada. Calliste found a doubly submerged split labour market, with three levels of stratification in this area of employment. While "white" trade unions were unable to restrict access to porter positions on the basis of race, they were able to impose differential pay scales. Consequently, Black porters received less pay than white porters, even though they were doing the same work. Furthermore, the labour market was doubly submerged because Black immigrant workers from the United States received even less pay than both Black and white Canadian porters. Throughout history, higher-paid workers have responded with racial hostility and joined movements to curtail immigration and thus do away with the source of cheap labour (Marger, 2000).

Proponents of the split-labour-market theory suggest that white workers benefit from racial and ethnic antagonisms. However, these analysts typically do not examine the interactive effects of race, class, and gender in the workplace.

Feminist Perspectives

Minority women (women of colour, immigrant women, and Aboriginal women) are doubly disadvantaged as a result of their gender. The term *gendered racism* refers to the interactive effect of racism and sexism in the exploitation of women of colour. According to social psychologist Philomena Essed

(1991), women's particular position must be explored within each racial or ethnic group, because their experiences will not have been the same as the men's in each grouping.

All workers are not equally exploited by capitalists. Gender and race or ethnicity are important in this exploitation. For example, jobs are race-typed and gender-typed. Consider a registered nurse and a custodian in a hospital. What race and gender are they likely to be? Did a white woman and a man of colour come to mind? Most jobs have similar race and gender designations. Often, the jobs people hold are linked to their class, race, and gender. Consequently, the effect of class on our life chances is inseparable from the effects of our gender and race or ethnicity. The split labour market, then, involves not only class but also race, ethnicity, and gender (Amott and Matthaei, 1991). Historically, the high-paying primary labour market has been monopolized by white men. People of colour and most white women more often hold lower-tier jobs (Arat-Koc, 1999). Below that tier is the underground sector of the economy, characterized by illegal or quasi-legal activities, such as drug trafficking, prostitution, and working in sweatshops, that do not meet minimum wage and safety standards. Many undocumented workers and some white women and people of colour attempt to earn a living in this sector (Amott and Matthaei, 1991).

Postmodern Perspectives

Conventional theories of race and ethnicity tend to see racial or ethnic identities as organized around social structures that are fixed and closed, such as nations, tribes, bands, and communities. As such, there is little movement in or out of these groups. Postmodern perspectives, in constrast, view ethnic and racial identities as largely a consequence of personal choice (agency) and subjective definition. These identities are constantly evolving and subject to the continuous interplay of history, power, and culture.

In postmodernism, "identity is not unitary or essential, it is fluid or shifting, fed by multiple sources and taking multiple forms (Kumar, 1997:98). Ethnic and racial identities are socially constructed and given meaning by our fragmented society. A postmodernist framework may ask how social actors come to understand who they are in "race" terms. This approach, which explores how racialized identities are constructed, analyzes an area that conventional theories of race and ethnicity have largely ignored. Central

to a postmodern perspective on race is the concept of *discourse*. Based on the work of Michael Foucault, discourse is used to refer to "different ways of structuring knowledge and social practice" (Fiske, 1994 c.f. Henry and Tator, 2006). Postmodernists view reality as constructed through a broad range of discourses, which includes all that is written, spoken, or otherwise represented through language and communication systems (Anderson, 2006:394). Postmodernists see science (which includes the social sciences) as constructed and as such do not see it as providing knowledge that is any more real than other sources of knowledge. Analysts using this perspective will therefore focus on *deconstructing—meaning analyzing the assumptions and meanings embedded in scientific works* (Anderson, 2006).

Postmodernist scholars, such as David Goldberg, use this perspective to shift the frame of analysis away from race relations to an intense examination (deconstruction) of racist discourse. *Racist discourse or racialized discourse* is defined as an identifiable repertoire of words, images, and practices through which racial power is directed against ethnic and racial minority groups. An analysis of racist discourse is central to understanding the ways in which a particular society gives a voice to racism and advances the interests of whites. Although this discourse may be expressed in many ways, including explanations, narratives, images, and social practices, they all serve to support, reinforce, and sustain patterns of domination and exclusion of particular minority group members (Henry and Tator, 2006:24). Frances Henry and Carol Tator (2006), have identified examples of racist discourse which serve to sustain or perpetuate racism in our society. For example, *"the discourse of denial"* suggests that racism simply does not exist in our Canadian democratic society. When racism is shown to exist, *the discourse of denial* will explain it away as an isolated incident rather than an indication of systemic racism. There are numerous examples of the discourse of denial in policing agencies across the country. Despite numerous complaints of racism directed at visible minority groups and Aboriginal persons, top police administrators continue to respond to allegations with "we do not have a problem with racism within our organization" or "I have never witnessed a racist incident." A second related discourse identified by Henry and Tator is *"the discourse of colour-blindness"* in which white people insist that they do not notice the skin colour of a racial-minority person. In doing so, white people also fail to "recognize that race is a part of the 'baggage' that people of colour carry with them, and the refusal to recognize racism as part of everyday values, policies, programs, and practices"(2006:25)

A postmodern perspective not only examines how identities of racial and ethnic minorities are formed but also asks the same question about white identities. For example

> [W]hite people are "raced" just as men are "gendered." And in a social context where white people have too often viewed themselves as non-racial or racially neutral, it is crucial to look at the "racialness" of the white experience. . . . Whiteness is first a location of structural advantage of race privilege. Second, a "standpoint," a place from which white people look at ourselves, at others, at society. Third, "whiteness" refers to a set of cultural practices that are usually unmarked and unnamed. (Frankenberg, 1993, c.f. Gann, 2000)

One of the most common criticisms of a postmodern analysis of race and ethnic relations applies to postmodernism in general; that is, postmodernism, given its high level of abstraction, has produced work that is extremely difficult to understand (Anderson, 2006). Postmodern perspectives have also been criticized because they offer no basis for evaluating race relations as either "good" or "bad." At best it implies a broad acknowledgement and acceptance of racial difference (Gann, 2000:16).

An Alternative Perspective: Critical Race Theory

Emerging out of scholarly law studies on racial and ethnic inequality, critical race theory derives its foundation from the U.S. civil rights tradition and the writing of persons such as Martin Luther King, Jr., W. E. B. Du Bois, Malcolm X, and César Chávez. The growth of critical race theory began in Canada during the 1980s. It is based on the same theoretical foundation as its American counterpart; that is, a growing dissatisfaction with the failure to acknowledge and recognize the critical roles that race and racism have played in the political and legal structures of Canadian society (Aylward, 1999).

Critical race theory has several major premises, including the belief that racism is such an ingrained feature of North American society that it appears to be ordinary and natural to many people (Delgado, 1995). As a result, civil rights legislation and affirmative action laws (formal equality) may remedy some of the more overt, blatant forms of racial injustice but have little

effect on subtle, business-as-usual forms of racism that people of colour experience as they go about their everyday lives. According to this approach, the best way to document racism and ongoing inequality in society is to listen to the lived experiences of people who have experienced such discrimination. In this way, we can learn what actually happens in regard to racial oppression and the many effects it has on people, including alienation, depression, and certain physical illnesses (Razack, 1998).

Central to this argument is the belief that *interest convergence* is a crucial factor in bringing about social change. According to the legal scholar Derrick Bell, white elites tolerate or encourage racial advances for people of colour *only* if the dominant-group members believe that their own self-interest will be served in so doing (cited in Delgado, 1995). From this approach, civil rights laws have typically benefited white North Americans as much (or more) as people of colour because these laws have been used as mechanisms to ensure that "racial progress occurs at just the right pace: change that is too rapid would be unsettling to society at large; change that is too slow could prove destabilizing" (Delgado, 1995: xiv).

Critical race theory is similar to postmodernist approaches in that it calls our attention to the fact that things are not always as they seem. Formal equality under the law does not necessarily equate to actual equality in society. This theory also makes us aware of the ironies and contradictions in civil rights law, which some see as self-serving laws. However, mainstream critics argue that critical race theory is unduly pessimistic because it largely ignores the strides that have been made toward racial equality in the United States. Concept Table 10.A outlines the key aspects of each sociological perspective.

ETHNIC GROUPS IN CANADA

How do racial and ethnic groups come into contact with one another? How do they adjust to one another and to the dominant group over time? Sociologists have explored these questions extensively; however, a detailed historical account of each group is beyond the scope of this chapter. As the Census Profile on page 301 indicates, Canada is a nation that has become increasingly multiethnic. Given the diversity of our population, imposing any

Concept Table 10.A SOCIOLOGICAL PERSPECTIVES ON RACE AND ETHNIC RELATIONS

PERSPECTIVE	FOCUS	THEORY/HYPOTHESIS
Symbolic Interactionist	Microlevel Contacts Between Individuals	Contact hypothesis

Functionalist	Macrolevel Intergroup Processes	1. Assimilation
		   a. cultural
		   b. biological
		   c. structural
		   d. psychological
		2. Ethnic pluralism
		   a. equalitarian pluralism
		   b. inequalitarian pluralism (segregation)

Conflict	Power/Economic Differentials Between Dominant and Subordinate Groups	1. Caste perspective 2. Class perspective 3. Internal colonialism 4. Split labour market
Feminist	Gendered Racism	Minority women are doubly disadvantaged as a result of their gender.
Postmodern	Racialized and Racist Discourse	Racist discourse serves to sustain and reinforce patterns of discrimination against racial and ethnic minorities.
Critical Race Theory	Racism as an Ingrained Feature of Society that Affects Everyone's Daily Life	Laws may remedy overt discrimination but have little effect on subtle racism. Interest convergence is required for social change.

kind of conceptual order on a discussion of ethnic groups in Canada is difficult. We will look briefly at some of the predominant ethnic groups in Canada. In the process, we will examine a brief history of racism with respect to each group.

Aboriginal Peoples

Canada's Aboriginal peoples are believed to have migrated to North America from Asia an estimated 40,000 years ago (Dyck, 2002). The term *Aboriginal* itself refers to the original or indigenous occupants of this country (Fleras and Elliott, 2003). Aboriginal peoples are an extremely diverse group with varying access to resources, development levels, and social health. Today, the terms *Native, First Nations,* or *Aboriginal* refer to approximately fifty-five sovereign peoples including the Inuit, Cree, Mi'kmaq, Blackfoot, Iroquois, and Haida. Other categories of Aboriginal peoples are status Indians (those Indians with legal rights under the *Indian Act*), nonstatus Indians (those without legal rights), Métis, and Inuit. Those who settled in the southern part of Canada, the Yukon, and the Mackenzie Valley can be termed *North American*

Indians. Those located in the eastern Arctic and northern islands, who were formerly referred to as Eskimos, are now referred to as *Inuit.* A third category, *Métis,* who live mostly on the Prairies, are descendants of Indian and non-Indian unions (primarily French settlers and Indian women).

When European settlers arrived on this continent, the Aboriginal inhabitants' way of life was changed forever. Experts estimate that between one and twelve million Aboriginal people lived in North America at this time; however, their numbers had been reduced to under 240,000 by 1900 (Churchill, 1994). What factors contributed to this drastic depopulation?

Genocide, Forced Migration, and Forced Assimilation

Aboriginal people have been the victims of genocide and forced migration. Many Native Americans either were massacred or died from European diseases (such as typhoid, smallpox, and measles) and starvation (Wagner and Stearn, 1945; Cook, 1973). In battle, Aboriginal people often were no match for the Europeans, who had the latest weaponry (Amott and Matthaei, 1991).

Europeans justified their aggression by stereotyping Aboriginals as "savages" and "heathens" (Frideres and Gadacz, 2001).

Entire nations were forced to move in order to accommodate the white settlers. The "Trail of Tears" was one of the most disastrous of the forced migrations to occur in North America. In the coldest part of the winter of 1832, more than half of the Cherokee Nation died during or as a result of their forced relocation from the southeastern United States to the Indian Territory in Oklahoma (Thornton, 1984). The colonization of the Aboriginal population was far less brutal in Canada than in the United States. However, it is not clear whether this more benign conquest left Aboriginals in Canada any better off than their counterparts in the United States in the long run (Weinfeld, 1995:48).

Indian rights were clearly defined in the Royal Proclamation of 1763, which divided up the territory acquired by Britain. In the large area called the Indian Territory, the purchase or settlement of land was forbidden without a treaty. This is sometimes called the principle of "voluntary cession" (Dyck, 1996:154). The government broke treaty after treaty as it engaged in a policy of wholesale removal of indigenous nations in order to clear the land for settlement by Anglo-Saxon "pioneers" (Green, 1977; Churchill, 1994). The 1867 *Constitution Act* gave jurisdiction over Indians and lands reserved for the Indians to the federal government. The Canadian government then passed the *Indian Act* of 1876, which provided for federal government control of almost every aspect of Indian life. The regulations under the act included prohibitions

against owning land, voting, and purchasing and consuming alcohol. Later provisions prevented Aboriginal people from leaving reserves without permission and a ticket from the agent (Frideres and Gadacz, 2001). It is clear that the *Indian Act* was designed to promote assimilation; Aboriginal peoples were to adopt the cultural attitudes and norms of the dominant culture and give up their own cultural traditions (including their values, customs, and language).

Aboriginal children were placed in residential boarding schools to facilitate their assimilation into the dominant culture. The Jesuits and other missionaries who ran these schools believed that Aboriginal peoples should not be left in their "inferior" natural state and considered it their mission to replace Aboriginal culture with Christian beliefs, values, rituals, and practices (Bolaria and Li, 1988). Many Aboriginal children who attended these schools were sexually, physically, and emotionally abused. They were not allowed to speak their language or engage in any of their traditional cultural practices. The coercive and oppressive nature of this educational experience is one of the most blatant examples of institutionalized racism (Henry et al., 1996:62).

Aboriginal Peoples Today   According to the 2001 census, close to 1 million people reported they were Aboriginal, including 608,850 North American Indian, 292,310 Métis, and 45,070 Inuit. These numbers represent approximately 3 percent of Canada's total population (Statistics Canada, 2003a). Figure 10.1 displays the composition of the Aboriginal population.

Figure 10.1   Aboriginal Identity Population, 2001*

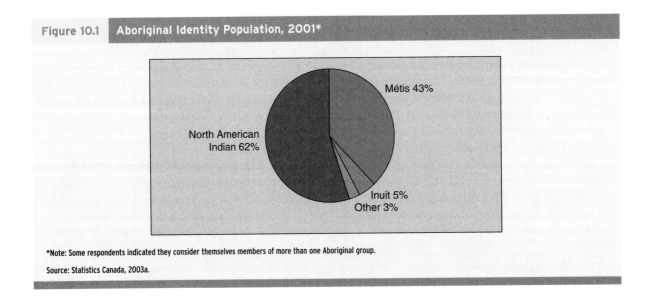

*Note: Some respondents indicated they consider themselves members of more than one Aboriginal group.

Source: Statistics Canada, 2003a.

There are several tribal groups, living in more than 600 bands. Although the majority of registered Indians live on reserves, the majority of all Aboriginal people live off reserves. The Aboriginal population is unevenly distributed across Canada, with the heaviest concentrations in western and northern Canada.

Aboriginal peoples are the most disadvantaged racial or ethnic group in Canada in terms of income, employment, housing, nutrition, and health (Statistics Canada, 2002c). The life chances of Aboriginal peoples who live on reservations are especially limited. They have the highest rates of infant mortality and death by exposure and malnutrition. They also have high rates of tuberculosis, alcoholism, and suicide (Statistics Canada, 2002l). The overall life expectancy of Aboriginal people in Canada is six years less than that of non-Aboriginals; this is largely due to poor health services and inadequate housing on reserves (Indian and Northern Affairs, 2005). Aboriginal peoples also

The North American Indigenous Games, held in Winnipeg in 2002, are a reflection of Aboriginal persons' sustained efforts to maintain their unique culture. For thousands of years before European contact, Aboriginal peoples held games throughout North America.

have had very limited educational opportunities (the functional illiteracy rate for Aboriginal peoples is 45 percent compared with the overall Canadian rate of 17 percent), and they have a very high rate of unemployment (twice the rate for non-Aboriginal Canadians). On reserves, the unemployment rate is about 29 percent, nearly three times the Canadian rate (Indian and Northern Affairs, 2005).

Despite the state's efforts to incorporate Aboriginal peoples into Canadian culture and society, many Aboriginal people have been successful in resisting oppression. National organizations like the Assembly of First Nations, Inuit Tapirisat, the Native Council of Canada, and the Métis National Council have been instrumental in bringing the demands of those they represent into the political and constitutional arenas. Of these demands, the major ones have been and still are self-government, Aboriginal rights, and the resolution of land claims (see Frideres and Gadacz, 2001). Meanwhile, Aboriginal women's groups, such as the Native Women's Association of Canada, have publicized the harmful conditions (including child sexual abuse, incest, and wife battering) that exist on reserves.

One of the first major successes in the quest for self-determination has been the creation of Nunavut (which means "our land"). The vision of Nunavut came to be in 1993 when the Nunavut Land Claims Agreement was signed. Under the terms of this agreement, the Inuit have received title to 350,000 square kilometres of land in the Northwest Territories, including mineral rights to 36,000 square kilometres. The agreement also provides financial compensation of $1.14 billion. Nunavut is a positive step for the Inuit in establishing their rights of self-determination over their unique culture.

The Québécois

The European colonization of Canada began with the exploration and settlement of New France. In 1608, the first permanent settlement in New France was established at Quebec City. At this time France's North American empire extended from Hudson Bay to Louisiana.

Following the British conquest of the French in Canada in the Seven Years' War (1756–1763), Canada became a British dominion and the French found themselves in an inferior position (Weinfeld, 1995). The French were able to maintain French civil law, language, and religion; however, the overall economic, social, and political power passed to English Canada.

The British North America Act (1867) formally acknowledged the rights and privileges of the French and British as the founding or charter groups of Canadian society. With Confederation, it was assumed that in the future French- and English-speaking groups would coexist and complement one another. However, during the period between Confederation and World War II, the French struggled for cultural survival because English-speaking Canadians controlled the major economic institutions in both English Canada and Quebec.

During the period known as the *Quiet Revolution* (1960–1966), Quebec nationalism grew sharply. Under the leadership of Premier Jean Lesage in 1960, Quebec began undergoing a rapid process of modernization. During this time, the authority of the Catholic church over the educational system was reduced as the Quebec government established a department of education. More French Canadians began pursuing higher education, particularly in business and science. The church also lost some of its influence over moral issues, which was reflected in a declining birth rate and an increase in common-law marriages. Finally, nonfrancophone immigrants were challenging French culture by choosing to learn English and having their children learn English, rather than French. The result? Francophones came to view their language and culture as endangered. As a result, they rejected their Canadian identity and adopted a distinctly Québécois identity.

In the 1960s Quebec nationalism grew and francophones in Quebec began to believe that their language and culture were threatened (see Chapter 14). In two referendums held in 1980 and 1995 Quebeckers rejected sovereignty, but the issue remains contentious.

French Canadians Today   Today, approximately 23 percent of the Canadian population is francophone, 85 percent of which is located in Quebec (Statistics Canada, 2002q). Many Quebec nationalists now see independence or separation as the ultimate protection against cultural and linguistic assimilation, as well as the route to economic power. As political scientist Rand Dyck comments,

> [G]iven its geographic concentration in Quebec and majority control of a large province, and given their modern-day self-consciousness and self-confidence, the French fact in Canada cannot be ignored. If English Canada wants Quebec to remain a part of the country, it cannot go back to the easy days of pre-1960 unilingualism. (1996:185)

French Canadians have at least forced Canada to take its second language and culture seriously, which is an important step toward attaining cultural pluralism.

Canada's Multicultural Minorities

Home to approximately five million foreign-born immigrants, Canada is well described as a land of immigrants. Approximately 80 percent of immigrants arriving in Canada today are members of a visible minority group (Statistics Canada, 2003b). Canada's policies toward some of these groups have been far from exemplary. In fact, initial Canadian immigration policies have been described as essentially racist in orientation, assimilationist in intent, and exclusionary in outcome (Fleras and Elliott, 2003). For example, the *Immigration Act* of 1869 excluded certain types of undesirables, such as criminals and the diseased, and imposed strict limitations on the Japanese, Chinese, and East Asians. A "racial pecking order" (Lupul, 1988) was established as a result of selecting potential immigrants on the basis of race and perceived capacity for assimilation (Walker, 1997). As much energy was expended in keeping out certain "types" as was put into encouraging others to settle (Whitaker, 1991). A preferred category was that of *white ethnics*—a term coined to identify immigrants who came from European countries other than England, such as Scotland, Ireland, Poland, Italy, Greece, Germany, Yugoslavia, and Russia and other former Soviet republics. Immigration from "white" countries was encouraged to ensure the British character of Canada. With the exception of visa formalities, this category of "preferred" immigrants was virtually exempt from entry restrictions. On the other hand, Jews and other Mediterranean populations required special permits for entry, and Asian populations were admitted grudgingly, mostly to serve as cheap labour for Canadian capitalist expansion. The restrictions regarding the Chinese, Japanese, and Jews highlighted the racist dimension of Canada's early immigration policies (Satzewich, 1998).

Chinese Canadians   The initial wave of Chinese immigration began in the 1850s, when Chinese men were attracted to emigrate to Canada by the promise of gold in British Columbia and by employment opportunities. Nearly 16,000 Chinese were brought to Canada at this time to lay track for the Canadian Pacific Railway. The work was brutally hard and

As more Chinese Canadians have made gains in education and employment, many have also made a conscious effort to increase awareness of Chinese culture and to develop a sense of unity and cooperation. This Chinese Dragon parade exemplifies this desire to maintain traditional celebrations.

dangerous, living conditions were appalling, food and shelter were insufficient, and due to scurvy and smallpox there was a high fatality rate. These immigrants were "welcomed" only as long as there was a shortage of white workers. However, they were not permitted to bring their wives and children with them or to have sexual relations with white women, because of the fear they would spread the "yellow menace" (Henry and Tator, 2006). After the railroad was built, the welcome mat was quickly rolled up.

The Chinese were subjected to extreme prejudice and were referred to by derogatory terms, such as *coolies, heathens,* and *Chinks*. Some were attacked by working-class whites who feared they would lose their jobs to Chinese immigrants. In 1885 the federal government passed its first anti-Chinese bill, the purpose of which was to limit Chinese immigration. Other hostile legislation included a range of racist exclusionary policies, such as ones prohibiting the Chinese from voting, serving in public office, serving on juries, participating in white labour unions, and working in the professions of law and pharmacy. In 1888, a head tax was imposed on all Chinese males arriving in Canada. In 1903, the tax was raised to $500 from $100 in a further attempt to restrict entry to Canada (Satzewich, 1998). Not until after World

War II were these discriminatory policies removed from the *Immigration Act.* After immigration laws were further relaxed in the 1960s, the second and largest wave of Chinese immigration occurred, with immigrants coming primarily from Hong Kong and Taiwan (Henry and Tator, 2006).

Japanese Canadians Japanese immigrants began arriving in Canada in large numbers after Chinese immigration tapered off. Like Chinese immigrants two decades earlier, the Japanese were viewed as a threat by white workers and became victims of stereotyping and discrimination.

In 1907, an organization known as the Asiatic Exclusion League was formed with the mandate of restricting admission of Asians to Canada. Following the arrival of a ship carrying more than a thousand Japanese and a few hundred Sikhs, the league carried out a demonstration that precipitated a race riot. A "gentlemen's agreement," negotiated in 1908, permitted entry only of certain categories of Japanese on a fixed quota basis.

Japanese Canadians experienced one of the most vicious forms of discrimination ever sanctioned by Canadian law. During World War II, when Canada was at war with Japan, nearly 23,000 people of Japanese ancestry (13,300 of whom were Canadian-born) were placed in internment camps because they were seen as a security threat (Takaki, 1993). They remained in the camps for more than two years, despite the total lack of evidence that they posed a danger to this country. Many of the camps were situated in remote locales in British Columbia, Alberta, and Manitoba; they had guard towers and were surrounded by barbed-wire fences. This action was a direct violation of the citizenship rights of Japanese Canadians. Only the Japanese were singled out for such harsh treatment; German immigrants avoided this fate even though Canada was at war with both Japan and Germany. Four decades after these events, the Canadian government issued an apology for its actions and agreed to pay $20,000 to each person who had been placed in an internment camp (Henry and Tator, 2006).

South Asians South Asians also had to deal with discriminatory immigration laws. One of these laws was the "continuous passage" rule of 1908, which specified that South Asians could immigrate only if they came directly from India and did not stop at any ports on the way. This law made it almost impossible for them to enter the country, since no ships made direct journeys from India. South Asians who did manage to immigrate to Canada faced hostile employers and distrustful citizens. Their property and businesses were frequently attacked, and they were denied citizenship and the right to vote in British Columbia until 1947 (Henry and Tator, 2006).

Jewish Canadians   In 1942, Canada closed its doors to Jews fleeing Hitler and the Holocaust. A ship carrying Jewish refugees from Europe attempted to land in Halifax and was denied entrance. During the 1930s, Canada admitted fewer Jewish refugees as a percentage of its population than any other Western country. Jews who did immigrate experienced widespread discrimination in employment, business, and education. Other indicators of anti-Semitism included restrictions on where Jews could live, buy property, and attend university. Signs posted along Toronto's beaches warned "No dogs or Jews allowed." Many hotels and resorts had policies prohibiting Jews as guests (Abella and Troper, 1982, quoted in Henry et al., 2000:80). Despite the discrimination and racism to which Jews were subjected, Jewish Canadians today have attained a level of education and income considerably above the Canadian average.

Immigration Trends from 1929 to the Present   The Great Depression, which began in 1929, prompted the implementation of restrictive measures to further limit new immigrants to those from the preferred groups. Changes to the *Immigration Act* in 1962 opened the door to immigration on a nonracial basis. Education, occupation, and language skills replaced race or national origin as the criteria for admission. In 1967, a *points system* was introduced whereby immigrants regardless of origin or colour were rated according to the totals of points given for the following: job training, experience, skills, level of education, knowledge of English or French, degree of demand for the applicant's occupation, and job offers (Henry & Tator, 2006). Although, as shown in Figure 10.2, this act opened the doors to those from previously excluded countries, critics have suggested that it maintained some of the same racist policies. In 2002, in response to the numerous concerns of continued exclusionary and racist immigration practices, the *Immigration and Refugee Protection Act* was implemented. This act recognizes three classes of immigrant: economic, family class, and refugee, and reflects a more open policy with selection criteria based on language skills, education, age, employment experience, and a category called "adaptability" (Henry and Tator, 2006:78).

Figure 10.2   **Place of Birth of Immigrants by Period of Immigration, 2001**

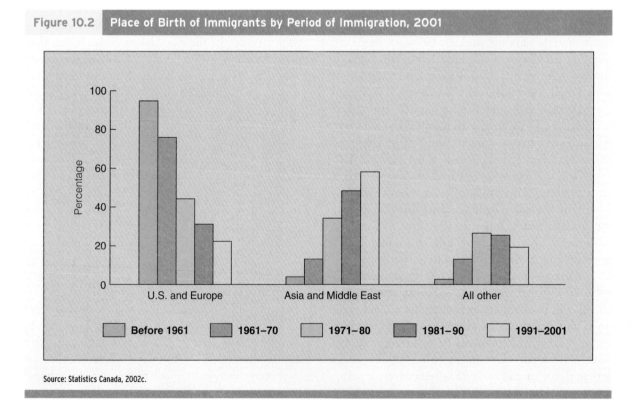

Source: Statistics Canada, 2002c.

RACIAL AND ETHNIC INEQUALITY IN THE FUTURE

Throughout the world, many racial and ethnic groups seek *self-determination*—the right to choose their own way of life. As many nations are currently structured, however, self-determination is impossible.

Worldwide Racial and Ethnic Struggles

The cost of self-determination is the loss of life and property in ethnic warfare. In recent years, the Cold War has given way to dozens of smaller wars over ethnic dominance. In Europe, for example, ethnic violence has persisted in Yugoslavia, Spain, Britain (between the Protestant majority and the Catholic minority in Northern Ireland), Romania, Russia, Moldova, and Georgia. Ethnic violence continues in the Middle East, Africa, Asia, and Latin America. Hundreds of thousands have died from warfare, disease (such as the cholera epidemic in war-torn Rwanda), and refugee migration.

Ethnic wars have a high price for survivors, whose life chances can become bleaker even after the violence subsides. In ethnic conflict between Abkhazians and Georgians in the former Soviet Union, for example, as many as two thousand people have been killed and more than eighty thousand displaced. More recently, ethnic hatred has devastated the province of Kosovo, which is located in Serbia—Yugoslavia's dominant republic—and brought about the deaths of thousands of ethnic Albanians. Even in the aftermath of the worst fighting and bloodshed, many refugees in Albania and North America search for relatives they have not seen or heard from for months and sometimes years. However, the Internet has provided some refugees with information regarding relatives and other concerns (Bennahum, 1999).

In the twenty-first century, the struggle between the Israeli government and various Palestinian factions over the future and borders of Palestine continues to make headlines. Discord in this region has heightened tensions among people not only in Israel and Palestine but also in North America and around the world as deadly clashes continue and political leaders are apparently unable to reach a lasting solution.

Growing Racial and Ethnic Diversity in Canada

Racial and ethnic diversity is increasing in Canada. This changing demographic pattern is largely the result of the elimination of overtly racist immigration policies and the opening up of immigration to low-income countries. Canada has evolved from a country largely inhabited by whites and Aboriginal peoples to a country made up of people from more than seventy countries. Today, almost two-thirds of racial-minority immigrants come from Asia. The number of Latin American immigrants is expected to grow fourfold in the new century (Henry et al., 2000). Almost all immigrants to Canada live in cities. Recent immigrants are especially attracted to Canada's three largest cities. The majority of recent immigrants have chosen to live in Toronto, Montreal, or Vancouver. Today, nearly half of the population of Toronto and nearly two-fifths of the population of Vancouver is composed of visible minorities. Furthermore, visible minorities make up more than 13 percent of the total population of Canada, in contrast to 6.3 percent in 1986 (Statistics Canada, 2003b).

What effect will these changes have on racial and ethnic relations? Several possibilities exist. On the one hand, conflict between whites and people of colour may become more overt and confrontational. Certainly, the concentration of visible minorities will mean that these groups will become more visible than ever in some Canadian cities. Increasing contact may lead to increased intergroup cohesion and understanding, or it may bring on racism or prejudice. Rapid political changes and the global economy have made people fearful about their future and may cause some to blame "foreigners" for their problems. Interethnic tensions among members of subordinate groups in urban areas may increase as subordinate groups continue to face economic deprivation and discrimination. People may continue to use *sincere fictions*—personal beliefs that reflect larger societal mythologies, such as "I am not racist" or "I have never discriminated against anyone"—even when these are inaccurate perceptions (Feagin and Vera, 1995). Concerns about violence, crime, welfare, education, housing, and taxes may be encompassed in the larger issue of race (Edsall and Edsall, 1992).

On the other hand, there is reason for cautious optimism. Throughout Canadian history, subordinate racial and ethnic groups have struggled to gain the freedom and rights that previously were withheld from them. Today, employment equity programs are alleviating some of the effects of past discrimination

BOX 10.4 YOU CAN MAKE A DIFFERENCE

Fighting Racism

What do you do when you encounter some form of racism in your daily life? Many do nothing for fear of creating awkwardness, reprisal, or other negative social consequences. Does this make you a racist? Race relations experts explain that although it may not be the desired effect, your silence may be interpreted a tacit approval of racism. You have the right, as well as the responsibility, to speak out.

If you are a victim of discrimination you can file a complaint with the Human Rights Commission. If another person files a complaint, you can support him or her by cooperating with the investigating officer. In addition, the New Brunswick Human Rights Commission suggests a number of ways in which you can fight racism:

In the community:

- Take part in activities marking the International Day for the Elimination of Racial Discrimination every March 21. For more information, go to www.march21.gc.ca.
- Join organizations dealing with issues of racism and human rights.
- Create a speakers bureau of persons willing to speak about racism and human rights.
- Explore ways in which community organizations can work together to promote positive race relations.

At your school:

- Object to racist jokes and insults.
- Organize an intercultural music or film festival.
- Invite guests to speak on racism and human rights.
- Show films on prejudice, stereotyping, discrimination, and racism.
- Examine the contents of television, film, radio, and newspapers for stereotypes. Identify and discuss the stereotypes.
- Find out about human rights organizations in your area and what role they play.
- Know the university or college's policy on all forms of racial discrimination.

In the workplace:

- Object to racist jokes and insults.
- Encourage dialogue on racism and human rights.
- Organize a lunchtime film series.
- Encourage human rights awareness at union meetings through guest speakers, films, or other presentations.
- Examine hiring practices to ensure equality of opportunity for all.
- Develop clear policy statements against all forms of racial discrimination and define ways to make them work through cooperation and consensus.

Source: Adapted from *"Say NO to Racism 2005,"* Government of New Brunswick Human Rights Commission

against minority groups as well as addressing systemic and institutional forms of racism that exist in employment. Movements made up of both whites and visible minorities continue to oppose racism in everyday life, to seek to heal divisions among racial groups, and to teach children about racial tolerance (Rutstein, 1993) (see Box 10.4, "You Can Make a Difference"). Many groups hope not only to affect their own countries but also to contribute to worldwide efforts to end racism (Ford, 1994). Norman Buchignani explains the need to end racism:

Racism is a moral issue, which reflects on Canadian society at large. Like sexism,

racism ties us morally and intellectually to centuries-old legitimations and patterns of subordination which simply have no morally justifiable place in today's world. The persistence of racism diminishes us all. (1991:200)

The challenge of trying to keep together a nation composed of people divided by ethnicity, language, and even region is a monumental task—one that will not be resolved in the near future (Rosenburg, 1995). Nevertheless, the elimination of racial–ethnic conflict should be an important government and public priority.

CHAPTER REVIEW

■ **How do race and ethnicity differ?**

A race is a category of people who have been singled out as inferior or superior, often on the basis of real or alleged physical characteristics, such as skin colour, hair texture, eye shape, or other subjectively selected characteristics. An ethnic group is a collection of people distinguished by others or by themselves, primarily on the basis of cultural or nationality characteristics.

■ **Why are race and ethnicity important?**

Race and ethnicity are ingrained in our consciousness. They often form the basis of hierarchical ranking in society and determine who gets what resources: employment, housing, education, and social services.

■ **What are majority and minority groups?**

A majority or dominant group is an advantaged group that has superior resources and rights in society. A minority or subordinate group is a disadvantaged group whose members are subjected to unequal treatment by the majority group. The terms *dominant* and *subordinate* reflect the importance of power in relationships.

■ **What is prejudice?**

Prejudice is a negative attitude based on preconceived notions about members of selected groups. Prejudice is often reinforced by stereotypes and is present in ethnocentric attitudes.

■ **What is discrimination, and how does it differ from prejudice?**

Discrimination involves actions or practices of dominant group members that have a harmful impact on members of a subordinate group. Whereas prejudice involves attitudes, discrimination involves actions. Discriminatory actions range from name-calling to violent actions. Discrimination can be either *de jure* (encoded in law) or *de facto* (informal).

■ **What is racism and what forms does it take?**

Racism refers to an organized set of beliefs about the innate inferiority of some racial groups combined with the power to discriminate on the basis of race. There are many different ways in which racism may manifest itself, including overt racism, polite racism, subliminal racism, institutional racism, and systemic racism.

■ **How do sociologists view racial and ethnic group relations?**

Interactionists suggest that increased contact between people from divergent groups should lead to favourable attitudes and behaviour when members of each group (1) have equal status, (2) pursue the same goals, (3) cooperate with one another to achieve goals, and (4) receive positive feedback when they interact with one another. Functionalists stress that members of subordinate groups become absorbed into the dominant culture. Conflict theorists focus on economic stratification and access to power in race and ethnic relations. Feminist analysts highlight the fact that women who are members of racial and ethnic minorities are doubly disadvantaged as a result of their gender. There is an interactive effect of racism and sexism on the exploitation of women of colour.

■ **How have the experiences of various ethnic groups in Canada differed?**

Aboriginal people suffered greatly from the actions of European settlers, who seized their lands and made them victims of forced assimilation strategies and migration. White Anglo-Saxon Protestants are the most privileged group in Canada, although social class and gender affect their life chances. White ethnics whose ancestors migrated from southern and eastern European countries gradually have made their way into the mainstream of Canadian society. The struggle of francophones, the majority of whom live in Quebec, to receive recognition of their language and culture has been ongoing and is reflected in the increasing identification of Québécois with the separatist movement.

■ **How have Canada's immigration policies past and present affected the composition of Canada's ethnic population?**

Canada's early immigration policies were described as racist and included exclusionary policies directed at Asian populations including Chinese, Japanese, and South Asians, as well as Jews. "White ethnics" who came from European countries comprised the preferred category of immigrants. Changes to the *Immigration Act* in 1962 involving the implementation of a points system opened the door to immigration on a nonracial basis. In 2002 the *Immigration and Refugee Protection Act* was implemented with selection criteria based on human capital attributes and skills of potential immigrants.

KEY TERMS

assimilation 310
authoritarian personality 303
discrimination 303
ethnic group 299
ethnic pluralism 310
ethnocentrism 302
genocide 306
institutionalized racism 307
internal colonialism 311
majority (dominant) group 301
minority (subordinate) group 301
overt racism 306
polite racism 307
prejudice 302
race 299
racial prejudice 302
racism 306
scapegoat 303
segregation 311
social distance 303
split labour market 312
stereotypes 302
subliminal racism 307
systemic racism 308
visible minority 301

NET LINKS

For highlights from the Report of the Royal Commission on Aboriginal Peoples, go to:
http://www.ainc-inac.gc.ca/ch/rcap/rpt/index_e.html

For additional information on First Nations peoples, go to the Aboriginal Web Links site at:
http://www.johnco.com/firstnat/#13

"The Crosspoint" is the Internet's largest collection of links in the field of human rights, antiracism, and anti-facism; see:
http://www.magenta.nl/crosspoint

For a thorough overview of anti-Semitism in Canada, review Dr. Karen Mock's article "Perspectives on Racism: Anti-Semitism in Canada":
http://www1.ca.nizkor.org/hweb/people/m/mock-karen/perspectives-on-racism.html

"Hate on the Internet" by Dr. K. Mock and Lisa Armony, B'nai B'rith Canada, outlines the growth of hate on the Internet, debates the pros and cons of Internet regulations of hate propaganda, and suggests other responses to the presence of hate on the Internet; go to:
http://www.media-awareness.ca/english/resources/articles/online_hate/hate_on_internet.cfm

QUESTIONS FOR CRITICAL THINKING

1. Do you consider yourself defined more by your race, your ethnicity, or neither of these concepts? Explain.
2. Given that minority groups have some common experiences, why is there such deep conflict between certain minority groups?
3. What would need to happen in Canada, both individually and institutionally, for a positive form of ethnic pluralism to flourish in the twenty-first century?
4. Is it possible for members of racial minorities to be racist?

SUGGESTED READINGS

For an in-depth analysis of race and ethnic relations, these texts are excellent:

W. W. Isajiw. *Understanding Diversity: Ethnicity and Race in the Canadian Context*. Toronto: Thompson Educational Publishing, 1999.

Carl E. James and Adrienne Shadd (eds.). *Talking About Identity: Encounters in Race, Ethnicity and Language*. Toronto: Between the Lines, 2001.

Stanley R. Barrett. *Is God a Racist? The Right Wing in Canada*. Toronto: University of Toronto Press, 1987.

Augie Fleras and Jean Leonard Elliott. *Unequal Relations: An Introduction to Race, Ethnic and Aboriginal Dynamics in Canada* 4th ed.). Scarborough, Ont.: Prentice-Hall, 2003.

Frances Henry, Carol Tator. *The Colour of Democracy: Racism in Canadian Society* (3rd ed.). Toronto: Thomson Nelson Canada, 2006.

Carl E. James. *Seeing Ourselves: Exploring Race, Ethnicity, and Culture* (2nd ed.). Toronto: Thompson Educational Publishing, 1999.

For additional information on the experiences of specific racial and ethnic groups:

Menno Boldt. *Surviving as Indians: The Challenge of Self-Government*. Toronto: University of Toronto Press, 1993.

Frideres, James S., and Rene R. Gadacz. *Aboriginal Peoples in Canada: Contemporary Conflicts* (6th ed.). Toronto. Prentice Hall, 2001.

ONLINE STUDY AND RESEARCH TOOLS

THOMSONNOW™ *Thomson NOW!*

Go to **http://hed.nelson.com** to link to ThomsonNOW for *Sociology in Our Times,* Fourth Canadian Edition, your online study tool. First take the **Pre-Test** for this chapter to get your personalized **Study Plan,** which will identify topics you need to review and direct you to the appropriate resources. Then take the **Post-Test** to determine what concepts you have mastered and what you still need work on.

INFOTRAC®

Infotrac College Edition is included free with every new copy of this text. Explore this online library for additional readings, review, and a handy resource for assignments. Visit **www.infotrac-college.com** to access this online database of full-text articles. Enter the key terms from this chapter to start your search.

Sex and Gender

Consider the story of this young Bishop's University student's struggle with anorexia:

"It was March 1995, I was seventeen and in my graduating year of high school when I decided that I wanted to lose weight–ten pounds, maybe fifteen, certainly not more than twenty. I was 5'8" and 155 pounds. I wanted to impress the boys in university and I thought being thin would help. So I went on a diet.

"People with eating disorders do not wake up one morning and say to themselves, 'I am not going to eat anymore' or 'I think I will start bingeing and purging.' Nobody called me fat or told me life would be perfect if I lost fifty pounds. I can't pinpoint one event that directly led to my disorder. I just needed something to depend on, something to think about and to put all my effort into. I just happened to find dieting at the wrong time. It was comforting to take a break from the changes and worries in my life to concentrate on what I was, or wasn't, going to eat that day. It was also nice to pat myself on the back every time I resisted eating.

"By June graduation I was down to 130 pounds. I was satisfied but afraid I might regain weight, so I kept dieting. When I entered university that fall, I weighed 120 pounds. I had heard about the Frosh 15, the fifteen pounds on average that university students supposedly gain in the first

year. I decided that I, dieter extraordinaire, would not become part of that statistic. . . . At Christmas I returned home to a horrified family. I wasn't just thin, I was emaciated. But aside from my looks I still seemed to have it all together. I was an honours student when I entered university and had an 82 percent average after my first semester. I had made lots of friends and had balanced my social and academic obligations. Except for the state of my health, I was a success story.

"When I went back to university in January, my life dissolved both emotionally and physically. I cried at least twice a day, although never in public. I couldn't get up for class. I couldn't even walk up the stairs without sitting down to take a rest. Every single moment was a fight between me and every cell in my body—cells that were begging me to give in and nourish them . . . I knew that I could not continue living that way but I saw no alternative. Losing the anorexia nervosa felt like losing everything" (Rutherford, 1998:107-108).

The story of this young woman is anything but unique. Her comments are similar to those found in numerous sociological studies, including recent research by sociologist Sharlene Hesse-Biber (1996), who found that many women in college and university were also extremely critical of their weight and shape. Many young women in Canada report feeling dissatisfied with their weight. For example, one study found that by the age of eighteen, 80 percent of girls of normal height and weight reported they would like to weigh less. Disordered eating attitudes and behaviour are particularly common among university and college women in Western countries. Recent evidence suggests that the prevalence of eating disorders is rising, and the age of onset for these disorders has fallen (Jones et al., 2001). As these young women are aware, people who deviate significantly from existing weight and appearance norms are often devalued and objectified by others. *Objectification* is the process of treating people as if they were objects or things, not human beings. We objectify people when we judge them on the basis of their physical appearance rather than on the basis of their individual qualities or actions (Schur, 1983). In our society, objectification of women is especially common (see Table 11.1).

Table 11.1 THE OBJECTIFICATION OF WOMEN

GENERAL ASPECTS OF OBJECTIFICATION	OBJECTIFICATION BASED ON CULTURAL PREOCCUPATION WITH "LOOKS"
Women are responded to primarily as "females," while their personal qualities and accomplishments are of secondary importance.	Women often are seen as the objects of sexual attraction, not full human beings—for example, when they are stared at.
Women are seen as being "all alike."	Women are seen by some as depersonalized body parts—for example, "a piece of ass."
Women are seen as being subordinate and passive, so things can easily be "done to a woman"—for example, discrimination, harassment, and violence.	Depersonalized female sexuality is used for cultural and economic purposes—such as in the media, advertising, fashion and cosmetics industries, and pornography.
Women are seen as easily ignored, dismissed, or trivialized.	Women are seen as being "decorative" and status-conferring objects, to be sought (sometimes collected) and displayed by men and sometimes by other women.
	Women are evaluated according to prevailing, narrow "beauty" standards and often feel pressure to conform to appearance norms.

Source: Schur, 1983.

Other studies have found that both men and women may have negative perceptions about their body size, weight, and appearance (Heywood and Dworkin, 2003). Many men compare themselves unfavourably to muscular bodybuilders and believe that they need to gain weight or muscle mass, which for some is associated with masculinity and power (Basow, 1992; Klein, 1993). For women, however, body image is an even greater concern. Women may compare themselves unfavourably to slender stars of film and television and believe that they need to lose weight. They are surrounded by images that define attractiveness as a very particular, thin, "perfect" ideal (Matthews, 2001). Men are less likely to let concerns about appearance affect how they feel about their own competence, worth, and abilities; among women, dislike of their bodies may affect self-esteem and feelings of self-worth (Fisher et al., 1995).

Why do women and men feel differently about their bodies? Cultural differences in appearance norms may explain women's greater concern; they are judged more harshly, and they know it (Abu-Laban and McDaniel, 2001). Throughout life, men and women receive different cultural messages about body image, food, and eating. Men are encouraged to eat, whereas women are made to feel guilty about food (Basow, 1992). Sharlene Hesse-Biber refers to this phenomenon as the *cult of thinness,* in which people worship the "perfect" body and engage in rituals, such as dieting and exercising, with "obsessive attention to monitoring progress—weighing the body at least once a day and constantly checking calories (1996:11). Moreover, the main criterion for joining the cult of thinness is being female (Hesse-Biber, 1996). Similarly, the authors of a recent study describing "the confident, empowered female athlete" as a new cultural icon acknowledge that eating disorders remain an "occupational hazard of appearance-based sports like figure skating, gymnastics, long-distance running, or even swimming . . ." (Heywood and Dworkin, 2003:48).

Body image is only one example of the many socially constructed differences between men and women—differences that relate to gender (a social concept) rather than to a person's biological makeup or sex. In this chapter, we examine the issue of gender: what it is and how it affects us. Before reading on, test your knowledge about gender and body image by taking the quiz in Box 11.1.

Chapter Focus Question: How do expectations about female and male appearance reflect gender inequality?

How do a society's resources and economic structure influence gender stratification?

What are the primary agents of gender socialization?

How does the contemporary workplace reflect gender stratification?

How do functionalist, conflict, feminist, interactionist, and postmodern perspectives on gender differ?

SEX: THE BIOLOGICAL DIMENSION

Whereas the word *gender* is often used to refer to the distinctive qualities of men and women (masculinity and femininity) that are culturally created, *sex* **refers to the biological and anatomical differences between females and males.** At the core of these differences is the chromosomal information transmitted at the moment a child is conceived. The mother contributes an X chromosome and the father either an X chromosome (which produces a female embryo) or a Y chromosome (which produces a male embryo). At birth, male and female infants are distinguished by *primary sex characteristics:* **the genitalia used in the reproductive process.** At puberty, an increased production of hormones results in the development of *secondary sex characteristics:* **the physical traits (other than reproductive organs) that identify an individual's sex.** For women, these include larger breasts, wider hips, and narrower shoulders, a layer of fatty tissue covering the body, and menstruation. For men, they include development of enlarged genitals, a deeper voice, greater height, a more muscular build, and more body and facial hair.

BOX 11.1 SOCIOLOGY AND EVERYDAY LIFE

How Much Do You Know About Body Image and Gender?

True	False	
T	F	1. Most people have an accurate perception of their own physical appearance.
T	F	2. The majority of men express dissatisfaction with some aspect of their bodies.
T	F	3. The prevalence of eating disorders has declined in North America during the last decade.
T	F	4. Physical attractiveness is a more central part of self-concept for women than for men.
T	F	5. Virtually no men have eating problems, such as anorexia and bulimia.
T	F	6. Thinness has always been the "ideal" body image for women.
T	F	7. Women bodybuilders have gained full acceptance in society.
T	F	8. Canada has laws prohibiting employment discrimination on the basis of weight.

Answers on page 330.

BOX 11.1 SOCIOLOGY AND EVERYDAY LIFE

Answers to the Sociology Quiz on Body Image and Gender

1. **False.** Many people do not have a very accurate perception of their own bodies. For example, many young girls and women think of themselves as fat when they are not. Some young boys and men tend to believe that they need well-developed chest and arm muscles, broad shoulders, and a narrow waist (Jones et al., 2001).

2. **True.** In recent studies, up to 95 percent of men believed they needed to improve some aspect of their bodies (Lips, 2001).

3. **False.** More than half of all adult women in North America are currently dieting, and more than three-quarters of normal-weight women think they are too fat. One study found that by the age of eighteen, 80 percent of girls of normal height and weight reported they would like to weigh less (Jones et al., 2001).

4. **True.** Women have been socialized to believe that being physically attractive is very important. Studies have found that weight and body shape are the central determinants of women's perception of their physical attractiveness (Kilbourne, 1994).

5. **False.** Some men do have eating problems such as anorexia and bulimia. These problems have been found especially among gay men and male fashion models and dancers (Tanofsky et al., 1997).

6. **False.** The "ideal" body image for women has changed a number of times. A positive view of body fat has prevailed for most of human history; however, over the last several decades in North America, this view has given way to "fat aversion" (Seid, 1994).

7. **False.** Although bodybuilding among women has gained some degree of acceptance, women bodybuilders still are expected to be very "feminine" and not to overdevelop themselves (George, 2005).

8. **False.** To date, Canada has no laws that specifically prohibit employment discrimination on the basis of weight (Ontario Human Right Commission, 2005).

Hermaphrodites/Transsexuals

Sex is not always clear-cut. Occasionally, a hormone imbalance before birth produces a **hermaphrodite—a person in whom sexual differentiation is ambiguous or incomplete.** Hermaphrodites tend to have some combination of male and female genitalia. In one case, for example, a chromosomally normal (XY) male was born with a penis just one centimetre long and a urinary opening similar to that of a female (Money and Ehrhardt, 1972). In another case, a newborn male had his penis irreversibly damaged during a circumcision and had his gender "reassigned" to female (see Box 11.2). Some people may be genetically of one sex but have the gender identity of the other. That is true for a **transsexual, a person who believes that he or she was born with the body of the wrong sex.** Some transsexuals take hormone treatments or have a sex change operation to alter their genitalia in order to achieve a body congruent with their own sense of sexual identity (Basow, 1992).

Western societies acknowledge the existence of only two sexes; some other societies recognize three—men, women, and *berdaches* (or *hijras* or *xaniths*), biological males who behave, dress, and work and are treated in most respects as women. The closest approximation to a third sex in Western societies is a **transvestite, a male who lives as a woman or a female who lives as a man but does not alter the genitalia.** Although transvestites are not treated as a third sex, they often "pass" for members of that sex because their appearance and mannerisms fall within the range of what is expected from members of the other sex (Lorber, 1994).

Transsexuality may occur in conjunction with homosexuality, but this is frequently not the case. Some researchers believe that both transsexuality and homosexuality have a common prenatal cause, such as a critically timed hormonal release due to stress in the mother or the presence of certain hormone-mimicking chemicals during critical steps of fetal development. Researchers continue to examine this issue and debate the origins of transsexuality and homosexuality.

BOX 11.2 CRITICAL THINKING

Gender Reassignment: "As Nature Made Him"

On April 27, 1966, in Winnipeg, Manitoba, an infant boy's routine circumcision went terribly wrong. Through a medical error, eight-month-old Bruce Reimer was left without a penis. The circumcision of his twin brother, Brian, had gone smoothly and his male genitalia remained intact. In desperation, the twins' parents consulted John Money, medical director of the Gender Identity Clinic at the world-renowned Johns Hopkins University. Based on his research, Money asserted that a person's gender identity and sexual orientation were not biologically determined but rather were the result of socialization. Tragically, Bruce Reimer became the "test case" used to prove this theory.

Dr. Money convinced Bruce's parents to have their son surgically transformed into a girl (he was renamed Brenda), based on his assurance that with appropriate parenting she would grow up to be a feminine, heterosexual woman (LeVay, 2000:1). John Money monitored Brenda and her identical twin, Brian, during their childhood, and he reported extensively in books, journals, and lectures that this "experiment" had been a complete success. According to Money, Brenda had grown up happily feminine, displaying many of the stereotypical traits associated with being female: she was shy, neat, and pretty, and she enjoyed playing dolls and cooking. Most important, Brenda's own gender identity was that of a female, supporting Money's theory that gender was malleable.

This "test case" gave Money enormous professional acclaim and success as it became one of the most famous cases in modern medicine and the social sciences. The case was cited repeatedly for thirty years as proof that our sense of being female or male is not inborn but primarily the result of how we are raised. The case also established a medical precedent for the gender reassignment of thousands of other newborns who were similarly injured during circumcision or who were born with ambiguous genitals.

This "experiment" was in fact a failure from the start and had disastrous results for the Reimer family. The truth was that "Brenda" did not see herself as female, nor did her peers. She preferred to play with her twin brother's toys. She was tormented at school, nicknamed "Cavewoman," and teased for her masculine qualities. Brenda failed at school and was frequently in fights. Finally, when Brenda was a teenager, after years of depression and a suicide attempt, her parents told her the truth about her gender reassignment. In response, Brenda assumed a male gender identity and underwent surgery to create a cosmetic penis. He changed his name to David (in reference to David and Goliath) and eventually married a woman who had three children.

Dr. Money failed to report this final outcome and claimed that he had lost track of the Reimer family, despite the fact that they had never moved (Nussbaum, 2003:1). In 1996, sexologist Milton Diamond from the University of Hawaii found David and revealed the truth to the medical community, destroying Money's professional reputation. The true facts of this case have been particularly helpful in dealing with the treatment of hermaphroditic infants, who in the past were "normalized" to female. Evidence now shows that many, like David, had rejected their medically created gender and had been traumatized by the medical intervention. Tragically, on May 4, 2004, David Reimer committed suicide at the age of thirty-eight.

What conclusions do you draw about gender identity from David Reimer's case? Consider the formation of your own gender identity. What factors have contributed to your being a female or a male? What role does society play in the formulation of gender identity, both in general and in your own life in particular?

Sources: LeVay, 2000; Nussbaum, 2003; and Colapinto, 2001.

Sexual Orientation

Sexual orientation refers to an individual's preference for emotional–sexual relationships with members of the opposite sex (heterosexuality), the same sex (homosexuality), or both (bisexuality) (Lips, 2001). Some scholars believe that sexual orientation is rooted in biological factors that are present at birth; others believe that sexuality has both biological and social components and is not preordained at birth.

The terms *homosexual* and *gay* are most often used in association with males who prefer same-sex relationships; the term *lesbian* is used in association with

No wonder many women are extremely concerned about body image; even billboards communicate cultural messages about appearance.

females who prefer same-sex relationships. Heterosexual individuals, who prefer opposite-sex relationships, are sometimes referred to as *straight*. However, it is important to note that heterosexual people are much less likely to be labelled by their sexual orientation than are people who are gay, lesbian, or bisexual.

What criteria do social scientists use to classify individuals as gay, lesbian, or homosexual? In a definitive study of sexuality in the mid-1990s, researchers at the University of Chicago established three criteria for identifying people as homosexual or bisexual: (1) *sexual attraction* to persons of one's own gender, (2) *sexual involvement* with one or more persons of one's own gender, and (3) *self-identification* as gay, lesbian, or bisexual (Michael et al., 1994). According to these criteria, then, having engaged in a homosexual act does not necessarily classify a person as homosexual. In fact, many respondents in the University of Chicago study indicated that although they had at least one homosexual encounter when they were younger, they were no longer involved in homosexual conduct and never identified themselves as gay, lesbian, or bisexual.

More recent studies have examined how sexual orientation is linked to identity. Sociologist Kristin G. Esterberg (1997) interviewed lesbian and bisexual women to determine how they "perform" lesbian or bisexual identity through daily activities, such as choice of clothing and hairstyles, as well as how they use body language and talk. According to Esterberg (1997), some of the women viewed themselves as being "lesbian from birth," whereas others had experienced shifts in their identities depending on social surroundings, age, and political conditions at specific periods in their lives. Another study looked at gay and bisexual men. Human development scholar Ritch C. Savin-Williams (2004) found that gay/bisexual youths often believe from an early age that they are different from other boys:

> The pattern that most characterized the youths' awareness, interpretation, and affective responses to childhood attractions consisted of an overwhelming desire to be in the company of men. They wanted to touch, smell, see, and hear masculinity. This awareness originated from earliest childhood memories; in this sense, they "always felt gay."

However, most of the boys and young men realized that these feelings were not typical of other males and were uncomfortable when others attempted to make them conform to the established cultural definitions of masculinity, such as showing a great interest in team sports, competition, and aggressive pursuits.

Recently, the term *transgender* was created to describe individuals whose appearance, behaviour, or self-identification does not conform to common social rules of gender expression. Transgenderism is sometimes used to refer to those who cross-dress, to transsexuals, and to others outside mainstream categories. Although some gay and lesbian advocacy groups oppose the concept of transgender as being somewhat meaningless, others applaud the term as one that might help unify diverse categories of people based on sexual identity. Various organizations of gays, lesbians, and transgender persons have been unified in their desire to reduce hate crimes and other forms of **homophobia—extreme prejudice directed at gays, lesbians, bisexuals, and others who are perceived as not being heterosexual.**

GENDER: THE CULTURAL DIMENSION

Gender **refers to the culturally and socially constructed differences between females and males found in the meanings, beliefs, and practices** associated with "femininity" and "masculinity." Although biological differences between women and men are very important, most "sex differences" actually are socially constructed "gender differences" (Gailey, 1987). According to sociologists, social and cultural processes, not biological "givens," are most important in defining what females and males are, what they should do, and what sorts of relations do or should exist between them (Ortner and Whitehead, 1981; Lott, 1994). Sociologist Judith Lorber (1994:6) summarizes the importance of gender:

> Gender is a human invention, like language, kinship, religion, and technology; like them, gender organizes human social life in culturally patterned ways. Gender organizes social relations in everyday life as well as in the major social structures, such as social class and the hierarchies of bureaucratic organizations.

Virtually everything social in our lives is *gendered:* people continually distinguish between males and females and evaluate them differentially (Mackie, 1995). Gender is an integral part of the daily experiences of both women and men (Mandell, 2001).

A microlevel analysis of gender focuses on how individuals learn gender roles and acquire a gender identity. **Gender role refers to the attitudes, behaviour, and activities that are socially defined as appropriate for each sex and are learned through the socialization process** (Lips, 2001). For example, in Canadian society, males traditionally are expected to demonstrate aggressiveness and toughness while females are expected to be passive and nurturing. **Gender identity is a person's perception of the self as female or male.** Typically established between eighteen months and three years of age, gender identity is a powerful aspect of our selfconcept (Lips, 2001). Although this identity is an individual perception, it is developed through interaction with others. As a result, most people form a gender identity that matches their biological sex: most biological females think of themselves as female, and most biological males think of themselves as male. Body consciousness is a part of gender identity. **Body consciousness is how a person perceives and feels about his or her body; it also includes an awareness of social conditions in society that contribute to this self-knowledge** (Thompson, 1994). Consider, for example, these comments by Steve Michalik, a former Mr. Universe:

> I was small and weak, and my brother Anthony was big and graceful, and my old man made no bones about loving him and hating me . . . The minute I walked in from school, it was, "You worthless little s—t, what are you doing home so early?" His favorite way to torture me was to tell me he was going to put me in a home. We'd be driving along . . . and we'd pass a building with iron bars on the windows, and he'd stop the car and say to me, "Get out. This is the home we're putting you in." I'd be standing there sobbing on the curb—I was maybe eight or nine at the time. (quoted in Klein, 1993:273)

As we grow up, we become aware, as Michalik did, that the physical shape of our bodies subjects us to the approval or disapproval of others. While being small and weak may be considered positive attributes for women, they are considered negative characteristics for "real men."

A macrolevel analysis of gender examines structural features, external to the individual, that perpetuate gender inequality. These structures have been referred to as *gendered institutions,* meaning that gender is one of the major ways by which social life is organized in all sectors of society. Gender is embedded in the images, ideas, and language of a society and is used as a means to divide up work, allocate resources, and distribute power. For example, every society uses gender to assign certain tasks—ranging from child rearing to warfare—to females and to males, and differentially rewards those who perform these duties.

These institutions are reinforced by a *gender belief system* that includes all of the ideas regarding masculine and feminine attributes that are held to be valid in a society. This belief system is legitimated by religion, science, law, and other societal values (Lorber, 1994, 2001). For example, gendered belief systems may change over time as gender roles change. Many fathers take care of young children today, and there is a much greater acceptance of this change in roles. However, popular stereotypes about men and women, as well as cultural norms about gender-appropriate appearance and behaviour, serve to reinforce gendered institutions in society (Mandell, 2001).

The Social Significance of Gender

Gender is a social construction with important consequences in everyday life. Just as stereotypes regarding race/ethnicity have built-in notions of superiority and inferiority, gender stereotypes hold that men and women are inherently different in attributes, behaviour, and aspirations. Stereotypes define men as strong, rational, dominant, independent, and less concerned with their appearance. Women are stereotyped as weak, emotional, nurturing, dependent, and anxious about their appearance.

The social significance of gender stereotypes is illustrated by eating problems. The three most common eating problems are anorexia, bulimia, and obesity. With *anorexia,* a person has lost at least 25 percent of body weight due to a compulsive fear of becoming fat (Ressler, 1998). With *bulimia,* a person binges by consuming large quantities of food and then purges the food by induced vomiting, laxatives, or fasting (Renzetti and Curran, 1992). A relatively new eating disorder—activity bulimia—may become more dangerous than both anorexia and bulimia. Activity bulimia is characterized by excessive exercising, usually attached to feelings of guilt about eating. The danger with this eating disorder is that it is virtually impossible to detect until serious health problems arise (Sharell, 1996). With *obesity,* individuals are 20 percent or more above their desirable weight, as established by the medical profession. For a 5-foot-4-inch (1.7-metre) woman, that is about twenty-five pounds (11 kilograms); for a 5-foot-10-inch (1.8-metre) man, about thirty pounds (13.5 kilograms) (Burros, 1994:1).

Sociologist Becky W. Thompson argues that, based on stereotypes, the primary victims of eating problems are presumed to be white, middle-class, heterosexual women. However, such problems also exist among women of colour, working-class women, lesbians, and some men. According to Thompson, explanations regarding the relationship between gender and eating problems must take into account a complex array of social factors, including gender socialization and women's responses to problems

For males, objectification and gender stereotyping may result in excessive body building.

such as racism and emotional, physical, and sexual abuse (Thompson, 1994; see also Heywood, 1998).

Bodybuilding is another gendered experience. *Bodybuilding* is the process of deliberately cultivating an increase in mass and strength of the skeletal muscles by means of lifting and pushing weights (Mansfield and McGinn, 1993). In the past, bodybuilding was predominantly a male activity; musculature connoted power, domination, and virility (Klein, 1993). Today, an increasing number of women engage in this activity. As gendered experiences, eating problems and bodybuilding have more in common than we might think. Historian Susan Bordo (1993) has noted that the anorexic body and the muscled body are not opposites; instead, they exist on a continuum because they are united against a "common platoon of enemies: the soft, the loose; unsolid, excess flesh." The *body* is objectified in both compulsive dieting and bodybuilding (Mansfield and McGinn, 1993:53).

Sexism

Sexism is the subordination of one sex, usually female, based on the assumed superiority of the other sex. Sexism directed at women has three components: (1) negative attitudes toward women, (2) stereotypical beliefs that reinforce, complement, or justify the prejudice, and (3) discrimination—acts that exclude, distance, or keep women separate (Lott, 1994).

Can men be victims of sexism? Although women are more often the target of sexist remarks and practices, men can be victims of sexist assumptions. As social psychologist Hilary M. Lips (1993:11) notes, "Sexism cuts both ways; for example, the other side of the prejudiced attitude that [usually bars] women from combat positions in the military is the attitude that it is somehow less upsetting to have male soldiers killed than to have female soldiers killed."

Like racism, sexism is used to justify discriminatory treatment. When women participate in what is considered gender-inappropriate endeavours in the workplace, at home, or in leisure activities, they often find that they are the targets of prejudice and discrimination. Obvious manifestations of sexism are found in the undervaluing of women's work, in hiring and promotion practices that effectively exclude women from an organization or confine them to the bottom of the organizational hierarchy, and in the denial of equal access for women to educational opportunities (Armstrong and Armstrong, 1994). Some people feel that pornography serves to perpetuate sexism by portraying women as objects. Women who attempt to enter nontraditional occupations (such as firefighting, welding, and steelworking) or professions (such as dentistry and architecture) often encounter hurdles that men do not face. Women may experience discrimination because they are perceived to be "out of place." Consider the following comments from a male steelworker in Hamilton regarding the hiring of female steelworkers:

> It's dirty, heavy, it's no climate for a woman. The men's world is a little rougher than the women's. Physically a man is in better shape. Men are more mechanically minded . . . There is nothing wrong with women, it's just that sometimes with heavy work . . . if you take the overall picture, masculinity has always been the man's. It doesn't mean that he has more brains because that is not true, but muscularity. I think that women should be outside. It is no place for women. I hate it. (Livingston and Luxton, 1995:190)

Sexism is interwoven with *patriarchy*—**a hierarchical system of social organization in which cultural, political, and economic structures are controlled by men.** By contrast, *matriarchy* **is a hierarchical system of social organization in which cultural, political, and economic structures are controlled by women;** however, few (if any) societies have been organized in this manner (Lengermann and Wallace, 1985). Patriarchy is reflected in the way men may think of their position as men as a given while women may deliberate on what their position in society should be. As sociologist Virginia Cyrus (1993:6) explains, "Under patriarchy, men are seen as 'natural' heads of households, political candidates, corporate executives, university presidents, etc. Women, on the other hand, are men's subordinates, playing such supportive roles as housewife, mother, nurse, and secretary." Gender inequality and a division of labour based on male dominance are nearly universal, as we will see in the following discussion of the origins of gender-based stratification.

GENDER STRATIFICATION IN HISTORICAL PERSPECTIVE

How do tasks in a society come to be defined as "men's work" or "women's work"? Three factors are important in determining the gendered division of labour in a society: (1) the type of subsistence base, (2) the supply of and demand for labour, and (3) the extent to which women's child-rearing activities are compatible with certain types of work. *Subsistence* refers to the means by which a society gains the basic necessities of life, including food, shelter, and clothing (Nielsen, 1990). You may recall that societies are classified, based on subsistence, as hunting and gathering societies, horticultural and pastoral societies, agrarian societies, industrial societies, and postindustrial societies.

Hunting and Gathering Societies

The earliest known division of labour between women and men is in hunting and gathering societies. While the men hunt for wild game, women gather roots and berries (Nielsen, 1990). A relatively equitable relationship exists because neither sex has the ability to provide all of the food necessary for survival. When wild game is nearby, both men and women may hunt (Basow, 1992). When it is far away, hunting becomes incompatible with child rearing (which women tend to do because they breast-feed their young), and women are placed at a disadvantage in terms of contributing to the food supply (Lorber, 1994). In most hunting and gathering societies, women are full economic partners with men; relations between them tend to be cooperative and relatively egalitarian (Chafetz, 1984; Bonvillain, 2001). Little social stratification of any kind is found because people do not acquire a food surplus.

A few hunting and gathering societies remain, including the Bushmen of Africa, the Aborigines of Australia, and the Yanomamö of South America.

Horticultural and Pastoral Societies

In horticultural societies, which first developed ten to twelve thousand years ago, a steady source of food becomes available. People are able to grow their own food because of hand tools, such as the digging stick and the hoe. Women make an important contribution to food production because hoe cultivation is compatible with child care. A fairly high degree of gender equality exists because neither sex controls the food supply (Basow, 1992).

When inadequate moisture in an area makes planting crops impossible, *pastoralism*—the domestication of large animals to provide food—develops. Herding primarily is done by men, and women contribute relatively little to subsistence production in such societies. In some herding societies, women have relatively low status; their primary value is their ability to produce male offspring so that the family lineage can be preserved and enough males will exist to protect the group against attack (Nielsen, 1990).

Social practices contribute to gender inequality in horticultural and pastoral societies. Male dominance is promoted by practices, such as menstrual taboos, bridewealth, and polygyny (Nielsen, 1990). *Polygyny*—the marriage of one man to multiple wives—contributes to power differences between women and men. A man with multiple wives can produce many children who will enhance his resources, take care of him in his "old age," and become heirs to his property (Nielsen, 1990). *Menstrual taboos* place women in a subordinate position by segregating them into menstrual huts for the duration of their monthly cycle. Even when women are not officially segregated, they are defined as "unclean." *Bridewealth*—the payment of a price by a man for a wife—turns women into property that can be bought and sold. The man gives the bride's family material goods in exchange for their daughter's exclusive sexual services and his sole claim to their offspring.

In contemporary horticultural societies, women do most of the farming while men hunt game, clear land, work with arts and crafts, make tools, participate in religious and ceremonial activities, and engage in war (Nielsen, 1990). A combination of horticultural and pastoral activities is found in some contemporary societies in Asia, Africa, the Middle East, and South America. These societies are characterized by more gender inequality than in hunting and gathering societies but less than in agrarian societies (Bonvillain, 2001).

Agrarian Societies

In agrarian societies, which first developed about eight to ten thousand years ago, gender inequality and male dominance become institutionalized. The most extreme form of gender inequality developed about five thousand years ago in societies in the fertile crescent around the Mediterranean Sea (Lorber, 1994). Agrarian societies rely on agriculture—farming done by animal-drawn or energy-powered plows and equipment. Because agrarian tasks require more labour and greater physical strength than horticultural ones, men become more involved in food production. It has been suggested that women are excluded from these tasks because they are viewed as too weak for the work and because child care responsibilities are considered incompatible with the full-time labour that the tasks require (Nielsen, 1990).

Why does gender inequality increase in agrarian societies? Scholars cannot agree on an answer; however, some suggest that it results from private ownership of property. When people no longer have to move continually in search of food, they can acquire a surplus. Men gain control over the disposition of the surplus and the kinship system, and this control serves men's interests (Lorber, 1994). The importance of producing "legitimate" heirs to inherit the surplus increases significantly, and women's lives become more secluded and restricted as men attempt to ensure the legitimacy of their children. Premarital virginity and marital fidelity are required; indiscretions are punished (Nielsen, 1990). However, some scholars argue that male dominance existed before the private ownership of property (Firestone, 1970; Lerner, 1986).

Four practices in agrarian societies contribute to the subordination of women. *Purdah,* found primarily among Hindus and Muslims, requires the seclusion of women, extreme modesty in apparel, and the visible subordination of women to men. Women must show deference to men by walking behind them, speaking only when spoken to, and eating only after the men have finished a meal (Nielsen, 1990).

Footbinding is the custom of thwarting the growth of a female's feet that was practised in China beginning around 1000 C.E. and continued into the early twentieth century. The toes of young girls are bent under and continually bound tighter to the soles of their feet. As a result, women may experience extreme pain as their toenails grow into their feet or develop serious infections due to lack of blood circulation (Dworkin, 1974).

Suttee (most common in parts of India) is the sacrificial killing of a widow upon the death of her husband. Although some women allegedly choose to make this sacrifice, others are tied to their husband's funeral pyre. The practice is justified on the basis that the widow's sins in a former life are responsible for her husband's death. However, the actual purpose is to ensure that the husband's male relatives, rather than the widow, inherit his property (Nielsen, 1990).

Genital mutilation is a surgical procedure performed on young girls as a method of sexual control (Nielsen, 1990). The mutilation involves cutting off all or part of a girl's clitoris and labia, and in some cases stitching her vagina closed until marriage (Simons, 1993b). Often justified on the erroneous belief that the Koran commands it, these procedures are supposed to ensure that women are chaste before marriage and have no extramarital affairs after marriage. Genital mutilation has resulted in the maiming of many females, some of whom have died as a result of hemorrhage, infection, or other complications. Genital mutilation is still practised in more than twenty-five countries.

In sum, male dominance is very strong in agrarian societies. Women are secluded, subordinated, and mutilated as a means of regulating their sexuality and protecting paternity. Most of the world's population currently lives in agrarian societies in various stages of industrialization. Issues concerning the rights of women in some of these societies became the subject of media attention after the 2001 terrorist attacks on the United States were linked to an organization with ties to the repressive Taliban regime in Afghanistan (see Box 11.3).

BOX 11.3 SOCIOLOGY IN GLOBAL PERSPECTIVE

Oppression, Resistance, and the Women of Afghanistan

It was a very emotional moment. After years the women of Afghanistan came out in the open. Under the Taliban we all wore burkas and did not know each other. Now we all know each other's faces. . . . I just want to tell the world that women should be able to speak out about their own problems.

−Soraya Parlika, a prominent Afghan activist, describing how she felt when many women removed their veils after the overthrow of the Taliban regime (qtd. in McCarthy, 2001: 46)

Although the plight of women and girls in Afghanistan was already a topic of concern for some international women's activist groups prior to the September 11, 2001, terrorist attacks, it was not until after this date that U.S. political leaders and the media highlighted the problems that many Afghan women had experienced for nearly a half decade under the Taliban. After the Taliban's takeover of that country in 1996, Afghan women were prohibited from most employment, walking alone on the streets, and teaching or studying in the schools. Residents were required to paint their windows black so that passersby could not see the face of any woman in the home (Lacayo, 2001). During the Taliban era, women were virtually imprisoned in their homes.

However, women had not always been so oppressed in Afghanistan. Prior to the Taliban takeover, Afghan women comprised 60 percent of the teachers and 50 percent of students at Kabul University; they had also been 40 percent of the doctors and 70 percent of the schoolteachers. After the takeover, many schools were closed because of a shortage of teachers and students, and women and girls were forced to wear a head-to-toe covering called a "burqa" (or "burka"), which has only a small mesh opening through which the person can see and breathe (NOW, 2002).

Although women lost virtually all of their rights under the repressive Taliban regime, journalists and other social analysts have documented how, even under these adverse conditions, some Afghan women subtly fought against the Taliban's oppression of women through acts of resistance. Some women ran secret home schools so that girls could continue their education, while other women operated clandestine businesses, such as beauty salons and laundries in an effort to obtain enough money to feed their children (Waldman, 2001).

What rights will emerge for the women of Afghanistan? It has been suggested by some analysts that people who live in North America are not able to fully understand the many factors that are involved in the struggle for women's rights in other countries. According to these observers, our beliefs about women's rights are linked to Western thinking and the ideas of feminist movements in Western Europe and North America, which are not applicable to people in other nations and cultures. According to Rina Amiri (2001:A21), senior associate for research with the Women Waging Peace Initiative at Harvard's Kennedy School of Government,

It has come to be assumed in much of the Muslim world that to be a proponent of women's rights is to be pro-Western. This enmeshing of gender and geopolitics has robbed Muslim women of their ability to develop a discourse on their rights independent of a cultural debate between the Western and Muslim worlds.

Many social scientists who specialize in international relations hope that such a discourse−free of cultural bias−will develop so that girls and women will not continue to experience the high levels of subordination that exist in many areas of the world today. Although not as oppressive as the rules established by the Taliban, these patterns of subordination may limit the human potential of more than half of the population of these regions.

Industrial Societies

An *industrial society* is one in which factory or mechanized production has replaced agriculture as the major form of economic activity (Nielsen, 1990:49). As societies industrialize, the status of women tends to decline further. Industrialization in Canada created a gap between the nonpaid work performed by women at home and the paid work that increasingly was performed by men and unmarried women (Krahn and Lowe, 1998; Armstrong and Armstrong, 1994).

In Canada, the division of labour between men and women in the middle and upper classes became much more distinct with industrialization. The men were responsible for being "breadwinners," while the women were seen as "homemakers." In this new "cult of domesticity" (also referred to as the "cult of true womanhood"), the home became a private, personal sphere in which women created a haven for the family (Mandell and Momirov, 1999). Those who supported the cult of domesticity argued that women were the natural keepers of the domestic sphere and that children were the mother's responsibility. Meanwhile, the "breadwinner" role placed enormous pressure on men to support their families—being a good provider was considered to be a sign of manhood. However, this gendered division of labour increased the economic and political subordination of women.

The cult of true womanhood not only increased white women's dependence on men but also became a source of discrimination against women of colour, based on both their race and the fact that many of them had to work in order to survive. Employed, working-class white women were similarly stereotyped; at the same time they became economically dependent on their husbands because their wages were so much lower.

Although industrialization was a source of upward mobility for many whites, most people of colour were left behind. For example, the cult of domesticity was distinctly white and middle or upper class. White families with sufficient means hired domestic servants to do much of the household work. In the early 1900s, many Black women (as well as white non-English-speaking European women) were employed as household servants (Das Gupta, 2000).

Postindustrial Societies

Postindustrial societies are ones in which technology supports a service- and information-based economy. In such societies, the division of labour in paid employment is increasingly based on whether people provide or apply information or are employed in service jobs, such as fast-food restaurant counter help or health care workers. For both women and men in the labour force, formal education is increasingly crucial for economic and social success. However, as some women have moved into the entrepreneurial, managerial, and professional occupations in society, many others have remained in the low-paying service sector, which affords few opportunities for upward advancement.

Will technology change the gendered division of labour in postindustrial societies? Scholars do not agree on the effects of computers, the Internet, the World Wide Web, cellular phones, and many newer forms of communications technology on the role of women in society. For example, some feminist writers had a pessimistic view of the impact of computers and monitors on women's health and safety, predicting that women in secretarial and administrative roles would experience an increase in eyestrain, headaches, risks of radiation, and other problems, such as carpal tunnel syndrome. However, some medical experts now believe that such problems extend to both men and women, as computers have become omnipresent in more people's lives. The term "24/7" has come to mean that a person is available "twenty-four hours a day, seven days a week" via cell phones, pocket pagers, fax machines, e-mail, and other means of communication, whether the individual is at the office or six thousand kilometres away on "vacation."

How does the division of labour change in families in postindustrial societies? For a variety of reasons, more households are headed by women with no adult male present. Chapter 15 ("Families and Intimate Relationships") discusses a number of reasons why the division of labour in household chores in some families now is between a woman and her children rather than between women and men. Consider, for example, that more than one-sixth (17 percent) of all Canadian children live with their mother only (as contrasted with just 3 percent who reside with their father only) (Statistics Canada, 2002o). This means that women in these households truly have a double burden, both from family responsibilities and the necessity of holding gainful employment in the labour force.

Even in single-person or two-parent households, programming "labour-saving" devices (if they can be afforded) often means that a person must have some leisure time to learn how to do the programming. According to analysts, leisure is deeply divided among gender lines, and women have less time to "play in the house" than do men and boys. Some Web sites seek to appeal to women who have economic resources but are short on time, making it possible for them to shop, gather information, "telebank," and communicate with others at all hours of the day and night.

In postindustrial societies, such as Canada, close to 60 percent of adult women are in the labour force, meaning that finding time to care for children, help aging parents, and meet the demands of the workplace will continue to place a heavy burden on women, despite living in an information- and service-oriented economy.

How people accept new technologies and the effect these technologies have on gender stratification are related to how people are socialized into gender roles. However, gender-based stratification remains rooted in the larger social structures of society, which individuals have little ability to control.

GENDER AND SOCIALIZATION

We learn gender-appropriate behaviour through the socialization process. Our parents, teachers, friends, and the media all serve as gendered institutions that communicate to us our earliest, and often most lasting, beliefs about the social meanings of being male or female and thinking and behaving in masculine or feminine ways. Some gender roles have changed dramatically in recent years; others remain largely unchanged over time.

Are children's toys a reflection of their own preferences and choices? How do toys reflect gender socialization by parents and other adults?

Many parents prefer boys to girls because of stereotypical ideas about the relative importance of males and females to the future of the family and society (Achilles, 1996). Although some parents prefer boys to girls because they believe old myths about the biological inferiority of females, research suggests that social expectations also play a major role in this preference. We are socialized to believe that it is important to have a son, especially as a first or only child. For many years, it was assumed that a male child could support his parents in their later years and carry on the family name.

Across cultures, boys are preferred to girls, especially when the number of children that parents can have is limited by law or economic conditions. For example, in China, which strictly regulates the allowable number of children to one per family, a disproportionate number of female fetuses are aborted (Basow, 1992). In India, the practice of aborting female fetuses is widespread, and female infanticide occurs frequently (Achilles, 1996). As a result, both India and China have a growing surplus of young men who will face a shortage of women their own age (Shenon, 1994).

In North America, some sex selection no doubt takes place through abortion. However, most women seek abortions because of socioeconomic factors, problematic relationships with partners, health-related concerns, and lack of readiness or ability to care for a child (or another child) (Lott, 1994).

Parents and Gender Socialization

From birth, parents act toward children on the basis of the child's sex. Baby boys are perceived to be less fragile than girls and tend to be treated more roughly by their parents. Girl babies are thought to be "cute, sweet, and cuddly" and receive more gentle treatment (MacDonald and Parke, 1986). When girl babies cry, parents respond to them more quickly, and parents are more prone to talk and sing to girl babies (Basow, 1992). However, one early study ("The Favored Infants," 1976) found that African American mothers "rubbed, patted, rocked, touched, kissed and talked to" boy babies more than girl babies.

Children's toys reflect their parents' gender expectations. Gender-appropriate toys for boys include computer games, trucks and other vehicles, sports equipment, and war toys, such as guns and soldiers (Richardson and Simpson, 1982). Girls' toys include Barbie dolls, play makeup, and homemaking items. Parents' choices of toys for their children are not likely to change in the near future (see Box 11.4).

BOX 11.4 SOCIOLOGY AND THE MEDIA

Red Jack: Revenge of the Brethren, Barbie Super Sports, and Gendered Play

To play *Red Jack: Revenge of the Brethren:*

You take the role of Nicholas Dove, a dreamer who lives in the doomed island of Lizard Point. As you walk into town on a stormy night, you come across a bunch of pirates who have docked to stock up on ale. As you converse with the various crew members, you realize that this is your way off this lowly island. You decide to go with the pirates, who are trying to find out who has been killing the Brethren (a renegade band of privateers, formerly led by Red Jack, who was killed because of an unknown traitor). You join the pirates and the two remaining Brethren to find the traitor. (IGN Entertainment, 2003)

To play *Barbie Super Sports:*

You decide whether you want to be Barbie or one of her friends—Christie, Kira or Teresa. Then, after choosing between in-line skating and snowboarding, you'll go shopping for a coordinating outfit and the appropriate sports-specific footgear (skates or boards). You then go to the sport's practice area and listen to Barbie as she tells you the requirements for the sport. For example, you may be required to race against the clock, collect pink balloons, jump over fountains in an oriental garden, or smash into snowmen on a slippery slope. At the end of each race, you are awarded tickets that can be traded for faster skates and snowboards.

—Based on a review of *Barbie Super Sports* by Jim Fleming (2000)

Do newer forms of media, including computer games, bring equal rewards to girls and boys in regard to gender socialization? One analyst answers this question by noting that male control of computers is supported by the vast libraries of games software with characteristics conventionally described as masculine: an emphasis on competition and violence

(Grint and Woolgar, 1997). In this case, the technology is physically flexible and can easily be used by both girls and boys, but the social construction of gender is reproduced by software programs, such as Barbie Super Sports and Red Jack: Revenge of the Brethren.

Through the magic of computer graphics, girls can experience the "perfect body" myth as they are exposed to Barbie's unrealistic measurements and her beautiful clothing even when skating or snowboarding. By contrast, boys playing Red Jack are engaged in a computer-animated tale of "villainous betrayal, supernatural curses, and buried treasure" (Herz, 1998a:D4). Children's and young people's encounters with Barbie or Red Jack are examples of *simulacra*, the term that postmodernist theorist Jean Baudrillard uses to describe a situation in which simulation replaces a reality that never existed. For example, instead of playing with a real person, or even a plastic Barbie doll with genuine nylon hair, girls in cyberspace amuse themselves with a virtual doll on a screen. Likewise, boys playing Red Jack seek "to uncover the traitor, revenge the great fallen pirate, dig up gold, get the girl and sail off into the Caribbean sunset" (Herz, 1998a:D4).

What influence will virtual Barbie and Red Jack have on young people? According to a Mattel spokesperson, girls who play with virtual Barbie will spend more time on the computer and gain similar skills and equal footing with boys in the job market (Herz, 1998b). Likewise, boys playing with Red Jack may learn "masculine" behaviour and problem-solving skills through their analysis of what the virtual actors should do next in their quest to gain the upper hand.

However, to further examine the issue of gendered play, think about these questions: What happens if a boy wants to play with Barbie computerized games? Is it different if a girl wants to play with a "male-oriented" game, such as Red Jack? What do you think?

A group of university students in a recent study was shown slides of toys and asked to decide which ones they would buy for girls and boys. Most said they would buy guns, soldiers, jeeps, carpenter tools, and red bicycles for boys; girls would get baby dolls, dishes, sewing kits, jewellery boxes, and pink bicycles (Fisher-Thompson, 1990).

Differential treatment leads to differential development. A doll or a stuffed animal in a girl's hand calls for "hugging, stroking, and tender loving care"; a ball

From an early age, a number of societal influences encourage us to learn gender-appropriate behaviour.

in a boy's hand "demands bouncing, throwing, and kicking" (Lott, 1994:40). When children are old enough to help with household chores, they often are assigned different tasks. Maintenance chores (such as mowing the lawn) are assigned to boys while domestic chores (such as shopping, cooking, and cleaning the table) are assigned to girls. Chores also may become linked with future occupational choices and personal characteristics. Girls who are responsible for domestic chores, such as caring for younger brothers and sisters, may learn nurturing behaviours that later translate into employment as a nurse or schoolteacher. Boys may learn about computers and other types of technology that lead to different career options.

Because most studies of gender socialization by parents focus on white, middle-class families, it is probably inappropriate to assume that the patterns of differential parental treatment of girls and boys hold true in all respects for other class and racial groups (Lips, 2001). For example, children from middle- and upper-income families are less likely to be assigned gender-linked chores than those from lower-income backgrounds. In addition, analysts have found that gender-linked chore assignments occur less frequently in African American families, where both sons and daughters tend to be socialized toward independence, employment, and child care (Bardwell, Cochran, and Walker, 1986; Hale-Benson, 1986). Sociologist Patricia Hill Collins (1991) suggests that African American mothers are less likely to socialize their

daughters into roles as subordinates; instead, they are likely to teach them a critical posture that allows them to cope with contradictions.

Just as appropriate "masculine" or "feminine" behaviour is learned through interaction with parents and other caregivers, inappropriate behaviour, such as eating problems, can be learned from parents. Nicole Annesi tells how she learned about binging and purging from her mother:

> I was seven years old the first time I was exposed to my mother's bulimia. It was after dinner one evening. After Mom and I cleared the table . . . she quickly disappeared into the bathroom . . . What was unusual about these visits was that they became consistent. After each meal Mom would visit the bathroom and come out a few minutes later looking pale, yet refreshed . . .
>
> So after the dishes were cleared away that evening, I disappeared into the bathroom. I hid in the tub, behind the navy blue, opaque curtain . . . like clockwork, in she came. I peered between the curtains to find my mother bent over the toilet, like she was going to get sick or something. And then I watched her . . . She placed a popsicle stick down her throat and made herself sick. How weird, I thought to myself. Mom comes into the bathroom every night to stick one of these doctor sticks down her throat! . . .
>
> I began to do some thinking myself . . . I knew when I got sick, afterwards my stomach would flatten out. I felt lighter. So one day after school I ate a bag of Pecan Sandies. I stuffed myself until I couldn't swallow. Afterwards I made my way to the upstairs bathroom and locked the door behind me. I turned on the faucet so that nothing could be heard . . . That day I became a seven-year-old bulimic. (Annesi, 1993:91–93)

Many parents are aware of the effect that gender socialization has on their children and make a conscientious effort to provide nonsexist experiences for them. For example, one study found that mothers with nontraditional views encourage their daughters to be independent (Brooks-Gunn, 1986). Many fathers also take an active role in socializing their sons to be thoughtful and caring individuals who do not live by traditional gender stereotypes. However, peers often make nontraditional gender socialization much more difficult for parents and children (see Rabinowitz and Cochran, 1994).

Peers and Gender Socialization

Peers help children learn prevailing gender role stereotypes, as well as gender-appropriate—and inappropriate—behaviour. During the school years, same-sex peers have a powerful effect on how children see their gender roles (Maccoby and Jacklin, 1987); children are more socially acceptable to their peers when they conform to gender stereotypes (Martin, 1989).

Male peer groups place more pressure on boys to do "masculine" things than female peer groups place on girls to do "feminine" things (Fagot, 1984). For example, girls wear jeans and other "boy" clothes, play soccer and softball, and engage in other activities traditionally associated with males. But, if a boy wears a dress, plays hopscotch with girls, and engages in other activities associated with being female, he will be ridiculed by his peers. This distinction between the relative value of boys' and girls' behaviours strengthens the cultural message that masculine activities and behaviour are more important and more acceptable (Wood, 1999).

During adolescence, peers often are more influential agents of gender socialization than adults. Peers are thought to be especially important in boys' development of gender identity (Maccoby and Jacklin, 1987). Male bonding that occurs during adolescence is believed to reinforce masculine identity (Gaylin, 1992) and to encourage gender-stereotypical attitudes and behaviour (Huston, 1985; Martin, 1989). For example, male peers have a tendency to ridicule and bully others about their appearance, size, and weight. One woman painfully recalled walking down the halls at school when boys would flatten themselves against the lockers and cry, "Wide load!" At lunchtime, the boys made a production of watching her eat lunch and frequently made sounds like pig grunts or moos (Kolata, 1993). Because peer acceptance is so important for both males and females during their first two decades, such actions can have very harmful consequences for the victims.

As young adults, men and women still receive many gender-related messages from peers. Among university students, for example, peers play an important role in career choices and the establishment of long-term, intimate relationships. Male peers may pressure other men to participate in "male bonding" rituals that are abusive of women (DeKeseredy and Kelly, 1995). For example, fraternity initiations may require pledges to participate in behaviour ranging from "showing their manhood"

to gang rapes (O'Sullivan, 1993). Some of the research suggests that male peers are often unable to show a man how to effectively interact intimately with other people (Tannen, 1990; DeKeseredy and Kelly, 1995).

Peer groups for both women and men on university campuses are organized largely around gender relations (Holland and Eisenhart, 1990). In a study that followed a number of women students at two universities, anthropologists Dorothy C. Holland and Margaret A. Eisenhart (1990) found that the peer system propelled women into a world of romance in which their attractiveness to men counted most; the women were subjected to a "sexual auction block." Although peers initially did not influence the women's choices of majors and careers, they did influence whether the women continued to pursue their initial goals, changed their course of action, or were "derailed" (Holland and Eisenhart, 1981, 1990).

If Holland and Eisenhart's research can be generalized to other colleges and universities, peer pressure often is at its strongest in relation to appearance norms. As other researchers have shown, peer pressure can strongly influence a person's body consciousness. Women in university often feel pressure to be very thin, as Karen explains:

"Do you diet?" asked a friend [in my first year of university], as I was stuffing a third home-made chocolate chip cookie in my mouth. "Do you know how many calories there are in that one cookie?"

Stopping to think for a moment as she and two other friends stared at me, probably wanting to ask me the same question, I realized that I really didn't even know what a calorie was . . .

From that moment, I'd taken on a new enemy, one more powerful and destructive than any human can be. One that nearly fought me to the death—my death . . .

I just couldn't eat food anymore. I was so obsessed with it that I thought about it every second . . . In two months, I'd lost thirty pounds . . . Everyone kept telling me I looked great . . .

I really didn't realize that anything was wrong with me . . . There were physical things occurring in my body other than not having my period anymore. My hair was falling out and was getting thinner . . . I would constantly get head rushes every time I stood up . . . When my friends would all go out to dinner or to a party I stayed home quite often, afraid that I might have to eat something, and afraid that my friends would find out that I didn't eat. (Twenhofel, 1993:198)

Feminist scholars have concluded that eating problems are not always psychological "disorders" (as they are referred to by members of the medical profession). Instead, eating (or not eating) may be a strategy for coping with problems, such as unrealistic social pressures about slenderness (see Orbach, 1978; Chernin, 1981; Hesse-Biber, 1996) and/or social injustices caused by racism, sexism, and classism in society (Thompson, 1994).

Teachers, Schools, and Gender Socialization

From kindergarten through university, schools operate as gendered institutions. Teachers provide important messages about gender through both the formal content of classroom assignments and informal interaction with students. Sometimes, gender-related messages from teachers and other students reinforce gender roles that have been taught at home; however, teachers also may contradict parental socialization. During the early years of a child's schooling, the teacher's influence is very powerful; many children spend more hours per day with their teachers than they do with their own parents.

Research conducted during the 1990s found extensive evidence of gender bias in virtually all educational settings. **Gender bias consists of showing favouritism toward one gender over the other.** Gender bias is displayed in a number of different ways in academic settings: through teacher–student interactions, biased or stereotyped resources, and responses to male and female interactions. Although there is evidence that girls are becoming more academically successful than boys, close examination of what goes on in our classrooms shows that girls and boys continue to be socialized in ways that work against gender equality (Chapman, 2003).

In the 1990s a book based on a study by Myra and David Sadker (1994) entitled *How Schools Shortchange Girls* (1994) suggested that girls were disadvantaged in the educational system and this was resulting in a diminished sense of self-esteem for young women. Sadker and Sadker found that teachers devoted more time, effort, and attention to boys than to girls. Male students received more praise for their contributions and were called on more frequently in class, even when they did not volunteer. Very often, the boys received additional attention because they called out in class, demanded help, or engaged in other disruptive behaviours (Sadker and Sadker, 1994).

Subsequent research on the marginalization of girls in the education system has produced contradictory evidence. For example, a survey of 1,300 students and more than 1,000 teachers reported that girls were more likely to have higher educational aspirations than boys, more likely to value a good education, and less likely to believe that their teachers didn't listen to them (Sommers, 2000). Another 1990 study conducted by the American Association of University Women provided evidence that both male and female students surveyed felt that their teachers systematically favoured girls. Specifically, they indicated that teachers thought girls were smarter than boys, more likely to get complimented by teachers, less likely to get disciplined, more likely to be called on in class, and more likely to get the teacher's attention (Sommers, 2000 cited in Brannigan, 2003:154).

Teachers also influence how students treat one another during school hours. Teachers may use sex segregation as a way of organizing students, resulting in unnecessary competition between females and males (Eyre, 1992). In addition, teachers may also take a "boys will be boys" attitude when females complain of sexual harassment. As a result, the school setting can become a hostile environment rather than a site for learning (Sadker and Sadker, 1994).

Evidence of gender bias is also found in the resources chosen for the classroom. Using textbooks that omit or minimize the contributions of women, trivialize the experiences of women, or reinforce gender stereotypes, further compounds gender bias in the school curriculum. Research conducted in the 1970s found extensive evidence of gender stereotyping in both elementary and high school curriculums. Women and girls were underrepresented in textbooks, and when they were represented they were stereotyped. Boys were stereotyped as well, but in more powerful and active roles. As Jane Gaskell describes:

Little girls in elementary texts played with dolls while their brothers played baseball: mothers wore aprons and baked cookies, while fathers drove off to work; adult women were princesses and witches, while men were doctors and farmers. (Gaskell, McLaren, and Novogradsky, 1995:102)

Figure 11.1 **University Degrees Awarded, by Sex, 2003**

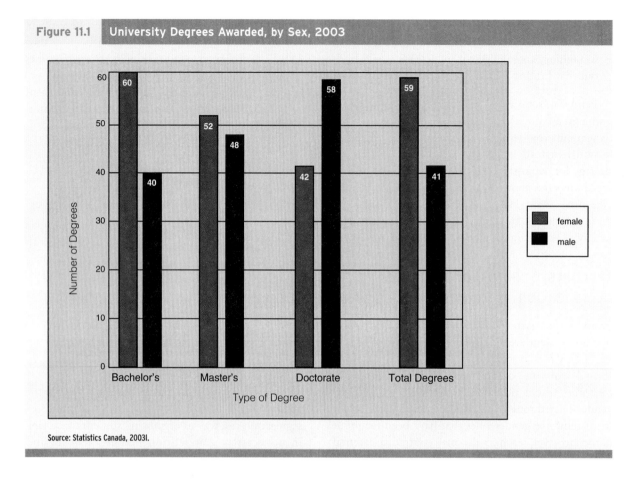

Source: Statistics Canada, 2003l.

As a result of research evidence of the destructive impact of gender bias in the classroom and political lobbying, positive changes have been made. Ministries of education across the country appointed advisory groups to screen resources being used in the classroom, issued nonsexist guidelines and developed and published alternative materials. As a result there are more diverse and less stereotyped materials used in classroom curriculum today, and more awareness of gender bias in teacher–student interactions (Gaskell et al., 1995). As one group of elementary school teachers who met in Toronto to discuss the effects of affirmative action strategies utilized in their school reported:

> Girls' lines and boys' lines were a thing of the past, now that the classroom housekeeping area was sex-integrated, that the *Paper Bag Princess* has become a modern classic, and that while school libraries had not ditched most sexist children's books, at least they had added numerous titles which portrayed girls and women in a positive light. (Gaskell et al., 1995:111)

We are beginning to see some results of these changes in the educational system. As shown in Figure 11.1, women represent just under 60 percent of degrees, diplomas, and certificates awarded by universities in Canada. The proportion awarded to women at the bachelor, master's, and doctorate levels was higher than ever before (Statistics Canada, 2003l). The mix of men and women in professions that in the past have been male dominated is now relatively equal. For example, women now make up more than half of all law and medicine students in Canadian universities. These recent trends should be reflected in further reductions in the wages gaps still seen in these professions.

Sports and Gender Socialization

Children spend more than half of their nonschool time in play and games, but the type of games played differs with the child's sex. Studies indicate that boys are socialized to participate in highly competitive, rule-oriented games with a larger number of participants than games played by girls. Girls have been socialized to play exclusively with others of their own age, in groups of two or three, in activities, such as hopscotch and jump rope, that involve a minimum of competitiveness (Adler et al., 1995).

In recent years, women have expanded their involvement in university and professional sports. However, most sports remain rigidly divided into female events and male events. How did the media coverage of the Canadian National Women's team gold win at the 2002 Olympics differ from the men's Olympic hockey coverage?

In recent years, women have expanded their involvement in university and professional sports. However, most sports remain rigidly divided into female events and male events. Other research shows that boys express more favourable attitudes toward games and sports that involve physical exertion and competition than girls do. Some analysts believe this difference in attitude is linked to ideas about what is gender-appropriate behaviour for boys and girls (Brustad, 1996).

For males, competitive sport becomes a means of "constructing a masculine identity, a legitimated outlet for violence and aggression, and an avenue for upward mobility" (Lorber, 1994:43). For females, being an athlete and a woman may constitute contradictory statuses. One study during the 1980s found that women college basketball players dealt with this contradiction by dividing their lives into segments. On the basketball court, the women "did athlete"; they pushed, shoved, fouled, ran hard, sweated, and cursed. Off the court, they "did woman"; after the game, they showered, dressed, applied makeup, and styled their hair, even if they were only getting on a van for a long ride home (Watson, 1987). However, researchers in a more recent study concluded that perceptions about women athletes may be changing. Specifically, ideas about what constitutes the ideal body image for girls and women are changing as more females become involved in physical fitness activities and athletic competitions (George, 2005). Young women and men in one poll rated the athletic female body higher than that of the anorexic model (Heywood and Dworkin, 2003).

Since the 1970s, when legislation was passed that mandated equal opportunities in academic and athletic programs for females, girls' and young women's

participation in athletics has increased substantially. More girls play soccer and softball and participate in other sports formerly regarded as "male" activities. However, even with these changes over the past three decades, only about 42 percent of high school and college athletes are female. According to sociologist Michael A. Messner (2002), girls and women have been empowered by their entry into sports; however, sex segregation of female and male athletes, as well as coaches, persists.

Most sports are rigidly divided into female and male events, and funding of athletic programs is often unevenly divided between men's and women's programs. Assumptions about male and female physiology and athletic capabilities influence the types of sports in which members of each sex are encouraged to participate. For example, women who engage in activities that are assumed to be "masculine" (such as bodybuilding) may either ignore their critics or attempt to redefine the activity or its result as "feminine" or womanly (Klein, 1993; Lowe, 1998). Some women bodybuilders do not want their bodies to get "overbuilt." They have learned that they are more likely to win women's bodybuilding competitions if they look and pose "more or less along the lines of fashion models" (Klein, 1993:179). In her study of more than 100 people connected with women's bodybuilding, the sociologist Maria R. Lowe (1998) found that "women of steel" (the female bodybuilders) live in a world where size and strength must regularly be balanced with a nod toward grace and femininity.

Cautious optimism is possible regarding the changing nature of sports and gender socialization based on several recent studies of women in sports (Heywood and Dworkin, 2003; Messner, 2002). Clearly, changes have occurred that might positively influence the gender socialization of both girls and boys; however, it appears that much remains to be done to bring about greater gender equity in the area of sport. One such area is how the media report on women's and men's sporting events and the attributes (such as physical attractiveness) that they highlight regarding female competitors while they emphasize the athletic skills of male competitors.

Mass Media and Gender Socialization

The media, including newspapers, magazines, television, and movies, are powerful sources of gender stereotyping. Although some critics argue that the media simply reflect existing gender roles in society, others point out that the media have a unique ability to shape ideas. Think of the impact that television might have on children if they spend one-third of their waking time watching it, as has been estimated.

From children's cartoons to adult shows, television programs offer more male than female characters. Furthermore, the male characters act in a strikingly different manner from female ones. Male characters in both children's programs and adult programs are typically aggressive, constructive, and direct, while some female characters defer to others or manipulate them by acting helpless, seductive, or deceitful (Basow, 1992). Because advertisers hope to appeal to boys, who constitute a significant proportion of the viewing audience for some shows, many programs feature lively adventure and lots of loud noise and violence. Until recently, even educational programs, such as *Sesame Street*, featured more characters with male names and masculine voices, and the audience was typically encouraged to participate in "boys' activities."

Although attempts have been made by media watchdogs and some members of the media to eliminate sexism in children's programming, adult daytime and prime-time programs (which children frequently watch) have received less scrutiny. Soap operas are a classic example of gender stereotyping. As media scholar Deborah D. Rogers (1995) has noted, even though more contemporary soaps feature career women, the cumulative effect of these programs is to reconcile women to traditional feminine roles and relationships. Whether the scene takes place at home or in the workplace, female characters typically gossip about romances or personal problems or compete for a man. Meanwhile, male characters are shown as superior beings who give orders and advice to others and do almost anything. In a hospital soap, for example, while female nurses gossip about hospital romances and their personal lives, the same male doctor who delivers babies also handles AIDS patients and treats trauma victims (Rogers, 1995). Prime-time television has provided better portrayals of women in medicine and in leadership positions in hospitals, but this change to more realistic depictions of women is not reflected throughout television programming.

How do the media serve to "construct" gender and our ideas about what is appropriate for women and men? Television and films influence our thinking about the appropriate behaviour of women and men in the roles they play in everyday life. Because it is often necessary for an actor to overplay a comic role to gain laughs from the viewing audience or to exaggerate a dramatic role to make a quick impression on the audience, the portrayal of girls and women may (either intentionally or inadvertently) reinforce old stereotypes or create new ones. Consider, for example, the growing number of women who are depicted as having careers or professions (such as law or medicine) in which they may earn more income and have more power than female characters had in the past. Some of these women may be portrayed as well-adjusted individuals; however, many women characters are still shown as overly emotional and unable to resolve their personal problems even as they are able to carry out their professional duties (the title character in *Judging Amy* is an example). Women characters who are supervisors or bosses are sometimes portrayed as loud, bossy, and domineering individuals. Mothers in situation comedies frequently boss their children around and may have a Homer Simpson–type husband who is lazy and incompetent or who engages in aggressive verbal combat with the woman throughout most of the program (*My Wife and Kids, The George Lopez Show,* and reruns of *Roseanne,* for example).

The competence of women to engage in certain kinds of activities, such as purchasing a vehicle, is often questioned and serves as the subject of laugh lines in popular situation comedies. One example is an episode of the ABC comedy *According to Jim.* In a Season 2 episode, "Car and Chicks," Jim (the lead male character, played by Jim Belushi) claims that women are not capable of getting a good deal on a car. Consequently, when Cheryl (his wife, played by Courtney Thorne-Smith) helps Dana (her unmarried sister, played by Kimberly Williams) select a new car to purchase, the vehicle turns out to be a lemon, and Dana begs Jim to "use his macho influence at the dealership to help her, but instead he allows sexy sales manager Gretchen (played by Cindy Crawford) to talk him into trading the family van in for a sports car—without consulting Cheryl," according to ABC's (2003) description.

Both married and single women are stereotyped in the media. The models for single women include the "sexy sales manager" in *According to Jim* and the sex-addicted Samantha in *Sex and the City*—for a number of years one of the most popular cable television programs. Programs such as this do not portray single career women as being self-supporting and emotionally balanced. Rather, they depict the single woman as incomplete without "a man," or they suggest that physical attractiveness and sexuality are commodities that women frequently use to their own advantage. As Betsy Israel, author of a recent book on single women, stated, "Single women have always been portrayed and depicted in the mass culture in a negative and nasty way that influenced the lives of many women, and at the same time was completely untrue, and these images, some of them 150 years old, are still being played out and the ideas are just being recycled" (qtd. in Hoban, 2002:A19).

Advertising—whether on television and billboards or in magazines and newspapers—further reinforces ideas about women and physical attractiveness. The intended message is clear to many people: If they embrace femininity and heightened sexuality, their personal and social success is assured; if they purchase the right products and services, they can enhance their appearance and gain power over other people. For example, one study of television commercials reflects that men's roles are portrayed differently from women's roles (Kaufman, 1999). Men are more likely to be away from home or are more likely to be shown working or playing outside the house rather than inside, where women are more likely to be located. There is also a far greater likelihood that women will be doing domestic tasks, such as cooking, cleaning, or shopping, whereas men are more likely to be taking care of cars or yards or playing games. As such, television commercials may act as agents of socialization, showing children and others what women's and men's designated activities are (Kaufman, 1999).

A study by the sociologist Anthony J. Cortese (1999) found that women—regardless of what they were doing in a particular ad—were frequently shown in advertising as being young, beautiful, and seductive. Although such depictions may sell products, they may also have the effect of influencing how we perceive ourselves and others with regard to issues of power and subordination. Women are bombarded with media images of ideal beauty and physical appearance (Cortese, 1999), and eating problems, such as anorexia and bulimia, are a major concern associated with many media depictions of the ideal body image for women. In both forms of eating disorders, distorted body image plays an important part, and this distorted image may be perpetuated by media depictions and advertisements. Clearly, the dramatic increase in eating problems in recent years cannot be attributed solely to advertising and the mass media; however, their potential impact on the gender socialization of young girls and women in establishing role models with whom to identify is extremely important (Kilbourne, 1994, 1999).

CONTEMPORARY GENDER INEQUALITY

According to feminist scholars, women experience gender inequality as a result of economic, political, and educational discrimination (Luxton, 1980; Smith, 1987; Eichler, 1997). Women's position in the Canadian workforce reflects their overall subordination in society.

Gendered Division of Paid Work

Where people are located in the occupational structure of the labour market has a major effect on their earnings (Kemp, 1994). The workplace is another example of a gendered institution. In industrialized countries, most jobs are segregated by gender and by race/ethnicity. Sociologist Judith Lorber (1994:194) gives this example:

In a workplace in New York City—for instance, a handbag factory—a walk through the various departments might reveal that the owners and managers are white men; their secretaries and bookkeepers are white and Asian women; the order takers and data processors are African American women; the factory hands are [Latinos] cutting pieces and [Latinas] sewing them together; African American men are packing and loading the finished product; and non-English-speaking Eastern European women are cleaning up after everyone. The workplace as a whole seems integrated by race, ethnic group, and gender, but the individual jobs are markedly segregated according to social characteristics.

Lorber notes that in most workplaces, employees are either gender segregated or all of the same gender. *Gender-segregated work* refers to the concentration of women and men in different occupations, jobs, and places of work (Reskin and Padavic, 2002). Gender-segregated work is most visible in occupations that remain more than 90-percent female (for example, secretary, registered nurse, and bookkeeper/auditing clerk) or more than 90-percent male (for example, carpenter, construction worker, mechanic, truck driver, and electrical engineer) (Statistics Canada, 2003d). In 2001, for example, more than 85 percent of all clerical staff in Canada were women; close to 90 percent of all engineers were men (Statistics Canada, 2003d). To eliminate gender-segregated jobs in North America, more than half of all men or all women workers would have to change occupations. Moreover, women are severely underrepresented at the top Canadian corporations, at only about 14 percent of the corporate officers in the *Financial Post 500* list (comprised of the 500 largest companies in Canada). Of these, only about 7 percent hold the highest corporate officer titles, and only nineteen women are the CEO (Catalyst, 2005). Despite some gains, "the story of women's advancement in corporate leadership in Canada continues to be one of disturbingly slow growth" (Catalyst, 2005:1). Based on current rates of change, the number of women reaching the top ranks of corporate Canada will not reach an acceptable level of 25 percent until the year 2025. See Table 11.2 for more on gender segregation in occupations.

Although the degree of gender segregation in parts of the professional labour market has declined since the 1970s (Sokoloff, 1992), racial–ethnic segregation has remained deeply embedded in the social structure. However, the relationship between visible minority status and occupational status is complex and varies by gender. Although visible-minority males are overrepresented in both lower- and higher-status occupations, nonwhite women are heavily overrepresented in lower-paying, low-skilled jobs (Krahn and Lowe, 1998).

Workplace gender segregation is not unique to Canada. For example, in Sweden—the country with the highest rate of women's paid labour force participation in the world—gender segregation is

---

Table 11.2   GENDER SEGREGATION BY OCCUPATION

PERCENTAGE OF WOMEN IN THE TEN HIGHEST-PAYING OCCUPATIONS

Judges	23%
Specialist physicians	26%
General practitioners and family physicians	26%
Dentists	18%
Senior managers (goods production, utilities, transportation, construction)	9%
Senior managers (financial, communications, other business)	17%
Lawyers	37%
Senior managers (trade, broadcasting, other services)	14%
Primary production managers	6%
Securities agents, investment dealers, traders	33%

PERCENTAGE OF WOMEN IN THE TEN LOWEST-PAYING OCCUPATIONS

Sewing machine operators	92%
Cashiers	84%
Ironing, pressing, and finishing occupations	70%
Artisans and craftspersons	52%
Bartenders	56%
Harvesting labourers	54%
Service station attendants	20%
Food service attendants and food preparers	75%
Food and beverage servers	76%
Babysitters, nannies, and parents' helpers	98%

Source: UN Platform for Action Committee, 2005.

even greater (Borchorst and Siim, 1987). Across cultures, men are less active than women in crossing the gender barrier in employment (Kauppinen-Toropainen and Lammi, 1993).

Labour market segmentation—the division of jobs into categories with distinct working conditions—results in women having separate and unequal jobs (Amott and Matthaei, 1996; Lorber, 1994). The pay gap between men and women is the best-documented consequence of gender-segregated work (Reskin and Padavic, 2002). Most women work in lower-paying, less-prestigious jobs, with little opportunity for advancement. Because many employers assume that men are the breadwinners, men are expected to make more money than women in order to support their families. For many years, women have been viewed as supplemental wage earners in a male-headed household, regardless of the women's marital status. Consequently, women have not been seen as legitimate workers but mainly as wives and mothers (Lorber, 1994, 2001).

Gender-segregated work affects both men and women. Men are often kept out of certain types of jobs. Those who enter female-dominated occupations often have to justify themselves and prove that they are "real men." They have to fight stereotypes (gay, "wimpy," and passive) about why they are interested in such work (Williams, 2004). Even if these assumptions do not push men out of female-dominated occupations, they affect how the men manage their gender identity at work. For example, men in occupations, such as nursing, emphasize their masculinity, attempt to distance themselves from female colleagues, and try to move quickly into management and supervisory positions (Williams, 2004).

Occupational gender segregation contributes to stratification in society. Job segregation is structural; it does not occur simply because individual workers have different abilities, motivations, and material needs. As a result of gender and racial segregation, employers are able to pay many men of colour and all women less money, promote them less often, and provide fewer benefits. If they demand better working conditions or wages, workers are often reminded of the number of individuals (members of Marx's "reserve army") who would like to have their jobs.

The Gender Wage Gap

Occupational segregation contributes to a second form of discrimination—the **wage gap, a term used to describe the disparity between women's and men's earnings.** It is calculated by dividing women's earnings by men's to yield a percentage, also known as the *earnings ratio* (Lowe, 1999). Male–female wage differences reveal that gender is a major source of inequality in the workforce. There has been some improvement in this earnings ratio in recent decades, but the progress has been slow. Today, women who work full time for the whole year still earn just over 70 cents for each dollar earned by their male counterparts (Statistics Canada, 2003d). A recent study found that the majority of this wage gap is explained by differences in worker characteristics, such as experience, type of occupation, and workplace characteristics (Drolet, 2002). Marital status has a dramatic impact on the wage gap. The wage gap is smallest between single, never-married men and women (96 percent) and biggest between married men and women (77 percent) (Drolet, 2001b). As shown in Figure 11.2, the gender wage gap exists for all levels of education. In 2000, young university educated women who worked full time for the full year earned 81 cents for every dollar earned by their male counterparts (Statistics Canada, 2003d). Although higher education clearly narrows the wage gap between men and women, a woman with a university degree still earns approximately $15,000 less than a man with a university degree. Once again, this gap is attributable to occupational segregation. The majority of female university students enrol in degree programs in education, health professions, fine arts, and the humanities, while males continue to dominate in the fields of science and engineering. Even within occupations that require specialized educational credentials, the wage gap does not disappear—for every dollar earned by men, women earned 65 cents as dentists, 68 cents as lawyers, and 77 cents as university professors (Statistics Canada, 2001f).

Because women's overall pay relative to men's has increased by about a penny a year for the past ten years, it might seem that women's earnings have taken a noticeable move upward. However, this decrease in the wage gap can be partially attributed to the fact that men's earnings have declined since the 1970s, while women's have climbed slowly (Drolet, 2001a).

Pay Equity and Employment Equity

A number of strategies have been implemented in an attempt to achieve greater gender equality in the labour market. *Pay equity* attempts to raise the value of the work traditionally performed by women. *Employment equity* strategies focus on ways to move women into higher-paying jobs traditionally held by men (Creese

| Figure 11.2 | The Wage Gap |

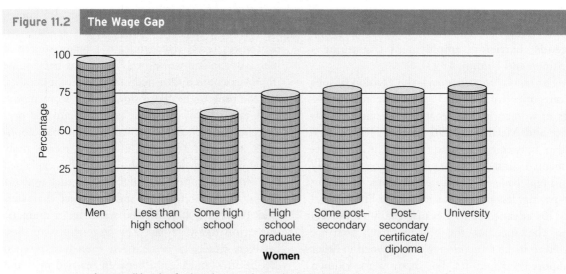

a. Across all levels of education, men's earnings are higher than the earnings of women. The wage gap does narrow slightly for women with higher levels of education.

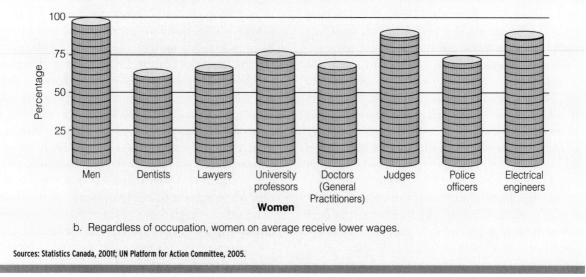

b. Regardless of occupation, women on average receive lower wages.

Sources: Statistics Canada, 2001f; UN Platform for Action Committee, 2005.

and Beagan, 1999). Since the 1980s, the federal government, some provincial governments, and a number of private companies have implemented pay equity and employment equity policies (Lowe, 1999).

Pay equity (or, as it is sometimes called, *comparable worth*) reflects the belief that wages ought to reflect the worth of a job, not the gender or race of the worker (Kemp, 1994). How can the comparable worth of different kinds of jobs be determined? One way is to compare the actual work of women's and men's jobs and see if there is a disparity in the salaries paid for each. To do this, analysts break a job into components—such as the education, training, and skills required, the extent of responsibility for others' work, and the working conditions—and then allocate points for each (Lorber, 1994). For pay equity to exist, men and women in occupations that receive the same number of points should be paid the same. In short, pay equity promotes the principle of equal pay for work of equal value.

A second strategy for addressing inequality in the workplace is *employment equity*—a strategy to eliminate the effects of discrimination and to fully open the competition for job opportunities to those who have been excluded historically (Krahn and Lowe, 1998). The target groups for employment equity are visible minorities, persons with disabilities, Aboriginal peoples, and women. In comparison with pay equity, which addresses wage issues only, employment equity covers a range of employment issues, such as recruitment, selection, training, development, and promotion. Employment equity also addresses issues pertaining to conditions of employment, such as compensation, layoffs, and disciplinary

What stereotypes are associated with men in female-oriented occupations? With women in male-oriented occupations? Do you think such stereotypes will change in the near future?

action (Boyd, 1995). Critics of employment equity policies have pointed out that the *Employment Equity Act* of 1995 has jurisdiction over a very small percentage of the population; it covers only federal government employers or companies that have contracts with the federal government. Although these policies represent a start in the right direction, male resistance and poor regulation and enforcement have resulted in minimal progress toward gendered employment equity.

Paid Work and Family Work

As previously discussed, the first big change in the relationship between family and work occurred with the Industrial Revolution and the rise of capitalism. The cult of domesticity kept many middle- and upper-class women out of the workforce during this period, primarily because working-class and poor women were the ones who had to deal with the work/family conflict. Today, however, the issue spans the entire economic spectrum. The typical married woman in Canada combines paid work in the labour force and family work as a homemaker (Sauvé, 2002).

Even with dramatic changes in women's workforce participation, the sexual division of labour in the family remains essentially unchanged. Most married women now share responsibility for the breadwinner role, yet many men do not accept their share of domestic responsibilities (Armstrong, 1993; Luxton,

1999; McQuillan and Belle, 1999; Statistics Canada, 2003c). The 1996 census was the first census to include questions on unpaid work. The results indicated that even when women work full-time in the paid workforce, most maintain primary responsibility for unpaid work, which includes child care, elder care, housework, shopping, and food preparation (Creese and Beagan, 1999). The most recent census has confirmed the burden of unpaid work continues to rest disproportionately on women (Statistics Canada, 2003c). Among couples without children, the woman does about 60 percent more housework than her male partner (see Figure 11.3). This gap is even more pronounced in families with children, in which women spend more than twice as much time on domestic work. Consequently, many women have a "double day" or "second shift" because of their dual responsibilities for paid and unpaid work (Hochschild, 1989, 2003) (see also Chapter 15). Working women have less time to spend on housework; if husbands do not participate in routine domestic chores, some chores simply do not get done or get done less often. Although the income that many women earn is essential for the economic survival of their families, they still must spend part of their earnings on family maintenance, such as daycare centres, fast-food restaurants, and laundry and housecleaning, in an attempt to keep up with their obligations.

Especially in families with young children, domestic responsibilities consume a great deal of time and energy. Although some kinds of housework can be put

Figure 11.3   The Second Shift: Hours of Housework per Week by Gender and Presence of Children

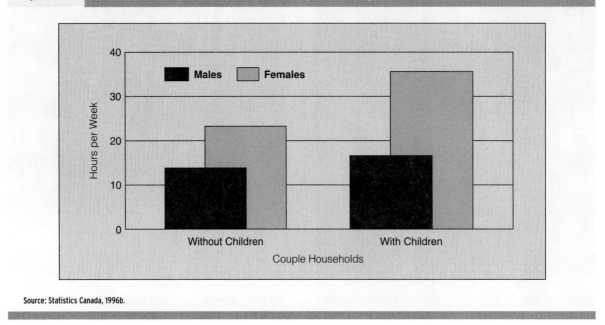

Source: Statistics Canada, 1996b.

off, the needs of children often cannot be ignored or delayed. When children are ill or school events cannot be scheduled around work, parents (especially mothers) may experience stressful role conflicts ("Shall I be a good employee or a good mother?"). Consider the following scenario of a mother trying to balance the often conflicting demands of working and parenting her young daughter:

> A few weeks ago, Camille Allen tried to get a jump on the day by leaving earlier than usual to her human resources job at the Canadian Imperial Bank of Commerce in Toronto. The change in timetable didn't suit her seven-year-old daughter, who burst into tears when her mother got ready to go. "She's not usually like that and her Dad was there, but she wanted me to take her to school," Allen says. "She wailed and wailed and I kind of peeled her off me at the front door." Allen, 41, got in her van and drove off with her daughter's cries still ringing in her head. "I got close to the highway and I thought, 'You know what? This just isn't worth it.' So I turned around, went home, waited around for half an hour and took her to school." (Chisholm et al., 1999)

Many working women care not only for themselves, their husbands, and their children but also for elderly parents or in-laws. Some analysts refer to these women as "the sandwich generation"—caught

between the needs of their young children and elderly relatives. Many women try to solve their time crunch by forgoing leisure time and sleep. When Arlie Hochschild interviewed working mothers, she found that they talked about sleep "the way a hungry person talks about food" (1989:9). Perhaps this is one reason that, in more recent research, Hochschild (1997) learned that some married women with children found more fulfillment at work and that they worked longer hours because they liked work better than facing the pressures of home. (See Chapter 15, "Families and Intimate Relationships," for a discussion on situations in which women are the sole earners in their families while their husbands take care of the household and children.)

What can be done to address the gendered division of unpaid work? Strategies include improved government supports, such as low-cost daycare and better maternity and paternity leave provisions. Employers also need to create more "family friendly" programs, such as on-site daycare, flextime, and family leave, as well as decreasing demands for overtime. Finally, although men are involved in a greater share of the unpaid work in the home than ever before, the division of labour is still far from equal. Until significant changes are made in the distribution of unpaid work, gender segregation in lower-paying jobs will likely remain a reality for most Canadian women (Creese and Beagan, 1999:208).

PERSPECTIVES ON GENDER STRATIFICATION

Sociological perspectives on gender stratification vary in their approach to examining gender roles and power relationships in society. Some focus on the roles of women and men in the domestic sphere; others note the inequalities arising from a gendered division of labour in the workplace. Still others attempt to integrate both the public and private spheres into their analyses.

Functionalist and Neoclassical Economic Perspectives

As shown earlier, functionalist theory views men and women as having distinct roles that are important for the survival of the family and society. The most basic division of labour is biological: men are physically stronger while women are the only ones able to bear and nurse children. Gendered belief systems foster assumptions about appropriate behaviour for men and women and may have an impact on the types of work women and men perform.

The Importance of Traditional Gender Roles

According to functional analysts, such as Talcott Parsons (1955), women's roles as nurturers and caregivers are even more pronounced in contemporary industrialized societies. While the husband performs the *instrumental* tasks of providing economic support and making decisions, the wife assumes the *expressive* tasks of providing affection and emotional support for the family. This division of family labour ensures that important societal tasks will be fulfilled; it also provides stability for family members.

This view has been adopted by a number of conservative analysts. George F. Gilder (1986) argues that traditional gender roles are important not only for individuals but also for the economic and social order of society. He asserts that relationships between men and women are damaged when changes in gender roles occur, and family life suffers as a consequence. According to Gilder, women provide for the socialization of the next generation; if they do not, society's moral fabric will decay, resulting in higher rates of crime, violence, and drug abuse. From this perspective, the traditional division of labour between men and women is the natural order of the universe (Kemp, 1994).

According to the human capital model, women earn less in the labour market because of their child-rearing responsibilities. What other explanations are offered for the lower wages that women receive?

The Human Capital Model

Functionalist explanations of occupational gender segregation are similar to neoclassical economic perspectives, such as the human capital model (Horan, 1978; Kemp, 1994). According to this model, individuals vary widely in the amount of human capital they bring to the labour market. *Human capital* is acquired by education and job training; it is the source of a person's productivity and can be measured in terms of the return on the investment (wages) and the cost (schooling or training) (Stevenson, 1988; Kemp, 1994).

From this perspective, what individuals earn is the result of their own choices (the kinds of training, education, and experience they accumulate, for example) and of the labour market need (demand) for and availability (supply) of certain kinds of workers at specific points in time. For example, human capital analysts argue that women diminish their human capital when they leave the labour force to engage in childbearing and child care activities. While women are out of the labour force, their human capital deteriorates from nonuse. When they return to work, women earn lower wages than men because they have fewer years of work experience and have "atrophied human capital" because their education and training may have become obsolete (Kemp, 1994:70).

Other neoclassical economic models attribute the wage gap to such factors as (1) the different amounts of energy men and women expend on their work (women who spend much energy on their family and household have less to put into their work), (2) the occupational choices women make (choosing female-dominated occupations so that they can spend more time with their families), and (3) the crowding of too many women into some occupations (suppressing wages because the supply of workers exceeds demand) (Kemp, 1994).

Evaluation of Functionalist and Neoclassical Economic Perspectives

Although Parsons and other functionalists did not specifically endorse the gendered division of labour, their analysis views it as natural and perhaps inevitable. However, critics argue that problems inherent in traditional gender roles, including the personal role strains of men and women and the social costs to society, are minimized by this approach. For example, men are assumed to be "money machines" for their families when they might prefer to spend more time in child-rearing activities. Also, the woman's place is assumed to be in the home, an assumption that ignores the fact that many women hold jobs due to economic necessity.

In addition, the functionalist approach does not take a critical look at the structure of society (especially the economic inequalities) that make educational and occupational opportunities more available to some than to others. Furthermore, it fails to examine the underlying power relations between men and women or to consider the fact that the tasks assigned to women and to men are unequally valued by society (Kemp, 1994). Similarly, the human capital model is rooted in the premise that individuals are evaluated based on their human capital in an open, competitive market where education, training, and other job-enhancing characteristics are taken into account. From this perspective, those who make less money (often men of visible minority groups and all women) have no one to blame but themselves. According to sociologist Alice Kemp (1994:76):

> If women have children to care for, it is a situation they freely chose and will have to work out for themselves. That jobs and professions have been structured to reflect men's lives and circumstances is seldom recognized; instead women are conceptualized as somehow different from men in their motivations and preference for income.

Critics note that, instead of blaming people for their choices, we must acknowledge other realities. Wage discrimination occurs in two ways: (1) The wages are higher in male-dominated jobs, occupations, and segments of the labour market, regardless of whether women take time for family duties, and (2) in any job, women and members of some minority groups will be paid less (Lorber, 1994).

Conflict Perspectives

According to many conflict analysts, the gendered division of labour within families and in the workplace results from male control of and dominance over women and resources. Differentials between men and women may exist in terms of economic, political, physical, and/or interpersonal power. The importance of a male monopoly in any of these arenas depends on the significance of that type of power in a society (Richardson, 1993). In hunting and gathering and horticultural societies, male dominance over women is limited because all members of the society must work in order to survive (Collins, 1971; Nielsen, 1990). In agrarian societies, however, male sexual dominance is at its peak. Male heads of household gain a monopoly not only on physical power but also on economic power, and women become sexual property.

Although men's ability to use physical power to control women diminishes in industrial societies, men still remain the heads of household and control the property. In addition, men gain more power through their predominance in the most highly paid and prestigious occupations and the highest elected offices. In contrast, women have the ability to trade their sexual resources, companionship, and emotional support in the marriage market for men's financial support and social status; as a result, however, women as a group remain subordinate to men (Collins, 1971; Nielsen, 1990).

All men are not equally privileged; some analysts argue that women and men in the upper classes are more privileged, because of their economic power, than men in lower-class positions and members of some minority groups (Lorber, 1994). In industrialized societies, persons who occupy elite positions in corporations, universities, the mass media, and government or who have great wealth have the most power (Richardson, 1993). However, most of these are men.

Conflict theorists in the Marxist tradition assert that gender stratification results from private ownership of the means of production; some men not only gain control over property and the distribution of goods but also gain power over women. According to Friedrich Engels and Karl Marx, marriage serves to enforce male dominance. Men of the capitalist class instituted monogamous marriage (a gendered institution) so that they could be certain of the paternity of their offspring, especially sons, whom they wanted to inherit their wealth. Feminist analysts have examined this theory, among others, as they have sought to explain male domination and gender stratification.

Feminist Perspectives

Feminism—**the belief that women and men are equal and that they should be valued equally and have equal rights**—is embraced by many men as well as women. Gender is viewed as a socially constructed concept that has important consequences in the lives of all people (Craig, 1992). According to sociologist Ben Agger (1993), men can be feminists and propose feminist theories; both women and men have much in common as they seek to gain a better understanding of the causes and consequences of gender inequality.

Although all feminist perspectives begin with the assumption that the majority of women occupy a subordinate position to men, they often diverge in terms of their explanations of how and why women are subordinated and the best strategies for achieving true equality for women (Chunn, 2000). Feminist perspectives vary in their analyses of the ways in which norms, roles, institutions, and internalized expectations limit women's behaviour. Taken together, they all seek to demonstrate how women's personal control operates even within the constraints of a relative lack of power (Stewart, 1994). Although subordination and oppression have significant consequences in women's lives, feminist theorists note that these are not the *only* features of women's lives (Fine, 1987, 1989). We will now look at the main types of feminist theory and examine the focus of each.

Liberal Feminism

In liberal feminism, gender equality is equated with equality of opportunity. Liberal feminists assume that women's inequality stems from the denial to them of equal rights (Mandell, 2001). Liberal feminism strives for sex equality through the elimination of laws that differentiate people by gender. Only when these constraints on women's participation are removed will women have the same chance of success as men. This approach notes the importance of gender-role socialization and suggests that changes need to be made in what children learn from their families, teachers, and the media about appropriate masculine and feminine attitudes and behaviour. Liberal feminists fight for better child care options, a woman's right to choose an abortion, and elimination of sex discrimination in the workplace.

Radical Feminism

According to radical feminists, male domination causes all forms of human oppression, including racism and classism (Tong, 1989). Radical feminists often trace the roots of patriarchy to women's childbearing and child-rearing responsibilities, which make them dependent on men (Firestone, 1970; Chafetz, 1984). In the radical feminist view, men's oppression of women is deliberate, and ideological justification for this subordination is provided by other institutions, such as the media and religion. For women's condition to improve, radical feminists claim, patriarchy must be abolished. If institutions currently are gendered, alternative institutions—such as women's organizations seeking better health care, daycare, and shelters for victims of domestic violence and sexual assault—should be developed to meet women's needs.

Socialist Feminism

Socialist feminists suggest that women's oppression results from their dual roles as paid *and* unpaid workers in a capitalist economy. In the workplace, women are exploited by capitalism; at home, they are exploited by patriarchy (Kemp, 1994). Women are easily exploited in both sectors; they are paid low wages and have few economic resources. Gendered job segregation is "the primary mechanism in capitalist society that maintains the superiority of men over women, because it enforces lower wages for women in the labour market" (Hartmann, 1976:139). As a result, women must do domestic labour either to gain a better-paid man's economic support or to stretch their own wages (Lorber, 1994). According to socialist feminists, the only way to achieve gender equality is to eliminate capitalism and develop a socialist economy that would bring equal pay and rights to women.

Multicultural Feminism

During what has been referred to as the "second wave of feminism" (1970–1990), the mainstream feminist movement was criticized for ignoring the experiences of poor women, women of colour, and women with disabilities. Feminism in its various forms described middle-class white women's experiences as the norm, and other women's experiences were treated as "different" (Cassidy, Lord, and Mandell, 2001). Recently, academics and activists have been attempting to address these criticisms and working to include the experiences of women of colour and Aboriginal women. Antiracist feminist perspectives are based on the belief that women of colour experience a different world than middle-class white women because of multilayered oppression based on race/ethnicity, gender, and class (Khayatt, 1994). Building on the civil rights and feminist movements of the late 1960s and early 1970s, contemporary feminists have focused on the cultural experiences of marginalized women, such as women of colour, immigrant women, and Native women. An assumption central to this analysis is that race, class, and gender are forces that simultaneously oppress some women (Hull, Bell-Scott, and Smith, 1982). The effects of these statuses cannot be adequately explained as "double" or "triple" jeopardy (class plus race plus gender) because these ascribed characteristics are not simply added to one another. Instead, they are multiplicative in nature (race times class times gender); different characteristics may be more significant in one situation than another. For example, a wealthy white woman (class) may be in a position of privilege as compared with people of colour (race) and men from lower socioeconomic positions (class), yet be in a subordinate position as compared to a white man (gender) from the capitalist class (Andersen and Collins, 1998). In order to analyze the complex relationship among these characteristics, the lived experiences of women of colour and other previously "silenced" people must be heard and examined within the context of particular historical and social conditions.

Feminists who analyze race, class, and gender suggest that equality will occur only when all women, regardless of race/ethnicity, class, age, religion, sexual orientation, or ability (or disability), are treated more equitably (Cassidy, Lord, and Mandell, 2001).

Postmodernist Feminism

One of the more recent feminist perspectives to emerge is *postmodernist feminism*. This perspective has been described as existing "both as a rebuke to all statements of claim made by other branches of feminist thought and as a perspective in its own right" (Nelson, 2006:93). Postmodernist feminism has emerged out of several shared assumptions of both feminist and postmodernist theory. Both perspectives are highly skeptical about existing knowledge. As discussed in previous chapters, postmodernists reject the idea that science can objectively measure and describe a world that is "out there." Consequently, postmodernists resist making generalizations and see the world as consisting of diverse, multiple, and unique experiences (Anderson, 2006:395).

Postmodernists view **discourses—all that is written, spoken, or otherwise represented through language and communication systems**—as constructs of social reality. In addition, discourse is viewed as a mechanism of social control. Similarly, feminist scholars recognize how socially constructed ideas and images have been used to create *gender ideology–specific representations of what it means to be male or female*, which is oppressive to women. As a result, both feminists and postmodernists strive to deconstruct our traditional understanding of what constitutes being female or male in society today.

Postmodern feminists argue that the various feminist theories—including liberal, Marxist, radical, and socialist—which advocate a single or limited number of causes for women's inequality and oppression are flawed, inadequate, and typically based upon suppression of female experiences. In keeping with the assumptions of postmodernist theory, postmodernist feminists resist making generalizations about "all women." Rather, they attempt to acknowledge the individual experiences and perspectives of women of all classes, races, ethnicities, abilities, sexualities, and ages. To postmodernist feminists, a singular feminist theory is impossible because there is no essential "woman." The category *woman* is seen as a social construct that is "a fiction, a non-determinable identity" (Cain, 1993 c.f. Nelson, 2006:94). Given that the category "woman" is regarded as socially constructed, the challenge of postmodernist feminism is to "deconstruct" these notions of the natural or essential woman. For example, the traditional sciences, in particular medicine, have viewed "reproduction" as a central construct of "woman." As Phoenix and Woolett (1991:7) have argued, "women continue to be defined in terms of their biological functions" such that "motherhood and particularly childbearing continues to be defined as the supreme route to physical and emotional fulfillment and as essential for all women." Postmodernist feminists challenge the concept of the reproductive woman as essential and highlight the oppressive nature of such so-called scientific knowledge.

Postmodernist feminists argue that there is nothing that is essentially male or female. In fact, they go so far as to challenge the idea of any real biological categories of male or female—suggesting, rather, that our understanding of biological differences between the sexes is of socially constructed categories that have emerged from specific cultural and historical contexts. Some scholars view the distinction between sex and gender as false because it is based on the assumption of biological differences as real (Anderson, 2006:395). In sum, the categories of male and female, and man and woman, are best understood by postmodernist feminists as fluid, artificial, and malleable. Critics have suggested that this understanding of gender contradicts the fundamental principle of other feminist perspectives; that is, a central focus on women. As one critic asks, "how can it ascribe to be feminist, since feminism is a theory that focuses on the unitary category 'woman'?" (Cain, 1993:76).

Feminist Perspectives on Eating Problems

As noted earlier, feminist analysts suggest that eating problems are not just individual "disorders" but relate to the issue of subordination (see Orbach, 1978; Fallon, Katzman, and Wooley, 1994). This analysis focuses on the relationship between eating problems and patriarchy (male dominance) in the labour force and family. Eating problems cannot be viewed solely as psychological "disorders" but rather are symbolic of women's personal and cultural oppression. Anorexia and bulimia reflect women's (and sometimes men's) denial of other problems, disconnection from other people, and disempowerment in society (Peters and Fallon, 1994:353).

Feminist scholars have begun to look at ways in which race/ethnicity may be linked to eating problems (Root, 1990). In contrast, most early research focused on the problems of white, middle- to upper-class females; women from minority groups were, at most, mentioned in a footnote (for example see Brumberg, 1988). In a study of women with eating problems, sociologist Becky Thompson (1992, 1994) found that more than half the women from minority groups had been victims of sexual abuse, racism, anti-Semitism, and/or homophobia. However, she suggests that it is impossible to determine a single explanation about socialization and eating problems among women of colour.

Eating problems also may be associated with social class and sexual orientation. For example, some lower-class women may view binge eating as a momentary reprieve from poverty and other worries. Some lesbians may develop eating problems in rebellion against cultural expectations that attempt to force heterosexuality or at least heterosexual values on them, in sharp contradiction to their own sexual identities (Thompson, 1994). Two feminist studies comparing lesbian and heterosexual women found that both groups are influenced by cultural pressures to be thin but that lesbians tend to be more satisfied with their bodies and to desire a somewhat higher ideal weight (Brand, Rothblum, and Solomon, 1992; Herzog et al., 1992). Gay men, on the other hand, may be more prone to eating problems because of the importance some place on low body weight and physical attractiveness (see Shisslak and Crago, 1992).

Evaluation of Conflict and Feminist Perspectives
Conflict and feminist perspectives provide insights into the structural aspects of gender inequality in society. While functionalist approaches focus on the characteristics of individuals, the conflict and feminist approaches emphasize factors external to individuals that contribute to the oppression of women. These approaches also examine the ways in which the workplace and the home are gendered.

Conflict theory has been criticized for emphasizing the differences between men and women without taking into account their commonalities. Feminist approaches have been criticized for their emphasis on male dominance without a corresponding analysis of the ways in which some men also may be oppressed by patriarchy and capitalism. Some theorists in men's studies have attempted to overcome this deficit by exploring how gender domination includes "men's subordination and denigration of other men as well as men's exploitation of women" (Brod, 1987; Kimmel and Messner, 1992; Lorber, 1994:4).

Symbolic Interactionist Perspectives

In contrast to functionalist, conflict, and feminist theorists, who focus primarily on macrolevel analysis of structural and systemic sources of gender differences and inequities, symbolic interactionists focus on a microlevel analysis that views a person's identity as a product of their social interactions. From this perspective people create, maintain, and modify gender as they go about their everyday lives. Candace West and Don Zimmerman (1991) utilized a symbolic interactionist perspective to explain what they refer to as "doing gender." An individual is "doing gender" whenever he or she interacts with another in a way that displays characteristics of a particular gender. This perspective views gender not as fixed in biology or social roles, but rather as something that is "accomplished" through interactions with others. They explain that

> Gender is not a set of traits, nor a variable, nor a role, but the product of social doings of some sort. What then is the social doing of gender? It is more that the continuous creation of the meaning of gender through human actions. We claim that gender itself is constituted through interaction. (1991:16)

In illustrating the concept of "doing gender," West and Zimmerman refer to a case study of Agnes, a transsexual raised as a boy until she adopted a female identity at age seventeen. Although Agnes eventually underwent a sex reassignment operation several years later, she had the challenging task of displaying herself as female even though she had never experienced the everyday interactions that women use to attach meaning to the concept of being female. Agnes had to display herself as a woman while simultaneously learning what it was to be a woman. To make matters more difficult, she was attempting to do so when most people at that age "do gender" virtually without thinking. As West and Zimmerman explain, this does not make Agnes's gender artificial:

> She was not faking what real women do naturally. She was obliged to analyze and figure out how to act within socially constructed circumstances and conceptions of femininity that women born with the appropriate biological credentials take for granted early on. . . . As with others who must "pass" . . . Agnes's case makes visible what culture has made invisible—the accomplishment of gender. (1991:18)

Can you think of ways in which you "do gender" in your daily interactions? Using a symbolic interactionist perspective helps us to understand how we create, sustain, or change the gender categories that constitute being a man or a woman in our society. They emphasize that socialization into gender roles is not simply a passive process whereby people simply internalize others' expectations, but rather they can choose to "do gender" to varying degrees. In doing so, we are able to continually change the social definition of gender (Messner, 2000, c.f. Anderson, 2006). The interactionist perspective has

been criticized for failing to address the power differences between men and women as well as the significant economic and political advantages that exist in the larger social structure (Anderson, 2006).

GENDER ISSUES IN THE FUTURE

In the past thirty years, women have made significant progress in the labour force (Creese and Beagan, 1999). Laws have been passed to prohibit sexual discrimination in the workplace and in schools. Affirmative action programs have made women more visible in education, government, and the professional world.

Many men have joined movements to raise their consciousness not only about men's concerns but also about the need to eliminate sexism and gender bias. Many men realize that what is harmful to women also may be harmful to men. For example, women's lower wages in the labour force suppress men's wages as well;

Concept Table 11.A THEORETICAL PERSPECTIVES ON GENDER

PERSPECTIVE	KEY TERMS	KEY ELEMENTS
Functionalist	Instrumental and Expressive Tasks	Division of labour by gender ensures stability.
Neoclassical Economic	Human Capital	Gender inequality in the labour market results from women's diminished human capital.
Conflict	Gendered Division of Labour	The gendered division of labour at home and work is the result of male control of women and resources.
Feminist Liberal Feminism	Equal Rights	Women's equality is equated with equality of opportunity.
Radical Feminism	Patriarchy	Patriarchy must be abolished for gender equality to be achieved.
Socialist Feminism	Gendered Job Segregation	Capitalism must be eliminated and a socialist economy established to obtain gender equality.
Multicultural Feminism	Double or Triple Jeopardy	Race, class, and gender simultaneously oppress women.
Postmodernist Feminism	Deconstructing Gender	Categories of male and female and man and woman are artificial and malleable. People create, maintain, and modify their gender through their everday interactions.

in a two-paycheque family, women who are paid less contribute less to the family's finances, thus placing a greater burden on men to earn more money.

In the midst of these changes, many gender issues remain unresolved. In the labour force, gender segregation may increase if the number of female-dominated jobs—such as information clerk, nurse's aide, and fast-food restaurant worker—continues to grow. If men lose jobs in the blue-collar sector as factories relocate to other countries or close entirely, they may seek jobs that primarily have been held by women. Although this situation might lead to less gender segregation, the loss of desirable jobs ultimately is not in anyone's interest (Reskin and Padavic, 1994:172). As men see the number and quality of "men's jobs" shrink, they also may become more resistant to women's entry into what have customarily been male jobs (Reskin and Padavic, 1994).

The pay gap between men and women should continue to shrink, but this may be due in part to decreasing wages paid to men (Drolet, 2001b). Employers and governments will continue to implement family-leave policies, but these will not relieve women's domestic burden in the family. The burden of the "double day" or "second shift" has led many women to work part time in an attempt to reconcile family–work contradictions. This choice increases or maintains occupational segregation, low pay with minimal or no benefits, and marginalized treatment (Gee, 2000). The burden of the "double day" or "second shift" will likely preserve women's inequality at home and in the workplace for another generation.

CHAPTER REVIEW

■ How do sex and gender differ?

Sex refers to the biological categories and manifestations of femaleness and maleness; *gender* refers to the socially constructed differences between females and males. In short, sex is what we (generally) are born with; gender is what we acquire through socialization.

■ How do gender roles and gender identity differ from gendered institutions?

Gender role encompasses the attitudes, behaviours, and activities that are socially assigned to each sex and that are learned through socialization. Gender identity is an individual's perception of self as either female or male. Gendered institutions are those structural features that perpetuate gender inequality.

■ How does the nature of work affect gender equality in societies?

In most hunting and gathering societies, fairly equitable relationships exist because neither sex has the ability to provide all of the food necessary for survival. In horticultural societies, hoe cultivation is compatible with child care, and a fair degree of gender equality exists because neither sex controls the food supply. In agrarian societies, male dominance is very apparent; agrarian tasks require more labour and physical strength, and women often are excluded from these tasks because they are viewed as too weak or too tied to child-rearing activities. In industrialized societies, a gap exists between nonpaid work performed by women at home and paid work performed by men and women. A wage gap also exists between men and women in the marketplace. In postindustrial societies, the division of labour in paid employment is increasingly based on whether people provide or apply information or are employed in service jobs.

■ What are the key agents of gender socialization?

Parents, peers, teachers and schools, sports, and the media are agents of socialization that tend to reinforce stereotypes of gender-appropriate behaviour.

■ What causes gender inequality in Canada?

Gender inequality results from economic, political, and educational discrimination against women. In most workplaces, jobs are either gender segregated or the majority of employees are of the same gender. Although the degree of gender segregation in the professional workplace has declined since the 1970s, racial and ethnic segregation remains deeply embedded.

■ How is occupational segregation related to the pay gap?

Many women work in lower-paying, less prestigious jobs than men. This occupational segregation leads to a disparity, or pay gap, between women's and men's earnings. Even when women are employed in the same job as men, on average they do not receive the same, or comparable, pay.

■ **How do functionalists and conflict theorists differ in their view of division of labour by gender?**

According to functional analysts, women's roles as caregivers in contemporary industrialized societies are crucial in ensuring that key societal tasks are fulfilled. Whereas the husband performs the instrumental tasks of economic support and decision making, the wife assumes the expressive tasks of providing affection and emotional support to the family. According to conflict analysis, the gendered division of labour within families and the workplace—particularly in agrarian and industrial societies—results from male control and dominance over women and resources.

■ **How do the various feminist perspectives explain gender inequality?**

Although feminist perspectives vary in their analyses of women's subordination, they all advocate social change to eradicate gender inequality. In liberal feminism, gender equality is connected to equality of opportunity. In radical feminism, male dominance is seen as the cause of oppression. According to socialist feminists, women's oppression results from their dual roles as paid and unpaid workers. Antiracist feminists focus on including knowledge and awareness of the lives of marginalized women in the struggle for equality.

KEY TERMS

body consciousness 333
discourses 356
employment equity 350
feminism 355
gender 332
gender bias 343
gender identity 333
gender role 333
hermaphrodite 330
homophobia 332
matriarchy 335
patriarchy 335
pay equity (comparable worth) 350
primary sex characteristics 329
secondary sex characteristics 329
sex 329
sexism 334
sexual orientation 331

transsexual 330
transvestite 330
wage gap 349

NET LINKS

Status of Women Canada (SWC) is a federal government agency that promotes gender equality and full participation of women in the economic, social, cultural, and political life of the country. SWC focuses on three areas: improving women's economic autonomy and well-being, eliminating violence against women and children, and advancing women's human rights; go to:
http://www.swc-cfc.gc.ca/index_e.html

Canadian Women's Internet Association (CWIA) contains hundreds of links to sites relevant to women, with a special focus on Canadian content; go to:
http://directory.womenspace.ca/directory.cgi

The National Organization for Men Against Sexism (NOMAS) has a profeminist stance that seeks to end sexism and an affirmative stance on the rights of gay men and lesbians. Go to:
http://www.nomas.org/sys-tmpl/door

MenWeb (*Men's Voices* magazine) is an e-zine that offers support and advocacy for men. Features articles on the men's movement and a national calendar of men's events, as well as links to other sites:
http://www.menweb.org

QUESTIONS FOR CRITICAL THINKING

1. Do the media reflect societal attitudes on gender, or do the media determine and teach gender behaviour? (As a related activity, watch television for several hours and list the roles women and men play in the shows and in the advertisements.)
2. Examine the various academic departments at your university. What is the gender breakdown of the faculty in selected departments? What is the gender breakdown of undergraduates and graduates in those departments? Are there major differences among the social sciences, science, and humanities departments? What can you come up with to explain your observations?
3. As discussed throughout this chapter, gender may be viewed as a social construction. "Doing gender," whether you are male or female, is something you have learned through a process of socialization. What changes would you have to make in your "gender performance" if you were to wake up one morning as the opposite gender?

SUGGESTED READINGS

These well-written books provide in-depth information on various issues raised in this chapter:

Sandra L. Bem. *The Lenses of Gender: Transforming the Debate on Sexual Inequality.* New Haven, Conn.: Yale University Press, 1993.

Michael S. Kimmel and Michael A. Messner (eds.). *Men's Lives.* New York: Macmillan, 1992.

Nancy Mandell (ed.). *Feminist Issues: Race, Class, and Sexuality* (3rd ed.). Toronto: Prentice-Hall, 2001.

Pat Armstrong and Hugh Armstrong. *The Double Ghetto: Canadian Women and Their Segregated Work.* Toronto: McClelland & Stewart, 1994.

For additional information on the bodybuilding subculture:

Alan M. Klein. *Little Big Men: Bodybuilding Subculture and Gender Construction.* Albany: State University of New York Press, 1993.

ONLINE STUDY AND RESEARCH TOOLS

THOMSONNOW™ Thomson NOW!

Go to **http://hed.nelson.com** to link to ThomsonNOW for *Sociology in Our Times,* Fourth Canadian Edition, your online study tool. First take the **Pre-Test** for this chapter to get your personalized **Study Plan,** which will identify topics you need to review and direct you to the appropriate resources. Then take the **Post-Test** to determine what concepts you have mastered and what you still need work on.

INFOTRAC®

Infotrac College Edition is included free with every new copy of this text. Explore this online library for additional readings, review, and a handy resource for assignments. Visit **www.infotrac-college.com** to access this online database of full-text articles. Enter the key terms from this chapter to start your search.

CHAPTER 12

Aging

"It all became clear one day, as I stood at the MAC makeup counter of a Toronto department store, trying to catch a salesperson's eye. The black-clad 20-somethings kept avoiding my steely gaze and waited on all of the younger women around me.

"I worried that perhaps I was in the middle of a dream or possibly even, invisible. When I finally grabbed a young man at the counter with a couple of piercings to his lower lip, he apologized. "I thought you were with your daughter," he said, pointing to one of the Goths beside me. God forbid a woman in her 40s should buy lipstick on her own.

"I realized then that part of me was starting to disappear. Unlike Alice, in Woody Allen's movie of the same name, who was given potions to make her invisible, all I had to do was continue to sit around and age and I, too, would start to fade away.

"I did what many women do when they first realize they're disappearing—I fought back. We can be perked up or puffed out. I coloured my hair, increased my daily dosage of makeup, bought bellbottoms (or are they flares now?). And started wearing my daughter's clothes.

"Cosmetic surgery was beyond my budget, though it has done much to make a liar out of Shakespeare's Duke Orsino, who claims in *Twelfth Night* that women are like roses, 'whose fair flower, Being once display'd, doth fall that very hour.'

"What I didn't realize initially is that invisibility runs deeper than just our skin." (Binks, 2003)

Vic Plowman's day begins at 5:30 a.m., with the chime of an alarm clock and his wife Lillian's now-familiar greeting: "Are you still here?"

"When you're 88 years old, the next day is never guaranteed. But with his survival confirmed, Mr. Plowman quickly shifts into work mode: He shaves, makes coffee and puts on a pressed white shirt and a carefully knotted tie—proper office attire is a tradition that has helped to carry him through seven decades of work."

Punctuality is another. By 6:45, he's in his Ford Focus, driving to his office in Oakville, Ont. His company is called GLN Farm and Forest Research—Mr. Plowman sometimes describes his job as "tree doctor." By 7 a.m., he's in the office, checking his e-mail, a newfangled invention he has come to love.

Mr. Plowman has been running this company for 47 years, but his enthusiasm is undimmed. "When you do something like this, it isn't work," he says. Each day presents a new challenge. At the moment, he's diagnosing the private forest of a Toronto business tycoon whose trees have been afflicted by a mysterious ailment. . . . He considers work his fountain of youth.

"People ask me why I want to keep working," he says. "But my question is, why would someone stop? If you have something interesting, that makes you go on." (Cheney, 2004:F4)

"When Morley Callaghan turned 80, his sons gave him a birthday party in a fine restaurant. During a graceful thank-you speech, the novelist said, 'Being 80 is like walking through a jungle: you never know what is going to pounce on you next.'

"I've been 80 for a few months now and I don't see it as a very big deal. My packaging is wearing out: my skin is too big for me and falls in folds, I have less hair, I am shorter and stooped, and my knees hurt on stairs. Plus a bit of cancer. But I'm still me; exactly me, irreducibly, for better and also for worse, me.

"When I was young, I expected that age would make me sage and I would become so serene that strangers would stop to take my pulse. I now realize that all age does is make you old.

"Almost all the invincible women of the 1950s are now widows. I am almost the only one of our gang with a living husband. After 60 years, our marriage is a mellow one. We seem to be bobbing on a sea of affection, and disagreements are rare. Perhaps we are maturing. Just in time." (Callwood, 2005:56)

 ventually, all of us will be affected by aging. *Aging* **is the physical, psychological, and social processes associated with growing**

older (Atchley, 1997). As the experiences of Georgie Binks, Vic Plowman, and June Callwood suggest, the psychological and social processes associated with aging can be at least as important as the physical processes in determining how we will spend our older years.

In some societies, including Canada, older people may be the targets of prejudice and discrimination based on myths about aging. For example, older people may be viewed as incompetent solely because of their age. Although some older people may need assistance from others and support from society, many others are physically, socially, and financially independent. In this chapter, we examine the sociological aspects of aging. We will also examine how older people seek dignity, autonomy, and empowerment in a society that often devalues people who do not fit the ideal norms of youth, beauty, physical fitness, and self-sufficiency. Before reading on, test your knowledge about aging and age-based discrimination by taking the quiz in Box 12.1.

QUESTIONS AND ISSUES

Chapter Focus Question: Given the fact that aging is an inevitable consequence of living (unless an individual dies young), why do many people in Canada devalue older persons?

How does functional age differ from chronological age?

How does age determine a person's roles and statuses in society?

What factors contribute to successful aging?

What actions can be taken to bring about a more equitable society for older people?

THE SOCIAL SIGNIFICANCE OF AGE

"How old are you?" This is one of the most frequently asked questions in our society. Beyond indicating how old or young a person is, age is socially significant because it defines what is appropriate for or expected of people at various stages. Moreover, while it is an ascribed status, age is one of the few ascribed statuses that changes over time. Thus behaviour that is considered appropriate at one stage of a person's life may be considered odd or unusual at another stage. For example, nobody thinks it is unusual if a person in her twenties goes in-line skating. However, if her

seventy-five-year-old grandfather does the same thing, he may receive some odd looks and even media coverage because he is defying norms regarding age-appropriate behaviour.

When people say "Act your age," they are referring to *chronological age*—**a person's age based on date of birth.** However, most of us actually estimate a person's age on the basis of *functional age*—**observable individual attributes, such as physical appearance, mobility, strength, coordination, and mental capacity that are used to assign people to age categories** (Atchley and Barusch, 2004). Because we typically do not have access to other people's birth certificates to learn their chronological age, we often use visible characteristics—such as youthful

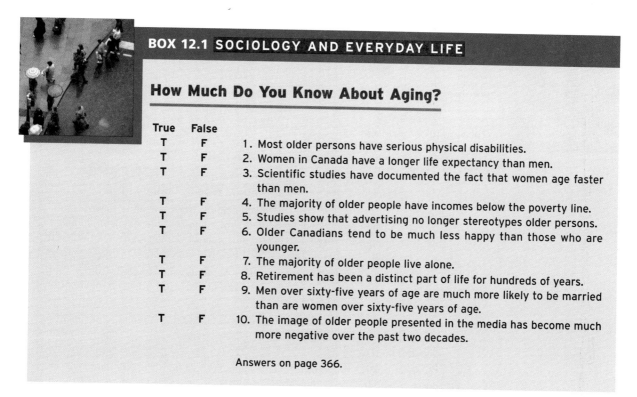

BOX 12.1 SOCIOLOGY AND EVERYDAY LIFE

How Much Do You Know About Aging?

True	False	
T	F	1. Most older persons have serious physical disabilities.
T	F	2. Women in Canada have a longer life expectancy than men.
T	F	3. Scientific studies have documented the fact that women age faster than men.
T	F	4. The majority of older people have incomes below the poverty line.
T	F	5. Studies show that advertising no longer stereotypes older persons.
T	F	6. Older Canadians tend to be much less happy than those who are younger.
T	F	7. The majority of older people live alone.
T	F	8. Retirement has been a distinct part of life for hundreds of years.
T	F	9. Men over sixty-five years of age are much more likely to be married than are women over sixty-five years of age.
T	F	10. The image of older people presented in the media has become much more negative over the past two decades.

Answers on page 366.

appearance or grey hair and wrinkled skin—as our criteria for determining whether someone is "young" or "old." As historian Lois W. Banner (1993:15) suggests, "Appearance, more than any other factor, has occasioned the objectification of aging. We define someone as old because he or she looks old." Feminist scholars have noted that functional age works differently for women and men—as they age, men may be viewed as distinguished or powerful whereas when women grow older they are thought to be "over the hill" or grandmotherly (Banner, 1993).

Trends in Aging

You are used to thinking about people getting older, but you may not have realized that societies can also age. Today, older Canadians make up more than one-tenth of the population. This makes Canada's population one of the oldest in the world, and population projections suggest that Canadian society will age even more in the next fifty years (see Figure 12.1).

In 1981, the median age (the age at which half the people are younger and half are older) in Canada was thirty. In 2001, it was thirty-eight. This substantial increase—eight years in two decades—is partly the result of the baby boomers (people born between 1946 and 1964) moving into middle age, and partly the result of more people living longer. As shown in

Many older persons seek dignity, autonomy, and empowerment in a society that values youth, beauty, physical fitness, and self-sufficiency.

BOX 12.1 SOCIOLOGY AND EVERYDAY LIFE

Answers to the Sociology Quiz on Aging

1. **False.** In Canada, 18 percent of people between the ages of sixty-five and seventy-four, and 24 percent of those seventy-five and over, report their activities are limited because of physical impairment (Statistics Canada, 2003p).

2. **True.** In 2002, female life expectancy (at birth) was eighty-two years, compared with seventy-seven years for males (Statistics Canada, 2004p).

3. **False.** No studies have documented that women age faster than men. However, some scholars have noted a "double standard" of aging that places older women at a disadvantage with respect to older men because women's worth in the North American culture is defined in terms of physical appearance.

4. **False.** The 1997 poverty rate for seniors was 18 percent, which is down from 33 percent reported in 1980. However, females are at a greater risk of living in poverty than males (Lindsay, 1999).

5. **False.** Studies have shown that advertisements frequently depict older people negatively—for example, as sickly or silly. However, this is changing (see Question 10).

6. **False.** Several surveys have shown that people sixty-five and over are actually more satisfied with their lives than are younger Canadians (Statistics Canada, 2003p).

7. **False.** The majority of older persons live with others. In Canada, only about 16 percent of men and 35 percent of women sixty-five and over live alone (Cranswick, 2003).

8. **False.** Retirement is a relatively modern invention. The first government pension plan was established in Germany in 1899. Canada adopted a pension system in 1927, but retirement was not common until after World War II, when benefits were improved.

9. **True.** In 1996, 79 percent of men and 43 percent of women over sixty-five were married. The reason for this is that women live longer than men. This means that men are unlikely to be widowed, while women are likely to outlive their spouses (Lindsay, 1999).

10. **False.** Analysis of books, magazines, advertisements, and television shows has shown that over the years media images of older people have become more positive and less likely to give stereotypical and negative portrayals (Novak and Campbell, 2006).

Figure 12.1   Projected Population by Age Group, Canada, 1992-2036

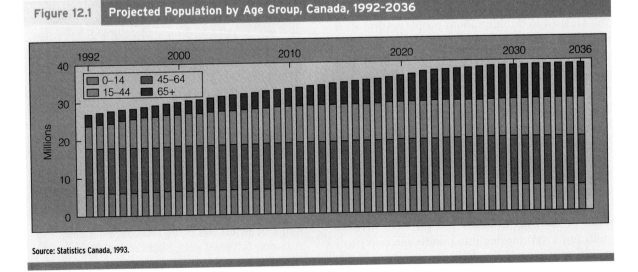

Source: Statistics Canada, 1993.

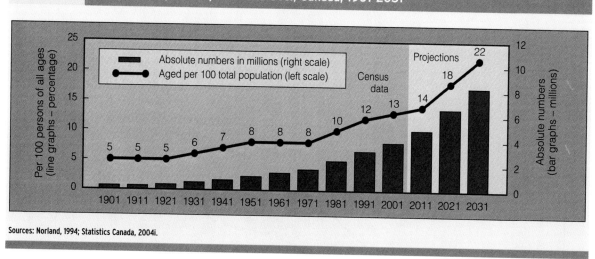

Figure 12.2 Population Aged Sixty-Five and Over, Canada, 1901-2031

Sources: Norland, 1994; Statistics Canada, 2004i.

Figure 12.2, the number of older people (age sixty-five and above) increased dramatically between 1901 and 1991 (McKie, 1994). The number of people aged eighty years and over increased by 40 percent in the decade between 1991 and 2001 (Cranswick, 2003).

Referred to by some analysts as the *greying of Canada,* the aging of the Canadian population resulted from an increase in life expectancy combined with a decrease in birth rates (McKie, 1994). **Life expectancy is the average length of time a group of individuals of the same age will live.** Based on the death rates in the year of birth, life expectancy shows the average length of life of a *cohort*—**a group of people born within a specified period of time.** Cohorts may be established on the basis of one-, five-, or ten-year intervals; they may also be defined by events taking place at the time of their birth, such as the "Depression era" babies or baby boomers (Moody, 1998). For the cohort born in 2002, for example, life expectancy at birth was 82 for females and 77 for males (Statistics Canada, 2004c). Figure 12.3 outlines the sex differences in life expectancy.

At the turn of the last century, about 5 percent of the Canadian population was over age sixty-five; in 1981, that number had risen to approximately 10 percent. As Figure 12.2 shows, in 1991, approximately 12 percent of the population was age sixty-five or over. By the year 2026, according to projections, about 21 percent of the population will be at least sixty-five (Cranswick, 2003).

Since the beginning of the twentieth century, life expectancy has steadily increased as industrialized nations developed better water and sewage systems, improved nutrition, and made tremendous advances in medical science. Economic development that

contributed to the lower death rate also was a force in lowering the birth rate. In industrialized nations, children came to be viewed as an economic liability: they could not contribute to the family's financial well-being and had to be supported.

The current distribution of the Canadian population is depicted in the "age pyramid" in Figure 12.4. If, every year, the same number of people are born as in the previous year and a certain number die in each age group, the plot of the population distribution should be pyramid-shaped. As you will note, however, Figure 12.4 is not a perfect pyramid, but rather reflects declining birth rates since the baby boom. This has resulted in fewer young people (see Chapter 19, "Population and Urbanization").

As a result of changing population trends, research on aging has grown dramatically in the past fifty years. *Gerontology* is the study of aging and older people. A subfield of gerontology, **social gerontology is the study of the social (nonphysical) aspects of aging,** including such topics as the societal consequences of an aging population and the personal experience of aging. According to gerontologists, age is viewed differently from society to society and changes over time.

Age in Historical Perspective

People are assigned to different roles and positions based on the age structure and role structure in a particular society. *Age structure* is the number of persons at each age level within the society; *role structure* is the number and type of positions available to them (Riley and Riley, 1994). Over the years, the age continuum has been chopped up into finer and finer points.

Figure 12.3   Evolution of Life Expectancy at Birth by Age and Sex, Canada, 1921-2002

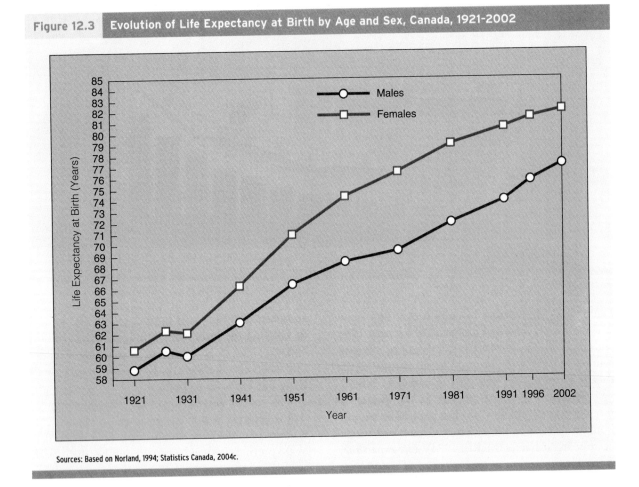

Sources: Based on Norland, 1994; Statistics Canada, 2004c.

Two hundred years ago, people divided the age spectrum into "babyhood," a *very* short childhood, and then adulthood. What we would consider "childhood" today was very different two hundred years ago, when agricultural societies needed a large number of strong arms and backs to work on the land to ensure survival. When most of the population had to be involved in food production, categories, such as toddlers, preschoolers, preteens, teenagers, young adults, the middle-aged, or older persons, did not exist.

If the physical labour of young persons is necessary for society's survival, then young persons are considered "little adults" and are expected to act like adults and do adult work. Older persons also are expected to continue to be productive for the benefit of the society for as long as they are physically able. In some hunting and gathering societies, older members may be abandoned or killed when they become a burden on others (Glascock and Feinman, 1981). In preindustrial societies, persons of all ages help with the work, and little training is necessary for the roles that they fill. During the seventeenth and eighteenth centuries in North America, for example, older individuals helped with

the work and were respected because they were needed—and because few people lived that long (Gratton, 1986). The presence of large numbers of older people is a modern phenomenon and their place in society is still evolving.

AGE AND THE LIFE COURSE IN CONTEMPORARY SOCIETY

In industrialized societies, the skills necessary for many roles are more complex and the number of unskilled positions is more limited. Consequently, children are expected to attend school and learn the necessary skills for future employment rather than perform unskilled labour. Further, older persons are expected to retire so that younger persons can take their places.

Figure 12.4 Age Pyramid of Population of Canada, 2006

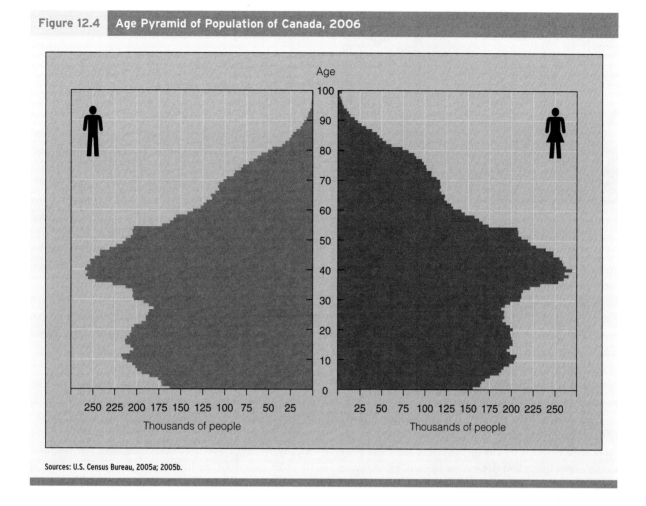

Sources: U.S. Census Bureau, 2005a; 2005b.

In North America, age differentiation is based on narrowly defined categories, such as infancy, childhood, adolescence, young adulthood, middle adulthood, and later adulthood. These narrowly defined age categories have had a profound effect on our perceptions of people's capabilities, responsibilities, and entitlements. What is considered appropriate for or expected of people at various ages is somewhat arbitrarily determined and produces *age stratification*—**the inequalities, differences, segregation, or conflict between age groups** (Atchley, 1997). We will now examine some of those strata.

Middle Adulthood

Prior to the twentieth century, life expectancy in Canada was not nearly as high as it is today, so the concept of middle adulthood—people between the ages of forty and sixty-five—did not exist until fairly recently. Normal changes in appearance occur during these years; although these changes have little relationship to a person's health or physical functioning, they are socially

significant to many people (Lefrançois, 1999). In going through these changes, people are experiencing *senescence* (primary aging) in the form of molecular and cellular changes in the body. Wrinkles and grey hair are visible signs of senescence. Less visible signs include arthritis and a gradual dulling of the senses of taste, smell, touch, and vision. Typically, reflexes begin to slow down, but the actual nature and extent of the changes vary greatly from person to person.

People may experience a change of life in this stage. Women undergo *menopause*—the cessation of the menstrual cycle caused by a gradual decline in the body's production of the "female" hormones estrogen and progesterone. Menopause typically occurs between the mid-forties and the early fifties and signals the end of a woman's childbearing capabilities. Some women may experience irregular menstrual cycles for several years, followed by hot flashes, retention of body fluids, swollen breasts, and other aches and pains. Other women may have few or no noticeable physical symptoms. The psychological aspects of menopause often are as important as any physical effects. In one study,

Today many retired persons have good health and the resources to enjoy an active life.

Anne Fausto-Sterling (1985) concluded that many women respond negatively to menopause because of negative stereotypes associated with menopausal and postmenopausal women. These stereotypes make the natural process of aging in women appear abnormal when compared with men's aging process. Actually, many women experience a new interest in sexual activity because they no longer have to worry about the possibility of becoming pregnant.

Men undergo a *climacteric* in which the production of the "male" hormone testosterone decreases. Some have argued that this change in hormone levels produces nervousness and depression in men. However, it is not clear whether these emotional changes are due to biological changes or to a more general "midlife crisis" in which men assess what they have accomplished (Benokraitis, 2002).

Along with primary aging, people in middle adulthood also experience *secondary aging*, which occurs as a result of environmental factors and lifestyle choices. For example, smoking, drinking heavily, and engaging in little or no physical activity are factors that affect the aging process. People who live in regions with high levels of environmental degradation and other forms of pollution are also at greater risk of aging more rapidly and having chronic illnesses and diseases associated with these external factors.

On the positive side, middle adulthood for most people represents the time during which (1) they have the highest levels of income and prestige, (2) they leave the problems of child rearing behind them and are content with their spouse of many years, and (3) they may have grandchildren who give them another tie to the future. Even so, persons in middle adulthood know that, given society's current structure, their status may begin to change significantly when they reach the end of that period of their lives. Formal recognition of this new status also occurs.

Many businesses and services offer reduced rates for seniors as early as age fifty-five.

Late Adulthood

Late adulthood is generally considered to begin at age sixty-five—the "normal" retirement age. *Retirement* is the institutionalized separation of an individual from an occupational position, with continuation of income through a retirement pension based on prior years of service (Atchley and Barusch, 2004). Retirement means the end of a status that long has been a source of income and a means of personal identity. Perhaps the loss of a valued status explains why many retired persons introduce themselves by saying, "I'm retired now, but I was a (banker, lawyer, plumber, supervisor, and so on) for forty years."

Some gerontologists subdivide late adulthood into three categories: (1) the "young-old" (ages 65–74), (2) the "old-old" (ages 75–85), and (3) the "oldest-old" (over age 85) (see Moody, 1998). Although these are somewhat arbitrary divisions, the "young-old" are less likely to suffer from disabling illnesses, while some of the "old-old" are more likely to suffer such illnesses (Belsky, 1990). A recent study found, however, that the prevalence of disability among those eighty-five and over has decreased over the last two decades due to better health care.

The rate of biological and psychological changes in older persons may be as important as their chronological age in determining how they are perceived by themselves and others. As adults grow older, their bones become more brittle; simply falling may result in broken bones that take longer to heal. With age, arthritis increases, and connective tissue stiffens joints. Wrinkled skin, "age spots," grey (or white) hair, and midriff bulge appear; however, people may use Oil of Olay, Clairol, or Buster's Magic Tummy Tightener in the hope of avoiding looking older (Atchley and Barusch, 2004).

Older persons also have increased chances of heart attacks, strokes, and cancer. Some diseases affect virtually only persons in late adulthood. Alzheimer's disease (a progressive and irreversible deterioration of brain tissue) is an example; about 55 percent of all organic mental disorders in the older population are caused by Alzheimer's (Atchley and Barusch, 2004). Persons with this disease have an impaired ability to function in everyday social roles. Eventually, they cease to be able to recognize people they have always known and lose all sense of their own identity. Finally, they may revert to a speechless, infantile state such that others must feed them, dress them, sit them on the toilet, and lead them around. The disease has no known cause and, currently, there is no cure. More than a quarter million Canadians suffer from Alzheimer's disease and related dementias. By the year 2030, it is estimated that this number will grow to three-quarters of a million.

The time and attention needed to care for someone who has Alzheimer's disease or who simply no longer can leave home without help can be staggering. Daniel Heinrichs, a full-time caregiver for his wife, explains what caring for Norah was like:

> My wife Norah was afflicted with Alzheimer's disease. She could no longer function as a person in our marriage. Slowly I had to take over the various duties she had performed. After that I took over her financial affairs. Then I had to care for her personally: choosing, buying, and looking after clothing, dressing and undressing her, combing her hair, and feeding her. Slowly our conversation ceased. She could not think rationally any more. She could not understand the words that were being used, and she did not know the names of objects she saw. She no longer knew who I was either. "Norah is gone, there is nothing left of your marriage. You need to look after yourself again," is advice that I have heard and felt. Fortunately, I did not yield to this advice. Despite all of Norah's disabilities, we continued to have a rich and enjoyable experience together. I learned to communicate with Norah in other ways. How I spoke the words said more than their actual meaning. She watched for the smile on my face and the fun in my voice. My disposition had more effect on her than my words. She let me put my arm around her and hold her hands whenever I desired, or needed to do so . . . Now Norah is gone, but I'm glad that I stayed with her ". . . till death do us part." (Heinrichs, 1996:48)

Caring for an older person with a physical disability or a cognitive impairment can be very stressful (Novak and Campbell, 2001). Feelings of caregiver burden can particularly affect spouses who face not only the stress of caregiving but also the pain of seeing their loved one decline.

Fortunately, most older people do not suffer from Alzheimer's and are not incapacitated by their physical condition. Only about 5 percent of older people live in nursing homes, about 10 percent have visual impairment, and about 50 percent have some hearing loss (Naeyaert, 1990; Novak, 1993). Although most older people experience some decline in strength, flexibility, stamina, and other physical capabilities, much of that decline does not result simply from the aging process and is avoidable; with proper exercise, some of it is even reversible (Lefrançois, 1999).

Along with physical changes come changes in the roles played by older adults. One that most people enjoy is being a grandparent. An extended family is a great source of pleasure for many older Canadians. Grandparenting is an interesting role because it "has no clearly defined responsibilities, expectations, or rights" (McPherson, 1998:209). This gives members of younger and older generations the opportunity to build relationships that are to their mutual benefit. Some of the benefits of having grandparents are described in the following comments by Grade 3 students about the role of a grandmother (Huyck, cited in McPherson, 1998:213):

> When they read to us they don't skip words and they don't mind if it is the same story.
>
> They don't have to be smart, only answer questions like why dogs hate cats, and how come God isn't married.
>
> Grandmas are the only grownups who have got time—so everybody should have a grandmother, especially if you don't have television.

Some of the physical and psychological changes that come with increasing age can cause stress. According to Erik Erikson (1963), older people must resolve a tension of "integrity versus despair." They must accept that the life cycle is inevitable, that their lives are nearing an end, and that achieving inner harmony requires accepting both one's past accomplishments and past disappointments. Mark Novak interviewed several older people about what he termed "successful aging." One respondent, Joanne, commented:

> For me getting older was very painful at first because I resisted change. Now I'm changed, and it's okay. I would say I have a new freedom . . . I thought I had no limits, but for me a great learning [experience] was recognizing my limits. It was a complete turnover, almost like a rebirth. I guess I've learned we're all weak really. At least we should accept that—being weak—and realize, "Hey, I'm only a fragile human being." (Novak, 1995:125)

Despite its negative aspects, aging has many positive dimensions and most older people are quite content with their lives. Many are financially secure, with home mortgages paid off and no children remaining at home. This gives them a great deal of personal freedom. Most report they are in good or excellent health (Norland, 1994). Northcott found that older Edmonton residents were actually happier with their lives than younger respondents (1982). A national study conducted by Health and Welfare Canada (1998) found that older people were much less likely than younger people to report that their lives were stressful and the vast majority (92 percent) reported that they were pretty happy or very happy. Finally, Connidis (1989) reports that married people over sixty-five have a higher level of satisfaction with their romantic relationships than married people of any other age.

Retirement

Retirement is a recent invention. The first national pension system was established by Otto von Bismark in Germany in 1889. In Canada, the *Old Age Pension Act* was introduced in 1927 to provide a basic income to needy retired people. This was the beginning of a shift in the burden of retirement from the individual to the state. However, people were still expected to look after themselves or to receive help from their families. Initially, pensions were given only to needy people over the age of seventy, and payments were minimal in the early days. Retirement did not become common until the amount paid to retirees by public pension plans increased. The pension system became more generous when coverage was made universal in 1951 and as benefits were improved between 1951 and 1975 (Northcott, 1982).

Pensions are one of the most important factors affecting retirement plans. Currently, all working people in Canada are covered by the Canada or Quebec Pension Plans, and all those over age sixty-five receive additional money through the Old Age Security pension, though some or all of this may be taxed back from higher-income recipients. About 1.4 million lower-income Canadians also receive the benefits of the Guaranteed Income Supplement program. These programs are responsible for the reduction in poverty among older people shown in Figure 12.5.

Many people also have their own company pension plans and others have invested in Registered Retirement Savings Plans (RRSPs). Most government workers belong to pension plans compared with only about one-third of those employed in the private sector (Statistics Canada, 1996a).

Retirement plays an increasingly important part in the lives of Canadians. When the first retirement laws were passed, the retirement age (usually seventy) was much higher than the average life expectancy. As a result, most people never retired, and for those who did, the retirement years were typically short. Today, fewer than 10 percent of seniors are still working (Statistics Canada, 2004i). Since the retirement age has been declining and life expectancy has been increasing, the retirement years will likely make up an increasing proportion of people's lives in the future. On the other hand, many people—like Vic Plowman, who is quoted in the Chapter Introduction—prefer to continue working after the normal retirement age of sixty-five. Most provinces no longer allow mandatory retirement, and many of the remaining provinces, including Ontario, are considering similar legislation. Do you feel that people should be forced to retire at sixty-five? What are the advantages and disadvantages of mandatory retirement?

Retirement can represent a major transition for people, as they lose a source of income, identity, lifestyle, and friends that they may have had for most of their adult lives. This is especially true of high-status workers who achieve a great deal of satisfaction from their jobs. Jack Culberg explains the difficulties of the transition:

> When you suddenly leave [the corporate jungle], life is pretty empty. I was sixty-five, the age people are supposed to retire. I started to miss it quite a bit. The phone stops ringing. The king is dead. You start wanting to have lunch with old friends. At the beginning, they're nice to you, but then you realize that they're busy, they're working. They've got a job

| Figure 12.5 | Low-Income Rate,* People Sixty-Five and Older, 1980-1999, Selected Years |

Poverty rates have steadily declined for all categories of older people. There are still dramatic differences between couples and unattached people, particularly females.

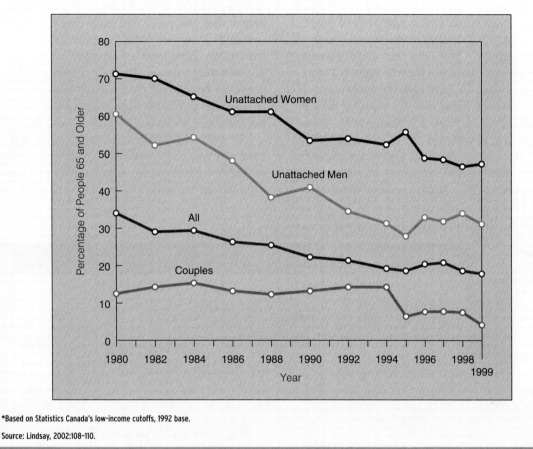

*Based on Statistics Canada's low-income cutoffs, 1992 base.

Source: Lindsay, 2002:108–110.

to do and just don't have the time to talk to anybody where it doesn't involve their business. I could be nasty and say, "Unless they make a buck out of it"—but I won't . . . You hesitate to call them. (quoted in Terkel, 1996:9–10)

As Culberg's statement indicates, people tend to think of age in narrowly defined categories and reaching "retirement age" places many of them out of the mainstream. To ease this transition, researchers suggest that people plan ways of remaining occupied and engaged in society. Those who are involved with activities, such as volunteer work and hobbies that can be continued after retirement, are happier and healthier than those who have few retirement interests and who withdraw from social life. Research has shown that people do adjust successfully to retirement and they have few problems adapting to their new social status and lifestyle (McPherson, 1998). Many retirees say they are busier after retirement than before; the difference is that they

stay busy doing things they choose to do rather than things they are obliged to do. Also, many organizations are encouraging older workers to make gradual transitions to retirement by staying in the labour force on a part-time basis. This allows the organization to retain the skills of senior employees and enables the individual to make the transition to retirement at a comfortable pace.

A Statistics Canada survey found that more than half of retirees would have liked to continue working, particularly if they were allowed more flexible working hours and more time off (Schellenberg and Silver, 2004). While the vast majority of seniors do retire by sixty-five, some, like Vic Plowman, prefer to stay on the job. Between 1996 and 2001 the number of seniors who were working increased at nearly twice the rate of the growth in the senior population. The average age of working seniors was older in 2001, and they were employed in a more diverse range of occupations.

Along with the difficulties of changing status from worker to retiree, the major threats to successful retirement are finances and health. Financially, the government provides most Canadians with sufficient resources to meet basic needs for food and shelter. However, if you want to travel, move to escape harsh winters, buy gifts for grandchildren, and do the other things that bring satisfaction to many retired people, you will need to save money to supplement the government pension. This can be done through employer-sponsored pension plans or registered retirement savings plans. In either case, the mathematics of compound interest mean that this must be done as early in life as possible. Unfortunately, many Canadians have not learned this lesson; a 1999 poll showed that 11 percent of Canadians actually expected to finance their retirement through lottery winnings (Dube, 1999). Since the odds of winning the

6/49 lottery are about 14 million to one, this is not really a sound financial plan. The same poll also pointed out the costs of neglecting retirement planning, as 38 percent of retired Canadians reported that they did not have sufficient funds to maintain the lifestyle they had envisioned when they retired.

Health is another major determinant of successful retirement. Poor health has many consequences. An individual may lose his or her freedom and independence because of illness. Poor health may also be isolating, as it limits the physical and social activities that are so important to older people.

The costs of pensions and health care have led to some concerns about whether Canada can afford the inevitable increase in the number of retired people. Consider the arguments in Box 12.2.

BOX 12.2 CRITICAL THINKING

Will There Be a Generational War Between the Old and the Young?

Canadians enjoy retirement, and why not? Most retirees are having the time of their lives: long, lazy summers at the cottage, gambling jaunts to Vegas in the winter, golf all year round . . .

Retirement as we know it—ten or twenty years of fun, partly at public expense, as a reward for showing up at work during our adult lives—is doomed. The happy coincidence of generous governments and the postwar economic and population boom that made it possible has come undone. The web of government-sponsored seniors' programmes that pays retirees largely from the taxes of those still working has become unsustainable . . .

Funding leisure in later life must become a personal responsibility, not a social obligation. Retirees must stop insisting that they have a right to siphon money from their kids to help make their golden years enjoyable. (Taylor, 1995:18)

Is Peter Shawn Taylor correct? Will our social welfare system go bankrupt when the baby boomers reach retirement age? Will young people be impoverished by their parents and grandparents? Let us look at how the system works and at its likely future.

Much of Canada's social welfare system has been designed to support the young and the old. An informal social contract between generations obliges the working-age population to support dependent children and older adults. In exchange, these workers received support during their own childhoods and could expect to receive support in their old age.

After World War II, governments in most industrial countries placed a priority on providing old-age pensions for seniors, and initially this effort was successful. However, in the mid-1970s people began to worry that increasing numbers of elderly and increasing entitlements would cause the collapse of the Old Age Security program (Myles, 1999).

This led people, such as Taylor, to suggest that the social contract between generations has been broken and that young people will have to pay far more to support older people than they will ever receive in return. The huge numbers of aging baby boomers, who themselves supported a relatively small number of older people and who are responsible for building up much of our national debt, will have to be supported in their old age by a much smaller number of workers.

The debate over the possibility of intergenerational conflict flourished during the 1980s and 1990s when unemployment rates were high, particularly for young people, and when massive social service cuts were pitting one group against the other. This was symbolized by seniors' activist Solange Denis, who confronted then-prime minister Brian Mulroney on Parliament Hill in 1985 and helped force him to back down on planned cuts to pensions. Because of their political power, older people suffered fewer cuts to social programs than other vulnerable groups, such as children and single-parent families (Gray, 1997).

The tension between the generations is increased by public images, such as the one in the quotation at the beginning of this box, that suggest older people are living the good life while younger people struggle to find jobs and to pay off student loans. Those concerned with this issue have suggested that benefits be cut, that the age for payment of government pensions be raised, or that monthly premiums be raised to ensure that sufficient funds are available when the baby boomers begin to retire. Others have proposed rationing health care to older people (Callahan, 1987).

Those readers who will not retire for several decades should not be too concerned about the gloomy future predicted by Taylor. Ellen Gee (2000) has described the alarmist view of the costs of aging as "voodoo demography." Several European countries already have high proportions of older persons and are able to support old-age-security programs without seeing signs of intergenerational hostility. Also, a number of factors should help to alleviate the problem before it turns into a crisis. First, because of declining fertility rates, fewer resources will be required to look after children and it will be easier to direct resources to older people (Desjardins, 1993). Second, the Canadian government has taken action that will lessen the future burden on our pension system. While many corporations have cut back on their pension benefits, the 1999 increase in Canada Pension Plan contributions will ensure that government pensions are still available for all Canadians in the future. Finally, many older persons will be well off and paying high levels of tax on their retirement income. Most seniors are debt-free and own their own homes (Statistics Canada, 2003q). Many give money and other kinds of support to other family members and contribute significant amounts of volunteer labour, so older people do not just take from their children and grandchildren.

With good planning, much can also be done to alleviate a possible crisis in health care. Measures, such as community support programs, are discussed in this chapter. Others include taking measures to improve health. In fact, older people have responded well to government health-promotion efforts focused on diet, exercise, and lifestyle, and have led the way in adopting healthier lifestyles. This should help reduce their use of the health care system. Health care officials can also deal with the problems of inappropriate referrals and repeat visits to doctors adding significant costs to the system by reducing their numbers without affecting public health. Finally, we can develop policies that address the fact that a large proportion of health care costs occur in the final six months of life. These costs include keeping the dying patient in an acute care facility, ordering tests, and using life support in order to prolong life even when it is clear that the patient is dying. Many dying patients could be well cared for in hospices or chronic care hospitals, rather than in more expensive acute care hospitals.

What do you think about this issue? Are you prepared to pay to support your parents and grandparents? How can people be persuaded to do necessary things, such as exercising and stopping smoking, that will reduce their need for health care? What should our politicians do to prepare Canada for the future?

How can you increase your chances of enjoying a long and happy retirement? The answer is that you should begin to look after your physical and financial health as early in life as possible. Proper diet, moderate drinking, not smoking, regular medical checkups, maintaining your fitness, and investing for your older years will help to ensure many years of successful retirement.

INEQUALITIES RELATED TO AGING

In previous chapters, we have seen how prejudice and discrimination may be directed toward individuals based on ascribed characteristics—such as ethnicity or gender—over which they have no control. The same holds true for age.

In some respects, older people are treated very well in Canada. Most have adequate incomes and all have access to publicly funded medical care. Housing for older people is often subsidized, and many businesses offer discounts for people who are over sixty-five. At the same time, however, many older people feel their biggest problem is that other people have negative views of aging and of the capabilities of older people.

Ageism

Stereotypes regarding older persons reinforce *ageism—* **prejudice and discrimination against people on the basis of age, particularly when they are older persons** (Butler, 1975). Ageism against older persons is rooted in the assumption that people become unattractive, unintelligent, asexual, unemployable, and mentally incompetent as they grow older (Comfort, 1976).

For many years, advertisers have bombarded women with messages about the importance of a youthful appearance. Increasingly, men, too, are being targeted by advertising campaigns that play on fears about the "ravages" of aging.

Ageism is reinforced by stereotypes, whereby people have narrow, fixed images of certain groups. One-sided and exaggerated images of older people are used repeatedly in everyday life. Older persons often are stereotyped as thinking and moving slowly; as bound to themselves and their past and, therefore, unable to change and grow; and as being unable to move forward and often moving backward (Belsky, 1990). They are viewed as cranky, sickly, and lacking in social value (Atchley and Barusch, 2004); as egocentric and demanding; as shallow and enfeebled; and as aimless and absent-minded (Belsky, 1990).

The media contribute to negative images of older persons, many of whom are portrayed as doddering, feebleminded, wrinkled, and laughable men and women, figuratively standing on their last legs (Lefrançois, 1999). This is especially true with regard to advertising. In one survey, 40 percent of respondents over age sixty-five agreed that advertising portrays older people as unattractive and incompetent (Pomice, 1990). According to the advertising director of one magazine, "Advertising shows young people at their best and most beautiful, but it shows older people at their worst" (quoted in Pomice, 1990:42). Of older persons who do appear on television, most are male; only about one in ten characters appearing to be age sixty-five or older is a woman, conveying a subtle message that older women especially are unimportant (Pomice, 1990).

Stereotypes also contribute to the view that women are "old" ten or fifteen years sooner than men (Bell, 1989). The multibillion-dollar cosmetics industry helps perpetuate the myth that age reduces the "sexual value" of women but increases it for men. Men's sexual value is defined more in terms of personality, intelligence, and earning power than physical appearance. For women, however, sexual attractiveness is based on youthful appearance. By idealizing this "youthful" image of women and playing up the fear of growing older, sponsors sell thousands of products that claim to prevent the "ravages" of aging. Many recent movies provide examples of how older male film stars represent wealth and virility, while their female co-stars are often half their age. Consider the on-screen and real-life relationship between Michael Douglas and the much younger Catherine Zeta-Jones.

In recent years, there appears to have been a change in the media coverage of older persons. Analysis of books, magazines, advertisements, and television shows has shown that media images of older people have recently become more positive (Kaufert and Lock, 1997; Novak, 1997). Features such as the "Aging Dangerously" segment on CBC radio's *This Morning* program draw attention to the contributions, talents, and stamina of older persons rather than offering stereotypical and negative portrayals. Because of the increasing consumer power of older persons, it is likely that this trend will continue in the future.

Despite some changes in media coverage of older people, many younger individuals still hold negative stereotypes of "the elderly." In one study, William C. Levin (1988) showed photographs of the same man (disguised to appear as ages 25, 52, and 73 in various photos) to a group of college students and asked them to evaluate these (apparently different) men for employment purposes. Based purely on the photographs, the "73-year-old" was viewed by many of the students as being less competent, less intelligent, and less reliable than the "25-year-old" and the "52-year-old."

These attitudes have serious consequences. Many older people who find themselves unemployed due to layoffs or plant closures often find it very difficult to find new jobs. Both employers and employment counsellors say that there is age-related bias against older workers (Underhill et al., 1997; Lipovenko, 1997). The situation is particularly difficult for workers who have never acquired the technological skills demanded by employers. Many of these people simply give up their search for employment when faced with discrimination by employers. Others are forced to accept low salaries or jobs that do not fully utilize their skills.

Although not all people act on appearances alone, Patricia Moore, an industrial designer, found that many do. At age twenty-seven, Moore disguised herself as an eighty-five-year-old woman by donning age-appropriate clothing and placing baby oil in her eyes to create the appearance of cataracts. With the help of a makeup artist, Moore supplemented the "aging process" with latex wrinkles, stained teeth, and a grey wig. For three years, "Old Pat Moore" went to various locations, including a grocery store, to see how people responded to her:

> When I did my grocery shopping while in character, I learned quickly that the Old Pat Moore behaved—and was treated—differently from the Young Pat Moore. When I was 85, people were more likely to jockey ahead of me in the checkout line. And even more interesting, I found that when it happened, I didn't say anything to the offender, as I certainly would at age 27. It seemed somehow, even to me, that it was okay for them to do this to the Old Pat Moore, since they were undoubtedly busier than I was anyway. And further, they apparently thought it was okay, too! After all, little old ladies have plenty of time, don't they? What it all added up to was that people feared I would be trouble, so they tried to have as little to do with me as possible. And the amazing thing is that I began almost to believe it myself . . . I think perhaps the worst thing about aging may be the overwhelming sense that everything around you is letting you know that you are not terribly important anymore. (Moore with Conn, 1985:75–76)

If we apply our sociological imagination to Moore's study, we find that "Old Pat Moore's" experiences reflect what many older persons already know—it is other people's *reactions* to their age, not their age itself, that places them at a disadvantage.

Wealth, Poverty, and Aging

Many of the positive images of aging and suggestions on how to avoid the most negative aspects of ageism are based on an assumption of class privilege.

Older people are seen as being able to afford travel, exercise classes, and social activities, such as ballroom dancing or golf, and it is often assumed that they have available the time and facilities to engage in pursuits that will "keep them young." However, many older people have meagre incomes, have saved little, or are in poor health. In addition, those who are isolated in rural areas or in low-income areas of central cities do not have the same opportunities to follow popular recommendations about successful aging (Stoller and Gibson, 1997:76). For these people, aging is not so much a matter of seeking to defy one's age but rather of simply surviving in a society where they do not have sufficient financial resources and where they are devalued because of their age. The consequences of a weak social safety network are shown in Box 12.3.

How have older Canadians as a group fared economically in recent decades? There is no easy answer to this question. The elderly comprise an extremely heterogeneous group. Some of Canada's wealthiest individuals are old. At the same time, a significant number of this country's older citizens are poor or near poor. The image of our elderly population living the "high life" on the backs of our younger population is a myth that serves only to perpetuate ageism.

In order to accurately assess the economic situation of older people, it is necessary to address two questions. First, has the economic situation of older Canadians improved? The answer is yes—rather dramatically. The income of people over the age of sixty-five has improved in the past two decades. In fact, the income for Canadians aged sixty-five and over rose by 18 percent between 1981 and 1997, while it actually declined for the rest of the population (Lindsay, 1999) after taking inflation into account.

The second question is whether older Canadians are able to maintain a satisfactory standard of living. The answer to this question is more complex. If we compare wealth (all economic resources of value, whether they produce cash or not) with income (available money or its equivalent in purchasing power), we find that older people tend to have more wealth but less income than younger people. For example, older people are more likely to own a home that has increased substantially in market value; however, some may not have the available cash to pay property taxes, to buy insurance, and to maintain the property (Moody, 1998).

It is important to remember that although the economic situation of seniors has improved, 15 percent

BOX 12.3 SOCIOLOGY IN GLOBAL PERSPECTIVE

Aging in Russia

Since the breakup of the Soviet Union in 1991, Russia has been struggling to make the transition from communism to capitalism. Faced with a crumbling economy and an ineffective government, and plagued by corruption and organized crime, the Russian economy has been failing, and the country has been unable to pay its debts or provide for its citizens. Under the communist regime, older persons were provided for by the state. While they were not particularly well-off by Canadian standards, they had basic medical care and the security of a state pension. Today, the health care system is in crisis and pensioners are in desperate financial trouble.

The political change in Russia had a dramatic impact on the structure of the Russian population (see the figure below). As the economic and political structure changed, birth rates dropped and death rates rose. Death rates are particularly high for working-age males, many of whom die prematurely because of accidents, homicide, and alcohol consumption. In 1994, mortality rates for males 15 to 64 were twice as high as they had been in 1986. For the first time in Russian history, the number of deaths was higher than the number of births (DaVanzo and Adamson, 1997).

The decline in births in the 1990s represents the continuation of a long-term trend that was interrupted by mid-1980s government incentives to have children during that period (DaVanzo and Adamson, 1997). The reduction in births means that the average age of the population is rising and

Birth and Death Rates in Russia, 1979–2004

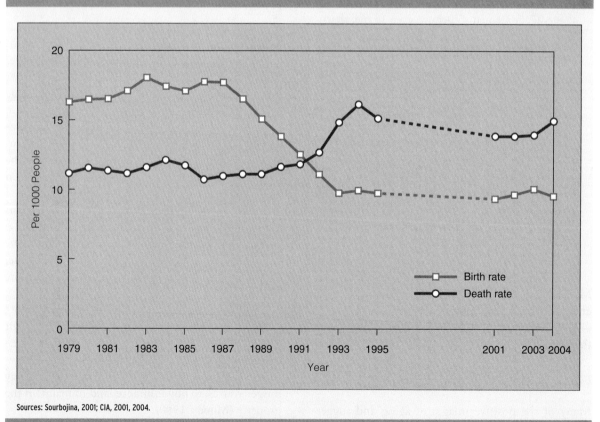

Sources: Sourbojina, 2001; CIA, 2001, 2004.

that fewer working-age people are supporting larger numbers of older persons. While the proportion of the population aged sixty-five and over is lower than that of many countries, including Canada, the average age of the Russian working population is among the highest in the world and will continue to increase over the next several decades.

As you read in Box 12.2, the increasing ratio of old persons to young persons is an issue in Canada, but Russia faces far greater difficulties. With its economy still very weak, continuing to provide services to older people will be very hard. The pension system is threatened by a reduction in workers' contributions because of high unemployment and because many employers have stopped making their required contributions to the plan (United Nations, 1997b). This dismal situation is made worse by the fact that part of the transition to capitalism involved removing price subsidies from food and other essential commodities. This means that while the value of pensions was dropping, the price of basic commodities was increasing.

Older people have also been hurt by the decline in Russia's health care system. DaVanzo and Adamson conclude that the system is in crisis:

> As the command economy crumbled, the public-health sector plunged into financial crisis. The system found itself in an emerging market environment without the capacity to function successfully in it. Left without proper funding, health-care facilities were forced to abandon new construction, renovation, and other basic investments. Cost cutting necessitated switching to cheaper technologies, which proved insufficient to maintain needed levels of care. Available funds were frequently diverted to current needs. As a result, the health status of

the Russian population is deteriorating, and diseases long thought to be eliminated or controlled . . . are now spreading again. (1997:6)

Under these conditions, older people will be victims of diseases, such as tuberculosis, that are now becoming epidemic in Russia, and also will not have adequate treatment for the diseases and disabilities that afflict the elderly in all societies.

The cause of Russia's difficulties was summed up by Natalia Rimachevskaya, a Russian delegate to a United Nations conference, who said: "[T]he old principles and social structures had been destroyed but nothing new had really been created" (United Nations, 1997b). As usual, the burden of difficulties such as these fall most heavily on those who are vulnerable, including children and older people. Rates of poverty have begun to decline in recent years, but for many Russians the situation remains desperate.

While older people in Russia are having a very difficult time, the situation may be even worse in other parts of the world (Novak and Campbell, 2001). Many developing countries will see a rapid increase in the percentage of people over 60. For example, the United Nations has predicted that by 2050, 30 percent of China's population and 24 percent Mexico's population will be over 60 (United Nations, 2002). Most developing countries do not have the formal support systems, such as pensions, housing, and health care, needed to properly care for older people. Africa may be particularly hard hit, as HIV/AIDS has decimated the working-age population. This means that older people may not have the family caregivers who have traditionally looked after their elders. The burden of the older people may be compounded by the fact that in many cases they have been left to care for their orphaned grandchildren.

of all people over the age of sixty-five have low incomes. Changes to government income transfer programs, expansion of tax-sheltered Registered Retirement Savings Plans, and increased investment returns have reduced the incidence of low income among older people in Canada since the early 1970s (Ng, 1994). Furthermore, while income has risen in the past few years for older people in general, certain groups still have incomes below the poverty line in old age. Older people from lower-income backgrounds, people who cannot speak English or French, people with limited education, Aboriginal people, and people in small towns tend to have low incomes. Very old

people, women, and unattached individuals (see Figure 12.5) often live below the poverty line.

Elder Abuse

Abuse and neglect of older persons has received increasing public attention in recent years, due both to the increasing number of older people and to the establishment of more vocal groups to represent their concerns. ***Elder abuse* refers to physical abuse, psychological abuse, financial exploitation, and medical abuse or neglect of people age sixty-five or older** (Patterson and Podnieks, 1995).

The elderly are often referred to as "hidden victims" of intimate violence (DeKeseredy, 1996). It is difficult to determine the extent of abuse of older persons. Many victims are understandably reluctant to talk about it. The 1999 General Social Survey interviewed more than 4,000 seniors who were living in private households and asked if they had experienced emotional, financial, physical, or sexual abuse in the previous five years (Dauvergne, 2003). Seven percent of seniors reported having experienced one of these forms of abuse from an adult child, caregiver, or spouse. Emotional abuse was the most common form reported, followed by financial abuse and physical and sexual abuse. Additional data were obtained from police records for 2000 (Dauvergne, 2003). According to these data, about 25 percent of reported offences were committed by family members. Common assault was the most frequently reported offence committed by family members, followed by uttering threats and more serious levels of assault. Robbery was the most commonly reported crime committed by a nonfamily member. While rates of victimization for seniors are lower than for the rest of the population, the consequences may be much more severe. For example, seniors may be dependent upon their caregivers and cannot readily escape a dangerous or threatening situation. In response to the problem of elder abuse, many Canadian jurisdictions have passed legislation to help protect seniors from victimization.

Although the risk of criminal victimization is much lower for individuals over the age of sixty-five than for their younger counterparts (Lindsay, 1999), older people report more fear of crime. For example, the 1993 General Social Survey found that people over sixty-five were more afraid of walking alone at night and being at home alone at night than people aged forty-five to sixty-four. Older women were much more likely to be fearful than older men. There are a number of factors that may lead to this fear. According to Novak, "loss of social networks due to retirement, widowhood, and staying home may lead to increased fear of crime" (1993:8). Furthermore, cases of abuse and neglect of older people are highly dramatized in the media because of their extremely disturbing nature. However, the media coverage may also serve to create a fear of victimization that does not fit the facts regarding elder abuse. Finally, the consequences of victimization may be more serious. A young person who is knocked down by a stranger may get up unharmed, while an older person may be seriously hurt in a similar incident.

SOCIOLOGICAL PERSPECTIVES ON AGING

Sociologists and social gerontologists have developed a number of explanations of the social effects of aging. Some of the early theories were based on a microlevel analysis of how individuals adapt to changing social roles. More recent theories have used a macrolevel approach to examine the inequalities produced by age stratification at the societal level.

Functionalist Perspectives on Aging

Functionalist explanations of aging focus on how older persons adjust to their changing roles in society. According to sociologist Talcott Parsons (1960), the roles of older persons need to be redefined by society. He suggested that devaluing the contributions of older persons is dysfunctional for society; older persons often have knowledge and wisdom to share with younger people.

How does society cope with the disruptions resulting from its members growing older and dying? According to **disengagement theory, older persons make a normal and healthy adjustment to aging when they detach themselves from their social roles and prepare for their eventual death** (Cumming and Henry, 1961). Gerontologists Elaine C. Cumming and William E. Henry (1961) noted that disengagement can be functional for both the individual and society. The withdrawal of older persons from the workforce, for example, provides employment opportunities for younger people. Disengagement also facilitates a gradual and orderly transfer of statuses and roles from one generation to the next; an abrupt change would result in chaos. Retirement, then, can be thought of as recognition for years of service and acknowledgment that the person no longer fits into the world of paid work (Williamson, Duffy Rinehart, and Blank, 1992). The younger workers who move into the vacated positions have received more up-to-date training—for example, the computer skills that are taught to most younger people today.

Critics of this perspective object to the assumption that all older persons want to disengage while they still are productive and gain satisfaction from their work. Disengagement may be functional for organizations but not for individuals. A corporation that has compulsory retirement may be able to replace higher-paid, older workers with lower-paid, younger workers, but retirement may not be beneficial for some older workers. Contrary to disengagement theory, a number of studies have found that activity in society is *more* important as people get older.

Symbolic Interactionist Perspectives on Aging

What does growing old mean to you? Do all people experience aging in the same way? Are there cultural differences in the aging experience? Those who study aging from the symbolic interactionist perspective look at how people deal with the aging process and at how this experience can vary under different circumstances. For example, culture provides broad ideas of what constitutes aging. Symbolic interactionist scholars show us that the experience of older people in a culture that respects them as sources of wisdom and stability is dramatically different from the experience in a culture in which they are seen as a drain on the resources of younger people.

Within their broader cultural context, individuals find different ways of dealing with aging. ***Activity theory* states that people tend to shift gears in late middle age and find substitutes for previous statuses, roles, and activities** (Havighurst, Neugarten, and Tobin, 1968).

Whether they invest their energies in grandchildren, travelling, hobbies, or new work roles, social activity among retired persons is directly related to longevity, happiness, and health (Palmore, 1981). Psychologist and newspaper columnist Eda LeShan observed a difference in the perceptions of people who do and do not remain active:

> The Richardsons came for lunch: friends we hadn't seen for twenty years . . . Helen and Martin had owned and worked together in a very fine women's clothing shop . . . Having some mistaken notion they were getting too old and should retire and "enjoy themselves," they sold the business ten years ago.
>
> During lunch, Larry and I realized we were dealing with two seriously depressed people, in excellent health but with no place to go. When Larry asked Helen what she'd been doing, she replied bitterly, "Who has anything to do?" Martin said sadly he was sorry he gave up tennis ten years ago; if he'd kept it up he could still play . . .

> We were embarrassed to indicate we were still so busy that we couldn't see straight. They seemed genuinely shocked that we had no plans to retire at seventy-one and seventy-four. (LeShan, 1994:221–222)

Studies have confirmed LeShan's suggestion that healthy people who remain active have a higher level of life satisfaction than do those who are inactive or in ill health (Havighurst, Neugarten, and Tobin, 1968). (For a discussion of how some seniors use technology to stay active and in touch with others, see Box 12.4.) Among those whose mental capacities decline later in life, deterioration is most rapid in people who withdraw from social relationships and activities.

A variation on activity theory is the concept of *continuity*—that people are constantly attempting to maintain their self-esteem and lifelong principles and practices and that they simply adjust to the feedback from and needs of others as they grow older (Williamson, Duffy Rinehart, and Blank, 1992). From this perspective, aging is a continuation of earlier life stages rather than a separate and unique period. Thus, values and behaviours that have been important to an individual previously will continue to be so as the person ages.

Other symbolic interactionist perspectives focus on role and exchange theories. Role theory poses the question, What roles are available for older people? Some theorists have noted that industrialized, urbanized societies typically do not have roles for older people (Cowgill, 1986). Analysts examining the relationship between ethnicity and aging have found that many older persons are able to find active roles within their own ethnic group. While their experiences may not be valued in the larger society, they are esteemed within their ethnic subculture because they provide a rich source of knowledge of ethnic lore and history. For example, Mildred Cleghorn, an eighty-year-old Aboriginal woman, passes on information to younger people by the use of dolls:

> I decided . . . to show that we were all not the same, by making dolls that said we were just as different as our clothes are different. I made four dolls . . . representing the four tribes there—then seven more . . . for the tribes living here. Now, over the years, I have a collection of forty-one fabric dolls, all different tribes. The trouble is there are thirty-two more to go! (quoted in Mucciolo, 1992:23)

BOX 12.4 SOCIOLOGY AND TECHNOLOGY

Seniors and Cyberspace

Do you know a grandparent or other older person who will not use a bank machine or who can't understand why there is so much fuss about computers? If so, this fits the stereotype many of us hold that seniors are far behind the rest of us in their use of technology. While older people are not usually among the first to adopt new technology, recent studies concerning their use of computers and the Internet have shown that while younger people have much higher rates of Internet usage, older people are catching up to other age groups (Silver, 2001; Statistics Canada, 2001c).

In the early days of personal computing few seniors used computers. Because many of them had retired, they did not learn to use computers on the job and the early technology was difficult to use. However, computers are now much more user-friendly, requiring neither lengthy training nor consultants on stand-by. There is even technology that enables older persons with disabilities, such as blindness or arthritis, to use computers.

Many seniors start using the Internet in order to communicate by e-mail with children and grand-children living in other parts of the country. However, they have many other uses. Chat rooms and other forms of e-mail can help replace friends who have died and keep in touch with those who have moved away. Internet shopping can help those who have difficulty going out. Surfing the Internet can help alleviate the boredom and reduce the loneliness felt by some older persons (McMellon and Schiffman, 2002). One senior describes her experience with the Internet:

> From my desk chair I now tracked elephants in Africa, listened to the national anthem of Greece, read the *New York Times* . . . But most of all, the people. Relatives and long-time, long-distance friends who used to be in touch only on holidays, were now "talking" with me regularly on the computer. I soon made myself

at home in a chat-room for seniors only and met people from all over the United States and beyond—"seniornetters" . . . who also had exchanged their typewriters for cyberspace.

> What a zany, caring bunch! It was obvious that the Internet was rescuing many seniors from what otherwise would be isolated lives. Some were house-bound due to illness or the illness of a spouse. Others sought relief from boredom, or relished just plain fun and good conversation. Friendships (yes, real ones), blossomed through this medium and, with appropriate precautions, I dared travel to meet in person some of those whom I had met online.

> My mother, nearing 90, remains convinced that the folks I meet via computer all belong to the Mafia and warns me regularly about "those Internet people." I try to break the news gently that I am one of "those Internet people." (Patterson, 1998)

Older people who are housebound can do their shopping, banking, and other tasks on the computer. Recent research has shown that Internet use may even have health benefits: a psychological study found that Internet-using older persons showed gains in a cognitive ability test that is part of the Geriatric Depression Scale (Philbeck, 1997). Unfortunately, some seniors may not be able to afford Internet connections and do not have access to schools and workplaces with computers.

Creative Retirement Manitoba claims to have established the first Web site specifically designed for seniors and retirees (http://www.crm.mb.ca). This site provides information for seniors in areas such as health and computer instruction. The organization also runs computer training programs for its members.

Some additional Web sites for seniors are:
http://www.seniornet.org/
http://www.hc-sc.gc.ca/seniors-aines/
http://www.eurolinkage.org/

Sources: Patterson, 1998; and Philbeck, 1997.

Cleghorn's unique knowledge about the various First Nations has been a valuable source of information for young Aboriginal people who otherwise might be unaware of the great diversity found among First Nations peoples. According to sociologist Donald E. Gelfand (1994), older people can "exchange" their knowledge for deference and respect from younger people.

What happens as we grow older? Activity theory assumes we will find substitutes for our previous roles and activities. Disengagement theory assumes we will detach ourselves from social roles and prepare for death. Which scenario do you prefer for your future?

Conflict Perspectives on Aging

Conflict theorists view aging as especially problematic in contemporary capitalistic societies. As people grow older, their power tends to diminish unless they are able to maintain wealth. Consequently, those who have been disadvantaged in their younger years become even more so in late adulthood. Women age seventy-five and over are among the most disadvantaged because they often must rely solely on government support payments, having outlived their spouses and sometimes their children (Harrington Meyer, 1990).

Underlying the capitalist system is an ideology that assumes that all people have equal access to the means of gaining wealth and that poverty results from individual weakness. When older people are in need, they may be viewed as not having worked hard enough or planned adequately for their retirement. The family and the private sector are seen as the "proper" agents to respond to their needs. To minimize the demand for governmental assistance, these services are made punitive and stigmatizing to those who need them (Atchley and Barusch, 2004). Class-based theories of inequality assert that government programs for older persons stratify society on the basis of class. Feminist approaches claim that these programs perpetuate inequalities on the basis of gender and ethnicity in addition to class (Harrington Meyer, 1994).

Just as older women are often more disadvantaged than older men, members of racial and ethnic minority groups may also suffer disadvantage. Some do not speak English, and because of racism and geographic isolation many have been excluded from the broader society. Many come from cultures in which older people are viewed with respect and have an important role to play, and may feel particularly distressed at the way they are treated in Canada. Aboriginal people who live on reserves often face poverty, poor housing, and second-class medical care. These living conditions lead to higher rates of disability and more health problems among Aboriginal older people than among the rest of the population (Frideres, 1994). One positive trend in Aboriginal communities is an enhanced role of elders, who are increasingly being used as a resource for mentoring, teaching, and filling other leadership roles. Taking on these important roles can help ease some of the stresses of aging (Novak and Campbell, 2001).

Conflict analysis draws attention to the diversity in the older population. Differences in social class, gender, and ethnicity divide older people just as they

Concept Table 12.A   THEORETICAL PERSPECTIVES ON AGING

PERSPECTIVE	THEORY	KEY ELEMENTS
Functionalist		
Parsons	Functional Theory	Devaluing the contributions of older persons is dysfunctional for societies because of the contribution older persons can make.
Cumming and Henry	Disengagement Theory	Older people make a normal and healthy adjustment to aging when they detach themselves from their social roles and prepare for their eventual death.
Symbolic Interactionist		
Havighurst et al.	Activity Theory	People tend to shift gears in late middle age and find substitutes for previous statuses, roles, and activities.
Cowgill	Role Theory	Aging will be more successful if cultures provide active roles for older people.
Conflict		
Harrington Meyer	Conflict Theory	As people grow older, their power tends to diminish unless they are able to maintain their health. Those who have been disadvantaged in their younger years become even more disadvantaged in late adulthood.
Feminist		
Hardy and Hazelrigg	Feminization of Poverty	Because many older women grew up in an era in which women were not treated as men's financial equals, they are much more likely than men to be poor in old age.
Postmodern		
Katz, Polivka	De-differentiation of Lifecourse Stages	Postmodern society has eroded the rigid stages of the lifecourse. Older people are now able to experiment with new identities with the assistance of anti-aging technologies.

do everyone else. Wealth cannot forestall aging indefinitely, but it can soften the economic hardships faced in later years. The conflict perspective adds to our understanding of aging by focusing on how capitalism devalues older people, especially women. Critics assert, however, that this approach ignores the fact that industrialization and capitalism have greatly enhanced the longevity and quality of life for many older persons.

Feminist Perspectives on Aging

Feminist theorists draw our attention to the way in which gender is a factor in social relations. In the field of aging, feminist scholars analyze the gender-based inequalities that affect older women:

One conclusion stands out from all the facts and figures [about aging and poverty]: Poverty in old age is largely a woman's problem, and is becoming more so every year. (National Council of Welfare, c.f. Novak, 1993:239)

The poverty rate for elderly women is double the poverty rate for elderly men. *Unattached* elderly women are at the greatest risk of poverty, with a rate that is double that of married elderly women (see Figure 12.5). In 2000, 43 percent of women living alone had incomes below the low-income cut-off, compared to 31 percent of men (Statistics Canada, 2003g). Why do women have such low incomes in old age? According to the National Council of Welfare, "after a lifetime spent taking care of their spouses and children, these women who had no opportunity to become financially self-sufficient are now abandoned by the generation that benefited most from their work" (quoted in Novak, 1993:239).

Although middle-aged and older women make up an increasing portion of the workforce, they are paid substantially less than men their age, receive raises at a slower pace, and still work largely in gender-segregated jobs (see Chapter 11). As a result, women do not garner economic security for their retirement years at the same rate that men do. These factors have contributed to the economic marginality of the current cohort of older women.

Gerontologists Melissa A. Hardy and Lawrence E. Hazelrigg (1993) found that gender was more directly related to poverty in older persons than was ethnicity, educational background, or occupational status. Hardy and Hazelrigg (1993) suggested that many women who are now age sixty-five or over spent their early adult lives as financial dependants of husbands or as working nonmarried women trying to support themselves in a culture that did not see women as the heads of households or sole providers of family income. Because they were not viewed as being responsible for the family's financial security, women were paid less. Therefore, older women may rely on inadequate income replacement programs originally designed to treat them as dependants. Furthermore, women tend to marry men who are older than they are, and women live longer than men. Consequently, nearly half of all women over age sixty-five are widowed and living alone on fixed incomes. The result? According to the National Council of Welfare, "after fifty years or so of unpaid, faithful service a women's only reward is likely to be poverty" (quoted in Novak, 1993:241).

Young women today will be much better equipped to deal with the financial pressures of old age as a result of a number of structural changes in Canadian society. The majority of women are working in the paid labour force, they have begun to enter male-dominated professions, and more of them belong to private pension plans.

Postmodern Perspectives on Aging

A central theme of postmodern theory is the notion that identity is a social construct; this implies that we can alter the way our culture thinks about aging—what theorists call our *cultural narratives*. Steven Katz has characterized the postmodern approach to aging as one in which the rigid stages of "childhood, middle age and old age are eroding under pressure from cultural directions that have accompanied profound changes in labor, retirement and the welfare state, and the globalization

of Western consumer economies and lifestyles" (1999:3). Katz's analysis emphasizes the role played by marketers of consumer products in portraying an ageless image of older people. Postmodern consumers do not want to buy products that are targeted to "old" people, so marketers have had to develop strategies that mask the dimension of age. Thus, at a time when the number of older persons is poised to increase dramatically, the physical aspects of aging are being concealed (Woodward, 1991). In the postmodern world, nobody should look or act as if they are old.

Technology has enabled us to change our appearance. No longer must we allow our bodies to visibly change if we choose to surgically mask the aging process. Meredith Jones (2004) has compared cosmetic surgery to postmodern architecture. In a world in which anti-aging technologies, such as Botox injections, breast implants, and hormone replacement therapy have been normalized, in which tattoos and piercings are common, and in which public figures including Michael Jackson and the French artist Orlan (www.orlan.net) have used plastic surgery to create faces that radically depart from the "normal," the postmodern notion that we can simply choose from a variety of ages and that we can alter that choice at will does not seem out of place. Jones illustrates this view by quoting Kathryn Morgan's idea of celebrating old age by:

> Bleaching one's hair white and applying wrinkle-inducing 'wrinkle-creams,' having one's face and breasts surgically pulled down (rather than lifted), and having wrinkles sewn and carved into one's skin. (Morgan, 1991:46 cited in Jones, 2004:99)

Unlike traditional societies in which well-defined roles and statuses are attached to older persons, the shifting of lifecourse stages in contemporary society has eroded the framework that helps older people to confirm who they are. Retirement at age sixty-five is no longer mandatory in most provinces, so there are not even clear signals about when people should move into a new role as a retired person. This blurring of identity can make it difficult for older people to define themselves, particularly when physiological changes make it difficult to conceal the aging process.

Newspaper columnist Margaret Wente has described the shock when she realized that her image of herself was being contradicted by the state of her health:

> Although I am (grudgingly) on the other side of 50, I like to think I'm in okay shape. Last summer I went hiking in the Rockies. The winter before that I went skiing at Whistler. I'm a crummy skier, but I'm working on it.

I'm no jock, but I have my fantasies. My husband's aunt climbed up to the base camp of Mount Everest when she was 65, and I've always thought that I could too, if I really wanted to."

[However, this future disappeared when Wente learned she had arthritis.] I despise the word arthritis. It doesn't match my image of myself. Arthritis is for the old and I am young. It's the antithesis of sexy. It's something your grandmother gets. It conjures up images of little old ladies with sensible shoes and canes, who shuffle across the street at the speed of snails.

That's not me. I'm more the Kim Cattrall type. I secretly believe that if I ever could take up a career as a femme fatale, I could move to London and live with a handsome chef who's 21 years younger than I am. That's what she did, and she's almost as old as I am. (Wente, 2005:A19).

Negotiating an identity as an older person may be particularly hard on lower-income people who cannot afford to participate in the consumer culture and to define themselves by what they buy and where they travel and who cannot afford cosmetic surgery and other anti-aging technologies (Polivka, 2000). As the media increasingly portray older people as active and youthful, those who cannot live up to this standard may feel they are to blame for their condition (Hodgetts et al., 2003). This problem will be magnified if the pressures of globalization and economic rationalization erode some of the supports that government provides for older people.

More positively, postmodern culture may provide older people with the freedom to experiment with new identities. Older people no longer have to fit into stereotyped roles, and as long as the pension and health care systems are sustained they can continue to shape their own identities. Affluent seniors in particular will be able to resist traditional aging through pharmaceuticals, cosmetic surgery, technology, and participation in the consumer culture. They will also be able to continue working, but will be able to arrange flexible worktimes and embark upon new paid or volunteer occupations that they find rewarding. Many older people now feel free to do things like taking up surfing at age eighty, and playing tennis at age ninety. Featherstone and Hepworth (1998) feel that these developments have the potential of extending the period of active living for many years before biology finally takes its toll and that older

What does the concept of nursing homes imply about the ability of residents to live out their lives with dignity and respect?

people should remain creative and engaged with life. This is a very different perspective than the functionalist view of old age as a time for gradual disengagement and preparation for death.

LIVING ARRANGEMENTS FOR OLDER ADULTS

Many frail, older people live alone or in a family setting where care is provided informally by family or friends. Relatives (especially women) provide most of the care (Glazer, 1990). Many women caregivers are employed outside the home; some are still raising a family. Recently, the responsibilities of informal caregivers have become more complex. For frail, older persons, for example, family members often are involved in nursing regimes—such as chemotherapy and tube-feeding— that previously were performed in hospitals (Glazer, 1990). Only a small percentage of older persons live in nursing homes or other special-care facilities. In 2001, about 10 percent of older women and 5 percent of older men were in these facilities (Cranswick, 2003). As one would expect, the older the people are, the more likely it is they will live in institutions. Very few people under seventy-five are in nursing homes, compared with 38 percent of women and 23 percent of men aged eighty-five and over (Cranswick, 2003). An increase in social supports and in community care has led to a significant decline in rates of institutionalization over the past three decades.

There has been a corresponding increase in the number of people aged sixty-five years or over who are receiving care in the community because of health problems. Many of these people are being cared for by relatives or friends. While most caregivers find this task to be rewarding, it does have a significant negative impact on many of them (Cranswick, 2003). If seniors are to be cared for in the community, mechanisms must be found to support the caregivers, many of whom are themselves seniors (Stobert and Cranswick, 2004).

Support Services, Homemaker Services, and Daycare

Not all older persons have the same degree of access to informal support. More than half a million seniors are living at home with a long-term disability. These dependent seniors receive most of their care informally from relatives and friends (Lafreniere et al., 2003); only 27 percent of the help time received came from formal sources who were paid to provide help. Those seniors who were living alone, who were older, and who had no children were less likely to receive informal care than seniors who lived with a spouse or with another person, who were younger, and who had children. Because these people had to rely on formal care, they received fewer hours of help than those with stronger networks that would also provide informal assistance. Declining family sizes over the past three decades mean that the baby boomers will likely require higher levels of formal care than the preceding generation of seniors.

Support services help older individuals cope with the problems in their day-to-day care. For older persons, homemaker services perform basic chores (such as light housecleaning and laundry); other services (such as Meals on Wheels) deliver meals to homes. Some programs provide balanced meals at set locations, such as churches, synagogues, or seniors' centres.

Daycare centres also have been developed to help older persons maintain as much dignity and autonomy as possible. These centres typically provide transportation, activities, some medical personnel (such as a licensed practical nurse) on staff, and nutritious meals.

Support services and daycare for older persons can be costly, but they are far less expensive than institutional care. Even intensive services that provide the support to allow older persons with serious physical problems to live in their homes may cost only 25 percent of that of a nursing home. More importantly, these services allow older persons to live in a familiar environment and to retain much of their independence.

A Victoria, British Columbia, program illustrates how a carefully planned program can save money and enhance the quality of life of older persons (Novak, 1997). The Quick Response Team (QRT) was designed to deal with patients who have been admitted to hospital because of medical emergencies, such as broken bones and strokes. After the emergency has been dealt with, the acute care hospital can do little more for the patient. Many patients are, however, unable to return home because they are unable to care for themselves. The QRT arranges for community support for these patients. The nature of these supports depends on the patient's needs and can include live-in homemaker services, transportation, home nursing, Meals on Wheels, physiotherapy, and household equipment, such as walkers and bath seats. Because it costs about $1,000 per day to keep a patient in an acute care hospital, programs, such as the QRT, can be a very cost-effective way of providing high-quality services to older persons.

Most of us rely on informal support networks to help us through difficult times. When our needs become greater or our informal supports weaken, as they do with some older persons, we need to find formal support networks to replace them. Programs, such as QRT, can be effective because they recognize that older persons often have multiple needs and several different types of support must be coordinated if they are to be effective.

Some people require home care because institutional care is not available. In some communities, waiting lists are long for desirable locations, so seniors must stay with relatives or other caregivers until space becomes available.

Nursing Homes

Nursing homes can be defined as any institution that offers medical care for chronically ill older people but that is not a hospital (Novak, 1997:148). They are the most restrictive environment for older persons.

Why do people live in nursing homes? Many nursing home residents have major physical and/or cognitive problems that prevent them from living in any other setting or do not have available caregivers in their family. Women are more likely to enter nursing homes because of their greater life expectancy, higher rates of chronic illness, and higher rates of widowhood. Seniors with lower incomes and educations were also more likely to be in institutions because they do not have the financial resources to live on their own (Trottier et al., 2000). Some of the facilities available to the poor do not offer high-quality care.

Some people adjust very well to life in a nursing home. However, for many others the transition to an institutional setting can be very stressful. Mortality rates are higher after admission to nursing homes. In part, this is due to the fact that the sickest older people enter these institutions. However, researchers have concluded that institutionalization itself can lower levels of well-being and can accelerate mortality (Novak, 1997). Cases of neglect, excessive use of physical restraints, overmedication of patients, and other complaints have been rampant in many of the homes. Author Betty Friedan (1993:516) stresses that even the best-run nursing homes "deny the person-hood of age [because they] reify the image of age as inevitable decline and deterioration."

One solution to this problem is to reduce the number of admissions to nursing homes by providing higher levels of support that will enable people to remain in the community. However, there will always be people whose physical or mental condition makes institutional care necessary. Gerontologists have found that nursing homes can do many things to reduce the negative effects of institutionalization by making life in the institution as much like life outside as possible (MacLean and Bonar, 1983). One is ensuring that patients are always treated with respect and allowed as much freedom of choice as possible. Patients should also have programs that allow them to remain active, and they should be allowed to maintain the daily, monthly, and yearly rhythms of life (Novak, 1997). It is also important for patients to have a normal social life and to have enough of their own possessions that the institution becomes their home and not just a place where they are forced to stay.

Contrasting views of nursing home life that illustrate some of these points are expressed by two nursing home residents (NACA, 1992):

My eyesight and ability to walk are very bad. I have a hard time getting around. But I am feeling alright because I have enough money, thanks to my pension, and I am in a home where people look after me. I don't have any family but like being here because everybody is a friend.

They take care of me here but they don't do it the same as I would myself. I can't take care of myself because I'm all crippled up. Sometimes I think this place is run more for the convenience of the staff than for the residents. I resent having to go to bed early just to suit them . . . I have only $90 a month to get by on. That is not very much. It is very hard for me to take a car or a bus to go anywhere.

Older persons and persons with disabilities both seek to be fully accepted as participants in everyday life, as this seniors' protest demonstrates.

DEATH AND DYING

Historically, death has been a common occurrence at all stages of the life course. Until the twentieth century, the chances that a newborn child would live to adulthood were very small. Poor nutrition, infectious diseases, accidents, and natural disasters took their toll on men and women of all ages. In contemporary, industrial societies, however, death is looked on as unnatural because it largely has been removed from everyday life. Most deaths now occur among older persons and in institutional settings. The association of death with the aging process has contributed to ageism in our society; if people can deny aging, they feel they can deny death (Atchley and Barusch, 2004).

In the past, explanations for death and dying were rooted in custom or religious beliefs; today, they have been replaced by medical and legal explanations and definitions, and ongoing medical and legal battles.

The Canadian courts have not yet successfully resolved a number of controversial issues that relate to the right to die with dignity. Should parents of incompetent persons in permanent vegetative states have the legal right to refuse medical treatment? Should individuals suffering from an incurable, terminal illness have the right to decide when their life should end? In 1993, the Supreme Court of Canada considered this question in the case of Sue Rodriguez, a British Columbia woman suffering from Lou Gehrig's disease. The court decided that the right to life, liberty, and security of the person (as outlined in the *Charter of Rights and Freedoms*) does not include the right to take action that will end one's life. Furthermore, the court decided that prohibition of physician-assisted suicide did not constitute cruel and unusual treatment. However, the lack of consensus over this complex issue was reflected in a strong dissenting vote expressed by four of the nine justices. Justice Beverley McLachlin wrote:

> The denial to Sue Rodriguez of a choice available to others cannot be justified. Such a denial deprived Sue Rodriguez of her security of the person (the right to make decisions concerning her own body which affect only her own body) in a way that offended the principles of fundamental justice. (quoted in Bolton, 1995:391)

After the Supreme Court declined her challenge for a legal physician-assisted suicide, Rodriguez took her own life with the help of an anonymous doctor and former NDP MP and right-to-die advocate Svend Robinson. Currently, the *Criminal Code* specifies that anyone who counsels or "aids and abets" a suicide is guilty of an indictable offence and subject to fourteen years in prison (McGovern, 1995). The patient's consent cannot be used as a defence.

A related issue concerns the legality of a doctor hastening the death of a terminally ill patient. Ethical guidelines allow doctors to remove life support with the consent of the patient or of the patient's family if the patient is incapable of responding. After life support is removed, doctors may administer painkilling drugs to make the patient comfortable even if these drugs may hasten death. However, Halifax doctor Nancy Morrison was charged with murder over her role in the 1996 death of a patient who was near death and in terrible pain. Dr. Morrison administered two drugs that were not painkillers, but which would stop the patient's heart. After a colleague reported the occurrence to police, the hospital was raided by sixty police officers and Dr. Morrison was arrested on a charge of first-degree murder. The charges were subsequently dismissed by a judge who did not think that the Crown could prove its charges. However, the case has led to a major debate about proper medical practice.

There is no national standard for determining when life support measures should be ended. Thousands of people are in some kind of permanent vegetative state today, and many thousands more are faced with terminal illnesses. As a result, many people have chosen to have a say in how their own lives might end by signing a *living will*—a document stating their wishes about the medical circumstances under which their life should be terminated. Most provinces recognize living wills. Many issues pertaining to the quality of life and to death with dignity may remain unresolved, but we can be sure that the debate about the right to die will continue. The number of deaths in Canada will increase from about 200,000 per year now to 500,000 per year in 2039 as the lives of the baby boomers end (Kettle, 1998).

How do people cope with dying? There are three widely known frameworks for explaining how people cope with the process of dying: the *stage-based approach,* the *dying trajectory,* and the *task-based approach.* The *stage-based approach* was popularized by psychiatrist Elisabeth Kübler-Ross (1969), who proposed five stages: (1) denial ("Not me!"), (2) anger ("Why me?"), (3) bargaining ("Yes me, but . . ."—negotiating for divine intervention), (4) depression and sense of loss, and (5) acceptance. She pointed out that these stages are not the same for all people; some of them may exist at the same time. Kübler-Ross (1969:138) also stated that "the one thing that usually persists through all these stages is hope."

Kübler-Ross's stages were attractive to the general public and the media because they provided common responses to a difficult situation. On the other hand, her stage-based model also generated a great deal of criticism. Some have pointed out that these stages have never been conclusively demonstrated or comprehensively explained.

The second approach, the *dying trajectory,* focuses on the perceived course of dying and the expected time of death. For example, a dying trajectory may be sudden, as in the case of a heart attack, or it may be slow, as in the case of lung cancer. According to the dying-trajectory approach, the process of dying involves three phases: the acute phase, characterized by the expression of maximum anxiety or fear; the chronic phase, characterized by a decline in anxiety as the person confronts reality; and the terminal phase, characterized by the dying person's withdrawal from others (Glaser and Strauss, 1968).

Finally, the *task-based approach* is based on the assumption that the dying person can and should go about daily activities and fulfil tasks that make the process of dying easier on family members and friends, as well as on the dying person. Physical tasks can be performed to satisfy bodily needs, whereas psychological tasks can be done to maximize psychological security, autonomy, and richness of experience. Social tasks sustain and enhance interpersonal attachments and address the social implications of dying. Spiritual tasks help people identify, develop, or reaffirm sources of spiritual energy and foster hope (Corr, Nabe, and Corr, 2003). In the final analysis, however, how a person dies is shaped by many social and cultural factors. According to social gerontologists Nancy Hooyman and H. Asuman Kiyak (1996:417), "the dying process is shaped by an individual's own personality and philosophy of life, by the specific illness, and by the social context (e.g., whether at home surrounded by family who encourage the expression of feelings, or isolated in a hospital)."

In recent years, the process of dying has become an increasingly acceptable topic for public discussion. Such discussions helped further the hospice movement in the 1970s (Weitz, 1995). A *hospice* is a homelike facility that provides supportive care for patients with terminal illnesses. The hospice philosophy asserts that people should participate in their own care and have control over as many decisions pertaining to their life as possible. Pain and suffering should be minimized, but artificial measures should not be used to sustain life. This approach is family based and provides support for family members and friends, as well as for the person who is dying (see Corr, Nabe, and Corr, 2003). Many hospitals have established palliative care units designed to make the process of dying more compassionate and humane.

AGING IN THE FUTURE

The size of the older population in Canada will increase dramatically in the next few decades. By the year 2031, there will be an estimated 8 million persons aged sixty-five and older, compared with 3.2 million in 1991. Because of decreasing birth rates, over the next sixty years most of the population growth will occur in the older age cohorts. More people will survive to age eighty-five, and more will even reach the ninety-five-and-over cohort (Norland, 1994). These estimates point out the importance of developing ways of assisting people to live full and productive lives as they grow older.

One of the most positive consequences of the "greying of Canada" is that there will be considerably less age segregation. The younger population today has limited contact with older people. When the elderly comprise one-quarter of the population, there will be much more interaction between individuals of all age groups. This increased information regarding older people and the effects of aging should lead to dramatic decreases in both ageism and negative stereotypes of old age (Dooley and Frankel, 1990).

Who will assist persons with needs they cannot meet themselves? Family members in the future may be less willing or able to serve as caregivers. Women, the primary caregivers in the past, are faced with not just double but *triple* workdays if they attempt to combine working full-time with caring for their children and assisting older relatives. Even "superwomen" have a breaking point—no one has unlimited time, energy, and will to engage in such demanding activities for extended periods of time. Also, the declining in family size over the past few decades means there will be fewer children to provide supports in the future.

As biomedical research on aging and disabilities continues, new discoveries in genetics may eliminate life-threatening diseases and make early identification of others possible. Advances in the diagnosis, prevention, and treatment of Alzheimer's disease may revolutionize people's feelings about growing older (Butler, 1987; Atchley and Barusch, 2004). Any major breakthrough that significantly extends life expectancy will also lead to changes in the way in which our society defines things like retirement and old age.

Advances in technology and improved design will continue to relieve some of the difficulties that come with aging. Just as eyeglasses, heart pacemakers, and accessible buses have improved life for older persons in the past, computers, robots, and household elevators will make things easier in the future. Even simple changes, such as buttons that can be done up with arthritic fingers, can make a major difference in the ability of older people to care for themselves.

If these advances occur, will they help everyone or just some segments of the population? This is a very important question for the future. As we have seen, many of the benefits and opportunities of living in a highly technological, affluent society are not available to all people. Classism, racism, sexism, and ageism all serve to restrict individuals' access to education, medical care, housing, employment, and other valued goods and services in society.

For older persons the issues discussed in this chapter are not merely sociological abstractions; they are an integral part of their everyday lives. Older people have resisted ageism by organizing politically, and with their increased numbers, older people will have far more political power in the future than they have had in the past.

Finally, your own actions will help to determine how aging affects Canadian society in the future. Results of the National Population Health Survey have confirmed the fact that personal choices play a major role in determining the health and happiness of people over sixty-five (Martel et al., 2005). As someone pursuing postsecondary education, you have already made a positive contribution to your future, as education and income are important factors in successful aging. The study also showed that people were at greater risk of losing their health in later life if they smoked, if they were overweight, or if they were inactive. While individuals will benefit if they continue their education and live healthy, active lifestyles, society will also benefit through a reduction in the costs of health care and the need for institutional or home care for elderly persons.

CHAPTER REVIEW

■ **What is aging, and what is the study of aging called?**

Aging refers to the physical, psychological, and social processes associated with growing older. Gerontology is the study of aging and older people. Social gerontology is the study of the social (nonphysical) aspects of aging, including the consequences of an aging population and the personal experience of aging.

■ **How do views of aging differ in preindustrial and industrialized societies?**

In preindustrial societies, people of all ages are expected to share the work, and the contributions of older people are valued. In industrialized societies, however, older people are often expected to retire so that younger people may take their place.

■ **What are ageism and elder abuse, and how are these perpetrated in society?**

Ageism is prejudice and discrimination against people on the basis of age, particularly against older persons. Ageism is reinforced by stereotypes of older people. Elder abuse includes physical abuse, psychological abuse, financial exploitation, and medical abuse or neglect of people aged sixty-five or older. Passive neglect is the most common form of abuse.

■ **How do functionalist and symbolic interactionist explanations of aging differ?**

Functionalist explanations of aging focus on how older persons adjust to their changing roles in society; gradual transfer of statuses and roles from one generation to the next is necessary for the functioning of society. Activity theory, a part of the symbolic interactionist perspective, states that people change in late middle age and find substitutes for previous statuses, roles, and activities. This theory asserts that people do not want to withdraw unless restricted by poor health or disability.

■ **What is the conflict perspective on aging and age-based inequality?**

Conflict theorists link the loss of status and power experienced by many older persons to their lack of ability to produce and maintain wealth in a capitalist economy.

■ **What are the most common living arrangements for older people?**

Many older persons live alone or in an informal family setting. Support services and daycare help older individuals who are frail or disabled cope with their day-to-day needs, although many older people do not have the financial means to pay for these services. Nursing homes are the most restrictive environment for older persons. Many nursing home residents have major physical and/or cognitive problems that prevent them from living in any other setting, or they do not have caregivers available in their family.

■ **How is death typically viewed in industrialized societies?**

In industrialized societies, death has been removed from everyday life and is often regarded as unnatural.

■ **What stages in coping with dying were identified by Elizabeth Kübler-Ross?**

Kübler-Ross proposed five stages of coping with dying: denial, anger, bargaining, depression, and acceptance.

KEY TERMS

activity theory 381
age stratification 369
ageism 375
aging 364
chronological age 364
cohort 367
disengagement theory 380
elder abuse 379
functional age 364
hospice 390
life expectancy 367
social gerontology 367

NET LINKS www

Several universities, including the University of Manitoba, have research centres focusing on aging. See how sociologists approach aging and pick up other Net links at:
http://www.umanitoba.ca/centres/aging/

For data about Canada's seniors, see Health Canada's "Seniors—Just for You" Web site:
http://www.hc-sc.gc.ca/jfy-spv/seniors-aines_e .html

The federal government is responsible for support programs for seniors. To learn about Canada's pension and old-age security programs; go to:
http://www.sdc.gc.ca/en/gateways/nav/ top_nav/program/isp.shtml

Go to the Web site of Canada's Association for the Fifty-Plus:
http://www.fifty-plus.net/carp/about/ main.cfm

You can watch how Canada's population has aged over the last century by looking at animated pyramids from Statistics Canada at:
http://www12.statcan.ca/english/census01/ products/analytic/Multimedia.cfm?M=1

QUESTIONS FOR CRITICAL THINKING

1. Is it necessary to have a mandatory retirement age?
2. How will the size of the older population in Canada affect society in the coming decades?
3. Analyze your grandparents (or other older persons you know well or even yourself if you are older) in terms of disengagement theory and activity theory. Which theory seems to provide the most insight? Why?
4. Find media examples presenting aging in a positive and a negative light.
5. What would you consider the ideal life expectancy? Why?
6. Should we increase the age at which Canadians should start to draw their own pensions? How would this affect your own retirement plans?

SUGGESTED READINGS

Texts and readers that give insightful coverage of aging and diversity include:

Robert C. Atchley. *Social Forces and Aging: An Introduction to Social Gerontology* (9th ed.). Belmont, Cal.: Wadsworth, 2000.

Susan McDaniel. *Canada's Aging Population.* Toronto: Butterworths, 1986.

Barry D. McPherson. *Aging as a Social Process: An Introduction to Individual and Population Aging.* Toronto: Harcourt Brace, 1998.

Harry R. Moody. *Aging: Concepts and Controversies* (2nd ed.). Thousand Oaks, Cal.: Pine Forge Press, 1998.

Mark Novak and Lori Campbell. *Aging and Society: A Canadian Perspective* (5th ed.). Toronto: Thomson Nelson, 2006.

Eleanor Palo Stoller and Rose Campbell Gibson. *Worlds of Difference: Inequality in the Aging Experience* (2nd ed.). Thousand Oaks, Cal.: Sage, 1997.

To learn more about aging in global perspective:

Steven M. Albert and Maria G. Cattell. *Old Age in Global Perspective: Cross-Cultural and Cross-National Views.* New York: G.K. Hall, 1994.

ONLINE STUDY AND RESEARCH TOOLS

THOMSONNOW™ Thomson NOW!

Go to **http://hed.nelson.com** to link to ThomsonNOW for *Sociology in Our Times,* Fourth Canadian Edition, your online study tool. First take the **Pre-Test** for this chapter to get your personalized **Study Plan,** which will identify topics you need to review and direct you to the appropriate resources. Then take the **Post-Test** to determine what concepts you have mastered and what you still need work on.

INFOTRAC®

Infotrac College Edition is included free with every new copy of this text. Explore this online library for additional readings, review, and a handy resource for assignments. Visit **www.infotrac-college.com** to access this online database of full-text articles. Enter the key terms from this chapter to start your search.

CHAPTER 13

The Economy and Work

Wilfred Popoff was the associate editor of Saskatoon's *Star Phoenix* until Conrad Black's Hollinger Corporation purchased the newspaper in early 1996 and immediately reduced the size of its staff. Popoff (1996:A22) describes how he, a senior employee with more than thirty years of service, was dismissed:

"I can only attribute my sudden firing, within several months of possible retirement, a dignified retirement I had seen so many others receive, to total abandonment of common civility, a phenomenon more and more prevalent today. You see, I was fired not because of anything I did or didn't do, but because of the need to cut costs in the quest for fantastic profits. And how the affair was stage-managed tells more than one wishes to know about the uncivil environment surrounding contemporary capitalism.

"On a Friday afternoon all employees, about 300 in all, received a terse letter from the boss commanding attendance at a meeting in a hotel the following morning. The arrangement was reminiscent of military occupations portrayed in countless movies. The vanquished are summoned to the market square where officers of the occupying army register all people and direct them to various camps. In our case the officers were employees of a consulting firm, also strangers, who directed employees to various rooms, separating survivors from those marked for elimination. Of course, I was in the second group, although none of us knew what fate awaited us. Eventually the boss entered, gripped the lectern and read a brief statement: We were all finished, the decision was final.

"Not only were we finished, our place of work a few blocks away had been locked up, incapacitating our entry cards, and was under guard. We could never go back except to retrieve our personal belongings, and this under the watchful eye of a senior supervisor and one of the newly retained guards. I felt like a criminal. In my time I had managed large portions of this company, had represented it the world over and, until the previous day, had authority to spend its money. Now I couldn't be trusted not to snitch a pencil or note pad ... The current phenomenon known as downsizing is threatening to hurt capitalism by depriving it of the very thing it needs most: a market. This, however, speaks to the stupidity of capitalism today, not its abandonment of civility. But perhaps there is a connection."

Many Canadians have faced unemployment over the past decade because of slow economic growth and deficit cutting by governments. However, Popoff and his colleagues at the *Star Phoenix* lost their jobs for another reason that has become very common: corporate cost-cutting.

Although the paper had been quite profitable under its previous owners, new owner Conrad Black wished to cut costs and increase profits so that he and other shareholders would receive a greater return on their investment. Firing staff is often the quickest route to short-term profits, so the termination consultants were called.

Unemployment shows the linkage between the economy and work. Changes in the economy affect the lives of most people. Those who lose their jobs will feel an acute sense of financial and personal loss.

For many people, work helps define who they are. The first question usually asked of someone with whom one is speaking for the first time is, Where do you work? or What do you do for a living? Job loss may cause people to experience financial crises that could include the loss of their cars and homes to bankruptcy and foreclosure, as well as bringing on personal problems, such as depression and divorce.

In this chapter, we will discuss the economy and the world of work—how people feel about their work, how the work world is changing, what impact these changes may have on university students and other current and future workers, and what connections there are between the work we do and the larger economic structure of our society and the global economy. We will also look at how workers have sought better wages and working conditions through unions and at how unions have affected work in contemporary society. Before reading on, test your knowledge about the economy, work, and workers by taking the quiz in Box 13.1.

QUESTIONS AND ISSUES

Chapter Focus Question: How is work in Canada affected by changes in the economy?

How do economics and sociology overlap?

What are the key assumptions of capitalism and socialism?

What contributes to job satisfaction and to work alienation?

Why does unemployment occur?

How do workers attempt to gain control over their work situation?

How will the nature of work change in the future?

■ THE ECONOMY

The *economy* is the social institution that ensures the maintenance of society through the production, distribution, and consumption of goods and services. *Goods* are tangible objects that are necessary (such as food, clothing, and shelter) or desired (such as DVD players and electric toothbrushes). *Services* are intangible activities for which people are willing to pay (such as dry cleaning, a movie, or medical care). *Labour* consists of the physical and intellectual services, including training, education, and individual abilities,

In the wake of the Industrial Revolution, many thoughtful observers were dismayed by the mechanization of work and its effects on the dignity of workers. Filmmaker Charlie Chaplin bitingly satirized the new relationship between workers and machines in the classic *Modern Times*.

that people contribute to the production process (Boyes and Melvin, 1994). *Capital* is wealth (money or property) owned or used in business by a person or corporation. Obviously, money, or financial capital, is needed to invest in the physical capital (such as machinery, equipment, buildings, warehouses, and factories) used in production.

The Sociology of Economic Life

While economists focus on the complex workings of economic systems (such as monetary policy, inflation, and the national debt), sociologists who study the economy focus on interconnections among the economy, other social institutions, and the social organization of work. At the macrolevel, sociologists may study the impact of multinational corporations on industrialized and developing nations. At the microlevel, sociologists might study people's satisfaction with their jobs. To better understand the Canadian economy, we will examine how economic systems came into existence and how they have changed over time.

Historical Changes in Economic Systems

In all societies, the specific method of producing goods is related to the technoeconomic base of the society. In each society, people develop an economic system, ranging from simple to very complex, for the sake of survival.

Preindustrial Economies Hunting and gathering, horticultural and pastoral, and agrarian societies are all preindustrial economic structures (previously discussed in Chapter 8, "Social Class"). Most workers engage in ***primary sector production—the extraction of raw materials and natural resources from the environment.*** These materials and resources typically are consumed or used without much processing.

The *production* units in hunting and gathering societies are small; most goods are produced by family members. The division of labour is by age and gender. The potential for producing surplus goods increases as people learn to domesticate animals and grow their

BOX 13.1 SOCIOLOGY AND EVERYDAY LIFE

How Much Do You Know About the Economy and the World of Work?

True	False	
T	F	1. Women are dramatically increasing their representation in the professions of law and medicine.
T	F	2. Sociologists have developed special criteria to distinguish professions from other occupations.
T	F	3. Workers' skills usually are upgraded when new technology is introduced in the workplace.
T	F	4. Many of the new jobs being created in the service sector pay poorly and offer little job security.
T	F	5. Women are more likely than men to hold part-time jobs.
T	F	6. Labour unions probably will not exist in the future.
T	F	7. It is possible for a person to start with no money and to build a personal fortune worth more than $110 billion in less than twenty years.
T	F	8. New office technology has made it possible for clerical workers to function with little or no supervision.
T	F	9. Unions were established in Canada with the full cooperation of industry and government, who recognized the need to protect the interests of workers.
T	F	10. Assembly lines are rapidly disappearing from all sectors of the Canadian economy.

Answers on page 398.

own food. In horticultural and pastoral societies, the economy becomes distinct from family life. The distribution process becomes more complex with the accumulation of a *surplus* such that some people can engage in activities other than food production. In agrarian societies, production is related primarily to producing food. However, workers have a greater variety of specialized tasks. For example, warriors are necessary to protect the surplus goods from theft by outsiders. Most commercial enterprises operate on a small scale, and

the vast majority of the population still lives in small rural communities. This changed dramatically with the advent of industrialization.

Industrial Economies   At the beginning of the twentieth century, the majority of workers in Canada and in most other countries were farmers (Drucker, 1994). However, industrialization brought about a sweeping transformation in the nature of work. By the end of the century, only 3 percent were

BOX 13.1 SOCIOLOGY AND EVERYDAY LIFE

Answers to the Sociology Quiz on the Economy and the World of Work

1. True.   In 1971, women received 9 percent of law degrees and 13 percent of medical degrees. By 2000, more than half of the new graduates in law and medicine were women (Law Society of Upper Canada, 2002; Association of Faculties of Medicine of Canada, 2005).

2. True.   Sociologists define professions by five characteristics that distinguish them from other occupations: (1) abstract, specialized knowledge, (2) autonomy, (3) self-regulation, (4) authority over clients and subordinate occupational groups, and (5) a degree of altruism.

3. False.   Jobs often are deskilled when new technology (such as bar code scanners or computerized cash registers) is installed in the workplace. Some of the workers' skills are no longer needed because a "smart machine" now provides the answers (such as how much something costs or how much change a customer should receive). Even when new skills are needed, the training is often minimal.

4. True.   Many of the new jobs being created in the service sector, such as nurse's aide, child care worker, hotel maid, and fast-food server, offer little job security and low pay.

5. True.   Women account for nearly 70 percent of part-time workers (Statistics Canada, 2003r).

6. False.   Sociologists who have examined organized labour generally predict that unions will continue to exist. However, their strength may wane in the global economy because companies having to deal with strong unions may move production to other countries where labour is less powerful.

7. True.   Bill Gates, founder of Microsoft, turned his idea for a computer operating system into a personal fortune that in 1999 was worth $110 billion (see the Bill Gates's Wealth Index at http://www.templetons.com/brad/billg.html). Since then, it has declined to about $50 billion, but he is still the richest person in the world.

8. False.   Clerical workers still work under supervision. However, they may not even know when they are being observed because of new technology. For example, a supervisor may examine a clerk's work on a computer network and an airline reservationist's supervisor may listen in on selected conversations with customers.

9. False.   The struggle to unionize in Canada was always difficult and often bloody. Governments often worked with employers to make union organizing difficult.

10. False.   Assembly lines still remain a fact of life for businesses ranging from fast-food restaurants to high-tech semiconductor plants.

agriculture workers, and other primary sector workers were equally rare. Industrialization dramatically changed the system of production and the distribution of goods and services. Drawing on new forms of energy (such as steam, gasoline, and electricity) and technology, factories became the primary means of producing goods. Wage labour became the dominant form of employment relationship. Workers sold their labour to others rather than working for themselves or with other members of their family. In a capitalist system, this means that the product belongs to the factory owner and not to those whose labour creates that product.

Most workers engage in **secondary sector production—the processing of raw materials into finished goods.** For example, steel workers process metal ore; auto workers then convert the steel into automobiles, trucks, and buses. In industrial economies, work becomes specialized and repetitive, activities become bureaucratically organized, and workers primarily work with machines instead of with one another.

This method of production is very different from craftwork, where individual artisans perform all steps in the production process. Think of the difference between a skilled artisan, who creates a wide variety of intricate metal castings from handmade sand mouldings, and a relatively unskilled foundry worker who operates a moulding machine.

The craft workers were forced out and their jobs were taken over by machines and by unskilled labourers. The work was broken up into simple tasks that labourers repeated hour after hour. This was much less costly than using craftspeople who completed a finished product because more goods are produced in a shorter time on an assembly line and because labourers received a lower wage than more skilled workers. However, workers lost control over their workplaces and some began to see themselves as part of the machinery, not as human beings.

In many countries, industrialization had a major impact on women's lives. In preindustrial times, much of the production took place within the household

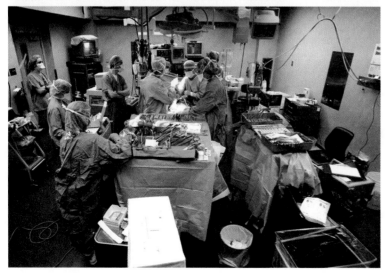

The nature of work is markedly different in the three main types of economies. In preindustrial economies, most workers are directly involved in extracting raw materials and natural resources from the environment. In industrial economies, production and distribution of goods are much more complex and work tends to become specialized and repetitive. In postindustrial economies, workers increasingly are involved in providing services, such as health care, rather than in manufacturing goods.

and men and women often worked together. Factories separated production from the household, causing a gendered division of labour. Men became responsible for the family's income and women for domestic tasks. In Canada, however, home-based production had never been widespread outside the agricultural sector. The resource-based economy was already male-oriented, so industrialization brought little change to the role of women (Cohen, 1993).

Working conditions were very harsh in the early days of industrialization. Hours were long, wages were low, and workers had no pensions, no vacation, and no overtime pay. The comments of a member of a parliamentary committee that investigated working conditions in the 1880s show how child labour was exploited:

> Many children of tender age, some of them not more than nine years old, were employed in cotton, glass, tobacco and cigar factories . . . Some of them worked from six o'clock in the morning till six in the evening, with less than an hour for dinner, others worked from seven in the evening till six in the morning. (quoted in Rinehart, 1996)

By 1950, unionized industrial workers had gained better working conditions, better wages, and significant political power. However, many of these gains were lost by the end of the century as manufacturing jobs disappeared in the *postindustrial economy*.

Postindustrial Economies During the first half of the twentieth century, Canada shifted from a primary sector economy to one focused on manufacturing and service industries. By 1951, 47 percent of Canadian workers were employed in the service sector, an additional 31 percent were employed in manufacturing, and the remaining 22 percent worked in primary industries. However, manufacturing has steadily declined in importance as technology (such as robots) replaced workers and as production has shifted offshore to low-wage countries, and we have moved to a service-based economy. By 2000, only 5 percent of workers remained in primary industries, while 21 percent were employed in manufacturing and construction. Fully 74 percent worked in service industries (Krahn and Lowe, 2002). We now have what has been called a *postindustrial economy*. A **postindustrial economy is based on the provision of services rather than goods.** The service sector includes a wide range of activities, such as fast-food service, transportation, communication, health care, education, real estate, advertising, sports, and entertainment.

The postindustrial economy has several characteristics:

1. *Information displaces property as the central focus of the economy.* Postindustrial economies are characterized by ideas, and computer software may become the infrastructure of the future.
2. *Workplace culture shifts away from factories and toward increased diversification of work settings, the workday, the employee, and the manager.* Although many people continue to be employed in traditional workplaces with set workdays, increasing numbers of these jobs are being affected by layoffs and outsourcing. Cutbacks have eliminated many middle-management jobs, so lower-level workers may now be doing more supervisory work than they did in factory settings.
3. *The traditional boundaries between work and home are being set aside.* Communications technology means that many workers can work away from the office and globalization means that some businesses operate 24 hours a day.

Challenging, well-paid jobs in the service sector have grown dramatically, and highly skilled "knowledge workers" in this sector have benefited from the postindustrial economy. However, these benefits have not been felt by those who do routine production work, such as manufacturing and data entry, and workers who provide personal services, including restaurant workers and sales clerks. The positions filled by these workers form a second tier where labour is typically unskilled and poorly paid. Many jobs in the service sector emphasize productivity, often at the expense of workers. Fast-food restaurants are a case in point, as the manager of a McDonald's explains:

> As a manager I am judged by the statistical reports which come off the computer. Which basically means my crew labour productivity. What else can I really distinguish myself by? . . . O.K., it's true, you can over spend your [maintenance and repair] budget; you can have a low fry yield; you can run a dirty store, every Coke spigot is monitored. Every ketchup squirt is measured. My costs for every item are set. So my crew labour productivity is my main flexibility . . . Look, you can't squeeze a McDonald's hamburger any flatter. If you want to improve your productivity there is nothing for a manager to squeeze but the crew. (quoted in Garson, 1989:33–35)

"McDonaldization" is built on many of the ideas and systems of industrial society, including bureaucracy and the assembly line (Ritzer, 1993) (see Box 13.2 and Chapter 6, "Groups and Organizations").

Class conflict and poverty may well increase in postindustrial societies (see Touraine, 1971; Thompson, 1983). Recently, researchers also have found that employment in the service sector remains largely gender segregated and that skills degradation, rather than skills upgrading, has occurred in many industries where women hold a large number of positions (Steiger and Wardell, 1995). Machines and offshore production

BOX 13.2 SOCIOLOGY IN GLOBAL PERSPECTIVE

McJobs: Assembling Burgers in the Global Economy

Yesterday I was meant to go home at midnight, after working 8 hours. But they were short-staffed and asked me to clean up until 2:30 a.m. I didn't want to but there was nothing I could do. Same thing happened night before. Lots of us are working 12 hours sometimes without proper breaks ... John hasn't had a day off for months—they keep ringing him up on his rest day—and a bloke who refused to come in one Saturday was reported to head office.

—Julie, a worker at a McDonald's in outer London (quoted in McSpotlight 1999)

"McJobs" at McDonald's and other fast-food restaurants worldwide have received both praise and criticism from employees and social analysts in recent years. One thing is clear: The franchise restaurants that constitute McDonald's global corporate chain are employers of more than a million people, primarily young workers and/or people of colour. When the first McDonald's restaurant opened in 1955, few people predicted that the kingdom of Ray Kroc, the company's founder, would grow to more than 30,000 restaurants, serving 50 million customers a day in 119 of the world's 191 countries (McDonald's, 2004).

Does McDonald's provide a service to communities by giving job opportunities to people who might otherwise be out of work? Those who view McDonald's employment practices favourably believe that this is indeed the case. Many young people have had their first jobs at McDonald's and were happy to receive some training and a paycheque. However, critics state that McDonald's and other fast-food restaurants intentionally hire young workers and members of minority groups that have experienced discrimination because they can be more easily exploited for corporate profits. From this perspective, McDonald's vast corporate profits are derived at the expense of workers who are paid low wages, given few breaks, and often required to work shifts that meet fluctuating demands of customers rather than providing a living wage and stable employment for workers. According to critics, this high-profile burger chain (along with others) is a net destroyer of jobs: It uses low wages and the huge size of its business to undercut local food outlets and thereby force them out of business (McSpotlight, 1999). McSpotlight (http://www.mcspotlight.org), a Web site critical of McDonald's, states that the restaurant chain "feeds" on foreign visitors, women, students, and ethnic minorities who, with few other opportunities, are forced to accept the poor wages and conditions (McSpotlight, 1999). By contrast, McDonald's spokespersons adamantly disagree. For example, the manager of a McDonald's restaurant in England stated that "We don't look at people's colour or nationality but their availability" (quoted in McSpotlight, 1999).

Would it be possible for McDonald's workers to organize and challenge this giant corporation? Labour union activists state that McDonald's crushes workers' attempts at unionization any time they arise in a nation. For example, Natalya Gracheva, an employee of McDonald's Russia, as the McDonald's joint venture in Russia is known, wanted to form a trade union in the company's factory outside Moscow. However, she quickly learned that the company would block all her efforts for pay raises and more rest periods (Charlton, 1999). By contrast, McDonald's spokespersons state that the franchise restaurants provide equitable compensation for their workers and that their employees are happy. McDonald's Russia responded to the complaints of Natalya Gracheva and others by forming a company-supervised "workers' council," and, in return, hundreds of employees agreed to sign a document stating that they did not want a union (Charlton, 1999).

As such disputes have arisen on a global basis, this question remains: Are corporations, such as McDonald's, good employers and good corporate citizens in the global community? What do you think?

have eliminated many of the well-paying manufacturing jobs that were formerly available to young people with low levels of education and training. These people now work in lower-paying service sector jobs. A Statistics Canada study showed that this change was particularly hard on young men between the ages of 18 and 24 with full-time jobs, whose earnings declined by 20 percent between 1977 and 1997 (Gadd, 1998). Over the same period, earnings for young women declined by 9 percent, but their incomes levelled off during the 1990s. Many young men have been stuck in entry-level jobs with few prospects for advancement or for additional training. It is too early to tell whether these young men will become more prosperous as they move on in their careers or whether the wage restructuring is permanent. However, analysts studying these data did not think that many would ever move into a more favourable job situation.

To gain a better understanding of how our economy works today, we now turn to an examination of contemporary economic systems and their interrelationship in an emerging global economy.

CONTEMPORARY ECONOMIC SYSTEMS

During the twentieth century, capitalism and socialism have been the principal economic models in industrialized countries. Sociologists often use two criteria—property ownership and market control—to distinguish between types of economies. Keep in mind, however, that no society has a purely capitalist or socialist economy.

Capitalism

Capitalism **is an economic system characterized by private ownership of the means of production, from which personal profits can be derived through market competition and without government intervention.** Most of us think of ourselves as "owners" of private property because we own a car, a stereo, or other possessions. However, most of us are not capitalists; we are consumers who *spend money* on the things we own, rather than *making money* from them. Capitalism is not simply the accumulation of wealth, but is the "use of wealth . . . as a means for gathering more wealth" (Heilbroner, 1985:35). Relatively few people control the means of production, and the rest are paid to work for these capitalists. "Ideal" capitalism has four distinctive features: (1) private ownership of the means of production, (2) pursuit of personal profit, (3) competition, and (4) lack of government intervention.

Private Ownership of the Means of Production Capitalist economies are based on the right of individuals to own income-producing property, such as land, water, mines, and factories, and to "buy" people's labour. The early Canadian economy was based on the sale of *staples*—goods associated with primary industries including lumber, wheat, and minerals. Economist Harold Innis (1984/1930) showed how the early Canadian economy was driven by the demands for raw materials by the colonial powers of France and Britain. This began early in Canada's history; in 1670, a British royal charter gave the privately held Hudson's Bay Company exclusive control over much of what is now Western Canada, which was the source of the very lucrative fur trade. This was *commercial capitalism,* in which fortunes were made by merchants who controlled the trade in these raw materials. Inventions, such as the steam engine and the spinning jenny, led to factory production and the dramatic transformation to *industrial capitalism.* Industrial capitalism did not just alter the production of goods and services, it changed the very nature of European and North American societies. Urbanization, the growth of the modern nation-state, and the struggle for democracy can all be traced to the growth of industrial capitalism (Krahn and Lowe, 1998).

In the early stages of industrial capitalism (1850–1890), virtually all of the capital for investment was individually owned, and a few individuals and families controlled all the major trade and financial organizations in Canada. Under early monopoly capitalism (1890–1940), most ownership rapidly shifted from individuals to huge *corporations*—**large-scale organizations that have legal powers, such as the ability to enter into contracts and buy and sell property, separate from their individual owners.** During this period, major industries came under the control of a few corporations owned by shareholders. For example, the automobile industry in North America came to be dominated by the "Big Three"—General Motors, Ford, and Chrysler. Industrial development in Canada lagged behind that of many other countries as business focused on exporting raw materials and importing finished products. Many of the industries that did establish themselves in Canada were branch plants of large American and British corporations whose profits flowed back to their home countries. By 1983, Canada received more direct foreign investment than any other country (Laxer, 1989). Economist Kari Levitt (1970) was among the first to show how this foreign private investment posed a threat to Canadian sovereignty as fundamental economic decisions were made outside the country and did not necessarily take Canadian interests into account. While foreign investment has declined (see Figure 13.1), many of our industries are still controlled by American parent corporations.

In advanced monopoly capitalism (1940–present), ownership and control of major industrial and business sectors have become increasingly concentrated. *Economic concentration* is the degree to which a relatively small number of corporations control a disproportionately large share of a nation's economic resources. There are about 400,000 corporations in Canada; the top 100 control 67 percent of Canadian business assets, while the other 399,900 account for the remaining 33 percent of these assets. The level of corporate concentration in Canada is far higher than that of our major trading partners, the United States, Germany, and Japan (Richardson, 1992).

Today, ***multinational corporations***—**large companies that are headquartered in one country and have** **subsidiaries or branches in other countries**—play a major role in the economies and governments of many nations. These corporations are not dependent on the labour, capital, or technology of any one country and may move their operations to countries where wages and taxes are lower and potential profits are higher. Corporate considerations of this kind help explain why many jobs formerly located in Canada have been moved to developing nations where workers will accept jobs at significantly less pay than would Canadians because there are few employment opportunities.

Pursuit of Personal Profit   A tenet of capitalism is the belief that people are free to maximize their individual gain through personal profit; in the process, the entire society will benefit from their activities (Smith, 1976/1776). Economic development is assumed to benefit both capitalists and workers, and the general public also benefits from public expenditures (such as for roads, schools, and parks) made possible through an increase in business tax revenues.

During the period of industrial capitalism, however, specific individuals and families (not the general public) were the primary recipients of profits.

Figure 13.1   **Percentage of Canadian Non-Financial Industries under Foreign Control**

Foreign control was at its peak in the early 1970s.

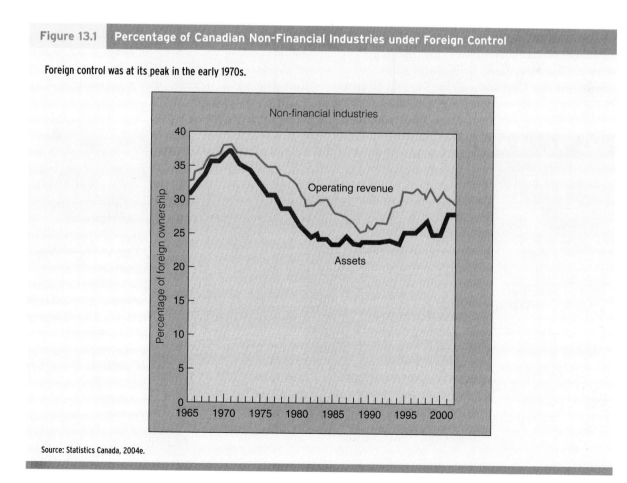

Source: Statistics Canada, 2004e.

For many generations, descendants of some of the early industrial capitalists have benefited from the economic deeds (and misdeeds) of their ancestors. For example, much of the Seagram distillery's fortune was based on the profits made from bootlegging during Prohibition.

Competition   In theory, competition acts as a balance to excessive profits. When producers vie with one another for customers, they must be able to offer innovative goods and services at competitive prices. However, from the time of early industrial capitalism, the trend has been toward less, rather than more, competition among companies; profits are higher when there is less competition. In early monopoly capitalism, competition was diminished by increasing concentration *within* a particular industry. For example, Microsoft Corp. so dominates certain areas of the computer software industry that it has virtually no competitors in those areas. In 2000, the U.S. government successfully prosecuted Microsoft for unlawfully trying to monopolize the Internet browser market.

How do large companies restrict competition? One way is by temporarily setting prices so low that weaker competitors are forced out of business. Ultramar, which owns 1,400 gasoline stations in Quebec and Atlantic Canada, started a gasoline price war that saw gas prices in Quebec fall from 63 to 19.9 cents per litre in 1996. One Nova Scotia independent station owner complained that Ultramar was charging him 50 cents a litre for wholesale gasoline, while it was retailing its own gasoline at a nearby station for 42.9 cents per litre. While this provides a temporary benefit to consumers, it reduces competition by forcing small retailers out of the market. The large companies recoup their losses when the competition has disappeared. Similarly, Netscape was dominant in the Internet browser market until Microsoft began giving its own browser away free in order to secure a larger share of the market for its own products.

What appears to be competition among producers *within* an industry actually may be "competition" among products, all of which are produced and distributed by relatively few corporations. Much of the beer in Canada is produced by Molson Coors and Labatt, which use a wide variety of different brand names for their products. An ***oligopoly exists when several companies overwhelmingly control an entire industry.*** An example is the music industry, in which a few giant companies are behind many of the labels and artists known to consumers (see Table 13.1).

Lack of Government Intervention   Proponents of capitalism say that ideally capitalism works best without government intervention in the marketplace. This policy of laissez-faire was advocated by economist Adam Smith in his 1776 treatise *An Inquiry into the Nature and Causes of the Wealth of Nations*. Smith argued that when people pursue their own selfish interests, they are guided "as if by

---

Table 13.1   THE MUSIC INDUSTRY'S BIG FOUR

These four foreign-owned companies share almost 90 percent of Canada's record business. They have a similar share of the market throughout much of the world.

COMPANY	PARENT COMPANY/COUNTRY	LEADING ARTISTS
Sony BMG	Japan/Germany	Avril Lavigne, Christina Aguilera, Bruce Springsteen, Beyoncé
Vivendi Universal	France/United States	Black Eyed Peas, U2, Eminem, The Tragically Hip
Warner Music	United States	Alanis Morissette, Barenaked Ladies, Madonna, Faith Hill
EMI	United Kingdom	The Rolling Stones, The Beastie Boys, Norah Jones, Coldplay

an invisible hand" to promote the best interests of society (see Smith, 1976/1776). Today, terms such as *market economy* and *free enterprise* often are used, but the underlying assumption is the same: that free market competition, not the government, should regulate prices and wages.

However the "ideal" of unregulated markets benefiting all citizens has seldom been realized. Individuals and companies in pursuit of higher profits have run roughshod over weaker competitors, and small businesses have grown into large monopolistic corporations. Accordingly, government regulations were implemented in an effort to curb the excesses of the marketplace brought about by laissez-faire policies. While its effectiveness can be debated, Canada has a Competitions Bureau with the mandate of ensuring that corporations compete fairly.

Ironically, much of what is referred to as government intervention has been in the form of aid to business. Canadian governments have always been intimately involved with business. To encourage settlement of the West, the government gave subsidies and huge tracts of land to the Canadian Pacific Railway to encourage the construction of a national railway. Many corporations receive government assistance in the form of public subsidies and protection from competition by tariffs, patents, and trademarks. Government intervention now includes billions of dollars in tax credits for corporations, large subsidies or loan guarantees to manufacturers, and subsidies and tariff protection for farmers. Overall, most corporations have gained much more than they have lost as a result of government involvement in the economy.

Socialism

Socialism is an economic system characterized by public ownership of the means of production, the pursuit of collective goals, and centralized decision making. Like "pure" capitalism, "pure" socialism does not exist. Karl Marx described socialism as a temporary stage en route to an ideal communist society. Although the terms *socialism* and *communism* are associated with Marx and often are used interchangeably, they are not identical. Marx defined communism as an economic system characterized by common ownership of all economic resources (Marshall, 1998). In *The Communist Manifesto* and *Das Kapital*, he predicted that the working class would become increasingly impoverished and alienated under capitalism. As a result, the workers would become aware of their own class interests, revolt against the capitalists, and overthrow the entire

system. After the revolution, private property would be abolished, and capital would be controlled by collectives of workers who would own the means of production. The government (previously used to further the interests of the capitalists) no longer would be necessary. People would contribute according to their abilities and receive according to their needs (Marx and Engels, 1967/1848; Marx, 1967/1867). Over the years, state control was added as an organizing principle for communist societies. "Ideal" socialism has three distinct features: (1) public ownership of the means of production, (2) pursuit of collective goals, and (3) centralized decision making.

Public Ownership of the Means of Production In a truly socialist economy, the means of production are owned and controlled by a collectivity or the state, not by private individuals or corporations. Prior to the early 1990s, the state owned all the natural resources and almost all the capital in the Soviet Union. In the 1980s, for example, state-owned enterprises produced more than 88 percent of agricultural output and 98 percent of retail trade, and owned 75 percent of the urban housing space (Boyes and Melvin, 1994). At least in theory, goods were produced to meet the needs of people. Access to housing and medical care was considered a right.

Leaders of the former Soviet Union and some Eastern European nations decided to abandon government ownership and control of the means of production because the system was unresponsive to the needs of the marketplace and offered no incentive for increased efficiency (Boyes and Melvin, 1994). Shortages and widespread unrest led to the reform movement headed by Soviet President Mikhail Gorbachev in the late 1980s.

Gasoline price wars benefit consumers. However, they may also be part of a strategy in which major companies put smaller competitors out of business.

Since the 1990s, Russia and other states in the former Soviet Union have attempted to privatize ownership of production. In *privatization,* resources are converted from state ownership to private ownership; the government takes an active role in developing, recognizing, and protecting private property rights (Boyes and Melvin, 1994). However, this has proven difficult, and the Russian economy almost completely collapsed in 1998. It has recovered somewhat, but it will be many years before the Russian economy is operating smoothly.

Pursuit of Collective Goals
Ideal socialism is based on the pursuit of collective goals, rather than on personal profits. Equality in decision making replaces hierarchical relationships (such as between owners and workers or political leaders and citizens). Everyone shares in the goods and services of society, especially necessities, such as food, clothing, shelter, and medical care, based on need, not on ability to pay. In reality, however, few societies pursue purely collective goals.

Centralized Decision Making
Another tenet of socialism is centralized decision making. In theory, economic decisions are based on the needs of society; the government is responsible for facilitating the production and distribution of goods and services. Central planners set wages and prices to ensure that the production process works. When problems, such as shortages and unemployment, arise, they can be dealt with quickly and effectively by the central government (Boyes and Melvin, 1994).

Centralized decision making is hierarchical. In the former Soviet Union, for example, broad economic policy decisions were made by the highest authorities of the Communist Party, who also held political power. The production units (the enterprises and farms) at the bottom of the structure had little voice in the decision-making process. Wages and prices were based on political priorities and eventually came to be completely unrelated to actual supply and demand. At the same time as some factories kept producing goods that nobody wanted, there were chronic shortages of other goods.

The collapse of state socialism in the former Soviet Union was due partly to the declining ability of the Communist Party to act as an effective agent of society and partly to the growing incompatibility of central planning with the requirements of a modern economy (see Misztal, 1993). While the socialist system as practised in the Soviet Union was not sustainable, privatization has proven difficult. More than a decade after centralized decision making was abolished in

Russia, people are still faced with soaring unemployment and crime rates, and the prices of goods and services have risen greatly. Organized criminal groups have muscled their way into business and trade; many workers feel their future is very dim. While the situation has begun to improve, the transition to a capitalist economy will take decades.

Mixed Economies

As we have seen, no economy is truly capitalist or socialist; most economies are mixtures of both. A *mixed economy* **combines elements of a market economy (capitalism) with elements of a command economy (socialism).** Sweden and France have mixed economies, sometimes referred to as *democratic socialism*—**an economic and political system that combines private ownership of some of the means of production, governmental distribution of some essential goods and services, and free elections.** Government ownership in Sweden, for example, is limited primarily to railroads, mineral resources, a public bank, and liquor and tobacco

One of the twentieth century's most important leaders was Mikhail Gorbachev, who began reforms that led to the end of the socialist economy in the former U.S.S.R.

operations (Feagin and Feagin, 1994). Compared with capitalist economies, however, the government in a mixed economy plays a larger role in setting rules, policies, and objectives.

The government also is heavily involved in providing services, such as medical care, child care, and transportation. In Sweden, for example, all residents have health insurance, housing subsidies, child allowances, paid parental leave, and daycare subsidies. National insurance pays medical bills associated with work-related injuries, and workplaces are specially adapted for persons with disabilities. Public funds help subsidize cultural institutions, such as theatres and orchestras ("General Facts on Sweden," 2005; Kelman, 1991). While Sweden has a very high degree of government involvement, all industrial countries have assumed many of the obligations to provide support and services to its citizens. However, there are very significant differences in the degree to which these services are provided among these countries. For example, Canada provides medical care to all its citizens, but more than 40 million Americans have no health insurance at all (see Chapter 18, "Health, Health Care, and Disability"). While Canada is much closer to a welfare state than the United States, the benefits provided by our government are less than those provided in most Western European countries.

PERSPECTIVES ON ECONOMY AND WORK

The Functionalist Perspective on the Economic System

Functionalists view the economy as a vital social institution because it is the means by which needed goods and services are produced and distributed. When the economy runs smoothly, other parts of society function more effectively. However, if the system becomes unbalanced, such as when demand does not keep up with production, a maladjustment occurs (in this case, a surplus). Some problems may be easily remedied in the marketplace (through "free enterprise") or through government intervention (such as buying and storing excess production of butter and cheese). However, other problems, such as periodic *peaks* (high points) and *troughs* (low points) in the business cycle, are more difficult to resolve. The *business cycle* is the rise and fall of economic activity relative to long-term growth in the economy (McEachern, 1994).

From this perspective, peaks occur when "business" has confidence in the country's economic future. During a peak, or *expansion* period, the economy thrives. Plants are built, raw materials are ordered, workers are hired, and production increases. In addition, upward social mobility for workers and their families becomes possible. For example, some workers hope their children will not have to follow their footsteps into the factory. Ben Hamper (1992:13) describes how GM workers felt:

> Being a factory worker in Flint, Michigan, wasn't something purposely passed on from generation to generation. To grow up believing that you were brought into this world to follow in your daddy's footsteps, just another chip-off-the-old-shoprat, was to engage in the lowest possible form of negativism. Working the line for GM was something fathers did so that their offspring wouldn't have to.

The dream of upward mobility is linked to peaks in the business cycle. Once the peak is reached, however, the economy turns down because too large a surplus of goods has been produced. In part, this is due to *inflation*—a sustained and continuous increase in prices (McEachern, 1994). Inflation erodes the value of people's money, and they no longer are able to purchase as high a percentage of the goods that have been produced. Because of this lack of demand, fewer goods are produced, workers are laid off, credit becomes difficult to obtain, and people cut back on their purchases even more, fearing unemployment. Eventually, this produces a distrust of the economy, resulting in a *recession*—a decline in an economy's total production that lasts six months or longer. To combat a recession, the government lowers interest rates (to make borrowing easier and to get more money back into circulation) in an attempt to spur the beginning of the next expansion period.

The Conflict Perspective on the Economic System

Conflict theorists view business cycles and the economic system differently. From a conflict perspective, business cycles are the result of capitalist greed. In order to maximize profits, capitalists suppress the wages of workers. As the prices of the products increase, the workers are not able to purchase them in the quantities that have been produced. The resulting surpluses cause capitalists to reduce production, close factories, and lay off workers, thus contributing to the growth of the reserve army of the unemployed, whose presence helps reduce the wages of the remaining workers. For example, many businesses have forced wages down by hiring large numbers of part-time workers and by negotiating pay cuts for full-time employees. Companies justify this on the grounds of meeting the lower wages paid by competitors. The practice of contracting out—governments and corporations hiring outside workers to do some jobs rather than using existing staff—has become a favourite cost-cutting technique. In today's economy, it is easy to find someone who will do the work more cheaply than existing employees whose seniority and wages have increased over time, often because of the efforts of unions.

Much of the pressure to reduce costs has come from shareholders, and many observers have seen the firing or deskilling of workers as symptoms of class warfare. The rich are benefiting at the expense of the poor. The rich have indeed thrived; those with large amounts of capital have seen their fortunes increase dramatically. However, the largest shareholders in many companies are pension plans, whose assets belong to workers from the private and public sectors; in essence, some workers have lost their jobs to enhance the retirement benefits of other workers. Bob Bertram, vice president of the Ontario Teachers Pension Plan, puts the matter very succinctly:

> We believe the board of directors is representing us as owners and they have a duty to maximize share wealth for us. If it's not going to be looking after our interests first and foremost, then we will invest elsewhere . . . Companies aren't put together to create jobs. The No.1 priority is creating shareholder wealth. (Ip, 1996:B1)

Alienation is an important part of conflict theory. Alienation occurs when workers' needs for self-identity and meaning are not met and when work is done strictly for material gain, with no accompanying sense of personal satisfaction. According to Marx, workers dislike having very little power and no opportunities to make workplace decisions. This lack of control contributes to an ongoing struggle between workers and employers. Job segmentation, isolation of workers, and the discouragement of any type of pro-worker organizations (such as unions) further contribute to feelings of helplessness and frustration. Some occupations may be more closely associated with high levels of alienation than others. Also, contemporary pressures to reduce the labour force and cut payroll costs have likely increased the levels of alienation of Canadian workers.

THE SYMBOLIC INTERACTIONIST PERSPECTIVE

The Meaning of Work

Symbolic interactionists have examined the meaning of work in people's lives and have studied the factors that contribute to job satisfaction. Does work play a role in defining our humanity, or is it just something we have to do to put bread on the table? Some critics view work as dehumanizing, oppressive, and alienating. In his book *The End of Work*, Jeremy Rifkin (1995) tells us that only by working less can people be free. He feels that less work and more leisure will lead to greater personal fulfillment and will allow people the time to rebuild communities that have been weakened by the pressures of work and the market economy.

Others take the view that people find both moral meaning and a sense of personal identity through their work. Sociologist Robert Wuthnow (1996) found that when people were asked about their most important reason for working, the most common response was "the money." However, when asked what they most preferred in a job, 48 percent chose "a feeling of accomplishment," and only 21 percent chose "high income." Wuthnow found that even for many lower-level employees, work is not just a source of money, but also a vital part of their identity. Work is important in several ways: people are connected to their communities through their work; they share personal friendships in their work settings; and work gives them a sense of accomplishment. Murial Johnson, one of Wuthnow's interview subjects, has three jobs but spends most of her work time as a security guard at a city convention centre. She takes pride in the job because she has been able to do it well. According to Wuthnow, Johnson

> says she has earned the "respect and liking" of other employees to the point that she is often called on to serve in a supervisory capacity. She takes pride in having organizational skills. When a big event takes place, or when there is a special crisis . . . she can be counted on to make things work. (Wuthnow, 1996:219)

However, Wuthnow also found that in a rapidly changing world, many people are redefining the relationship between work and other parts of their lives and this can create uncertainty and dissatisfaction.

This redefinition is also apparent in a study by Arlie Hochschild (1997). Hochschild found that many of the women she interviewed found more satisfaction with work than with other parts of their lives. Many worked long hours because they liked to work, not because of economic necessity. In fact, many used work as a refuge from the stresses and strains of the contemporary family. Of course, these long hours spent at work, whether out of choice or necessity, only make family problems worse (see Chapter 15, "Families and Intimate Relationships").

In an interesting contrast to Rifkin's view of a better future in which work plays a less important role in people's lives, William Julius Wilson (1996) studied inner-city neighbourhoods to see what happens when work actually disappears. He found that the impact has been devastating to individuals and to the community. To Wilson, a person without work is incomplete. They lack the system of concrete goals and expectations, and the daily discipline and regularities that work provides. Without work, it is difficult for the urban poor to take control of their lives.

However, even proponents of the view that work has moral meaning recognize that not all jobs allow the same degree of satisfaction and personal fulfillment. Assembly-line work can be particularly alienating:

> Basically, I stand there all day and slash the necks of chickens. You make one slash up on the skin of the neck and then you cut around the base of the neck so the next person beside you can crop it . . . The chickens go in front of you on the line and you do every other chicken or whatever. And you stand there for eight hours on one spot and do it. (Armstrong and Armstrong, 1983:128)

Job Satisfaction

According to symbolic interactionists, work is an important source of self-identity for many people; it can help people feel positive about themselves or it can cause them to feel alienated. A study based on Canada's General Social Survey found that men and women who enjoyed their work reported a much higher quality of life than those who disliked their jobs (Frederick and Fast, 2001).

Job satisfaction refers to people's attitudes toward their work, based on (1) their job responsibilities, (2) the organizational structure in which they work, and (3) their individual needs and values (Hodson and Sullivan, 2002). Studies have found that worker satisfaction is highest when employees have some degree of control over their work, when they are part of the decision-making process, when they are not too closely supervised, and when they feel that they play an important part in the outcome (Kohn et al., 1990). The reasons contract administrator Beth McEwen gives for liking her job, for example, bear this out:

> I've worked for employers who couldn't care if you were gone tomorrow—who let you think your job could be done by anyone because 100,000 people out there are looking for work. But here, there's always someone to help you if you need assistance, and they're open to letting you set out your own job plan that suits what they're after and what you're trying to accomplish. They know every person goes about a job in a different way. (quoted in Maynard, 1987:121)

Job satisfaction often is related to both intrinsic and extrinsic factors. Intrinsic factors pertain to the nature of the work itself, while extrinsic factors

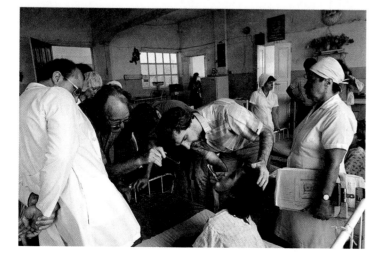

Professionals are expected to share their knowledge and display concern for others. These surgeons have volunteered their services to people in Ecuador.

include such things as vacation and holiday policies, parking privileges, on-site daycare centres, and other amenities that contribute to workers' overall perception that their employer cares about them.

FEMINIST PERSPECTIVES ON WORK AND LABOUR

In all societies, some tasks are assigned to people based on their gender and their age. For example, in hunting and gathering societies women typically have the role of caring for young children and men look after the hunting. In industrial economies, men in what is defined as the working age are involved in wage labour, while women and males who are too young or too old for paid jobs look after household tasks. This situation has been changing slowly, and as Wallerstein has noted, "Much political activity of the last 100 years has been aimed at overcoming the gender specificity of these definitions" (2004:34).

The relationship between gender and work has been an important research area for feminist researchers. According to Amy Wharton, feminist theory in this area "implies that work and the social practices that compose it are organized in ways that create and reproduce gender distinctions and inequalities" (2000:179). She has identified the three major themes of this research: "(1) characteristics of housework and so-called women's work more generally; (2) economic inequality between men and women; and (3) structural and institutional bases of gender in the workplace" (2000:167).

Women's Work

Early feminist scholarship in this field drew attention to the fact that the home was a workplace and that women did a great deal of unpaid work at home. This research was done at a time when many women were full-time housewives and when the prevailing model of a working career was a male who worked steadily from graduation until retirement to support his family. Society assigned women the task of staying at home, caring for children, and supporting the husband's career. Some of the early research pointed out that while homemakers were full-time workers, they were often in a financially precarious position because their contribution was not recognized when their husbands died or when they were divorced. Programs, such as Employment Insurance and the Canada Pension Plan, were not available to provide support for women who had not been in the paid labour force. Other research at this time focused on the type of work done by women, which was largely in stereotypical "women's" fields, such as nursing and office and clerical work. Women rarely held high-level positions, even in female-dominated occupations; for example, most elementary school teachers were women, but most principals were men. Women were greatly underrepresented in the prestigious professions, such as medicine, law, and dentistry.

When women did work, they arranged their jobs and work hours to ensure that their work did not interfere with their husbands' careers and that they could care for their children (Nelson, 2006). Women in Canada are still much more likely than men to choose to work part time (Statistics Canada, 2003r). One of the most important early studies was done by Hochschild (1989), who showed that working women faced a "second shift" when they got home because they were also primarily responsible for household tasks and child-rearing (see also Chapters 11 and 15).

Gender Inequality in Wages

While housewives often suffered economically because their labour was not recognized by society, women who were in the paid labour force also suffered from discrimination. Men were seen as the primary breadwinners for their families, so the financial needs of women were not recognized. Women were predominantly in low-wage jobs, they were often paid less than men doing the same work, and a "glass ceiling" limited their access to managerial positions (see Chapter 11, "Sex and Gender"). This analysis highlighted the structural problems facing women in the workforce. Structural factors, such as the segregation of women into lower-income segments of the labour force, mean that it is very difficult for them to achieve equality. While labour force segregation and the gender wage gap did decline, its persistence led to campaigns by feminist scholars and activists to ensure pay equity and affirmative action hiring. Canada's *Charter of Rights and Freedoms* and provincial pay equity legislation has provided legal support for these actions.

The Structural Sources of Gender Bias

The work of Rosabeth Kanter (1977) raised important concerns about the impact of structural factors in the workplace. Kanter's research showed that employees whose gender or race made them a minority in their workplace faced difficulties because of their status as "tokens." They were often singled out as representatives of their gender or race, were often excluded from formal and informal work groups, and lacked support from their peers. In many situations, such as police and fire departments, their male colleagues felt they lacked basic qualities, such as strength and courage, that were important in doing the job effectively. As a result of these factors, many of the women who were among the first to move into new roles had a very difficult time. According to Kanter, once the proportion of minorities reached a "tipping point" of 15 or 20 percent, the pressures on the minority would be reduced and the work environment would be normalized.

Subsequent research has supported some of Kanter's work, but has suggested that women suffer from more than just token status. Christine Williams (1989) found that women in traditionally male jobs face far more hostility than do men entering female-dominated occupations. The female police officer is more likely to hear derogatory comments from male police than the male nurse will hear from female nurses. While the situation has improved over the last few decades, male hostility toward women in nontraditional jobs still persists. In 2005, Neil French, one of the world's most successful advertising executives, resigned his job because of the controversy created by a speech in Toronto in which he said that there were few successful women creative directors in the advertising business because they couldn't commit themselves to the job:

> You can't be a great creative director and have a baby and keep spending time off every time your kids are ill. You can't do the job. Somebody has to do it and the guy has to do it the same way that I've had to spend months and months flying around the world and not seeing my kid. You think that's not a sacrifice? Of course it's a sacrifice. I hate it. But that's the job and that's what I do in order to keep my family fed. (McArthur, 2005)

Thus, social structure is not gender neutral. Rather "gender is embodied in social structures and other forms of social organization" (Wharton, 2000:175). Occupational gender assignments almost always reflect male superiority. For example, nurses (almost exclusively female until recently) were subordinate to doctors (who were almost always male), and the role of paralegals (female) was to provide support to lawyers (male). Just as in households, women were assigned the caretaker roles in the occupational world and men were in charge (Pierce, 1995). These gendered institutions have persisted because their structures and practices have become an integral part of the society, so once an occupation has been defined as a "male" or "female" one it is very difficult to change. Change is also resisted by those who benefit from the gender bias; if women are given equal access to male-dominated occupations and to high-paying, high-status managerial positions, these jobs will be less available to men.

The analysis of feminist scholars has contributed to the significant changes that have occurred in the workplace over the past thirty years. Most occupations and professions are now much more open to women and, while the glass ceiling still persists, women are now much more likely to hold managerial positions than they did in the past. Progress has been made in equalizing wages, though again some differences still remain (see Chapter 11). The area of gender and work is an area where feminist scholarship has made a major contribution to social change.

THE SOCIAL ORGANIZATION OF WORK

Occupations

Occupations **are categories of jobs that involve similar activities at different work sites** (Reskin and Padavic, 1994). There are hundreds of different types of occupations. Historically, occupations have been classified as blue collar and white collar. Blue-collar workers primarily were factory and craftworkers who did manual labour; white-collar workers were office workers and professionals. However, contemporary workers in the service sector do not easily fit into either of these categories; neither do the so-called pink-collar workers, primarily women, who are employed in occupations such as preschool teacher, dental assistant, secretary, and clerk (Hodson and Sullivan, 2002).

Professions

What occupations are professions? Athletes who are paid for playing sports are referred to as "professional athletes." Dog groomers, pest exterminators, automobile mechanics, and nail technicians (manicurists) also refer to themselves as professionals. Although sociologists do not always agree on exactly which occupations are professions, most do agree that the term *professional* includes most doctors, natural scientists, engineers, computer scientists, accountants, economists, social scientists, psychotherapists, lawyers, policy experts of

Concept Table 13.A THEORETICAL PERSPECTIVES ON WORK

PERSPECTIVE	KEY TERMS	KEY ELEMENTS
Functionalist The economic cycle	The Economic Cycle	The business cycle is the rise and fall of economic activity relative to long-term growth in the economy. This system is largely self-correcting, though government intervention may be necessary.
Symbolic Interactionist Rifkin	The End of Work	Only by working less can people be free. Less work and more leisure time will lead to greater personal fulfilment and stronger communities.
Wuthnow, Hochschild	Work Is Important to Identity	Even for lower-level employees, work is important to one's sense of identity. However, work may conflict with other parts of one's life.
Conflict Marx	Alienation Theory	Work in capitalist societies is characterized by conflict between workers and employers. Work is alienating when workers' needs for self-identity and meaning are not met and when work is done strictly for material gain, with no accompanying sense of personal satisfaction. Workers have little control over their work environments.
Feminist Wharton	Women's Work Is Devalued	Work is gendered. Women are not paid as highly as men; work in the home is typically assigned to women; and these gender biases persist because they are an integral part of a patriarchal society.

various sorts, professors, at least some journalists and editors, some clergy, and some artists and writers.

Characteristics of Professions
Professions are high-status, knowledge-based occupations. Sociologists use five criteria to determine which occupations classify as professions (Freidson, 1970, 1986; Larson, 1977):

1. *Abstract, specialized knowledge.* Professionals have abstract, specialized knowledge of their field, based on formal education and interaction with colleagues. Education provides the credentials, skills, and training that allow professionals to have job opportunities and to assume positions of authority within organizations (Brint, 1994).

2. *Autonomy.* Professionals are autonomous in that they can rely on their own judgment in selecting the relevant knowledge or the appropriate technique for dealing with a problem.

3. *Self-regulation.* In exchange for autonomy, professionals theoretically are self-regulating. All professions have licensing, accreditation, and regulatory associations that set professional standards and that require members to adhere to a code of ethics as a form of public accountability.

4. *Authority.* Because of their authority, professionals expect compliance with their directions and advice. Their authority is based on mastery of the body of specialized knowledge and on their profession's autonomy: professionals do not expect the client to argue about the professional advice rendered.

5. *Altruism.* Ideally, professionals have concern for others. The term *altruism* implies some degree of self-sacrifice whereby professionals go beyond self-interest or personal comfort so that they can help a patient or client (Hodson and Sullivan, 2002). Professionals also have a responsibility to protect and enhance their knowledge and to use it for the public interest.

In the past, job satisfaction among professionals generally has been very high because of relatively high levels of income, autonomy, and authority. In the future, some professionals may become the backbone of a postindustrial society, while others may suffer from "intellectual obsolescence" if they cannot keep up with the knowledge explosion (Leventman, 1981).

Many professions exist under legislation that gives their members a monopoly on the provision of particular services, and these professions use their power to resist attempts by others to provide these services. For example, in the health care field, doctors have used their professional associations to protect their right to control the practice of medicine. Chiropractors, midwives, and other alternative health care practitioners have been fighting for decades to have governments recognize their right to practise and to be paid under provincial health care legislation. The role of nurse practitioners is currently under debate in several provinces as health care officials look for cheaper ways of providing health care services. Similarly, lawyers actively opposed the attempt by companies of nonlawyers to represent people accused of traffic offences.

Women have made significant gains in most traditionally male-dominated professions in Canada. The gains will continue to grow as women continue to increase their representation in professional schools. In 1971, women received 9 percent of law degrees and 13 percent of medical degrees (see Figure 13.2).

Figure 13.2 Gender Differences in Medical School Enrolment

In 1993-1994, women outnumbered men in first-year medical school enrolment for the first time.

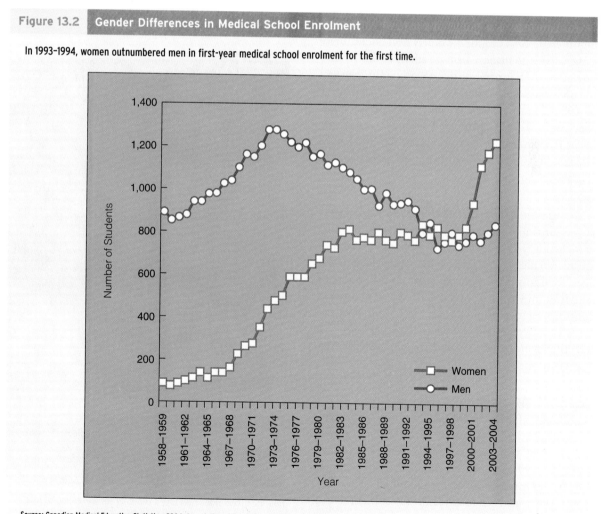

Source: Canadian Medical Education Statistics, 2004, Association of Faculties of Medicine of Canada.

By 2000, more than half the graduates in law and medicine were women, and females made up 30 percent of the lawyers in Ontario (Law Society of Upper Canada, 2002). In 2003, 30 percent of the physicians in Canada were women (Canadian Institute for Health Information, 2004c).

Upper-Tier Jobs: Managers and Supervisors

A wide variety of occupations are classified as "management" positions. The generic term *manager* often is used to refer to executives, managers, and administrators (Hodson and Sullivan, 2002). At the upper level of a workplace bureaucracy are *executives,* who control the operation of their organizations. *Administrators* often work for governmental bureaucracies or organizations dealing with health, education, or welfare (such as hospitals, colleges and universities, and nursing homes) and usually are appointed. *Managers* typically have responsibility for workers, physical plants, equipment, and the financial aspects of a bureaucratic organization. Women have increasingly gained access to management positions at this level.

In 2003, 35 percent of those working in managerial positions were women, compared with 29 percent in 1987. However, only 24 percent of senior managers were women, compared with 36 percent of lower-level managers (Statistics Canada, 2003r). In 1971, only 6 percent of managers were women (Statistics Canada, 1994).

Management in Bureaucracies   Managers are essential in contemporary bureaucracies in which work is highly specialized and authority structures are hierarchical (see Chapter 6). Upper-level managers typically are responsible for coordination of activities and control of workers. Lack of worker control over the labour process was built into the earliest factory systems through techniques known as scientific management (Taylorism) and mass production (Fordism).

Scientific Management (Taylorism)   At the beginning of the twentieth century, industrial engineer Frederick Winslow Taylor revolutionized management with a system he called *scientific management.* In an effort to increase productivity in factories, Taylor did numerous *time-and-motion* studies of workers he considered to be reasonably efficient. From these studies, he broke down each task into its most minute components to determine the "one best way"

of doing each of them. Workers then were taught to perform the tasks in a concise series of steps. Skilled workers became less essential since unskilled workers could be trained by management to follow routinized procedures. The process of breaking up work into specialized tasks and minute operations contributed to the *deskilling* of work and shifted much of the control of knowledge from workers to management (Braverman, 1974). As this occurred, workers increasingly felt powerless (Westrum, 1991).

The *differential* piece-rate system, a central component of scientific management in which workers were paid for the number of units they produced, further contributed to the estrangement between workers and managers. Workers felt distrustful and overworked because managers often increased the number of pieces required when workers met their quotas. Overall, scientific management amplified the divergent interests of management and workers rather than lessening them (Zuboff, 1988). Management became even more removed from workers with the advent of mass production.

Robots at this Honda factory exemplify the deskilling of jobs through automation. What are managers' responsibilities in workplaces such as this?

Mass Production through Automation (Fordism)

Fordism, named for Henry Ford, the founder of the Ford Motor Company, incorporated hierarchical authority structures and scientific management techniques into the manufacturing process (Collier and Horowitz, 1987). Assembly lines, machines, and robots became a means of *technical control* over the work process (Edwards, 1979). The *assembly line,* a system in which workers perform a specialized operation on an unfinished product as it is moved by conveyor past their workstation, increased efficiency and productivity. On Ford's assembly line, for example, a Model T automobile could be assembled in one-eighth the time formerly required. Ford broke the production process of the Model T into 7,882 specific tasks (Toffler, 1980).

This fragmentation of the labour process meant that individual workers had little to do with the final product. There is a huge difference between a craftsperson helping to build a complete automobile and an assembly-line worker repeating the same task hundreds of times each shift. The assembly line also allowed managers to control the pace of work by speeding up the line when they wanted to increase productivity. As productivity increased, however, workers began to grow increasingly alienated as they saw themselves becoming robot-like labourers (Collier and Horowitz, 1987). However, dramatically increased productivity allowed Ford to give pay raises, which kept workers relatively content, while his own profits steadily rose. Without mass consumers there could be no mass production; Ford recognized that better wages would allow the workers to buy his products.

The role of contemporary managers has been strongly influenced by the development of the assembly line and mass production techniques, which made it possible to use interchangeable parts in a variety of products. According to George Ritzer (2000), the assembly line and machine technology have even come to dominate work settings, such as fast-food restaurants. Burger King, for example, uses a conveyor belt to cook hamburgers, and food is produced in assembly line fashion. McDonald's has a soft-drink dispenser with a sensor that shuts off when the cup is full so that the employee does not have to make this decision (Ritzer, 2000). What do managers do in such a highly rationalized, technically controlled setting? Their task is limited because the restaurant's system is designed to be error-free. George Cohon, the former president of McDonald's of Canada, describes how the system works:

A McDonald's outlet is a machine that produces, with the help of unskilled machine attendants, a highly polished product. Through painstaking attention to total design and facilities planning, everything is built integrally into the technology of the system. The only choice open to the attendant is to operate it exactly as the designers intended. (*Globe and Mail,* 1990:B80)

Of course, managers also hire workers, settle disputes, and take care of other tasks, but in many work settings, automation has dramatically deskilled their jobs (Garson, 1989; Zuboff, 1988; Ritzer, 2000).

Lower-Tier and Marginal Jobs

Positions in the lower tier of the service sector are characterized by low wages, little job security, few chances for advancement, and higher unemployment rates. Typical lower-tier positions include janitor, waitress, messenger, sales clerk, typist, file clerk, farm labourer, and textile worker.

According to the employment norms of this country, a job should (1) be legal, (2) be covered by government work regulations, such as minimum standards of pay, working conditions, and safety standards, (3) be relatively permanent, and (4) provide adequate pay with sufficient hours of work each week to make a living (Hodson and Sullivan, 2002). However, many lower-tier service sector jobs do not meet these norms and therefore are marginal. **Marginal jobs differ from the employment norms of the society in which they are located.** Examples in the Canadian labour market are service and household workers.

Occupational segregation by race and gender is clearly visible in personal service industries, such as restaurants and fast-food chains. Women and visible minorities are disproportionately represented in marginal jobs, such as waitperson, fast-food server, or cleaner—jobs that do not meet societal norms for minimum pay, benefits, or security.

Service and Household Workers   Service workers often are viewed by customers as subordinates or personal servants. Frequently, they are required to wear a uniform that reflects their status as a clerk, food server, maid, or porter. Occupational segregation by gender (see Chapter 11) and by age is clearly visible in personal service industries. Women are more likely than men to be employed in this sector. Younger workers are also more likely than older people to work in this sector, as they pay for their studies with part-time work or use these low-level positions as a means of entering the labour force.

Household service work has shifted. Once done by domestics who worked full-time with one employer, it is now usually performed by part-time workers who may work several hours a week in each of several different homes. Household work is marginal: it lacks regularity, stability, and adequacy. The jobs are excluded from most labour legislation, the workers are not unionized, and employers sometimes flout the rules and regulations that do apply. The jobs typically have few benefits.

Globalization of Marginal Jobs   Some manufacturing jobs also may be marginalized, especially those in peripheral industries, such as garment or microelectronics manufacturing, that operate in markets where prices are subject to sudden, intense fluctuations and where labour is a significant part of the cost of the goods sold (Hodson and Sullivan, 2002). Companies, such as sportswear manufacturer Nike, have moved much of their production to low-wage countries in Asia and Latin America (see Chapter 9, "Global Stratification").

To gain the same benefits of "cheap labour," some Canadian companies hire women who have recently migrated to this country. While many work for low wages in factories, their lack of language and job skills and the shortage of affordable child care makes these women vulnerable to companies that will hire them as *homeworkers*; that is, they perform the work these companies require at home. As such, they are not protected by employment standards legislation. Many expensive fashion labels sell clothing that is made by homeworkers who are paid less than the minimum wage. A 1991 study of Chinese-Canadian garment workers in Toronto found that their hourly wages averaged $4.50, they did not get vacation pay or overtime, and their employers did not make contributions on their behalf to unemployment insurance or to the Canada Pension Plan (Dagg and Fudge, 1992).

Contingent Work

***Contingent work* is part-time work or temporary work** that offers advantages to employers but that can be detrimental to the welfare of workers. Contingent work is found in every segment of the workforce, including colleges and universities, where tenure-track positions are fewer in number than in the past and a series of one-year, non–tenure-track appointments at the lecturer or instructor level has become a means of livelihood for many faculty members. The federal government is part of this trend, as is private enterprise. For example, the health care field continues to undergo significant change as governments try to cut health costs. Nurses, personal care homeworkers, and others in this field increasingly are employed through temporary agencies as their jobs are contracted out.

Employers benefit by hiring workers on a part-time or temporary basis. They are able to cut costs, maximize profits, and have workers available only when they need them. As some companies have cut their workforce,

Workers in developing nations—often women or young girls—make or assemble a number of products sold in North America and other developed nations. Workers in China make many Nike products; in the United States, Nike employees are primarily involved in nonmanufacturing work, including research, design, and retailing.

or downsized, they have replaced regular employees who had higher salaries and full benefits packages with part-time and hourly employees who receive lower wages and no benefits. Although some people voluntarily work part time (such as through job sharing and work sharing), many people are forced to do so because they lack opportunities for full-time employment. Between 1976 and 2000, the percentage of jobs that were filled by part-time employees increased from 13 to 18 percent (Krahn and Lowe, 2002).

Most part-time workers are young people, many who are working while attending school. Women are much more likely to hold part-time jobs than men are. In 2003, women accounted for 69 percent of part-time workers. About 75 percent of women and 70 percent of men (Statistics Canada, 2003r) who worked part-time did so voluntarily.

Temporary workers make up the fastest-growing segment of the contingent workforce, and the number of agencies that "place" them has increased dramatically in the last decade. The agencies provide workers on a contract basis to employers for an hourly fee; workers are paid a portion of this fee.

Men and women were equally likely to hold temporary employment. Temporary workers usually have lower wages and fewer benefits than permanent, full-time employees in the same field. Many employers enjoy the flexibility provided by temporary employees. In examining this perspective, Zeidenberg (1990) interviewed Kathy Sayers, the co-owner of a Vancouver technical writing company that relies heavily on temporary employees, and found, in the case of this enterprise, that

> When the [economic] downturn hits, International Wordsmith will be ready and able to retrench quickly and wait out the storm. It won't have a big payroll to cut, nor high overhead costs. "It takes a load off your mind and lets you sleep easier," says Sayers, "when your company has a plan to deal with a change in the economic weather." When the economy perks up . . . the partners will quickly hire more temporary employees for stints lasting weeks or months. (Zeidenberg, 1990:31)

While employers find it easier to cope with changes in the economy using such methods, their temporary employees have no economic security and can find themselves quickly unemployed during economic hard times. Temporary workers also earned 16 percent less per hour than permanent workers in 2003 (Galarneau, 2005).

Secretaries Unlimited

**Let us do the work
so
you get the work done**

We screen them
We hire them
We send them to you

Hiring contingent workers can increase the profitability of many corporations. Other companies make their profits by furnishing these contingent workers to the corporations. What message does this ad convey to corporate employees?

Unemployment

To many Canadians, unemployment rates are just numbers we see in the news every month. However, behind the statistics lie countless individual tragedies. The story of Wilfred Popoff in the chapter introduction shows the personal devastation of losing a job. When an entire community is affected, the consequences can be far-reaching. A 1998 newspaper article on unemployment in Port Hardy, British Columbia, began with the statement "This picturesque Vancouver Island coastal town is on a deathwatch" (Howard, 1998:A4). Already high, the suicide rate increased dramatically in the town following the closing of a copper mine, a reduction in logging activity, and a sharp decline in salmon stocks. With a population of only 5,500, Port Hardy had five suicides and twenty-four attempted suicides in a nine-month period. Those who killed themselves were young to middle-aged adults—in other words, members of the group whose prospects were most affected by the community's poor employment prospects. While suicide is the most serious consequence of a community's loss of jobs, hundreds of communities, particularly in the Maritimes and Newfoundland, are disappearing due to the loss of so many of their young people to other provinces, as traditional resource-related jobs in the fishery and mining industries have disappeared.

There are three major types of unemployment—cyclical, seasonal, and structural. *Cyclical unemployment* occurs as a result of lower rates of production during recessions in the business cycle. Although massive lay-offs initially occur, some of the workers eventually will be rehired, largely depending on the length and severity of the recession. *Seasonal unemployment* results from shifts in the demand for workers based on conditions such as the weather (in agriculture, the construction industry, and tourism) or the season (holidays and summer vacations). Both of these types of unemployment tend to be relatively temporary in nature.

By contrast, structural unemployment may be relatively permanent. *Structural unemployment* arises because the skills demanded by employers do not match the skills of the unemployed or because the unemployed do not live where the jobs are located (McEachern, 1994). This type of unemployment often occurs when a number of plants in the same industry are closed or new technology makes certain jobs obsolete. For example, workers previously employed in the Nova Scotia coal industry or in the Ontario steel industry found that their job skills did not transfer to other types of industries when their mines and plants closed.

The ***unemployment rate* is the percentage of unemployed persons in the labour force actively seeking jobs.** The unemployment rate is not a complete measure of unemployment because it does not include those who have become discouraged and have stopped looking for work, nor does it count students, even if they are looking for jobs. Unemployment rates vary by year, region, gender, race, age, and with the presence of a disability.

■ *Yearly variations.* The Canadian unemployment rate reached a post–World War II high in the early 1980s, when it climbed above 11 percent. For most of the 1990s the rate was above 10 percent. In November 2005, 6.4 percent of the workforce was unemployed, the lowest level in almost thirty years.

■ *Regional differences.* Canada's regions have widely different rates of unemployment. Newfoundland has traditionally been the highest, with rates that are now above 15 percent. Rates in the other Atlantic provinces and in Quebec are also usually higher than the Canadian average.

■ *Gender.* In 2003, the unemployment rate for men was 8.0 percent, compared with 7.2 percent for women. Females have had lower unemployment rates than men since 1990 (Statistics Canada, 2003r).

■ *Race.* Data from the 1996 census showed that visible minorities (a category that does not include Aboriginals) had an unemployment rate that was higher than the national average. However, despite higher levels of education, their average employment income was lower than for Canadians overall (Kazemipur and Halli, 2001). In 2005, Aboriginal Canadians had rates of unemployment that were more than double the national average. However, employment rates for Aboriginal people have been increasing, particularly for those who have postsecondary education (Statistics Canada, 2005f).

■ *Age.* Youth have higher rates of unemployment than older persons. Unemployment rates for people aged 15 to 24 are as much as double the overall unemployment rate. The gap between youth and other workers has grown since 1990 (Statistics Canada, 2003r).

■ *Presence of a disability.* People with disabilities were much less likely to be employed than other Canadians. According to a study conducted in 2001, the unemployment rate of adults aged 25 to 64 with disabilities was almost double that of people without disabilities, and those with disabilities were nearly twice as likely to have had an annual incomes of less than $15,000 (Statistics Canada, 2004h). Even those with jobs were often underemployed in jobs below their qualifications.

Canada's unemployment rates have historically been higher than those of most other industrial countries. They declined substantially at the end of the last decade, but still remain higher than those of the United States and Japan. However, unemployment has risen to unusually high levels in many European countries in recent years, and Canada's rates are low compared to the rates in some of these countries.

Labour Unions

Workers have used a number of methods to improve their work environment and gain some measure of control over their own work-related activities. Many have joined labour unions to gain strength through collective actions. A ***labour union* is a group of employees who join together to bargain with an employer or a group of employers over wages, benefits, and working conditions.**

During the period of monopoly capitalism, as industries, such as automobile and steel manufacturing shifted to mass production, workers realized that they needed more power to improve poor working conditions. The suppression of the Winnipeg General Strike in 1919 and the employment crisis during the Depression of the 1930s had devastated unions. Those that remained were largely based in the United States and usually organized to benefit specific trades, such as bricklayers and carpenters. One of the most important events in Canadian labour history was the United Automobile Workers (UAW) strike against General Motors in 1937 in Oshawa, Ontario (Abella, 1974). At the beginning of 1937, there was no union at the Oshawa plant, and workers had suffered their fifth consecutive wage cut while General Motors had announced record profits. When the company announced that the assembly line would be speeded up to produce thirty-two units per hour instead of the twenty-seven it had been producing, the men stopped work and organizers started a Canadian chapter of the UAW.

An unusual feature of the strike was the involvement on behalf of GM of the premier of Ontario, Mitchell Hepburn. He hoped to crush the strike and stop the spread of industrial unions in Ontario. His fear of unions is clear from the following statement, which he made at a press conference (Abella, 1974:106):

> We now know what these [union] agitators are up to. We are advised only a few hours ago that they are working their way into the lumber camps and pulp mills and our mines. Well, that has got to stop and we are going to stop it! If necessary we'll raise an army to do it.

Hepburn did raise an army. He recruited hundreds of men into the provincial police; the newcomers were irreverently called "Hepburn Hussars" and "Sons of Mitches." Despite the premier's efforts, the union won the strike and received a contract that became a model for unions throughout Canada. This also marked the beginning of *industrial unionism* in Canada, in which all workers in a particular industry, covering a wide variety of different trades, belonged to a single union. This gave the workers a great deal of bargaining power, because a strike could shut down an entire industry.

Industrial unions faced a long struggle to organize. Relations between workers and managers were difficult and violence against workers was often used to fight unionization. Ultimately, organizers were successful, and unions have been credited with gaining an eight-hour workday and a five-day work week, health and retirement benefits, sick leave and unemployment insurance, and workplace health and safety standards for many employees.

Union membership has grown dramatically over the last century, particularly during the two world wars, when labour shortages and economic growth made union expansion easy, and in the 1970s when governments allowed public servants to unionize (Krahn and Lowe, 1998). However, union membership declined during the 1980s and 1990s as economic recessions and massive layoffs in government and industry have reduced the numbers of unionized workers and severely weakened the bargaining power of unions. Between 1981 and 2004 the percentage of workers who belonged to unions declined from 38 percent to 31 percent (Morisette et al., 2005). You have seen that jobs have shifted from manufacturing and manual work to the service sector, where employees have been less able to unionize. While white-collar workers in the public sector, such as teachers and civil servants, have successfully organized, white-collar workers in the private sector remain largely unorganized. For example, only 4 percent of workers in banks and other financial services belong to unions. Women now make up nearly half of all union membership and have accounted for most of the growth in union membership over the past

Unions have been negatively portrayed in the media. This stereotyping can make it more difficult for unions to obtain support from the public.

decade. In 2004, 31 percent of all female paid workers were unionized, the same percentage as for male paid workers (Morisette et al., 2005).

The rate of union membership among workers in Canada is higher than in Japan and the United States, but far lower than in most Western European countries. About 90 percent of all workers in Sweden belong to unions, as do 50 percent in Great Britain, almost 40 percent in Germany, and about 33 percent in Switzerland. Thirty years ago, the union membership rate in the United States was the same as in Canada, but it is now less than half. American industry has been very anti-union, and state and federal laws have not protected the rights of workers to unionize.

In most industrialized countries, collective bargaining by unions has been dominated by men. However, in many countries, including Sweden, Germany, and Austria, women workers have made important gains as a result of labour union participation. Higher rates of unionization among Canadian women are a major factor in explaining the fact that male and female wages are more equal in Canada than in the U.S. (Human Resources Development Canada, 2000).

Difficult times may lie ahead for unions: the growing diversity of the workforce, the increase in temporary and part-time work, the threat of global competition, the ease with which jobs can be moved from one country to another, the replacement of jobs with technology, and the increasing popularity of new patterns of work (such as telecommuting) where workers have little contact with one another are just a few of the challenges that lie ahead.

Immediately after the employees of this Wal-Mart store in Jonquière, Quebec obtained certification as a union, Wal-Mart officials closed it down. Such actions have discouraged Wal-Mart employees in other communities from attempting to unionize.

Governments are contracting out jobs that were held by unionized employees. For example, to save money the City of Winnipeg is replacing its unionized garbage collectors with a private company whose employees will not likely be union members, and who will be paid much lower wages. As our economy becomes increasingly service-based, an important challenge for unions will be organizing the lower tier of service sector workers. Companies like McDonald's and Wal-Mart have strongly resisted attempts to organize unions. Both companies have shut down stores where staff have sought to unionize. In 2005, Wal-Mart closed a store in Jonquière, Quebec in which staff had obtained union certification. The closure put 176 employees out of work.

The next decade will be a critical time for the labour movement. How do you think union leaders can change their organizations to meet the new realities of the world of work?

THE GLOBAL ECONOMY IN THE FUTURE

Will the nature of work change during your lifetime? What are Canada's future economic prospects? What about the global economy? Although sociologists do not have a crystal ball with which to predict the future, some general trends can be suggested.

The End of Work?

Corporations around the world eliminated millions of jobs in the 1990s for a variety of different reasons. Some employers cut jobs because of their belief that they needed to reduce their costs because the globalization of trade means that competition can now come from anywhere in the world. Downsizing has also become fashionable, and even profitable companies feel pressure to reduce costs. Perhaps most importantly, technology has enabled workers to be replaced with machines. Because of these trends, economist and futurist Jeremy Rifkin (1995) thinks that work as we know it is coming to an end. Rifkin feels that we are moving into a postindustrial, information-based economy in which factory work, clerical work, middle management, and many other traditional jobs are falling victim to technology. Bank machines and Internet banking are replacing tellers, robots are replacing factory workers, and electronic scanners are replacing cashiers. Even jobs associated with the postindustrial economy, such as computer programming and working in call centres, are being lost to workers in low-wage countries, such as India. When agriculture became mechanized, displaced workers found jobs in industry, and when industry turned to computers, service jobs were available. However, Rifkin feels that the information age does not hold the same potential for jobs. Some *knowledge workers*—the engineers, technicians, and scientists who are leading us into the information age—will gain, but there may be little work for the rest of us (see Box 13.3, "The Digital Divide"). We will have an elite workforce, not a mass workforce. The elites will be well paid; Microsoft's Bill Gates is but one of a number of people who have made astonishing fortunes in the computer industry. However, the majority have not received the benefits of the postindustrial society. Many people do not have jobs, and those with jobs have seen declines in their purchasing power. Nathan Gardels fears that the unemployed face economic irrelevance: "We don't need what they have and they can't buy what we sell" (quoted in Rifkin, 1995:215).

Two questions arise from Rifkin's analysis. First, what does society do with the millions of people who may not be needed by employers? Second, how do we persuade the top 20 percent, who are receiving the benefits of productivity gains, to share them with the bottom 80 percent who are bearing the burden of change?

What incentives exist to encourage those benefiting from increased productivity to change? While the number of jobs in Canada increased throughout this decade, many of the new jobs were rather poorly paid, particularly for new employees (Statistics Canada, 2005g). Decades ago, Henry Ford recognized that only well-paid workers could buy his cars. Many economists blame the depression of the 1930s on the failure of business leaders to recognize that they had to share the benefits of increased productivity with their workers (Rifkin, 1995). The same threat may now exist if people do not have adequate incomes; nobody will be able to purchase the goods and services created by our new technology. Henry Ford paid his employees wages that were good for his time. However, service economy employers, such as Wal-Mart and McDonald's, keep their prices down and their profits up by paying their employees very low wages. While Henry Ford wanted his employees to be able to buy his cars, the Walton family (which runs Wal-Mart and whose members make up five of the ten richest people in the world) pays wages that are so low that its employees can shop only at low-cost stores, such as Wal-Mart.

Increased inequality may also destabilize society. As British journalist Victor Keegan has observed, "A world in which the majority of people are disenfranchised will not be a pleasant or safe place for the rich minority" (1996:D4). The United States, which has the greatest disparity between rich and poor in the industrialized world, now incarcerates about 2 percent of its adult male population, yet still has a much higher crime rate than most other industrialized countries. Rifkin argues that the rich can either use some of their gains to create a fortress economy or they can use the same money to prevent it. Edward Luttwak has contrasted these two different approaches to the distribution of wealth:

> When I go to a gas station in Japan, five young men wearing uniforms jump on my car. They not only check the oil but also wash the tires and wash the lights. Why is that? Because government doesn't allow oil companies to compete by price, and therefore they have to compete by service . . . I pay a lot of money for the gas.
>
> Then I come to Washington, and in Washington gas is much cheaper. Nobody washes the tires, nobody does anything for me, but here, too, there are five young men . . . standing around, unemployed, waiting to rob my car. I still have to pay for them, through my taxes, through imprisonment, through a failed welfare system . . . But in Japan at least they clean my car. (1996:24)

Also, the public, unions, and some politicians have begun to protest the growing trend toward paying executives enormous salaries while their workers are being laid off or having their wages cut. Public pressure may eventually force a redistribution of the costs and benefits of the shift to a new economy. Blaming World War II on economic crises, policymakers built a postwar economy designed to promote both growth and equity (Epstein, 1996). The resulting decades of stability and prosperity may help serve as a model for the future.

Many disagree with Rifkin's view that work is coming to an end. They argue that while the nature of work has changed in our postindustrial society, there are now more jobs, not fewer. In North

America, millions of new jobs have been created over the past decade, and some futurists feel that this technology-led growth will continue. Certainly, job growth has been strong in Canada. Also, the retirement of people from the baby boom generation (see Chapter 19, "Population and Urbanization") will mean that millions of jobs will be open for younger workers. However, Rifkin's scenario is a plausible one and his work points out the way in which fundamental changes in our economy can affect all of us.

The Canadian Economy

Many of the trends we have examined in this chapter will produce dramatic changes in the organization of the economy and work in the next century. Canadian industry will continue to compete with companies around the globe for a share of international trade and the jobs that go with this trade. As globalization and the technological revolution continue, workers increasingly may be fragmented into two major labour market divisions: (1) those who work in the innovative, primary sector and (2) those whose jobs are located in the growing secondary, marginal sector (see Box 13.3, "The Digital Divide"). Knowledge will increasingly become the factor that differentiates the rich from the poor. In the innovative sector, increased productivity will be the watchword as corporations respond to heightened international competition. In the marginal sector, alienation may grow as temporary workers, sometimes professionals, look for

BOX 13.3 SOCIOLOGY AND TECHNOLOGY

The Digital Divide

Many people feel that in our postindustrial society, knowledge will be what differentiates the rich from the poor. Because of the key role played by technology, access to computers and to the Internet is critical to gaining this knowledge. However, this access is affected by social class—the "digital divide" refers to the gap between children and adults from lower-class backgrounds, who have less access to computers, and those from higher classes. Access is also affected by place of residence, as computers and Internet access are more prevalent in cities than in rural areas. Governments, community organizations, and corporations are placing more and more information on the Internet and less in other channels of communication, so the digital divide is becoming more and more important. For example, if the number of job vacancies posted on the Internet continues to increase, those without computer access will also not have access to these jobs. Also, if government policy information is channelled through the Internet, those without access will not be able to participate in policy decisions.

There are several ways of reducing the digital divide. Increasing the number of computers and improving computer instruction in the schools would help ensure that all young people are on an equal footing. Community computer networks, or FreeNets, provide Internet access to those who cannot afford commercial access charges. Libraries are now a major access provider, and many provinces have offered funding to provide Internet access through their library systems. The federal government has funded a Community Access Program with the goal of providing Internet access in 5,000 rural and remote communities.

The digital divide also has international implications. Some observers feel that Internet lines and data-transmission facilities may soon be a better indicator of development than roads, bridges, and railroad lines. In a knowledge-based global economy the countries that develop the fastest will be those that build a strong communications infrastructure (or what some call an "infostructure") and provide high-technology training for their workforce. Countries that lack this communications technology and expertise will be bypassed in the global economy. Not surprisingly, the industrialized countries are in the best position to benefit from the information-based economy, as people in these countries have far greater access to modern communications technology than do residents of poorer nations.

Sources: Ditchburn, 1998; and Tapscott, 1998.

avenues of upward mobility or at least a chance to make their work life more tolerable.

Labour unions will be increasingly less able to help workers, because in a global economy work can quickly be moved to areas where wages are low. Unions must find ways to recruit knowledge workers and workers engaged in nontraditional forms of work, such as telecommuting. The participation of women in the labour force will continue to increase, and women will continue to make inroads into the professions and senior levels of management. Part-time work, job sharing, and work from the home—the "electronic cottage"—will likely continue to grow.

Global Economic Interdependence and Competition

Borderless markets and industries defy political boundaries. For example, Japanese cars are produced in Canada and the United States using components that can be made virtually anywhere in the world. Capital and jobs can move very rapidly, so governments have much less power to intervene in markets.

Most futurists predict that multinational corporations will become even more significant in the global economy. As they continue to compete for world market share, these corporations will become even less aligned with the values of any one nation. Those who advocate increased globalization typically focus on its potential impact on high-income countries, not on the effect it may have on the 80 percent of the world's population that resides in middle-income and low-income countries. Persons in low-income countries may become increasingly resentful when they are bombarded with media images of Western affluence and consumption. Billions of "have nots" may feel angry at the "haves"—including the employees and managers of multinational companies living and working in their midst (Kennedy, 1993).

The chasm between rich and poor nations probably will widen as high-income countries purchase fewer raw materials from low-income countries and more products and services from one another. This change will take place because raw materials of all sorts are no longer as important to manufacturers in high-income nations.

In recent years, the average worker in Canada and other developed countries has benefited from global economic growth more than have workers in less developed and developing countries. More than a billion of the world's people live in abject poverty. For many, this means attempting to survive on less than $370 a year (Kennedy, 1993). In 1996 a United Nations report showed that the total wealth of the world's 358 billionaires equalled the combined incomes of the poorest 45 percent of the world's population—2.3 billion people (United Nations Development Programme, 1996). While some countries, including many in Southeast Asia and Latin America, will begin to enter the developed world, others, particularly in Africa, will continue to fall farther behind the rest of the world (see Chapter 9, "Global Stratification").

The impact of globalization on Canada has been the subject of an interesting debate, part of which concerns whether our economy has benefited from agreements, such as the North American Free Trade Agreement (NAFTA), which involves Canada, the United States, and Mexico. We know that the economies of Canada and the United States are becoming more closely linked. The amount of trade is steadily increasing and the border has become almost irrelevant to business. Those looking for opportunities to expand business are increasingly looking south rather than east or west. For example, the Manitoba government placed a high priority on building a four-lane highway south to the United States, while parts of the Trans-Canada Highway in Manitoba still had only two lanes. This is symbolic of the fact that most of our provincial economies are more dependent on exports to other countries than on exports to other provinces.

The economic consequences of NAFTA will not be known for decades. Critics complained that NAFTA would bring an end to medicare and to our social safety net and would dramatically reduce environmental standards. During the first few years following the 1989 implementation of the agreement with the United States that preceded NAFTA, a great number of manufacturing jobs were lost, just as opponents of the deal had predicted. However, these were also years when Canada's economy was in a recession, and when high interest rates and the high value of the Canadian dollar made our exports uncompetitive. More recently, as a result of low interest rates, a low dollar, and more competitive industry, Canada is exporting far more to the United States than we import, and export-related jobs are creating economic growth. We do not know if the future will bring increased prosperity to all three countries, or whether factors, such as the low wages paid to workers in Mexico and the southern United States, will result in jobs permanently moving out of Canada.

Regardless of the impact of globalization on individual countries, the process will almost inevitably continue. A global workplace is emerging in which telecommunications networks will link workers in distant locations, and the skills of some professionals will transcend the borders of their own countries. For example, there is a demand for the services of international law specialists, engineers, and software designers across countries. One result of this has been a "brain drain" of skilled technical specialists to the United States, where jobs are plentiful, wages are higher, and taxes lower. One area that has been particularly hard-hit is medicine. There are currently almost 10,000 Canadian doctors living in the United States, and from 1994 to 1996, 17,000 Canadian nurses also moved there. Even as nations become more dependent on one another, they also will become more competitive in the economic sphere.

The need to stay competitive with low-wage countries has had an impact on all Canadians. By threatening to close plants and move elsewhere, corporations have forced drastic wage cuts. Even more significantly, there is great pressure on governments to adjust taxation and social policies so business remains competitive. Business leaders argue that if Canada's tax rates are higher than those of other countries, particularly those of our main trading partner, the United States, corporations will not locate here and we will steadily lose jobs and people. This international pressure limits the freedom of our government to act in the best interests of all its citizens. It would be very difficult for the Canadian government to raise taxes on business or on wealthy Canadians in order to redistribute income to the poor because this would make us less competitive with the low tax rates of the United States. This means that governments are steadily losing the ability to set national policies in the face of opposition from global market forces and from multinational corporations that operate without concern for national boundaries. The impact of globalization has been particularly acute in countries that lack the resources to provide a basic manufacturing infrastructure and a minimally trained labour force. In many of these countries, there has been an almost complete collapse of jobs, and people can barely maintain a subsistence standard of living

(see Chapter 9, "Global Stratification"). These fears have led to massive protests in many countries against the globalization of trade.

Corporate Responsibility

The growing power of corporations and the globalization of trade raise issues about the social role of corporations. To whom should corporations be responsible? Do businesses owe anything to the communities in which they operate? Should corporations spend resources helping to build a better society or should they be responsible only for raising wealth for their shareholders? This issue is of concern to the general public. Surveys in many countries have shown that a large majority feel social responsibility is important and prefer to do business with responsible corporations. However, a 1997 Angus Reid poll showed that 45 percent of Canadians felt that corporations were becoming less responsible (Pratt, 1997).

Milton Friedman, winner of the Nobel Prize for economics, has set out one side of this issue. Friedman (1970) believes that the only responsibility of business is to engage in activities designed to increase its profits:

> There is one and only one social responsibility of business—to use its resources and engage in activities designed to increase its profits so long as it stays within the rules of the game. (1970:125)

According to this view, corporations should not be concerned about their social responsibilities but only about maximizing the money they make for shareholders. Thus, investing in communities, training workers, protecting the environment, and producing safe products should not be of concern unless doing these things will make the corporation more profitable. Businesses that maximize their profits will provide the jobs and investment that are essential to strong communities. However, it is up to other organizations, including government and the voluntary sector, to ensure that other community needs are looked after.

Others feel that corporate responsibility should go beyond enriching shareholders. Courtney Pratt, the former president of Canadian resources company Noranda, has strongly advocated that corporations exercise greater social responsibility (1997). He argues that corporations must be concerned with profit, but that they should also be committed to creating a better society. According to Pratt, there is no conflict between profits and taking an active role in improving society; he feels business can "do well by doing good" (1997:4). Only by helping build strong communities can businesses ensure that they have effective employees and the kind of economically prosperous society that provides a good climate for business.

As globalization reduces the power of governments, corporate citizenship will become an important issue in the future. If corporations are only economic entities and do not contribute to the public good, it will be much more difficult to resolve social issues, such as youth unemployment, income disparities, and the full participation of women and minorities in Canadian society.

CHAPTER REVIEW

■ What is the primary function of the economy?

The economy is the social institution that ensures the maintenance of society through the production, distribution, and consumption of goods and services.

■ What are the three sectors of economic production?

In primary sector production, workers extract raw materials and natural resources from the environment and use them without much processing. Industrial societies engage in secondary sector production, which is based on the processing of raw materials (from the primary sector) into finished goods. Postindustrial societies engage in tertiary sector production by providing services rather than goods.

■ How do the three major contemporary economic systems differ?

Over the last century, capitalism, socialism, and mixed economies have been the main economic systems in industrialized countries. Capitalism is characterized by ownership of the means of production, pursuit of personal profit, competition, and limited government intervention. Socialism is characterized by public ownership of the means of production, the pursuit of collective goals, and centralized decision making. In mixed economies, elements of a capitalist, market economy are combined with elements of a command, socialist economy.

■ What are the functionalist, conflict, and symbolic interactionist perspectives on the economy and work?

According to functionalists, the economy is a vital social institution because it is the means by which needed goods and services are produced and distributed.

Business cycles represent the necessary rise and fall of economic activity relative to long-term economic growth. Conflict theorists view business cycles as the result of capitalist greed. In order to maximize profits, capitalists suppress the wages of workers who, in turn, cannot purchase products, making it necessary for capitalists to reduce production, close factories, lay off workers, and adopt other remedies that are detrimental to workers and society. Symbolic interactionists focus on the microlevel of the economic system, particularly on the social organization of work and its effects on workers' attitudes and behaviour. Feminist researchers have documented the ways in which women are discriminated against in the world of work.

■ How do occupations differ in the primary and secondary labour market?

The primary labour market consists of well-paying jobs with good benefits that have some degree of security and the possibility of advancement. The secondary labour market consists of low-paying jobs with few benefits and very little job security or possibility of advancement.

■ What is a labour union?

A labour union is a group of employees who join together to bargain with an employer or a group of employers over wages, benefits, and working conditions.

■ How has globalization affected Canadian workers?

The need to stay competitive with low-wage countries has kept wages down. If workers insist on higher wages, companies can simply close their factories and move production to another country. On the positive side, increased trade has created jobs in Canada.

KEY TERMS

capitalism 402

contingent work 416

corporations 402

democratic socialism 406

economy 396

labour union 418

marginal jobs 415

mixed economy 406

multinational corporations 403

occupations 411

oligopoly 404

postindustrial economy 400

primary sector production 397

professions 412

secondary sector production 399

socialism 405

unemployment rate 418

NET LINKS

For a left-wing perspective on economic and labour issues, go to the Canadian Centre for Policy Alternatives at:

http://www.policyalternatives.ca/

For a right-wing perspective on economic and labour issues, go to the Fraser Institute at:

http://www.fraserinstitute.ca/

The Canadian government has a one-stop guide to the Canadian economy at

http://canadianeconomy.gc.ca/english/ economy/

LaborNet uses computer communications as a means of building an international labour movement; see:

http://www.labornet.org/

For a wide range of information on labour and the labour force in Canada, go to the Web site of Human Resources and Skills Development Canada (the government department responsible for employment matters) at:

http://www.hrsdc.gc.ca/

QUESTIONS FOR CRITICAL THINKING

1. If you were the manager of a computer software division, how might you encourage innovation among your technical employees? How might you encourage efficiency? If you were the manager of a fast-food restaurant, how might you increase job satisfaction and decrease job alienation among your employees?

2. Why does a smaller proportion of workers belong to unions than was the case a generation ago?

Do you think unions can regain their earlier role or will they continue to decline in importance? Explain why you feel this way.

3. Table 13.1 shows the four companies that control the recorded music industry in the industrialized world. In the 1960s there were hundreds of record companies, but these four have now taken almost all the important artists into their corporate empires. Can you think of how this corporate concentration affects the kind of music that you and your friends listen to?

4. Many occupations will change or disappear in the future. Think of a specific occupation or profession and consider its future. For example, what will be the role of the librarian when books, journals, and abstracts are all instantly accessible on the Internet?

SUGGESTED READINGS

A very good general book on the sociology of work is:

Harvey J. Krahn and Graham S. Lowe. *Work, Industry, and Canadian Society*. 4th ed. Scarborough, Ont.: Nelson Canada, 2002.

These books provide more information about capitalism:

Peter L. Berger. *The Capitalist Revolution: Fifty Propositions About Prosperity, Equality, and Liberty*. New York: Basic Books, 1986.

Harry Braverman. *Labor and Monopoly Capital: The Degradation of Work in the Twentieth Century*. New York: Monthly Review Press, 1974.

Karl Marx. *Selected Writings in Sociology and Social Philosophy*. Thomas B. Bottomore and Maximilian Rubel (eds.). New York: McGraw-Hill, 1964.

Books that provide interesting insights on the sociology of work include:

Patrick Burman. *Killing Time, Losing Ground: Experiences of Unemployment*. Toronto: Wall and Thompson, 1988.

Barbara Garson. *The Electronic Sweatshop: How Computers Are Transforming the Office of the Future into the Factory of the Past*. New York: Penguin Books, 1989.

Ben Hamper. *Rivethead: Tales from the Assembly Line*. New York: Time Warner, 1992.

Studs Terkel. *Working: People Talk About What They Do All Day and How They Feel About What They Do*. New York: Ballantine Books, 1985.

Scholarly works on labour unions include:

Irving Abella. *On Strike: Six Key Labour Struggles in Canada 1919–1949*. Toronto: James Lewis and Samuel, 1974.

Berch Berberoglu (Ed.). *The Labor Process and the Control of Labor: The Changing Nature of Work Relations in the Late Twentieth Century.* Westport, Conn.: Praeger, 1993.

ONLINE STUDY AND RESEARCH TOOLS

THOMSONNOW™ ThomsonNOW!

Go to **http://hed.nelson.com** to link to ThomsonNOW for *Sociology in Our Times,* Fourth Canadian Edition, your online study tool. First take the **Pre-Test** for this chapter to get your personalized **Study Plan,** which will identify topics you need to review and direct you to the appropriate resources. Then take the **Post-Test** to determine what concepts you have mastered and what you still need work on.

INFOTRAC®

Infotrac College Edition is included free with every new copy of this text. Explore this online library for additional readings, review, and a handy resource for assignments. Visit **www.infotrac-college.com** to access this online database of full-text articles. Enter the key terms from this chapter to start your search.

Power, Politics, and Government

Compared with most other nations, Canada has had a very peaceful political history. However, there have been instances of political violence. During the 1960s and early 1970s, a group called the Front de Libération du Québec (FLQ) committed a number of terrorist acts, which culminated in the kidnapping of a British diplomat and the murder of a Quebec cabinet minister. One of the intellectual leaders of the FLQ was Pierre Vallières. In *White Niggers of America*, a book he wrote in prison following his arrest for the murder of a woman who died in one of the terrorist bomb attacks carried out by the FLQ, Vallières outlined some of the grievances of the Quebec separatists:

"In writing this book I claim to do no more than bear witness to the determination of the workers of Quebec to put an end to three centuries of exploitation, of injustices borne in silence, of sacrifices accepted in vain, of insecurity endured with resignation; to bear witness to their new and increasingly energetic determination to take control of their economic, political, and social affairs and to transform into a more just and fraternal society this country, Quebec, which is theirs, this country where they have always been the overwhelming majority of citizens and producers of the 'national' wealth, yet where they never have enjoyed the economic power and social freedom to which their numbers and labor entitle them" (1971:17).

While this sounds much like the rhetoric of present-day separatists, the FLQ was different because its members also adhered to a revolutionary Marxist ideology, which they used to justify their violence. Vallières, who saw himself as a political prisoner rather than as a "common criminal," described the two goals of his movement in this way:

"The FLQ is . . . the armed avant-garde of the exploited classes of Quebec: the workers, the farmers, the petty white-collar workers, the students, the unemployed, and those on welfare—that is, at least 90 percent of the population. The FLQ is struggling not only for the political independence of Quebec, but also and inseparably for the revolution, a total revolution which will give all power to the workers and students in a free, self-administering, and fraternal society. Only a total revolution will make it possible for the Québécois, in collaboration with the other peoples of the earth, to build a Quebec that is truly free, truly sovereign" (1971:258-259).

While few now share Vallières's views about the need for a violent revolution, many Quebeckers still dream of independence. Feeling their culture threatened by the influence of English-speaking North America, separatists believe they can fulfil their destiny only as a distinct "people" through political independence. While the separatists lost the October 1995 referendum by the narrowest of margins and were supported by a large majority of French-speaking voters, the feelings of Quebeckers remain ambivalent. For example, a poll conducted after the referendum found that two-thirds of Quebeckers wanted their province to remain part of Canada. However, the same poll showed that 55 percent would vote for separation. These data reflect Quebec comedian Yvon Deschamps's perception that what Québécois really want is an independent Quebec within a strong and united Canada. They also suggest that some flexibility from the other provinces concerning Quebec's place in Canada would ensure that our country stays together, as many Quebeckers would clearly prefer constitutional reform to separation.

Interestingly, Vallières himself reflected these two different strains of Québécois political thought. After his release from prison, he disavowed violence and became a member of the separatist Parti Québécois. However, he left that party, feeling it had become too conservative in economic matters. Late in his life, Vallières was horrified by the ethnic violence in the former

Yugoslavia and prior to his death in 1998 he rejected separatism, fearing it would lead to ethnic and linguistic apartheid.

This chapter is about political and state institutions. Political institutions are concerned with the exercise of power, and state institutions are the means through which that power is exercised. Modern nations face tremendous political challenges. Resolving the place of

Quebec in (or out of) Confederation is but one of the political issues facing Canadians. In this chapter, we will discuss some of these issues and describe the political system through which Canadians will deal with them. We will also examine other systems of government. Before reading on, test your knowledge about political issues and state institutions by taking the quiz in Box 14.1.

QUESTIONS AND ISSUES

Chapter Focus Question: Can the aspirations of Aboriginal people and French-speaking Quebeckers be accommodated within the Canadian political system?

What is the relationship between power and authority? Why do people accept authority?

What are the major political systems?

Whose interests are reflected in political decisions?

How is government shaped by political parties and political attitudes?

Why is nationalism such an important force in the world today?

What is the place of democracy in the twenty-first century?

Tension between anglophone and francophone Montrealers increased after the 1995 referendum. Many separatists were angry at the English and ethnic voters who refused to support independence.

Over the past few decades, indicators of political participation, such as the percentage of people who vote in elections, have been steadily declining, and many Canadians, particularly young people, seem to feel that

politics is irrelevant to their lives. However, politics is vitally important to all of us, and many things about your future will be affected by political decisions. At the extreme, we can look at "failed states," such as Somalia and Haiti, where politics has failed and where people live miserable lives on the edge of starvation. Even in Canada, political decisions affect almost all aspects of our lives. Political analyst Michael Parenti (1996:7–8) has described the impact of politics as follows:

> The taxes and prices we pay and the jobs available to us, the chances that we will live in peace or perish in war, the costs of education and the availability of scholarships, the safety of the airliner or highway we travel on, the quality of the food we eat and the air we breathe, the availability of affordable housing and medical care, the legal protections against racial and sexual discrimination—all the things that directly affect the quality of our lives are influenced in some measure by politics.

Thus politics has a major impact on our daily lives. During much of the 1990s, the trend was to reduce the role government played in our lives; many of the functions of government were cut or contracted out to private companies. However, disasters, such as the destruction of the World Trade Center and the deaths related to water contamination in Walkerton,

Ontario, were reminders of the important role that governments must play in protecting the public from harm.

POLITICS, POWER, AND AUTHORITY

Politics **is the social institution through which power is acquired and exercised by some people and groups.** In contemporary societies, the government is the primary political system. *Government* **is the formal organization that has the legal and political authority to regulate the relationships among members of a society and between the society and those outside its borders.** Some social scientists refer to government as the *state*—**the political entity that possesses a legitimate monopoly over the use of force within its territory to achieve its goals.**

Power and Authority

Power **is the ability of persons or groups to carry out their will despite opposition from others** (Weber, 1968/1922). Through the use of persuasion, authority, or force, some people are able to get others to acquiesce to their demands. Consequently, power is a *social relationship* that involves both leaders and followers. Power also is a dimension in the structure of social stratification. Persons in positions of power control valuable resources of society—including wealth, status, comfort, and safety—and are able to influence the actions of others by awarding or withholding those resources (Dye and Zeigler, 1993).

The most basic form of power is force or military might. Initially, force may be used to seize and hold power. Max Weber suggested, however, that force is not the most effective long-term means of gaining compliance, because those who are being ruled do not accept as legitimate those who are doing the ruling. Consequently, most leaders do not want to base their

BOX 14.1 SOCIOLOGY AND EVERYDAY LIFE

How Much Do You Know About Political Issues and State Institutions?

True	False	
T	F	1. Organizations in which authority is based on the charismatic qualities of particular leaders can be unstable, and these kinds of organizations often fail.
T	F	2. In Canada, our constitutional right to freedom of speech means that any kind of pornography or hate literature can be legally distributed.
T	F	3. While authoritarian governments still exist in many countries, democratic government has become more widespread throughout the world during the past fifteen years.
T	F	4. In Canada, members of the governing party are free to vote against the government in Parliament whenever they wish.
T	F	5. Canada's Aboriginal peoples have been able to vote in federal elections since 1867, the year of Confederation.
T	F	6. All citizens have an equal say in government decisions.
T	F	7. Canada has had a female prime minister.
T	F	8. Canada is one of the few nations in the world that has had as its official opposition in Parliament a political party dedicated to the breakup of the country.
T	F	9. A higher proportion of Canadians vote in federal elections than do the citizens of other industrialized countries.
T	F	10. Under most proposals for Aboriginal self-government, Aboriginal groups in Canada would have total control over their territory and would be considered sovereign nations.

Answers on page 432.

Answers to the Sociology Quiz on Political Issues and State Institutions

1. **True.**   Many political and religious movements that are held together by the personal qualities of their leader fail when the leader dies, retires, or is found to be "ordinary."

2. **False.**   While the *Canadian Charter of Rights and Freedoms* does guarantee the freedom of speech, all freedoms are subject to "reasonable limits." Our courts have interpreted this to allow governments some powers of censorship.

3. **True.**   The movement toward democratic government sped up dramatically with the fall of the Berlin Wall in 1989 and the subsequent breakup of the Soviet Union. A number of countries in Africa and in Central and South America have also become democracies since that time.

4. **False.**   In the United States, members of Congress who belong to the same party as the president often vote against the president. However, in Canada party discipline is often imposed on those who vote against their leader.

5. **False.**   Aboriginal people did not have voting rights in federal elections until 1960.

6. **False.**   Special interest groups and various elites in society have far more influence on government policy than do average citizens.

7. **True.**   Kim Campbell was prime minister of Canada in 1993. When Brian Mulroney retired from politics, Campbell took over the leadership of the Progressive Conservative Party and automatically became prime minister. However, she was defeated in an election held a few months later, so we have still never had a woman elected prime minister.

8. **True.**   In 1993, the Bloc Québécois won the second highest number of seats in the federal election and become the official opposition. The main purpose of the Bloc is to promote the separation of Quebec from Canada (http://www.danielturp.org).

9. **False.**   Canada's voter turnout rate is higher than that of the United States, but lower than that of most other industrialized countries.

10. **False.**   Some Aboriginal groups, including some Quebec Mohawks, do argue that they have the status of sovereign nations, but most Aboriginal people have a more limited view of self-government (Boldt, 1993).

power on force alone; they seek to legitimize their power by turning it into *authority*—**power that people accept as legitimate rather than coercive.**

Ideal Types of Authority

Under what circumstances are people most likely to accept authority as legitimate and adhere to it? People have a greater tendency to accept authority as legitimate if they are economically or politically dependent on those who hold power. They also may accept authority more readily if it reflects their own beliefs and values (Turner, Beeghley, and Powers, 1995). *Legitimation* refers to the process by which power is institutionalized and given a moral

foundation to justify its existence. Weber outlined three *ideal types* of authority—charismatic, traditional, and rational-legal—each of which has a different basis of legitimacy and a different means of administration.

Charismatic Authority   According to Weber, ***charismatic authority*** **is power legitimized on the basis of a leader's exceptional personal qualities** or the demonstration of extraordinary insight and accomplishment, which inspire loyalty and obedience from followers. To Weber, charismatic individuals are able to "identify themselves with the central facts or problems of people's lives [and through the force of their personalities] communicate their inspirations to others and lead them in new directions" (Turner, Beeghley, and Powers, 1995:214–215).

From Weber's perspective, a charismatic leader may be either a tyrant or a hero. Thus, charismatic authority has been attributed to such diverse historical figures as Jesus Christ, Napoleon, Julius Caesar, Adolf Hitler, Winston Churchill, and Martin Luther King, Jr. Among the most charismatic leaders in Canadian politics have been former Prime Minister Pierre Trudeau and Lucien Bouchard, the former premier of Quebec. Bouchard's personal appeal almost led to a separatist victory in the 1995 referendum, which, under the distinctly uncharismatic Jacques Parizeau, looked to be heading for an overwhelming defeat.

Since women seldom are permitted to assume positions of leadership in patriarchal political and social structures, they are much less likely to become charismatic leaders. Famous women who had charismatic appeal include Joan of Arc, Mother Teresa, Indira Gandhi of India, Evita Perón of Argentina, and Margaret Thatcher of the United Kingdom. Kim Campbell's strong performance as Minister of Justice and her personality gave her a charismatic appeal, which, in turn, helped her win the leadership of the Progressive Conservative Party and become Canada's first woman prime minister. However, the fleeting nature of such appeal was illustrated in the 1993 election when the campaign performance of Campbell and her party was too weak to overcome the negative feelings Canadians held about the government of her predecessor, Brian Mulroney. The Conservatives were reduced to only two seats in Parliament and their future as a party was threatened.

Charismatic authority generally tends to be temporary and unstable; it derives primarily from individual leaders (who may change their minds, leave, or die) and from an administrative structure usually limited to a small number of faithful followers. For this reason, charismatic authority often becomes routinized. The *routinization of charisma* **occurs when charismatic authority is succeeded by a bureaucracy controlled by a rationally established authority or by a combination of traditional and bureaucratic authority** (Turner, Beeghley, and Powers, 1995). According to Weber (1968/1922:1148), "It is the fate of charisma to recede . . . after it has entered the permanent structures of social action." However, charisma cannot always be successfully transferred to organizations. Many organizations, particularly religious ones, fail when the leader departs.

Traditional Authority   In contrast to charismatic authority, ***traditional authority*** **is power that is legitimized by respect for long-standing custom.** In preindustrial societies, the authority of traditional leaders, such as kings, queens, pharaohs, emperors, and religious dignitaries, usually is grounded in religious beliefs and established practices. For example, British kings and queens historically have traced their authority from God. Members of subordinate classes obey a traditional leader's edicts out of economic and political dependency and sometimes personal loyalty. However, custom and religious beliefs are sufficient to maintain traditional authority only as long as people share similar backgrounds and accept this type of authority as legitimate.

As societies industrialize, traditional authority is challenged by a more complex division of labour and by the wider diversity of people who now inhabit the area as a result of migration. In industrialized societies, people do not share the same viewpoint on many issues and tend to openly question traditional authority. As the division of labour

Pierre Trudeau was one of Canada's most charismatic politicians. When he died sixteen years after retiring from the prime minister's office, hundreds of thousands of people left their homes to pay their respects to him and his family. Shown here is his son Justin Trudeau on the train carrying his father's body from Ottawa to Montreal for burial.

becomes more complex, political and economic institutions become increasingly interdependent (Durkheim, 1933/1893).

Weber predicted that traditional authority would inhibit the development of capitalism. He stressed that capitalism cannot fully develop when rules are not logically established, when officials follow rules arbitrarily, and when leaders are not technically trained (Weber, 1968/1922; Turner, Beeghley, and Powers, 1995). Weber believed that capitalism worked best in systems of rational-legal authority.

Gender, race, and class relations are closely intertwined with traditional authority. Weber noted that traditional authority is often based on a system of patriarchy in which men are assumed to have authority in the household and in other small groups. Political scientist Zillah R. Eisenstein (1994) suggests that *racialized patriarchy*—the continual interplay of race and gender—reinforces traditional structures of power in contemporary societies. According to Eisenstein (1994:2), "Patriarchy differentiates women from men while privileging men. Racism simultaneously differentiates people of color from whites and

Concept Table 14.A   WEBER'S THREE TYPES OF AUTHORITY

Max Weber's three types of authority are shown here in global perspective. Charismatic authority is exemplified by former prime minister Indira Gandhi of India. Nepal's King Gyanendra provides an example of traditional authority sanctioned by custom. Canadian Members of Parliament represent rational-legal authority, which depends on established rules and procedures.

	DESCRIPTION	**EXAMPLES**	
Charismatic	Based on leaders' personal qualities Temporary and unstable	Napoleon Adolf Hitler Indira Gandhi	
Traditional	Legitimized by long-standing custom Subject to erosion as traditions weaken	Authority resides in traditional leader supported by larger social structures, as in old British monarchy Patriarchy (rule by men occupying traditional positions of authority, as in the family)	
Rational-legal	Legitimized by rationally established rules and procedures Authority resides in the office, not the person	Modern British Parliament Canadian prime minister, Parliament, federal bureaucracy	

privileges whiteness. These processes are distinct but intertwined." Although racialized patriarchy has been increasingly challenged, many believe that it remains a reality in both preindustrial and industrialized nations.

Rational-Legal Authority According to Weber, ***rational-legal authority* is power legitimized by law or written rules and regulations.** Rational-legal authority is also called *bureaucratic authority*. As you will recall from Chapter 6, bureaucracies are characterized by a clear-cut division of labour, hierarchy of authority, formal rules, impersonal enforcement of rules, and job security based on a person's technical qualifications. In rational-legal authority, power is legitimized by procedures; if leaders obtain their positions in a procedurally correct manner (such as by election or appointment), they have the right to act.

In Canada, our political system gives rational-legal authority to the office of the prime minister, for example, by specifying the procedures by which persons hold the office as well as its duties and limitations. Rational-legal authority also is held by other elected or appointed government officials and by officers in a formal organization. However, authority is invested in the *office,* not in the *person* who holds the office. For example, when the Conservatives lost the 1993 federal election, Kim Campbell passed on the power of the office of prime minister to Jean Chrétien and no longer had any involvement in government.

In a rational-legal system, bureaucracy is the apparatus responsible for creating and enforcing rules in the public interest. Weber believed that rational-legal authority was the only means by which to attain "efficient, flexible, and competent regulation under a rule of law" (Turner, Beeghley, and Powers, 1995:218). Weber's three types of authority are summarized in Concept Table 14.A.

GLOBAL POLITICAL SYSTEMS

Political systems as we know them today have evolved slowly. In the earliest societies, politics was not an entity separate from other aspects of life. As we will see, however, all groups have some means of legitimizing power.

Hunting and gathering societies do not have political institutions as such because they have very little division of labour or social inequality. Leadership and authority are centred in the family and clan. Individuals acquire leadership roles due to personal attributes, such as great physical strength, exceptional skills, or charisma (Lenski, Lenski, and Nolan, 1991).

Political institutions first emerged in agrarian societies as they acquired surpluses and developed greater social inequality. Elites took control of politics and used custom or traditional authority to justify their position. When cities developed circa 3500–3000 B.C.E., the *city-state*—a city whose power extended to adjacent areas—became the centre of political power. Both the Roman and Persian empires comprised a number of city-states, each of which had its own monarchy. Thus, in these societies, political authority was decentralized. After each of these empires fell, the individual city-states lived on.

Nation-states, as we know them, began to develop in Spain, France, and England between the twelfth and fifteenth centuries (see Tilly, 1975). A *nation-state* is a unit of political organization that has recognizable national boundaries and citizens who possess specific legal rights and obligations. Nation-states emerge as countries develop specific geographic territories and acquire greater ability to defend their borders. Improvements in communication and transportation make it possible for people in a larger geographic area to share a common language and culture. As charismatic and traditional authority are superseded by rational-legal authority, legal standards come to prevail in all areas of life, and the nation-state claims a monopoly over the legitimate use of force (Kennedy, 1993).

Queen Elizabeth II, shown visiting Sheridan College in Oakville, Ontario, is Canada's head of state.

Approximately 190 nation-states currently exist throughout the world. The four main types of political systems found in nation-states are monarchies, authoritarian systems, totalitarian systems, and democracies.

Monarchies

A *monarchy* **is a political system in which power resides in one person or family and is passed from generation to generation through lines of inheritance.** Monarchies are most common in agrarian societies and are associated with traditional authority patterns. However, the relative power of monarchs has varied across nations, depending on religious, political, and economic conditions. *Absolute monarchs* claim a hereditary right to rule (based on membership in a noble family) or a divine right to rule (in other words, a God-given right to rule that legitimizes the exercise of power). In *limited monarchies,* rulers depend on powerful members of the nobility to retain their thrones. Unlike absolute monarchs, limited monarchs are not considered to be above the law. In *constitutional monarchies,* the royalty serve as symbolic rulers or heads of state while actual authority is held by elected officials in the national parliaments. In such present-day monarchies as the United Kingdom, Sweden, Japan, and the Netherlands, members of royal families primarily perform ceremonial functions.

Authoritarian Systems

An *authoritarian political system* **is one controlled by rulers who deny popular participation in government.** A few authoritarian regimes have been absolute monarchies in which rulers claimed a hereditary right to their position. Today, Saudi Arabia and Kuwait are examples of authoritarian absolute monarchies. *Dictatorships,* in which power is gained and held by a single individual, also are authoritarian in nature. Pure dictatorships are rare: all rulers need the support of the military and the backing of business elites to maintain their position. *Military juntas* result when military officers seize power from the government, as has happened in recent years in Nigeria, Pakistan, and Haiti. Some countries, such as Myanmar, have been under military rule for many years. Authoritarian regimes may be relatively short-lived. Some nations may move toward democracy while others may become more totalitarian.

Totalitarian Systems

A *totalitarian political system* **is one in which the state seeks to regulate all aspects of people's public and private lives.** One example of a totalitarian regime was the National Socialist (Nazi) party in Germany during World War II, where military leaders sought to control all aspects of national life, not just government operations.

To keep people from rebelling, totalitarian governments enforce conformity. People are denied the right to assemble for political purposes; access to information is strictly controlled; and secret police enforce compliance, creating an environment of constant fear and suspicion. North Korea is one contemporary example of a totalitarian regime; another was the Taliban regime that ruled Afghanistan until it was forced out by an American-led coalition following the September 11, 2001 terrorist attacks in the United States. The Taliban regime maintained absolute control over the Afghan people in most of that country. For example, it required that all Muslims take part in prayer five times each day and that men attend prayer at mosques, where women were forbidden (Marquis, 2001). All facets of daily life were regulated according the Taliban leaders' interpretation of Muslim law. Although the totalitarian nature of the Taliban regime was difficult for many people, it was particularly oppressive for women, who were viewed by this group as being "biologically, religiously and prophetically" inferior to men (McGeary, 2001:41). The regime banned women from public life and essentially kept them isolated at home. It was overthrown because of its support for Osama bin Laden, who was permitted to run al-Qaeda terrorist training camps in Afghanistan. As a totalitarian regime, the Taliban leadership was officially recognized by only three other governments, despite controlling most of Afghanistan.

Democracies

A *democracy* **is a political system in which the people hold the ruling power either directly or through elected representatives.** In an ideal-type democracy, people would actively and directly rule themselves. *Direct participatory democracy* requires that citizens be able to meet regularly to debate and decide the issues of the day. Historical examples of direct democracy might include ancient Athens or a town meeting in colonial New England; however, the extent to which such meetings actually reflected the wishes of most people has been the subject of scholarly debate. Moreover, the impracticality of involving an entire citizenry in direct decision making becomes evident in nations containing millions of adults. If all thirty million people in Canada came together in one place for a meeting, for example, they would occupy an area of thirty square kilometres, and a single round of five-minute speeches would require hundreds of years. At this rate, people would be born, grow old, and die while waiting for a single decision to be made. Even an electronic town hall meeting in which people were linked through the telephone, television, or the Internet would be enormously complicated to organize.

In most democratic countries, including Canada, people have a voice in the government through *representative democracy,* whereby citizens elect representatives to serve as bridges between themselves and the government. In a representative democracy, elected representatives are supposed to convey the concerns and interests of those they represent, and the government is expected to be responsive to the wishes of the people. Elected officials are held accountable to the people through elections.

The specific form of representative democracies also varies. Canada is a *constitutional monarchy* whose head of state is the Queen, a hereditary ruler who is represented in Canada by the governor general. The governor general is appointed by the Queen but recommended by the prime minister, and has a role that is largely ceremonial, as our elected parliament actually governs the country. By contrast, the United States and France are *republics,* whose heads of state are elected and share governing power with the legislature.

Another major difference between Canada and the United States is that our system is a *parliamentary* one in which the prime minister is the leader of the party that wins the most seats in the House of Commons. This system is based on parliamentary discipline, which ensures that the policies favoured by the prime minister will become law. If government members oppose these policies they have the opportunity to debate them in private caucus meetings, but they are normally bound to support the government. Party discipline can be harsh; in 2004, Prime Minister Paul Martin expelled outspoken member of parliament Carolyn Parrish from the Liberal Party for making comments that were contrary to Party policy. By contrast, U.S. legislators often oppose their party's program.

When Canada adopted the British parliamentary system, the Fathers of Confederation also implemented an important feature of the American system—both Canada and the United States are *federations,* with a division of power between the central government and provincial or state governments. Many other countries, including Israel and Italy, are *unitary states,* which means they have a single central political authority. While John A. Macdonald, our first prime minister, would have preferred a centralized unitary state, this was opposed by Quebec and the Maritimes, which wished to protect their distinctive identities. *The British North America Act* of 1867 established the distribution of powers between federal and provincial governments.

Some countries have one-party democracies that appear to be democratic because they hold periodic elections. However, the outcome of these elections is a foregone conclusion because voters get to select from candidates belonging to only one party. For example, in the former Soviet Union all candidates belonged to the communist party; in North Korea, all candidates were from the party led by dictator Kim Jong-il.

During the past two decades, democracy has spread very rapidly, particularly in formerly communist states. Communism was a one-party system that often maintained its power through repressive means. Since the fall of the Berlin Wall in 1989, the countries of the former Soviet bloc in Eastern Europe, as well as others, such as Nicaragua and Zambia, have established democratic governments. While communist governments remain in a number of countries, including China and Cuba, pressures for democratization are strong around the globe. Between 1990 and 2005, the number of countries that are considered free based upon their human rights and civil liberties has increased from 65 to 89, and 119 countries are electoral democracies (Freedom House, 2005). However, new democracies may be fragile: Pakistan was taken over by the military in 1999, and Zimbabwe has become what the United Nations has called a "pseudo" democracy as President Robert Mugabe turned to authoritarian rule in order to maintain power. In 2005, Freedom House reclassified Russia from Partly Free to Not Free because of governmental interference in elections and control of the media.

If nothing else, the economic and social success of the democratic states serves as a model for those wishing to reform their own governments. Historically and today, capitalism is best served by a democratic system, and most countries initiating reforms are moving to capitalism. Full control over property and free markets are necessary and these are not compatible with an absolutist state. The global revolution in communications has also facilitated democratization. Nondemocratic governments may wish to keep their citizens cut off from developments elsewhere in the world. However, satellite television, fax machines, and the Internet make it impossible to completely control or close off communications, and global culture, including democratic ideals, continues to spread.

PERSPECTIVES ON POWER AND POLITICAL SYSTEMS

Is political power in Canada concentrated in the hands of the few or distributed among the many? Sociologists and political scientists have suggested many different answers to this question; however, two prevalent models of power have emerged: pluralist and elite.

Functionalist Perspectives: The Pluralist Model

The pluralist model is rooted in a functionalist perspective, which assumes that people share a consensus on central concerns, such as freedom and protection from harm, and that the government serves important functions in society that no other institution can fulfil. According to Émile Durkheim (1933/1893), the purpose of government is to socialize people to become good citizens, to regulate the economy so that it operates effectively, and to provide the necessary services for citizens. Contemporary functionalists state the four main functions of government are as follows: (1) maintaining law and order, (2) planning and directing society, (3) meeting social needs, and (4) handling international relations, including warfare.

If government at national, provincial, and local levels is responsible for these functions, what role do people play in the political system? What keeps the government from becoming all-powerful? What happens when people do not agree on specific issues or concerns? Functionalists suggest that divergent viewpoints lead to a system of political pluralism in which the government functions as an arbiter between competing interests and viewpoints. According to the *pluralist model*, **power in political systems is widely dispersed throughout many**

competing interest groups (Dahl, 1961). Many of these are *special interest groups*—**political coalitions made up of individuals or groups that share a specific interest they wish to protect or advance with the help of the political system** (Greenberg and Page, 1996). Examples of special interest groups include the Business Council on National Issues, the Canadian Labour Congress, the National Action Committee on the Status of Women, and the Assembly of First Nations.

From a pluralist perspective, representative democracy (coupled with the checks and balances provided by the legal system, and the division of governmental powers between a central government and smaller units, such as provinces and municipalities) ensures that no one group can overpower the others and that individual rights are protected.

In addition to direct contact with legislators, special interest groups such as the "gun lobby" try to influence policymaking by mobilizing constituents and stirring up public opinion. Recent years have seen a proliferation of single-issue groups like those on both sides of the gun-control issue. The strong feelings of gun owners are shown in this Ottawa rally.

Special Interest Groups Special interest groups help people advocate their own interests and further their causes. Of the thousands of special interest groups in Canada, some (such as consumer groups) seek a collective good while others (such as the cigarette manufacturers' lobby) have a relatively narrow focus. Broad categories of special interest groups include banking, business, education, energy, the environment, health, labour, persons with a disability, religious groups, retired persons, women, and those espousing a specific ideological viewpoint; obviously, many groups overlap in interests and membership. Within each of these categories are numerous subgroups. In education, for example, different special interest groups represent teachers, parents, school administrators, universities, professors, vocational and technical schools, and students. Despite their claims to objectivity, members of the media also represent interest groups. Box 14.2 shows how the media portray different sides in the separatism debate.

Advocates of the pluralist model point out that special interest groups provide a voice for people who otherwise might not be heard by elected officials at the national, provincial, and local level. However, many special interest groups have specific economic stakes in public policy. Professional groups (such as the Canadian Bankers' Association) wield power with policymakers on issues that they feel may affect their economic well-being (such as increased competition in the banking industry). As discussed in Chapter 13, labour unions have asserted their claims in the hope of protecting the jobs of their members and gaining maximum wages and benefits.

Some feel that pressure group activity is increasingly replacing individual and party activity in Canada's political system. Our country is so large and so diverse that we have always had a highly pluralistic society, and political scientist Rand Dyck (2004) predicts that pluralism will become even more important in the future. Our ethnic diversity is growing (see Chapter 10), and groups representing women, French-speaking Quebeckers, Aboriginal peoples, ethnic Canadians, and many others are challenging the elitism of the past. Interest groups are now part of our political culture and their influence has been enhanced through legislation, such as the *Charter of Rights and Freedoms,* which guarantees them a voice in political affairs.

While a pluralistic system ensures the voice of many groups will be heard, it does not always work as fairly as political theorists might wish. For example, there are many more groups representing business interests than there are groups representing the interests of the lower class (Dyck, 1996). While this does not mean that government actions always reflect the interests of the powerful, it does mean that the weak must work much harder to be heard. Another potential problem with a highly pluralistic system is that if people turn away from broad social values to those of particular economic, cultural, racial, and gender groups—a process known as *identity politics*—society may become too fragmented.

Over the past two decades, special interest groups have become more involved in "single-issue politics," in which political candidates often are supported or rejected solely on the basis of their views on a specific issue—such as abortion, gun control, gay and lesbian rights, or the environment. Single-issue groups derive their strength from the intensity of their beliefs; leaders have little room to compromise on issues. Some of these groups have been very effective; about two decades ago, a quickly organized group of seniors was able to make the government back down on its plans to change the law that provided automatic cost-of-living increases to old-age pensioners.

Interest groups have also been effective on the international level. In recent years, Canada played a major role in passing two important international agreements. The first was to ban the use of landmines; the second was to set up a permanent war crimes tribunal. While these agreements were signed by governments, citizens' groups in many different countries were instrumental in convincing those governments to take action. The 1997 Nobel Peace Prize was awarded to one of these groups, the International Campaign to Ban Landmines, which coordinated the activities of over 1,000 nongovernmental organizations in more than sixty countries. These efforts culminated in the landmines treaty that was signed in Ottawa in 1997.

Conflict Perspectives: Elite Models

Although conflict theorists acknowledge that the government serves a number of important purposes in society, they assert that it exists for the benefit of wealthy or politically powerful elites who use it to impose their will on the masses. According to the ***elite model,*** **power in political systems is concentrated in the hands of a small group of elites and the masses are relatively powerless.**

BOX 14.2 SOCIOLOGY AND THE MEDIA

The Media and Separatism

The mass media have a major influence on politics. Most of us are aware that the media can distort events; this is particularly true of television, which is Canadians' main source of political information. Television news is very brief—items rarely last more than a minute or two—and producers try to show pictures that are interesting, exciting, and visually appealing. This means that any political messages must be short and simple. Since most political issues are very complex, they are inevitably oversimplified and distorted by television.

Media bias is a particular problem when reporters favour one side of a political debate. This has been the case in the battle over Quebec separatism. Many of those who work in Quebec's French-language media are ardent nationalists and their stories reflect their political views. Another problem is that owners can impose their views on reporters. For example, Pierre Péladeau was one of Quebec's wealthiest and most influential publishers. When he was accused of rebuking the staff of one of his papers for their stories praising Jews, Péladeau's defence was that he was not anti-Semitic, but that he wanted his papers to focus on stories about francophones. Since Quebec Jews are typically English-speaking, stories about them should not take up too much space in his papers.

On the other side, most of the English-language media are very much opposed to the sovereignty of Quebec and their work reflects a pro-unity position. That the French and English media in Quebec can differ dramatically in their reporting of the same event was shown in their coverage of a June 1996 rally of federalists on Parliament Hill in Ottawa. *The Gazette,* Montreal's leading English-language newspaper, reported that 12,000 people had attended a federalist "love-in." Their front-page photo showed a girl in front of the flag-waving crowd. In the girl's hand was a sign saying "Separation: It's Over." Contrast this with *Le Devoir,* a French-language paper, which reported that 6,000 people had attended the rally. On the front page was a photo of a protester wearing a Lucien Bouchard mask and carrying a cane. Another man appeared to be kicking him in the leg. (Bouchard, a leader of the separatist

■ In 1989, a group of protesters in Brockville, Ontario, stomped on the Quebec provincial flag. A film and photographs of this event played a prominent role in the 1995 referendum campaign. However, the pro-separatist media did not balance this coverage by showing pictures of the many Canadian flags that have been burned by Quebec nationalists.

forces, had recently had his leg amputated.) The spin the media put on events, as in this case, makes it difficult to separate reality from media bias.

The importance of the media in the battle for the hearts, minds, and votes of Quebeckers is indicated by the ongoing controversy over the role of the Canadian Broadcasting Corporation (CBC) in the unity debate. In 1967, the Liberal government gave the CBC the explicit mandate of promoting national unity and the Canadian identity. This led at times to political interference by the federal government in coverage by Radio-Canada, the French-language network of the CBC. While national unity has since been removed from the CBC's mission, the media remain an important part of our national debate.

Sources: Panitch and Swartz, 1993; Wieler, 1986.

Early Italian sociologists Vilfredo Pareto (1848–1923) and Gaetano Mosca (1858–1941) were among the first to show that concentration of power may be inevitable within societies. Pareto first used the term *elite* to refer to "the few who rule the many" (Marshall, 1998). Similarly, Karl Marx claimed that under capitalism, the government serves the interests of the ruling (or capitalist) class that controls the means of production.

From this perspective, a few of the "best and brightest" among the masses may rise to elite positions by acquiring the requisite education, experience, leadership skills, and other attributes of the elite (Dye and Zeigler, 2003). However, those who do not share the attitudes, political philosophy, gender, or race of the elites will not succeed in this way. The pluralist and elite models are compared in Figure 14.1.

C. Wright Mills and the Power Elite

Sociologist C. Wright Mills (1959a) was among the first to formulate and test ideas concerning power

elites. The ***power elite*** is composed of leaders at the top of business, the executive branch of the federal government, and the military. Of these three, Mills speculated that the "corporate rich" (the highest-paid officers of the biggest corporations) were the most powerful because of their unique ability to parlay the vast economic resources at their disposal into political power. At the middle level of the pyramid, Mills placed the legislative branch of government, special interest groups, and local opinion leaders. The bottom (and widest layer) of the pyramid is occupied by the unorganized masses who are relatively powerless and vulnerable to economic and political exploitation.

Mills emphasized that individuals who make up the power elite have similar class backgrounds and interests; many of them also interact on a regular basis. Members of the power elite are able to influence many important decisions, including federal spending. Other researchers (Hunter, 1953)

Figure 14.1   Pluralist and Elite Models

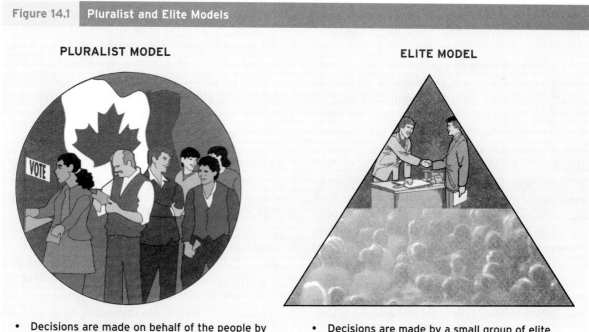

PLURALIST MODEL

- Decisions are made on behalf of the people by leaders who engage in bargaining, accommodation, and compromise.
- Competition among leadership groups makes abuse of power by any one group difficult.
- Power is widely dispersed and people can influence public policy by voting.
- Public policy reflects a balance among competing interest groups.

ELITE MODEL

- Decisions are made by a small group of elite people.
- Consensus exists among the elite on the basic values and goals of society.
- Power is highly concentrated at the top of a pyramid-shaped social hierarchy.
- Public policy reflects the values and preferences of the elite.

have identified elites who control decision making at local community levels; so, the view of elite domination can be extended to all levels of government.

G. William Domhoff and the Ruling Class

According to G. William Domhoff (1978), the *ruling class* is made up of the corporate rich, who make up less than 1 percent of the population. Domhoff uses the term *ruling class* to signify a relatively fixed group of privileged people who wield sufficient power to constrain political processes and serve underlying capitalist interests. By contrast, *governing power* refers to the everyday operation of the political system; who *governs* is much less important than who *rules*.

Like Mills, Domhoff asserted that individuals in the upper echelon are members of a business class that owns and controls large corporations. The intertwining of the upper class and the corporate community produces economic and social cohesion. Economic interdependence among members of the ruling class is rooted in common stock ownership and is visible in interlocking corporate directorates that serve as a communication network (Domhoff, 1983; Clement, 1975). Members of the ruling class also are socially linked with one another. They attend the same schools, belong to the same clubs, and frequently socialize together. Consider the example of Power Corporation, which is controlled by Paul Desmarais, who is a close friend of former Prime Ministers Brian Mulroney and Jean Chrétien—in fact, Desmarais's son is married to Chrétien's daughter. Prime Minister Paul Martin used to work for Power Corporation, and a wide variety of senior politicians and government bureaucrats move back and forth between senior Power Corporation positions and government service. With these contacts, Desmarais certainly has no difficulty in having his views heard by those responsible for Canada's governmental policy. Fox and Ornstein (1986) have documented an extensive network of links between large corporations and the federal cabinet, the Senate, and the federal bureaucracy. These links grew over the three decades they studied. They found far fewer links between provincial governments and the corporate world.

According to Domhoff (1983), the corporate rich influence the political process in three ways. First, they affect the candidate selection process by helping to finance campaigns and providing favours to political candidates. Second, through participation in the special interest process, the corporate rich are able to obtain favours, tax breaks, and favourable regulatory rulings. Finally, the corporate rich in Canada may gain access to the policymaking process through their appointments to governmental bodies, such as the Senate. While the economic elites are not in agreement on all issues, they do agree on the need to ensure an economic climate that favours their continuing accumulation of wealth. Fox and Ornstein conclude that the state is not simply an instrument or tool of the capitalists, but that there are important structural connections between the state and corporations that often help capitalists shape legislation to their benefit.

Today, some members of the ruling class influence international politics through their involvement in banking, business services, and law firms that have a strong interest in overseas sales, investments, or raw materials extraction (Domhoff, 1990). The power of transnational corporations has become an important factor in class analyses of the modern state.

Class Conflict Perspectives

Most contemporary elite models are based on the work of Karl Marx; however, there are divergent viewpoints about the role of the state within the Marxist (or class conflict) perspective. On the one hand, *instrumental Marxists* argue that the state invariably acts to perpetuate the capitalist class. From this perspective, capitalists control the government through special interest groups, lobbying, campaign financing, and other types of "influence peddling" to get legislatures and the courts to make decisions favourable to their class (Miliband, 1969; Domhoff, 1970). In other words, the state exists only to support the interests of the dominant class (Marger, 1987).

On the other hand, *structural Marxists* contend that the state is not simply a passive instrument of the capitalist class. Because the state must simultaneously preserve order and maintain a positive climate for the accumulation of capital, not all decisions can favour the immediate wishes of the dominant class (Quadagno, 1984; Marger, 1987). For example, at various points in the history of this country, the state has had to institute social welfare programs, regulate business, and enact policies that favour unions in order to placate people and maintain "law and order." Ultimately, however, such actions serve the long-range interests of the capitalists by keeping members of subordinate groups from rebelling against the dominant group (O'Connor, 1973).

Critique of Pluralist and Elite Models

Pluralist and elite models each make a unique contribution to our understanding of power. The pluralist model emphasizes that many different groups, not just elected officials, compete for power and advantage in society. This model also shows how coalitions may shift over time and how elected officials may be highly responsive to public opinion on some occasions. However, critics counter that research shows that our system has only the appearance of pluralism and that it is, in fact, remarkably elitist for a society that claims to value ordinary people's input. A wide disparity exists between the resources and political clout of big business and those of interest groups that represent infants and children or persons with disabilities, for example. According to critics, consensus is difficult, if not impossible, in populations consisting of people from different classes, religions, and racial–ethnic and age groups.

Mills's power elite model highlights the interrelationships of the economic, political, and military sectors of society and makes us aware that the elite may be a relatively cohesive group. Similarly, Domhoff's ruling class model emphasizes the role of elites in setting and implementing policies that benefit the capitalist class. Power elite models call our attention to a central concern in contemporary Canadian society: the ability of democracy and its ideals to survive in the context of the increasingly concentrated power held by capitalist oligarchies (see Chapter 13).

One important critique of elite models is that social change does not always favour the dominant groups in our society. For example, women have won many battles over the past two decades despite the degree of control that males have had over the corporate and political spheres. The success of the women's movement supports the pluralist claim that non-elites can organize to force change.

Feminist Perspectives

Political theorists have focused much of their attention on class issues. British sociologist Mary McIntosh (1978) was among the first to argue that gender issues were also important. McIntosh felt that the state supported a system in which women were controlled in the household, where they performed unpaid labour that helped supply a cheap workforce for the capitalist system. Until they achieved some political power, women would inevitably be subordinated by the patriarchal state.

Women have long been excluded from the political process. The *Elections Act* of 1903 said that "No woman, criminal, or lunatic can vote," and Canadian women were not permitted to vote in federal elections until 1918. Most provinces began allowing women to vote at around this time, though in Quebec women were not enfranchised until 1940. With the vote, women also received the right to run for election. However, few ran, and even fewer were successful. Only 27 women were elected to the federal Parliament between 1921 and 1968. As late as 1980, only 5 percent of members of parliament (MPs) were women. Since that time, significant progress has been made; 21.1 percent of the members of parliament elected in 2004 were women (see Table 14.1), a figure that is similar to that of most provincial legislatures (the exception being Quebec, where about 30 percent of legislators were women) (Equal Voice, 2005). But women have not yet reached the highest political positions. While Canada has had one woman prime minister (Kim Campbell) and two provincial premiers, only one of these three, Catherine Callbeck of Prince Edward Island, was actually elected to the position. Women have been much more successful at the municipal level; many of Canada's mayors are women. The low representation of women in Canadian political office is typical of most Western countries. The major exception is the Scandinavian countries, where women make up more than 35 percent of the membership of the national parliaments. The issue is not simply one of representation. The absence of women in our legislatures has meant that many gender-related issues have

Table 14.1 PERCENTAGE OF WOMEN IN PARLIAMENT, SELECTED COUNTRIES, 2005	
Rwanda	48.4
Sweden	45.3
Norway	38.2
Finland	37.5
Denmark	36.9
Netherlands	36.7
South Africa	32.8
Australia	24.7
Canada	**21.1**
United Kingdom	18.1
United States	15.2
France	12.2
Italy	11.5

Source: Inter-Parliamentary Union, 2005.

not received sufficient attention. Issues, such as daycare policy, pay equity, the feminization of poverty, and violence against women and children, have only recently begun to receive the attention they deserve. In theory, male legislators, whose constituents are more than 50 percent women, could have pursued these issues. But for many years they did not.

Interactionist Perspectives on the Political Process

Symbolic interactionists have not done much work in the area of politics and government. However, the perspective is a useful one because politics is very much a human process and the insights of interactionism can help to understand why people behave the way they do in the political arena. The work of Joseph Gusfield on the importance of symbolic action in the political process shows how the interactionist perspective can be applied to the study of politics and government.

Gusfield and Symbolic Crusades
In 2005 many interest groups, including the Catholic Church and various family organizations, spent a great deal of time and money trying to defeat the federal Liberal government's same-sex marriage legislation. At the same time, in the United States, the National Rifle Association was fighting proposed laws that would prevent people whose names were listed on terrorist watch lists from buying weapons. To many of us, these battles might not seem worth the effort. Allowing gays and lesbians to marry should not affect other Canadians, especially because at the time the legislation was being considered same-sex marriage was already permitted in eight provinces and territories representing more than 90 percent of the Canadian population and could not be regulated by the federal government without invoking the notwithstanding clause in the *Charter of Rights and Freedoms.* In the security-conscious United States, denying suspected terrorists access to weapons would seem a prudent thing to do and it is difficult to see any social benefit in allowing them to legally purchase guns. However, for many North Americans these issues were vitally important.

Why do interest groups spend so much time and energy on issues such as same-sex marriage and gun control? A number of years ago Joseph Gusfield (1963) asked this question about the temperance movement. He was interested in learning why people became intensely involved in trying to ban the consumption of alcohol. The temperance movement was very active in North America in the early part of the twentieth century and was temporarily successful in having alcohol sales prohibited for a period of several years throughout the United States and in most Canadian provinces. Gusfield concluded that the movement was a *symbolic crusade* in which the recognition of the crusaders' values by the government was at least as important as achieving the instrumental goal of a society in which alcohol use was prohibited. During a period when the United States was becoming urbanized, many of those involved in the temperance movement were rural Protestants who felt that their importance in American society was declining and that their values were being replaced with an urban-oriented value system that was much more indulgent. For many, this change threatened their honoured place in American society as well as their religious and moral values. "In response, many in [the Protestant group] fought to reassert the dominance of their lifestyle by pressing for adherence to its values regarding alcohol consumption. However, the movement's alcohol orientation did not simply highlight preferences regarding liquid refreshments; more important, it provided the symbolic means for proclaiming one's membership in a status group that valued self-control and industriousness. Furthermore, the inability to enforce Prohibition was of small consequence to the crusaders. What these crusaders defined as important was that other rival status groups had to modify their drinking habits according to 'our' law" (Snow, 2003:141).

Gusfield's work helps us to understand the dynamics of the legislative process. Not all laws are passed for symbolic reasons; many are deemed necessary in order to keep society running smoothly. For example, the federal government increased Canada Pension Plan premiums in order to ensure the plan will have enough assets to pay for the pensions of future generations. However, many other laws have a symbolic component, and passage of these laws reassures various groups that their views are important and have been recognized by the government. Political campaigns rely heavily on symbolism to appeal emotionally to voters because these symbols have the power to bring people together and to unite them behind a political movement (Hall, 1972). For example, in the early 1990s the newly formed Reform Party ran as outsiders from the rural West who would bring a new style of taxpayer-friendly government to Ottawa. Their campaign literature and advertisements portrayed members of the old-line parties as pigs who were lined up at a money trough to receive huge pensions when their political careers ended. Perhaps not surprisingly, virtually all members of the Reform Party who were elected eventually chose to join that rich pension plan once they got to Ottawa, indicating that they themselves recognized their campaign promises were intended only to be understood at a symbolic level as a protest against the urban Easterners who dominated political life in Canada. Can you think of other political positions or laws that are primarily symbolic? Can you think of others that are intended to accomplish some actual change in society and have little symbolic impact?

Postmodern Perspectives on Government

Postmodern scholars have made a significant contribution to our understanding of government by broadening the concept to include the means by which the state, and organizations working above and below the interests of the state, influences the behaviour of the citizenry. They refer to this as *governmentality* or *governance.* Rather than taking the traditional view that governments and other organizations rule through top-down commands, postmodernists, such as Foucault (1991), have asserted that the state actually seeks to control people in a less repressive fashion by providing them with incentives and by enlisting members of the community to encourage conforming behaviour. Ideally, conformity becomes part of each individual's self-identity so people essentially govern themselves.

This concept of governance has been applied in a wide variety of contexts. For example, Tannis Peikoff (2000) used Foucault's framework to analyze the nonstate techniques of governance that were used to control Aboriginal people in the Red River settlement during the mid-1800s. Her research focused on Anglican missionaries who were not part of the government but who played a very significant role in the colonization of Aboriginal people. The missionaries sought to convert the Aboriginal people to Christianity and a Christian way of life, and to help them establish an indigenous Anglican clergy who would lead their own congregations. This would require a break with traditional forms of Aboriginal spirituality and profound changes in existing practices in areas such as family life and education.

The missionaries were surprised to find strong resistance to their attempts to convert Aboriginal people to Christianity and to convince them to shift to European values and practices in other parts of their lives. While the missionaries had no direct power over Aboriginal people, they sought to overcome this resistance by breaking down their traditional way of life, their spirituality, and their sense of self in order to change them

from "barbarous Indians" into good Christians. Some of the methods they used included trying to discredit Aboriginal spiritual leaders and trying to convince parents that their children were at risk unless they agreed to religious conversion. This was illustrated by the comments of the missionary William Cockran to the parents of a child who has just died:

> Trifle not with the Master of Life, or He will touch you again. You have more children; you have an only son; perhaps he shall be next, who shall be taken if your reformation is not effected by the present warning. (Peikoff, 2000:105)

Ultimately, the efforts of the missionaries were not very successful and they decided that they should focus on trying to educate the children. When this tactic also failed, they began to establish residential schools where they could isolate children from their families and from their cultural traditions in order to resocialize them.

The notion of governance can also be used to help to understand processes at a very different level from the interaction of missionaries with Cree and Ojibwa people. For example, you read in Chapter 7 how new technologies of surveillance allow the state and private organizations to increase their control over members of the public. Sociologists have also begun to study governance issues related to globalization. Several chapters in this text have described how globalization involves a level of organization above the nation-state. However, our governmental systems are based on the independence of individual nations, so questions arise concerning how decisions are made at a global level and how people can be persuaded to follow those decisions. After the

When people move from one country to another, they learn new political attitudes, values, and behaviour. This citizenship ceremony was held in Quebec City during National Citizenship Week. What role do you think these new Canadians will play in Quebec politics?

September 11, 2001 attacks on the United States and subsequent acts of terrorism in other countries, many people have begun to link domestic security to larger issues of global governance. As a result, there has been a marked increase in transnational security linkages and collaborative interventions in internal conflicts, such as civil wars, as well as in conflict between states. James Sheptycki (1998) is among those who are studying the ways in which various forms of military intervention, peacekeeping missions, financial aid, institutional reform, and international trade regulations are part of the search for global security through global governance. It would be difficult to analyze such a complicated web of interactions between sovereign nations and international bodies without using a postmodern theoretical framework.

Concept Table 14.B	THEORETICAL PERSPECTIVES ON POLITICS	
PERSPECTIVE	**THEORY**	**KEY ELEMENTS**
Functionalist		
Durkheim	Consensus Theory	Citizens share a consensus on central concerns and government plays key functions that no other institution could fulfil.
Dahl	Pluralist Theory	Power in political systems is widely distributed among many competing interest groups.
Symbolic Interactionist		
Gusfield		Some political interest groups engage in symbolic crusades in which the recognition of the crusaders' values by the government was at least as important as achieving the instrumental goals of the movement.
Conflict		
Marx	Marxist Theory	The government serves the interests of the ruling (or capitalist) class that controls the means of production.
Mills	Power Elite Theory	Most decisions in society were made by power elites who control business, government, and the military.
Domhoff	Ruling Class Theory	Societies are ruled by a small, interconnected group of people who have power over the politicians who actually govern the country.
Feminist		
McIntosh	Feminist Approach	Historically, the state has excluded women from the political process. Women will inevitably be subordinated by the patriarchal state until they achieve real political power.
Postmodern		
Foucault	Governance Theory	The state does not just control through exercising top-down commands. The state also controls people by making conformity part of each individual's self-identity. People essentially govern themselves.

POLITICS AND GOVERNMENT IN CANADA

The Canadian political process consists of formal elements, such as the duties of the prime minister and the legislative process, and informal elements, such as the role of political parties in the election process. We now turn to an examination of these informal elements, including political parties, political socialization, and political participation.

Political Parties

A *political party* is an organization whose purpose is to gain and hold legitimate control of government; it usually is composed of people with similar attitudes, interests, and socioeconomic status. A political party (1) develops and articulates policy positions, (2) educates voters about issues and simplifies the choices for them, and (3) recruits candidates who agree with those policies, helps those candidates win office, and holds the candidates responsible for implementing the party's policy positions.

The party that wins the most seats in an election forms the government; the party with the next largest number of seats becomes the official Opposition. Since Confederation, two political parties, the Liberals and the Progressive Conservatives (now the Conservative Party, after a merger with the Canadian Alliance party in 2004), have dominated the Canadian political system. Although one party may control the government for several terms, at some point the voters elect the other party and control shifts. From time to time, other parties have gained some strength. At various times, the New Democratic Party (NDP) and the Social Credit Party had some political strength, but neither had enough seats to form the official Opposition. However, in the 1993 election, the Progressive Conservatives, who had been in power for nine years, were reduced to only two seats. The Bloc Québécois, a party that favours Quebec separation, became the official Opposition, and the Reform Party, which mainly represented politically disaffected Western Canadians, also won significant representation. These two new parties retained their representation in the 1997 election, though this time the Reform Party became the Opposition. Since that election, the Reform Party changed its name to the Canadian Alliance and then merged with the Progressive Conservatives in an attempt to help unite right-wing opposition to the Liberals.

Ideal Type versus Reality   Ideally, political parties offer clear alternatives to the electorate—alternatives that reflect the aspirations, concerns, and viewpoints of the population. For several reasons, this is usually not the case. First, the two major parties rarely offer voters clear policy alternatives. Most Canadian voters view themselves as being close to the centre of the political spectrum (extremely liberal being the far left of that spectrum and extremely conservative being the far right). Although the definitions of liberal and conservative vary over time, *liberals* tend to focus on equality of opportunity and the need for government regulation and social safety nets. By contrast, *conservatives* are more likely to emphasize economic restraint and freedom from government interference (Greenberg and Page, 1996). However, because most voters consider themselves moderates, neither party has much incentive to move very far from the middle. Parties like the NDP, which chooses to maintain some ideological purity, run the risk of being marginalized and are very unlikely to win a national election. The Reform Party (later the Canadian Alliance Party) recognized that it would likely never gain power so it has dropped much of its right-wing platform and merged with the Progressive Conservative Party in an attempt to broaden its appeal. While these parties have not won electoral power, they have been successful in having their ideas implemented. During the 1960s and 1970s, many of the social policies advocated by the NDP were implemented by Liberal and Progressive Conservative governments. More recently, the Reform/Canadian Alliance was much more successful in having its deficit-cutting agenda implemented by federal and provincial governments than it was in convincing Canadians it should be given the power to run the country.

This staying near the centre of the political spectrum and the co-optation of opposing parties' policy ideas mean that Canadian elections tend to be fought over issues of leadership rather than of fundamental political principles. The most notable recent exception to this is instructive. A major issue of the 1988 election was the Canada–U.S. Free Trade Agreement, a pact removing the barriers to the sale of goods and services between Canada and the United States. The Progressive Conservatives, who ultimately won the election, strongly supported the Canada–U.S. Free Trade Agreement, while their main opponents, the Liberals, opposed it. However, when the Liberals did eventually take power in 1993, they quickly "studied" the North American Free Trade Agreement (NAFTA), the successor to the earlier pact, which was also negotiated by the Conservatives and opposed by the Liberals, expressed their support for it, and since then have been ardent free traders, seeking to expand NAFTA to Chile.

The second reason why the two major political parties do not offer clear alternatives that reflect the viewpoints of the population is that most political parties are dominated by active elites who are not representative of the general population. Many represent special interests and tend to come from the upper echelons of society. Thus the poor, women, and racial minorities have not been included in drafting party policy or in selecting party leaders. One study (Lele et al., 1979) looked at attendance at Liberal, Progressive Conservative, and NDP conventions and found that none of them had participation that was representative of the Canadian population. Similarly, Members of Parliament are disproportionately male and from the upper and middle classes (Guppy et al., 1987). Many people involved in politics today tend to work outside the traditional party structure, often in single-issue interest groups. Organizations, such as the National Action Committee for the Status of Women, Greenpeace, and various Aboriginal groups, have been very effective in advancing their agendas and in getting grassroots involvement without attaching themselves to a particular political party.

Politics and the People

Why do some people vote and others do not? How do people come to think of themselves as being conservative, moderate, or liberal? Key factors include individuals' political socialization, attitudes, and participation.

Political Socialization *Political socialization* **is the process by which people learn political attitudes, values, and behaviour.** For young children, the family is the primary agent of political socialization, and children tend to learn and hold many of the same opinions as their parents. By the time children reach school age, they typically identify with the political party (if any) of their parents (Burnham, 1983). As they grow older, other agents of socialization including peers, teachers, and the media begin to affect children's political beliefs. Over time, these other agents may cause people's political attitudes and values to change, and they may cease to identify with the political party of their parents. Even for adults, political socialization continues through the media, friends, neighbours, and colleagues in the workplace.

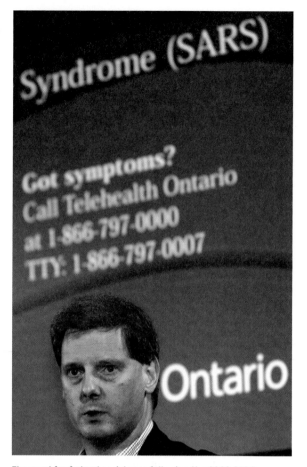

The need for federal assistance following the 2003 SARS outbreak in Ontario demonstrates the need for a strong central government in our complex society.

Political Attitudes In addition to the socialization process, people's socioeconomic status affects their political attitudes, values, beliefs, and behaviour. For example, individuals who are very poor or who are unable to find employment tend to believe that society has failed them and therefore are often indifferent toward the political system (Zipp, 1985; Pinderhughes, 1986). Believing that casting a ballot would make no difference to their own circumstances, they do not vote.

In general, voters tend to select candidates and political parties based on social and economic issues they consider important to their lives. *Social issues* are those relating to moral judgments or civil rights, ranging from abortion rights to equal rights for homosexuals. Conservatives tend to believe in limiting individual rights on social issues and to oppose social programs that they see as promoting individuals on the basis of minority status rather than merit. Based on these distinctions, Liberals and New Democrats are more likely to seek passage of social programs that make the government a more active participant in society, promoting social welfare and equality. By contrast, Conservative Party members are more likely to act according to the belief that government should limit its involvement in social issues.

Economic issues fall into two broad categories: (1) the amount that should be spent on government programs and (2) the extent to which these programs should encourage a redistribution of income and assets. Those holding liberal political views believe that without government intervention, income and assets would become concentrated in the hands of even fewer people and that the government must act to redistribute wealth, thus ensuring that everyone gets a "fair slice" of the economic "pie." In order to accomplish this, they envision that larger sums of money must be raised and spent by the government on such programs. Conservatives contend that such programs are not only unnecessary but also counterproductive. That is, programs financed by tax increases decrease people's incentive to work and to be innovative, and make people dependent on the government.

You will remember that the main parties tend toward the centre and that their policies are often not ideologically distinct on either social or economic issues. The Progressive Conservatives, who ideologically favoured spending restraint, ran up the largest budget *deficits* in Canadian history before they were voted out of office in 1993. The Liberals, on the other hand, after winning the election, implemented the largest budget *cuts* in Canadian history in order to reduce the deficit, despite the impact of these cuts on the social programs that have traditionally received their support. The immediate demands of political reality are often more important in determining government policy than is political philosophy.

Social class is correlated with political attitudes. People in the upper classes tend to be more conservative on economic issues and more liberal on social issues. Upper-class conservatives generally favour equality of opportunity but do not want their own income and assets taxed heavily to abolish poverty or societal problems that they believe some people bring upon themselves. Most of Canada's social programs faced opposition from corporate and upper-class interests, and some of these groups led the call for cuts to these programs in the 1990s. By contrast, Canadians in the lower classes tend to be conservative on social issues, such as capital punishment or abortion rights, but liberal on economic issues, such as increasing the minimum wage and expanding social programs.

Despite these tendencies, there is probably less of a connection between voting behaviour and social class in Canada than in many other industrialized countries.

The Liberal Party has typically attracted voters from all classes, while the NDP gets a high proportion of its support from skilled and unskilled labour. Even so, more voters from the skilled and unskilled labour classes usually vote for other parties than they do for the New Democrats. In fact, Canadian voters tend to be somewhat fickle at the polls and frequently switch parties. For example, comparing the 1988 and 1993 federal elections, more voters switched parties than voted for the same party they had chosen in the earlier election (Pammett, 1993).

Why is the association between class and voting so low in Canada? Canadian voters appear to be influenced more by individual leaders or particular issues and events than by loyalties to a particular party's philosophy. This conclusion is supported by the results of one study (Clarke et al., 1991) in which it was found that class, gender, ethnicity, religion, community size, and age all had some effect on Canadians' voting preferences, but much less than such political variables as prior voting record, concern about immediate issues, and the image of the party leader.

Another reason for the weak connection between class and voting is that the mainstream parties, particularly the Liberals, have been able to incorporate many of the reforms suggested by more class-based parties into their own platforms. For example, government medical care, which was introduced in Saskatchewan by the CCF (Co-operative Commonwealth Federation) party—now the New Democratic Party—was subsequently adopted by the Liberals, who implemented it at the national level.

Finally, Rick Ogmundson (1975) explained the weak link between class and voting as resulting from what he called the *subjective class vote*. Using survey data, he found that people often believed they were voting for a party that reflected their interests, even though more objective measures of the party's position indicated that this was not the case. According to Ogmundson and Ng (1982), the subjective class vote in Canada was about as high as it was in the United Kingdom, which is usually thought to have a high degree of class politics. Ogmundson's work is supported by research showing that support for the NDP was more strongly related to belief in class ideology, including support for unions and an egalitarian philosophy than it was to the actual class position of the voters (Nakhaie and Arnold, 1996).

Political Participation   Democracy has been defined as a government "of the people, by the people, and for the people." Accordingly, it would stand to reason that "the people" would actively participate in their government at any or all of four levels: (1) voting, (2) attending and taking part in political meetings, (3) actively participating in political campaigns, and (4) running for or holding political office. Participation is important as elections are the means through which citizens can make their views known to politicians. Participation also helps to legitimate the political process; those who vote share a responsibility for, and an interest in, the outcome of the election. In Canada, the participation rate for federal elections has declined from 75 percent in 1988 to 61 percent in 2004. The participation rate is slightly higher for provincial elections and much lower for municipal elections. While our 61-percent participation rate means that most Canadians do get involved in the electoral process, many Western industrial countries have even higher rates. For example, in many Western European countries, participation rates are normally 80 to 90 percent. The United States has one of the lowest voter participation rates of all Western nations. However, rates of voting are increasing, particularly among young people, and the participation rate was 59 percent in the 2004 U.S. presidential election.

Why do many eligible voters in North America stay away from the polls? During any election, some voting-age persons do not go to the polls due to illness, disability, lack of transportation, or absenteeism. However, these explanations do not account for why many other people do not vote. According to some analysts, people may not vote because they are satisfied with the status quo or because they are apathetic and uninformed, and being uninformed, they lack a basic understanding of both public issues and the basic process of government. Surveys of voters typically show that the majority of Canadians have little knowledge of the candidates or the issues. This lack of knowledge makes it difficult for many people to cast a meaningful ballot, so they simply stay away from the polls.

By contrast, others argue that people stay away from the polls because they feel alienated from politics at all levels of government—federal, provincial, and local. They believe that government does not care about issues that concern them and that only the elites or special interest groups have any influence.

Voting rates are particularly low among young Canadians. Less than 40 percent of people between 18 and 24 voted in the 2000 federal election. Why do you think young people show so little interest in the formal political process?

Trying to explain the declining political participation of Canadians, political scientist Neil Nevitte (2000) has concluded that the way in which Canadians relate to their structures of governance has changed over the last two decades. For Nevitte, the institutions of democratic governance that were designed in the industrial age no longer reflect the way in which citizens are connected to the state. Changes in values and structures have led to changes in the way citizens relate to their governments. In addition to lower rates of voting, signs of stress in the political systems of a number of Western democracies included lower levels of attachment to political parties and shifting patterns of support for political parties. In Canada, public confidence in political institutions, particularly in the federal Parliament, has eroded. Only one in ten Canadians says that he or she is "very satisfied" with government; one-third report "little satisfaction" with

Many young people are not interested in the formal political process because they feel that politicians do not respond to their concerns. Some have turned to alternate forms of political action. These demonstrators marched the streets of Calgary to protest against the 2002 G8 Economic Summit in Kananaskis, Alberta.

government. A majority of people (53 percent) feel they have little say in the actions of the government (Nevitte, 2000). Young people are particularly negative about government and have a weaker attachment to Canada.

At the same time as their attachment to government is declining, citizens are becoming more involved in alternate forms of political behaviour, such as demonstrations, boycotts, and other forms of political expression. The antiglobalization movement is a good example of political action taken outside the regular political system. Frustrated by the determination of most Western governments to pursue an agenda of globalized free trade through agreements, such as NAFTA and rules of the World Trade Organization (WTO), thousands of activists from around the globe have organized major protests during meetings of world leaders. In Canada, we have seen these demonstrations in Quebec City, Ottawa, and Calgary (during the G8 Summit meetings in Kananaskis).

These demonstrations, along with others involving people with a wide range of causes, have shown that many people are still interested in political matters but feel that the political system cannot or will not respond to their concerns. This raises a challenge to Canada's political parties to find ways of relating more effectively with their constituents in order to reconnect citizens to the political process.

MAJOR POLITICAL ISSUES IN CANADA: SEPARATISM AND ABORIGINAL SELF-GOVERNMENT

The Quiet Revolution and Quebec Nationalism

Because of our former status as a British colony and the dissatisfaction of many Quebec nationalists with the current political structure, constitutional matters have been much more prominent in Canada than in most other countries. The following review of events from the early 1960s onward will set the stage for the very close results of the 1995 referendum on separation. They are events that even after the referendum continue to play a major role in the political, economic, and social life in Canada.

The constitutional crises of recent years were set in motion by the Quiet Revolution, which began in Quebec in the 1960s. The term of Premier Jean Lesage (1960–1966) saw a dramatic change. Prior to 1960, Quebec had been a very traditional society. The Catholic church and the family were at the core of French Canadian society, and economic power was in the hands of English Canadians. In a very short time Quebec underwent a dramatic transformation into a secular, urban society with a modern educational system, public health and welfare programs, and a provincially controlled electric power system. A new sense of nationalism was used as a core ideology to justify the expanded role of the state. This nationalism was clearly expressed in the 1962 Liberal campaign slogan *maîtres chez nous* ("masters in our own house"). Economic and social reform would strengthen French culture. The state would replace the church at the heart of Quebec society. To pursue its agenda of renewal, the Quebec government began demanding, and receiving, more control over matters traditionally managed by the federal government.

As Quebec became more like the rest of North America in most other respects, language came to be its major distinguishing factor, assuming both a real and a symbolic role in the province's political future. English was the language of business in the province, and French Canadian owners and managers were rare. In a series of legislative steps beginning in the 1960s, the provincial government moved to ensure that French became the language of business. The goal was stated clearly in the White Paper (that is, a government policy document) that preceded a major piece of language legislation, Bill 101, which was adopted in 1977:

> The Quebec that we wish to build will be essentially French. The fact that the majority of the population is French will be distinctly visible: at work, in communications, in the country. It is also a country where the traditional division of powers, especially in matters concerning the economy, will be modified: the use of French will not be generalized simply to hide the predominance of foreign powers over Francophones; this usage will accompany, will symbolize a reconquest by the Francophone majority of Quebec of the hold which returns to it on the levers of the economy. (cited in Cook, 1995:133)

By any measure, the Quiet Revolution has been a success. A large body of legislation now protects the French language in Quebec. Regulations requiring immigrant children to attend French-language schools and restrictions on the use of English on commercial signs have reinforced the dominant role of the French language in Quebec. Quebeckers have gained control over the economy and other major social institutions, including culture, politics, and government.

While the transformation of Quebec was remarkably rapid, it was not rapid enough for some. Nationalist groups, which began to emerge in the 1960s, saw independence as the only means by which Quebec could fulfil its destiny. At the same time, another vision was offered by Quebeckers like Pierre Trudeau who felt that Quebec's aspirations could best be fulfilled within Canada. For Trudeau, cultural survival did not depend on political sovereignty. A strong federal government, which actively promoted bilingualism, was the best guarantee that French would survive in a predominantly English North America. As prime minister, Trudeau in 1969 brought in the *Official Languages Act,* which made the federal public service bilingual. This provided opportunities for francophones and helped ensure that Canadians in all parts of the country could receive services in either language. The government also began to encourage French immersion programs in schools in English Canada.

These changes met with vociferous resistance among some English Canadians. Consider matters from the perspective of those opposed to bilingualism. As Quebec was becoming more autonomous and less bilingual, the need for bilingualism was being promoted throughout the rest of the country (Dyck, 2004). Unilingual anglophone civil servants had to learn French if they wished to be promoted, and bilingualism was clearly a major part of the federal political agenda. Many felt that Quebec was blackmailing the federal government at the expense of the other provinces. With extreme Quebec nationalists on one side and those in

the rest of Canada who were tired of "having French forced down their throats" on the other, the stage was set for several decades of constitutional debate.

Since the 1995 referendum, which the separatists lost by a narrow margin of 50.6 percent to 49.4 percent, separatist sentiment gradually waned in Quebec. However, in 2005 findings of the Gomery Inquiry into bribery and corruption by the federal Liberals in Quebec led to outrage among many Quebeckers, and support for sovereignty once again began to climb.

Aboriginal Self-Government

Canada's constitutional debate has largely focused on the role of our "two founding peoples"—the English and the French. Aboriginal peoples have strongly objected to this view of Canadian history. Anthropologist Olive Dickason, a Métis, has pointed out that when the Europeans first came to North America, fifty-five Aboriginal First Nations were already on the continent. Each of these nations had its own government, territory, culture, and language. But Aboriginal objections to the notion of two founding peoples do not focus only on the historical issue of which groups were here first. The more important concern is which groups will have political power in the future. Quebec claims a special status that entitles it to certain powers to govern its own people, and also certain rights within the federation, such as having three Quebec members of the Supreme Court. Aboriginal peoples also claim a unique status based on their position as Canada's First Nations and have, because of that position, pursued their right to self-government.

While the issue of self-government is extremely complex, some background will help in understanding the broad issues involved. In 1763, the

Aboriginal leaders have played a prominent role in Canadian politics during the past decade. As questions of self-government, Aboriginal rights, and land claims have been considered, two of the most important leaders have been Grand Chief Phil Fontaine (left) of the Assembly of First Nations and Elijah Harper (right), who was formerly a member of the Manitoba legislature and the federal parliament.

British government issued a royal proclamation that formed the basis for the negotiation of treaties with Aboriginal groups. Without a background in European law, Aboriginal peoples did not realize that title to the land had passed to the Crown. They were, however, still entitled to the use and benefit of that land through their "aboriginal title" (Boldt, 1993). Following Confederation, Aboriginal peoples came under the control of the government. The mechanism for this control, the *Indian Act,* was passed in 1876 and gave government bureaucrats almost total control over Aboriginal peoples. The act even went so far as to define a "person" as "an individual other than an Indian" (Hamilton and Sinclair, 1991).

The consequences of the *Indian Act* were profound. For example, Aboriginal children were forced to attend residential schools (which meant that generations of children were not raised by their families); traditional religious practices were restricted;

Aboriginal people did not fully control their own land and could not sell agricultural products off the reserve; and the government imposed a "pass system," which restricted the right of Aboriginal peoples to travel off their reserves. Aboriginal peoples did not have full voting rights in federal elections until 1960. As sociologist Menno Boldt has observed, contemporary "Indian powerlessness has its roots in Canada's Indian policies" (1993:xvii).

In the 1960s, the federal government began to review its policies concerning Aboriginal peoples. A White Paper, tabled in 1969, proposed assimilation of Aboriginal peoples. Treaties were to be dropped, reserves were to become like neighbouring non-Aboriginal communities, and Aboriginal rights and Aboriginal land titles were to be discarded. The "Aboriginal problem" would disappear, it was thought, if Aboriginal people became, in Pierre Trudeau's words, "Canadians as all other Canadians"

BOX 14.3 SOCIOLOGY IN GLOBAL PERSPECTIVE

Terrorism in Canada

Some of you may have been surprised to read about political terrorism in Canada in the chapter introduction. While most Canadians rightly feel that Canada is a very peaceful country, there have been a significant number of terrorist incidents here over the past fifty years.

Using a database developed by the federal government's National Security Coordination Centre as well as other sources, Anthony Kellett (2004) studied acts of terrorism that occurred in Canada between 1960 and 1992. Defining terrorism as "comprising acts of serious violence, planned and executed clandestinely, and committed with clear intention to achieve political ends" (2004:286), Kellett found more than 400 incidents and thirteen deaths during this period. While this might seem like a large number, it is much lower than in many European countries where groups like the Irish Republican Army and the Basque separatist group ETA have been active for many years.

Almost 85 percent of the incidents in the database used by Kellett involved Canadian-based groups attacking domestic targets, while the remainder involved either foreign terrorists or foreign targets in Canada. Incidents, such as the Air India bombing (refer to Box 6.2), in which an explosive was put on a plane in Canada but detonated outside the country, were excluded from the database. The number of incidents peaked in the 1960s, when several secessionist groups were active in Quebec and the Sons of Freedom Doukhobor sect was engaged in bombings and other acts of terrorism in British Columbia. Together, these groups accounted for most of the terrorist attacks in the database, which largely explains why 97 percent of the total number of attacks occurred in the provinces of Quebec and British Columbia.

You read earlier about the role played by Pierre Vallières in events in Quebec. Terrorist acts began in the early 1960s and ended about a decade later. Kellett estimates that only about 100 people were ever members of the FLQ. Most FLQ members were young and single, and many were students. Like many contemporary terrorist groups, members financed their political activities by engaging in crimes, such as credit card fraud and robbery.

While the FLQ had many similarities to other terrorist organizations, the Sons of Freedom Doukhobors were quite unique. Members of the Sons of Freedom, one branch of the pacifist Christian Doukhobor group that came to Canada in the late nineteenth century, rejected any government involvement in their lives. They refused to send their children to school, pay taxes, or register births and deaths. While most Doukhobors eventually accepted the role of government, some members of the Sons of Freedom sect did not. There were many clashes between sect members and the government, and in the 1950s the B.C. government took children away from their communities and forced them to live in residential schools until they were 15 years of age. The protests of the sect against the government and against other Doukhobors finally culminated in an intense period between 1960 and 1962 when there were 107 incidents of arson and bombings of public facilities, such as schools, power lines, bridges, and the property of other Doukhobors. The terrorist acts largely ended when many of the perpetrators were imprisoned.

In addition to the political attacks in Quebec and the religious terrorism of some members of the Sons of Freedom, the only other category that had a substantial number of terrorist incidents between 1960 and 1989 was that of emigré groups. These included attacks by anti-Castro Cubans on Cuban targets in Canada, attacks on Turks in Canada by Armenian groups, and several attacks by Sikh militants supporting the formation of an independent Sikh state in India.

Since 1989, there have been a relatively small number of terrorist incidents. They have been committed in support of a wide range of causes including the environmental movement, animal rights, the anti-abortion movement, and the civil war in the former Yugoslavia.

As noted above, the database used by Kellett did not include incidents involving terrorist attacks that were supported in Canada but that took place elsewhere. The most important of these was the Air India bombing, in which a bomb placed on an aircraft in Vancouver took the lives of 329 people. Another disaster was narrowly averted in 1999, when a U.S. customs agent apprehended Ahmed Ressam as he attempted to cross into the United States from Canada with a car loaded with explosives. Ressam, allegedly a member of a Montreal-based al-Qaeda cell, intended to detonate his car bomb at the Los Angeles airport on January 1, 2000. Many terrorist groups, including the Irish Republican Army and the Sri Lankan Tamil Tigers, continue to collect funds in Canada from supporters who have emigrated from their home countries.

Combating terrorism is now a major government priority, partly because of the potential direct threat to Canada from al-Qaeda and other groups, but also because our American neighbours, concerned about terrorists moving south into the U.S., are demanding increased counterterrorism measures in Canada along with increased border security. After the September 11, 2001 attacks on the World Trade Center and the Pentagon, homeland security became the most important U.S. foreign policy concern (Harvey, 2004). This shift in U.S. priorities was stated by Charles Krauthammer:

On September 11, American foreign policy acquired seriousness. It also acquired a new organizing principle: We have an enemy, radical Islam; it is a global opponent of worldwide reach, armed with an idea, and with the tactics, weapons, and ruthlessness necessary to take on the world's hegemon; and its defeat is our supreme national objective, as overriding a necessity as were the defeats of fascism and Soviet communism. (quoted in Harvey, 2004:41).

Given that the most important part of our foreign policy involves our relationship with the United States, control of terrorism raises serious issues about Canada's ability to maintain its own sovereignty in the face of American demands for increased security in Canada. Can we maintain independent policies in areas, such as immigration regulations, military funding, and border control, if doing so affects our relationship with our largest trading partner?

■ Jacques Rose, Paul Rose, Francis Simard, and Bernard Lortie were the members of the Chenier cell of the FLQ who kidnapped and murdered Quebec cabinet minister Pierre Laporte in 1970.

(Boldt, 1993). Reaction to this paper marked a watershed in Aboriginal politics. A national campaign, which ultimately forced the government to drop its proposals, became a countrywide movement and several pan-Indian organizations, including the Assembly of First Nations, were formed (Hamilton and Sinclair, 1991). Rather than accepting the federal government's assimilationist model, Aboriginal leaders embraced nationalism. Self-government, Aboriginal rights, and land claims became the rallying points of the movement.

Some Aboriginal leaders, particularly among the Mohawks, view their bands as separate nations that have sovereign control over their lands. However, most proponents of Aboriginal self-government take the more limited view that their First Nations status gives them the "inherent" right to self-government within the Canadian federation (Boldt, 1993). They feel their status as Canada's first people, who were never conquered and who signed voluntary treaties with the Crown, entitles them to the right of self-determination and to protection of their culture and customs. These rights are not *granted* by the Canadian government, but are inherently theirs. On the other hand, the positions of the federal and the provincial governments have been that the right to self-determination could be extended only as powers delegated to Aboriginal people by government through legislation or constitutional change. Further, the powers that would be granted by government would extend only to powers now held by municipal governments rather than the much broader powers sought by Aboriginal peoples. It is difficult to predict where the current process of ending the colonial rule of Aboriginals will lead. One major change occurred in 1999, when Inuit took over government of the newly created Nunavut Territory, encompassing more than 350,000 square kilometres of land in the Eastern Arctic. Another major move toward self-government came in 1999 with the signing of a treaty with the Nisga'a people, who had been seeking recognition of Aboriginal title to their land for more than a hundred years. This treaty gave the Nisga'a a large land settlement in northwestern British Columbia and significant powers of self-government similar to those of municipal governments.

While the federal government accepted the inherent nature of Aboriginals' right to self-government in 1995 and is committed to eventually dismantling the Department of Indian Affairs and Northern Development, the future form of self-government is not at all clear—not even among Aboriginal people themselves. Also, many problems must be solved along the way, including decisions about how the growing number of urban Aboriginals will be included, the applicability of the *Canadian Charter of Rights and Freedoms* to Aboriginal communities, and sources of funding for this new order of government. The possible separation of Quebec also creates some interesting issues. While the separatists argue strongly for their right to self-determination and their recognition as a "people," they do not accept that Aboriginal people in the resource-rich northern part of Quebec have the same right.

Future developments in self-government will be guided by the 1996 report of the Royal Commission on Aboriginal Peoples. The principles that guided the work of the commission are the reality of societal and cultural difference; the right to self-government; the nature of Aboriginal nationhood; and the requirement for adequate land, resources, and self-reliant Aboriginal economies. The commission concluded that history and law give all Aboriginal peoples of Canada the inherent right to govern themselves. By virtue of this right, Aboriginal peoples are entitled to negotiate freely the terms of their relationship with Canada and to establish governmental structures that they consider appropriate for their needs. This report has set the stage for future negotiations between federal and provincial governments and First Nations.

POLITICAL ISSUES FOR THE FUTURE

Economic agreements, such as the North American Free Trade Agreement and the European Union, are helping to create a single market for capital and services, and will inevitably lead to closer relationships between the countries involved. At the same time, budget cuts have reduced the role of governments in providing services to their citizens, and globalization of financial markets has dramatically reduced the ability of governments to control their own economic destinies, as many economic decisions are made by international organizations, such as the World Trade Organization and the World Intellectual Property Organization. Multinational corporations, some of which are larger economic entities than many of the world's countries, also have an impact on global economic policy that may not reflect the interests of any nation-state. This has led many people to ask if the governments of modern nation-states will become obsolete. Although there has been some erosion of the powers of developed nations and an increase in the transnational nature of politics and the economy, scholars like Paul Kennedy (1993:134) argue that

> the nation-state remains the primary locus of identity for most people; regardless of who their employer is and what they do for a living, individuals pay taxes to the state, are subject to its laws, serve (if need be) in its armed forces, and can travel only by having its passport. Moreover, as new challenges emerge . . . people turn instinctively (at least in the democracies) to their own governments to find "solutions."

However, the nature of the new challenges facing many governments makes it increasingly difficult for them to control events. For example, how do nations deal with terrorism within their borders, such as the 2001 attacks on the World Trade Center and the Pentagon that resulted in the deaths of almost 3,000 people, and the terrorist attacks carried out in England by the Irish Republican Army? In the aftermath of tragedies such as these, governments' responsibility for protecting citizens but not violating their basic freedoms is widely examined in national debates that inevitably will continue into the future.

Likewise, how are nations to deal with the proliferation of arms and nuclear weapons in other countries? Will some of the missiles and warheads fall into the hands of terrorists? What should be done with the masses of nuclear waste being produced? No easy answers are forthcoming. International agencies, such

as the United Nations, the World Bank, and the International Monetary Fund, face many of the same problems that individual governments do—including severe economic constraints and extreme differences of opinion among participants. Without some form of effective international control, it will be impossible to ensure that future generations are protected from environmental threats, such as global warming and water and air pollution.

While international agreements are necessary, it is likely that these agreements will be reached in different ways and involve different participants from those in the past. The way in which hundreds of groups came together with governments to create the treaty banning land mines is increasingly becoming a model for involving more grassroots organizations in such negotiations. The Internet has made it much easier for such widely scattered organizations to work effectively together.

Another issue that will continue to trouble many countries is nationalism. Can Canada make an accommodation with Quebec? How will European countries adapt to the loss of national powers within the European Community? Will groups continue to make war to support their nationalistic aspirations? (Some of the more troubling aspects of nationalism are discussed in Box 14.4.) The issues surrounding nationalism must be resolved if we are to continue to move toward the dream of a peaceful world.

This century will be a challenging one for politicians and for the citizens they represent. Can countries, such as Russia and Mexico, with their weak

BOX 14.4 SOCIOLOGY IN GLOBAL PERSPECTIVE

Nationalism Around the World

Historian Ramsay Cook has observed that "Everyone belongs somewhere. Yet much of the conflict in the history . . . of mankind has been about who belongs where" (Cook, 1995:9). Cook goes on to discuss the role of nationalism in justifying one's place in the world. Nationalism, he says, is a "doctrine asserting that humanity is naturally divided into groups with common characteristics and that by virtue of those collective traits they have a right to exercise control—sovereignty—over the particular place" (1995:9). Most

Canadians have heard Lucien Bouchard and other Quebec separatists state that the Québécois constitute a "people" who must have sovereignty over their territory if their destiny is to be fulfilled. The desire for separation from Canada in Quebec is a manifestation of nationalism.

Quebec nationalists are not the only people trying to take control of what they see as their territory. Punjabis in India, Tamils in Sri Lanka, and Palestinians in the Middle East are just a few of the hundreds of nationalist groups active in the world today. Authority or justification for their claims is usually given to or provided by God, language, culture, or history. However, what ultimately decides things is power. This power may be political—the Czech Republic and Slovakia separated after a democratic vote—but more typically, it is military, as with the Iraqis and the Turks who have forcefully prevented the Kurds from establishing a separate homeland.

Nationalism can be a unifying force—many countries, including Germany and Italy, were formed in the late nineteenth century through the unification of smaller states with similar language and cultural backgrounds. Diverse groups were brought together under a common flag. However, nationalism can also be divisive—and often deadly. Societies based on national identity can easily become intolerant of those who do not share the same ethnicity, religion, or culture. Millions have died at the hands of oppressive nationalists. Historically, most wars have been between countries; today they are almost all within countries. Wars, such as the American-led invasion of Iraq, are the exception, while conflicts, such as the genocides in Sudan and Eastern Congo, are much more common and much more deadly in terms of lives lost (http://genocidewatch.org).

Successful nationalist movements often carry with them the seeds of their own destruction. Yugoslavia is a case in point. Prior to 1989, the diverse elements of the country had been held together by the communist regime. However, when the communist domination of Eastern Europe ended, the Croats and Muslims in Yugoslavia decided to break away from the Serb-dominated communist government and created the independent states of Croatia and Bosnia-Herzegovina. However, after years of living within the common boundaries of Yugoslavia, each of the new countries had significant ethnic minorities within its borders. These minorities in turn claimed their independence and the ensuing carnage has cost hundreds of thousands of lives and has added the words "ethnic cleansing" to our vocabulary. Ethnic cleansing is a chilling final solution to the minority problem—you simply kill or expel every man, woman, and child of a different religious or cultural background who has the misfortune of remaining within your territory. Internal conflicts such as these can be extremely complex. In the former Yugoslavia, each of the major groups—Serbs, Croats, and the Muslims of Bosnia-Herzegovina—has participated in ethnic cleansing in the areas under its control.

War has become a means of expressing national identities, and grievances dating back hundreds or even thousands of years have become the justification for brutal mass murder. As large nation-states become less relevant in an era of globalization and homogenization, they lose their ability to unify. People search for a collective identity at the local level. Unfortunately, this identity is often grounded on exclusion—those who are not "like us" are not tolerated. Where this will lead is uncertain. It is difficult to imagine the nationalist process continuing indefinitely. Fewer than 200 countries now exist; if every linguistic group became a nation, there would be about 8,000 countries.

International organizations, such as the United Nations, have intervened in an attempt to control these internal conflicts and to stop the killing and expulsions. However, these peacekeeping missions have had limited success. Intra-state conflicts, such as those in Somalia, Yugoslavia, Haiti, Guatemala, Angola, Mozambique, Kosovo, and East Timor, have left intractable problems even after the fighting was stopped. Devastated economies, a collapse of civil institutions, humanitarian emergencies involving refugees, and the difficulties of people returning to destroyed villages and towns have perpetuated cycles of conflict and human suffering. Disorder and bloodshed often continue long after the major conflict has ended, and militias or criminal gangs may exploit the weak social order. Often, the factions responsible for the original conflict are waiting for the opportunity to resume their activities. At least initially, these countries are often in a state that may not be full-scale war but which certainly is not peace.

In order to deal with protracted social conflict of this sort, peacekeeping has become more complex and has involved more types of organizations. While conflict between neighbouring countries might be managed by creating buffer zones, this tactic cannot be used when the conflict is between individuals and groups that share the same territory. Therefore, peacekeeping doctrine has evolved to include peacemaking, humanitarian operations, peace enforcement, and peace-building (Linden et al., forthcoming). The military cannot handle all these tasks alone, so many different types of organizations, including aid organizations, are now routinely involved in these missions.

The new peacekeeping environment requires cooperation among military, police, and civilian agencies to help create a self-sustaining peace. The Brahimi Report (United Nations, 2000), which is the United Nations' reassessment of its peacekeeping procedures, emphasizes that peace-building is likely to be required in most future operations. The elements of peace-building include "reintegrating former combatants into civilian society, strengthening the rule of law (for example, through training and restructuring of local police, and judicial and penal reform); improving respect for human rights through the monitoring, education and investigation of past and existing abuses; providing technical assistance for democratic development (including electoral assistance and support for free media); and promoting conflict resolution and reconciliation techniques" (United Nations, 2000:3).

democracies, cope with the conflicts inherent in the transition to a market economy? Will politicians around the globe be able to manage the changes that lie ahead when actions occurring elsewhere may profoundly affect their cultures, economies, and political systems? Even countries that wish to close themselves off to outside influences must still be involved in global trade and will be unable to control what is seen, read, and heard by their citizens because of the communications revolution. Can they restore people's faith in the ability of the political system to deal with issues, such as jobs, crime, and social services, before voters become too cynical and critical to care which party manages their country?

CHAPTER REVIEW

■ **What is power?**

Power is the ability of persons or groups to carry out their will even when opposed by others.

■ **What is the relationship between power and politics?**

Politics is the social institution through which power is acquired and exercised by some people or groups. Government is the formal organization that has the legal and political authority to regulate the relationships among members in a society.

■ **What are the three types of authority?**

Max Weber identified three types of authority. Charismatic authority is based on a leader's exceptional personal qualities. Traditional authority is based on respect for custom. Rational-legal authority is based on law or written rules and regulations.

■ **What are the main types of political systems?**

There are four main types of contemporary political systems. In a monarchy, one person is the ruler of the nation. In authoritarian systems, rulers tolerate little or no public opposition and generally cannot be removed from office by legal means. In totalitarian systems, the state seeks to regulate all aspects of society and to monopolize all societal resources in order to control completely both public and private life. In a democracy, the powers of the government are derived from the consent of all the people.

■ **What are the pluralist and elite perspectives on power?**

According to the pluralist (functionalist) model, power is widely dispersed throughout many competing interest groups. People influence policy by voting, joining special interest groups and political campaigns, and forming new groups. According to the elite (conflict) model, power is concentrated in a small group of elites, while the masses are relatively powerless.

KEY TERMS

authoritarian political system 436
authority 432
charismatic authority 432
democracy 436
elite model 439
government 431
monarchy 436
pluralist model 438
political party 447
political socialization 448
politics 431
power 431
power elite 441
rational-legal authority 435
routinization of charisma 433
special interest groups 438
state 431
totalitarian political system 436
traditional authority 433

NET LINKS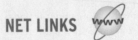

Each of Canada's major political parties has a Web site:
Bloc Quebecois: http://www .blocquebecois.org

Conservative Party: http://www.conservative.ca

Green Party: http://www.greenparty.ca

Liberal Party: http://www.liberal.ca

New Democratic Party: http://www.ndp.ca

An important development on the road to Aboriginal self-government is the Royal Commission on Aboriginal Peoples, at:
http://www.ainc-inac.gc.ca/ch/rcap/index_e.html

The International Institute for Democracy and Electoral Assistance has a Web site that discusses women in politics. It has some interesting material on the representation of women in parliaments; go to:
http://www.idea.int/women/

For a Canadian perspective on women in politics, go to:
http://www.equalvoice.ca

For a large collection of Canadian government information on the Internet, go to:
http://canada.gc.ca

The University of Lethbridge Department of Political Science has a very good educational Web site covering a range of Canadian political issues at:
http://mapleleafweb.com

QUESTIONS FOR CRITICAL THINKING

1. Who is ultimately responsible for decisions and policies that are made in a democracy, such as Canada, the people or their elected representatives?
2. In Canada's parliamentary system, politicians are elected by the people but normally must follow the policies of their party. Do you think this system needs to change? What are costs and benefits of this system?
3. How does your school (or workplace) reflect a pluralist or elite model of power and decision making?
4. Do you locate yourself politically on the left or on the right? How does this affect the way you look at political issues?
5. Can you apply Weber's three types of authority to people who have an influence on Canada?
6. Go to the Genocide Watch Web site (http://www.genocidewatch.org). What do you think the world community could do to intervene in these tragic situations?

SUGGESTED READINGS

These books examine politics from a sociological perspective:

G. William Domhoff. *The Power Elite and the State: How Policy Is Made in America.* New York: Aldine de Gruyter, 1990.

Anthony M. Orum. *Introduction to Political Sociology: The Social Anatomy of the Body Politic* (3rd ed.). Englewood Cliffs, N.J.: Prentice-Hall, 1988.

In-depth information about politics and government is provided in this political science text:

Rand Dyck. *Canadian Politics: Critical Approaches* (3rd ed.). Toronto: Nelson Canada, 2003.

Two books that are helpful in understanding Aboriginal political issues are:

Menno Boldt. *Surviving as Indians: The Challenge of Self-Government.* Toronto: University of Toronto Press, 1993.

Olive Dickason. *Canada's First Nations.* Toronto: McClelland and Stewart, 1992.

For a good overview of Quebec separatism and related issues, you can read:

Ramsay Cook. *Canada, Quebec and the Uses of Nationalism* (2nd ed.). Toronto: McClelland and Stewart, 1995.

Marcel Rioux. *Quebec in Question.* Toronto: James Lorimer and Company, 1971.

ONLINE STUDY AND RESEARCH TOOLS

THOMSONNOW™

Go to **http://hed.nelson.com** to link to ThomsonNOW for *Sociology in Our Times,* Fourth Canadian Edition, your online study tool. First take the **Pre-Test** for this chapter to get your personalized **Study Plan,** which will identify topics you need to review and direct you to the appropriate resources. Then take the **Post-Test** to determine what concepts you have mastered and what you still need work on.

INFOTRAC®

Infotrac College Edition is included free with every new copy of this text. Explore this online library for additional readings, review, and a handy resource for assignments. Visit **www.infotrac-college.com** to access this online database of full-text articles. Enter the key terms from this chapter to start your search.

Families and Intimate Relationships

The following is a brief excerpt from an article entitled "Out Family Values" by Professor James Miller from the University of Western Ontario:

The family I live in as a father is also the family I live *out* in as a gay man. I call it an "out family" for three reasons: its openness to homosexual membership; its opposition to heterosexist conformity (the prejudicial assumption of heterosexuality as normal and proper); and its overtness within the contemporary lesbian and gay movement.

Mine is a family that opens out, steps out, and stands out. It opens out to people traditionally excluded from the charmed circle of Home; it steps out beyond the polite and policed borders of the Normal; and it stands out as a clear new possibility on the horizon of what used to be called—in the heady days following Pierre Trudeau's decriminalization of homosexuality in Canada (1969)—the Just Society. Against the drone of current conservative rhetoric urging decent citizens to protect "family values" from homefront activists like me, I shall try to spell out here the distinctive qualities that my family has discovered in itself to meet the challenges of living in a pervasively homophobic culture that would rather we closed down, stepped in, and stood back.... When I first came out to my children in January of 1990, they immediately wanted

to know whether they were gay, too. Not necessarily, I told them, trying to allay their time-honoured fears without compromising my newfound sense of pride. Yet was I not outing them by outing myself? For better or worse, I realized my *uncloseted* gayness was bound to be socially projected onto all who lived with me. Whatever my children's sexual orientations might be, their close association with me would effectively *gay* them in the eyes of straight society and *queer* their cultural outlook. So look out, I warned them, the World likes to see things straight.

They have taken my warning to heart by setting the record straight about me and them ("Our Dad's gay, but we're probably not") for any curious soul who comes into our domestic space. . . . An out family must learn to speak about itself in unaccustomed ways, develop its own outlandish frontier lingo, for its members are always proudly, if at times also painfully, aware of their strategic positioning outside the normative vision of heterosexual monogamy . . . . My out family bravely resists the exclusionary pressures of heterosexist institutions and their defenders simply by existing as such, by brazenly occupying hallowed spaces like "family rooms" and "family cottages" and even "family restaurants" where we're not supposed to exist (Miller, 2003:104).

James Miller's family is one of millions around the globe redefining what the concept of family means in our modern society. Fifty years ago, the majority of Canadian families consisted of two adults in a permanent union that produced three to five children. Other kinds of families were the exception. Today, when we think of families, we think of diversity and change, and exceptions are the rule. The experiences of the family in the above narrative certainly are not unique. Other variations on what has been described as a "traditional" family are also common. Separation and divorce, remarriage, and blended or reconstituted families are a reality for many Canadians. Despite these changes, family life continues to be a source of great personal satisfaction and happiness. A recent opinion poll of Canadians indicated that more than 97 percent of respondents believed that family life was essential to their personal well-being (Bibby, 2004).

In this chapter, we examine the diversity and complexity of families and intimate relationships. Pressing social issues, such as same-sex marriage, divorce, child care, and new reproductive technologies, will be used as examples of how families and intimate relationships continue to change in the new century. Before reading on, test your knowledge about the changing family by taking the quiz in Box 15.1.

QUESTIONS AND ISSUES

Chapter Focus Question: How is social change affecting the Canadian family?

Why is it difficult to define family?

How do marriage patterns vary around the world?

What are the key assumptions of functionalist, conflict, feminist, symbolic interactionist, and postmodernist perspectives on families?

What significant trends affect many Canadian families today?

Despite the idealized image of "the family," North American families have undergone many changes in the past century as exemplified by the case of Carol Hoard and newborn K.C., who was conceived after his father Ron died from a heart attack. The new reproductive technologies available today raise many questions about how we define "a family."

FAMILIES IN GLOBAL PERSPECTIVE

Defining *Family*

What is a family? Although we all have a family of some form or another, and we all understand the concept of family, it is not an easy concept to define. More than ever, this term means different things to different people. As the nature of family life and work has changed in high-, middle-, and low-income nations, the issue of what constitutes a family has been widely debated. For example, Hutterite families in Canada live in communal situations, in which children from about the age of three spend most of their days in school. The children also eat their meals in a communal dining hall, away from their parents. In this case, the community is the family as opposed to a traditional nuclear family.

Some Aboriginal families in Canada also tend to have a much broader idea of family membership. Children are often cared for by relatives in the extended family. A social worker may define a family as consisting of parents and children only. Some Aboriginal parents may be perceived as neglecting their children, when the parents feel they are safe and well cared for by "their family"—that is, by uncles, grandparents, or other relatives (Ward, 1998).

Similarly, gay men and lesbians often form unique family forms. Many gay men and lesbians have *families we choose*—**social arrangements that include intimate relationships between couples and close familial relationships with other couples and with other adults and children** (Kirby and Robinson, 1998). In the following example, a young woman speaks about her family of choice:

> When I go to have a kid, I'm not gonna have my sisters as godparents. I'm gonna have people around me, that are gay. No, I call on my inner family—my community, or whatever—to help me with my life. So there's definitely a family. (quoted in Weston, 1991:108)

In a society as diverse as Canada, talking about "a family" as though a single type of family exists or ever did exist is inaccurate. In reality, different groups will define their family lives in unique ways, depending on a number of factors, such as their socioeconomic background, immigrant status, religious beliefs, or cultural practices and traditions (Baker, 2005).

For many years, a standard sociological definition of *family* has been a group of people who are related to one another by bonds of blood, marriage, or adoption and who live together, form an economic unit, and bear and raise children (Benokraitis, 1999). Many people believe that this definition should not be expanded—that social approval should not be extended to other relationships simply because the persons in those relationships wish to consider themselves a family. However, others challenge this definition because it simply does not match the reality of family life in contemporary society (Eichler, 1981; Lynn, 1996; Bibby, 2004). Today's families include many types of living arrangements and relationships, including single-parent households, unmarried couples, lesbian and gay couples, and multiple generations (such as grandparents, parents, and children) living in the same household. Historically, the state has played a significant role in determining what a family is, and family benefits have been available only to those families that fit a strictly legal definition of family. More recently, a number of legal challenges have been launched in Canada regarding the definitions of *marriage* and *spouse* by same-sex couples who, because they were not recognized as legally married, were denied the rights and benefits accorded to other families. To accurately reflect these changes in family life, we need an encompassing definition of what constitutes a family. Accordingly, we will define *families* as **relationships in which people live together with commitment, form an economic unit and care for any young, and consider their identity to be significantly attached to**

BOX 15.1 SOCIOLOGY AND EVERYDAY LIFE

How Much Do You Know About the Changing Family in Canada?

True	False	
T	F	1. Today, people in Canada are more inclined to get married than at any time in history.
T	F	2. Men are as likely as women to be single parents.
T	F	3. One out of every two marriages ends in divorce.
T	F	4. The incidence of reported spousal assault has increased dramatically in the past decade.
T	F	5. People marry at a much later age now than they did several decades ago.
T	F	6. Nearly 25 percent of all marriages are dual-earner marriages.
T	F	7. Same-sex couples cannot legally adopt children in Canada.
T	F	8. People who marry young are more likely to divorce than those who marry later in life.

Answers on page 464.

the group. Sexual expression and parent–children relationships are a part of most, but not all, family relationships (based on Benokraitis, 1999; Lamanna and Riedmann, 2003).

In our study of families, we will use our sociological imagination to see how our personal experiences are related to the larger happenings in our society. At the microlevel, each of us has our own "biography," based on our experience within a family; at the macrolevel, our families are embedded in a specific social context that has a major impact on them (Aulette, 1994). We will examine the institution of the family at both of these levels, starting with family structure and characteristics.

Family Structure and Characteristics

In preindustrial societies, the primary form of social organization is through kinship ties. *Kinship* **refers to a social network of people based on common ancestry, marriage, or adoption.** Through kinship networks, people cooperate so that they can acquire the basic necessities of life, including food and shelter.

Kinship systems can also serve as a means by which property is transferred, goods are produced and distributed, and power is allocated.

In industrialized societies, other social institutions fulfill some of the functions previously taken care of by the kinship network. For example, political systems provide structures of social control and authority, and economic systems are responsible for the production and distribution of goods and services. Consequently, families in industrialized societies serve fewer and more specialized purposes than do families in preindustrial societies. Contemporary families are primarily responsible for regulating sexual activity, socializing children, and providing affection and companionship for family members.

Families of Orientation and Procreation

During our lifetime, many of us will be members of two different types of families—a family of orientation and a family of procreation. The *family of orientation* **is the family into which a person is born and in which early socialization usually takes place.** Although most people are related to members of their family of orientation by blood ties, those who

BOX 15.1 SOCIOLOGY AND EVERYDAY LIFE

Answers to the Sociology Quiz on the Changing Family in Canada

1. **False.** According to census data, the marriage rate has gone down by about one-third since 1960. In 2002, the marriage rate was 4.7 per 1,000 population, well below the most recent peak in 1988 of 7.0 per 1,000 population (Statistics Canada, 2004g).

2. **False.** Eighty-one percent of single-parent families in Canada are headed by a mother (Statistics Canada, 2002o).

3. **False.** Current estimates are that about one-third of marriages will end in divorce (Statistics Canada, 2002o).

4. **True.** This trend is in part the result of the implementation of "zero tolerance" policies, which direct that charges be laid in all domestic violence cases (Linden, 2004).

5. **True.** In 2001 the average first time marrying age was 28 for women and 30 for men. In 1971, it was 22 for women and 25 for men (Statistics Canada, 2003n).

6. **False.** Approximately 70 percent of all marriages in Canada are dual-earner marriages—marriages in which both spouses are in the labour force (Statistics Canada, 2003g).

7. **False.** In seven Canadian provinces and territories, the courts have ruled that forbidding same-sex couples to adopt is a violation of the *Charter of Rights and Freedoms* (Ambert, 2005a).

8. **True.** Those who marry at an early age have a higher rate of divorce than those marrying later (Baker, 2005).

are adopted have a legal tie that is patterned after a blood relationship (Aulette, 1994). The *family of procreation* is the family that a person forms by having or adopting children (Benokraitis, 2002). Both legal and blood ties are found in most families of procreation. The relationship between a husband and wife is based on legal ties; however, the relationship between a parent and child may be based on either blood ties or legal ties, depending on whether the child has been adopted (Aulette, 1994).

Although many young people leave their family of orientation as they reach adulthood, finish school, and/or get married, recent studies have found that many people maintain family ties across generations, particularly as older persons have remained actively involved in relationships with their adult children. Author Betty Friedan explains how an intergenerational pattern of "extended family" has emerged in her own family:

> With my own children . . . I have noticed an interesting development. In their twenties and thirties, they started coming back home again—Thanksgiving, Passover, summers—bringing wives, husbands, their own children now, to my house in Sag Harbor. I relished the renewed sense of family which they clearly wanted again and enjoyed. I realized that they were confident enough now, in their grown-up selves, in their busy careers and the rich texture of their marriages ... that they did not need to defend themselves anymore against their childish need for mother. (Friedan, 1993:297)

Extended and Nuclear Families Sociologists distinguish between extended and nuclear families based on the number of generations that live within a household. An *extended family* is a family unit composed of relatives in addition to parents and children who live in the same household. These families often include grandparents, uncles, aunts, or other relatives who live in close proximity to the parents and children, making it possible for family members to share resources. In horticultural and agricultural societies, extended families are extremely important; having a large number of family members participate in food production may be essential for survival. Today, extended family patterns are found in Latin America, Africa, Asia, and some parts of Eastern and Southern Europe (Busch, 1990).

A *nuclear family* is a family composed of one or two parents and their dependent children, all of whom live apart from other relatives. A traditional definition specifies that a nuclear family is made up of a "couple" and their dependent children; however, this definition became outdated as a significant shift occurred in the family structure. As shown in the Census Profile (see page 466), in 2001, about 48 percent of all households were composed of married couples with children under the age of 18. The second-largest family type, at 29 percent, were married couples without children living at home. This group consisted of childless couples and couples whose children no longer lived at home (empty-nesters) (Statistics Canada, 2003n).

Nuclear families are smaller than they were twenty years ago; whereas the average family size in 1971 was 3.7 persons, in 2001 it was 3 persons (Statistics Canada, 2002d). This decrease has been largely attributed to decisions to postpone or forgo childbearing and to increases in separation and divorce rates.

Marriage Patterns

Across cultures, families are characterized by different forms of marriage. *Marriage* is a legally recognized and/or socially approved arrangement between two or more individuals that carries certain rights and obligations and usually involves sexual activity.

In Canada, the only legally sanctioned form of marriage is *monogamy—a marriage to one person at a time.* For some people, marriage is a lifelong commitment that ends only with the death of a partner.

Members of some religious groups believe that marriage is literally "forever"; if one spouse dies, the surviving spouse is precluded from marrying anyone else. For others, marriage is a commitment of indefinite duration. Through a pattern of marriage, divorce, and remarriage, some people practise *serial monogamy*—a succession of marriages in which a person has several spouses over a lifetime but is legally married to only one person at a time.

Polygamy is the concurrent marriage of a person of one sex with two or more members of the opposite sex (Marshall, 1998). The most prevalent form of polygamy is *polygyny*—the concurrent marriage of one man with two or more women. Polygyny has been practised in a number of Islamic societies, including in some regions of contemporary Africa and southern Russia. Government officials in Africa estimate that 20 percent of Zambian marriages today are polygynous (Chipungu, 1999). How many wives and children might a polygynist have at one time? According to one report, Rodger Chilala of southern

CENSUS ✦ PROFILE

Changes to the family structure include a decline in marriages, an increase in common-law unions, and an increase in single-parent families.

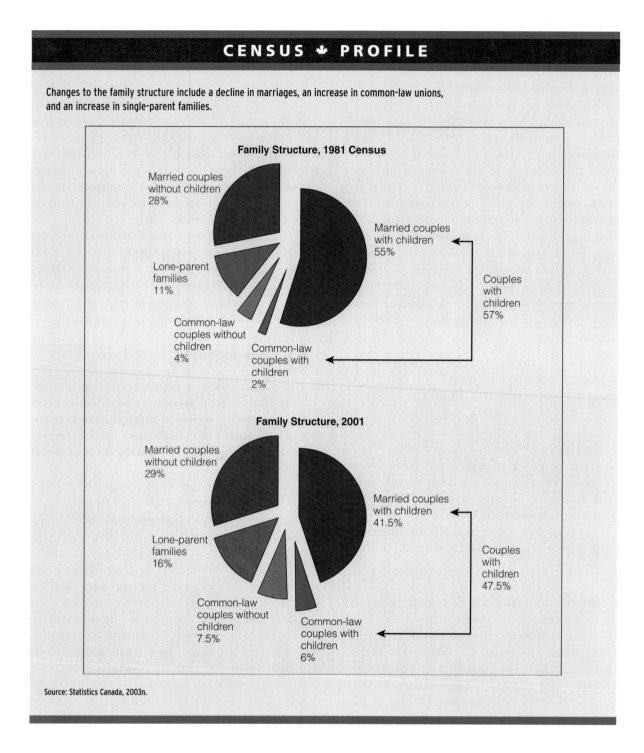

Family Structure, 1981 Census

Married couples without children
28%

Lone-parent families
11%

Common-law couples without children
4%

Common-law couples with children
2%

Married couples with children
55%

Couples with children
57%

Family Structure, 2001

Married couples without children
29%

Lone-parent families
16%

Common-law couples without children
7.5%

Common-law couples with children
6%

Married couples with children
41.5%

Couples with children
47.5%

Source: Statistics Canada, 2003n.

Zambia claimed to have fourteen wives and more than forty children; he stated that he previously had twenty-four wives but found that he could not afford the expenses associated with that many spouses (Chipungu, 1999). Polygyny is also allowed in southern Russia, where efforts are underway to revive Islamic traditions (ITA/TASS, 1999). Some analysts believe that the practice of polygamy contributes to the likelihood that families will live in poverty (Chipungu, 1999).

The second type of polygamy is ***polyandry***—**the concurrent marriage of one woman with two or more men.** Polyandry is very rare; when it does occur, it is typically found in societies where men greatly outnumber women because of high rates of female infanticide or where marriages are arranged between two brothers and one woman ("fraternal polyandry"). According to recent research, polyandry is never the only form of marriage in a society: Whenever polyandry occurs, polygyny co-occurs (Trevithick, 1997). Although Tibetans are the most frequently studied population where polyandry exists, anthropologists have also identified the Sherpas, Paharis, Sinhalese, and various African groups as sometimes practising polyandry (Trevithick, 1997). A recent anthropological study of Nyinba, an ethnically Tibetan population living in northwestern Nepal, found that fraternal polyandry (two brothers sharing the same wife) is the normative form of marriage and that the practice continues to be highly valued culturally (Levine and Silk, 1997). Despite the fact that some polyandrous marriages fail, societies such as this pass on the practice from one generation to the next (Levine and Silk, 1997).

Patterns of Descent and Inheritance

Even though a variety of marital patterns exist across cultures, virtually all forms of marriage establish a system of descent so that kinship can be determined and inheritance rights established. In preindustrial societies, kinship is usually traced through one parent (unilineally). The most common pattern of unilineal descent is *patrilineal descent*—**a system of tracing descent through the father's side of the family.** Patrilineal systems are set up in such a manner that a legitimate son inherits his father's property and sometimes his position upon the father's death. In nations, such as India, where boys are seen as permanent patrilineal family members and girls are seen only as temporary family members, girls tend to be considered more expendable than boys (O'Connell, 1994). Recently, some scholars

have concluded that cultural and racial nationalism in China is linked to the idea of patrilineal descent being crucial to the modern Chinese national identity (Dikotter, 1996).

Even with the less common pattern of *matrilineal descent*—**a system of tracing descent through the mother's side of the family**—women may not control property. However, inheritance of property and position usually is traced from the maternal uncle (mother's brother) to his nephew (mother's son). In some cases, mothers may pass on their property to daughters.

By contrast, in industrial societies, kinship usually is traced through both parents (bilineally). The most common form is *bilateral descent*—**a system of tracing descent through both the mother's and father's sides of the family.** This pattern is used in Canada for the purpose of determining kinship and inheritance rights; however, children typically take the father's last name.

Power and Authority in Families

Descent and inheritance rights are intricately linked with patterns of power and authority in families. A *patriarchal family* is **a family structure in which authority is held by the eldest male (usually the father).** The male authority figure acts as head of the household and holds power and authority over the women and children as well as over other males. A *matriarchal family* is **a family structure in which authority is held by the eldest female (usually the mother).** In this case, the female authority figure acts as head of the household. Although there has been

While the relationship between husband and wife is based on legal ties, relationships between parents and children may be established either by blood ties or by legal ties.

a great deal of discussion about matriarchal societies, scholars have found no historical evidence to indicate that true matriarchies ever existed.

The most prevalent pattern of power and authority in families is patriarchy. Across cultures, men are the primary (and often sole) decision makers regarding domestic, economic, and social concerns facing the family. The existence of patriarchy may give men a sense of power over their own lives, but it also can create an atmosphere in which some men feel greater freedom to abuse women and children (O'Connell, 1994). According to some feminist scholars and journalists, hostility and violence perpetrated by men against women and children is the result of patriarchal attitudes, economic hardship, rigid gender roles, and societal acceptance of aggression (Lynn and O'Neill, 1995; Smith, 1996). Moreover, some economists believe that the patriarchal family structure (along with prevailing market conditions and public policy) limits people's choices in employment

(Woolley, 1998). According to this view, the patriarchal family structure has remained largely unchanged in this country, even as familial responsibilities in the paid labour market have undergone dramatic transformation. In the postindustrial age, for example, gender-specific roles may have been reduced; however, women's choices remain limited by the patriarchal tradition in which women do most of the unpaid labour, particularly in the family. Despite dramatic increases in the number of women in the paid work force, there has been a lack of movement toward gender equity, which would equalize women's opportunities (Woolley, 1998). This issue is not limited to Canada and the United States. The patriarchal family places a heavy burden on women around the globe as they attempt to meet the needs of their families (see Box 15.2).

An *egalitarian family* **is a family structure in which both partners share power and authority equally.** In egalitarian families, issues of power and

BOX 15.2 SOCIOLOGY IN GLOBAL PERSPECTIVE

Fukugan Shufu: Changing Terminology and Family Life in Japan

I work until 8 in the evening, but there are plenty of times when I work much later. That's just the social reality in Japan. There are some other women in my milieu, but most of them have just one child and don't plan for more.

—Haruko Takachi, a postal manager in Tokyo, explaining why she is glad her child was accepted into a government-run nursery school (qtd. in French, 2003: A3)

Haruko Takachi is an example of the working woman in Japan who faces dual responsibilities in the workplace and in her family. Even with a significant increase in the number of employed women, a study by the Japanese prime minister's office found that most people still viewed household chores, such as cleaning, washing, cooking, and cleaning up after meals, as the wife's responsibility (White, 2002). However, according to the anthropologist Merry Isaacs White (2002), who has extensively studied family life in Japan, women's roles are becoming much more complex, and families in Japan are as diverse and sometimes as divisive as families elsewhere.

Although Japanese women make up 41 percent of all workers in Japan, the increase in their numbers in the paid work force is only one of many changes that have affected families in that country. Today, more Japanese women who marry are keeping their maiden names. However, this practice—known as *bessei*, or "separate names"—may create additional problems for many of them because they may be hassled by employers, refused passport documents, or denied access to their husband's insurance benefits (White, 2002). Along with the practice of separate names, more couples are choosing to cohabit or to not register their marriage with the government.

New terminology reflects some of the changes in women's roles within the Japanese family. *Fukugan shufu* (meaning many-faced housewife) refers to a "housewife who does not stay home but instead has created a busy collage of a life of activities" (White, 2002:93-94). If the traditional Japanese wife was the "indoor housewife" (*oku-sama*) who devoted her time to domestic tasks and child care, the "outdoor housewife" (*soto-sama*) is now busy pursuing leisure activities such as playing tennis, attending lectures, or taking pottery classes. The term *tenuki okusan*—meaning the "no-hands" housewife—is used to describe women who typically are not employed but choose to pick up prepared meals or foods from local shops to serve for dinner (White, 2002:94).

While these new terms reflect changes in the role of more-affluent married women in Japan, another phrase describes what many young women think of as an ideal husband—*baba nuki, kaa tsuki* ("without grandma, with car"). As White (2002:83) explains, "Mothers-in-law represented the oppression and immobility of the old-style family; cars represented the free-wheeling youthful style of the modern couple." This thinking represents a significant shift from the past, when it was assumed that the dutiful

daughter-in-law would look after elderly parents (Ikegami, 1998; Kakuchi, 1998). As younger women have sought greater freedom and felt less commitment to traditional marriage and family patterns, some analysts in Japan have expressed concern about the future of the family and who will take care of the aging population in that nation. Perhaps more than anything else, people in Japan and other nations are forced to admit that the previously held idealized views of the traditional Japanese family as a paragon of homogeneity, stability, and dutiful compliance are not an accurate depiction of what family life is actually like in Japan today.

Can you see similarities in discussions about "family values" in Canada and the controversy over changing family values in Japan? Why or why not?

Sources: Based on Ikegami, 1998: Jung, 1994; Kitano et al., 1992; White, 2002.

authority may be frequently negotiated as the roles and responsibilities within the relationship change over time. Recently, a trend toward more egalitarian relationships has been evident in a number of countries as women have sought changes in their legal status and increased educational and employment opportunities. Some degree of economic independence makes it possible for women to delay marriage or to terminate a problematic marriage (Ward, 1998). However, one study of the effects of egalitarian values on the allocation and performance of domestic tasks in the family found that changes were relatively slow in coming. According to the study, fathers were more likely to share domestic tasks in nonconventional families where members held more egalitarian values. Similarly, children's gender-role stereotyping was more closely linked to their parents' egalitarian values and nonconventional lifestyles than to the domestic tasks they were assigned (Weisner, Garnier, and Loucky, 1994).

THEORETICAL PERSPECTIVES ON FAMILIES

The *sociology of family* is the subdiscipline of sociology that attempts to describe and explain patterns of family life and variations in family structure. Functionalist perspectives emphasize the functions that

families perform at the macrolevel of society, while conflict and feminist perspectives focus on families as a primary source of social inequality. By contrast, symbolic interactionists examine microlevel interactions that are integral to the roles of different family members. Finally, postmodern theorists emphasize the fact that families today are diverse and variable.

Functionalist Perspectives

Functionalists emphasize the importance of the family in maintaining the stability of society and the well-being of individuals. According to Émile Durkheim, marriage is a microcosmic replica of the larger society; both marriage and society involve a mental and moral fusion of physically distinct individuals (Lehmann, 1994). Durkheim also believed that a division of labour contributed to greater efficiency in all areas of life—including marriages and families—even though he acknowledged that this division imposed significant limitations on some people.

Talcott Parsons was a key figure in developing a functionalist model of the family. According to Parsons (1955), the husband/father fulfils the *instrumental role* (meeting the family's economic needs, making important decisions, and providing leadership), while the wife/mother fulfils the *expressive role* (running the household, caring for children, and meeting the emotional needs of family members).

Contemporary functionalist perspectives on families derive their foundation from Durkheim and Parsons. Division of labour makes it possible for families to fulfill a number of functions that no other institution can perform as effectively. In advanced industrial societies, families serve four key functions:

1. *Sexual regulation.* Families are expected to regulate the sexual activity of their members and thus control reproduction so that it occurs within specific boundaries. At the macrolevel, incest taboos prohibit sexual contact or marriage between certain relatives. For example, virtually all societies prohibit sexual relations between parents and their children and between brothers and sisters. However, some societies exclude remotely related individuals, such as second and third cousins from such prohibitions. Sexual regulation of family members by the family is supposed to protect the *principle of legitimacy*—the belief that all children should have a socially and legally recognized father (Malinowski, 1964/1929).

2. *Socialization.* Parents and other relatives are responsible for teaching children the necessary knowledge and skills to survive. The smallness and intimacy of families makes them best suited for providing children with the initial learning experiences they need.

3. *Economic and psychological support.* Families are responsible for providing economic and psychological support for members. In pre-industrial societies, families are economic production units; in industrial societies, the economic security of families is tied to the workplace and to macrolevel economic systems. In recent years, psychological support and emotional security have been increasingly important functions of the family (Chafetz, 1989).

4. *Provision of social status.* Families confer social status and reputation on their members. These statuses include the ascribed statuses with which individuals are born, such as race/ethnicity, nationality, social class, and sometimes religious affiliation. One of the most significant and compelling forms of social placement is the family's class position and the opportunities (or lack thereof) resulting from that position. Examples of class-related opportunities include access to quality health care, higher education, and a safe place to live.

Functionalist explanations of family problems examine the relationship between family troubles and a decline in other social institutions. Changes in the economy, in religion, in the educational system, in the law, or in government programs all can contribute to family problems. Functionalists assert that erosion

Functionalist theorists believe that families serve a variety of important functions that no other social institution can adequately fulfill. In contrast, conflict and feminist analysts believe that the functionalist perspective is idealistic and inadequate for explaining problems in contemporary families.

of family values may occur when the institution of religion becomes less important in everyday life. Likewise, changes in law (such as recognition of "no fault" divorce) contribute to high rates of divorce and dramatic increases in single-parent households. According to some functionalists, children are the most affected by these trends because they receive less nurturance and guidance from their parents (see Popenoe, 1993).

Conflict Perspectives

Both conflict and feminist analysts view functionalist perspectives on the role of the family in society as idealized and inadequate. Rather than operating harmoniously and for the benefit of all members, families are sources of social inequality and conflict over values, goals, and access to resources and power (Benokraitis, 2002).

The foundation of conflict views of the family appeared in the works of Frederich Engels, a friend and colleague of Karl Marx. In his classic work *The Origin of the Family, Private Property and the State* (1972), which was first published in 1884, Engels argued that the family in a capitalist society is an exploitive social institution that is primarily responsible for the oppression of women. Conflict theorists view the relationship between husbands and wives as similar to the relationship between capitalists and their workers. Women are dominated by men in the home in the same manner that workers are dominated by capitalists and managers in factories. Just as workers exchange their labour for a wage, so do wives exchange their domestic labour for the economic support of their husbands. While childbearing and care for family members in the home contributes to capitalism, these activities also reinforce the subordination of women through unpaid (and often devalued) labour. As a result, husbands—like capitalists—enjoy more power and privilege within the family. Engels predicted that the oppression of women would end when women moved out of the private sphere of the home and into the paid workforce. As discussed in Chapter 11 ("Sex and Gender"), women's oppression has not disappeared as a result of the dramatic increases in the number of women in the paid workforce. In many ways, it has become more prevalent as women struggle with issues of gender inequality in pay and benefits, job advancement, and balancing career and home responsibilities. Other conflict analysts are concerned with the effect that class conflict has on the family. The exploitation of the lower classes by the upper classes contributes to family problems, such as high rates of divorce and overall family instability.

Feminist Perspectives

The contributions of feminist theorists have resulted in radical changes in the sociological study of families. Feminist theorists have been primarily responsible for redefining the concept of "the family" by focusing on the diversity of family arrangements. Some feminist scholars reject the "monolithic model of the family" (Eichler, 1981:368), which idealizes one family form—the family with a male breadwinner and stay-at-home wife and children—as the normal household arrangement. Feminist theorists argue that limiting our concept of family to this traditional form means ignoring or undervaluing diverse family forms, such as single-parent families, childless families, gay or lesbian families, and stepfamilies (Mackie, 1995:50). Roles within the family are viewed by feminist theorists as primarily socially constructed rather than biologically determined. Feminist scholars have challenged a number of common assumptions about family life and the roles we fulfill within families. For example, they question whether all "real" women want to be mothers, or whether the inequality between traditional husbands and wives is "natural" (Duffy et al., 1989:11).

In contrast to conflict theory, which focuses on class and property arrangements as the source of inequality within the family, feminist perspectives on inequality focus on *patriarchy*—**a hierarchical system of social organization in which cultural, political, and economic structures are controlled by men.** From this viewpoint, men's domination over women existed long before private ownership of property and capitalism (Mann, 1994). Women's subordination is rooted in patriarchy and men's control over women's labour power (Hartmann, 1981). Although the division of labour may appear to be an equal pooling of contributions within the family unit, feminist scholars view women as giving much but receiving less in return. According to sociologist Patricia Mann, "Male power in our society is expressed in economic terms even if it does not originate in property relations; women's activities in the home have been undervalued at the same time as their labor has been controlled by men" (1994:42). The power discrepancy and economic dependency created in a patriarchal family system was demonstrated in sociologist Meg Luxton's study of families in Flin Flon, Manitoba. Consider this husband's comments: "You'd never work like I do. That's hard work, real work that earns money. And that money keeps you alive. Don't you forget it" (Luxton, 1980:164). As these comments reveal, men may feel that they have earned special privileges as a result of their breadwinner status. On the other hand, a woman's economic dependence means that her needs become secondary in the family (Luxton, 1980).

Many women resist male domination. Women can control their reproductive capabilities through contraception and other means, and they can take control of their labour power from their husbands by working for wages outside the home (Mann, 1994). However, men are often reluctant to relinquish their status as family breadwinner. Why? Although only 15 percent of families in Canada are supported solely by a male breadwinner (Bradbury, 1996), many men continue to construct their ideal of masculinity around this cultural value (Livingston and Luxton, 1995).

Feminist perspectives on families primarily focus on the problems of dominance and subordination inherent in relationships. Specifically, feminist theorists have acknowledged what has been described as the "dark side of the family," focusing research efforts on issues, such as child abuse, wife abuse, and violence against the elderly. Feminist explanations take into account the unequal political relationship between women and men in families and outside of families (Ambert, 2001; Comack, 1996b; Smith, 1985).

Feminist analysis of families provides not only a theoretical perspective, but also a broad movement for social change. Supported by a variety of advocacy groups and networks, feminists have brought women's private problems, such as wife abuse, and the financial difficulties of economically dependent wives, into the public arena (Ambert, 2001). Feminist sociology seeks to enhance the status of women in society by validating the contributions, experiences, and viewpoints of women in all institutions, including the family (Gee, 1994).

Symbolic Interactionist Perspectives

Early symbolic interactionists viewed the communication process in families as integral to the roles that different family members play. Symbolic interactionists examine the roles of husbands, wives, and children as they act out their own part and react to the actions of others. From this perspective, what people think, as well as what they say and do, is very important in understanding family dynamics.

According to sociologists Peter Berger and Hansfried Kellner (1964), interaction between marital partners contributes to a shared reality. Although newlyweds bring separate identities to a marriage, over time they construct a shared reality as a couple. In the process, the partners redefine their past identities to be consistent with new realities. Development of a shared reality is a continuous process, taking place not only in the family but also in any group in which the couple participates together. Divorce is the reverse of this process; couples may start with a shared reality and, in the process of uncoupling, gradually develop separate realities (Vaughan, 1985).

Symbolic interactionists explain family relationships in terms of the subjective meanings and everyday interpretations people give to their lives. Sociologist Jessie Bernard (1982/1973) pointed out that women and men experience marriage differently and that a marriage contains two marriages: "his marriage" and "her marriage." While a husband may see his marriage very positively, his wife may feel less positive about her marriage, and vice versa. Researchers have found that husbands and wives may give very different accounts of the same event, and their two "realities" frequently do not coincide (Safilios-Rothschild, 1969).

How do symbolic interactionists view problems within the family? Some focus on the terminology used to describe these problems, examining the extent to which words convey assumptions or "realities" about the nature of the problem. For example, violence between men and women in the home often is referred to as *spouse abuse* or *domestic violence*. However, these terms imply that women and men play equal roles in the perpetration of violence in families, overlooking the more active part men usually play in

such aggression. In addition, the term *domestic violence* suggests that this is the "kind of violence that women volunteer for, or inspire, or provoke" (Jacobs, 1994:56). Some scholars and activists use terms such as *wife battering* or *wife abuse* to highlight the gendered nature of such behaviour (see Macleod, 1987). However, others argue that *battered woman* suggests a "woman who is more or less permanently black and blue and helpless" (Jacobs, 1994:56).

Analysts using an interactionist approach note that definitions concerning family violence not only are socially constructed but also have an effect on how people are treated. In one study of a shelter for battered women, analysts found that workers made decisions about whom to assist and how to assist them based on their own understanding of what constitutes a "real" battered woman (Loseke, 1992). In fact, the term "stitch rule" is used by some shelter workers in reference to the police practice in some jurisdictions that advises against arrest of an accused unless the victim had sustained injuries that required stitches (Straus and Ramirez, 2004).

Other symbolic interactionists have examined ways in which individuals communicate with one another and interpret these interactions. According to Lenore Walker (1979), females are socialized to be passive and males are socialized to be aggressive long before they take on the adult roles of battered and batterer. However, even women who have not been socialized by their parents to be helpless and passive may be socialized into this behaviour by abusive husbands. Three factors contribute to the acceptance of the roles of batterer and battered: (1) low self-esteem on the part of both people involved, (2) a limited range of behaviours (he only knows how to be jealous and possessive/she only knows how to be dependent and eager to make everyone happy), and (3) a belief by both in stereotypic gender roles (she should be feminine and pampered/he should be aggressive and dominant). Other analysts suggest that this pattern is changing as more women are gaining paid employment and becoming less dependent on their husbands or male companions for economic support.

Postmodern Perspectives

Although postmodern theorists disparage the idea that a universal theory can be developed to explain social life, a postmodern perspective might provide insights on questions such as this: How is family life different in the Information Age? Social scientist David Elkind (1995) describes the postmodern family as *permeable*—capable of being diffused or invaded in such a manner that an entity's original purpose is modified or changed. According to Elkind (1995), if the nuclear family is a reflection of the age of modernity, the permeable family reflects the postmodern assumptions of difference, particularity, and irregularity. Difference is evident in the fact that the nuclear family is now only one of many family forms. Similarly, the idea of romantic love under modernity has given way to the idea of consensual love: Individuals agree to have sexual relations with others whom they have no intention of marrying or, if they marry, do not necessarily see the marriage as having permanence. Maternal love has also been transformed into shared parenting, which includes not only mothers and fathers but also caregivers, who may be either relatives or nonrelatives (Elkind, 1995).

Today, many people value the autonomy of the individual family member more highly than the family unit. As Elkind (1995:13) states, "If the nuclear home was a haven, the permeable home is more like a busy railway station with people coming in for rest and sustenance before moving out on another track."

Urbanity is another characteristic of the postmodern family. The boundaries between the public sphere (the workplace) and the private sphere (the home) are becoming more open and flexible. In fact, family life may be negatively affected by the decreasing distinction between what is work time and what is family time. As more people are becoming connected "24/7" (twenty-four hours a day, seven days a week), the boss who before would not have called at 11:30 p.m. or when an employee was on vacation may send an e-mail asking for an immediate response to some question that has arisen while the person is away with family members (Leonard, 1999). According to some postmodern analysts, this is an example of the "power of the new communications technologies to integrate and control labour despite extensive dispersion and decentralization" (Haraway, 1994:439).

Social theorist Jean Baudrillard's idea that the simulation of reality may come to be viewed as "reality" by some people can be applied to family interactions in the Information Age. Does the ability to contact someone anywhere and any time of the day or night provide greater happiness and stability in families? Or is "reach out and touch someone" merely an ideology promulgated by the consumer society? Journalists have written about the experience of watching a family gathering at an amusement park, restaurant, mall, or other location only to see family members pick up their cell phones to receive or make calls to individuals not present, rather than spending "face time" with those family members who are present. Similarly, the Internet provides many people with the opportunity to send e-mail messages, birthday cards, flowers, or other presents to friends and family around the world. However, e-mail and chat groups also provide new avenues for miscommunication, whereby people may be offended by the comments, particularly sharp retorts, made by others. As one journalist stated, "E-mail allows us to act before we can think—the perfect tool for a culture of hyperstimulation" (Leonard, 1999:60). This journalist acknowledges that he has used e-mail to do everything from coping with the pressures of new fatherhood to arguing with his mother:

> [E-mail] saved me time and money without ever requiring me to leave the house; it salvaged my social life, allowed me to conduct interviews as a reporter and kept a lifeline open to my far-flung extended family. Indeed, I finally knew for sure that the digital world was viscerally potent when I found myself in the middle of a bitter fight with my mother—on e-mail. Again, new medium, old story. (Leonard, 1999:59)

Some analysts paint a bleak future for families in the age of the "integrated circuit." Social scientist Donna Haraway (1994:443) provides one scenario of the postmodern family:

> Women-headed households, serial monogamy, flight of men, old women alone, technology of domestic work, paid homework, reemergence of home sweat-shops, home-based businesses and telecommuting, electronic cottage, urban homelessness, migration, module architecture, reinforced (simulated) nuclear family, intense domestic violence.

However, Haraway believes that we should not demonize technology but should instead embrace the difficult task of "reconstructing the boundaries of daily life, in partial connections with others, in communication with all our parts" (Haraway, 1994:452).

Even as postmodern perspectives call our attention to cyberspace, consumerism, and the hyper-real, it is important to recall that there is a growing "digital divide" and a "new kind of cyber class warfare," as some journalists refer to it, going on in North America and around the world (Alter, 1999). New economic trends that are making the richest Canadians even richer are making the poorest one-fifth of Canadians even poorer. Although three quarters of all Canadians own computers and 60 percent of all households have Internet access, many families are left out as the gap in Internet access between the technological "haves" and "have-nots" continues to widen (Moscovitch, 1998; Canadian Internet Project, 2004).

Concept Table 15.A THEORETICAL PERSPECTIVES ON FAMILIES

PERSPECTIVE	FOCUS	KEY POINTS	PERSPECTIVE ON FAMILY PROBLEMS
Functionalist	Role of families in maintaining stability of society and individuals' well-being	In modern societies, families serve the functions of sexual regulation, socialization, economic and psychological support, and provision of social status.	Family problems are related to changes in social institutions, such as the economy, religion, education, and law/government.
Conflict	Families as sources of conflict and social inequality	Families both mirror and help perpetuate social inequalities based on class and gender.	Family problems reflect social patterns of dominance and subordination.
Feminist	Families are patriarchal institutions	Women's subordination is rooted in patriarchy and men's control over women's labour power.	Family problems, such as child abuse, wife abuse, and elder abuse are the result of attempts to control women and perpetuate gender inequality.
Symbolic Interactionist	Family dynamics, including communication patterns and subjective meanings people assign to events	Interactions within families create a shared reality.	How family problems are perceived and defined depends on patterns of communication, the meanings people give to roles and events, and individuals' interpretations of family interactions.
Postmodern	Permeability of families	In postmodern societies, families are diverse and fragmented. Boundaries between workplace and home are blurred.	Family problems are related to cyberspace, consumerism, and the hyper-real in an age increasingly characterized by high-tech "haves" and "have-nots."

Concept Table 15.A summarizes these sociological perspectives on the family. Taken together, these perspectives on the social institution of families help us understand both the good and bad sides of familial relationships. Now we shift our focus to love, marriage, intimate relationships, and family issues in Canada.

DEVELOPING INTIMATE RELATIONSHIPS AND ESTABLISHING FAMILIES

It has been said that North Americans are "in love with love." Why is this so? Perhaps the answer lies in the fact that our ideal culture emphasizes *romantic*

love, which refers to a deep emotion, the satisfaction of significant needs, a caring for and acceptance of the person we love, and involvement in an intimate relationship (Lamanna and Riedmann, 2003). Although the methods we employ to pursue romance may have changed, we are certainly no less enthralled with the idea (see Box 15.3, "Cyberdating: Love and Intimacy Online").

Love and Intimacy

How have Canadians viewed love and intimacy in the past? During the Industrial Revolution in the late nineteenth century, people came to view work and home as separate spheres in which different feelings and emotions were appropriate (Coontz, 1992). The public sphere of work—men's sphere—emphasized self-reliance and independence. In contrast, the

In Canada, the notion of romantic love is deeply intertwined with our beliefs about how and why people develop intimate relationships and establish families. Not all societies share this concern with romantic love.

private sphere of the home—women's sphere—emphasized the giving of services, the exchange of gifts, and love. Accordingly, love and emotions became the domain of women, and work and rationality the domain of men (Lamanna and Riedmann, 2003).

Although the roles of women and men have changed dramatically over the last century, men and women still do not always share the same perspectives about romantic love. According to sociologist Francesca Cancian (1990), women tend to express their feelings verbally, whereas men tend to express their love through nonverbal actions, such as running an errand for someone or repairing a child's broken toy.

Love, intimacy, and sexuality are closely intertwined. Intimacy may be psychic ("the sharing of minds") or sexual, or both. Although sexuality is an integral part of many intimate relationships, perceptions about sexual activities vary from one culture to the next and from one era to another. For example, kissing is found primarily in Western cultures; many African and Asian cultures view kissing negatively (Reinisch, 1990).

BOX 15.3 SOCIOLOGY AND TECHNOLOGY

Cyberdating: Love and Intimacy Online

A recent survey by Internet demographers reported that the number of Internet users over the age of 16 in Canada and the U.S. has reached close to 80 million. Global use is estimated at between 120 million and 140 million people (Merkle and Richardson, 2000). Canada is, per capita, the most "wired" country in the world, followed by the United States and Australia (Moscovitch, 1998). Because of the availability of this new technology, our interpersonal relationships have also been transformed. Relationships that previously involved face-to-face interaction or some other form of direct personal contact are now mediated through new forms of technology (such as e-mail, voice mail, and fax). As a result, on any given day, we can "interact" with numerous people in our professional and personal lives and yet never have any contact with them. As the pace of our daily lives continues to accelerate and free time becomes an increasingly scarce commodity, it becomes necessary to explore new avenues for social interaction.

The Internet is one such avenue (Merkle and Richardson, 2000). One of the newest trends in finding a partner is doing so online. Today, couples are hooking up and finding mates via the Internet. In other words, the Internet is being used to establish romantic relationships—what is most commonly referred to as *cyberdating.*

Although at first glance it may be disturbing that a society may increasingly turn to the Internet as a medium for engaging in interpersonal and romantic relationships, there may be many advantages to this new form of dating.

How does one go about cyberdating? It is relatively easy. Sign on with one of many cyberdating services and provide the relevant personal information, such as your history, hobbies and interests, and preferences in a mate. (Most sites offer the option of adding a photo to your profile.) Then the sites go to work with software that matches the information you provide with the data for those who share similar interests.

Who uses these sites? You name it: teenagers, seniors, heterosexuals, homosexuals, single parents, and, yes, university and college students. One online research firm estimates the number of regular users of Internet dating services at four million (Brym and Lenton, 2001). Although cyberdating is most popular with North American users, it is becoming popular globally. In China, the practice is challenging the tradition of parents selecting their child's spouse. In Britain, an estimated one in five singles used the Net or dating agencies to find romantic partners. One expert predicts this number will "explode over the next five years as globalization brings American-length workdays to the rest of the world" (Stone, 2001:46).

A recent study examined attitudes toward and involvement in the use of the Internet to find a mate. A telephone survey of 1,200 Canadians revealed the popularity of this new venue for dating. Specifically, the study reported the following:

1. Four main social forces appear to be driving the rapid growth of online dating:
   - A growing proportion of the population comprises singles, the main pool for online dating.
   - Career and time pressures are increasing, so people are looking for more efficient ways of meeting others for intimate relationships.
   - Single people are more mobile because of the demands of the job market, so it is more difficult for them to meet people for dating.
   - Workplace romance is on the decline because of growing sensitivity about sexual harassment.
2. Between 1.1 million and 1.2 million Canadians have visited an online dating site.
3. The potential for online dating services in Canada is an additional 2.5 million to 2.8 million adults.
4. In Canada, Internet users are younger, better educated, more likely to be employed in the paid labour force, and urban.

5. Most people use online dating services mainly to find dates and establish a long-term relationship, not to flirt online, find a marriage partner, or find a sexual partner.
6. People use online dating services mainly because they:
   - create the opportunity to meet people on would otherwise never meet.
   - offer privacy and confidentiality.
   - are more convenient than other ways of trying to meet people.
7. The main perceived disadvantage of online dating is that people sometimes do not tell the truth about themselves.
8. A quarter of online daters have misrepresented themselves online. There were almost no differences between men and women in their propensity to misrepresent themselves.
9. Online dating seems to be safer than conventional dating. Thus, although 10 percent of people who went out on a date with someone they met online reported being frightened at least once, this was not sufficiently serious to change their favourable attitude toward online dating. Moreover, the experience of conventional daters is almost certainly worse than that of online daters.
10. Embarrassment is not a major factor inhibiting Canadians from using online dating services. The main inhibiting factors are control-related (some people believe it is too risky) and pragmatic (some people do not believe it is effective, others think there are better ways to meet people for dating, and still others have simply not yet found a suitable date). However, if a friend has used an online dating service, and especially if the friend's experience was positive, these inhibitions are considerably reduced (Brym and Lenton, 2001:3).

What do you think about using the Internet to find a date or to find a romantic partner? What are the potential hazards of this new form of relationship building?

For more than forty years, the work of biologist Alfred C. Kinsey was considered the definitive research on human sexuality, even though some of his methodology had serious limitations. Recently, the work of Kinsey and his associates has been superseded by the National Health and Social Life Survey conducted by the National Opinion Research Center at the University of Chicago. Based on interviews with more than 3,400 men and women aged 18 to 59, this random survey tended to reaffirm the significance of the dominant sexual ideologies. Most respondents reported that they engaged in heterosexual relationships, although 9 percent of the men said they had had at least one homosexual encounter resulting in orgasm. While 6.2 percent of men and 4.4 percent of women said that they were at least somewhat attracted to others of the same gender, only 2.8 percent of men and 1.4 percent of women identified themselves as gay or lesbian.

According to the study, persons who engaged in extramarital sex found their activities to be more thrilling than those with their marital partner, but they also felt guilty. Persons in sustained relationships, such as marriage or cohabitation, found sexual activity to be the most satisfying emotionally and physically.

Cohabitation

Cohabitation **refers to a couple's living together without being legally married.** Many couples choose to live together before marrying or as an alternative to marriage. Although cohabitation or living together is a relatively new alternative to traditional marriage in Canada, in some parts of the world, especially Africa, Latin America, and Sweden, it has been practised for hundreds of years (Cunningham and Antill, 1995).

Attitudes about cohabitation have changed in the past three decades; this is reflected in Figure 15.1. In Canada, cohabitation has become increasingly popular. The census defines *common-law partners*

as two persons of the opposite sex who are not legally married but live together as husband and wife. The growth of common-law families is the strongest of all family structures. Since the early 1980s, the number of persons living common-law has nearly doubled, going from 700,000 in 1981 to 1.2 million in 2001 (Statistics Canada, 2002o). Almost half of these common-law-couple families included children, whether born to the current union or brought to the family from previous unions. The proportion of people in common-law unions varies considerably by province. In Quebec, one in three couples lives common-law, making it the province with the highest rate of common-law families.

The increase in cohabitation is thought to be associated with many recent social changes influencing family behaviours and attitudes. These include the massive entry of women into the labour market, the dissociation between sexuality and marriage and between fertility and marriage, the decline in religious practice, and the redefinition of the roles and expectations of spouses (Turcotte and Bélanger, 1997).

| Figure 15.1 | Proportion of Common-Law Families Grows While It Declines for Married Families, Canada |

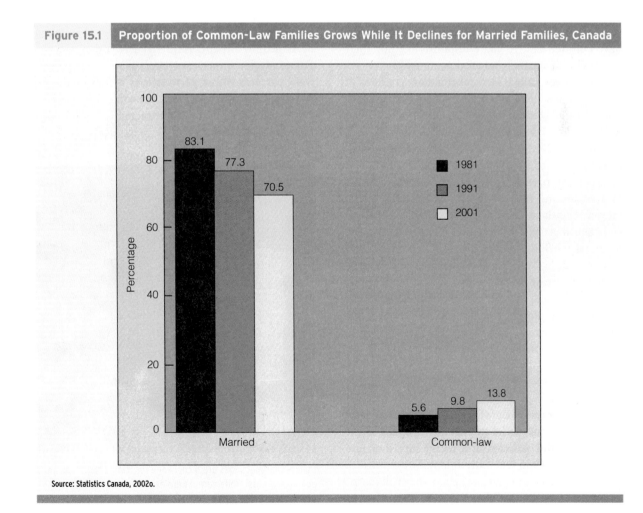

Source: Statistics Canada, 2002o.

Those most likely to cohabit are young adults between the ages of 25 and 29. Based on the Statistics Canada census data, one out of every six Canadians in this age group lives in a common-law union (Statistics Canada, 2002e). Cohabitation is even more common among Canadian university and college students, an estimated 25 percent of whom report having cohabited at some time. While "living together" is often a prelude to marriage for young adults, common-law unions are also becoming a popular alternative both to marriage and to remarriage following divorce or separation (Stout, 1994; Dumas, 1997; Statistics Canada, 2002e).

For couples who plan to get married eventually, cohabitation usually follows the *two-stage marriage* pattern set out by anthropologist Margaret Mead, who argued that dating patterns in North America are not adequate preparation for marriage and parenting responsibilities. Instead, Mead suggested that marriage should occur in two stages, each with its own ceremony and responsibilities. In the first stage, the *individual marriage,* two people would make a serious commitment to each other but agree not to have children during this stage. In the second stage, the *parental marriage,* the couple would decide to have children and to share responsibility for their upbringing (Lamanna and Riedmann, 2003).

Today, some people view cohabitation as a form of "trial marriage." For others, however, cohabitation is not a first step toward marriage. Some people who have cohabited do eventually marry the person with whom they have been living, whereas others do not. A recent study of 11,000 women found that there was a 70-percent marriage rate for women who remained in a cohabiting relationship for at least five years. However, of the women in that study who cohabited and then married their partner, 40 percent became divorced within a ten-year period (Bramlett and Mosher, 2001). Whether these findings will be supported by subsequent research remains to be seen. But we do know that studies over the past decade have supported the proposition that couples who cohabit before marriage do not necessarily have a stable relationship following marriage (Ambert, 2005b).

Marriage

Despite the prevalence of divorce in our society, marriage continues to be an extremely popular institution. This was reflected in a recent survey of just over 2,000 respondents interviewed nationwide. Ninety percent of respondents believe they will marry for life, and only three in ten indicated that it was possible that their marriages could fail (Bibby, 2004). Are these unrealistic expectations? Not at all. Despite debates regarding the demise of the institution of marriage, the fact remains that the majority of Canadians will marry at some point in their lives. Furthermore, although marriages today experience many problems, for better or worse the majority of marriages in Canada do last a lifetime (Vanier Institute of the Family, 1998).

Why do people get married? Couples get married for a variety of reasons. Some do so because they are "in love," desire companionship and sex, want to have children, feel social pressure, are attempting to escape from a bad situation in their parents' home, or believe that they will have more money or other resources if they get married. These factors notwithstanding, the selection of a marital partner actually is fairly predictable. Most people in Canada tend to choose marriage partners who are similar to themselves. **Homogamy refers to the pattern of individuals marrying those who have similar characteristics, such as race/ethnicity, religious background, age, education, or social class.** However, homogamy provides only the general framework within which people select their partners; people are also influenced by other factors. For example, some researchers claim that people want partners whose personalities match their own in significant ways. As a result, people who are outgoing and friendly may be attracted to people with

Dual-earner marriages are a challenge for many children as well as their parents. While parents are at work, latchkey children often are at home alone.

those same traits. However, other researchers claim that people look for partners whose personality traits differ from but complement their own.

Regardless of the individual traits of marriage partners, research indicates that communication and emotional support are crucial to the success of marriages. Common marital problems include lack of emotional intimacy, poor communication, and lack of companionship. One study concluded that for many middle- and upper-income couples, women's paid work was critical to the success of their marriages. People who have a strong commitment to their work have two distinct sources of pleasure—work and family. For members of the working class, however, work may not be a source of pleasure. For all women and men, balancing work and family life is a challenge (Daly, 2000).

Housework and Child Care Responsibilities

Thirty years ago, most Canadian families relied on one wage-earner. Today, approximately 70 percent of all families in Canada are *dual-earner families—***families in which both partners are in the labour force.** More than half of all employed women hold full-time, year-round jobs. Even when their children are very young, most working mothers work full-time. Moreover, as discussed in Chapter 11, many married women leave their paid employment at the end of the day and go home to perform hours of housework and child care. Difficulty in balancing work and family is the defining feature of family life today. Parents must make difficult decisions—decisions often driven by economic necessity—between the amount of time they spend at work and the amount of time they can be at home with their children (Daly, 2000). Sociologist Arlie Hochschild (1989, 2003) refers to this as the *second shift—***the domestic work that employed women perform at home after they complete their workday on the job.** Thus, many women today contribute to the economic well-being of their families and also meet many, if not all, of the domestic needs of family members by cooking, cleaning, shopping, taking care of children, and managing household routines. According to Hochschild, the unpaid housework women do on the second shift amounts to an extra month of work each year. Furthermore, women assume more responsibility for housework as the number of children in the family increases. This pattern is consistent regardless of whether the woman is employed full-time or part-time (Statistics Canada,

2003c). Across race, class, and culture, numerous studies have confirmed that domestic work remains primarily women's work (Canadian Council on Social Development, 1996). Hochschild states that continuing problems regarding the second shift in many families are a sign that the gender revolution has stalled:

> The move of masses of women into the paid workforce has constituted a revolution. But the slower shift in ideas of "manhood," the resistance of sharing work at home, the rigid schedules at work make for a "stall" in this gender revolution. It is a stall in the change of institutional arrangement of which men are the principal keepers. (2003:28)

As Hochschild points out, the second shift remains a problem for many women in dual-earner marriages.

In recent years, more husbands have attempted to share some of the household and child care responsibilities, especially in families in which the wife's earnings are essential to family finances. In contrast, husbands who see themselves as the primary breadwinners are less likely to share housework with their wives. Even when husbands share some of the household responsibilities, however, they typically spend much less time at these activities than do their wives (Statistics Canada, 2003c). Women and men perform different household tasks, and the deadlines for

Juggling housework, child care, and a job in the paid workforce are all part of the average day for many women. Why does sociologist Arlie Hochschild believe that many women work a "second shift"?

their work vary widely. Recurring tasks that have specific times for completion (such as bathing the child or cooking a meal) tend to be the woman's responsibility, whereas men are more likely to do the periodic tasks that have no highly structured schedule (such as mowing the lawn or changing the oil in the car) (Hochschild, 1997; Daly, 2000). Many men are also more reluctant to perform undesirable tasks, such as scrubbing the toilet or diapering a baby, or to give up leisure pursuits in order to contribute more time to household tasks.

Couples with more egalitarian ideas about women's and men's roles tend to share more equally in food preparation, housework, and child care (Wright et al., 1992). For some men, the shift to a more egalitarian household occurs gradually, as Wesley, whose wife works full-time, explains:

> It was me taking the initiative, and also Connie pushing, saying "Gee, there's so much that has to be done." At first I said, "But I'm supposed to be the breadwinner," not realizing she's also the breadwinner. I was being a little blind to what was going on, but I got tired of waiting for my wife to come home to start cooking, so one day I surprised the hell out [of] her and myself and the kids, and I had supper waiting on the table for her. (quoted in Gerson, 1993:170)

Women employed full-time who are single parents probably have the greatest burden of all; they have complete responsibility for the children and the household, often with little or no help from ex-husbands or relatives.

In Canada, millions of parents rely on child care so that they can work and so that their young children can benefit from early educational experiences that will help in their future school endeavours. For millions more parents, after-school care for school-age children is an urgent concern. The children need productive and safe activities to engage in while their parents are working (Friendly et al., 2002). Although child care is often unavailable or unaffordable for many parents, those children who are in day care for extended hours often come to think of child-care workers and other caregivers as members of their extended families because they may spend nearly as many hours with them as they do with their own parents. For children of divorced parents and other young people living in single-parent households, the issue of child care is often a pressing concern because of the limited number of available adults and lack of financial resources.

CHILD-RELATED FAMILY ISSUES AND PARENTING

Not all couples become parents. Those who decide not to have children often consider themselves to be "child-free," whereas those who do not produce children through no choice of their own may consider themselves "childless."

Deciding to Have Children

Cultural attitudes about having children and about the ideal family size began to change in North America in the late 1950s. On average, women are now having 1.5 children. However, rates of fertility differ across racial and ethnic categories. For example, Aboriginal women have a total fertility rate of 2.9 (Canadian Criminal Justice Association, 2005).

Advances in birth control techniques over the past four decades—including the birth control pill and contraceptive patches and shots—now make it possible for people to decide whether or not they want to have children and how many they wish to have, and to determine (at least somewhat) the spacing of their births. However, sociologists suggest that fertility is linked not only to reproductive technologies but also to women's beliefs that they do or do not have other opportunities in society that are viable alternatives to childbearing (Lamanna and Riedmann, 2003).

Today, the concept of reproductive freedom includes both the desire *to have* or *not to have* one or more children. According to sociologists Leslie King and Madonna Harrington Meyer (1997), many North American women spend up to half of their lives attempting to control their reproductivity. Other analysts have found that women, more often than men, are the first to choose a child-free lifestyle (Seccombe, 1991). However, the desire not to have children often comes in conflict with our society's *pronatalist bias,* which assumes that having children is the norm and can be taken for granted, whereas those who choose not to have children believe they must justify their decision to others (Lamanna and Riedmann, 2003).

However, some couples experience involuntary infertility, whereby they want to have a child but they are physically unable to do so. **Infertility is defined as an inability to conceive after one year of unprotected sexual relations.** Infertility has become increasingly common in recent years.

Research suggests that fertility problems originate in females in approximately 30 to 40 percent of cases and with males in about 40 percent of cases; in the other approximately 20 percent of the cases, the cause is unknown (Gabriel, 1996). A leading cause of infertility is sexually transmitted diseases, especially those cases that develop into pelvic inflammatory disease (Gold and Richards, 1994). It is estimated that about half of infertile couples who seek treatments, such as fertility drugs, artificial insemination, and surgery to unblock fallopian tubes can be helped; however, some are unable to conceive despite expensive treatments such as in vitro fertilization, which costs as much as $11,000 per attempt (Gabriel, 1996).

According to sociologist Charlene Miall (1986), women who are involuntarily childless engage in "information management" to combat the social stigma associated with childlessness. Their tactics range from avoiding people who make them uncomfortable to revealing their infertility so that others will not think of them as "selfish" for being childless. People who are involuntarily childless may choose to become parents by adopting a child.

Adoption

Adoption is a legal process through which the rights and duties of parenting are transferred from a child's biological and/or legal parents to new legal parents. This procedure gives the adopted child all of the rights of a biological child. In most adoptions, a new birth certificate is issued, and the child has no future contact with the biological parents. In Canada, adoption is regulated provincially. Therefore, adopted persons' access to information regarding their "biological parents" varies, as does their desire to access this information (Jackson, 1993).

Matching children who are available for adoption with prospective adoptive parents can be difficult. The available children have specific needs, and the prospective parents often set specifications on the type of child they want to adopt. Although thousands of children are available for adoption each year in North America, many prospective parents seek out children in developing nations, such as Romania, South Korea, and India. The primary reason is that the available children in Canada are thought to be "unsuitable." They may have disabilities or illnesses, or their undesirability may be due to their being non-white (most prospective parents are white) or too old (Zelizer, 1985). In addition, fewer infants are available for adoption today than in the past because better means of contraception exist, abortion is more

readily available, and more single parents decide to keep their babies. Consequently, the demand for adoptive children is growing, while the supply of children available for adoption is shrinking. In Canada, there are three applicants for each public adoption and almost as many for private adoptions. Today, international adoptions are increasing in number. Canadian parents are now often raising children from races and cultural origins different from their own (Vanier Institute of the Family, 2000).

New Reproductive Technologies

The availability of a variety of reproductive technologies is having a dramatic impact on traditional concepts of the family and parenthood. Since the first "test tube" baby was born in 1978, there has been an explosion of research, clinical practice, and experimentation in the area of reproductive technology. Procedures used in the creation of new life, such as artificial insemination and in vitro fertilization, are referred to as methods of assisted reproduction (Achilles, 1996). These procedures, in particular, have raised some controversial ethical issues in terms of what role medical science should play in the creation of human life (Eichler, 1996).

Artificial insemination is the oldest, simplest, and most common type of assisted reproduction. The most common form of artificial insemination is *intrauterine insemination,* which involves a physician inserting sperm directly into the uterus near the time of ovulation. Inseminations may be performed with donor sperm.

There are several complex issues concerning the moral, legal, and social implications of intrauterine insemination with donor sperm. In most cases the woman is given no information about the donor and the donor is not told if a pregnancy has occurred. The result of this anonymity is that neither mother nor the individuals conceived through donor insemination will have access to information regarding the biological father. With the exception of Quebec and the Yukon, the laws in all provinces and territories do not provide legal protection for the participants in this procedure. In Quebec, a child born through intrauterine insemination is legally considered to be the child of the *social* father, that is, the father who reared the child; in the Yukon, donors are protected from possible action by offspring or donor sperm recipients (Achilles, 1996).

The term *test-tube baby* is often used incorrectly to describe babies conceived through *in vitro fertilization.* An actual test-tube baby would require conception, gestation, and birth to occur outside of a woman's body. To date, this technology has not been developed (Achilles, 1996). In vitro (Latin for "in glass") fertilization involves inducing ovulation, removing the egg(s) from a woman, fertilizing the egg(s) with the sperm in a petri dish, and then implanting the fertilized egg(s) (embryos) into the woman. Critics of in vitro fertilization have suggested that the success rate of this procedure is no better than the probability of an infertile couple's having a child without medical intervention.

Another alternative available to couples with fertility problems is the use of a surrogate, or substitute, mother to carry a child for them. There are two types of surrogacy. In *traditional surrogacy*, the surrogate is artificially inseminated with the father's sperm. In this case, the egg is the surrogate's. The child is biologically related to the surrogate and the father. This type of surrogacy is typically used in cases where the woman is infertile or when there is a risk of passing on a serious genetic disorder from mother to child. In the second type of surrogacy, *gestational surrogacy*, the sperm and the eggs from the infertile couple are transferred to the surrogate using an assisted reproductive technology (such as in vitro fertilization). With gestational surrogacy, the surrogate carries the child but is not biologically or genetically related to it. The genetic parents are the man and woman whose eggs and sperm were donated to the surrogate.

All of this may be very confusing. One of the many reasons we have so much difficulty with these new reproductive technologies is because they are just that—new. They are new to our society and also new to our concept of the family. In fact, we have yet to develop accurate terminology to incorporate all of these new alternatives. Consider the comments of sociologist Christine Overall:

> Thanks to reproductive technology, a baby could, potentially, have five different parents: its genetic mother and genetic father, who supply the ovum and the sperm; its carrying mother, who gestates the embryo produced by the union of the ovum and sperm; and finally, its social mother and father, the individuals who rear the child produced by the carrying mother. (Overall, 1991:473)

In light of all the assisted reproductive technologies available, what does the term "parent" mean? How many "parents" does the child have? Is "mother" an accurate term for the gestational surrogate mother? The practice of surrogate motherhood also raises important questions about the position of women in society and about women's relationships to men and to their offspring (Overall, 1991).

To date, there is no comprehensive federal or provincial legislation governing human reproductive technologies and related research in Canada. However, legislation has been drafted that proposed banning several reproductive technologies, such as surrogate motherhood. The proposed bill also prohibits sex selection for nonmedical reasons; buying and selling human eggs, sperm, and embryos; and attempts to create animal–human hybrids. The laws pertaining to surrogacy are still evolving and so far are inadequate in addressing the complexities of these new family relationships. The issues raised by legislation in this area are complex and emotional, not just scientific and technical, and also have legal, social, moral, and ethical implications. However, these new reproductive technologies have enabled some infertile couples to become parents. For them, the benefits far outweigh the costs.

Single-Parent Households

Single parenting is not a new phenomenon in Canada. However, one of the most significant changes in Canadian families is the dramatic increase in single-parent families. Today, there are more than 1 million single parents in Canada. The vast majority (over 80 percent) of them are headed by women (Statistics Canada, 2002d). In the past, most single-parent families were created when one parent died. Today, the major causes of single parenthood for women are divorce and separation. Demographers estimate that just over one-third of Canadian women and just under one-quarter of men will be single parents at some point in their lives (Desrosier and LeBourdais, 1999a, 1999b).

Even for a person with a stable income and a network of friends and family to help with child care, raising a child alone can be an emotional and financial burden. According to sociologists Sara McLanahan and Karen Booth (1991), children in mother-only families are more likely than children in two-parent families to have poor academic achievement, higher school absentee and dropout rates, higher early marriage and parenthood, higher divorce rates, and more drug and alcohol abuse. Does living in a one-parent family cause all of this? Certainly not! Many other factors—including poverty, discrimination, unsafe neighbourhoods, and high crime rates—contribute to these problems.

Lesbian mothers and gay fathers are counted in some studies as single parents; however, they often share parenting responsibilities with same-sex partners. Due to *homophobia*—**a hatred and fear of homosexuals and lesbians**—lesbian mothers and gay fathers are more likely to lose custody to a heterosexual parent in divorce cases (Arnup, 1995b; Epstein, 1996; Robinson et al., 1998). In any case, many lesbians and gay men in Canada and the United States are parents. Some became parents through previous heterosexual marriages, others are single lesbians or gay men who have adopted children on their own, and still others are gay couples who have adopted children. Very little research exists on gay fathers; what does exist tends to show that noncustodial gay fathers try to maintain good relationships with their children (Bozett, 1988).

Single fathers who do not have custody of their children may play a relatively limited role in the lives of those children. Others struggle to maintain a relationship with their children. Author Robert Mason Lee describes how important his relationship with his daughter is to him, despite the fact that he is separated from her as a result of divorce:

> A man's love affair with his daughter has more in common with his love for a woman than most would care to admit—although not sexual, it is physical, passionate, and true. She calls me up just to say her "kiss box" is empty. We spend long hours on the phone making smooching noises. We bring to each other our most intimate concerns, a fervent heart, absolute trust. I like nothing better than to watch her when she's sleeping. I indulge her shamelessly. (Mason Lee, 1998:A14)

While some single fathers remain actively involved in their children's lives, others may become less involved, spending time with their children around recreational activities and on special occasions. Sometimes this limited role is by choice, but more often it is caused by workplace demands on time and energy, the location of the ex-wife's residence, and the limitations placed on the visitation arrangements.

Currently, men head close to one-fifth of lone-parent families; among many of the men, a pattern of "involved fatherhood" has emerged (Gerson, 1993). For example, in a study of men who became single fathers because of their wives' deaths, desertion, or relinquishment of custody, sociologist Barbara Risman (1987) found that the men had very strong relationships with their children.

Remarriage

Remarriage has been described as "the triumph of hope over experience" (Spencer, 1993:223). Most people who divorce get remarried (Bibby, 2004), and most divorced people remarry others who have been divorced. For example, approximately one in five men and women who were legally married during the early 1990s had been married before (Statistics Canada, 1997a). Remarriage rates, however, vary by gender and age. At all ages, a greater proportion of men than women remarry, often relatively soon after their divorce (an estimated 76 percent of men and 64 percent of women will remarry) (Ambert, 2005b). Among women, the older a woman is at the time of divorce, the lower the likelihood of her remarrying. Women who have not graduated from high school and have young children tend to remarry relatively quickly; by contrast, women with a university degree and without children are less likely to remarry (Nett, 1993). Some of these remarriages involve children from a previous relationship, thus creating stepfamilies or *blended families,* which consist of a husband

In recent years, many more fathers and mothers alike have been confronting the unique challenges of single parenting.

and wife, children from previous marriages, and children (if any) from the new marriage. There were just over 500,000 stepfamilies in 2001, accounting for almost 12 percent of all couples with children (Statistics Canada, 2002c).

At least initially, levels of family stress in stepfamilies may be fairly high because of rivalry among the children and hostility directed toward stepparents or ex-spouses (Ambert, 2001). Issues surrounding custody and visitation can precipitate extensive psychological, economic, and legal stresses on new blended families. The following is a quote from a woman recalling the problems created by visiting stepchildren:

> His kids kept coming here because he didn't want to visit them at their place, of course, because he hated his ex-wife. We had six kids here at times and his are the rough type; after they'd gone, the whole house was a mess for us to clean and the fridge was empty and I had to pay. (Ambert, 2001:284)

Elizabeth Church (1996) explains that although stepfamilies may look like instant families they need to go through a complex process of negotiation, compromise, and redefinition of boundaries to become a family. It is estimated that the developmental process of becoming an integrated stepfamily takes approximately two to four years. A significant factor in this new family unit is that for some of its members the family is the third type of family structure they have been a part of (a nuclear never-divorced family, a single-parent family, and a stepfamily). As Church explains, part of becoming a stepfamily involves integrating often very different customs, rules, and family rituals. One of the stepfamilies in her study describes their new stepfamily Christmas:

> The first couple of years after we got married, we had two Christmas trees, one in the living room and one in the rec room. Once they [Angie's biological children and stepchildren] got older, I could say no to them, "It's really a big hassle," but the first couple of years, there was so much decoration and everybody wanted everything—my kids wanted this because we had always had it on our tree, and the other ones wanted that because they had it on their tree. (Church, 1996:95)

In spite of these problems, however, many blended families succeed. The family that results from divorce and remarriage typically is a complex binuclear family in which children may have a biological parent and a stepparent, biological siblings and stepsiblings, and an array of other relatives including aunts, uncles, and cousins (Church, 1996).

According to sociologist Andrew Cherlin (1992), the norms governing divorce and remarriage are ambiguous. Because there are no clear-cut guidelines, people must make decisions about family life (such as whom to invite to birthday celebrations or weddings) based on their own beliefs and feelings about the people involved.

TRANSITIONS AND PROBLEMS IN FAMILIES

Families go through many transitions and experience a wide variety of problems ranging from separation and divorce to unplanned pregnancy to family violence. These all-too-common experiences highlight two important facts about families: (1) for good or ill, families are central to our existence, and (2) the reality of family life is far more complicated than the idealized image found in the media and in many political discussions. Whereas some families provide their members with love, warmth, and satisfying emotional experiences, other families may be hazardous to the individual's physical and mental well-being. Because of this dichotomy in family life, sociologists have described families as both a "haven in a heartless world" (Lasch, 1977) and a "cradle of violence" (Gelles and Straus, 1988).

Family Violence

Violence between men and women in the home is often referred to as spouse abuse or domestic violence. *Spouse abuse* refers to the violence or mistreatment that a woman or man may experience at the hands of a marital, common-law, or same-sex partner. Forms of spousal abuse include physical abuse, sexual abuse, and economic/financial abuse (Department of Justice, 2002a). As discussed in Chapter 4, *child abuse* refers to physical or sexual abuse and/or neglect by a parent or caregiver.

How much do we know about violence in families? Violence against spouses and children is clearly an extreme form of family dysfunction. However, sociologists have difficulty studying family violence because it is often hidden from outsiders and not reported to law-enforcement authorities. This is particularly true in cases of child abuse, because the powerlessness of children in the family ensures that most incidents remain hidden (Rodgers and Kong, 1996). Statistics on the incidence of familial child abuse capture only those cases that come to the attention of official agencies. Data on the extent of spousal assault in Canada are more extensive and are based on police reports and findings from self-report studies, such as the 2005 General Social Survey on Victimization (GSS). Reports from these sources of information indicate that

- Three in ten women currently or previously married have experienced at least one incident of physical or sexual violence at the hands of a marital partner.
- In almost 40 percent of violent marriages, the children heard or saw assaults on a parent. In more than half of these cases, their mothers were physically injured.
- Women and men living in common-law relationships are much more likely to experience violence at the hands of their spouse than are legally married women.

Many experts suggest that the prevalence of family violence may be much higher than those figures, given that surveys, studies, and police reports can not possibly capture all incidents of violence and abuse. For example, research has shown that many abuse victims do not—or cannot—report their experiences to the police, although there are some signs that reporting is increasing (Department of Justice, 2002b).

Children who are raised in an environment of violence suffer profoundly, even if they are not the direct targets. Their own physical and emotional needs are often neglected and they may learn by example to deal with conflict through violence (Dauvergne and Johnson, 2001).

Only within the last few decades have various forms of family violence been defined as intolerable criminal offences. Historically, domestic abuse was seen as a private family matter. For centuries the law permitted the male head of the house to use force against his wife and children.

Why has our society been slow to respond to the problem of family violence, whether in the form of child abuse, spouse abuse, or both? Until recently, individuals and law enforcement officials have followed a policy of *nonintervention,* which was based on a strong reluctance to interfere in other people's family matters. Police reacted to calls for assistance with frustration or apathy, viewing responses to "domestic" calls as a waste of valuable time and resources. The general perception was that battered women could simply leave an abusive relationship if they wanted to.

Although public awareness of domestic violence has increased in recent years, society is far from finding an effective solution for this pressing social problem.

The women's movement was largely responsible for bringing the issue of wife abuse into the public and political arenas in the 1970s. During the same period, child sexual abuse was "discovered" and found to be much more extensive than ever imagined (Rodgers and Kong, 1996:116). This growing awareness led to the organization of shelters for victims of family violence and to changes in the criminal justice system's response to spousal assault and child abuse. The first step in providing protection against domestic violence occurred in the early 1980s, when police forces across Canada were given directives making it mandatory for them to lay charges where there are reasonable grounds to believe an assault has occurred. Before these policies were implemented, the onus was on the abused spouse to lay charges. Many victims of spousal abuse refused to have their spouses charged because they feared provoking them to further violence. In 1983, the sexual assault laws were changed so that men could be charged with sexually assaulting their wives. At the same time, the *Canada Evidence Act* was revised to permit wives to testify against their husbands (Johnson, 1996). Finally, in order to provide better protection to children, the legislation was enacted encompassing a range of sexual offences against children (Rodgers and Kong, 1996).

Despite legislative changes and efforts to change attitudes, violence continues to be a much-too-common occurrence in families. The research indicates that many incidents of child and spousal abuse remain hidden in the private domain of the family home. According to criminologist Holly Johnson

> Unlike crimes that occur outside the milieu of the family, victims are living with their assailants; they often have strong emotional, financial, and physical bonds; many share children; and very often they want the relationship to continue. All of these factors create complications for both victims and police officers called to the scene of the crime. (1996:215)

In short, there are no easy solutions to a problem as complex as family violence.

Although differences in power and privilege between women and men do not inevitably result in violence, gender-based inequalities can still produce sustained marital conflicts. In any case, a common consequence of marital strife and unhappiness is divorce.

Divorce

Divorce is the legal process of dissolving a marriage that allows former spouses to remarry if they so choose. Prior to 1968 it was difficult to obtain a divorce in Canada. A divorce was granted only on the grounds of adultery. In 1968, the grounds for divorce were expanded to include marital breakdown (i.e., desertion, imprisonment, or separation of three or more years) and marital offences (physical or mental cruelty). As shown in Figure 15.2, the divorce rate increased dramatically as a result of the wider grounds for divorce. In 1985, the *Divorce Act* introduced "no fault" provisions that made marital breakdown the sole ground for divorce. In addition, the waiting period for divorce on the grounds of marriage breakdown was reduced to one year. Once again the divorce rate jumped following the implementation of a shorter waiting period. The amendments resulted in a record 96,200 divorces in 1987. Under no-fault divorce laws, proof of "blameworthiness" is no longer necessary. However, when children are involved, the issue of "blame" may assume greater importance in the determination of parental custody.

Have you heard statements such as "One out of every two marriages ends in divorce"? Statistics might initially appear to bear out this statement. In 2002,

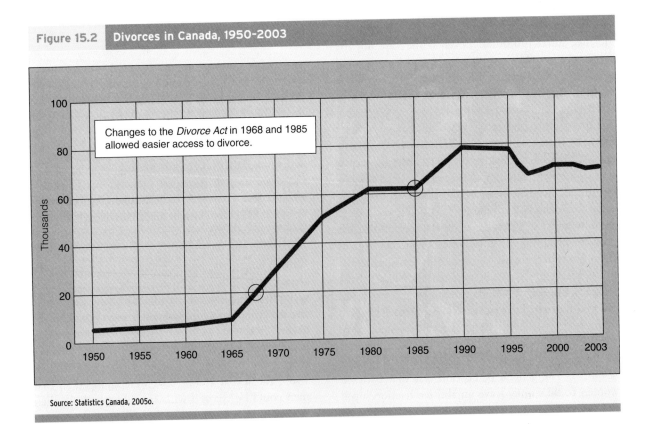

Figure 15.2   Divorces in Canada, 1950–2003

Changes to the *Divorce Act* in 1968 and 1985 allowed easier access to divorce.

Source: Statistics Canada, 2005o.

for example, 146,738 Canadian couples married and 70,155 divorces were granted (Statistics Canada, 2004g). However, comparing the number of marriages with the number of divorces from year to year can be misleading. The couples who are divorced in any given year are very unlikely to come from the group that married that year. In addition, in years when the economy is in a recession, people may delay getting married but not divorced (McVey and Kalbach, 1995). Some people also may go through several marriages and divorces, thus skewing the divorce rate. The likelihood of divorce goes up with each subsequent marriage in the serial monogamy pattern.

In order to accurately assess the probability of a marriage ending in divorce, it is necessary to use what is referred to as a *cohort approach*. This approach establishes probabilities based on assumptions about how the various age groups (cohorts) in society might behave, given their marriage rate, their age at first marriage, and their responses to various social, cultural, and economic changes. Canadian estimates based on a cohort approach are that 35 to 40 percent of marriages will end in divorce (Statistics Canada, 2000b).

Causes of Divorce   Why do divorces occur? As you will recall from Chapter 2, sociologists look for correlations (relationships between two variables) in attempting to answer questions such as this. Existing research has identified a number of factors at both the macro- and microlevel that make some couples more or less likely to divorce. At the macrolevel, societal factors contributing to higher rates of divorce include changes in social institutions, such as religion, the family, and the legal system. Some religions have taken a more lenient attitude toward divorce, and the social stigma associated with divorce has lessened. Further, as we have seen in this chapter, the family institution has undergone a major change that has resulted in less economic and emotional dependency among family members—and thus reduced a barrier to divorce. And, as Figure 15.2 demonstrates, the liberalization of divorce laws in Canada has had a dramatic impact on the divorce rate.

At the microlevel, a number of factors contribute to a couple's "statistical" likelihood of becoming divorced. Some of the primary risk factors for divorce include (Ambert, 2005b)

- youthful marriage
- low incomes and poverty as well as rapid upward social mobility
- cohabitation prior to marriage
- remarriage

- parents who are divorced or have unhappy marriages
- low religiosity
- the presence of children (depending on their gender and age at the beginning of the marriage)

The interrelationship of these and other factors is complicated. For example, the effect of age is intertwined with economic resources; persons from families at the low end of the income scale tend to marry earlier than those at more affluent income levels. Thus, the question becomes whether age itself is a factor or whether economic resources are more closely associated with divorce.

Consequences of Divorce   Divorce may have a dramatic economic and emotional impact on family members. Few children want their parents to divorce, no matter how unhappy the marriage is. Divorce for children results in the most significant changes they have experienced in their lifetimes—new relationships with each parent, often new residences, changing schedules to accommodate visitation privileges, and, in some cases, a new parental figure. Author Robert Mason Lee describes his daughter's reaction to her parents' divorce:

> The adult world of falling in and out of love, of emotions blowing fire and ice, of uncoupling and recoupling, is unknown to her. For some years it was fun to have two houses, two families, two Santas. But now she wishes that all her houses would be united. (Mason Lee, 1998:A14)

The exact number of children affected by divorce in Canada is difficult to determine because no official information is available on out-of-court custody decisions. In 2000, approximately 40,000 Canadian children were involved in custody disputes. In just over 50 percent of those cases, the mother was awarded custody (Statistics Canada, 2002i). Parental joint custody is also an option for some divorcing couples. When joint custody is a voluntary arrangement and when there is motivation to make it work, it has benefits for both children and parents (Ambert, 2005a). Joint custody allows the children to maintain regular contact with both parents, which can ease the adjustment to the marriage breakup and give parents more time to adjust to their new lives. However, this arrangement may also create unique problems for children. Siblings—six-year-old Kimberley, eight-year-old Ann Marie, and eleven-year-old Philippe talk about the impact of divorce on their lives:

Kimberley: I remember Daddy used to tuck me in at night and I remember I was still waiting and he didn't because that was when he first divorced.

Ann Marie: Now we are living far from Daddy and we only get to see him a little bit of time.

Philippe: The divorce is bad because I don't always like to go from one to the other and back again. I like being with both at the same time. It gets complicated. (quoted in Doyle Driedger, 1998:41)

For most children, divorce is a difficult experience. In fact, Rhonda Freeman, director of *Families in Transition,* a Toronto divorce support service, comments, "In 25 years, I have yet to meet a child who has no effects" (quoted in Doyle Driedger, 1998:40). Today, more than one-third of all divorced mothers have below-poverty-level incomes. As discussed in previous chapters, divorce is one of the major factors contributing to the feminization of poverty, because many divorced mothers attempt to support themselves and their children on low-wage jobs and whatever child support, if any, they get from their ex-husbands (Ambert, 2005a).

Divorce changes relationships not only for the couple involved but also for other relatives. In some divorces, grandparents feel that they are the big losers. To see their grandchildren, the grandparents have to keep in touch with the parent who has custody. In-laws are less likely to be welcome and may be seen as being on the "other side" simply because they are the parents of the ex-spouse. Recently, some grandparents have sued for custody of minor grandchildren. They generally have not been successful except in cases where questions existed about the emotional stability of the biological parents or the suitability of a foster care arrangement.

The consequences of divorce are not entirely negative. There is no doubt that some children are better off after their parents divorce. Sociologist Susan McDaniel emphasizes that "Many are relieved that they no longer live in abusive families, with fear and violence and squabbling" (quoted in Doyle Driedger, 1998:40). For some people, divorce may be an opportunity to terminate destructive relationships. For others, it may represent a means to achieve personal growth by enabling them to manage their lives and social relationships and establish their own identity. Consider the comments of this separated, single mother of two:

It was amazing once I got my affairs in order and got my apartment. It was like the clouds parted and the sun came out. It was so amazing. I think it was the best thing that I ever did for myself. Through that whole marriage I don't think I had

this much self-esteem. Everybody says, Oh, it's a tragedy. It's not a tragedy. It's a growing thing. It probably could have happened sooner. I'm glad it didn't happen later. I probably would have been a wreck. (quoted in Lynn, 1996:56)

Elizabeth Church (1996) suggests that, given the divorce rate in Canada, divorce should no longer be viewed as a deviant act, but should, rather, be considered a normal part of many people's lives. She stresses that viewing divorce in this way does not deny that divorce and remarriage cause significant upheaval. Both divorce and remarriage are generally very painful and difficult events for some members of the family (Church, 1996).

■ DIVERSITY IN FAMILIES

Gay and Lesbian Families

Lesbians and gay men grow up in families, establish long-lasting, committed, emotional relationships, and sometimes become parents. Nevertheless, until recently, discussions of gay and lesbian relationships and families have been excluded from discussions of the family. In fact, these relationships were considered by many as threatening to notions of the traditional family. Lesbians and gay men were viewed as existing entirely outside families, and many people felt that recognition of gay and lesbian relationships would result in the demise of "the family." Notions of the family that are limited to unions between members of the opposite sex are examples of *heterosexism*—**an attitude in which heterosexuality is considered the only valid form of sexual behaviour, and gay men, lesbians, and bisexuals are considered inferior to heterosexual people.**

In Canada, the law grants particular rights, benefits, and privileges only to heterosexual relationships, especially legally married partners. Until recently, gay and lesbian couples have been prohibited from sponsoring their partner's immigration to Canada, obtaining custody of their children, jointly adopting children, or receiving spousal benefits and survivors' pensions. Until July 2005, same-sex couples were prohibited from legally marrying. This lack of recognition has had emotional, legal, and economic consequences for same-sex families (O'Brien and Weir, 1995). The issue of same-sex marriages has become a hotly debated and divisive issue for the Canadian public (see Box 15.4).

Adoption is a complex legal process for most parents; it can be even more complicated for gay and lesbian couples.

In contrast to stereotypes of same-sex relationships as short-term, promiscuous, and noncommittal, research on homosexual relationships indicates that partnerships lasting twenty years or more are not uncommon (Ambert, 2005a). In fact, the breakup rates of married or cohabiting heterosexual couples and lesbian and gay couples have been found to be approximately equal. However, studies have found that lesbian and gay relationships are more egalitarian than heterosexual relationships. This finding is in part attributable to the fact that in virtually all lesbian and gay relationships both partners are wage earners (Ambert, 2005a).

An increasing number of lesbians and gay males form families with children. The 2001 census was the first to collect data on same-sex partnerships. A total of 34,200 couples identified themselves as same-sex common-law couples. Of these, 15 percent of female same-sex couples were living with children, compared to 3 percent of male couples (Statistics Canada, 2002o). In many cases, lesbian mothers and gay fathers may have children from a previous marriage or relationship. However, not all children in same-sex families are products of previous heterosexual relationships. Lesbians may become pregnant through *alternative insemination* (sexual relations as a means of getting pregnant or artificial insemination) (Epstein, 2003). Lesbian mothers and gay fathers may also form families through fostering or adoption. Unlike many heterosexual families in which both mother and father have genetic links to their children, gay and lesbian families always have a nonbiological parent. These nonbiological parents are often not regarded as parents either socially or legally. For example,

nonbiological parents may not be granted admission to parent–teacher interviews, or may be denied permission to make important medical decisions for their children if the biological parent is unavailable. Anne, a lesbian mother, describes one of her encounters with the medical profession:

> You can tell the doctor three times, "Talk to me like I'm his mother; so is she," and they don't get it. Sometimes they really say, "I don't know what you're talking about." [And we'll answer,] "We're two lesbians, we're both the mother." "Huh. No, I'll talk to the one with the dress, that's safe." (quoted in Epstein, 1996:123)

Many people believe that being parented by same-sex couples is emotionally unhealthy for children and can cause them confusion about their own sexuality. However, the research has shown that the children of lesbians and gay men are as well adjusted as children who grow up in heterosexual households. In addition, these children experience no psychological damage, and they are no more likely to be homosexual than are children raised by heterosexual parents (Ambert, 2005a). According to Rachel Epstein (2003), there can be positive effects of being raised by lesbian or gay parents, such as a greater appreciation of diversity and increased tolerance, since the child is taught to accept social differences in others.

Increasingly, younger lesbians and gay males are acknowledging their homosexuality and seeking acceptance from parents and other relatives. The reactions of family members range from support and acceptance to anger, denial, and rejection. These negative responses have led some researchers to conclude that families can be hazardous to the

BOX 15.4 CRITICAL THINKING

Lesbian and Gay Marriages: The State of the Union

On June 10, 2003, the Ontario Court of Appeal ruled that Canada's legal definition of marriage is unconstitutional and redefined it as "the voluntary union for life of two persons to the exclusion of all others." In her ruling, the judge further explained that "the existing common law rule is inconsistent with the constitutional values in modern Canadian society and offends the equality rights of gays and lesbians" (Kome, 2002:1).

In response to this ruling, Prime Minister Jean Chretien announced that the federal government would rewrite the legal definition of marriage to recognize same-sex marriages. At the same time, Chretien promised to protect freedom of religion by allowing officials of religious groups to refuse to conduct ceremonies if they conflict with their religious beliefs. This change in legislation effectively means the legalization of same-sex marriage across the country. Canada is the fourth country in the world to sanction gay and lesbian marriages (Ambert, 2003).

This change in law is the result of decades of lobbying by women's groups, such as the Women's Legal Education and Action Fund and the National Association of Women and the Law, who built case law that resulted in a broader definition of equality. Several high-profile court challenges preceded the 2003 decision. For example, in 1995 joint custody was awarded in three Ontario cases where lesbians were co-parents. In these cases, the courts ruled that forbidding adoptions by same-sex couples was a violation of their *Charter* rights (Ward, 1998). In the same year, the Supreme Court of Canada ruled that sexual orientation must be included as a prohibited ground for discrimination under all Canadian human rights acts. In 1998, a B.C. court ruled that both biological and nonbiological parents in same-sex families have the same parental rights. In 2000, the Supreme Court conferred common-law status on cohabiting same-sex couples. In other words, gay and lesbian couples were considered spouses in law. If same-sex couples already had the same legal rights as heterosexual common-law couples, then, why the need for marriage? The answer, according to the couples who launched the court challenges in Ontario, B.C., and Quebec, is that they wanted full equality with heterosexual couples. This includes the right to legally marry. As one appellant explains:

> Instead of being recognized as an equal family, we are considered to have an "alternative lifestyle." We are not very alternative. We are very ordinary. We'd like to be married because it's the ordinary thing to do with the feelings and commitments we share. (Kome, 2002:1)

Do you agree with this woman's comments? Not since the abortion issue was debated in the 1980s has any issue been so hotly debated in the public forum. Both our legal and our social definitions of family, marriage, and parenthood are socially constructed. Currently, the Canadian public is struggling to redefine these concepts. A consensus, however, remains elusive. A recent survey found that 53 percent of respondents are in favour of gay and lesbian couples marrying; 40 percent were opposed (Department of Justice, 2002d:6). As these results show, a significant number of Canadians are still opposed to same-sex marriage and same-sex family formation. Even for those who support same-sex marriages there remain many questions and concerns. Some of the concerns are related to the quality of homosexual unions—for example, are they as long-lasting and committed? Many are concerned about the ability of lesbians and gay men to parent and the effect that living in same-sex families may have on their children. Others argue that allowing same-sex couples to marry will devalue the institution of marriage (Ambert, 2003:2). What do you think? What other questions and concerns are you aware of?

Note: Sociology of the family expert Anne-Marie Ambert has written a comprehensive article on this topic that is available at http://www.vifamily.ca/library/cft/samesex_05.html.

emotional and physical well-being of gay and lesbian youth. This hazard is reflected in the alarmingly high suicide rates for gay adolescents. Many families will continue to deny their child's sexual orientation years after they have come out. One lesbian woman describes how her partner's family describes her:

> Her family didn't acknowledge our relationship. I would always be introduced as Chris's friend, or *our* friend even, but nothing real. But you understand that, you live with that. It became more of a personal issue when there was a kid there and I got referred to as the aunt or the live-in nanny. It would be sort of a joke, just to deal with her [mother's] own discomfort, I expect. (Epstein, 1996:122)

An encouraging sign of change is the growing number of parents who are accepting their child's sexual orientation. Canadian organizations, such as Parents and Friends of Lesbians and Gays, work to educate parents about homosexuality and assist gay youth in maintaining positive relationships with their families (O'Brien and Weir, 1995).

Diversity Among Singles

While marriage at increasingly younger ages was the trend in Canada during the first half of the twentieth century, by the 1960s the trend had reversed, and many more adults were remaining single. In 1971, close to half of Canadians aged twenty to twenty-four were already married. In 2001, almost 90 percent of Canadians aged twenty to twenty-four were single (Statistics Canada, 2002e). Currently, approximately 25 percent of households in Canada are one- or single-person households. However, this estimate includes people who are divorced, widowed, and those who have never married. Given the fact that nine out of ten Canadians marry at some time in their lives, single status is often temporary. Only an estimated 10 percent of the population will remain single throughout their lives (Nett, 1993).

Some never-married singles remain single by choice. Reasons include more opportunity for a career (especially for women), the availability of sexual partners without marriage, the belief that the single lifestyle is full of excitement, and the desire for self-sufficiency and freedom to change and experiment (Stein, 1976, 1981). Some scholars have concluded that individuals who prefer to remain single hold more individualistic values and are less

Secondary-school systems are being pressured to address issues of family diversity in the classroom. In Surrey, British Columbia, in 2002, a battle was fought over the censorship of books about same-sex families.

family-oriented than those who choose to marry. Friends and personal growth tend to be valued more highly than marriage and children (Alwin, Converse, and Martin, 1985; Nett, 1993).

Other never-married singles remain single out of necessity. For some people, being single is an economic necessity: they simply cannot afford to marry and set up their own household. Structural changes in the economy have limited the options of many working-class young people. Even some university and college graduates have found that they cannot earn enough money to set up a household separate from that of their parents. Consequently, a growing proportion of young adults are living with one or both parents (Boyd and Norris, 1999).

Aboriginal Families

It is difficult to discuss Aboriginal families given the fact that Aboriginal peoples in Canada are by no means a homogeneous group. Aboriginal peoples are composed of many distinct nations with different histories, cultures, economic bases, and languages (Das Gupta, 1995). However, in all Aboriginal families the extended family was seen as central to both the individual and the community. The concept of family was defined very broadly. For example, to the Ojibwa, *family* referred to individuals who worked together and were bound together by responsibility and friendship as well as kinship ties. Family size averaged between twenty and twenty-five persons (Shkilnyk, 1985). A bandmember describes the economic cooperation and sharing that once existed within the Ojibwa family:

> Trapping kept the family together because everyone in the family had something to do; the man had to lay traps and check them; the woman skinned the animals, cooked, and looked after the kids. The grandparents helped with the kids; they taught them manners, how to behave, and told them stories about our people. The kids, if they were old enough, had work to do. (Shkilnyk, 1985:81)

Under this cooperative family system, Aboriginal families were extremely successful in ensuring the survival and well-being of their members.

Four hundred years after contact with the European settlers, the current state of family disruption is evident when you consider the following data. The proportion of Aboriginal children who are removed from their homes as a result of parental abuse or neglect is ten times that of non-Aboriginal children; the proportion of Aboriginal children who commit suicide is seven times the rate of non-Aboriginal children; wife abuse among Aboriginal peoples is said to be at least seven times the national average; and mass disclosures of previously hidden sexual and physical abuse of Aboriginal children are being made (Timpson, 1995:9).

How did this happen? Sociologist Tania Das Gupta (1995) explains that the destruction of the traditional Aboriginal family was the result of interventionist strategies employed by the Canadian church and state. Families were displaced from their traditional lands, moved to reserves, and denied access to the resources that were central to the economic survival of the extended family unit. Aboriginal children were removed from their families and placed in residential schools (where they were often sexually and physically abused) or adopted by non-Aboriginal families. Generations of Aboriginal children were separated from their families and their communities, and this separation also served to sever links with Aboriginal culture and languages.

After generations of cultural and spiritual destruction, Aboriginal peoples are now reclaiming their culture. They have also united behind the goal of self-government, especially in the areas of social services and child welfare (Das Gupta, 1995). Aboriginal peoples believe in maintaining the ties between children and their natural parents, as well as caring for children within their Aboriginal communities. This they see as essential to the rebuilding of Aboriginal families in Canada. Many Aboriginal communities are striving to return to the practices and values that traditionally nourished Aboriginal family life: respect for women and children, mutual responsibility, and, above all, the general creed of sharing and caring (Royal Commission of Aboriginal Peoples, 1995:81).

FAMILY ISSUES IN THE FUTURE

As we have seen, families and intimate relationships have changed dramatically over the last century. Some people believe the family as we know it is doomed. Others believe that a return to traditional values will save this important social institution and create greater stability in society. Family diversity is perceived by some as an indication that Canadian families are in "decline" or "crisis." However, as sociologist Ellen Gee reminds us, "Family diversity is the norm in Canadian society, past and present. Only for a short period in history . . . did Canadian families approach uniformity, centered around near-universal marriage and parenthood, family 'intactness' and highly differentiated gender roles" (1995:80). The diversity in Canadian families has simply taken on new forms, with increases in common-law unions, gay and lesbian families, and single-parent and blended families.

One of the most notable changes in the past fifty years has been the increase in dual-wage-earner families. The labour force participation rate of women, particularly married women, has increased dramatically. However, regardless of women's labour force participation, women are still primarily responsible for child care and domestic chores (Canadian Council on Social Development, 1996).

The absence of adequate affordable child care and inflexible work hours and parental leave policies means that work is structured in ways that are not "user friendly" for family life (Gee, 1995:102). A challenge for families in the future is to find ways to reconcile family and work contradictions. As gender roles continue to change, we can expect to see a greater degree of egalitarianism within the family.

Despite the fact that most Canadian families are made up of two wage earners, many families are still unable to make ends meet. The result is that close to one million Canadian children live in families with incomes below the poverty line. Children living with a single-parent mother are the hardest hit—they are five times more likely to live in poverty than those living with two parents. Given that, Canada has the second highest rate of child poverty among industrialized countries. The situation of poor families is unlikely to change in the near future without significant changes in government support and tax incentives for families with children.

One of the most disturbing issues concerning the family, and one that will continue to affect the quality and stability of family relationships in the future, is family violence. The latter part of the twentieth century has been marked by the "discovery" of the dark side of the family—child abuse (including physical, sexual, and emotional abuse), wife abuse, and elder abuse. Armed with the knowledge that the family is not immune to this violence, the challenge of this new century is to find effective strategies to reduce the incidence of family violence.

The final issue to consider is the impact of new reproductive technologies on families. As Margrit Eichler comments, "There is probably no other recent social development which has a potentially more far-reaching impact on the very nature of the family, on our understandings as to what it means to be a parent, and on the rights and obligations attached to this status" (1988a:280). New reproductive technologies have the capacity to revolutionize family life. Whether or not people will choose to take advantage of the possibilities, and whether or not governments will allow certain services to be delivered, remains to be seen (Baker, 2005).

Regardless of problems facing families in this century, the family remains the central institution in the lives of most Canadians. A recent national opinion poll found that more than three-quarters of Canadians regard the family as the most important thing in their lives—more important than their career or religion. Ninety-two percent of the respondents with young children at home indicated that the family is becoming *more* important to them. Finally, an overwhelming majority demonstrated their faith in the family by indicating that they want to marry and have children (although fewer children) (Bibby, 2004). Individuals in families are now freer to establish the kinds of family arrangements that best suit them.

CHAPTER REVIEW

■ What is a family?

Families may be defined as relationships in which people live together with commitment, form an economic unit and care for any young, and consider their identity to be significantly attached to the group.

■ What pattern of marriage is legally sanctioned in Canada?

Monogamy is a marriage to one person at a time. In Canada, monogamy is the only form of marriage sanctioned by law.

■ What are the functionalist, conflict, feminist, symbolic interactionist, and postmodern perspectives on families?

Functionalists emphasize the importance of the family in maintaining the stability of society and the well-being of the individuals. Functions of the family include sexual regulation, socialization, economic and psychological support, and provision of social status. Conflict and feminist perspectives view the family as a source of social inequality and an arena for conflict over values, goals, and access to resources and power.

Symbolic interactionists explain family relationships in terms of the subjective meanings and everyday interpretations people give to their lives. Postmodern analysts view families as permeable, reflecting the individualism, particularity, and irregularity of social life in the Information Age.

■ How are Canadian families changing?

Families are changing dramatically in Canada. Cohabitation has increased significantly in the past two decades. With the increase in dual-earner marriages, women increasingly have been burdened by the "second shift"—the domestic work that employed women perform at home after they complete their workday on the job. The number of single-parent families has also increased dramatically in recent decades.

■ What is divorce, and what are some of its causes?

Divorce is the legal process of dissolving a marriage. At the macrolevel, changes in social institutions may contribute to an increase in divorce rates; at the microlevel, factors contributing to divorce include age at marriage, economic resources, religiosity, and parental marital happiness. Divorce has contributed to greater diversity in family relationships, including stepfamilies or blended families and the complex binuclear family.

KEY TERMS

bilateral descent 467
cohabitation 477
dual-earner families 479
egalitarian family 468
extended family 465
families 463
families we choose 463
family of orientation 464
family of procreation 465
heterosexism 488
homogamy 478
homophobia 483
infertility 480
kinship 464
marriage 465
matriarchal family 467
matrilineal descent 467
monogamy 465
nuclear family 465
patriarchal family 467
patriarchy 471
patrilineal descent 467

polyandry 466
polygamy 465
polygyny 465
second shift 479
sociology of family 469

NET LINKS

The Vanier Institute of the Family provides the most comprehensive information on Canadian families; see:
http://www.vifamily.ca

PFLAG (Parents and Friends of Lesbians and Gays) is a national organization promoting the health and well-being of gay, lesbian, and bisexual persons and their families and friends; see:
http://www.pflagcanada.ca

For more information on family violence in Canada, and the programs and government strategies in place to address it, go to:
http://canada.justice.gc.ca/en/ps/fm/

QUESTIONS FOR CRITICAL THINKING

1. In your own thinking, what constitutes an ideal family? How might functionalist, conflict, feminist, symbolic interactionist, and postmodern perspectives describe the ideal family?

2. Suppose you wanted to find out about women's and men's perceptions about love and marriage. What specific issues might you examine? What would be the best way to conduct your research?

3. Based on your understanding of the term *family*, should the following be considered families? Why or why not?

   ■ man, women, no children; married but living apart

   ■ woman, woman, child of one woman; living together. Women are a same-sex couple.

   ■ man, his biological child and woman (not his wife) with whom he has a sexual relationship; living together

   ■ four adults; sharing household for many years. None are a same-sex couple.

4. Do you think reproductive technology should be allowed to help people pre-select the sex of a fetus? Why or why not? Do you think pre-selection of sex would have an impact on the number of children couples had? What effect might this have on the sex ratio in Canada and other countries?

5. Do you think it's beneficial to expose children to diverse family forms in elementary schools through the use of teaching tools such as *Asha's Mums* or *One Dad, Two Dad, Brown Dad, Blue Dad*?

SUGGESTED READINGS

These comprehensive textbooks offer in-depth information on families and intimate relationships:

Anne-Marie Ambert. *Families in the New Millennium.* Toronto: Allyn and Bacon, 2001.

Margrit Eichler. *Family Shifts: Families, Policies, and Gender Equality.* Don Mills, Ont.: Oxford University Press, 1997.

Marion Lynn. *Voices: Essays on Canadian Families.* 2nd ed. Scarborough Ont.: Nelson, 2003.

Nancy Mandell and Ann Duffy. *Canadian Families: Diversity, Conflict, and Change.* 3rd ed. Scarborough, Ont.: Nelson, 2005.

Margaret Ward. *The Family Dynamic: A Canadian Perspective.* 3rd ed. Toronto: Nelson, 2002.

ONLINE STUDY AND RESEARCH TOOLS

THOMSONNOW™ Thomson NOW!

Go to **http://hed.nelson.com** to link to ThomsonNOW for *Sociology in Our Times,* Fourth Canadian Edition, your online study tool. First take the **Pre-Test** for this chapter to get your personalized **Study Plan,** which will identify topics you need to review and direct you to the appropriate resources. Then take the **Post-Test** to determine what concepts you have mastered and what you still need work on.

INFOTRAC®

Infotrac College Edition is included free with every new copy of this text. Explore this online library for additional readings, review, and a handy resource for assignments. Visit **www.infotrac-college.com** to access this online database of full-text articles. Enter the key terms from this chapter to start your search.

Education

Consider the following comments from a parent of three university students:

"I picked up a university education on the weekend.

"I did it with a rented U-Haul trailer, enough room, almost, for the yearly needs of two first-year students at a small university a few hours from Ottawa.

"We took them down in September; it required two U-Hauls: one for their clothes, CDs, snowboards, skateboards, hockey equipment, birdfeeders, posters, computers, and—oh, yes—pen and paper in case they ever needed to take a few notes; and one trailer, of course, for the money to get them through a year of higher Canadian education.

"It is really quite simple. You remortgage the house, cash in your RRSPs, take back the beer bottles, fill up the U-Haul with hard cash, add a couple of shovels and tell the kids to fill up the first black hole when they reach campus.

"I do not begrudge this state of affairs. We are among the extremely fortunate in that we can help out and besides, who could ever put a price on seeing all those slim, healthy young men and women hugging and weeping openly as they say their goodbyes in the residence parking lot while their overweight, sweating, near-cardiac arrest parents do all the heavy lifting?

"Still, one cannot help but think of the changes that have come about since we became the first generation in Canada who were given to take higher education as a basic rite of passage, thanks to the world of student loans and generous grants you never even had to consider paying back.

"Going to school was a simple project. You worked in the summer, socked away your $1,000; you got your student loan of $600, your student grant of $600, and that was it. Sometimes you ran unbelievably short—I will spare you my own horror stories—but you survived and, one day, you went out into the world owing a couple of thousand dollars in student loans which you soon paid off and never again thought about.

"Never again, that is, until your own kids were suddenly headed off to similar schools.

"At one point, no one would ever dare question the value of an education, and even today it makes one feel slightly queasy to do so, but there are just too many stories hanging around to ignore it. We have three at university this year, and one suspects even Bill Gates would blanch at the costs, even with the kids themselves contributing." (MacGregor, 2002)

More than ever before, education—in particular, higher education—is regarded as the key to success. Most young Canadians today will attend university, correct? Although you may be one of the fortunate ones, the answer to this question is no. Increasingly, a university education is becoming a valuable life asset that only a few can afford to obtain. The most recent statistics indicate that only 23 percent of Canadians aged 25 to 64 have a university degree (Statistics Canada, 2003e). Given the costs associated with attaining this higher level of education, these numbers should come as no surprise. The national chairperson of the Canadian Federation of Students recently commented, "University education has been placed out of reach for many lower-income families. The rise in tuition fees throughout the last decade has increasingly restricted access to universities to only the wealthiest Canadians" (Boyko, 2002). According to a recent Statistics Canada study, students from families in the highest-income group are two-and-a-half times more likely to attend university than those whose families come from the lowest-income group (Statistics Canada, 2001g). What effects will this increasing stratification have on our society?

It is not only in the system of higher education that we are witnessing unequal access to "intellectual capital." Parents can contribute directly to a young child's educational success by providing a supportive environment for learning or indirectly by paving the way for a higher level of educational attainment. Increasingly, we hear of parents opting out of the public school system, placing their children in private schools, charter schools, home-schooling, or "supplementing" their education with specialized extracurricular programming—computer camps, mini-universities, or private tutoring—in an effort to make sure their child "makes it." It is apparent that only parents with the financial resources (that is, middle- or upper-income families) can afford these programs.

Does this mean that education is stratified by social class? What effect will this have on students from low-income families? Education is one of the most significant social institutions in Canada and other high-income nations. Although most social scientists agree that schools are supposed to be places where people acquire knowledge and skills, not all of them agree on how a wide array of factors—including class, race, gender, age, religion, and family background—affects individuals' access to educational achievement or to the differential rewards that accrue at various levels of academic achievement. Canada has become a "schooled society" (Guppy and Davies, 1998), and the education system has become a forum for competition. All children in Canada have an equal opportunity to participate in elementary and secondary public schools. Does this mean that all students have an equal opportunity to succeed in school? In this chapter, we will explore the issue of educational inequality in Canada as well as look at other problems facing contemporary elementary, secondary, and higher education. Before reading on, test your knowledge about education in Canada by taking the quiz in Box 16.1.

QUESTIONS AND ISSUES

Chapter Focus Question: How do race, class, and gender affect people's access to and opportunities in education?

How do educational goals differ in various countries?

What are the key assumptions of functionalist, conflict, symbolic interactionist, and postmodern perspectives on education?

What major problems are being faced by Canadian schools today?

The first schools in Canada, typically one-room schoolhouses, combined children of all ages. Attendance was sparse, as other priorities, such as working the farm, took precedence.

AN OVERVIEW OF EDUCATION

Education **is the social institution responsible for the systematic transmission of knowledge, skills, and cultural values within a formally organized structure.** Education is a powerful and influential force in contemporary societies. As a social institution, education imparts values, beliefs, and knowledge considered essential to the social reproduction of individual personalities and entire cultures (Bourdieu and Passeron, 1990). Education grapples with issues of societal stability and social change, reflecting society even as it attempts to shape it. Early socialization is primarily informal and takes place within our families and friendship networks. Socialization then passes to the schools and other, more formalized organizations created for the specific purpose of educating people. Today, education is such a significant social institution that an entire subfield of sociology—the *sociology of education*—is devoted to its study.

How did education emerge as such an important social institution in contemporary, industrialized nations? To answer this question, we begin with a brief examination of education in historical–global perspective.

EDUCATION IN HISTORICAL-GLOBAL PERSPECTIVE

Education serves an important purpose in all societies. At the microlevel, people must acquire the basic knowledge and skills they need to survive in society. At the macrolevel, the social institution of education is an essential component in maintaining and perpetuating the culture of a society across generations. *Cultural transmission*—**the process by which children and recent immigrants become acquainted with the dominant cultural beliefs, values, norms, and accumulated knowledge of a society**—occurs through informal and formal education. However, the process of cultural transmission differs in preliterate, preindustrial, and industrial nations.

Informal Education in Preliterate Societies

Preliterate societies have no written language and are characterized by very basic technology and a simple division of labour. Daily activity often centres on the struggle to survive against natural forces, and the

BOX 16.1 SOCIOLOGY AND EVERYDAY LIFE

How Much Do You Know About Education in Canada?

True	False	
T	F	1. Canada has the largest population with postsecondary education of any developed nation.
T	F	2. Most students use the Internet as a learning tool in the classroom.
T	F	3. Children of parents with high levels of education are more likely to pursue postsecondary education.
T	F	4. Aboriginal peoples are underrepresented among postsecondary graduates.
T	F	5. In the past decade, the number of jobs requiring a university degree or postsecondary diploma has increased dramatically.
T	F	6. Students from low-socioeconomic-status families are more likely to have difficulty in school.
T	F	7. More young men than young women in Canada have university degrees.
T	F	8. By international standards, expenditures on primary and secondary education in Canada are low.

Answers on page 500.

earliest forms of education are survival-oriented. People in these societies acquire knowledge and skills through *informal education*—**learning that occurs in a spontaneous, unplanned way.** Through direct informal education, parents and other members of the group provide information about how to gather food, find shelter, make tools, and get along with others. For example, a boy might learn skills, such as hunting, gathering, fishing, and farming, from his father, whereas a girl might learn from her mother how to plant, gather, and prepare food, or how to take care of younger sisters and brothers. Such informal education often occurs through storytelling or ritual ceremonies that convey cultural messages and provide behavioural norms. Over time, the knowledge shared through informal education may become the moral code of the group.

Formal Education in Preindustrial, Industrial, and Postindustrial Societies

Although *preindustrial societies* have a written language, few people know how to read and write, and formal education is often reserved for the privileged. Education becomes more formalized in preindustrial and industrial societies. *Formal education* **is learning that takes place within an academic setting, such as a school, which has a planned instructional process and teachers who convey specific knowledge, skills, and thinking processes to students.** Perhaps the earliest formal education occurred in ancient Greece and Rome, where philosophers, such as Socrates, Plato, and Aristotle, taught elite males the necessary skills to become thinkers and orators who could engage in the

BOX 16.1 SOCIOLOGY AND EVERYDAY LIFE

Answers to the Sociology Quiz on Education in Canada

1. **True.** According to recent census figures, Canada has the highest proportion of educated people among thirty industrialized countries, with 41 percent of the working-age population holding a degree or diploma. That is followed by 37 percent in the United States and 36 percent in Ireland (Statistics Canada, 2003e).

2. **True.** In a recent survey, 88 percent of elementary school students and 97 percent of high school students attended schools with Internet access for instructional purposes (Statistics Canada, 1999a).

3. **True.** Young adults (aged twenty-six to thirty-five) were three times more likely to earn postsecondary credentials if their parents had a postsecondary education than if their parents had not completed high school (de Broucker and Lavallée, 2000).

4. **True.** Only 8 percent of Aboriginal persons between the ages of twenty-five and sixty-four have a university degree—well below the 23 percent of Canadians in the general population who hold a university degree. However, 15 percent of Aboriginal persons in the same age category have a college diploma; this number is not far below the Canadian average of 18 percent (Statistics Canada, 2003e).

5. **True.** Since 1990, the number of jobs requiring a university degree or postsecondary diploma has increased by 1.3 million. The number of jobs available for people without these credentials has decreased by 800,000. In short, the more education you have, the more likely it is that you will find a job (Statistics Canada, 2003e).

6. **True.** For example, students from the lowest socioeconomic group score lower on tests of academic performance, are more likely to have to repeat a grade, are more likely to require remedial education, and are more likely not to complete high school (Council of Ministers of Education, 2002).

7. **False.** In 2001, exactly one-half of university graduates aged twenty-five and over were women (Statistics Canada, 2003e).

8. **True.** In 2001, Canada was ranked nineteenth out of thirty developed countries for its spending on primary and secondary schooling (Statistics Canada, 2003e).

art of persuasion (Ballantine, 1997). During the Middle Ages, the first colleges and universities were developed under the auspices of the church. The history of education in Canada began with attempts by Jesuit priests and missionaries to "civilize" Aboriginal children and the children of the colonists. During this time, the church was central to the institution of education. Many of Canada's oldest universities and colleges were founded by churches.

The Renaissance and the Industrial Revolution had a profound effect on education. During the Renaissance, the focus of education shifted from human depravity to the importance of developing well-rounded and liberally educated people. With the rapid growth of industrial capitalism and factories during the Industrial Revolution, it became necessary for workers to have basic skills in reading, writing, and arithmetic. However, from the Middle Ages until the end of World War I, only the sons of the privileged classes were able to attend European universities. Agriculture was the economic base of society, and literacy for people in the lower classes was not deemed important.

As societies industrialize, the need for formal education of the masses increases significantly. In Canada, the school reformers of the late 1800s began to view education as essential to the country's economic growth (Gilbert, 1989). Ontario school reformer Egerton Ryerson promoted free schooling for all children, arguing that sending rich and poor children to the same schools would bring people closer together and create more harmony (Tepperman, 1994). By the early 1900s, mass education had taken hold in Canada, as the provinces established free, tax-supported elementary schools that were readily available to children throughout the country. ***Mass education* refers to providing free, public schooling for wide segments of a nation's population.**

As industrialization and bureaucratization intensified, managers and business owners demanded that schools educate students beyond Grade 3 or 4 so that well-qualified workers would be available for rapidly emerging "white-collar" jobs in management and clerical work (Bailyn, 1960). In addition to educating the next generation of children for the workplace, public schools were also supposed to serve as the primary agents of socialization for millions of European immigrants arriving in Canada seeking economic opportunities and a better life. By the 1920s, educators had introduced the "core" curriculum: courses such as mathematics, social sciences, natural sciences, and English. This core is reflected in the contemporary "back to basics" movement, which calls for teaching the "three R's" (reading, 'riting, and 'rithmetic) and enforcing stricter discipline in schools.

Contemporary education in Canada attempts to meet the needs of the industrial and postindustrial society by teaching a wide diversity of students myriad topics ranging from history and science to computer skills, how to balance a chequebook, and AIDS prevention. According to sociologists, many functions performed by other social institutions in the past are now under the auspices of the public schools. For example, full-day kindergartens, lunch programs, and after-school programs for school-age children are provided by many school divisions because of the growing numbers of working parents who need high-quality, affordable care for their children. Within the regular classroom, many teachers feel that their job description encompasses too many divergent tasks. According to Ruth Prale, an elementary reading specialist,

> A teacher today is a social worker, surrogate parent, a bit of disciplinarian, a counselor, and someone who has to see to it that they eat. Many teachers

Schools in Japan emphasize conformity even at an early age. Many Japanese people believe that high-quality education is a crucial factor in their country's economic success.

are mandated to teach sex education, drug awareness, gang awareness. And we're supposed to be benevolent. And we haven't come to teaching yet! (quoted in Collins and Frantz, 1993:83)

At all levels of education in Canada, from kindergarten through graduate school, controversy exists over *what* should be taught, *how* it should be taught, and *who* should teach it. Do other countries have similar questions regarding their educational systems? Let's take a brief look at how educational systems are organized in Japan and Bosnia.

Contemporary Education in Other Nations

In this section, we will examine schools in two nations that frequently show up in the media. Because Canada, the United States, and Japan are often compared to each other in the global marketplace, social analysts frequently compare the educational systems of these high-income countries. Similarly, since Bosnia is known for racial–ethnic factions and problems with racism, social analysts often examine how Bosnian schools handle ethnic and religious discord.

Education in Japan   Like other countries, Japan did not make public education mandatory for children until the country underwent industrialization. During the Meiji Period (1868–1912), feudalism was eliminated, and Japan embarked on a new focus on youth and "bureaucratic" universal education (White, 1994). In hopes of catching up with the West, Japanese officials created an educational system and national educational goals. Education was viewed as a form of economic and national development and as a means of identifying talent for a new technological elite (White, 1994).

Today, Japanese educators, parents, students, and employers all view education as a crucial link in Japan's economic success. Japanese schools not only emphasize conformity and nationalism; they also highlight the importance of obligation to one's family and of learning the skills necessary for employment. Beginning at about three years of age, many Japanese toddlers are sent to "cram schools" (*jukus*) to help them qualify for good preschools.

In both cram schools and public schools, students learn discipline and thinking skills, along with physical activities, such as karate and gymnastics, to improve agility. By the time children reach elementary school, they are expected to engage in cooperative activities with their classmates. In some schools, children are responsible for preparing, serving, and cleaning up after the midday meal. At the end of the day, children may be seen cleaning the chalkboards and even mopping the floors, all as a part of the spirit of cooperation they are being taught.

In Japan, the middle-school years are especially crucial: students' futures are based on the academic status track on which they are placed while in middle school. Moreover, the kind of job they will hold in the future depends on the university or vocational–technical school they attend, which in turn depends on the high school they attend. By the third year of middle school, most students are acutely aware of their academic future and how their lives and friendships change as they go through the educational process. As one former student recalled:

> Middle school was fun; I was with my friends and I could throw myself into sports and I didn't have to study very hard. I couldn't be sure which of my friends would be with me in high school. Now that I am in high school, I know these will be my friends for life—they've been with me through very tough times. (White, 1994:77)

Up until high school, the student population of a school typically reflects the neighbourhoods in which children live. However, at the high school level, entrance to a particular school is based on ability: some Japanese students enter vocational schools that teach them skills for the workplace; others enter schools that are exclusively for the university-bound. Many analysts have noted the extent to which most Japanese vocational schools provide state-of-the-art equipment and instruction in fields with wide employment opportunities. Consequently, graduates of most vocational high schools do not have problems finding relatively well-paid employment upon graduation.

Typically, the instruction in Japanese high schools for the university-bound is highly structured, and all students are expected to respond in unison to questions posed by the teacher. Students are expected to be fluent in more than one language; many Japanese high schools teach English, particularly vocabulary and sentence construction. Science and math courses are challenging, and Japanese students often take courses, such as algebra and calculus, several years before their North American counterparts. Students must be prepared for a variety of university entrance examinations because each college and university gives its own test, and all tests occur within a few weeks of each other.

Girls and young women in Canada would likely feel stifled by the lack of educational opportunities experienced by their counterparts in Japan. Although there have been some changes, many parents and educators still believe that a good junior college education is all that young women need in order to be employable and marriageable (White, 1994). At the college and university level, the absence of women as students and professors is especially pronounced. Although a woman recently became the first-ever female president of a state-run university (Nara Women's University) in Japan, women account for under 5 percent of all presidents of colleges and universities (Findlay-Kaneko, 1997). Moreover, lack of child care facilities within the universities remains a pressing problem for women students and faculty in Japanese higher education.

Young men also experience extreme pressures in the Japanese system. In fact, high rates of school truancy occur as tens of thousands of students balk at going to school, and still others experience school-related health problems, such as stomach ulcers, allergy disorders, and high blood pressure (White, 1994).

Education in Bosnia

To understand education in contemporary Bosnia, it is important to consider the country's recent history. Located in Eastern Europe and frequently the topic of Canadian newspaper headlines because of ongoing ethnic strife, the nation of Bosnia-Herzegovina has sought to maintain its schools throughout violent clashes among its three principal ethnic groups: Muslims, Eastern Orthodox Serbs, and Roman Catholic Croats.

Despite the existence of a formal peace agreement between these groups since 1995, animosities remain strong.

Recently, journalists and social scientists have found that each of the principal ethnic groups has taken control over how its children are educated and how cultural ideas are presented to them. Many schools identify and educate students by their ethnic background. For example, in history classes, students are segregated into ethnically distinct classrooms and taught different versions of history, language, and art, depending on their own ethnic and religious identity (Hedges, 1997). The fact that schools with integrated classrooms have seen an increase in conflicts between students from different ethnic groups undoubtedly contributes to this. According to one Serbian sociologist, his teenage daughter came home in tears because of comments made in her class about the Serbian "aggressors": "She would not return to school for 10 days. Many of her friends now cross the line at the edge of the city to take classes in schools run by the Bosnian Serbs to avoid ridicule and harassment" (quoted in Hedges, 1997:A4).

What will happen in the future is unknown. However, the case of Bosnian education illustrates how difficult it is for teaching and learning to take place in an environment where there is little consensus about a shared sense of values, history, and what is important for the future. How much consensus exists in Canada regarding education? Let's examine that question, using the functionalist, conflict, feminist, symbolic interactionist, and postmodern perspectives.

What values are these children being taught? Is there a consensus about what today's school should teach? Why or why not?

SOCIOLOGICAL PERSPECTIVES ON EDUCATION

Sociologists have divergent perspectives on the purpose of education in contemporary society. Functionalists believe that education contributes to the maintenance of society and provides people with an opportunity for self-enhancement and upward social mobility. Conflict theorists argue that education perpetuates social inequality and benefits the dominant class at the expense of all others. Symbolic interactionists focus on classroom dynamics and the effect of self-concept on grades and aspirations. Postmodern theorists view the education system as a social institution characterized by permeability. Each of these perspectives can provide valuable insights.

Functionalist Perspectives

Functionalists view education as one of the most important components of society. According to Émile Durkheim, education is crucial for promoting social solidarity and stability in society: education is the "influence exercised by adult generations on those that are not yet ready for social life" (Durkheim, 1956:28) and helps young people travel the great distance that it has taken people many centuries to cover. In other words, we can learn from what others already have experienced. Durkheim also asserted that *moral education* is very important because it conveys moral values—the foundation of a cohesive social order. He believed that schools are responsible for teaching a commitment to the common morality.

From this perspective, students must be taught to put the group's needs ahead of their individual desires and aspirations. Contemporary functionalists suggest that education is responsible for teaching social values. The 1994 Royal Commission on Learning outlined three purposes of schooling: first, to ensure for all students high levels of literacy by building on basic reading, writing, and problem-solving skills; second, to develop an appreciation of learning, the wish to continue learning, and the ability and commitment to do so; and finally, to prepare students for responsible citizenship, including developing "basic moral values, such as a sense of caring and compassion, respect for the human person and anti-racism, a commitment to peace and non-violence, honesty and justice" (Osborne, 1994:4).

Functionalists emphasize that "shared" values should be transmitted by schools from kindergarten through university. However, not all analysts agree on what those shared values should be, or what functions education should serve in contemporary societies. In analyzing the values and functions of education, sociologists using a functionalist framework distinguish between manifest and latent functions. Manifest functions and latent functions are compared in Figure 16.1.

Manifest Functions of Education   Some functions of education are *manifest functions*—previously defined as open, stated, and intended goals or consequences of activities within an organization or institution. Education serves five major manifest functions in society:

1. *Socialization.* From kindergarten through university, schools teach students the student role, specific academic subjects, and political socialization. In kindergarten, children learn the appropriate attitudes and behaviour for the student role (Ballantine, 1997). In primary and secondary schools, students are taught specific subject matter appropriate to their age, skill level, and previous educational experience. At the university level, students focus on more detailed knowledge of subjects they have previously studied and are exposed to new areas of study and research. Throughout their schooling, students receive political socialization in the form of history and civics lessons.

2. *Transmission of culture.* Schools transmit cultural norms and values to each new generation and play an active part in the process of assimilation, whereby recent immigrants learn dominant cultural values, attitudes, and behaviours so that they can be productive members of society. However, questions remain as to *whose* culture is being transmitted. Because of the great diversity in Canada today, it is virtually impossible to define a single culture.

3. *Social control.* Schools are responsible for teaching values, such as discipline, respect, obedience, punctuality, and perseverance. Schools teach conformity by encouraging young people to be good students, conscientious future workers, and law-abiding citizens. The teaching of conformity rests primarily with classroom teachers.

4. *Social placement.* Schools are responsible for identifying the most qualified people to fill the positions available in society. As a result, students are channelled into programs based on individual

Figure 16.1   Manifest and Latent Functions of Education

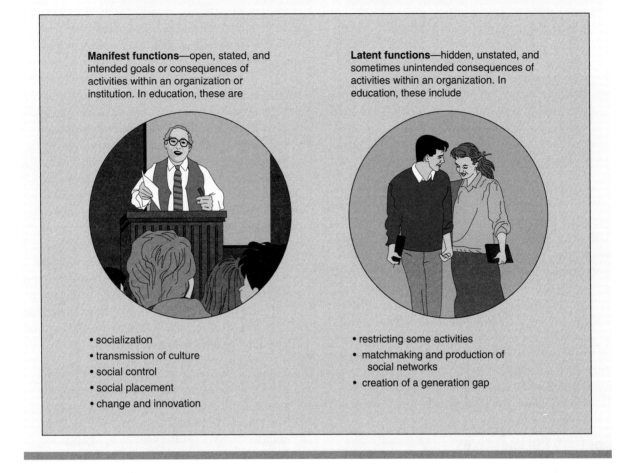

Manifest functions—open, stated, and intended goals or consequences of activities within an organization or institution. In education, these are

- socialization
- transmission of culture
- social control
- social placement
- change and innovation

Latent functions—hidden, unstated, and sometimes unintended consequences of activities within an organization. In education, these include

- restricting some activities
- matchmaking and production of social networks
- creation of a generation gap

ability and academic achievement. Graduates receive the appropriate credentials to enter the paid labour force.

5. *Change and innovation.* Schools are a source of change and innovation. As student populations change over time, new programs are introduced to meet societal needs; for example, sex education, drug education, and multicultural studies have been implemented in some schools to help students learn about pressing social issues. Innovation in the form of new knowledge is required in colleges and universities. Faculty members are required to engage in research and to share the results with students, colleagues, and others.

Latent Functions of Education   All social institutions, including education, have *latent functions*— previously defined as hidden, unstated, and sometimes unintended consequences of activities within an

organization or institution. Education serves at least three latent functions:

1. *Restricting some activities.* Early in the twentieth century, all provinces passed *mandatory education laws* that require children to attend school until they reach a specified age (usually the age of sixteen) or complete a minimum level of formal education (generally completion of Grade 8). The assumption was that an educated citizenry and workforce are necessary for the smooth functioning of democracy and capitalism. Out of these laws grew one latent function of education, which is to keep students off the street and out of the full-time job market for a number of years, thus helping keep unemployment within reasonable bounds (Braverman, 1974).

2. *Matchmaking and production of social networks.* Because schools bring together people of similar ages, social class, and race/ethnicity, young

people often meet future marriage partners and develop social networks that may last for many years.

3. *Creation of a generation gap.* Students may learn information in school that contradicts beliefs held by their parents or their religion. Debates over the content of textbooks and library books typically centre on information that parents deem unacceptable for their children. When education conflicts with parental attitudes and beliefs, a generation gap is created if students embrace the newly acquired perspective.

Functionalists acknowledge that education has certain dysfunctions. Some analysts argue that education systems in Canada are not promoting the high-level skills in reading, writing, science, and mathematics that are needed in the workplace and the global economy. However, a new international report that assesses the skill level of students nearing the end of their compulsory education ranked Canadian students among the best in the world when it comes to reading, mathematics, and science. Canadian fifteen-year-old students ranked second in reading, third in mathematics, and fifth in science among thirty-two participating countries (Organisation for Economic Co-operation and Development, 2004).

Conflict Perspectives

Conflict theorists do not believe that public schools reduce social inequality in society; rather, they believe that schools often perpetuate class, racial–ethnic, and gender inequalities as some groups seek to maintain their privileged position at the expense of others (Apple, 1980; Ballantine, 1997; Curtis, Grabb, and Guppy, 1999).

Cultural Capital and Class Reproduction

Although many factors—including intelligence, family income, motivation, and previous achievement—are important in determining how much education a person will attain, conflict theorists argue that access to high-quality education is closely related to social class. From this approach, education is a vehicle for reproducing existing class relationships. According to French sociologist Pierre Bourdieu, the school legitimates and reinforces the social elites by engaging in specific practices that uphold the patterns of behaviour and the attitudes of the dominant class. Bourdieu asserts that students from diverse class backgrounds come to school with differing amounts of *cultural capital*—**social assets that include values, beliefs, attitudes, and competencies in language and culture** (Bourdieu and Passeron, 1990). Cultural capital involves "proper" attitudes toward education, socially approved dress and manners, and knowledge about books, art, music, and other forms of high and popular culture. Middle- and upper-income parents endow their children with more cultural capital than do working-class and poverty-level parents. Because cultural capital is essential for acquiring an education, children with less cultural capital have fewer opportunities to succeed in school. For example, standardized tests that are used to group students by ability and to assign them to classes often measure students' cultural capital rather than their "natural" intelligence or aptitude. Thus, a circular effect occurs: Students with dominant cultural values are more highly rewarded by the educational system; in turn, the educational system teaches and reinforces those values that sustain the elite's position in society.

In her study of working-class women who returned to school after dropping out, sociologist Wendy Luttrell (1997:113–114) concluded that schools play a critical role in class reproduction and determining people's self-concept and identity:

School denied but at the same time protected certain students' unearned advantages related to class, gender, and skin color in ways that made the women doubt their own value, voice, and abilities . . . [When] the women were degraded by teachers and school officials for their speech, styles of dress, deportment, physical appearance, skin color, and forms of knowledge, they learned to recognize as "intelligent" or "valuable" only the styles, traits, and knowledge possessed by the economically advantaged students[:] . . . white, middle-class . . . behaviors and [appearance] . . . and urban or suburban mannerisms and styles of speech. Most important, [it was assumed that] those who possessed such cultural capital [were] entitled to their superior positions.

Tracking and Social Inequality

Closely linked to the issue of cultural capital is how tracking in schools is related to social inequality. Conflict theorists who study ability grouping focus on how the process of tracking affects students' educational performance. Ability grouping, which is based on the assumption that it is easier to teach students with similar abilities, is often used in elementary schools. However, class-based factors also affect which children are most likely to be placed in "high," "middle," or "low" groups, often referred to by such innocuous terms as "Blue Birds," "Red Birds," and "Yellow Birds."

In middle school, junior high, and high school, most students experience *tracking*—**the assignment of students to specific courses and educational programs based on their test scores, previous grades, or both.** Ruben Navarrette, Jr. (1997:274–275) talks about his experience with tracking:

One fateful day, in the second grade, my teacher decided to teach her class more efficiently by dividing it into six groups of five students each. Each group was assigned a geometric symbol to differentiate it from the others. There were the Circles. There were the Squares. There were the Triangles and Rectangles.

I remember something else, an odd coincidence. The Hexagons were the smartest kids in the class. These distinctions are not lost on a child of seven. Even in the second grade, my classmates and I knew who was smarter than whom. And on the day on which we were assigned our respective shapes, we knew that our teacher knew, too.

As Hexagons, we would wait for her to call on us, then answer by hurrying to her with books and pencils in hand. We sat around a table in our "reading group," chattering excitedly to one another and basking in the intoxication of positive learning. We did not notice, did not care to notice, over our shoulders, the frustrated looks on the faces of Circles and Squares and Triangles who sat quietly at their desks, doodling on scratch paper or mumbling to one another.

We knew also that, along with our geometric shapes, our books were different and that each group had different amounts of work to do. The Circles had the easiest books and were assigned to read only a few pages at a time. Not surprisingly, the Hexagons had the most difficult books of all, those with the biggest words and the fewest pictures, and we were expected to read the most pages.

The result of all of this education by separation was exactly what the teacher had imagined that it would be: Students could, and did, learn at their own pace without being encumbered by one another. Some learned faster than others. Some, I realized only [later], did not learn at all.

Numerous studies have found that ability grouping and tracking affects students' academic achievements and career choices (Oakes, 1985). Education scholar Jeannie Oakes found that tracking affects students' perceptions of classroom goals and achievements, as the following statements from high- and low-track students suggest:

I want to be a lawyer and debate has taught me to dig for answers and get involved. I can express myself. (High-Track English)

To understand concepts and ideas and experiment with them. Also to work independently. (High-Track Science)

To behave in class. (Low-Track English)

To be a better listener in class. (Low-Track English)

I have learned that I should do my questions for the book when he asks me to. (Low-Track Science)

Perceptions of the students on the "low tracks" reflect the impact that years of tracking and lowered expectations can have on people's educational and career aspirations. Often, the educational track—vocational or university-bound—on which high school students are placed has a significant influence on their future educational and employment opportunities. Although the stated purpose of tracking systems is to permit students to study subjects that are suitable to their skills and interests, most research reveals that this purpose has not been achieved (Oakes, 1985). Moreover, some social scientists believe that tracking is one of the most obvious mechanisms through which poor and minority students receive a diluted academic program, making it much more likely that they will fall even further behind their white, middle-class counterparts (see Miller, 1995).

Awareness of these effects has resulted in numerous destreaming initiatives across the country. For example, in 1993, the Ontario Ministry of Education and Training began a destreaming program of one grade per year starting with Grade 9. These initiatives were met with some opposition by parents, teachers, and school boards, who were concerned that children will receive lower-quality education in destreamed classrooms. However, the benefits of destreaming may outweigh the costs when we consider the perceptions and lowered expectations of students on the "low tracks," brought on by years of tracking.

Instead of enhancing school performance, tracking systems may result in students dropping out of school or ending up in dead-end situations because they have not taken the courses required to go to university.

The Hidden Curriculum   According to conflict theorists, the *hidden curriculum* **is the transmission of cultural values and attitudes, such as conformity and obedience to authority, through implied demands found in rules, routines, and regulations of schools** (Snyder, 1971). Although students from all social classes are subjected to the hidden curriculum, working-class and poverty-level students may be affected the most adversely (Cookson and Hodges Persell, 1985; Polakow, 1993; Ballantine, 1997). When teachers are from a higher-class background than their students, they tend to use more structure in the classroom and to have lower expectations for students' academic achievement. In a study of five elementary schools located in different communities, significant differences were found in the manner in which knowledge was transmitted to students even though the curriculum was organized similarly (Anyon, 1980). Schools for working-class students emphasize procedures and rote memorization without much decision making, choice, and explanation of why something is done a particular way. Schools for middle-class students stress the processes (such as figuring and decision making) involved in getting the right answer. Schools for affluent students focus on creative activities in which students express their own ideas and apply them to the subject under consideration. Schools for students from elite families work to develop students' analytical powers and critical thinking skills, applying abstract principles to problem solving.

Through the hidden curriculum, schools make working-class and poverty-level students aware that they will be expected to take orders from others, arrive

According to conflict theorists, the hidden curriculum in schools makes low-income students aware that they will be expected to follow rules when they work for others throughout their adult lives.

at work on time, follow bureaucratic rules, and experience high levels of boredom without complaining (Richer, 1988). Over time, these students may be disqualified from higher education and barred from obtaining the credentials necessary for well-paid occupations and professions (Bowles and Gintis, 1976). Educational credentials are extremely important in societies that emphasize *credentialism*—**a process of social selection in which class advantage and social status are linked to the possession of academic qualifications** (Collins, 1979; Marshall, 1998). According to conflict theorists, credentialism is not driven by an actual need for increased knowledge, but rather by the desire on the part of the members of professional groups to protect their own vested interests—namely income, prestige, autonomy, and power. Credentialism is closely related to meritocracy—previously defined as a social system in which status is assumed to be acquired through individual ability and effort (Young, 1994). Persons who acquire the appropriate credentials for a job are assumed to have gained the position through what they know, not who they are or whom they know. According to conflict theorists, the hidden curriculum determines in advance that the most valued credentials will primarily stay in the hands of the elites. Therefore, Canada is not actually as meritocratic as some might claim.

Feminist Perspectives

Gender Bias and the Hidden Curriculum

According to feminist theorists, gender bias is embedded in both the formal and hidden curriculums of schools. Although girls and young women in Canada have a greater opportunity for education than those living in developing nations, feminist scholars maintain that their educational opportunities are not equal to those of boys and young men of their social class (see Gaskell et al., 1995). For many years, reading materials, classroom activities, and treatment by teachers and peers contributed to a feeling among many young girls and young women that they were less important than male students. Over time, this kind of differential treatment undermines females' self-esteem and discourages them from taking certain courses, such as math and science, that are usually dominated by male teachers and students (Orenstein, 1995; Gaskell et al., 1995). For example, teachers tend to give girls less attention while encouraging boys to be problem solvers and asking them more complex questions. As a result, females tend to take fewer courses in math and science or drop them because of lack of interest (Fennema and Leder, 1990). The gender bias in education is evident at the postsecondary level, as shown in Table 16.1.

In recent years, some improvements have taken place in girls' education as more females have enrolled in advanced-placement or honours courses and in academic areas—such as math and science—where they had previously lagged behind. However, girls are still not enrolled in higher-level science (such as physics) and computer sciences in the same numbers as are boys. Girls and young women continue to make up only a small percentage of students in computer science and computer design classes, and the gender gap grows even wider from Grades 8 to 11. Some feminist analysts report that the hidden curriculum works against young women in that some educators do not provide females with as much information about economic trends and the relationships among curriculum, course-taking choices, and career options as they do to male students from middle- and upper-income families.

Some feminist analysts suggest that girls receive subtle cues from teachers and parents that lead them to attribute success to *effort;* boys learn to attribute success to their *intelligence* and *ability.* Conversely, girls attribute their own failure to lack of ability; boys attribute failure to lack of effort (Sadker and Sadker, 1994). Other analysts argue that girls—and some boys—who are high achievers may be the victims of *anti-intellectualism*—hostility or opposition toward persons assumed to have great mental ability or toward subject matter thought to necessitate significant intellectual ability or knowledge for its comprehension.

Canada is not unique in its lack of educational equality for women. As discussed in Box 16.2, literacy rates for women in low-income countries reflect the belief that women do not need to read or possess knowledge that might contribute to their country's social and economic development.

Table 16.1 CANADIAN UNIVERSITY GRADUATES' TOP TEN FIELDS OF STUDY, BY SEX, 2001*

MEN

Engineering	15.38
Business and commerce	9.99
Elementary, secondary, pre-primary teaching	8.22
Financial management	7.16
Computer science and applied mathematics	4.48
Economics	3.49
Law and jurisprudence	3.36
Medicine	2.98
Psychology	2.16
History	1.96
All other subjects	40.84
Total	100.00

WOMEN

Elementary, secondary, pre-primary teaching	20.08
Nursing	6.49
Business and commerce	6.06
Financial management	5.19
Psychology	4.83
Medical-related subjects	3.20
English language and literature	3.01
Social work and social services	2.80
Sociology	2.68
Engineering	2.36
All other subjects	43.30
Total	100.00

*University graduates aged 25 to 64.

Source: Statistics Canada, 2003e.

BOX 16.2 SOCIOLOGY IN GLOBAL PERSPECTIVE

Women's Literacy in Low-Income Countries

Education is a powerful agent of progress. Literacy is the most basic and necessary of learning skills.

—Maria Luisa Jauregui de Gainza, literacy specialist, UNESCO (quoted in Ballara, 1992)

An estimated 875 million adults are illiterate worldwide. Nearly two-thirds of them are women.

In 1969, the year man took his first step on the moon, four out of five women in Africa could not read or write. It is estimated that today nearly half of all African women are still illiterate.

More than 100 million children, including at least 60 million girls, have no access to primary schooling.

Since 1985, there are more female students enrolled in higher education than male students in most industrialized countries. In contrast, in the world's least developed countries, only one in four students of higher education are women (World Literacy of Canada, 2005a).

Functional illiteracy refers to a lack of basic literacy and numeracy skills that are essential for proper functioning—such as the ability to read or write or to make sense of written material (Ballara, 1992:1). Organizations, such as the United Nations, believe that the education of women in low-income countries is a high priority not only for national development but also for the well-being of children and families.

An estimated 95 percent of all illiterate people are concentrated in the developing nations of Southeast Asia and sub-Saharan Africa. Here, one-third of all women are illiterate, as compared with one-fifth of the men. In the countries with lowest incomes, 79 percent of adult women are illiterate. Even with organizations, such as the United Nations Educational, Scientific and Cultural Organization (UNESCO), attempting to eradicate illiteracy, the problem remains.

Many factors stand in the way of women's literacy, including religious beliefs that subordinate women and emphasize a traditional gendered division of labour, such as "care of children, maintenance of the household, care of older family members and the ill, servicing their husband and his relevant kin, maintenance of the network of familial ties, and servicing of the community" (Ballara, 1992:x). Religions that confine women's activities to domestic tasks and stress their role as wives and mothers often limit their access to education and produce feelings of low self-esteem and isolation.

Ultimately, the main reason why most women (and men) are illiterate is poverty; daily survival becomes far more important than learning how to read or compute math problems. Some analysts have found that schools in the poorest developing nations are becoming even more impoverished. Some countries have a two-tier system: (1) in rural areas, a grossly inadequate school system that may be state-run or attached to a local temple or mosque, where religious education is often the primary goal; and (2) in urban areas, a better school system that may be patterned after Western schools, such as those found in England or France, and that serves the children of the nation's elite population.

Is there hope for the future? Media campaigns and numerous projects are actively seeking to promote literacy. Perhaps a greater awareness of the problem is the first step toward eradication of it. Are the problems of women in developing nations in any way related to your life? Using your sociological imagination, can you think of ways in which their "fate" might be intertwined with yours?

Sources: Based on Ballara, 1992; Ballantine, 1997; World Literacy of Canada, 2005b.

Symbolic Interactionist Perspectives

Unlike functionalist analysts, who focus on the functions and dysfunctions of education, and conflict theorists, who focus on the relationship between education and inequality, symbolic interactionists focus on classroom communication patterns and educational practices, such as labelling, that affect students' self-concept and aspirations.

Labelling and the Self-Fulfilling Prophecy

Chapter 7 explained that *labelling* is the process whereby a person is identified by others as possessing a specific characteristic or exhibiting a certain pattern of behaviour (such as being deviant). According to symbolic interactionists, the process of labelling is directly related to the power and status of those persons who do the labelling and those who are being labelled. In schools, teachers and administrators are empowered to label children in various ways, including grades, written comments on classroom behaviour, and placement in classes. For example, based on standardized test scores or classroom performance, educators label some children as "special ed" or low achievers, whereas others are labelled as average or "gifted and talented." For some students, labelling amounts to a *self-fulfilling prophecy*—previously defined as an unsubstantiated belief or prediction resulting in behaviour that makes the originally false belief come true (Merton, 1968). A classic form of labelling and self-fulfilling prophecy occurs through the use of IQ (intelligence quotient) tests, which claim to measure a person's inherent intelligence, apart from any family or school influences on the individual. In many school systems, IQ tests are used as one criterion in determining student placement in classes and ability groups.

Using Labelling Theory to Examine the IQ Debate

The relationship between IQ testing and labelling theory has been of special interest to sociologists. In the 1960s, two social scientists conducted an experiment in an elementary school where they intentionally misinformed teachers about the intelligence test scores of students in their classes (Rosenthal and Jacobson, 1968). Despite the fact that the students were randomly selected for the study and had no measurable differences in intelligence, the researchers informed the teachers that some of the students had extremely high IQ test scores, whereas others had average to below-average scores. As the researchers observed, the teachers began to teach "exceptional" students in a different manner from other students. In turn, the "exceptional" students began to outperform their "average" peers and to excel in their classwork. This study called attention to the labelling effect of IQ scores.

However, experiments such as this also raise other important issues: What if a teacher (as a result of stereotypes based on the relationship between IQ and race) believes that some students of colour are less capable of learning? Will that teacher (often without realizing it) treat such students as if they are incapable of learning? In their controversial book *The Bell Curve: Intelligence and Class Structure in American Life*, Richard J. Herrnstein and Charles Murray (1994) argue that intelligence is genetically inherited and that people cannot be "smarter" than they are born to be, regardless of their environment or education. According to Herrnstein and Murray, certain racial–ethnic groups differ in average IQ and are likely to differ in "intelligence genes" as well. For example, they point out that, on average, people living in Asia score higher on IQ tests than white Americans, and that African Americans score 15 points lower on average than white Americans. Based on an all-white sample, the authors also concluded that low intelligence leads to social pathology, such as high rates of crime, dropping out of school, and ending up poor. In contrast, high intelligence typically leads to success and family background plays only a secondary role.

Many scholars disagree with Herrnstein and Murray's research methods and conclusions. Two major flaws found in their approach were as follows: (1) the authors used biased statistics that underestimate the impact of hard-to-measure factors, such as family background, and (2) they used scores from the Armed Forces Qualification Test, an exam that depends on how much schooling people have completed. Thus, what the authors claim is immutable intelligence is actually acquired skills (Weinstein, 1997). Despite this refutation, the idea of inherited mental inferiority tends to take on a life of its own when people want to believe that such differences exist (Duster, 1995; Hauser, 1995; Taylor, 1995). According to researchers, many African American and Mexican American children were placed in special education classes on the basis of IQ scores when the students were not fluent in English and thus could not understand the directions given for the test. Moreover, when children are labelled as "special ed" students or as being "learning disabled," these terms are social constructions that may lead to stigmatization and become a self-fulfilling prophecy (Carrier, 1986; Coles, 1987).

Labelling students based on IQ scores has been an issue throughout the twentieth century. Immigrants from Southern and Eastern Europe—particularly from Italy, Poland, and Russia—who arrived in this country at the beginning of the twentieth century typically had lower IQ scores on average than did Northern European immigrants who had arrived earlier from nations such as Great Britain. For many of the white ethnic students, IQ testing became a self-fulfilling prophecy: teachers did not expect them to do as well as children from a Northern European (WASP) family background and thus did not encourage them or give them an opportunity to overcome language barriers or other educational obstacles. Although many students persisted and achieved an education, the possibility that differences in IQ scores could be attributed to linguistic, cultural, and educational biases in the tests was largely ignored (Feagin and Feagin, 1997). Debates over the possible intellectual inferiority of white ethnic groups are unthinkable today, but arguments pertaining to African Americans and IQ continue to surface.

A self-fulfilling prophecy can also result from labelling students as gifted. Gifted students are considered to be those with above-average intellectual ability, academic aptitude, creative or productive thinking, or leadership skills (Ballantine, 1999). When some students are labelled as better than others, they may achieve at a higher level because of the label. Ironically, such labelling may also result in discrimination against these students. For example, according to law professor Margaret Chon (1995:238), the "myth of the superhuman Asian" creates a self-fulfilling prophecy for some Asian American students:

> When I was in college, I applied to the Air Force ROTC program . . . I was given the most complete physical of my life [and] I took an intelligence test. When I reported back to the ROTC staff, they looked glum. What is it? I thought. Did the physical turn up some life-threatening defect? . . . It turned out I had gotten the highest test score ever at my school . . . Rather than feeling pleased and flattered, I felt like a sideshow freak. The recruiters were not happy either. I think our reactions had a lot to do with the fact that I did not resemble a typical recruit. I am a woman of East Asian, specifically Korean, descent . . . They did not want me in ROTC no matter how "intelligent" I was.

According to Chon, painting Asian Americans as superintelligent makes it possible for others to pretend they do not exist: "Governments ignore us because we've already made it. Schools won't recruit us because we do so well on the SATs . . . Asian Americans seem almost invisible, except when there is a grocery store boycott—or when we're touted as the model minority" (Chon, 1995: 239–240).

Labelling and the self-fulfilling prophecy are not unique to U.S. and Canadian schools. Around the globe, students are labelled by batteries of tests and teachers' evaluations of their attitudes, academic performance, and classroom behaviour. Other problems in education, ranging from illiteracy and school discipline to unequal school financing and educational opportunities for students with disabilities, are concerns in elementary and secondary education in many countries.

Postmodern Perspectives

Postmodern theories often highlight *difference* and *irregularity* in society. From this perspective, education—like the family—is a social institution characterized by its permeability. In contemporary schools, a wide diversity of family kinship systems is recognized, and educators attempt to be substitute parents and promulgators of self-esteem in students. Urbanity is reflected in multicultural and anti-bias curriculums that are initially introduced in early childhood education. Similarly, autonomy is evidenced in policies, such as voucher systems, under which parents have a choice about which schools their children will attend. Since the values of individual achievement and competition have so permeated contemporary home and school life, social adjustment (how to deal with others) has become of little importance to some people (Elkind, 1995).

How might a postmodern approach describe higher education? Postmodern views of higher education might incorporate the ideas of the sociologist George Ritzer (1998), who believes that "McUniversity" can be thought of as a means of educational consumption that allows students to consume educational services and eventually obtain "goods," such as degrees and credentials:

> Students (and often, more importantly, their parents) are increasingly approaching the university as consumers; the university is fast becoming little more than another component

of the consumer society . . . Parents are, if anything, likely to be even more adept as consumers than their children and because of the burgeoning cost of higher education more apt to bring a consumerist mentality to it. (Ritzer, 1998:151–152)

Savvy college and university administrators are aware of the permeability of higher education and the "students-as-consumers" model:

[Students] want education to be nearby and to operate during convenient hours—preferably around the clock. They want to avoid traffic jams, to have easy, accessible and low cost parking, short lines, and polite and efficient personnel and services. They also want high-quality products but are eager for low costs. They are willing to shop—placing a premium on time and money. (Levine, 1993:4)

To attract new students and enhance current students' opportunities for consumption, many campuses have student centres equipped with amenities, such as food courts, ATMs, video games,

Olympic-sized swimming pools, and massive rock-climbing walls. "High-tech" or "wired" campuses are also a major attraction for student consumers, and virtual classrooms make it possible for some students to earn postsecondary credits without having to look for a parking place at the traditional bricks-and-mortar campus.

The permeability of contemporary universities may be so great that eventually it will be impossible to distinguish higher education from other means of consumption. For example, Ritzer (1998) believes that officials of "McUniversity" will start to emphasize the same kinds of production values as CNN or MTV, resulting in a simulated world of education somewhat like postmodernist views of Disneyland. Based on Baudrillard's fractal stage, where everything interpenetrates, Ritzer (1998:160) predicts that we may enter a "trans-educational" era: "Since education will be everywhere, since everything will be educational, in a sense nothing will be educational." Based on a postmodern approach, what do you believe will be the predominant means by which future students will consume educational services and goods at your college or university?

Concept Table 16.A SOCIOLOGICAL ANALYSIS OF EDUCATION

PERSPECTIVE	KEY TERMS	KEY ELEMENTS
Functionalist	Manifest and latent functions; moral education	Education to the maintenance of society by transmitting "shared" social values–provides for self-enhancement and upward mobility.
Conflict	Cultural capital; tracking; hidden curriculum	Education perpetuates social inequality and benefits; reproduces existing class relationships at the expense of those students in the lower classes.
Feminist	Gender bias	Gender bias exists throughout all levels of education; reading materials, classroom activities, and student-teacher interactions teach female students they are less important.
Symbolic Interactionist	Labelling, self-fulfilling prophecy	Classroom communication patterns and educational practices, such as labelling based on standardized tests, affect a student's self concept and lead to self-fulfilling prophecies.
Postmodern	Family kinship; urbanity; autonomy	Education is social institution characterized by permeability.

BOX 16.3 SOCIOLOGY AND TECHNOLOGY

The Technology Revolution in the Classroom: Equalizing Opportunity

Technology itself is not new, but its importance as an educational issue has exploded in the past few years as computers have moved into classrooms and workplaces. No longer simply an object of study for those who want to pursue "technical" careers, technology–particularly computer technology–has become an essential educational tool. Like reading or writing, it is now recognized as a prerequisite for student success. Word processing, simulations, and computerized data analysis have become as standard in schools as typewriters and adding machines a generation ago. In fact, the technological revolution is moving at such a rapid pace that any review of "current" activities is certain to be obsolete by the time it is read.

Canada was one of the first countries in the world to link its entire student body to the information highway. In 1995, Newfoundland and Labrador became the first province with full Internet access, linking all schools to the World Wide Web and the Internet; by 1977, virtually all schools in the country had access to the Internet via the SchoolNet national electronic network. Despite overall reductions in education budgets, most provinces have introduced systematic plans to expand the role of technology in the curriculum, primarily through the acquisition of computer hardware and software for classroom use.

A number of provinces have set specific targets for classroom computer acquisition, and Industry Canada's "Computers in the Schools" program has moved thousands of used computers, software, and other technologies from industry into Canadian classrooms.

Once in place, computers are being used to train teachers as well as students and to offer computer training and Internet access to the community. Human Resources Development Canada has set up the Office of Learning Technologies (OLT) expressly to provide funding support to innovative learning opportunities using new technologies. At the college and university level, many students are taking courses online and many corporations use the Internet to provide training to their employees.

Proponents of computers in schools see them as a powerful tool for levelling the playing field in Canadian classrooms. Their capacity to retrieve information is nearly limitless, and equally available in urban, rural, and remote locations; they can be equipped with features that allow many children with disabilities to work alongside their classmates; and they increase understanding within Canada and internationally by allowing students to connect with individuals and classrooms across the country and around the world.

Nevertheless, there are those who have reservations about the expanding role of computer technology in schools. Some parents and teachers continue to fear that, in the face of reduced school budgets, students may find themselves facing machines more frequently than teachers. They also express concern about the quality and suitability of information available on the Internet. Educators stress the importance of teaching students the skills to evaluate that information, since, at this point, the Internet does not impose standards equivalent to those of the publishing industry or exercise the judgment of a school librarian.

Source: Excerpted with permission from Dunning, 1997.

CURRENT ISSUES IN EDUCATION

Public schools in Canada today are a microcosm of many of the issues and problems facing the country. Canada is the only advanced industrialized country without a federal educational system—a fact that has made it difficult to coordinate national educational and teaching standards. Each province enacts its own laws and regulations, with local school boards frequently making the final determination regarding curriculum. Accordingly, no general standards exist as to what is to be taught to students or how, although many provinces have now adopted standards for what (at a minimum) must be learned in order to graduate from high school. France has an education ministry that is officially responsible for every elementary school in the nation. Japan has a centrally controlled curriculum; in England, national achievement tests are administered by the government and students must pass them in order to advance to the next level of education (Lemann, 1997).

Inequality in Public Schools versus Private Schools

Often, there is a perceived conflict between public schools and private schools for students and financial resources. However, far more students and their parents are dependent on public schools than on private ones for providing a high-quality education. Enrolment in Canadian elementary and secondary education (kindergarten through Grade 12) totals approximately 5.4 million students. More than 90 percent of elementary and secondary students are educated in public schools. About 6 percent of all students are educated in private schools, and approximately 1 percent of all students attend private schools with tuition of more than $5,000 a year (Statistics Canada, 2000c).

Private secondary boarding schools tend to be reserved for students from high-income families and for a few lower-income or minority students who are able to acquire academic or athletic scholarships that cover their tuition, room and board, and other expenses. The average cost for seven-day tuition and room and board at secondary boarding schools is nearly $20,000 a year, whereas the cost of day-school tuition can be as high as $8,000.

An important factor for many parents whose children attend private secondary schools is the emphasis on academics that they believe exists in private (as opposed to public) schools. Another is the moral and ethical standards that they believe private secondary schools instil in students. Overall, many families believe that private schools are a better choice for their children because they are more academically demanding, more motivating, more focused on discipline, and without many of the inadequacies found in public schools (Peterson's Educational Center, 1996). However, according to some social analysts, there is little to substantiate the claim that private schools (other than elite academies attended by the children of the wealthiest and most influential families) are inherently better than public schools (Institute for Social Research, 1995).

Dropping Out

Although the overall school dropout (or school leaver) rate has significantly decreased in recent decades, about 12 percent of people under the age of 20 still leave school before earning a high school diploma. Ethnic and class differences are important factors in the data on dropout rates. For example, Aboriginal students have a dropout rate of more than 40 percent. Recent immigrants to Canada were much less likely to drop out before they had completed high school. The dropout rate also varies by region— Prince Edward Island and Quebec had the highest proportion of school dropouts in 1999 at 16 percent, while Saskatchewan had the lowest at 7 percent (Statistics Canada, 2002s).

Why do students drop out? According to the recent Youth in Transition Survey, poor academic performance is only one characteristic shared by many youth who had dropped out of school. The dropouts were less engaged in school both academically and socially. They were less likely to have close friends who pursued education past high school, and were more likely to have skipped classes, to drink alcohol regularly, and to use drugs frequently (Statistics Canada, 2002s). Some students may drop out of school partly because their teachers have labelled them troublemakers. Some students are repeatedly expelled from school before they actually become dropouts. In a study by sociologist Howard Pinderhughes, one of the respondents—Rocco—discusses his reasons for leaving school:

> I never liked school. The teachers all hated my guts because I didn't just accept what they had to say. I was kind of a wiseass, and that got me in trouble. But that's not why they kept kicking me out of school. Either I didn't come to school or I got in fights when I did come. It got so I got a reputation that people heard about and there was always some kid challengin' me. (quoted in Pinderhughes, 1997:58)

Other students may view school as a waste of time. Another respondent in Pinderhughes's study— Ronnie—explains why he dropped out:

> I thought [school] was a big waste of time. I knew older guys who had dropped out of the tenth grade and within a couple of years were makin' cash money as a mechanic or carpenter. My brothers did the same

thing. I didn't think I was learnin' no skill that I could get a job in school. I wasn't very good in school. It was pretty damn boring. So I left. (quoted in Pinderhughes, 1997:58)

Female dropouts also identified boredom and a preference for work as important reasons for leaving school. However, they also cited problems with school work and pregnancy/marriage as factors involved in their decision to quit school (Statistics Canada, 2002s).

Students who drop out of school may be skeptical about the value of education in improving their job opportunities. Upon leaving school, many dropouts have high hopes of making money and enjoying their new freedom. However, these feelings often turn to disappointment when they find that few jobs are available and that they do not meet the educational requirements for any of the "good" jobs that exist (Pinderhughes, 1997). Increasingly, high school completion or higher is the minimum level of education needed for entry-level jobs.

Although critics of the public education system point to high dropout rates as proof of failure in the public education system, these rates have steadily declined in Canada since the 1950s, when more than 70 percent of students did not complete high school (Luciw, 2002).

Academic Standards and Functional Illiteracy

Across Canada, thousands of parents are expressing their concerns that the public school system is doing a poor job of teaching their children (Osborne, 1999). Although parents may have always been difficult to please, an increasing number are dissatisfied with the quality of their children's education. A recent opinion poll shows that Canadians are fairly evenly divided as to whether schools are getting better or worse, with the exception of people in Ontario and the Atlantic provinces. Respondents from the Atlantic provinces were the most optimistic, with 61 percent indicating that schools were getting better. In contrast, close to 60 percent of Ontario residents indicated they felt the academic standards in their schools were declining. The same opinion poll also shows that Canadian parents have high expectations of the education system and want more emphasis on the fundamentals of English and math, particularly in high school (Smyth, 2001).

How do students feel about the quality of their education? A survey of 500 university students indicated that 52 percent of respondents felt that high school had not prepared them properly for university. Postsecondary institutions and employers were also disillusioned with the level of preparedness they were finding in high school graduates (Canadian Education Association, 1999). The result is that many universities across the country have implemented remedial math and English classes to bring students up to the skill level they need to complete their degrees.

Much of the blame for declining standards in the 1980s and early 1990s has been directed at educational reforms focusing on *child-centred education*— a system of learning that encourages children to progress at their own rate. Critics of child-centred education argue that because this system did not impose clear standards it is unaccountable and produces students who cannot read and write. Critics of child-centred teaching methods also pointed to the declining skill level of students.

As further evidence of declining academic standards, social analysts cite the rate of functional illiteracy in this country. **Functional illiteracy is the inability to read and/or write at the skill level necessary for carrying out everyday tasks.** Everyday tasks include reading a newspaper, filling out a form, or following written instructions. Seventeen percent of adult Canadians do not have the skills to handle most of the written material they see every day; that is, they are functionally illiterate. An additional 24 percent can use reading materials only to carry out simple reading tasks. They do not have the reading skills to cope with unfamiliar and more complex reading materials. In other words,

Illiteracy is a problem across all age categories. Today, many adults are enrolled in classes that will help them learn to read, write, and speak English.

they can read, but not well (ABC Canada Literacy Foundation, 2001). Overall, Canada has a high rate of adult literacy compared with the seven other countries surveyed in the International Adult Literacy Survey (Organisation for Economic Co-operation and Development and Statistics Canada, 2000). However, Canada also had the largest proportion of youth with poor literacy skills (10 percent). To learn what you can do to combat this problem, see Box 16.4.

BOX 16.4 YOU CAN MAKE A DIFFERENCE

Mentoring in a Literacy Program

Are you surprised that so many young Canadians continue to struggle with reading and writing? University and college students from across the country are addressing this issue personally by volunteering in youth and child literacy mentor programs. Following are the comments of one university student who participates in a literacy program in Ontario:

> My name is Yolanda. I am twenty-two years old and am entering my fourth year at the University of Guelph. I am a volunteer as a tutor at an elementary school in Guelph. I got involved with Frontier College at a volunteer fair that was being held at the university. I was actually there with the Heart & Stroke Foundation looking for volunteers myself. The Frontier College display was just down from mine and it sounded like it would be a great experience without being a huge time commitment. So I signed up and ended up tutoring a girl in grade 3.
>
> There are quite a few moments I could share, some amusing, others frustrating!! But I think I felt the most proud during one of my last sessions with Brittany. As we worked through the tasks that the teacher had assigned us for the day, I began to notice a considerable improvement in Brittany's reading! Some of the words that she struggled with before now came much easier for her. I couldn't help but feel proud knowing that the time we spent together contributed to this improvement!

Frontier College is a national volunteer-based organization that relies upon volunteers from communities in all parts of the country to deliver its programs. Each program area recruits, trains, and places volunteers at various times through the year, depending on need. Trained volunteers work with adolescent and adult literacy learners, including prison inmates, people with physical disabilities, and others marginalized by society, to improve their reading and writing skills. Volunteers also help recent immigrants to Canada improve their English, encourage young children and their families to read together, and work side-by-side with migrant farm workers during the day and tutor them in English and literacy at night.

Are You Qualified to Be a Literacy Tutor?

You do not need to be a teacher or have a teaching background to be a Frontier College tutor. Everyone has the capacity to help another person improve their literacy or English language skills. Frontier College will provide you with comprehensive training and follow-up support.

Volunteer Screening

Frontier College adheres to the principle of duty of care toward its clients. For that reason, it carries out a careful screening of all volunteers. This is also to ensure that this is the right volunteer job for you, so that you will have a positive experience as a tutor. Screening includes all or some of the following: attending an information session, completing an application form, a personal interview, personal reference checks, and a police record check (paid for by Frontier College and as of September 2003 conducted every two years on new volunteers). For more information about volunteering in your area visit http://www.frontiercollege.ca/english/canada/canada.htm.

Source: Frontier College, 2005.

Table 16.2 NATIONS WITH LOWEST LITERACY RATES	
COUNTRY	LITERACY RATE
Niger	14%
Burkina Faso	19%
Somalia	24%
Eritrea	25%
Nepal	28%
Mali	31%
Sierra Leone	31%
Afghanistan	32%
Senegal	33%
Cambodia	35%

Source: CIA, 2001.

Illiteracy is a global problem as well as a national one (see Table 16.2). As a result of the concerns with declining standards and illiteracy, school boards across the country have been revising their curriculum to place a greater emphasis on the core subject areas of reading, mathematics, and science. Educators are also returning to more objective criteria and expectations and to more traditional teaching methods. The curriculum in most provinces has specified outcomes and objectives for age and grade levels. Some provinces are also moving away from the practice of passing children from grade to grade with their peers regardless of their achievement level. Educators in the public school system are also returning to an emphasis on testing and evaluation. In addition to increasing the amount of testing at the classroom level, the majority of provinces have introduced tests to assess systemwide performance levels. Final exams in high school, which were virtually eliminated in the 1970s and 1980s, are now mandatory in nine provinces (Canadian Education Association, 1999). Given their dissatisfaction with the public school system, some parents are moving away from traditional public schools and trying alternatives, such as home-schooling or charter schools. Sociologists also have concluded that more research is needed on how gender bias affects both female and male students and that more forums are needed in schools and elsewhere to allow people to discuss how education contributes to sexism and a limited view of masculinity and femininity that directly affects individuals and their academic accomplishments (see Thorne, 1993; Eder, 1995; Orenstein, 1995).

Equalizing Opportunities for Students with Disabilities

Another recent concern in education has been how to provide better educational opportunities for students with disabilities.

As we will see in Chapter 18, the term *disability* has a wide range of definitions (see Shapiro, 1993). For the purposes of this chapter, disability is regarded as any physical and/or mental condition that limits students' access to, or full involvement in, school life. As recently as 1994, eleven-year-old Emily Eaton, a Grade 4 student, was placed in a segregated classroom in a public school in a small community in Ontario because teachers and school board officials had decided that her severe cerebral palsy made it extremely difficult for her to learn in a regular classroom environment. Her parents disagreed, believing that the regular classroom was the best learning environment for their daughter. The courts agreed with the parents, finding that "Emily had a constitutional right to attend school with fully able children [and that] segregating Emily because of her disability—against her parents' wishes and without establishing that she would be better off in a segregated classroom—was no different than segregating her on the basis of race or gender" (Chisholm, 1995:53).

As this case demonstrates, the barriers facing students with disabilities are slowly being removed or surmounted by new legislation (Nagler, 1997). Today, most people with disabilities are no longer prevented from experiencing the full range of academic opportunities. Under various provincial human rights guidelines and the *Charter of Rights and Freedoms,* all children with disabilities are guaranteed a free and appropriate public education. This means that local school boards must make the necessary efforts and expenditures to accommodate special-needs students.

Many schools have attempted to *mainstream* children with disabilities by *inclusion programs* (Nagler, 1997). Inclusion means that children with disabilities work with a wide variety of people; over the course of a day, children may interact with their regular education teacher, the special education teacher, a speech therapist, an occupational therapist, a physical therapist, and a resource teacher, depending on the child's individual needs. Today, more than 70 percent of children with disabilities are integrated into mainstream schools. Only fifteen years ago, more than 80 percent of these children were placed in segregated schools. This dramatic change reflects growing acceptance of the fact that children with a range of disabilities often thrive in an integrated learning environment.

Although much remains to be done, recent measures to enhance education for children with disabilities has increased the inclusion of many young people who were formerly excluded or marginalized in the educational system (see Box 16.3). But the problem of equal educational opportunities does not end at the elementary and high school level for students with disabilities. If these students complete high school and continue on to university, they find new sets of physical and academic barriers that limit their access to higher education. Sociology professor Mark Nagler, who has cerebral palsy, recalls the academic barriers he faced when obtaining his Ph.D.:

> My parents made me aware that many people would make fun of my condition and that both kids and adults might create embarrassing situations . . . The former chairperson of a Sociology Graduate Department at a prominent university told me I should go home and live with my parents as I would never make it as a professor. Twenty-eight years later I am still proving him wrong. (Nagler, 1997:6)

Author Connie Panzarino (1994:219), who was born with the rare disease spinal muscular atrophy type III, explains how difficult it was to attend university without being able to take a shower:

> I received a letter from the Disabled Students Office informing me that the administration had to indefinitely put off installing wheelchair-accessible showers. "How the Hell am I supposed to stay healthy if I can't stay clean?" I thought to myself . . . Several of the disabled students had already fallen while trying to take showers or baths in the undersized, nonregulation tubs in our bathrooms. My Hoyer bathtub lift would not fit into these tubs.

But, as other students with disabilities have learned, a little activism sometimes resolves the problem. After Panzarino called a "shower strike" in which students with and without disabilities refused to bathe until something was done about the showers, the university constructed accessible showers for each wheelchair-accessible dorm room (Panzarino, 1994). Today, building codes have

been changed to require educational institutions to be accessible (Nagler, 1997). Many colleges and universities have provided relatively inexpensive accommodations to make facilities more accessible to students with disabilities. Despite these efforts, students with disabilities continue to be underrepresented at the postsecondary level. Statistics indicate that although persons with disabilities made up 7 percent of the total postsecondary student population in 1991, they represented less than 4 percent of university graduates. They did, however, account for 6.5 percent of community college graduates (Wannell and Caron, 1994).

The Cost of Postsecondary Education

Who attends college or university? What sort of college or university do they attend? Even for students who complete high school, access to colleges and universities is determined not only by prior academic record but also by the ability to pay.

Postsecondary education has been described as the dividing line of the modern labour market. Today more than ever before, employers want employees with a university degree, college diploma, or some other form of postsecondary educational certificate. As shown in Figure 16.2, for most Canadians higher education will result in higher earnings. However, in order to obtain a university education, students must have the necessary financial resources. What does a university education cost? In Canada, postsecondary education is funded by the federal and provincial governments, and by parents and students through personal savings. As governments cut their funding to higher education, an increasing financial burden is falling on the shoulders of students and their parents. To make matters worse, the cost of attending university has increased dramatically over the past twenty years. Increases in tuition fees have outstripped the rate of inflation every year since 1983. A prominent investment company estimated the cost of one year of undergraduate studies at almost $9,000. The Canadian Federation of Students indicated that the cost may be closer to $15,000 when living expenses are included. According to the Federation chairman, "More than ever, getting into the system depends not just on ability, but on how much money a person has" (Farren, 1998:45). Despite the soaring cost of postsecondary education, the percentage of young people attending university

| Figure 16.2 | Levels of Earning and Education, 2001 |

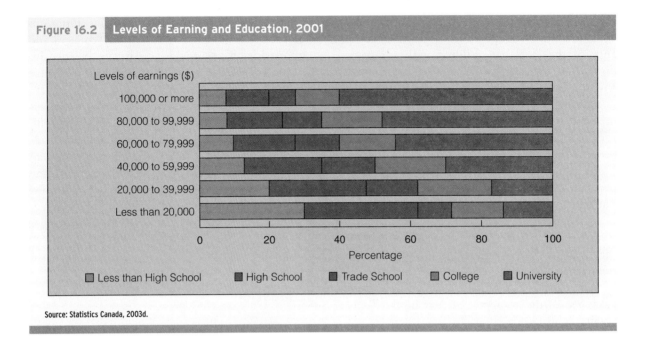

Source: Statistics Canada, 2003d.

Soaring costs at both public and private institutions of higher education are a pressing problem for today's university students and their parents. What factors have contributed to the higher overall costs of obtaining a university degree?

continued to rise in the first years of the 1990s. However, undergraduate enrolment has declined over the past seven consecutive years, an indication that for some students the cost of a university education has become prohibitive.

How do students afford this increasingly costly education? The 2001–2002 Student Financial Survey explored this question with a sample of 1,500 recent students. Both college and university graduates identified employment earnings and student loan programs as their primary sources of funding. Parents ranked a close third for university graduates. Scholarships, fellowships, grants, and bursaries were rarely identified as a significant source of funding. Approximately one-third of college and university students indicated that they relied on student loans to finance their education. Close to 30 percent of students surveyed anticipated debt of over $10,000 once their education was completed (EKOS Research Associates, 2003).

A substantial proportion of postsecondary students choose community college because of the lower costs. However, the overall enrolment of low-income students in community colleges has dropped as a result of increasing costs and also because many students must work full-time or part-time to pay for their education. Many Canadian colleges have implemented three- and four-year degree-granting programs that are an excellent

Today, computers are essential learning tools in most Canadian classrooms. Proponents of computers in schools see them as a powerful way to equalize opportunities for all students. What do you think are the negative aspects of using computers to teach in schools?

option but may be cost and time prohibitive for low-income students. In contrast, students from more affluent families are more likely to attend prestigious public universities or private colleges outside of Canada, where tuition fees alone may be more than $20,000 per year.

According to some social analysts, a university education is a bargain—even at about $90 a day for private schools or $35 for public schools—because for their money students receive instruction, room, board, and other amenities such as athletic facilities and job placement services. However, other analysts believe that the high cost of a university education reproduces the existing class system: Students who lack money may be denied access to higher education, and those who are able to attend college or university tend to receive different types of education based on their ability to pay. For example, a community college student who receives an associate's degree or completes a certificate program may be prepared for a position in the middle of the occupational status range, such as a dental assistant, computer programmer, or auto mechanic (Gilbert, 1998). In contrast, university graduates with four-year degrees are more likely to find initial employment with firms where they stand a chance of being promoted to high-paying management and executive positions. Although higher education may be a source of upward mobility for talented young people from poor families, the Canadian system of higher education is sufficiently stratified

that it may also reproduce the existing class structure (Gilbert, 1998; Barlow and Robertson, 1994; Davies, 1999).

EDUCATION IN THE FUTURE

This chapter ends as it began, by noting that education will remain an important institution in this century. Also remaining, however, will be the controversies that we have discussed—controversies that your generation will attempt to resolve. Questions will remain about what should be taught, not only in terms of preparing your children for their adult lives and the world of work but also with regard to the values to which you want your child exposed. The debate over what should be taught is not limited to moral issues; rather, it includes the entire curriculum. If, as critics assert, academic achievement in Canada compares unfavourably with the level of achievement by students in many other countries, what can be done to change the situation?

In recent decades, the Canadian public has been demanding greater accountability for student outcomes (Osbourne, 1999). A number of policy initiatives have been introduced in the public school system that should result in an improvement in the quality of education. At the elementary and secondary level there has been a shift toward increased emphasis on curriculum standards and more testing and provincial exams. In addition, *compensatory education programs,* including preschool, remedial, and extra education programs, which provide additional learning assistance to disadvantaged children, have been designed to address the effects of poverty, deprivation, and disadvantage on school performance (Guppy, 1995). Although these programs were tried and failed twenty years earlier, more recent compensatory programs have produced more favourable results.

Some elected officials, business leaders, and educators have shifted their focus to other ways of improving education. Some are advocating school-voucher programs, which give parents the choice of what school their child will attend. This strategy would make it possible for low-income children to leave behind the problems of the particular public schools and find better educational opportunities elsewhere. The question remains, however: What happens to those who remain in the inferior public schools?

Will distance learning courses change the face of the typical college or university classroom? What do you believe education will be like in the future?

The charter school movement has as its focus the creation of public schools that are free from many of the bureaucratic rules that often limit classroom performance. These schools operate under a charter contract negotiated by the school's organizers (often parents or teachers) and the local school board that oversees the provisions of the contract. A charter school is freed from the day-to-day bureaucracy of a larger school board and may provide more autonomy for individual students and teachers. However, critics of the charter school movement argue that it takes money away from conventional schools.

A final alternative, home-schooling, has been chosen by some parents who hope to avoid the problems of public school while providing a high-quality education for their children. Today, an estimated 70,000 children are educated in home-school programs. An association of home-schoolers now provides communication links for parents and children, and technological advances in computers and the Internet have made it possible for parents and children involved in home-schooling to access information and communicate with one another. However, critics question the knowledge and competence of typical parents to educate their own children at home, particularly in rapidly changing academic subjects, such as science and computer technology.

Increasingly, information technologies are being accepted as an integral part of education. Since 1993, the federal government has spent more than $25 million to create the SchoolNet system—a student-friendly Web site that links students with experts in a variety of fields, as well as with students and teachers across the country. The objective of SchoolNet was to bring every school in Canada online by the year 2000; the effects of the introduction of computer technologies to the classroom remain to be seen. While some experts argue that it will transform the way students learn, others view "high tech" teaching as simply the latest panacea in education.

What will education be like in the future? School enrolments will continue to grow and diversify as baby boomers continue to have children, and immigration to Canada creates an increasingly diverse population of students. The challenge lies in finding ways to facilitate learning in a pluralistic school system—by meeting the distinct cultural, linguistic, and religious traditions of a diverse student population.

A further challenge for educational systems in the future is to make education more accessible to all disadvantaged groups in Canadian society. Considerable progress has been made in diminishing the educational disparities among women and men and among most visible minority groups. Although differences remain in terms of types of education and fields of study, women now have outcomes superior to men on many measures of educational attainment. Similarly, the educational attainment of many visible minority groups is among the highest in Canada. However, although Aboriginal peoples and persons with disabilities have improved their educational levels in recent decades, progress remains slow (see Census Profile on page 523). Finally, social class continues to be the most persistent and enduring source of educational inequality at all levels of education, from preschool through university.

CENSUS ✦ PROFILE

Persons Aged 25 to 64 Reporting Aboriginal Identity Show Improved Levels of Educational Attainment

	1996	2001
Less than high school	45.20	38.71
High school	21.39	22.85
Trades	14.10	15.61
College	13.21	15.06
University	6.11	7.71
Part-time	9.34	7.84

Source: Statistics Canada 2003e.

Recent trends suggest that access to education is becoming more restricted as a result of funding cuts at both the provincial and federal levels. Course availability is diminished as school curricula are pared down to "core" subjects, and the specialized services of speech pathologists, physiotherapists, and psychologists are being cut, leaving some children—such as children with special needs, children from low-income families, and children from new immigrant families—without the services they need to help them achieve their full potential in the school system (Canadian Council on Social Development, 2001). At the postsecondary level, tuition fees are rising at a rate that has made university and college educations unaffordable for low-income students. If education is one of the key factors in promoting individual and collective prosperity, then we must strive to improve educational opportunities to all Canadians (Guppy and Davies, 1998).

CHAPTER REVIEW

■ What is education?

Education is the social institution responsible for the systematic transmission of knowledge, skills, and cultural values within a formally organized structure.

■ What is the functionalist perspective on education?

According to functionalists, education has both manifest functions (socialization, transmission of culture, social control, social placement, and change and innovation) and latent functions (keeping young people off the streets and out of the job market, matchmaking and producing social networks, and creating a generation gap).

■ What is the conflict perspective on education?

From a conflict perspective, education is used to perpetuate class, racial–ethnic, and gender inequalities through tracking, ability grouping, and a hidden curriculum that teaches subordinate groups conformity and obedience.

■ What is the interactionist perspective on education?

Interactionists examine classroom dynamics and study ways in which practices, such as labelling, may become a self-fulfilling prophecy for some students, such that these students come to perform up—or down—to the expectations held for them by teachers.

■ What percentage of students drop out before completing high school?

Approximately 12 percent of people under the age of 24 left school before earning a high school diploma. There are, however, significant ethnic and class differences in dropout rates.

■ **Are academic standards in the Canadian education system declining? Why?**

According to both parents and recent international tests of math, science, and English, Canadian students are failing to make the grade in comparison with other industrialized countries. Much of the blame for these declining standards has been directed at child-centred education—a system of learning that encourages children to progress at their own rate.

■ **What is functional illiteracy, and what is the rate of functional illiteracy in Canada?**

Functional illiteracy is the inability to read and/or write at the skill level necessary for carrying out everyday tasks. The International Adult Literacy Survey indicated that 16 percent of adult Canadians are functionally illiterate. Furthermore, Canada has the highest rate of youth with poor literacy skills among the leading industrialized nations.

■ **What controversies persist in education?**

Gender bias in the classroom, unequal educational opportunities for students with disabilities, and the soaring cost of a university education are among the pressing issues in education in Canada today.

KEY TERMS

credentialism 508
cultural capital 506
cultural transmission 499
education 499
formal education 500
functional illiteracy 516
hidden curriculum 508
informal education 500
mass education 501
tracking 507

NET LINKS

The National Adult Literacy Database is a national database of adult literacy programs, resources, services, and activities across Canada. It also links with other services and databases in North America and overseas; go to:
http://www.nald.ca/

The Canadian Teachers' Federation is an excellent source of information on teaching in Canada as well as current issues facing schools; see:
http://www.ctf-fce.ca/

The Canadian Federation of Students represents about half a million students at more than sixty universities, colleges, and technical institutes across Canada. Its Web site has been established to offer students, the general public, media, and government officials information on the issues facing college and university students today; go to:
http://www.cfs-fcee.ca/

The Council of Ministers of Education is the national voice of education in Canada. Its Web site contains valuable articles covering educational issues on the provincial, national, and international levels; go to:
http://www.cmec.ca/

QUESTIONS FOR CRITICAL THINKING

1. What are the major functions of education for individuals and for societies?
2. Why do some theorists believe that education is a vehicle for decreasing social inequality whereas others believe that education reproduces existing class relationships?
3. Why does so much controversy exist over what should be taught in Canadian public schools?
4. How are the values and attitudes you learned from your family reflected in your beliefs about education?

SUGGESTED READINGS

These books provides more information about the sociology of education:

Jeanne H. Ballantine. *The Sociology of Education: A Systematic Analysis* (4th ed.). Englewood Cliffs, N.J.: Prentice-Hall, 1997.

Ratna Ghosh and Douglas Ray. *Social Change and Education in Canada* (3rd ed.). Toronto: Nelson, 1995.

Comprehensive discussions on problems in today's schools may be found in the following studies:

Maude Barlow and Heather-Jane Robertson. *Class Warfare: The Assault on Canada's Schools.* Toronto: Key Porter Books, 1994.

Neil Guppy and Scott Davies. *Education in Canada: Recent Trends and Future Challenges.* Ottawa: Statistics Canada, 1998.

ONLINE STUDY AND RESEARCH TOOLS

THOMSONNOW™ *Thomson NOW!*

Go to **http://hed.nelson.com** to link to ThomsonNOW for *Sociology in Our Times,* Fourth Canadian Edition, your online study tool. First take the **Pre-Test** for this chapter to get your personalized **Study Plan,** which will identify topics you need to review and direct you to the appropriate resources. Then take the **Post-Test** to determine what concepts you have mastered and what you still need work on.

INFOTRAC®

Infotrac College Edition is included free with every new copy of this text. Explore this online library for additional readings, review, and a handy resource for assignments. Visit **www.infotrac-college.com** to access this online database of full-text articles. Enter the key terms from this chapter to start your search.

Religion

For most of Canada's history, religion played a major role in the development and maintenance of educational institutions. Religious instruction was considered an essential component of "becoming educated." Which religion was to be taught was relatively simple—it was Christianity in either its Catholic or Protestant form. Today, things are not that simple—while the majority of Canadians are Christians, with Catholics making up 43 percent and Protestants 29 percent, other religions, such as Hinduism, Islam, Buddhism, Confucianism, Sikhism, and others too numerous to mention, are now part of our Canadian mosaic (Statistics Canada, 2003j). Currently, there is no consensus among Canadians regarding the role religion should play in education.

Should students receive religious instruction in the classroom? If so, which religions should be included? Should prayer be offered in schools? Should participation in prayer be voluntary or compulsory? In our multi-ethnic society, these questions are becoming increasingly difficult to answer. Some parents feel that religious instruction is necessary, suggesting that secularization in the public school system is contributing to a declining morality.

Albertans Dick and Joanne Barendregt teach their children at home. While homeschooling is relatively common in Canada,

the Barendregts are part of a growing network of parents who disobey the law by not registering their children or allowing provincial officials to monitor their children's education because they feel this would interfere with their religious freedom. The couple decided to educate their children at home after they found that one of their children's textbooks had a section on evolution that conflicted with their religious views.

Joanne Barendregt feels that "in two or three years, they're going to regulate what we feed our children . . . and after that it will be our reproductive systems." She goes on to say that "we feel the highest calling a girl can have is to be a wife and mother first. We teach that that is their purpose . . . We are not changing. You [society] have changed. You're trying to destroy our [religious] heritage." Her husband says they will not register with the government because "we will not have a partnership with a government that promotes and allows homosexuality to continue, and abortion" (Mitchell, 1999:A7).

The Barendregts feel that religious instruction is a vital part of education. However, others feel that the educational system must be separate from religion and that the curriculum should be based on secular concerns.

Proponents of this point of view suggest that in our multicultural society no religion should be espoused or endorsed. How can schools teach religious values that might conflict with the values and customs of a significant number of students? How might students and teachers who come from diverse religious and cultural backgrounds feel about instruction or organized prayer in public schools? Rick Nelson, a teacher in the public school system, explains his concern about the potential impact of religion in his classroom:

"I think it really trivializes religion when you try to take such a serious topic with so many different viewpoints and cover it in the public schools. At my school we have teachers and students who are Hindu. They are really devout, but they are not monotheistic. I am not opposed to individual prayer by students. But when there is a group prayer, who's going to lead the group?" (CNN, 1994).

T his argument is only one in a lengthy history of debates about the appropriate relationship between religion and other social institutions. In education, for example, controversies have arisen over topics such as the teaching of creationism versus evolutionism, moral education, sex education, school prayer, and the subject matter of textbooks and library books.

What role does religion play in Canada's school systems today? The simple answer is that religion plays almost no role in the public school system. Most of those who wish to combine education with religious instruction must do so through private schooling. However, education falls within provincial jurisdiction, and some provinces provide public funding to Roman Catholic separate schools (Holmes, 1998). For example, Saskatchewan and Ontario fully fund Roman Catholic schools, but do not support schools operated by members of other religious denominations. On the other hand, Manitoba and British Columbia do not use religion as a criterion, but provide funding to a wide variety of

private schools (many of which are religious schools) based on academic criteria. Ontario's situation is quite interesting, as the teaching of the Christian religion in the public school system, which was once mandatory, is now forbidden. At the same time, Roman Catholic schools are fully funded. This means that the Protestant majority cannot teach its religion in the public schools, while the Catholic minority has its own funded system. All other minorities and Protestants who wish a religious-based education receive no provincial support (Holmes, 1998).

As the issue of religious education suggests, religion can be a highly controversial topic. One group's deeply held beliefs or cherished religious practices may be a source of irritation to another. Religion is a source of both stability and conflict throughout the world (Kurtz, 1995). In this chapter, we examine how religion influences life in Canada and in other areas of the world. Before reading on, test your knowledge about how religion affects public education in this country by taking the quiz in Box 17.1.

QUESTIONS AND ISSUES

Chapter Focus Question: What is the relationship between society and religion, and what role does religion play in people's everyday lives?

What are the key components of religion?

How do functionalist, conflict, interactionist, and feminist perspectives on religion differ?

What are the central beliefs of the world's religions?

How do religious bodies differ in organizational structure?

What is the future of religion in Canada?

Debates about what children should be taught in schools have taken place throughout the history of Canadian public education. The issue of teaching creationism versus evolution in science classrooms is only one example of the intersection of religion and education.

THE SOCIOLOGICAL STUDY OF RELIGION

What is religion? *Religion* **is a system of beliefs, symbols, and rituals, based on some sacred or supernatural realm, that guides human behaviour, gives meaning to life, and unites believers into a community** (Durkheim, 1995/1912). For many people, religious beliefs provide the answers to the difficult questions about the meaning of life and death. Religion is one of the most significant social institutions in society. As such, it consists of a variety of elements, including beliefs about the sacred or supernatural, rituals, and a social organization of believers drawn together by their common religious tradition (Kurtz,

1995). This system of beliefs seeks to bridge the gap between the known and the unknown, the seen and the unseen, and the sacred ("holy, set apart, or forbidden") and the secular (things of this world). Most religions attempt to answer fundamental questions such as those regarding the meaning of life and how the world was created. Most religions also provide comfort to persons facing emotional traumas, such as illness, suffering, grief, and death. According to Lester Kurtz (1995:9), religious beliefs are typically woven into a series of narratives, including stories about how ancestors and other significant figures had meaningful experiences with supernatural powers. Moreover, religious beliefs are linked to practices that bind people together and to rites of passage, such as birth, marriage, and death. People with similar religious beliefs and practices often bind themselves together in a moral community (such as a church, mosque, temple, or synagogue) where they can engage in religious beliefs and practices with similarly minded people.

Given the diversity and complexity of religion, how is it possible for sociologists to study this social institution? Most sociologists studying religion are committed to the pursuit of "disinterested scholarship," meaning that they do not seek to make value judgments about religious beliefs or to determine whether particular religious bodies are "right" or "wrong." However, many acknowledge that it is impossible to completely rid themselves of those values and beliefs into which they were socialized (Bruce, 1996). Therefore, for the most part, sociologists study religion by using sociological methods, such as historical analysis, experimentation, participant observation, survey research, and content analysis that can be verified and replicated (Roberts, 1995b). As a result, most studies in the sociology of religion focus on tangible elements that can be *seen,* such as written texts, patterns of behaviour, or individuals' opinions about religious matters, and that can be studied using standard sociological research

BOX 17.1 SOCIOLOGY AND EVERYDAY LIFE

How Much Do You Know About the Impact of Religion on Education in Canada?

True	False	
T	F	1. Provincial governments in Canada do not fund separate religious schools.
T	F	2. Parents who home-school their children for religious reasons are free to teach the children whatever curriculum they wish.
T	F	3. The federal government has limited control over how funds are spent by school districts because most of the money comes from the provinces; thus, questions of religion in the schools are decided at the provincial level.
T	F	4. Enrolment in parochial schools has decreased in Canada as interest in religion has waned.
T	F	5. In Canada, the public school system recognizes only Christian religious holidays by giving students those days off.
T	F	6. The number of children from religious backgrounds other than Christian and Judaic has grown steadily in schools over the past three decades.
T	F	7. Debates over textbook content focus only on elementary education because of the vulnerability of young children.
T	F	8. Increasing numbers of parents are instructing their own children through home-schooling because of their concerns about what public schools are (or are not) teaching their children.
T	F	9. Prayer in public schools in Canada is offered on a voluntary basis.
T	F	10. Most Canadians feel that the public schools should teach children about all the major religions of the world.

Answers on page 530.

BOX 17.1 SOCIOLOGY AND EVERYDAY LIFE

Answers to the Sociology Quiz on Religion and Education

1. **False.**   Schools operated by the Catholic church are provincially funded in several provinces, and others fund a variety of private schools, including religious ones.

2. **False.**   Every province monitors home-schoolers to ensure compliance with its *Education Act*. However, as suggested by the Barendregts in the chapter introduction, enforcement of the law may be lax in some provinces.

3. **True.**   Under the terms of the *British North America Act*, education is a provincial responsibility. Public-school revenue comes from local funding through property taxes and provincial funding from a variety of sources. The federal government is responsible for maintaining schools for Aboriginal people, running a military college, funding adult education programs, and overseeing educational programs in federal penitentiaries.

4. **False.**   In recent years, just the opposite has happened. As parents have begun feeling that their children were not receiving the type of education the parents desired for them in public schools, parochial schools have flourished. Most religions have established their own parochial schools.

5. **True.**   This is normally the case, although, as you will learn, some schools have also recognized Jewish holidays. However, this has resulted in conflict, as other religious groups also want to see their religious holidays formally recognized. While other religious holidays may not be recognized by closing the school, it is normal practice not to force students to write exams on their holy days.

6. **True.**   Although about 72 percent of Canadians aged 18 and over describe their religion as one of the forms, or denominations, of Christianity, the number of those who either adhere to no religion or who are Jewish, Muslim/Islamic, Sikh, Buddhist, or Hindu has increased significantly (Statistics Canada, 2003j).

7. **False.**   Attempts to remove textbooks occur at all levels of schooling. One case involved the removal of Chaucer's "The Miller's Tale" and Aristophanes' *Lysistrata* from a high school curriculum (Johnson, 1994). Parents in many communities have tried to prevent teachers from using *Harry Potter* books in the classroom because they feel the books promote witchcraft.

8. **True.**   Some parents choose home-schooling for religious reasons. Others embrace it for secular reasons, including fear for their children's safety and concerns about the quality of public schools.

9. **True.**   If a public school in Canada wishes to have prayers, parents must sign consent forms for their children to participate.

10. **True.**   A national survey found that 56 percent of Canadians felt public schools should teach children about all the major religions of the world, while 31 percent felt that students should not be taught about any religion (Opinion Canada, 2004).

tools. According to Keith A. Roberts (1995:28), beliefs constitute only a small part of a sociological examination of religion:

> The sociological approach focuses on religious groups and institutions (their formation, maintenance, and demise), on the behavior of individuals within these groups (e.g., social processes that affect conversion, ritual behavior), and on conflicts between religious groups (such as Catholic vs. Protestant, Christian vs. [Muslim],

mainline denomination vs. cult). For the sociologist, beliefs are only one small part of religion.

Recently, more scholars have started examining religion from a global perspective to determine "ways in which religious ideas are performed on the world stage" (Kurtz, 1995:16). As Kurtz (1995:211) points out, conflicts in the global village are often deeply intertwined with religious differences: "In the twentieth century, the twin crises of modernism and multiculturalism . . . added a religious dimension to many ethnic, economic, and political battles, providing cosmic justifications for the most violent struggles."

How does the sociological study of religion differ from the theological approach? Unlike the sociological approach, which focuses primarily on the visible aspects of religion, *theologians* study specific religious doctrines or belief systems, including answers to questions, such as: What is the nature of God or the gods? and What is the relationship among supernatural power, human beings, and the universe? Many theologians primarily study the religious beliefs of a specific religion (such as Christianity, Judaism, Buddhism, or Hinduism), denomination (such as Catholic or Anglican), or religious leader so that they can interpret this information for laypersons who seek answers for seemingly unanswerable questions about the meaning of life and death.

Religious Belief and Ritual

Religion seeks to answer important questions such as why we exist, why people suffer and die, and what happens when we die. Sociologist Peter Berger (1967) referred to religion as a *sacred canopy*—a sheltering fabric hanging over people that gives them security and provides answers for the questions of life. However, this sacred canopy requires that people have *faith*—**unquestioning belief that does not require proof or scientific evidence.** Science and medicine typically rely on existing scientific evidence to respond to questions of suffering, death, and injustice, whereas religion seeks to explain such phenomena by referring to the sacred. According to Émile Durkheim (1995/1912), the *sacred* **refers to those aspects of life that are extraordinary or supernatural**—in other words, those things that are

Devout Muslims around the world kneel in prayer at specific times of day. Muslims are among the fastest-growing religious groups in North America.

set apart as "holy." People feel a sense of awe, reverence, deep respect, or fear for that which is considered sacred. Across cultures and in different eras, many things have been considered sacred, including invisible gods, spirits, specific animals or trees, altars, crosses, holy books, and special words or songs that only the initiated could speak or sing (Collins, 1982). Those things that people do not set apart as sacred are referred to as the *profane*—**the everyday, secular, or "worldly" aspects of life** (Collins, 1982). Sacred beliefs are rooted in the holy or supernatural, whereas secular beliefs have their foundation in scientific knowledge or everyday explanations. For example, in the educational debate over creationism and evolutionism, advocates of creationism view their belief as founded in sacred (biblical) teachings, but advocates of evolutionism argue that their beliefs are based on provable scientific facts.

In addition to beliefs, religion also comprises symbols and rituals. According to anthropologist Clifford Geertz (1966), religion is a set of cultural symbols that establishes powerful and pervasive moods and motivations to help people interpret the meaning of life and establish a direction for their behaviour. People often act out their religious beliefs in the form of *rituals*—**regularly repeated and carefully prescribed forms of behaviour that symbolize a cherished value or belief** (Kurtz, 1995). Rituals range from songs and prayers to offerings and sacrifices that worship or praise a supernatural being, an ideal, or a set of supernatural principles. For example, Muslims bow toward Mecca, the holy city of Islam, five times a day at fixed times to pray to God, and Christians participate in the celebration of communion to commemorate the life, death, and resurrection of Jesus Christ. Rituals differ from everyday actions in that they involve very strictly determined behaviour. The rituals involved in praying or in observing communion are carefully orchestrated and must be followed with precision. According to Randall Collins (1982:34), "In rituals, it is the forms that count. Saying prayers, singing a hymn, performing a primitive sacrifice or a dance, marching in a procession, kneeling before an idol or making the sign of the cross—in these, the action must be done the right way."

Rituals are one of the sets of rules that are part of religious life. The importance of rituals and other religious regulations can be understood if you recall that the purpose of religion is to provide explanations of fundamental questions, such as death and the meaning of life. Rodney Stark has pointed out that religions do more for humans than "supply them with answers to questions of ultimate meaning. The assumption that the supernatural exists raises a new

Throughout the world, people seek the meaning of life through traditional and non-traditional forms of religion. These Italian spiritual seekers are meeting together at a Mayan ruin in quest of harmonic convergence.

question: *What does the supernatural want or expect from us?"* (1998:386). Thus religions also provide the faithful with rules about how they must act if they are to please the gods. These rules can be justified in religious terms, and those who share the religious faith see them as legitimate.

Categories of Religion

Although it is difficult to establish exactly when religious rituals first began, anthropologists have concluded that all known groups over the past hundred thousand years have had some form of religion (Haviland, 1993). Religions have been classified into four main categories based on their dominant belief: simple supernaturalism, animism, theism, and transcendent idealism (McGee, 1975). In very simple preindustrial societies, religion often takes the form of *simple supernaturalism*—**the belief that supernatural forces affect people's lives either positively or negatively.** This type of religion does not acknowledge specific gods or supernatural spirits but focuses instead on impersonal forces that may exist in people or natural objects. For example, simple supernaturalism has been used to explain mystifying events of nature, such as sunrises and thunderstorms, and ways that some objects may bring a person good or bad luck. By contrast, *animism* **is the belief that plants, animals, or other elements of the natural world are endowed with spirits or life forces that have an impact on events in society.** Animism is associated with early hunting and gathering societies in which everyday life is not separated from the elements of the natural world (Albanese, 1992).

The third category of religion is *theism*—**a belief in a god or gods.** Horticultural societies were among the first to practise *monotheism*—**a belief in a**

single, supreme being or god who is responsible for significant events, such as the creation of the world.** Three of the major world religions—Christianity, Judaism, and Islam—are monotheistic. By contrast, Shinto and a number of the indigenous religions of Africa are forms of *polytheism*—**a belief in more than one god.** The fourth category of religion, transcendent idealism, is a *nontheistic religion*—**a religion based on a belief in divine spiritual forces, such as sacred principles of thought and conduct, rather than a god or gods.** Transcendent idealism focuses on principles, such as truth, justice, affirmation of life, and tolerance for others, and its adherents seek an elevated state of consciousness in which they can fulfil their true potential.

SOCIOLOGICAL PERSPECTIVES ON RELIGION

Religion as a social institution is a powerful, deeply felt, and influential force. Sociologists study the social institution of religion because of the importance that religion holds for many people. They also want to know more about the influence of religion on society, and vice versa. For example, some people believe that the introduction of prayer or religious instruction in public schools would have a positive effect on the teaching of values, such as honesty, compassion, courage, and tolerance, because these values could be given a moral foundation. However, society has strongly influenced the practice of religion in Canada as a result of court rulings and laws that have limited religious activities in public settings, including schools.

The major sociological perspectives have different outlooks on the relationship between religion and society. Functionalists typically emphasize the ways in which religious beliefs and rituals can bind people together. Conflict explanations suggest that religion can be a source of false consciousness in society. Interactionists focus on the meanings that people give to religion in their everyday lives. Feminists look at the ways in which women's religious experiences differ from those of men. Postmodern theorists examine the changing nature and role of religion in the twenty-first century.

The Functionalist Perspective on Religion

Durkheim on Religion   Émile Durkheim was one of the first sociologists to emphasize that religion is essential to the maintenance of society. He suggested that religion was a cultural universal found in all societies because it met basic human needs and served important societal functions.

For Durkheim, the central feature of all religions is the presence of sacred beliefs and rituals that bind people together in a collectivity. In his studies of the religion of the Australian Aborigines, for example, Durkheim found that each clan had established its own sacred totem, which included kangaroos, trees, rivers, rock formations, and other animals or natural creations. To clan members, their totem was sacred; it symbolized some unique quality of their clan. People developed a feeling of unity by performing ritual dances around their totem, which caused them to abandon individual self-interest. Durkheim suggested that the correct performance of the ritual gives rise to religious conviction. Religious beliefs and rituals are *collective representations*—group-held meanings that express something important about the group itself (McGuire, 1992:177). Because of the intertwining of group consciousness and society, functionalists suggest that religion is functional because it meets basic human needs.

Functions of Religion   From a functionalist perspective, religion has three important functions in any society: (1) providing meaning and purpose to life, (2) promoting social cohesion and a sense of belonging, and (3) providing social control and support for the government.

Meaning and Purpose   Religion offers meaning for the human experience. Some events create a profound sense of loss on both an individual basis (such as injustice, suffering, and the death of a loved one) and a group basis (such as famine, earthquake, economic depression, or subjugation by an enemy). Inequality may cause people to wonder why their own personal situation is no better than it is. Most religions offer explanations for these concerns. Explanations may differ from one religion to another, yet each tells the individual or group that life is part of a larger system of order in the universe (McGuire, 1997). Some (but not all) religions even offer hope of an afterlife for persons who follow the religion's tenets of morality in this life. Such beliefs help make injustices in this life easier to endure.

In a study of religious beliefs among baby boomers (born between 1946 and 1964), religion and society scholar Wade Clark Roof (1993) found that a number of people had returned to organized religion as part of a personal quest for meaning. Roof notes that they were looking "for something to believe in, for answers to questions about life," as reflected in this woman's comments:

> Something was missing. You turn around and you go, is this it? I have a nice husband, I have a nice house; I was just about to finish graduate school. I knew I was going to have a very marketable degree. I wanted to do it. And you turn and you go, here I am. This is it. And there were just things that were missing. I just didn't have stimulation. I didn't have the motivation. And I guess when you mentioned faith, I guess that's what was gone. (quoted in Roof, 1993:158)

Social Cohesion and a Sense of Belonging   By emphasizing shared symbolism, religious teachings and practices help promote social cohesion. An example is the Christian ritual of communion, which not only commemorates a historical event but also allows followers to participate in the unity ("communion") of themselves with other believers (McGuire, 1997). All religions have some forms of shared experience that rekindle the group's consciousness of its own unity.

Religion has played an important part in helping members of subordinate groups develop a sense of social cohesion and belonging. For example, in the late 1980s and early 1990s, Russian Jewish immigrants to Canada found a sense of belonging in their congregations. Even though they did not speak the language of their new country, they had religious rituals and a sense of history in common with others in the congregation. Korean immigrants are forming their own congregations in Canada. In Calgary, the Baptist minister at a church with a congregation made up of 1,500 Korean Calgarians commented, "The church is more than a Christian institution, it is also a means of cultural fellowship. It is a place to feel comfortable. They are in a strange country and here there is friendship" (Nemeth et al., 1993:33). Shared experiences such as these strengthen not only the group but also the individual's commitment to the group's expectations and goals (McGuire, 1997).

Social Control and Support for the Government

How does religion help bind society together and maintain social control? All societies attempt to maintain social control through systems of rewards and punishments. Sacred symbols and beliefs establish powerful, pervasive, long-lasting motivations based on the concept of a general order of existence (Geertz, 1966). In other words, if individuals consider themselves to be part of a larger order that holds the ultimate meaning in life, they will feel bound to one another (and to past and future generations) in a way that otherwise might not be possible (McGuire, 1997).

Religion also helps maintain social control in society by conferring supernatural legitimacy on the norms and laws in society. In some societies, social control occurs as a result of direct collusion between the dominant classes and the dominant religious organizations. Niccolò Machiavelli, an influential sixteenth-century statesman and author, wrote that it was "the duty of princes and heads of republics to uphold the foundations of religion in their countries, for then it is easy to keep their people religious, and consequently well conducted and united" (quoted in McGuire, 1997:235). As discussed in Chapter 14, absolute monarchs often have claimed that God gave them the right to rule.

The Conflict Perspective on Religion

Karl Marx on Religion   While most functionalists feel that religion serves a positive role in society, many conflict theorists, including Karl Marx, view religion negatively. For Marx, *ideologies*—"systematic views of the way the world ought to be"—are embodied in religious doctrines and political values (Turner, Beeghley, and Powers, 1995:135). These ideologies also serve to justify the status quo and to retard social change. The capitalist class uses religious ideology as a tool of domination to mislead the workers about their true interests. For this reason, Marx wrote his now famous statement that religion is the "opiate of

the masses." People become complacent because they have been taught to believe in an afterlife in which they will be rewarded for their suffering and misery in this life. Although these religious teachings soothe the masses' distress, any relief is illusory. Religion unites people under a "false consciousness," according to which they believe they have common interests with members of the dominant class (Roberts, 1995b).

From a conflict perspective, religion also tends to promote strife between groups and societies. The conflict may be *between* religious groups (for example, anti-Semitism), *within* a religious group (for example, when a splinter group leaves an existing denomination), or between a religious group and *the larger society* (for example, conflict over religion in the classroom described at the beginning of the chapter and in Box 17.2). Conflict theorists assert that, in attempting to provide meaning and purpose in life while at the same time promoting the status quo, religion is used by the dominant classes to impose their own control over society and its resources (McGuire, 1992).

Max Weber's Response to Marx   Whereas Marx believed that religion retarded social change, Weber argued just the opposite. For Weber, religion could be a catalyst to produce social change. In *The Protestant Ethic and the Spirit of Capitalism* (1976/1904–1905), Weber asserted that the religious teachings of John Calvin were directly related to the rise of capitalism. Calvin emphasized the doctrine of *predestination*—the belief that, even before they are born, all people are divided into two groups, the saved and the damned. Only God knows who will go to heaven (the elect) and who will go to hell. Because people cannot know whether they will be saved, they look for earthly signs that they are

The shared experiences and beliefs associated with religion have helped many groups maintain a sense of social cohesion and a feeling of belonging in the face of prejudice and discrimination.

BOX 17.2 CRITICAL THINKING

A Legal Challenge to Religious Holidays in Schools

Like millions of other young Canadians, 14-year-old Aysha Bassuny returned to school in September 1994. However, the Ottawa Board of Education delayed the start of her school year for two days so that Jewish students could observe the Jewish New Year—Rosh Hashanah. Bassuny was one of many in Ottawa's Islamic community who were upset that the board refused to consider extending them a similar courtesy by closing schools for two Muslim holy days. "It's not fair," said Bassuny, a Grade 10 student at suburban Brookfield High School, who wears the traditional Islamic head scarf, the hijab. "I have to miss school for my holy days and the Jewish kids don't. You cannot have it for one group and not the other."

In July 1995, Islamic Schools Federation of Ontario, which represents independent Muslim schools, launched a lawsuit against the Ottawa Board of Education alleging that the rights of Muslims to freedom of conscience and religion under the *Charter of Rights* have been undermined by the board's actions. The lawsuit argued that schools with significant numbers of Muslim students should be required to observe two important Islamic holidays. The Islamic Schools Federation chose to sue the Ottawa Board of Education as a test case, believing that a victory there would set a precedent for the rest of the country.

The dispute began in April 1994, when the Ottawa board agreed to what seemed at the time to be a modest request from Ottawa's Jewish community—to delay the start of the school year so that Jewish students could observe Rosh Hashanah without missing the first two days of school. According to Jewish community leader Ron Singer, the request was entirely reasonable, because it did not mean a permanent change in the school year: the Jewish calendar is based on the cycles of the moon, and Rosh Hashanah coincides with the opening of school only once every forty years.

On the other side of the issue, the lawyer for the Islamic Schools Federation of Ontario said that the problem was "the recognition of two religions, Christian and Jewish, and the rejection of another, Muslim."

Those involved in the dispute recognized that, if taken to its logical extreme, the rapid growth of Canada's Muslim, Buddhist, Hindu, and Sikh communities could lead to a school year with as many as fifteen religious holidays. At the time, one school board member conceded that it was "a tough problem," and one that an increasingly multicultural society would be unable to avoid. Ultimately, the lawsuit was rejected by the Ontario Divisional Court and in July 1997 the Ontario Appeal Court refused to hear an appeal. This means that Ontario schools are not required to recognize the holidays of minority religious groups. Do you think it is fair that Christian holidays are recognized while the holidays of other religions are not?

Source: Fisher, 1994.

---

among the elect. According to the Protestant ethic, those who have faith, perform good works, and achieve economic success are more likely to be among the chosen of God. As a result, people work hard, save their money, and do not spend it on worldly frivolity; instead they reinvest it in their land, equipment, and labour (Chalfant, Beckley, and Palmer, 1994).

The spirit of capitalism grew in the fertile soil of the Protestant ethic. As people worked ever harder to prove their religious piety, structural conditions in Europe led to the Industrial Revolution, free markets, and the commercialization of the economy—developments that worked hand in hand with Calvinist religious teachings. From this viewpoint, wealth was an unintended consequence of religious piety and hard work.

With the contemporary secularizing influence of wealth, people often think of wealth and material possessions as the major (or only) reason to work. Although no longer referred to as the "Protestant" ethic, many people still refer to the "work ethic" in somewhat the same manner that Weber did.

Like Marx, Weber was acutely aware that religion could reinforce existing social arrangements, especially the stratification system. The wealthy can use religion to justify their power and privilege: it is a sign of God's approval of their hard work and morality. As for the poor, if they work hard and live a moral life, they will be richly rewarded in another life. The Hindu belief in reincarnation is an example of religion reinforcing the stratification system. Because a person's social position in the current life is the result of behaviour in a former life, the privileges of the upper class must be protected so that each person may enjoy those privileges in another incarnation.

Does Weber's thesis about the relationship between religion and the economy withstand the test of time? Recently, sociologist Randall Collins reexamined Weber's assertion that the capitalist breakthrough occurred just in Christian Europe and concluded that this belief is only partially accurate. According to Collins, Weber was correct that religious institutions are among the most likely places within agrarian societies for capitalism to begin. However, Collins believes that the foundations for capitalism in Asia, particularly Japan, were laid in the Buddhist monastic economy in late medieval Japan. Collins (1997:855) states that "the temples were the first entrepreneurial organizations in Japan: the first to combine control of the factors of labor, capital, and land so as to allocate them for enhancing production." Due to an ethic of self-discipline and restraint on consumption, high levels of accumulation and investment took place in medieval Japanese Buddhism. Gradually, secular capitalism emerged from temple capitalism as new guilds arose that were independent of the temples, and the gap between the clergy and everyday people narrowed through property transformation brought about by uprisings of the common people and wars with outside entities. Moreover, the capitalist dynamic in the monasteries was eventually

According to Marx and Weber, religion serves to reinforce social stratification in a society. For example, according to Hindu belief, a person's social position in his or her current life is a result of behaviour in a former life.

transferred to the secular economy, opening the way to the Industrial Revolution in Japan. From the works of Weber and Collins, we can conclude that the emergence of capitalism through a religious economy happened in several parts of the world, not just one, and that it occurred in both Christian and Buddhist forms (Collins, 1997).

The Symbolic Interactionist Perspective on Religion

Thus far, we have been looking at religion primarily from a macrolevel perspective. Symbolic interactionists focus their attention on a microlevel analysis that examines the meanings that people give to religion in their everyday life.

Religion as a Reference Group   For many people, religion serves as a reference group to help them define themselves. For example, religious symbols have meaning for many people. The Star of David holds special significance for Jews, just as the crescent moon and star do for Muslims and the cross does for Christians. For individuals, a symbol may have a certain meaning beyond that shared by the group. For instance, a symbol given to a child may have special meaning when he or she grows up and faces war or other crises. It may not only remind the adult of a religious belief but also create a feeling of closeness with a relative who is now deceased. It has been said that the symbolism of religion is so very powerful because it "expresses the essential facts of our human existence" (Collins, 1982:37).

Religious Conversion   John Lofland and Rodney Stark (1965) wanted to find out why people converted to nontraditional religious movements. They wished to know what would attract people to a small movement outside the religious mainstream, and why some movements were successful at attracting people while others failed. In the early 1960s, Lofland and Stark became acquainted with a small religious movement that had been brought to the San Francisco area from Korea. They called the movement the Divine Precepts, but later revealed that the group was actually the Unification Church, better known as "the Moonies" after their founder, Sun Myung Moon.

As participant observers, Lofland and Stark spent a great deal of time with the group, observing their activities and conducting interviews. Based on this research experience, they developed a seven-step theory of conversion. Their research suggested that the most important personal characteristics that made conversion more likely were

1. Some important tension or strain in their lives. These tensions included financial problems, marital issues, sexual identity problems, and issues involving mental and physical disabilities.

2. A religious problem-solving perspective. Many other people experience the same types of strain, but may take direct action (such as divorce or declaring bankruptcy), go to a psychiatrist, or get involved with political movements rather than seeking to solve their problems through spiritual means.

3. Their self-definition as religious seekers who actively sought to resolve their problems through some system of religious meaning. Some of the converts had tried a wide variety of different religious alternatives before encountering the Divine Precepts.

These background factors were present before the potential converts came to the Divine Precepts. Lofland and Stark found that several situational factors also increased the likelihood of conversion. These factors were

4. An individual had come to a turning point in his or her life at the time of encountering the Divine Precepts. A number of the future converts had just failed or dropped out of school, while others had moved, lost a job, or had experienced some other major life change. This turning point not only increased the level of tension experienced by the individual, but also gave the people the opportunity to turn to something new.

5. Close personal ties with a member of the Divine Precepts. While many religious seekers heard the message of the Divine Precepts, only those who also developed an affective bond with a member underwent conversion. One of the converts, who had recently recovered from a serious illness, described the process:

I felt as if I had come to life from a numb state and there was spiritual liveliness and vitality within me by being among this group. As one feels when he comes from a closed stuffy room into the fresh air, or the goodness and warmth after freezing coldness was how my spirit witnessed its happiness. Although I could not agree with the message intellectually I found myself one with it spiritually. I reserved my conclusions and waited for guidance from God. (Lofland and Stark, 1965:871)

6. A lack of ties with people outside the group. Few of those who converted had strong ties outside the group.

7. Exposure to very intensive interaction with Divine Precepts members. The Divine Precepts recognized this and strongly encouraged those who had verbally converted to move into a shared residence with other group members. This helped to secure their total commitment to the movement.

Later in this chapter, you will read about some of the cultural and structural factors that have encouraged the growth of new religious movements in North America over the past three decades. You might consider how these macrosociological factors might affect the individual conversion process described by Lofland and Stark.

Feminist Perspectives on Religion

His Religion and Her Religion Not all people interpret religion in the same way. In virtually all religions, women have much less influence on the establishment of social definitions of appropriate gender roles both within the religious community and in the larger community (McGuire, 1997). Therefore, women and men may belong to the same religious group, but their individual religion will not necessarily be a carbon copy of the group's entire system of beliefs. In fact, according to McGuire (1997), women's versions of particular religions probably differ markedly from men's versions. For example, whereas an Orthodox Jewish man may focus on his public ritual roles and his discussion of sacred texts, Orthodox Jewish women have few ritual duties and are more likely to focus on their responsibilities in the home. Consequently, the meaning of being Jewish may be different for women than for men.

Religious symbolism and language typically create a social definition of the roles of men and women. For example, religious symbolism may depict the higher deities as male and the lower deities as female. Sometimes, females are depicted as negative, or evil, spiritual forces. For example, the Hindu goddess Kali represents men's eternal battle against the evils of materialism (Daly, 1973). Historically, language has defined women as being nonexistent in the world's major religions. Phrases such as "for all men" in Catholic and Anglican services gradually have been changed to "for all," but some churches retain the traditional liturgy. Although there has been resistance, especially by women, to some of the terms, overall inclusive language is less common than older male terms for God (Briggs, 1987).

Many women resist the subordination they have experienced in organized religion and object to its patriarchal nature. Some advocate a break from traditional religions, while others seek to reform religious language, symbols, and rituals to eliminate the elements of patriarchy (Renzetti and Curran, 1992).

Women in the Ministry

> I believe in God, the Father Almighty, Creator of Heaven and Earth, and in Jesus Christ, His only Son. (MacDonald, 1996:47)
>
> A woman can't represent Christ. Men and women are totally different—that's not my fault—and Jesus chose men for his disciples. (MacDonald, 1996:47)

These quotations relate to two issues that are becoming increasingly important to women in today's society: the gender inclusiveness of Christianity and Judaism and the absence of women in significant roles within religious institutions. These contentious issues are leading many women to reject mainstream religion in search of a spirituality that reflects the experiences of both women and men. In churches, synagogues, and other places of worship, women are demanding an end to the traditions that do not reflect their historical role and their religious commitment. Some women are choosing alternative spiritual belief systems, while others are working from within the church to create change. The battles have been intense, and the issue of the role of women has polarized some churches. In 1992, the Church of England allowed the ordination of women priests. In response, a British vicar made a point of telling the media that he would "burn the bloody bitches" (MacDonald, 1996:47).

Despite opposition, some advances have been made. Twenty-five percent of ordained United Church ministers and approximately 10 percent of Anglican priests in Canada are women (Nason-Clark, 1993). The Baptist and Presbyterian churches in Canada have begun to ordain women as well. However, once ordained, these women still face an uphill battle: they continue to be offered junior positions, are paid lower wages, and are not promoted to more prestigious posts (Nason-Clark, 1993). Not all religions are resistant to women in the clergy. For example, Reform Judaism has ordained women as rabbis since the early 1970s. Aboriginal Canadian religions have traditionally given status to women in spiritual leadership.

According to Raymond Currie and John Stackhouse (1996), there is little doubt that the future role of religion will depend significantly on the ability of religious institutions to respond to the changing role of women in society.

Interestingly, while women are a distinct minority among religious leaders, they make up a substantial majority of the faithful. Rodney Stark has concluded that "in every sizable religious group in the Western world, women outnumber men, usually by a considerable margin" (2004:61). This gender difference begins in adolescence, so it is not explained by the fact that women live longer than men.

The Postmodern Perspective on Religion

The Secularization Debate   One of the most important debates among those who study the sociology of religion deals with the question of whether the world is becoming more secular and less religious or whether we are seeing a renewal of religious belief. The view that modern societies are becoming more secular and that religion has less impact on other social institutions than in the past goes back to the work of Weber, Durkheim, and Marx. For example, Weber felt that as societies became modernized, the role of religion as the sole source of authority would inevitably diminish as other social institutions— particularly economic and political ones—became dominant. Jeffrey Hadden has briefly summarized the *secularization* perspective:

> Once the world was filled with the sacred—in thought, practice, and institutional form. After the Reformation and the Renaissance, the forces of modernization swept across the globe and secularization . . . loosened the dominance of the sacred. In due course, the sacred shall disappear altogether except, possibly, in the private realm. (1987:598)

Proponents of this view link modernization with secularization. These theorists predict that while the church and the state were once closely linked, as the world becomes more rational and bureaucratized and as knowledge becomes more science-based the role and influence of religion will decline. According to Fukuyama, Weber's prediction has proven accurate in many ways: "rational science-based capitalism has spread across the globe, bringing material advancement to large parts of the world and welding it together into the iron cage we call globalization" (2005:2). As you will read later in this chapter, religion has become much less important in Canada and in almost all Western industrial countries other than the United States. Church membership in these countries has dramatically declined over the past 50 years, and while many people still report an interest in spiritual matters they do not pursue these interests through the organized church.

However, we have certainly not seen the end of religion, which is still flourishing in many parts of the world and is at least surviving in others. Most critics of secularization theory concede that in most Western industrialized countries the separation between church and state has increased and church attendance has declined. However, at the same time religion is actually becoming more important in some parts of the world. Religion remains strong in Islamic societies, even in countries, such as Turkey and Pakistan, which have begun to modernize. In the former Soviet bloc, where religion had been forbidden by the government, there has been a dramatic resurgence in religious participation since the end of the communist era. Pentecostal churches are growing very rapidly in South America. Finally, the United States, perhaps the world's most modernized society, is still a very religious country, showing that modernization does not inevitably cause a decline in religiosity. Norris and Inglehart (2004) have shown that there are now more people with religious beliefs in the world than ever before and that the proportion of the world's population that holds these beliefs is now growing because of high birth rates in religious countries. Because of this, some sociologists, such as Rodney Stark, strongly disagree with secularization theory: "After nearly three centuries of utterly failed prophecies and misrepresentations of both past and present, it seems time to carry the secularization doctrine to the graveyard of failed theories, and there to whisper ['rest in peace']" (Stark, 1999:270).

Jeff Haynes (1997) has looked at this situation from the postmodern perspective and concludes that both sides in this debate are partially correct. While the process of secularization continues in much of the industrialized West, the postmodern condition has led people in many low-income countries to turn to religion. The structural conditions of postmodernism, including the negative consequences of globalization (see Chapter 9, "Global Stratification") and its perceived threats to the moral order can destabilize local values and traditions. Ironically, instead of leading to secularization, these conditions can lead to a strengthening of faith as some people resist these threats by turning to religion. Proponents of secularization would not likely have predicted the role played by religion in global politics in the past three decades. Religion has been critical in such major political events as the fall of the Shah of Iran in 1979; the ongoing conflicts between India and Pakistan and between Israel and the Palestinians; the violent break-up of the former Yugoslavia; and the Republican victories in the United States in 2000 and 2004.

Haynes explains the coexistence of secularization in some parts of the world and the spread of religion elsewhere by hypothesizing that secularization will continue, except in circumstances where religion "finds or retains work to do other than relating people to the supernatural . . . only when religion does something other than mediate between man and God does it retain a high place in people's attentions and in their politics" (1997:713). Thus in countries where organized religion fills other functions for adherents it will flourish, and in countries, such as Canada, where religion retains only its pre-modern spiritual role, it will continue to stagnate or to decline.

Haynes concludes that religion will retain or increase its importance in societies where it helps to defend culture against perceived threats from outside or from the threat of internal cultural change. Global capitalism has weakened national sovereignty and carries with it only the values of the marketplace. Many people view their own governments as part of the enemy (Juergensmeyer, 2003). The comments of Joanne Barendregt in the chapter introduction show how even some Canadians feel threatened by this social change. Islamic militant Sayyid Qutb, who was tortured and executed by Egyptian police in 1966, stated his disgust with the Westernization of the Arab world, which he felt was destroying his basic Islamic values:

> Humanity today is living in a large brothel! One has only to glance at its press, films, fashion shows, beauty contests, ballrooms, wine bars, and broadcasting stations! Or observe its mad lust for naked flesh, provocative postures, and sick, suggestive statements in the literature, the arts and the mass media! (Ruthven, 2004:37)

One of the ways in which people can deal with these threats is by turning to fundamentalist beliefs (see Box 17.3 for a discussion of the role of fundamentalist beliefs in religious terrorism). These beliefs do more than mediate between people and their God. To people who feel their values and identities are under threat from globalization, poverty, immorality, religious pluralism, or corrupt government, religious fundamentalism provides certainty in an otherwise uncertain world. According to Haynes, "For many people, especially in the Third World, postmodernism is synonymous with poverty, leading the poor especially to be receptive to fundamentalist arguments which supply a mobilising ideology" (1997:719). In large part, these fundamentalist religious institutions are based on strong local community organizations.

Thus they not only fill people's spiritual needs and provide a moral code that protects them from the consequences of globalization, but they also provide adherents with the support of a strong moral community that can replace older structures that have been weakened by rapid social change.

BOX 17.3 SOCIOLOGY IN GLOBAL PERSPECTVE

Religious Terrorism

Religious terrorism has become a major threat in postmodern societies. While the world has a long history of religious wars among states and there were many earlier examples of religious terrorism, the phenomenon has seen a resurgence over the past two decades (Hoffman, 1995). Following the September 11 attacks on the United States and subsequent bombings in Madrid, Bali, London, Saudi Arabia, and elsewhere, much of the world's attention is now focused on Islamic terrorists, including Osama bin Laden and his followers. However, all the world's major religious traditions—as well as many minor religious movements—have been linked with terrorism. Among the questions that interest sociologists are What are the causes of religious terrorism? How does it differ from other types of terrorist activities?

A list of just a few of the terrorist attacks over the past twenty-five years that have involved at least some religious influence shows that violent extremism is not limited to any one faith. In Northern Ireland, the Catholic Irish Republican Army (IRA) has exploded hundreds of bombs and killed hundreds of civilians in an attempt to free Northern Ireland from British rule. In 1994, a Jewish right-wing settler, Dr. Baruch Goldstein, shot and killed more than thirty Palestinians who were praying at the Tomb of the Patriarchs in Hebron. On the other side of the Israeli-Palestinian conflict, hundreds of Israelis have been killed by Palestinian suicide bombers. In Canada and the United States, there have been numerous bombings of abortion clinics and several doctors who perform abortions have been killed or wounded. Some of these attacks have been carried out by Christian ministers, and others were supported by militant Christian groups. The largest domestic terrorism incident in the U.S. was the bombing by Timothy McVeigh of the Oklahoma City federal building, which killed 168 people. McVeigh was inspired by the white supremacist book *The Turner*

Diaries, which condemned the dictatorial secularism that it alleged had been imposed on the United States by a Jewish and liberal conspiracy, and by a religious group called Christian Identity that shares these values and beliefs (Juergensmeyer, 2003). Militant Sikhs, fighting for an independent homeland, committed many acts of terrorism including the assassination of Indian Prime Minister Indira Ghandi by her own bodyguards. Sikh extremists were also responsible for Canada's worst act of terrorism, the Air India bombing that killed 329 people (see Chapter 14, "Power, Politics, and Government"). In 1995, members of the apocalyptic Japanese Buddhist Aum Shinrikyo sect released sarin nerve gas into the Tokyo subway system. This was the first attempt by religious terrorists to use a weapon of mass destruction. While the attack killed twelve people, thousands more would have died if the terrorists had been able to find a more effective way of vapourizing the sarin gas.

There are significant differences in the motivation behind these different attacks. For example, the bombing campaign of the IRA has a very strong political component, while members of Aum Shinrikyo had few overt political goals. However, in each of the examples the religious ideology of the terrorists helps to define the enemy and provides a justification for killing innocents.

According to Bruce Hoffman there are important differences between religious and secular terrorism. Most importantly:

> For the religious terrorist, violence first and foremost is a sacramental act or divine duty executed in direct response to some theological demand or imperative. Terrorism assumes a transcendental dimension, and its perpetrators are thereby unconstrained by the political, moral, or practical constraints that seem to affect other terrorists.... Thus, religion serves as a legitimizing force—conveyed by sacred text or imparted via clerical authorities claiming to speak for the divine. (1995:272).

Secular terrorists have to appeal to a broader constituency, so their acts are often restrained by their fear of alienating potential supporters. Religious terrorists must please only themselves and their god, and can justify attacks against all "nonbelievers." Finally, purely religious terrorists are not seeking modifications of an existing system, such as a change in the ruling government. Rather, they wish to completely transform the social order and to achieve total victory. Unlike groups, such as the IRA, who combine their religious ideology with specific and limited political goals, Osama bin Laden is not trying to replace governments, but to destroy the enemy and transform the world:

> It is no secret that warding off the American enemy is the top duty after faith and that nothing should take priority over it . . . jihad has become [obligatory] upon each and every Muslim. . . . The time has come when all the Muslims of the world, especially the youth, should unite and soar . . . and continue jihad till

these forces are crushed to naught, all the anti-Islamic forces are wiped off the face of this earth and Islam takes over the whole world and all the other false religions. (quoted in Juergensmeyer, 2003:431).

The fact that it is almost impossible to negotiate with religious terrorists and the loose networked form of contemporary terrorist organizations (refer to Box 6.4) makes them very difficult to control. This likely means that there will be no quick end to the religious terrorism now affecting the world.

While religious terrorism is a serious threat, we should keep the role of religion in perspective by remembering that the mass genocides of the twentieth century, including the Holocaust, Stalin's purges, China's Cultural Revolution, and Pol Pot's massacre in Cambodia, were committed in the name of political ideology, not religion.

Haynes' theory is supported by data from the World Values Survey. Several indicators of religiosity are strongly correlated with a country's level of development (see Figure 17.1). Respondents in agrarian countries (including Nigeria, Tanzania, and Zimbabwe) are twice as likely as those in industrialized, high-income countries to attend religious services at least weekly and to pray daily, and three times as likely to say that religion is "very important" in their lives (Norris and Inglehart, 2004). The major exceptions to this pattern are the United States and Ireland, which are both very wealthy and very religious countries.

Figure 17.1   Religiosity by Type of Society

The level of development of a country is strongly related to the religiosity of its citizens.

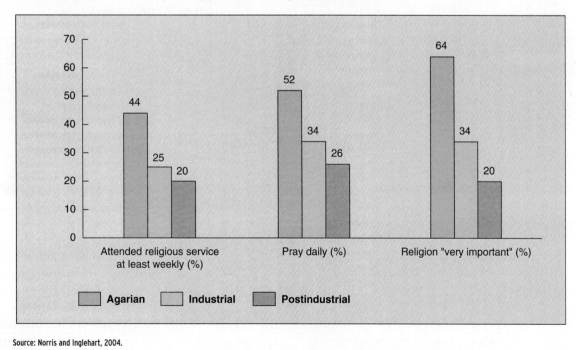

Source: Norris and Inglehart, 2004.

Concept Table 17.A **THEORETICAL PERSPECTIVES ON RELIGION**

PERSPECTIVE	THEORY	KEY ELEMENTS
Functionalist		
Durkheim	Functions of Religion	Religion has three important functions in any society: (1) providing meaning and purpose to life; (2) promoting social cohesion; (3) providing social control and support for the government.
Weber	The Protestant Ethic and the Spirit of Capitalism	The religious teachings of Calvinist Protestantism were directly related to the rise of capitalism.
Conflict		
Marx	Conflict Theory	The capitalist class uses religious ideology as a tool of domination to mislead the workers about their true interests. Religion can also promote strife between groups and societies.
Symbolic Interactionist		
Lofland and Stark	Conversion Theory	Conversion to nontraditional religious movements was more likely if individuals had certain predisposing background factors and if they had come to a turning point in life; had close personal ties to members of the group; a lack of ties to people outside the group; and intensive interaction with group members.
Feminist		
McGuire	His Religion and Her Religion	Religious symbolism and language typically create a social definition of the roles of men and women. Typically, these definitions subordinate women to men.
Postmodern		
Haynes	Religion as Oppositional Ideology	The postmodern condition stimulates a turning to religion under certain circumstances. While secularization continues in much of the industrialized West, in lower-income countries religion often functions as a mobilizing oppositional ideology.

TYPES OF RELIGIOUS ORGANIZATIONS

Religious groups vary widely in their organizational structure. While some groups are large and somewhat bureaucratically organized, others are small and have a relatively informal authority structure. Some require total commitment from their members; others expect members to have only a partial commitment. Sociologists have developed typologies or ideal types of religious organization to enable them to study a wide variety of religious groups. The most common categorization sets forth four types: ecclesia, church, sect, and cult.

Ecclesia

Some countries have an official or state religion known as the *ecclesia*—**a religious organization that is so integrated into the dominant culture that it claims as its membership all members of a society.** Membership in the ecclesia occurs as a result of being born into the society, rather than by any conscious decision on the part of individual members. The linkages between the social institutions of religion and government often are very strong in such societies. Although no true ecclesia exists in the contemporary world, the Anglican church (the official church of England), the Lutheran church in Sweden and Denmark, the Catholic church in Spain, and Islam in Iran and Pakistan come fairly close.

The Church-Sect Typology

To help explain the different types of religious organizations found in societies, Ernst Troeltsch (1960/1931) and his teacher, Max Weber (1963/1922), developed a typology that distinguishes between the characteristics of churches and sects (see Table 17.1). Unlike an ecclesia, a church is not considered to be a state religion. However, it may still have a powerful influence on political and economic arrangements in society. A *church* is a **large, bureaucratically organized religious body that tends to seek accommodation with the larger society in order to maintain some degree of control over it.** Church membership is largely based on birth; children of church members typically are baptized as infants and become lifelong members of the church. Older children and adults may choose to join the church, but they are required to go through an extensive training program that culminates in a ceremony similar to the one that infants go through. Leadership is hierarchically arranged, and clergy generally have many years of formal education. Churches have very restrained services that appeal to the intellect rather than the emotions (Stark, 1992). Religious services are highly ritualized; they are led by clergy who wear robes, enter and exit in a formal processional, administer sacraments, and read services from a prayer book or other standardized liturgical format.

Midway between the church and the sect is a *denomination*—**a large, organized religion characterized by accommodation to society but frequently lacking the ability or intention to dominate society** (Niebuhr, 1929). Denominations have a trained ministry, and while involvement by lay members is encouraged more than in the church, their participation usually is limited to particular activities, such as readings or prayers. This form of organization is most likely to thrive in societies characterized by *religious pluralism*—a situation in which many religious groups exist because they have a special appeal to specific segments of the population. Because of its diversity, Canada has more denominations than most other countries.

A *sect* **is a relatively small religious group that has broken away from another religious organization to renew what it views as the original version of the faith.** Unlike churches, sects offer members a more personal religion and an intimate relationship with a supreme being, who is depicted as taking an active interest in the individual's everyday life. Whereas churches use formalized prayers, often from a prayer book, sects have informal prayers composed at the time they are given. Whereas churches typically appeal to members of the upper classes, and denominations to members of the middle and upper classes, sects

Table 17.1 CHARACTERISTICS OF CHURCHES AND SECTS		
CHARACTERISTIC	**CHURCH**	**SECT**
Organization	Large, bureaucratic organization, led by a professional clergy	Small, faithful group, with high degree of lay participation
Membership	Open to all; members usually from upper and middle classes	Closely guarded membership, usually from lower classes
Type of Worship	Formal, orderly	Informal, spontaneous
Salvation	Granted by God, as administered by the church	Achieved by moral purity
Attitude toward Other Institutions and Religions	Tolerant	Intolerant

Christians around the world have been drawn to cathedrals such as Notre-Dame de Paris (built between 1163 and 1257) to worship God and celebrate their religious beliefs.

seek to meet the needs of people who are low in the stratification system (Stark, 1992).

According to the church–sect typology, as members of a sect become more successful economically and socially, they tend to focus more on this world and less on the next. If some members of the sect do not achieve financial success, they may feel left behind as other members and the ministers shift their priorities. Eventually, this process will weaken some organizations, and people will split off to create new, less worldly versions of the group, which will be more committed to "keeping the faith." Those who defect to form a new religious organization may start another sect or form a cult (Stark and Bainbridge, 1981).

Cults/New Religious Movements

A *cult* is a religious group with practices and teachings outside the dominant cultural and religious traditions of a society. Even though many of the world's major religions, including Islam, Christianity, and Buddhism, and denominations, such as Mormonism, began as cults, the term now has a negative connotation for many people outside the field of sociology. Because of this, some sociologists use the term *new religious movement* (or *novel religious movement* to reflect that fact that not all of these movements are new) to refer to these groups (Barrett, 2001). Cult leadership is based on charismatic characteristics of the individual, including an unusual ability to form attachments with others (Stark, 1992). An example is the religious movement started by Reverend Sun Myung Moon, a Korean electrical engineer who believed that God had revealed to him that Judgment Day was rapidly approaching. Out of this movement, the Unification church, or "Moonies," grew and flourished, recruiting new members through their personal attachments to present members (Stark, 1992). Some recent cult leaders have not fared well, including Jim Jones, whose ill-fated cult ended up committing mass suicide in Guyana, and David Koresh of the also ill-fated Branch Davidians in Waco, Texas.

Are all cults short-lived? Over time, most cults disappear. However, others undergo transformation into sects or denominations. For example, cult leader Mary Baker Eddy's Christian Science church has become an established denomination with mainstream methods of outreach. Some researchers view cults as a means of reviving religious practice when existing churches do not provide satisfaction to those seeking a spiritual home.

Earlier in this chapter, we discussed Lofland and Stark's theory of why people join new religious movements. Sociologists have also been interested in

This mass wedding ceremony of thousands of brides and grooms brought widespread media attention to the Reverend Sun Myung Moon and the Unification church, which many people view as a religious cult.

the question of why these movements continue to emerge and specifically why there have been so many new religious movements in North America over the past several decades. Lorne Dawson (1998) has suggested that these movements have been a response to several kinds of cultural and social change:

1. *Changes in values.* Some researchers believe that new religious movements represent a response to a rapid change in social values. During the 1960s, many young people were involved in social protest movements that focused on important issues, such as civil rights, feminism, and the Vietnam War. Many also participated in alternative lifestyle experiments, which often involved drug use and alternative living arrangements, such as communes. Mainstream religions did not seem to address the concerns of these young people, and many found religion irrelevant or turned to nontraditional forms of worship. As this generation aged, its members found that while many of their battles had resulted in lasting change, they were faced with the need to build their adult lives in an imperfect and morally ambiguous world. Some of the new religious movements became attractive to the baby boomers because they offered the purpose and meaning that has always been part of religion, but at the same time also allowed the baby boomers to retain the expressive values that had been such an important part of their lives during the 1960s.

2. *Changes in social structure.* Participation in new religious movements may also be a way of dealing with changes in social structure. Some feel that contemporary society has seen a decline in "mediating institutions"—institutions, such as the extended family, neighbourhoods, schools, and voluntary organizations, that link the individual to the broader society. As people become more mobile and as cities become larger and more anonymous, these organizations no longer play the critical role in socialization that they did in the past. The nuclear family has had to take on more of these functions, but some young people experience difficulties adjusting once they have left the family and moved to university or into the world of work. Some sociologists feel that new religious movements may provide a substitute for the family that helps young people make the transition to adulthood.

3. *Changes in the role and character of religious institutions.* Some sociologists feel that new religious movements have grown as a response to the decline in traditional religious denominations in North America. In some parts of our secular society, churches have lost many of their roles to other institutions. Further, religious pluralism has increased as our society has become more diverse, so society no longer provides a clear and consistent religious message. Thus new religious movements can play a role that was once filled by traditional denominations.

TRENDS IN RELIGION IN CANADA

Canada's Religious Mosaic

Canada has been described as a "monopolized mosaic." Until the end of the nineteenth century, Canada was a country with a religious population made up almost entirely of Protestants and Catholics. The Roman Catholic church was the dominant religious force during the early settlement of Canada, a situation that continued well into the nineteenth century. With the arrival of the United Empire Loyalists from the American colonies in the 1780s, the Protestant population in Canada became larger than the French-Catholic population. The turning point, with respect to the dominance of the Protestant churches, occurred after World War II. Their combined share declined from 51 percent in 1951 to 36 percent in 1991, and the most rapid decline occurred during the 1980s (McVey and Kalbach, 1995). Changes in the population of the major religious groups in Canada are illustrated in Figure 17.2. In 2001, Catholics, at 43 percent of the population, were the largest religious group in Canada.

Other religions than Christianity were practised in Canada prior to European colonization. Aboriginal peoples were excluded from the earliest census collections. Even so, in 1891, almost 2 percent of Canadians reported practising religions other than Christianity. In 2001, more than 10 percent of Canadians were affiliated with "other" religions, including Eastern Orthodox, Judaism, and Eastern non-Christian religions, such as Islam, Buddhism, Hinduism, Sikhism, and parareligious groups

| Figure 17.2 | Religious Affiliation in Canada |

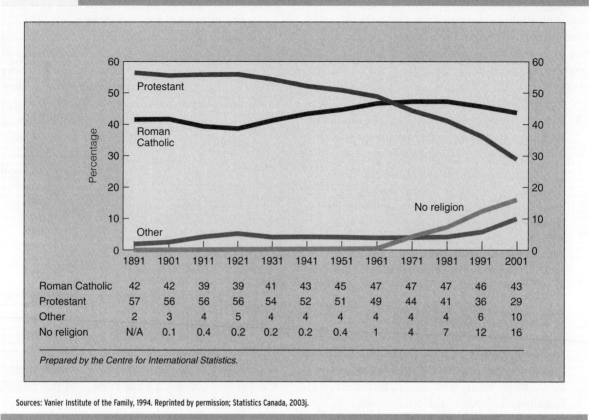

	1891	1901	1911	1921	1931	1941	1951	1961	1971	1981	1991	2001
Roman Catholic	42	42	39	39	41	43	45	47	47	47	46	43
Protestant	57	56	56	56	54	52	51	49	44	41	36	29
Other	2	3	4	5	4	4	4	4	4	4	6	10
No religion	N/A	0.1	0.4	0.2	0.2	0.2	0.4	1	4	7	12	16

Prepared by the Centre for International Statistics.

Sources: Vanier Institute of the Family, 1994. Reprinted by permission; Statistics Canada, 2003j.

(see Figure 17.3). Eastern non-Christian religious populations have grown significantly since the 1960s as a result of the liberalization of immigration laws in Canada, as have the numbers of those who fall under the category "no religion," going from 56,679 in 1951 to almost 4.8 million in 2001 (Statistics Canada, 2003j). Does this mean that Canadians are rejecting religion? An answer to this question can be found by examining other recent trends in religion in Canada.

Religiosity

As we have seen, religion in Canada is very diverse. Pluralism and religious freedom are among the cultural values most widely espoused. However, is Canada a religious society? The answer depends on how you look at things. Nationally, attendance at religious services, public confidence in religious leadership, and religious influence have all gradually declined since the late 1940s.

Religious affiliation has been tracked through the census, the annual General Social Survey (GSS), and opinion polls. Over the past fifty years, attendance at religious services has declined precipitously (Clark, 1998). A 1946 Gallup poll reported that 67 percent of Canadian adults had attended religious services during the previous week. By 2001, the General Social Survey found that attendance at weekly religious services had declined to only 20 percent (Clark, 2003). A generation ago, most Canadians attended religious services; today only a small minority attend.

In recent years, different denominations have seen different rates of decline (Clark, 1998). The 1996 GSS found that 24 percent of Roman Catholics attended weekly services, a marked drop from 37 percent attendance in 1986. Nearly one in three Roman Catholics did not attend church at all in 1996, compared with one in seven in 1986. During the same period, attendance in the mainline Protestant churches (United, Anglican, Presbyterian, and Lutheran) dropped from 17 percent to 14 percent. However, members of conservative Protestant denominations (Baptist, Pentecostal) have maintained 50 percent to 60 percent attendance rates. While 30 percent of Canadians claim affiliation with the mainline Protestant denominations compared

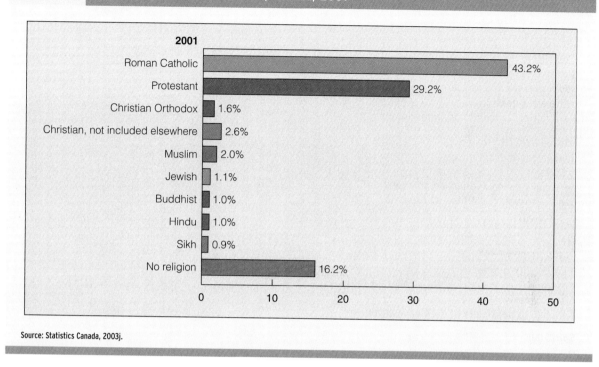

Figure 17.3   Major Religious Denominations, Canada, 2001

2001

Roman Catholic — 43.2%
Protestant — 29.2%
Christian Orthodox — 1.6%
Christian, not included elsewhere — 2.6%
Muslim — 2.0%
Jewish — 1.1%
Buddhist — 1.0%
Hindu — 1.0%
Sikh — 0.9%
No religion — 16.2%

(axis: 0 10 20 30 40 50)

Source: Statistics Canada, 2003j.

with 8 percent for the conservative denominations, the latter now have more people who are regular participants than do the mainline churches (Posterski and Barker, 1993). Most other religions (including Judaism, Hinduism, Buddhism, and Sikhism) have also seen serious declines in the percentage of people attending services, although some have seen a stabilization or even an increase in the number of members because of immigration.

While attendance rates have declined for all age groups, the drop has been particularly large for younger people. Thirty-four percent of those 65 years of age and over regularly attend religious services, compared with only 12 percent of 15- to 24-year-olds. This loss of young members does not bode well for the future of Canadian religions, as the vast majority of regular adult attendees had also been regular attenders in childhood. This means that as older members die, there will likely be fewer and fewer people taking their places in the pews. According to recent surveys conducted by Reginald Bibby (2002), the decline in attendance at religious services has stopped, but it remains to be seen if attendance will ever begin to return to previous levels.

However, despite the decline in involvement with the religious institutions, the vast majority of Canadians still report a religious affiliation and affirm that they believe in God. Both of these measures, though, have also declined in recent years. In 1961, only 1 percent of Canadians reported no religious affiliation; by 2001, this had increased to 16 percent (Statistics Canada, 2003j). In 1975, 89 percent of Canadians reported that they believed in God, compared with 81 percent in 1995 (Bibby, 1995b). Despite these declines, the vast majority of Canadians still have religious affiliations and beliefs. This view is further supported by a 1993 poll that found that 75 percent of Canadians expressed a belief in the death and the resurrection of Jesus, the basic tenet of Christianity. Almost one-third of the adult population claimed to pray daily and more than half reported reading the Bible or other religious literature at least occasionally (Nemeth et al., 1993). Bibby found that 76 percent of Canadian young people identified with a religious group in 2000 (Bibby, 2001).

Table 17.2 shows some of Bibby's other findings concerning the spiritual beliefs and practices of Canadians. In addition to their religious beliefs, Canadians also show an interest in other aspects of spirituality. Table 17.2 shows that most Canadians believe that some people have psychic powers; that supernatural and evil forces exist; that there is life after death; and that some people have extrasensory perception. A significant minority believe that astrology has some merit; that it is possible to make contact with the spirit world; and that they have experienced God.

Table 17.2   SPIRITUAL BELIEFS AND INVOLVEMENT OF CANADIANS, 2000

"I BELIEVE..."	ADULTS	TEENS
Conventional	**Percentage Agreeing**	
God exists	81%	73%
God or a higher power cares about you	73	68
In life after death	68	78
Have felt presence of God/higher power	47	36
Less Conventional		
In near-death experiences	68	76
In ESP	66	59
Personally have experienced precognition	58	63
Can have contact with the spirit world	45	43
In astrology	35	57
"I..."		
Group Involvement		
Identify with a group	86	76
Am committed to Christianity or another faith	55	48
Attend weekly	21	22
Am open to possibility of greater involvement	57	43
Spirituality		
Have spiritual needs	73	48
Find spirituality very important	34	30
Pray privately weekly or more often	47	33

Source: Bibby, 2001.

The results of these surveys lead us to an interesting paradox. Attendance at religious services has dramatically declined despite the fact that most Canadians report some religious affiliation, express a belief in God, and believe in other spiritual aspects of life. It should be noted that people have not rejected the religious institutions completely. Most still rely on organized religion for services, such as baptisms, weddings, and funerals, and recent surveys suggest that this will continue in the future (Bibby, 2002). However, they are not regular participants in religious activities, choosing instead to adopt what Bibby calls "religious fragments"—isolated beliefs, isolated practices, and isolated services (1987). They receive spiritual sustenance from their religions, but they also draw from alternatives, such as astrology, extrasensory perception, and New Age practices, such as crystals, that serve as adjuncts to traditional religious practice. Theologian Tom Harpur sums up this approach to religion:

There is a huge spiritual quest going on. There's a lot of attempts at quick fixes and spiritual junk food as well. But even the silly fringe is part of

it . . . People seem intuitively aware that something is missing in their lives, and there's a reaction against traditional religion. (quoted in MacDonald, 1996:42)

Why Have Canadians Turned Away from the Church?

Bibby concludes that people have moved from religious commitment to religious consumption. These religious consumers look at the church as simply one of many different options for solving their spiritual or worldly problems. Even those with a high degree of religious commitment may not feel church attendance is the best way to express that commitment. As one of Bibby's respondents commented:

I've been through a great deal in life and my faith is very strong. But I believe that one is closer to God in their own home and garden than a church. I see going to church these days as "keeping up with the Joneses." (Bibby, 1987:83)

No simple explanations can account for this change. It is apparent, though, that organized religion no longer seems relevant to the lives of many Canadians. Comments of two participants in one of Bibby's studies illustrate this view: "I don't see religion as having much power at all in today's affairs," and "The major issues of the day seem to me to have little to do with religion and morality; economic and political factors are far more important" (1993:59). Our culture has become more individualistic and people are less likely to accept without question the dictates of the church.

When it has tried to address contemporary issues, the church has often had problems. For example, several Protestant denominations have had major conflicts over the role of homosexuals in the church. Debates over issues ranging from the tolerance of homosexuality to the ordination of homosexual ministers have led to splits within local congregations and to major divisions at the national level. Not only have these moral issues been divisive, but they have also distracted the churches from other activities. Some churches, notably the United Church, have tried to become more socially relevant by focusing on social justice issues, but this strategy has not attracted new members (Bibby, 1993) and may have driven older members away from the church.

Many women have also felt marginalized by the church, and their alienation may have contributed to the decline in attendance. While the role of women in Canadian society has changed dramatically over the past thirty years, some churches are still very patriarchal organizations. These practices can be difficult or impossible to change, as traditional gender roles are part of the core religious ideology of some churches. Many people hold gendered images of God (Renzetti and Curran, 1998). We also know that in many denominations only males are allowed to become priests or ministers and women are expected to play a very traditional role supporting the males who are leaders of their religion. The quotation from Joanne Barendregt in the opening to this chapter illustrates the fundamentalist view that a woman's sacred duty is submission to her husband. While some women welcome this role, this subordination is seen as unacceptable by many others who do not feel comfortable in a male-dominated church. The failure by many denominations to address the concerns of women may have serious consequences, as women are normally more likely to participate in church activities than are men.

The image of the church has also suffered from thousands of charges of child sexual abuse by ministers and priests. While these incidents have taken place in a wide variety of contexts, the abuse was most pervasive in residential settings, such as the church-run schools that were established for Aboriginal children during the first half of the twentieth century. Over 125,000 children attended these schools before the system was closed in the 1980s, and by 1999 more than one thousand abuse complaints had been laid against church officials who worked in the schools (Cheney et al., 1998). The problem was not limited to the abuse of Aboriginal youth; the first major scandal grew out of offences committed by members of the Christian Brothers order at Newfoundland's Mount Cashel orphanage. The image of the church was further damaged by the fact that in many cases senior church officials knew about the problem, did little or nothing to stop it, and tried to cover it up. Few church leaders have been willing to take responsibility for the problem or even to apologize to those whose lives were destroyed by people who were entrusted with their physical and spiritual care. These incidents make it more difficult for the churches to speak credibly on moral issues. Many critics have linked abuse within the Roman Catholic church to its patriarchal structure and its celibate male priesthood and have called into question these fundamental principles of the church.

Finally, we can look at the special case of Quebec. According to S.D. Clark (1962), in few countries of the Western world has religion had more influence on the nature of community as it has in Canada. The early development of French and English Canada was strongly influenced by religious principles. This was particularly apparent in Quebec, where all social institutions came under the influence of the Roman Catholic church. For example, much of the education system was directly run by the church. Throughout most of Quebec's history, the Catholic church was politically powerful and dominated the province's social and moral life.

However, following the Quiet Revolution in the mid-1960s (see Chapter 14, "Power, Politics, and Government"), the influence of the Roman Catholic church in Quebec dwindled rapidly. Weekly church attendance dropped from a remarkable high of 90 percent in the 1940s (Bibby, 1993) to less than 30 percent by 1990 and continues to decline (Clark, 2003). As Quebec was transformed into a secular society, the church lost its influence in fields such as education and social services. The decline of the church represented a break with the past that was accompanied by such major shifts as the birth of the separatist political movement. Policies of the Roman Catholic church, such as the prohibitions on birth control, premarital sex, abortion, and divorce and the refusal to ordain women priests, also turned people away. The reduced influence of the church is shown by the fact that the province with the highest proportion of Roman Catholics (Quebec) also has Canada's highest rate of common-law marriage (see Chapter 15, "Families and Intimate Relationships").

Fundamentalism

The rise of a new fundamentalism has occurred at the same time as a number of mainline denominations have been losing membership. The term *religious fundamentalism* refers to a traditional religious doctrine that is conservative, is typically opposed to modernity, and rejects "worldly pleasures" in favour of other-worldly spirituality. In Canada, fundamentalism has been gaining popularity, primarily among Protestants, but also among Roman Catholics and Jews. Whereas "old" fundamentalism usually appealed to people from lower-income, rural backgrounds, the "new" fundamentalism appears to have a much wider following among persons from all socio-economic levels, geographical areas, and occupations. "New-right" fundamentalists have been especially critical of *secular humanism*—a belief in the perfectibility of human beings through their own efforts rather than through a belief in God and a religious conversion. As you read in the chapter introduction, fundamentalists feel that instead of offering children a proper Christian education, the public schools are teaching things that seem to the child to prove that their parents' lifestyle and religion are inferior and perhaps irrational (Carter, 1994:52). The new-right fundamentalists claim that banning the teaching of Christian beliefs in the classroom while teaching things that are contrary to their faith is an infringement on their freedom of religion (Jenkinson, 1979). As we have seen in this chapter, the debate continues over what should be taught and what practices (such as Bible reading and prayer) should be permitted in public schools. The selection of textbooks and library materials is an especially controversial issue. Starting in the 1960s, books considered to have racist and sexist biases were attacked by civil rights activists and feminists. Soon thereafter, challenges were brought by conservative religious groups to protest the use of books that they alleged had "factual inaccuracies" (such as a criticism of the free enterprise system) or morally objectionable subject matter or language (see Hefley, 1976; Shor, 1986; Wong, 1991; Bates, 1994). For example, a small group of parents in Ontario recently convinced the Durham Regional School Board to restrict the classroom reading of the *Harry Potter* books because the novels contain references to witchcraft and magic. This debate, along with the message of fundamentalism, has been transformed into an international issue because of the growth of the electronic church and the Internet, as discussed in Box 17.4.

Does Religion Make a Difference?

Research looking at the impact of religion on attitudes and behaviour has had mixed results. Bibby (1998) concluded that religiosity has little impact on personal characteristics, such as happiness and contentment. While religion may help some people to be happy and content, many others find the same level of satisfaction through other means. He also found that people with strong religious beliefs were no different from other Canadians in terms of relationships with other people, compassion, and tolerance of others (Bibby, 1995a). However, a recent Statistics Canada study found that weekly church attendees were much more likely to feel satisfied with their lives and much less likely to feel their lives were stressful than nonattenders (Clark, 1998).

Religiosity also affects other aspects of behaviour. All religions have ethical codes that govern personal and social behaviour. While it would be naive to equate religious with "good" and nonreligious with "bad," there is some evidence that religious commitment does influence people's conduct with regard to a variety of what might be called moral issues. For example, religiosity does reduce involvement in delinquent and criminal behaviour (Linden, 2000). However, this relationship is complex—it is greatest where there is a strong religious community (Stark et al., 1982); to some extent it is mediated by one's relationships with family and friends (Elifson et al., 1983); and it has more impact on behaviour that is not universally condemned by other segments of society, such as illegal drug use, than on behaviour, such as theft and assault, that most other social institutions also disapprove of (Linden and Currie, 1977).

Religiosity is also associated with marital stability. Weekly church attenders place more importance on marriage and children than those who do not attend church, although the differences are not large. Church attenders also have longer and happier marriages than nonattenders, and the marriages of church attenders are less than half as likely to break down than the marriages of nonattenders. Attenders are also much less likely to have lived common-law prior to marriage (Clark, 1998).

BOX 17.4 SOCIOLOGY AND TECHNOLOGY

In the Media Age: The Electronic Church and the Internet

In a single telecast, I preach to millions more than Christ did in His entire lifetime.

—Billy Graham (quoted in Roberts, 1995b:360)

Television and the Internet are having an impact on religion in the United States and Canada. Although television has been used as a medium of communication by ministers since the 1950s, the *electronic church* has far surpassed most people's wildest estimates by becoming a multimillion-dollar industry with audiences ranging from 10 million to 130 million in the United States.

When religious services were first televised, many were church services conducted by a local congregation and carried by a regional television station primarily for the benefit of shut-ins and those who had no "church home" in the community. In the 1950s and early 1960s, the few nationally televised religious programs featured people, such as the Rev. Bishop Fulton J. Sheen, an established spokesperson for the Roman Catholic church, or evangelists, such as Billy Graham, who were televised conducting a revival or "crusade" in some remote part of the world.

By comparison, most contemporary televangelists are entrepreneurs whose success hinges on presenting a message that "sells well" and generates the extremely large sums of money needed to keep the "television ministry" profitable. Rather than attempting to change viewers' beliefs, many televangelists attempt simply to confirm them. In the 1970s and 1980s, televangelists, such as Jerry Falwell, Oral Roberts, Jim and Tammy Faye Bakker, James Robison, Jimmy Swaggart, and Pat Robertson, offered audiences a sense of belonging; for a certain sum of money, people could become "members" of the "700 Club" or "partners" in the "P.T.L. (Praise the Lord) Club" with Jim and Tammy Faye Bakker. Even while some televangelists were discredited because of sexual or financial misconduct or, as in the case of Jim Bakker, convicted of felonies, others took their place not only to proclaim the "gospel" but also to become spokespersons for a conservative political agenda.

While televangelists have a great deal of impact in the United States, they have not been as successful in Canada. According to Reginald Bibby (1998), fewer than 5 percent of Canadians regularly watch religious services on television, which is much less than the 29 percent who watched or listened to services on television and radio in 1958. Further, most of those who did watch religious programs on television also attended church services regularly. This means that television has not become an electronic church replacing more traditional forms of worship. Only a few televangelists, such as David Mainse, have become nationally known in Canada, and none have any political influence.

By comparison, the Internet is just beginning to have an impact on religion. Some religious groups now have begun to use it to spread their message. For example, the Catholic Information Center on the Internet (http://www.catholic.net) was established to provide a wide range of services, including a review of recent Church-related news stories; discussions of church teachings; and a solicitation to inactive Catholics to become reinvolved with the church. While the Internet is a good way for mainline churches to get their message out, it also provides a means for newer spiritual groups to try to attract new followers. For example, the Fishgoat's Leaves of Wonder site (http://users.whtvcable.com/adjatti/flow/) provides information about Wicca and magick for those who might have an interest in paganism.

While the Internet may be a useful tool for religious groups, it raises new questions and concerns for some religious groups because controlling what young people read on the Internet is almost impossible. Some religious groups have begun pressing for limits to the type of information available on this network, or at least to limits on young people's access to certain types of information. How do you think religious organizations should respond to this problem? Is censorship of the Internet either possible or desirable?

Sources: Based on Hadden and Swann, 1981; Frankl, 1987; Hadden and Shupe, 1988; McGuire, 1992; Kosmin and Lachman, 1993; Tidwell, 1993; Bates, 1994; and Roberts, 1995b.

What about the impact of religion on health? In many small-scale societies, the same individual—the healer or *shaman*—was responsible for both physical and spiritual needs. After many years of separateness or even conflict, some people are once more trying to reintegrate medicine and religion. The increasing popularity of alternative medicine has led to an openness to nontraditional approaches, and opinion polls show that many people (including some doctors) believe that religious faith can help cure disease and, therefore, use prayer as medical therapy (Sloan et al., 1999).

Many researchers have attempted to test the relationship between religion and medical outcomes. In a somewhat humorous attempt to test the hypothesis, the eminent British scientist Sir Francis Galton sought to determine if prayer could increase longevity. He assumed that nobody in England received more prayers for longevity than the British royal family. People sang "God Save the Queen [or King]" and regularly expressed concerns for their rulers in their prayers. Recognizing that the upper-class lifestyle of royalty made them more likely to live longer, Galton knew he had to compare them with other wealthy people. He selected for his comparison group wealthy lawyers, determining that nobody would pray that lawyers live longer lives. Contrary to his hypothesis, he found that the lawyers lived longer and concluded that prayer had little efficacy in this regard.

Other, more serious studies have found that priests, monks, and nuns have less illness and live longer than members of the general population. However, these studies lack validity because they do not control for the lower exposure of those in religious orders to a variety of risk factors. Similarly, studies of Israelis living on secular and religious kibbutzim that found that the religious Jews lived longer than those who were nonreligious did not control for risk factors, such as smoking, blood cholesterol, and marital status (Sloan et al., 1999).

In their review of several dozen studies in this area, Sloan and his colleagues (1999) concluded that the evidence of an association between religiosity and health is weak and inconsistent. However, if it does not affect physical health, there is evidence that religion can play a role in comforting the sick. For example, one study found that 40 percent of a group of hospitalized adults reported that their religious faith was the most important factor in their ability to cope with their illness (Johns Hopkins, 1998).

RELIGION IN THE FUTURE

Religious debates, particularly over issues such as secularization and fundamentalism, no doubt will continue well into the future. However, in many parts of the world we are seeing not only the creation of new religious forms, but also a revitalization of traditional forms of religious life (Kurtz, 1995).

One example of this change is *liberation theology*—the Christian movement that advocates freedom from political subjugation within a traditional perspective and the need for social transformation to benefit the poor and downtrodden (Kurtz, 1995). Although liberation theology initially emerged in Latin America as people sought to free themselves from the historical oppression of that area, this perspective has been embraced by a wide variety of people, ranging from Africans and African American Christians to German theologians and some feminists.

Another change in the nature of theology is found in some feminist movements that have turned to pagan religions and witchcraft as a means of countering what they consider the patriarchal structure and content of the world's religions. For instance, the *Goddess movement* encompasses a variety of counter-cultural beliefs based on paganism and feminism rooted in acknowledgment of the legitimacy of female power as a "beneficent and independent power" (Christ, 1987:121).

What significance will religion have in the future? Religion will continue to be important in the lives of many people. Moreover, the influence of religion may be felt even by those who claim no religious beliefs of

Storefront missions such as this seek to win religious converts and offer solace to people in low-income central-city areas.

their own. In many nations, the rise of *religious nationalism* has led to the blending of strongly held religious and political beliefs. The rise of religious nationalism is especially strong in the Middle East, where Islamic nationalism has spread rapidly and where the daily lives of people, particularly women and children, have been strongly affected (Juergensmeyer, 1993). Similarly, in Canada the influence of religion will be evident in ongoing political battles over social issues, such as school prayer, abortion, gay and lesbian rights, and family issues. On the one hand, religion may unify people; on the other, it may result in tensions and confrontations among individuals and groups.

We began this chapter with a discussion of the place of religion in our educational system. It is clear that this role is diminishing. Numerous recent incidents have forced the issue of what is acceptable in schools and what is not. For example, to promote a multicultural environment, several schools in Toronto decided to exclude all references to Christian symbols or doctrine from their annual Christmas celebrations. One Toronto high school renamed its Christmas assembly a "holiday assembly" and eliminated all references to Christianity. Another school banned the singing of religious Christmas carols on the grounds that references to Christianity would upset the non-Christian children (more than 30 percent of Toronto's school population). As discussed in Box 17.2, the issue of which religious holidays are recognized in public schools is being played out in the courts. The overall effect of such incidents has been the increased secularization of the public school system. For example, in 1990, the Ontario Court of Appeal ruled against religious instruction in public elementary schools because it violates an individual's rights to freedom of religion (Fleras and Elliott, 1992). In 1995, Newfoundlanders voted to eliminate church-run schools in favour of a public, nondenominational education system. Newfoundland was at that time the only province in Canada that still had a church-run educational system.

The changing role of religion in education is but one example of the declining influence of organized religion in Canadian society. In many respects, the church in Canada is facing a bleak future. Despite an interest in the supernatural and a continued identification with religious traditions, church attendance and church membership continue to decline. In addition to these problems, which it shares with most other denominations, the Roman Catholic church faces an additional difficulty in that the number of priests and nuns has declined dramatically. Fewer than two hundred men enter the priesthood in Canada each year, a figure that is only one-sixth the number of those who entered in 1962. More than half of Canadian nuns and priests are over 65 years of age (Jackman, 1999). These facts make it plain that this is an organization in decline and that church renewal, including the attracting of young new members, will be difficult.

One might think that with Canada's high rate of immigration from a wide variety of countries (see Chapter 10, "Race and Ethnicity") membership in religions, such as Islam and Hinduism would be growing rapidly. However, this has not been the case for two reasons. First, many immigrants are Christian and are adding to the ethnic and religious diversity within the dominant religious groups (Posterski and Barker, 1993). Second, growth has been slowed because many young people from these other faith groups have been marrying outside their faith (Bibby, 1998). Children resulting from these marriages may attend Protestant or Catholic churches, or the family may drop all participation in religious activities.

Some see hope for the future in our aging population (see Chapter 12, "Aging"). They feel that as the baby boomers age, they are likely to search for spiritual meaning and some may turn back to the religions of their youth. However, the baby boomers are used to institutions that respond to their demands, while the mainstream churches may prove to be unresponsive. As a result, they may look for the answers and the support they need elsewhere. Thus far there is little evidence that the church is meeting these needs, and membership continues to stagnate.

As we have seen in this chapter, the debate continues over what religion is, what it should do, and what its relationship to other social institutions, such as education, should be. It will be up to your generation to understand other religions and to work for greater understanding among the diverse people who make up our country and the world. But some religious leaders see reason for hope, as one scholar explains:

> [People] know that religion, for all its institutional limitations, holds a vision of life's unity and meaningfulness, and for that reason it will continue to have a place in their narrative. In a very basic sense, religion itself was never the problem, only social forms of religion that stifle the human spirit. The sacred lives on and is real to those who can access it. (Roof, 1993:261)

CHAPTER REVIEW

■ **What is religion, and what purpose does it serve in society?**

Religion is a system of beliefs, symbols, and rituals, based on some sacred or supernatural realm, that guides human behaviour, gives meaning to life, and unites believers into a community.

■ **What is the functionalist perspective on religion?**

According to functionalists, religion has three important functions in any society: (1) providing meaning and purpose to life, (2) promoting social cohesion and a sense of belonging, and (3) providing social control and support for the government.

■ **What is the conflict perspective on religion?**

From a conflict perspective, religion can have negative consequences in that the capitalist class uses religion as a tool of domination to mislead workers about their true interests. However, Max Weber believed that religion could be a catalyst for social change.

■ **What is the symbolic interactionist perspective on religion?**

Symbolic interactionists focus on a microlevel analysis of religion, examining the meanings people give to religion and the meanings they attach to religious symbols in their everyday life.

■ **What are the major types of religious organizations?**

Religious organizations can be categorized as ecclesia, churches, denominations, sects, and cults.

■ **What impact does religion have on attitudes and behaviour?**

Research looking at the impact of religion on attitudes and behaviour has had mixed results. Religiosity reduces involvement in delinquent and criminal behaviour, though this relationship is complex. Religious people have longer and happier marriages than nonreligious people. Religion and prayer appear to have little impact on health, though they play a strong role in comforting the sick.

■ **Will religion continue as a major social institution?**

Religion in Canada is clearly in decline and the prognosis for the future is not bright. However, Canadians still have a strong interest in spiritual matters and continue to identify with the church. If it is to take advantage of these factors, the church must find new ways to become relevant to the daily lives of Canadians.

KEY TERMS

animism 532
church 543
cult 544
denomination 543
ecclesia 543
faith 531
liberation theology 552
monotheism 532
nontheistic religion 532
polytheism 532
profane 531
religion 528
rituals 531
sacred 531
sect 543
simple supernaturalism 532
theism 532

NET LINKS

For links related to research on religion, go to the Virtual Religion Index at:
http://virtualreligion.net/vri/

To see the Web site of the World Council of Churches, go to:
http://www.wcc-coe.org/wcc/english.html

Much of civilization's greatest art was commissioned by religious organizations. Visit the Vatican's Sistine Chapel with its ceiling painted by Michelangelo at:
http://www.wga.hu/index.html

Read about the PBS documentary on the first Christians at:
http://www.pbs.org/wgbh/pages/frontline/shows/religion/

QUESTIONS FOR CRITICAL THINKING

1. What are the major functions of religion and education for individuals and for societies? Why do these functions overlap in Canada? How would you design a research project to study the effects of

fundamentalist religion on everyday life? What kinds of data would be most accessible?

2. How is religion a force for social stability? How is it a force for social change?

3. If Durkheim, Marx, and Weber were engaged in a discussion about religion, on what topics might they agree? On what topics would they disagree?

4. Will religion continue as a major social institution in Canada? What factors lead people to turn away from religion? What factors promote a renewed or continued interest in religion?

5. In 2004 a Canadian university was criticized for not providing prayer space for Muslim students. Do you think that secular universities should be required to provide on-campus prayer space for all observant students?

SUGGESTED READINGS

These books provide more information on religion in Canada:

Reginald Bibby. *Fragmented Gods: The Poverty and Potential of Religion in Canada.* Toronto: Irwin, 1987.

W.E. Hewitt (ed.). *The Sociology of Religion: A Canadian Focus.* Toronto: Butterworths, 1993.

Useful books on the world's religions include the following:

Lester Kurtz. *Gods in the Global Village: The World's Religions in Sociological Perspective.* Thousand Oaks, Cal.: Pine Forge, 1995.

Warren Matthews. *World Religions.* St. Paul, Minn.: West, 1995.

Arvind Sharma (ed.). *Our Religions.* San Francisco: HarperSanFrancisco, 1993.

Huston Smith. *The World's Religions: Our Great Wisdom Traditions.* San Francisco: HarperSanFrancisco, 1991.

ONLINE STUDY AND RESEARCH TOOLS

THOMSONNOW™ Thomson NOW!

Go to **http://hed.nelson.com** to link to ThomsonNOW for *Sociology in Our Times,* Fourth Canadian Edition, your online study tool. First take the **Pre-Test** for this chapter to get your personalized **Study Plan,** which will identify topics you need to review and direct you to the appropriate resources. Then take the **Post-Test** to determine what concepts you have mastered and what you still need work on.

INFOTRAC®

Infotrac College Edition is included free with every new copy of this text. Explore this online library for additional readings, review, and a handy resource for assignments. Visit **www.infotrac-college.com** to access this online database of full-text articles. Enter the key terms from this chapter to start your search.

Health, Health Care, and Disability

Rae Lewis-Thornton describes her experience with HIV/AIDS in the following way:

"The day I found out [I was HIV positive] I was so calm . . . I walked out of the . . . Red Cross office and into the . . . sunshine, flagged a cab and went back to work. I worked late that night . . . I was 24. I'd just been given a death sentence . . . I am the quintessential Buppie. I'm young . . . Well educated. Professional. Attractive. Smart. I've been drug and alcohol-free all my life. I'm a Christian. I've never been promiscuous. Never had a one-night stand. And I am dying of AIDS.

"I've been living with the disease for nine years, and people still tell me that I am too pretty and intelligent to have AIDS. But I do. I discovered I was HIV-positive when I tried to give blood at the office. I have no idea who infected me or when it happened. Still, there is one thing I am absolutely certain of; I am dying now because I had one sexual partner too many. And I'm here to tell you one is all it takes" (Lewis-Thornton, 1994:63).

As we begin the twenty-first century, AIDS is among the most significant global/human problems we face, taking its toll on individuals, families, cities, and nations. The disease known as AIDS (acquired immune-deficiency syndrome) is caused by HIV, the human immunodeficiency virus, which gradually destroys the immune system by attacking the white blood cells, making the person with HIV more vulnerable to other types of illnesses.

While we do not know the actual number of people infected with HIV—some countries do not have adequate diagnostic equipment or centralized reporting systems—the United Nations estimated that 40 million people were infected with HIV/AIDS (including 2.2 million children under 15) and that 3.1 million people died of AIDS in 2004 (UNAIDS, 2004). Some countries are being devastated by HIV/AIDS; in Botswana and Zimbabwe, more than 25 percent of the adult population is infected. In Canada, over 56,000 people had tested positive for HIV (Public Health Agency of Canada, 2004), and more than 14,000 had died of AIDS by 2002 (Health Canada, 2002b). Map 18.1 outlines the global distribution of the virus.

AIDS is also a significant global/human problem because it may be a major species-threatening phenomenon with a potentially devastating impact on the world's population. This threat is particularly significant in sub-Saharan Africa. In 2004, the region experienced 6,300 deaths from AIDS each day, and there were 3.1 million new cases of the disease (UNAIDS, 2004). Half of all new infections are among 15- to 24-year-olds, and many newborns are being infected by their mothers, which means that the disease will destroy much of Africa's hope for the future. The average life expectancy in many countries has dropped by as much as seventeen years, and the cost of providing even minimal treatment for the disease is taking away many of the hard-won economic gains some countries have achieved in the past decade. Clearly, the problem of AIDS illustrates

how sociology can be applied to what, at first glance, appears to be a purely medical phenomenon. As sociologist Karen Grant explains, AIDS is a social phenomenon as much as a disease: "AIDS demonstrates that disease not only affects health, but one's definition of self, relations with others, and behaviours. As well, AIDS has had a significant impact on social institutions. The health-care system has been most directly affected, requiring assessments of the adequacy of research, treatment modalities, and health care facilities. Legal scholars and legislators have wrestled with issues of privacy and human rights protections for people with AIDS. AIDS has resulted in social and sexual mores and lifestyles being reassessed" (Grant, 1993:395).

In this chapter, we will explore the dynamics of health and health care. In the process, we will periodically focus on HIV/AIDS and its impact on society. While we will use HIV/AIDS as an example throughout this chapter, you should be aware that globally several other causes of death are more common. In 1997, there were 52 million deaths around the world. About 2.5 million of them were due to HIV/ AIDS, compared with 17.3 million due to infectious and parasitic diseases, 15.3 million caused by circulatory diseases, 6.2 million due to cancer, 2.9 million as a result of respiratory diseases, and 3.6 million due to perinatal conditions (World Health Organization, 1998). Before reading on, test your knowledge about HIV/AIDS by taking the quiz in Box 18.1.

QUESTIONS AND ISSUES

Chapter Focus Question: What effect has HIV/AIDS had on the health of the global population?

Why is HIV/AIDS referred to as a global/ human problem?

In what ways do sociological factors influence health and disease?

How do functionalist, symbolic interactionist, conflict, feminist, and postmodern theories differ in their analyses of health?

How does social inequality affect health and health care?

What are some of the consequences of disability?

What is the state of the health care system in Canada today and how could it be improved?

| Map 18.1 | Number of HIV-Positive People Around the World in 2004 |

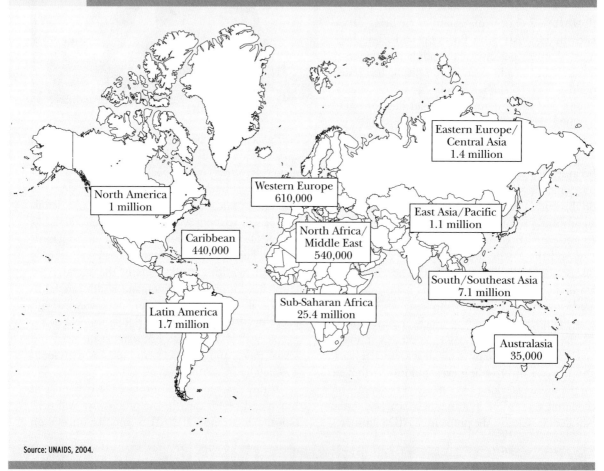

Eastern Europe/ Central Asia 1.4 million

North America 1 million

Western Europe 610,000

East Asia/Pacific 1.1 million

Caribbean 440,000

North Africa/ Middle East 540,000

South/Southeast Asia 7.1 million

Latin America 1.7 million

Sub-Saharan Africa 25.4 million

Australasia 35,000

Source: UNAIDS, 2004.

BOX 18.1 SOCIOLOGY AND EVERYDAY LIFE

How Much Do You Know About HIV/AIDS?

True	False	
T	F	1. Worldwide, most people with AIDS are gay men.
T	F	2. In Canada, you can be sent to prison if you knowingly transmit HIV.
T	F	3. HIV, the virus that transmits AIDS, is spreading rapidly among women in some nations.
T	F	4. Nearly 50 percent of people who are HIV-positive worldwide are under the age of 25.
T	F	5. Bill Gates, the Microsoft founder who is among the world's richest
T	F	people, is one of the leaders in the fight against AIDS.
T	F	6. People can get AIDS from sharing toilets, toothbrushes, eating utensils, or razors.
T	F	7. People infected with HIV may not show any physical symptoms for ten years or longer and can infect others without realizing it.
T	F	8. AIDS is now a curable disease.
T	F	9. In Canada, the majority of new HIV cases occur among homosexual men.
T	F	10. One of the major concerns of AIDS activists is reducing the stigmatization of HIV/AIDS victims.

Answers on page 560.

HEALTH AND MEDICINE

What does the concept of health mean to you? If you were asked whether you are healthy, how would you respond? Although the definition of health may appear obvious, consensus on it remains elusive. Health was once considered to be simply the absence of disease. The World Health Organization (WHO) provides a more inclusive definition of *health,* **calling it the state of complete physical, mental, and social well-being**. Health, as the WHO's definition makes clear, has several dimensions; physical, social, and psychological factors are all important. It does not, therefore, depend solely on the absence of disease or sickness. Health is also socially defined and therefore varies over time and between cultures (Farley, 1992). For example, in our society obesity is viewed as unhealthy, while in other times and places it has signalled prosperity and good health.

Medicine **is an institutionalized system for the scientific diagnosis, treatment, and prevention of illness**. Medicine forms a vital part of the broader concept of *health care,* **which is any activity intended to improve health**. In North American culture, medicine typically is used when there is a failure in health. When people become sick, they seek medical attention to make them healthy again. As the definition of medicine suggests, medicine and health can go hand in hand. Medicine and the larger category of health care have undergone many changes over time. Most recently, the field of *preventive medicine—***medicine that emphasizes a healthy lifestyle in order to prevent poor health before it occurs, is receiving increasing attention** (Appelbaum and Chambliss, 1997).

SOCIOLOGICAL PERSPECTIVES ON HEALTH AND MEDICINE

The Functionalist Perspective on Health: The Sick Role

Functionalists view society as a complex, stable system. Therefore, the normal state of affairs is for people to be healthy and to contribute to their

BOX 18.1 SOCIOLOGY AND EVERYDAY LIFE

Answers to the Sociology Quiz on HIV/AIDS

1. **False.** Although AIDS has taken a devastating toll on the gay population in North America, the World Health Organization estimates that about 75 percent of the people with AIDS worldwide were infected through heterosexual intercourse.

2. **True.** No specific law forbids this behaviour. However, in 1995, a Newfoundland man who knowingly infected nineteen women was sentenced to eleven years and three months in jail after pleading guilty to a charge of criminal negligence causing bodily harm. Also, in 1998, the Supreme Court of Canada ruled that a person could be charged with assault if they did not tell their sexual partners they had HIV/AIDS or other sexually transmitted diseases.

3. **True.** HIV has been spreading rapidly among women. Estimates place the number of HIV-infected women in the world at 17.6 million, compared with 19.6 million men (UNAIDS, 2004). In Canada, women accounted for 25 percent of newly diagnosed HIV cases in 2002 (Public Health Agency of Canada, 2004).

4. **True.** AIDS is found disproportionately among young people, a consequence of the fact that they are more likely either to engage in sexually promiscuous behaviour and/or to be intravenous drug users. Twenty-seven percent of HIV cases in Canada were found among people ages fifteen to twenty-nine (Public Health Agency of Canada, 2004).

5. **True.** Through the Bill and Melinda Gates Foundation, Gates has given billions of dollars to the campaign against AIDS. One of his priorities is to develop a vaccine that would immunize people against HIV/AIDS. Gates is funding a University of Manitoba project studying Kenyan prostitutes who have not contracted AIDS despite repeated exposure. Understanding their immunity may help to find a vaccine (http://www.gatesfoundation.org/default.htm).

6. **False.** AIDS is caused by HIV (human immunodeficiency virus), which is transmitted to men or women through unprotected (vaginal, anal, or oral) sexual intercourse with an infected partner (either male or female), through sharing a contaminated hypodermic needle with someone who is infected, through exposure to contaminated blood or blood products (usually from a transfusion), and through the passing on of the virus by an infected woman to her child during pregnancy, childbirth, or breast-feeding.

7. **True.** Without an HIV antibody test (which indicates whether a person's body has begun making antibodies in response to the virus), it may be impossible for an individual to tell whether he or she has been infected with HIV. And, for those who have taken this test, it can take from three to six months from the time a person is infected for the virus to show up on the test.

8. **False.** AIDS is a fatal disease. While new drug treatments have extended the lives of many people with AIDS, there is no cure.

9. **False.** In 2002, 40 percent of newly diagnosed HIV infections occurred among men who have sex with men, 31 percent were attributed to heterosexual transmission, and 23 percent were due to injection drug use (Public Health Agency of Canada, 2004).

10. **True.** Many AIDS victims have suffered hostility and discrimination as a result of their illness. Educational programs and political lobbying by AIDS activists have tried to reduce this stigmatization.

Microsoft founder Bill Gates is one of the leaders in the global fight against AIDS.

society. Talcott Parsons viewed illness as dysfunctional both for the individual who is sick and for the larger society (Parsons, 1951). Sick people may be unable to fulfil their necessary social roles, such as parenting, maintaining a home, or working in the paid labour force. Thus illness can cause the social system to malfunction. Societies must, therefore, establish boundaries that define who is legitimately sick. Furthermore, those who are sick are expected to get well so that they can once again contribute to the healthy functioning of the social system. According to Parsons, all societies have a *sick role*—**patterns of behaviour defined as appropriate for people who are sick**. The characteristics of the sick role are:

1. The sick person is temporarily exempt from normal social responsibilities. For example, when you are sick you are not expected to go to work or school.
2. The sick person is not responsible for his or her condition. Individuals should not be blamed or punished, because sickness is not their fault.
3. The sick person must want to get well. The sick role is considered to be a temporary role. The person who does not do everything possible to return to a healthy state is no longer a legitimately sick person and may be considered a hypochondriac or a malingerer.

4. The sick person should seek competent help and cooperate with health care practitioners to hasten his or her recovery.
5. Physicians are the "gatekeepers" who maintain society's control over people who enter the sick role.

Critics of Parsons's model, and more generally of the functionalist view of health and illness, argue that it places too much responsibility for illness upon the sick people themselves, neglecting the fact that often the actions of other people may be the cause of someone's illness. For example, a child may be born with fetal alcohol syndrome as a result of the mother consuming alcohol while pregnant. Individuals living in poverty may become sick because of inadequate food and shelter (see Chapter 8, "Social Class").

Critics of the sick role theory also point out that it is more applicable to individuals with acute illnesses than to those with either chronic illnesses or disabilities that may not be reversible. *Acute illness* **is illness of limited duration from which the patient recovers or dies.** Examples include chicken pox, the flu, pneumonia, and appendicitis. The term *chronic illness* **is applied to a long-term or permanent condition that may or may not be fatal.** Examples of chronic conditions are multiple sclerosis, muscular dystrophy, arthritis, and cystic fibrosis. Patients with terminal conditions, such as Lou Gehrig's disease, who want to get well once they have been diagnosed, may be criticized for both failing to accept the reality of their situation and failing to adapt to daily limitations and disabilities (Nancarrow Clarke, 1996). Also, contrary to the functionalist view, individuals may be blamed for their illness, as people who contract HIV or lung cancer often are.

Symbolic Interactionist Theory: The Social Construction of Illness

Interactionists attempt to understand the specific meanings and causes that we attribute to particular events. In studying health, interactionists focus on the fact that the meaning that social actors give their illness or disease will affect their self-concept and their relationships with others. The interactionist approach is illustrated by society's response to AIDS.

We often try to explain disease by blaming it on those who are ill. This reduces the uncertainty of

This AIDS memorial in Toronto is a striking reminder that AIDS has taken a toll on individuals, families, cities, and nations. In some countries, AIDS is a significant cause of population mortality.

those of us who fear the disease. Nonsmokers who learn that a cancer victim had a two-pack-a-day habit feel comforted that the guilty have been punished and that the same fate is unlikely to befall them. Because of the association of their disease with promiscuous homosexuality and intravenous drug use, victims of AIDS have particularly suffered from blame. How is a person's self-concept affected when they are diagnosed with AIDS? How does this diagnosis affect the relationships the person has with others in his or her social world?

In the case of AIDS, the social definition of the illness has had as profound an impact on the AIDS patient as the medical symptoms. According to Giddens (1996:123), AIDS is an example of illness as stigma. As indicated in Chapter 5, a *stigma* is any physical or social attribute or sign that so devalues a person's social identity that it disqualifies that person from social acceptance. Unlike other illnesses—the ones that provoke sympathy or compassion—an illness that is seen primarily as infectious is perceived as dishonourable or shameful. The result is that sufferers are rejected by the healthy population. Children with AIDS have been driven from their schools; homes of people with AIDS have been burned by those afraid of getting the disease; employees have been fired; and medical professionals have refused treatment to AIDS patients. All of this has happened despite the fact that AIDS cannot be transmitted by casual, everyday contact. However, as the case of AIDS clearly demonstrates, the social definition of an illness is not always based on medical fact. The incidents of hostility and discrimination directed at individuals with AIDS nevertheless have a profound impact on their

self-concept, social relationships, and ability to cope with the illness. The role of the media in shaping the way in which society defines an illness is discussed in Box 18.2.

The Social Definition of Health and Illness: The Process of Medicalization

Most of us would agree that conditions, such as heart disease, tuberculosis, and cancer, are illnesses because of their biological characteristics. However, even in these cases, there is a subjective component to the way illness is defined. This subjective component is very important when we look at conditions that are more ambiguous than cancer or a broken bone. For example, a child who has difficulty learning may be diagnosed as having attention deficit disorder (ADD); a man who occasionally behaves strangely may be called mentally ill; and a woman going through menopause may be defined as having a hormonal deficiency disease. Alternatively, we could view these conditions as part of the range of normal human behaviour. The child might be seen as a poor student, the man as a bit odd, and the woman as a person going through the normal aging process. The way we view these individuals will depend on our cultural perspectives, which can change over time.

The term *medicalization* **refers to the process whereby an object or a condition becomes defined by society as a physical or psychological illness.** This process usually entails the application of medical technology in the diagnosis and treatment of the condition (Grant, 1993). Conrad and Schneider (1992) found that medicalization is typically the result of a lengthy promotional campaign conducted by interest

BOX 18.2 SOCIOLOGY AND THE MEDIA

AIDS in the News

At the age of 13, Ryan White learned that he had contracted HIV through blood products used to treat his hemophilia. When school officials told White he could not return to school because of his HIV, he fought back and eventually was readmitted. White also temporarily became a celebrity.

> We had been in the news so much that reporters were practically part of the family. They came from all over the place, even Japan. I felt like I was growing up with some of them. They followed us into the bathroom to see if we were telling the truth when we said we shared toothpaste and glasses. They stood by the kitchen sink and asked Mom if she was doing dishes by hand so she could use bleach on mine . . .
> We talked to some reporters more often than we visited with our friends and relatives.
> (quoted in White and Cunningham, 1992:120–121)

Why did journalists pay so much attention to Ryan White and his plight?

Journalists have the ability to transform events—such as White's illness and battle with the school—into news. However, HIV poses unique problems for journalists. Gay men (a stigmatized category) were among the first to be identified with the problem. To report on HIV transmitted by gay men, journalists must refer to blood, semen, sex, and death, all of which are viewed by some media elites as being beyond good taste. Because of these problems, some journalists divided persons with HIV into two categories: "innocent victims," such as Ryan White, who acquire the virus through blood transfusions or other means considered beyond their control, and "sources" of the problem, including gay and bisexual men, intravenous drug users, and prostitutes. This way of thinking suggests that we

> withhold compassion from those whose behaviours may have caused or contributed to their deaths. On these grounds we would never mourn the passing of a heart attack victim who did not exercise, worked under stress, or ate foods high in cholesterol. Persons with lung cancer owing to smoking should be disdained; persons with back injuries from lifting should be despised; the person who sees the ice but nonetheless slips on it should be left in agony where he landed . . . This is more than logically ridiculous. It is morally reprehensible. (Fisher, 1993:27–30)

The novel that was the basis for the hit play *Rent* dealt with gay victims of AIDS. However, producers of the play changed the focus to a heterosexual couple with AIDS because they felt the audience would not accept a play that was primarily about homosexuals (Gideonse, 1998).

Do you think media coverage of HIV/AIDS divides people into innocent victims and guilty parties? What role should the media play, if any, in disseminating information about HIV/AIDS to the public?

Sources: Based on Molotch and Lester, 1974; Colby and Cook, 1991; White and Cunningham, 1992; Fisher, 1993; Hernandez, 1994.

---

groups, often culminating in legislative or other official changes that institutionalize a medical treatment for the new "disease." The interest groups may include scientists acting on the results of their research; those who have the disease and who may be seeking either a cure or a socially acceptable excuse for their behaviour; and members of the medical industry interested in increasing their profits.

Conrad and Schneider (1980) emphasize that many behaviours that were at one time defined as "badness" have been redefined as "sicknesses" or "illnesses." Peter Conrad (1975) describes how the disruptive behaviour of children in schools became medicalized. Until a medical condition was established and given the name attention deficit/hyperactivity disorder (ADHD), children who had difficulty sitting still, concentrating, or who were impulsive and full of energy were labelled "active" or "energetic," or they were called "problem children" (Conrad, 1975). In the early 1970s, the medical profession started to intervene in treating these "deviant" children. The "discovery" of the illness now known as attention deficit disorder (ADD) coincided with the development of Ritalin, a drug that suppresses hyperactive behaviours. As a result, medication became the accepted treatment for this condition. For schools, the social construction of this illness results in fewer disruptive students and more manageable classrooms. Furthermore, it creates a large new patient population for the medical profession and a profitable new market for the pharmaceutical industry. For the children whose

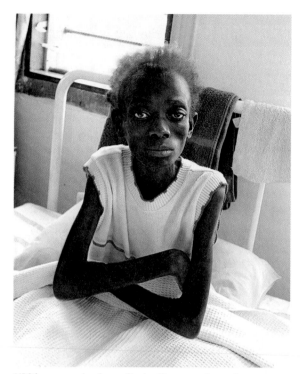

AIDS is a severe burden on the health-care systems of poor countries. Sixteen-year-old Lucy Bwanali died in a hospice far from her home in northern Zambia because the palliative care system cannot meet the needs of the huge numbers of people who are dying of the disease.

problem behaviour is organically based, Ritalin enables them to concentrate and function better in the classroom. However, for children whose disruptive behaviour is a reflection of their acting "like children" rather than symptomatic of ADD, it results in unnecessary medication.

Just as conditions can be medicalized, so can they be *demedicalized*. For many years, homosexuality was defined as a mental illness, and gays and lesbians were urged to seek psychiatric treatment. Conrad and Schneider (1992) have described the successful fight by gay activists to convince the American Psychiatric Association to remove homosexuality from the association's psychiatric diagnostic manual. At the same time, women's groups have been trying to demedicalize childbirth and menopause, and to redefine them as natural processes rather than as illnesses.

Feminist Perspectives on Health and Illness

Feminist scholars have studied many different aspects of health and the health care system. One of the earliest problems they identified was the fact that most medical research was centred on males and that diseases that primarily affected females were ignored.

Other researchers have studied the discrimination against women who work in a health care system that has traditionally been dominated by male doctors. Women have been relegated to subservient roles and have had few opportunities to get access to leadership roles within the system. Some of the most interesting and important work by feminist scholars has been done on the ways in which the process of medicalization has had a particular impact on women.

The Medicalization of Women's Lives

You learned about the concept of medicalization in the discussion of the interactionist perspective. This has been a particular focus of feminist researchers, because women's health issues, such as those having to do with childbirth, menopause, PMS, and contraception, have been particularly susceptible to medicalization—and this process has not necessarily served the interests of women. For example, for most of human history women's health needs, including pregnancy and childbirth, were looked after by other women in their communities (Findlay and Miller, 2002). The era of women looking after women ended when the male profession of medicine successfully challenged midwives and other traditional health practitioners and claimed exclusive jurisdiction over a broad range of conditions that were redefined as medical problems. Medical doctors won this struggle despite the fact that traditional practices often had more favourable outcomes than those of the new profession of medicine. Findlay and Miller conclude that healing became "men's work," and that while this helped to raise the status of the profession of medicine, it was accomplished at the cost of reducing women's control over their own bodies.

Medicalization had a profound effect on the practices of childbirth, child-rearing, and mothering and contributed to forcing women into the stereotyped role of full-time mother. Feminist researchers have also questioned the role that medicine is playing in shaping the ways in which women view their physical appearance: "Certain sociocultural forces invite an excessive concern for 'feminine beauty,' and medical rhetoric itself acts to exacerbate the already powerful cultural demands on women to overemphasize their bodily appearance" (Findlay and Miller, 2002:197). A 1989 paper by the American Society for Plastic and Reconstructive Surgery provides a rather extreme example of this medical rhetoric. This society, the major professional organization representing plastic surgeons, wanted the U.S. government to loosen its restrictions on the use of breast implants. The society based its case on the view that having small breasts constituted a disease. It alleged that this disease (called *micromastia*) resulted in "feelings of inadequacy, lack of self-confidence, distortion of body image, and a total lack of well-being due to a lack of self-perceived femininity" (cited in Weitz, 1996:123). Of course, this "disease" could be cured if the victims received expensive, potentially dangerous breast implants from the plastic surgeons. In Chapter 11, "Sex and Gender," you learned about the low self-esteem felt by women that is often the result of sexism. It is not difficult to imagine the harm that the plastic surgeons' lobbying effort encouraging women to think of their biologically normal bodies as "diseased" might have on some women's self-image. For example, press reports of a Penticton, B.C. contest in which thirty-six women competed for a chance to win breast implants said that many of the losers had "lost a chance at gaining self-confidence" (Carmichael, 2005). The fact that breast size is still a measure of these young women's sense of self-worth, and that many aspects of physical appearance have come under medical control, is a clear indication of the degree to which women's appearance has become medicalized.

Findlay and Miller feel that there are negative consequences to the medicalization of women's lives: it individualizes and depoliticizes their problems, and by blaming them on the women "leaves the dominant patriarchal conceptions of femininity untouched" (2002:201). Medicalization also forces women to conform to a set of traditional social norms, and it "limits women's options—in behaviour, in appearance, and in relationships" (2002:201). However, they believe that the medical model is so dominant in industrial societies that women will not be be able to develop an alternative. Rather, they will continue to make incremental changes that will reduce some of the negative effects of medicalization while retaining the benefits of the modern medical system. Women have made great headway in reestablishing midwifery and natural childbirth methods that return some of the control over the birthing process to the mother. Women have also forced the medical profession to share more information and to empower clients in many other ways.

Postmodern Analysis: The Clinical Gaze

In *The Birth of the Clinic* (1994/1963), postmodern theorist Michel Foucault questioned existing assumptions about medical knowledge and the power that doctors have gained over other medical personnel and everyday people. Foucault asserted that truth in medicine—like in all other areas of life—is a social construction, in this instance one that doctors have created. Foucault believed that doctors gain power through the *clinical* (or "observing") *gaze,* which they use to gather information. Doctors develop the clinical gaze through their observation of patients; as the doctors begin to diagnose and treat medical conditions, they also start to speak "wisely" about everything. As a result, other people start to believe that doctors can "penetrate illusion and see . . . the hidden truth" (Shawver, 1998).

According to Foucault, the prestige of the medical establishment was further enhanced when it became possible to categorize all illnesses within a definitive network of disease classification under which physicians can claim that they know why patients are sick. Moreover, the invention of new tests made it necessary for physicians to gaze upon the naked body, to listen to the human heart with an instrument, and to run tests on the patient's body fluids. Patients who objected were criticized by the doctors for their "false modesty" and "excessive restraint" (Foucault, 1994/1963:163). As the new rules allowed for the patient to be touched and prodded, the myth of the doctor's diagnostic wisdom was further enhanced, and "medical gestures, words, gazes took on a philosophical density that had formerly belonged only to mathematical thought" (Foucault, 1994/1963:199). For Foucault, the formation of clinical medicine was merely one of the more visible ways in which the fundamental structures of human experience change throughout history.

Foucault's work provides new insights on medical dominance, but it has been criticized for its lack of attention to alternative viewpoints. Among these is the possibility that medical breakthroughs and new technologies actually help physicians become wiser and more scientific in their endeavours. Another criticism is that Foucault's approach is based upon the false assumption that people are passive individuals who simply comply with doctors' orders—he does not take into account that people (either consciously or unconsciously) may resist the myth of the "wise doctor" and not follow "doctors' orders" (Lupton, 1997).

Conflict Theory: Inequalities in Health and Health Care

The conflict approach to health and illness emphasizes the political, economic, and social forces that affect health and the health care system and the

In the summer of 1997, 650 people met in Kingston, Ontario, for the first World Conference on Breast Cancer. The major political goal of the conference was "to do for breast cancer what happened to AIDS in the 1980s—to put breast cancer on the centre stage" (Driedger, 1997).

Alzheimer's disease is a tragedy for the afflicted individuals and for their families. As our population ages, such debilitating conditions will also increasingly place a burden on our health care system and on the taxpayers who fund it.

inequities that result from these forces. Among the issues of concern for conflict theorists are the ability of all citizens to obtain health care; the impact of race, class, and gender on health and health care; the relative power of doctors compared with other health workers; the dominance of the medical model of health care; and the role of profit in the health care system.

While we will consider several of these issues later in this chapter, the role of conflict in the provision of health care is clearly illustrated in the debate over the allocation of money for research and treatment for different diseases. There is competition among those concerned with different diseases; money spent doing research on cancer cannot be spent on heart disease. Conflict also exists among those who take different approaches to research and treatment of a particular disease. Should funds be spent on treatment or prevention? Should nontraditional treatment methods be studied or is the medical model the only legitimate way of responding to disease?

Understandably, groups representing victims of particular types of diseases have lobbied governments and medical groups to give their problem a higher priority and more funding. Thus the priority given to research, prevention, and medical care for particular types of diseases may reflect the power of lobby groups as well as the seriousness of the problem. AIDS activists have been particularly successful in having their concerns reflected in policy. Gay men have worked together to form a lobby that has had a powerful impact on securing government support and funding for AIDS research and treatment. As you will learn from reading Box 18.3, AIDS activists have also been very concerned with reducing the stigmatization of HIV/AIDS victims.

Women with breast cancer saw that AIDS research received about ten times the funding of breast cancer research and have also organized to increase their share of research funding.

SOCIAL FACTORS IN HEALTH: AGE, SEX, AND SOCIAL CLASS

We often think of health in only physical terms. However, the health of any group is a product of the interaction of a wide range of physiological, psychological, spiritual, historical, sociological,

Concept Table 18.A   THEORETICAL PERSPECTIVES ON HEALTH AND ILLNESS

PERSPECTIVE	THEORY	KEY ELEMENTS
Functionalist		
Parsons	Functional Theory	Illness is dysfunctional both for the individual who is sick and for the larger society. All societies have a sick role—patterns of behaviour defined as appropriate for people who are sick.
Symbolic Interactionist		
Conrad and Schneider	Medicalization Theory	All illnesses have a subjective component. Medicalization is the process whereby an object or a condition becomes defined by society as a physical or psychological illness.
Feminist		
Findlay and Miller	Medicalization of Womens' Lives	Medicalization blames women for their problems. It also forces women to conform to traditional role expectations and limits their freedom of behaviour, appearance, and relationships.
Conflict		
Inequalities in Health Care	Inequalities in Health Care	Among the issues for conflict theorists are the ability of all citizens to obtain health care; the impact of race, class, and gender on health care; the relative power of doctors and the medical model in the health care system; and the role of profit in the health care system.
Postmodern		
Foucault	The Clinical Gaze	Doctors have gained and maintained power through the clinical gaze, which they use to gather information. This helps them to create a mystique that convinces the public that doctors have special knowledge and hence should be granted special powers.

cultural, economic, and environmental factors (Waldram et al., 1995). In this section, we will see how these factors affect the health of people of different ages, genders, and classes in Canada. A basic premise of conflict theory is that groups compete with one another for access to scarce resources. Conflict theorists would predict that because of this competition, the quality of health and health care will vary by age, sex, and class. As with other social issues you have studied so far, there are dramatic differences in the health of people in these different social categories.

Age

Rates of illness and death are highest among the old and the very young. Mortality rates drop shortly after birth and begin to rise significantly during the middle

BOX 18.3 SOCIOLOGY AND THE LAW

AIDS and Public Health

In 1993, London, Ontario, resident Charles Ssenyonga was charged with criminal negligence causing bodily harm and aggravated sexual assault for knowingly passing AIDS on to several women. At least twenty women had contracted HIV through having unprotected sex with him. Ssenyonga died during his trial, so we don't know what verdict would have been rendered, though in a similar case a Newfoundland man received a sentence of eleven years after pleading guilty to criminal negligence causing bodily harm for knowingly infecting women with HIV/AIDS. Canada has no specific law against knowingly infecting others with a sexually transmittable disease, though such laws do exist in several other countries.

Ssenyonga knew in 1985 that he likely had HIV. On several occasions doctors suggested he get tested for HIV; however, he refused and was having unprotected sex with multiple partners. In early 1989, two of his victims reported him to public health authorities. The local health unit advised Ssenyonga to be tested. In March of 1989, both Ssenyonga and the health department received confirmation of his infection. A restraining order forbidding him to have sex was issued at the request of public health officials. Despite this, he continued to infect more women. The public health system could not protect Ssenyonga's victims from HIV/AIDS.

Controlling the spread of HIV has been very controversial. The normal steps taken in dealing with infectious diseases include routine testing for infection, reporting the names of those who have positive tests, tracing contacts to determine who might have been infected, and informing them they have been exposed to the disease. Quarantine has even been used to prevent the spread of disease. In Ontario, twelve diseases including syphilis, gonorrhea, and tuberculosis are defined as virulent, and people with these diseases can be forced to stay in a hospital or jail for up to four months for treatment. However, HIV/AIDS is not included in this category. Because it is incurable, health authorities have reasoned, it does not make sense to force victims to have treatment. When Dr. Richard Schabas, Ontario's medical officer of health, suggested classifying HIV/AIDS as

a virulent disease in order to control rare, irresponsible victims like Ssenyonga who knowingly spread the disease, AIDS activists burned Dr. Schabas in effigy and he was given police protection when he received death threats.

Why is HIV/AIDS treated differently from other serious communicable diseases? One reason is the societal reaction to victims of the disease. Homosexual men have had justifiable fears that AIDS testing and reporting would result in discrimination against them. For example, some U.S. school districts wished to use HIV tests to identify and fire gay teachers, and insurance companies were anxious to cancel the policies of victims. Most Canadian provincial human rights codes do not protect homosexuals from discrimination in matters such as housing and employment. To AIDS activists and civil libertarians, Dr. Schabas's suggestion that AIDS victims could be involuntarily detained raised the possibility of homophobic governments locking up large numbers of gay men simply because they were ill.

Clearly there are weaknesses in our current system of controlling AIDS. However, the argument has been made that actions like mandatory testing and reporting or quarantining some AIDS victims will drive those at risk of AIDS underground, thus increasing the chances of further transmission. If there were a chance that HIV-positive people could be publicly identified, those at risk might choose to avoid the health care system altogether. In addition, coercive control measures would be costly in financial as well as human terms, and would not likely be effective as a general public health measure (Hodgson, 1989).

What are your views on this issue? Should all known partners of HIV victims be informed of their risk? Because medical advances such as AZT treatment can slow the progress of HIV, should more effort go into identifying those with HIV so that they can be treated? Can attitudes be changed so that the consequences of being labelled an HIV/AIDS victim are less severe? Should it be a crime to knowingly spread HIV, or should the problem be dealt with outside the criminal courts?

Sources: Callwood, 1995; Burr, 1997; Weston and Jeffery, 1994.

years. After 65, rates of chronic illness and mortality increase rapidly. This has obvious implications for individuals and their families, but also has an impact on Canadian society.

Canada is an aging society (see Chapter 19, "Population and Urbanization"). Today, about 12 percent of the population is age sixty-five or over; by 2036, this will double to about 25 percent. Because health care costs are high for some older people, these costs will begin to rise dramatically after 2010 when the first baby boomers turn sixty-five. This concern with future costs is one of the factors behind the current attempts by provincial and federal governments to restructure the operation of health care. For example, the number of cases of one of the most debilitating conditions among the elderly, *senile dementia*—**a term for diseases, such as Alzheimer's, that involve a progressive impairment of judgment and memory**—is forecast to triple by 2031 to nearly 800,000 people (Lipovenko, 1997). Many of these people will require costly institutional care unless changes are made to improve the support available for home care and group homes.

Sex

Prior to the twentieth century, women had shorter life expectancies than men because of high mortality rates during pregnancy and childbirth. Preventive measures have greatly reduced this cause of female mortality and women now live longer than men. Females born in Canada in 2002 could expect to live about 82 years, compared with 77 years for males (Statistics Canada, 2004c). Ingrid Waldron (1994) has identified three factors leading to this sex difference in mortality rates. First, differences in gender roles in our society mean that females are less likely than males to engage in risky behaviour, such as drinking alcohol and using drugs, driving dangerously, and engaging in violent activities, such as fights. Males are also more likely than females to work in dangerous occupations, such as commercial fishing, mining, and construction. Second, females are more likely to make use of the health care system and so may have problems identified at an earlier, more treatable stage than men, who are more reluctant to consult doctors. Third, it is likely that biological differences contribute, as females have higher survival rates than males at every stage from fetus to old age.

Some health experts have predicted that as the social roles played by females become more like those of males, the mortality gap will narrow. Women in traditionally male-dominated occupations, such as farming and policing, face the same risks as their male counterparts, and the number of such women is steadily increasing. Also, as female rates of behaviour, such as smoking and illicit drug use, approach those of males, females have begun to pay the price in illness and early death. About three decades ago smoking among women began to increase steadily. Predictably, rates of lung cancer among women have tripled since 1975, while rates for men are dropping because men began reducing their smoking rates in the 1960s (Canadian Cancer Society, 2005). Also, Leviathan and Cohen (1985) studied life expectancy in Israeli kibbutz society, where the social roles of men and women are very similar. They found that sex differences in mortality on the kibbutz were only 4.5 years, compared with 7.1 years for the general population of Israel.

Because women live longer than men, many of us assume that women are also healthier. In fact, while men die sooner, women have higher rates of disease and disability. While men at every age have higher rates of fatal diseases, women have higher rates of nonfatal chronic conditions (Waldron, 1994).

One of the interesting issues relating to women's health concerns the lack of medical research on women. For example, many of the largest and most influential studies of diseases that affect both sexes, such as heart disease, have excluded women. Despite this limitation, these studies have become the basis for the diagnosis and treatment of both sexes, even though there may be differences between them. Protests by women's groups have led to change in this area, and some funding agencies now require researchers to include both men and women subjects unless there are clear reasons for limiting the study to one sex. However, the fact remains that a great deal of existing medical knowledge is based on the earlier male-centred research.

Social Class

The poor have worse health and die earlier than the rich. This is also true of poor and rich countries, as illness and mortality rates are far higher in low-income countries than in high-income countries. In Canada, males living in the highest-income neighbourhoods have a life expectancy of almost five more years than males in the lowest-income neighbourhoods. For women the difference is about two years (Statistics Canada, 2002m). There are similar differences between people in the highest- and lowest-income neighbourhoods for other health indicators. For example, in 1996, the infant mortality rate in Canada's poorest urban neighbourhoods was more than 50 percent higher than that in the richest neighbourhoods (Statistics Canada, 2002m).

In 1994–1995 and 1996–1997, the National Population Health Survey found that low-income Canadians were much more likely to experience major chronic diseases, such as emphysema, high blood pressure, and stomach ulcers, than those with middle- and upper incomes. People under 75 in the low-income group in 1994–1995 were also twice as likely to die as those with higher incomes (Statistics Canada, 1998b). The National Longitudinal Survey of Children and Youth found that children from low-income families were more than twice as likely as those from families in the highest income category to have functional health problems (see Figure 18.1).

While poverty is correlated with poor health regardless of the nature of the health care system, good health care policy can help reduce its effects. Providing the poor with access to medical advice and treatment through universal medicare is one way of

doing this. A five-year study comparing cancer survival rates for the poorest one-third of Toronto residents, who all had government-funded health care, with their counterparts in Detroit, who typically had little or no health insurance, shows the impact of ensuring the poor have adequate health care (Gorey et al., 1997). Survival rates were higher in Toronto for twelve of the fifteen most common types of cancer. For many of these types of cancer, survival rates after five years were 50 percent higher among the poor in Toronto than among those in Detroit. The benefits of government-funded care go particularly to the poor, as this study found no differences among middle- or high-income patients in the two countries.

This conclusion was supported by a recent survey comparing Americans and Canadians. Americans were more likely to report having health care needs that were not being met (largely because of a very high rate of unmet needs among those without insurance) and poor Americans were 33 percent more likely than poor Canadians to report having current health problems.

If access to medical care does improve the health of the poor, why then are Canada's poor still less

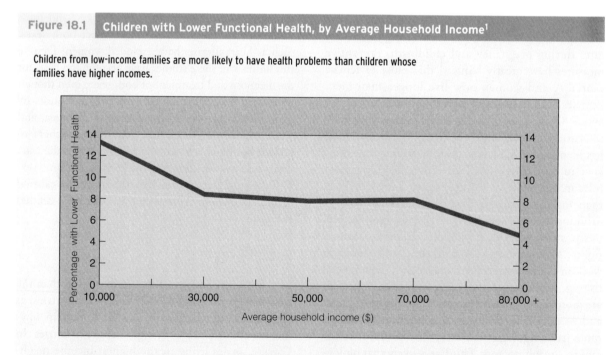

Figure 18.1   Children with Lower Functional Health, by Average Household Income[1]

Children from low-income families are more likely to have health problems than children whose families have higher incomes.

[1]Statistics Canada has based functional health on eight attributes: vision, hearing, speech, mobility, dexterity, cognition, emotion, and pain and discomfort.

Note: Two-parent families with children aged 4–11.

Sources: Canadian Council on Social Development, 1996, 1998.

healthy than its middle and upper classes? The answer is that medical care cannot compensate for the other disadvantages of poverty, such as poor housing, hazardous employment, inadequate diet, greater exposure to disease, and the psychological stresses of poverty. The poor are more likely to engage in unhealthy behaviours, such as smoking and excessive drinking, and are also more likely to become injured or sick because of these conditions. Thus their health is worse despite the availability of care once the medical problem has occurred. The poor may also lack knowledge of preventive strategies and services. For example, college- or university-educated women are twice as likely as women who have not graduated from high school to have mammograms. This means that less educated women are at higher risk of dying of breast cancer. Finally, when they are ill the poor are less likely to visit doctors than are wealthier people (Roos et al., 2004).

While differences remain between rich and poor, it is encouraging to note that the gap in life expectancy between people living in the highest- and lowest-income neighbourhoods has declined substantially over the past thirty years (Statistics Canada, 2002m). One reason for this is that the difference in infant mortality rates between high- and low-income neighbourhoods declined from 9.8 deaths per 1,000 births in 1971 to 2.4 deaths per 1,000 births in 1996.

RACE, CLASS, AND HEALTH: CANADA'S ABORIGINAL PEOPLES

We have looked at some aspects of the relationship between class and health. The experience of Canada's Aboriginal peoples clearly illustrates how the disadvantages of race interact with those of class to cause health problems. While the economic disadvantages and the prejudice suffered by Aboriginal people are worse than they are for most other groups of Canadians, the poverty and discrimination that affect Aboriginal people's health also affect the health of some other minority groups. For example, in the United States the infant mortality rate for Blacks is 250 percent higher than for whites and overall life expectancy is nearly 10 years lower for Blacks (Lavizzo-Mourey et al., 2005).

Health Problems Among Aboriginal Peoples in Canada

Aboriginal people have a history of serious health problems that begins with their early contact with Europeans. *Epidemics—sudden, significant increases in the numbers of people contracting a disease*—of contagious diseases, such as tuberculosis, measles, smallpox, and influenza, broke out in the early years of this contact. These epidemics were partly due to the fact that Aboriginals had no immunity to these European diseases. They were also caused by new patterns of trade that led to contact with more diverse groups of people than had occurred before European settlement. A critical mass of population is necessary to sustain an epidemic, and trade led to higher population densities around trading posts. Tuberculosis epidemics were particularly devastating in the late nineteenth century, as Aboriginal people were moved to reserves. Crowded and lacking proper sanitation and hygiene facilities, the reserves were ideal settings for the spread of disease, and mortality rates for tuberculosis remained high until the 1950s. The epidemics were very dramatic, but death rates from diseases, such as typhoid fever, and puerperal fever caused by poor sanitation in the settlements were also high (Waldram et al., 1995).

While their mortality rates have improved significantly since the middle of the twentieth century, Aboriginal people still die earlier than other Canadians. Infant mortality rates among Aboriginal people have declined by 71 percent since 1979, but are still nearly twice the Canadian average (*National Post*, 2003). Life expectancy is seven years less than average for First Nations men and five years less for First Nations women, who also have higher than average rates of hospital admission and disease (Canadian Institute for Health Information, 2004b). While infectious diseases among Aboriginals have been brought under control (though their rates remain higher than those of other Canadians), their health problems are now chronic diseases, such as heart disease, respiratory problems, and diabetes. HIV/AIDS is now beginning to affect the Aboriginal community. The B.C. Aboriginal HIV/AIDS Task Force reported that while Aboriginal people made up less than 5 percent of the province's population, they made up 16 percent of those testing HIV-positive. The problem was particularly acute for Aboriginal women, who were eight times more likely to contract HIV than were non-Aboriginal women.

What are the reasons for the poorer health of Aboriginal people? A major factor is poverty. You have seen in Chapter 8, "Social Class," that Aboriginal people are among the poorest in Canada and suffer from the poor nutrition and other social conditions that go with poverty. The complexity of these problems is shown in a study of the food supply of three northern Manitoba Cree communities (Campbell et al., 1997). The use of traditional food obtained from fishing and hunting was common but limited by the fact that 50 percent of the respondents did not have an active hunter or fisher in the household. Because the communities are isolated, food is up to twice as expensive as in the more accessible communities of Thompson and Winnipeg. The costs of a well-balanced diet may be too high for some families who do not have an adequate supply of traditional food, so health problems due to nutritional deficiencies are a concern.

Many of the diseases that affect Aboriginal people can also be traced to the inadequate housing, crowding, and poor sanitary conditions common on reserves and in other communities where they live. The isolation of many Aboriginal communities is also a factor; an illness that could be easily treated in a city hospital can be fatal in a community 800 kilometres from the nearest doctor.

Aboriginal people also have high rates of violent death and suicide. Rates of homicide are six times higher than the Canadian average for Aboriginal men and four times higher for women; rates of suicide are three times higher for men and twice as high for women than the Canadian averages (Mao et al., 1992). Rates of adolescent suicide are particularly high; the images of gasoline-sniffing young Innu from Davis Inlet in Labrador that many of us saw on television were a vivid and haunting illustration of this problem. Accidental death rates are also higher: Aboriginal people are three times more likely than other Canadians to die as a result of motor vehicle accidents and twice as likely to die by drowning (Wotherspoon, 1994). These kinds of accidental deaths are often associated with the high rates of alcohol and drug abuse that are serious problems in many Aboriginal communities. These problems in turn are a consequence of the marginal role Aboriginal people play in Canadian society.

Finally, the legacy of colonialism still affects Aboriginal people's health problems. Anastasia Shkilnyk (1985), who studied the Ojibwa community of Grassy Narrows in northwestern Ontario, attributes the high rates of suicide and violent death and health problems on the reserve to colonial actions, such as the destruction of Aboriginal language and religion, the family breakdown caused by enforced attendance at residential schools, and the forced relocation of the community by the Department of Indian Affairs. Environmental destruction by local industries that dumped methyl mercury into the lakes and rivers around the reserve was another contributor. This toxic substance had a direct impact on the health of Grassy Narrows residents and also had an indirect impact by destroying the traditional fishery that was the foundation of the community's way of life.

Aboriginal Healing Methods

Aboriginal cultural and healing traditions are holistic and deal with the interactions between spirit, mind, and body. However, the Western medical model of medicine has been as dominant in Aboriginal communities as it has in the rest of Canada. Janice Acoose-Pelletier describes the problems this has created:

> When a Native person is admitted to a hospital, a number of other problems arise because we have our own ways of dealing with illness and care of the sick. Most hospitals don't recognize this or simply don't care . . . Non-native medical personnel do not understand that healing, to many Native people, concerns whole communities or families . . . To become well and whole again, the sick person must have faith and confidence in the healing process. For Native people, this is difficult and frustrating because in many cases they can't even communicate with doctors . . . Doctors are just not aware of the cultural differences between Natives and non-Natives regarding disease and care of the sick. (cited in Anderson, 1994:320–321)

Though traditional healing practices fell into disuse for many years, they are now becoming popular again for several reasons. First, medical and government authorities have responded to Aboriginal demands that culturally appropriate healing methods should be available. The introduction and acceptance of these methods, however, has been mixed. Some hospitals and clinics now have Aboriginal healers and combine traditional and Western treatment methods. For example, a plaque in a Kenora, Ontario, hospital reads: "We believe traditional Native healing and culture have a place in our provision of health care services to the Native people" (Waldram et al., 1995).

Second, Aboriginal groups are gaining greater control over the delivery of medical services in their communities. These changes are almost certainly indicators of a future in which there will be greater involvement of Aboriginal people in the health care system and more integration of the traditional and Western medical traditions.

Research suggests there is evidence that this restoration of Native control over their health care will lead to improved health among Aboriginal people (Canadian Institute for Health Information, 2004b). Researchers in many parts of the world, moreover, have found that many traditional medicines are effective, and pharmaceutical companies now market many products (including Aspirin) with the same chemical composition as traditional herbal remedies.

■ DISABILITY

What is a disability? There are many different definitions. In business and government, it often is defined in terms of work—for instance, "an inability to engage in gainful employment." Medical professionals tend to define it in terms of organically based impairments—the problem being entirely within the body (Albrecht, 1992). However, not all disabilities are visible to others nor do they necessarily limit people physically. An alternative definition of ***disability*** **is a physical or health condition that reduces a person's ability to perform tasks he or she would normally do at a given stage of life and that may result in stigmatization or discrimination against the person.** In other words, the notion of disability is based not only on physical conditions but also on social attitudes and the social and physical environments in which people live. All too often, people with disabilities are treated as if they were not fully human. Laurie Krever Karmona, the mother of a daughter with cerebral palsy, experienced this herself when she was temporarily forced to use a wheelchair:

> My sister wheeled me to my local Shoppers Drug Mart where I shop at least once a week. I recognize the clerks and, I thought, they recognize me. When we got to the cashier, she asked my sister, "Does she have an Optimum card?" and then, "How does she wish to pay for her purchases?" I was looking around for the "she" until I realized she meant me . . The equation, I realize, goes something like this: one sprained ankle plus one broken ankle must equal one totally brain-injured person. (Karmona, 2001:A16)

According to Blackford (1996), the social system and its planners have failed to provide the universal access that would allow people with disabilities to participate fully in all aspects of life. For example, in

Does life expectancy take on a different meaning for persons with chronic disabilities? While he was still in college, British theoretical physicist Stephen Hawking learned he had Lou Gehrig's disease (amyotrophic lateral sclerosis). Hawking nevertheless went on to develop a quantum theory of gravity that forever changed our view of the universe, and as a result he is considered one of the leading figures in modern cosmology.

an elevator, the buttons may be beyond the reach of persons using a wheelchair. In this context, disability derives from the fact that certain things have been made inaccessible to some people (Weitz, 1995). Michael Oliver (1990) used the term *disability oppression* to describe the barriers that exist for disabled persons in Canadian society. These include economic hardship (from such things as the additional costs of accessibility devices, transportation, and attendant care; or employment discrimination), inadequate government assistance programs, and negative social attitudes toward disabled persons. According to disability rights advocates, disability must be thought of in terms of how society causes or contributes to the problem—not in terms of what is "wrong" with the person with a disability.

Sociological Perspectives on Disability

How do sociologists view disability? Those using the functionalist framework often apply Parsons's sick role model, which is referred to as the *medical model* of disability. According to the medical model, people with disabilities become, in effect, chronic patients under the supervision of doctors and other medical personnel, subject to a doctor's orders or a program's rules and not to their own judgment (Shapiro, 1993). From this perspective, disability is deviance. The deviance framework is also apparent in some symbolic interactionist perspectives. According to symbolic interactionists, people with a disability experience *role ambiguity* because many people equate disability with deviance (Murphy et al., 1988). By labelling individuals with a disability as "deviant," other people can avoid them or treat them as outsiders. Society marginalizes people with a disability because they have lost old roles and statuses and are labelled as "disabled" persons. According to Eliot Freidson (1965), how the people are labelled results from three factors: (1) their degree of responsibility for their impairment, (2) the apparent seriousness of their condition, and (3) the perceived legitimacy of the condition. Freidson concluded that the definition of and expectations for people with a disability are socially constructed factors.

Finally, from a conflict perspective, persons with a disability are members of a subordinate group in conflict with persons in positions of power in the government, in the health care industry, and in the rehabilitation business, all of whom are trying to control their destinies (Albrecht, 1992). Those in positions of power have created policies and artificial barriers

Steven Fletcher, the Parliamentary Health Critic for the Conservative Party, is the first quadriplegic to be elected to Canada's House of Commons. After being injured in an automobile accident, Fletcher began his political career by serving two terms as President of the University of Manitoba's Students' Union while completing his MBA degree.

that keep people with disabilities in a subservient position (Asch, 1986; Hahn, 1987). Moreover, in a capitalist economy, disabilities are big business. When people with disabilities are defined as a social problem and public funds are spent to purchase goods and services for them, rehabilitation becomes a commodity that can be bought and sold by the medical–industrial complex (Albrecht, 1992). From this perspective, persons with a disability are objectified. They have an economic value as consumers of goods and services that will allegedly make them "better" people. Many persons with a disability endure the same struggle for resources faced by people of colour, women, and older persons. Individuals who hold more than one of these ascribed statuses, combined with experiencing disability, are doubly or triply oppressed by capitalism.

Disability in Contemporary Society

An estimated 3.6 million people aged 15 and over, representing 12 percent of the adult population in Canada, report having one or more physical or mental disabilities (Statistics Canada, 2004h). This number is increasing for several reasons. First, with advances in medical technology, many people who formerly would have died from an accident or illness now survive, although with an impairment. Second, as more people live longer, they are more likely to experience diseases (such as arthritis) that may have disabling consequences (Albrecht, 1992). Third, persons born with serious disabilities are more likely to survive infancy because of medical technology. However, fewer than 15 percent of persons with a disability today were born with it; accidents and disease account for most disabilities in this country.

Although anyone can become disabled, some people are more likely to be or to become disabled than others. Aboriginal people have higher rates of disability than other Canadians, especially rates of more serious disabilities; persons with lower incomes also have higher rates of disability (Bolaria and Bolaria, 1994). However, "disability knows no socioeconomic boundaries. You can become disabled from your mother's poor nutrition or from falling off your polo pony," says Patrisha Wright, a spokesperson for the Disability Rights Education and Defense Fund (quoted in Shapiro, 1993:10).

For persons with chronic illness and disability, life expectancy may take on a different meaning. Knowing that they likely will not live out the full life expectancy for persons in their age cohort, they may come to "treasure each moment," as does James Keller, a baseball coach:

> In December 1992, I found out I have Lou Gehrig's disease—amyotrophic lateral sclerosis, or ALS. I learned that this disease destroys every muscle in the body, that there's no known cure or treatment and that the average life expectancy for people with ALS is two to five years after diagnosis.
>
> Those are hard facts to accept. Even today, nearly two years after my diagnosis, I see myself as 42-year-old career athlete who has always been blessed with excellent health. Though not an hour goes by in which I don't see or hear in my mind that phrase "two to five years," I still can't quite believe it. Maybe my resistance to those words is exactly what gives me the strength to live with them and the will to make the best of every day in every way. (Keller, 1994)

Environment, lifestyle, and working conditions all may contribute to either temporary or chronic disability. For example, air pollution in automobile-clogged cities leads to a higher incidence of chronic respiratory disease and lung damage, which may result in severe disability in some people. Eating certain types of food and smoking cigarettes increase the risk for coronary and cardiovascular diseases (Albrecht, 1992). In contemporary industrial societies, workers in the second tier of the labour market (primarily recent immigrants, white women, and visible minorities) are at the greatest risk for certain health hazards and disabilities. Employees in data processing and service-oriented jobs also may be affected by work-related disabilities, such as arthritis, lower-back pain, and carpal tunnel syndrome.

In 2001, one in eight Canadians experienced "limitations in their everyday activities because of physical, psychological or health conditions" (Statistics Canada, 2004h). Among adults the most common form of disabilities are mobility-related (2.5 million people) followed by chronic pain (2.4 million people), agility difficulties (2.3 million people), hearing difficulties (1 million people), vision difficulties (590,000 people), and speech-related difficulties (360,000 people).

Living with disabilities is a long-term process. For infants born with certain types of congenital (present at birth) problems, their disability first acquires social significance for their parents and caregivers. In a study of children with disabilities in Israel, sociologist Meira Weiss (1994) challenged the assumption that parents automatically bond with infants, especially those born with visible disabilities. She found that an infant's appearance may determine how parents view the child. Parents are more likely to be bothered by external, openly visible disabilities than by internal or disguised ones; some of the parents are more willing to consent to or even demand the death of an "appearance-impaired" child (Weiss, 1994). According to Weiss, children born with internal (concealed) disabilities at least initially are more acceptable to parents because they do not violate the parents' perceived body images of their children. Weiss's study provides insight into the social significance people attach to congenital disabilities.

Many disability rights advocates argue that persons with a disability have been kept out of the mainstream of society. They have been denied equal opportunities in education by being consigned to special education classes or special schools. For example, people who grow up deaf often are viewed as disabled. However, many members of the deaf community instead view themselves as a "linguistic minority" that is part of a unique culture (Lane, 1992; Cohen, 1994). They believe they have been restricted from entry into schools and the workforce, not due to their own limitations, but by societal barriers. Why are disabled persons excluded? Susan Wendell offers an explanation:

> In a society which idealizes the body, the physically disabled are often marginalized. People learn to identify with their own strengths (by cultural standards) and to hate, fear, and neglect their

own weaknesses. The disabled are not only de-valued for their de-valued bodies; they are constant reminders to the able-bodied of the negative body—of what the able-bodied are trying to avoid, forget, and ignore . . . In a culture which loves the idea that the body can be controlled, those who cannot control their bodies are seen (and may see themselves) as failures. (1995:458)

Among persons who acquire disabilities through disease or accidents later in life, the social significance of their disability can be seen in how they initially respond to their symptoms and diagnosis, how they view the immediate situation and their future, and how the illness and disability affect their lives. According to Wendell:

> Disabled people can participate in marginalizing ourselves. We can wish for bodies we do not have, with frustration, shame, self-hatred. We can feel trapped in the negative body; it is our internalized oppression to feel this. Every (visibly or invisibly) disabled person I have talked to has felt this; some never stop feeling it. (1995:458)

When confronted with a disability, most people adopt one of two strategies—avoidance or vigilance. Those who use the avoidance strategy deny their condition so as to maintain hopeful images of the future and elude depression; for example, some individuals refuse to participate in rehabilitation following a traumatic injury because they want to pretend that it does not exist (Weitz, 1995). By contrast, those using the vigilant strategy actively seek knowledge and treatment so that they can respond appropriately to the changes in their bodies (Weitz, 1995).

The combination of a disability and society's reaction to the disability has an impact on the lives of many people. The disabled often suffer from stereotyping. For example, movies often depict villains as individuals with disabilities (think of *Nightmare on Elm Street*, in which the villain was turned into a hateful, sadistic killer because of disfigurement resulting from a fire, and the villains in the *Batman* movies). Charitable organization fundraising campaigns may contribute to the perception of the disabled as persons who are to be pitied. Prejudice against persons with disabilities may result in either subtle or overt discrimination. According to Asch (2004:11):

> Many commentators note that people with disabilities are expected to play no adult social role whatsoever; to be perceived as always, in every social interaction, a recipient of help and never a provider of assistance; and to be more disliked by nondisabled others if they are clearly competent than if they are perceived as incompetent at a task.

This attitude is part of the reason why they have difficulty finding employment. While the role of disabled persons in the Canadian labour force has expanded in recent years, compared with nondisabled adults a much smaller proportion of the disabled population is employed. A Statistics Canada survey found that only about 25 percent of working-age people who had received care at home because of a long-term health problem or physical limitation were in the labour force. The care-receivers who had jobs were younger, better educated, and healthier than those who did not (Cranswick, 1999). Overall, the unemployment rate of adults aged twenty-five to sixty-four with disabilities was almost double that of people without disabilities, and those with disabilities were nearly twice as likely to have had 2001 annual incomes of less than $15,000 (Statistics Canada, 2004h).

Greater inclusion of people with disabilities is a challenge Canadians must accept if we are to achieve our goal of equality for all citizens. This is not just a matter for governments. While legislation is important, social attitudes also must change. Adrienne Asch, who is a blind university professor, says that even her close friends do not treat her in the same way as they treat others. For example, they "do not feel comfortable accepting my offers to pick up food as part of a dinner we plan to have; . . . or who would prefer that a high-school-age stranger take care of their six-year-old son for an evening than have me do it, even though I have known their son and their home ever since his birth" (2004:11). Thus it isn't just a matter of ending discrimination against people with disabilities, but rather of ensuring full integration into mainstream society.

SOCIAL DEVELOPMENT AND HEALTH: A GLOBAL PERSPECTIVE

Earlier in this chapter you learned how poverty and colonialism have affected the health of Canada's Aboriginal people. These factors also operate on a global scale. For example, Hunt (1989) attributes the rapid spread of diseases, such as HIV/AIDS in Africa, to the underdevelopment and dependency that is the legacy of colonialism. While one of the specific causes of HIV transmission is Africa's labour market that concentrates male migrant workers in a few locations far from their families, the underlying roots of this health problem lie in the economic and social marginalization of most African people.

The difference between rich and poor countries is dramatically reflected in infant mortality rates. While about 5 out of every 1,000 infants in Canada die before their first birthday, infant mortality rates in the world's poorest countries are far higher. Rwanda, Haiti, and Pakistan, for instance, have infant mortality rates of 91, 73, and 72 per 1,000 live births (CIA, 2005). Life expectancy is correspondingly low; for persons born in Canada in 2002, life expectancy at birth was about 80 years, compared with less than 45 years in many poor African nations. Most deaths in less-developed countries are caused by infectious and parasitic diseases that are now rare in the industrialized world.

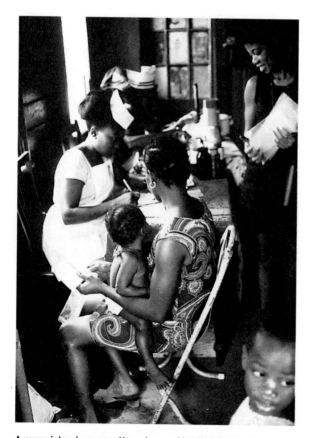

A nurse interviews a mother at a rural health clinic in Sierra Leone. With the support of the World Health Organization, these clinics were established to reduce infant mortality and to improve the health of mothers and their children.

While statistics paint a grim picture of health in the developing world, a World Health Organization report on the health of the world's children puts the situation in even starker terms (2005). More than eleven million children each year die of the childhood diseases of measles, diarrhea, malaria, pneumonia, and malnutrition. As Monica Sharma and James Tulloch tell us, "Children in rich countries do not die from the common, preventable diseases of childhood. Children in poor countries do" (Sharma and Tulloch, 1997:1).

Tremendous progress has nevertheless been made in saving the lives of children (see Figure 18.2). Steps, such as immunization, oral rehydration therapy for diarrhea, and iodizing salt, save as many as five million children each year. Sharma and Tulloch say this progress "must be ranked as one of the great achievements of the second half of the twentieth century" (1997:2). However, almost eleven million children die before the age of five in low-income countries. Millions of these deaths could be prevented through simple measures, such as improved sanitation, clean water, improved preventive measures, such as immunization, and the provision of better local health services.

Of course, not only children in poor countries are dying. Each year, 529,000 women die of complications arising from pregnancy and childbirth. Virtually all of these deaths take place in poor countries (World Health Organization, 2005).

As we have noted, AIDS is becoming an epidemic in low-income countries but little has been done to prevent its spread there. (See Box 18.4 for more on the spread of AIDS in Africa, particularly Uganda.) Unfortunately, the new methods of treatment that have successfully extended the lives of those with AIDS in the high-income countries are unaffordable in low-income countries, where average annual incomes are only a fraction of the cost of these treatments. Financial considerations also mean that drug companies are not interested in developing cures for diseases, such as malaria, as residents of poor countries where these diseases are epidemic cannot afford to pay high prices for such drugs.

Despite these problems, tremendous progress has been made in saving the lives of children and adults. Over the past 50 years, the average life expectancy in the world has increased from 46 years in 1955 to 65 years in 2002 (World Health Organization, 2003). Life expectancy at birth has risen to more than 70 years in 84 countries, up from only 55 countries in 1990. Life expectancy in low-income nations increased on average from 55 to 62 years and

Figure 18.2 | **Infant Mortality Rate Change Over Period 1990-2003**

To reduce child deaths, infants must survive.

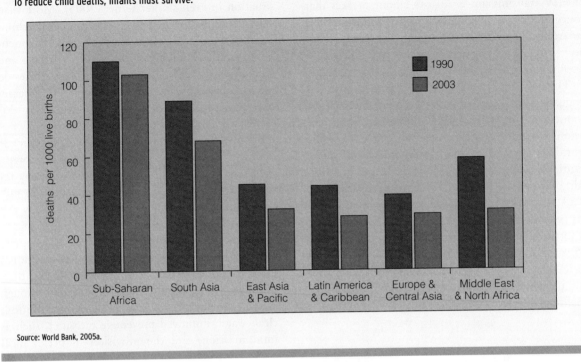

Source: World Bank, 2005a.

mortality of children under five years of age dropped from 149 to 85 per 1,000 live births. This increase has been attributed to a number of factors, one of the most important of which is the development of a safe water supply. The percentage of the world's population with access to safe water nearly doubled between 1990 and 2000 (United Nations Development Programme, 2003).

Health Care in Canada

For many years, the United Nations ranked Canada as one of the three best places in the world to live. This prestigious designation is in part based on an assessment of Canada's national health care system. Though it is cherished by Canadians and envied by many in other countries, Canada's health care system is struggling to recover from major cutbacks made during the 1990s. In 1996, government funding for health care fell for the first time since the birth of medicare (Canadian Press, 1997). In the early 1990s, medical school enrolments were reduced, and nurses and other health care workers were laid off. As a result of these and other cuts,

waiting times for surgery and other medical procedures increased. Public opinion polls show how these changes led to public concern about medical care, a concern that continues today. An international health survey found that in 1988 only 5 percent of Canadians felt their health care system required major rebuilding. As shown in Figure 18.3, by 2001, 18 percent felt that major changes were needed (Blendon, et al., 2002).

In this survey, 26 percent of Canadians said their access to health care had gotten worse in the previous two years. More than twice as many respondents reported long waiting times for elective surgery than had reported this problem in a similar survey conducted in 1998. Just over half the respondents felt that the quality of care was excellent or very good, which is similar to the results of surveys in the United States, England, Australia, and New Zealand. Lower-income Canadians were less likely to report that they had received satisfactory care.

Despite these problems, there is some cause for optimism about the future of our health care system in that Canadians still highly value their system and are determined to ensure its survival. Public pressure

BOX 18.4 SOCIOLOGY IN GLOBAL PERSPECTIVE

The AIDS Epidemic in Africa

RAKAI, UGANDA: From the shadows of this mud hut, the gaunt and weary young man stares outside at the pigs playing in the dust under the banana palms. His chest is covered with open sores; skin rashes have left his ebony arms looking as if they are covered in chalk; his army fatigues hang loosely around his waist.

Outside, Charles Lawanga glances toward his ailing second son and lowers his voice. Last year, when the Ugandan army gave him his medical furlough, his son was sick, but at least he could walk, says Lawanga.

Lawanga's brows are furrowed; he has the face of a man who is watching his son die. His eyes sharpen when he hears that an American journalist knows many of the Western doctors working on the disease. He knows that the United States is a country of immense wealth, and that the medicine that will save his country and his son will probably come from there. Tears gather in his brown eyes, and he asks, "When will it come? When will there be the cure?" (Shilts, 1988:621)

In the mid-1990s, Uganda had the highest number of recorded HIV cases in Africa—around 1.5 million. AIDS has touched virtually all families in this country. However, Uganda has become the first African country to make major gains in the fight against HIV/AIDS. One of the key indicators is the infection rate of pregnant women: Between 1992 and 1998 this rate dropped from 31 percent to 14 percent in the capital city of Kampala and from 21 percent to 8 percent in the rest of the country. The rate among men attending clinics for sexually transmitted diseases dropped from 46 percent to 20 percent over the same period (Global Health Council, 2002).

The fight against HIV/AIDS was led by Uganda's President Museveni personally. The government involved a broad array of partners from all sectors of society to implement a program involving sex education in the schools that encouraged abstinence but also promoted condom use for those who were sexually active; quick treatment of other sexually transmitted diseases; and same-day results for HIV tests and immediate counselling for those who were tested. Uganda developed the ABC approach to AIDS prevention: Abstinence; Be faithful to one partner; and use Condoms. This program was implemented through grassroots organizations throughout the country and received funding from the World Bank and from the United States (Avert, 2005).

Unfortunately, few other countries have followed Uganda's lead. Successful programs in Thailand and Senegal have also been based on encouraging condom use and discouraging risky sexual behaviour, such as casual sex and sex with prostitutes (Global Health Council, 2002). However, many countries deny they have a problem, while in other countries public discussion of sexual behaviour is so taboo that governments and other leaders refuse to address rising infection rates. Even in Uganda, programs are at risk because U.S.-based funding organizations are discouraging the promotion of condoms and advocating "abstinence-only" programs. President Museveni has recently condemned condom use as immoral and the safe-sex advertising campaign and the free distribution of condoms have been drastically curtailed. There is clear evidence that condom use is a vital component of successful AIDS prevention programs and that abstinence-only programs do not work, so the ideology of the faith-based organizations that are delivering U.S. funding is jeopardizing the lives of millions of Ugandans (Avert, 2005; New York Times, 2005).

---

has stopped the erosion of health services. The provinces have put new money into health care, and the federal government has placed health care funding at the top of the spending priority list. However, health care costs are increasing rapidly, and major changes must be made to the health care system if quality care is to remain affordable.

Universal Health Care

Canadians have not always had a **universal health care system; that is, one in which all citizens receive medical services paid for through taxation revenues.** Prior to the early 1960s, Canadians had a "user pay" system, in which people had to pay for

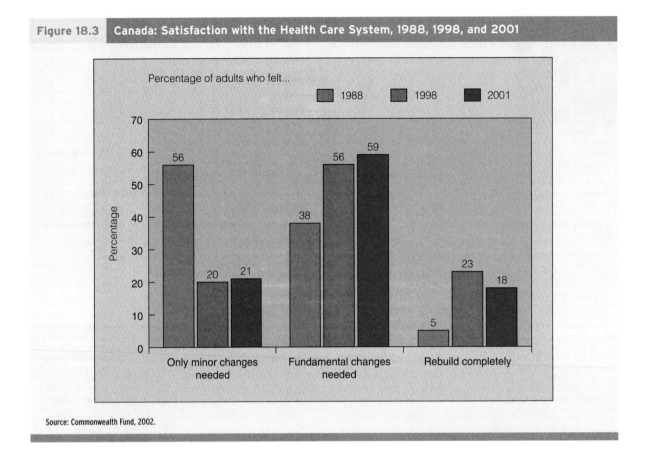

Figure 18.3   Canada: Satisfaction with the Health Care System, 1988, 1998, and 2001

Source: Commonwealth Fund, 2002.

health care directly out of their pockets. Individuals who did not have health insurance and who required expensive medical procedures or long-term care or who developed a chronic illness often suffered severe financial losses. Today, under our universal system, if you are sick, you have the right to receive medical care regardless of your ability to pay. Individuals do not pay doctor or hospital costs directly, but they are responsible for at least part of the costs of other medical services, such as prescription drugs and ambulances.

While the idea of universal health care was first introduced in Canada by Liberal Party leader Mackenzie King in 1919, it took almost five decades for this platform proposal to be implemented. This long delay was due in part to the fact that, constitutionally, health care is a provincial responsibility, and all changes had to be approved by the provinces. Legislation providing universal hospital insurance— but not fees for doctors' services—was passed in 1958. Responding to concerns about the quality of health care in Canada, in 1961 the federal government established the Royal Commission on Health Services. The commission identified many problems

in Canada's health care system, including high infant mortality, high incidence of sickness, insufficient numbers of trained personnel, gaps in health insurance, and inequality in health care for the poor (Jarvis, 1994). The commission recommended that the provincial and federal governments introduce a program to remove the economic barriers that prevented many Canadians from accessing necessary medical care.

Acting on its own, in 1962 the government of Saskatchewan implemented a provincial health insurance plan despite opposition from doctors, who went on strike in protest against the program. The strike was not successful, as the vast majority of citizens supported the government, which maintained health services by importing doctors from Great Britain. The Saskatchewan program proved itself to be viable in the years that followed the strike, and by 1972 all Canadian provinces and territories had coverage for medical and hospital services.

Shirley Douglas, the daughter of Tommy Douglas, the premier who brought in medicare (and the mother of actor Kiefer Sutherland), provides a description of the hostility that accompanied the introduction of a universal hospitalization plan in 1947 in Saskatchewan:

> There was such a fear in the business community. And the people were bewildered, too. The letters in the newspapers and editorials were vicious. You had the radio stations and all the newspapers across the entire province dead set against it. "It's all Communist," people would say. "My doctor just told me that after the election I won't be able to go to him any more." It took a lot of faith to trust us. It was amazing that the '48 election was won. (Douglas, 2000:195)

Health care is a provincial responsibility, and each province has its own medical insurance plan. However, the federal government contributes a significant amount of money to the provinces for health care and enforces basic standards that each province must follow. Provincial plans must meet the following five requirements:

1. *Universality*—all Canadians should be covered on uniform terms and conditions;
2. *Comprehensiveness*—all necessary medical services should be guaranteed, without dollar limit, and should be available solely on the basis of medical need;
3. *Accessibility*—reasonable access should be guaranteed to all Canadians;
4. *Portability*—benefits should be transferable from province to province; and
5. *Public administration*—the system should be operated on a nonprofit basis by a public agency or commission. (Grant, 1993:401)

Although Canada's health care system continues to rank among the best in the world, it has its critics. The system has been subjected to drastic cuts in funding that have led to reduced resources and services. Canada still spends 10 percent of its gross domestic product on health care. While this figure is low in comparison with the rate in the United States (see Table 18.1), it is higher than in most other industrialized countries and amounts to a sizable expenditure. For example, Canada's 2003 health care expenditures were $121 billion (Canadian Institute for Health Information, 2004a). Of this amount, $85 billion came from government funding, while the remainder came from individuals and medical insurance companies for services not covered by medicare.

Related to the issue of increasing costs and declining resources is the problem of overutilization of health care services by the Canadian public. Utilization surveys have indicated that Canadians began to use health services more extensively following the introduction of medicare. According to Karen Grant:

> Canadians have an almost insatiable appetite for medical services, because they do not pay for health services when received, and because they have no knowledge of the actual costs of care, they inappropriately use the system. Frequenting emergency rooms for routine care is perhaps the most common illustration of this problem. (Grant, 1993:401)

While members of the public may not always make the most economical choices, many of the costs of our system are controlled by doctors, who prescribe

Table 18.1 LIFE SPAN AND HEALTH CARE EXPENDITURE

COUNTRIES IN ORDER OF LIFE EXPECTANCY	LIFE EXPECTANCY AT BIRTH, 2003, IN YEARS	TOTAL EXPENDITURE ON HEALTH, % OF GDP, 2003	EXPENDITURE ON HEALTH, PER CAPITA, 2003[1]
Japan	81.8	7.9	2,588
Australia	80.3	9.3	3,266
Canada	79.7	9.9	3,634
France	79.4	10.1	3,513
U.K.	78.5	7.7	2,700
Germany	78.4	11.1	3,625
U.S.	77.2	15.0	6,818

[1]Adjusted for cost of living differences. Converted to Canadian dollars at CAD$1.21 = US$1.00.

Source: OECD, 2005.

drugs, admit patients to hospitals, determine patients' lengths of stay in hospital, order tests and examinations, determine the course of treatment that will be used, and recommend follow-up visits. Since patients will do almost anything to ensure their health and since they do not pay directly, they have no incentive to question doctors' recommendations. On the other hand, doctors have a financial interest in providing more treatment. Reducing the economic control of doctors while ensuring that treatment decisions are made on medical, not economic, grounds is one of the major challenges of taxpayer-funded health care systems.

A final criticism of the Canadian health care system is its costly and often wasteful focus on hospitals and doctors. From the beginning, there has been an imbalance in our national health care system in its emphasis on acute care and its lack of recognition of and funding for community care (Crichton et al., 1997). Cheaper forms of noninstitutional health care, such as home-care services, are not subject to national standards, so these services vary widely from province to province and may not be available even when they are the most cost-effective type of care. Thus, people who need minimal care may be taking up expensive acute care hospital beds costing more than $1,000 per day because community alternatives are not available. The focus on physicians and hospitals can also be costly because it comes at the expense of preventive measures.

One of the consequences of cutbacks to Canada's health care system during the 1990s has been hospital overcrowding. These patients are waiting for treatment in a hospital emergency room.

Health Care in the United States

The United States is the only industrialized country without a health care system that provides universal coverage to all its citizens. In fact, the United States does not really have a health care system at all; what it has is a mixture of private and public health care providers with no centralized control. While Canada and Western European countries treat health care as a basic human right, the United States sees it as a market commodity. Most Americans receive health care coverage through private insurance programs that are sometimes paid for or subsidized by their employers. However, many Americans cannot afford to buy insurance and others may be denied coverage because of medical conditions. Some of those who do not have insurance may be covered by government-funded Medicare and Medicaid programs. Medicare covers Americans over 65 and some people with permanent disabilities. Medicaid provides coverage to a minority of those below the poverty line. Approximately 15 percent of the U.S. population— 44 million people—have no medical coverage. An even larger number are inadequately covered and the expenses incurred in treating a serious medical condition, such as cancer, a heart attack, or long-term disability, can lead to financial ruin. Medical expenses are the leading cause of personal bankruptcy in the United States (Himmelstein et al., 2005).

Despite the lack of universal coverage, per capita health care costs in the United States are much higher than in Canada. In 2003, for example, adjusted per capita costs in the United States of $6,818 were

Government home-care workers march at the Manitoba legislature in April 1997, protesting the provincial government's plans to contract out their services to private companies. Public opposition to this privatization convinced the government to scale back its plans to a small trial project. Later in the year, the government found that privatization would not save any money and returned all responsibility for home care to government workers.

roughly double the per capita cost of $3,634 in Canada for that year (see Table 18.1). Much of this difference is due to the efficiency of Canada's national nonprofit government insurance system compared with the fragmented U.S. system with its large number of different health care insurers and providers, each eager to maximize profits and each adding its overhead costs to the final bill. The salaries of health care workers, particularly doctors, are much lower in Canada than in the United States. A recent study compared the costs of heart bypass surgery in Canada and the U.S. (Eisenberg et al., 2005). The same operation cost twice as much in the United States ($20,673 in the U.S. and $10,373 in Canada), even though the success rate for the procedure was the same in both countries.

In an effort to address the inadequacies of the existing system, a national health care reform plan was proposed by the Clinton administration in 1993 (Weitz, 1996). However, a massive lobbying effort by the health care industry, fearful of losing some of its profits, ensured that this proposal was not successful. Even if it had been adopted, coverage provided by the plan would have fallen far short of Canadian standards.

In the debate over health care reform, many U.S. politicians and health care lobbyists were highly critical of Canada's "socialized" health care. They claimed that Clinton's plan would lead to the treatment delays and inferior care alleged to characterize the Canadian system. Are these critics correct? Do Canadians have an inferior system that forces people to travel to the United States to get proper treatment? The answer to these questions is no. Despite the higher costs of U.S. health care, Canadians are healthier than Americans and have better access to health care. Canada has a lower rate of infant mortality and longer life expectancy than the United States; these two indicators are often used as broad measures of the quality of health care. A wide variety of studies demonstrates the superiority of our health care system. Earlier in this chapter, you read about a study showing that poor Canadians had much higher cancer survival rates than poor Americans. Another study comparing the outcomes of ten different surgical procedures for elderly persons in Manitoba with those in the New England states reported that long-term survival rates were higher in Canada than in the United States for nine of the ten procedures studied (Roos et al., 1992). Finally, Manuel and Mao (2002) compared death rates in Canada and the U.S. for several diseases that can be treated effectively through public health and medical intervention. These diseases include asthma,

cervical cancer, hypertension and cerebrovascular disease, tuberculosis, and maternal mortality. While mortality from these diseases—termed "avoidable mortality" by the researchers—declined in both Canada and the U.S. between 1980 and 1996, the rate of decline was higher in Canada. For diseases like cervical cancer, tuberculosis, and asthma, where family doctors can play a significant preventive role, death rates were far higher in the U.S. than in Canada. This study provides additional evidence to support the view that health care outcomes are better in Canada despite the much higher rate of health care spending in the U.S. These differences are recognized by the public; Americans are much more likely than Canadians to say that their health care system needs to be completely rebuilt (Blendon et al., 2002).

APPROACHES TO HEALTH CARE

The Medical Model of Illness

The medical model has been the predominant way of thinking about illness in Western industrialized societies for many years. The medical model can best be described by considering its five basic assumptions: that illness is "(1) deviation from normal, (2) specific and universal, (3) caused by unique biological forces, (4) similar to the breakdown of a machine whose parts can be repaired, and (5) defined and treated through a neutral scientific process" (Weitz, 1996:129). One consequence of this model has been that our society has vested great power in the hands of doctors, who are seen to be the experts in diagnosing and treating illness. Doctors have gone to great lengths to protect this view and their role at the centre of the health care system. For example, they have actively resisted those with conflicting views, such as midwives, advocates of natural healing methods, and those more concerned with preventing disease than with treating it.

Alternative Approaches

Despite the many successes of modern medicine, such as heart pacemakers, arthroscopic surgery, and lung transplants, the medical model of illness is losing some of its dominance. While medical care is an important part of the health care system, Canadians are recognizing that their health needs cannot be met by medical services alone and that more medical care does not necessarily lead to better health (Grant, 1993). In 1986, the federal government explicitly adopted a health promotion policy, which emphasized prevention of disease, and promoted healthy lifestyles and an increase in informal and community based care (Crichton et al., 1997). The cost crisis in medicare has led the federal government to implement programs in support of this approach that emphasize environment and lifestyle in health promotion. For example, education about the hazards of smoking combined with more effective legislation against the use and advertising of tobacco products can improve public health and save the money now used to treat victims of smoking-related diseases, such as emphysema and lung cancer. Responsibility for health care is shifting away from the government and the health care system and toward the individual and the family.

Issues of cost and benefit to patients have also led to a move toward community-based care in most provinces. Programs, such as home care, community health clinics, and alternative care for the elderly have

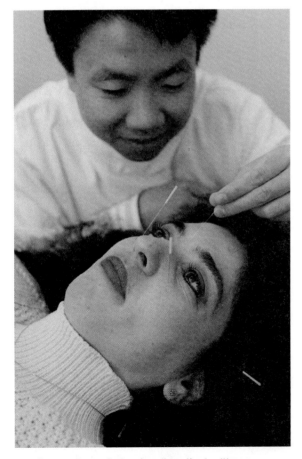

Canadians are increasingly using alternative health care methods, such as acupuncture.

saved costs by reducing the need for more expensive hospital care (Crichton et al., 1997). Many of these community programs also enhance people's quality of life by allowing them to remain in their communities.

The popularity of the holistic health care movement is a further indication of the move toward a new definition of health. Holism has a long history and reflects the orientations of many ancient therapeutic systems including that of Canadian Aboriginal peoples. Modern scientific medicine has been widely criticized for its focus on diseases and injuries rather than on the prevention of illness and the promotion of overall well-being. Advocates of holistic medicine say the medical model looks at problems in a mechanical fashion without considering their context, while the holistic approach emphasizes the interdependence of body, mind, and environment.

Holism is adaptable to more traditional medical practice and is being adopted by some medical doctors and nurses as well as by practitioners of alternative health care, including chiropractors, osteopaths, acupuncturists, and naturopathic doctors. Supporters of the holistic health movement encourage people to take greater individual responsibility for their health and health care, especially with regard to diseases and disabilities that are the products of lifestyle. This approach also urges health care providers to pay more attention to clients in diagnosing and treating illness and to develop a greater sensitivity to cultural differences in the ways in which people define and react to illness.

The holistic approach also emphasizes the role of social factors in illness. This view is now beginning to receive support in research done by traditional practitioners. For example, authors of an article published in the *Journal of the American Heart Association* found that middle-aged men with high levels of despair had a 20 percent greater chance of developing atherosclerosis—narrowing of the arteries—than more optimistic men with similar physiological risk factors. This was a difference in the risks for heart disease as great as that between a nonsmoker and a pack-a-day smoker (Cable News Network, 1997). Research on the health of older adults has also shown that nonmedical factors, such as isolation, the death of a family member or a friend, and the loss of status after retirement have a major influence on health. Thus, programs for the elderly must deal with these issues as well as with physical problems (Crichton et al., 1997).

Alternative approaches will continue to challenge traditional medicine's preoccupation with illness and disease and its focus on treatment by conventional biomedical means (Alix, 1995). The National Population Health Survey found that many Canadians were making use of alternative medicine. While about 20 percent of those surveyed said they had consulted an alternative practitioner within the previous year, very few of them said they had relied exclusively on an alternative practitioner within the previous year (Statistics Canada, 2005e). Thus it seems that alternative medicine is being used as a complement to traditional medicine rather than as a replacement. Of the groups surveyed, college- and university-educated young adults were most likely to use alternative health care. Also, women were more likely than men to use alternative health care.

While its use appears to be growing, some types of alternative medicine are being criticized. Psychologist Barry Beyerstein has recently repeated the most pointed criticism, saying that some of the claims of alternative medical practice have not been empirically verified. He blames the acceptance of such claims on the fact that most people know little about science:

> . . . even an elementary understanding of chemistry should raise strong doubts about the legitimacy of homeopathy; a passing familiarity with human anatomy would suggest that "subluxations" of the vertebrae cannot cause all the diseases that chiropractors believe they do; and a quite modest grasp of physiology should make it apparent that a coffee enema is unlikely to cure cancer. But when consumers have not the foggiest idea of how bacteria, viruses, carcinogens, oncogenes, and toxins wreak havoc on bodily tissues, then shark cartilage, healing crystals, and pulverized tiger penis seem no more magical than the latest breakthrough from the biochemistry laboratory. (1997:150)

Beyerstein does, however, see some benefits in alternative medicine. It has, he says, added a comforting human component to a medical world that has become increasingly impersonal and technological. Many alternative healers offer sound advice about prevention and a healthy lifestyle, and some alternative practices do have strong scientific backing. However, he fears that some alternatives can divert sick people from more effective treatment. Consumers of health care will need to be sufficiently well informed about the variety and nature of the options available to make sound treatment choices in the future. These options will certainly grow in number as alternative therapies become more widely accepted and as some become integrated with conventional medicine.

HEALTH CARE ISSUES IN THE FUTURE

Health and health care have changed dramatically in this century, and will continue to change in the years to come. Scientific developments, such as the mapping of human genes and the new reproductive technologies, have already begun to affect our lives. These changes will improve the lives of many but will also create some very difficult social and ethical problems that will continue to be debated for years to come. To give but one example, the ability to determine the sex of our children may lead to an imbalance between males and females. This would have a major impact on courtship and marriage as some in the larger sex group would have no chance to marry, while those in the smaller group would be very much in demand. Can you predict some of the possible consequences this might have on family structure and social relationships?

Unless there is a major shift in the economy, Canadians will likely see continued increases in funding to the health care system. However, the evolution from hospital-based care to prevention and community care will continue. This change can potentially be a positive one. For example, most of you have many years to live before you reach old age, but think ahead to that time. If you become unable to perform some household tasks, such as cooking and cleaning, would you prefer to sell your home and move into institutional care, or to receive daily home-care visits that would enable you to continue living independently? The political power of the aging baby boomers (see Chapter 12) and the cost of caring for growing numbers of elderly people will force governments to give more serious attention to home-care programs.

However, there is one worry—the shift to community-based health care will not improve matters unless governments put adequate resources into community care. The deinstitutionalization of the mentally ill in the 1970s and 1980s illustrates this danger. Ending the warehousing of mentally ill people in institutions was a good thing. However, rather than providing sufficient funding for community services for the deinstitutionalized patients, governments spent the savings on other things. As a result, many former patients became a burden on their communities and were themselves put at risk because the proper support was not available. If home care is not properly funded, the burden of care will be transferred from the state to relatives who already have busy lives (Armstrong et al., 1997). More than one in eight Canadians is already providing care to people with long-term health problems. Many of these caregivers have reported that providing this help has hurt their jobs, finances, or health (Statistics Canada, 1997b). While many of the caregivers surveyed were willing and able to provide support, government assistance will be necessary for those caregivers who lack the resources to do it alone and for individuals who do not have a network of family and friends to assist them.

As medical costs continue to take up an increasing share of government and personal revenues, we will continue to see a debate over the level of health care that Canadians will receive and the type of services that are funded by the government. There has been a great deal of pressure from some provinces to privatize many of the services that are now provided by the government. Proponents of privatization claim that it would provide services more cheaply and reduce waiting lists for diagnostic tests and treatment. Those who oppose privatization feel that it would be the first step in the move toward a two-tier health care system, in which those who can afford to pay would receive a different level of service than those who cannot pay for private treatment.

While the health of Canadians will likely continue to improve in the future, at the global level there is great cause for concern. You have already read about the impact of AIDS on people living in low-income nations and about the precarious health of many of the world's children. Medical authorities now also fear the return of infectious diseases, such as cholera, malaria, and tuberculosis, that were once controlled

BOX 18.5 YOU CAN MAKE A DIFFERENCE

Improving Your Own Health

You have read in this chapter that the Canadian government has adopted an approach to health that emphasizes the prevention of disease and the adoption of healthy lifestyles. Rather than just spending money to cure the sick, the preventive approach invests in keeping people healthy. This not only will improve each individual's quality of life, but also will help to reduce health care costs. There is a large body of research that demonstrates how bad lifestyle choices can increase the risk of illness and reduce life expectancy. Nearly everyone is aware of the health consequences of smoking, but fewer know about recent research on obesity, a problem that is increasing so quickly it may lead to a reduction in the life expectancy of Canadians for the first time in more than 100 years.

Statistics Canada recently reported the results of a study in which the height and weight of a large sample of Canadians were directly measured by researchers (Statistics Canada, 2005b). The study looked at changes in obesity over the twenty-five-year period between 1979 and 2004. In 2004, 8 percent of Canadian children were classed as obese compared with only 3 percent in 1979. In 2004, 23 percent of adults (5.5 million people) were considered obese compared with 14 percent in 1979. This is not simply a matter of aesthetics; obesity is related to many life-shortening diseases including diabetes and heart disease. The incidence of these ailments can be reduced through changes in diet and in levels of exercise.

There are many things you can do to improve your own health. By doing some of these things you will also have an impact on the people around you. For example, if you do not smoke, your children will be unlikely to do so and will not suffer the effects of secondhand smoke while they are growing up. You can learn about a wide variety of health issues, such as alcohol and drug use, school health, fitness, nutrition, tobacco reduction, and workplace health from the Health Canada Web site:

http://www.hc-sc.gc.ca/

For specific information on smoking, you can visit the National Clearinghouse on Tobacco and Health at:

http://www.ncth.ca

A good source of nutritional information is the award-winning Web site run by Jean Fremont of Simon Fraser University:

http://www.sfu.ca/~jfremont/

There are many things that you can do to improve your own health; these changes not only will improve your own life, but also will contribute to reduced health care costs.

by antibiotics and vaccines, and by public health programs like improved sanitation. The reasons for the renewed threat from these diseases include environmental change, the public health consequences of poverty in the developing world, and the fact that global travel has helped bacteria and viruses move easily from one place to another (Taylor, 1997). For example, health authorities are concerned that **avian influenza, which has been epidemic among domestic birds in several Asian countries, may spread to humans and become a pandemic that will kill millions of people.**

The resurgence of diseases, such as malaria and tuberculosis, and the rapid spread of HIV/AIDS, show that health is a social issue as much as it is a medical one. Social factors, such as economic inequality, geographic mobility, societal values, human settlement patterns, and the overuse of pesticides and antibiotics all contribute to the spread of disease. Improving the health of the world's population will require social change as well as improved ways of treating the sick. Box 18.5, "Improving Your Own Health," suggests ways in which you can help to ensure you stay healthy in the future.

CHAPTER REVIEW

■ What is health?

Health is often defined as a state of complete physical, mental, and social well-being.

■ What is the relationship between health care, medicine, and preventive medicine?

Medicine is an institutionalized system for the scientific diagnosis, treatment, and prevention of illness. Medicine forms a vital part of the broader concept of health care, which is any activity intended to improve health. Preventive medicine is medicine that emphasizes a healthy lifestyle that will prevent poor health before it occurs.

■ What are the functionalist, symbolic interactionist, conflict, feminist, and postmodern perspectives on health and health care?

Functionalists view society as a complex, stable system; therefore, the normal state of affairs is for people to be healthy and to contribute to their society. Illness is seen as dysfunctional for both the individual who is sick and for society. Sickness may result in an inability on the part of the sick person to fulfil his or her necessary social roles. Symbolic interactionists attempt to understand the specific meanings and causes that we attribute to particular events. In studying health, interactionists focus on the fact that the meaning that social actors give their illness or disease will affect their self-concept and their relationships with others. The interactionist approach is illustrated by society's response to AIDS. The conflict approach to health and illness considers the political and social forces that affect health and the health care system, and the inequities that

result from these forces. Among the issues of concern for conflict theorists are the ability of all citizens to obtain health care; the impact of race, class, and gender on health and health care; the relative power of doctors compared with that of other health care workers; the dominance of the medical model of health care; and the role of profit in the health care system. Feminist scholars have studied a variety of issues including the male-centred focus of medical research; discrimination against women working in the health care system; and the manner in which the process of medicalization has affected the lives of women. Finally, postmodern theorists have examined the nature of the power relationships in the medical system that have given power and privilege to doctors.

■ How do age, sex, and social class affect health?

Rates of illness and death are highest among the old and the very young. Mortality rates drop shortly after birth and begin to rise significantly during the middle years. After 65, rates of chronic illness and mortality increase rapidly. While in earlier times women had shorter life expectancies than men because of high mortality rates due to complications arising from pregnancy and childbirth, women now live longer than men. Females born in Canada in 2002 could expect to live about 82 years, compared with 77 years for males. However, women have higher rates of disease and disability. While men at every age have higher rates of fatal disease, women have higher rates of nonfatal chronic conditions. The poor have worse health and die earlier than the rich. Illness and mortality rates are far higher for low-income countries than for high-income countries. Within the industrialized world, citizens of those countries with the most equal distribution of income (Norway and Sweden) have the best health as measured by life expectancy.

■ What is a disability?

A disability is a physical or health condition that reduces a person's ability to perform tasks he or she would normally do at a given stage of life and that may result in stigmatization or discrimination against the person.

■ What is the difference between a universal health care system and one in which the user pays for health services?

Canadians have a universal health care system in which all Canadians receive medical services that are paid for through the tax system. If you are sick, you have the right to receive medical care regardless of your ability to pay. Prior to the early 1960s, Canadians had a "user pay" system, which meant that many people had to pay for health care directly out of their pockets. Individuals without health insurance who required expensive medical procedures, long-term care, or who developed a chronic illness often suffered severe financial losses. The United States has a user pay system.

KEY TERMS

acute illness 561
avian influenza 587
chronic illness 561
disability 573
epidemic 571
health 559
health care 559
medicalization 562
medicine 559
preventive medicine 559
senile dementia 569
sick role 561
universal health care system 579

NET LINKS

Read about a wide variety of diseases, including HIV/AIDS, at the Web site of the Centers for Disease Control and Prevention:
http://www.cdc.gov/hiv/pubs/facts.htm

Health Canada has established a comprehensive database on health and health care issues called the Canadian Health Network; see
http://www.canadian-health-network.ca/

For recent information about the problems of HIV/AIDS, see the Web site of the Joint United Nations Programme on HIV/AIDS:
http://www.unaids.org/

Learn about global health issues and some possible solutions at the Web site of the World Health Organization:
http://www.who.int/en/

The Web site of the Society for Women's Health Research discusses the sex differences between women and men that affect the prevention, diagnosis, and treatment of disease.
http://www.womenshealthresearch.org/

For the latest information about health care in Canada, see the Canadian Institute for Health Information site:
http://secure.cihi.ca/cihiweb/splash.html

This article by Gail Fawcett entitled "Canada's Untapped Workplace Resource: People with Disabilities" deals with the issue of barriers to employment faced by disabled persons; go to:
http://www.ccsd.ca/perception/214/ per_214a.htm

The Council of Canadians with Disabilities advocates for the right of Canadians with disabilities to be centrally involved in the decision-making processes that affect their lives, and for the removal of barriers to their full participation in matters affecting their lives. The organization has a Web site at:
http://www.ccdonline.ca/

QUESTIONS FOR CRITICAL THINKING

1. How do you think governments should balance their needs for financial savings and the public need for high-quality health care? Should everyone receive unlimited health services regardless of cost, or should priorities be set based on provincial and federal budgets?
2. What is the best way for society to deal with diseases, such as lung cancer and HIV/AIDS that sometimes can be controlled by changing people's behaviour?
3. What is the role of alternative therapies in health care? Have you or your friends or relatives made use of alternative treatments?
4. In your view, what constitutes a disability? How do you think that Canadians and Canadian government policies need to change so that disabled persons can participate more fully in society?

SUGGESTED READINGS

Terry Albert and Gregory Williams. *The Economic Burden of HIV/AIDS in Canada.* Ottawa: Canadian Policy Research Networks, 1998.

Gary L. Albrecht. *The Disability Business: Rehabilitation in America.* Newbury Park: Sage, 1992.

B. Singh Bolaria and Harley D. Dickinson. *Health, Illness, and Health Care in Canada.* Toronto: Nelson, 2002.

Pat Armstrong and Hugh Armstrong. *Wasting Away: The Undermining of the Canadian Health Care System.* Toronto: Oxford University Press, 1996.

Juanne Nancarrow Clarke. *Health, Illness and Medicine in Canada.* 3rd ed. Toronto: Oxford University Press, 2000.

Garrett, Laurie. *Betrayal of Trust: The Collapse of Global Public Health.* New York: Hyperion, 2000.

James B. Waldram, D. Ann Herring, and T. Kue Young. *Aboriginal Health in Canada: Historical, Cultural, and Epidemiological Perspectives.* Toronto: University of Toronto Press, 1995.

Rose Weitz. *The Sociology of Health, Illness, and Health Care: A Critical Approach.* Belmont: Wadsworth, 1996.

ONLINE STUDY AND RESEARCH TOOLS

THOMSONNOW™

Go to **http://hed.nelson.com** to link to ThomsonNOW for *Sociology in Our Times,* Fourth Canadian Edition, your online study tool. First take the **Pre-Test** for this chapter to get your personalized **Study Plan,** which will identify topics you need to review and direct you to the appropriate resources. Then take the **Post-Test** to determine what concepts you have mastered and what you still need work on.

INFOTRAC®

Infotrac College Edition is included free with every new copy of this text. Explore this online library for additional readings, review, and a handy resource for assignments. Visit **www.infotrac-college.com** to access this online database of full-text articles. Enter the key terms from this chapter to start your search.

Population and Urbanization

Moving to a new country and a new culture can be difficult, but the transition is easier for those who have support from others who share the same experiences. Consider the descriptions of the contrasting lives of two women—one described and one quoted—below. The following excerpt is from an interview with the child of a Sikh woman:

"My mother had it hard when I was growing up. We had a small rented farm in the Okanagan Valley, where there were then very few Sikhs. I made friends with Canadians at school. Since I knew English fluently I often talked with the neighbours, as did my father. Mother wasn't so lucky. She never learned English well enough to communicate easily, so never really had any good Canadian friends. There were so few other Sikh families around that she had little contact with them either. For her, the family was everything" (Buchignani, Indra, and Srivastiva, 1985:76).

In the next excerpt a woman who moved from Hong Kong to a Canadian city with a large middle-class Chinese community talks about her Chinese friends in Canada:

"I feel we have more in common with each other. We often get together and reminisce about our lives in Hong Kong. We also laugh about our ignorance of Canadian culture and the little faux pas that we get ourselves into. Other times, we exchange information about schools, dentists, and other practical knowledge. Or we marvel at the high price we now pay for little things, such as cooking wares and stockings. I have a feeling of solidarity when I talk to these people. They understand where I'm coming from" (Man, 1996:290).

The presence of others from one's former home plays a large role in determining where new immigrants settle in Canada. This has meant that cities, such as Toronto and Vancouver, have very high proportions of recent immigrants, while other communities have almost none. This is just one example of the impact that immigration has on our society. However, immigration is just one of the *demographic factors* that are changing Canada and the rest of the world. The phenomena of births, deaths, and the movement of people interact to affect us all in very complex ways.

In this chapter, we will explore the dynamics of population growth and urban change. In the process, we will periodically focus on immigration and its importance to Canadian society. Before reading on, test your knowledge about the causes and consequences of immigration by taking the quiz in Box 19.1.

DEMOGRAPHY: THE STUDY OF POPULATION

Although population growth has slowed in Canada, the world's population of 6.5 billion in 2005 is increasing by 74 million people per year. By 2050, there will be an estimated 9.2 billion people in the world (U.S. Census Bureau, 2005). Virtually all of this growth will come in the lower-income nations. The population in many of the high-income nations may actually decrease over this period. This means that people in different parts of the world face dramatically different futures. While many people in low-income countries face starvation because of rapidly increasing populations, Canadians have a

much different problem. Because of very low birth rates, our population is aging and there are concerns about how a relatively small number of young workers will support large numbers of elderly people.

Why does the population grow rapidly in some nations? What are the consequences of low birth rates in industrialized countries? What impact does immigration have on immigrants and on the country of destination? What effect is the AIDS crisis having on world population? How large will our cities be in twenty years? These questions are of interest to scholars who specialize in the study of **demography—the subfield of sociology that examines population size, composition, and distribution.** Many sociological studies use demographic analysis as a component in the research design because all aspects of social life are affected by the nature of population.

Increases or decreases in population can have a powerful impact on the social, economic, and political structures of societies. Demographers define *population* as a group of people who live in a specified geographic area. Changes in populations occur as a result of three processes: *fertility* (births), *mortality* (deaths), and *migration* (movement from one place to another).

Fertility

Fertility **is the actual level of childbearing for an individual or a population.** The level of fertility in a society is based on biological and social factors. The primary biological factor is the number of women of childbearing age (usually between ages 15 and 45). Other biological factors affecting fertility include the general health and level of nutrition of women of childbearing age. Social factors influencing the level

Canada has a long history of immigration. In this photo, the Netherlands' ambassador welcomes a shipload of Dutch immigrants to Canada in 1947.

of fertility include the roles available to women in a society and prevalent viewpoints regarding what constitutes the "ideal" family size.

Based on biological capability alone, most women could produce twenty or more children during their childbearing years. Women do not have this many children because people's biological capabilities are limited by social factors, such as practising voluntary abstinence and refraining from sexual intercourse until an older age, as well as by contraception, voluntary sterilization, abortion, and infanticide (Davis and Blake, 1956). Additional social factors affecting fertility include significant changes in the number of available partners for sex and/or marriage (as a result of war, for example), increases in the numbers of women of childbearing age in the workforce, and high rates of unemployment.

In some countries, governmental policies also affect the fertility rate. For example, China's two-decades-old policy of allowing only one child per family in order to limit population growth will result in that country's population starting to decline in 2042, according to United Nations population projections (Beech, 2001). Some of the consequences of this policy are discussed later in the chapter.

The birth rate in China has dropped dramatically and is now below replacement level. However, Weeks (2002) concludes that the decline in fertility is due more to socioeconomic development than it is to the one-child policy. Over time, China will be faced with a declining fertility rate combined with a rapidly aging population, many of whom will be dependent on younger people for their care and incomes.

The most basic measure of fertility is the *crude birth rate*—**the number of live births per 1,000 people in a population in a given year.** In 2003, the crude birth rate in Canada was almost 11 per 1,000, compared with a post–World War II high of 28 per 1,000 in 1956 and around 40 per 1,000 at the time of Confederation. This measure is referred to as a "crude" birth rate because it is based on the entire population and is not "refined" to incorporate significant variables affecting fertility, such as age, marital status, religion, or race/ethnicity.

In most parts of the world, women are having fewer children. Crude birth rates are very low in Germany (8 per 1,000), Italy and Japan (both 9 per 1,000); about the same as Canada in France and the United Kingdom (11 per 1,000); and just over 14 per 1,000 in the United States (CIA, 2005). However, families are much larger in low-income, agricultural regions of the world where children's labour is essential to a family's economic survival, and child mortality rates in

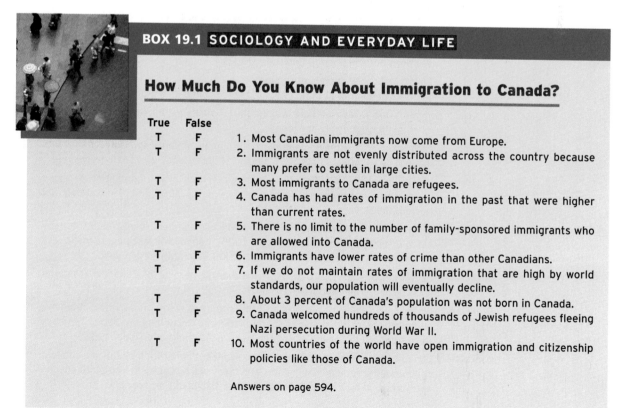

BOX 19.1 SOCIOLOGY AND EVERYDAY LIFE

How Much Do You Know About Immigration to Canada?

True	False	
T	F	1. Most Canadian immigrants now come from Europe.
T	F	2. Immigrants are not evenly distributed across the country because many prefer to settle in large cities.
T	F	3. Most immigrants to Canada are refugees.
T	F	4. Canada has had rates of immigration in the past that were higher than current rates.
T	F	5. There is no limit to the number of family-sponsored immigrants who are allowed into Canada.
T	F	6. Immigrants have lower rates of crime than other Canadians.
T	F	7. If we do not maintain rates of immigration that are high by world standards, our population will eventually decline.
T	F	8. About 3 percent of Canada's population was not born in Canada.
T	F	9. Canada welcomed hundreds of thousands of Jewish refugees fleeing Nazi persecution during World War II.
T	F	10. Most countries of the world have open immigration and citizenship policies like those of Canada.

Answers on page 594.

those regions are still very high. Countries with high crude birth rates (more than 40 per 1,000) include Nigeria, Somalia, and Afghanistan (CIA, 2005).

Mortality

The primary cause of world population growth in recent years has been a decline in ***mortality*—the incidence of death in a population.** The simplest measure of mortality is the ***crude death rate*—the number of deaths per 1,000 people in a population in a given year.** Mortality rates have declined dramatically in most countries in the last two hundred years. In 1867, the crude death rate in Canada was 21 deaths per 1,000—half what it had been one hundred years earlier. By 2005, the death rate had dropped to 7 per 1,000. This decline has been due to the fact that infectious diseases, such as malaria,

polio, cholera, tetanus, typhoid, and measles, have been virtually eliminated by improved nutrition, sanitation, and personal hygiene and by vaccination. As the burden of communicable diseases has steadily declined, the major causes of death in the developed world are now chronic and degenerative diseases, such as heart disease and cancer.

While mortality rates have dropped significantly in the low- and middle-income nations, they are still two or three times higher than those of high-income nations. In many countries, infectious diseases remain the leading cause of death; in some areas, mortality rates are increasing rapidly as a result of HIV/AIDS and a resurgence of tuberculosis (see Chapter 18, "Health, Health Care, and Disability").

In addition to the crude death rate, demographers often measure the ***infant mortality rate*— the number of deaths of infants under one year**

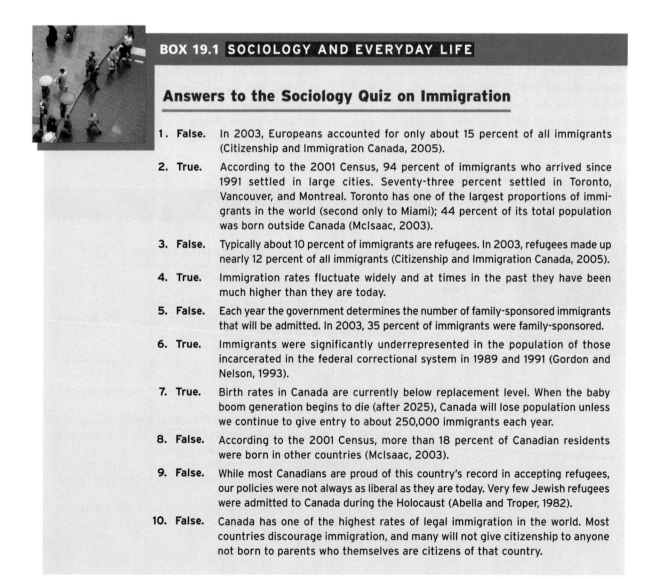

BOX 19.1 SOCIOLOGY AND EVERYDAY LIFE

Answers to the Sociology Quiz on Immigration

1. **False.** In 2003, Europeans accounted for only about 15 percent of all immigrants (Citizenship and Immigration Canada, 2005).

2. **True.** According to the 2001 Census, 94 percent of immigrants who arrived since 1991 settled in large cities. Seventy-three percent settled in Toronto, Vancouver, and Montreal. Toronto has one of the largest proportions of immigrants in the world (second only to Miami); 44 percent of its total population was born outside Canada (McIsaac, 2003).

3. **False.** Typically about 10 percent of immigrants are refugees. In 2003, refugees made up nearly 12 percent of all immigrants (Citizenship and Immigration Canada, 2005).

4. **True.** Immigration rates fluctuate widely and at times in the past they have been much higher than they are today.

5. **False.** Each year the government determines the number of family-sponsored immigrants that will be admitted. In 2003, 35 percent of immigrants were family-sponsored.

6. **True.** Immigrants were significantly underrepresented in the population of those incarcerated in the federal correctional system in 1989 and 1991 (Gordon and Nelson, 1993).

7. **True.** Birth rates in Canada are currently below replacement level. When the baby boom generation begins to die (after 2025), Canada will lose population unless we continue to give entry to about 250,000 immigrants each year.

8. **False.** According to the 2001 Census, more than 18 percent of Canadian residents were born in other countries (McIsaac, 2003).

9. **False.** While most Canadians are proud of this country's record in accepting refugees, our policies were not always as liberal as they are today. Very few Jewish refugees were admitted to Canada during the Holocaust (Abella and Troper, 1982).

10. **False.** Canada has one of the highest rates of legal immigration in the world. Most countries discourage immigration, and many will not give citizenship to anyone not born to parents who themselves are citizens of that country.

Women tend to have more children in agricultural regions of the world, such as Kenya, where children's labour is essential to the family's economic survival and child mortality rates are very high.

of age per 1,000 live births in a given year. The infant mortality rate is an important reflection of a society's level of preventive (prenatal) medical care, maternal nutrition, childbirth procedures, and neonatal care for infants, and it is often used by sociologists as a measure of the level of a country's social development. The impact of modernization on infant mortality rates has been dramatic. In 1921, the infant mortality rate in Canada was 102 deaths per 1,000 live births; by 2002 it had declined to 5.4 per 1,000 live births (Statistics Canada, 2004c). This can be compared with rates of 7 per 1,000 in the United States, 5 in the United Kingdom, and 3 in Japan (CIA, 2005).

Countries with high birth rates also have high infant mortality rates. For example, the infant mortality rates for Afghanistan, Pakistan, and Nigeria were (respectively) 163, 72, and 99 per 1,000 live births in 2005 (CIA, 2005).

Infant mortality rates are high among Canada's Aboriginal population, who suffer severe social disadvantages compared with the rest of the population and who often lack access to health care services (see Chapter 18, "Health, Health Care, and Disability"). In 1996, the infant mortality rate for Aboriginal people was 11.6, compared with 6.1 for the total population of Canada (Indian and Northern Affairs Canada, 2000).

Our declining mortality rates have led to substantial increases in *life expectancy,* which is an estimate of the average lifetime in years of people born in a specific year. For persons born in Canada in 2002, for example, life expectancy at birth was about eighty years (Statistics Canada, 2004c). This life expectancy is among the highest in the world. Within Canada, life expectancy is lower for Aboriginal people. On average, Aboriginals live about six fewer years than the non-Aboriginal population, though this difference has been reduced from ten years in 1981 (Cooke et al., 2004). Life expectancy also varies by sex; for example, females born in Canada in 2002 could expect to live about eighty-two years as compared with seventy-seven years for males (Statistics Canada, 2004c).

Migration

Migration **is the movement of people from one geographic area to another for the purpose of changing residency.** Migration involves two types of movement: immigration and emigration. *Immigration* **is the movement of people into a geographic area to take up residency,** while *emigration* **is the movement of people out of a geographic area to take up residency elsewhere.**

Migration affects the size and distribution of population in a given area. In Canada, people are not evenly distributed throughout the country; most Canadians live in densely populated areas while much of the country is sparsely populated. *Density* is the number of people living in a specific geographic area. Density may be measured by the number of people who live per room, per block, or per square kilometre.

Migration may be either international (movement between two nations) or internal (movement within national boundaries).

Internal Migration
Internal migration has occurred throughout Canada's history and has significantly changed the distribution of our population over time. In the late nineteenth and early twentieth centuries, a major population shift occurred as Canada was transformed from a rural to an urban nation. At the time of Confederation, about 80 percent of the population resided in rural areas; today, almost 80 percent are urban. While Canada is now an urban country, the degree of urbanization among the provinces varies, ranging from 85 percent of the population of Ontario to only 45 percent of Prince Edward Island residents (Transport Canada, 2002).

Along with movement from rural to urban areas, we have also seen extensive migration from one province to another. The booming economies of Alberta and Ontario have drawn migrants from

Political unrest, violence, and war are "push" factors that encourage people to leave their country of origin. Shown here are a shipload of Liberian refugees awaiting political asylum in Ghana, and Bosnian refugees fleeing Serb-held parts of Sarajevo. Civil wars cause massive population movement.

BOX 19.2 SOCIOLOGY IN GLOBAL PERSPECTIVE

Immigration Policies of Canada and Other Countries

Canadian immigration laws and policies are among the most open in the world. Each year Canada accepts just under 1 percent of our population as immigrants and all have the right to obtain citizenship. Israel takes in up to 2 percent of its population annually, while the other two leading destination countries for immigrants, Australia and the United States, each accept less than one-half of a percent of their populations. Most of the world's countries accept few or no immigrants, though many do accept refugees, at least on a temporary basis. Receiving countries react to immigration in three different ways.

The first is *differential exclusion*, according to which immigrants are allowed in certain areas of society, chiefly the labour market, but denied access to other areas, such as health care, education, and social benefits. Immigrants in these countries are primarily refugees and guest workers who are admitted for specified periods to do work that members of the resident population cannot or will not perform. Germany, for example, imports workers from many countries, especially Turkey. Until 2000, citizenship was based on ethnicity. German ancestry entitled an immigrant to automatic citizenship. However, naturalization of non-Germans was extremely rare. The result of this was the marginalization of people who were essentially permanent residents but who could not become citizens. Before the change in law, almost none of the eight million residents of Germany who were born elsewhere or who were children of guest workers were allowed to become citizens. Japan, which has strongly emphasized the need for ethnic purity, has similar policies, but has treated its immigrant workers much more harshly than has Germany. Ethnic Koreans, many of whom are third- and fourth-generation Japanese, have suffered severe discrimination.

The second immigration model is *assimilationist*, whereby immigrants are incorporated into the host society through a one-sided process of change. Immigrants are expected to become the same as the majority. Canada used to follow this policy, but today France probably follows this model the most closely. Immigrants to France can obtain citizenship after five years of residence, and children born in France automatically become citizens at 18 years of age unless they give up this right. All citizens are expected to accept the French language and culture. This is sometimes referred to as the "melting-pot approach."

The third model is *pluralism,* according to which immigrants are encouraged to form ethnic communities that can have equal rights while retaining their diversity in language, culture, and other matters. Citizenship is readily given to legal immigrants, and even to children of visitors and illegal immigrants. Canada has a multicultural policy that actively supports the retention of ethnic languages and cultures.

Source: Castles, 1995.

provinces with fewer job opportunities. For decades, people from the Atlantic provinces have moved west in search of work. The impact of this migration can be seen in Fort McMurray, Alberta, which has seen very rapid growth because of the development of the oil sands. This city is effectively Newfoundland's fifth largest community. One in every three of Fort McMurray's 60,000 residents is a Newfoundlander (Sytnick, 1998; Regional Municipality of Wood Buffalo, 2005). Other reasons for internal migration are climate and lower living costs, which tend to be particularly important for retired persons.

International Migration   People migrate either voluntarily or involuntarily. *Pull* factors, such as a democratic government, religious freedom, employment opportunities, or a more temperate climate, may draw voluntary immigrants into a country. *Push* factors, such as political unrest, violence, war, famine, plagues, and natural disasters, may encourage people to leave one area and relocate elsewhere. Involuntary, or forced, migration usually occurs as a result of political oppression, such as when Jews fled Nazi Germany in the 1930s or when Afghans fled the

Taliban regime in the late 1990s. Slavery is the most striking example of involuntary migration; the ten to twenty million Africans transported forcibly to the Western Hemisphere prior to 1800 did not come by choice.

Most of Canada's 32 million people are immigrants or the descendants of immigrants. Thus, immigration has been a critical factor in the country's growth and development. Our immigration policy is one of the most open in the world, and we have much higher rates of legal immigration than almost any other country. Immigrants make up more than 18 percent of Canada's population (Statistics Canada, 2003b). This compares with 10 percent for the United States and 4 percent for Britain. Australia, with 21 percent of its population born elsewhere, is one of the few countries in which the percentage is higher than in Canada. Japan (1.2 percent) and Spain (1.5 percent) have two of the lowest percentages of foreign-born residents (Coppel et al., 2001). For a discussion of differences in immigration policies, see Box 19.2.

Figure 19.1 shows that Canadian immigration levels throughout the last century have fluctuated a great deal. Economic conditions, wars, pressures

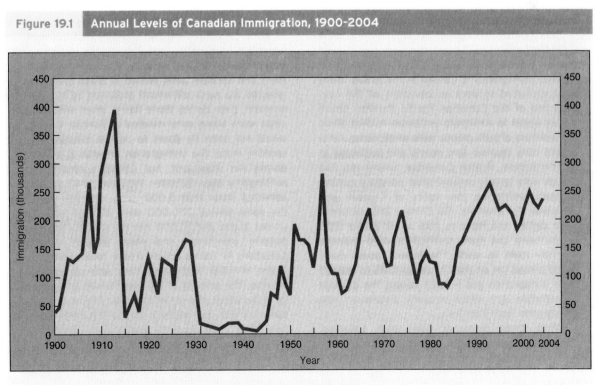

Figure 19.1   Annual Levels of Canadian Immigration, 1900–2004

Sources: Dumas, 1990; Beaujot, Basavarajappa, and Verrm, 1988; Citizenship and Immigration Canada, 2005.

from refugees, and changes in government policies have all contributed to these shifts. Following the end of an economic depression in 1896, the government began to promote immigration to encourage settlement of the West. In the years before World War I, as many as 400,000 people per year immigrated to Canada, a number which has never been exceeded. Most of these immigrants were European and many of them settled the farms, towns, and cities of the Prairie provinces. The beginning of World War I caused a precipitous decline in immigration. While numbers rose again after the war, the Great Depression and World War II meant very low levels of immigration for almost twenty years. During this period, more people left Canada than arrived here. Immediately after World War II, immigration rates

again climbed. Canada built a large industrial capacity during the war, and the postwar economy was very strong. Skilled foreign workers were needed to help with the expansion. Political instability and economic difficulty in Europe meant that many people were willing to leave to find a better life elsewhere. The postwar immigration peak in 1956–1957 was the result both of Canada's acceptance of great numbers of refugees who were escaping the unsuccessful Hungarian Revolution and of its providing a home for British subjects leaving Egypt following the Suez crisis.

As discussed in Chapter 10 ("Race and Ethnicity"), Canada's immigration regulations permitted discrimination on the basis of racial and ethnic origin until the early 1960s (see Box 19.3). At

BOX 19.3 SOCIOLOGY AND THE LAW

Immigration and the Law in Canada

Canadians can be proud of having welcomed immigrants from around the globe. However, the record has not always been fair; at times in the past our immigration policy has been exclusionary and racist.

Shortly after the turn of the last century, some Canadians began to express concerns about immigration from East Asia and South Asia. The first Chinese immigrated to Canada in the 1850s; many were recruited to work as labourers on the construction of the Canadian Pacific Railway. South Asians began to immigrate to Canada in 1903. While the numbers of both groups were small, these immigrants were treated very poorly and subjected to discrimination. British Columbia, where the two groups were largely concentrated, passed a number of laws restricting the rights of Chinese and Japanese. For example, the Chinese and Japanese were denied the right to vote in 1872 and 1895 respectively, and many restrictions were imposed on their right to work. The federal government levied a head tax on the Chinese in 1885 to restrict their immigration and in 1923 passed the *Chinese Immigration Act*, which virtually disallowed new immigration from East Asia.

While these measures now seem appalling, Canada's behaviour was no worse than that of most other Western countries, which also had very

restrictive immigration policies. Many leading scientists of the day backed the view that Anglo-Saxons were biologically superior, and the admission of other races was seen as a danger to white democracies.

Many Canadians are also unaware that for many years our immigration policy restricted the admission of Jews. This was because of anti-Jewish sentiment and because Jews settled in urban areas and rejected the rural settlement preferred by the government. Even during World War II, when millions of Jews were being exterminated in Europe, Canada would not open its doors to Jewish refugees. No country made the immigration of Jews a priority during the Holocaust, but Canada's record was particularly poor. Between 1933 and 1945 Canada admitted fewer than 5,000 Jews, whereas during the same period 200,000 were allowed into the United States and 70,000 into the United Kingdom. Despite significant and vocal support among Canadians for taking action to save Jewish refugees, Prime Minister Mackenzie King and his cabinet refused. The attitude of the government is summed up in the words of a senior Canadian official who was speaking with journalists in early 1945. When asked how many Jews would be admitted to Canada following the war, his response was "None is too many" (Abella and Troper, 1982:xxi).

Sources: Based on Abella and Troper, 1982; Ghosh and Kanungo, 1992.

various times, Chinese, Japanese, and South Asians were prohibited from immigrating to Canada, and the 1953 *Immigration Act* allowed the government to bar entry on the grounds of race, ethnicity, or even "peculiar customs, habits, modes of life or methods of holding property" (Beaujot, 1991:109). Preference was given to whites, particularly those of British origin. These discriminatory restrictions were lifted in 1962, and the face of immigration changed dramatically. Compare the source countries of immigrants arriving in 1957 with those of immigrants who came in 2003, as shown in Table 19.1. Whereas, in 1957, the vast majority of immigrants were whites from northern Europe, in 2001 immigrants to Canada came from all over the world and represented many different ethnic groups and cultures. While this diversity would not have been possible under the old rules, the factors "pushing" immigrants have also changed. For the past thirty years, most Western European countries have had very strong economies, low unemployment rates, and stable governments. Living under these conditions, people have had little reason to emigrate. At the same time, conditions in many other parts of the world are less favourable, so emigration to Canada is seen positively.

For most of the past decade, the number of immigrants coming to Canada has remained relatively stable at between 200,000 and 250,000 persons. This is the result of government policy aimed at achieving a stable population in the future in the face of declining birth rates and an aging population.

Population Composition

Changes in fertility, mortality, and migration affect the *population composition—the biological and social characteristics of a population,* including age, sex, ethnic origin, marital status, education, occupation, income, and size of household.

One measure of population composition is the *sex ratio—the number of males for every hundred females in a given population.* A sex ratio of 100 indicates an equal number of males and females. If the number is greater than 100, there are more males than females; if it is less than 100, there are more females than males. In Canada, the sex ratio in 2001 was 96, which means there were about 96 males per 100 females. Although approximately 105 males are born for every 100 females, higher male mortality rates mean there are more females than males in the population. This difference is particularly great among people over 65 years of age, with 75 senior men to every 100 senior women (Statistics Canada, 2002h).

For demographers, sex and age statistics are significant population characteristics. They are key predictors of fertility and mortality rates, and the age distribution of a population has a direct bearing on the demand for schooling, health, employment, housing, and pensions. The distribution of a population can be depicted in a *population pyramid—a graphic representation of the distribution of a population by sex and age.* Population pyramids are a series of bar graphs divided into five-year age cohorts; the left side of the pyramid shows the

Table 19.1   CANADIAN IMMIGRANTS' COUNTRIES OF ORIGIN, 1957 AND 2003

	1957			2003	
Rank	**Country**	**% of Total Immigration**	**Rank**	**Country**	**% of Total Immigration**
1.	U.K.	38.6	1.	China	16.3
2.	Hungary	11.2	2.	India	11.1
3.	Germany	10.0	3.	Pakistan	5.6
4.	Italy	9.8	4.	Philippines	5.4
5.	Netherlands	4.2	5.	South Korea	3.2
6.	U.S.	3.9	6.	U.S.	2.7
7.	Denmark	2.7	7.	Iran	2.6
8.	France	2.0	8.	Romania	2.5
9.	Austria	2.0	9.	U.K.	2.4
10.	Greece	1.9	10.	Sri Lanka	2.0

Sources: Zgodzinski; 1996; Statistics Canada, 1997e; Citizenship and Immigration Canada, 2005.

number or percentage of males in each age bracket; the right side provides the same information for females.

The age/sex distribution in Canada and other developed nations no longer has the appearance of a pyramid, but rather is more rectangular (see France in Figure 19.2) or diamond-shaped (see Canada in Figure 19.2). This shows a population that has a low birth rate and an increasing number of older people. You can see in Figure 19.2 that a developing nation such as Mexico has a population distribution that fits the classic population pyramid. Mexico has high fertility and mortality rates, which means a large number of children and few older people. The population pyramid for Russia has some unusual features that have been caused by catastrophic events, such as the two World Wars, the Civil War of 1917–1922, famine in the 1920s and 1930s, and the recent dramatic decline in birth rates. For example, the large number of males killed during World War II gave

Figure 19.2 Population Pyramids for Russia, Mexico, Canada, and France, 2006

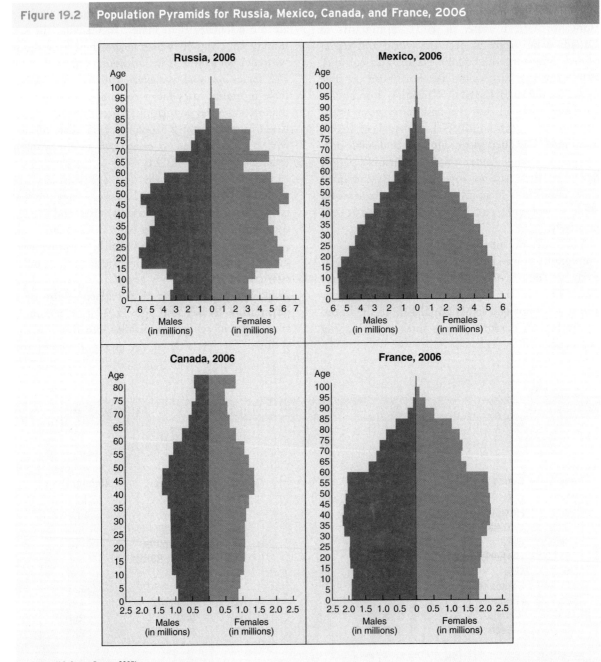

Source: U.S. Census Bureau, 2005b.

Russia the lowest male-to-female ratio in the world. The irregularities in Russia's population pyramid will affect patterns of population growth and aging for decades to come (Institut National d'Etudes Demographiques, 1995).

As societies modernize, there is a time lag between the decrease in the death rate and a corresponding decrease in the birth rate. During this time lag, populations often grow very rapidly. The rate of population growth in a society is determined by a combination of fertility, mortality, and migration. The age and sex composition of the population affects each of these processes. If a large number of young people are in their prime reproductive years, the crude birth rate will rise because a large number of children will be produced relative to the total population. This is why the population of China will continue to grow even though the birth rate is below replacement level.

The Baby Boom and the Baby Bust

One very simple fact will help you understand many things about Canadian society: every year you get one year older, and, more importantly, so does everyone else. Until recently, the age structure of the population was something of a hidden factor. While age differences among individuals were obvious, researchers and planners often failed to recognize the impact of changes in the *age structure* of the population.

One of the most significant demographic changes in Canadian history was the *baby boom*—the dramatic increase in births that occurred between 1946 and 1966. The boom was caused by young couples who married and began having large families in the years immediately following the war. The high birth rates of the baby boom were followed by the *baby bust,* which saw birth rates fall to the very low levels where they remain today. While many demographic changes take place over a long period of time, the baby boom was a rapid reversal of a long-term downward trend in birth rates. This increase is shown in Figure 19.3. You can see that the long-term decline in birth rates was interrupted for twenty years following the end of World War II. By the end of the boom in 1966, one-third of all the people in Canada had been born in the preceding fifteen years.

The baby boom and the baby bust have had a dramatic impact on the age structure, which can be seen

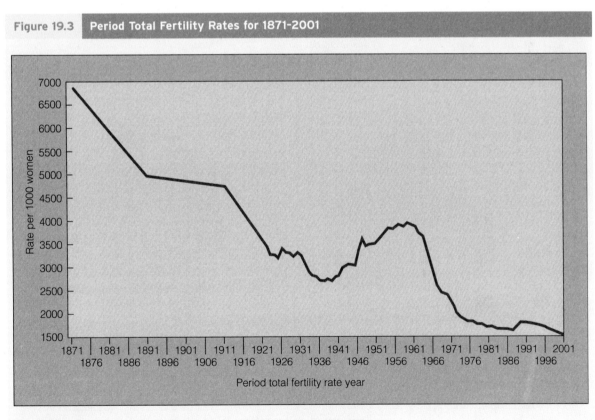

Figure 19.3 **Period Total Fertility Rates for 1871-2001**

Sources: Romaniuc, 1994:121–22; Beaujot and McQuillan, 1982:54; Dumas, 1990:18; Statistics Canada, 2003o, 2005a.

in the series of population pyramids in Figure 19.4. The top pyramid shows the population of Canada toward the end of the baby boom in 1961. There are large numbers of young people because of the boom. The relatively small number of people aged 15 to 24 is the result of low birth rates during the Depression and World War II. In the 1981 pyramid, we can see the consequences of the baby boom and the drop in fertility rates that followed. This drop is called the "baby bust." The pyramid for 2006 shows an increased

Figure 19.4   Population by Age and Sex, Canada, 1961 and 1981 (Census), 2006 and 2031

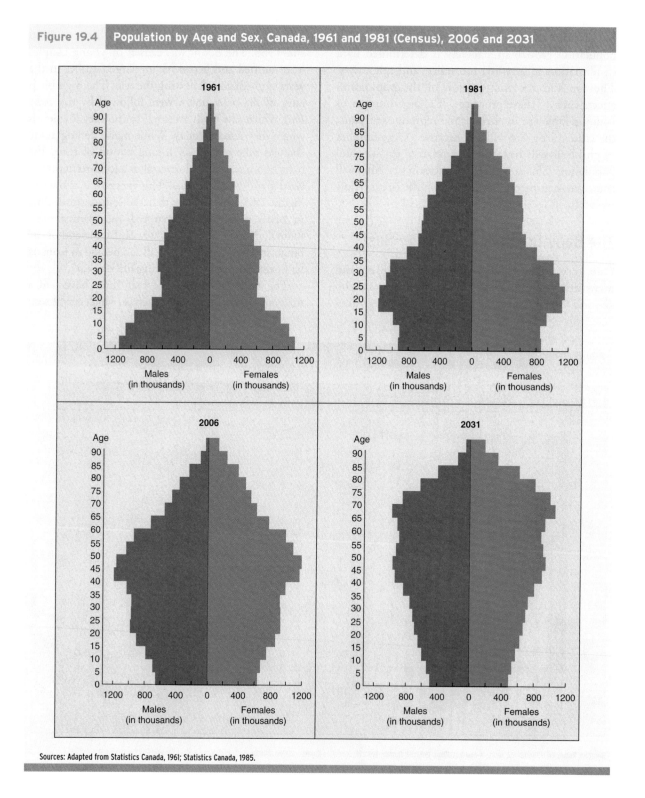

Sources: Adapted from Statistics Canada, 1961; Statistics Canada, 1985.

number of older people as the oldest baby boomers approach 60. Finally, in the 2031 pyramid, mortality has begun to affect the baby boomers, and the survivors are now 65 to 85 years of age.

The baby boom has had a profound impact on virtually every aspect of our society. To understand the impact of the baby boom, think of it as a twenty-year bulge in the population pyramid. Each year, this bulge moves one year up the pyramid as the baby boom cohort ages. You can easily track this bulge in the population pyramids in Figure 19.4. Some demographers have used the analogy of a pig that has been swallowed by a python to describe the way in which the baby boom generation has moved up the population pyramid. It is interesting to compare Canada's demographic structure with those of other countries. For example, you can see from Figure 19.2 that Mexico, which is a developing society, has a constant baby boom—it is continually adding young people to its population as its population rapidly expands. On the other hand, France did not have a baby boom after World War II, so its age structure is quite different from Canada's. The age structure of many European countries is much like that of France. Besides Canada, the only other countries that had a sustained baby boom were Australia, the United Kingdom, and the United States.

The baby boom has transformed society in many different ways. Beginning in the late 1940s, many businesses saw their markets expand. Manufacturers of baby food, diapers, and children's toys flourished, and obstetricians were in great demand. As the baby boom cohort aged, school construction increased dramatically and teaching jobs were plentiful. By the mid-1960s, university enrolments began to climb and many new universities opened to meet the demand. You will recall from Chapter 7 ("Crime and Deviance") that crime rates also began to increase at this time. This is because the baby boomers had entered the 15 to 24 age group, during which criminal behaviour is most common. In the mid-1970s house prices rose quickly in most Canadian cities, as the baby boomers began to settle down and raise families.

Because of the baby bust, many of these changes reversed themselves in the 1980s. Schools that had been built to house the soaring numbers of children in the 1960s were forced to close twenty years later, and school boards spent decades dealing with an oversupply of teachers. By the 1990s, both university enrolments and crime rates had begun to decline. In most parts of Canada, house prices dropped or remained stable for much of the 1990s. Radio stations that had catered to the baby boomers when they were young began to play "golden oldies" to keep this large audience. Corporations that had targeted youthful consumers have begun to reorient their products and their advertising to appeal to an older market. Clothing manufacturers are now offering their products in "relaxed fit" sizes as middle-aged spread begins to hit the baby boomers, and fast food chains are developing products to appeal to older people. The sight of a television commercial showing Ronald McDonald on a golf course is a sure sign of the consumer power of the baby boom generation. In fact, golf and other modestly active forms of recreation, such as travel, gardening, and birdwatching, are replacing more active sports like tennis and downhill skiing in popularity as the baby boomers begin to slow down in middle age.

What of the future? The baby boom cohort is now well into middle age, and the first of its members will reach 65 in the year 2011. As you have read in Chapter 12 ("Aging"), our society will soon begin to have a much higher proportion of older persons than it does today. In 1971, about 8 percent of Canadians were 65 and over; by 2011, the percentage will be 16 percent; and by 2036, it will likely stabilize at almost 25 percent. There will be about 9 million Canadians over 65, compared with the current 3.7 million.

The aging of our population will lead to changes in a number of areas. Since the elderly are the biggest users of health care, governments are trying to get health costs under control before the baby boomers start reaching the age at which they will begin to have serious health concerns. Those responsible for the Canada Pension Plan have increased premiums and decreased some benefits so the plan can stay in operation.

One final trend worth noting is the *baby boom echo*—the children of the baby boomers. You can see this echo in Figure 19.4, which shows a relatively large cohort following about twenty years behind the baby boom. Even though the baby boomers had far fewer children than their parents (about 1.66 children per family, compared with more than 3 children for their parents), there were so many of them that their children are having a significant impact. The leading edge of the echo generation were about 25 years old in 2006, so they will have an impact on such things as university enrolments, the job market, and the housing market over the next two decades.

The Baby Boom and Immigration Policy

One consequence of our current low birth rate is possible depopulation. Fertility of 2.1 children per woman is needed to ensure the replacement of a population. Two children will replace the parents, and the additional 0.1 compensates for deaths that occur before potential parents reach reproductive age. This level of fertility will eventually lead to a stable population with zero population growth except for that caused by migration. In Canada, our fertility is near its all-time low of 1.5 children per woman, which will not provide replacement of our population (Statistics Canada, 2005a). If this level of fertility remains constant for the next several decades, Canada will begin losing population when the baby boomers begin to die. You can see this in the 2031 population pyramid in Figure 19.4. At present, besides losing population through death, we also lose about 60,000 each year to emigration.

As Figure 19.1 shows, since the 1990s Canada has admitted between 200,000 and 250,000 immigrants annually. This number was chosen because demographers have calculated that to stabilize the population we need about 250,000 immigrants a year. Thus, the baby bust has had an important impact on our immigration policies.

POPULATION GROWTH IN A GLOBAL CONTEXT

While Canada does not face any population pressures, in many other countries the population is growing very rapidly. What are the consequences of global population growth? Scholars do not agree on the answer to this question. Some biologists have warned that the earth is a finite ecosystem that cannot support the 9.2 billion people expected on the planet by 2050; however, some economists have predicted that free-market capitalism is capable of developing innovative ways to solve such problems, and religious opponents of birth control assure us that God will provide. This debate is not a new one; for several centuries, strong opinions have been voiced about the effects of population growth on human welfare.

The Malthusian Perspective

English clergyman and economist Thomas Robert Malthus (1766–1834) was one of the first scholars to systematically study the effects of population. According to Malthus, the population, if left unchecked, would exceed the available food supply. He argued that the population would increase in a geometric (exponential) progression (2, 4, 8, 16 . . .),

while the food supply would increase only by an arithmetic progression (1, 2, 3, 4 . . .). In other words, a *doubling effect* occurs: two parents can have four children, sixteen grandchildren, and so on, but food production increases by only one acre at a time. Thus, population growth inevitably surpasses the food supply, and the lack of food ultimately ends population growth and perhaps eliminates the existing population (Weeks, 2002). Even in a best-case scenario, overpopulation results in poverty.

However, Malthus suggested that this disaster might be averted by either positive or preventive checks on population. *Positive checks* are mortality risks, such as famine, disease, and war; *preventive checks* are limits to fertility. For Malthus, the only acceptable preventive check was *moral restraint*; people should practise sexual abstinence before marriage and postpone marriage as long as possible in order to have only a few children.

The Marxist Perspective

According to Karl Marx and Friedrich Engels, the food supply is not threatened by over population. Technologically, it is possible to produce the food and other goods needed to meet the demands of a growing population. Writing from a conflict perspective, Marx and Engels viewed poverty as a consequence of the exploitation of workers by the owners of the means of production.

From this perspective, overpopulation occurs because capitalists want to have a surplus of workers (an industrial reserve army) so as to suppress wages and force workers concerned about losing their livelihoods to be more productive. Marx believed that overpopulation would contribute to the eventual destruction of capitalism. Unemployment would make the workers dissatisfied, resulting in a class consciousness based on their shared oppression and in the eventual overthrow of the system. In a socialist regime, enough food and other resources would be created to accommodate population growth.

Marx and Engels made a significant contribution to the study of demography by suggesting that poverty, not overpopulation, is the most important issue with regard to food supply in a capitalist economy. Although Marx and Engels offer an interesting counterpoint to Malthus, some scholars argue that the Marxist perspective is self-limiting because it attributes the population problem solely to capitalism. In actuality, nations with socialist economies have demographic trends similar to those in capitalist societies.

The Neo-Malthusian Perspective

More recently, *neo-Malthusians* (or "new Malthusians") have re-emphasized the dangers of overpopulation. To neo-Malthusians, the earth is "a dying planet" with too many people, too little food, and environmental degradation. From the time of Christ to 1840, the doubling time of the population was 1,250 years, while at current growth rates the earth's population will double every 55 years (Weeks, 2002). Overpopulation and rapid population growth result in global environmental problems ranging from global warming and rainforest destruction to famine and vulnerability to epidemics such as AIDS (Ehrlich, Ehrlich, and Daily, 1995). Environmental problems will worsen as countries, such as India and China, with their large populations, modernize and begin to use resources at a rate closer to that of industrialized countries.

Throughout history, population growth and epidemic diseases have interacted to shape human destiny. Figure 19.5 shows the dramatic impact of AIDS on the population structure of Botswana. People are extremely vulnerable to disease if they already are debilitated from inadequate nutrition, unclean water supplies, poor medical care, and lack of sanitation.

Are the neo-Malthusians correct? Will population increases leave many populations vulnerable to mass death through starvation and disease? Some possible outcomes are found in the work of Thomas Homer-Dixon, a University of Toronto political scientist

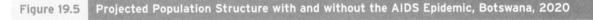

Figure 19.5 Projected Population Structure with and without the AIDS Epidemic, Botswana, 2020

The population pyramid in countries with high rates of HIV/AIDS, such as Botswana, has an unusual "chimney" shape. Few older people survive, which means that many children will be orphaned, there will be few teachers to educate young people, and there will be a very small adult labour force to produce wealth for the country. Average life expectancy will be less than thirty years.

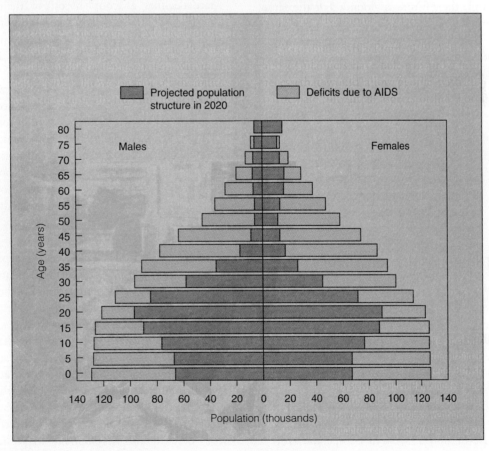

Source: U.S. Census Bureau, *World Population Profile 2000.*

who is often placed in the neo-Malthusian camp. Homer-Dixon feels that increases in population and resource consumption will lead to significant environmental changes, including scarcities of soil and water, and climatic instability (1993). The strains caused by these scarcities may lead to unrest, including war, revolution, ethnic violence, and riots. The gloominess of this scenario is tempered by the fact that Homer-Dixon does not feel that population disaster is inevitable. Human social and technical ingenuity can overcome or at least delay the consequences of population increase. For example, despite decades of predictions that China will be unable to support its population, the average caloric intake in China has been rising as the country has massively increased its production of food. Unfortunately, there is no guarantee that solutions to the predicted problems will be found. Ingenuity is itself a function of a country's social institutions, and in many countries these institutions are too fragmented or too lacking in human and physical resources to solve their problems. In addition, political turmoil has been an obstacle; unrest has kept many countries in sub-Saharan Africa from progressing and, without major reform, their future is gloomy. For the same reasons, Homer-Dixon is more pessimistic about the future of India than of China because, he feels, India's social institutions are endangered by religious and caste cleavages. Also, India's population, which was nearly 1.1 billion in 2005, is growing much more rapidly than China's, so any economic gains may be lost to increased population. On the other hand, India has been developing a globally competitive workforce and has greatly improved its standard of living. Ultimately, the future of humanity will depend on both national and international action to solve the problems created by population growth and environmental damage.

Demographic Transition Theory

Some scholars who disagree with the neo-Malthusian viewpoint suggest that the theory of demographic transition offers a more accurate picture of future population growth. **Demographic transition is the process by which some societies have moved from high birth and death rates to relatively low birth and death rates as a result of technological development.** Although demographic transition theory initially was applied to population changes brought about by the Industrial Revolution in Western Europe and North America, it recently has emerged as a dominant perspective in contemporary demography (Weeks,

2002). Demographic transition is linked to four stages of economic development (see Figure 19.6):

- *Stage 1: Preindustrial societies.* Little population growth occurs because high birth rates are offset by high death rates. Children are viewed as an economic asset because of their ability to work, but infant and child mortality rates are high due to lack of sanitation and poor nutrition. Life expectancy is around thirty years.

- *Stage 2: Early industrialization.* Significant population growth occurs because birth rates remain relatively high while death rates decline. Improvements in health, sanitation, and nutrition produce a substantial decline in infant mortality rates. Overpopulation is likely to occur because more people are alive than the society has the ability to support. However, social institutions continue to promote high fertility. Many developing nations—especially in Africa, Asia, and Latin America—currently are in this stage.

- *Stage 3: Advanced industrialization and urbanization.* Very little population growth occurs because both birth rates and death rates are low. The birth rate declines as couples control their fertility through contraceptives and become less likely to adhere to religious directives against their use. Children are not viewed as an economic asset; they consume income rather than producing it. Societies in this stage attain zero population growth—the point at which no population increase occurs from year to year.

- *Stage 4: Postindustrialization.* Birth rates continue to decline as more women gain full-time employment and the cost of raising children continues to increase. The population grows very slowly, if at all, because the decrease in birth rates is coupled with a stable death rate.

Debate continues as to whether this evolutionary model accurately explains the stages of population growth in all societies. Advocates note that demographic transition theory highlights the relationship between technological development and a slowing of population growth—a relationship that makes Malthus's predictions obsolete. Scholars also point out that demographic transitions occur at a faster rate in currently low-income nations than they previously did in the nations that already are industrialized. Critics suggest that demographic transition theory best explains development in Western societies. Many low-income countries may never achieve a steady growth in social and economic wealth unless

BOX 19.4 SOCIOLOGY AND THE MEDIA

Immigration and the Media

Just after the turn of the last century, a great deal of hostility was directed at nonwhite immigrants. The media actively promoted this racism by publishing inflammatory articles about racial minorities. These articles not only affected public opinion, but also were used by legislators to justify laws that targeted minority immigrants. The writing of Judge Emily Murphy of Edmonton, the first woman judge in the British Empire, was particularly influential. Her series of five articles, published in *Maclean's* magazine, shaped Canada's drug laws throughout the 1920s; their effects live on in our present narcotics legislation. These articles also shaped the attitudes of Canadians toward nonwhite immigrants by attributing the drug problem to Chinese and Black "villains" who, according to Judge Murphy, were trying to spread the drug habit in order to seduce white women and to destroy the Anglo-Saxon way of life.

Judge Murphy felt that nonwhite immigrants were a threat to the Canadian way of life. Her articles in *Maclean's* were illustrated with photographs of opium smokers (almost all of whom were women and/or nonwhite men) and cartoons (which were also racially demeaning). Each article featured a caricature of a Chinese opium smoker with smoke coming out of each ear. She saw the Chinese drug peddler as one who was perhaps unknowingly carrying out the wishes of his superiors who were trying to bring about the "downfall of the white race." The "Negroes coming into Canada," she wrote "have similar ideas."

The same conspiratorial view was advanced by other media. For example, in 1911, the Montreal *Herald* responded to the immigration of 58 Black women domestics from Guadeloupe by reporting that the "dark-skinned domestics were the advanced guard for others to follow" (Calliste, 1993:94).

That these views were so freely expressed in the media certainly made it easy for politicians and members of the public to follow the same racist line. The views, moreover, help explain why Canada had racially based immigration policies for much of the last century.

These photographs appeared in Judge Murphy's book *The Black Candle* (1922), which, like her articles published in *Maclean's* in the 1920s, were used by legislators to justify laws that targeted minority immigrants.

■ An opium addict

■ The keeper of an opium den

Sources: Based on Murphy, 1922; and Cook, 1969.

Figure 19.6 The Demographic Transition

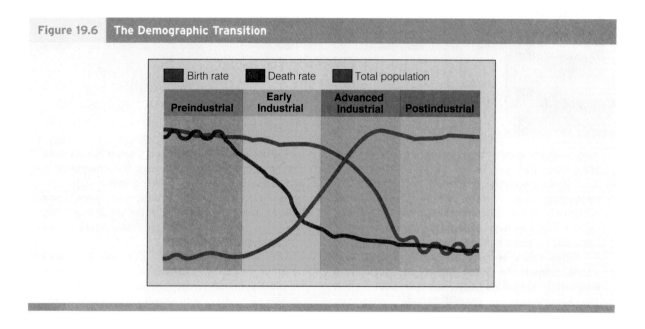

fertility levels first decline, so other routes to population control must be found.

Timothy Weiskel (1994) has pointed out that we should not expect that low-income countries will follow the same path as Western nations, as they have very different demographic histories and their population dynamics operate within very different historical, cultural, and economic circumstances. Weiskel notes that women's status and education, along with active family planning programs, have been more important than overall economic growth as causes of declining fertility.

The increased education of women in low-income nations is one of the reasons the rate of population growth in these countries has slowed in recent decades. Once the average education of women gets beyond Grade 8, fertility rates decline. The global fertility rate is now 2.7 births per woman, compared with 5 births per woman in the early 1950s. This decline has been most dramatic in Latin America and the Caribbean, where fertility rates have dropped by almost 50 percent to 2.6 over the past twenty-five years. However, rates remain at 5.7 per woman in sub-Saharan Africa (UNICEF, 2005).

Demography and Public Policy

China: One Child per Family

China's one-child policy is an example of public policy that is based on demographic knowledge. The Chinese government recognized that with more than one billion people, the country could not continue to sustain high birth rates. To avoid the consequences of overpopulation suggested by Malthus, they developed a number of policies to convince couples to have only one child. This is a very harsh measure (if successful, it would mean that Chinese society would no longer have brothers, sisters, aunts, uncles, or cousins), which conflicts with both the strong value placed on the family in Chinese society and with the practical need for several children to help support the parents in old age. However, the government decided that the health of the nation was more important than the rights of Chinese citizens to have the number of children they wished.

The one-child policy has helped to reduce China's birth rate, but it has also had some other serious long-term consequences. First, because there are more parents and grandparents than there are children, Chinese society will age quickly. Over the next thirty-five years, the average age will increase from thirty-two to forty-four (Khan, 2004). This means that the working-age population will have a heavy burden caring for their aging parents. Unlike Canada, China does not have a well-funded government pension system, so families will bear a major share of the burden. The second consequence is caused by the preference for sons in Chinese families. Traditionally, male children have been responsible for supporting their parents through their old age so males are preferred by most families. With the one-child policy this means that the single child should be a son, and many parents have used ultrasound tests to enable them to have sex-selective abortions. As a result, the sex ratio moved from 107 boys to each 100 girls in 1982 to 121 boys for each 100 girls in 1996 (Hudson and den Boer, 2004). This means that in the future there will be tens of millions more males than females, so about one in six men will find it impossible to marry. It is difficult to predict what role these men will play, since lifelong bachelorhood has not been a common social role in China (Eberstadt, 2004). In addition, because young single males have the highest rates of crime and other types of deviance, it is possible that the presence of large numbers of them may lead to an increase in misconduct in the future. The Chinese government is trying to encourage families to have more girls—for example, rural families are permitted have a second child if the first is a girl—but even if they are successful there will be at least one generation with a great excess of males

Demography and Quebec Language Policy

We have discussed some of the ways the baby boom has affected Canadian public policy. While many government policies are related to population trends, it might surprise you to learn that demographic analysis has played a large part in French–English politics over the past three decades.

Traditionally, Quebec has constituted about one-third of Canada's population. For many years, it had a higher birth rate than the other provinces. This meant increasing numbers of French-speaking Quebeckers—what some have called "the revenge of the cradle"—and it ensured a strong political voice for Quebec and helped maintain the dominance of the French language in Quebec. However, following the Quiet Revolution in the 1960s in Quebec (see Chapter 14, "Power, Politics, and Government"), the influence of the Catholic church diminished and the province became increasingly secular. The birth rate declined dramatically to a level far lower than that of most other provinces, reaching a low of 1.4 children per family in 1985 (Romaniuc, 1994). Like the rest of Canada, Quebec sought to make up for this shortage of births by increasing immigration. However, to the dismay of the Quebec government, many immigrants to Quebec chose to learn English rather than French. The French-speaking population continued to drop and, in response, the government passed Bill 101,

BOX 19.5 YOU CAN MAKE A DIFFERENCE

Helping with the Resettlement of Immigrants

Each year, nearly 250,000 immigrants arrive in Canada. For some, it is a relatively easy transition. People with relatives in Canada, with resources, and with a good knowledge of English or French may have no difficulties creating new lives in this country. However, many others, particularly those who come as refugees, may be faced with very serious problems adjusting to their new home. Those who come with only a few possessions, who have no marketable job skills, and who do not speak one of Canada's official languages may need help getting established.

While the government does provide some funding to help with resettlement, many of the programs rely heavily on volunteers. The Citizenship and Immigration Canada Web site (http:www.cic.gc.ca/english/newcomer/involve/index.html) describes a number of roles that you can play in helping newcomers to Canada. Most larger communities in Canada have local organizations that serve immigrants and that can help you to get involved. You can find these organizations through the Citizenship and Immigration Canada Web site or by phoning them at 1-888-242-2100.

- **Hosting a Newcomer.** The Host Program allows volunteers to meet with new immigrants for several hours each week in order to provide them with support, friendship, and an introduction to the community.
- **Refugee Sponsorship.** The Private Sponsorship of Refugees Program allows groups and individuals to sponsor refugees. The commitment to supply needs, such as accommodation, clothing, and food, must be for at least a year. One of the sponsorship programs allows Canadians to sponsor people with special needs who might otherwise not be allowed into Canada. These include refugees, such as women at risk, victims of trauma and torture, and people with medical conditions.
- **Host a Citizenship Ceremony.** Groups and organizations can act as hosts for ceremonies at which immigrants receive their Canadian citizenship.

Your university or college may also be looking for volunteers to work with international students. This could be a mutually rewarding way of learning about other cultures and languages.

which restricted the use of English and which required immigrants to send their children to French-language schools. Much of the nationalism in Quebec can be explained by Quebeckers' fears that the French language and culture will disappear in the vast North American sea of English. In 1996, Quebec's share of the Canadian population dropped below 25 percent for the first time since Confederation.

While the French–English question will remain with us in some form for some time, demographic trends may create other sources of policy debate and political division. For example, most of the political and economic power in Canada has been centred in Ontario and Quebec. With the shift in jobs and population to Western Canada (British Columbia and Alberta together now have more jobs than Quebec), we can anticipate that the West will continue to demand that its interests be reflected more broadly in national policies.

URBANIZATION AND THE GROWTH OF CITIES

Urban sociology **is a subfield of sociology that examines social relationships and political and economic structures in the city.** According to urban sociologists, a *city* is a relatively dense and permanent settlement of people who secure their livelihood primarily through nonagricultural activities. The census term that defines our cities is *census metropolitan area,* or CMA. A CMA is "an area consisting of one or more adjacent municipalities situated around a major urban core. To form a census metropolitan area, the urban core must have a population of at least 100,000" (Statistics Canada, 2002k). Canada has 27 CMAs, which in 2004 ranged in size from about 5.2 million people in Toronto to 127,000 in Saint John.

Although cities have existed for thousands of years, only about 3 percent of the world's population lived in cities two hundred years ago, as compared with almost 50 percent today. In Canada, the population is even more concentrated: almost 80 percent of us live in areas defined as urban; about 60 percent in CMAs; and about 30 percent in the three major metropolitan areas of Toronto, Montreal, and Vancouver. Canada has become steadily more urbanized since Confederation, when our population was roughly 16 percent urban (Stone, 1967). To understand the process by which increasing numbers of people have become urban residents, we first need to examine how cities developed over time.

Preindustrial Cities

The largest preindustrial city was Rome; by 100 C.E., it may have had a population of 650,000 (Chandler and Fox, 1974). With the fall of the Roman Empire in 476 C.E., the nature of European cities changed. Seeking protection and survival, those persons who lived in urban settings typically did so in walled cities containing no more than 25,000 people. For the next 600 years, the urban population continued to live in walled enclaves, as competing warlords battled for power and territory. Slowly, as trade increased, cities began to tear down their walls. Some walled cities still exist; Quebec City is the only walled city on this continent.

Preindustrial cities were limited in size by a number of factors. For one thing, crowded conditions and a lack of adequate sewage facilities increased the hazards from plagues and fires, and death rates were high. For another, food supplies were limited. In order to generate food for each city resident, at least fifty farmers had to work in the fields (Davis, 1949), and animal power was the only means of bringing food to the city. Once foodstuffs arrived in the city, there was no effective way to preserve them. Finally, migration to the city was difficult because people were bound to the land through systems of serfdom and slavery and because travel was arduous.

In spite of these problems, many preindustrial cities had a sense of *community*—a set of social relationships operating within given spatial boundaries or locations that provide people with a sense of identity and a feeling of belonging. The cities were full of people from all walks of life, both rich and poor, and they felt a high degree of social integration. You will recall that Ferdinand Tönnies (1940/1887) described such a community as a *Gemeinschaft*—a society in which social relationships are based on personal bonds of friendship and kinship and on intergenerational stability, such that people have a commitment to the entire group and feel a sense of togetherness. In this type of society, the person who sells you groceries may also be your neighbour, an elder in your church, and a relative by marriage. When you visit the store, your grocery purchase will be handled in a very personal fashion. By contrast, an industrial city was classified by Tönnies as a *Gesellschaft*—a society characterized by impersonal and specialized relationships, with little long-term commitment to the group or consensus on values (see Chapter 5). In *Gesellschaft* societies, even neighbours are "strangers" who feel they have little in common with one another. Your transaction at the grocery store will be handled much more formally in this type of society.

Canadian communities arose as settlement extended to new parts of this large country. Until the building of the Canadian Pacific Railway, much of Canada was accessible only by water, so most of our settlements, including those that have grown into large cities, were in areas with access to waterways. Transportation routes were particularly important for a colony whose main function was sending large quantities of raw materials, such as timber, wheat, and beaver pelts, overseas to European markets.

Industrial Cities

The Industrial Revolution changed the nature of the city. Factories sprang up rapidly as production shifted from the primary, agricultural sector to the secondary, manufacturing sector. With the advent of factories came many new employment opportunities not available to people in rural areas. In fact, factories required a concentration of population to act as a labour force. Emergent technology, including new forms of transportation and agricultural production, made it easier for people to leave the countryside and move to the city. Between 1700 and 1900, the population of many European cities mushroomed. Although the Industrial Revolution did not start in North America until the mid-nineteenth century, the effect was similar. Between 1871 and 1911, the population of Toronto grew by 700 percent and that of Montreal by 450 percent (Nader, 1976). By 1911, both cities had roughly 500,000 people and were on their way to becoming major metropolises. A **metropolis is one or more central cities and their surrounding suburbs that dominate the economic and cultural life of a region. A *central city* is the densely populated centre of a metropolis.**

The growth of cities during the industrial period was something of a mixed blessing. As cities grew in size and density, overcrowding, poor sanitation, and lack of a clean water supply often led to the spread of epidemic diseases and contributed to a high death rate. In Europe, mortality rates were higher in cities than in rural areas until the nineteenth century, and this remains the case in many cities in the low-income countries today.

Postindustrial Cities

Since the 1950s, postindustrial cities have emerged in technologically advanced countries, the economies of which have gradually shifted from secondary (manufacturing) production to tertiary (service and information-processing) production. As more traditional industries, such as textile manufacturing, steel producing, and many different types of light manufacturing, have become obsolete or moved to other countries with lower wages, cities have had to either change or face decline. For example, cities in New Brunswick were economically devastated in the 1980s and 1990s by the loss of many jobs in traditional industries, such as shipbuilding and railroad maintenance, as well as in resource industries associated with the fishing industry. The province counteracted these losses by moving into the technologically based field of telephone call centres, which perform tasks such as telephone marketing and airline-reservation handling.

Postindustrial cities are dominated by "light" industry, such as computer software manufacturing; information-processing services, such as airline and hotel reservation services; educational complexes; medical centres; convention and entertainment centres; and retail trade centres and shopping malls. Most families do not live in close proximity to a central business district. Technological advances in communication and transportation make it possible for middle- and upper-income individuals and families

Toronto's Highway 401 at rush hour illustrates the development of postindustrial cities in which people commonly commute long distances to work. Smog is one of the problems that comes with urbanization.

to have more work options and to live greater distances from the workplace. Some futurists feel that communications technology, along with the retirement plans of the baby boomers, may soon lead to a degree of de-urbanization. People who do not have to be physically present in the city centre each day may find a rural or semirural lifestyle an attractive alternative to the commuting and high housing prices that are a part of life in a large city.

PERSPECTIVES ON URBANIZATION AND THE GROWTH OF CITIES

Functionalist Perspectives: Ecological Models

Functionalists examine the interrelations among the parts that make up the whole. Therefore, in studying the growth of cities, they emphasize the life cycle of urban growth. Like the social philosophers and sociologists before him, University of Chicago sociologist

Robert Park (1915) based his analysis of the city on *human ecology*—the study of the relationship between people and their physical environment. According to Park (1936), economic competition produces certain regularities in land-use patterns and population distributions. Applying Park's idea to the study of urban land-use patterns, sociologist Ernest W. Burgess (1925) developed the concentric zone model to explain why some cities expand radially from a central business core.

Concentric Zone Model Burgess's *concentric zone model* is a description of the process of urban growth that views the city as a series of circular areas or zones, each characterized by a different type of land use, that developed from a central core (see Figure 19.7a). *Zone 1* is the central business district and cultural centre (retail stores, financial institutions, hotels, and theatres, for example), in which high land prices cause vertical growth in the form of skyscrapers. *Zone 2* is the zone of transition. As the city expanded, houses formerly occupied by wealthy families were divided into rooms that now are rented to recent immigrants and poor persons; this zone also contains wholesale light manufacturing and marginal business (such as secondhand stores,

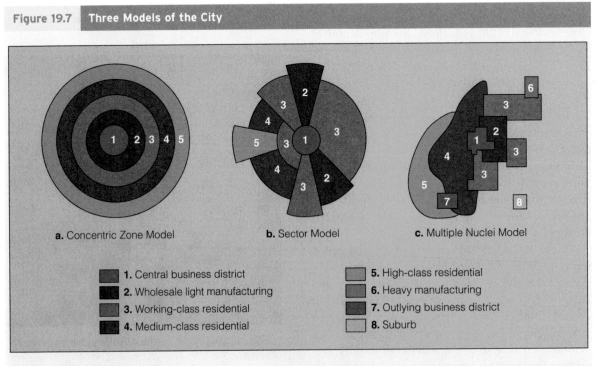

Figure 19.7   Three Models of the City

a. Concentric Zone Model   **b.** Sector Model   **c.** Multiple Nuclei Model

1. Central business district
2. Wholesale light manufacturing
3. Working-class residential
4. Medium-class residential
5. High-class residential
6. Heavy manufacturing
7. Outlying business district
8. Suburb

Source: Adapted from Harris and Ullman, 1945.

pawnshops, and taverns). *Zone 3* contains working-class residences and shops and ethnic enclaves, such as Little Italy. *Zone 4* is composed of homes for affluent families, single-family residences of white-collar workers, and shopping centres. *Zone 5* is a ring of small cities and towns populated by persons who commute to the city to work and by wealthy people living on estates.

Two important ecological processes are involved in the concentric zone theory: invasion and succession. *Invasion* **is the process by which a new category of people or type of land use arrives in an area previously occupied by another group or land use** (McKenzie, 1925). For example, Burgess noted that recent immigrants and low-income individuals "invaded" Zone 2, formerly occupied by wealthy families. *Succession* **is the process by which a new category of people or type of land use gradually predominates in an area formerly dominated by another group or activity** (McKenzie, 1925). In Zone 2, for example, when some of the single-family residences were sold and subsequently divided into multiple housing units, the remaining single-family owners moved out because the "old" neighbourhood had changed. As a result of their move, the process of invasion was complete and succession had occurred.

Invasion and succession theoretically operate in an outward movement: those who are unable to "move out" of the inner rings are those without upward social mobility, so the central zone ends up being primarily occupied by the poorest residents—except when gentrification occurs. *Gentrification* **is the process by which members of the middle and upper-middle classes move into the central city area and renovate existing properties.** Centrally located, naturally attractive areas are the most likely candidates for gentrification. To urban ecologists, gentrification is the solution to revitalizing the central city. To conflict theorists, gentrification creates additional hardships for the poor by depleting the amount of affordable housing available and "pushing" them out of the area (Flanagan, 1999).

The concentric zone model demonstrates how economic and political forces play an important part in the location of groups and activities, and it shows how a large urban area can have internal differentiation (Gottdiener, 1985). However, the model is most applicable to older cities that experienced high levels of immigration early in the twentieth century (Queen and Carpenter, 1953). No city, including Chicago (on which the model is based), entirely conforms to this model.

The Sector Model   In an attempt to examine a wider range of settings, urban ecologist Homer Hoyt (1939) studied the configuration of 142 cities. Hoyt's *sector model* emphasizes the significance of terrain and the importance of transportation routes in the layout of cities. According to Hoyt, residences of a particular type and value tend to grow outward from the centre of the city in wedge-shaped sectors, with the more expensive residential neighbourhoods located along the higher ground near lakes and rivers or along certain streets that stretch in one direction or another from the downtown area (see Figure 19.7b). By contrast, industrial areas tend to be located along river valleys and railroad lines. Middle-class residential zones exist on either side of the wealthier neighbourhoods. Finally, lower-class residential areas occupy the remaining space, bordering the central business area and the industrial areas.

The Multiple Nuclei Model   According to the *multiple nuclei model* developed by urban ecologists Chauncey Harris and Edward Ullman (1945), cities do not have one centre from which all growth radiates, but rather they have numerous centres of development based on specific urban needs or activities (see Figure 19.7c). As cities began to grow rapidly, they annexed formerly outlying and independent townships that had been communities in their own right. In addition to the central business district, other nuclei developed around activities, such as an educational institution, a medical complex, or a government centre. Residential neighbourhoods may exist close to or far away from these nuclei. A wealthy residential area may be located near a high-priced shopping centre, for instance, while less-expensive housing must locate closer to industrial and transitional areas of town. This model fits some urban areas such as Toronto, which has large nuclei, such as the business district of North York. It also applies to a number of communities, such as Edmonton, which have nuclei around universities.

Differences Between Canadian and U.S. Cities   The models of urban growth discussed above were developed to explain the growth of U.S. cities. They do not fit preindustrial cities (most of which have their slums on the outskirts of the city rather than in the central core), nor do they fit cities, such as those in Europe, that were relatively large before they industrialized. Because they developed on the same continent and at about the same time, there are many similarities between Canadian and

American cities, but the models probably do not apply as well to Canadian cities, which differ from U.S. cities in the following important ways (Gillis, 1995; Wolfe, 1992):

1. Canadian cities are higher in density, which means they have less urban sprawl. It is cheaper to provide services in compact cities, and commuting to work is far easier.

2. The core areas of Canadian cities are much healthier than those in the United States. In many U.S. cities, residents have moved to the suburbs to avoid crime, high taxes, and other inner-city problems. This has created what some observers refer to as "doughnut cities," with poor central core areas that have no industry, no job opportunities, poor schools, deteriorated housing, and no tax base to help improve things. The strength of our urban core areas is a major reason Canadian cities have much lower crime rates than American cities.

3. Urban Canadians rely on public transit more than do Americans, though both countries are far behind European cities in public transit use. Because of this, our cities are less divided by freeways than those in the U.S.

4. Racial tension has been far less pronounced in Canada than in the United States, where it has led to many problems including urban riots and "white flight" to the suburbs.

5. Canadian and U.S. public housing policies have been very different. With a few exceptions, such as Toronto's Regent Park and Montreal's Jeanne Mance, governments in Canada have not built large-scale, high-rise developments. Public housing in Canada has taken the form of small, infill projects in established neighbourhoods. These are small housing developments typically consisting of small apartment buildings or row housing. Thus we have not faced the problem of large numbers of economically disadvantaged people crowded into areas that can easily be neglected by the rest of society.

Conflict Perspectives: Political Economy Models

Conflict theorists argue that cities do not grow or decline by chance. Rather, they are the product of specific decisions made by members of the capitalist class and political elites. These far-reaching decisions regarding land use and urban development benefit the members of some groups at the expense of others

(see Castells, 1977/1972). Karl Marx suggested that cities are the arenas in which the intertwined processes of class conflict and capital accumulation take place; class consciousness and worker revolt were more likely to develop when workers were concentrated in urban areas (Flanagan, 1999).

Capitalism and Urban Growth   According to political economy models, urban growth is influenced by capital investment decisions, power and resource inequality, class and class conflict, and government subsidy programs. Members of the capitalist class choose corporate locations, decide on sites for shopping centres and factories, and spread the population that can afford to purchase homes into sprawling suburbs located exactly where the capitalists think they should be located (Feagin and Parker, 1990).

Business involvement in urban development is nothing new. Winnipeg became a major transportation centre because of its location at the junction of the Red and Assiniboine Rivers. However, because of Winnipeg's flooding problems, the small community of Selkirk was originally chosen for the route of the Canadian Pacific Railway (CPR). After several years of intense lobbying by Winnipeg's political and business leaders, along with promises of subsidies to the CPR, the line was built through Winnipeg in 1881. According to Bellan (1978), Sir Donald Smith, the man who drove the last spike to finish the transcontinental railway, was instrumental in having the route shifted to Winnipeg. A key figure in building the CPR, Smith was also the largest shareholder in the Hudson's Bay Company, which owned a large block of land in the centre of Winnipeg. During the land boom that followed the announcement of the railway's new route, the Hudson's Bay Company made millions of dollars selling this land.

Today, a small number of financial institutions and developers finance and construct most of Canada's major and many of its smaller urban development projects, including skyscrapers, shopping malls, and suburban housing projects across the country. These decision makers set limits on the individual choices of the ordinary citizen with regard to real estate, just as they do with regard to other choices (Feagin and Parker, 1990). They can make housing more affordable or totally unaffordable for many people. Ultimately, their motivation rests not in benefiting the community, but rather in making a profit; the cities they produce reflect this mindset.

One of the major results of these urban development practices is *uneven development*—the tendency of some neighbourhoods, cities, or regions to grow and prosper while others stagnate and decline (Perry and Watkins, 1977). An example of this is the movement of middle- and upper-class people to the suburbs, which reduces the tax base of the city core. Conflict theorists argue that uneven development reflects inequalities of wealth and power in society. The problem not only affects areas in a state of decline but also produces external costs, even in "boom" areas, that are paid for by the entire community. Among these costs are increased pollution, traffic congestion, and rising rates of crime and violence. According to Mark Gottdiener (1985:214), these costs are "intrinsic to the very core of capitalism, and those who profit the most from development are not called upon to remedy its side effects."

Feminist Perspectives

Feminist perspectives have only recently been incorporated in urban studies (Garber and Turner, 1995). From this perspective, urbanization reflects the workings not only of the political economy but also of patriarchy.

Gender Regimes in Cities

According to Lynn Appleton (1995), different kinds of cities have different *gender regimes*—prevailing ideologies of how women and men should think, feel, and act; how access to social positions and control of resources should be managed; and how relationships between men and women should be conducted. The higher density and greater diversity found in central cities serve as a challenge to the patriarchy found in the home and workplace in lower-density, homogeneous areas such as suburbs and rural areas because central

According to conflict theorists, members of the capitalist class make decisions that limit the choices of ordinary citizens, such as how affordable or unaffordable their housing will be. However, scenes like this show that tenants may become active participants in class conflict over the usage of urban space.

cities offer a broader range of lifestyle choices, some of which do not involve traditional patriarchal family structures. For example, cities are more likely than suburbs to support a subculture of economically independent females. Thus the city may be a forum for challenging patriarchy; all residents who differ in marital status, paternity, sexual orientation, class, and/or race/ethnicity tend to live in close proximity to one another and may hold and act upon a common belief that both public and private patriarchy should be eliminated (Appleton, 1995).

Gender and City Life

Do women and men experience city life differently? Many feminists feel that cities reflect the partriarchy of the broader society in that fear of crime committed by males has effectively limited the access of females to public space (Koskela, 1997). According to Elizabeth Wilson (1991), some men view the city as *sexual space* in which women are categorized as prostitutes, lesbians, temptresses, or virtuous women in need of protection, based on their sexual desirability and accessibility. Wilson suggests that affluent, dominant-group women are more likely to be viewed as virtuous women in need of protection by their own men or police officers. Cities offer a paradox for women: on the one hand, they offer more freedom than is found in comparatively isolated rural, suburban, and domestic settings; on the other, women may be in greater physical danger in the city. For Wilson, the answer to women's vulnerability in the city is not found in offering protection to them, but rather in changing people's attitudes so that they no longer believe they can treat women as sexual objects because of the impersonality of city life (Wilson, 1991). This view was supported by research conducted by Ross Macmillan and colleagues, who found that the experience of sexual harassment by strangers is a major predictor of fear of victimization among a national sample of Canadian women (Macmillan, Nierobisz, and Welsh, 2000).

Michelson (1994) has highlighted another dimension of the vulnerability of women in cities. Women with children are much more likely to be in the paid workforce than they were several decades ago. When women were more likely to stay home, they spent much of their time in the company of immediate neighbours and rarely ventured from their neighbourhoods at night without their husbands. Employed women have a much different city experience. Much of their time is now spent with people on the job and they are more often alone outside their immediate neighbourhoods at different hours.

For many women in this situation, travelling to and from work is perceived as dangerous. Michelson cites a Statistics Canada study showing that 80 percent of women fear entering parking garages and 76 percent fear using public transportation after dark. Women feel particularly vulnerable if they have to walk alone after dark because of work or school. Our cities have not yet adapted well to these major social changes in the lives of women.

Symbolic Interactionist Perspectives: The Experience of City Life

Symbolic interactionists examine the *experience* of urban life. How does city life affect the people who live in a city? Some analysts feel cities create a positive social environment; others are more negative about the effect of urban living on the individual.

Simmel's View of City Life

According to German sociologist Georg Simmel (1950/1902–1917), urban life is highly stimulating and it shapes people's thoughts and actions. Urban residents are influenced by the quick pace of city life and the pervasiveness of economic relations in everyday life. Due to the intensity of urban life, people become somewhat insensitive to events and individuals around them. When city life requires you to interact with hundreds of different people every day, you cannot become personally involved with each of them, so most of your contacts will be impersonal. Urbanites are wary of one another because most interactions in the city are economic rather than social. Simmel suggests that attributes, such as punctuality and exactness, are rewarded but that friendliness and warmth in interpersonal relations are viewed as personal weaknesses. Some people act in a reserved way to cloak deeper feelings of distrust or dislike toward others. However, Simmel did not view city life as completely negative; he also pointed out that urban living could have a liberating effect on people because they had opportunities for individualism and autonomy (Flanagan, 1999).

Urbanism as a Way of Life

Based on Simmel's observations on social relations in the city, early Chicago School sociologist Louis Wirth (1938) suggested that urbanization is a "way of life." *Urbanism* refers to the distinctive social and psychological patterns of life typically found in the city. According to Wirth, the size, density, and heterogeneity of urban populations typically result in an elaborate division of labour and in spatial segregation of people by race/ethnicity, social class, religion, and/or lifestyle. In the city, primary group ties largely are replaced by secondary relationships; social interaction is fragmented, impersonal, and often superficial ("Hello! Have a nice day"). Even though people gain some degree of freedom and privacy by living in the city, they pay a price for their autonomy, losing the group support and reassurance that comes from primary group ties.

From Wirth's perspective, people who live in urban areas are alienated, powerless, and lonely. A sense of community is obliterated and replaced by "mass society"—a large-scale, highly institutionalized society in which individuality is supplanted by mass messages, faceless bureaucrats, and corporate interest.

Simmel and Wirth share an *environmental determinism* that assumes that the physical environment of the city determines the behaviour of urban dwellers. Their work has contributed to the commonly held view that cities are cold, anonymous, and unfriendly places (Kennedy, 1983). However, other researchers claim that the rural–urban contrast is too simplistic and ignores the wide diversity of lifestyles found in urban areas. This view has led to research into the reasons for the different ways in which urban residents have responded to their environment.

Gan's Urban Villagers

In contrast to Wirth's gloomy assessment of urban life, sociologist Herbert Gans (1982/1962) suggested that not everyone experiences the city in the same way. Based on research conducted in the west end of Boston, Gans concluded that many residents develop strong loyalties and a sense of community in central city areas that outsiders may view negatively. People make choices about the lifestyle they wish to lead based on their personal characteristics, the most important of which are social class and stage in the life cycle. According to Gans, there are five major categories of adaptation among urban dwellers. *Cosmopolites* are students, artists, writers, musicians, entertainers, and professionals who live in the city because they want to be close to its cultural facilities. *Unmarried people and childless couples* live in the city because they want to be close to work and entertainment. *Ethnic villagers* live in ethnically segregated neighbourhoods; some are recent immigrants who feel most comfortable within their own group. The *deprived* are poor individuals with dim future prospects; they have very limited education and few, if any, other resources. The *trapped* are urban dwellers who can find no escape from the city; this group includes persons left behind by the process of invasion and succession, downwardly mobile individuals who have lost their former position in society, older persons who have nowhere else to go, and individuals addicted to alcohol or other drugs. Transient people in the inner city are most likely to suffer the urban ills described by Wirth, but this is because of residential instability and not simply an inevitable result of urbanization. Gans concluded that the city is a pleasure and a challenge for some urban dwellers and an urban nightmare for others.

How Do We Live in Cities? Social Interaction in a World of Strangers

People who live in small rural communities usually know most other residents and recognize those who are strangers. The city, on the other hand, is a world of strangers. How do people manage to live in such

These photographs represent three of the ways people adapt to city life described by Herbert Gans. Cosmopolites choose to live in the city to enjoy cultural facilities, such as Toronto's Roy Thomson Hall (top left). Ethnic villagers live in the tightly knit neighbourhood enclaves, such as this Chinese neighbourhood in Richmond, British Columbia (top right). Trapped residents can find no escape from the city, as exemplified by this homeless person in Toronto (bottom).

a world, in which they know nothing about most of the people they encounter in the course of a day? Lyn Lofland has addressed this question:

> The answer to the question of how city life was to be possible, then, is this. *City life was made possible by an 'ordering' of the urban populace in terms of appearance and spatial location such that those within the city could know a great deal about one another simply by looking.* (Lofland, 1973:22; emphasis in original)

Erving Goffman (1971) was one of the first sociologists to study the way people handled social interaction in cities. Our largest cities contain huge numbers of people, and without some orderly process it would be difficult to simply make our way down a crowded street. While there are no formal rules, people are able to maintain an orderly flow of pedestrian traffic with few collisions. The next time you are walking on a busy sidewalk, try to consciously think of the "rules of the road." Now see how the trained eye of a symbolic interactionist analyzes pedestrian routing practices:

> When an individual determines that a simple check is not sufficient, as when a collision course is apparent or there is no clear indication of the other's course, then additional assurances are likely to be sought. He can ostentatiously take or hold a course, waiting to do this until he can be sure that the other is checking him out. If he wants to be still more careful, he can engage in a 'checked-body-check'; after he has given a course indication, he can make sure the signal has been picked up by the other, either by meeting the other's eyes (although not for engagement) or by noting the other's direction of vision, in either case establishing that his own course gesture has not likely been overlooked. In brief, he can check up on the other's eye check on him, the assumption here being that other can be relied on to act safely providing only that he has perceived the situation. Finally, a brief face engagement may be initiated in which one party signals what he proposes they do and the other party signals agreement. (A strategic device here is to signal a collaborative routing in which the other has a slight advantage, thus usually assuring agreement.) (Goffman, 1971:13)

Avoiding collisions is just one simple example of the cooperation and mutual trust that exists among urban strangers. Tracy Nielsen (2005) has described how informal interaction in public places helps to build community. As a lesbian, Nielsen is aware of the risks of being publicly identified and stigmatized in a world dominated by heterosexuals. On the other hand, passing as heterosexual is a denial of one's own identity. Also, lesbians are particularly interested in being visible to other lesbians. Nielsen says that the gay/lesbian subculture has developed signalling and receiving behaviour referred to as "gaydar" to identify one another even if the other is not necessarily out. Just as the pedestrian routing practices described in Goffman involve a mutual exchange of information between individuals, gaydar also involves interaction between sender and receiver in the course of very brief social interaction. While outward appearance is part of mutual recognition, one of the women interviewed by Nielsen says that appearance is only the beginning:

> I believe there are a thousand hidden cues that we give to one another that we then interpret as a feeling. But there is a feeling I get when I discover another lesbian. I am having a hard time narrowing it down. . . . It's a look, a feeling, a vibe that they send you that says, I see you, I recognize you. (Nielsen, 2005:92)

According to Nielsen, this recognition is important because even if it is just for a very brief moment, the recognition bonds the women together in a larger community and is an affirmation of solidarity in a world that may sometimes be hostile to non-heterosexuals.

The well-known urban theorist Jane Jacobs reminded us nearly fifty years ago that urban order and safety are not maintained by the police, but by "an intricate, almost unconscious, network of voluntary controls and standards among the people themselves, and enforced by the people themselves" (1961:32). Jacobs feels that urban dwellers will be safest where communities are rich in the kinds of street-level businesses, such as bars, stores, and restaurants, that keep the streets full of people who will watch over one another. For Jacobs, the most successful cities will be those designed to encourage this civil interaction.

There is, then, a diversity in the life experience of urban dwellers that depends on a wide variety of factors, such as age, social class, gender, sexual orientation, marital status, and type of residence. The same is likely true of rural residents; the romantic view of rural society held by the early urban sociologists may have been nostalgia for a mythical past. In reality, urban life is not as bad, nor rural life as good, as Wirth and his colleagues assumed.

Postmodern Perspectives: The Postmodern City

Decentred Cities   While Chicago was the model for the modernist city, Los Angeles is seen by some as the model of the postmodern city: "an interminable urbanised area with no coherent form, no hierarchical structure, no centre and no unity; [and a diverse mixture of races and ethnicities]. . ." (Fahmi, 2001:5). While the modernist city was represented by *concentric circles* that characterized how land-use patterns changed in an orderly way as one moved out from the urban core, the postmodern city is signified by a "*collage* of . . . consumption-oriented landscapes devoid of conventional centers" (Dear and Flusty, 1998:66) with a haphazard pattern of development (see Figure 19.8). The key processes that led to these changes are globalization and the economic restructuring caused by the transition from the industrial era to the information economy. Cities like Los Angeles have no urban cores, but grow in clusters over a large geographical area. Postmodern business enterprises are typically smaller than the older industrial factories, so they can be scattered across the metropolis. Knowledge industries that are part of the global economy can locate anywhere around a major population centre and related businesses and population growth will follow. Shopping and entertainment industries also contribute to the decentred city. Huge malls and entertainment centres, such as theme parks and casinos, are built on the edges of urban areas because of land costs and then attract housing and other service businesses. There is little planned development, as land developers and business owners shape the city to suit their own interests.

Table 19.2 compares the spatial characteristics of the industrial city and the postmodern city. While Chicago in 1900 had a densely populated central downtown core and patterns of land use that changed as one moved out from that core, Los Angeles in 2000 was a sprawling urban area with many different city cores. Unlike Chicago's slaughterhouses and factories, the businesses of contemporary cities are much more flexible and much less tied to the services of a central hub. Like Los Angeles, Chicago drew large numbers of immigrants. However, Chicago's immigrants moved from one part of the city to another as the fortunes of their ethnic and racial groups rose and fell, while contemporary cities, including Los Angeles, are much more diverse and minority populations have a greater influence throughout the entire urban area. Dear and Flusty (1998) point out that sprawling metropolitan areas, such as Los Angeles, have a huge negative impact on the environment in the form of air pollution from the personal vehicles that are essential to life in the postmodern city to the destruction of natural habitat as urban expansion erases the natural environment.

The Fantasy City   With the decline of manufacturing industries that used to be located in the city centres, urban planners have had to look at ways of reversing the flight to the suburbs and of keeping their downtowns alive. Many have turned to the entertainment industry to help to restore their cities and have tried to create what John Hannigan (1998) has termed the "fantasy city." Restaurants and bars, gambling casinos, movie theatres, sports arenas and stadiums, and arts centres bring people downtown from the suburbs in the evenings and also encourage people to live in downtown areas. Perhaps the best example of a fantasy city is Las Vegas, one of the world's most popular tourist destinations. Its main attractions are gambling and nightclub entertainment, and its built environment is totally artificial. Many of its large hotels attempt to simulate other cities. The Paris Las Vegas hotel has replicas of the Eiffel Tower and the Arc de Triomphe, while New York, New York has a façade that simulates the skyline of the real New York City, complete with replicas

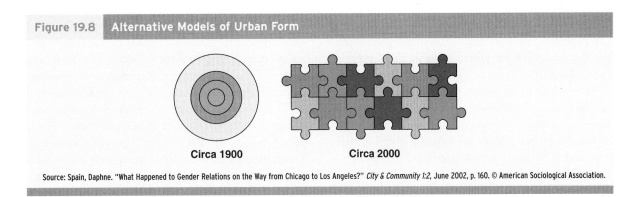

Figure 19.8   Alternative Models of Urban Form

Circa 1900   Circa 2000

Source: Spain, Daphne. "What Happened to Gender Relations on the Way from Chicago to Los Angeles?" *City & Community 1:2*, June 2002, p. 160. © American Sociological Association.

Table 19.2   SPATIAL CHARACTERISTICS OF URBAN FORM

	CIRCA 1900	CIRCA 2000
Prototype	Industrial city	Informational metropolis
Number of centres	One	Two or more
Location of activities	Mixed	Separated
Density of population	High	Low
Direction of development	Vertical	Horizontal

Source: Spain, Daphne. "What Happened to Gender Relations on the Way from Chicago to Los Angeles?" *City & Community 1:2*, June 2002, p. 160. © American Sociological Association.

of the Statue of Liberty and the Empire State Building. Unlike the real cities of Paris and New York, they are not grounded in their locations and their history but rather are standardized, branded businesses, like Disneyland and McDonald's, that provide an experience that can be recreated anywhere their owners wish to put them. These simulated travel experiences provide consumers with a social experience that is quite different from that of their suburban homes, but they provide controlled environments that eliminate many of the risks of real travel. Nothing need be left to chance for travellers: you are unlikely to be mugged in Disneyland, where the behaviour of visitors is tightly controlled; you know what the cheeseburgers will taste like in any of the world's 143 Hard Rock Cafés; and people enjoying an all-inclusive Club Med vacation at Columbus Isle, Bahamas may never meet anybody or see anything outside the gates of the resort.

Franchises and branding are important components of the fantasy city experience. Even when people do travel to real cities, many choose to go to globally branded franchises. For example, some visitors to London prefer to celebrate their trip by wearing Hard Rock Café London T-shirts rather than shirts with logos representing something that is unique to London. Hannigan says this branded merchandise enhances the status of the tourist: "They are . . . regarded as 'passports,' proclaiming not only that you have been somewhere interesting but that you have consumed a highly rated experience" (1998:70).

The urban entertainment phenomenon has a number of negative consequences. As cities become more and more alike because of their franchised entertainment attractions, we lose the diversity that is provided by more locally grounded experiences. The experience of enjoying a very inexpensive café au lait and beignets at the Café du Monde, which has

been located next to the Mississipi River in the French Quarter of New Orleans since 1862, is very different from a visit to one of the world's many Starbucks outlets. Hannigan also points out that many of the entertainment facilities are built with public money. In many cases the public money is never recovered, but private corporations, such as sports teams, reap huge financial benefits from new facilities. The stadium built in Montreal for the 1976 Olympics had huge overruns in construction costs and taxpayers paid a special levy until 2005 to pay for these excess costs. Finally, these entertainment facilities, as well as other developments, such as enclosed walkways, isolate many of the urban poor from the rest of city life. The middle class are protected while the underclass do not have access to the privatized space.

The Disappearance of Public Space   A major trend in the postmodern city is the disappearance of public space. Rather than being open and accessible to all, cities are becoming private places. We shop in malls or in isolated big-box shopping areas, and many of us live in gated communities. Why do some people feel this is a problem? Think of West Edmonton Mall, which covers 48 acres and has more than 800 businesses, two indoor amusement parks, and a marine mammal park. On an average day 60,000 people visit the mall, and security personnel respond to more than 40,000 calls each year (Murphy and Clarke, 2005). In some ways it is like the downtown centre in a major city. However, it has one fundamental difference from a city centre: the mall and its 20,000-car parking lot are private space. The most recent generation of malls, such as the new Village, which is part of Park Royal shopping centre in Vancouver, are actually reproductions of streets with shops accessible from outdoors rather than through enclosed malls. While they look like public territory,

This is the Village at Park Royal in West Vancouver. While it looks like a normal city street, it is actually private property.

these inviting "public" streets are actually on private property. While we all have free access to public space, any of us can be denied entrance to private space even if that space is open to the public. In the West Edmonton Mall or any other private shopping centre, if you wish to just sit on a bench for hours, play a game with your friends, stage a political protest, or do many other things that are encouraged or tolerated in public spaces, you may be prohibited access to the property. The major factor that determines what takes place within a mall is what will make a profit, so commercial interests are paramount. In many cities, these large malls have drawn stores and shoppers away from the downtown business centre, so the street space that is still available for public access may no longer have the interest and vitality it once did.

Gated residential communities are created by developers so they can offer potential residents a feeling of safety, privacy, and luxury they might not have in non-gated residential areas. Gated communities for the wealthy convey the idea of exclusivity and privilege, while those aimed at the middle class typically focus on such features as safety for children and the ability to share amenities such as "community" recreational facilities with the other residents. Regardless of the social and economic reasons given for the development of gated communities, they reflect a growing divide between public and private space in urban areas. Unlike medieval walled cities in which all citizens were protected by the walls, the benefits of the protection go only to those who pay for it. Gated communities do more than simply restrict access to the residents' homes. They also limit the use of once-public spaces, making it impossible for others to use the roads, parks, and open space

contained within the enclosed community (Low, 2003). Those inside the gates are no longer full participants in broader urban life.

To many, the essence of city life is its public space: "one of the most important social characteristics of cities is the provision of public spaces in which relative strangers can interact and observe each other, debate and learn politically, and grow psychologically from diverse contacts" (Calhoun, 1986:341). The exclusivity and restrictiveness of the privatized space in our postmodern cities can lead to a fragmentation that can have a negative impact on the vitality of the city itself as well as on those who are denied access inside the gates.

Concept Table 19.A examines the different theoretical perspectives on urban growth and urban living.

POPULATION AND URBANIZATION IN THE FUTURE

Rapid global population growth is inevitable. Although death rates have declined in many low-income nations, there has not been a corresponding decline in birth rates. Between 1985 and 2025, 93 percent of all global population growth will have occurred in Africa, Asia, and Latin America; 83 percent of the world's population will live in those regions by 2025 (Petersen, 1994).

Predicting changes in population is difficult. Natural disasters, such as earthquakes, volcanic eruptions, hurricanes, tornados, floods, and so on, obviously cannot be predicted. A cure for diseases caused by HIV may be found; however, HIV/AIDS may reach epidemic proportions in more nations. A number of diseases, such as tuberculosis, which had been controlled by antibiotics, are now returning in a form that is resistant to the drugs usually used for treatment.

Whatever the impact of disease, developing nations will have an increasing number of poor people. While the world's population will *double,* the urban population will *triple* as people migrate from rural to urban areas in search of food, water, and jobs. Of all developing regions, Latin America is becoming the most urbanized; four mega-cities—Mexico City (20 million), Buenos Aires (12 million), Lima (7 million), and Santiago (5 million)—already contain more than half of this region's population and continue to grow rapidly. By 2010, Rio de Janeiro and Sao Paulo are

Concept Table 19.A   PERSPECTIVES ON URBANISM AND THE GROWTH OF CITIES

PERSPECTIVE	MODEL THEORIES	KEY ELEMENTS
Functionalist: Ecological Models		
Burgess	Concentric Zone Model	Due to invasion, succession, and gentrification, cities are a series of circular zones, each characterized by a particular land use.
Hoyt	Sector Model	Cities consist of wedge-shaped sectors, based on terrain and transportation routes, with the most-expensive areas occupying the best terrain.
Harris and Ullman	Multiple Nuclei Model	Cities have more than one centre of development, based on specific needs and activities.
Conflict: Political Economy Models		
Marx	Capitalism and Urban Growth	Members of the capitalist class choose locations for skyscrapers and housing projects, limiting individual choices by others.
Symbolic Interactionist: The Experience of City Life		
Simmel	View of City Life	Due to the intensity of city life, people become somewhat insensitive to individuals and events around them.
Wirth	Urbanism as a Way of Life	The size, density, and heterogeneity of urban population result in elaborate division of labour and space.
Gans	Urban Villagers	Five categories of adaptation occur among urban dwellers, ranging from cosmopolites to trapped city dwellers.
Feminist		
Appleton	Gender Regimes in Cities	Different cities have different prevailing ideologies regarding access to social positions and resources for men and women.
Wilson, Michelson	Gender and City Life	Cities offer women a paradox: more freedom, yet greater potential danger.
Postmodern		
Dear and Flusty	Decentred Cities	The postmodern city has many centres with low density and urban sprawl. They have more private space and greater diversity. They are becoming centres for consuming and entertainment.
Hannigan	Fantasy City	City planners have attempted to bring people back to the city centre by establishing urban entertainment districts that often include branded, risk-free attractions.

expected to have a combined population of about 40 million people living in a 500-kilometre-long *megalopolis*—**a continuous concentration of two or more cities and their suburbs that have grown until they form an interconnected urban area** (Petersen, 1994). These huge cities will have a profound impact on the environment because of air pollution, greenhouse gas emissions, sewage and waste disposal, and water consumption.

The speed of social change means that areas that we currently think of as being relatively free from such problems will be characterized by depletion of natural resources and greater air and water pollution (see Ehrlich and Ehrlich, 1991). At the same time, if social and environmental problems become too great in one nation, those who can afford it may simply move to another country. For example, many affluent residents of Hong Kong acquired business interests and houses in the United States, Canada, and other countries before Hong Kong's reversion to China in 1997. As people become "world citizens" in this way, their lives are not linked to the stability of any one city or nation. However, this option is limited only to the wealthiest of citizens.

In a best-case scenario for the future, the problems brought about by rapid population growth in low income nations will be remedied by new technologies that make goods readily available to people. International trade agreements, such as NAFTA (the North American Free Trade Agreement) and GATT (the General Agreement on Tariffs and Trade), will remove trade barriers and make it possible for all nations to engage fully in global trade. People in developing nations will benefit by gaining jobs and opportunities to purchase goods at lower prices. Of course, the opposite also may occur: people may be exploited as inexpensive labour, and their country's natural resources may be depleted as transnational corporations buy up raw materials without contributing to the long-term economic stability of the nation.

In the longer term, global population growth may not be as great a problem as some had feared. Fertility rates have dropped dramatically in most countries, and in all industrialized countries except the United States they are now far below the replacement level of 2.1 children per family. Spain now has a fertility rate of 1.1 children per family (down from 2.8 in 1978), Italy of 1.2, France and Germany of 1.3, and Canada of 1.5. The rate in the United States is just above the replacement level, at 2.13. This means that without dramatically increased rates of immigration, the population will fall in these countries (except the United States). According to the United Nations (2005b), by 2050 the population in 51 countries, including Germany, Italy, and Japan, will be lower than it was in 2005. While we know that fertility rates have also dropped significantly in poorer countries, they have not stabilized and we do not know how low they will drop. Some demographers believe that rates will continue to decline until most countries are below replacement level. This would mean that eventually the world's population could begin to decline.

While we cannot predict future trends with any degree of certainty, we do know that even if population growth stabilizes or begins to decline by the middle of this century, increased standards of living around the world will continue to be a drain on the earth's resources. People in industrialized countries use far more water, energy, and other natural resources than their poorer counterparts in other countries. Thus it seems inevitable that environmental issues will become more important in the future, even if population growth does not continue.

Some futurists predict that environmental activism will increase dramatically as people see irreversible changes in the atmosphere and experience first-hand the effects of environmental hazards and pollution on their own health and well-being. These environmental problems will cause a realization that overpopulation is a world problem, a problem that will be most apparent in the world's weakest economies and most fragile ecosystems. Futurists suggest that we must "leave the old ways and invent new ones" (Petersen, 1994:340). What aspects of our "old ways" do you think we should discard? Can you help invent new ways?

CHAPTER REVIEW

■ What is demography?

Demography is the study of the size, composition, and distribution of the population.

■ What demographic processes result in population change?

Population change is the result of fertility (births), mortality (deaths), and migration.

■ What is the Malthusian perspective?

More than two hundred years ago, Thomas Malthus warned that overpopulation would result in poverty, starvation, and other major problems that would limit the size of the population. According to Malthus, the population would increase geometrically, while the food supply would increase only arithmetically, resulting in poverty and a critical food shortage.

■ **What are the views of Karl Marx and the neo-Malthusians on overpopulation?**

According to Karl Marx, poverty is the result of capitalist greed, not overpopulation. More recently, neo-Malthusians have re-emphasized the dangers of overpopulation and encouraged zero population growth—the point at which no population increase occurs from year to year.

■ **What are the stages in demographic transition theory?**

Demographic transition theory links population growth to four stages of economic development: (1) the preindustrial stage, with high birth rates and death rates, (2) early industrialization, with relatively high birth rates and a decline in death rates, (3) advanced industrialization and urbanization, with low birth rates and death rates, and (4) postindustrialization, with additional decreases in the birth rate coupled with a stable death rate.

■ **What is the political economy/conflict perspective on urban growth?**

According to political economy models/conflict perspectives, urban growth is influenced by capital investment decisions, power and resource inequality, class and class conflict, and government subsidy programs.

■ **What is the feminist perspective on urbanization?**

Feminists feel that different cities have different gender regimes—prevailing ideologies of how women and men should think, feel, and act; how access to social positions and control of resources should be managed; and how relationships between men and women should be conducted.

■ **How do symbolic interactionists view urban life?**

Symbolic interactionist perspectives focus on how people experience urban life. Some analysts view the urban experience positively; others believe that urban dwellers become insensitive to events and people around them.

■ **How do postmodernist theorists view city life?**

The postmodern city has many centres because of low density and urban sprawl; it has more private space and greater diversity. Some cities are trying to attract people back to the city centres by establishing urban entertainment districts.

KEY TERMS

NET LINKS

Watch the world's population grow on the World Population Clock:
http://opr.princeton.edu/popclock/

To look up demographic information on births, deaths, and infant mortality, go to the World Factbook at:
http://www.odci.gov/cia/publications/ factbook/

For the latest revision to world population estimates, go to:
http://www.un.org/popin/

For information about the United Nations' Sustainable Cities Program see:
http://www.unchs.org/programmes/ sustainablecities/

QUESTIONS FOR CRITICAL THINKING

1. What impact does a high rate of immigration have on culture and personal identity in Canada?
2. If you were designing a study of growth patterns for the city in which you live (or one you know well), which theoretical model(s) would provide the most useful framework for your analysis?
3. What do you think everyday life in Canadian cities, suburbs, and rural areas will be like in 2020? Where would you prefer to live? What,

if anything, does your answer reflect about the future of our cities?

4. How do you think the aging baby boomers will change Canadian society over the next twenty years? How will these developments compare with a country, such as Iran, that has a much younger population?

SUGGESTED READINGS

These texts provide in-depth information on the topics in this chapter:

Roderic Beaujot. *Population Change in Canada: The Challenges of Policy Adaptation.* Toronto: McClelland and Stewart, 1991.

Harry Hiller. *Urban Canada: Sociological Perspectives.* Don Mills: Oxford University Press, 2005.

Peter McGahan. *Urban Sociology in Canada* (3rd ed.). Toronto: Harcourt Brace, 1995.

Wayne W. McVey Jr. and Warren E. Kalbach. *Canadian Population.* Scarborough: Nelson Canada, 1995.

The following books discuss global overpopulation and urban growth issues:

Paul Ehrlich and Anne Ehrlich. *The Population Explosion.* New York: Touchstone/Simon & Schuster, 1991.

Thomas Homer-Dixon. *Environmental Scarcity and Global Security.* Foreign Policy Association, Headline Series, Number 300. Ephrata, Penn.: Science Press, 1993.

World Resources Institute. *World Resources 1996–97.* Washington: World Resources Institute, 1996.

ONLINE STUDY AND RESEARCH TOOLS

THOMSONNOW™ Thomson NOW!

Go to **http://hed.nelson.com** to link to ThomsonNOW for *Sociology in Our Times,* Fourth Canadian Edition, your online study tool. First take the **Pre-Test** for this chapter to get your personalized **Study Plan,** which will identify topics you need to review and direct you to the appropriate resources. Then take the **Post-Test** to determine what concepts you have mastered and what you still need work on.

INFOTRAC®

Infotrac College Edition is included free with every new copy of this text. Explore this online library for additional readings, review, and a handy resource for assignments. Visit **www.infotrac-college.com** to access this online database of full-text articles. Enter the key terms from this chapter to start your search.

CHAPTER 20

Collective Behaviour

Brett Solomon is coordinator of the International Youth Parliament, Community Aid Abroad in Australia. He shares his thoughts on activism and social change:

"Five years ago I began working at Oxfam Community Aid Abroad. It was there I developed the idea of the International Youth Parliament (IYP). IYP is an international forum where hundreds of young people from over 150 countries exchange ideas, strategies, and the implementations of their Action Plans. These Action Plans were developed in working groups at IYP 2000, when all of the Action Partners converged on Sydney for the first meeting of the Parliament.

"I have spent a lot of time overseas and seen the many ways people, particularly the young, live in poverty without the ability to influence the direction of their lives. This was, and remains to be, of grave concern to me. I knew that to effect social change, civil society had to be involved on the ground; that change had to come from the bottom, and that young people had to be involved in this change.

"I believe the current state of the globe is not inevitable. It is the result of decisions made by institutions, national governments, corporations and individuals. IYP gives young people the tools to work with their peers from around the world and effect change at the grassroots level. There

is a dynamic environment of dialogue among IYP Action Partners, dealing with issues ranging from young people and AIDS in Africa, to labour conditions in Indonesia. Nothing is unworthy of discussion.

"In so many societies, at home and abroad, youth are silenced or overlooked because of culture or myths about their involvement in development and governance. But young people have rights; foremost, to an education, a livelihood, to health care and to freedom of association. But also young people have the right to be involved as part of the solution, not the problem.

"Effective Development is a complex process in which young people's voices and actions for positive social change are necessary, or things will continue as in the past. If we don't change direction, we will end up where we are headed.

"My vision is a world without poverty in which people, particularly young people, have rights that are respected and implemented. It is about economic and social rights, as well as cultural and political rights. Where they have the power to express their own political voice and have access to education and medicine. A world

where a young woman working in a factory has a job that provides for a sustainable life. A world in which not only the rich, but the broader population, have access to fresh water, not because they can pay for it, but because it is their right as citizens of the world. I also envision a world in which difference is respected and celebrated" (Greenpeace, 2005).

Like other nations, Canada has a long history of positive social change resulting from grassroots activism. Over the past century, continuing streams of progressive grassroots movements have contested capitalist exploitation and other forms of oppression in Canada, and mobilized for greater human rights. The first half of the century saw the democratic demands of trades workers for collective-bargaining rights, suffragettes for women's rights, farmers for cooperative marketing, and popular educators for public broadcasting. These movements played key roles in shaping the political culture of the last half-century. The diversity we experience today in this country is a product of these past social movements (Livingston, 2002).

More recently, we have seen images in the news of controversial responses to acts of various protest groups. In 1990, Native American Mohawks and the Canadian Armed Forces engaged in a two-and-a-half-month armed standoff in a confrontation over Native land claims in Oka, Quebec. In 1993, Clayoquot Sound became a high-profile battleground in which the logging industry was pitted against a coalition of environmental groups. In 1997, at the Asia–Pacific Economic Cooperation (APEC) summit, student protesters at the University of British Columbia were pepper-sprayed by police. In 2003, a weekend of worldwide anti-war demonstrations brought millions of people throughout the world to the streets in support of a peaceful solution to the crisis between Iraq and the United States. The individuals involved in all of these incidents are social activists in one form or another. What they all have in common is their pursuit of social change. ***Social change*** **is the alteration, modification, or transformation of public policy, culture, or social institutions over time;** such change is usually brought about by collective behaviour and social movements.

In this chapter, we will discuss collective behaviour, social movements, and social change. Throughout the chapter, we will use environmental activism as an example of all three topics. Before reading on, test your knowledge about collective behaviour, social change, and environmental issues by taking the quiz in Box 20.1.

QUESTIONS AND ISSUES

Chapter Focus Question: Can collective behaviour and social movements make people aware of important social issues, such as environmental issues, workers' rights, and social justice?

What causes people to engage in collective behaviour?

What are some common forms of collective behaviour?

How can different types of social movements be distinguished from one another?

What draws people into social movements?

What factors contribute to social change?

In 2003, between six and ten million people are thought to have marched for peace in up to sixty countries—the largest demonstrations of their kind since the Vietnam War.

COLLECTIVE BEHAVIOUR

Collective behaviour is voluntary, often spontaneous activity that is engaged in by a large number of people and typically violates dominant group norms and values. Unlike the *organizational behaviour* found in corporations and voluntary associations (such as labour unions and environmental organizations), collective behaviour lacks an official division of labour, hierarchy of authority, and established rules and procedures. Unlike *institutional behaviour* (in education, religion, or politics, for example), it lacks institutionalized norms to govern behaviour. Collective behaviour can take various forms, including crowds, mobs, riots, panics, fads, fashions, and public opinion.

According to Steven M. Buechler (2000), early sociologists studied collective behaviour because they lived in a world that was responding to the processes of modernization, including urbanization, industrialization, and proletarianization of workers. Contemporary forms of collective behaviour, particularly social protests, are variations on themes that originated during the transition from feudalism to capitalism and the rise of modernity in Europe (Buechler, 2000). Today, some forms of collective behaviour and social movements are directed toward public issues, such as air pollution, water pollution, and the exploitation of workers in global sweatshops by transnational corporations (see Shaw, 1999).

Conditions for Collective Behaviour

Collective behaviour occurs as a result of some common influence or stimulus that produces a response from a collectivity. A *collectivity* is a relatively large number of people who mutually transcend, bypass, or subvert established institutional patterns and structures. Three major factors contribute to the likelihood that collective behaviour will occur: (1) structural factors that increase the chances of people responding in a particular way, (2) timing, and (3) a breakdown in social control mechanisms and a corresponding feeling of normlessness (McPhail, 1991; Turner and Killian, 1993). A common stimulus is an important factor. For example, in the case of Clayoquot Sound, the issue of clear-cut logging was part of a larger issue of environmental destruction. In the words of one commentator, "Clayoquot is a symbol, a cause, one of those local battles that becomes a flashpoint of a larger war" (Fulton and Mather, 1993:20). The clear-cut logging issue came at

BOX 20.1 SOCIOLOGY AND EVERYDAY LIFE

How Much Do You Know About Collective Behaviour, Social Movements, and Social Change?

True	False	
T	F	1. The environmental movement in North America started in the 1960s.
T	F	2. A number of social movements in North America are becoming globalized.
T	F	3. Environmental groups may engage in civil disobedience or use symbolic gestures to call attention to their issue.
T	F	4. People are most likely to believe rumours when no other information is readily available on a topic.
T	F	5. Influencing public opinion is a very important activity for many social movements.
T	F	6. Social movements are more likely to flourish in democratic societies.
T	F	7. Most social movements in Canada seek to improve society by changing some specific aspect of the social structure.
T	F	8. Policing agencies have become more aggressive in the past decade in their response to protest movements engaging in civil disobedience.

Answers on page 630.

a time when people were becoming more concerned about social issues and beginning to see that they could empower themselves through grassroots activism. Similarly, protest was inevitable at the FTAA Summit in Quebec. The exclusive focus on economic issues made it an obvious target for protesters increasingly concerned about the human rights and social costs of economic globalization.

Timing and a breakdown in social control mechanisms also are important in collective behaviour. Since the 1960s, most urban riots in Canada and the United States have begun in the evenings or on weekends when most people are off work (McPhail, 1971). For example, the 1992 Los Angeles riots erupted in the evening after the verdict in the Rodney King beating trial had been announced. As rioting, looting, and arson began to take a toll on certain areas of Los Angeles, a temporary breakdown in formal social

control mechanisms occurred. In some areas of the city, law enforcement was inadequate to quell the illegal actions of rioters, some of whom began to believe that the rules had been suspended. In the aftermath of the riot in Montreal following their 1993 Stanley Cup victory, the Montreal Canadiens were protected by hundreds of police officers and a riot squad in an effort to prevent any further breakdown of social control. Similarly, hundreds of protesters were arrested in Quebec City in what law-enforcement personnel indicated was an effort to prevent any breakdown in social control.

Dynamics of Collective Behaviour

To better understand the dynamics of collective behaviour, let us briefly examine three basic questions. First, how do people come to transcend, bypass,

BOX 20.1 SOCIOLOGY AND EVERYDAY LIFE

Answers to the Sociology Quiz on Collective Behaviour, Social Movements, and Social Change

1. False. The environmental movement in North America is the result of more than 100 years of collective action. The first environmental organization in North America was the American Forestry Association (now American Forests), which originated in 1875 (Worster, 1985).

2. True. For example, protestors at the second People's Summit of the Americas included voices of unions, environmental organizations, women's groups, human rights organizations, indigenous groups, and student associations from all over the world (Ericson and Doyle, 1999).

3. True. Environmental groups have held sit-ins, marches, boycotts, and strikes, which sometimes take the form of civil disobedience (Marx and McAdam, 1994).

4. True. Rumours are most likely to emerge and circulate when people have very little information on a topic that is important to them. For example, rumours abound in times of technological disasters when people are fearful and often willing to believe the worst.

5. True. Many social movements, including grassroots environmental activism, attempt to influence public opinion so that local decision makers will feel obliged to correct a specific problem through changes in public policy (Adams, 1991).

6. True. Having a democratic process available is important for dissenters. Grassroots movements have utilized the democratic process to bring about change even when elites have sought to discourage such activism (Adams, 1991).

7. True. Most social movements are reform movements that focus on improving society by changing some specific aspect of the social structure. Examples include human rights movements and the disability rights movement (Marx and McAdams, 1994).

8. True. Recent incidents involving aggressive police tactics to control nonviolent protesters at the APEC Summit in Vancouver in 1997 and the Summit of the Americas in Quebec City in 2001 clearly demonstrated this fact (Ericson and Doyle, 1999).

or subvert established institutional patterns and structures? The Friends of Clayoquot Sound initially tried to work within established means through provincial government environment officials. However, they quickly learned that their problems were not being solved through these channels; as the problem appeared to grow worse, organizational responses became more defensive and obscure. Accordingly, some activists began acting outside of established norms by holding protests, establishing blockades, and (on one occasion) storming the B.C. legislature and almost breaking into the assembly. Some situations are more conducive to collective behaviour than others. When people can communicate quickly and easily with one another, spontaneous behaviour is more likely (Turner and Killian, 1993). When people are gathered together in one general location (whether lining the streets or assembled in a stadium), they are more likely to respond to a common stimulus.

Second, how do people's actions compare with their attitudes? People's attitudes (as expressed in public opinion surveys, for instance) are not always reflected in their political and social behaviour. Issues pertaining to the environment are no exception. For example, people may indicate in survey research that they believe the quality of the environment is very important, but the same people may not turn out on election day to support propositions that protect the environment or candidates who promise to focus on environmental issues. Likewise, individuals who indicate on a questionnaire that they are concerned about increases in ground-level ozone—the primary component of urban smog—often drive single-occupant, oversized vehicles that government studies have shown to be "gas guzzlers" that contribute to lowered air quality in urban areas. As a result, smog levels increase, contributing to human respiratory problems and dramatically reduced agricultural crop yields (Voynick, 1999).

Third, why do people act collectively rather than independently? As sociologists Ralph H. Turner and Lewis M. Killian (1993:12) note, people believe that there is strength in numbers: "the rhythmic stamping of feet by hundreds of concert-goers in unison is different from isolated, individual cries of 'bravo.'" Likewise, people may act as a collectivity when they believe it is the only way to fight those with greater power and resources. Collective behaviour is not just the sum of a large number of individuals acting at the same time; rather, it reflects people's joint response to some common influence or stimulus.

Distinctions Regarding Collective Behaviour

People engaging in collective behaviour may be divided into crowds and masses. A *crowd* is a relatively large number of people who are in one another's immediate vicinity (Lofland, 1993). In contrast, a *mass* is a large number of people who share an interest in a specific idea or issue but who are not in one another's immediate vicinity (Lofland, 1993). To further distinguish between crowds and masses, think of the difference between a riot and a rumour: people who participate in a riot must be in the same general location; those who spread a rumour may be thousands of kilometres apart, communicating by telephone or through the Internet.

Collective behaviour also may be distinguished by the dominant emotion expressed. According to sociologist John Lofland (1993:72), the *dominant emotion* refers to the "publicly expressed feeling perceived by participants and observers as the most prominent in an episode of collective behaviour." Lofland suggests that fear, hostility, and joy are three fundamental emotions found in collective behaviour; however, grief, disgust, surprise, or shame also may predominate in some forms of collective behaviour.

Types of Crowd Behaviour

When we think of a crowd, many of us think of *aggregates,* previously defined as a collection of people who happen to be in the same place at the same time but who have little else in common. However, the presence of a relatively large number of people in the same location does not necessarily produce collective behaviour. Sociologist Herbert Blumer (1946) developed a typology in which crowds are divided into four categories: casual, conventional, expressive, and acting. Other scholars have added a fifth category, protest crowds.

Casual and Conventional Crowds   *Casual crowds* are relatively large gatherings of people who happen to be in the same place at the same time; if they interact at all, it is only briefly. People in a shopping mall or on a bus are examples of casual crowds. Other than sharing a momentary interest, such as a watching a busker perform on the street or observing the aftermath of a car accident, a casual crowd has nothing in common. The casual crowd plays no active part in the event—such as the car accident—which

would have occurred whether or not the crowd was present; it simply observes.

Conventional crowds are made up of people who specifically come together for a scheduled event and thus share a common focus. Examples include religious services, graduation ceremonies, concerts, and university lectures. Each of these events has established schedules and norms. Because these events occur regularly, interaction among participants is much more likely; in turn, the events would not occur without the crowd, which is essential to the event.

Expressive and Acting Crowds

Expressive crowds provide opportunities for the expression of some strong emotion (such as joy, excitement, or grief). People release their pent-up emotions in conjunction with other persons experiencing similar emotions. Examples include worshippers at religious revival services; mourners lining the streets when a celebrity, public official, or religious leader has died; and nonrioting crowds at a sporting event.

Acting crowds are collectivities so intensely focused on a specific purpose or object that they may erupt into violent or destructive behaviour. Mobs, riots, and panics are examples of acting crowds, but casual and conventional crowds may become acting crowds under some circumstances. A *mob* **is a highly emotional crowd whose members engage in, or are ready to engage in, violence against a specific target—a person, a category of people, or physical property.** Mob behaviour in this country has included fire bombings, effigy hangings, and hate crimes. Mob violence tends to dissipate relatively

Sometimes acts of civil disobedience become violent even though it is not the intent of the parties involved. During what is referred to as the Oka crisis, a police officer was shot and killed and several people on both sides of the blockade were injured.

quickly once a target has been injured, killed, or destroyed. Sometimes, actions, such as effigy hanging, are used symbolically by groups that otherwise are not violent. For example, during the 1990 Oka crisis on the Kanehsatake reserve in Quebec, local non-Aboriginal residents burned an effigy of a Mohawk to emphasize their displeasure with the blockade of the Mercier Bridge to Montreal.

Compared with mob action, riots may be of somewhat longer duration. A *riot* **is violent crowd behaviour that is fuelled by deep-seated emotions but not directed at one specific target.** Riots often are triggered by fear, anger, and hostility; however, not all riots are caused by deep-seated hostility and hatred. People may be expressing joy and exuberance when rioting occurs. Examples include celebrations after sports victories, such as those that occurred in Montreal following a Stanley Cup win and in Vancouver following a playoff victory.

A *panic* **is a form of crowd behaviour that occurs when a large number of people react to a real or perceived threat with strong emotions and self-destructive behaviour.** The most common type of panic, known as entrapment, occurs when people seek to escape from a perceived danger, fearing that few (if any) of them will be able to get away from that danger. For example, in 1994 a firebomb on a New York City subway engulfed a car in flames. Many people were knocked to the ground by the crush of people (Gonzales, 1994). Panic sometimes occurs, however, when people attempt to gain access to an event or a location, as was the case at a concert by the British rock group The Who in Cincinnati in 1979. Seating was on a first-come, first-served basis, and when the doors opened people surged into the arena and began to fall over one another. Unaware of the press of bodies in front of them, those farther back heard the band warming up and began to panic for fear that they would not get a seat. This type of panic is referred to as *exclusion panic*. When people started to realize what was happening, they experienced an overwhelming emotion of fear. Eleven people were killed in the ensuing pile-up.

Panic also can arise in response to events that people believe are beyond their control—such as a major disruption in the economy. Although instances of panic are relatively rare, they receive massive media coverage because they provoke strong feelings of fear in readers and viewers, and the number of casualties may be large.

Protest Crowds

Sociologists Clark McPhail and Ronald T. Wohlstein (1983) added protest crowds to the four types of crowds identified by Blumer. *Protest*

Convergence theory is based on the assumption that crowd behaviour involves shared emotions, goals, and beliefs. An example is the Anti-War Protest held in locations throughout the world on the anniversary of the war in Iraq, which was attended by thousands of people.

crowds engage in activities intended to achieve specific political goals. Examples include sit-ins, marches, boycotts, blockades, and strikes. Some protests sometimes take the form of **civil disobedience—nonviolent action that seeks to change a policy or law by refusing to comply with it.** Acts of civil disobedience may become violent, as in a confrontation between protesters and police officers; in this case, a protest crowd becomes an *acting crowd*. Such was the case in Quebec when protestors tore down a section of the chainlink fence built to protect visiting heads of state. Apparently, some protests can escalate into violent confrontations even though that is not the intent of the organizers (see Box 20.2).

As you will recall, collective action often puts individuals in the position of doing things as a group that they would not do on their own. Does this mean that people's actions are produced by some type of "herd mentality"? Some analysts have answered this question affirmatively; however, sociologists typically do not agree with that assessment.

Explanations of Crowd Behaviour

What causes people to act collectively? How do they determine what types of action to take? One of the earliest theorists to provide an answer to these questions was Gustave Le Bon, a French scholar who focused on crowd psychology in his contagion theory.

Contagion Theory
Contagion theory focuses on the social–psychological aspects of collective behaviour; it attempts to explain how moods, attitudes, and behaviour are communicated rapidly and why

they are accepted by others (Turner and Killian, 1993). Le Bon (1841–1931) argued that people are more likely to engage in antisocial behaviour in a crowd because they are anonymous and feel invulnerable. Le Bon (1960/1895) suggested that a crowd takes on a life of its own that is larger than the beliefs or actions of any one person. Because of its anonymity, the crowd transforms individuals from rational beings into a single organism with a collective mind. In essence, Le Bon asserted that emotions, such as fear and hate, are contagious in crowds because people experience a decline in personal responsibility; they will do things as a collectivity that they would never do when acting alone.

Le Bon's theory is still used to explain crowd behaviour. However, critics argue that the "collective mind" has not been documented by systematic studies.

Social Unrest and Circular Reaction
Robert E. Park was the first U.S. sociologist to investigate crowd behaviour. Park believed that Le Bon's analysis of collective behaviour lacked several important elements. Intrigued that people could break away from the powerful hold of culture and their established routines to develop a new social order, Park added the concepts of social unrest and circular reaction to contagion theory. According to Park, social unrest is transmitted by a process of *circular reaction*—the interactive communication between persons such that the discontent of one person is communicated to another who, in turn, reflects the discontent back to the first person (Park and Burgess, 1921).

BOX 20.2 CRITICAL THINKING

Coercive Policing of Protest Movements: Summit of the Americas, Quebec City, 2001; APEC, Vancouver, 1997

From April 20 to 22, 2001, the Summit of the Americas was held in Quebec City. The focus of the summit, which was attended by thirty-four heads of state, was the eventual implementation of the Free Trade Area of the Americas (FTAA). The FTAA promises to extend the North American Free Trade Agreement (NAFTA) to the entire Western hemisphere, further widening inequality between and within countries. In response to the somewhat clandestine negotiating process of the FTAA and to its potential harmful effects on the environment, human rights, health, education, and labour, thousands of protesters converged on the city to voice their opposition.

In preparation for this protest, Canadian authorities organized the largest deployment of police in recent history. This show of force included four levels of police and the armed forces, totalling nearly ten thousand officers. A three-metre-high, 3.8-kilometre-long concrete and chainlink fence, which would later come to be known as the wall of shame, was built around the downtown core of Quebec City to protect the delegates. The cost of security operations was estimated to have exceeded $100 million.

It comes as no surprise that these security measures resulted in many clashes between the protesters and the police at or near the fence. From Friday, April 20, through Sunday, April 22, police discharged more than 5,000 tear gas canisters on people in the streets and fired more than 900 rubber and plastic bullets into crowds or directly at individuals, often at close range (Chang et al., 2001). Following are the recollections of one of the protesters:

> So many little things stick out in my mind about what happened on the streets of Quebec City. I'll never be able to forget the face of the riot cop who stepped out of formation shooting a tear gas canister, point blank, into the lap of a mediating man or the medic who held my hand as I walked in a daze through a cloud of tear gas. I'll never forget the couch that was set on fire and the ten-storey-high cloud of tear gas that rained down afterwards. I probably won't be allowed to forget the plastic bullet that hit me in the leg, nearly breaking it. I'll also never forget the camaraderie and

> love I felt from all those people out in the streets; as my friend Nicola described it, I now trust punks dressed all in black more than I trust the cops. And I won't let myself forget the reason I was out there—to stop the FTAA; to stop exploitation of the earth, of indigenous peoples, of workers ....
>
> It started off so peacefully, about a hundred of us sitting in the alley (Cote Ste-Genevieve, I think) in front of a section of the fence that had been torn down. My friend Sokia and I were talking about leaving, seeing if anything exciting was happening at Cote d'Abraham. And then the police advanced. Sokia and I screamed at people to sit down and link arms but everybody ran. We just sat there with our arms linked. The RCMP shot off what they called smoke bombs, but I never felt smoke that burned like pepper spray. They yelled at us to move. We refused. They dragged us away from the gate. Sokia jumped on top of me in case they started beating us. I just screamed. They shocked him with a stun gun while he was still on top of me, and then they took him away ... They did everything they could to make me forget I was human, to make me feel worthless, to make me turn my back on my principles. Though they tried to break us, we all have come out stronger, more militant and more dedicated to changing the world. When will they learn? (Liberty, 2001:103-106)

On November 27, 1997, eighteen heads of state met in Vancouver for the fifth Asia–Pacific Economic Cooperation (APEC) Summit. The event at the University of British Columbia campus was a celebration of economic globalization, or "free and open trade and investment" in the Pacific region. Also present at this event were "antiglobalization" groups protesting human rights and welfare problems involving several of the participating countries. It was this "civil disobedience" and the response of the police in controlling the protesters that became the focus of a national incident, an incident that precipitated a public inquiry and an ongoing public debate regarding the increasingly coercive styles of policing protests.

What happened at this particular event? About 3,000 protesters gathered on the UBC campus as the APEC representatives met. Some of the protesters attempted to scale a chainlink fence and were pepper-sprayed. The protesters then agreed to allow some of their members to be arrested, voluntarily. At the end of the APEC leaders' meeting, one of the motorcade routes was blocked by a group of protesters sitting across the roadway. The news media captured the RCMP officer (now euphemistically referred to as Sergeant Pepper) in charge of removing the protesters warning them:

> "Ladies and gentlemen, my name's Staff-Sergeant Stewart. I am clearing this roadway. You have one opportunity to move up that road and clear it off, or you will be arrested. I am going to use force, whatever force I deem necessary. I do not intend to fool around. I intend to clear this road, and I intend to clear it now. Put the dogs on the side. You are going that way!" (CBC, 1997)

Immediately following this warning, the officer began pepper-spraying the protesters who were already complying with his command and dispersing. He also pepper-sprayed a CBC cameraman in the face and then proceeded to cover his camera lens to prevent any further filming. Dozens of protesters, mostly students, were injured, along with several journalists. According to one news source, "Police used their bicycles as battering rams and charged into the crowd, spraying everyone within range" (Ericson and Doyle, 1999).

Not surprisingly, these incidents became the focus of a media circus. The dramatic coverage of the incidents that appeared on the news shocked Canadians. The use of pepper-spray to attack nonviolent protesters seemed un-Canadian. It looked more like something that police in less democratic countries would do (Pue, 2000). Following the events in Quebec City several lawsuits were filed against the RCMP, the prime minister, and the government of Canada addressing numerous violations—freedom of expression, liberty, and security, the right not to be arbitrarily detained, the right to be protected from assault and wrongful arrest, and freedom from defamation. A formal inquiry was conducted by the RCMP Public Complaints Commission that lasted several months and cost taxpayers millions of dollars (Ericson and Doyle, 1999).

There was, however, a less obvious and certainly unintended result of the attempts by police to suppress these non-violent protests, one that is alluded to in the narrative at the beginning of this chapter. When police and the state attempt to repress a protest using coercive methods, they may in fact serve to escalate, solidify, and promote the organization of social movements. As social activist Mick Lowe (2002:4) explains in his discussion of the antiglobalization movement:

> The movement is galvanized by overt suppression. Far from intimidating veterans and discouraging newcomers, every rubber bullet fired, every swing of the police truncheon serves to stimulate the growth of the still fledgling movement. Police over-reaction, real or perceived, becomes our most valuable recruiting tool, it is like pouring water over a grease fire.

Not only are social movements promoted nationally, but, as sociologists Richard Ericson and Aaron Doyle conclude in their extensive case analysis of the events at the APEC Summit, the publicity over the attempted repression of protest at international events such as this can also serve to fuel the globalization of social movements. As they explain, "mass-mediated dramatizations of the repression of international protest may help tie together the concerns of publics dispersed around the globe, and fuel the increasing globalization of social movements" (Ericson and Doyle, 1999:603).

Given the aggressive response to the protesters witnessed by the Canadian public, it comes as no surprise that many citizens may choose not to participate in social protest movements. How far do you think you would be prepared to go in support of a social movement that is important to you? Would you risk assault? detention? criminal conviction?

Convergence Theory   *Convergence theory* focuses on the shared emotions, goals, and beliefs many people bring to crowd behaviour. Because of their individual characteristics, many people have a predisposition to participate in certain types of activities (Turner and Killian, 1993). From this perspective, people with similar attributes find a collectivity of like-minded persons with whom they can express their underlying personal tendencies. Although people may reveal their "true selves" in crowds, their behaviour is not irrational; it is highly predictable to those who share similar emotions or beliefs.

Convergence theory has been applied to a wide array of conduct, from lynch mobs to environmental movements. In social psychologist Hadley Cantril's (1941) study of a lynching in the United States, he found that the participants shared certain common attributes: they were poor and working-class whites who felt that their own status was threatened by the presence of successful African Americans. Consequently, the characteristics of these individuals made them susceptible to joining a lynch mob even if they did not know the target of the lynching.

Convergence theory adds to our understanding of certain types of collective behaviour by pointing out how individuals may have certain attributes—such as racial hatred or fear of environmental problems that directly threaten them—that initially bring them together. However, this perspective does not explain how the attitudes and characteristics of individuals who take some collective action differ from those who do not.

Emergent Norm Theory   Unlike contagion and convergence theories, *emergent norm theory* emphasizes the importance of social norms in shaping crowd behaviour. Drawing on the interactionist perspective, sociologists Ralph Turner and Lewis Killian (1993:12) asserted that crowds develop their own definition of a situation and establish norms for behaviour that fit the occasion:

> Some shared redefinition of right and wrong in a situation supplies the justification and coordinates the action in collective behaviour. People do what they would not otherwise have done when they panic collectively, when they riot, when they engage in civil disobedience, or when they launch terrorist campaigns, because they find social support for the view that what they are doing is the right thing to do in the situation.

According to Turner and Killian (1993:13), emergent norms occur when people define a new situation as highly unusual or see a longstanding situation in a new light.

Sociologists use the emergent-norm approach to determine how individuals in a given collectivity develop an understanding of what is going on, how they construe these activities, and what type of norms are involved. For example, in a study of audience participation, sociologist Steven E. Clayman (1993) found that members of an audience listening to a speech applaud promptly and independently but wait to coordinate their booing with other people; they do not wish to "boo" alone.

Some emergent norms are permissive—that is, they give people a shared conviction that they may disregard ordinary rules, such as waiting in line, taking turns, or treating a speaker courteously. Collective activity, such as mass looting, may be defined (by participants) as taking what rightfully belongs to them and punishing those who have been exploitative. For example, following the Los Angeles riots of 1992, some analysts argued that Korean Americans were targets of rioters because they were viewed by Latinos and African Americans as "callous and greedy invaders" who became wealthy at the expense of members of other racial–ethnic groups (Cho, 1993). Thus, rioters who used this rationalization could view looting and burning as a means of "paying back" Korean Americans or of gaining property (such as TV sets and microwave ovens) from those who had already taken from them. Once a crowd reaches some agreement on the norms, the collectivity is supposed to adhere to them. If crowd members develop a norm that condones looting or vandalizing property, they will proceed to cheer for those who conform and ridicule those who are unwilling to abide by the collectivity's new norms.

Emergent-norm theory points out that crowds are not irrational. Rather, new norms are developed in a rational way to fit the needs of the immediate situation. However, critics note that proponents of this perspective fail to specify exactly what constitutes a norm, how new ones emerge, and how they are so quickly disseminated and accepted by a wide variety of participants. One variation of this theory suggests that no single dominant norm is accepted by everyone in a crowd; instead, norms are specific to the various categories of actors rather than to the collectivity as a whole (Snow, Zurcher, and Peters, 1981). For example, in a study of football victory celebrations, sociologists David Snow, Louis Zurcher, and Robert Peters (1981) found that each week

What type of crowd behaviour occurred during the tragic flooding in New Orleans? Which explanation of crowd behaviour would you use to explain what occurred?

behavioural patterns were changed in the postgame revelry, with some being modified, some added, and some deleted.

Mass Behaviour

Not all collective behaviour takes place in face-to-face collectivities. *Mass behaviour* **is collective behaviour that takes place when people (who often are geographically separated from one another) respond to the same event in much the same way.** For people to respond in the same way, they typically have common sources of information, and this information provokes their collective behaviour. The most frequent types of mass behaviour are rumours, gossip, mass hysteria, fads, fashions, and public opinion. Under some circumstances, social movements constitute a form of mass behaviour. However, we will examine social movements separately because they differ in some important ways from other types of dispersed collectivities.

Rumours and Gossip   *Rumours* **are unsubstantiated reports on an issue or subject** (Rosnow and Fine, 1976). Rumours may spread through an assembled collectivity, but they may also be transmitted among people who are dispersed geographically. Although they may initially contain a kernel of truth, as they spread, rumours may be modified to serve the interests of those repeating them. Rumours thrive when tensions are high and little authentic information is available on an issue of great concern.

People are willing to give rumours credence when no offsetting information is available. Once rumours begin to circulate, they seldom stop unless compelling information comes to the forefront that either proves the rumour false or makes it obsolete.

In industrialized societies with sophisticated technology, rumours come from a wide variety of sources and may be difficult to trace. Print media (newspapers and magazines) and electronic media (radio and television), fax machines, cellular networks, satellite systems, and the Internet facilitate the rapid movement of rumours around the globe. In addition, modern communications technology makes anonymity much easier. In a split second, messages (both factual and fictitious) can be disseminated to thousands of people through e-mail, computerized bulletin boards, and newsgroups on the Internet. (For more on this, see Box 20.3, "Urban Legends: Don't Believe Everything You Read.")

Whereas rumours deal with an issue or a subject, *gossip* **refers to rumours about the personal lives of individuals.** Charles Horton Cooley (1962/1909) viewed gossip as something that spread among a small group of individuals who personally knew the person who was the object of the rumour. Today, this often is not the case; many people enjoy gossiping about people they have never met. Tabloid newspapers and magazines, such as the *National Enquirer* and *People,* and television "news" programs that purport to provide "inside" information on the lives of celebrities are sources of contemporary gossip, much of which has not been checked for authenticity.

Mass Hysteria and Panic   *Mass hysteria* **is a form of dispersed collective behaviour that occurs when a large number of people react with strong emotions and self-destructive behaviour to a real or perceived threat.** Does mass hysteria actually occur? Although the term has been widely used, many sociologists believe this behaviour is best described as panic with a dispersed audience. You will recall that panic is a form of crowd behaviour that occurs when a large number of people react with strong emotions and self-destructive behaviour to a real or perceived threat.

An example of mass hysteria or panic with a widely dispersed audience was actor Orson Welles's 1938 Halloween-evening radio dramatization of H. G. Wells's science fiction classic *The War of the Worlds.* A CBS radio dance music program was interrupted suddenly by a news bulletin informing the audience that Martians had landed in New Jersey and were in the process of conquering the earth. Some listeners became extremely frightened even though an announcer had indicated before, during, and after the performance that the broadcast was a fictitious dramatization. According to some reports, as many as one million of the estimated ten million listeners

BOX 20.3 SOCIOLOGY AND TECHNOLOGY

Urban Legends: Don't Believe Everything You Read

Consider the following story:

> Hi All—
>
> I think you all know that I don't send out hoaxes and don't do the reactionary thing and send out anything that crosses my path. This one, however, is a friend of a friend and I've given it enough credibility in my mind that I'm writing it up and sending it out to all of you.
>
> My friend's friend was dating a guy from Afghanistan up until a month ago. She had a date with him around 9/6 and was stood up. She was understandably upset and went to his home to find it completely emptied. On 9/10, she received a letter from her boyfriend explaining that he wished he could tell her why he had left and that he was sorry it had to be like that. The part worth mentioning is that he BEGGED her not to get on any commercial airlines on 9/11 and to not go to any malls on Halloween. As soon as everything happened on the 11th, she called the FBI and has since turned over the letter.
>
> This is not an e-mail that I've received and decided to pass on. This came from a phone conversation with a long-time friend of mine last night.

This rumour is an example of an *urban legend*—an unsubstantiated story containing a sensational or unusual plot that is widely circulated and believed. According to urban legend expert Jan Harold Brunvand, the Internet has become a popular medium for transmitting urban legends. As he explains:

> the Internet has increased the speed at which some of these stories are circulated. Just like "that" they are all over . . . Judging from the e-mail I get there are still plenty of people sophisticated in the use of computers who are falling for the most incredible legends that pop up. (CNN, 1999)

Internet rumours and hoaxes including the above-quoted e-mail abounded in the wake of the tragic events of September 11, 2001. The FBI conducted an inquiry into the source of this e-mail and determined that this particular rumour is false. Other disturbing examples of September 11 urban legends include:

- Photo manipulations, a new type of Internet development. For example, one photograph shows a tourist standing on the rooftop observation deck of the World Trade Center. The man is oblivious to a commercial jet that appears to be approaching impact just below. The ability to manipulate photos represents a new way to blur the lines between truth and fiction.
- Bogus news accounts linking Osama bin Laden to the production of gum arabic, an emulsifier in soft drinks.
- E-mail reports that a deadly "Klingerman virus" is being dispersed via U.S. mail on blue sponges sent to random American homes.

The stories in urban legends are either completely false, or, if they do have some basis in fact, the events being related occurred in the distant past. Urban legends are typically believed because they call up fears or concerns that are real, such as the unpredictable terrorist attacks of September 11, or because they describe embarrassing situations that we can imagine ourselves in, or because they relate to some aspect of modern life that we accept but find somewhat disturbing.

The Internet has made communication of urban legends faster and easier. In fact, it has been described as the perfect environment for fostering urban legends. Why do we believe these outrageous stories? Paul Gliser, author of *Digital Literacy*, explains that for many Internet users any information provided via the computer has instant credibility:

> There's lingering public perception . . . of the computer's ferocious accuracy: computers don't make mistakes. Couple that with the general public's sense of the Internet as having been developed by the academic-scientific community, under government auspices, as a high-level information source, and you do indeed have some people accepting far too quickly, any information that appears on a computer screen simply because it does appear on a screen. (Cited in Ferrell, 1997:4)

Jan Harold Brunvald also points out that people believe urban legends because they are not "that incredible." They are about familiar places like shopping malls, familiar experiences like travelling, or worries and fears that are common to most of us (Brunvand, 2001).

According to David Emery, who investigates and debunks urban legends and Internet hoaxes, another reason why Internet folklore is so readily accepted is that other sources of information are increasingly regarded with suspicion:

> One reason rumour-mongering is rampant is that we don't always trust authorities to tell us the truth. Sometimes we don't even trust the media to tell us the truth, and so you see rumours functioning as a sort of shadow news whereby people share—or think they are sharing—the untold truth. A lot of people have an itchy forward finger, not even bothering to think twice before shooting off unverified

rumours to everyone they know. For almost every falsehood transmitted on the Net, the truth is also there to be found. The challenge, I think, is for people to accept the personal responsibility that implies. (Christie, 2001:A1)

Have you received any urgent e-mails lately warning of deadly anthrax viruses, or Nostradamus prophecies, or Microsoft's Wingdings font? Again, these are Internet urban legends. The world of urban legends is growing so rapidly via the Internet that there are now dozens of Web sites devoted just to debunking these stories. To read about some of the more common urban legends or to verify whether the e-mail you received about Bin Laden's shares in Snapple drinks is true, explore some of the following urban legend sites:

http://www.snopes2.com
http://www.scambusters.org
http://urbanlegends.about.com/od/internet/a/current_netlore.htm

believed that this astonishing event had occurred. Thousands were reported to have hidden in their storm cellars or to have gotten in their cars so that they could flee from the Martians (see Brown, 1954). In actuality, the program probably did not generate mass hysteria, but rather created panic among gullible listeners. Others switched stations to determine if the same "news" was being broadcast elsewhere. When they discovered that it was not, they merely laughed at the joke being played on listeners by CBS. In 1988, on the fiftieth anniversary of the broadcast, a Portuguese radio station rebroadcast the program and, once again, panic ensued.

Fads and Fashions

A *fad* **is a temporary but widely copied activity enthusiastically followed by large numbers of people.** Some examples of fads are the *Harry Potter* books and movies, skateboarder fashions, X-Box and PS2 video gaming, and iPods. Can you think of others? Fads can be embraced by widely dispersed collectivities; news networks, such as CBC Newsworld, may bring the latest fad to the attention of audiences around the globe. North America has witnessed a number of fads. One especially remembered by faculty who have been on university and college campuses for several decades was the 1970s fad of "streaking"—students taking off their clothes and running naked in public. Regardless of how it may sound, this activity was not purely spontaneous. Streakers had to calculate and plan their activity so that an audience (often including members

of the media) would be present. Streaking had no meaning if it was not widely publicized; for this reason, some students chose graduation ceremonies and other highly visible occasions for their streaking escapades. Other fads, such as exercise regimes and health practices, tend to be taken more seriously.

Fashions tend to last longer than fads. ***Fashion*** **may be defined as a currently valued style of behaviour, thinking, or appearance.** Fashion also applies to art, drama, music, literature, architecture, interior design, and automobiles, among other things. However, most sociological research on fashion has focused on clothing, especially women's apparel (Davis, 1992).

Trading Yu-Gi-Oh! cards is one of the many fads that have swept North America in recent years. What role does advertising play in determining what will become a fad?

In preindustrial societies, clothing styles remained relatively unchanged. With the advent of industrialization, however, items of apparel became readily available at low prices because of mass production. Fashion became more important as people embraced the "modern" way of life and advertising encouraged "conspicuous consumption."

Georg Simmel, Thorstein Veblen, and French sociologist Pierre Bourdieu all have viewed fashion as a means of status differentiation among members of different social classes. Simmel (1904) suggested a classic "trickle-down" theory (although he did not use those exact words) to describe the process by which members of the lower classes emulate the fashions of the upper class. As the fashions descend through the status hierarchy, they are watered down and "vulgarized" so that they are no longer recognizable to members of the upper class, who then regard them as unfashionable and in bad taste (Davis, 1992). Veblen (1967/1899) asserted that fashion served mainly to institutionalize conspicuous consumption among the wealthy. Almost eighty years later, Bourdieu (1984) similarly (but most subtly) suggested that "matters of taste," including fashion sensibility, constitute a large share of the "cultural capital" (or social assets) possessed by members of the dominant class.

Herbert Blumer (1969) disagreed with the trickle-down approach, arguing that "collective selection" best explains fashion. Blumer suggested that people in the middle and lower classes follow fashion because it is *fashion,* not because they desire to emulate members of the elite class. Blumer thus shifts the focus on fashion to collective mood, states, and choices: "Tastes are themselves a product of experience . . . They are formed in the context of social interaction, responding to the definitions and affirmation given by others. People thrown into areas of common interaction and having similar runs of experience develop common tastes" (quoted in Davis, 1992:116). Perhaps one of the best refutations of the trickle-down approach is the way in which fashion today often originates among people in the lower social classes and is mimicked by the elites. The mid-1990s so-called grunge look was a prime example of this.

Public Opinion

Public opinion **consists of the political attitudes and beliefs communicated by ordinary citizens to decision makers** (Greenberg and Page, 1996). It is measured through polls and surveys, which utilize research methods, such as interviews and questionnaires, as described in Chapter 2. Many people are not interested in all aspects of public policy but are concerned about issues they believe are relevant to themselves. Even on a single topic, public opinion will vary widely based on race/ethnicity, religion, region, social class, education level, gender, age, and so on.

Scholars who examine public opinion are interested in the extent to which the public's attitudes are communicated to decision makers and the effect (if any) that public opinion has on policy making (Turner and Killian, 1993). Some political scientists argue that public opinion has a substantial effect on decisions at all levels of governments (see Greenberg and Page, 1996); others strongly disagree. For example, Thomas Dye and Harmon Zeigler (1993:158) argue that

> Opinions flow downward from elites to masses. Public opinion rarely affects elite behaviour, but elite behaviour shapes public opinion. Elites are relatively unconstrained by public opinion for several reasons. First, few people among the masses have opinions on most policy questions confronting the nation's decision makers. Second, public opinion is very unstable; it can change in a matter of weeks in response to "news" events precipitated by elites. Third, elites do not have a clear perception of mass opinion. Most communications decision makers receive are from other elites—newsmakers, interest-group leaders, influential community leaders—not from ordinary citizens.

From this perspective, polls may create the appearance of public opinion artificially; pollsters may ask questions that those being interviewed had not even considered before the survey.

As the masses attempt to influence elites and vice versa, a two-way process occurs with the dissemination of *propaganda*—**information provided by individuals or groups that have a vested interest in furthering their own cause or damaging an opposing one.** Although many of us think of propaganda in negative terms, the information provided can be correct and can have positive effects on decision making.

In recent decades, grassroots environmental activists have attempted to influence public opinion. In a study of public opinion on environmental issues, sociologist Riley E. Dunlap (1992) found that public awareness of the seriousness of environmental problems and support for environmental protection increased dramatically between the late 1960s and the early 1990s. It is less clear, however, that public opinion translates into action by either decision makers in government and industry or individuals (for example, in their willingness to adopt a more ecologically sound lifestyle).

Initially, most grassroots environmental activists attempt to influence public opinion so that local decision makers will feel the necessity of correcting a specific problem through changes in public policy. Although activists usually do not start out seeking broader social change, they often move in that direction when they become aware of how widespread the problem is in the larger society or on a global basis. One of two types of social movements often develops at this point—one focuses on NIMBY ("not in my backyard"), while the other focuses on NIABY ("not in anyone's backyard") (Freudenberg and Steinsapir, 1992). An example of a NIMBY social movement occurred when Toronto proposed the building of a large landfill to handle the city's garbage. Residents of the municipalities identified as possible sites for the landfill protested vigorously and demonstrated the "not in my backyard" approach by counterproposing that the garbage be shipped by rail to abandoned mines in northern Ontario. Ultimately much of the garbage was sent over the border to a dump in Michigan.

■ SOCIAL MOVEMENTS

Although collective behaviour is short-lived and relatively unorganized, social movements are longer lasting and more organized and have specific goals or purposes. A *social movement* **is an organized group that acts consciously to promote or resist change through collective action** (Goldberg, 1991). Because social movements have not become institutionalized and are outside the political mainstream, they offer "outsiders" an opportunity to have their voices heard.

Social movements are more likely to develop in industrialized societies than in preindustrial societies, where acceptance of traditional beliefs and practices makes such movements unlikely. Diversity and a lack of consensus (hallmarks of industrialized nations) contribute to demands for social change, and people who participate in social movements typically lack power and other resources to bring about change without engaging in collective action. Social movements are most likely to spring up when people come to see their personal troubles as public issues that cannot be solved without a collective response.

Social movements make democracy more available to excluded groups (see Greenberg and Page, 1996). Historically, people in North America have worked at the grassroots level to bring about changes even when

elites sought to discourage activism (Adams, 1991). For example, in the United States, the civil rights movement brought into its ranks African Americans who had never been allowed to participate in politics (see Killian, 1984). The women's suffrage movement gave voice to women, who had been denied the right to vote (Rosenthal et al., 1985).

Most social movements rely on volunteers to carry out the work. Women traditionally have been strongly represented in both the membership and leadership of many grassroots movements (Levine, 1982; Freudenberg and Steinsapir, 1992).

The prototype of the grassroots, locally based environmental group is the Homeowners' Association formed in the 1970s by some of the residents of the Love Canal neighbourhood in Niagara Falls, New York, whose properties had been contaminated by toxic waste buried on it thirty years earlier by a local chemical company. Action taken by the association included protest marches, demonstrations, press conferences, political lobbying, legal injunctions, and a hostage taking. Finally, in 1980, U.S. president Jimmy Carter declared a state of emergency at Love Canal, and 700 families living close to the canal were relocated at government expense (Gibbs, 1982).

The Love Canal activists set the stage for other movements that have grappled with the kind of issues that sociologist Kai Erikson (1994) refers to as a "new species of trouble." Erikson describes the "new species" as environmental problems that "contaminate rather than merely damage . . . they pollute, befoul, taint, rather than just create wreckage . . . they penetrate human tissue indirectly rather than just wound the surfaces by assaults of a more straightforward kind . . . And the evidence is growing that they scare human beings in new and special ways, that they elicit an uncanny fear in us" (Erikson, 1991:15). The chaos Erikson (1994:141) describes is the result of technological disasters—"meaning everything that can go wrong when systems fail, humans err, designs prove faulty, engines misfire, and so on."

A recent example of such a disaster occurred in Japan, where more than 300,000 residents living within ten kilometers of the nuclear plant at Tokaimura were told to stay indoors in the aftermath of three workers' mishandling of stainless-steel pails full of uranium, which caused the worst nuclear accident in Japan's history (Larimer, 1999). Although no lives were immediately lost, workers in the plant soaked up potentially lethal doses of radiation; radioactive material also leaked from the plant into the community. The fifty-two nuclear power plants in Japan have been plagued by other accidents and radiation leaks, causing concern for many people around the globe (Larimer, 1999).

Social movements provide people who otherwise would not have the resources to enter the game of politics a chance to do so. We are most familiar with those movements that develop around public policy issues considered newsworthy by the media, ranging from abortion and women's rights to gun control and environmental justice. However, a number of other types of social movements exist as well.

Types of Social Movements

Social movements are difficult to classify; however, sociologists distinguish among movements on the basis of their *goals* and the *amount of change* they seek to produce (Aberle, 1966; Blumer, 1974). Some movements seek to change people, while others seek to change society.

Reform Movements   Grassroots environmental movements are an example of *reform movements,* which seek to improve society by changing some specific aspect of the social structure. Members of reform movements usually work within the existing system to attempt to change existing public policy so that it more adequately reflects their own value system. Examples of reform movements (in addition to the environmental movement) include labour movements, animal rights movements, antinuclear movements, Mothers Against Drunk Driving, and the disability rights movement.

Sociologist Lory Britt (1993) suggested that some movements arise specifically to alter social responses to and definitions of stigmatized attributes. From this perspective, social movements may bring about changes in societal attitudes and practices, while at the same time causing changes in participants' social emotions. For example, the civil rights, gay rights, and Aboriginal rights movements helped replace shame with pride (Britt, 1993). Consider the comments of Mohawk warrior Mike Myers, who participated in the standoff at Oka:

> For the moment, we have to endure persecution. But, in the long course of history, the face of Canada will be politically, socially, economically, and spiritually changed. Back in favour of our people. At least we will be able to leave the earth knowing that while we were here we did all that we could to set in motion a better future for our great-grandchildren. And so for me that's what Kanehsatake is about. (Obomsawin, 1993)

Revolutionary Movements   Movements seeking to bring about a total change in society are referred to as *revolutionary movements.* These movements usually do not attempt to work within the existing system; rather, they aim to remake the system by replacing existing institutions with new ones. Revolutionary movements range from utopian groups seeking to establish an ideal society to radical terrorists who use fear tactics to intimidate those with whom they disagree ideologically (see Alexander and Gill, 1984; Berger, 1988; Vetter and Perlstein, 1991).

Terrorism is the calculated unlawful use of physical force or threats of violence against persons or property in order to intimidate or coerce a government, organization, or individual for the purpose of gaining some political, religious, economic, or social objective. Movements based on terrorism often use tactics, such as bombings, kidnappings, hostage taking, hijackings, and assassinations (Vetter and Perlstein, 1991). Over the past thirty years, terrorism has become a global phenomenon. Suicide bombings in warring Israel and Palestine have become weekly occurrences. The year 2000 showed that terrorism continues to pose an ongoing threat to the international community. The many threats that surrounded the new millennium heightened fears of terrorist attacks. The September 11, 2001, terrorist attacks on the World Trade Center and the Pentagon and the crash of a jetliner in Pennsylvania constituted the worst incident of domestic terrorism in U.S. history.

Canada is not immune to terrorist activity. In the late 1960s, the Front de Libération du Québec (FLQ), a small group of extremists on the fringe of the separatist movement, carried out 200 bombings. In addition, Sikh separatists are believed to be responsible for the 1985 bombing of an Air India jet that was travelling to India from Canada. This disaster was the biggest mass killing in Canadian history. Of the 329 people who died, 278 were Canadians. After the terrorist attacks of September 11, 2001, the world has focused on the "war on terrorism" in an attempt to prevent further terrorist activities and to ensure that persons who participate in such conduct are punished.

Religious Movements   Social movements that seek to produce radical change in individuals typically are based on spiritual or supernatural belief systems. Also referred to as *expressive movements, religious movements* are concerned with renovating or renewing people through "inner change." Fundamentalist religious groups seeking to convert nonbelievers to their belief system are an example of this type of movement. Some religious movements are *millenarian*—that is, they forecast that "the end is near" and assert that an immediate change in behaviour is imperative. Relatively new religious movements in industrialized Western societies have included the Hare Krishna sect, the Unification Church, Scientology, and the Divine Light Mission, all of which tend to appeal to the psychological and social needs of young people seeking meaning in life that mainstream religions have not provided for them.

Alternative Movements   Movements that seek limited change in some aspect of people's behaviour are referred to as *alternative movements*. For example, in the early twentieth century, the Woman's Christian Temperance Union attempted to get people to abstain from drinking alcoholic beverages. Some analysts place "therapeutic social movements," such as Alcoholics Anonymous, in this category; however, others do not, due to their belief that people must change their lives completely in order to overcome alcohol abuse (see Blumberg, 1977). More recently, a variety of "New Age" movements have directed people's behaviour by emphasizing spiritual consciousness combined with a belief in reincarnation and astrology. Such practices as vegetarianism, meditation, and holistic medicine often are included in the self-improvement category. Beginning in the 1990s, some alternative movements have included the practice of yoga (usually without its traditional background in Hindu religion) as a means by which the self can be liberated and union can be achieved with the supreme spirit or universal soul.

Resistance Movements   Also referred to as *regressive movements, resistance movements* seek to prevent change or to undo change that already has occurred. Virtually all of the proactive social movements previously discussed face resistance from one or more reactive movements that hold opposing viewpoints and want to foster public policies that reflect their own viewpoints. Examples of resistance movements are groups organized to oppose free trade, gun control, and restrictions on smoking. Perhaps the most widely known resistance movement, however, includes many who label themselves as "pro-life" advocates—such as Operation Rescue, which seeks to close abortion clinics and make abortion illegal under all circumstances (Gray, 1993; Van Biema, 1993). Protests by some radical anti-abortion groups in Canada and the United States have grown violent, resulting in the deaths of

These "pro-lifers" demonstrating outside of the Morgentaler abortion clinic in Toronto are members of a resistance movement. They are seeking to prevent or undo change advocated by another social movement: the "pro-choice" movement.

several doctors and clinic workers and creating fear among health professionals and patients seeking abortions (Belkin, 1994).

Stages in Social Movements

Do all social movements go through similar stages? Not necessarily, but there appear to be identifiable stages in virtually all movements that succeed beyond their initial phase of development.

In the *preliminary* (or incipiency) *stage,* widespread unrest is present as people begin to become aware of a problem. At this stage, leaders emerge to agitate others into taking action. In the *coalescence stage,* people begin to organize and to publicize the problem. At this stage, some movements become formally organized at local and regional levels. In the *institutionalization* (or bureaucratization) *stage,* an organizational structure develops, and a paid staff (rather than volunteers) begins to lead the group. When the movement reaches this stage, the initial zeal and idealism of members may diminish as administrators take over management of the organization. Early grassroots supporters may become disillusioned and drop out; they also may start another movement to address some as yet unsolved aspect of the original problem. For example, some environmental organizations—such as the Sierra Club, the Canadian Nature Federation, and the National Audubon Society—that started as grassroots conservation movements currently are viewed by many people as being unresponsive to local environmental problems (Cable and Cable, 1995). As a result, new movements have arisen.

SOCIAL MOVEMENT THEORIES

What conditions are most likely to produce social movements? Why are people drawn to these movements? Sociologists have developed several theories to answer these questions.

Relative Deprivation Theory

According to relative deprivation theory, people who are satisfied with their present condition are less likely to seek social change. Social movements arise as a response to people's perception that they have been deprived of their "fair share" (Rose, 1982). Thus, people who suffer relative deprivation are more likely to feel that change is necessary and to join a social movement in order to bring about that change. *Relative deprivation* refers to the discontent that people may feel when they compare their achievements with those of similarly situated persons and find that they have less than they think they deserve (Orum and Orum, 1968). Karl Marx captured the idea of relative deprivation in this description: "A house may be large or small; as long as the surrounding houses are small it satisfies all social demands for a dwelling. But let a palace arise beside the little house, and it shrinks from a little house to a hut" (quoted in Ladd, 1966:24). Movements based on relative deprivation are most likely to occur when an upswing in the standard of living is followed by a period of decline, such that people have *unfulfilled rising expectations*—newly raised hopes of a better lifestyle that are not fulfilled as rapidly as they expected or are not realized at all.

Although most of us can relate to relative deprivation theory, it does not fully account for why people experience social discontent but fail to join a social movement. Even though discontent and feelings of deprivation may be necessary to produce certain types of social movements, they are not sufficient to bring movements into existence. In fact, sociologist Anthony Orum (1974) found the best predictor of participation in a social movement to be prior organizational membership and involvement in other political activities.

Value-Added Theory

The value-added theory developed by sociologist Neal Smelser (1963) is based on the assumption that certain conditions are necessary for the development of a social movement. Smelser called his theory the "value-added" approach, based on the concept (borrowed from the field of economics) that each step in the production process adds something to the finished product. For example, in the process of converting iron ore into automobiles, each stage "adds value" to the final product (Smelser, 1963). Similarly, Smelser asserted, the following six conditions are necessary and sufficient to produce social movements when they combine or interact in a particular situation.

1. *Structural conduciveness.* People must become aware of a significant problem and have the opportunity to engage in collective action. According to Smelser, movements are more likely to occur when a person, class, or agency can be singled out as the source of the problem; when channels for expressing grievances either are not available or fail; and when the aggrieved have a chance to communicate among themselves.
2. *Structural strain.* When a society or community is unable to meet people's expectations that something should be done about a problem, strain occurs in the system. The ensuing tension and conflict contributes to the development of a social movement based on people's belief that the problems would not exist if authorities had done what they were supposed to do.
3. *Spread of a generalized belief.* For a movement to develop, there must be a clear statement of the problem and a shared view of its cause, effects, and possible solution.
4. *Precipitating factors.* To reinforce the existing generalized belief, an inciting incident or dramatic event must occur. With regard to technological disasters, some gradually emerge from a longstanding environmental threat, while others involve a suddenly imposed problem.
5. *Mobilization for action.* At this stage, leaders emerge to organize others and give them a sense of direction.
6. *Social control factors.* If there is a high level of social control on the part of law-enforcement officials, political leaders, and others, it becomes more difficult to develop a social movement or engage in certain types of collective action.

Value-added theory takes into account the complexity of social movements and makes it possible to use Smelser's assertions to test for the necessary and sufficient conditions that produce such movements.

Resource Mobilization Theory

Smelser's value-added theory tends to underemphasize the importance of resources in social movements. By contrast, *resource mobilization theory* focuses on the process through which members of a social movement gather, trade, use, and occasionally waste resources as they seek to advance their cause (Oberschall, 1973; McCarthy and Zald, 1977). Resources include money, members' time, access to the media, and material goods, such as property and equipment. Assistance from outsiders is essential for social movements. Reform movements, for example, are more likely to succeed when they gain the support of political and economic elites (Oberschall, 1973).

Resource mobilization theory is based on the belief that participants in social movements are rational people. According to sociologist Charles Tilly (1973, 1978), movements are formed and dissolved, and mobilized and deactivated, based on rational decisions about the goals of the group, available resources, and the cost of mobilization and collective action. In other words, social movements do not develop because of widespread discontent but because organizations exist that make it possible to express discontent by concerted social action (Aminzade, 1973; Gamson, 1990). Based on an analysis of fifty-three U.S. social protest groups ranging from labour unions to peace movements between 1800 and 1945, sociologist William Gamson (1990) concluded that the organization and tactics of a movement strongly influence its chances of success. However, critics of this theory note that this theory fails to account for social changes brought about by groups with limited resources.

Social Constructionist Theory: Frame Analysis

Recent theories based on a symbolic interactionist perspective focus on the importance of the symbolic presentation of a problem to both participants and the general public (see Snow et al., 1986; Capek, 1993). Social constructionist theory is based on the assumption that social movements are an interactive, symbolically defined, and negotiated process that involves participants, opponents, and bystanders (Buechler, 2000).

Research based on this perspective often investigates how problems are framed and what names they are given. This approach reflects the influence of sociologist Erving Goffman's *Frame Analysis* (1974), in which

he suggests that our interpretation of the particulars of events and activities is dependent on the framework from which we perceive them. According to Goffman (1974:10), the purpose of frame analysis is "to try to isolate some of the basic frameworks of understanding available in our society for making sense out of events and to analyze the special vulnerabilities to which these frames of reference are subject." In other words, various "realities" may be simultaneously occurring among participants engaged in the same set of activities. Sociologist Steven M. Buechler (2000:41) explains the relationship between frame analysis and social movement theory:

> Framing means focusing attention on some bounded phenomenon by imparting meaning and significance to elements within the frame and setting them apart from what is outside the frame. In the context of social movements, framing refers to the interactive, collective ways that movement actors assign meanings to their activities in the conduct of social movement activism. The concept of framing is designed for discussing the social construction of grievances as a fluid and variable process of social interaction— and hence a much more important explanatory tool than resource mobilization theory has maintained.

Sociologists have identified at least three ways in which grievances are framed. First, *diagnostic framing* identifies a problem and attributes blame or causality to some group or entity so that the social movement has a target for its actions. Second, *prognostic framing* pinpoints possible solutions or remedies, based on the target previously identified. Third, *motivational framing* provides a vocabulary of motives that compel people to take action (Benford, 1993; Snow and Benford, 1988). When successful framing occurs, the individual's vague dissatisfactions are turned into well-defined grievances, and people are compelled to join the movement in an effort to reduce or eliminate those grievances (Buechler, 2000).

Beyond motivational framing, additional frame alignment processes are necessary in order to supply a continuing sense of urgency to the movement. *Frame alignment* is the linking together of interpretive orientations of individuals and social movement organizations so that there is congruence between individuals' interests, beliefs, and values and the movement's ideologies, goals, and activities (Snow et al., 1986). Four distinct frame alignment processes occur in social movements: (1) *frame bridging* is the process by which movement organizations reach individuals who already share the same worldview as the organization; (2) *frame amplification* occurs when movements appeal to deeply held values and beliefs in the general population and link those to movement issues so that people's pre-existing value commitments serve as a "hook" that can be used to recruit them; (3) *frame extension* occurs when movements change to boundaries of an initial frame to incorporate other issues that appear to be of importance to potential participants; and (4) *frame transformation* refers to the process whereby the creation and maintenance of new values, beliefs, and meanings induce movement participation by redefining activities and events in such a manner that people believe they must become involved in collective action (Buechler, 2000). Some or all of these frame alignment processes are used by social movements as they seek to define grievances and recruit participants.

Sociologist William Gamson (1995) believes that social movements borrow, modify, or create frames as they seek to advance their goals. For example, social activism regarding nuclear disasters involves differential framing over time. When the Fermi reactor in the United States had a serious partial meltdown in 1966, there was no sustained social opposition. However, when Pennsylvania's Three Mile Island nuclear power plant experienced a similar problem in 1979, the situation was defined as a technological disaster. At that time, social movements opposing nuclear power plants grew in number, and each intensified its efforts to reduce or eliminate such plants. This example shows that people react toward something on the basis of the meaning that thing has for them, and such meanings typically emerge from the political culture, including the social activism, of that specific era (Buechler, 2000).

Frame analysis provides new insights on how social movements emerge and grow when people are faced with problems such as technological disasters, where greater ambiguity typically exists, and when people are attempting to "name" the problems associated with things, such as nuclear or chemical contamination. However, frame analysis has been criticized for its "ideational biases" (McAdam, 1996). According to the sociologist Doug McAdam (1996), frame analyses of social movements have looked almost exclusively at ideas and their formal expression, whereas little attention has been paid to other significant factors, such as movement tactics, mobilizing structures, and changing political opportunities that influence the work of movements. In this context, *political opportunity* means government structure, public policy, and political

conditions that set the boundaries for change and political action. These boundaries are crucial variables in explaining why various social movements have different outcomes (Meyer and Staggenborg, 1996; Gotham, 1999).

New Social Movement Theory

New social movement theory looks at a diverse array of collective actions and the manner in which those actions are based in politics, ideology, and culture. It also incorporates sources of identity, including race, class, gender, and sexuality, as sources of collective action and social movements. Examples of "new social movements" include ecofeminism and environmental justice movements. Ecofeminism emerged in the late 1970s and early 1980s out of the feminist, peace, and ecology movements. Prompted by the near-meltdown at the Three Mile Island nuclear power plant, ecofeminists established World Women in Defense of the Environment. Ecofeminism is based on the belief that patriarchy is a root cause of environmental problems. According to ecofeminists, patriarchy not only results in the domination of women by men but also contributes to a belief that nature is to be possessed and dominated, rather than treated as a partner (see Ortner, 1974; Merchant, 1983, 1992; Mies and Shiva, 1993).

Another "new social movement" focuses on environmental justice and the intersection of race and class in the environmental struggle. Stella M. Capek (1993) investigated a contaminated landfill in the Carver Terrace neighbourhood of Texarkana, Texas, and found that residents were able to mobilize for change and win a federal buyout and relocation by symbolically linking their issue to a larger *environmental justice* framework. Since the 1980s, the emerging environmental justice movement has focused on the issue of **environmental racism—the belief that a disproportionate number of hazardous facilities (including industries such as waste disposal/treatment and chemical plants) are placed in low-income areas populated primarily by people of colour** (Bullard and Wright, 1992). These areas have been left out of most of the environmental cleanup that has taken place in the last two decades (Schneider, 1993). Capek concluded that linking Carver Terrace with environmental justice led to it being designated as a cleanup site. She also views this as an important turning point in new social movements: "Carver Terrace is significant not only as a federal buyout and relocation of a minority community, but also as a marker of the emergence of environmental racism as a major new component of environmental social movements in the United States" (Capek, 1993:21).

Sociologist Steven M. Buechler (2000) has argued that theories pertaining to twenty-first-century social movements should be oriented toward the structural, macrolevel contexts in which movements arise. These theories should incorporate both political and cultural dimensions of social activism:

> Social movements are historical products of the age of modernity. They arose as part of a sweeping social, political, and intellectual change that led a significant number of people to view society as a social construction that was susceptible to social reconstruction through concerted collective effort. Thus, from their inception, social movements have had a dual focus. Reflecting the political, they have always involved some form of challenge to prevailing forms of authority. Reflecting the cultural, they have

always operated as symbolic laboratories in which reflexive actors pose questions of meaning, purpose, identity, and change. (Buechler, 2000:211)

Concept Table 20.A summarizes the main theories of social movements.

As we have seen, social movements may be an important source of social change. Throughout this text, we have examined a variety of social problems that have been the focus of one or more social movements during the past hundred years. In the process of bringing about change, most movements initially develop innovative ways to get their ideas across to decision makers and the public. Some have been successful in achieving their goals; others have not. As the historian Robert A. Goldberg (1991) has suggested, gains made by social movements may be fragile, acceptance brief, and benefits minimal and easily lost. For this reason, many groups focus on preserving their gains while simultaneously fighting for those they believe they still desire.

Concept Table 20.A   SOCIAL MOVEMENT THEORIES

THEORY	KEY COMPONENTS
Relative Deprivation	People who are discontent when they compare their achievements with those of others consider themselves relatively deprived and join social movements in order to get what they view is their "fair share," especially when there is an upswing in the economy followed by a decline.
Value-Added	Certain conditions are necessary for a social movement to develop: (1) structural conduciveness, such that people are aware of a problem and have the opportunity to engage in collective action; (2) structural strain, such that society or the community cannot meet people's expectations for taking care of the problem; (3) growth and spread of a generalized belief as to causes and effects of and possible solutions to the problem; (4) precipitating factors or events that reinforce the beliefs; (5) mobilization of participants for action; and (6) social control factors, such that society comes to allow the movement to take action.
Resource Mobilization	A variety of resources (money, members, access to media, and material goods, such as equipment) are necessary for a social movement; people participate only when they feel the movement has access to these resources.
Social Constructionist: Frame Analysis	Based on the assumption that social movements are an interactive, symbolically defined, and negotiated process involving participants, opponents, and bystanders, frame analysis is used to determine how people assign meaning to activities and processes in social movements.
New Social Movement	The focus is on sources of social movements, including politics, ideology, and culture. Race, class, gender, sexuality, and other sources of identity are also factors in movements, such as ecofeminism and environmental justice.

SOCIAL CHANGE IN THE FUTURE

In this chapter, we have focused on collective behaviour and social movements as potential forces for social change in contemporary societies. A number of other factors also contribute to social change, including the physical environment, population trends, technological development, and social institutions.

The Physical Environment and Change

Changes in the physical environment often produce changes in the lives of people; in turn, people can make dramatic changes in the physical environment, over which we have only limited control. Throughout history, natural disasters have taken their toll on individuals and societies. Major natural disasters—including ice storms, floods, and tornadoes—can devastate an entire population. Even comparatively "small" natural disasters change the lives of many people. As sociologist Kai Erikson (1976, 1994) has suggested, the trauma that people experience from disasters may outweigh the actual loss of physical property—memories of such events can haunt people for many years.

Some natural disasters are exacerbated by human decisions. For example, floods are viewed as natural disasters, but excessive development may contribute to a flood's severity. As office buildings, shopping malls, industrial plants, residential areas, and highways are developed, less land remains to absorb rainfall. When heavier-than-usual rains and snowfall occur, flooding becomes inevitable; some regions in Canada have remained under water for days and even weeks in recent years. Clearly, humans cannot control the rain, but human decisions can worsen the consequences.

People also contribute to changes in the earth's physical condition. Through soil erosion and other degradation of grazing land, often at the hands of people, an estimated 24 billion tons of the earth's topsoil is lost annually. As people clear forests to create farmland and pastures and to acquire lumber and firewood, the earth's tree cover continues to diminish. As hundreds of millions of people drive motor vehicles, the amount of carbon dioxide in the environment continues to rise each year, possibly resulting in global warming.

Just as people contribute to change in the physical environment, human activities also must be adapted to changes in the environment. For example, we are being warned to stay out of the sunlight because of increases in ultraviolet rays, a cause of skin cancer, which has resulted from the increasing depletion of the ozone layer. If this prediction is accurate, the change in the physical environment will dramatically affect those who work or spend their leisure time outside.

Population and Change

Changes in population size, distribution, and composition affect the culture and social structure of a society and change the relationships among nations. As discussed in Chapter 19, the countries experiencing the most rapid increases in population have a less developed infrastructure to deal with those changes. How will nations of the world deal with population growth as the global population continues to move toward seven billion? Only time will provide a response to this question.

Immigration to Canada has created an increasingly multiethnic population. The changing makeup of the Canadian population has resulted in children from more diverse cultural backgrounds entering school, producing a demand for new programs and changes in curriculums. An increase in the number of women in the workforce has created a need for more child care; an increase in the older population has created a need for services such as home care and placed increasing demands on programs, such as the Canada Pension Plan.

Technology and Change

Technology is an important force for change; in some ways, technological development has made our lives much easier. Advances in communication and transportation have made instantaneous worldwide communication possible but also have brought old belief systems and the status quo into question as never before. Today, we increasingly are moving information instead of people—and doing it almost instantly (Petersen, 1994). Advances in science and medicine have made significant changes in people's lives. The lightbulb, the automobile, the airplane, the assembly line, and the high-tech developments of the last few decades—all have contributed to dramatic changes. Individuals in high-income nations have benefited from the use of the technology; those in low-income nations may have paid a disproportionate share of the cost of some of these inventions and discoveries.

Scientific advances will continue to affect our lives, from the foods we eat to our reproductive

The twenty-first century will continue to see passionate debates over the changes people make to the earth's physical condition.

capabilities. Genetically engineered plants have been developed and marketed in recent years, and biochemists are creating potatoes, rice, and cassava with the same protein value as meat (Petersen, 1994). Advances in medicine have made it possible for those formerly unable to have children to procreate; women well beyond menopause now are able to become pregnant with the assistance of medical technology. Advances in medicine also have increased the human lifespan, especially for white and middle- or upper-class individuals in high-income nations; they also have contributed to the declining death rate in low-income nations, where birth rates have not yet been curbed.

Just as technology has brought about improvements in the quality and length of life for many, it has created the potential for new disasters, ranging from global warfare to localized technological disasters at toxic waste sites. As sociologist William Ogburn (1966) suggested, when a change in the material culture occurs in society, a period of *cultural lag* follows in which the nonmaterial (ideological) culture has not caught up with material development. The rate of technological advance at the level of material culture today is mind-boggling. Many of us can never hope to understand technological advances in the areas of artificial intelligence, holography, virtual reality, biotechnology, and robotics.

One of the ironies of twenty-first-century high technology is the increased vulnerability that results from the increasing complexity of such systems. As futurist John L. Petersen (1994:70) notes, "The more complex a system becomes, the more likely the chance of system failure. There are unknown secondary effects and particularly vulnerable nodes." He also asserts that most of the world's population will not participate in the technological revolution that is occurring in high-income nations (Petersen, 1994).

Technological disasters may result in the deaths of tens of thousands of people, especially if we think of modern warfare as a technological disaster. Nuclear energy, which can provide power for millions, also can be the source of a nuclear war that could devastate the planet. As a U.S. government study on even limited nuclear war concluded:

> Natural resources would be destroyed; surviving equipment would be designed to use materials and skills that might no longer exist; and indeed some regions might be almost uninhabitable. Furthermore, pre-war patterns of behaviour would surely change, though in unpredictable ways. (U.S. Congress, 1979, quoted in Howard, 1990:320)

Even when lives are not lost in technological disasters, families are uprooted and communities cease to exist as people are relocated. In many cases, the problem is not solved; people simply are moved away from its site.

Social Institutions and Change

Many changes have occurred in the family, religion, education, the economy, and the political system over the last century. As we saw in Chapter 15, the size and composition of families in Canada changed

BOX 20.4 YOU CAN MAKE A DIFFERENCE

Can You Make a Difference?

Although you may feel compelled to become involved in addressing some of the many social issues identified in this text, it is not uncommon to feel that one individual is not capable of having any impact. Following are the comments from environmental activists responding to the question we all often ask ourselves: "Can I make a difference?" You may or may not have heard of the people profiled here. They are ordinary people, making a difference. People like this are all over the world (Greenpeace, 2005). Their stories serve to inspire and motivate us all to get active.

Benedict Southworth is a past campaigns manager for Greenpeace Australia Pacific:

TRADE UNIONS: THE MOVEMENT THAT BROUGHT YOU THE WEEKEND!

This bumper sticker slogan from the USA is a reminder that much of the quality of life we take for granted (like the weekend) came about because of individuals standing up and taking action.

When I was a student my first response to the scale of the problems facing the world was to head to the nearest bar. There I asked myself: "Why aren't THEY doing anything about it and why aren't THEY forcing them to do something." Then I realised I could either stay in the bar or do something myself.

I still believe the answer to both questions is that THEY are US. Social change will only occur if action takes place at all levels. As individuals, we contribute to the problem; as citizens, we have the power to force change in the economic and political systems to establish a world that is able to sustain life in all its diversity.

Since then I've been involved in all sorts of campaigns, from working with communities on local pollution problems, to planning large national campaigns on waste and transport run by environmental non-government organisations:

There is no such thing as only one way to do it.

We are powerful when the personal meets the political.

Be thankful for all the people who have helped.

All too often we are tempted to believe there is only one way that change can be achieved. In fact, the diversity of the environment movement

allows us to choose how we want to work. What makes us powerful is our ability to combine all the different ways of working and the different issues into an overwhelming and unstoppable movement for change.

Jan Douglas works with the Wongatha Aboriginal Corporation in central Western Australia.

"Can you make a difference?" is something most activists—and certainly me—ask themselves fairly regularly. The enormity of the injustices which we confront often makes it impossible to imagine that our individual actions can effect change. The bottom line for me is that I believe individual action, like apathy, is cumulative.

Julie Eaton is waste minimisation officer for Manly Council.

I could tell you a million stories. I could tell you about the developer who consistently lops down 100-year-old native trees on the sly because they block views. I could talk about the jetski renegade who wrapped up an endangered Little Penguin in his motor—hit and run. I could let you know about the rats who sneak out at night to dump liquid waste into local creeks. But there are a squillion other stories about ordinary people living as heroes.

Once we accept that everything we do has an impact somewhere along the line, we find ourselves face to face with everyday choices. It's in these choices that the power of making a difference lies. Small actions and choices can have exponential, influential and exceptional effects. Never underestimate the difference you can make.

If you would like to become in some way involved in environmental or social activism, one place to start is Greenpeace's Activism "How To resources online: http://www.greenpeace.ca/e/resource/activism.php.

Greenpeace Australia's Guide to Community Campaigns

The Greenpeace Australia Web site has all the information you need to start making a difference in your community. From planning your campaign to managing volunteers to how to speak to the media, this site explains exactly how to start and run a community campaign that will make a difference: http://www .greenpeace.org.au/getactive/index.html.

NonviolenceHelp

This site draws together some of the available online resources on the history, theory, and practise of nonviolence. It is both an introduction to

nonviolent social change and a resource for trainers and activists: http://nonviolence.org.au

Friends of the Earth Guide to Organizing

This is another good site from our friends at Friends of the Earth, explaining how to work with others in your community to protect the planet: http://www.foe.org.

Source: Greenpeace, 2005.

---

with the dramatic increase in the number of single-person and single-parent households. Changes in families have produced changes in the socialization of children, many of whom spend large amounts of time in front of a television set or in child care facilities outside their own homes. Although some political and religious leaders have advocated a return to "traditional" family life, many scholars have argued that such families never worked quite as well as some might wish to believe.

Public education has changed dramatically in Canada over the last century. This country was one of the first to provide "universal" education for students regardless of their ability to pay. As a result, Canada has had one of the most highly educated populations and one of the best public education systems in the world. However, some feel that the education system is not meeting the needs of some students, namely, those who are failing to learn to read and write or those who are dropping out. As the nature of the economy changes, schools almost inevitably will have to change, if for no other reason than the demands from leaders in business and industry for an educated workforce that allows Canadian companies to compete in a global economic environment.

Political systems have experienced tremendous change and upheaval in some parts of the world over the last century. Canada's government seems unable to determine what its priorities should be, even as the country faces serious economic and social problems. As the centralized federal government becomes less able to respond to the needs and problems of the country, federal political leaders likely will seek to decentralize services and programs by putting more of the burden onto provincial and municipal governments. Unfortunately, these governments are no better

equipped to deal with problems, such as poverty and homelessness, environmental pollution, and decaying infrastructures.

Although we have examined changes in the physical environment, population, technology, and social institutions separately, they all operate together in a complex relationship, sometimes producing large, unanticipated consequences. In the twenty-first century, we need new ways of conceptualizing social life at both the macro- and microlevels. The sociological imagination helps us think about how personal troubles—regardless of our race/ethnicity, class, gender, age, sexual orientation, or physical abilities and disabilities—are intertwined with the public issues of our society and the global community of which we are a part. Using our sociological imagination also encourages us to think creatively about ways to contribute personally to the social issues identified in this text (see Box 20.4).

A FEW FINAL THOUGHTS

In this text, we have covered a substantial amount of material, examined different perspectives on a wide variety of social issues, and suggested different methods by which to deal with them. The purpose of this text is not to encourage you to take any particular point of view; rather, it is to allow you to understand different viewpoints and ways in which they may be helpful to you and to society in dealing with the issues of the twenty-first century. Possessing that understanding, we can hope that the future will be something we can all look forward to—producing a better way of life, not only in this country but worldwide.

C H A P T E R   R E V I E W

■ **What is the relationship between social change and collective behaviour?**

Social change is the alteration, modification, or transformation of public policy, culture, or social institutions over time; it usually is brought about by collective behaviour, which is relatively spontaneous, unstructured activity that typically violates established social norms.

■ **When is collective behaviour likely to occur?**

Collective behaviour occurs when some common influence or stimulus produces a response from a relatively large number of people.

■ **What is a crowd?**

A crowd is a relatively large number of people who are in one another's immediate vicinity. Sociologist Howard Blumer divided crowds into four categories: (1) casual crowds, (2) conventional crowds, (3) expressive crowds, and (4) acting crowds (including mobs, riots, and panics). A fifth type of crowd is a protest crowd.

■ **What causes crowd behaviour?**

Social scientists have developed several theories to explain crowd behaviour. Contagion theory asserts that a crowd takes on a life of its own as people are transformed from rational beings into part of an organism that acts on its own. A variation on this is circular reaction—people express their discontent to others, who communicate back similar feelings, resulting in a conscious effort to engage in the crowd's behaviour. Convergence theory asserts that people with similar attributes find other like-minded persons with whom they can release underlying personal tendencies. Emergent norm theory asserts that, as a crowd develops, it comes up with its own norms that replace more conventional norms of behaviour.

■ **What are the primary forms of mass behaviour?**

Mass behaviour is collective behaviour that occurs when people respond to the same event in the same way even if they are not geographically close to one another. Rumours, gossip, mass hysteria, fads and fashions, and public opinion are forms of mass behaviour.

■ **What are the major types of social movements, and what are their goals?**

A social movement is an organized group that acts consciously to promote or resist change through collective action; such movements are most likely to be formed when people see their personal troubles as public issues that cannot be resolved without a collective response. Reform movements seek to improve society by changing some specific aspect of the social structure. Revolutionary movements seek to bring about a total change in society— sometimes by the use of terrorism. Religious movements seek to produce radical change in individuals based on spiritual or supernatural belief systems. Alternative movements seek limited change to some aspect of people's behaviour. Resistance movements seek to prevent change or to undo change that already has occurred.

■ **How do social movements develop?**

Social movements typically go through three stages: (1) a preliminary stage (unrest results from a perceived problem), (2) coalescence (people begin to organize), and (3) institutionalization (an organization is developed and paid staff replaces volunteers in leadership positions).

■ **How do relative deprivation theory, value-added theory, and resource mobilization theory explain social movements?**

Relative deprivation theory asserts that, if people are discontented when they compare their accomplishments with those of others similarly situated, they are more likely to join a social movement than are people who are relatively content with their status. Value-added theory asserts that six conditions must exist in order to produce social movements: (1) a perceived source of a problem, (2) a perception that the authorities are not resolving the problem, (3) a spread of the belief to an adequate number of people, (4) a precipitating incident, (5) mobilization of other people by leaders, and (6) a lack of social control. Resource mobilization theory asserts that successful social movements can occur only when they gain the support of political and economic elites, without whom they do not have access to the resources necessary to maintain the movement.

■ **What is the primary focus of research based on frame analysis and new social movement theory?**

Research based on frame analysis often highlights the social construction of grievances through the process of social interaction. Various types of framing occur as problems are identified, remedies are sought, and people feel compelled to take action. Like frame analysis, new social movement theory has been used in research that looked at technological disasters and cases of environmental racism.

KEY TERMS

civil disobedience 633
collective behaviour 629
crowd 631
environmental racism 646
fad 639
fashion 639
gossip 637
mass 631
mass behaviour 637
mass hysteria 637
mob 632
panic 632
propaganda 640
public opinion 640
riot 632
rumours 637
social change 628
social movement 641
terrorism 642

NET LINKS

The Sierra Club is a public interest organization that concentrates on influencing public policy decisions to conserve the natural environment; go to:
http://www.sierraclub.org/

Envirolink is an objective online information clearinghouse providing information about hundreds of environmental action groups. The Web site presents the latest environmental news, education resources, government links, career resources, articles, publications, and much more.
http://www.envirolink.org/

The Canadian Nature Federation is a national voice for the protection of nature, its diversity, and the processes that sustain it. Its site has information of environmental threats, endangered species, community education, and bird conservation; go to:
http://www.cnf.ca/index.html

Web Networks is a nonprofit organization dedicated to serving the needs of the social change community in Canada. This site contains *Web Networks Community*, a comprehensive listing of social change groups and individuals across Canada; go to:
http://www.web.net/

QUESTIONS FOR CRITICAL THINKING

1. What types of collective behaviour in Canada do you believe are influenced by inequalities based on race/ethnicity, class, gender, age, or disabilities? Why?
2. Which of the four explanations of crowd behaviour (contagion theory, social unrest and circular reaction, convergence theory, and emergent norm theory) do you believe best explains crowd behaviour? Why?
3. How would you analyze the environmental movement in terms of the value-added theory? What about the relative deprivation and resource mobilization theories?
4. Using the sociological imagination that you have gained in this course, what are some positive steps that you believe might be taken in Canada to make our society a better place for everyone in this century? What types of collective behaviour and/or social movements might be required in order to take those steps?

SUGGESTED READINGS

For more in-depth information on collective behaviour and social movements, both of these texts are excellent:

Russell L. Curtis, Jr., and Benigno E. Aguirre. *Collective Behaviour and Social Movements*. Boston: Allyn & Bacon, 1993.

Ralph H. Turner and Lewis M. Killian. *Collective Behaviour* (4th ed.). Englewood Cliffs, N.J.: Prentice-Hall, 1993.

These books provide additional insights on environmental hazards and the social movements that were launched to combat them:

Sherry Cable and Charles Cable. *Environmental Problems, Grassroots Solutions: The Politics of Grassroots Environmental Conflict*. New York: St. Martin's Press, 1995.

Jen Chang, Bethany Or, Eloginy Tharmendran, Emmie Tsumara, Steve Daniels, and Darryl Leroux, eds. *RESIST! A Grassroots Collection of Stories, Poetry, Photos and Analysis from the FTAA Protests in Québec City and Beyond.* Halifax: Fernwood Publishing, 2001.

Kai Erikson. *A New Species of Trouble: Explorations in Disaster, Trauma, and Community.* New York: Norton, 1994.

ONLINE STUDY AND RESEARCH TOOLS

THOMSONNOW™

Go to **http://hed.nelson.com** to link to ThomsonNOW for *Sociology in Our Times,* Fourth Canadian Edition, your online study tool. First take the **Pre-Test** for this chapter to get your personalized **Study Plan,** which will identify topics you need to review and direct you to the appropriate resources. Then take the **Post-Test** to determine what concepts you have mastered and what you still need work on.

INFOTRAC®

Infotrac College Edition is included free with every new copy of this text. Explore this online library for additional readings, review, and a handy resource for assignments. Visit **www.infotrac-college.com** to access this online database of full-text articles. Enter the key terms from this chapter to start your search.

absolute poverty A level of economic deprivation in which people do not have the means to secure the most basic necessities of life.

achieved status A social position that a person assumes voluntarily as a result of personal choice, merit, or direct effort.

activity theory The proposition that people tend to shift gears in late middle age and find substitutes for previous statuses, roles, and activities.

acute illness Illness of limited duration from which the patient recovers or dies.

age stratification The inequalities, differences, segregation, or conflict between age groups.

ageism Prejudice and discrimination against people on the basis of age, particularly when they are older persons.

agents of socialization Those persons, groups, or institutions that teach people what they need to know in order to participate in society.

aggregate A collection of people who happen to be in the same place at the same time but have little else in common.

aging The physical, psychological, and social processes associated with growing older.

alienation A feeling of powerlessness and estrangement from other people and from oneself.

altruism Behaviour intended to help others and done without any expectation of personal benefit.

analysis The process through which data are organized so that comparisons can be made and conclusions drawn.

animism The belief that plants, animals, or other elements of the natural world are endowed with spirits or life forces that have an impact on events in society.

anomie Émile Durkheim's designation for a condition in which social control becomes ineffective as a result of the loss of shared values and a sense of purpose in society.

anticipatory socialization The process by which knowledge and skills are learned for future roles.

ascribed status A social position that is conferred on a person at birth or received involuntarily later in life.

assimilation A process by which members of subordinate racial and ethnic groups become absorbed into the dominant culture.

asymmetrical warfare Attacks by small groups of people who usually do not represent states or governments upon much larger and stronger opponents.

authoritarian personality Characterized by excessive conformity, submissiveness to authority, intolerance, insecurity, a high level of superstition, and rigid, stereotypic thinking.

authoritarian political system A political system controlled by rulers who deny popular participation in government.

authority Power that people accept as legitimate rather than coercive.

avian influenza A virus affecting birds that is believed to have the potential to spread to humans and to become a pandemic that will kill millions of people around the world.

bilateral descent A system of tracing descent through both the mother's and father's sides of the family.

body consciousness How a person perceives and feels about his or her body; it also includes an awareness of social conditions in society that contribute to this self-knowledge.

bourgeoisie (or capitalist class) Karl Marx's term for the class comprised of those who own and control the means of production.

bureaucracy An organizational model characterized by a hierarchy of authority, a clear division of labour, explicit rules and procedures, and impersonality in personnel matters.

bureaucratic personality A psychological construct that describes those workers who are more concerned with following correct procedures than they are with doing the job correctly.

capitalism An economic system characterized by private ownership of the means of production, from which personal profits can be derived through market competition and without government intervention.

category A number of people who may never have met one another but who share a similar characteristic.

central city The densely populated centre of a metropolis.

charismatic authority Power legitimized on the basis of a leader's exceptional personal qualities.

chronic illness Term applied to long-term or permanent conditions that may or may not be fatal.

chronological age A person's age based on date of birth.

church A large, bureaucratically organized religious organization that tends to seek accommodation with the larger society in order to maintain some degree of control over it.

civil disobedience Nonviolent action that seeks to change a policy or law by refusing to comply with it.

class The relative location of a person or group within a larger society, based on wealth, power, prestige, or other valued resources.

class conflict Karl Marx's term for the struggle between the capitalist class and the working class.

class system A type of stratification based on the ownership and control of resources and on the kinds of work people do.

classism The belief that persons in the upper or privileged class are superior to those in the lower or working class, particularly in regard to values, behaviour, and lifestyles.

cohabitation The sharing of a household by a couple who live together without being legally married.

cohort A category of people who are born within a specified period in time or who share some specified characteristic.

collective behaviour   Voluntary, often spontaneous activity that is engaged in by a large number of people and typically violates dominant group norms and values.

commonsense knowledge   A form of knowing that guides ordinary conduct in everyday life.

complete observation   Research in which the investigator systematically observes a social process but does not take part in it.

conflict perspective   The sociological approach that views groups in society as engaged in a continuous power struggle for control of scarce resources.

conformity   The process of maintaining or changing behaviour to comply with the norms established by a society, subculture, or other group.

content analysis   The systematic examination of cultural artifacts or various forms of communication to extract thematic data and draw conclusions about social life.

contingent work   Part-time or temporary work.

control group   Subjects in an experiment who are not exposed to the independent variable but later are compared to subjects in the experimental group.

core nation   According to world systems theory, a dominant capitalist centre characterized by high levels of industrialization and urbanization and a high degree of control over the world economy.

corporate crime   An illegal act committed by corporate employees on behalf of the corporation and with its support.

corporation   A large-scale organization that has legal powers (such as the ability to enter into contracts and buy and sell property) separate from its individual owner or owners.

counterculture   A group that strongly rejects dominant societal values and norms and seeks alternative lifestyles.

credentialism   A process of social selection in which class advantage and social status are linked to the possession of academic qualifications.

crime   Behaviour that violates criminal law and is punishable with fines, jail terms, and other sanctions.

crowd   A relatively large number of people who are in one another's immediate vicinity.

crude birth rate   The number of live births per 1,000 people in a population in a given year.

crude death rate   The number of deaths per 1,000 people in a population in a given year.

cult   A religious group with practices and teachings outside the dominant cultural and religious traditions of a society.

cultural artifacts   Products of individual activity, social organizations, technology, and cultural patterns.

cultural capital   Pierre Bourdieu's term for people's social assets, including their values, beliefs, attitudes, and competencies in language and culture.

cultural imperialism   The extensive infusion of one nation's culture into other nations.

cultural lag   William Ogburn's term for a gap between the technical development of a society (material culture) and its moral and legal institutions (nonmaterial culture).

cultural relativism   The belief that the behaviours and customs of a society must be viewed and analyzed by the culture's own standards.

cultural transmission   The process by which children and recent immigrants become acquainted with the dominant cultural beliefs, values, norms, and accumulated knowledge of a society.

cultural universals   Customs and practices that occur across all societies.

culture   The knowledge, language, values, customs, and material objects that are passed from person to person and from one generation to the next in a human group or society.

culture shock   The disorientation that people feel when they encounter cultures radically different from their own.

deductive approach   Research in which the investigator begins with a theory and then collects information and data to test the theory.

democracy   A political system in which people hold the ruling power, either directly or indirectly.

democratic socialism   An economic and political system that combines private ownership of some of the means of production, governmental distribution of some essential goods and services, and free elections.

demographic transition   The process by which some societies have moved from high birth and death rates to relatively low birth and death rates as a result of technological development.

demography   A subfield of sociology that examines population size, composition, and distribution.

denomination   A large, organized religion characterized by accommodation to society but frequently lacking the ability or intention to dominate society.

dependency theory   The perspective that global poverty can at least partially be attributed to the fact that low-income countries have been exploited by high-income countries.

dependent variable   A variable that is assumed to depend on or be caused by one or more other (independent) variables.

descriptive study   Research that attempts to describe social reality or provide facts about some group, practice, or event.

deviance   Any behaviour, belief, or condition that violates cultural norms in the society or group in which it occurs.

differential association theory   The proposition that individuals have a greater tendency to deviate from societal norms when they frequently associate with persons who are more favourable toward deviance than conformity.

diffusion   The transmission of cultural items or social practices from one group or society to another.

disability   A health condition that reduces a person's ability to perform tasks he or she would normally do at a given stage of life and that may result in stigmatization or discrimination against the person.

discourses All that is written, spoken, or otherwise represented through language and communication systems.

discovery The process of learning about something previously unknown or unrecognized.

discrimination Actions or practices of dominant group members (or their representatives) that have a harmful impact on members of a subordinate group.

disengagement theory The proposition that older persons make a normal and healthy adjustment to aging when they detach themselves from their social roles and prepare for their eventual death.

dramaturgical analysis The study of social interaction that compares everyday life to a theatrical presentation.

dual-earner family A family in which both partners are in the labour force.

dyad A group consisting of two members.

dysfunctions A term referring to the undesirable consequences of any element of a society.

ecclesia A religious organization that, is so integrated into the dominant culture that it claims as its membership all members of a society.

economy The social institution that ensures the maintenance of society through the production, distribution, and consumption of goods and services.

education The social institution responsible for the systematic transmission of knowledge, skills, and cultural values within a formally organized structure.

egalitarian family A family structure in which both partners share power and authority equally.

ego According to Sigmund Freud, the rational, reality-oriented component of personality that imposes restrictions on the innate pleasure-seeking drives of the id.

elder abuse A term used to describe physical abuse, psychological abuse, financial exploitation, and medical abuse or neglect of people age 65 or older.

elite model A view of society in which power in political systems is concentrated in the hands of a small group of elites and the masses are relatively powerless.

emigration The movement of people out of a geographic area to take up residency elsewhere.

empirical approach Research that attempts to answer questions through a systematic collection and analysis of data.

employment equity A strategy to eliminate the effects of discrimination and to make employment opportunities available to groups who have been excluded.

environmental racism The belief that a disproportionate number of hazardous facilities are placed in low-income areas populated largely by people of colour.

epidemic Sudden, significant increase in the numbers of people contracting a disease.

ethnic group A collection of people distinguished, by others or by themselves, primarily on the basis of cultural or nationality characteristics.

ethnic pluralism The coexistence of a variety of distinct racial and ethnic groups within one society.

ethnicity The cultural heritage or identity of a group based on factors such as language or country of origin.

ethnocentrism The tendency to regard one's own culture and group as the standard, and thus superior, whereas all other groups are seen as inferior.

ethnography A detailed study of the life and activities of a group of people by researchers who may live with that group over a period of years.

ethnomethodology The study of the commonsense knowledge that people use to understand the situations in which they find themselves.

experiment A research method involving a carefully designed test in which the researcher studies the impact of certain variables on subjects' attitudes or behaviour.

experimental group Subjects in an experiment who are exposed to the independent variable.

explanatory study Research that attempts to explain relationships and to provide information on why certain events do or do not occur.

extended family A family unit composed of relatives in addition to parents and children who live in the same household.

fad A temporary but widely copied activity followed enthusiastically by large numbers of people.

faith Unquestioning belief that does not require proof or scientific evidence.

families we choose Social arrangements that include intimate relationships between couples and close relationships with other couples, and with other adults and children.

family A relationship in which people live together with commitment, form an economic unit and care for any young, and consider their identity to be significantly attached to the group.

family of orientation The family into which a person is born and in which early socialization usually takes place.

family of procreation The family that a person forms by having or adopting children.

fashion A currently valued style of behaviour, thinking, or appearance.

feminism The belief that all people—both women and men—are equal and that they should be valued equally and have equal rights.

feminist perspective The sociological approach that focuses on the significance of gender in understanding and explaining inequalities that exist between men and women in the household, in the paid labour force, and in the realms of politics, law, and culture.

feminization of poverty The trend in which women are disproportionately represented among individuals living in poverty.

fertility The actual level of childbearing for an individual or a population.

field research The study of social life in its natural setting: observing and interviewing people where they live, work, and play.

folkways Informal norms or everyday customs that may be violated without serious consequences within a particular culture.

formal education Learning that takes place within an academic setting, such as school, which has a planned instructional process and teachers who convey specific knowledge, skills, and thinking processes to students.

formal organization A highly structured group formed for the purpose of completing certain tasks or achieving specific goals.

functional age A term used to describe observable individual attributes, such as physical appearance, mobility, strength, coordination, and mental capacity, that are used to assign people to age categories.

functional illiteracy The condition in which reading and writing skills are inadequate to carry out everyday activities.

functionalist perspective The sociological approach that views society as a stable, orderly system.

Gemeinschaft (guh-MINE-shoft) A traditional society in which social relationships are based on personal bonds of friendship and kinship and on intergenerational stability.

gender The culturally and socially constructed differences between females and males found in meanings, beliefs, and practices associated with "femininity" and "masculinity."

gender bias Behaviour that shows favouritism toward one gender over the other.

gender identity A person's perception of the self as female or male.

gender role Attitudes, behaviour, and activities that are socially defined as appropriate for each sex and are learned through the socialization process.

gender socialization The aspect of socialization that contains specific messages and practices concerning the nature of being female or male in a specific group or society.

generalized other George Herbert Mead's term for the child's awareness of the demands and expectations of the society as a whole or of the child's subculture.

genocide The deliberate, systematic killing of an entire people or nation.

gentrification The process by which members of the middle and upper-middle classes move into the central city area and renovate existing properties.

Gesellschaft (guh-ZELL-shoft) A large, urban society in which social bonds are based on impersonal and specialized relationships, with little long-term commitment to the group or consensus on values.

global interdependence A relationship in which the lives of all people are intertwined closely and any one nation's problems are part of a larger global problem.

goal displacement A process that occurs in organizations when the rules become an end in themselves and organizational survival becomes more important than achievement of goals.

gossip Rumours about the personal lives of individuals.

government The formal organization that has the legal and political authority to regulate the relationships among members within a society and between the society and those outside its borders.

gross national income All the goods and services produced in a country in a given year, plus the income earned outside the country by individuals or corporations.

groupthink The process by which members of a cohesive group arrive at a decision that many individual members privately believe is unwise.

health The state of complete physical, mental, and social well-being.

health care Any activity intended to improve health.

hermaphrodite A person in whom sexual differentiation is ambiguous or incomplete.

heterosexism The belief that heterosexuality is the only valid form of sexual behaviour.

hidden curriculum The transmission of cultural values and attitudes, such as conformity and obedience to authority, through implied demands found in rules, routines, and regulations of schools.

high-income economies Countries with an annual per capita Gross National Income over $9,386.

homogamy The pattern of individuals marrying those who have similar characteristics, such as race/ethnicity, religious background, age, education, or social class.

homophobia Extreme prejudice directed at gays, lesbians, bisexuals, and others who are perceived as not being heterosexual.

hospice A homelike facility that provides supportive care for patients with terminal illnesses.

hypothesis In research studies, a tentative statement of the relationship between two or more concepts or variables.

id Sigmund Freud's term for the component of personality that includes all of the individual's basic biological drives and needs that demand immediate gratification.

ideal culture The values and standards of behaviour that people in a society profess to hold.

ideal type An abstract model that describes the recurring characteristics of some phenomenon.

illegitimate opportunity structures Circumstances that provide an opportunity for people to acquire through illegitimate activities what they cannot achieve through legitimate channels.

immigration The movement of people into a geographic area to take up residency.

impression management (or presentation of self) A term for people's efforts to present themselves to others in ways that are most favourable to their own interests or image.

income The economic gain derived from wages, salaries, income transfers (governmental aid), and ownership of property.

independent variable A variable that is presumed to cause or determine a dependent variable.

inductive approach Research in which the investigator collects information or data (facts or evidence) and then generates theories from the analysis of that data.

industrialization The process by which societies are transformed from dependence on agriculture and handmade products to an emphasis on manufacturing and related industries.

infant mortality rate The number of deaths of infants under 1 year of age per 1,000 live births in a given year.

infertility A medical term used to describe one year of attempting to achieve pregnancy without success.

informal education Learning that occurs in a spontaneous, unplanned way.

informal structure A term used to describe the aspect of organizational life in which participants' day-to-day activities and interactions ignore, bypass, or do not correspond with the official rules and procedures of the bureaucracy.

ingroup A group to which a person belongs and with which the person feels a sense of identity.

institutionalized racism A term used to describe the rules, procedures, and practices that directly and deliberately prevent minorities from having full and equal involvement in society.

intergenerational mobility The social movement (upward or downward) experienced by family members from one generation to the next.

internal colonialism According to conflict theorists, a practice that occurs when members of a racial or ethnic group are conquered or colonized and forcibly placed under the economic and political control of the dominant group.

interview A research method using a data collection encounter in which an interviewer asks the respondent questions and records the answers.

intragenerational mobility The social movement (upward or downward) experienced by individuals within their own lifetime.

invasion The process by which a new category of people or type of land use arrives in an area previously occupied by another group or land use.

invention The process of reshaping existing cultural items into a new form.

iron law of oligarchy According to Robert Michels, the tendency of bureaucracies to be ruled by a few people.

job deskilling A reduction in the proficiency needed to perform a specific job that leads to a corresponding reduction in the wages paid for that job.

juvenile delinquency The violation of a law or the commission of a status offence by young people less than a specific age.

karoshi A Japanese term referring to employees who die from overwork.

kinship A social network of people based on common ancestry, marriage, or adoption.

labelling theory The proposition that deviants are those people who have been successfully labelled as such by others.

labour union An organization of employees who join together to bargain with an employer or a group of employers over wages, benefits, and working conditions.

language A system of symbols that expresses ideas and enables people to think and communicate with one another.

latent functions Unintended functions that are hidden and remain unacknowledged by participants.

laws Formal, standardized norms that have been enacted by legislatures and are enforced by formal sanctions.

liberation theology Christian movement that advocates freedom from political subjugation within a traditional perspective and the need for social transformation to benefit the poor and downtrodden.

life chances Max Weber's term for the extent to which persons have access to important scarce resources, such as food, clothing, shelter, education, and employment.

life expectancy The average length of time a group of individuals of the same age will live.

looking-glass self Charles Horton Cooley's term for the way in which a person's sense of self is derived from the perceptions of others.

low-income cutoff The income level at which a family may be in "straitened circumstances" because it spends considerably more on the basic necessities of life (food, shelter, and clothing) than the average family.

low-income economies Countries with an annual per capita Gross National Income of $765 or less.

lower-middle-income economies Countries with an annual per capita Gross National Income between $766 and $3,035.

macrolevel analysis Sociological theory and research that focuses on whole societies, large-scale social structures, and social systems.

majority (dominant) group An advantaged group that has superior resources and rights in a society.

manifest functions Open, stated, and intended goals or consequences of activities within an organization or institution.

marginal job A position that differs from the employment norms of the society in which it is located.

marriage A legally recognized and/or socially approved arrangement between two or more individuals that carries certain rights and obligations and usually involves sexual activity.

mass A large collection of people who share an interest in a specific idea or issue but who are not in another's immediate physical vicinity.

mass behaviour Collective behaviour that takes place when people (who often are geographically separated from one another) respond to the same event in much the same way.

mass education Free, public schooling for wide segments of a nation's population.

mass hysteria A form of dispersed collective behaviour that occurs when a large number of people react with strong emotions and self-destructive behaviour to a real or perceived threat.

master status A term used to describe the most important status a person occupies.

material culture A component of culture that consists of the physical or tangible creations (such as clothing, shelter, and art) that members of a society make, use, and share.

matriarchal family A family structure in which authority is held by the eldest female (usually the mother).

matriarchy A hierarchical system of social organization in which cultural, political, and economic structures are controlled by women.

matrilineal descent A system of tracing descent through the mother's side of the family.

means of production Karl Marx's term for tools, land, factories, and money for investment that form the economic basis of a society.

mechanical solidarity Émile Durkheim's term for the social cohesion that exists in preindustrial societies, in which there is a minimal division of labour and people feel united by shared values and common social bonds.

medicalization The process whereby an object or a condition becomes defined by society as a physical or psychological illness.

medicine An institutionalized system for the scientific diagnosis, treatment, and prevention of illness.

megalopolis A continuous concentration of two or more cities and their suburbs that have grown until they form an interconnected urban area.

meritocracy A hierarchy system in which all positions are rewarded based on people's ability and credentials.

metropolis One or more central cities and their surrounding suburbs that dominate the economic and cultural life of a region.

microlevel analysis Sociological theory and research that focuses on small groups rather than large-scale social structures.

migration The movement of people from one geographic area to another for the purpose of changing residency.

minority (subordinate) group A disadvantaged group whose members, because of physical or cultural characteristics, are subjected to unequal treatment by the dominant group and who regard themselves as objects of collective discrimination.

mixed economy An economic system that combines elements of a market economy (capitalism) with elements of a command economy (socialism).

mob A highly emotional crowd whose members engage in, or are ready to engage in, violence against a specific target, which may be a person,

a category of people, or physical property.

modernization theory A perspective that links global inequality to different levels of economic development and suggests that low-income economies can move to middle- and high-income economies by achieving self-sustained economic growth.

monarchy A political system in which power resides in one person or family and is passed from generation to generation through lines of inheritance.

monogamy Marriage to one person at a time.

monotheism Belief in a single, supreme being or god who is responsible for significant events, such as the creation of the world.

moral crusades Public and media awareness campaigns that help generate public and political support for moral entrepreneurs' causes.

moral entrepreneurs People or groups who take an active role in trying to have particular behaviours defined as deviant.

mores Strongly held norms with moral and ethical connotations that may not be violated without serious consequences in a particular culture.

mortality The incidence of death in a population.

multinational corporations Large companies that are headquartered in one country and have subsidiaries or branches in other countries.

network enterprise Separate businesses, which may be companies or parts of companies, join together for specific projects that become the focus of the network.

new international division of labour theory The perspective that commodity production is being split into fragments that can be assigned to whichever part of the world can provide the most profitable combination of capital and labour.

nonmaterial culture A component of culture that consists of the abstract or intangible human creations of society (such as attitudes, beliefs, and values) that influence people's behaviour.

nontheistic religion A religion based on a belief in divine spiritual forces, such as sacred principles of thought and conduct, rather than a god or gods.

nonverbal communication The transfer of information between persons without the use of speech.

normative approach The use of religion, custom, habit, tradition, or authority to answer important questions.

norms Established rules of behaviour or standards of conduct.

nuclear family A family made up of one or two parents and their dependent children, all of whom live apart from other relatives.

objective Free from distorted subjective (personal or emotional) bias.

occupation A category of jobs that involve similar activities at different work sites.

occupational (or white-collar) crime A term used to describe illegal activities committed by people in the course of their employment or in dealing with their financial affairs.

oligopoly The situation that exists when several companies overwhelmingly control an entire industry.

operational definition An explanation of an abstract concept in terms of observable features that are specific enough to measure the variable.

organic solidarity Émile Durkheim's term for the social cohesion that exists in industrial (and perhaps postindustrial) societies, in which people perform very specialized tasks and feel united by their mutual dependence.

organized crime A business operation that supplies illegal goods and services for profit.

outgroup A term used to describe a group to which a person does not belong and toward which the person may feel a sense of competitiveness or hostility.

overt racism Racism that may take the form of public statements about the "inferiority" of members of a racial or ethnic group.

panic A form of crowd behaviour that occurs when a large number of people react with strong emotions and self-destructive behaviour to a real or perceived threat.

participant observation A research method in which researchers collect systematic observations while being part of the activities of the group they are studying.

patriarchal family A family structure in which authority is held by the eldest male (usually the father).

patriarchy A hierarchical system of social organization in which cultural, political, and economic structures are controlled by men.

patrilineal descent A system of tracing descent through the father's side of the family.

pay equity (comparable worth) The belief that wages ought to reflect the worth of a job, not the gender or race of the worker.

peer group A group of people who are linked by common interests, equal social position, and (usually) similar age.

peripheral nations According to world systems theory, nations that are dependent on core nations for capital, have little or no industrialization, and have uneven patterns of urbanization.

personal space The immediate area surrounding a person that the person claims as private.

perspective An overall approach to or viewpoint on some subject.

pink-collar occupation Relatively low-paying, nonmanual, semiskilled positions primarily held by women.

pluralist model An analysis of political systems that views power as widely dispersed throughout many competing interest groups.

polite racism A term used to describe an attempt to disguise a dislike of others through behaviour that outwardly is nonprejudicial.

political crime Illegal or unethical acts involving the usurpation of power by government officials, or illegal or unethical acts perpetrated against the government by outsiders seeking to make a political statement, undermine the government, or overthrow it.

political party An organization whose purpose is to gain and hold legitimate control of government.

political socialization The process by which people learn political attitudes, values, and behaviour.

politics The social institution through which power is acquired and exercised by some people and groups.

polyandry The concurrent marriage of one woman with two or more men.

polygamy The concurrent marriage of a person of one sex with two or more members of the opposite sex.

polygyny The concurrent marriage of one man with two or more women.

polytheism Belief in more than one god.

popular culture The component of culture that consists of activities, products, and services that are assumed to appeal primarily to members of the middle and working classes.

population In a research study, those persons about whom we want to be able to draw conclusions.

population composition In demography, the biological and social characteristics of a population.

population pyramid A graphic representation of the distribution of a population by sex and age.

positivism A belief that the world can best be understood through scientific inquiry.

postindustrial economy An economy that is based on the provision of services rather than goods.

postmodern perspectives The sociological approach that attempts to explain social life in modern societies that are characterized by postindustrialization, consumerism, and global communications.

power According to Max Weber, the ability of people or groups to achieve their goals despite opposition from others.

power elite C. Wright Mills's term for a small clique composed of the top corporate, political, and military officials.

prejudice A negative attitude based on faulty generalizations about members of selected groups.

prestige The respect or regard with which a person or status position is regarded by others.

preventive medicine Medicine that emphasizes a healthy lifestyle in order to prevent poor health before it occurs.

primary deviance A term used to describe the initial act of rule breaking.

primary group Charles Horton Cooley's term for a small, less specialized group in which members engage in face-to-face, emotion-based interactions over an extended period of time.

primary sector production The sector of the economy that extracts raw materials and natural resources from the environment.

primary sex characteristics The genitalia used in the reproductive process.

profane A term used to describe the everyday, secular, or "worldly," aspects of life.

profession A high-status, knowledge-based occupation.

proletariat (or working class) Karl Marx's term for those who must sell their labour because they have no other means to earn a livelihood.

propaganda Information provided by individuals or groups that have a vested interest in furthering their own cause or damaging an opposing one.

public opinion The political attitudes and beliefs communicated by ordinary citizens to decision makers.

punishment An action designed to deprive a person of things of value (including liberty) because of some offence the person is thought to have committed.

questionnaire A research instrument containing a series of items to which subjects respond.

race A term used by many people to specify groups of people distinguished by physical characteristics, such as skin colour; also, a category of people who have been singled out as inferior or superior, often on the basis of real or alleged physical characteristics, such as skin colour, hair texture, eye shape, or other subjectively selected attributes.

racial prejudice Beliefs that certain racial groups are innately inferior to others or have a disproportionate number of negative traits.

racism A set of ideas that implies the superiority of one social group over another on the basis of biological or cultural characteristics, together with the power to put these beliefs into practice in a way that denies or excludes minority women and men.

random sample   A selection in which everyone in the target population has an equal chance of being chosen; in other words, choice occurs by chance.

rationality   The process by which traditional methods of social organization, characterized by informality and spontaneity, are gradually replaced by efficiently administered formal rules and procedures (bureaucracy).

rational-legal authority   Power legitimized by law or written rules and procedures. Also referred to as *bureaucratic authority*.

reactivity   The tendency of experiment participants to change their behaviour in response to the presence of the researcher or to the fact that they know they are being studied.

real culture   The values and standards of behaviour that people actually follow (as contrasted with ideal culture).

reference group   A term used to describe a group that strongly influences a person's behaviour and social attitudes, regardless of whether that individual is an actual member.

relative homelessness   Being housed in a dwelling that fails to meet basic living standards.

relative poverty   A level of economic deprivation in which people may be able to afford basic necessities but still are unable to maintain an average standard of living.

reliability   In sociological research, the extent to which a study or research instrument yields consistent results.

religion   A system of beliefs, symbols, and rituals, based on some sacred or supernatural realm, that guides human behaviour, gives meaning to life, and unites believers into a community.

replication   In sociological research, the repetition of the investigation in substantially the same way that it originally was conducted.

representative sample   A selection from a larger population that has the essential characteristics of the total population.

research   The process of systematically collecting information for the purposes of testing an existing theory or generating a new one.

research methods   Specific strategies or techniques for conducting research.

resocialization   The process of learning a new set of attitudes, values, and behaviours different from those in one's previous background and experiences.

respondent   A person who provides data for analysis through an interview or questionnaire.

riot   Violent crowd behaviour that is fuelled by deep-seated emotions but is not directed at one specific target.

rituals   Regularly repeated and carefully prescribed forms of behaviour that symbolize a cherished value or belief.

role   A set of behavioural expectations associated with a given status.

role conflict   A situation in which incompatible role demands are placed on a person by two or more statuses held at the same time.

role exit   A situation in which people disengage from social roles that have been central to their self-identity.

role expectation   A term used to describe a group's or society's definition of the way a specific role ought to be played.

role performance   How a person actually plays a role.

role strain   The strain experienced by a person when incompatible demands are built into a single status that the person occupies.

role-taking   The process by which a person mentally assumes the role of another person in order to understand the world from that person's point of view.

routinization of charisma   A term for the process by which charismatic authority is succeeded by a bureaucracy controlled by a rationally established authority or by a combination of traditional and bureaucratic authority.

rumour   An unsubstantiated report on an issue or subject.

sacred   A term used to describe those aspects of life that are extraordinary or supernatural.

sample   The people who are selected from the population to be studied.

sanction   A reward for appropriate behaviour or a penalty for inappropriate behaviour.

Sapir–Whorf hypothesis The proposition that language shapes the view of reality of its speakers.

scapegoat   A person or group that is incapable of offering resistance to the hostility or aggression of others.

second shift   Arlie Hochschild's term for the domestic work that employed women perform at home after they complete their workday on the job.

secondary analysis   A research method in which researchers use existing material and analyze data that originally was collected by others.

secondary deviance   A term used to describe the process whereby a person who has been labelled deviant accepts that new identity and continues the deviant behaviour.

secondary group   A larger, more specialized group in which the members engage in more impersonal, goal-oriented relationships for a limited period of time.

secondary sector production   The sector of the economy that processes raw materials (from the primary sector) into finished goods.

secondary sex characteristics   The physical traits (other than reproductive organs) that identify an individual's sex.

sect   A relatively small religious group that has broken away from another religious organization to renew what it views as the original version of the faith.

secularization   Movement of a group or society from a religious to a civil orientation.

segregation   A term used to describe the spatial and social separation of categories of people by race/ethnicity, class, gender, and/or religion.

self-concept   The totality of our beliefs and feelings about ourselves.

self-fulfilling prophecy   A situation in which a false belief or prediction produces behaviour that makes the originally false belief come true.

semiperipheral nation   According to world systems theory, a nation that is more developed than peripheral nations but less developed than core nations.

senile dementia A term for diseases, such as Alzheimer's, that involve a progressive impairment of judgment and memory.

sex A term used to describe the biological and anatomical differences between females and males.

sex ratio A term used by demographers to denote the number of males for every hundred females in a given population.

sexism The subordination of one sex, usually female, based on the assumed superiority of the other sex.

sexual orientation A person's preference for emotional–sexual relationships with members of the opposite sex (heterosexuality), the same sex (homosexuality), or both sexes (bisexuality).

sick role Patterns of behaviour defined as appropriate for people who are sick.

significant others Those persons whose care, affection, and approval are especially desired and who are most important in the development of the self.

simple supernaturalism The belief that supernatural forces affect people's lives either positively or negatively.

small group A collectivity small enough for all members to be acquainted with one another and to interact simultaneously.

social bond theory The proposition that the likelihood of deviant behaviour increases when a person's ties to society are weakened or broken.

social change The alteration, modification, or transformation of public policy, culture, or social institutions over time.

social construction of reality The process by which our perception of reality is shaped largely by the subjective meaning that we give to an experience.

social control Systematic practices developed by social groups to encourage conformity and to discourage deviance.

social Darwinism The belief that those species of animals (including human beings) best adapted to their environment survive and prosper, whereas those poorly adapted die out.

social devaluation A situation in which a person or group is considered to have less social value than other individuals or groups.

social distance A term used to describe the extent to which people are willing to interact and establish relationships with members of racial and ethnic groups other than their own.

social exclusion The process by which certain individuals and groups are systematically barred from access to positions that would enable them to have an autonomous livelihood in keeping with the social standards and values of a given social context.

social facts Émile Durkheim's term for patterned ways of acting, thinking, and feeling that exist outside any one individual.

social gerontology The study of the social (nonphysical) aspects of aging.

social group A group that consists of two or more people who interact frequently and share a common identity and a feeling of interdependence.

social institution A set of organized beliefs and rules that establish how a society will attempt to meet its basic social needs.

social interaction The process by which people act toward or respond to other people.

social marginality The state of being part insider and part outsider in the social structure.

social mobility The movement of individuals or groups from one level in a stratification system to another.

social movement An organized group that acts consciously to promote or resist change through collective action.

social network A series of social relationships that link an individual to others.

social solidarity The state of having shared beliefs and values among members of a social group, along with intense and frequent interaction among group members.

social stratification The hierarchical arrangement of large social groups based on their control over basic resources.

social structure The stable pattern of social relationships that exist within a particular group or society.

socialism An economic system characterized by public ownership of the means of production, the pursuit of collective goals, and centralized decision making.

socialization The lifelong process of social interaction through which individuals acquire a self-identity and the physical, mental, and social skills needed for survival in society.

societal consensus A situation whereby the majority of members share a common set of values, beliefs, and behavioural expectations.

society A large social grouping that shares the same geographical territory and is subject to the same political authority and dominant cultural expectations.

sociobiology The systematic study of how biology affects social behaviour.

socioeconomic status (SES) A combined measure that attempts to classify individuals, families, or households in terms of indicators, such as income, occupation, and education, to determine class location.

sociological imagination C. Wright Mills's term for the ability to see the relationship between individual experiences and the larger society.

sociology The systematic study of human society and social interaction.

sociology of family The subdiscipline of sociology that attempts to describe and explain patterns of family life and variations in family structure.

special interest groups Political coalitions comprised of individuals or groups that share a specific interest that they wish to protect or advance with the help of the political system.

split labour market A term used to describe the division of the economy into two areas of employment: a primary sector or upper tier, composed of higher-paid (usually dominant group) workers in more secure jobs; and a secondary sector or lower tier, composed of lower-paid (often subordinate group) workers in jobs with little security and hazardous working conditions.

state   The political entity that possesses a legitimate monopoly over the use of force within its territory to achieve its goals.

status   A socially defined position in a group or society characterized by certain expectations, rights, and duties.

status set   A term used to describe all the statuses that a person occupies at a given time.

status symbol   A material sign that informs others of a person's specific status.

stereotype   An overgeneralization about the appearance, behaviour, or other characteristics of all members of a group.

stigma   According to Erving Goffman, any physical or social attribute or sign that so devalues a person's social identity that it disqualifies that person from full social acceptance.

strain theory   The proposition that people feel strain when they are exposed to cultural goals that they are unable to obtain because they do not have access to culturally approved means of achieving those goals.

street crime   All violent crime, certain property crimes, and certain morals crimes.

subculture   A group of people who share a distinctive set of cultural beliefs and behaviours that differ in some significant way from that of the larger society.

subliminal racism   A term used to describe an unconscious criticism of minorities.

succession   The process by which a new category of people or type of land use gradually predominates in an area formerly dominated by another group or activity.

superego   Sigmund Freud's term for the human conscience, consisting of the moral and ethical aspects of personality.

survey   A research method in which a number of respondents are asked identical questions through a systematic questionnaire or interview.

symbol   Anything that meaningfully represents something else.

symbolic crusade   Activity by an interest group in which the recognition of the crusaders' values by the government was at least as important as achieving their stated goal.

symbolic interactionist perspective   The sociological approach that views society as the sum of the interactions of individuals and groups.

systemic racism   A term that refers to the practices, rules, and procedures of social institutions that have the unintended consequence of excluding minority group members.

taboo   A more that is so strong that its violation is considered to be extremely offensive and even unmentionable.

technology   The knowledge, techniques, and tools that make it possible for people to transform resources into usable forms, and the knowledge and skills required to use them after they are developed.

terrorism   Acts of serious violence, planned and executed clandestinely, and committed in order to achieve political ends.

theism   A belief in a god or gods.

theory   A set of logically interrelated statements that attempts to describe, explain, and (occasionally) predict social events.

total institution   Erving Goffman's term for a place where people are isolated from the rest of society for a set period of time and come under the control of the officials who run the institution.

totalitarian political system   A political system in which the state seeks to regulate all aspects of people's public and private lives.

tracking   The assignment of students to specific courses and educational programs based on their test scores, previous grades, or both.

traditional authority   Power that is legitimized on the basis of long-standing custom.

transsexual   A person who believes that he or she was born with the body of the wrong sex.

transvestite   A male who lives as a woman or a female who lives as a man but does not alter the genitalia.

triad   A group composed of three members.

triangulation   Using several different research methods, data sources, investigators, and/or theoretical perspectives in the same study.

upper-middle-income economies   Countries with an annual per capita Gross National Income between $3,036 and $9,385.

unemployment rate   The percentage of unemployed persons in the labour force actively seeking jobs.

universal health care system   System in which all citizens receive medical services paid for through taxation revenues.

unstructured interview   A research method involving an extended, open-ended interaction between an interviewer and an interviewee.

urban sociology   A subfield of sociology that examines social relationships and political and economic structures in the city.

urbanization   The process by which an increasing proportion of a population lives in cities rather than in rural areas.

validity   In sociological research, the extent to which a study or research instrument accurately measures what it is supposed to measure.

value   A collective idea about what is right or wrong, good or bad, and desirable or undesirable in a particular culture.

value contradiction   A situation in which values conflict with one another or are mutually exclusive.

variable   In sociological research, any concept with measurable traits or characteristics that can change or vary from one person, time, situation, or society to another.

visible minority   Refers to an official government category of nonwhite, non-Caucasian individuals.

wage gap   A term used to describe the disparity between women's and men's earnings.

wealth   The value of all of a person's or family's economic assets, including income, personal property, and income-producing property.

world systems theory   The perspective that the capitalist world economy is a global system divided into a hierarchy of three major types of nations—core, semiperipheral, and peripheral—in which upward or downward mobility is conditioned by the resources and obstacles that characterize the international system.

REFERENCES

ABC Canada. 2005. "Learning a Living: First Results of the Adult Literacy and Life Skills (ALL) Survey." Retrieved August 10, 2005. Available: http://www.abc-canada.org/media_room/media/all_summary_may_05.pdf.

ABC Canada Literacy Foundation. 2001. "Who Wants to Learn." Available: http://www.abc-canada.org.

Abella, Irving. 1974. *On Strike: Six Key Labour Struggles in Canada 1919–1949.* Toronto: James Lewis and Samuel.

Abella, Irving, and Harold Troper. 1982. *None Is Too Many.* Toronto: Lester and Orpen Dennys.

Aberle, D.F., A.K. Cohen, A.K. Davis, M.J. Leng, Jr., and F.N. Sutton. 1950. "The Functional Prerequisites of Society." *Ethics,* 60(January):100–111.

Aberle, David F. 1966. *The Peyote Religion Among the Navaho.* Chicago: Aldine.

Abu-Laban, Sharon McIrvin, and Susan A. McDaniel. 2001. "Beauty, Status and Aging." In N. Mandell (ed.), *Feminist Issues* (3rd ed.). Scarborough: Prentice-Hall.

Achenbaum, W. Andrew. 1978. *Old Age in the New Land: The American Experience Since 1870.* Baltimore: John Hopkins University Press.

Achilles, Rona. 1996. "Assisted Reproduction: The Social Issues." In E.D. Nelson and B.W. Robinson (eds.), *Gender in the 1990s.* Scarborough, Ont.: Nelson Canada, 346–364.

Adams, Michael. 1998. *Sex in the Snow: Canadian Social Values at the End of the Millennium.* Toronto: Penguin.

Adams, Tom. 1991. *Grass Roots: How Ordinary People Are Changing America.* New York: Citadel Press.

Adler, Patricia A., Steven J. Kless, and Peter Adler. 1995. "Socialization to Gender Roles: Popularity Among Elementary School Boys and Girls." In E.D. Nelson and B.W. Robinson (eds.), *Gender in the 1990s.* Scarborough, Ont.: Nelson.

Adler, Patricia A., and Peter Adler. 1994. *Constructions of Deviance: Social Power, Context, and Interaction.* Belmont, Cal.: Wadsworth.

———. 1998. *Peer Power: Preadolescent Culture and Identity.* New Brunswick, N.J.: Rutgers University Press.

Adorno, Theodor, et al. 1950. *The Authoritarian Personality.* New York: Harper & Row.

Agger, Ben. 1993. *Gender, Culture, and Power: Toward a Feminist Postmodern Critical Theory.* Westport, Conn.: Praeger.

Aiello, John R., and S.E. Jones. 1971. "Field Study of Proxemic Behavior of Young School Children in Three Subcultural Groups." *Journal of Personality and Social Psychology,* 19:351–356.

Albanese, Catherine L. 1992. *America, Religions and Religion.* Belmont, Cal.: Wadsworth.

Albas, Cheryl, and Daniel Albas. 1988. "Emotion Work and Emotion Rules: The Case of Exams." *Qualitative Sociology,* 11(4):259–275.

———. 1989. "Aligning Actions: The Case of Subcultural Proxemics." *Canadian Ethnic Studies,* 21(2):74–81.

Albrecht, Gary L. 1992. *The Disability Business: Rehabilitation in America.* Newbury Park, Cal.: Sage.

Alexander, Jeffrey C. 1985. *Neofunctionalism.* Beverly Hills, Cal.: Sage.

Alexander, Peter, and Roger Gill (eds.). 1984. *Utopias.* London: Duckworth.

Alireza, Marianne. 1990. "Lifting the Veil of Tradition." *Austin American-Statesman* (September 23):C1, C7.

Alix, Ernest K. 1995. *Sociology: An Everyday Life Approach.* Minneapolis: West Publishing.

Allahar, Anton. 1989. *Sociology and the Periphery: Theories and Issues.* Toronto: Garamond.

Allport, Gordon. 1958. *The Nature of Prejudice* (abridged ed.). New York: Doubleday/Anchor.

Altemeyer, Bob. 1981. *Right-Wing Authoritarianism.* Winnipeg: University of Manitoba Press.

———. 1988. *Enemies of Freedom: Understanding Right-Wing Authoritarianism.* San Francisco: Jossey-Bass.

Alter, Jonathan. 1999. "Bridging the Digital Divide." *Newsweek* (September 20):55.

Alwin, Duane, Philip Converse, and Steven Martin. 1985. "Living Arrangements and Social Integration." *Journal of Marriage and the Family,* 47:319–334.

Ambert, Anne-Marie. 1992. *The Effect of Children on Parents.* New York: Haworth.

———. 2001. *Families in the New Millennium.* Toronto: Allyn and Bacon.

———. 2003. "Same-Sex Couples and Same-Sex Families: Relationships, Parenting, and Issues of Marriage." Vanier Institute of the Family. Retrieved August 21, 2003. Available: http://vifamily.ca/library/cft/samesex.html.

———. 2005a. *Same Sex Couples and Same Sex Families: Relationships, Parenting and Issues of Marriage.* Vanier Institute of the Family. Retrieved August 21, 2005. Available: http://www.vifamily.ca/library/cft/samesex_05.html.

———. 2005b. "Divorce: Facts, Figures and Consequences. Vanier Institute of the Family. Retrieved September 13, 2005. Available: http://www.cfc-efc.ca/docs/vanif/00005_en.htm.

American Sociological Association. 2005. "The Future of Sociology."

Aminzade, Ronald. 1973. "Revolution and Collective Political Violence: The Case of the Working Class of Marseille, France, 1830–1871." Working Paper #86, Center for Research on Social Organization. Ann Arbor: University of Michigan, October 1973.

Amiri, Rina. 2001. "Muslim Women as Symbols—and Pawns." *New York Times* (Nov. 27):A21.

Amott, Teresa, and Julie Matthaei. 1991. *Race, Gender, and Work: A Multicultural Economic History of Women in the United States.* Boston: South End Press.

———. 1996. *Race, Gender, and Work: A Multicultural Economic History of Women in the United States* (Rev. ed.). Boston: South End.

Andersen, Margaret, L. 2006. *Thinking About Women: Sociological Perspectives on Sex and Gender.* (7th ed.). Boston: Pearson.

Andersen, Margaret L., and Patricia Hill Collins, eds. 1998. *Race, Class, and Gender: An Anthology* (3rd ed.). Belmont, Cal.: Wadsworth.

Anderson, Alan B. 1994. "The Health of Aboriginal People in Saskatchewan: Recent Trends and Policy Implications." In. B. Singh Bolaria and Rosemary Bolaria (eds.), *Racial Minorities, Medicine and Health.* Halifax: Fernwood Publishing, 313–322.

Anderson, Elijah. 1990. *Streetwise: Race, Class, and Change in an Urban Community.* Chicago: University of Chicago Press.

———. 1994. "The Code of the Streets." *Atlantic Monthly* (May): 80–94.

———. 1999. *The Code of the Streets: Decency, Violence, and the Moral Life of the Inner City.* New York: Norton.

Anderson, Karen. 1996. *Sociology: A Critical Introduction.* Scarborough, Ont.: Nelson Canada.

Anderssen, Gerald F. 1998. *Highlights of the 1998 Multinational Comparisons of Health Care.* New York: The Commonwealth Fund.

Angier, Natalie. 1993. "'Stopit!' She Said. 'Nomore!'" *New York Times Book Review* (April 25):12.

Angus Reid. 1991. *Multiculturalism and Canadians: Attitude Study, 1991.* National Survey Report submitted to the Department of Multiculturalism and Citizenship.

Annesi, Nicole. 1993. "Like Mother, Like Daughter." In Leslea Newman (ed.), *Eating Our Hearts Out: Personal Accounts of Women's Relationship to Food.* Freedom, Cal.: Crossing Press, 91–95.

Anyon, Jean. 1980. "Social Class and the Hidden Curriculum of Work." *Journal of Education,* 162:67–92.

APA Online. 2000. "Psychiatric Effects of Violence." *Public Information. APA Fact Sheet Series.* Washington D.C.:

American Psychological Association. Retrieved April 5, 2000. Available: http://www.psych.org/psych/htdocs/public_info/media_violence.html.

Appelbaum, R.P., and W.P. Chambliss. 1997. *Sociology* (2nd ed.). New York: Addison-Wesley Longman.

Apple, Michael W. 1980. "Analyzing Determinations: Understanding and Evaluating the Production of Social Outcomes in Schools." *Curriculum Inquiry,* 10:55–76.

Appleton, Lynn M. 1995. "The Gender Regimes in American Cities." In Judith A. Garber and Robyne S. Turner (eds.), *Gender in Urban Research.* Thousand Oaks, Cal.: Sage, 44–59.

Arat-Koc, Sedef. 1999. "Foreign Domestic Workers and the Law." In Elizabeth Comack (ed.), *Locating Law: Race, Class, and Gender Connections.* Halifax, N.S.: Fernwood Publishing, 125–151.

Arendt, Hannah. 1973a. *On Revolution.* London: Penguin.

Armstrong Pat. 1993. "Work and Family Life: Changing Patterns." In G.N. Ramu (ed.), *Marriage and the Family in Canada Today* (2nd ed.). Scarborough, Ont.: Prentice-Hall, 127–145.

Armstrong, Pat, and Hugh Armstrong. 1983. *A Working Majority: What Women Must Do for Pay.* Ottawa: Canadian Government Publishing Centre.

———. 1994. *The Double Ghetto: Canadian Women and Their Segregated Work.* Toronto: McClelland and Stewart.

Armstrong, Pat, Hugh Armstrong, Jacqueline Choiniere, Eric Mykhalovsky, and Jerry P. White. 1997. *Medical Alert: New Work Organizations in Health Care.* Toronto: Garamond Press.

Arnold, Regina A. 1990. "Processes of Victimization and Criminalization of Black Women." *Social Justice,* 17(3):153–166.

Arnup, Katherine. 1995a. *Lesbian Parenting: Living with Pride and Prejudice.* Charlottetown, PEI: Gynergy Books.

———. 1995b. "We Are Family: Lesbian Mothers in Canada." In E.D. Nelson and B.W. Robinson (eds.), *Gender in the 1990s.* Scarborough, Ont.: Nelson Canada, 330–345.

Arquilla, John, and David Ronfeldt. 2001. *Networks and Netwars.* Santa Monica: RAND Corporation.

Asch, Adrienne. 1986. "Will Populism Empower Disabled People?" In Harry G. Boyle and Frank Reissman (eds.), *The New Populism: The Power of Empowerment.* Philadelphia: Temple University Press, 213–228.

———. 2004. "Critical Race Theory, Feminism, and Disability." In Bonnie G. Smith and Beth

Hutchison (eds.), *Gendering Disability*. New Brunswick, N.J.: Rutgers University Press, 9–44.

Asch, Solomon E. 1955. "Opinions and Social Pressure." *Scientific American,* 193(5):31–35.

———. 1956. "Studies of Independence and Conformity: A Minority of One Against a Unanimous Majority." *Psychological Monographs,* 70(9) (Whole No. 416).

Association of Faculties of Medicine of Canada. 2005. *Canadian Medical Education Statistics 2004.* Ottawa: Association of Faculties of Medicine of Canada.

Atchley, Robert C. (ed.). 1997. *Social Forces and Aging* (2nd ed.). Belmont, Cal.: Wadsworth.

Atchley, Robert C., and Amanda Barusch. 2004. *Social Forces and Aging: An Introduction to Social Gerontology* (10th ed.). Belmont, Calif.: Wadsworth.

Aulette, Judy Root. 1994. *Changing Families.* Belmont, Cal.: Wadsworth.

Avert. 2005. "HIV and AIDS in Uganda." Retrieved July 22, 2005. Available: http://www.avert.org/ aidsuganda.htm.

Aylward, Carol A. 1999. *Canadian Critical Race Theory: Racism and the Law.* Fernwood Publishing: Halifax.

Axtell, Roger E. 1991. *Gestures: The Do's and Taboos of Body Language around the World.* New York: Wiley.

Babbie, Earl. 2001. *The Practice of Social Research* (9th ed.). Belmont, Cal.: Wadsworth.

Bahr, Howard M., and Theodore Caplow. 1991. "Middletown as an Urban Case Study." In Joe R. Feagin, Anthony M. Orum, and Gideon Sjoberg (eds.), *A Case for the Case Study.* Chapel Hill: University of North Carolina Press, 80–120.

Bailyn, Bernard. 1960. *Education in the Forming of American Society.* New York: Random House.

Baker, Maureen. 2005. *Families: Changing Trends in Canada* (5th ed.). Toronto: McGraw-Hill Ryerson.

Baker, Robert. 1993. "'Pricks' and 'Chicks': A Plea for 'Persons.'" In Anne Minas (ed.), *Gender Basics: Feminist Perspectives on Women and Men.* Belmont, Cal.: Wadsworth, 66–68.

Ballantine, Jeanne H. 1993. *The Sociology of Education: A Systematic Analysis* (3rd ed.). Englewood Cliffs, N.J.: Prentice-Hall.

———. 1997. *The Sociology of Education: A Systematic Analysis* (4th ed.). Englewood Cliffs, N.J.: Prentice-Hall.

Ballara, Marcela. 1992. *Women and Literacy.* Prepared for the UN/NGO Group on Women and Development. Atlantic Highlands, N.J.: Zed Books.

Bane, Mary Jo. 1986. "Household Composition and Poverty: Which Comes First?" In Sheldon H. Danziger and Daniel H. Weinberg (eds.), *Fighting Poverty: What Works and What Doesn't.* Cambridge, M.A.: Harvard University Press.

Banner, Lois W. 1993. *In Full Flower: Aging Women, Power, and Sexuality.* New York: Vintage.

Bardwell, Jill R., Samuel W. Cochran, and Sharon Walker. 1986. "Relationship of Parental Education, Race, and Gender to Sex Role Stereotyping in Five-Year-Old Kindergarteners." *Sex Roles,* 15:275–281.

Barlow, Hugh D. 1987. *Introduction to Criminology* (4th ed.). Boston: Little, Brown.

Barlow, Maude and Heather-Jane Robertson. 1994. *Class Warfare: The Assault on Canada's Schools.* Toronto: Key Porter Books.

Barnard, Chester. 1938. *The Functions of the Executive.* Cambridge, Mass.: Harvard University Press.

Baron, Dennis. 1986. *Grammar and Gender.* New Haven, Conn.: Yale University Press.

Baron, Stephen. 1994. *Street Youth and Crime: The Role of Labour Market Experiences.* Unpublished Ph.D. diss., University of Alberta.

———. 1997. "Canadian Male Skinhead: Street Gang or Street Terrorists." *Canadian Review of Sociology and Anthropology,* 34(2):125–154.

Barrett, David V. 2001. *The New Believers.* London: Cassell and Company.

Barrett, Stanley R. 1987. *Is God a Racist? The Right Wing in Canada.* Toronto: University of Toronto Press.

Basow, Susan A. 1992. *Gender Stereotypes and Roles* (3rd ed.). Pacific Grove, Cal.: Brooks/Cole.

Bates, Stephen. 1994. *Battleground: One Mother's Crusade, the Religious Right, and the Struggle for Our Schools.* New York: Owl/Henry Holt.

Baudrillard, Jean. 1983. *Simulations.* New York: Semiotext.

Baxter, J. 1970. "Interpersonal Spacing in Natural Settings." *Sociology,* 36(3): 444–456.

Beare, Margaret. 1996a. *Criminal Conspiracies: Organized Crime in Canada.* Scarborough, Ont.: Nelson Canada.

———. 1996b. "Organized Crime and Money Laundering." In Robert A. Silverman, James J. Teevan, and Vincent F. Sacco (eds.), *Crime in Canadian Society* (5th ed.). Toronto: Harcourt Brace and Co., 187–245.

Beaujot, Roderic. 1991. *Population Change in Canada:* The Challenges of Policy Adaptation. Toronto: McClelland and Stewart.

Beaujot, Roderic, K.G., Basavarajappa, and Ravi B.P. Verma. 1988. *Current Demographic Analysis: Income and Immigrants in Canada.* Cat. no. 91-527. Ottawa: Minister of Supply and Services.

Beaujot, Roderic and Kevin McQuillan. 1982. *Growth and Dualism: The Demographic Development of Canadian Society.* Toronto: Gage.

Becker, Howard S. 1963. *Outsiders: Studies in the Sociology of Deviance.* New York: Free Press.

Beech, Hannah. 2001. "China's Lifestyle Choice." *Time* (August 6):32.

Beeghley, Leonard. 1996. *The Structure of Social Stratification in the United States* (2nd ed.). Boston: Allyn & Bacon.

———. 2000. *The Structure of Social Stratification in the United States* (3rd ed.). Boston: Allyn & Bacon.

Belkin, Lisa. 1994. "Kill for Life?" *New York Times Magazine* (October 30):47–51, 62–64, 76, 80.

Bell, Inge Powell. 1989. "The Double Standard: Age." In Jo Freeman, *Women: A Feminist Perspective* (4th ed.). Mountain View, Cal.: Mayfield, 236–244.

Bellan, Ruben. 1978. *Winnipeg First Century: An Economic History.* Winnipeg: Queenston House Publishing.

Belsky, Janet. 1990. *The Psychology of Aging: Theory, Research, and Interventions* (2nd ed.). Pacific Grove, Cal.: Brooks/Cole.

Benford, Robert D. 1993. "'You Could Be the Hundredth Monkey': Collective Action Frames and Vocabularies of Motive Within the Nuclear Disarmament Movement." *Sociological Quarterly,* 34:195–216.

Bennahum, David S. 1999. "For Kosovars, an On-Line Phone Directory of People in Exile." *New York Times* (July 15):D7.

Bennett, Holly. 1997. "A Good Spanking or a Bad Habit?" *Today's Parent* (June 1997):51–52. Retrieved November 20, 2002. Available: http://www.todaysparent.com/ behaviour/article.jsp?cId=51.

Benokraitis, Nijole V. 1999. *Marriages and Families: Changes, Choices, and Constraints* (3rd ed.). Englewood Cliffs, N.J.: Prentice-Hall.

———. 2002. *Marriages and Families: Changes, Choices, and Constraints* (4th ed.). Upper Saddle River, N.J.: Prentice-Hall.

Benokraitis, Nijole V., and Joe R. Feagin. 1986. *Modern Sexism: Blatant, Subtle, and Covert Discrimination.* Englewood Cliffs, N.J.: Prentice-Hall.

Benson, Susan Porter. 1983. "The Customers Ain't God: The Work Culture of Department Store Saleswomen, 1890–1940." In Michael H. Frisch and Daniel J. Walkowitz, *Working Class America: Essays on Labor, Community, and American Society.* Urbana: University of Illinois Press, 185–211.

Benzie, Robert. 2002. "Flaherty Vows to Make Homelessness a Crime: 'Call It Tough Love If You Will.'" *National Post* (February 15). Online at http://www.nationalpost.com.

Bergen, Raquel Kennedy. 1993. "Interviewing Survivors of Marital Rape." In Claire M. Renzetti and Raymond M. Lee (eds.), *Researching Sensitive Topics.* Newbury Park: Sage, 97–211.

Berger, Bennett M. 1988. "Utopia and Its Environment." *Society* (January/February):37–41.

Berger, Peter. 1963. *Invitation to Sociology: A Humanistic Perspective.* New York: Anchor.

———. 1967. *The Sacred Canopy: Elements of a Sociological Theory of Religion.* New York: Doubleday.

Berger, Peter, and Hansfried Kellner. 1964. "Marriage and the Construction of Reality." *Diogenes,* 46:1–32.

Berger, Peter, and Thomas Luckmann. 1967. *The Social Construction of Reality: A Treatise in the Sociology of Knowledge.* Garden City, N.Y.: Anchor Books.

Bernard, Jessie. 1982. *The Future of Marriage.* New Haven, Conn.: Yale University Press (orig. pub. 1973).

Betschwar, Karl. 2002. "Role Reversal: The Stay-at-Home Dad's Perspective." Retrieved June 30, 2003. Available: http://www.homedad.org.uk/ feature_twins.html.

Beyerstein, Barry. 1997. "Alternative Medicine: Where's the Evidence?" *Canadian Journal of Public Health,* 88 (May/June):149–150.

Bibby, Reginald W. 1987. *Fragmented Gods: The Poverty and Potential of Religion in Canada.* Toronto: Irwin.

———. 1993. *Unknown Gods: The Ongoing Story of Religion in Canada.* Toronto: Stoddart.

———. 1995a. *The Bibby Report: Social Trends Canadian Style.* Toronto: Stoddart.

———. 1995b. *Mosaic Madness: The Potential and Poverty of Canadian Life.* Toronto: Stoddart.

———. 1998. "Religion." In Robert J. Brym (ed.), *New Society: Sociology for the 21st Century* (2nd ed.). Toronto: Harcourt Brace Canada, 128–152.

———. 2001. *Canada's Teens: Today, Yesterday, and Tomorrow.* Toronto: Stoddart.

———. 2002. *Restless Gods: The Renaissance of Religion in Canada.* Toronto: Stoddart.

———. 2004. "The Future Families Project: A Survey of Hopes and Dreams." Vanier Institute of the Family. Retrieved September 13, 2005. Available: http://www.vifamily.ca/ library/future/future.html.

Binks, Georgie. 2003. "Are Older Women Invisible?" CBC News Viewpoint. www.cbc.ca.

Bissoondath, Neil. 1994. *Selling Illusions: The Cult of Multiculturalism in Canada.* Toronto: Penguin.

Bittner, Egon. 1980. *Popular Interests in Psychiatric Remedies: A Study in Social Control.* New York: Ayer.

Blackford, Karen A. 1996. "Families and Parental Disability." In Marion Lynn (ed.), *Voices: Essays on Canadian Families.* Scarborough, Ont.: Nelson Canada, 161–163.

Blau, Peter M., and Otis Dudley Duncan. 1967. *The American Occupational Structure.* New York: Wiley.

Blau, Peter M., and Marshall W. Meyer. 1987. *Bureaucracy in Modern Society* (3rd ed.). New York: Random House.

Blauner, Robert. 1972. *Racial Oppression in America.* New York: Harper & Row.

Blendon, Robert, Cathy Schoen, Catherine DesRoches, Robin Osborn, Kimberly Scoles, and Kinga Zappert. 2002. "Inequities in Health Care: A Five Country Survey." *Health Affairs*, 21:182–191.

Bluestone, Barry, and Bennett Harrison. 1982. *The Deindustrialization of America*. New York: Basic Books.

Blumberg, Leonard. 1977. "The Ideology of a Therapeutic Social Movement: Alcoholics Anonymous." *Journal of Studies on Alcohol*, 38:2122–2143.

Blumer, Herbert G. 1946. "Collective Behavior." In Alfred McClung Lee (ed.), *A New Outline of the Principles of Sociology*. New York: Barnes & Noble, 167–219.

———. 1969. *Symbolic Interactionism: Perspective and Method*. Englewood Cliffs, N.J.: Prentice-Hall.

———. 1974. "Social Movements." In R. Serge Denisoff (ed.), *The Sociology of Dissent*. New York: Harcourt Brace Jovanovich, 74–90.

Bogardus, Emory S. 1925. "Measuring Social Distance." *Journal of Applied Sociology*, 9:299–308.

———. 1968. "Comparing Racial Distance in Ethiopia, South Africa, and the United States." *Sociology and Social Research*, 52(2):149–156.

Bolaria, B. Singh, and Rosemary Bolaria. 1994. "Inequality and Differential Health Risks of Environmental Degradation." In Bolaria and Bolaria (eds.), *Racial Minorities, Medicine and Health*. Halifax, N.S.: Fernwood, 85–97.

Bolaria, S., and P. Li. 1988. *Racial Oppression in Canada* (2nd ed.). Toronto: Garamond.

Bolaria, S., B. Singh, and T. Wotherspoon. 1991. "Income, Inequality, Poverty, and Hunger." In B. Singh Bolaria (ed.), *Social Issues and Contradictions in Canadian Society*. Toronto: Harcourt Brace.

Boldt, Menno. 1993. *Surviving as Indians: The Challenge of Self-Government*. Toronto: University of Toronto Press.

Bologh, Roslyn Wallach. 1992. "The Promise and Failure of Ethnomethod-ology from a Feminist Perspective: Comment on Rogers." *Gender & Society*, 6(2):199–206.

Bolton, M. Anne. 1995. "Who Can Let You Die?" In Mark Novak (ed.), *Aging in Society: A Canadian Reader*. Scarborough, Ont.: Nelson Canada, 385–392.

Bonacich, Edna. 1972. "A Theory of Ethnic Antagonism: The Split Labor Market." *American Sociological Review*, 37:547–549.

———. 1976. "Advanced Capitalism and Black–White Relations in the United States: A Split Labor Market Interpretation." *American Sociological Review*, 41:34–51.

Bonger, Willem. 1969. *Criminality and Economic Conditions* (abridged ed.). Bloomington: Indiana University Press (orig. pub. 1916).

Bonvillain, Nancy. 2001. *Women & Men: Cultural Constructs of Gender* (3rd ed.). Upper Saddle River, N.J.: Prentice Hall.

Borchorst, A., and B. Siim. 1987. "Women and the Advanced Welfare State—A New Kind of Patriarchal Power?" In A. Showstack-Sasson (ed.), *Women and the State*. London: Hutchinson, 128–157.

Bordo, Susan. 1993. *Unbearable Weight: Feminism, Western Culture, and the Body*. Berkeley: University of California Press.

Bourdieu, Pierre. 1984. *Distinction: A Social Critique of the Judgement of Taste*. Trans. Richard Nice. Cambridge, Mass.: Harvard University Press.

Bourdieu, Pierre, and Jean-Claude Passeron. 1990. *Reproduction in Education, Society and Culture*. Newbury Park, Cal.: Sage.

Bowles, Samuel. 1977. "Unequal Education and the Reproduction of the Social Division of Labor." In Jerome Karabel and A.H. Halsey (eds.), *Power and Ideology in Education*. New York: Oxford University Press, 137–153.

Bowles, Samuel, and Herbert Gintis. 1976. *Schooling in Capitalist America: Education and the Contradictions of Economic Life*. New York: Basic Books.

Boyd, Monica. 1995. "Gender Inequality: Economic and Political Aspects." In Robert J. Brym, *New Sociology: Sociology for the 21st Century*. Toronto: Harcourt Brace and Company.

Boyd, Monica, and Doug Norris. 1999. "The Crowded Nest: Young Adults at Home." *Canadian Social Trends* (Spring). Ottawa: Statistics Canada, 2–5.

Boyes, William, and Michael Melvin. 1994. *Economics* (2nd ed.). Boston: Houghton Mifflin.

Boyko, Ian. 2002. "Low Income Families Excluded from Universities: Report" (December 7). Ottawa: Canadian Federation of Students.

Bozett, Frederick. 1988. "Gay Fatherhood." In Phyllis Bronstein and Carolyn Pape Cowan (eds.), *Fatherhood Today: Men's Changing Role in the Family*. New York: Wiley, 60–71.

Bradbury, Bettina. 1996. "The Social and Economic Origins of Contemporary Families." In Maureen Baker (ed.), *Families: Changing Trends in Canada*. Toronto: McGraw-Hill Ryerson, 55–103.

Bramlett, Matthew D., and William D. Mosher. 2001. "First Marriage Dissolution, Divorce, and Remarriage: United States." DHHS publication no. 2001–1250 01–0384 (5/01). Hyattsville, MD: Department of Health and Human Services.

Brand, Pamela A., Esther D. Rothblum, and L.J. Solomon. 1992. "A Comparison of Lesbians, Gay Men, and Heterosexuals on Weight and Restrained Eating." *International Journal of Eating Disorders*, 11:253–259.

Brannigan, Augustine. 2003. *The Rise and Fall of Social Psychology*. Unpublished manuscript.

———. 2004. *The Rise and Fall of Social Psychology: The Use and Misuse of the Experimental Method*. Hawthorne, N.Y.: Aldine.

Brantingham, Paul J., Shihing Mu, and Aruind Verma. 1995. "Patterns in Canadian Crime." In Margaret A. Jackson and Curt T. Griffiths (eds.), *Canadian Criminology*. Toronto: Harcourt Brace and Company, 187–245.

Braun, Denny. 1991. *The Rich Get Richer: The Rise of Income Inequality in the United States and the World*. Chicago: Nelson-Hall.

Braverman, Harry. 1974. *Labor and Monopoly Capital: The Degradation of Work in the Twentieth Century*. New York: Monthly Review Press.

Briggs, Sheila. 1987. "Women and Religion." In Beth B. Hess and Myra Marx Ferree (eds.), *Analyzing Gender: A Handbook of Social Science Research*. Newbury Park, Cal.: Sage, 408–441.

Brint, Steven. 1994. *In an Age of Experts: The Changing Role of Professionals in Politics and Public Life*. Princeton, N.J.: Princeton University Press.

Britt, Lory. 1993. "From Shame to Pride: Social Movements and Individual Affect." Paper presented at the 88th Annual Meeting of the American Sociological Association, Miami (August).

Brod, Harry, ed. 1987. *The Making of Masculinities*. Boston: Allen & Unwin.

Bronfenbrenner, Urie. 1990. "Five Critical Processes for Positive Development." From "Discovering What Families Do" in *Rebuilding the Nest: A New Commitment to the American Family*. Retrieved June 29, 1999. Available: http://www.montana.edu/wwwctf/process.html.

Brooks Gardner, Carol. 1989. "Analyzing Gender in Public Places: Rethinking Goffman's Vision of Everyday Life." *American Sociologist*, 20 (Spring):42–56.

Brooks-Gunn, Jeanne. 1986. "The Relationship of Maternal Beliefs About Sex Typing to Maternal and Young Children's Behavior." *Sex Roles*, 14:21–35.

Brown, Robert W. 1954. "Mass Phenomena." In Gardner Lindzey (ed.), *Handbook of Social Psychology*, vol. 2. Reading, Mass.: Addison-Wesley, 833–873.

Brown, Russell. 2003. "Illusions of Choice: The Selling of *American Idol* and *The Matrix Reloaded*." Retrieved June 21, 2003. Available: http://www.thesimon.com/article_of_week/281.

Bruce, Steve. 1996. *Religion in the Modern World*. New York: Oxford University Press.

Brumberg, Joan Jacobs. 1988. *Fasting Girls: The Emergence of Anorexia Nervosa as a Modern Disease*. Cambridge, Mass.: Harvard University Press.

Brunvand, Jan Harold. 2001. *Too Good to be True: The Colossal Boook of Urban Legends*. New York: W.W. Norton and Co.

Brustad, Robert J. 1996. "Attraction to Physical Activity in Urban Schoolchildren: Parental Socialization and Gender Influence." *Research Quarterly for Exercise and Sport*, 67:316–324.

Brym, Robert, and Bonnie Fox. 1989. *From Culture to Power: The Sociology of English Canada*. Toronto: Oxford University Press.

Brym, Robert, and Rhonda L. Lenton. 2001. "Love Online: A Report on Digital Dating in Canada." A Report on Surveys. Funded by MSN.ca. Retrieved August 26, 2003. Available: http://www.soc-canada.com/loveonline.pdf.

Buchignani, Norman. 1991. "Some Comments on the Elimination of Racism in Canada." In Ormond McKague (ed.), *Racism in Canada*. Saskatoon: Fifth House, 199–205.

Buchignani, Norman, Doreen M. Indra, and Ram Srivastiva. 1985. *Continuous Journey: A Social History of South Asians in Canada*. Toronto: McClelland and Stewart.

Buechler, Steven M. 2000. *Social Movements in Advanced Capitalism: The Political Economy and Cultural Construction of Social Activism*. New York: Oxford University Press.

Bullard, Robert B., and Beverly H. Wright. 1992. "The Quest for Environmental Equity: Mobilizing the African-American Community for Social Change." In Riley E. Dunlap and Angela G. Mertig (eds.), *American Environmentalism: The U.S. Environmental Movement, 1970–1990*. New York: Taylor & Francis, 39–49.

Buntain-Ricklefs, J.J., K.J. Kemper, M. Bell, and T. Babonis. 1994. "Punishments: What Predicts Adult Approval." *Child Abuse and Neglect*, 18:945–955.

Burciaga, Jose Antonio. 1993. *Drink Cultura*. Santa Barbara, Cal.: Capra.

Burawoy, Michael. 1991. "Introduction." In Michael Burawoy, Alice Burton, Ann Arnett Ferguson et al. (eds.), *Ethnography Unbounded: Power and Resistance in the Modern Metropolis*. Berkeley: University of California Press, 1–7.

Burgess, Ernest W. 1925. "The Growth of the City." In Robert E. Park and Ernest W. Burgess (eds.), *The City*. Chicago: University of Chicago Press, 47–62.

Burman, Patrick. 1998. *Killing Time, Losing Ground: Experiences of Unemployment*. Toronto: Wall and Thompson.

Burnham, Walter Dean. 1983. *Democracy in the Making: American Government and Politics*. Englewood Cliffs, N.J.: Prentice-Hall.

Burns, Tom. 1992. *Erving Goffman*. New York: Routledge.

Burr, Chandler. 1997. "The AIDS Exception: Privacy Versus Public Health." *The Atlantic Monthly* (June): 57–67.

Burros, Marian. 1994. "Despite Awareness of Risks, More in U.S. Are Getting Fat." *New York Times* (July 17):1, 8.

Busch, Ruth C. 1990. *Family Systems: Comparative Study of the Family.* New York: P. Lang.

Butler, Robert N. 1975. *Why Survive? Being Old in America.* New York: Harper & Row.

———. 1987. "Future Trends." In George L. Maddox, Robert C. Atchley, and Raymond J. Corsini (eds.), *The Encyclopedia of Aging.* New York: Springer, 265–267.

Buvinic´, Mayra. 1997. "Women in Poverty: A New Global Underclass." *Foreign Policy* (Fall):38–53.

Cable News Network. 1997. "Study: Despair Increases Health Risks in Middle-Aged Men." CNN Web site: August 26, 1997. Available: http://www.cnn.com.

Cable, Sherry, and Charles Cable. 1995. *Environmental Problems, Grassroots Solutions: The Politics of Grassroots Environmental Conflict.* New York: St. Martin's Press.

Cain, P.A. 1993. "Feminism and the Limits of Equality." In D.K. Weisberg (ed.), *Feminist Legal Theory: Foundations.* Philadelphia: Temple University Press, 237–247.

Calhoun, Craig. 1986. "Computer Technology, Large-Scale Social Integration and the Local Community." *Urban Affairs Quarterly,* 22(2):329–349.

Callahan, Daniel. 1987. *Setting Limits: Medical Goals in an Aging Society.* New York: Simon and Schuster.

Calliste, Agnes. 1987. "Sleeping Car Porters in Canada: An Ethically Submerged Split Labour Market." *Canadian Ethnic Studies,* 19:1–20.

———. 1993/94. "Race, Gender, and Canadian Immigration Policy: Blacks from the Caribbean, 1900–1932." *Journal of Canadian Studies,* 28(4):131–148.

Callwood, June. 1995. *Trial Without End.* Toronto: Albert A. Knopf.

———. 2005. "On Turning 80." *Chatelaine* (May):56.

Campaign 2000. 2002a. "Breaking the Cycle of Poverty for Higher Risk Populations." In *Putting Promises into Action: A Report on a Decade of Child and Family Poverty in Canada.* Retrieved November 21, 2002. Available: http://campaign2000.ca/ rc/unsscMAY02/un8.html.

———. 2002b. "Canada Falling Behind on International Stage." Retrieved August 7, 2002. Available: http://www .campaign2000.ca/rc/unsscMAY02/ un10.html.

———. 2002c. "A Decade of Decline." In *Putting Promises into Action: A Report on a Decade of Child and Family Poverty in Canada.* Retrieved November 21, 2002. Available: http://campaign2000 .ca/rc/unsscMAY02/un8.html.

———. 2002d. "Developing a National Plan of Action for Canada's Children." Retrieved August 8, 2002. Available: http://campaign2000.ca/rc/ unsscMAY02/unplan.html.

———. 2003. "Honouring Our Promises: Meeting the Challenge to End Child and Family Poverty—2003 Report Card on Child Poverty in Canada." Retrieved August 20, 2005. Available: http://www.campaign2000 .ca/rc/rc03/NOV03ReportCard.pdf.

Campbell, Marian L., Ruth M.F. Diamant, Brian D. Macpherson, and Judy Halladay. 1997. "The Contemporary Food Supply of Three Northern Manitoba Cree Communities." *Canadian Journal of Public Health,* 88 (March/April):105–108.

Canada Mortgage and Housing Corporation. 1998. "Survey of Canadians' Attitudes Toward Homelessness." Available: http://www.cmhc-schl.gc.ca/ Research/ Homeless/F_public.html

Canadian Association of Food Banks. 2005. Retrieved August 22, 2005. Available: http://www.cafb-acba.ca/ english/GetInvolved.html.

Canadian Business. 2004. "The Rich 100: 2003–2004 Edition." Retrieved August 12, 2005. Available: http://www. canadianbusiness.com/rich100/ index.htm#.

Canadian Cancer Society. 2005. *Canadian Cancer Statistics 2005.* Retrieved July 21, 2005. Available: http://www.cancer.ca/ vgn/images/portal/cit_86751114/48/28/ 401594768cw_2005stats_en.pdf.

Canadian Council on Social Development. 1996. *The Progress of Canada's Children 1996.* Ottawa: Canadian Council on Children Development.

———. 2001. "Children and Youth with Special Needs." (November). Ottawa: Canadian Council on Social Development.

———. 2002a. "Disability Information Sheet: Number 5." Retrieved August 8, 2002. Available: http://www.ccsd .ca/drip/research/dis5/dis5.pdf.

———. 2002b. "Percentage and Numbers of Persons in Poverty: Canada, 1990 and 1999." Ottawa: Canadian Council on Social Development.

———. 2002c. "Percentage and Number of Persons in Low Income/Poverty, by Age, Sex and Family Characteristics, Canada, 1990 and 1999." Ottawa: Canadian Council on Social Development. Retrieved June 25, 2002. Available: http://www.ccsd.ca/ factsheets/fs_pov9099.htm.

———. 2003. "How the Poverty Line is Calculated." Retrieved May 20, 2003. Available: http://www.ccsd.ca/ facts.html.

Canadian Council on Social Development. 1998. *The Progress of Canada's Children: 1998 Highlights.* Ottawa: Canadian Council on Social Development.

Canadian Criminal Justice Association. 2005. "Aboriginal Peoples and the Criminal Justice System." Retrieved September 14, 2005. Available: http:// www.ccja-acjp.ca/en/aborit.html.

Canadian Education Association. 1999. "Educational Trends in Canada." Available: http://www.acea.ca/ trends.html.

Canadian Institute of Child Health. 1994. *The Health of Canada's Children* (2nd ed.). Ottawa: Canadian Institute of Child Health.

Canadian Institute for Health Information. 2004a. *Health Care in Canada 2004.* Ottawa: Author. Retrieved July 21, 2005. Available: http://www.cihi.ca.

———. 2004b. *Improving the Health of Canadians.* Ottawa: Retrieved July 22, 2005. Available: http://www.cihi.ca.

———. 2004c. *Full-Time Equivalent Physicians,Canada.* 2002–2003. Ottawa: Author. Retrieved July 23, 2005. Available: http://www.cihi .cahttp://secure.cihi.ca/cihiweb/ dispPage.jsp?cw_page=AR_17_E.

Canadian Internet Project, 2004. Retrieved November 25, 2005. Available: http:// www.canadianinternetproject.ca/en/ documents/Canada%20Online% 20Final%20English%20Version% 2010302005.pdf.

Canadian Press. 1997. "Health-Care Bill Falls, Report Says." *Winnipeg Free Press* (August 12):A14.

Canadian Public Health Association. 1997. "Position Paper on Homelessness and Health." Available: http://www .cpha.ca/cpha.docs/homeless.eng.html.

Cancian, Francesca M. 1990. "The Feminization of Love." In C. Carlson (ed.), *Perspectives on the Family: History, Class, and Feminism.* Belmont, Cal.: Wadsworth, 171–185.

Canetto, S.S., and Isaac Sakinofsky. 1998, "The Gender Paradox in Suicide." *Suicide and Life-Threatening Behavior,* 28:1–22.

Canter, R.J., and S.S. Ageton. 1984. "The Epidemiology of Adolescent Sex-Role Attitudes." *Sex Roles,* 11:657–676.

Cantor, Muriel G. 1980. *Prime-Time Television: Content and Control.* Newbury Park, Cal.: Sage.

———. 1987. "Popular Culture and the Portrayal of Women: Content and Control." In Beth B. Hess and Myra Marx Ferree, *Analyzing Gender: A Handbook of Social Science Research.* Newbury Park, Cal.: Sage, 190–214.

Cantril, Hadley. 1941. *The Psychology of Social Movements.* New York: Wiley.

Capek, Stella M. 1993. "The 'Environmental Justice' Frame: A Conceptual Discussion and Application." *Social Problems,* 40(1):5–23.

Carmichael, Amy. 2005. "And the Booby Prize Goes to ..." Retrieved January 13, 2006. Available: http://www.theglobe.ca/ servlet/story/RTGAM.20050724. wimplants0724/BNStory/National/.

Carrier, James G. 1986. *Social Class and the Construction of Inequality in American Education.* New York: Greenwood.

Carroll, John B., ed. 1956. *Language, Thought, and Reality: Selected Writings of Benjamin Lee Whorf. Cambridge,* Mass.: MIT Press.

Carter, Stephen L. 1994. *The Culture of Disbelief: How American Law and Politics Trivializes Religious Devotion.* New York: Anchor/Doubleday.

Cashmore, E. Ellis. 1996. *Dictionary of Race and Ethnic Relations* (4th ed.). London: Routledge.

Cassidy, B., R. Lord, and N. Mandell. 2001. "Silenced and Forgotten Women: Race, Poverty, and Disability." In Nancy Mandell (ed.), *Feminist Issues: Race, Class, and Society* (3rd ed.). Toronto: Prentice-Hall, 75–107.

Castells, Manuel. 1977. *The Urban Question.* London: Edward Arnold (orig. pub. 1972 as *La Question Urbaine,* Paris).

———. 1998. *End of Millennium.* Malden, Mass.: Blackwell.

———. 2000a. *The Rise of the Network Society* (2nd ed.). Oxford: Blackwell Publishers.

———. 2000b. "Materials for an Exploratory Theory of the Network Society." *British Journal of Sociology* (January/March):5–24.

———. 2004. "Informationalism and the Network Society." In Manuel Castells (ed.), *The Network Society.* Cheltenham: Edward Elgar, 3–45.

Castles, Stephen. 1995. "Trois Siècles de Dépopulation Amerindienne." In L. Normandeau and V. Piche (eds.), *Les Populations Amerindienne et Inuit du Canada.* Montreal: Presse de l'Université de Montréal.

Catalyst Canada. 2005. "2004 Catalyst Census of Women Corporate Officers and Top Earners of Canada." Retrieved September 22, 2005. Available: http://www.catalystwomen.org/ bookstore/files/fact/2004%20Canadian %20COTE%20Census%20Fact% 20Sheet.pdf.

Cavender, Gray. 1995. "Alternative Theory: Labeling and Critical Perspectives." In Joseph F. Sheley (ed.), *Criminology: A Contemporary Handbook* (2nd ed.). Belmont, Cal.: Wadsworth, 349–371.

Cavender, Nick. 2001. "It's a Dad's Life." Retrieved June 20, 2003. Available: http://www.homedad .org.uk/feature_dadslife.html.

CBC. 1997. *The National* (December 18).

———. 2004. "Firefighter Claims Union Turning Members Against Her." Retrieved February 4, 2005. Available: http://www.cbc.ca/ story/news/national/2004/11/04/ firefighter041104.html.

Chafetz, Janet Saltzman. 1984. *Sex and Advantage: A Comparative, Macro-Structural Theory of Sex Stratification.* Totowa, N.J.: Rowman & Allanheld.

———. 1989. "Marital Intimacy and Conflict: The Irony of Spousal Equality." In Jo Freeman (ed.), *Women: A Feminist Perspective* (4th ed.). Mountain View, Cal.: Mayfield, 149–156.

Chagnon, Napoleon A. 1992. *Yanomamö: The Last Days of Eden.* New York: Harcourt Brace Jovanovich (rev. from 4th ed., *Yanomamö: The Fierce People,* by Holt, Rinehart & Winston).

Chalfant, H. Paul, Robert E. Beckley, and C. Eddie Palmer. 1994. *Religion in Contemporary Society* (3rd. ed.). Ithaca, Ill.: Peacock.

Chambliss, William J. 1973. "The Saints and the Roughnecks." *Society,* 11:24–31.

Chandler, Tertius, and Gerald Fox. 1974. *3000 Years of Urban History.* New York: Academic Press.

Chang, Jen, Bethany Or, Eloginy Tharmendran, Emmie Tsumura, Steve Daniels, and Darryl Leroux. 2001. *RESIST! A Grassroots Collection of Stories, Poetry, Photos and Analysis from the FTAA Protests in Québec City and Beyond.* Compiled by Jen Chang, Bethany Or, Eloginy Tharmendran, Emmie Tsumura, Steve Daniels and Darryl Leroux. Halifax: Fernwood Publishing.

Chapman, Amanda. 2003. "Gender Bias in Education." *Multicultural Pavilion: Exchange Research Room.* Retrieved September 20, 2003. Available: http://www.edchange.org/multicultural/papers/genderbias.html.

Charlton, Angela. 1999. "Natalya Gracheva is giving McDonald's Heartburn." Associated Press (June 23). Retrieved Sept. 7, 1999. Available: http://www.mcspotlight.org/media/press/apny_23june99.html.

Cheney, Peter. 2004. "They'll Bop Till They Drop." *The Globe and Mail.* (February 28):F4–F5.

Cheney, Peter, Robert Matas, and David Roberts. 1998. "Abuse Claims Against Churches Surge." *The Globe and Mail* (June 9):A1, A5.

Cherlin, Andrew J. 1992. *Marriage, Divorce, Remarriage.* Cambridge, Mass.: Harvard University Press.

Chernin, Kim. 1981. *The Obsession: Reflections on the Tyranny of Slenderness.* New York: Harper & Row.

Chidley, Joe. 1995. "Spreading Hate on the Internet." *Maclean's* (May 8):3.

Chipungu, Joel. 1999. "Polygamy is Alive and Well in Zambia." African News Service (July 22). Retrieved September 11, 1999. Available: http://www.comtexnews.com.

Chisholm, Patricia. 1995. "Schooling for the Disabled." *Maclean's* (March 27): 52–54.

Chisholm, Patricia, Sharon Doyle Driedger, Susan McClelland. 1999. "The Mother Load." *Maclean's* (March 1). Available: http://www.macleans.ca/pub-doc/1999/03/01.

Cho, Sumi K. 1993. "Korean Americans vs. African Americans: Conflict and Construction." In Robert Gooding-Williams (ed.), *Reading Rodney King, Reading Urban Uprising.* New York: Routledge, 196–211.

Chon, Margaret. 1995. "The Truth About Asian Americans." In Russell Jacoby and Naomi Glauberman (eds.), *The Bell Curve Debate: History, Documents, Opinions.* New York: Times Books, 238–240.

Chossudovsky, Michel. 1997. *The Globalization of Poverty.* Penang: Third World Network.

Christ, Carol P. 1987. *Laughter of Aphrodite: Reflections on a Journey to the Goddess.* San Francisco: Harper & Row.

Christians, Clifford G.G., Kim B. Rotzoll, and Mark Fackler. 1987. *Media Ethics.* New York: Longman.

Christie, B. 2001. "Attack Hoax Makes Rounds on the Web." *The Bakersfield Californian* (September 18):A1.

Chunn, Dorothy E. 2000. "Politicizing the Personal: Feminism, Law, and Public Policy." In Nancy Mandell and Ann Duffy (eds.), *Canadian Families: Diversity, Conflict, and Change* (2nd ed.). Toronto: Harcourt, 225–259.

Church Council on Justice and Corrections. 1996. *Satisfying Justice.* Ottawa: Church Council on Justice and Corrections.

Church, Elizabeth. 1996. "Kinship and Stepfamilies." In Marion Lynn (ed.), *Voices: Essays on Canadian Families.* Scarborough, Ont.: Nelson Canada, 81–106.

Churchill, Ward. 1994. *Indians Are Us? Culture and Genocide in Native North America.* Monroe, Maine: Common Courage Press.

CIA (Central Intelligence Agency). 2001. *The World Factbook 2001.* Washington, D.C.: Office of Public Affairs.

———. 2004. *The World Factbook 2004.* Washington D.C.: Office of Public Affairs.

———. 2005. *The World Factbook 2005.* Washington D.C.: Office of Public Affairs. Available: http://www.cia.gov/cia/publications/factbook/index.html.

"Citizen's Forum on Canada's Future: Report to the People and Government of Canada." 1991. Ottawa: Privy Council Office.

Citizenship and Immigration Canada. 2005. *Facts and Figures: Immigration Overview.* Ottawa: Author. Retrieved July 14, 2005. Available: http://www.cic.gc.ca/english/pub/facts2003/overview/1.html.

Clark, S.D. 1962. *The Developing Canadian Community.* Toronto: University of Toronto Press.

Clark, Warren. 1998. "Religious Observance: Marriage and Family." *Canadian Social Trends.* Autumn 2–7. Ottawa: Statistics Canada.

———. 2003. "Pockets of Belief: Religious Attendance in Canada." *Canadian Social Trends* (Spring):2–5.

Clarke, Harold D., Jane Jenson, Lawrence LeDuc, John H. Pammett. 1991. *Absent Mandate: The Politics of Discontent in Canada* (2nd ed.). Toronto: Gage.

Clayman, Steven E. 1993. "Booing: The Anatomy of a Disaffiliative Response." *American Sociological Review,* 58(1):110–131.

Clement, Wallace. 1975. *The Canadian Corporate Elite.* Toronto: McClelland and Stewart.

Clement, Wallace and John Myles. 1994. *Relations of Ruling: Class and Gender in Postindustrial Societies.* Montreal: McGill-Queen's University Press.

Cleveland, Gordon, and Michael Krashinsky. 2003. "Eight Myths about Early Childhood Education and Care." Retrieved June 14, 2005. Available: http://www.childcarecanada.org/pubs/other/FF/FactandFantasy.pdf.

Cloward, Richard A., and Lloyd E. Ohlin. 1960. *Delinquency and Opportunity: A Theory of Delinquent Gangs.* New York: Free Press.

CNN. 1994. "Both Sides: School Prayer." (November 26).

———. 1999. Chatpage "Jan Harold Brunvand." Retrieved September 27, 2002. Available: http://www.cnn.com/COMMUNITY/transcripts/jan.harold.brunvand.html.

———. 2005. "Leadership Vacuum Stymied Aid Offers." CNN.com. Retrieved September 16, 2005. Available: http://edition.cnn.com/2005/US/09/15/katrina.response/index.html.

Coakley, J. J. 1998. *Sport in Society: Issues and Controversies* (6th ed.). New York: McGraw-Hill.

Cohen, Leah Hager. 1994. *Train Go Sorry: Inside a Deaf World.* Boston: Houghton Mifflin.

Cohen, Marjorie Griffin. 1993. "Capitalist Development, Industrialization, and Women's Work." In Graham S. Lowe and Harvey J. Krahn (eds.), *Work in Canada.* Scarborough, Ont.: Nelson Canada, 142–144.

Colapinto, John.. 2001. *As Nature Made Him: The Boy Who Was Raised as a Girl.* NewYork: HarperCollins.

Colby, David C., and Timothy E. Cook. 1991. "Epidemics and Agendas: The Politics of Nightly News Coverage of AIDS." *Journal of Health Politics, Policy and Law,* 16(2):215–249.

Coles, Gerald. 1987. *The Learning Mystique: A Critical Look at "Learning Disabilities."* New York: Pantheon.

Collier, Peter, and David Horowitz. 1987. *The Fords: An American Epic.* New York: Summit Books.

Collins, Catherine, and Douglas Frantz. 1993. *Teachers: Talking Out of School.* Boston: Little, Brown.

Collins, Patricia Hill. 1990. *Black Feminist Thought: Knowledge, Counsciousness, and the Politics of Empowerment.* London: HarperCollins Academic.

———. 1991. "The Meaning of Motherhood in Black Culture." In Robert Staples (ed.), *The Black Family: Essays and Studies.* Belmont, Cal.: Wadsworth, 169–178. Orig. pub. in *SAGE: A Scholarly Journal on Black Women,* 4 (Fall 1987):3–10.

Collins, Randall. 1971. "A Conflict Theory of Sexual Stratification." *Social Problems,* 19(1):3–21.

———. 1979. *The Credential Society: An Historical Sociology of Education.* New York: Academic Press.

———. 1982. *Sociological Insight: An Introduction to Non-Obvious Sociology.* New York: Oxford University Press.

———. 1994. *Four Sociological Traditions.* New York: Oxford University Press.

———. 1997. "An Asian Route to Capitalism: Religious Economy and the Origins of Self-Transforming Growth in Japan." *American Sociological Review,* 62: 843–865.

Coltrane, Scott. 1992. "The Micropolitics of Gender in Nonindustrial Societies." *Gender and Society* 6:86–107.

Comack, Elizabeth. 1996a. "Women and Crime." In R. Linden (ed.), *Criminology: A Canadian Perspective* (3rd ed.). Toronto: Harcourt Brace, 139–175.

———. 1996b. *Women in Trouble.* Halifax: Fernwood Publishing.

———. 2000. "Women and Crime." In R. Linden (ed.), *Criminology: A Canadian Perspective* (4th ed.). Toronto: Harcourt Brace.

———. 2004. "Feminism and Criminology." In Rick Linden (ed.), *Criminology: A Canadian Perspective* (5th ed.) Toronto: Thomson, 164–195.

Comfort, Alex. 1976. "Age Prejudice in America." *Social Policy,* 7(3):3–8.

Commission on Systemic Racism in the Ontario Criminal Justice System. 1995. *Report of the Commission on Systemic Racism in the Ontario Criminal Justice System.* Toronto: Queen's Printer for Ontario.

Commonwealth Fund. 2002. "Canadian Adults' Health Care System Views and Experiences." *Commonwealth Fund 2001 International Health Policy Survey.* New York: Commonwealth Fund. Retrieved December 17, 2002. Available: http://www.cmwf.org/programs/international/can_sb_552.pdf.

Condry, Sandra McConnell, John C. Condry, Jr., and Lee Wolfram Pogatshnik. 1983. "Sex Differences: A Study of the Ear of the Beholder." *Sex Roles,* 9:697–704.

Connidis, Ingrid. 1989. *Family Ties and Aging.* Toronto: Butterworths.

Conrad, Peter. 1975. "The Discovery of Hyperkinesis." *Social Problems* 23, (October):12–21.

Conrad, Peter, and Joseph W. Schneider. 1980. "The Medical Control of Deviance: Conquests and Consequences." In Julius A. Roth (ed.), *Research in the Sociology of Health Care: A Research Annual,* 1. Greenwich, Conn.: Jai Press, 1–53.

———. 1992. *Deviance and Medicalization: From Badness to Sickness.* Philadelphia: Temple University Press.

Cook, Ramsay. 1995. *Canada, Quebec and the Uses of Nationalism* (2nd ed.). Toronto: McClelland and Stewart.

Cook, Sherburn F. 1973. "The Significance of Disease in the Extinction of the New England Indians." *Human Biology,* 45:485–508.

Cook, Shirley J. 1969. "Canadian Narcotics Legislation, 1908–1923: A Conflict Model Interpretation." *Canadian Review of Sociology and Anthropology,* 6(1):36–46.

Cooke, Martin, Daniel Beavon, and Mindy McHardy. 2004. *Measuring the Well-Being of Aboriginal People: An Application of the United Nations' Human Development Index to Registered Indians in Canada, 1981–2001.* Ottawa: Indian and Northern Affairs Canada.

Cookson, Peter W., Jr., and Caroline Hodges Persell. 1985. *Preparing for Power: America's Elite Boarding Schools.* New York: Basic Books.

Cooley, Charles Horton. 1922. *Human Nature and Social Order*. New York: Scribner (orig. pub. 1902).

———. 1962. *Social Organization*. New York: Schocken Books (orig. pub. 1909).

———. 1998. "The Social Self—The Meaning of 'I.'" In Hans-Joachim Schubert (ed.), *On Self and Social Organization—Charles Horton Cooley*. Chicago: University of Chicago Press, 155–175. Reprinted from *Charles Horton Cooley, Human Nature and the Social Order*. New York: Schocken, 1902.

Coontz, Stephanie. 1992. *The Way We Never Were: American Families and the Nostalgia Trap*. New York: Basic Books.

Coppel, Jonathan, Jean-Christophe Dumond, and Ignazio Visco. 2001. "Trends in Immigration and Economic Consequences." OECD Economics Department Working Papers 284, OECD Economics Department. Paris: OECD.

Corr, Charles A., Clyde M. Nabe, and Donna M. Corr. 2003. *Death and Dying, Life and Living* (4th ed.). Pacific Grove, Calif.: Brooks/Cole.

Corrado, Raymond R. 1996. "Political Crime in Canada." In Rick Linden (ed.), *Criminology: A Canadian Perspective* (3rd ed.). Toronto: Harcourt Brace and Company, 459–493.

Corsaro, William A. 1985. *Friendship and Peer Culture in the Early Years*. Norwood: N.J.: Ablex.

———. 1992. "Interpretive Reproduction in Children's Peer Cultures." *Social Psychology Quarterly*, 55(2):160–177.

———. 1997. *Sociology of Childhood*. Thousand Oaks, Cal.: Pine Forge.

Cortese, Anthony. 1999. *Provocateur: Images of Women and Minorities in Advertising*. Latham, Md.: Rowman & Littlefield.

Cose, Ellis. 1993. *The Rage of a Privileged Class*. New York: HarperCollins.

Coser, Lewis A. 1956. *The Functions of Social Conflict*. Glencoe, Ill.: Free Press.

Coughlin, Ellen K. 1993. "Author of Noted Study on Black Ghetto Life Returns with a Portrait of Homeless Women." *The Chronicle of Higher Education* (March 31):A7–A8.

Council of Ministers of Education. 2002. *Education Indicators in Canada: Report of the Pan-Canadian Education Indicators Program, 1999*. Toronto: Council of Ministers of Education.

Cowgill, Donald O. 1986. *Aging Around the World*. Belmont, Cal.: Wadsworth.

Craig, Steve. 1992. "Considering Men and the Media." In Steve Craig (ed.), *Men, Masculinity, and the Media*. Newbury Park, Cal.: Sage, 1–7.

Cranswick, Kelly. 1999. "At Work Despite a Chronic Health Problem." *Canadian Social Trends* (Spring):11–15. Ottawa: Statistics Canada.

———. 2003. *General Social Survey Cycle 16: Caring for an Aging Society*. Ottawa: Statistics Canada.

Crawford, Elizabeth. 2003. "Campus Castoffs." *Chronicle of Higher Education* (June 20):A6.

Creese, Gillian, and Brenda Beagan. 1999. "Gender at Work: Seeking Solutions for Women's Equality." In Curtis, James, Edward Grabb, and Neil Guppy (eds.), *Social Inequality in Canada: Patterns, Problems, and Policies*. Scarborough: Prentice Hall, 199–221.

Creswell, John W. 1998. *Qualitative Inquiry and Research Design: Choosing Among Five Traditions*. Thousand Oaks, Cal.: Sage.

Crichton, Anne, Ann Robertson, Christine Gordon, and Wendy Farrant. 1997. *Health Care: A Community Concern?* Calgary: University of Calgary Press.

CTV. 2005. "Blacks Stopped More Often by Police, Study Finds." Retrieved July 12, 2005. Available: http://www.ctv.ca/servlet/ArticleNews/story/CTVNews/1117145635847_112554835?s_name=&no_ads=.

Cumming, Elaine C., and William E. Henry. 1961. *Growing Old: The Process of Disengagement*. New York: Basic Books.

Cunningham, J., and J.K. Antill. 1995. "Current Trends in Non-Marital Cohabitation: In Search of the POSSLQ." In J.T. Wood and S. Duck (eds.), *Under-studied Relationships: Off the Beaten Track*. Thousand Oaks, Cal.: Sage, 148–172.

Currie, Raymond, and John Stackhouse. 1996. "Religious Institutions." In L. Tepperman, J.E. Curtis, and R.J. Richardson (eds.), *Sociology*. Toronto: McGraw-Hill Ryerson, 482–519.

Curtis, James, and Edward Grabb. 1999. "Social Status and Beliefs About What's Important for Getting Ahead." In James Curtis, Edward Grabb, and Neil Guppy (eds.), *Social Inequality in Canada: Patterns, Problems and Policies* (3rd ed.). Scarborough: Prentice-Hall, 330–346.

Curtis, James E., and Ronald D. Lambert. 1994. "Culture." In R. Hagedorn (ed.), *Sociology* (5th ed.). Toronto: Holt Rinehart and Winston, 57–86.

Curtis, James E., Edward Grabb, and Neil Guppy (eds.). 1999. *Social Inequality in Canada: Patterns, Problems, Policies* (3rd ed.). Scarborough, Ont.: Prentice Hall.

Curtiss, Susan. 1977. *Genie: A Psycho-linguistic Study of a Modern Day "Wild Child."* New York: Academic Press.

Cyrus, Virginia. 1993. *Experiencing Race, Class, and Gender in the United States*. Mountain View, Cal.: Mayfield.

Dagg, Alexandra, and Judy Fudge. 1992. "Sewing Pains: Homeworkers in the Garment Trade." *Our Times* (June):22–25.

Dahl, Robert A. 1961. *Who Governs?* New Haven, Conn.: Yale University Press.

Dahrendorf, Ralph. 1959. *Class and Class Conflict in an Industrial Society*. Stanford, Cal.: Stanford University Press.

Daly, Kathleen, and Meda Chesney-Lind. 1998. "Feminism and Criminology." *Justice Quarterly*, 5:497–533.

Daly, Kerry. 2000. *It Keeps Getting Faster: Changing Patterns of Time in Families*. Ottawa: Vanier Institute of the Family.

Daly, Martin, Margo Wilson, and Shawn Vasdev. 2001. "Income Inequality and Homicide Rates in Canada and the United States." *Canadian Journal of Criminology*, 43:219–236.

Daly, Mary. 1973. *Beyond God the Father*. Boston: Beacon Press.

Darley, John M., and Thomas R. Shultz. 1990. "Moral Rules: Their Content and Acquisition." *Annual Review of Psychology*, 41:525–556.

Dart, Bob. 1999. "Kids Get More Screen Time Than School Time." *Austin American-Statesman* (June 28): A1, A5.

Das Gupta, Tania. 1995. "Families of Native Peoples, Immigrants, and People of Colour." In Nancy Mandell and Ann Duffy (eds.), *Canadian Families: Diversity, Conflict and Change*. Toronto: Harcourt Brace, 141–174.

———. 2000. "Families of Native People, Immigrants, and People of Colour." In Nancy Mandell and Ann Duffy (eds.), *Canadian Families: Diversity, Conflict, and Change* (2nd ed.). Toronto: Harcourt, 146–187.

Dauvergne, Mia. 2003. "Family Violence Against Seniors." *Canadian Social Trends* (Spring):10–14. Ottawa: Statistics Canada.

———. 2004. "Homicide in Canada, 2003." *Juristat*, Vol. 24, No. 8. Ottawa: Statistics Canada.

Dauvergne, Mia, and Holly Johnson. 2001. "Children Witnessing Family Violence." *Juristat*, 21(6). Cat. no. 85-002-XPE Ottawa: Statistics Canada.

DaVanzo, Julie, and David Adamson. 1997. "Russia's Demographic 'Crisis': How Real Is It?" *Rand Issue Paper*. Rand Corporation: Center for Russian and Eurasian Studies. Available: http://www.rand.org/publications/IP/IP162.

Davies, Scott. 1999. "Stubborn Disparities: Explaining Class Irregularities in Schooling." In Curtis, James, Edward Grabb, and Neil Guppy (eds.), *Social Inequality in Canada: Patterns, Problems and Policies*. Scarborough, Ont.: Prentice Hall, 138–150.

Davis, Fred. 1992. *Fashion, Culture, and Identity*. Chicago: University of Chicago Press.

Davis, Kingsley. 1940. "Extreme Social Isolation of a Child." *American Journal of Sociology*, 45(4):554–565.

———. 1949. *Human Society*. New York: Macmillan.

Davis, Kingsley, and Judith Blake. 1956. "Social Structure and Fertility: An Analytical Framework." *Economic Development and Cultural Change*, 4 (April):211–235.

Davis, Kingsley, and Wilbert Moore. 1945. "Some Principles of Stratification." *American Sociological Review*, 7 (April): 242–249.

Dawson, Lorne L. 1998. *Comprehending Cults: The Sociology of New Religious Movements*. Toronto: Oxford University Press.

Dean, L.M., F.N. Willis, and J.N. la Rocco. 1976. "Invasion of Personal Space as a Function of Age, Sex and Race." *Psychological Reports*, 38(3) (pt. 1):959–965.

Dear, Michael, and Steven Flusty. 1998. "Postmodern Urbanism." *Annals of the Association of American Geographers*, 88(1):50–72.

de Broucker, Patrice, and Laval Lavalleé. 2000. "Getting Ahead in Life: Does Your Parents' Education Count?" *Canadian Social Trends*, 3:143–147.

Deegan, Mary Jo. 1988. *Jane Addams and the Men of the Chicago School, 1892–1918*. New Brunswick, N.J.: Transaction.

deGroot-Maggetti, Greg. 2002. *A Measure of Poverty in Canada: A Guide to the Debate About Poverty Lines*. Toronto: Public Justice Resource Centre.

DeKeseredy, Walter S. 1996. "Patterns of Family Violence." In Maureen Baker (ed.), *Families: Changing Trends in Canada*. Whitby, Ont.: McGraw-Hill Ryerson, 249–272.

DeKeseredy, Walter S., and Katherine Kelly. 1995. "Sexual Abuse in Canadian University and College Dating Relationships: The Contribution of Male Peer Support." *Journal of Family Violence*, 10(1):41–53.

Delgado, Richard. 1995. "Introduction." In Richard Delgado (ed.), *Critical Race Theory: The Cutting Edge*. Philadelphia: Temple University Press, xiii–xvi.

Denton, Margaret A., and Alfred A. Hunter. 1995. "What Is Sociology?" In Lorne Tepperman and R.J. Richardson (eds.), *The Social World* (3rd ed.). Toronto: McGraw-Hill Ryerson, 1–32.

Denzin, Norman K. 1989. *The Research Act* (3rd ed.). Englewood Cliffs, N.J.: Prentice Hall.

Department of Justice. 1994. "Minister of Justice Introduces Sentencing Reform Bill." Ottawa: Press Release (June 13).

Department of Justice. 2002. "Child Abuse: A Fact Sheet from the Department of Justice." Ottawa: Author.

———. 2002a. "Spousal Abuse: A Fact Sheet from the Department of Justice Canada." Ottawa: Department of Justice. Retrieved May 16, 2002. Available: http://canada.justice.gc.ca/en/ps/fm/spouseafs.html.

———. 2002b. "Family Violence." Ottawa: Department of Justice. Retrieved May 16, 2002. Available: http://canada.justice.gc.ca/en/ps/fm/overview.html.

———. 2002c. "Child Abuse: A Fact Sheet from the Department of Justice Canada." Ottawa: Department of Justice Canada.

———. 2002d. "Marriage and Legal Recognition of Same-Sex Unions." Ottawa: Department of Justice.

Derber, Charles. 1983. *The Pursuit of Attention: Power and Individualism in Everyday Life.* New York: Oxford University Press.

Desai, Sabra. 2001. "But You Are Different." In Carl E. James and Adrianne Shadd (eds.), *Talking About Identity: Encounters in Race, Ethnicity, and Language* (2nd ed.). Toronto: Between the Lines, 241–249.

Desjardins, B. 1993. *Population Ageing and the Elderly.* Cat. no. 91-533E. Ottawa: Minister of Industry, Science and Technology.

Desrosier, Heather Juby, and Celine LeBourdais. 1999a. "Female Family Paths." In Peron et al., *Canadian Families Approach the Year 2000.* Ottawa: Statistics Canada, 124.

———. 1999b. "Male Family Paths." In Peron et al., *Canadian Families Approach the Year 2000.* Ottawa: Statistics Canada, 180.

Deutschmann, Linda B. 2002. *Deviance and Social Control* (3rd ed.) Toronto: Nelson Canada.

Dikotter, Frank. 1996. " 'Race' and Nation: The Formation of Identity in Twentieth-Century China." *Journal of International Affairs* (Winter): 590–605.

DiMaggio, Paul. 1987. "Classification in Art." *American Sociological Review,* 52:440–455.

DiMaggio, Paul, and Michael Useem. 1978. "Social Class and Arts Consumption: The Origins and Consequences of Class Differences in Exposure to the Arts in America." *Theory and Society,* 5(2):141–161.

Dishman, Chris. 2001. "Terrorism, Crime, and Transformation." *Studies in Conflict and Terrorism,* 24:43–58.

Ditchburn, Jennifer. 1988. "Info-Poor Nations Lose Out, Group Told." *The Globe and Mail* (August 19):A7.

Dodds, Peter Sheridan, Roby Muhamad, and Duncan J. Watts. 2003. "An Experimental Study of Search in Global Networks." *Science,* 301:827–829.

Dollard, John, et al. 1939. *Frustration and Aggression.* New Haven: Conn.: Yale University Press.

Domhoff, G. William. 1974. *The Bohemian Grove and Other Retreats.* New York: Harper and Row.

———. 1978. *The Powers That Be: Processes of Ruling Class Domination in America.* New York: Random House.

———. 1983. *Who Rules America Now? A View for the '80s.* Englewood Cliffs, N.J.: Prentice-Hall.

———. 1990. The Power Elite and the State: How Policy Is Made in America. New York: Aldine De Gruyter.

Doob, Anthony, and Julian V. Roberts. 1983. *An Analysis of the Public's View of Sentencing.* Ottawa: Department of Justice Canada.

Dooley, Stephen, and B. Gail Frankel. 1990. "Improving Attitudes Toward Elderly People: Evaluation of an Intervention Program for Adolescents." *Canadian Journal on Aging,* 9:400–409.

Douglas, Shirley. 2000. "A Politician Who Gave People Hope." *Maclean's* (January 1):195.

Doyle Driedger, Sharon. 1998. "Divorce." *Maclean's* (April 20):39–44.

Driedger, Sharon Doyle. 1997. "Radical Responses." *Maclean's* (July 28):46–47.

Drolet, Marie. 2001a. "The Male-Female Wage Gap." *Perspectives on Labour and Income: The Online Edition* 2(12) (December). Cat. no. 75-001-X1E. Ottawa: Statistics Canada. Retrieved October 15, 2002. Available: http://www.statcan.ca/english/ indepth/75-001/online/01201/hi-fs_200112_01_a.html.

———. 2001b. "The Persistent Gap: New Evidence on the Canadian Gender Wage Gap." Cat. no. 11F0019MPE-157. Ottawa: Statistics Canada.

———. 2002. "Can the Workplace Explain Canadian Gender Pay Differentials?" *Canadian Public Policy,* Special Issue 2002.

Drucker, Peter. 1994. "The Age of Social Transformation." *The Atlantic Monthly* (November):53–80.

———. 2005. "Trading Places." *The National Interest* (Spring):1–13. Retrieved March 25, 2005. Available: www.nationalinterest.org.

D'Sousa, Dinesh. 1996. *The End of Racism: Principles for a Multicultural Society.* New York: Free Press.

Du Bois, W.E.B. 1967. *The Philadelphia Negro: A Social Study.* New York: Schocken Books (orig. pub. 1899).

Dube, Francine. 1999. "One in 10 Canadians Plan to Retire on Lottery Winnings." *National Post* (January 15): A1.

Duffy, Ann, et al. (eds.). 1989. *Few Choices: Women, Work and Family.* Toronto: Garamond Press.

Dumas, Jean. 1990. *Rapport sur l'état de la population du Canada.* Cat. no. 91-209. Ottawa: Minister of Supply and Services.

———. 1997. "Report on the Demographic Situation in Canada, 1996." Cat. no. 91-209-XPE, 121–186. Ottawa: Minister of Industry.

Duncan, Otis Dudley. 1968. "Social Stratification and Mobility: Problems in Measurement of Trend." In E.B. Sheldon and W.E. Moore (eds.), *Indicators of Social Change.* New York: Russell Sage Foundation.

Dunlap, Riley E. 1992. "Trends in Public Opinion Toward Environmental Issues: 1965–1990." In Riley E. Dunlap and Angela G. Mertig (eds.), *American Environmentalism: The U.S. Environmental Movement, 1970–1990.* New York: Taylor & Francis, 89–113.

Dunning, Paula. 1997. *Education in Canada: An Overview.* Toronto: Canadian Education Association.

Durkheim, Émile. 1933. *Division of Labor in Society.* Trans. George Simpson. New York: Free Press (orig. pub. 1893).

———. 1956. *Education and Sociology.* Trans. Sherwood D. Fox. Glencoe, Ill.: Free Press.

———. 1964a. *The Rules of Sociological Method.* Trans. Sarah A. Solovay and John H. Mueller. New York: Free Press (orig. pub. 1895).

———. 1964b. *Suicide.* Trans. John A. Sparkling and George Simpson. New York: Free Press (orig. pub. 1897).

———. 1995. *The Elementary Forms of Religious Life.* Trans. Karen E. Fields. New York: Free Press (orig. pub. 1912).

Durning, Alan. 1993. "Life on the Brink." In William Dan Perdue (ed.), *Systemic Crisis: Problems in Society, Politics, and World Order.* Fort Worth: Harcourt Brace, 274–282.

Durrant, Joan. 2002. "Physical Punishment and Physical Abuse." *B.C. Institute Against Family Violence Newsletter* (Winter):1–7.

Durrant, Joan E., Anders G. Broberg, Linda Rose-Krasnor. 2000. "Predicting Mothers' Use of Physical Punishment During Mother–Child Conflicts in Sweden and Canada." In Paul D. Hastings, Caroline C. Piotrowski, *Conflict as a Context for Understanding Maternal Beliefs About Child Rearing and Children's Misbehavior: New Directions for Child and Adolescent Development.* Hoboken, N.J.: Jossey-Bass.

Duster, Troy. 1995. "Symposium: The Bell Curve." *Contemporary Sociology: A Journal of Reviews,* 24(2):158–161.

Dworkin, Andrea. 1974. *Woman Hating.* New York: Dutton.

Dyck, Rand. 1996. *Canadian Politics: Critical Approaches* (2nd ed.). Scarborough, Ont.: Nelson Canada.

———. 2002. *Canadian Politics* (2nd ed., concise). Scarborough, Ont.: Nelson.

———. 2004. *Canadian Politics: Critical Approaches* (4th ed.). Toronto: Thomson Nelson.

Dye, Thomas R., and Harmon Zeigler. 1993. *The Irony of Democracy: An Uncommon Introduction to American Politics* (9th ed.). Belmont, Cal.: Wadsworth.

Ebaugh, Helen Rose Fuchs. 1988. *Becoming an EX: The Process of Role Exit.* Chicago: University of Chicago Press.

Eberstadt, Nicholas. 2004. "Power and Population in Asia." *Policy Review Online.* Retrieved December 24, 2004. Available: http://www.policyreview.org/feb04/eberstadt.html.

Eccles, Jacquelynne S., Janis E. Jacobs, and Rena D. Harold. 1990. "Gender Role Stereotypes, Expectancy Effects, and Parents' Socialization of Gender Difference." *Journal of Social Issues,* 46:183–201.

Economic Council of Canada. 1991. *New Faces in the Crowd: Economic and Social Impacts, Immigration.* Ottawa: Economic Council of Canada.

The Economist. 1997. "The Anti-Management Guru." (May 4).

Eder, Donna. 1985. "The Cycle of Popularity: Interpersonal Relations Among Female Adolescents." *Sociology of Education,* 58 (July):154–165.

———. 1995. *School Talk: Gender and Adolescent Culture* (with Catherine Colleen Evans and Stephen Parker). New Brunswick, N.J.: Rutgers University Press.

Edgerton, Robert B. 1992. *Sick Societies: Challenging the Myth of Primitive Harmony.* New York: Free Press.

Edsall, Thomas Byrne, with Mary D. Edsall. 1992. *Chain Reaction: The Impact of Race, Rights, and Taxes on American Politics.* New York: Norton.

Edwards, Harry. 1973. *Sociology of Sport.* Homewood, Ill.: Dorsey.

Edwards, Richard. 1979. *Contested Terrain.* New York: Basic Books.

———. 1993. "An Education in Interviewing." In C.M. Renzetti and R.M. Lee (eds.), *Researching Sensitive Topics.* Newbury Park: Sage, 181–196.

Ehrenreich, Barbara. 2001. *Nickel and Dimed: On (Not) Getting By in America.* New York: Metropolitan.

Ehrlich, Paul R., and Anne H. Ehrlich. 1991. *The Population Explosion.* New York: Touchstone/Simon & Schuster.

Ehrlich, Paul R., Anne H. Ehrlich, and Gretchen C. Daily. 1995. *The Stork and the Plow: An Equity Answer to the Human Dilemma.* Connecticut: Yale University Press.

Eichler, Margrit. 1981. "The Inadequacy of the Monolithic Model of the Family." *Canadain Journal of Sociology,* 6: 367–388.

———. 1988a. *Families in Canada Today* (2nd ed.). Toronto: Gage.

———. 1988b. *Nonsexist Research Methods: A Practical Guide.* Boston: Allen & Unwin.

———. 1996. "The Impact of New Reproductive and Genetic Technologies on Families." In Maureen Baker (ed.), *Families: Changing Trends in Canada.* Toronto: McGraw-Hill Ryerson, 104–108.

———. 1997. *Family Shifts: Families, Policies, and Gender Equality.* Don Mills, Ont.: Oxford University Press.

Eighner, Lars. 1993. *Travels with Lizbeth.* New York: St.Martins.

Eisenberg, Mark, Kristian Filion, Arik Azoulay, Anya Brox, Seema Haider, and Louise Pilote. 2005. *Archives of Internal Medicine,* 165:1506–1513.

Eisenstein, Zillah V. 1994. *The Color of Gender: Reimaging Democracy.* Berkeley: University of California Press.

EKOS Research Associates. 2003. *Making Ends Meet: The 2001–2002 Student Financial Survey.* Montreal, Que.: Canadian Millennium Scholarship Foundation.

Elifson, Kirk W., David M. Petersen, and C. Kirk Hadaway. 1983. "Religiosity and Delinquency: A Contextual Analysis." *Criminology,* 21: 505–527.

Elkin, Frederick, and Gerald Handel. 1989. *The Child and Society: The Process of Socialization* (5th ed.). New York: Random House.

Elkind, David. 1995. "School and Family in the Postmodern World." *Phi Delta Kappan* (September): 8–21.

Elliott, D.S., and A. Ageton. 1980. "Reconciling Differences in Estimates of Delinquency." *American Sociological Review*, 45(1):95–110.

Emling, Shelley. 1997. "Haiti Held in Grip of Another Drought." *Austin American-Statesman* (September 19):A17, A18.

Engels, Friedrich. 1972. *The Origins of the Family, Private Property, and the States*. Ed. Eleanor Burke Leacock. New York: International (orig. pub. 1884).

Epstein, Cynthia Fuchs. 1988. *Deceptive Distinctions: Sex, Gender, and the Social Order*. New Haven, Conn.: Yale University Press.

Epstein, Ethan B. 1996. "Workers and the World Economy." *Foreign Affairs*, 75(May/June):16–37.

Epstein, Rachel. 1996. "Lesbian Families." In Marion Lynn (ed.). *Voices: Essays on Canadian Families*. Scarborough, Ont.: Nelson Canada.

Epstein, Rachel. 2003. "Lesbian Families." In Marion Lynn (ed.). *Voices: Essays on Canadian Families* (2nd ed.). Scarborough, Ont.: Nelson Canada, 76–102.

Equal Voice. 2005. "The Facts Ma'am: Some Facts About Women in Politics in Canada." Retrieved June 9, 2005. Available: http://www.equalvoice.ca/research.html.

Ericson, Richard, and Aaron Doyle. 1999. "Globalization and the Policing of Protest: The Case of APEC 1997." *British Journal of Sociology*, 50(4) (December):589–609.

Erikson, Eric H. 1963. *Childhood and Society*. New York: Norton.

Erikson, Kai T. 1962. "Notes on the Sociology of Deviance." *Social Problems*, 9:307–314.

———. 1976. *Everything in Its Path: Destruction of Community in the Buffalo Creek Flood*. New York: Simon & Schuster.

———. 1991. "A New Species of Trouble." In Stephen Robert Couch and J. Stephen Kroll-Smith (eds.), *Communities at Risk: Collective Responses to Technological Hazards*. New York: Peter Land, 11–29.

———. 1994. *A New Species of Trouble: Explorations in Disaster, Trauma, and Community*. New York: Norton.

Esbensen, Finn-Aage, and David Huizinga. 1993. "Gangs, Drugs, and Delinquency in a Survey of Urban Youth." *Criminology*, 31(4):565–589.

Esping Anderson, Gosta. 2000. "Two Societies, One Sociology, and No Theory." *British Journal of Sociology* (January/March):59–77.

Essed, Philomena. 1991. *Understanding Everyday Racism*. Newbury Park, Cal.: Sage.

Esterberg, Kristen G. 1997. *Lesbians and Bisexuals: Constructing Communities, Constructing Self*. Philadelphia: Temple University Press.

Etter, Commander Barbara. 2002. "Critical Issues in Hi-Tech Crime." Paper Presented at the "Embracing the Future Together" Commonwealth Investigations Conference.

Evans, Glen, and Norman L. Farberow. 1988. *The Encyclopedia of Suicide*. New York: Facts on File.

Evans, John, and Alexander Himelfarb. 1996. "Counting Crime." In Rick Linden (ed.), *Criminology: A Canadian Perspective* (3rd ed.). Toronto: Harcourt Brace and Company, 61–94.

———. 2004. "Counting Crime." In Rick Linden (ed.), *Criminology: A Canadian Perspective* (5th ed.). Toronto: Thomson, 55–87.

Evans, Peter B., and John D. Stephens. 1988. "Development and the World Economy." In Neil J. Smelser (ed.), *Handbook of Sociology*. Newbury Park, Cal.: Sage, 739–773.

Eyre, Linda. 1992. "Gender Relations in the Classroom: A Fresh Look at Coeducation." In J. Gaskell and A. McLaren (eds.), *Women and Education*. Calgary: Detselig.

Fabes, Richard A., and Carol L. Martin. 1991. "Gender and Age Stereotypes of Emotionality." *Personality and Social Psychology Bulletin*, 17:532–540.

Fagot, Beverly I. 1984. "Teacher and Peer Reactions to Boys' and Girls' Play Styles." *Sex Roles*, 11:691–702.

Fahmi, Wael Salah. 2001. " 'Honey, I Shrunk the Space': Planning in the Information Age." Paper Presented at the 37 International Planning Congress. Utrecht: The Netherlands.

Fallon, Patricia, Melanie A. Katzman, and Susan C. Wooley. 1994. *Feminist Perspectives on Eating Disorders*. New York: Guilford Press.

Farb, Peter. 1973. *Word Play: What Happens When People Talk*. New York: Knopf.

Farley, John E. 1992. *Sociology* (2nd ed.). Englewood Cliffs, N.J.: Prentice-Hall.

Farren, Sandra. 1998. "Money Matters." *The Maclean's Guide to Canadian Universities, 1998*, 44–47.

Fausto-Sterling, Anne. 1985. *Myths of Gender: Biological Theories About Women and Men*. New York: Basic Books.

"The Favoured Infants." 1976. *Human Behaviour* (June):49–50.

Fawcett, G. 1996. *Living with Disability in Canada: An Economic Portrait*, Cat. no. SDDP-020-10-96-E. Ottawa: Canadian Council on Social Development.

Fawcett, Gail. 2000. *Bringing Down the Barriers: The Labour Market and Women with Disabilities in Ontario*. Ottawa: Canadian Council on Social Development. Retrieved June 27, 2002. Available: http://www.ccsd.ca/pubs/2000/wd/intro.htm.

Feagin, Joe R. 1991. "The Continuing Significance of Race: Antiblack Discrimination in Public Places." *American Sociological Review*, 56 (February):101–116.

Feagin, Joe R., and Clairece Booher Feagin. 1994. *Social Problems: A Critical Power-Conflict Perspective* (4th ed.). Englewood Cliffs, N.J.: Prentice-Hall.

———. 1997. *Social Problems : A Critical Power-Conflict Perspective*. (5th ed). Englewood Cliffs, N.J.: Prentice Hall.

———. 1999. *Racial and Ethnic Relations* (6th ed.). Upper Saddle River, N.J.: Prentice Hall.

———. 2003. *Racial and Ethnic Relations*. (7th ed.). Upper Saddle River, N.J.: Prentice Hall.

Feagin, Joe R., and Robert Parker. 1990. *Building American Cities: The Urban Real Estate Game* (2nd ed.). Englewood Cliffs, N.J.: Prentice-Hall.

Feagin, Joe R., and Melvin P. Sikes. 1994. *Living with Racism: The Black Middle-Class Experience*. Boston: Beacon.

Feagin, Joe R., and Hernán Vera. 1995. *White Racism: The Basics*. New York: Routledge.

Feagin, Joe R., Anthony M. Orum, and Gideon Sjoberg (eds.). 1991. *A Case for the Case Study*. Chapel Hill: University of North Carolina Press.

Featherstone, Mike, and Mike Hepworth. 1998. "Aging, the Lifecourse and the Sociology of Embodiment". In Graham Scamble and Paul Higgs (eds.), *Community, Medicine and Health*. New York: Routledge, 147–175.

Fennema, Elizabeth, and Gilah C. Leder (eds.). 1990. *Mathematics and Gender*. New York: Teachers College Press.

Ferguson, Sue. 2004. "Stressed Out." *Maclean's*, 117(47):30–33.

Ferrell, Keith. 1997. *Truth, Lies, and the Internet*. CNET (October 9). Available: www.cnet.com/content/Features/Dlife/Truth/index.html.

Findlay, Deborah A., and Leslie J. Miller. 1994. "Through Medical Eyes: The Medicalization of Women's Bodies and Women's Lives." In B. Singh Bolaria and Harley D. Dickinson (eds.), *Health, Illness and Health Care in Canada*. (2nd ed.). Toronto: Harcourt Brace, 276–306.

Findlay, Deborah and Leslie Miller. 2002. "Through Medical Eyes: The Medicalization of Women's Bodies and Women's Lives." In B. Singh Bolaria and Harley D. Dickinson (eds.), *Health, Illness, and Health Care in Canada* (3rd ed.). Toronto: Nelson,185–210.

Findlay-Kaneko, Beverly. 1997. "In a Breakthrough for Japan, a Woman Takes Over at a National University." *Chronicle of Higher Education* (June 20): A41–A42.

Fine, Michelle. 1987. "Silencing and Nurturing Voice in an Improbable Context: Urban Adolescents in Public Schools." In Henry A. Giroux and Peter McLaren (eds.), *Schooling and the Politics of Culture*. Albany: SUNY Press.

———. 1989. "Coping with Rape: Critical Perspectives on Consciousness." In Rhoda Kesler Unger (ed.), *Representations: Social Constructions of Gender*. Amityville, N.Y.: Baywood, 186–200.

Fine, Michelle, and Lois Weis. 1998. *The Unknown City: The Lives of the Poor and Working Class Young People*. Boston: Beacon.

Firestone, Shulamith. 1970. *The Dialectic of Sex*. New York: Morrow.

Fisher, Luke. 1994. "A Holy War Over Holidays." *Maclean's* (August 12):26.

Fisher, M., N. Golden, D. Katzman, R.E. Kreipe, J. Rees, J. Schebendach, G. Sigman, S. Ammerman, and H.M. Hoberman. 1995. "Eating Disorders in Adolescents: A Background Paper." *Journal of Adolescent Health*, 16:420–437.

Fisher, Mary. 1993. "Tap Moral Courage to Mold Opinions." *Masthead*, 45(3):27–30.

Fisher-Thompson, Donna. 1990. "Adult Sex-Typing of Children's Toys." *Sex Roles*, 23:291–303.

Fjellman, Stephen M. 1992. *Vinyl Leaves: Walt Disney World and America*. Boulder, Col.: Westview.

Flanagan, William G. 1999. *Urban Sociology: Images and Structure* (3rd ed.). Needham Heights, Mass.: Allyn & Bacon.

Fleming, Jim. 2000. "Barbie Super Sports." Retrieved July 13, 2003. Available: http://www.gradingthemovies.com/html/games/barbie_sports.shtml.

Fleras, Augie, and Jean Leonard Elliott. 1992. *Multiculturalism in Canada*. Scarborough, Ont.: Nelson.

———. 1996. *Unequal Relations: An Introduction to Race, Ethnic and Aboriginal Dynamics in Canada* (2nd ed.). Scarborough, Ont.: Prentice Hall.

———. 1999. *Unequal Relations: An Introduction to Race, Ethnic and Aboriginal Dynamics in Canada* (3rd ed.). Scarborough: Prentice-Hall Canada.

———. 2003. *Unequal Relations: An Introduction to Race, Ethnic and Aboriginal Dynamics in Canada* (4th ed.). Scarborough: Prentice-Hall Canada.

Fleras, Augie, and Jean Lock Kunz. 2001. *Media and Minorities: Representing Diversity in a Multicultural Canada*. Toronto: Thompson Educational Publishing.

Forbes. 2002. "The World's Richest People." Retrieved June 25, 2002. Available: http://www.forbes.com.

Forcese, Dennis. 1986. *The Canadian Class Structure*. Toronto: McGraw-Hill Ryerson.

Ford, Clyde W. 1994. *We Can All Get Along: 50 Steps You Can Take to Help End Racism*. New York: Dell.

Foucault, Michel. 1979. *Discipline and Punish: The Birth of the Prison*. New York: Vintage.

———. 1991. "Governmentality." In Buchell et al. (eds.). *The Foucalt Effect*. Hemel Hempstead: Harvester Wheatsheaf.

———. 1994. *The Birth of the Clinic: An Archaeology of Medica Perception*. New York: Vintage (orig. pub. 1963).

Fox, John, and Michael Ornstein. 1986. "The Canadian State and Corporate Elites in the Post-War Period." *Canadian Review of Sociology and Anthropology*, 23: 481–506.

Fox, Mary Frank. 1989. "Women and Higher Education: Gender Differences in the Status of Students and Scholars." In Jo Freeman (ed.), *Women: A Feminist Perspective.* Mountain View, Cal.: Mayfield, 217–235.

Frank, Andre Gunder. 1969. *Latin America: Underdevelopment or Revolution?* New York: Monthly Review Press.

———. 1981. *Reflections on the World Economic Crisis.* New York: Monthly Review Press.

Frankenberg, Ruth. 1993. *White Women, Race Matters: The Social Construction of Whiteness.* Minneapolis: University of Minnesota Press.

Frankl, Razelle. 1987. *Televangelism: The Marketing of Popular Religion.* Carbondale: Southern Illinois University Press.

Frederick, Judith A., and Janet E. Fast. 2001. "Enjoying Work: An Effective Strategy in the Struggle to Juggle." *Canadian Social Trends* (Summer): 8–11.

Freedom House. 2005. "Freedom in the World Country Rankings." Retrieved June 11, 2005. Available: http://www.freedomhouse.org/ratings/index.htm.

Freidson, Eliot. 1965. "Disability as Social Deviance." In Marvin B. Sussman (ed.), *Sociology and Rehabilitation.* Washington, D.C.: American Sociology Association, 71–99.

———. 1970. *Profession of Medicine.* New York: Dodd, Mead.

———. 1986. *Professional Powers.* Chicago: University of Chicago Press.

French, Howard W. 2003. "Japan's Neglected Resource: Female Workers." *New York Times* (July 25):A3.

Freud, Sigmund. 1924. *A General Introduction to Psychoanalysis* (2nd ed.). New York: Boni & Liveright.

Freudenberg, Nicholas, and Carl Steinsapir. 1992. "Not in Our Backyards: The Grassroots Environmental Movement." In Riley Dunlap and Angela G. Mertig (eds.), *American Environmentalism: The U.S. Environmental Movement, 1970–1990.* New York: Taylor and Francis, 27–37.

Frideres, James. 1994. "The Future of Our Past: Native Elderly in Canadian Society." In National Advisory Council on Aging, *Aboriginal Seniors' Issues,* 17–37. Cat. no. H71-2/1-15-1994E. Ottawa: Minister of Supply and Services.

———. 1998. *Aboriginal Peoples in Canada: Contemporary Conflicts* (5th ed.). Scarborough: Prentice-Hall.

Frideres, James S., and Rene R. Gadacz. 2001. *Aboriginal Peoples in Canada: Contemporary Conflicts* (6th ed.). Scarborough, Ont.: Prentice-Hall.

Friedan, Betty. 1993. *The Fountain of Age.* New York: Simon & Schuster.

Friedman, Milton. 1970. "The Social Responsibility of Business Is to Increase Its Profits." *New York Times Magazine* (September 13):33.

Friedman, Thomas L. 2005. *The World Is Flat.* New York: Farrar, Straus and Giroux.

Friendly, Martha, Jane Beach, and Michelle Turiano. 2002. "Early Childhood Education and Care in Canada 2001." Childcare Resource and Research Unit, December 2002. Retrieved September 14, 2005. Available: http://www.childcarecanada.org/ECEC2001/.

Fukuyama, Francis. 2005. "The Calvinist Manifesto." *The New York Times Review of Books.* Retrieved March 13, 2005. Available: www.nytimes.com/200/03/13/books/review/013/FUKUYA.

Fulton, E. Kaye, and Ian Mather. 1993. "A Forest Fable." *Maclean's* (August 16):20.

Fuse, Toyama. 1997. *Suicide, Individuality, and Society.* Toronto: Canadian Scholars' Press.

Gabor, Thomas. 1994. *Everybody Does It! Crime by the Public.* Toronto: University of Toronto Press.

Gabriel, Trip. 1996. "High-Tech Pregnancies Test Hope's Limit." *New York Times* (January 7):1, 10–11.

Gadd, Jane. 1998. "Young Men Across Canada Earning Less, Report Says." *The Globe and Mail* (July 29):A5.

Gailey, Christine Ward. 1987. "Evolutionary Perspectives on Gender Hierarchy." In Beth B. Hess and Myra Marx Ferree (eds.), *Analyzing Gender: A Handbook of Social Science Research.* Newbury Park, Cal.: Sage, 32–67.

Galarneau, Diane. 2005. "Earnings of Temporary Versus Permanent Employees." *Perspectives on Labour and Income,* 6 (January):5.

Galbi, Douglas. 2002. "Rapid Development of Communications Capabilities in Low-Income Countries." Presentation at the World Bank. Retrieved August 14, 2005. Available: http://www.galbithink.org/wbp2_files/v3_document.htm.

Galloway, Gloria. 1999. "Number of Racist Canadians Falling." *National Post.* Online. Retrieved March 1, 1999.

Gamson, William. 1990. *The Strategy of Social Protest* (2nd ed.). Belmont, Cal.: Wadsworth.

———. 1995. "Constructing Social Protest." In Hank Johnston and Bert Klandermans (eds.), *Social Movements and Culture.* Minneapolis: University of Minnesota Press, 85–106.

Gann, R. 2000. "Postmodern Perspectives on Race and Racism: Help or Hindrance?" Retrieved September 2, 2005. Paper for the *Political Studies Association-UK, 10–13 April 2000.* Ebsco host database.

Gans, Herbert. 1974. *Popular Culture and High Culture: An Analysis and Evaluation of Tastes.* New York: Basic Books.

———. 1982. *The Urban Villagers: Group and Class in the Life of Italian Americans* (updated and expanded ed.; orig. pub. 1962). New York: Free Press.

Garber, Judith A., and Robyne S. Turner. 1995. "Introduction." In Judith A. Garber and Robyne S. Turner (eds.), *Gender in Urban Research.* Thousand Oaks, Cal.: Sage, x–xxvi.

Garcia Coll, Cynthia T. 1990. "A Message to a Future Child About the Danger of Gangs." *Austin American-Statesman* (August 17):A6.

Garfinkel, Harold. 1967. *Studies in Ethnomethodology.* Englewood Cliffs, N.J.: Prentice-Hall.

Gargan, Edward A. 1996. "An Indonesian Asset Is Also a Liability." *New York Times* (March 16):17, 18.

Garreau, Joel. 1993. "GAK Attack." *Austin American-Statesman* (January 9): D1, D6.

Garson, Barbara. 1989. *The Electronic Sweatshop: How Computers Are Transforming the Office of the Future into the Factory of the Past.* New York: Penguin.

Gaskell, Jane, Arlene McLaren, and Myra Novogradsky. 1995. "What Is Worth Knowing? Defining the Feminist Curriculum." In E.D. Nelson and B.W. Robinson (eds.), *Gender in the 1990s: Images, Realities and Issues.* Scarborough: ITP Nelson, 100–118.

Gaylin, Willard. 1992. *The Male Ego.* New York: Viking/Penguin.

Gecas, Viktor. 1982. "The Self-Concept." In Ralph H. Turner and James F. Short, Jr. (eds.), *Annual Review of Sociology, 1982.* Palo Alto, Cal.: Annual Reviews, 1–33.

Gee, Ellen. 1994. "What Is Family?" In R. Hagedorn (ed.), *Sociology.* Toronto: Harcourt Brace, 369–398.

——— 2000. "Voodoo Demography, Population Aging, and Social Policy." In E.M. Gee and G.M. Guttman (eds.), *The Overselling of Population Aging: Apocalyptic Demography, Intergenerational Challenges, and Social Policy.* Don Mills, Ont.: Oxford University Press.

Geertz, Clifford. 1966. "Religion as a Cultural System." In Michael Banton (ed.), *Anthropological Approaches to the Study of Religion.* London: Tavistock, 1–46.

Gelfand, Donald E. 1994. *Aging and Ethnicity: Knowledge and Services.* New York: Springer.

Gelles, Richard J., and Murray A. Straus. 1988. *Intimate Violence: The Definitive Study of the Causes and Consequences of Abuse in the American Family.* New York: Simon & Schuster.

General Facts on Sweden. 2005. Retrieved July 23, 2005. Available: http://www.finansforbundet.se/Resource.phx/plaza/content/material/internationelelteu.htx.pdf.material.3.pdf.

George, Molly. 2005. "Making Sense of Muscle: The Body Experiences of Collegiate Women Athletes." *Sociological Inquiry,* 75(3):317–345.

Gerber, Linda. 1990. "Multiple Jeopardy: A Socioeconomic Comparison of Women Among the Indian, Metis, and Inuit Peoples of Canada." *Canadian Ethnic Studies,* 22(3):22–34.

Gerbner, George, Larry Gross, Michael Morton, and Nancy Signorielli. 1987. "Charting the Mainstream: Television's Contributions to Political Orientations." In Donald Lazere (ed.), *American Media and Mass Culture: Left Perspectives.* Berkeley: University of California Press, 441–464.

Gereffi, Gary. 1994. "The International Economy and Economic Development." In Neil J. Smelser and Richard Swedberg (eds.), *The Handbook of Economic Sociology.* Princeton, N.J.: Princeton University Press, 206–233.

Gergen, Kenneth J. 1991. *The Saturated Self: Dilemmas of Identity in Contemporary Life.* New York: Basic Books.

Gerschenkron, Alexander. 1962. *Economic Backwardness in Historical Perspective.* Cambridge, Mass.: Harvard University Press.

Gerson, Kathleen. 1993. *No Man's Land: Men's Changing Commitment to Family and Work.* New York: Basic Books.

Ghosh, Ratna, and Rabindra Kanungo. 1992. *South Asian Canadians: Current Issues in the Politics of Culture.* Montreal: Shastri Indo-Canadian Institute.

Gibbs, Lois Marie, as told to Murray Levine. 1982. *Love Canal: My Story.* Albany: SUNY Press.

Giddens, Anthony. 1996. *Introduction to Sociology* (2nd ed.). New York: W.W. Norton & Co.

Gideonse, Ted. 1998. "Review: Author Sees Distortion in Marketing of Gays." Available: http://www.salonmagazine.com.

Gilbert, Dennis L. 1998. *The American Class Structure in an Age of Growing Inequality* (5th ed.). Belmont, Cal.: Wadsworth.

Gilbert, Dennis, and Joseph A. Kahl. 1998. *The American Class Structure: A New Synthesis* (5th ed.). Belmont, Cal.: Wadsworth.

Gilbert, S.N. 1989. "The Forgotten Purpose and Future of University Education." *Canadian Journal of Community Mental Health,* 8(2):103–122.

Gilder, George F. 1986. *Men and Marriage.* New York: Pelican.

Gilligan, Carol. 1982. *In a Different Voice: Psychological Theory and Women's Development.* Cambridge, Mass.: Harvard University Press.

Gillis, A.R. 1995. "Urbanization." In Robert J. Brym (ed.), *New Society: Sociology for the 21st Century.* Toronto: Harcourt Brace and Company, 13.1–13.40.

Glascock, A.P., and S.L. Feinman. 1981. "Social Asset or Social Burden: Treatment of the Aged in Non-Industrial Societies." In C.L. Fry (ed.), *Dimensions: Aging, Culture, and Health.* New York: Praeger.

Glaser, Barney, and Anselm Strauss. 1967. *The Discovery of Grounded Theory.* Chicago: Aldine.

———. 1968. *Time for Dying.* Chicago: Aldine.

Glazer, Nona. 1990. "The Home as Workshop: Women as Amateur Nurses and Medical Care Providers." *Gender & Society,* 4:479–499.

Global Health Council. 2002. *Health: A Key to Prosperity. Success Stories in Developing Countries.* Retrieved July 22, 2005. Available: http://www.globalhealth.org/sources/view.php3?id=390.

The Globe and Mail Report on Business Magazine. 1990. (October):B80.

Goffman, Erving. 1956. "The Nature of Deference and Demeanor." *American Anthropologist,* 58:473–502.

———. 1959. *The Presentation of Self in Everyday Life.* New York, N.Y.: Doubleday.

———. 1961a. *Asylums: Essays on the Social Situation of Mental Patients and Other Inmates.* Chicago: Aldine.

———. 1961b. *Encounters: Two Studies in the Sociology of Interaction.* Indianapolis, Ind.: Bobbs-Merrill.

———. 1963a. *Behavior in Public Places: Notes on the Social Structure of Gatherings.* New York: Free Press.

———. 1963b. *Stigma: Notes on the Management of Spoiled Identity.* Englewood Cliffs, N.J.: Prentice-Hall.

———. 1967. *Interaction Ritual: Essays on Face to Face Behavior.* Garden City, N.Y.: Anchor Books.

———. 1971. *Relations in Public.* New York: Basic Books.

———. 1974. *Frame Analysis: An Essay on the Organization of Experience.* Boston: Northeastern University Press.

Gold, Rachel Benson, and Cory L. Richards. 1994. "Securing American Women's Reproductive Health." In Cynthia Costello and Anne J. Stone (eds.), *The American Woman 1994–95.* New York: Norton.

Goldberg, Robert A. 1991. *Grassroots Resistance: Social Movements in Twentieth Century America.* Belmont, Cal.: Wadsworth.

Golden, Anne. 1999. *Taking Responsibility for Homelessness: An Action Plan for Toronto.* Report to the Mayor's Homelessness Action Task Force. Toronto: City of Toronto.

Golden, Stephanie. 1992. *The Women Outside: Meanings and Myths of Homelessness.* Berkeley: University of California Press.

Gonzales, David. 1994. "Frenzied Passengers, Their Hair and Clothes in Flames, Flee Burning Train." *New York Times* (December 22):A12.

Goode, William J. 1960. "A Theory of Role Strain." *American Sociological Review,* 25:483–496.

Goodman, Peter S. 1996. "The High Cost of Sneakers." *Austin American-Statesman* (July 7):F1, F6.

Gordon, David. 1973. "Capitalism, Class, and Crime in America." *Crime and Delinquency,* 19:163–186.

Gordon, Milton. 1964. *Assimilation in American Life: The Role of Race, Religion, and National Origins.* New York: Oxford University Press.

Gordon, Robert M., and Jacquelyne Nelson. 1993. *Census '93: The Report of the 1993 Census of Provincial Correctional Centres in British Columbia.* Victoria: Ministry of the Solicitor General.

Gorey, Kevin, Eric J. Holowaty, Gordon Fehringer, Ethan Laukkanen, Agnes Moskowitz, David J. Webster, and Nancy L. Richter. 1997. "An International Comparison of Cancer Survival: Toronto, Ontario, and Detroit, Michigan, Metropolitan Areas." *American Journal of Public Health,* 87:1156–1163.

Gotham, Kevin Fox. 1999. "Political Opportunity, Community Identity, and the Emergence of a Local Anti-Expressway Movement." *Social Problems,* 46:332–254.

Gottdiener, Mark. 1985. *The Social Production of Urban Space.* Austin: University of Texas Press.

———. 1997. *The Theming of America.* Boulder, Col.: Westview.

Gouldner, Alvin W. 1970. *The Coming Crisis of Western Sociology.* New York: Basic Books.

Grameen Bank. 2005. "Grameen Bank." Retrieved December 30, 2005. Available: http://www.grameen-info.org/bank/index.html.

Granovetter, Mark. 1994. *Getting a Job: A Study in Contacts and Careers.* Cambridge, Mass.: Harvard University Press.

Grant, Karen. 1993. "Health and Health Care." In Peter S. Li and B. Singh Bolaria (eds.), *Contemporary Sociology: Critical Perspectives.* Toronto: Copp-Clark Pitman, 394–409.

Gratton, Bruce. 1986. "The New History of the Aged." In David Van Tassel and Paul N. Stearns (eds.), *Old Age in a Bureaucratic Society.* Westport, Conn.: Greenwood Press, 3–29.

Gray, Charlotte. 1997. "Are We in Store for Some Intergenerational Warfare?" *Canadian Medical Association Journal,* 157:1123–1124.

Gray, Paul. 1993. "Camp for Crusaders." *Time* (April 19):40.

Green, Donald E. 1977. *The Politics of Indian Removal: Creek Government and Society in Crisis.* Lincoln: University of Nebraska Press.

Greenberg, Edward S., and Benjamin I. Page. 1996. *The Struggle for Democracy* (2nd ed.). New York: HarperCollins.

Greenfeld, Karl Taro. 1999. "What Glass Ceiling?" *Time* (August 2):72.

Greenpeace. 2005. "You Can Make a Difference." Retrieved July 18, 2005. Available: http://www.greenpeace.org.au/getactive/difference/people_t.html#Solomon.

Greenspan, Edward. 1982. "The Role of the Defence Lawyer in Sentencing." In Craig L. Boydell and Ingrid Connidis (eds.), *The Canadian Criminal Justice System.* Toronto: Holt, Rinehart and Winston, 200–210.

Griffiths, Curt T., and Simon N. Verdun-Jones. 1994. *Canadian Criminal Justice* (2nd ed.). Toronto: Harcourt Brace and Company.

Grint, Keith, and Steve Woolgar. 1997. *The Machine at Work: Technology, Work, and Organization.* Cambridge: Polity.

Guppy, Neil. 1995. "Education and Schooling." In L. Tepperman, J.E. Curtis, and R.J. Richardson (eds.), *Sociology.* Toronto: McGraw-Hill Ryerson, 450–478.

Guppy, Neil, and Scott Davies. 1998. *Education in Canada: Recent Trends and Future Challenges.* Ottawa: Statistics Canada.

Guppy, Neil, Sabrina Freeman, and Shari Buchan. 1987. "Representing Canadians: Changes in the Economic Backgrounds of Federal Politicians, 1965–1984." *Canadian Review of Sociology and Anthropology,* 24:417–430.

Gusfield, Joseph. 1963. *Symbolic Crusade: Status Politics and the American Temperance Movement.* Urbana: University of Illinois Press.

Haas, Jack. 1977. "Learning Real Feelings: A Study of High Steel Ironworkers' Reactions to Fear and Danger." *Sociology of Work and Occupations,* 4 (May):147–170.

Haas, J., and W. Shaffir. 1995. "Giving Medical Students a Cloak of Competence." In L. Tepperman and James Curtis (eds.), *Everyday Life.* Toronto: McGraw-Hill Ryerson.

Hackler, James C. 1994. *Crime and Canadian Public Policy.* Scarborough, Ont.: Prentice Hall.

Hadden, Jeffrey. 1987. "Toward Desacralizing Secularization Theory." *Social Forces,* 65:587–611.

Hadden, Jeffrey K., and Charles K. Swann. 1981. *Prime Time Preachers: The Rising Power of Televangelism.* Reading, Mass.: Addison-Wesley.

Hadden, Richard W. 1997. *Sociological Theory: An Introduction to the Classical Tradition.* Peterborough, Ont.: Broadview.

Hagan, John. 2004. "Corporate and White-Collar Crime." In Rick Linden (ed.), *Criminology: A Canadian Perspective* (5th ed.). Toronto: Thomson, 480–515.

Hagan, John, and Bill McCarthy. 1992. "Streetlife and Delinquency." *British Journal of Sociology,* 43(4):533–561.

Hagan, John, and Bill McCarthy. 1998. *Mean Streets: Youth Crime and Homelessness.* Cambridge, U.K: Cambridge University Press.

Hahn. Harlan. 1987. "Civil Rights for Disabled Americans: The Foundation of a Political Agenda." In Alan Gartner and Tom Joe (eds.), *Images of the Disabled, Disabling Images.* New York: Praeger, 181–203.

Haines, Valerie A. 1997. "Spencer and His Critics." In Charles Camic (ed.), *Reclaiming the Sociological Classics: The State of the Scholarship.* Malden, Mass.: Blackwell, 81–111.

Halberstadt, Amy G., and Martha B. Saitta. 1987. "Gender, Nonverbal Behavior, and Perceived Dominance: A Test of the Theory." *Journal of Personality and Social Psychology,* 53:257–272.

Hale-Benson, Janice E. 1986. *Black Children: Their Roots, Culture, and Learning Styles* (rev. ed.). Provo, Utah: Brigham Young University Press.

Hall, Edward. 1966. *The Hidden Dimension.* New York: Anchor/Doubleday.

Hall, Peter M. 1972. "A Symbolic Interactionist Analysis of Politics." *Sociological Inquiry,* 42: 35–75.

Halle, David. 1993. *Inside Culture: Art and Class in the American Home.* Chicago, Ill.: University of Chicago Press.

Hamilton, Allen C. and C. Murray Sinclair. 1991. *Report of the Aboriginal Justice Inquiry of Manitoba,* Winnipeg: Queen's Printer, vol. 1. Winnipeg: Queen's Printer.

Hamper, Ben. 1992. *Rivethead: Tales from the Assembly Line.* New York: Warner Books.

Hannigan, John. 1998. *Fantasy City: Pleasure and Profit in the Postmodern Metropolis.* London: Routledge.

Hartnagel, Timothy. 2004. "Correlates of Criminal Behaviour." In Rick Linden (ed.), *Criminology: A Canadian Perspective* (5th ed.). Toronto: Thomson, 120–163.

Haraway, Donna. 1994. "A Cyborg Manifesto: Science, Technology, and Socialist-Feminism in the Late Twentieth Century." In Anne C. Herrmann and Abigail J. Stewart (eds.), *Theorizing Feminism: Parallel Trends in the Humanities and Social Sciences.* Boulder, Colo.: Westview, 427–457.

Harding, Sandra. 1986. *The Science Question in Feminism.* Ithaca, N.Y.: Cornell University Press.

Hardy, Melissa A., and Lawrence E. Hazelrigg. 1993. "The Gender of Poverty in an Aging Population." *Research on Aging,* 15(3):243–278.

Hargrave, Connie. 2005. "Homelessness in Canada: From Housing to Shelters to Blankets." SHARE International Archives. Retrieved June 1, 2005. Available: http://www.shareintl.org/archives/homelessness/hl-ch_Canada.htm.

Harlow, Harry F., and Margaret Kuenne Harlow. 1962. "Social Deprivation in Monkeys." *Scientific American,* 207(5):137–146.

———. 1977. "Effects of Various Mother-Infant Relationships on Rhesus Monkey Behaviors." In Brian M. Foss (ed.), *Determinants of Infant Behavior,* vol. 4. London: Methuen, 15–36.

Harman, Lesley. 1989. *When a Hostel Becomes a Home: Experiences of Women.* Toronto: Garamond Press.

Harrington Meyer, Madonna. 1990. "Family Status and Poverty Among Older Women: The Gendered Distribution of Retirement Income in the United States." *Social Problems,* 37:551–563.

———. 1994. "Gender, Race, and the Distribution of Social Assistance: Medicaid Use Among the Frail Elderly." *Gender & Society,* 8 (1):8–28.

Harris, Chauncey D., and Edward L. Ullman. 1945. "The Nature of Cities." *Annals of the Academy of Political and Social Sciences* (November):7–17.

Harris, Marvin. 1974. *Cows, Pigs, Wars, and Witches.* New York: Random House.

———. 1985. *Good to Eat: Riddles of Food and Culture.* New York: Simon & Schuster.

Harrison, Janine. 2001. "Welfare Reports Document Increasing Homelessness in Australia." *World Socialist Web Site.* Retrieved September 11, 2001. Available: http://wsws .orgarticles/2001/jun2001/home-j07 _prn.shtml.

Harrison, Algea O., Melvin N. Wilson, Charles J. Pine, Samuel Q. Chan, and Raymond Buriel. 1990. "Family Ecologies of Ethnic Minority Children." *Child Development,* 61(2):347–362.

Hartmann, Heidi. 1976. "Capitalism, Patriarchy, and Job Segregation by Sex." *Signs: Journal of Women in Culture and Society,* 1 (Spring):137–169.

———. 1981. "The Unhappy Marriage of Marxism and Feminism." In Lydia Sargent (ed.), *Women and Revolution.* Boston: South End Press.

Hartnagel, Timothy F. 2000. "Correlates of Crime." In R. Linden (ed.), *Criminology: A Canadian Perspective* (4th ed.). Toronto: Harcourt Brace.

Harvey, Frank P. 2004. *Smoke and Mirrors: Globalized Terrorism and the Illusion of Multilateral Security.* Toronto: University of Toronto Press.

HateWatch. 2000. "Hate on the Internet." Retrieved December 18, 2002. Available: http://www.hatewatch .org/hate_internet/index.jsp.

Hauchler, Ingomar, and Paul M. Kennedy (eds.). 1994. *Global Trends: The World Almanac of Development and Peace.* New York: Continuum.

Hauser, Robert M. 1995. "Symposium: The Bell Curve." *Contemporary Sociology: A Journal of Reviews,* 24(2):149–153.

Hauser, Robert M., and David L. Featherman. 1976. "Equality of Schooling: Trends and Prospects." *Sociology of Education,* 49:99–120.

Havighurst, Robert J., Bernice L. Neugarten, and Sheldon S. Tobin. 1968. "Disengagement and Patterns of Aging." In Bernice L. Neugarten (ed.), *Middle Age and Aging.* Chicago: University of Chicago Press, 161–172.

Haviland, William A. 1993. *Cultural Anthropology* (7th ed.). Orlando, Fla.: Harcourt Brace Jovanovich.

Haynes, Jeff. 1997. "Religion, Secularisation and Politics: A Postmodern Conspectus." *Third World Quarterly,* 18:709–728.

Health Canada. 1997. *For the Safety of Canadian Children and Youth: From Injury Data to Preventative Measures,* Cat. no. H39-412/1997E. Ottawa: Health Programs and Services Branch.

———. 1999. "Social Inequality in the Health of Canadians." In James Curtis, Edward Grabb, and Neil Guppy (eds.), *Social Inequality in Canada: Patterns, Problems and Policies* (3rd ed.). Scarborough: Prentice-Hall, 300–314.

———. 2002a. *Adult Survivors of Child Sexual Abuse.* National Clearinghouse on Family Violence. Ottawa: Health Canada. Available: http://www.hc-sc .gc.ca/hppb/ familyviolence/pdfs/ adsurexa.pdf.

———. 2002b. *HIV and AIDS in Canada: Surveillance Report to June 30, 2002.* Ottawa: Health Canada, Centre for Infectious Disease Prevention and Control.

Health and Welfare Canada. 1998. *Active Health Report: The Active Health Report on Seniors.* Ottawa: Minister of Supply and Services.

Hedges, Chris. 1997. "In Bosnia's Schools, 3 Ways Never to Learn from History." *New York Times* (November 25): A1, A4.

Hefley, James C. 1976. *Textbooks on Trial.* Wheaton, Ill.: Victor Books.

Heilbron, Johan. 1995. *The Rise of Social Theory.* Trans. Sheila Gogol. Minneapolis: University of Minnesota Press.

Heilbroner, Robert. 1985. *The Nature and Logic of Capitalism.* New York: W.W. Norton and Company.

Heinrichs, Daniel. 1996. *Caring for Norah.* Winnipeg: Daniel Heinricks Publishing.

Henley, Nancy. 1977. *Body Politics: Power, Sex, and Nonverbal Communication.* Englewood Cliffs, N.J.: Prentice-Hall.

Henry, Frances and Carol Tator. 2006. *The Colour of Democracy: Racism in Canadian Society* (3rd ed.). Toronto: Thomson Nelson.

Henry, Frances, Carol Tator, Winston Mattis, and Tim Rees. 1996. "The Victimization of Racial Minorities in Canada. In Robert J. Brym (ed.), *Society in Question: Sociological Readings for the 21st Century.* Toronto: Harcourt Brace and Company, 133–144.

———. 2000. *The Colour of Democracy: Racism in Canadian Society* (2nd ed). Toronto: Harcourt Canada.

Henry, Frances, and Effie Ginzberg. 1984. *Who Gets Work: A Test of Racial Discrimination in Employment.* Toronto: Urban Alliance on Race Relations and the Social Planning Council of Toronto.

Heritage, John. 1984. *Garfinkel and Ethnomethodology.* Cambridge, Mass.: Polity.

Herman, Nancy. 1996. "'Mixed Nutters,' 'Looney Tuners,' and 'Daffy Ducks.'" In Earl Rubington and Martin S. Weinberg (eds.), *Deviance: The Interactionist Perspective* (6th ed.). Boston: Allyn and Bacon, 254–266.

Hernandez, Debra Gersh. 1994. "AIDS Fades: The Epidemic Swells But Reporters Complain Editors Have Lost Interest." *Editor & Publisher,* 127(34):16–18.

Herrnstein, Richard J., and Charles Murray. 1994. *The Bell Curve: Intelligence and Class Structure in American Life.* New York: Free Press.

Herz, J.C. 1998a. "New Title on the Cutlass Edge of Software." *New York Times* (September 3): D4.

———. 1998b. "Puzzling Over the Allure of Virtual Barbie." *New York Times* (March 19): D4.

Herzog, David B., K.L. Newman, Christine J. Yeh, and M. Warshaw. 1992. "Body Image Satisfaction in Homosexual and Heterosexual Women." *International Journal of Eating Disorders,* 11:391–396.

Heshka, Stanley, and Yona Nelson. 1972. "Interpersonal Speaking Distances as a Function of Age, Sex, and Relationship." *Sociometry,* 35(4):491–498.

Hesse-Biber, Sharlene. 1996. *Am I Thin Enough Yet? The Cult of Thinness and the Commercialization of Identity.* New York: Oxford University Press.

Hettne, Bjorn. 1995. *Development Theory and the Three Worlds* (2nd ed.). Essex: Longman.

Heywood, Leslie. 1998. *Pretty Good for a Girl.* New York: The Free Press.

Heywood, Leslie, and Shari L. Dworkin. 2003. *Built to Win: The Female Athlete as Cultural Icon.* Minneapolis: University of Minnesota Press.

Himmelstein, David, Elizabeth Warren, Deborah Thorne, and Steffie Woolhandler. 2005. "Marketwatch: Illness and Injury as Contributors to Bankruptcy." *Health Affairs,* 24 (March/April): 570.

The Hindu. 1998. "The Idea of Human Development." (October 25):25.

Hirschi, Travis. 1969. *Causes of Delinquency.* Berkeley: University of California Press.

Hirschi, Travis, and Michael Gottfredson. 1983. "Age and the Explanation of Crime." *American Journal of Sociology,* 89(3):552–584.

Hoban, Phoebe. 2002. "Single Girls: Sex But Still No Respect." *New York Times* (Oct. 12):A19, A21.

Hochschild, Arlie Russell. 1983. *The Managed Heart: Commercialization of Human Feeling.* Berkeley: University of California Press.

———. 1989. *The Second Shift: Working Parents and the Revolution at Home.* New York: Viking/Penguin.

———. 1997. *The Time Bind: When Work Becomes Home and Home Becomes Work.* New York: Metropolitan Books.

———. 2003. *The Commercialization of Intimate Life: Notes from Home and Work.* Berkeley: University of California Press.

Hoddinott, Susan. 1998. "Something to Think About: Please Think About This." Report on a National Study of Access to Adult Basic Education Programs and Services in Canada. Ottawa: Ottawa Board of Education.

Hodge, Robert W., Paul Siegel, and Peter Rossi. 1964. "Occupational Prestige in the United States, 1925–63." *American Journal of Sociology,* 70 (November): 286–302.

Hodgetts, Darrin, Kerry Chamberlain, and Graeme Bassett. 2003. "Between Television and the Audience: Negotiating Representations of Ageing." *Health: An Interdisciplinary Journal for the Social Study of Health, Illness and Medicine,* 7(4):417–438.

Hodgson, Doug. 1989. "The Legal and Public Policy Implications of Human Immunodeficiency Virus Antibody Testing in New Zealand." In *Legal Implications of AIDS.* Auckland: Legal Research Foundation, 39–95.

Hodson, Randy, and Robert E. Parker. 1988. "Work in High Techology Settings: A Review of the Empirical Literature." *Research in the Sociology of Work,* 4:1–29.

Hodson, Randy, and Teresa A. Sullivan. 2002. *The Social Organization of Work* (3rd ed.). Belmont, Cal.: Wadsworth.

Hoecker-Drysdale, Susan. 1992. *Harriet Martineau: First Woman Sociologist.* Oxford, England: Berg.

Hoffman, Bruce. 1995. " 'Holy Terror': The Implications of Terrorism Motivated by a Religious Imperative." *Studies in Conflict and Terrorism,* 18:271–284.

———. 2003. "Al Qaeda, Trends in Terrorism, and Future Potentialities: An Assessment." *Studies in Conflict and Terrorism,* 26:429–442.

Holland, Dorothy C., and Margaret A. Eisenhart. 1981. *Women's Peer Groups and Choice of Career.* Final report for the National Institute of Education. ERIC ED 199 328. Washington, D.C.

———. 1990. *Educated in Romance: Women, Achievement, and College Culture.* Chicago: University of Chicago Press.

Holmes, Mark. 1998. *The Reformation of Canada's Schools: Breaking the Barriers to Parental Choice.* Montreal: McGill-Queen's University Press.

Homer-Dixon, Thomas. 1993. *Environmental Scarcity and Global Security.* Foreign Policy Association, Headline Series, Number 300. Ephrata, Penn.: Science Press.

Hoover, Kenneth R. 1992. *The Elements of Social Scientific Thinking.* New York: St. Martin's Press.

Hooyman, Nancy R.R., and H. Asuman Kiyak. 1996. *Social Gerontology: A Multidisciplinary Perspective* (4th ed.). Boston: Allyn & Bacon.

Horan, Patrick M. 1978. "Is Status Attainment Research Atheoretical?" *American Sociological Review,* 43:534–541.

Horsburgh, Susan. 2003. "Daddy Day Care." *People* (June 23):79–81.

Hou, Feng, and T.R. Balakrishnan. 1999. "The Economic Integration of Visible Minorities in Contemporary Canadian Society." 214–225.

Howard, Michael E. 1990. "On Fighting a Nuclear War." In Francesca M. Cancian and James William Gibson (eds.), *Making War, Making Peace: The Social Foundations of Violent Conflict.* Belmont, Cal.: Wadsworth, 314–322.

Howard, Ross. 1998. "No Way Out for Despairing Port Hardy." *The Globe and Mail* (June 15):A4.

Hoyt, Homer. 1939. *The Structure and Growth of Residential Neighborhoods in American Cities.* Washington, D.C.: Federal Housing Administration.

HRSDC. (Human Resources and Skills Development Canada.) 2003. "Winnipeg Annual Labour Market Perspectives, 2003." Retrieved June 14, 2005. Available: http://www .hrsdc.gc.ca/asp/gateway.asp?hr=/en/ mb/lmireports/ perspectives2003- 3.shtml&hs=mb0.

Hudson, Valerie M., and Andrea den Boer. 2004. *Bare Branches: Security Implications of Asia's Surplus Male Population.* Cambridge, Mass.: MIT Press.

Hughes, Everett C. 1945. "Dilemmas and Contradictions of Status." *American Journal of Sociology,* 50:353–359.

Hull, Gloria T., Patricia Bell-Scott, and Barbara Smith. 1982. *All the Women Are White, All the Blacks Are Men, But Some of Us Are Brave.* Old Westbury, N.Y.: Feminist.

Humphreys, Laud. 1970. *Tearoom Trade: Impersonal Sex in Public Places.* Chicago: Aldine.

Hunt, Charles W. 1989. "Migrant Labor and Sexually Transmitted Diseases: AIDS in Africa." *Journal of Health and Social Behaviour.* 30:353–73.

Hunter, Floyd. 1953. *Community Power Structure.* Chapel Hill, N.C.: University of North Carolina Press.

Hurst, Charles E. 1998. *Social Inequality: Forms, Causes, and Consequences* (3rd ed.). Boston: Allyn and Bacon.

Huston, Aletha C. 1985. "The Development of Sex Typing: Themes from Recent Research." *Developmental Review,* 5:2–17.

Huyssen, Andreas. 1984. *After the Great Divide.* Bloomington: Indiana University Press.

Hyde, Mary, and Carol La Prairie. 1987. "American Police Crime Prevention." Working paper. Ottawa: Solicitor General.

Ibrahim, Youseff M. 1990. "Saudi Tradition: Edicts from Koran Produce Curbs on Women." *New York Times* (November 6):A6.

IGN Entertainment. 2003. "Review of Red Jack: Revenge of the Brethren." Retrieved July 19, 2003. Available: http://pc.ign.com/articles/160/160369p1.html.

Ikegami, Naoki. 1998. "Growing Old in Japan." *Age and Ageing* (May):277–283.

Indian and Northern Affairs Canada. 2000. *Comparison of Social Conditions, 1991 and 1996.* Ottawa: Indian and Northern Affairs Canada.

———. 2005. "Some Fast Fasts on the Funding of Aboriginal Programs." Retrieved September 8, 2005. Available: http://www.ainc-inac.gc.ca/nr/prs/j-a2000/mar7_e.html.

Innis, Harold. 1984. *The Fur Trade in Canada.* Toronto: University of Toronto Press (orig. pub. 1930).

Internet World Stats. 2005. "Internet Usage Statistics: The Big Picture." Retrieved August 14, 2005. Available: http://www.internetworldstats.com/stats.htm.

Interfaith Social Assistance Reform Coalition. 1998. *Our Neighbours' Voices: Will We Listen?* Toronto: James Lorimer & Company.

Inter-Parliamentary Union. 2005. "Women in National Parliaments." Retrieved May 30, 2005. Available: http://www.ipu.org/wmn-e/world.htm.

Institute for Social Research. Centre for Research in Higher Education. 1995. "York Student Experience Study: Do Private High Schools Make A

Difference." *Bulletin 8* (October 15). Available: http:/www.isr.yorku.ca.isr/bulletins/bullet8.asp.

Institut National d'Etudes Demographiques. 1995. From Julie DaVanzo and David Adamson. 1997. "Russia's Demographic 'Crisis': How Real Is It?" *Rand Issue Paper,* July 1997. Santa Monica: Rand Center for Russian and Eurasian Studies.

Ip, Greg. 1996. "Shareholders vs. Job Holders." *The Globe and Mail* (March 23):B1.

Isajiw, Wsevolod W. 1999. *Understanding Diversity: Ethnicity and Race in the Canadian Context.* Toronto: Thompson Educational Publishing.

ITAR/TASS News Agency. 1999. "Polygamy Allowed in Southern Russia" (July 21). Retrieved September 11, 1999. Available: http://www.comtexnews.com.

Jackman, Philip. 1999. "The Greying of Canada's Sisters and Brothers." *The Globe and Mail.* February 23: A24.

Jackson, Beth E. 1993. "Constructing Adoptive Identities: The Accounts of Adopted Adults." Unpublished masters thesis, University of Manitoba.

Jacobs, Gloria. 1994. "Where Do We Go from Here? An Interview with Ann Jones." *Ms.* (September/October):56–63.

Jacobs, Jane. 1961. *The Death and Life of Great American Cities.* New York: Vintage Books.

James, Carl E. 1998. " 'Up to No Good': Black on the Streets and Encountering the Police." In Vic Satzewich (ed.), *Racism and Social Inequality in Canada.* Toronto: Thompson Educational Publishing, 157–176.

———. 1999. *Seeing Ourselves: Exploring Ethnicity, Race and Culture.* Toronto: Thompson Educational Publishing.

———. 2001. *Seeing Ourselves: Exploring Ethnicity, Race, and Culture.* (2nd ed.). Toronto: Thompson Educational Publishing.

Jameson, Fredric. 1984. "Postmodernism, or, the Cultural Logic of Late Capitalism." *New Left Review,* 146:59–92.

Jamieson, Alison. 2001. "Transnational Organized Crime: A European Perspective." *Studies in Conflict and Terrorism,* 24:377–387.

Janigan, Mary. 2000. "The Wealth Gap." *Maclean's* (August 28): 42–46.

Janis, Irving. 1972. *Victims of Groupthink.* Boston: Houghton Mifflin.

———. 1989. *Crucial Decisions: Leadership in Policymaking and Crisis Management.* New York: Free Press.

Jankowski, Martin Sanchez. 1991. *Islands in the Street: Gangs and American Urban Society.* Berkeley: University of California Press.

Jarvis, George K. 1994. "Health, Health Care and Dying." In W. Meloff and D. Pierece (eds.), *An Introduction to Sociology.* Scarborough: ITP Nelson, 342–375.

Jary, David, and Julia Jary. 1991. *The Harper Collins Dictionary of Sociology.* New York: HarperPerennial.

Jenkinson, Edward B. 1979. *Censors in the Classroom: The Mind Benders.* Carbondale: Southern Illinois University Press.

Jensen, Mike. 2002. "The African Internet: A Status Report." Retrieved August 14, 2005. Available: http://www3.sn.apc.org/africa/afstat.htm.

Jewell, K. Sue. 1993. *From Mammy to Miss America and Beyond: Cultural Images and the Shaping of US Social Policy.* New York: Routledge.

Johns Hopkins. 1998. "Can Religion be Good Medicine?" *The Johns Hopkins Medical Letter* (November 3).

Johnson, Allan. 1995. *The Blackwell Dictionary of Sociology.* Malden, Mass.: Blackwell.

———. 2005. "The Perspective of Sociology." In Bruce Ravelli (ed.), *Exploring Canadian Sociology: A Reader.* Toronto: Pearson, 8–13.

Johnson, Claudia. 1994. *Stifled Laughter: One Woman's Story About Fighting Censorship.* Golden, Colorado: Fulcrum.

Johnson, Earvin "Magic," with William Novak. 1992. *My Life.* New York: Fawcett Crest.

Johnson, Holly. 1996. *Dangerous Domains: Violence Against Women in Canada.* Scarborough, Ont.: Nelson Canada.

Johnson, L.A. 1974. *Poverty in Wealth.* Toronto: New Hogtown Press.

Jones, Jennifer M., Susan Bennett, Marion P. Olmsted, Margaret L. Lawson, and Gary Rodin. 2001. "Disordered Eating Attitudes and Behaviours in Teenaged Girls: A School-Based Study." *Canadian Medical Association Journal,* 165:547–552.

Jones, Meredith. 2004. "Architecture of the Body: Cosmetic Surgery and Postmodern Space." *Space and Culture,* 7(1):90–101.

Juergensmeyer, Mark. 1993. *The New Cold War? Religious Nationalism Confronts the Secular State.* Berkeley: University of California Press.

———. 2003. *Terror in the Mind of God.* Berkeley: University of California Press.

Jung, John. 1994. *Under the Influence: Alcohol and Human Behavior.* Pacific Grove, Cal.: Brooks/Cole.

Kaczor, Bill. 2005. "Fla. Pilots 'Counseled' for Rescues." washingtonpost.com (September 7). Retrieved September 12, 2005. Available: http://www.washingtonpost.com/wp-dyn/content/article/2005/09/07/AR2005090701352.html.

Kakuchi, Suvendrini. 1998. "Population: Japan Desperate for a Baby Boom." World News: InterPress Service. Retrieved September 21,1999. Available: http://www.oneworld.org/ips2/nov/japan.html.

Kanter, Rosabeth Moss. 1977. *Men and Women of the Corporation.* New York: Basic Books.

———. 1983. *The Change Masters: Innovation and Entrepreneurship in the American Corporation.* New York: Simon & Schuster.

Kantrowitz, Barbara. 2003. "Hoping for the Best, Ready for the Worst." *Newsweek* (May 12):50–51.

Karmona, Laurie Krever. 2001. "Who Me, Disabled?" *The Globe and Mail* (October 18):A16.

Karp, David A., and William C. Yoels. 1976. "The College Classroom: Some Observations on the Meanings of Student Participation." *Sociology and Social Research,* 60:421–439.

Kaspar, Anne S. 1986. "Consciousness Re-evaluated: Interpretive Theory and Feminist Scholarship." *Sociological Inquiry,* 56(1):30-49.

Katz, Michael B. 1989. *The Undeserving Poor: From the War on Poverty to the War on Welfare.* New York: Pantheon.

Katz, Stephen. 1999. *Old Age as Lifestyle in an Active Society.* Doreen B. Townsend Center Occasional Papers. Berkeley: University of California. Retrieved May 30, 2005. Available: http://townsendcenter.berkeley.edu/pubs/OP19_Katz.pdf.

Katzer, Jeffrey, Kenneth H. Cook, and Wayne W. Crouch. 1991. *Evaluating Information: A Guide for Users of Social Science Research.* New York: McGraw-Hill.

Kaufert, S.R., and M. Lock. 1997. "Medicalization of Women's Third Age." *Journal of Psychosomatic Obstetrics and Gynaecology,* 18:81–86.

Kaufman, Gayle. 1999. "The Portrayal of Men's Family Roles in Television Commercials." *Sex Roles,* 313:439–451.

Kauppinen-Toropainen, Kaisa, and Johanna Lammi. 1993. "Men in Female-Dominated Occupations: A Cross-Cultural Comparison." In Christine L. Williams (ed.), *Doing "Women's Work": Men in Nontraditional Occupations.* Newbury Park, Cal.: Sage, 91–112.

Kazemipur, Abdolmohammad and Shiva Halli. 2001. "The Changing Colour of Poverty in Canada." *Canadian Review of Sociology and Anthropology,* 38(2):217–238.

Keegan, Victor. 1996. "A World Without Bosses—Or Workers." *The Globe and Mail* (August 24):D4.

Keister, Lisa A. 2000. *Wealth in America: Trends in Wealth Inequality.* Cambridge, U.K.: Cambridge University Press.

Keller, James. 1994. "I Treasure Each Moment." *Parade Magazine* (September 4):4–5.

Kelman, Steven. 1991. "Sweden Sour? Downsizing the 'Third Way.'" *New Republic* (July 29):19–23.

Kellett, Anthony. 2004. "Terrorism in Canada, 1960–1992." In Jeffrey Ian Ross (ed.), *Violence in Canada: Sociopolitical Perspectives* (2nd ed.). New Brunswick, N.J.: Transaction Press, 284–312.

Kelly, John, and David Stark. 2002. "Crisis, Recovery, Innovation: Responsive Organization After September 11." Paper Presented at the Reginald H. Jones Center's 3rd Annual Conference on the Internet and

Strategy "The Internet and the 21st Century Firm." Philadelphia: The Wharton School.

Kemp, Alice Abel. 1994. *Women's Work: Degraded and Devalued.* Englewood Cliffs, N.J.: Prentice-Hall.

Kennedy, Leslie W. 1983. *The Urban Kaleidoscope: Canadian Perspectives.* Toronto: McGraw-Hill Ryerson.

Kennedy, Leslie, Robert Silverman, and David Forde. 1991. "Homicide in Urban Canada." *Canadian Journal of Sociology,* 16:397–410.

Kennedy, Paul. 1993. *Preparing for the Twenty-First Century.* New York: Random House.

Kenny, Charles. 2003. "Development's False Divide." *Foreign Policy* (January/February):76–77.

Kephart, William M. 1982. *Extraordinary Groups.* New York: St. Martin's Press.

Kerbo, Harold. 2000. *Social Stratification and Inequality: Class Conflict in Historical, Comparative, and Global Perspective* (4th ed.). New York: McGraw-Hill.

Kerstetter, Steve. 2002. *Rags and Riches: Wealth Inequality in Canada.* Ottawa: Canadian Centre for Policy Alternatives.

Kettle, John. 1998. "Death Still Looks Like a Healthy Business." *The Globe and Mail* (May 7):B15.

Khan, Joseph. 2004. "The World: China's Time Bomb; The Most Populous Nation Faces a Population Crisis." *New York Times* (May 30), section 4, page 1.

Khayatt, Didi. 1994. "The Boundaries of Identity at the Intersection of Race, Class and Gender." *Canadian Woman Studies,* 14(2) (Spring).

Kidron, Michael, and Ronald Segal. 1995. *The State of the World Atlas.* New York: Penguin.

Kilbourne, Jean. 1994. "Still Killing Us Softly: Advertising and the Obsession with Thinness." In Patricia Fallon, Melanie A. Katzman, and Susan C. Wooley (eds.), *Feminist Perspectives on Eating Disorders.* New York: Guilford, 395–454.

———. 1999. *Deadly Persuasion: The Addictive Power of Advertising.* New York: Simon & Schuster.

Killian, Lewis. 1984. "Organization, Rationality, and Spontaneity in the Civil Rights Movement." *American Sociological Review,* 49:770–783.

Kimmel, Michael S., and Michael A. Messner (eds.). 1992. *Men's Lives* (2nd ed.). New York: Macmillan.

King, Gary, Robert O. Keohane, and Sidney Verba. 1994. *Designing Social Inquiry: Scientific Inference in Qualitative Research.* Princeton, N.J.: Princeton University Press.

King, Leslie, and Madonna Harrington Meyer. 1997. "The Politics of Reproductive Benefits: U.S. Insurance Coverage of Contraceptive and Infertility Treatments." *Gender and Society,* 11(1):8–30.

Kirby, S.L., and A. Robinson. 1998. *Lesbian Struggles for Human Rights in Canada: Report to the Secretary of State on the Status of Women.* Ottawa.

Kirby, Sandra, and Kate McKenna. 1989. *Experience Research Social Change: Methods from the Margins.* Toronto: Garamond.

Kirmayer. Laurence J. 1994. "Suicide Among Canadian Aboriginal Peoples." *Transcultural Psychiatric Research Review,* 31:7.

Kitano, Harry, Iris Chi, Siyon Rhee, C.K. Law, and James E. Lubben. 1992. "Norms and Alcohol Consumption: Japanese in Japan, Hawaii, and California." *Journal of Studies on Alcohol,* 53(1):33–39.

Klein, Alan M. 1993. *Little Big Men: Bodybuilding Subculture and Gender Construction.* Albany: SUNY Press.

Klein, Naomi. 2000. *No Logo.* Toronto: Vintage Canada.

Kleinfeld, Judith S. 2002. "The Small World Problem." *Society* (January/February):61–66.

Klockars, Carl B. 1979. "The Contemporary Crises of Marxist Criminology." *Criminology,* 16:477–515.

Kluckhohn, Clyde. 1961. "The Study of Values." In Donald N. Barrett (ed.), *Values in America.* South Bend, Ind.: University of Notre Dame Press, 17–46.

Knox, Paul L., and Peter J. Taylor, eds. 1995. *World Cities in a World-System.* Cambridge, England: Cambridge University Press.

Knudsen, Dean D. 1992. *Child Maltreatment: Emerging Perspectives.* Dix Hills, N.Y.: General Hall.

Kohlberg, Lawrence. 1969. "Stage and Sequence: The Cognitive-Developmental Approach to Socialization." In David A. Goslin, *Handbook of Socialization Theory and Research.* Chicago: Rand McNally, 347–480.

Kohn, Melvin L. 1977. *Class and Conformity: A Study in Values* (2nd ed.). Homewood, Ill.: Dorsey Press.

Kohn, Melvin L., Atsushi Naoi, Carrie Schoenbach, Carmi Schooler, and Kazimierz M. Slomczynski. 1990. "Position in the Class Structure and Psychological Functioning in the United States, Japan, and Poland." *American Journal of Sociology,* 95:964–1008.

Kolata, Gina. 1993. "Fear of Fatness: Living Large in a Slimfast World." *Austin American-Statesman* (January 3):C1, C6.

Kome, Penney. 2002. "Canada Court Tells Parliament to OK Gay Marriages." Women's eNews. Retrieved August 23, 2003. Available: http://www .womensnews.org/article/cfm/dyn/ aid/987/context/archive.

Korsmeyer, Carolyn. 1981. "The Hidden Joke: Generic Uses of Masculine Terminology." In Mary Vetterling-Braggin (ed.), *Sexist Language: A Modern Philosophical Analysis.* Totowa, N.J.: Littlefield, Adams, 116–131.

Korte, Charles and Stanley Milgram. 1970. "Acquaintance Networks Between Racial Groups: Application of the Small World Method." *Journal of Personality and Social Psychology,* 15 (101–108).

Korten, David C. 1996. *When Corporations Rule the World.* West Hartford, Conn.: Kumarian Press.

Koskela, Hille. 1997. "Bold Walk and Breakings: Women's Spatial Confidence versus Fear of Violence." *Gender, Place and Culture,* 4(3):301–320.

Kosmin, Barry A. and Seymour P. Lachman. 1993. *One Nation Under God: Religion in Contemporary American Society.* New York: Crown.

Kozol, Jonathan. 1988. *Rachael and Her Children: Homeless Families in America.* New York: Fawcett Columbine.

———. 1991. *Savage Inequalities: Children in America's Schools.* New York: Crown.

Krahn, Harvey J., and Graham S. Lowe. 1998. *Work, Industry, and Canadian Society* (3rd ed.). Scarborough, Ont.: Nelson Canada.

———. 2002. *Work, Industry and Canadian Society* (4th ed.). Toronto: Nelson Thomson Learning.

Kramnick, Isaac, ed. 1995. *The Portable Enlightenment Reader.* New York: Penguin.

Krebs, Valdis E. 2002. "Mapping Networks of Terrorist Cells." *Connections,* 24(3):43–52.

Kübler-Ross, Elisabeth. 1969. *On Death and Dying.* New York: Macmillan.

Kumar, K. 1997. "The Post-Modern Condition." In A.H. Halsey, H. Lauder, P. Brown, and A.S. Wells (eds). *Education: Culture, Economy, and Society.* Oxford University Press.

Kurian, George. 1991. "Socialization in South Asian Immigrant Youth." In S.P. Sharma, A.M. Erwin, and D. Meintel (eds.), *Immigrants and Refugees in Canada.* Saskatoon: University of Saskatchewan.

Kurtz, Lester. 1995. *Gods in the Global Village: The World's Religions in Sociological Perspective.* Thousand Oaks, Cal.: Sage.

Kvale, Steinar. 1996. *Interviews: An Introduction to Qualitative Research Interviewing.* Thousand Oaks, Cal.: Sage.

Laberge, Danielle. 1991. "Women's Criminality, Criminal Women, Criminalized Women?: Questions in and for a Feminist Perspective." *Journal of Human Justice,* 2(2):37–56.

Lacayo, Richard. 2001. "About Face: An Inside Look at How Women Fared Under Taliban Oppression and What the Future Holds for Them Now." *Time* (Dec. 5):36–49.

Ladd, E.C., Jr. 1966. *Negro Political Leadership in the South.* Ithaca, N.Y.: Cornell University Press.

Lafreniere, Sylvie A., Yves Carriere, Laurent Martel, and Alain Belanger. 2003. "Dependent Seniors at Home: Formal and Informal Help." *Health Reports,* 14(August):31–39.

Lamanna, Marianne, and Agnes Riedmann. 2003. *Marriages and Families: Making Choices and Facing Change* (8th ed.). Belmont, Cal.: Wadsworth.

Lane, Harlan. 1992. *The Mask of Benevolence: Disabling the Deaf Community.* New York: Vintage Books.

Langdon, Steven. 1999. *Global Poverty, Democracy and North-South Change.* Toronto: Garamond Press.

Lankenau, S.E. 1999. "Panhandling Repertoires and Routines for Overcoming the Non-Person Treatment." *Deviant Behaviour: An Interdisciplinary Journal,* 20:183–206.

Lapchick, Richard E. 1991. *Five Minutes to Midnight: Race and Sport in the 1990s.* Lanham, Md.: Madison Books.

Lapsley, Daniel K. 1990. "Continuity and Discontinuity in Adolescent Social Cognitive Development." In Raymond Montemayor, Gerald R. Adams, and Thomas P. Gullota (eds.), *From Childhood to Adolescence: A Transitional Period? (Advances in Adolescent Development,* vol. 2). Newbury Park, Cal.: Sage.

Larimer, Tim. 1999. "The Japan Syndrome." *Time* (October 11):50–51.

Larson, Magali Sarfatti. 1977. *The Rise of Professionalism: A Sociological Analysis.* Berkeley: University of California Press.

Lasch, Christopher. 1977. *Haven in a Heartless World.* New York: Basic Books.

Lash, Scott, and John Urry. 1994. *Economies of Signs and Space.* London: Sage.

Lashmar, Paul. 2004. "It's All for Your Own Good." *The Guardian* (September 25).

Latané, Bibb, and John M. Darley. 1970. *The Unresponsive Bystander: Why Doesn't He Help?* New York: Appleton Century Crofts.

Latouche, Serge. 1992. "Standard of Living." In Wolfgang Sachs (ed.), *The Development Dictionary.* Atlantic Highlands, N.J.: Zed Books, 250–263.

Lavigne, Yves. 1987. *Hell's Angels: Taking Care of Business.* Toronto: Ballantine Books.

Lavizzo-Mourey, Risa, William Richardson, Robert Ross, and John Rowe. 2005. "A Tale of Two Cities." *Health Affairs,* 24:313–315.

Law Reform Commission of Canada. 1974. *The Native Offender and the Law.* Ottawa: Information Canada.

Law Society of Upper Canada. 2002. "The Changing Face of the Legal Profession." Fact Sheets. Retrieved December 7, 2002. Available: http://www.lsuc.on.ca/news/factst/ changeface.jsp.

Laxer, Gordon. 1989. *Open for Business: The Roots of Foreign Ownership in Canada.* Don Mills: Oxford University Press.

Le Bon, Gustave. 1960. *The Crowd: A Study of the Popular Mind.* New York: Viking (orig. pub. 1895).

Lee, Kevin K. 2000. "Urban Poverty in Canada: A Statistical Profile." Ottawa: Canadian Council on Social Development.

Leenaars, Antoon A., Susan Wenckstern, Isaac Sakinofsky, Ronald J. Dyck, Michael J. Kral, and Roger C. Bland. 1998. *Suicide in Canada.* Toronto: University of Toronto Press.

Lefrançois, Guy R. 1999. *The Lifespan* (6th ed.). Belmont, Cal.: Wadsworth.

Lehmann, Jennifer M. 1994. *Durkheim and Women*. Lincoln: University of Nebraska Press.

Leidner, Robin. 1993. *Fast Food, Fast Talk: Service Work and the Routinization of Everyday Life*. Berkeley: University of California Press.

Lele, J., G.C. Perlin, and H.G. Thorburn. 1979. "The National Party Convention." In H.G. Thorburn (ed.), *Political Parties in Canada*. Scarborough, Ont.: Prentice Hall, 89–97.

Lemann, Nicholas. 1997. "Let's Guarantee the Key Ingredients." *Time* (October 27):96.

Lemert, Charles. 1997. *Postmodernism Is Not What You Think*. Malden, Mass.: Blackwell.

Lemert, Edwin M. 1951. *Social Pathology*. New York: McGraw-Hill.

Lengermann, Patricia Madoo, and Jill Niebrugge-Brantley. 1998. *The Women Founders: Sociology and Social Theory, 1830–1930*. New York: McGraw-Hill.

Lengermann, Patricia Madoo, and Ruth A. Wallace. 1985. *Gender in America: Social Control and Social Change*. Englewood Cliffs, N.J.: Prentice-Hall.

Lenski, Gerhard. 1966. *Power and Privilege: A Theory of Social Stratification*. New York: McGraw-Hill.

Lenski, Gerhard, Jean Lenski, and Patrick Nolan. 1991. *Human Societies: An Introduction to Macrosociology* (6th ed.). New York: McGraw-Hill.

Lenzer, Gertrud, ed. 1998. *The Essential Writings: Auguste Comte and Positivism*. New Brunswick, N.J.: Transaction.

Leonard, Andrew. 1999. "We've Got Mail—Always." *Newsweek* (September 20): 58–61.

LeShan, Eda. 1994. *I Want More of Everything*. New York: New Market Press.

Letkemann, Peter. 1973. *Crime as Work*. Englewood Cliffs, N.J.: Prentice-Hall.

LeVay, Simon. 2000. "As Nature Made Him: The Boy Who Was Raised as a Girl. Book Review" *Psychology Today* (May). Retrieved September 25, 2003. Available: http://findarticles.com/m1175/3_33/62215090/pl/article.

Leventman, Paula Goldman. 1981. *Professionals Out of Work*. New York: Free Press.

Leviathan, U., and J. Cohen. 1985. "Gender Differences in Life Expectancy among Kibbutz Members." *Social Science and Medicine*, 21:545–551.

Levin, William C. 1988. "Age Stereotyping: College Student Evaluations." *Research on Aging*, 10(1):134–148.

Levine, Adeline Gordon. 1982. *Love Canal: Science, Politics, and People*. Lexington, Mass.: Lexington Books.

Levine, Arthur. 1993. "Student Expectations of College." *Change* (September/October): 4.

Levine, Nancy E., and Joan B. Silk. 1997. "Why Polyandry Fails: Sources of Instability in Polyandrous Marriages." *Current Anthropology* (June): 375–399.

Levitt, Kari. 1970. *Silent Surrender: the Multinational Corporation in Canada*. Toronto: Macmillan of Canada.

Lewis, Paul. 1998. "Marx's Stock Resurges on a 150-Year Tip." *New York Times* (June 27):A17, A19.

Lewis-Thornton, Rae. 1994. "Facing AIDS." *Essence* (December):63–130.

Leyton, Elliott. 1979. *The Myth of Delinquency: An Anatomy of Juvenile Nihilism*. Toronto: McClelland and Stewart.

———. 1997. *Dying Hard: The Ravages of Industrial Carnage*. Toronto: Oxford University Press.

Liberty. 2001. "You Could See the Shame on Their Faces." In *RESIST! A Grassroots Collection of Stories, Poetry, Photos and Analysis from the FTAA Protests in Québec City and Beyond*. Compiled by Jen Chang, Bethany Or, Eloginy Tharmendran, Emmie Tsumura, Steve Daniels and Darryl Leroux. Halifax: Fernwood Publishing, 103–107.

Liebow, Elliot. 1993. *Tell Them Who I Am: The Lives of Homeless Women*. New York: Free Press.

Linden, Rick. 1994. "Deviance and Crime." In Lorne Tepperman, James E. Curtis, and R.J. Richardson (eds.), *The Social World* (3rd ed.). Whitby, Ont.: McGraw-Hill Ryerson, 188–226.

———. 2000. *Criminology: A Canadian Perspective* (4th ed.) Toronto: Harcourt Brace and Company.

———. 2004. *Criminology: A Canadian Perspective* (5th ed.). Toronto: Nelson.

Linden, Rick and Raymond C. Currie. 1977. "Religiosity and Drug Use: A Test of Social Control Theory." *Canadian Journal of Criminology and Corrections*, 19:346–355.

Linden, Rick, and Cathy Fillmore. 1981. "A Comparative Study of Delinquency Involvement." *Canadian Review of Sociology and Anthropology*, 18:343–361.

Linden, Rick, David Last, and Christopher Murphy. Forthcoming. "Obstacles on the Road to Peace and Justice: The Role of Civilian Police in Peacekeeping." In James Sheptycki (ed.), *Crafting Global Policing*.

Lindsay, Colin. 1999. *A Portrait of Seniors in Canada* (3rd ed.). Cat. no. 89-519-XPE. Ottawa: Statistics Canada.

Lindsay, Colin. 2002. *Poverty Profile, 1999*. Ottawa: Statistics Canada.

Linton, Ralph. 1936. *The Study of Man*. New York: Appleton-Century-Crofts.

Lipovenko, Dorothy. 1997. "Older People Looking for Work Often Face Frowns, Study Says." *The Globe and Mail* (November 19):A6.

Lippa, Richard A. 1994. *Introduction to Social Psychology*. Pacific Grove, Cal.: Brooks/Cole.

Lips, Hilary M. 1989. "Gender-Role Socialization: Lessons in Femininity." In Jo Freeman (ed.), *Women: A Feminist Perspective* (4th ed.). Mountain View, Cal.: Mayfield, 197–216.

———. 1993. *Sex and Gender: An Introduction* (2nd ed.). Mountain View, Cal.: Mayfield.

———. 2001. *Sex and Gender: An Introduction* (4th ed.). New York: McGraw-Hill.

Lipton, Eric, Christopher Drew, Scott Shane, and David Rohde. 2005. "Breakdowns Marked Path from Hurricane to Anarchy." NYTimes.com (September 11). Retrieved September 12, 2005. Available: http://www.nytimes.com/2005/09/11/national/nationalspecial/11response.html?pagewanted=1&ei=5070&en=b1231d972456e252&ex=1126670400.

Livingston, D.W. 2002. "Universities and the Left." *Canadian Dimension* (May/June), 36(3). Lorber, Judith (ed.). 2001. *Gender Inequality: Feminist Theories and Politics* (2nd ed.). Los Angeles: Roxbury.

Livingston, D.W., and Meg Luxton. 1995. "Gender Consciousness at Work: Modification of the Male Breadwinner Norm Among Steelworkers and Their Spouses." In E.D. Nelson and B.W. Robinson (eds.), *Gender in the 1990s*. Scarborough, Ont.: Nelson Canada, 172–200.

Lochhead, Clarence, and Vivian Shalla. 1996. "Delivering the Goods: Income Distribution and the Precarious Middle Classes." *Perception*, 20(1). Canadian Council on Social Development. Retrieved June 27, 2002. Available: http://www.ccsd.ca/deliver.html.

Lofland, Lyn. 1973. *A World of Strangers: Order and Action in Urban Public Space*. New York: Basic Books.

Lofland, John. 1993. "Collective Behavior: The Elementary Forms." In Russell L. Curtis, Jr., and Benigno E. Aguirre (eds.), *Collective Behavior and Social Movements*. Boston: Allyn & Bacon, 70–75.

Lofland, John, and Rodney Stark. 1965. "Becoming a World-Saver: A Theory of Conversion to a Deviant Perspective." *American Sociological Review*, 30(6): 862–875.

Lombardo, William K., Gary A. Cretser, Barbara Lombardo, and Sharon L. Mathis. 1983. "For Cryin' Out Loud—There Is a Sex Difference." *Sex Roles*, 9:987–995.

Lorber, Judith. 1994. *Paradoxes of Gender*. New Haven, Conn.: Yale University Press.

———. 2001. *Gender Inequality: Feminist Theories and Politics* (2nd ed.), Los Angeles: Roxbury.

Loseke, Donileen. 1992. *The Battered Woman and Shelters: The Social Construction of Wife Abuse*. Albany: SUNY Press.

Lott, Bernice. 1994. *Women's Lives: Themes and Variations in Gender Learning* (2nd ed.). Pacific Grove, Cal.: Brooks/Cole.

Low, Setha. 2003. *Behind the Gates: Life, Security, and the Pursuit of Happiness in Fortress America*. New York: Routledge.

Lowe, Graham S. 1999. "Labour Markets, Inequality, and the Future of Work." In Curtis, James, Edward Grabb and Neil Guppy (eds.), *Social Inequality in Canada: Patterns, Problems, and Policies*. Scarborough, Ont.: Prentice Hall, 113–128.

Lowe, Maria R. 1998. *Women of Steel: Female Bodybuilders and the Struggle for Self-Definition*. New York: New York University Press.

Lowe, Mick. 2002. "It Takes a Moment to Change the World: Reflections on Quebec City and Beyond." *Straight Goods* (March 18).

Luciw, Roma. 2002. "Dropout Rate Falls to 12% as Students Focus on Future." *The Globe and Mail* (Jan. 24). Available: http://www.globeandmail.com.

Lummis, C. Douglas. 1992. "Equality." In Wolfgang Sachs (ed.), *The Development Dictionary*. Atlantic Highlands, N.J.: Zed Books, 38–52.

Lupton, Deborah. 1997. "Foucault and the Medicalization Critique." In Alan Petersen and Robin Bunton (eds.), *Foucault: Health and Medicine*. London: Routledge, 94–110.

Lupul, M.R. 1988. "Ukrainians: The Fifth Cultural Wheel in Canada." In Ian H. Angus (ed.), *Ethnicity in a Technological Age*. Edmonton: Canadian Institute of Ukrainian Studies, University of Alberta, 177–192.

Luttrell, Wendy. 1997. *School-Smart and Mother-Wise: Working-Class Women's Identity and Schooling*. New York: Routledge.

Luttwak, Eugene. 1996. Quoted in Kenneth Kidd, "Social Contracts." *The Globe and Mail Report on Business Magazine* (September):24.

Luxton, Meg. 1980. *More Than a Labour of Love*. Toronto: Women's Press.

———. 1995. "Two Hands for the Clock: Changing Patterns of Gendered Division of Labour in the Home." In E.D. Nelson and B.W. Robinson (eds.), *Gender in the 1990s*. Scarborough, Ont.: Nelson Canada, 288–301.

———. 1999. *Work, Family, and Community: Key Issues and Directions for Future Research*. Ottawa: Canadian Council on Social Development.

Lynd, Robert S., and Helen M. Lynd. 1929. *Middletown*. New York: Harcourt.

———. 1937. *Middletown in Transition*. New York: Harcourt.

Lynn, Marion (ed.). 1996. *Voices: Essays on Canadian Families*. Scarborough, Ont.: Nelson Canada.

Lynn, Marion, and Eimear O'Neill. 1995. "Families, Power and Violence." In Nancy Mandell and Ann Duffy (eds.), *Canadian Families: Diversity, Conflict and Change*. Toronto: Harcourt Brace and Company, 271–305.

Lyons, John. 1998. "The Way We Live: Central Plains." *Winnipeg Free Press* (June 7):B3.

Maccoby, Eleanor E., and Carol Nagy Jacklin. 1987. "Gender Segregation in Childhood." *Advances in Child Development and Behavior*, 20:239–287.

MacDonald, Kevin, and Ross D. Parke. 1986. "Parental-Child Physical Play: The Effects of Sex and Age of Children and Parents." *Sex Roles,* 15:367–378.

MacDonald, Marci. 1996. "The New Spirituality." *Maclean's* (October 10):44–48.

MacGregor, Roy. 2002. "Questioning the Value of an Education." *National Post* (April 25). Available: http://www.nationalpost.com.

Mack, Raymond W., and Calvin P. Bradford. 1979. *Transforming America: Patterns of Social Change* (2nd ed.). New York: Random House.

Mackie, Marlene. 1995. "Gender in the Family: Changing Patterns." In Nancy Mandell and Ann Duffy (eds.), *Canadian Families: Diversity, Conflict, and Change* (2nd ed.). Toronto: Harcourt Brace, 17–43.

MacKinnon, Catherine. 1982. "Feminism, Marxism, Method and the State: An Agenda for Theory." In N.O. Keohane et al. (eds), *Feminist Theory: A Critique of Ideology.* Chicago: University of Chicago Press, 1–30.

MacLean, M.J. and R. Bonar. 1983. "The Normalization Principle and the Institutionalization of the Elderly." *Canada's Mental Health,* 31:16–18.

Macleod, Linda. 1987. *Battered But NOT Beaten: Preventing Wife Battering in Canada.* Ottawa: Canadian Advisory Council on the Status of Women.

Macmillan, Ross, Annettte Nierobisz, and Sandy Welsh. 2000. "Experiencing the Streets: Harassment and Perceptions of Safety Among Women." *Journal of Research in Crime and Delinquency,* 37(3).

Maggio, Rosalie. 1988. The Non-Sexist Word Finder: A Dictionary of Gender-Free Usage. Boston: Beacon Press.

Malinowski, Bronislaw. 1922. *Argonauts of the Western Pacific.* New York: Dutton.

———. 1964. "The Principle of Legitimacy: Parenthood, the Basis of Social Structure." In Rose Laub Coser (ed.), *The Family: Its Structure and Functions.* New York: St. Martin's Press (orig. pub. 1929).

Man, Guida. 1996. "The Experience of Middle-Class Women in Recent Hong Kong Chinese Immigrant Families in Canada." In Marion Lynn (ed.), *Voices: Essays on Canadian Families.* Toronto: Nelson Canada, 271–300.

Mandell, Nancy (ed.). 2001. *Feminist Issues: Race, Class, and Sexuality* (3rd ed.). Toronto, Ont.: Prentice-Hall.

Mandell, Nancy, and Julianne Momirov. 1999. "Family Histories." In Nancy Mandell and Ann Duffy (eds.), *Canadian Families: Diversity, Conflict, and Change* (2nd ed.). Toronto: Harcourt Brace, 17–43.

Mann, Patricia S. 1994. *Micro-Politics: Agency in Postfeminist Era.* Minneapolis: University of Minnesota Press.

Mansfield, Alan, and Barbara McGinn. 1993. "Pumping Irony: The Muscular and the Feminine." In Sue Scott and

David Morgan (eds.), *Body Matters: Essays on the Sociology of the Body.* London: Falmer Press, 49–58.

Mantell, David Mark. 1971. "The Potential for Violence in Germany." *Journal of Social Issues,* 27(4):101–112.

Manuel, Douglas G., and Yang Mao. 2002. "Avoidable Mortality in the United States and Canada, 1980–1996." *American Journal of Public Health,* 92(9):1481–1484.

Mao, Y., B.W. Moloughney, R. Semenciw, and H. Morrison. 1992. "Indian Reserve and Registered Indian Mortality in Canada." *Canadian Journal of Public Health,* 83:350–353.

Marchak, Patricia. 1975. *Ideological Perspectives on Canadian Society.* Toronto: McGraw-Hill.

Marger, Martin N. 1987. *Elites and Masses: An Introduction to Political Sociology* (2nd ed.). Belmont, Cal.: Wadsworth.

———. 2000. *Race and Ethnic Relations: American and Global Perspectives* (5th ed.). Belmont, Cal.: Wadsworth.

———. 2003. *Race and Ethnic Relations: American and Global Perspectives* (6th ed.). Belmont, Cal.: Wadsworth.

Marion, Russ, and Mary Uhl-Bien. 2003. "Complexity Theory and Al-Qaeda: Examining Complex Leadership." *Emergence,* 5(1):54–76.

Markoff, John. 2000. "Napster Debate About More Than Music." *The Globe and Mail* (May 9): B14.

Marquis, Christopher. 2001. "An American Report Finds the Taliban's Violation of Religious Rights 'Particularly Severe.'" *New York Times* (Oct. 27):B3.

Marshall, Gordon (ed.). 1998. *The Concise Oxford Dictionary of Sociology* (2nd ed.). New York: Oxford University Press.

Marshall, Katherine. 1995. "Dual Earners: Who's Responsible for Housework?" In E.D. Nelson and B.W. Robinson, *Gender in the 1990s.* Scarborough, Ont.: Nelson Canada, 302–308.

Marshall, S.L.A. 1947. *Men Against Fire.* New York: Morrow.

Martel, Laurent, Alain Belanger, Jean-Marie Berthelot, and Yves Carriere. *Healthy Today, Healthy Tomorrow? Findings From the National Population Health Survey.* Ottawa: Statistics Canada.

Martin, Carol L. 1989. "Children's Use of Gender-Related Information in Making Social Judgments." *Developmental Psychology,* 25:80–88.

Martin, Michael T., and Howard Cohen. 1980. "Race and Class Consciousness: A Critique of the Marxist Concept of Race Relations." *Western Journal of Black Studies,* 4(2):84–91.

Martin, Nick. 1996. "Aboriginal Speech Dying." *Winnipeg Free Press* (March 29): A8.

Martineau, Harriet. 1962. *Society in America* (edited, abridged). Garden City, N.Y.: Doubleday (orig. pub. 1837).

———. *How to Observe Morals and Manners.* In Michael R. Hill (ed.). New Brunswick, N.J.: Transaction. (Orig. Pub. 1838).

Martinussen, John. 1997. *Society, State and Market: A Guide to Competing Theories of Development.* Halifax: Fernwood Books.

Marx, Gary, and Douglas McAdam. 1994. *Collective Behavior and Social Movements: Process and Structure.* Englewood Cliffs, N.J.: Pearson Education.

Marx, Karl. 1967. *Capital: A Critique of Political Economy.* Friedrich Engels (ed.). New York: International Publishers (orig. pub. 1867).

Marx, Karl, and Friedrich Engels. 1967. *The Communist Manifesto.* New York: Pantheon (orig. pub. 1848).

———. 1970. *The German Ideology,* Part 1. Ed. C.J. Arthur. New York: International (orig. pub. 1845–1846).

Mason Lee, Robert. 1991. *Death and Deliverance.* Toronto: Macfarlane Walter and Ross.

———. 1998. "I'll Be Home for Christmas." *The Globe and Mail* (December 24).

Matthews, Beverly J. 2001. "The Body Beautiful: Adolescent Girls and Images of Beauty." In Lori G. Beaman (ed.), *New Perspectives on Deviance: The Construction of Deviance in Everyday Life.* Scarborough: Prentice-Hall, 208–219.

Maynard, Rona. 1987. "How Do You Like Your Job?" *The Globe and Mail Report on Business Magazine* (November):120–25.

McAdam, Doug. 1996. "Conceptual Origins, Current Problems, Future Directions." In Doug McAdam, John McCarthy, and Meyer N. Zald (eds.), *Comparative Perspectives on Social Movements.* New York: Cambridge University Press, 23–40.

McArthur, Keith. 2005. "Criticism of Women's Fitness for Top Jobs Causes International Stir." *The Globe and Mail* (October 21):A1.

McCall, George J., and Jerry L. Simmons, 1978. *Identities and Interactions: An Explanation of Human Associations in Everyday Life.* New York: Free Press.

McCarthy, Terry. 2001. "Stirrings of a Woman's Movement." *Time* (Dec. 3):46.

McCarthy, John D., and Mayer N. Zald. 1977. "Resource Mobilization and Social Movements: A Partial Theory." *American Journal of Sociology,* 82:1212–1241.

McCormick, Chris. 1995. *Constructing Danger: The Mis/Representation of Crime in the News.* Halifax: Fernwood Publishing.

McDonald's. 2004. *2004 Summary Annual Report.* Retrieved July 24, 2005. Available: http://www.mcdonalds.com/corp/invest/pub/2004_Summary _Annual_Report.html.

McEachern, William A. 1994. *Economics: A Contemporary Introduction.* Cincinnati: South-Western.

McGeary, Johanna. 2001. "The Taliban Troubles." *Time* (October 1):36–42.

McGee, Reece. 1975. *Points of Departure.* Hinsdale, Ill.: Dryden Press.

McGovern, Celeste. 1995. "Dr. Death Speaks." *Alberta Report/Western Report,* 22 (January 9):33.

McGuire, Meredith B. 1992. *Religion: The Social Context* (2nd ed.). Belmont, Cal.: Wadsworth.

———. 1997. *Religion: The Social Context* (4th ed.). Belmont, Cal.: Wadsworth.

McIntosh, Mary. 1978. "The State and the Oppression of Women." In Annette Kuhn and Ann Marie Wolpe (eds.), *Feminism and Materialism.* London: Routledge and Kegan Paul.

McIsaac, Elizabeth. 2003. "Immigrants in Canadian Cities: Census 2001— What Do the Data Tell Us?" *Policy Options* (May):58–63.

McKenzie, Roderick D. 1925. "The Ecological Approach to the Study of the Human Community." In Robert Park, Ernest Burgess, and Roderick D. McKenzie, *The City.* Chicago: University of Chicago Press.

McKie, Craig. 1994. "Population Aging: Baby Boomers into the 21st Century." *Canadian Social Trends.* Toronto: Thompson Educational Publishing, 3–7.

McLanahan, Sara, and Karen Booth. 1991. "Mother-Only Families." In Alan Booth (ed.), *Contemporary Families: Looking Forward, Looking Backward.* Minneapolis: National Council on Family Relations, 405–428.

McMellon, C.A., and L.G. Schiffman. 2002. "Cybersenior Empowerment: How Some Older Individuals are Taking Control of Their Lives." *Journal of Applied Gerontology,* 21(2):157–75.

McPhail, Clark. 1971. "Civil Disorder Participation: A Critical Examination of Recent Research." *American Sociological Review,* 36:1058–1073.

———. 1991. *The Myth of the Maddening Crowd.* New York: Aldine de Gruyter.

McPhail, Clark, and Ronald T. Wohlstein. 1983. "Individual and Collective Behavior within Gatherings, Demonstrations, and Riots." In Ralph H. Turner and James F. Short, Jr. (eds.), *Annual Review of Sociology,* 9. Palo Alto, Cal.: Annual Reviews, 579–600.

McPherson, Barry D. 1998. *Aging as a Social Process: An Introduction to Individual and Population Aging.* Toronto: Harcourt Brace.

McPherson, J. Miller, and Lynn Smith-Lovin. 1982. "Women and Weak Ties: Differences by Sex in the Size of Voluntary Organizations." *American Journal of Sociology,* 87 (January):883–904.

———. 1986. "Sex Segregation in Voluntary Associations." *American Sociological Review,* 51 (February):61–79.

McQuillan, Kevin, and Marilyn Belle. 1999. "Who Does What? Gender and the Division of Labour in Canadian Households." In Curtis, James E., Edward Grabb, and Neil Guppy (eds.), *Social Inequality in Canada: Patterns, Problems, Policies* (3rd ed.). Scarborough, Ont.: Prentice Hall, 186–198.

McSpotlight. 1999. "McDonald's and Employment." Retrieved September 7, 1999. Available: http://www .mcspotlight.org/issues/rants/ employment.html.

McVey, Wayne W., and Warren E. Kalbach. 1995. *Canadian Population.* Scarborough, Ont.: Nelson Canada.

Mead, George Herbert. 1962. *Mind, Self, and Society.* Chicago: University of Chicago Press (orig. pub. 1934).

Medved, Michael. 1992. *Hollywood vs. America: Popular Culture and the War on Traditional Values.* New York: HarperPerennial.

Mehrotra, Santosh, and Richard Jolly. 2000. *Development with a Human Face: Experiences in Social Achievement and Economic Growth.* Oxford: Clarendon Press.

Melchers, Ronald. 2003. "Do Toronto Police Engage in Racial Profiling?" *Canadian Journal of Criminology and Criminal Justice,* 45(July):347–366.

Merchant, Carolyn. 1983. *The Death of Nature: Women, Ecology, and the Scientific Revolution.* San Francisco: Harper & Row.

———. 1992. *Radical Ecology: The Search for a Livable World.* New York: Routledge.

Merkle, Erich R., and Rhonda A. Richardson. 2000. "Digital Dating and Virtual Relating: Conceptualizing Computer-Mediated Romantic Relationships." *Family Relations,* 49(2) (April):187–211.

Merton, Robert King. 1938. "Social Structure and Anomie." *American Sociological Review,* 3(6):672–682.

———. 1949. "Discrimination and the American Creed." In Robert M. MacIver (ed.), *Discrimination and National Welfare.* New York: Harper & Row, 99–126.

———. 1968. *Social Theory and Social Structure* (enlarged ed.). New York: Free Press.

Messner, Michael A. 2000. "Barbie Girls versus Sea Monsters: Children Constructing Gender." In Margaret L. Andersen (ed.), *Thinking About Women: Sociological Perspectives on Sex and Gender* (7th ed.). Boston: Pearson, 765–784.

———. 2002. *Taking the Field: Women, Men and Sports.* Minneapolis: University of Minnesota Press.

Meyer, David S., and Suzanne Staggenborg. 1996. "Movements, Countermovements, and the Structure of Political Opportunity." *American Journal of Sociology,* 101:1628–1660.

Miall, Charlene. 1986. "The Stigma of Involuntary Childlessness." *Social Problems,* 33(4):268–282.

Michael, Robert T., John H. Gagnon, Edward O. Laumann, and Gina Kolata. 1994. *Sex in America.* Boston: Little, Brown.

Michels, Robert. 1949. *Political Parties.* Glencoe, Ill.: Free Press (orig. pub. 1911).

———. 1994. "Cities and Urbanization." In Lorne Tepperman, James Curtis, and R.J. Richardson (eds.), *The Social World* (3rd ed.). Toronto: McGraw-Hill, 672–709.

Mies, Maria, and Vandana Shiva. 1993. *Ecofeminism.* Highlands, N.J.: Zed Books.

Mihorean, Steve, and Stan Lipinski. 1992. "International Incarceration Patterns, 1980–1990." *Juristat,* 12(3). Ottawa: Statistics Canada.

Milgram, Stanley. 1963. "Behavioral Study of Obedience." *Journal of Abnormal and Social Psychology,* 67:371–378.

———. 1967. "The Small World Problem." *Psychology Today,* 2:60–67.

———. 1974. *Obedience to Authority.* New York: Harper & Row.

Miliband, Ralph. 1969. The State in Capitalist Society. New York: Basic Books.

Miller, Casey, and Kate Swift. 1991. *Words and Women: New Language in New Times* (updated). New York: HarperCollins.

———. 1993. "Who Is Man?" In Anne Minas, *Gender Basics: Feminist Perspectives on Women and Men.* Belmont, Cal.: Wadsworth, 68–75.

Miller, Dan E. 1986. "Milgram Redux: Obedience and Disobedience in Authority Relations." In Norman K. Denzin (ed.), *Studies in Symbolic Interaction.* Greenwich, Conn.: JAI Press, 77–106.

Miller, James. 2003. "Out Family Values." In Marion Lynn (ed.). *Voices: Essays on Canadian Families* (2nd ed.). Scarborough, Ont.: Nelson Canada, 103–130.

Miller, L. Scott. 1995. *An American Imperative: Accelerating Minority Educational Advancement.* New Haven, Conn: Yale University Press.

Mills, C. Wright. 1956. *White Collar.* New York: Oxford University Press.

———. 1959a. *The Sociological Imagination.* London: Oxford University Press.

———. 1959b. *The Power Elite.* Fair Lawn, N.J.: Oxford University Press.

Minister of Indian Affairs and Northern Development. 2000. "Comparison of Social Conditions, 1991 and 1996: Registered Indians, Registered Indians Living on Reserve and the Total Population in Canada." Ottawa: Minister of Indian Affairs and Northern Development.

Misztal, Barbara A. 1993. "Understanding Political Change in Eastern Europe: A Sociological Perspective." *Sociology,* 27(3):451–471.

Mitchell, Alanna. 1997. "Native Life in Canada: Seed Money for Grassroots Entrepreneurs." *The Globe and Mail* (July 22).

———. 1999. "Home Schooling Goes AWOL." *The Globe and Mail* (February 2):A1, A7.

Molotch, Harvey, and Marilyn Lester. 1974. "News as Purposive Behavior: On the Strategic Use of Routine Events, Accidents and Scandals." *American Sociological Review,* 39:101–112.

Money, John, and Anke A. Ehrhardt. 1972. *Man and Woman, Boy and Girl.* Baltimore: Johns Hopkins University Press.

Moody, Harry R. 1998. *Aging: Concepts and Controversy* (2nd ed.). Thousand Oaks, Cal.: Pine Forge Press.

Moore, Patricia, with C.P. Conn. 1985. *Disguised.* Waco, Tex.: Word Books.

Moore, Wilbert E. 1968. "Occupational Socialization." In David A. Goslin (ed.), *Handbook on Socialization Theory and Research.* Chicago: Rand McNally, 861–883.

Morisette, Rene, Grant Schellenberg, and Anick Johnson. 2005. "Diverging Trends in Unionization." *Perspectives on Labour and Income* 6(April):5–12. Catalogue Number 75-001-XIE. Ottawa: Statistics Canada.

Morselli, Henry. 1975. *Suicide: An Essay on Comparative Moral Statistics.* New York: Arno Press (orig. pub. 1881).

Moscovitch, Arlene. 1998. "Electronic Media and the Family." *Contemporary Family Trends.* Ottawa: Vanier Institute of the Family. Retrieved November 20, 2002. Available: http://www.vifamily .ca/cft/media/media.htm.

Mucciolo, Louis. 1992. *Eighty something: Interviews with Octogenarians Who Stay Involved.* New York: Birch Lane Press.

Mukerji, Chandra, and Michael Schudson. 1991. *Rethinking Popular Culture: Contemporary Perspectives in Cultural Studies.* Berkeley: University of California Press.

Murdie, Robert. 1999. "The Housing Careers of Polish and Somali Newcomers in Toronto's Rental Market." Paper presented at the 4th International Metropolis Conference (October), Washington, D.C. Retrieved November 27, 2002. Available: http:// www.library.utoronto.ca/hnc/publish/ careers.pdf.

Murdock, George P. 1945. "The Common Denominator of Cultures." In Ralph Linton (ed.), *The Science of Man in the World Crisis.* New York: Columbia University Press, 123–142.

Murphy, Christopher, and Curtis Clarke. 2005. "Policing Communities and Communities of Policing: A Comparative Study of Policing and Security in Two Canadian Communities." In Dennis Cooley (ed.), *Re-Imagining Policing in Canada.* Toronto: University of Toronto Press, 209–259.

Murphy, Emily F. 1922. *The Black Candle.* Toronto: Thomas Allan.

Murphy, Robert E., Jessica Scheer, Yolanda Murphy, and Richard Mack. 1988. "Physical Disability and Social Liminality: A Study in Rituals of Adversity." *Social Science and Medicine,* 26:235–242.

My dans, Seth. 1997. "Its Mood Dark as the Haze, Southeast Asia Aches." *New York Times* (October 26):3.

Myles, John. 1999. "Demography or Democracy? The 'Crisis' of Old-Age Security." In Curtis, James E., Edward Grabb, and Neil Guppy (eds.), *Social Inequality in Canada: Patterns, Problems, Policies* (3rd ed.). Scarborough, Ont.: Prentice Hall.

Myrdal, Gunnar. 1970. *The Challenge of World Poverty: A World Anti-Poverty Program in Outline.* New York: Pantheon/Random House.

NACA. 1992. *The NACA Position on Canada's Oldest Seniors: Maintaining the Quality of Their Lives.* Ottawa: National Advisory Council on Aging, 54–55.

Nader, George A. 1976. *Cities of Canada,* vol. 2. *Profiles of Fifteen Metropolitan Centres.* Toronto: Macmillan of Canada.

Naeyaert, Kathleen. 1990. *Living with Sensory Loss: Vision.* Ottawa: National Advisory Council on Aging.

Nagler, Mark. 1997. *Yes You Can: A Guide for Parents of Children with Disabilities.* Toronto: Stoddart.

Naim, Moises. 2003. "The Five Wars of Globalization." *Foreign Policy,* 134:28–37.

Naiman, Joanne. 2000. *How Societies Work: Class, Power, and Change in a Canadian Context.* Concord, Ont.: Irwin.

Nairne, Doug. 1998. "Good Samaritan Feels That He Was Victimized Twice." *Winnipeg Free Press* (June 4):A4.

Nakhaie, M. Reza, and Robert Arnold. 1996. "Class Position, Class Ideology, and Class Voting: Mobilization of Support for the New Democratic Party in the Canadian Election of 1984." *Canadian Review of Sociology and Anthropology,* 33(2):181–212.

Nancarrow Clarke, Juanne. 1996. *Health, Illness and Medicine in Canada* (2nd ed.). Toronto: Oxford University Press.

NAPO (National Anti-Poverty Association). 2002. "Governments targeting poor people instead of poverty." October 17 2002. Retrieved December 14, 2002. Available: http://www .napo-onap.ca/media_room.htm.

———. 2005. "Towards a National Poverty Elimination Strategy." Retrieved September 12, 2005. Available: http://www.napo-nap.ca/en/issues/NAPO%202005% 20finance%20committee%20 submission.pdf.

Nason-Clark, Nancy. 1993. "Gender Relations in Contemporary Christian Organizations." In W.E. Hewitt (ed.), *The Sociology of Religion: A Canadian Focus.* Toronto: Butterworths, 215–234.

National Council of Welfare. 2002. *Poverty Profile 1999.* Ottawa: National Council of Welfare.

National Media Archive. 1997. "TV Coverage Down: Murder Rate Up Slightly." *On Balance,* 10(7). Vancouver: The Fraser Institute.

National Opinion Research Center. 1989. *General Social Survey.* Chicago: National Opinion Research Center.

National Opinion Research Center. 1996. *General Social Surveys, 1972–1996: Cumulative Codebook.* Chicago: National Opinion Research Center.

National Post. 2003. "Quality of Life and Quality of Service." Toronto: National Post (A8).

Navarrette, Ruben, Jr. 1997. "A Darker Shade of Crimson." In Diana Kendall (ed.), *Race, Class, and Gender in a Diverse Society.* Boston, Mass.: Allyn and Bacon, 274–279. Reprinted from Ruben Navarrette, Jr., *A Darker Shade of Crimson.* New York: Bantam, 1993.

Neal, Lainie, ed. 2004. *Voices of Survivors.* Winnipeg: North End Women's Centre.

Nelson, Adie. 2006. *Gender in Canada* (3rd ed.). Toronto: Pearson Prentice Hall.

Nelson, Margaret K., and Joan Smith. 1999. *Working Hard and Making Do: Surviving in Small Town America.* Berkeley: University of California Press.

Nemeth, Mary, Nora Underwood, and John Howse. 1993. "God Is Alive." *Maclean's* (April 12):32–36.

Nett, Emily M. 1993. *Canadian Families: Past and Present* (2nd ed.). Toronto: Butterworths.

Nettler, Gwynn. 1984. *Explaining Crime* (3rd ed.). Toronto: McGraw-Hill.

Nevitte, Neil. 2000. "Value Change and Reorientations in Citizen-State Relations." *Canadian Public Policy,* 26 (Supplement):73–94.

Newman, Katherine S. 1988. *Falling from Grace: The Experience of Downward Mobility in the American Middle Class.* New York: Free Press.

———. 1993. *Declining Fortunes: The Withering of the American Dream.* New York: Basic Books.

———. 1999. *No Shame in My Game: The Working Poor in the Inner City.* New York: Knopf and the Russell Sage Foundation.

New York Times. 2002b. "Text: Senate Judiciary Committee Hearing, June 6, 2002." Retrieved June 9, 2002. Availalbe: http://www.nytimes.com/2002/06/06../06TEXT-INQ2.html.

———. 2005. "The Missing Condoms." NYTimes.com. Retrieved September 4, 2005. Available: http://www.nytimes.com/2005/09/04/opinion/04sun2.html.

Ng, Edward. 1994. "Children and Elderly People: Sharing Public Income Resources." In Craig McKie (ed.), *Canadian Social Trends.* Toronto: Thompson Educational Publishing Company, 249–252.

Niebuhr, H. Richard. 1929. *The Social Sources of Denominationalism.* New York: Meridian.

Nielsen, Joyce McCarl. 1990. *Sex and Gender in Society: Perspectives on Stratification* (2nd ed.). Prospects Heights, Ill.: Waveland Press.

Nielsen, T.M. 2005. "Streets, Strangers, and Solidarity." In Bruce Ravelli (ed.), *Exploring Canadian Sociology: A Reader.* Toronto: Pearson, 89–98.

Nisbet, Robert. 1979. "Conservatism." In Tom Bottomore and Robert Nisbet (eds.), *A History of Sociological Analysis.* London: Heineman, 81–117.

Norland, J.A. 1994. *Profile of Canada's Seniors,* Cat. no. 96–312E. Scarborough, Ont.: Statistics Canada and Prentice-Hall.

Norris, Mary Jane. 1998. "Canada's Aboriginal Languages." *Canadian Social Trends* (Winter):8–16.

Norris, Pippa, and Ronald Inglehart. 2004. *Sacred and Secular: Religion and Politics Worldwide.* Cambridge: Cambridge University Press.

Northcott, Herbert, C. 1982. "The Best Years of Your Life." *Canadian Journal on Aging,* 1:72–78.

Novak, Mark. 1993. *Aging and Society: A Canadian Perspective.* Scarborough, Ont.: Nelson Canada.

———. 1995. "Successful Aging." In *Aging and Society: A Canadian Reader.* Scarborough, Ont.: Nelson Canada.

———. 1997. *Aging and Society* (3rd ed.). Toronto: ITP Nelson.

Novak, Mark, and Lori Campbell. 2001. *Aging and Society: A Canadian Perspective* (4th ed.). Scarborough: Nelson Thomson Learning.

———. 2006. *Aging and Society: A Canadian Perspective* (5th ed.). Toronto: Thomson Nelson.

NOW (National Organization for Women). 2002. "Stop the Abuse of Women and Girls in Afghanistan!" Retrieved July 14, 2002. Available: http://www.nowfoundation.org/_global/taliban.html.

Nussbaum, Emily. 2003. "Nature vs. Nurture." Retrieved October 6, 2003. Available: http://btosearch.barnesandnoble.com/booksearch.

Oakes, Jeannie. 1985. *Keeping Track: How High Schools Structure Inequality.* New Haven, Conn.: Yale University Press.

Oberschall, Anthony. 1973. *Social Conflict and Social Movements.* Englewood Cliffs, N.J.: Prentice-Hall.

Obomsawin, Alanis. 1993. *Kanehsatake: 270 Years of Resistance* [motion picture]. Montreal: National Film Board of Canada.

O'Brien, Carol-Anne, and Lorna Weir. 1995. "Lesbians and Gay Men Inside and Outside Families." In Nancy Mandell and Ann Duffy (eds.), *Canadian Families.* Toronto: Harcourt Brace and Company, 111–139.

O'Connell, Helen. 1994. *Women and the Family.* Prepared for the UN-NGO Group on Women and Development. Atlantic Highlands, N.J.: Zed Books.

O'Connor, James. 1973. *The Fiscal Crisis of the State.* New York: St. Martin's Press.

Odendahl, Teresa. 1990. *Charity Begins at Home: Generosity and Self-Interest Among the Philanthropic Elite.* New York: Basic.

OECD. 2005. *OECD Health Data 2005.* Paris: OECD. Retrieved July 21, 2005. Available: http://www.oecd.org/document/30/0,2340,en_2649_34631_12968734_1_1_1,00.html.

Ogburn, William F. 1966. *Social Change with Respect to Culture and Original Nature.* New York: Dell (orig. pub. 1922).

Ogden, Russell D. 1994. *Euthanasia and Assisted Suicide in Persons with Acquired Immunodeficiency Syndrome (AIDS) or Human Immunodeficiency Virus (HIV).* Pitt Meadows, B.C.: Perreault Goedman.

Ogmundson, Rick. 1975. "Party Class Images and the Class Vote in Canada." *American Sociological Review,* 40:506–512.

Ogmundson, Rick, and M. Ng. 1982. "On the Inference of Voter Motivation: A Comparison of the Subjective Class Vote in Canada and the United Kingdom." *Canadian Journal of Sociology,* 7:41–59.

Oliver, Michael. 1990. *The Politics of Disablement: A Sociological Approach.* New York: St. Martin's Press.

Ontario Human Rights Commission. 2005. "Policy on Height and Weight Requirements" Retrieved September 17, 2005. Available: http://www.ohrc.on.ca/en_text/publications/height-weight-policy.shtml.

Opinion Canada. 2004. "Fewer Canadians Believe Religious Practice is Important." *Facts and Figures,* 6(27):September 16.

Orbach, Susie. 1978. *Fat Is a Feminist Issue.* New York: Paddington.

O'Reilly-Fleming, Thomas. 1993. *Down and Out in Canada: Homeless Canadians.* Toronto: Canadian Scholars' Press.

Orenstein, Peggy, in association with the American Association of University Women. 1995. *School Girls: Young Women, Self-Esteem, and the Confidence Gap.* New York: Anchor/Doubleday.

Organisation for Economic Co-operation and Development. 2004.

Organisation for Economic Co-operation and Development, and Statistics Canada. 2000. *Literacy in the Information Age: Final Report of the International Adult Literacy Survey.* Ottawa.

Ortner, Sherry B. 1974. "Is Female to Male as Nature Is to Culture?" In Michelle Rosaldo and Louise Lamphere (eds.), *Women, Culture, and Society.* Stanford, Cal.: Stanford University Press.

Ortner, Sherry B., and Harriet Whitehead (eds.). 1981. *Sexual Meanings: The Cultural Construction of Gender and Sexuality.* Cambridge, Mass.: Cambridge University Press.

Orum, Anthony M. 1974. "On Participation in Political Protest Movements." *Journal of Applied Behavioral Science,* 10:181–207.

Orum, Anthony M., and Amy W. Orum. 1968. "The Class and Status Bases of Negro Student Protest." *Social Science Quarterly,* 49 (December):521–533.

Osborne. 1994. Royal Commission on Learning. *For the Love of Learning: Report of the Royal Commission on Learning.* Vol. 4. Toronto: Queen's Printer, 4–5.

Osborne, Ken. 1999. *Education: A Guide to the Canadian School Debate— Or, Who Wants What and Why.* Toronto: Penguin Books.

Ostrower, Francie. 1997. *Why the Wealthy Give: The Culture of Elite Philanthropy.* Princeton, N.J.: Princeton University Press.

O'Sullivan, Chris. 1993. "Fraternities and the Rape Culture." In Emile Buchwald et al. (eds.), *Transforming a Rape Culture.* Minn.: Milkweed Ltd.

Overall, Christine. 1991. "Reproductive Technology and the Future of the Family." In Jean E. Veevers (ed.), *Continuity and Change in Marriage and the Family.* Toronto: Holt, Rinehart and Winston, 466–477.

Owen, Bruce. 1996. "Harassment Ends in Firings." *Winnipeg Free Press* (March 23).

Oxfam. 2001. *Rigged Trade and Not Much Aid: How Rich Countries Help to Keep the Least Developed Countries Poor.* London: Oxfam.

Page, Charles H. 1946. "Bureaucracy's Other Face." *Social Forces,* 25 (October):89–94.

Palmore, Erdman. 1981. *Social Patterns in Normal Aging: Findings from the Duke Longitudinal Study.* Durham, N.C.: Duke University Press.

Palys, Ted. 1997. *Research Decisions: Quantitative and Qualitative Perspectives.* Toronto: Harcourt Brace.

Palys, Ted, and John Lowman. 1998. "Abandoning 'the Highest Ethical Standards': Research Ethics at SFU." *The Bulletin,* 11(1).

Pammett, Jon H. 1993. "Tracking the Votes." In Alan Frizell et al. (eds.), *The Canadian General Election of 1993.* Ottawa: Carleton University Press.

Panitch, Leo, and Donald Swartz. 1993. *Assault on Trade Union Freedoms* (2nd ed.). Toronto: Garamond.

Panzarino, Connie. 1994. *The Me in the Mirror.* Seattle, Wash.: Seal Press.

Parenti, Michael. 1994. *Land of Idols: Political Mythology in America.* New York: St. Martin's Press.

———. 1996. *Democracy for the Few* (5th ed.). New York: St. Martin's.

Park, Robert E. 1915. "The City: Suggestions for the Investigation of Human Behavior in the City." *American Journal of Sociology,* 20:577–612.

———. 1928. "Human Migration and the Marginal Man." *American Journal of Sociology,* 33.

———. 1936. "Human Ecology." *American Journal of Sociology,* 42:1–15.

Park, Robert E., and Ernest W. Burgess. 1921. *Human Ecology.* Chicago: University of Chicago Press.

Parker, Robert Nash. 1995. "Violent Crime." In Joseph F. Sheley, *Criminology: A Contemporary Handbook* (2nd. ed.). Belmont, Cal.: Wadsworth, 169–185.

Parrish, Dee Anna. 1990. *Abused: A Guide to Recovery for Adult Survivors of Emotional/Physical Child Abuse.* Barrytown, N.Y.: Station Hill Press.

Parsons, Lee. 2003. "Food Bank Use Continues to Rise." Retrieved August 12, 2003. Available: http://www.wsws.org/articles/2003/oct2003/food-o22.shtml.

Parsons, Talcott. 1951. *The Social System.* Glencoe, Ill.: Free Press.

———. 1955. "The American Family: Its Relations to Personality and to the Social Structure." In Talcott Parsons and Robert F. Bales (eds.), *Family, Socialization and Interaction Process.* Glencoe, Ill.: Free Press, 3–33.

———. 1960. "Toward a Healthy Maturity." *Journal of Health and Social Behavior,* 1:163–173.

Parsons, Talcott, and Edward A. Shils, eds. 1951. *Toward a General Theory of Action.* Cambridge, Mass.: Harvard University Press.

Patterson, Christopher, and Elizabeth Podnieks. 1995. "A Guide to the Diagnosis and Treatment of Elder Abuse." In Mark Novak (ed.), *Aging and Society: A Canadian Reader.* Scarborough, Ont.: Nelson Canada.

Patterson, Naomi. 1998. "Old Dogs Must Learn New Tricks in the Modern Era." *SeniorNet* (Winter/Spring). Available: http://www. Seniornet.org/ newsline/olddogs.shtml.

PBS. 1992. "Sex, Power and the Workplace."

———. 2001. "Crossing Borders: How Terrorists Use Fake Passports, Visas, and Other Identity Documents." Retrieved July 12, 2005. Available: http://www.pbs.org/wgbh/pages/ frontline/shows/trail/etc/fake.html.

Pearce, Diana. 1978. "The Feminization of Poverty: Women, Work, and Welfare." *Urban and Social Change Review,* 11 (1/2):28–36.

Pearson, Judy C. 1985. *Gender and Communication.* Dubuque, Iowa: Brown.

Peikoff, Tannis. 2000. *Anglican Missionaries and Governing the Self: An Encounter with Aboriginal Peoples in Western Canada.* Unpublished Ph.D. dissertation, University of Manitoba.

Perrow, Charles. 1984. *Normal Accidents.* New York: Basic Books.

———. 1986. *Complex Organizations: A Critical Essay* (3rd ed.). New York: Random House.

Perrucci, Robert, and Earl Wysong. 1999. *The New Class Society.* Lanham, M.D.: Rowman & Littlefield.

Perry, David C., and Alfred J. Watkins, eds. 1977. *The Rise of the Sunbelt Cities.* Beverly Hills, Cal.: Sage.

Peter, Karl A. 1987. *The Dynamics of Hutterite Society.* Edmonton: University of Alberta Press.

Peters, John F. 1985. "Adolescents as Socialization Agents to Parents." *Adolescence,* 20 (Winter):921–933.

Peters, Linda, and Patricia Fallon. 1994. "The Journey of Recovery: Dimensions of Change." In Patricia Fallon, Melanie A. Katzman, and Susan C. Wooley (eds.), *Feminist Perspectives on Eating Disorders.* New York: Guilford Press, 339–354.

Petersen, John L. 1994. *The Road to 2015: Profiles of the Future.* Corte Madera, Cal.: Waite Group Press.

Peterson's Educational Center. 1996. "Report on Private Secondary Education 1996–97." Retrieved

November 23, 1997. Available: http://www.peterson.com/research/ reports/privateschools.html.

Pheonix, A. and A.Woollett. 1991. "Motherhood, Social Construction, Politics, and Psychology." In A. Pheonix, A Woollett, and E. Lloyd (eds.), *Motherhood: Meanings, Practices and Ideologies.* London: Sage.

Philbeck, Joyce. 1997. "Seniors and the Internet." *Cybersociology,* 2. Available: http://www.socio.demon.co.uk/ magazine/magazine.html.

Philp, Margaret. 1997. "Poverty Crusade Gets Personality." *The Globe and Mail* (September 20):A1.

Piaget, Jean. 1932. *The Moral Judgment of the Child.* London: Routledge and Kegan Paul.

———. 1954. *The Construction of Reality in the Child.* Trans. Margaret Cook. New York: Basic Books.

Picot, Garnett, and John Myles. 2004. "Income Inequality and Low Income in Canada." *Horizons* (December) 7(2):9–18.

Pierce, Jennifer. 1995. *Gender Trials: Emotional Lives in Contemporary Law Firms.* Berkeley: University of California Press.

Pietilä, Hilkka, and Jeanne Vickers. 1994. *Making Women Matter: The Role of the United Nations.* Atlantic Highlands, N.J.: Zed Books.

Pinderhughes, Dianne M. 1986. "Political Choices: A Realignment in Partisanship Among Black Voters?" In James D. Williams (ed.), *The State of Black America 1986.* New York: National Urban League, 85–113.

Pinderhughes, Howard. 1997. *Race in the Hood: Conflict and Violence Among Urban Youth.* Minneapolis: University of Minnesota Press.

Pines, Maya. 1981. "The Civilizing of Genie." *Psychology Today,* 15 (September):28–29, 31–32, 34.

Pohl, Rudy. 2002. "Poverty in Canada." Ottawa: Ottawa Innercity Ministries. Retrieved June 25, 2002. Available: http://www.ottawainnercityministries .ca/homepage/homelessness2InCanada_ Part2.htm.

Polakow, Valerie. 1993. *Lives on the Edge: Single Mothers and Their Children in the Other America.* Chicago: University of Chicago Press.

Polanyi, Karl. 1944. *The Great Transformation: The Political and Economic Origins of Our Time.* New York: Beacon.

Polivka, Larry. 2000. "Postmodern Aging and the Loss of Meaning." *Journal of Aging and Identity,* 5:225–235.

Pomice, Eva. 1990. "Madison Avenue's Blind Spot." In Karin Swisher (ed.), *The Elderly: Opposing Viewpoints.* San Diego: Greenhaven Press, 42–45.

Ponting, J.R. 1997. *First Nations in Canada: Perspectives on Opportunity, Empowerment and Self-Determination.* Toronto: McGraw-Hill Ryerson.

Popenoe, David. 1993. "American Family Decline, 1960–1990: A Review and Appraisal." *Journal of Marriage and the Family,* 55(3):527–543.

Popoff, Wilfred. 1996. "One Day You're Family; the Next Day You're Fired." *The Globe and Mail* (March 14):A22.

Porter, John. 1965. *The Vertical Mosaic: An Analysis of Social Class and Power in Canada.* Toronto: University of Toronto Press.

Posterski, Donald C., and Irwin Barker. 1993. *Where's a Good Church?* Winfield, B.C.: Wood Lake Books.

Postone, Moishe. 1997. "Rethinking Marx (in a Post-Marxist World)." In Charles Camic (ed.), *Reclaiming the Sociological Classics: The State of the Scholarship.* Malden, Mass.: Blackwell, 45–80.

Pratt, Courtney. 1997. "Business Accountability: Shareholders, Stake-holders or Society?" Address to the Canadian Club of Toronto (September 29).

President's Commission. 1986. *Report of the President's Commission on the Space Shuttle Challenger Accident.* Washington: U.S. Government Printing Office.

Prus, Robert. 1996. *Symbolic Interaction and Ethnographic Research: Intersubjectivity and the Study of Human Lived Experience.* Albany: State University of New York Press.

Pryor, John B., and Kathleen McKinney. 1995. "Research Advances in Sexual Harassment: Introduction and Overview." *Basic and Applied Social Psychology,* 17:421–424.

Public Health Agency of Canada. 2004. *Epi Update 2004.* Ottawa: Public Health Agency of Canada. Retrieved July 20, 2005. Available: http://www .phac-aspc.gc.ca/publicat/epiu-aepi/ epi_update_may_04/10_e.html.

Public Safety and Emergency Preparedness Canada. 2004. Corrections and Conditional Release Statistical Overview. Ottawa: Author.

Pue, W. Wesley, ed. 2000. *Pepper in Our Eyes: The APEC Affair.* Vancouver: UBC Press, 77–84.

Quadagno, Jill S. 1984. "Welfare Capitalism and the Social Security Act of 1935." *American Sociological Review,* 49:632–647.

Queen, Stuart A., and David B. Carpenter. 1953. *The American City.* New York: McGraw-Hill.

Quigley, Tim. 1994. "Some Issues in the Sentencing of Aboriginal Offenders." Cited in Royal Commission on Aboriginal Peoples Report, 1996, *Bridging the Cultural Divide.* Ottawa: Minister of Supply and Services Canada.

Quinney, Richard. 1979. *Class, State, and Crime.* New York: McKay.

———. 1980. *Class, State, and Crime* (2nd ed.). New York: Longman.

Quinton, Rhonda. 1989. "Liability of Search and Rescuers." Unpublished paper, Faculty of Law, University of Victoria.

Qvortrup, Jens. 1990. *Childhood as a Social Phenomemon.* Vienna: European Centre for Social Welfare Policy and Research.

Rabinowitz, Fredric E., and Sam V. Cochran. 1994. *Man Alive: A Primer of Men's Issues.* Pacific Grove, Cal.: Brooks/Cole.

Radcliffe-Brown, A.R. 1952. *Structure and Function in Primitive Society.* New York: Free Press.

Raphael, Dennis. 2001. *Inequality Is Bad for Our Hearts: Why Low Income and Social Exclusion Are Major Causes of Heart Disease in Canada.* Toronto: North York Heart Health Network.

Razack, Sherene H. 1998. *Looking White People in the Eye.* Toronto: University of Toronto Press.

Reckless, Walter C. 1967. *The Crime Problem.* New York: Meredith.

Reed, Christopher. 1998. "No Fingerprints Puts Man Under Society's Thumb." *The Globe and Mail* (April 23):A11.

Rees, T. 1991. "Racial Discrimina-tion and Employment Agencies." *Currents: Readings in Race Relations,* 7(2):16–19.

Regional Municipality of Wood Buffalo. 2005. *2005 Municipal Census.* Fort McMurray: Author.

Reich, Robert. 1993. "Why the Rich Are Getting Richer and the Poor Poorer." In Paul J. Baker, Louis E. Anderson, and Dean S. Dorn (eds.), *Social Problems: A Critical Thinking Approach* (2nd ed.). Belmont, Cal.: Wadsworth, 145–149. Adapted from *The New Republic,* May 1, 1989.

Reiman, Jeffrey H. 1979. *The Rich Get Richer and the Poor Get Prison.* New York: Wiley.

———. 1984. *The Rich Get Richer and the Poor Get Prison* (2nd ed.). New York: Wiley.

Reinharz, Shulamit. 1992. *Feminist Methods in Social Research.* New York: Oxford University Press.

Reinisch, June. 1990. *The Kinsey Institute New Report on Sex: What You Must Know to Be Sexually Literate.* New York: St. Martin's Press.

Reitz, J. 2001. "Immigrant Skill Utilization in the Canadian Labour Market: Implications for Human Capital Research." *Journal of International Migration and Integration,* 2(3).

Reitz, Jeffery G. and Raymond Breton. 1994. *The Illusion of Difference: Realities of Ethnicity in Canada and the United States.* Toronto: C.D. Howe Institute.

Renzetti, Claire M., and Daniel J. Curran. 1992. *Women, Men, and Society.* Boston: Allyn and Bacon.

———. 1995. *Women, Men, and Society* (3rd ed.). Boston: Allyn and Bacon.

———. 1998. *Living Sociology.* Boston: Allyn and Bacon.

Reskin, Barbara F., and Irene Padavic. 1994. *Women and Men at Work.* Thousand Oaks, Cal.: Pine Forge Press.

Reskin, Barbara F., and Irene Padavic. 2002. *Women and Men at Work* (2nd ed.). Thousand Oaks, Cal.: Pine Forge Press.

Ressler, A. 1998. "'A Body to Die For': Eating Disorders and Body-Image Distortion in Women." *International Journal of Fertility and Women's Medicine,* 43:133–138.

Richard, Justice K. Peter. 1997. *The Westray Story: A Predictable Path to Disaster,* Executive Summary. Halifax: Government of Nova Scotia.

Richardson, John G., and Carl H. Simpson. 1982. "Children, Gender and Social Structure: An Analysis of the Content of Letters to Santa Claus." *Child Development*, 53:429–436.

Richardson, Laurel. 1993. "Inequalities of Power, Property, and Prestige." In Virginia Cyrus (ed.), *Experiencing Race, Class, and Gender in the United States*. Mountain View, Cal.: Mayfield, 229–236.

Richardson, R. Jack. 1992. "Free Trade: Why Did It Happen?" *Canadian Review of Sociology and Anthropology*, 29:307–328.

Richer, Stephen. 1988. "Equality to Benefit from Schooling: The Issue of Educational Opportunity." In D. Forcese and S. Richer (eds.), *Social Issues: Sociological Views of Canada*. Toronto: Prentice Hall, 262–86.

Richler, Mordecai. 1992. *Oh Canada! Oh Quebec!* Toronto and New York: Knopff.

Rifkin, Jeremy. 1995. *The End of Work*. New York: G.P. Putnam's Sons.

Rigler, David. 1993. "Letters: A Psychologist Portrayed in a Book About an Abused Child Speaks Out for the First Time in 22 Years." *New York Times Book Review* (June 13):35.

Riley, Matilda White, and John W. Riley, Jr. 1994. "Age Integration and the Lives of Older People." *The Gerontologist*, 34(1):110–115.

Rinehart, James W. 1996. *The Tyranny of Work: Alienation and the Labour Process* (3rd ed.). Toronto: Harcourt Brace.

Risman, Barbara J. 1987. "Intimate Relationships from a Microstructural Perspective: Men Who Mother." *Gender & Society*, 1:6–32.

Ritzer, George. 1993. *The McDonaldization of Society: An Investigation into the Changing Character of Contemporary Social Life*. Thousand Oaks, Cal.: Pine Forge Press.

———. 1996. *Sociological Theory* (4th ed.). New York: McGraw-Hill.

———. 1997. *Postmodern Society Theory*. New York: McGraw-Hill.

———. 1998. *The McDonaldization Thesis*. London: Sage.

———. 2000. *The McDonaldization of Society*. Thousand Oaks, Calif.: Pine Forge.

Roberts, Keith A. 1995b. *Religion in Sociological Perspective*. Belmont, Cal.: Wadsworth.

Roberts, Lance W., and Rodney A. Clifton. 1999. "Multiculturalism in Canada: A Sociological Perspective." In Peter S. Li (ed.), *Race and Ethnic Relations in Canada* (2nd ed.). Toronto: Oxford University Press.

Robertshaw, Corinne. 2003. "Strike Down S.43." *Law Times*. June 16, 2003. Retrieved June 16, 2005. Available: http://repeal43.org/constitution.html#scchearing.

Robertson, Ian. 1977. *Sociology*. New York: Worth Publishers.

Robinson, David, Frank J. Porporino, William A. Millson, Shelley Trevethan, and Barry McKillop. 1998. "A One-Day Snapshot of Inmates in Canada's Adult Correctional Facilities." *Juristat*, 18(8). Ottawa: Statistics Canada.

Rodgers, Kain, and Rebecca Kong. 1996. "Crimes Against Women and Children in the Family." In Leslie Kennedy and Vincent Sacco (eds.), *Crime Counts: A Criminal Event Analysis*. Scarborough, Ont.: Nelson Canada, 115–132.

Roethlisberger, Fritz J., and William J. Dickson. 1939. *Management and the Worker*. Cambridge, Mass.: Harvard University Press.

Rogers, Deborah D. 1995. "Daze of Our Lives: The Soap Opera as Feminine Text." In Gail Dines and Jean M. Humez (eds.), *Gender, Race, and Class in Media: A Text-Reader*. Thousand Oaks, Calif.: Sage, 325–331.

Rollins, Judith. 1985. *Between Women: Domestics and Their Employers*. Philadelphia: Temple University Press.

Romaniuc, Anatole. 1994. "Fertility in Canada: Retrospective and Prospective." In Frank Trovato and Carl F. Grindstaff (eds.), *Perspectives on Canada's Population*. Toronto: Oxford University Press, 214–229.

Roof, Wade Clark. 1993. *A Generation of Seekers: The Spiritual Journeys of the Baby Boom Generation*. San Francisco: HarperSanFrancisco.

Roos, Leslie, Elliott Fisher, Ruth Brazauskas, Sandra Sharp, and Evelyn Shapiro. 1992. "Health and Surgical Outcomes in Canada and the United States." *Health Affairs*, 11: 56-73.

Roos, Noralou, Evelyn Forget, and Gerard Beirne. 2004. "Health Care User Fees: Clinic Charges are Wrong Way to Go." *Winnipeg Free Press*, (January 20):A11.

Root, Maria P.P. 1990. "Disordered Eating in Women of Color." *Sex Roles*, 22(7/8):525–536.

Rose, Jerry D. 1982. *Outbreaks*. New York: Free Press.

Rosenburg, Michael. 1995. "Ethnic and Race Relations." In L. Tepperman, J.E. Curtis, and R.J. Richardson (eds.), *Sociology*. Toronto: McGraw-Hill Ryerson, 302–344.

Rosenfeld, Alvin, and Nicole Wise. 2000. *The Over-Scheduled Child: Avoiding the Hyper-Parenting Trap*. New York: St. Martin's Griffin.

Rosenthal, Naomi, Meryl Fingrutd, Michele Ethier, Roberta Karant, and David McDonald. 1985. "Social Movements and Network Analysis: A Case Study of Nineteenth-Century Women's Reform in New York State." *American Journal of Sociology*, 90:1022–1054.

Rosenthal, Robert, and Lenore Jacobson. 1968. *Pygmalion in the Classroom: Teacher Expectation and Student's Intellectual Development*. New York: Holt, Rinehart, and Winston.

Rosnow, Ralph L., and Gary Alan Fine. 1976. *Rumor and Gossip: The Social Psychology of Hearsay*. New York: Elsevier.

Ross, David P., and Paul Roberts. 1997. "Does Family Income Affect the Healthy Development of Children?" *Perception*, (21)1:1–5. Ottawa: Canadian Council on Social Development.

Ross, David P., Katherine Scott, and Peter Smith. 2000. *The Canadian Fact Book on Poverty, 2000*. Ottawa: Canadian Council on Social Development.

Ross, David P., E. Richard Shillington, and Clarence Lochhead. 1994. *The Canadian Fact Book on Poverty*. Ottawa: Canadian Council on Social Development.

Ross, Rupert. 1996. *Returning to the Teachings: Exploring Aboriginal Justice*. Toronto: Penguin Books.

Rossi, Alice S. 1980. "Life-Span Theories and Women's Lives." *Signs*, 6(1):4–32.

Rossides, Daniel W. 1986. *The American Class System: An Introduction to Social Stratification*. Boston: Houghton Mifflin.

Rostow, Walt W. 1971. *The Stages of Economic Growth: A Non-Communist Manifesto* (2nd ed.). Cambridge: Cambridge University Press (orig. pub. 1960).

———. 1978. *The World Economy: History and Prospect*. Austin, Tex.: University of Texas Press.

Roth, Guenther. 1988. "Marianne Weber and Her Circle." In Marianne Weber, *Max Weber: A Biography*. New Brunswick, N.J.: Transaction.

Royal Commission on Aboriginal Peoples. 1995. *Choosing Life: Special Report on Suicide Among Aboriginal Peoples*. Ottawa: Canada. Communications Group Publishing.

Rubin, Lillian B. 1994. *Families on the Fault Line*. New York: HarperCollins.

Ruiz-Duremdes, Sharon. n.d. "An Open Letter to My Children (On the National Situation)." Anglican Church of Canada. Unpublished.

Rutherford, Leanna. 1998. "An Anorexic's Recovery." *Canadian Living* (October): 107–110.

Ruthven, Malise. 2004. *Fundamentalism: The Search for Meaning*. Oxford: Oxford University Press.

Rutstein, Nathan. 1993. *Healing in America*. Springfield, Mass.: Whitcomb.

Rymer, Russ. 1993. *Genie: An Abused Child's Flight from Silence*. New York: HarperCollins.

Sadker, Myra, and David Sadker. 1994. *Failing at Fairness: How America's Schools Cheat Girls*. New York: Scribner.

Sacks, Nancy E., and Catherine Marrone. 2004. *Gender and Work in Today's World*. Cambridge, MA: Westview Press.

Safilios-Rothschild, Constantina. 1969. "Family Sociology or Wives' Family Sociology? A Cross-Cultural Examination of Decision-Making." *Journal of Marriage and the Family*, 31(2): 290–301.

Samovar, Larry A., and Richard E. Porter. 1991a. *Communication Between Cultures*. Belmont, Cal.: Wadsworth.

———. 1991b. *Intercultural Communication: A Reader* (6th ed.). Belmont, Cal.: Wadsworth.

Samuelson, Paul A., and William D. Nordhaus. 1989. *Economics* (13th ed.). New York: McGraw-Hill.

Sapir, Edward. 1961. *Culture, Language and Personality*. Berkeley: University of California Press.

Sargent, Margaret. 1987. *Sociology for Australians* (2nd ed.). Melbourne, Australia: Longman Cheshire.

Sarick, Lila. 1999. "Record Numbers Turn to Food Banks to Cope, National Survey Shows." *Globe and Mail* (September 29):A3.

Sassen, Saskia. 1991. *The Global City: New York, London, Tokyo*. Princeton, N.J.: Princeton University Press.

———. 1995. "On Concentration and Centrality in the Global City." In Paul L. Knox and Peter J. Taylor (eds.), *World Cities in a World System*. Cambridge, England: Cambridge University Press.

Satzewich, Vic, ed. 1998. *Racism and Social Inequality in Canada: Concepts, Controversies and Strategies for Resistance*. Toronto: Thompson Educational Publishing.

Saulnier, Beth. 1998. "Small World." *Cornell Magazine Online*. Available: http://cornell-magazine.cornell.edu/Archive/JulyAugust98/JulyWorld.html.

Saunders, Eileen. 1999. "Theoretical Approaches to the Study of Women." In Curtis, James, Edward Grabb, and Neil Guppy (eds.), *Social Inequality in Canada: Patterns and Policies*. Scarborough: Prentice Hall, 168–185.

Sauvé, Roger. 2001. *Wealth: How Many Millionaires Does It Take to Buy "Everything" and More?* Ottawa: Vanier Institute of the Family. Retrieved June 25, 2002. Available: http://www.vifamily.ca/wealth/four.htm.

———. 2002. "The Dreams and Reality: Assets, Debts, and Net Worth." People Patterns Consulting. Retrieved August 16, 2005. Available http://www.vifamily.ca.

———. 2003. "Rich Canadians, Poor Canadians, and Everyone in Between." *Transition Magazine*, 32(4).

———. 2003b. "The Current State of Family Finances—2003 Report." People Patterns Consulting. Retrieved August 12, 2005. Available http://www.vifamily.ca/library/cft/state03.html#3_million.

Savin-Williams, Ritch C. 2004. "Memories of Same-Sex Attractions." In Michael S. Kimmel and Michael A. Messner (eds.), *Men's Lives* (6th ed.). Boston: Allyn & Bacon, 116–132.

Schaefer, Richard T. 1993. *Racial and Ethnic Groups*. New York: HarperCollins.

———. 1995. *Race and Ethnicity in the United States*. New York: HarperCollins.

Schafer, A. 1998. *Down and Out in Winnipeg and Toronto: The Ethics of Legislating Against Panhandling*. Ottawa: Institute of Social Policy.

Schama, Simon. 1989. *Citizens: A Chronicle of the French Revolution.* New York: Knopf.

Schellenberg, Grant, and David P. Ross. 1997. *Left Poor by the Market: A Look at Family Poverty and Earnings.* Ottawa: Canadian Council on Social Development.

Schellenberg, Grant, and Cynthia Silver. 2004. "You Can't Always Get What You Want: Retirement Preferences and Experiences." *Canadian Social Trends,* Winter:2–7.

Schemo, Diana Jean. 1996. "Indians in Brazil, Estranged from Their Land, Suffer an Epidemic of Suicide." *New York Times* (August 25):7.

Schlesinger, Ben. 1998. *Strengths in Families: Accentuating the Positive Contemporary Family Trends.* Ottawa: Vanier Institute of the Family.

Schneider, Keith. 1993. "The Regulatory Thickets of Environmental Racism." *New York Times* (December 19):E5.

Schur, Edwin M. 1965. *Crimes Without Victims: Deviant Behavior and Public Policy.* Englewood Cliffs, N.J.: Prentice-Hall.

———. 1983. *Labeling Women Deviant: Gender, Stigma, and Social Control.* Philadelphia: Temple University Press.

Schutz, Alfred. 1967. *The Phenomenology of the Modern World.* Evanston: Northwestern University Press. (Originally published in 1932).

Scott, Robert A. 1969. T*he Making of Blind Men: A Study of Adult Socialization.* New York: Russell Sage Foundation.

Scully, Diana. 1990. *Understanding Sexual Violence: A Study of Convicted Rapists.* Boston: Unwin Hyman.

Searles, Neil. 1995. *Physician Assisted Suicide in Manitoba.* Manitoba Association of Rights and Liberties.

Seccombe, Karen. 1991. "Assessing the Costs and Benefits of Children: Gender Comparisons Among Childfree Husbands and Wives." *Journal of Marriage and the Family,* 53(1):191–202.

Seegmiller, B.R., B. Suter, and N. Duviant. 1980. *Personal, Socioeconomic, and Sibling Influences on Sex-Role Differentiation.* Urbana: ERIC Clearinghouse of Elementary and Early Childhood Education, ED 176 895, College of Education, University of Illinois.

Seid, Roberta P. 1994. "Too 'Close to the Bone': The Historical Context for Women's Obsession with Slenderness." In Patricia Fallon, Melanie A. Katzman, and Susan C. Wooley (eds.), *Feminist Perspectives on Eating Disorders.* New York: Guilford Press, 3–16.

Serbin, Lisa A., Phyllis Zelkowitz, Anna-Beth Doyle, Dolores Gold, and Bill Wheaton. 1990. "The Socialization of Sex-Differentiated Skills and Academic Performance: A Mediational Model." *Sex Roles,* 23:613–628.

Shadd, Adrienne. 1991. "Institutionalized Racism and Canadian History: Notes of a Black Canadian." In Ormond McKague (ed.), *Racism in Canada.* Saskatoon: Fifth House, 1–5.

———. 1994. "Where Are You Really From?" In Carl E. James and Adrienne Shadd (eds.), *Talking About Difference.* Toronto: Between the Lines Press, 9–15.

Shapiro, Joseph P. 1993. *No Pity: People with Disabilities Forging a New Civil Rights Movement.* Toronto: Time Books/Random House.

Shapiro, Susan P. 1990. "Collaring the Crime, Not the Criminal: Reconsidering the Concept of White-collar Crime." *American Sociological Review,* 55:346–365.

Sharell, Janine. 1996. "Exercise Bulimia: Too Much of a Good Thing." *CNN Interactive: Food and Health* (May 20, 1996). Retrieved November 22, 2002. Available: http://www.cnn.com/ HEALTH/9605/20/exercise .bulimia.

Sharma, Monica, and James Tulloch. 1997. "Commentary: Unfinished Business." *Progress of Nations 1996.* New York: The United Nations. Retrieved December 7, 2002. Available: http://www.unicef.org/ pon96/heunfini.htm.

Shaw, Randy. 1999. *Reclaiming America: Nike, Clean Air, and the New National Activism.* Berkeley: University of California Press.

Shawver, Lois. 1998. "Notes on Reading Foucault's *The Birth of the Clinic.*" Retrieved October 2, 1999. Available: http://www.california.com/~rathbone/ foucbc.htm.

Sheen, Fulton J. 1995. *From the Angel's Blackboard: The Best of Fulton J. Sheen.* Ligouri, Missouri: Triumph.

Sheley, Joseph F. 1991. *Criminology: A Contemporary Handbook.* Belmont, Cal.: Wadsworth.

Shenon, Philip. 1994. "China's Mania for Baby Boys Creates Surplus of Bachelors." *New York Times* (August 16):A1, A4.

Sheptycki, James. 1998. "Policing, Postmodernism, and Transnation-alism." *British Journal of Criminology,* 38(3):485–503.

Sher, Julian, and William Marsden. 2003. *How the Biker Gangs Are Conquering Canada.* Toronto: Alfred A. Knopf.

Shilts, Randy. 1988. *And the Band Played On: Politics, People, and the AIDS Epidemic.* New York: Penguin.

Shisslak, Catherine M., and Marjorie Crago. 1992. "Eating Disorders Among Athletes." In Raymond Lemberg (ed.), *Controlling Eating Disorders with Facts, Advice, and Resources.* Phoenix: Oryx Press, 29–36.

Shkilnyk, Anastasia M. 1985. *A Poison Stronger Than Love: The Destruction of an Ojibwa Community.* New Haven: Yale University Press.

Shor, Ira. 1986. *Culture Wars: School and Society in the Conservative Restoration 1969–1984.* Boston: Routledge & Kegan Paul.

Sikorsky, Robert. 1990. "Highway Robbery: Canada's Auto Repair Scandal." *Reader's Digest* (February):55–63.

Silver, Cynthia. 2001. "Older Surfers." *Canadian Social Trends,* Winter:9–12.

Silverman, Robert, and Leslie Kennedy. 1993. *Deadly Deeds: Murder in Canada.* Scarborough, Ont.: Nelson Canada.

Simmel, Georg. 1904. "Fashion." *American Journal of Sociology,* 62 (May 1957):541–558.

———. 1950. *The Sociology of Georg Simmel.* Trans. Kurt Wolff. Glencoe, Ill.: Free Press (orig. written 1902–1917).

———. 1990. *The Philosophy of Money.* Ed. David Frisby. New York: Routledge (orig. pub. 1907).

Simon, David R., and D. Stanley Eitzen. 1993. *Elite Deviance* (4th ed.). Boston: Allyn & Bacon.

Simons, Marlise. 1993a. "Homeless Find a Spot in France's Heart." *New York Times* (December 9):A4.

———. 1993b. "Prosecutor Fighting Girl-Mutilation." *New York Times* (November 23):A4.

Simpson, George Eaton, and Milton Yinger. 1972. *Racial and Cultural Minorities: An Analysis of Prejudice and Discrimination* (4th ed.). New York: Harper & Row.

Simpson, Sally S. 1989. "Feminist Theory, Crime, and Justice." *Criminology,* 27:605–632.

Sloan, R.P., E. Bagiella, and T. Powell. 1999. "Religion, Spirituality, and Medicine." *The Lancet,* Vol. 353:664–667.

Smandych, Russell. 1985. "Marxism and the Creation of Law: Re-Examining the Origins of Canadian Anti-Combines Legislation." In Thomas Fleming (ed.), *The New Criminologies in Canada: State, Crime and Control.* Toronto: Oxford University Press, 87–99.

Smelser, Neil J. 1963. *Theory of Collective Behaviour.* New York: Free Press.

———. 1988. "Social Structure." In Neil J. Smelser (ed.), *Handbook of Sociology.* Newbury Park, Cal.: Sage, 103–129.

Smith, Adam. 1976. *An Inquiry into the Nature and Causes of the Wealth of Nations.* Ed. Roy H. Campbell and Andrew S. Skinner. Oxford, England: Clarendon Press (orig. pub. 1776).

Smith, Allen C., III, and Sheryl Kleinman. 1989. "Managing Emotions in Medical School: Students' Contacts with the Living and the Dead." *Social Science Quarterly,* 52(1):56–69.

Smith, Dorothy. 1974. "Women's Perspective as a Radical Critique of Sociology." *Sociological Inquiry,* (44):7–13.

———. 1985. "Women, Class and Family." In Varda Burstyn and Dorothy Smith (eds.), *Women, Class and the State.* Toronto: Garamond.

———. 1987. *The Everyday World as Problematic: A Feminist Sociology.* Toronto: University of Toronto Press.

Smith, Michael D. 1996. "Patriarchal Ideology and Wife Beating." In Robert J. Brym (ed.), *Society in Question: Sociological Readings for the 21st Century.* Toronto: Harcourt Brace, and Company.

Smith, R. Jeffrey. 2003. "Mistakes of NASA Toted Up." *The Washington Post,* (July 13):A1.

Smyke, Patricia. 1991. *Women and Health.* Atlantic Highlands, N.J.: Zed Books.

Smyth, Julie. 2001. "Prepare Them for Work and Create Good Citizens, Too." *State of Education Quarterly Report.* Edition 2. *National Post* (September 8). Available: http:// quarterlyreport.nationalpost.com/ stateofeducation/edupoll.html.

Snider, Laureen. 1988. "Commercial Crime." In Vincent F. Sacco (ed.), *Deviance, Conformity and Control in Canadian Society.* Scarborough, Ont.: Prentice Hall, 231–283.

Snow, David A. 2003. "Observations and Comments on Gusfield's Journey." *Symbolic Interaction,* 26:141–149.

Snow, David A., and Leon Anderson. 1991. "Researching the Homeless: The Characteristic Features and Virtues of the Case Study." In Joe R. Feagin, Anthony M. Orum, and Gideon Sjoberg (eds.), *A Case for the Case Study.* Chapel Hill: University of North Carolina Press, 148–173.

———. 1993a. "Researching the Home-less: The Characteristic Features and Virtues of the Case Study." In Joe R. Feagin, Anthony M. Orum, and Gideon Sjoberg (eds.), *A Case for the Case Study.* Chapel Hill: University of North Carolina Press, 148–173.

———. 1993b. *Down on Their Luck: A Case Study of Homeless Street People.* Berkeley: University of California Press.

Snow, David A., and Robert Benford. 1988. "Ideology, Frame Resonance, and Participant Mobilization." In Bert Klandermans, Hanspeter Kriesi, and Sidney Tarrow (eds.), *International Social Movement Reserch,* vol. 1, *From Structure to Action.* Greenwich, Conn.: JAI, 133–155.

Snow, David A., E. Burke Rochford, Jr., Steven K. Worden, and Robert D. Benford. 1986. "Frame Align-ment Processes, Micromobilization, and Movement Participation." *American Sociological Review,* 51:464–481.

Snow, David A., Louis A. Zurcher, and Robert Peters. 1981. "Victory Celebrations as Theater: A Dra-maturgical Approach to Crowd Behavior." *Symbolic Interaction,* 4(1):21–41.

Snyder, Benson R. 1971. *The Hidden Curriculum.* New York: Knopf.

Snyder, Trish, and Terri Foxman. 1998. "The Global Marketing Hall of Shame." *Canadian Inflight Magazine* (July): 42–560.

Sokoloff, Natalie. 1992. *Black Women and White Women in the Professions.* New York: Routledge.

Sommers, C.H. 2000. "The War Against Boys: How Misguided Feminism Is Harming Our Young Men." *Atlantic Monthly*, 285)5):59–74.

Sorokin, Pitirim. 1950. *Altruistic Love*. Boston: The Boston Press.

South, Scott J., Charles M. Bonjean, Judy Corder, and William T. Markham. 1982. "Sex and Power in the Federal Bureaucracy." *Work and Occupations*, 9(2):233–254.

Sowell, Thomas. 1981. *Ethnic America*. New York: Basic.

Spain, Daphne. 2002. "What Happened to Gender Relations on the Way from Chicago to Los Angeles?" *City & Community* 1(June):155–169.

Spence, Jan. 1997. "Homeless in Russia: A Visit with Valery Sokolov." Share International. Retrieved September 15, 2001. Available: http://www.shareintl .org/archives/homelessness/ hl-jsRussia.htm.

Spencer, Metta. 1993. *Foundations of Modern Sociology* (6th ed.). Scarborough, Ont.: Prentice Hall.

Stackhouse, John. 1998. "Village Phones Ring Up Profit." *The Globe and Mail* (July 6):A1, A8.

———. 1999. "Foreign Aid Cuts Assailed for Harming Children." *The Globe and Mail* (February 23):A1, A12.

Stamler, Rodney T. 2004. "Organized Crime." In Rick Linden (ed.), *Criminology: A Canadian Perspective* (5th ed.). Toronto: Thomson, 444–479.

Stannard, David E. 1992. *American Holocaust: Columbus and the Conquest of the New World*. New York: Oxford University Press.

Stark, Rodney. 1992. *Sociology* (4th ed.). Belmont, Cal.: Wadsworth.

———. 1998. *Sociology* (7th ed.). Belmont: Wadsworth Publishing.

———. 1999. "Secularization: R.I.P." *Sociology of Religion*, 60:249–273.

———. 2004. *Exploring the Religious Life*. Baltimore: The Johns Hopkins Press.

Stark, Rodney, and William Sims Bainbridge. 1981. "American-Born Sects: Initial Findings." *Journal for the Scientific Study of Religion*, 20:130–149.

Stark, Rodney, Daniel P. Doyle, and Lori Kent. 1982. "Religion and Delinquency: The Ecology of a 'Lost' Relationship." *Journal of Research in Crime and Delinquency*, 19:4–24.

Statistics Canada. 1961. *1961 Census Bulletin* 1.2-2.

———. 1985. *Population Projections for Canada, Provinces and Territories 1984–2006*. Cat no. 91-520. Ottawa: Statistics Canada.

———. 1993. *Canadian Social Trends*. Ottawa: Statistics Canada.

———. 1994. *Women in the Labour Force*. Ottawa: Ministry of Industry, Science, and Technology.

———. 1996a. *Canada's Retirement Income Programs: A Statistical Overview*. Ottawa: Ministry of Industry.

———. 1996b. *General Social Survey*. Cat. no. 11–612.

———. 1997a. "1996 Census: Marital Status, Common-law Unions and Families." *The Daily* (October 14), Cat. no. 11-001E.

———. 1997b. "1996 Census: Mother Tongue, Home Language and Knowledge of Languages." *The Daily* (December 2). Ottawa: Minister of Supply and Services. Available: http://www.statcan.ca/Daily/English/ 971202/d971202.htm.

———. 1997c. "Breast Cancer Mortality and Mammography." *The Daily* (July 28). Ottawa: Minister of Supply and Services.

———. 1997d. "Family Income After Separatism." *The Daily* (April 9).

———. 1997e. "1996 Census: Immigration and Citizenship." *The Daily* (November 4). Cat. no. 11-001E.

———. 1997f. "The Social Context of Young Children." *Canadian Social Trends* (Winter). Cat. no. 11-008-XPE.

———. 1998a. "Canadian Crime Statistics, 1997." *Juristat* 18(11):12. Cat. no. 85-002-XPE. Ottawa: Statistics Canada.

———. 1998b. "Deaths, 1996." *The Daily* (April 16).

———. 1999a. "Computer Technology in Schools." *The Daily* (October 1). Retrieved December 10, 1999. Available: http://www.statcan.ca:80/Daily/ English/991012/d991012a.htm.

———. 1999b. "National Longitudinal Survey of Children and Youth." Ottawa: Special Surveys Division and Human Resources Development Canada.

———. 1999c. "National Longitudinal Survey of Children and Youth: School Component." *The Daily* (October 14). Retrieved June 3, 2005. Available: http://www.statcan.ca:80/Daily/ English/991014/d99104a.htm.

———. 2000a. "Criminal Victimization." *The Daily* (November 2). Retrieved January 14, 2005. Available: http://www.statcan.ca/Daily/English/ 001102/d001102a.htm.

———. 2000b. "Divorces." *The Daily* (September 28).

———. 2000c. "Enrolment in Elementary and Secondary Schools." Cat. no. 81-229-X1B. Ottawa: Statistics Canada.

———. 2001a. *2001 Census*. Available: http://www.12.statcan.ca/english/ census01/products/analytic/ companion/age/pyramid.cfm.

———. 2001b. "Alternative Health Care Practitioners." *The Daily* (December 13).

———. 2001c. "General Social Survey: Internet Use." *The Daily* (March 26). Retrieved December 15, 2002. Available: http://www.statcan.ca/Daily/ English/010326/d010 326a.htm.

———. 2001d. "Homicide Statistics." *The Daily* (October 31). Ottawa: Statistics Canada.

———. 2001e. "Measuring Student Knowledge and Skills: The Performance of Canada's Youth in Reading, Mathematics, and Science." *The Daily* (December 4).

———. 2001f. "Number of Earners Who Worked Full Year, Full-Time in 1995 in the 25 Highest-Paying and 25 Lowest-Paying Occupations and Their Average Earnings by Sex." Retrieved March 10, 2003. Available: http://www.statcan.ca/english/census96/ may12/ t2.htm.

———. 2001g. "Participation in Postsecondary Education and Family Income." *The Daily* (December 7).

———. 2002a. "Aboriginal Peoples of Canada: A Demographic Profile." *2001 Census Analysis Series*. Cat. no. 96F0030X1E200107.

———. 2002b. "Births." *The Daily* (September 26).

———. 2002c. "Canada's Ethnocultural Portrait: The Changing Mosaic." *2001 Census Analysis Series*. Cat. no. 96F0030X1E200108.

———. 2002d. "Census: Families, Number and Average Size." Cat. no. 91-213-XPB.

———. 2002e. "Changing Conjugal Life in Canada." *The Daily* (July 11). Available: http://www.statcan.ca/ Daily/English/020711/d020711a.htm.

———. 2002f. "Crime and Statistics in Canada, 2001." Cat. no. 85-00XPE. *Juristat* 22(6). Ottawa: Statistics Canada.

———. 2002g. "Crime Statistics, 2001." *The Daily* (July 17).

———. 2002h. "Deaths." *The Daily* (May 7).

———. 2002i. "Divorces." *The Daily* (December 2). Retrieved March 15, 2003. Available: http://www.statcan .ca/Daily/English/021202/d021202f .htm.

———. 2002j. "Family Income." *The Daily* (October 30). Retrieved October 30, 2002. Available: http://www .statcan.ca/Daily/English/021030/ d021030a.htm.

———. 2002k. "Geographic Units: Census Metropolitan Area and Census Agglomeration." Ottawa: Statistics Canada. Retrieved July 15, 2005. Available: http://www12.statcan.ca/ english/census01/Products/Reference/ dict/geo009.htm.

———. 2002l. "Health of the Off-Reserve Aboriginal Population." *The Daily* (August 27). Retrieved February 21, 2003. Available: http://www .statcan.ca/Daily/English/020827/ d020827a.htm.

———. 2002m. "Impact of Income and Mortality in Urban Canada." *The Daily* (September 26).

———. 2002n. "Participation and Activity Limitation Survey: A Profile of Disability in Canada." *The Daily* (December 3).

———. 2002o. *Profile of Canadian Families and Households: Diversification Continues*. Cat. no. 96F0030X1E2001003. Retrieved December 13, 2002. Available: http://www12.statcan.ca/english/ census01/products/analytic/ companion/fam/canada.cfm.

———. 2002p. *Profile of the Canadian Population by Age and Sex: Canada Ages*. Cat. no. 96 F0030XIE2001002.

Retrieved May 5, 2003. Available: http://www.12.statcan.ca/english/ census01/products/analytic/ companion/age/contents.cfm.

———. 2002q. "Profile of Languages in Canada: English, French, and Many Others." *2001 Census: Analysis Series*. Cat. no. 96F0030XIE2001005.

———. 2002r. *Women in Canada: Work Chapter Updates*. Cat. no. 89F0133XIE. Ottawa: Statistics Canada.

———. 2002s. "Youth in Transition Survey." *The Daily* (January 23).

———. 2002t. "Uniform Crime Reporting Survey." *Juristat* Cat. No. 85-00.

———. 2002u. "Homicide Survey." Policing Services Program, Canadian Centre for Justice Statistics, *Juristat* Cat. No. 85-00.

———. 2003a. "2001 Census: Ethic Origins, 2001." Cat. no. 96F0030XIE200108. Ottawa: Statistics Canada.

———. 2003b. "Census of Population: Immigration, Birthplace and Birthplace of Parents, Citizenship, Ethnic Origin, Visible Minorities and Aboriginal Peoples." *The Daily* (January 21). Retrieved February 20, 2003. Available: http://www .statcan.ca/Daily/English/030121/ do30121a/htm.

———. 2003c. "The Changing Profile of Canada's Labour Force." *2001 Census Analysis Series*. Cat. no. 96F0030XIE200109. Retrieved March 15, 2003. Available: http:// www.statcan.ca/english/IPS/Data/ 96F003XIE200109.htm.

———. 2003d. "Earnings of Canadians: Making a Living in the New Economy." Cat. no. 96F0030XIE2001013. Retrieved March 8, 2003. Available: http://www12.statcan.ca/english/ census01/products/analytic/ companion/earn/contents.cfm.

———. 2003e. "Education in Canada: Raising the Standard." *2001 Census: Analysis Series*. Cat. no. 96F0030XIE2001012. Retrieved March 11, 2003. Available: http:// www.statcan.ca/English/census01/ Products/Analytic/companion/ educ/pdf/96F0030XIE2001012.pdf.

———. 2003f. "Ethnic Origin, Sex, and Single and Multiple Responses for Population Canada." Catalogue 97F00101XCB01001. Retrieved February 20, 2003. Available: http:// www.statcan.ca/english/census01/ products/standard/themes/ListProducts .cfm?Temporal=2001&APATH= 3&THEME=44&FREE=0.

———. 2003g. "Income of Canadian Families." *2001 Census: Analysis Series*. Cat. no. 96F0030XIE2001014. Ottawa: Ministry of Industry.

———. 2003h. "Marriages." *The Daily* (February 6). Retrieved March 3, 2003. Available: http://www.statcan.ca/Daily/ English/030206/d030206c.htm.

———. 2003i. "Population by Mother Tongue, Provinces, and Territories." Retrieved February 19, 2003. Available: http://www.statcan .ca/english/Pgdb/demo18a.htm.

———. 2003j. "Religions in Canada." *2001 Census: Analysis Series.* Cat. no. 96F0030XIE2001015. Ottawa: Ministry of Industry.

———. 2003k. "University Qualifications Granted by Field of Study, by Sex." CANSIM cross-classified table 00580602. Retrieved May 5, 2003. Available: http://www .statcan.ca/english/Pgdb/healtheduc .21.htm.

———. 2003l. "Census of Population: Income of Individuals, Families, and Households; Religion." *The Daily* (May 13). Retrieved May 26, 2003. Available: http://www.statcan.ca/ Daily/English/030513/d030513a.htm.

———. 2003m. *Income of Individuals, Families, and Households Highlight Tables.* Cat. no. 97F0024XIE2001014 Retrieved August 20, 2005. Available: http://www12.statcan.ca/english/ census01/products/highlight/Income/ Index.cfm?Lang=E.

———. 2003n. "Marriages." *The Daily* (November 20). Retrieved September 13, 2005. Available: http://www .statcan.ca/Daily/English/031120/ d031120c.htm.

———. 2003o. *Report on the Demographic Situation in Canada 2002.* Cat. no. 91-209-XPE. Ottawa: Ministry of Industry.

———. 2003p. "Satisfaction with Life, by Age Group and Sex, Household Population Aged 15 and Over, Canada Excluding Territories, 2002." *Canadian Community Health Survey: Mental Health and Well-Being* 2002, Table 21. Cat. no. 82-617-X1I. Ottawa: Ministry of Industry.

———. 2003q. "Study: Finances in the Golden Years." *The Daily* (November 17).

———. 2003r. "Women in Canada: Work Chapter Updates 2003." Cat. no. 89F0133XIE. Ottawa: Statistics Canada. Retrieved July 23, 2005. Available: http://www.statcan.ca/ english/freepub/89F0133XIE/ 89F0133XIE2003000.pdf.

———. 2003s. "Crime Statistics, 2003." *Juristat* 24(6).

———. 2004a. "Adult Correctional Services in Canada, 2002/03." *Juristat.* Ottawa: Canadian Centre for Justice Statistics.

———. 2004b. "Crime Statistics." *The Daily* (July 28). Retrieved February 3, 2005. Available: http://www.statcan .ca/Daily/English/040728/d040728a .htm.

———. 2004c. "Deaths." *The Daily* (September 27).

———. 2004d. "Family Income." *The Daily* (May 20). Retrieved August 18, 2005. Available: http://www.statcan .ca/Daily/English/040520/d040520b .htm.

———. 2004e. "Foreign Control in the Canadian Economy." *The Daily* (November 2).

———. 2004f. "Low-income in Census Metropolitan Areas." *The Daily* (April 7). Retrieved August 18, 2005. Available: http://www.statcan.ca/ Daily/English/040407/d040407a.htm.

———. 2004g. "Marriages." *The Daily* (December 21). Retrieved September 13, 2005. Available: http://www .statcan.ca/Daily/English/041221/ d041221d.htm.

———. 2004h. "Profile of Disability in 2001." *Canadian Social Trends* Spring: 16–20. Ottawa: Statistics Canada.

———. 2004i. "Seniors at Work: An Update." *The Daily* (February 25).

———. 2005a. "Births." *The Daily* (July 12).

———. 2005b. "Canadian Community Health Survey: Obesity Among Children and Adults." *The Daily* (July 6).

———. 2005c. "Crime Statistics in Canada, 2004." *Juristat* 25(5). Ottawa, Statistics Canada.

———. 2005d. "Divorces." *The Daily* (March 9). Retrieved September 14, 2005. Available: http://www.statcan.ca/ Daily/English/050309/d050309b.htm.

———. 2005e. "Health Reports: The Use of Alternative Health Care." *The Daily* (March 15).

———. 2005f. "Labour Force Survey: Western Canada's Off-Reserve Aboriginal Population." *The Daily* (June 13). Ottawa: Statistics Canada.

———. 2005g. "Study: Are Good Jobs Disappearing in Canada?" *The Daily* (January 26).

Steiger, Thomas L., and Mark Wardell. 1995. "Gender and Employment in the Service Sector." *Social Problems,* 42(1): 91–123.

Stein, Joel. 2003. "The Singin', Dancin' American Idyll. Time.com. Retrieved June 21, 2003. Available: http://www .time.com/time/magazine/printout/ 0.8816,458781,00.html.

Stein, Peter J. 1976. *Single.* Englewood Cliffs, N.J.: Prentice-Hall.

———, ed. 1981. *Single Life: Unmarried Adults in Social Context.* New York: St. Martin's Press.

Steinbacher, Roberta, and Helen Bequaert Holmes. 1987. "Sex Choice: Survival and Sisterhood." In Gena Corea et al. (eds.), *Man-made Women: How New Reproductive Technologies Affect Women.* Bloomington: Indiana University Press, 52–63.

Stevenson, Mary Huff. 1988. "Some Economic Approaches to the Persistence of Wage Differences Between Men and Women." In Ann H. Stromberg and Shirley Harkess (eds.), *Women Working: Theories and Facts in Perspective* (2nd ed.). Mountain View, Cal.: Mayfield, 87–100.

Stewart, Abigail J. 1994. "Toward a Feminist Strategy for Studying Women's Lives." In Carol E. Franz and Abigail J. Stewart (eds.), *Women Creating Lives: Identities, Resilience, and Resistance.* Boulder, Col.: Westview, 11–35.

Stier, Deborah S., and Judith A. Hall. 1984. "Gender Differences in Touch: An Empirical and Theoretical Review." *Journal of Personality and Social Psychology,* 47(2):440–459.

Stobert, Susan and Kelly Cranswick. 2004. "Looking After Seniors: Who Does What for Whom?" *Canadian Social Trends.* Autumn: 2-6.

Stoller, Eleanor Palo, and Rose Campbell Gibson. 1997. *Worlds of Difference: Inequality in the Aging Experience* (2nd ed.). Thousand Oaks, Cal.: Sage.

Stone, Brad. 2001. "Love Online." *Newsweek Magazine* 19 Feb 2001: 46–51.

Stone, Leroy O. 1967. *Urban Development in Canada: 1961 Census Monograph.* Ottawa: Queen's Printer.

Stout, Cam. 1994. "Common Law: A Growing Alternative." In C. McKie (ed.), *Canadian Social Trends,* vol. 2. Toronto: Thompson Educational Publishing, 179–182.

Straus, Murray A., and I. Luis Ramirez. 2004. "Criminal History and Assault of Dating Partners: The Role of Type of Prior Crime, Age of Onset, and Gender." *Violence and Victims,* 19(4), 414–434. Retrieved September 10, 2005. Available: http://pubpages .unh.edu/~mas2/ID03-PR13.pdf.

Straus, M.A. and C. Smith. 1992. "Family Patterns and Child Abuse." In M.A. Straus and R.J. Gelles (eds.), Physical Violence in American Families: Risk Factors and Adaptations to Violence in 8145 Families. New Brunswick, N.J.: Transaction.

Strogatz, Steven H., and Duncan J. Watts. 1998. "Collective Dynamics of 'Small-World' Networks," *Nature,* 393:440–442.

Suicide Information & Education Centre. 2002. "About Suicide: Frequently Asked Questions." Retrieved September 7, 2002. Available: http://www.suicideinfo .ca/faq/suicide/faq.asp?faqID=2.

Sumner, William G. 1959. *Folkways.* New York: Dover (orig. pub. 1906).

Sutherland, Edwin H. 1939. *Principles of Criminology.* Philadelphia: Lippincott.

———. 1949. *White Collar Crime.* New York: Dryden.

Sutin, Laura. 2002. "At Home with the Kids: Balancing the Child Care Equation," *Transition,* Winter 2001–2002:14.

Swidler, Ann. 1986. "Culture in Action: Symbols and Strategies." *American Sociological Review,* 51 (April):273–286.

Sytnick, Patricia. 1998. "A District Society in the Tar Sands." *The Globe and Mail* (February 23):A2.

Takaki, Ronald. 1993. *A Different Mirror: A History of Multicultural America.* Boston: Little, Brown.

Tannen, Deborah. 1990. *You Just Don't Understand: Women and Men in Conversation.* New York: Morrow.

———. 1993. "Commencement Address, State University of New York at Binghamton." Reprinted in *Chronicle of Higher Education* (June 9):B5.

———. 1995. "Wears Jump Suit. Sensible Shoes. Uses Husband's Last Name." In E.D. Nelson, and B.W. Robinson (eds.), *Gender in the 1990s: Images, Realities, and Issues.* Scarborough, Ont.: Nelson Canada, 3–7.

Tanner, Julian. 2001. *Teenage Troubles: Youth and Deviance in Canada.* Toronto: ITP Nelson.

Tanofsky, M.B. et al. 1997. "Comparison of Men and Women with Binge Eating Disorder," *International Journal of Eating Disorders,* 21(1):49.

Tapscott, Don. 1998. *Growing Up Digital: The Rise of the Net Generation.* New York: McGraw-Hill.

Tator, Carol, and Frances Henry. 1999. "South Pacific Perspective Based on Denigrating Stereotypes." *The Toronto Star* (January 3).

Tavris, Carol. 1993. *The Mismeasure of Woman.* New York: Touchstone.

Taylor, Charles. 1989. *Sources of the Self.* Cambridge: Cambridge University Press.

Taylor, Payl. 1997. "Fatal Viruses Return with a Vengeance." *The Globe and Mail* (April 12):A1.

Taylor, Peter Shawn. 1995. "Grandma! Grandpa! Back to Work." *Saturday Night* (June):18–23, 96.

Taylor, Steve. 1982. *Durkheim and the Study of Suicide.* New York: St. Martin's Press.

Tepperman, Lorne. 1994. *Choices and Chances: Sociology for Everyday Life* (2nd ed.). Toronto: Harcourt Brace and Company.

Terkel, Studs. 1996. *Coming of Age: The Story of Our Century by Those Who've Lived It.* New York: St. Martin's Griffin.

Thomas, D. 1992. *Criminality Among the Foreign Born: Analysis of Federal Prison Population.* Ottawa: Immigration and Employment Canada.

Thomas, William I., and Dorothy Swaine Thomas. 1928. *The Child in America.* New York: Knopf.

Thompson, Becky W. 1992. "'A Way Outa No Way': Eating Problems Among African-American, Latina, and White Women." *Gender & Society,* 6(4):546–561. Revised article, "Food, Bodies, and Growing Up Female: Childhood Lessons About Culture, Race, and Class." In Patricia Fallon, Melanie A. Katzman, and Susan C. Wooley (eds.), *Feminist Perspectives on Eating Disorders.* New York: Guilford Press, 1994, 355–378.

———. 1994. *A Hunger So Wide and So Deep: American Women Speak Out on Eating Problems.* Minneapolis: University of Minnesota.

Thompson, Paul. 1983. *The Nature of Work.* London: Macmillan.

Thornberry, T.P., and M. Farnworth. 1982. "Social Correlates of Criminal Involvement." *American Sociological Review,* 47(4):505–518.

Thorne, Barrie, Cheris Kramarae, and Nancy Henley. 1983. *Language, Gender, and Society.* Rowley, Mass.: Newbury House.

Thorne, Barrie. 1993. *Gender Play: Girls and Boys in School.* New Brunswick, N.J.: Rutgers University Press.

Thornton, Russell. 1984. "Cherokee Population Losses During the Trail of Tears: A New Perspective and a New Estimate." *Ethnohistory,* 31:289–300.

Tidwell, Gary L. 1993. *Anatomy of a Fraud: Inside the Finances of the P.T.L. Ministries.* New York: Wiley.

Tilly, Charles. 1973. "Collective Action and Conflict in Large-Scale Social Change: Research Plans, 1974–78." Center for Research on Social Organization. Ann Arbor: University of Michigan, October.

———, ed. 1975. *The Formation of National States in Western Europe.* Princeton, N.J.: Princeton University Press.

———. 1978. *From Mobilization to Revolution.* Reading, Mass.: Addison-Wesley.

Timpson, Joyce. 1995. "Four Decades of Literature on Native Canadian Child Welfare: Changing Themes." *Child Welfare,* 74:525.

Tiryakian, Edward A. 1978. "Émile Durkheim." In Tom Bottomore and Robert Nisbet (eds.), *A History of Sociological Analysis.* New York: Basic Books, 187–236.

Titmuss, Richard. 1971. *The Gift Relationship: From Human Blood to Social Policy.* New York: Vintage Books.

Tittle, Charles W., William J. Villemez, and Douglas A. Smith. 1978. "The Myth of Social Class and Criminality." *American Sociological Review,* 43(5):643–656.

Tjepkema, Michael. 2002. "The Health of the Off-Reserve Aboriginal Population." Statistics Canada. Retrieved August 2, 2005. Available: http://www.statcan.ca/english/freepub/82-003-SIE/2002001/pdf/82-003-SIE2002004.pdf.

Toffler, Alvin. 1980. *The Third Wave.* New York: Bantam.

Tong, Rosemarie. 1989. *Feminist Thought: A Comprehensive Introduction.* Boulder, Col.: Westview Press.

Tönnies, Ferdinand. 1940. *Fundamental Concepts of Sociology (Gemeinschaft und Gesellschaft).* Trans. Charles P. Loomis. New York: American Book Company (orig. pub. 1887).

Toronto Disaster Relief Committee. 2004. "Homelessness is a National Disaster." Retrieved July 3, 2005. Available: http://www.tdrc.net/1aboutTDRC.htm.

Toronto Healthy City Office. 1998. *Homeless Voices.* Toronto: City of Toronto.

Touraine, Alain. 1971. *Post Industrial Society.* New York: Random House.

Transport Canada. 2002. "Urbanization by Province/Territory." Retrieved July 13, 2005. Available: http://www.tc.gc.ca/pol/en/T-Facts3/main.asp?id=10&table=05-Table10&file=economy&Lang=&title=ECONOMY%20%20-%20Demography#graph.

Trevithick, Alan. 1997. "On a Panhuman Preference for Moandry: Is Polyandry an Exception?" *Journal of Comparative Family Studies* (September): 154–184.

Trocmé, Nico, Bruce MacLaurin, Barbara Fallon, Joanne Daciuk, Diane Billingsley, Marc Tourigny, Micheline Mayer, John Wright, Ken Barter, Gale Burford, Joe Hornick, Richard Sullivan, and Brad McKenzie. 2001. *Canadian Incidence Study of Reported Child Abuse and Neglect: Final Report.* Ottawa: Health Canada.

Troeltsch, Ernst. 1960. *The Social Teachings of the Christian Churches,* vols. 1 and 2. Trans. O. Wyon. New York: Harper & Row. (orig. pub. 1931).

Trottier, Helen, Laurent Martel, Christian Houle, Jean-Marie Berthelot, and Jacques Legare. 2000. "Living at Home or in an Institution: What Makes the Difference for Seniors?" *Health Reports,* 11(Spring):49–61.

Tuggle, Justin L. and Malcolm D. Holmes. 2000. "Blowing Smoke: Status Politics and the Smoking Ban." In Patricia A. Adler and Peter Adler (eds.), *Constructions of Deviance.* Belmont, Cal.: Wadsworth, 159–168.

Tumin, Melvin. 1953. "Some Principles of Stratification: A Critical Analysis." *American Sociological Review,* 18 (August):387–393.

Turcotte, Peter, and Alain Bélanger. 1997. "Moving in Together." *Canadian Social Trends* (Winter). Cat. no. 11-008-XPE, 7–10. Ottawa: Statistics Canada.

Turner, Jonathan, Leonard Beeghley, and Charles H. Powers. 1995. *The Emergence of Sociological Theory* (3rd ed.). Belmont, Cal.: Wadsworth.

———. 1998. *The Emergence of Sociological Theory* (4th ed.). Belmont, Cal.: Wadsworth.

Turner, Jonathan H., Royce Singleton, Jr., and David Musick. 1984. *Oppression: A Socio-History of Black–White Relations in America.* Chicago: Nelson-Hall (reprinted 1987).

Turner, Ralph H., and Lewis M. Killian. 1993. "The Field of Collective Behavior." In Russell L. Curtis, Jr., and Benigno E. Aguirre (eds.), *Collective Behavior and Social Movements.* Boston: Allyn & Bacon, 5–20.

Twenhofel, Karen. 1993. "Do You Diet?" In Leslea Newman (ed.), *Eating Our Hearts Out: Personal Accounts of Women's Relationship to Food.* Freedom, Cal.: Crossing Press.

Tyre, Peg, and Daniel McGinn. 2003. "She Works, He Doesn't." *Newsweek* (May 12):45–52.

UNAIDS. 2002. *AIDS Epidemic Update 2002.* Geneva: Joint United Nations Program on HIV/AIDS and World Health Organization.

———. 2004. *Global Summary of the HIV and AIDS Epidemic.* New York: United Nations. Retrieved July 20, 2005. Available: http://www.unaids.org/en/resources/epidemiology/epicore.asp.

Underhill, Susan, Victor Marshall, and Sylvie Deliencourt. 1997. *Options 45+: HRCC Survey Final Report.* Ottawa: One Voice.

UN Platform for Action Committee. 2005. "Women and the Economy." Retrieved September 22, 2005. Available: http://unpac.ca/economy/wagegap3.html.

UNICEF. 2002. *The State of the World's Children.* New York: UNICEF.

———. 2005. "Fertility and Contraceptive Use." UNICEF Statistics. Retrieved July 15, 2005. Available: http://www.childinfo.org/eddb/fertility/.

UNICEF Innocenti Research Centre. 2000. "A League Table of Child Poverty in Rich Nations." (Innocenti Report Card No. 1, June). Florence, Italy: UNICEF Innocenti Research Centre.

United Nations. 1997a. "Global Change and Sustainable Development: Critical Trends." United Nations Department for Policy Coordination and Sustainable Development. Online (January 20).

———. 1997b. *Report of the Workshop on Managing the Social Consequences of Structural Change.* New York: Economic and Social Council.

———. 2000. *Report of the Panel on United Nations Peace Operations.* New York: Author.

———. 2001a. "A World Fit for Children." Preparatory Committee for the Special Session of the General Assembly on Children. Revised draft outcome document A/AC-256/CRP.6/Rev. 3 (June). New York: United Nations.

———. 2001b. "We the Children: End-Decade Review of the Follow-up to the World Summit for Children." Report of the Secretary General. A/S-27/3 (May 4). New York: United Nations.

———. 2002. *World Population Ageing 1950–2050.* New York: United Nations Population Division. Retrieved May 23, 2005. Available: http://www.un.org/esa/population/publications/worldageing19502050/countriesorareas.htm.

United Nations Development Programme. 1996. *Human Development Report, 1996.* New York: Oxford University Press.

———. 1997. *Human Development Report, 1997.* New York: Oxford University Press.

———. 1998. *Human Development Report, 1998.* New York: Oxford University Press.

———. 1999. *Human Development Report 1999: Globalization with a Human Face.* New York: Oxford University Press. Available: http://hdr.undp.org.

———. 2001. *Human Development Report 2001: Making Technologies Work for Development.* New York: Oxford University Press. Available: http://hdr.undp.org.

———. 2003. *Human Development Report, 2003.* New York: Oxford University Press. Retrieved July 20, 2005. Available: http://hdr.undp.org/reports/global/2003/.

———. 2004. *Human Development Report, 2004.* New York: Oxford University Press. Retrieved August 10, 2005. Available: http://hdr.undp.org/reports/global/2004/.

———. 2005. *Human Development Report, 2005.* New York: Oxford University Press. Retrieved December 30, 2005. Available: http://hdr.undp.org/reports/global/2005/.

United Nations DPCSD. 1997. "Report of Commission on Sustainable Development, April 1997." New York: United Nations Department for Policy Coordination and Sustainable Development. Online.

University of Winnipeg. 2002. "Careers in Sociology." Department of Sociology.

Ursel, Jane. 1996. *Submission to the Commission of Inquiry into the Deaths of Rhonds LaVoie and Roy Lavoie.* Winnipeg.

U.S. Census Bureau. 2000. *World Population Profile 2000.* Washington, U.S. Census Bureau.

———. 2005a. *World Population Information.* Washington: U.S. Census Bureau. Retrieved July 14, 2005. Available: http://www.census.gov/ipc/www/world.html.

———. 2005b. "IDB Population Pyramids." Retrieved July 15, 2005. Available: http://www.census.gov/ipc/www/idbpyr.html.

U.S. Congress, Office of Technology Assessment. 1979. "The Effects of Nuclear War." Report quoted in Michael E. Howard, 1990, "On Fighting a Nuclear War." In Francesca M. Cancian and James William Gibson (eds.), *Making War, Making Peace: The Social Foundations of Violent Conflict.* Belmont, Cal.: Wadsworth, 314–322.

Vallières, Pierre. 1971. *White Niggers of America.* Toronto: McClelland and Stewart.

Van Biema, David. 1993. "But Will It End the Abortion Debate?" *Time* (June 14):52–54.

Vanier Institute of the Family. 1998. "Families: Change and Continuity." Available: http://www.cfc-efc.ca/docs/00000329.htm.

———. 2000. *Profiling Canada's Families II.* Retrieved March 3, 2003. Available: http://www.vifamiliy.ca/profiling/p2introe.htm.

———. 2002. *Family Facts.* Ottawa: Vanier Institute of the Family.

Vanneman, Reeve, and Lynn Weber Cannon. 1987. *The American Perception of Class.* Philadelphia: Temple University Press.

Vaughan, Diane. 1985. "Uncoupling: The Social Construction of Divorce." In James M. Henslin (ed.), *Marriage and Family in a Changing Society* (2nd ed.). New York: Free Press, 429–439.

Vaughan, Ted R., Gideon Sjoberg, and Larry T. Reynolds, eds. 1993. *A Critique of Contemporary American Sociology.* Dix Hills, N.Y.: General Hall.

Veblen, Thorstein. 1967. *The Theory of the Leisure Class.* New York: Viking (orig. pub. 1899).

Vetter, Harold J., and Gary R. Perlstein. 1991. *Perspectives on Terrorism.* Pacific Grove, Cal.: Brooks/Cole.

Vigil, James. 1990. "Cholos and Gangs: Culture Change and Street Youth in Los Angeles." In Ronald C. Huff (ed.), *Gangs in America*. Newbury Park, Cal.: Sage.

Voynick, Steve. 1999. "Living with Ozone." *The World*, 1 (July):192–199.

Wagner, Elvin, and Allen E. Stearn. 1945. *The Effects of Smallpox on the Destiny of the American Indian*. Boston: Bruce Humphries.

Waldman, Amy. 2001. "Behind the Burka: Women Subtly Fought Taliban." *New York Times* (Nov. 19):A1, B4.

Waldram, James B., D. Ann Herring, and T. Kue Young. 1995. *Aboriginal Health in Canada: Historical, Cultural, and Epidemiological Perspectives*. Toronto: University of Toronto Press.

Waldron, Ingrid. 1994. "What Do We Know About the Causes of Sex Differences in Mortality? A Review of the Literature." In Peter Conrad and Rochelle Kern (eds.), *The Sociology of Health and Illness: Critical Perspectives*. New York: St. Martin's Press, 42–54.

Walker, James W. St. G. 1997. *"Race": Rights and the Law in the Supreme Court of Canada*. Waterloo: Wilfrid Laurier Press.

Walker, Lenore. 1979. *The Battered Woman*. New York: Harper & Row.

Wallace, Walter L. 1971. *The Logic of Science in Sociology*. New York: Aldine de Gruyter.

Wallerstein, Immanuel. 1979. *The Capitalist World-Economy*. Cambridge, England: Cambridge University Press.

———. 1984. *The Politics of the World Economy*. Cambridge, England: Cambridge University Press.

———. 1991. *Unthinking Social Science: The Limits of Nineteenth-Century Paradigms*. Cambridge, England: Polity Press.

———. 2004. *World Systems Analysis: An Introduction*. Durham: Duke University Press.

Wannell, Ted, and Nathalie Caron. 1994. "A Look at Employment Equity Groups Among Recent Postsecondary Graduates: Visible Minorities, Aboriginal Peoples and the Activity Limited." Cat. 11F0019MPE, no. 69. Ottawa: Statistics Canada.

Ward, Margaret. 1998. *The Family Dynamic: A Canadian Perspective* (2nd ed.). Scarborough: ITP Nelson.

Ward, Mike. 1996. "Firm Fined $6,000 After Man Killed in Unsafe Workplace." *Winnipeg Free Press* (March 7).

Warner, W. Lloyd, and Paul S. Lunt. 1941. *The Social Life of a Modern Community*. New Haven, Conn.: Yale University Press.

Warr, Mark. 1995. "America's Perceptions of Crime and Punishment." In Joseph F. Sheley, *Criminology: A Contemporary Handbook* (2nd ed.). Belmont, Cal.: Wadsworth, 15–31.

Warren, J.S. 1986. "Air India Litigation." Letter to Mr. John Sims. Document used in investigation of Air India crash. Retrieved March 24,

2005. Available: http://www.cbc.ca/ news/background/airindia/documents/ tab25.pdf.

Waters, Malcolm. 1995. *Globalization*. London and New York: Routledge.

Watson, Tracey. 1987. "Women Athletes and Athletic Women: The Dilemmas and Contradictions of Managing Incongruent Identities." *Sociological Inquiry*, 57 (Fall):431–446.

Webb, Eugene, et al. 1966. *Unobtrusive Measures: Nonreactive Research in the Social Sciences*. Chicago: Rand McNally.

Weber, Max. 1947. *The Theory of Social and Economic Organization*. Trans. A.M. Henderson and Talcott Parsons; ed. Talcott Parsons. New York: Oxford University Press.

———. 1963. *The Sociology of Religion*. Trans. E. Fischoff. Boston: Beacon Press (orig. pub. 1922).

———. 1968. *Economy and Society: An Outline of Interpretive Sociology*. Trans. G. Roth and G. Wittich. New York: Bedminster Press (orig. pub. 1922).

———. 1976. *The Protestant Ethic and the Spirit of Capitalism*. Trans. Talcott Parsons. Introduction by Anthony Giddens. New York: Scribner (orig. pub. 1904–1905).

Weeks, John R. 2002. *Population: An Introduction to Concepts and Issues* (8th edition). Belmont, Cal.: Wadsworth/Thomson Learning.

Weigel, Russell, and P.W. Howes. 1985. "Conceptions of Racial Prejudice: Symbolic Racism Revisited." *Journal of Social Issues*, 41:124–132.

Weinfeld, Morton. 1995. "Ethnic and Race Relations." In R. Brym (ed.), *New Society: Sociology for the 21st Century*. Toronto: Harcourt Brace and Company, 4.1–4.29

Weinstein, Michael M. 1997. "'The Bell Curve,' Revisited by Scholars." *New York Times* (October 11):A20.

Weintraub, J. 2000. "Where's Bill Cosby When You Need Him?" *National Post* (July 24).

Weiskel, Timothy. 1994. "Vicious Circles." *Harvard International Review* 16:12–20.

Weisner, Thomas S., Helen Garnier, and James Loucky. 1994. "Domestic Tasks, Gender Egalitarian Values and Children's Gender Typing in Conventional and Nonconventional Families." *Sex Roles* (January): 23–55.

Weiss, Meira. 1994. *Conditional Love: Parents' Attitudes Toward Handicapped Children*. Westport, Conn.: Bergin & Garvey.

Weitz, Rose. 1993. "Living with the Stigma of AIDS." In Delos H. Kelly (ed.), *Deviant Behavior: A Text-Reader in the Sociology of Deviance* (4th ed.). New York: St. Martin's Press, 222–236.

———. 1995. *A Sociology of Health, Illness, and Health Care*. Belmont, Cal.: Wadsworth.

———. 1996. *The Sociology of Health, Illness, and Health Care: A Critical Approach*. Belmont, Cal.: Wadsworth.

Weitzman, Lenore. 1999. "Poverty After Divorce—The Divorce

Revolution: The Unexpected Social and Economic Consequences for Women and Children in America." In M. Reza Nakhaie (ed.), *Debates on Social Inequality: Class, Gender, and Ethnicity*. Toronto: Harcourt Canada, 204–213.

Wendell, Susan. 1995. "Toward a Feminist Theory of Disability." In E.D. Nelson and B.W. Robinson (eds.), *Gender in the 1990s*. Scarborough, Ont.: Nelson Canada, 455–465.

Wente, Margaret. 2005. "The Footprint of My Future." *The Globe and Mail*. (June 4):A19.

West, Candice and Don H. Zimmerman. 1991. "Doing Gender." In J. Lorber and Susan A. Farrell (eds.), *The Social Construction of Gender*. Sage Publications: London.13–37.

Weston, Kath. 1991. *Families We Choose: Lesbians, Gays, Kinship*. New York: Columbia University Press.

Weston, Marianne, and Bonnie Jeffery. 1994. "AIDS: The Politicizing of a Public Health Issue." In B. Singh Bolaria and Harley D. Dickinson (eds.), *Health, Illness, and Health Care in Canada* (2nd ed.). Toronto: Harcourt Brace and Company, 721–738.

Westrum, Ron. 1991. *Technologies and Society: The Shaping of People and Things*. Belmont, Cal.: Wadsworth.

Wharton, Amy. 2000. "Feminism at Work." *The Annals of the American Academy of Political and Social Science*, 571(September):167–182.

Whitaker, Barbara. 1997. "Earning It; If You Can't Beat Dilbert, Hire Him." *New York Times* (June 29):C12.

Whitaker, Reg. 1991. *Double Standard: The Secret Story of Canadian Immigration*. Toronto: Lester and Orpen Dennys.

White, Merry. 1994. *The Material Child: Coming of Age in Japan and America*. Berkeley: University of California Press.

———. *Perfectly Japanese: Making Families in an Era of Upheaval*. Berkeley: University of California Press.

White, Richard W. 1992. *Rude Awakening: What the Homeless Crisis Tells Us*. San Francisco: ICS Press.

White, Ryan, and Anne Marie Cunningham. 1992. *Ryan White: My Own Story*. New York: Signet/ Penguin.

Whorf, Benjamin Lee. 1956. *Language, Thought and Reality*. John B. Carroll (ed.). Cambridge, Mass.: MIT Press.

Whyte, William Foote. 1988. *Street Corner Society: Social Structure of an Italian Slum*. Chicago: University of Chicago Press (orig. pub. 1943).

———. 1989. "Advancing Scientific Knowledge Through Participatory Action Research." *Sociological Forum*, 4:367–386.

Whyte, William H., Jr. 1957. *The Organization Man*. Garden City, N.Y.: Anchor.

Wieler, Joseph M. 1986. "The Role of Law in Labour Relations." In Ivan Bernier and Andree Lojoie (eds.), *Labour Law and Urban Law in Canada*. Toronto: University of Toronto Press.

Williams, Christine L. 1989. *Gender Differences at Work*. Berkeley: University of California Press.

Williams Jr., Robin M. 1970. *American Society: A Sociological Interpretation* (3rd ed.). New York: Knopf.

Williams, Stephen. 2004. *Karla, A Pact with the Devil*. Toronto: Seal.

Williamson, Robert C., Alice Duffy Rinehart, and Thomas O. Blank. 1992. *Early Retirement: Promises and Pitfalls*. New York: Plenum Press.

Wilson, Beth, and Carly Steinman. 2000. *Hunger Count 2000: A Surplus of Hunger*. Toronto: Canadian Association of Food Banks.

Wilson, David (ed.). 1997. "Globalization and the Changing U.S. City." *Annals of the American Academy of Political and Social Sciences*, 551, special issue (May).

Wilson, Edward O. 1975. *Sociobiology: A New Synthesis*. Cambridge, Mass.: Harvard University Press.

Wilson, Elizabeth. 1991. *The Sphinx in the City: Urban Life, the Control of Disorder, and Women*. Berkeley: University of California Press.

Wilson, William Julius. 1996. *When Work Disappears: The World of the New Urban Poor*. New York: Knopf.

Winn, Maria. 1985. *The Plug-in Drug: Television, Children, and the Family*. New York: Viking.

Wirth, Louis. 1938. "Urbanism as a Way of Life." *American Journal of Sociology*, 40:1–24.

Wirth, Louis. 1945. "The Problem of Minority Groups." In Ralph Linton (ed.), *The Science of Man in the World Crisis*. New York: Columbia University Press, 38.

Wiseman, Jacqueline. 1970. *Stations of the Lost: The Treatment of Skid Row Alcoholics*. Chicago: University of Chicago Press.

Wolf, Daniel. 1996. "A Bloody Biker War." *Maclean's* (January 15):10–11.

Wolfe, Jeanne M. 1992. "Canada's Livable Cities." *Social Policy*, 23:56–63.

Wollstonecraft, Mary 1974. *A Vindication of the Rights of Woman*. New York: Garland (orig pub. 1797).

Wong, Sandra L. 1991. "Evaluating the Content of Textbooks: Public Interests and Professional Authority." *Sociology of Education*, 64:11–18.

Wood, Darryl S., and Curt T. Griffiths. 1996. "Patterns of Aboriginal Crime." In Robert A. Silverman, James J. Teevan, and Vincent F. Sacco (eds.), *Crime in Canadian Society* (5th ed.). Toronto: Harcourt Brace and Company, 222–223.

Wood, Julia T. 1999. *Gendered Lives: Communication, Gender, and Culture* (3rd ed.). Belmont, Cal.: Wadsworth.

Wooden, Wayne S. 1995. *Renegade Kids, Suburban Outlaws: From Youth Culture to Delinquency*. Belmont, Cal.: Wadsworth.

Woodward, Kathleen. 1991. *Aging and Its Discontents: Freud and Other Fictions*. Bloomington: Indiana University Press.

Woolley, Frances. 1998. "Work and Household Transactions." Ottawa: Canadian Policy Research Networks.

World Bank. 2003. *World Development Indicators 2003.* New York: Author. Retrieved August 8, 2005. Available: http://www.worldbank.org/data/wdi2003/.

———. 2004. "Millennium Development Goals: Global Data Monitoring System. Promote Gender Equality and Empower Women." New York: Author. Retrieved August 12, 2005. Available: http://ddp-ext .worldbank.org/ext/MDG/gdmis.do.

———. 2005a. "World Development Indicators 2005." New York: Author. Retrieved July 22, 2005. Available: http://www.worldbank.org/data/wdi2005/.

———. 2005b. "Data and Statistics: Country Classification." New York: Author. Retrieved August 9, 2005. Available: http://www.worldbank .org/data/countryclass/countryclass .html.

World Health Organization. 1998. *Fifty Facts from the World Health Report 1998.* Available: www.who.int/whr/1998/factse.htm.

World Health Organization. 2002. "Suicide Rates (per 100,000), by Gender, Canada, 1950–1997." Retrieved October 5, 2002. Available: http://www5.who.int/mental_health/download.cfm?id=000000029.

———. 2003. *World Health Report 2003.* New York: Author. Retrieved July 20, 2005. Available: http://www.who.int/whr/2003/overview/en/.

———. 2004. *World Health Report 2004.* New York: Author. Retrieved August 10, 2005. Available: http://www.who.int/whr/2004/en/.

———. 2005. *World Health Report 2005.* New York: Author. Retrieved July 20, 2005. Available: http://www.who.int/whr/2005/en/index.html.

World Literacy of Canada. 2005a. "Facts and Figures." Retrieved September 15, 2005. Available: http://www.worldlit.ca/facts.html.

———. 2005b. World Literacy of Canada, 1995 "Learning About Literacy." Retrieved November 15, 2005. Available: http://www.worldlit.ca/literacy.html.

Worster, Donald. 1985. *Natures Economy: A History of Ecological Ideas.* New York: Cambridge University Press.

Wortley, Scott, and Julian Tanner. 2003. "Data, Denials, and Confusion: The Racial Profiling Debate in Toronto." *Canadian Journal of Criminology and Criminal Justice,* 45(July):367–390.

Wotherspoon, Terry. 1994. "Colonization, Self-Determination, and the Health of Canada's First Nations Peoples." In B. Singh Bolaria and Rosemary Bolaria (eds.), *Racial Minorities, Medicine and Health.* Halifax: Fernwood Publishing, 247–267.

Wouters, Cas. 1989. "The Sociology of Emotions and Flight Attendants: Hochschild's Managed Heart." *Theory, Culture & Society,* 6:95–123.

Wresch, William. 1996. *Disconnected: Haves and Have-Nots in the Information Age.* New Brunswick, N.J.: Rutgers University Press.

Wright, Erik Olin. 1978. "Race, Class, and Income Inequality." *American Journal of Sociology,* 83(6): 1397.

———. 1979. *Class Structure and Income Determination.* New York: Academic Press.

———. 1985. *Class.* London: Verso.

———. 1997. *Class Counts: Comparative Studies in Class Analysis.* Cambridge, U.K.: Cambridge University Press.

Wright, Erik Olin, Karen Shire, Shu-Ling Hwang, Maureen Dolan, and Janeen Baxter. 1992. "The Non-Effects of Class on the Gender Division of Labor in the Home: A Comparative Study of Sweden and the U.S." *Gender & Society,* 6(2):252–282.

Wuthnow, Robert. 1996. *Poor Richard's Principle: Recovering the American Dream Through the Moral Dimension of Work, Business, and Money.* Princeton, N.J.: Princeton University Press.

Yinger, J. Milton. 1960. "Contraculture and Subculture." *American Sociological Review,* 25 (October):625–635.

———. 1982. *Countercultures: The Promise and Peril of a World Turned Upside Down.* New York: Free Press.

Young, K., and L. Curry. 1997. "Beyond White Pride: Identity, Meaning, and Contradiction in the Canadian Skinhead Subculture." *Canadian Review of Sociology and Anthropology,* 34(2):176–206.

Young, Michael Dunlap. 1994. *The Rise of the Meritocracy.* New Brunswick, N.J.: Transaction (orig. pub. 1958).

Yunus, Muhammad. 1997. "Empowerment of the Poor: Eliminating the Apartheid Practiced by Financial Institutions." Paper presented to the State of the World Forum, San Francisco.

Zavella, Patricia. 1987. *Women's Work and Chicano Families: Cannery Workers of the Santa Clara Valley.* Ithaca, N.Y.: Cornell University Press.

Zeidenberg, Jerry. 1990. "The Just-in-Time Workforce." *Small Business* (May):31–34.

Zeitlin, Irving M. 1997. *Ideology and Development of Sociological Theory* (6th ed.). Upper Saddle River, N.J.: Prentice Hall.

Zelizer, Viviana. 1985. *Pricing the Priceless Child: The Changing Social Value of Children.* New Haven, Conn.: Yale University Press.

Zgodzinski, Rose. 1996. "Where Immigrants Come From." *The Globe and Mail* (June 20).

Zimmerman, Don H. 1992. "They Were All Doing Gender, But They Weren't All Passing: Comment on Rogers." *Gender & Society,* 6(2):192–198.

Zipp, John F. 1985. "Perceived Representativeness and Voting: An Assessment of the Impact of 'Choices' vs. 'Echoes.' " *The American Political Science Review,* 60:3:738–759.

Zuboff, Shoshana. 1988. *In the Age of the Smart Machine.* New York: Basic Books.

Zurcher, Louis. 1968. "Social-Psychological Functions of Ephemeral Roles: A Disaster Work Crew." *Human Organization,* 27 (Winter):281–298.

———. 1983. *Social Roles: Conformity, Conflict, and Creativity.* Beverly Hills, Cal.: Sage.

Chapter 17

p. 527: © Lindsay Hebberd/Corbis; **p. 528:** © Gabe Palmer/Corbis; **p. 531:** CP/AP; **p. 532:** Bob Daemmrich Photography Inc.; **p. 534:** © Bettmann/Corbis; **p. 535:** Nicholas Monu/Shutterstock.com; **p. 536:** Mark O'Neill/Canada Wide; **p. 544:** Left: © Steve Vidler/Superstock, Right: AP Photo/Ahn Young-joon; **p. 552:** John Neubauer/Photo Edit.

Chapter 18

p. 557: CP/AP/Eraldo Peres; **p. 561:** © Reuters/Corbis; **p. 562:** Maclean's; **p. 563:** Nancy R. Cohen/Photodisc Green/Getty Images; **p. 564:** Maclean's, May 13, 2002, p. 69; **p. 566:** Top: CP/Kingston Whig Standard/Michael Lea, Bottom: CP/Edmonton Journal/Bruce Edwards; **p. 573:** Patrick Guis/ Gamma Liaison; **p. 574:** CP/Tom Hanson; **p. 577:** UN/DPI; **p. 582:** Left: CP/Winnipeg Free Press/Jeff Debooy, Right: AP Photo/Gary Kazanjian; **p. 584:** CP/Tim Clark.

Chapter 19

p. 591: CP/Chris Schwartz; **p. 592:** CP; **p. 595:** © Howard Davies/Corbis; **p. 596:** Left: CP/AP/David Gottenfelder, Right: CP/AP/Rikard Larma; **p. 607:** Top: Nancy R. Cohen/Photodisc Green/Getty Images; Bottom Left: Emily F. Murphy, The Black Candle, © Coles Publishing, 1922, Bottom Right: Emily F. Murphy, The Black Candle, © Coles Publishing, 1922; **p. 611:** Charla Jones/Toronto Star; **p. 615:** P. Power/Toronto Star; **p. 617:** Top Left: Gary Cralle/Stone, Top Right: Norm Betts/Canada Wide, Bottom: Norm Betts/Canada Wide; **p. 621:** Rick Linden.

Chapter 20

p. 627: © Raymond Gehman/Corbis; **p. 628:** © Reuters/Corbis; **p. 632:** CP/Shaney Komulainen; **p. 633:** © Gunes Kocetepe/Corbis; **p. 634:** Top: Nicholas Monu/ Shutterstock.com, Bottom: CP/Chuck Stoody; **p. 637:** AP Photo/Eric Gray; **p. 639:** Jorg Carstensen/dpa/Landov; **p. 643:** CP; **p. 649:** CP/Frank Gunn.

TEXT CREDITS

Chapter 1
p. 5: J. Katzer et al. *Evaluating Information: A Guide for Users of Social Science.* Reprinted by permission of The McGraw-Hill Companies, Inc.; **p. 18:** From Sociological Illiteracy to Sociological Imagination, by Judith Shapiro, *The Chronicle of Higher Education*, March 31, 2000, p. A68.

Chapter 2
p. 32: Reprinted with permission from *Death and Deliverance*, by Robert Mason Lee (Macfarlane Walter & Ross, Toronto, 1992), pp. 229–231; **p. 45:** Latané and Darley, 1970. Reprinted by permission of Prentice Hall.

Chapter 3
p. 81: Reprinted by permission from Trish Snyder and Terri Foxman, authors of "The Global Marketing Hall of Shame" published in *Canadian Inflight Magazine* (July, 1998), 42–50; **p. 82:** Statistics Canada, 2003a; Statistics Canada, 2003j; "Household Income, 1995," adapted with permission from the Statistics Canada website at www.statcan.ca/english/census96/may12/t6can.htm.

Chapter 4
p. 116: Adapted from the Statistics Canada publication, "Age and Sex: Highlight Tables, 2001 Census," Catalogue 97F0024XIE, July 15, 2002, available at: http://www12.statcan.ca/english/census01/products/highlight/AgeSex/HighlightsTables.cfm?Lang=E.

Chapter 5
p. 124: Rusty Neal for the National Anti-Poverty Organization, 2004 "Voices: Women, Poverty and Homelessness in Canada" National Anti-Poverty Organization http://www.napo-onap.ca/en/resources/Voices_English_04232004.pdf. Retrieved June 2/05; **p. 131:** Abridged from Lesley Harman, *When a Hostel Becomes a Home*, Garamond Press, Toronto, 1989. Reprinted with the permission of Fernwood Publishing; **p. 134:** Hagan and McCarthy, 1998: 222. Reprinted with the permission of Cambridge University Press.

Chapter 6
p. 179: Marion, Russ and Mary Uhl-Bien. 2003. A Complexity Theory and Al-Qaeda: Examining Complex Leadership. @ *Emergence* 5(1): 54-76; **p. 180:** "Mapping Networks of Terrorist Cells," by Valdis E. Krebs. *Connections* 24 (3): 43–52. Copyright (c) 2002, Valdis Krebs–mapped and measured with InFlow 3.0 software.

Chapter 8
p. 228: *Our Neighbours' Voices: Will We Listen?* by The Interfaith Social Assistance Reform Coalition. Toronto: James Lorimer & Co. Ltd. Reprinted with permission; **p. 234:** Sauve, 2003. Reprinted by permission of People Patterns Consulting; **p. 252:** UNICEF Innocenti Research centre, Florence, Italy. Innocenti Report Card No. 1, June 2000. "A League Table of Child Poverty in Rich Nations." Reprinted by permission of UNICEF, Innocenti Research Centre.

Chapter 9
p. 282: Mehrotra S, Jolly R, eds. *Development with a human face: experiences in social achievement and economic growth.* Oxford: Oxford University Press, 2000.

Chapter 10
p. 296: From, "I've never had a black teacher before" by Carl E. James, in *Talking About Identity: Encounters in Race, Ethnicity, and Language*, Carl E. James and Adrienne Shadd (eds.) Between the Lines, Toronto, 2001, pp. 153–154; **p. 304:** Fleras and Kunz, 2001. Reprinted by permission of Thompson Educational Publishing; **p. 306:** Fleras and Elliot, 1996: 84. Reprinted by permission of Prentice Hall.

Chapter 11
p. 326: Rutherford, 1998, reprinted by permission of the author; **p. 328:** Schur, *Labelling Women Deviant*, © 1983. Reproduced with permission of The McGraw-Hill Companies.

Chapter 13
p. 394: Popoff, 1996, reprinted by permission of the author.

Chapter 16
p. 507: From *A Darker Shade of Crimson* by Ruben Navarrette, Jr. Copyright © 1993 by Ruben Navarette Jr. Used by permission of Bantam Books, a division of Random House, Inc.

Chapter 17
p. 548: Bibby, Reginald W. 2001. Canada's Teens: Today, Yesterday, and Tomorrow. Toronto: Stoddart.

Chapter 18
p. 563: From *Ryan White: My Own Story* by Ryan White and Ann Marie Cunningham, copyright © 1991 by Jeanne White and Ann Marie Cunningham. Used by permission of Dial Books for Young Readers, A Division of Penguin Young Readers Group, a Member of Penguin Group (USA) Inc., 345 Hudson Street, New York, NY 10014. All rights reserved; **p. 570:** Prepared by the Canadian Council on Social Development, using the National Longitudinal Survey of Children and Youth, 1994–1995. Reprinted by permission.